OXFORD HANDBOOK OF

CRIME AND CRIMINAL JUSTICE

THE OXFORD HANDBOOKS IN CRIMINOLOGY AND CRIMINAL JUSTICE

General Editor: Michael Tonry, University of Minnesota

THE OXFORD HANDBOOKS IN CRIMINOLOGY AND CRIMINAL JUSTICE offer authoritative, comprehensive, and critical overviews of the state of the art of criminology and criminal justice. Each volume focuses on a major area of each discipline, is edited by a distinguished group of specialists, and contains specially commissioned, original essays from leading international scholars in their respective fields. Guided by the general editorship of Michael Tonry, the series will provide an invaluable reference for scholars, students, and policy makers seeking to understand a wide range of research and policies in criminology and criminal justice.

Other titles in this series:

Crime and Public Policy
Michael Tonry

Juvenile Crime and Juvenile Justice
Barry C. Feld & Donna M. Bishop

Crime Prevention
Brandon C. Welsh & David P. Farrington

Sentencing and Corrections
Joan Petersilia & Kevin R. Reitz

THE OXFORD HANDBOOK OF

CRIME
AND
CRIMINAL
JUSTICE

MICHAEL TONRY

OXFORD
UNIVERSITY PRESS

OXFORD
UNIVERSITY PRESS

Oxford University Press is a department of the University of Oxford.
It furthers the University's objective of excellence in research, scholarship,
and education by publishing worldwide.

Oxford   New York
Auckland   Cape Town   Dar es Salaam   Hong Kong   Karachi
Kuala Lumpur   Madrid   Melbourne   Mexico City   Nairobi
New Delhi   Shanghai   Taipei   Toronto

With offices in
Argentina   Austria   Brazil   Chile   Czech Republic   France   Greece
Guatemala   Hungary   Italy   Japan   Poland   Portugal   Singapore
South Korea   Switzerland   Thailand   Turkey   Ukraine   Vietnam

Oxford is a registered trade mark of Oxford University Press
in the UK and certain other countries.

Published in the United States of America by
Oxford University Press
198 Madison Avenue, New York, NY 10016

Library of Congress Cataloging-in-Publication Data
The Oxford handbook of crime and criminal justice / [edited by] Michael Tonry.
p.   cm. — (Oxford handbooks)
Includes bibliographical references and index.
ISBN 978-0-19-539508-2 (hardcover : alk. paper); 978-0-19-933828-3 (paperback)
1. Criminal justice, Administration of—United
States—Handbooks, manuals, etc. 2. Crime—United States—Handbooks, manuals, etc. I. Tonry, Michael H.
HV9950.O94   2011
364.973—dc22   2010030266

Printed in the United States of America
on acid-free paper

Contents

....

List of Contributors

ROBERT APEL is associate professor of criminal justice at the University at Albany, State University of New York.

BRANDON K. APPLEGATE is associate professor of criminology and criminal justice at the University of South Carolina.

ERIC P. BAUMER is the Allen E. Liska Professor of Criminology at Florida State University.

DONNA M. BISHOP is professor of criminology and criminal Justice at Northeastern University.

SANDRA M. BUCERIUS is assistant professor of criminology at the University of Toronto.

JONATHAN P. CAULKINS is Stever Chair of Operations Research at Carnegie Mellon University's Heinz College and Qatar Campus.

AARON CHALFIN is a PhD student in the Goldman School of Public Policy at the University of California, Berkeley.

FRANCIS T. CULLEN is Distinguished Research Professor of Criminal Justice and Sociology at the University of Cincinnati.

KATHLEEN DALY is professor of criminology and criminal justice at Griffith University.

DAVID P. FARRINGTON is Professor of Psychological Criminology at the University of Cambridge.

BARRY C. FELD is Centennial Professor of Law at the University of Minnesota Law School.

ROSEMARY GARTNER is professor of criminology and sociology at the University of Toronto.

YVONNE JEWKES is professor of criminology at the University of Leicester, UK.

BRIAN D. JOHNSON is associate professor of criminology and criminal justice at the University of Maryland.

MARK A.R. KLEIMAN is professor of public policy at the University of California, Los Angeles (UCLA).

CANDACE KRUTTSCHNITT is a professor of sociology at the University of Toronto.

SANJA KUTNJAK IVKOVIĆ is associate professor of criminal justice at the Michigan State University.

STEPHEN D. MASTROFSKI is University Professor in the Department of Criminology, Law and Society at George Mason University.

MATT MATRAVERS is professor of political philosophy and Director of the School of Politics, Economics and Philosophy at the University of York.

CANDACE McCOY is a professor at the Graduate Center, City University of New York, and teaches in the doctoral program in CUNY's John Jay College of Criminal Justice.

OJMARRH MITCHELL is an assistant professor in the Department of Criminology at the University of South Florida.

DANIEL S. NAGIN is the Teresa and H. John Heinz III University Professor of Public Policy and Statistics, Carnegie Mellon University.

RAYMOND PATERNOSTER is professor of criminology in the Department of Criminology at the University of Maryland, College Park.

JOAN PETERSILIA is the Adelbert H. Sweet Professor of Law at Stanford Law School and Co-director of the Stanford Criminal Justice Center (SCJC).

STAN C. PROBAND is an independent criminologist.

GITANA PROIETTI-SCIFONI is research assistant in the Key Centre for Ethics, Law, and Governance at Griffith University.

STEVEN RAPHAEL is Professor of Public Policy, Goldman School of Public Policy at the University of California, Berkeley.

MICHAEL D. REISIG is professor of criminology and criminal justice at Arizona State University.

LAWRENCE W. SHERMAN is Wolfson Professor of Criminology at the University of Cambridge and Distinguished University Professor at the University of Maryland.

PAULA SMITH is assistant professor of criminal justice and Director of the Corrections Institute at the University of Cincinnati.

CASSIA SPOHN is a professor in the School of Criminology and Criminal Justice at Arizona State University.

MICHAEL TONRY is professor of law and public policy at the University of Minnesota Law School.

CHARLES F. WELLFORD is Professor of Criminology and Criminal Justice at the University of Maryland.

BRANDON C. WELSH is associate professor of criminology at Northeastern University and senior research fellow at the Netherlands Institute for the Study of Crime and Law Enforcement at Free University in Amsterdam.

JAMES J. WILLIS is assistant professor in the Department of Criminology, Law & Society at George Mason University.

OXFORD HANDBOOK OF

CRIME AND CRIMINAL JUSTICE

CHAPTER 1

....

CRIME AND CRIMINAL JUSTICE

....

MICHAEL TONRY

CRIMINAL justice systems in developed Western countries are much alike in form, structure, and function. They encompass written criminal codes; professional police, prosecution, and judicial systems; and a variety of pretrial, community, and custodial corrections programs and institutions. Details vary. In most countries, judges and prosecutors are nonpartisan civil servants; in the United States and Switzerland, many prosecutors and judges are elected or appointed by politicians. Prosecutors in some countries are governed by the "equality principle," in others by the "expediency principle." In equality principle systems, prosecutors in theory do not exercise discretion and prosecute all cases in which they believe crimes can be proven. In expediency principle systems, prosecutors may choose whether to prosecute a case on the basis of a range of practical and policy considerations. English-speaking common-law countries operate "adversarial" systems in which lawyers for the state and the defendant present evidence and try to persuade the judge how to interpret and apply the law. Judges—and sometimes juries—in theory are blank slates and consider only the evidence presented and are mostly passive receivers of information. Continental European civil-law countries operate "inquisitorial" systems in which judges dominate the fact-finding and trial processes, and lawyers play less active roles. Nonetheless, at day's end, in fundamental ways all systems are similar: defendants must be proven guilty beyond a reasonable doubt, and when they are, judges must determine an appropriate sentence choosing from a range of options that is much the same everywhere.

Juvenile systems vary more widely. Some countries including the United States, Canada, and England and Wales operate juvenile courts that are in effect criminal courts for young offenders, and many young offenders are transferred to criminal courts and sentenced as if they were adults. Some countries, most notably in Sweden and Finland and to a large extent in Belgium, do not have special courts for juveniles, and set the age of criminal responsibility at fifteen (in Belgium except for homicide, eighteen). This means that criminal or juvenile courts have no role in responding to serious wrongdoing by young offenders; social welfare, educational, and mental health agencies must deal with them. Germany has special youth courts for young offenders up to age eighteen, young offenders may not be transferred to adult courts, and most eighteen- to twenty-year-olds are handled as if they were younger than eighteen. In New Zealand, almost every young offender must be dealt with by a restorative justice-style conference either to determine the punishment or to recommend the punishment to the judge. In Scotland, "children's hearings" operate instead of juvenile courts and are by law directed not to punish wrongdoing but to look for resolutions that will promote the child's welfare.

Although the broad outlines of criminal justice systems are much the same, there are important differences in detail. This handbook deals mostly with the American criminal justice system. It is important, however, to remember that American approaches, policies, and institutions are not the only, or often the best, ways to address particular issues or problems.

In three respects the American system is unique. The first is its acute politicization. Since the mid-1960s crime and punishment have often been treated as major ideological and partisan issues in American elections (Beckett 1997). Candidates have regularly run for office accusing their opponents of being "soft on crime" and promising to adopt harsher policies or to apply existing policies in harsher ways. Candidates for election as county prosecutors have been especially prone to do this, but some candidates for judgeships have done it too. This stands in stark contrast to other developed countries. Nowhere else but in Switzerland are judges or prosecutors elected—they are usually career civil servants—and in Switzerland they act as if they were nonpartisan civil servants. And in no other country but England and Wales did crime and punishment become major political issues on a continuing basis in elections for legislatures and executive branch positions such as president, governor, or mayor (Tonry 2004a, 2004b). A major consequence of these differences is that American judges and prosecutors often take public opinion, or their personal re-election prospects and political self-interest, into account in setting policies or in making decisions about the handling of particular cases. In other countries, doing either of those things would be seen as unethical and inconsistent with judicial system officials' obligation to consider each case impartially, strictly on its own merits, and not to be influenced by extraneous considerations.

The second major difference, a consequence of the first, is that compared with other developed countries American legislatures have enacted laws of unmatched severity, or that are unprecedentedly insensitive to the interests of alleged and actual offenders. One notable example of notoriously severe laws is California's three-strikes-and-you're-out law, which requires a minimum prison sentence ranging from twenty-five years to life following conviction for the third time of a felony—no matter how minor (Zimring, Hawkins, and Kamin 2001). Twenty-five other states have three-strikes laws. No other Western country has anything comparable. Another example are life-without-possibility-of-parole laws (LWOPs)—most states have them—which mean what they literally say and have been applied to offenders as young as twelve. A few other countries have such laws, usually very narrowly defined, and affecting a handful of prisoners. In 2008, 41,000 people were serving LWOPs, 7,000 of them for offenses committed by people who were minors at the time (Nellis and King 2009). A third example is the proliferation since 1970 of mandatory minimum sentence laws, which require imposition of designated minimum prison sentences, sometimes of a few years' duration but often measured in decades. Only a few other countries have such laws, and the sentences they mandate are much shorter than in the United States (Tonry 2009).

The most notable laws insensitive to offenders' interests involve voting, other disabilities of current and former prisoners, and sex offenders. The United States is one of a handful of countries that forbid current and many former prisoners to vote; forty-eight of the fifty American states do not allow prisoners to vote, and many deny the vote to all or most former prisoners and to people on parole (Manza and Uggen 2006). Most other countries—England and Wales is a major exception—set up polling booths within prisons and allow all former prisoners to vote. While in prison, American inmates are denied Social Security benefits to which they would otherwise be entitled. They also are denied access to federal social welfare programs—conspicuously to federal student loan and grant programs that might enable them to obtain job skills or college educations, which would make going straight after release more likely. After release, many states make ex-prisoners ineligible to practice many professions and trades, including such improbable ones as being a hairdresser or a plumber. Throughout the United States "Megan's Laws" require convicted sex offenders to register with the police and make knowledge of where they live publicly available. Many forbid prisoners to live in particular places. This often has the effect in some cases of making it impossible for them to live anywhere in entire towns and cities (Wright 2009). "Dangerous offender" laws in some states allow states to continue to imprison sex offenders and some violent offenders after their prison terms have expired. No other country has anything like Megan's Laws' registration and notification requirements, and only a few—again England and Wales is the major exception—allow confinement of dangerous offenders after their prison terms have been completed.

The third major difference is that American punishments are far harsher than those in other Western countries. No other country retains capital punishment or regularly uses LWOPs or lengthy mandatory minimum sentence laws. As a result, the U.S. imprisonment rate of nearly 800 per 100,000 residents dwarfs imprisonment rates elsewhere. Rates in Scandinavia vary between 60 and 75 per 100,000 residents, rates in most Western European countries (e.g., Belgium, Germany, France, Italy, the Netherlands) are around 100, and rates in other English-speaking countries range between 100 and 150 (International Centre for Prison Studies 2010).

When all those things are put together, it can be seen that the American criminal justice system is structurally similar to those of other Western countries, but the punishments it imposes are often vastly harsher. A sizable literature has tried to explain why (e.g., Garland 2001; Tonry 2004b; Simon 2007). Higher crime rates and harsher public attitudes are not the answer; U.S. crime rates other than for murder are no higher than in other Western countries and public attitudes are not harsher (Roberts et al. 2002). The most persuasive answers focus on the politicization of criminal justice policy, the influence of evangelical Protestant moral beliefs, and the history of American race relations (nearly half the people in prison and on death row are black, and nearly a quarter are Hispanic) (Tonry 2011).

This chapter provides an overview of the American criminal justice system, though not in detail. Separate chapters in this handbook do that. Section I discusses patterns of crime and victimization rates and trends since the 1960s and 1970s. The most noteworthy trend is that crime has been declining—for most offenses substantially—since 1991. Section II describes the organization of the justice system. Section III discusses punishment patterns and trends. The most noteworthy are the extraordinary increase in imprisonment since 1973 and the overrepresentation of black people among prisoners. Section IV looks back on the earlier sections and tries to tie them together.

I. Crime Rates and Trends

In 1992, the year after American crime rates peaked and began a steep and continuing decline that continued at least through 2010, 89 percent of Americans believed crime rates were rising and 3 percent believed they were falling. In 2009, 74 percent still believed crime rates were rising and only 15 percent believed they were falling. In 2000 and 2001, roughly the same percentages of people—in the 40 percent range—believed crime was rising as believed it was falling, but the customary imbalance soon reappeared (*Sourcebook of Criminal Justice Statistics Online*, table 2.33.2009).

Why ordinary people so misperceive what is happening is not a mystery. Although major newspapers run stories at least four times a year—when FBI quarterly reports on crime rates are released—reporting the latest declines, television and films continue to trade in fictional crime stories, and mass media continue to run stories on the latest horrifying crime. Ordinary citizens do not read or pay much attention to FBI data or know much about the workings of police or courts, so they generalize from what they do know.

Nonetheless, there is no reasonable doubt that crime rates have long been falling and have fallen a lot (Goldberger and Rosenfeld 2008). This is shown by police data on reported crimes, by U.S. Bureau of the Census data on crimes reported to interviewers by victims, and by medical records on admissions to emergency rooms of hospitals. The same thing is happening in all the major English-speaking countries and in most or all Western European countries—as shown by their police, victimization, and medical data systems.

This section briefly discusses American police and victimization data, reports findings from the International Crime Survey, an international survey carried out in most developed (and many less-developed) countries, and discusses the reasons that have been offered to explain the near ubiquitous declines.

Figure 1.1 shows rates per 100,000 U.S. residents for murder, rape, robbery, and aggravated assault for the period 1960–2008. The data come from the Federal Bureau of Investigation's Uniform Crime Reports. Figure 1.2 shows similar data for the same period for burglary, theft, and motor vehicle theft.[1] For all seven crimes, there were rapid and steep increases in crime rates through the early 1980s, declines through 1985 or 1986, increases through 1991–92, and substantial declines since. Some of the early increases are attributable to increased professionalization of police records-keeping, increased availability of computerized data systems, and increased reporting of crimes to the police by citizens. For rape and aggravated assault, for example, reduced tolerance of sexual offending and domestic violence caused substantial increases in citizen reports during the 1970s and 1980s. Some crime rates have been affected by improved crime prevention technologies (e.g., ignition locks for motor vehicles since the early 1980s) and insurance company requirements that thefts be reported to the police as a condition of insurance policy claims.

Nonetheless, it is clear that crime rates increased greatly through 1981 and again in the late 1980s, but have fallen substantially since. This is best shown by the changes in the murder rate. Dead bodies provide incontrovertible evidence, which is collected by both police and health authorities. The police and public health data are independently confirmed by data from the National Crime Victimization Survey (NCVS) shown in figures 1.3 (violent offenses) and 1.4 (property offenses). The NCVS is a national survey, which has been conducted since 1973 by the U.S. Bureau of the Census for the Bureau of Justice Statistics of the U.S. Department of Justice. Members of 40,000–60,000 U.S. households are interviewed every six months for three years about crime victimization. The victimization patterns documented before 1993 are somewhat different from those shown by police data in the 1970s and 1980s; they generally showed declines in victimization in the 1970s, which continued. Figures 1.3 and 1.4 cover the period

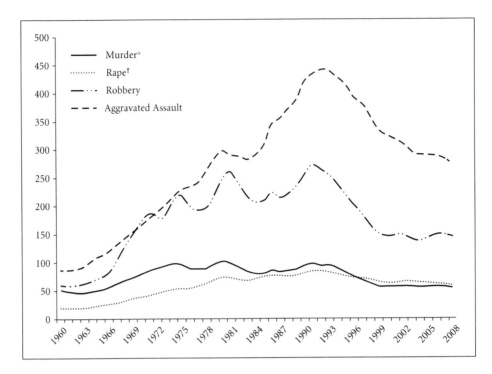

Figure 1.1. Violent Crime Rates per 100,000 Resident Population, 1960–2008
Murder rates per 100,000 have been multiplied by ten. Incidents of rape per 100,000
have been multiplied by two.
Source: Sourcebook of Criminal Justice Statistics, table 3.106
(Bureau of Justice Statistics, 2008, http://albany.edu/sourcebook/csv/t31062008.csv).

1993–2008. Major modifications of the NCVS in 1992 make the data from earlier periods not fully comparable to the data beginning in 1993. The victimization data strongly confirm the pattern of steep declines in crime rates shown for official police data in figures 1.1 and 1.2.

The difference in patterns shown by police and victimization data before 1993 occurs partly because the victim surveys identify many more criminal events than are reported to the police. The NCVS asks whether crimes are reported, and for many offenses fewer than half are, usually because the crime was not very serious, because it was not completed, because it was committed by a family member or a friend, or because the victim believed the police would or could do nothing about it. However, the rates at which victims said they reported crimes to the police increased during the 1970s and 1980s, which is one reason why police data showed increases at a time when victimization rates declined. It is also possible, and not implausible, that crime rates overall were falling in the 1970s and late 1980s even though rates for the most serious crimes reported to the police (and we know that overall more were reported) were increasing. In the late 1980s, for example, many

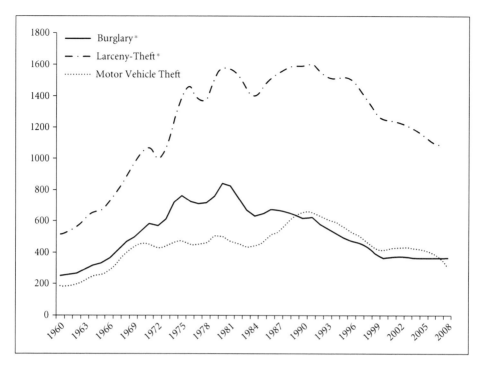

Figure 1.2.   Property Crime Rates per 100,000 Resident Population, 1960–2008
Burglary and larceny-theft rates per 100,000 have been divided by two.
Source: Sourcebook of Criminal Justice Statistics, table 3.106 (Bureau of Justice Statistics, 2008,
http://albany.edu/sourcebook/csv/t31062008.csv).

observers believe that the combination of rapid expansion of the crack cocaine market, easier access to especially lethal firearms, and the entry of gangs into drug
selling caused a major increase in violent crime, which fell when drug markets stabilized (Blumstein 1993).

The Since the late 1980s, and particularly since the early 1990s when major changes
were made to the NCVS to improve its accuracy, NCVS data have tracked the FBI's
police data. They confirm that crimes rates have long been falling, and have fallen
substantially.

The same patterns exist in many countries. Canadian crime patterns and trends
have closely followed U.S. trends and patterns since 1960 (Webster and Doob 2007,
fig. 1.4). So have those of England and Wales (Newburn 2007, figs. 1.5 and 1.6) and
all of the Scandinavian countries (Lappi-Seppälä 2007, fig. 1.6), among many others
(Eisner 2008).

One confirmation of the trend toward declining crime rates in most countries
can be seen in data from the International Crime Victims Survey (ICVS). The ICVS
has been carried out approximately every five years since 1989 and asks representative

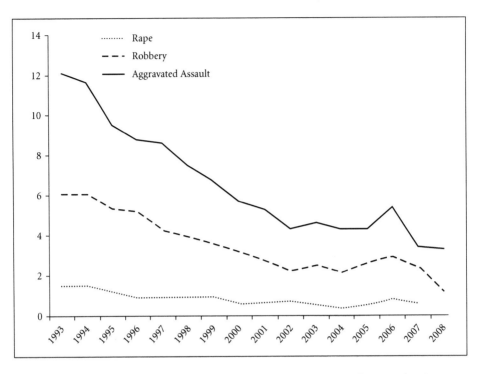

Figure 1.3.   Violent Offenses, Victimization Rates per 1000 Persons Aged 12 and Over, 1993–2008

Source: Sourcebook of Criminal Justice Statistics (Bureau of Justice Statistics, various years).

samples of the populations of participating countries about crimes they have experienced in the preceding year. Table 1.1 shows data from countries that participated in at least four of the five surveys on the percentages of respondents who reported victimization by any crime. The percentage of U.S. participants reporting that they have been crime victims has declined every year since 1989, which parallels the patterns shown in FBI (figs. 1.1 and 1.2) and NCVS (figs. 1.3 and 1.4) data. For other countries the peak years are later, but all show declines since the early or mid-1990s, and in most cases the declines closely parallel declines in the individual countries shown by other sources of data.

No one has a good explanation for the declines in crime rates in many countries. American scholars tend to see explanations in improved policing and rising imprisonment rates (e.g., Blumstein and Wallman 2005; Goldberger and Rosenfeld 2008). These things, however, while not irrelevant are not a major part of the explanation. They cannot explain why crime rates fell equally steeply elsewhere, such as in Canada and the Scandinavian countries, none of which significantly changed their policing systems nor significantly increased their prison populations. Some

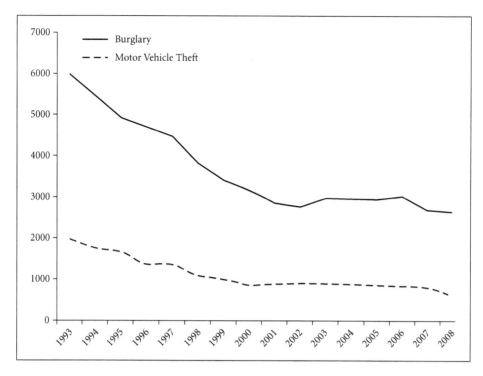

Figure 1.4.   Property Offenses, Victimization Rates per 1000 Persons Aged 12
and Over, 1993–2008
Source: Sourcebook of Criminal Justice Statistics (Bureau of Justice
Statistics, various years).

scholars outside the United States attribute the decline to increased public and private investment in crime prevention technology and hardware (e.g., van Dijk 2010).
Only a few countries, however, most notably the Netherlands, greatly increased
investment in crime prevention, and the United States did not. This also cannot
explain the ubiquitous decline.

II. THE CRIMINAL JUSTICE SYSTEM

Among developed countries, the United States has much the most complex and
fragmented criminal justice system. The President's Commission on Law Enforcement and Administration of Justice (1967) long ago observed that to describe it as
a "system" at all is at least an exaggeration and probably a misnomer. Each of the
federal government, the fifty states, the District of Columbia, Puerto Rico, and

miscellaneous smaller territories has a separate criminal justice system. Within each jurisdiction, institutions and authority are highly fragmented. Before I describe typical institutions and processes, looks at other countries' systems may be helpful to provide a basis for comparisons.

England and Wales has a unified political system in which judges are appointed on the basis of nonpartisan, meritocratic criteria; the heads of the judicial, prosecution, probation, and prison systems are appointed by the government of the day; police chiefs are appointed by governing boards of the forty-three police forces; and individual prosecutors, police officers, and prison, probation, and parole managers and line staff are civil servants. The heads of agencies who are appointed by elected officials are almost always people with relevant specialist backgrounds and experience. There is a single body of criminal law and procedure for the entire country, and a single hierarchically organized judicial system that applies it. Each police force has a designated territory. Except for the police, the other major criminal justice organizations—the Crown Prosecution Service, the Prison Service, the Probation Service, the Parole Board, and the Youth Justice Board—are headquartered in London and are operated as national organizations according to national policies. The police forces, though locally organized, are overseen by a unit of the Home Office and are subject to regulations and procedures set by the Home Office. Local chief prosecutors, prison wardens (called governors), and heads of probation offices are appointed by senior officials in the national office. No criminal justice officials are elected, and only the heads of national agencies are directly appointed by elected politicians. All very tidy. Similar descriptions could be given for many countries including those in Denmark, Finland, Norway, Sweden, Ireland, and Scotland. Systems in Italy, France, and elsewhere are not very different.

Other countries besides the United States have federal legal systems. They include Australia, Canada, and Germany. Canada provides the closest and most familiar comparison. Canada, like England and Wales, has a single body of criminal law and procedure and a single hierarchically organized judicial system, which applies it. No criminal justice officials are elected. Judges are appointed by the governments (federal or provincial depending on the level of the court), but those appointed are generally from lists of candidates found to be appropriate by nonpartisan independent committees. The heads of agencies who are appointed by elected officials are almost always people with relevant specialist backgrounds and experience.

To this point, Canada closely resembles England and Wales. The differences result from federalism. Canada has ten provinces and three territories. Policing is generally seen as the responsibility of the municipalities (but is regulated by provincial statutes). Smaller municipalities are generally policed by a provincial police force (in two provinces) or by the Royal Canadian Mounted Police as a result of contracts between the province and the federal government. Criminal cases are dealt with in trial courts organized at provincial levels (appeals are initially heard by appellate courts in each province and ultimately by the Supreme Court of Canada), but all apply the same national criminal laws and procedures. Pretrial detention, prison sentences less than two years, and probation and other community penalties are handled by provincial institutions. Prison sentences of two years and longer are served in federal prisons. Parole release is managed by federal or provincial parole boards. Supervision is carried out by federal or provincial officials, depending on where the sentence was served. Provincial judges are selected by the government in power. The details of the procedure vary somewhat from province to province (and with the federal government), but all involve open application processes, interviews, and meritocratic selection. Heads of corrections agencies are typically civil servants appointed by the relevant government (provincial or federal). Lower-ranking managers and line staff are civil servants. Prosecutors (Crown attorneys) are civil servants who are selected in a manner similar to all civil servants (applications, competitions, interviews, and merit selection committees).

In the United States, by contrast, there are overlapping federal and state criminal justice systems, each with its own constitution and criminal laws and procedures. Ultimately, all are governed by U.S. Supreme Court interpretations of the U.S. Constitution. The federal system has its own police agencies, trial and appellate courts, prosecutors' offices, and correctional systems. Judges and chief prosecutors are appointed by the president, usually on the basis of partisan political considerations and sometimes subject to ideological litmus tests. The heads of the FBI, the U.S. Bureau of Prisons, the U.S. Probation System, and the U.S. Parole Commission are appointed by the president, usually from among people who have relevant specialist backgrounds and expertise. Lower-ranking managers and line staff are civil servants.

Each state and equivalent jurisdiction has its own constitution, criminal law and procedure, and a hierarchically organized system of courts.[2] Appellate judges are sometimes elected in statewide elections and sometimes appointed by the governor. Each state has a state police system and a state prison system, and most have a state parole system. Heads of those systems are appointed by the governor, sometimes from among professionally qualified people and sometimes not.

So far this description is not very different from those of other countries, setting aside the multiplicity of constitutions and criminal laws and procedures. Two other considerations generate enormous complexity. First, much of the state criminal justice systems is organized, operated, and staffed at county levels.[3] Local county jails house pretrial detainees (called "remand prisoners" in most other countries) and usually convicted prisoners serving terms shorter than one year; county prosecutors handle prosecutions; and county correctional agencies manage probation and other community penalty programs. Second, most county-level judges, nearly all prosecuting attorneys (sometimes called district or county attorneys), and all sheriffs are elected at the county level. The sheriff, a uniquely American public official patterned on prerevolutionary English functionaries who no longer exist, typically manages a county police force (called sheriff's deputies) and

Table 1.1. Victimization Rates, All Offenses, Various Countries, 1989–2004/5

	1989	1992	1996	2000	2004/5
Australia	23.3	24.0	*	25.2	16.3
Belgium	13.4	15.2	*	17.5	17.7
Canada	22.4	24.0	21.8	20.5	17.2
England and Wales	15.2	23.9	25.4	22.3	21.8
Estonia	*	27.6	28.3	26.0	20.2
Finland	13.0	17.2	16.2	16.6	12.7
France	16.4	***	20.8	17.2	12.0
Netherlands	21.9	25.7	26.0	20.2	19.7
Poland	*	24.6	20.5	19.1	15.0
Scotland	13.9	19.6	*	17.5	13.3
Sweden	*	18.7	22.0	22.6	16.1
Switzerland	13.0	*	21.6	15.6	18.1
USA	25.0	22.2	21.5	17.6	17.5

Source: van Dijk, Jan, John van Kesteren, and Paul Smit. 2005. "Criminal Victimisation in International Perspective: Key findings from the 2004–2005 ICVS and EU ICS." Appendix 9, Table 1. http://rechten.uvt.nl/icvs/pdffiles/ICVS2004_05.pdf.

runs the county jail. In some places, for example Los Angeles County, the sheriff's deputies constitute a police force comparable in size and diversity of function to those of sizable cities.

This distinctive American pattern of county-level criminal justice system agencies, processes, and elected officials is important. It means that county prosecutors and sheriffs are politically and fiscally accountable not to state officials but to county voters and county legislatures (usually called county boards). And it means that the costs of court operations, prosecutors' offices, and county jails and other corrections programs must be appropriated by county boards from funds raised from local taxpayers.

As a practical matter, the combination of locally elected officials and locally funded operations means that the vast majority of criminal justice system operations are fundamentally local. If prosecutors want to enforce laws in idiosyncratic ways, or defy state officials, they can, and they are accountable only to local voters. Conversely, if state officials want to implement new statewide correctional programs, they can do so only if local officials are prepared to cooperate. Often they will not be prepared to cooperate, either because local funds are unavailable to support the new programs or because they do not believe the new program is a good idea.

Finally, and critically, the election of judges and prosecutors exposes them to pressures and temptations from which their nonpartisan and civil service peers in other countries are largely immune. Routine local political pressures and periods of public emotion precipitated by political campaigns or shocking crimes create pressures to resolve individual cases differently than would otherwise happen. The need to be re-elected, or to build a reputation to be used in campaigns for higher office, often leads to a politicization of criminal justice policies and practices and sentences in individual cases, which is uncommon—in many countries unheard of and unthinkable—in other countries' legal systems.

Even setting aside the problems of politicization, the combination of elected officials and divisions of function between state and county levels of government creates criminal justice systems (or nonsystems) of bewildering complexity. Policies, practices, and programs vary enormously between counties within a state. Effective establishment and implementation of statewide programs and policies for courts, prosecution, and community corrections are exceedingly difficult and often impossible.

Subject to the caveats that the criminal justice system is exceedingly complex and varies from place to place, it is possible to describe basic common processes. Although most states operate state police systems, their functions concentrate on highway patrol and provision of specialized services to small local departments that lack them (for examples, crime laboratories or specialized homicide or drugs units). Most police services are provided by municipal departments and in the unincorporated areas of counties or in small towns without police forces by sheriff's deputies. Most towns and cities with more than a few thousand residents operate municipal police forces ranging from some of the largest in the world with 30,000–40,000 officers to a handful. Police chiefs are generally appointed by mayors or city or town councils. Although in earlier eras, police chiefs, at least in big cities, were appointed largely for political reasons, these days most are selected from among qualified professionals. In many countries, police forces are subsidiary to prosecutors as law enforcement officials and their operations, especially their investigations in individual cases, are closely supervised. In the United States police operate almost entirely autonomously.

American prosecutors operate under the "expediency principle" discussed earlier: they possess near absolute discretion whether to prosecute people believed to have committed crimes, and for what. In most jurisdictions, 95–98 percent of people charged with crimes plead guilty, usually at the end of plea negotiations. Sometime "charge bargaining" occurs—for example, the defendant pleads guilty to one burglary charge on condition that three other charges be dismissed. Other times "sentence bargaining" occurs—for example, the defendant pleads guilty on condition that he or she receive a particular sentence, or a sentence not more severe than whatever was agreed. Sometimes more exotic bargains occur, such as "fact bargains" in which the prosecutor agrees not to inform the judge of a fact (such as use of a gun) that might lead to a severer or mandatory penalty. This is sometimes referred to as "swallowing the gun."

Of the small percentage of cases that are tried, nearly all are heard by a judge sitting alone. Defendants have a constitutional right to demand a jury trial but few do so. Probably as many occur in television programs and films as occur in real life.

Judges' sentencing powers vary widely. In some states, judges have authority to impose any sentence the statutes authorize, sometimes ranging between probation and a maximum prison sentence of many years. In some states, judges are supposed to sentence according to sentencing guidelines that specify a range of appropriate sentences for run-of-the-mill cases; in out-of-the-ordinary cases, judges can impose some other sentence not authorized by the guidelines. In such cases, the defendant can usually file an appeal to a higher court to obtain a review of the adequacy of the reasons the judge gave in justifying the extraordinary sentence. In every state some crimes—many in some places—are subject to a mandatory minimum sentence that requires imposition of a prison sentence of at least a designated minimum number of years. Three-strikes laws requiring a minimum sentence of twenty-five years to life and LWOP sentences are the extreme examples.

Depending both on state laws and available local and state resources, a range of sentences are available to judges. Short prison sentences are served in county jails, long ones in state prisons. Probation sentences are available everywhere. These range from nominal punishments in which the offender need only call the probation office every few months or send in a postcard explaining what he is doing, to intensive forms of probation involving close supervision, frequent drug tests, electronic monitoring, and requirements to pay restitution and participate in treatment programs. Fines are often imposed in minor cases. Some jurisdictions operate community service and house arrest programs. Many counties now operate drug, mental health, and family violence courts that couple close supervision with participation in treatment programs.

In many states, parole systems operate. Prisoners can apply for release before the expiration of their terms, and sometimes are released. For most of the twentieth century through the mid-1970s, every state operated a parole release system and most prisoners were released by it. Since the 1970s, some states have abolished parole release altogether, and all have become much more conservative about releasing prisoners. Half the states adopted "truth-in-sentencing" laws requiring offenders convicted of specified offenses to serve at least 85 percent of the announced sentence. Prisoners serving mandatory minimum sentences are ineligible for parole release before the minimum has been served. LWOP prisoners are never eligible. Governors and the U.S. president have power to pardon prisoners altogether and to shorten sentences by commuting them, but they seldom use those powers.

Prison officials also have power to shorten some prisoners' sentences (but usually not those serving mandatory minimum or LWOP sentences). Until the 1970s, nearly every state and the federal system operated "good time" (time off for good behavior) systems; prisoners typically received three days credit for every two days served and could thus routinely shorten their sentences by a third. Other sentence credits—for extraordinary services or treatment program participation—were often also available. Good time credits have since been eliminated in some states and cut back in most. They cannot affect mandatory minimum sentences, and are constrained by truth-in-sentencing laws.

Compared with the English and Welsh, and Canadian, criminal justice systems, the American systems are much more organizationally complex. They are also much more vulnerable to politicization, improper political influence on handling of individual cases, and personal idiosyncrasies of individual judges and prosecutors. These are among the reasons why the American system is the world's most punitive and the imprisonment rate is the world's highest.

III. Punishment Patterns and Trends

Punishment methods, patterns, and trends vary enormously between countries. All use a mix of prison terms, community penalties such as probation and community service, and fines, but the details vary greatly. Some, most conspicuously the United States, Russia, and South Africa, rely extremely heavily on imprisonment and confine more than 500 of their residents per 100,000 population. Other countries, notably Switzerland and the Scandinavian countries, imprison few of their residents, at rates usually below 75 per 100,000. Some countries, most extensively Germany and in Scandinavia, rely heavily on fines, often "day fines." The number of day fines is scaled to the seriousness of the crime, and the daily amount is based on the offender's daily income and personal wealth. All countries use probation and other community penalties extensively. Only the United States among Western countries continues to use capital punishment (although thirteen states, mostly in the Northeast and upper Midwest plus Alaska and Hawaii, do not).

The United States is the world's premiere imprisoner. Table 1.2 shows imprisonment rates for 2009–10 in the major English-speaking countries and Western Europe, South Africa, and Russia. The U.S. rate dwarfs those of any country except Russia. It is ten times higher than the rates in Scandinavia and Switzerland and five to seven times those of the other European and English-speaking countries.

It was not always so. In 1970 the U.S. imprisonment rate was 160 per 100,000, lower than in some other Western countries (e.g., Finland) and not greatly higher than most. Beginning in 1973, things began to change. According to annual statistical reports published by the Bureau of Justice Statistics, the imprisonment rate and the number of prisoners increased every year from 1973 through 2009. Figure 1.5 shows the imprisonment rate for state and federal inmates for those years, and the rate for state, federal, and county inmates since 1990. Before 1990, data from county jails were not available for every year. Usually jail inmates make up about one-third of the total, so increasing the rate in your mind's eye by a third for

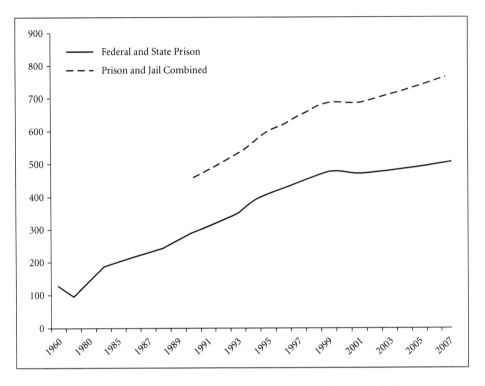

**Figure 1.5. Imprisonment Rates per 100,000 Resident Population,
United States, 1960–2008**

Sources: Sourcebook of Criminal Justice Statistics (Bureau of Justice Statistics [BJS], various
years); *Jail Inmates* (BJS, various years); *Prison and Jail Inmates at Midyear* (BJS, various
years); *Prisoners in [Various years] This* (BJS, various years); *Sourcebook of Criminal Justice
Statistics Online*, table 6.29 (BJS,2008, http//albany.edu/sourcebook/csv/t31062008.csv).

the earlier years gives a reasonable approximation of the total imprisonment rates
for those years.

Comparative analyses of punishment usually focus on capital punishment and
imprisonment in the United States, but this understates the severity of American
sentencing. Table 1.3 shows the total number of people under control of the criminal
justice system in the even years between 1980 and 2008, and separately for jails,
prisons, probation, and parole.

Several patterns leap from the table. First, the 7.3 million people under criminal justice system control in 2008 constituted 2.5 percent of the U.S. population
(then under 300 million), and nearly 6 percent of the population between the
ages of sixteen and sixty, the age group most likely to be affected. Second,
although imprisonment rates are high in the United States, less than a third of
the people under control were in confinement. The majority were on probation.
Third, the numbers in jail and prison grew by a factor of five after 1980, and those

on probation and parole by a factor of four. Fourth, even during the years since 1991 when crime rates have fallen continuously, the numbers of people controlled by the justice system continued to increase rapidly—by 50–75 percent, depending on the category. Even in the face of twenty years of declining crime rates, criminal punishment since 1990 became harsher and intruded more deeply into the lives of more people.

The criminal justice system affects black Americans disproportionately. Throughout the first decade of the twentieth century nearly a third of black men in their twenties have been under criminal justice system control. A black baby boy born in 2001 faced a one in three likelihood of spending some time as an inmate in a state or federal prison. The starkest disparities concern imprisonment. Figure 1.6 shows the black and white percentages of state and federal inmates since 1950. Fewer than a third of prisoners in 1950 were black. The percentage of black prisoners rose rapidly during the 1970s after "law and order" became a high-visibility political issue, peaking at 50 percent in the 1980s and fluctuating in the mid-40 percents since then.

Table 1.2. Prison Population Rate per 100,000 National Population, 2009–2010

USA	756
Russia	629
South Africa	335
Latvia	288
Estonia	259
Lithuania	234
Poland	221
New Zealand	185
Czech Republic	182
England & Wales	153
Scotland	152
Hungary	149
Australia	129
Canada	116
Netherlands	100
France	96
Austria	95
Belgium	93
Germany	89
Switzerland	76
Ireland	76
Sweden	74
Norway	69
Finland	64
Denmark	63

Source: Walmsley, Roy. 2010. "World Prison Population List." 8th ed. London, U.K.: Kings College London, International Centre for Prison Studies. http://www.kcl.ac.uk/depsta/law/research/icps/downloads/wppl-8th_41.pdf.

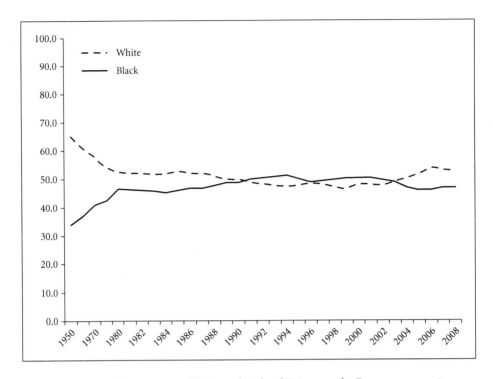

Figure 1.6. Percentages of State and Federal Prisoners, by Race, 1950–2008
Sources: for 1950—80: Cahalan (1986); for 1980—2008: Prisoners (BJS, various years).
Until the late 1990s, race was broken down by BJS into three categories: white, black,
and other. In recent years, has added Hispanic as a separate racial/ethnic category
which includes black and white people, thereby reducing "black" percentages. To various
statistics, thus complicating linear representations of the data. We have adopted the
approach taken in Tonry (2005). To allow continuity of presentation, "Hispanic" prisoners
have been disaggregated by race for each year since 1999. In 1990 and 1995, BJS reported
data with and without a separate Hispanic category. Approximately one-fourth of
Hispanics were counted as black in those years. The category of "two or more races"
has been redistributed evenly between blacks and whites.

The causes of this stark disparity are complex. Black people have constituted
12–13 percent of the U.S. population since 1980. When imprisonment rates are calculated relative to black and white population numbers, the rate of imprisonment
for black Americans is six to seven times higher than the rate for whites. To a small
extent these stark disparities occur because arrest rates for serious violent crimes
are higher for blacks than for whites. To a much greater extent they result from
drug arrest policies that target inner-city crack dealers, racial profiling by the
police, and enactment of laws in the 1980s and 1990s prescribing lengthy prison
sentences for drug and violent crimes for which blacks are disproportionately
arrested (Tonry 2011).

Table 1.3. US Population under Control of Adult Criminal Justice System
Institutions, 1980–2008, Alternate Years

	Total Estimated Correction Population	Probation	Jail	Prison	Parole
1980	1,840,400	1,118,097	182,288	319,598	220,438
1982	2,192,600	1,357,264	207,853	402,914	224,604
1984	2,689,200	1,740,948	233,018	448,264	266,992
1986	3,239,400	2,114,621	272,735	526,436	325,638
1988	3,714,100	2,356,483	341,893	607,766	407,977
1990	4,350,300	2,670,234	405,320	743,382	531,407
1992	4,762,600	2,811,611	441,781	850,566	658,601
1994	5,141,300	2,981,022	479,800	990,147	690,371
1996	5,490,700	3,164,996	518,492	1,127,528	679,733
1998	6,134,200	3,670,441	592,462	1,224,469	696,385
2000	6,445,100	3,826,209	621,149	1,316,333	723,898
2002	6,758,800	4,024,067	665,475	1,367,547	750,934
2004	6,995,100	4,143,792	713,990	1,421,345	771,852
2006	7,211,400	4,237,023	766,010	1,492,973	798,202
2008	7,308,200	4,270,917	785,556	1,518,559	828,169

Source: Bureau of Justice Statistics. 2006. *Sourcebook of Criminal Justice Statistics*. "Adults on probation, in jail or prison, and on parole United States, 1980–2006, Table 6.1." Washington D.C.: U.S. Department of Justice, Bureau of Justice Statistics. Bureau of Justice Statistics. *Sourcebook of Criminal Justice Statistics Online, 2006*, Table 6.1, available at http://www.albany.edu/sourcebook/csv/t612006csv. Glaze, Lauren E., Thomas P. Bonczar, and Matthew S. Cooper. 2009. *Probation and Parole in the United States 2008*. Washington D.C.: U.S. Department of Justice, Bureau of Justice Statistics.

IV. WHY?

We tend to be least aware of the things around us. What is, is. When it changes, it tends to do so gradually, almost imperceptibly. Although the American criminal justice system as seen from outside is extraordinarily severe—the world's most severe with China as the only rival candidate—most Americans probably do not see it that way. Those under the age of forty have always lived in a country with capital punishment; three-strikes, LWOPs, and Megan's laws; and one of the world's highest imprisonment rates.

It was not always this way. Americans over sixty who pay attention to such things can remember a time when the U.S. Supreme Court was famous world-wide for decisions strengthening defendants' procedural protections, when capital punishment seemed to be falling into disuse and for six years was not used at all, when American jurisdictions were leaders in devising alternatives to imprisonment, and above all, when the U.S. imprisonment rate was not markedly higher than those of other countries to which the United States would ordinarily be compared.

Things changed radically, and we are only beginning to understand why. Explanations initially offered were soon shown to be inadequate. The first thought in most people's minds is that U.S. punishment laws and patterns became harsher than those elsewhere because American crime rates were higher or were increasing more rapidly (Bennett, DiIulio, and Walters 1996). A related idea is that American public opinion was more punitive than elsewhere and less supportive of rehabilitative, preventative, and social welfare approaches. A more sophisticated idea is that large-scale changes in the world such as globalization, increased population diversity, and increased awareness of the risks of everyday life made Americans anxious, and in need of scapegoats to blame. As a result, a "culture of control" came into existence. Criminals were nominated for the role of scapegoat (Garland 2001).

The difficulty with the first two ideas is that they are based on a fundamental misunderstanding of the evidence. American crime rates, except for homicide, have traditionally *not* been higher than those in other countries, and in recent decades have typically been lower (Tonry 2004*b*). And, as the figures in section I show, American crime trends since 1970 have been paralleled by those in most Western countries, including America's nearest and culturally most similar neighbor, Canada (Webster and Doob 2007). In addition, American public opinions about the causes of crime, the purposes of punishment, and severity of punishment are almost indistinguishable from those of citizens in other English-speaking countries (Roberts et al. 2002).

The problem with the culture-of-control idea is that, if it is right, it should apply to every developed Western country. No country has been immune from the economic uncertainties and restructuring associated with globalization, from increases in population diversity and mobility, or from increased awareness of what some academics call "ontological insecurity" associated with increased awareness and sensitivity to risks ranging from job loss and crime through environmental calamity and terrorist mayhem. If those influences made American laws and practices much more severe, and also those in England and Wales since 1993, they should have had the same effect everywhere.

They did not. In the face of comparable rises in crime rates in the 1970s and 1980s, and comparable declines since the early and mid-1990s, countries responded in dramatically different ways. Crime trends were much the same in Finland, Germany, and the United States from 1965 to 1990 (basically up: murder rates increasing two to three times and overall violence rates three to four times), but the policy responses were radically different. The American imprisonment rate tripled (from about 160 per 100,000 to 500), the Finnish rate declined by two-thirds (from 165 to 60), and the German rate, after falling 20 percent in the early 1970s, remained stable between 90 and 100 per 100,000 through 1990 and since (Tonry 2004*b*). The American rate since 1990 has increased by another 60 percent, to nearly 800 per 100,000, and the other countries' rates have basically stabilized at the 1990 level.

The only conclusion that can be drawn is that countries have the imprisonment rates and punishment policies they choose. Finnish policy makers chose to reduce their imprisonment rate (Törnudd 1993; Lappi-Seppälä 2007), German to hold theirs stable (Weigend 2001), and American to drive theirs up (Tonry 2004b). The next question in each case is, why? The answers no doubt will be found in basic features of each country's history and culture.

There have been a few attempts at answers. Garland's "culture of control" argument is unconvincing since it seems at best a plausible hypothesis for the United States, and England and Wales (Garland 2001), but if it is correct it should apply to most or all developed countries, and patently it does not. Jonathan Simon's "governing through crime" argument—that politicians have discovered crime and punishment to be subjects with which to mobilize public fears and resentments and to win votes, while offending no powerful voting blocs—made sense in America from 1970 to 2000, but it does not explain why American policies were so boringly similar to those elsewhere before that (Simon 2007). My latest explanatory effort (Tonry 2011) focuses on various developments in American history and their continuing aftereffects, which have created a contemporary culture unprecedentedly punitive toward offenders. These include the development of a post–Revolutionary War constitutional system in which judges and prosecutors are elected at local levels (and thus politically independent and susceptible to influence by short-term public emotional reactions), a history of race relations in which in each era devices have been created to maintain white political and economic domination of blacks, and a continuing influence of Protestant moral attitudes—sometimes harsh, judgmental, and emotional—that have been powerful since the earliest days in Massachusetts Bay Colony. All of these analyses, however, are at early stages. Readers may well be able to come up with better and more persuasive ones.

NOTES

1. The numbers in figure 1.1 for murder have been multiplied by ten, and those for rape by two, so that all four violent crimes can be shown in one figure. Similarly, numbers in figure 1.2 for theft and burglary have been halved.

2. From this point, with apologies to the District of Columbia, Puerto Rico, and the territories, I use the term "states" but mean also to refer to those other governments.

3. However, there are always exceptions. A few states, including Alaska, Delaware, and Vermont, operate unified corrections systems in which prisons, probation, and parole throughout the state are managed by a single state agency. In other states, for example Minnesota, correctional services in some counties are provided by state agencies and in other counties are provided by county agencies. A few states, including Alaska and Delaware, have state prosecution systems; in most prosecution is a county function.

REFERENCES

Beckett, Katherine. 1997. *Making Crime Pay*. New York: Oxford University Press.

Bennett, William J., John J. DiIulio, and John P. Walters. 1996. *Body Count: Moral Poverty—and How to Win America's War against Crime and Drugs*. New York: Simon and Schuster.

Blumstein, Alfred. 1993. "Racial Disproportionality of U.S. Prison Populations Revisited." *University of Colorado Law Review* 64:743–60.

Blumstein, Alfred, and Joel Wallman, eds. 2005. *The Crime Drop in America*, rev. ed. New York: Cambridge University Press.

Eisner, Manuel. 2008. "Modernity Strikes Back? A Historical Perspective on the Latest Increase in Interpersonal Violence (1960–1990)." *International Journal of Conflict and Violence* 2:268–316.

Garland, David. 2001. *Culture of Control: Crime and Social Order in Contemporary Society*. Chicago: University of Chicago Press.

Goldberger, Arthur S., and Richard Rosenfeld, eds. 2008. *Understanding Crime Trends*. Washington, DC: National Academies Press.

International Centre for Prison Studies. 2010. "*World Prison Population List*." 7th ed. London: Kings College London.

Lappi-Seppälä, Tapio. 2007. "Penal Policy in Scandinavia." In *Crime, Punishment, and Politics in Comparative Perspective*, edited by Michael Tonry. Vol. 36 of *Crime and Justice: A Review of Research*, edited by Michael Tonry. Chicago: University of Chicago Press.

Manza, Jeff, and Christopher Uggen. 2008. *Locked Out: Felon Disenfranchisement and American Democracy*. New York: Oxford University Press.

Nellis, Ashley, and Ryan S. King. 2009. *No Exit: The Expanding Use of Life Sentences in America*. Washington, DC: The Sentencing Project.

Newburn, Tim. 2007. "'Tough on Crime': Penal Policy in England and Wales." In *Crime, Punishment, and Politics in Comparative Perspective*, edited by Michael Tonry. Vol. 36 of *Crime and Justice: A Review of Research*, edited by Michael Tonry. Chicago: University of Chicago Press.

President's Commission on Law Enforcement and Administration of Justice. 1967. *The Challenge of Crime in a Free Society*. Washington, DC: U.S. Government Printing Office.

Roberts, Julian V., Loretta J. Stalans, David Indermaur, and Mike Hough. 2002. *Penal Populism and Popular Opinion*. New York: Oxford University Press.

Simon, Jonathan. 2007. *Governing Through Crime: How the War on Crime Transformed American Democracy and Created a Culture of Fear*. New York: Oxford University Press.

Sourcebook of Criminal Justice Statistics Online. "Attitudes Toward Level of Crime." Table 2.33.2009. http://www.albany.edu/sourcebook/pdf/t2332009.pdf.

Tonry, Michael. 2004a. *Punishment and Politics: Evidence and Emulation in the Making of English Crime Control Policy*. Cullompton, Devon, UK: Willan.

———. 2004b. *Thinking about Crime: Sense and Sensibility in American Penal Culture*. New York: Oxford University Press.

———. 2009. "The Mostly Unintended Effects of Mandatory Penalties: Two Centuries of Consistent Findings." In *Crime and Justice: A Review of Research*, vol. 38, edited by Michael Tonry. Chicago: University of Chicago Press.

———. 2011. *Punishing Race: A Continuing American Dilemma*. New York: Oxford University Press.

Törnudd, Patrik. 1993. *Fifteen Years of Declining Prisoner Rates*. Research Communication no. 8. Helsinki: National Research Institute of Legal Policy.

van Dijk, Jan. 2010. "The European Crime Falls. Security Driven?" *Criminology in Europe* 9(1):5, 12–13.

Webster, Cheryl, and Anthony Doob. 2007. "Punitive Trends and Stable Imprisonment Rates in Canada." In *Crime, Punishment, and Politics in Comparative Perspective*, edited by Michael Tonry. Vol. 36 of *Crime and Justice: A Review of Research*, edited by Michael Tonry. Chicago: University of Chicago Press.

Weigend, Thomas. 2001. "Sentencing in Germany." In *Sentencing and Sanctions in Western Countries*, ed. Michael Tonry and Richard Frase. New York: Oxford University Press.

Wright, Richard, ed. 2009. *Sex Offender Laws: Failed Policies, New Directions*. New York: Springer.

Zimring, Franklin E., Gordon Hawkins, and Sam Kamin. 2001. *Punishment and Democracy: Three Strikes and You're Out in California*. New York: Oxford University Press.

CHAPTER 2

CRIME TRENDS

ERIC P. BAUMER

UNTIL fairly recently, there has been fleeting fascination about crime trends among the public, policymakers, and scholarly community. Aside from occasional rich descriptions and discussions of long-term temporal crime patterns by historians (e.g., Gurr 1981; Spierenburg 1996; Lane 1997; Eisner 2001; Roth 2009), detailed attention to crime trends during the past century typically has emerged as an after-thought during major social and economic shifts or, even more often, as the result of such shifts. It is perhaps not surprising then, that one would be hard-pressed to find an article or essay specifically on crime trends in previous scholarly volumes of this type.

The discourse about crime trends has been transformed, however, in the after-math of what some have called the "Great American Crime Decline," an umbrella phrase that refers to a substantial fall in crime rates in the United States during the 1990s that, it appears, also occurred in other parts of the world (Zimring 2006; Eisner 2008; Rosenfeld and Messner 2009). The interest level in tracking temporal crime patterns has grown during the past decade, with articles, books, confer-ences, national symposiums, panels, and roundtables of various sorts devoted to describing and explaining recent crime trends and, to a lesser extent, formulating educated guesses about trends that might emerge around the corner (e.g., for reviews, see LaFree 1998; Blumstein and Wallman 2006; Goldberger and Rosen-feld 2008). It seems appropriate to take stock on what we know, lay out some of the key analytical issues, and outline the most pertinent issues about which we need further study.

We do not yet know enough to be comfortable in drawing definitive conclu-sions about either the description of crime trends or their explanation, but we know quite a bit more about the former than the latter. In part, this is because during the past few decades several scholars have devoted considerable time and energy to describing crime trends in America and elsewhere. Drawing on their work, we see that while it is sometimes difficult to estimate precisely the actual volume of crime at specified times, a fairly coherent portrait emerges about the general direction in which crime has moved.

The historical record for crime trends is limited primarily to estimates of homicide rates; data on other crimes have been inconsistently recorded over time and are largely nonexistent in any systematic fashion prior to the twentieth century. Eisner (2001, 2008) has assembled the most comprehensive collection of homicide rate estimates as part of his History of Violence Database. Drawing from Eisner's published data (2001, 629), figure 2.1 displays long-term homicide rate trends for selected European regions and nations. Homicide rates were quite high in the thirteenth and fourteenth centuries, but declined substantially from then until the seventeenth century, and then generally continued to decline more gradually from that point through the middle part of the twentieth century. A variety of arguments have been put forth to explain these trends. Some of the observed long-term decline, of course, is likely due to advances in medical technologies that limited the lethality of assaults or other interpersonal conflicts (e.g., Spierenburg 1996). Aside from this, however, most historians suggest that the magnitude of declines in homicide observed over this period were far greater than one would expect if merely medical advancements were responsible. Some scholars attribute the residual

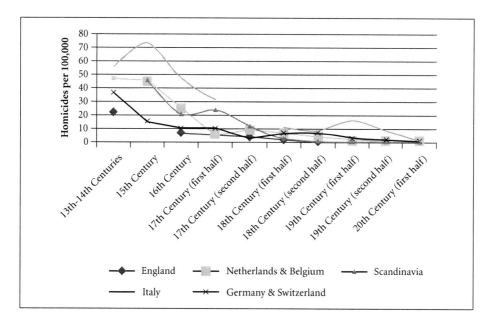

Figure 2.1. Estimated Long-Term Homicide Trends in Selected European Nations, 13th Century–Mid-20th Century.

declines to a process by which levels of internal and external social control increased and aggression lessened generally (e.g., Oestreich 1968, 1982; Gurr 1981; Spierenburg 1996), while others point to a related rise in moral individualism that lessened the incidence of retributive violence in particular (Eisner 2001).

Comparatively little is known about the volume of homicide in America prior to the twentieth century. Lane (1997) suggests that murder rates were relatively low in Colonial America and during the Early Republic years, but estimates reported by Roth (2009) indicate significant variation across this period, with very high rates of homicide during the first three decades of the seventeenth century followed by quickly falling and ultimately much lower rates. Homicide rates in several European nations appear to have fallen to approximately 5 per 100,000 by the early nineteenth century. Some estimates for parts of the United States during that period are roughly comparable, but there are very few estimates of homicide offending rates for this period. Most of the available evidence comes in the form of homicide arrests or indictments, which contain an unknown amount of error for estimating homicide offending rates (e.g., Lane 1979; Gurr 1981). Still, the best available information suggests that, aside from the early decades of the seventeenth century, rates of homicide in Colonial America and into the turn of the nineteenth century were relatively low by contemporary American standards, which Lane (1997, 66) attributes primarily to high levels of prosperity, full employment, and strong doses of collective regulation in public spaces.

More is known about homicide offending trends in America from the nineteenth century on than there is known about actual levels. Though it is difficult to discern a clear picture of homicide trends for the first half of the nineteenth century and there is important variation across places (Roth 2009), evidence reviewed by Gurr (1981), Lane (1997), and Monkkonen (2001, 2005) points to relatively stable and possibly declining homicide rates during this period, interrupted by significant spikes in lethal violence around the time of the American Civil War. This is seen in figure 2.2, which summarizes data on homicide trends for New York City from the beginning of the eighteenth century to the middle of the twentieth century, and Chicago and the United States as a whole for a shorter portion of this period. Monkkonen shows comparable data for Los Angeles dating back to the early nineteenth century, which exhibited a significant increase in homicide during the 1850s and 1860s (2005, 172, fig. 2.1). Data on arrests and indictments also show similar trends during the Antebellum and Civil War eras for other areas too, including Suffolk County and Boston (Gurr, 1981). Most observers have pointed to a "U-shaped" trajectory in homicide rates in America from the post–Civil War period through the late 1920s, a pattern also noticeable in figure 2.2. The quality and breadth of data on American homicide trends increased significantly with the creation of the Uniform Crime Reporting (UCR) program in the early 1930s. Based on these data and other records from selected cities, figure 2.2 shows that there was a steady decline in homicide rates between approximately 1930 and the late 1950s (see also McDowall and Loftin 2005).

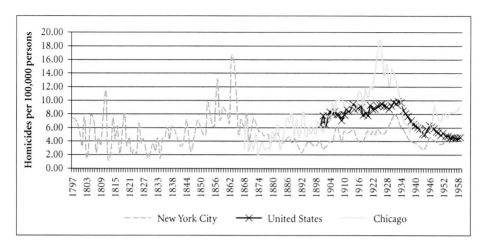

Figure 2.2. Long-Term Homicide Trends in the U.S. and Selected Areas
Source: Monkkonen 2001b.

Historians who attend to the mid-nineteenth-century rise in lethal violence in some American communities generally point to the birth of the revolver, heavy immigration to the United States, major growth in cities, and rising anxieties that ultimately coalesced into the Civil War (Gurr 1981; Lane 1997). The significant and roughly fifty-year decline in lethal violence in America that follows has been attributed by Lane to fundamental economic and social changes associated with the urban industrial revolution (1997, 184–86). In particular, he suggests that the major economic transformations that occurred during this period translated into a more disciplined population, "increasing sobriety," and "regular, predictable, cooperative behavior." In essence, murder rates fell as the American population "grew less free-swinging and more sober, regimented, and introspective." The thin amount of attention devoted to crime trends during the early part of the twentieth century is disappointing, and the literature thus provides little by way of explanation (e.g., Gurr 1981). Lane (1997) expresses some skepticism about the existence of a significant rise in violence during this period, noting that observed increases are probably to some extent confounded with changes in and expansions of recording practices. Nonetheless, Lane acknowledges that there was a notable rise in gun use in homicides during this period, and he makes indirect linkages of this trend to the proliferation of organized crime and social upheavals of those years.

The empirical record is notably clearer for crime trends during the contemporary era, defined here as approximately 1960 and beyond. We not only have more comprehensive official records on homicides and other crimes in several nations, but also for the most recent few decades, some data on crime trends based on victim reports to provide additional insights. The two most general trends that emerge

from these data on crime trends in the contemporary era are (1) there was a significant increase in crime, especially lethal violence, that emerged in the early 1960s
and continued through the end of the 1970s in the United States and the mid-1990s
in many European nations; and (2) there have been significant decreases in most
forms of street crime in many nations since the early to mid-1990s.

Figures 2.3 and 2.4 depict this pattern visually for several European nations.
Figure 2.3 draws from Eisner's (2008) History of Violence Database and shows
average homicide rates by decade from the 1960s through the first half of the 2000s.
Figure 2.4 displays estimated rates of overall victimization from the first five sweeps
of the International Crime Victimization Survey (ICVS), a period that spans the late
1980s through the mid-2000s.

The story is slightly more complicated in the United States, but the same general
pattern shown for Europe of significant increases in crime rates starting in the early
1960s, and significant declines beginning in the early to mid-1990s, holds. Figure 2.5
shows homicide rate trends for America from 1960 to 2008 as recorded by law
enforcement agencies in the Uniform Crime Reporting (UCR) program. Figure 2.6
shows UCR trends for violent and property crime for the same period, as well as
roughly comparable data from the annual victimization surveys that were first
fielded on a national scale in this country in the early 1970s (i.e., the National Crime
Survey 1973–1991 and the National Crime Victimization Survey 1992–2008).

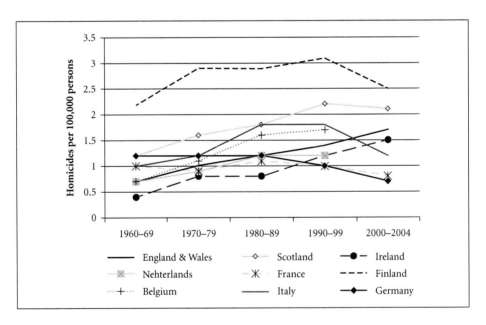

Figure 2.3. Homicide Trends in Selected European Nations,
1960–2004
Source: Eisner 2008, Figure 3.

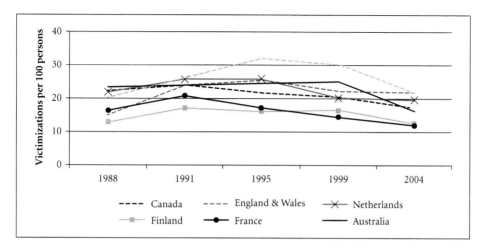

Figure 2.4. Overall Victimization Trends for Selected Nations,
ICVS 1988–2004.
Source: van Kesteren 2008.

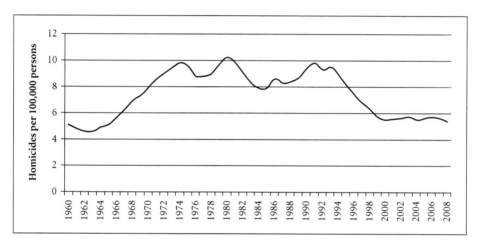

Figure 2.5. U.S. Trends in UCR Homicide Rates, 1960–2008
Source: Bureau of Justice Statistics 2010*b*.

Detailed assessments of the UCR trends confirm that there were substantial increases in violence and property crime in America from the early 1960s through the mid-1970s, and significant declines from the early 1990s through at least the early years of the 2000s. But the increase in UCR crime rates in the latter part of the 1970s and 1980s evident in figure 2.6 is confounded somewhat by changes in police recording practices, and careful assessments of this period suggest that the increases in violent crime that began in the 1960s slowed considerably and, for property

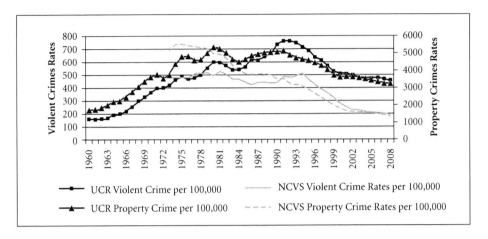

Figure 2.6. US Trends in Violent and Property Crime Rates, 1960–2008

Source: Bureau of Justice Statistics 2010a.

crime, clearly did not continue during this period (see Jencks 1991; O'Brien 2003). Some notable exceptions to this, though, are the noticeable short-term fluctuations such as a significant spike in youth homicide, robbery, and gun crimes from the mid-1980s through the early 1990s (Blumstein and Wallman 2006).

Observers of US trends during the contemporary era have tended to offer short-run "period-specific" explanations, attributing the rise in violence in the 1960s and 1970s to an increase in the size of youth cohorts and a decline in institutional legitimacy; the rise in youth homicide in the mid- to late 1980s primarily to the emergence and proliferation of crack cocaine use and marketing; and highlighting the potential casual role of numerous factors for the more widespread crime decline that began in the early 1990s, with special prominence to increased use of incarceration, shifts in policing, and economic expansion. Those who have studied crime trends more broadly tend to offer up more integrative explanations for post-1960 crime increases, which include some of the factors highlighted in the American case (e.g., demographic factors), but also point to broader cultural components (Fukuyama 1999; Eisner 2003, 2008; Thome and Birkel 2007). These scholars acknowledge the important demographic shifts that yielded larger cohorts of people in high-crime age groups, but also suggest that the 1960s signaled a cultural shift in Western societies characterized by increased individualism, egoism, reduced self-constraint, and weakened external social bonds, all of which increased the tendency for violent forms of self-expression. The more recent countertrend of declining homicide observed since the early to mid-1990s is viewed by at least some as evidence of cultural shifts away from these features (e.g., Eisner 2008).

There are four major patterns in terms of crime trends during the past several centuries:

- Long-term decline in lethal violence in several European regions occurred from approximately the thirteenth through the mid-twentieth century. It has been attributed largely to increasing forms of civility and regulation of individuals, public spaces, and situations that are conducive to violence.
- General decline in lethal violence occurred in America during the nineteenth century and first half of the twentieth century with two notable countertrends: increases in the 1850s and 1860s, and increases during the first two decades of the 1900s. The former has been associated with the rise of the urban industrial revolution in America and the discipline it brought to people's lives; the two noted significant departures from this downward trend in violence have been associated with heavy doses of immigration and rapid social change that disrupted life in major urban centers.
- Increases in violence occurred beginning in the 1960s were gradual and fairly consistent in much of Europe through the early 1990s. Increases were sharper initially in America but also shorter-lived, reaching a plateau in the mid- to late 1970s and fluctuating in the 1980s with a steep increase in youth violence during the latter half of the decade. The abrupt increases in violence observed in many societies in the 1960s has been attributed to demographic shifts that yielded substantial increases in young persons, and to cultural changes that translated into increased individualism, declining institutional legitimacy, and reduced social controls.
- General and widespread decline in many forms of street crime has occurred in both America and Europe during the 1990s and at least part of the 2000s. It has been linked theoretically to a large number of factors, which empirical research has yet to sort through in terms of causal prominence.

In this chapter, I put some of the trends just summarized in proper context by laying out key methodological considerations. I then describe in more detail what we know in terms of the description and explanation of historical and contemporary crime trends, closing with some comments on the most pertinent needs for future knowledge.

In section I, I discuss key methodological issues that are germane to understanding some of the parameters for developing a sound knowledge base on temporal crime patterns. It might appear simple enough to count the number of crimes, convert them to a meaningful rate, and record such information over time, but in reality there are a host of impediments to doing so and some important considerations in how this has been and is done need to be kept in mind, even for purposes of simply describing how crime has changed over a specified time frame in a given place. The complexities multiply further when we move from *description* of crime trends (section IA) to the *explanation* of crime trends (section IB). Issues of theoretical and empirical specification, measurement properties, and statistical modeling choices emerge as important for shaping the conclusions we draw, and so some attention to those issues is vital for forming a clear portrait of what we know about crime trends. After describing key considerations in the development of a sound body of knowledge on crime trends, I survey in section II the landscape of what we currently know, focusing initially on the description and explanation of crime trends in the United States and elsewhere through the late 1950s (sections IIA and IIB), then addressing comparable themes since that time, which I label as the "contemporary period" (sections IIC and IID).

A final matter that warrants some attention concerns the *forecasting* of crime trends. From a policy standpoint, there is clearly some value to describing and explaining current and/or past crime trends, but that value presumably pales in comparison to valid and reliable information on the anticipated future direction of crime trends. Yet, there is relatively little by way of a serious program of research on crime forecasting in America or elsewhere. In the concluding section of the chapter, I outline some of the problems and prospects for moving in that direction in future research.

I. Key Issues

If we waited for error-free data we would not get very far in describing and explaining crime trends. There are several pertinent issues to bear in mind.

A. Methodological Considerations

Others have written at length about the validity and reliability of crime rate estimates and other important methodological considerations in describing, explaining, and forecasting crime (e.g., O'Brien 1985; Lane 1997; Cantor and Lynch 2000; Monkkonon 2001a; Eisner 2001, 2003; Baumer 2008; Goldberger and Rosenfeld 2008). Comprehensive introductions to the key issues can be found in those sources, but some general comments are in order here because they help to orient the discussion of past research and needed future research that follows.

Describing crime trends accurately requires full information on the number of crimes that have occurred across multiple times and on the population at risk for crime during those periods. Developing good estimates of these components of crime rates has proven challenging in historical research, especially in work geared toward estimating crime trends before the twentieth century. Such research often has had to rely on incomplete and disconnected historical records of various sorts (e.g., coroner's reports, court records, other government documents) that lack uniformity not only in how crime is defined but how both crime and people are counted across time and place (see also Spierenburg 1996; Lane

1997). These data challenges have limited historical research on crime trends largely to homicide, but from careful assessments and comparisons by historians we now have well-organized quantitative data from which to draw inferences about long-term trajectories in violence across multiple nations. These include the *History of Homicide Database* (Eisner 2003), which provides excellent coverage across many nations, and the *Historical Violence Database*, which also has a broad geographic reach but is particularly useful for tracking historical homicide rates for America (Roth et al. 2008). Although one cannot do much by way of retrospectively assessing the validity and reliability of the homicide estimates contained in such composite databases, the availability of multiple sources of data for proximate nations during the same period provides some protection against drawing erroneous inferences about trends that merely represent shifts in data reporting or recording.

Describing crime trends from the early part of the twentieth century on has been less troublesome, but it is still not without problems. The two main sources for America are the Uniform Crime Reports (UCR) and the National Vital Statistics System (NVSS). The UCR program was established in 1930 and has consistently collected from several thousand local police agencies data on crimes known to the police and arrests made by the police. Some notable strengths of the UCR data are that they provide information about the volume of crime and arrests across time for both lethal and nonlethal crimes, and they can be used to generate data for the nation as a whole and for various sub-national areas (e.g., states, counties, and cities). There is a well-noted limitation that UCR data include information only on crimes that come to the attention of the police and crimes and arrests that are recorded by the police. Importantly, there is some evidence that both citizen reporting and police recording rates have changed over time (e.g., O'Brien 1996, 2003; Baumer and Lauritsen 2010), which incorporate temporal patterns that are important to keep in mind when interpreting observed changes in crime rate trends. Some additional considerations in using the UCR to study long-term crime trends point to changes in data collection methods in the late 1950s, which altered the comparability of the data with prior periods (OMB 1974), and there were also declining participation rates among local law enforcement agencies during the last few decades of the twentieth century with the emergence of the National Incident Based Reporting System (NIBRS) (Maltz 1999). The other major source of long-term American crime trends in the United States is the NVSS. This data source is limited to lethal violence, but it also provides data at the national and local (county) levels. This source has been in place since 1900, although during the first three decades of the twentieth century the geographic coverage was spotty, and complete coverage of the nation was not established until the early 1930s (Eckberg 1995).

More recently these data sources have been supplemented by the Supplementary Homicide Reports (SHRs) and the National Crime Surveys (referred to as the National Crime Survey prior to 1992 and the National Crime Victimization Survey

[NCVS] from 1992 on). Both were fully implemented by the early to mid-1970s (O'Brien 1985; Riedel 1990), so their relevance to crime trends is limited to the past four decades. The SHR is further restricted to homicides, as its name implies, but it is a significant extension of the UCR homicide data because it provides detailed information on the age, race, and sex of disputants and the circumstances associated with the homicide incident, features that permit a more precise analysis of trends in lethal violence in America. Like the UCR more generally, SHR data can be used to yield estimates of homicide both for that nation as a whole and for sub-areas—states, counties, and cities. The NCVS is limited primarily to national estimates for the most part (but see Lauritsen and Schaum 2005). However, it provides data on trends in rates of nonlethal violence that can be disaggregated by age, race, sex, and a variety of other attributes of victims and offenders (Cantor and Lynch 2000).

Data on crime trends outside America during the past century is much more varied in terms of quality and temporal coverage. Differences across nations in data recording by officials charged with counting crimes have restricted most of the large-scale data collection efforts and the resulting research to homicide, a crime for which there is less variability in definitions and recording practices. Four often cited composite sources of data on international crime trends are (1) the World Health Organization (WHO), (2) the International Police Organization (Interpol), (3) United Nations Survey of Crime Trends and Operations of Criminal Justice Systems (UNCS), and (4) the European Sourcebook of Crime and Criminal Justice Statistics. These sources vary in the nations and time frames covered, in addition to the specific content (e.g., crimes) they include. In depth overviews on the advantages and disadvantages of these sources can be found in Neapolitan (1997), Marshall and Block (2004), and Stamatel (2006). In general, most of the cross-national and international research on crime trends during the past century has relied either on the WHO data on homicide mortality (e.g., LaFree and Tseloni 2006), integrated sources such as the *History of Violence Database* (Eisner 2008) and the *International Homicide Index* (Marshall and Block 2004), or localized sources for a single or small group of specific nations (e.g., Spierenburg 1996; Finch 2001; O'Donnell 2005; Roberts and LaFree 2005; Pridemore and Chamlin 2006; Johnson 2008; McAra 2008; Savolainen, Lehti, and Kivivuori 2008; Rosenfeld and Messner 2009).

As in the United States, during the last few decades of the twentieth century the available official data on crime trends increasingly was supplemented by victimization data. Major initiatives such as the British Crime Survey (BCS), the Canadian National Survey on Criminal Victimization, and the International Crime Victimization Survey (ICVS) were initiated during the 1980s and now provide periodic victim-based estimates of trends in nonlethal crimes across much of Europe and selected other parts of the world. Like the NCVS, these sources tend to provide considerably more detail than official sources on crime trends disaggregated by victim, offender, and incident attributes.

B. Methodological Considerations

Most descriptions of crime trends in America and elsewhere tend to agree on the basic trajectories that crime has taken during the past several centuries, at least with respect to major swings that likely reflect significant change in the volume of crime and not just minor fluctuations due to shifts in recording practices or other methodological nuisances. There is much less consensus, or at least certainty, in explaining these major crime shifts. In part this is because the data and nonexperimental methods at our disposal for addressing the subject are highly imperfect. But, beyond these realities, there are some notable features of the research literature on crime trends that operate as impediments.

Three significant obstacles to forming more definitive explanations of crime trends are (1) the body of relevant research is relatively small, (2) the typical focus of individual studies tends to be relatively narrow, and (3) there is a lack of uniformity in data, specifications, and methods. While the latter two problems are common features of research literatures in many areas of criminology, in the area of crime-trends research they are compounded by the first problem. Variability in approaches and foci across studies can sometimes yield good outcomes, most notably a body of research that forms a whole from different types of data and efforts, and points to general conclusions that, despite notable exceptions, fit the key observations. But when the body of work is relatively small, as is the literature on crime trends, this is less likely to occur. Indeed, the literature on crime trends tends to focus on a limited set of potential causal variables while other potentially relevant factors are often omitted, and there has been significant variability in approaches across a small body of research. The geographic areas sampled, time periods covered, control variables included, and statistical methods employed differ across studies, in research both on cross-national and American crime trends. The end result is that the pertinent literature can be read as providing support for just about all the hypothesized explanations for changes in crime rates during a given period if we relax our expectations for empirical and theoretical specifications—or none of them if we keep the bar high.

II. EXISTING KNOWLEDGE

The literature on crime trends diverges in meaningful ways depending on whether the focus is on historical or contemporary crime patterns. The state of knowledge also diverges within both historical and contemporary focused research on both *descriptions* and *explanations* of those trends.

A. Historical Trends

There appears to be a general consensus that there has been a significant long-term decline in lethal violence and perhaps other crimes worldwide over the past several centuries, through approximately the mid-twentieth century (Gurr 1981; Spieren-burg 1996; Lane 1997; Eisner 2001, 2003). Eisner (2003, 2008) provides comprehensive overviews of long-term homicide trends for several European regions, dating back to the thirteenth century for England, and the sixteenth and seventeenth centuries for other regions. Eisner's analysis reveals a high degree of support for there being a long-term decrease in lethal violence from medieval times through the middle of the twentieth century. However, Eisner also highlights some notable fluctuations. Among other things, there were significant spikes in homicide in some regions in the late sixteenth century and again in the late eighteenth century; the magnitude of the decline occurred later and was less steep in some places (e.g., Italy), and not all nations—most notably, Finland—exhibited the familiar long-term homicide decline (see also LaFree and Drass 2001; Savolainen, Lehti, and Kivivuori 2008).

The historical record in America is much shorter, but it is nonetheless fragmentary. Roth (2009) documents very high homicide rates in many corners of America during the first three decades of the 1600s. After this period, however, Lane (1997) pieces together some persuasive evidence that points to three major trends in homicide from America's earliest days through the middle of the twentieth century. First, he notes that murder rates declined through much of the seventeenth and eighteenth centuries as America began to mature and claimed its independence. Indeed, it appears that homicide rates in America declined much as they did elsewhere during this period, a decline that stretched well into the early part of the nineteenth century. Yet, a second pattern Lane (1997) documents is a significant reversal of this trend from the early 1830s until the early to mid-1860s. As Lane (1997, 92) summarized, during the so-called antebellum era in America "the homicide rate rose markedly . . . [making this period] . . . the most disorderly and bloodiest in our history." A third dimension of Lane's (1997) account of the historical record of homicide in America reveals that after the Civil War, homicide rates began to decline steadily and, he argues, continued to decline with an occasional fluctuation to the contrary for nearly a century, through the mid- to late 1950s. More recent historical research in select American cities generally affirms Lane's claims of a significant spike in homicide rates during the antebellum period but paints a somewhat different portrait of homicide trends during the early decades of the twentieth century. Adler's (2001) research in Chicago and Monkkonon's (2001a, 2005) studies in New York City and Los Angeles suggest some notable, albeit short-term, spikes in lethal violence during this period. Most sources agree, nonetheless, that homicide rates declined significantly from approximately the mid-1930s through the late 1950s (see also McDowall and Loftin 2005).

B. Explaining Historical Trends

The descriptions of historical crime trends raise several provocative questions about potential *explanations*. For instance, why were levels of homicide relatively high in many parts of Europe in the fourteenth and fifteenth centuries? Why has there been a steady, even if occasionally interrupted, long-term decline in lethal criminal violence over the past several centuries since then? What can explain the significant shorter-term spikes in homicide experienced in some nations, most notably in major European centers in the late sixteenth century and late eighteenth century, and the sharp rise in homicide in America in the middle of the nineteenth century? Finally, how can we account for some of the outliers to the general conclusion of a long-term move toward lower levels of homicide during the past few centuries, such as Finland, which experienced relatively flat rates during the eighteenth and nineteenth centuries and very large increases during the early decades of the twentieth century?

A modest but engaging literature has grappled with these questions, but the inherent nature of retrospective historical accounts makes it difficult to arrive at definitive answers (Lane 1997). Eisner (2001) provides an especially vivid overview of explanations that have been given for the long-term decline in homicide observed in many parts of Europe from approximately the fourteenth century on (see also Monkkonon 2005). Most observers point to advances in medical technologies as likely playing a key role in reducing the lethality of interpersonal conflicts, though precise estimates have not been proposed and few consider this to explain the bulk of the observed declines. Instead, a common explanation borrows from Norbert Elias's (1978) concept of the "civilizing process," arguing that broad cultural and social processes were at work, which created more civilized populations with greater self-control and who were less apt to resort to violence to resolve conflicts (e.g., Gurr 1981; Spierenburg 1996). Other popular explanations suggest that increasing formal and informal social controls led to greater regulations of and on individuals (Oestreich 1968, 1982) or that shifts in social solidarity were key (Roth 2009). Finally, Eisner (2001, 632–33) integrates insights from Durkheim to sketch out an additional explanation, namely that the long-term decline in homicide observed in much of Europe, especially from the seventeenth century on, might reflect "a liberation of the individual from collective obligations . . . and a rise in moral individualism" which may have in turn reduced retributive violence often associated with maintaining group-based honor codes.

Most discussions of long-term crime trends have focused on the gradual multicentury secular decline in homicide across Europe, but some attention also has been given to narrower periods and interesting fluctuations around the trend. Commenting on the widespread declines in homicide from approximately 1850–1950, Eisner (2008, 303) favors an explanation in which culture "assumes a leading role." He suggests that, during this period, there was a "diffusion, throughout

Europe, of a cultural model of the conduct of life . . . [that included] . . . three main elements: an emphasis on *self-control* as an ideal of personality; *domesticity and familialism* as guidelines for private life; and *respectability* as the yardstick for public appearance." Explanations also have been offered for exceptions to the rule. For example, Finland has long been discussed as an outlier in European homicide trends, especially during the late nineteenth and early twentieth century period when homicide rates increased threefold in the small Scandinavian nation while rates fell consistently elsewhere on the Continent (LaFree and Drass 2001). Savolainen et al. (2008, 76) suggest that this divergent trend in Finland was due to unique and abrupt economic shifts in the nation. The combination of a strong demand for ships and Finland's ability to provide necessary raw materials to meet it (e.g., lumber and tar) translated into "a labor market that created communities with large concentrations of able-bodied young men employed as lumberjacks." This imbalanced sex-ratio, Savolainen et al. argue, coupled with an ample supply of alcohol, yielded significant increases in lethal violence.

Less attention has been given to long-term violence trends in America and, specifically, the apparent decline in homicide from the Colonial era through the early decades of the nineteenth century, the sharp rise in homicide rates during the antebellum period, and the steady decline in homicide from the Reconstruction era to the late 1950s. But some persuasive explanations have been put forth in each case. Lane (1997, 66) notes that while in some ways Colonial America had characteristics that might conduce to high levels of violence, it was also characterized by prosperity, full employment, and rapid growth, all of which served to regulate interpersonal contacts in public spaces and kept the murder rate low and declining. He echoes a similar theme when speculating about the reasons for the approximately century-long decline in homicide that began in the aftermath of the American Civil War. As for the sharp increase in homicide sandwiched between these periods, Lane notes that, while it is difficult to discern clear causal associations from the historical record, levels of crime and homicide in America rose for about two decades starting in about 1840, a trend characterized by the birth of the revolver, heavy immigration to the United States, major growth in cities, and political tensions that ultimately coalesced into the Civil War. The scant attention devoted to crime trends during the early part of the twentieth century is disappointing, and the literature thus provides little by way of explanation (e.g., Gurr 1981). Again, Lane (1997) suggests that where lethal violence did increase during this period, it is likely related to a notable rise in gun use in violent incidents, and he also posits indirect links to the proliferation of organized crime and social upheavals of the period.

Overall, historical research on crime trends has generated some rich descriptions of long-term outcomes across distinct periods and socio-cultural contexts. The historical record and this research provides an immensely important backdrop for contemporary studies.

C. Contemporary Trends

In the period after 1960, much better information is available. There appears to be general agreement that the long-term decline in homicide in much of Europe and the general decline in homicide observed in America since the Reconstruction era, with especially sharp declines during the 1940s and 1950s, had reversed by the late 1950s and early 1960s. With some notable exceptions (i.e., Japan, Finland), the evidence points to relatively uniform increases in lethal criminal violence across a wide variety of nations from the early 1960s through the early 1990s (LaFree 1998; Hicks and Allen 1999; Monkkonon 2001a, 2005; LaFree 2005; Thome and Birkel 2007; Eisner 2008). LaFree and Drass (2002) document that many nations experienced crime booms during this period, while rates in others were less consistent but generally headed upward. In America there was an abrupt and lengthy increase in all major forms of serious violent and property crime from the mid-1960s through the late 1970s (LaFree 1998). This trend was followed by a significant reduction in most forms of crime during the first half of the 1980s and a comparable and significant increase in most forms of crime (save for adult homicide and burglary, which continued to decline) between the mid-1980s and early 1990s, especially youth homicide, robbery, and motor vehicle theft, which resumed their upward trend alongside the emergence and proliferation of crack-cocaine beginning in the mid-1980s and extending through the early 1990s (Blumstein 1995; Baumer et al. 1998; McDowall and Loftin 2005; Blumstein and Wallman 2006; Rosenfeld and Goldberger 2008). Comparisons of police-based and victim-based data during this period suggest that a portion of the noted increase during the 1980s in police-derived measures of nonlethal violence and property crime was due to enhanced reporting of crimes to the police by citizens (Baumer and Lauritsen, 2010) and increased crime recording by police (O'Brien 2003). But trends in rates of serious violence clearly paralleled the significant rise in homicide during the mid- to late 1980s, and viewing police-based and victimization data together show that this cannot be easily dismissed merely as an artifact of crime reporting and recording changes (Rand, Lynch, and Cantor 1997).

Eisner (2008) shows similar trends for more than a dozen European nations, which affirms his earlier conclusion that the available evidence indicates that "all European countries (with the exception of Finland) have experienced a period of unbroken increase in homicide rates between the early 1960s and mid-1990s" (Eisner 2001, 630). In Finland, there were abrupt increases in the late 1960s and the 1970s, but relatively stable rates from then until the mid-1990s (Savolainen, Lehti, and Kivivuori 2008). There is additional evidence that, in several European nations, after at least a century of exceptionally low levels, police-recorded robberies increased substantially from the early 1960s through the early to mid-1990s (Eisner 2008, 306). Victim-based survey data on crime were not available for most European nations until the tail end of this period (e.g., the late 1980s), but the longest-standing such survey (the British Crime Survey, first fielded in 1982) indicates that in England and Wales crime rates rose steadily from the early 1980s through the early 1990s (Walker et al. 2009). There was one clear exception to the noted pattern, though. There is consensus that Japan bucked the general trend of significantly escalating homicide rates between 1960 and the early 1990s: homicide (and robbery) fell dramatically in that country (Roberts and LaFree 2005; Johnson 2008).

In the aftermath of the significant rise in youth homicide and overall rates of robbery and motor vehicle theft during the late 1980s and early 1990s in America, some observers began to warn of an impending "blood bath" and flood of "super-predators" that would soon hit the streets (Dilulio 1996; Fox 1996). What had already commenced in the United States, however, was the start of what would a decade later be dubbed "The Great American Crime Decline" (Zimring 2006). From the early 1990s through at least the early part of the 2000s, rates of all seven "index crimes" routinely tracked by the police in America (homicide, rape, robbery, assault, burglary, larceny, and auto theft) dropped significantly, on the order of 25–40 percent depending on the crime in question (Zimring 2006). Data from the NCVS reveal even greater declines in nonlethal violence and property crime during this period.

Many US scholars, however, overlooked that the significant downturn in crime during the 1990s did not occur only in America (Zimring 2006; van Dijk 2007; van Dijk, van Kesteren and Smit 2007; Eisner 2008; Rosenfeld and Messner 2009; Walker et al. 2009). Zimring (2006) highlights that Canada experienced declines of most forms of crime during the 1990s that paralleled those in the United States. Several sources indicate significant crime declines in many European nations as well, though perhaps with a somewhat later starting point. Walker et al. (2009) illustrate with data from the BCS that in England and Wales most forms of serious crime as reported by survey respondents have fallen by 40 percent since 1995. Data from the ICVS reveal a similar pattern for the dozen or so nations for which a continuous series has been collected since the late 1980s (van Dijk 2007; van Kesteren and Smit 2007). There are comparatively fewer analyses of cross-national trends in police-recorded data, but Barclay and Tavares (2003) revealed significant declines in police-based burglary and motor vehicle theft rates for several European nations. Additionally, Eisner's (2008, 310–11) data on homicide indicate that since the early 1990s "homicide rates in most European countries have been falling, in some cases quite dramatically." Eisner singles out significant drops in homicide from the early 1990s on in Austria, Germany, Italy, France, Switzerland, and Portugal. Mouzos (2003) adds Australia to the mix as well, documenting that homicide rates fell by about 43 percent from the early 1990s through the middle of the 2000s. While there were certainly exceptions—e.g., crime rates in Japan (Roberts and LaFree 2005) and Finland (Lehti and Kivivuori 2005, and homicide rates in the United Kingdom and Ireland (Eisner 2008)—there appears to have been a fairly broad decline in crime from the early 1990s on that occurred across several continents and was relatively large in magnitude.

Depending on how you look at it, or perhaps from where you look at it, the decade of the 2000s has been either a continuation of the 1990s with respect to prevailing crime trends or a largely uneventful decade with crime rates holding steady with a few temporary notable shifts. In the United States, the significant crime declines observed in the 1990s appeared to have leveled off during the early years of the 2000s, though crime continued to decline in some major US cities for several years beyond this point and rose temporarily around mid-decade in others (Police Executive Research Forum 2006, 2007). Overall, the conclusion that best fits with the data on crime trends during the 2000s is that they have been relatively flat for the most part (Rosenfeld and Oliver 2008). A similar pattern is evident in England and Wales during the 2000s, where crime rates continue to decline for the early part of the decade and then stabilized and remained relatively flat (Walker et al. 2009; Smith et al. 2010). Crime trends in other nations for the 2000s are more difficult to pin down and piece together, but when data from the 2004/2005 ICVS are lined up with previous installments of this survey, they paint a picture of crime trends during the first half of the 2000s for a wide range of nations that looks much like the trends observed in the United States and in England and Wales (van Dijk, van Kesteren, and Smit 2008).

D. Explaining Contemporary Trends

At least three perplexing questions emerge from the observed crime trends in America and elsewhere during the contemporary era: Why did crime rates, and especially homicide rates, increase so substantially in many societies from approximately the early 1960s through the early 1990s? What can explain the widespread decline in most forms of serious crime beginning in the early to mid-1990s and extending well into the 2000s? What are we to make of the relatively flat crime rate trends in the 2000s, a period dubbed by one American news magazine as the "Decade from Hell" (Serwer 2009) and, by many measures, an era filled with forces often considered to customarily yield important shifts in crime (e.g., abrupt increases in unemployment, mass layoffs, unprecedented levels of home foreclosure, a global economic recession, severely dampened consumer sentiment)? The second question has attracted the greatest attention from the scholarly and policy communities because it emerged during a time when more than just a few scholars were studying crime trends. The first question has yielded a great deal of persuasive speculation but has proved to be something of a mystery. We are only beginning to grapple with the third question.

1. *The Early 1960s through the Early 1990s*

Those who have attempted to offer up explanations for the significant increase in serious crime that began in the early 1960s have approached the matter in two distinct ways. Some have taken a broad vantage point and, despite some noticeable fluctuations in crime trends between the early 1960s and early 1990s, have focused on the general upward trend and have posed general explanations for that pattern (e.g., Eisner 2003, 2008). Others, and especially those evaluating American crime trends, have taken a more segmented approach, breaking the period in question into two distinct eras—roughly the twelve- to fifteen-year period starting in the early 1960s and ending in the mid- to late 1970s, and then the crack cocaine era, which stretched from about 1986 to 1992 (e.g., LaFree 1998). Not surprisingly, the different approaches have emphasized divergent forces.

Several studies of US post–World War II crime rates have focused on specific variables (such as unemployment rates, inequality, and related economic indicators; incarceration rates; and the quantity and quality of youth cohorts) rather than on testing or proposing a general theoretical explanation (e.g., Cantor and Land 1985; Cook and Zarkin 1985; Marvell and Moody 1994; LaFree and Drass 1996; O'Brien, Stockard, and Isaacson 1999; Messner, Raffalovich, and McMillian 2001; Arvanites and Defina 2006; Spelman 2008). This research has tended to focus on the post–World War II period, in general, rather than on the increases of the 1960s and 1970s specifically. The collective findings from this research are variable and contingent on empirical specification and other study design features (e.g., unit of analysis, temporal period covered, and methods used). Good overviews can be found in LaFree (1998), Greenberg (2001), Stemen (2007), and Rosenfeld (2009).

Although few would question that the upturn in crime rates in America during the 1960s and 1970s was a major turning point in the volume of crime experienced in the United States, there has been a disappointingly small amount of systematic empirical research directed at explaining it. What has been done suggests that changes in age structure were one significant factor in the rise in crime during the 1960s and 1970s. Crime is disproportionately committed by teenagers and young adults (e.g., those fifteen to twenty-nine), so it stands to reason that where there are more of that age cohort, higher crime rates will follow for purely demographic reasons as long as rates of offending for subsequent cohorts do not decline over time. Available evidence suggests that age structure shifts accounted for one-fifth to one-half of the observed increase in crime in America (see Sagi and Wellford 1968; Cohen and Land 1987; Marvell and Moody 1991; Levitt 1999), though an important limitation of this research is that it makes untested assumptions about cohort-specific offending rates.

In any event, there is also persuasive evidence that the dramatic increase in American crime rates during the 1960s and 1970s reflected more than simply demographic change; crime rates among both youthful and older cohorts increased during the 1960s and 1970s (LaFree 1998), suggesting that something about this period provided a social context more conducive to crime than was the case earlier in the twentieth century. Cohen and Felson (1979) make a compelling case that among the key elements of the shifting social context in America during this time was a substantial movement in various technological advances, coupled with daily activities away from the home, both of which yielded more plentiful and more attractive opportunities for crime. Others have pointed to the limited economic opportunities and the rise of an underclass (e.g., Greenberg 1977; Murray 1994).

LaFree (1998) acknowledges these factors but also argues that a decline in the legitimacy of several key social institutions may have been especially instrumental in driving the observed increases in American crime rates in the 1960s and 1970s. More specifically, LaFree (1998) suggests that growing distrust of government, rising inflation and inequality, and the breakdown of traditional family forms worked to both increase motivations for criminal behavior and to reduce levels of social control over such impulses. LaFree provides a good dose of persuasive data to support these claims.

A general conclusion that emerges from research on American crime trends during the 1960s and 1970s, however, is that it is difficult to draw definitive inferences from the available evidence because the body of empirical research directly relevant is thin and not very strong from the standpoint of identifying the specific causal role that given factors may have played.

There was a comparatively greater volume of research directed at American crime trends in the 1980s and early 1990s, and some consensus about why youth violence—especially homicides and robberies committed with firearms—increased sharply during this period. The emergence and proliferation of a crack cocaine epidemic was a major social phenomenon in the United States during this era (Blumstein and Wallman 2006). There has long been a suspected link between crime rates and drug use and market activity, and given the coincidental timing of changes in youth violence and crack cocaine activity during the 1980s, many observers have attributed trends in the former to trends in the latter. Baumer et al. (1998) speculated, for example, that the psychopharmacological properties and low per unit cost of crack cocaine drove a persistent need for cash to support its use, which in turn led would-be property offenders increasingly to turn away from burglary to crimes such as robbery that tend to yield cash more quickly.

Focusing more on drug market dynamics, Blumstein (1995) argued that the emergence and proliferation of crack cocaine in many inner cities in the mid-1980s transformed drug markets in fundamental ways that ultimately stimulated and spread violence. Part of the crack market–violence link lies with the nature of crack cocaine distribution (i.e., a strong demand for it, a low per unit cost, and a high volume of transactions), but Blumstein suggests that the distinctive feature that made crack markets particularly violent in the late 1980s and early 1990s was their youthful age structure: as the demand for crack grew and the adult sellers who dominated markets were arrested and imprisoned, crack markets became staffed largely by young and inexperienced street sellers. As these teenage crack sellers armed themselves to manage the daily risks brought on by their jobs, so did other young people who also had to navigate the increasingly dangerous environments in which crack markets flourished. This fueled lethal firearm violence among young people in the late 1980s, says Blumstein, because the young persons in and around crack markets at that time were reckless and irresponsible (much more so than older folks), they lacked the necessary maturity and skills to resolve conflicts in nonphysical ways, and they used guns with little restraint (1995, 29–31).

Although it is difficult to measure drug use and drug market activity in aggregate research, and probably impossible to distinguish between these two dimensions of the drug scene, there is some persuasive evidence on the link between the prevalence of crack cocaine activity (i.e., crack use and crack market activity) and the rise in youth violence during the 1980s and early 1990s (e.g., Baumer et al. 1998; Blumstein and Rosenfeld 1998; Cork 1999; Ousey and Lee 2002, 2004). The relatively few studies that have examined the issue generally show that cities with higher levels and greater increases in crack use and market activity experienced larger increases in violence during the 1980s (e.g., Baumer et al. 1998; Cork 1999; Grogger and Willis 2000; Fryer et al. 2006).

Baumer (2008) criticizes this research for overlooking the potential significance of drug market "age structure" indicators and suggests the research might overstate the magnitude of the link between crack and violence during the 1980s, in general because it omits many other potentially important factors that changed over time and are thought to be connected to recent crime trends. Baumer's (2008) city-level analysis suggests that three indicators of illicit drug market activity and drug use (cocaine/heroin arrest rates, cocaine mortality rates, and the percent of cocaine arrests involving persons under age eighteen) account for between 20 and 40 percent of the observed increases in overall homicide, gun homicide, and youth homicide, and 10 percent of the increases in robbery rates between 1984 and 1992. His analysis also points to the relevance of other factors, though, that have not been given much weight in most discussions of crime trends during this period, such as the rise in cohabitation and changes in the prevalence of births to teenage mothers in an earlier period. Additionally, incarceration rates emerged as a primary significant contributor to the decline in burglary and adult homicide observed in America during the 1980s, accounting for more than half of the observed declines in both of these crimes (see also Blumstein and Rosenfeld 1998).

These arguments, however, cannot explain similar trends elsewhere. As in the United States, general increases in violence—especially robbery and homicides in public spaces involving male perpetrators who were not acquainted—began to occur in many European nations during the early 1960s and continued until the early 1990s (Eisner 2008). The shared nature of post–World War II crime increases has stimulated some integrative explanations that are comparable to perspectives applied to explain the American experience but which also include broader cultural components (Fukuyama 1999; Eisner 2003, 2008; Thome and Birkel 2007). Eisner (2008) provides a useful summary of these perspectives, while also adding his own slightly modified version. In essence, these scholars suggest that in the 1950s and 1960s there was a cultural shift in Western societies characterized by increased individualism, egoism, reduced self-constraint, and weakened external social bonds, all of which increased the tendency for violent forms of self-expression. Such an explanation for contemporary crime trends has interesting parallels with some of the arguments about longer-term historical shifts. However, it shares with those earlier historical explanations a very limited systematic empirical basis from which one could affirm or refute competing insights.

2. The Widespread Crime Decline of the 1990s

What can explain the widespread decline in most forms of serious crime in America and many European nations beginning in the early to mid-1990s and extending well into the 2000s?

Are these patterns the result primarily of modifications to the quantity and quality of policing and incarceration? Or did the declines occur because of reductions in illicit drug involvement and alcohol consumption, declining lead exposure, shifts in abortion laws, demographics (e.g., age structure and immigration), or improvements in the economy (e.g., unemployment and wages)? As it turns out, it depends on whom you ask.

Each of the earlier-mentioned arguments has received some support in the empirical literature or has advocates prepared to make a plausible case irrespective of what the available scientific evidence suggests. I have argued elsewhere (Baumer 2008) that the existing empirical research is not of sufficient breadth or depth to provide definitive evidence on which factors mattered a lot, which mattered relatively little, and importantly, which mattered the most (see also Travis and Waul 2002).

There have been many good ideas presented about why crime *probably* declined significantly in the 1990s in the manner it did (Travis 1998; Blumstein and Rosenfeld 1998; Blumstein and Wallman 2006; Zimring 2006), and there have been some sophisticated empirical investigations of the matter. But because of the relatively small body of systematic empirical research, the relatively narrow focus of much of that research (e.g., studies that focus primarily on policing or incarceration while leaving other possible causes underspecified theoretically and empirically)[1], and high degree of variability in analytical methods applied across studies (e.g., variables considered, units of analysis employed, and the types of models estimated)[2], it is difficult to draw definitive conclusions and easy to make strong claims for the importance of given factors even when the scientific evidence appears to be quite weak. It is perhaps not surprising then, that recent overviews of the scientific evidence about the 1990s crime drop in America have reached different conclusions. Consider, for example, the overviews provided in two widely cited sources (Levitt 2004; Zimring 2006), summarized here in table 2.1.

As the table illustrates, assessments of the same literature yield an agreement between Levitt (2004) and Zimring (2006) that rising incarceration rates were one of the keys to crime declines in America during the 1990s (see also Spelman 2006).

Table 2.1. Contrasting Conclusions About Factors Associated with
the 1990s Crime Decline

A. Levitt (2004)

Factors That Probably Were Significant	Factors That Probably Did Not Matter Much
Increases in incarceration rates	Improving economic conditions
Increases in police per capita	Changes in policing focus
Decline in crack	Smaller youth cohorts
1970s abortion legalization	

B. Zimring (2006)

Factors That Probably Were Significant	Factors That Probably Did Not Matter Much
Increases in incarceration rates	1970s abortion legalization
Improving economic conditions	Decline in crack (except youth violence)
Smaller youth cohorts	Increases in police per capita (except NYC)
Regional cyclical factors	Changes in policing focus (except NYC)

But that is the only commonality between them. Both assessments are much more contextualized than presented here—neither strongly denies the potential importance of factors not included on their "likely important" list—but the discrepancy in view of recent literature is telling. There simply is not enough good-quality empirical research on the 1990s crime decline to develop a list of factors that can be defended strongly.

Subsequent studies have not resolved the matter but have added to our knowledge base on the American experience during the 1990s. A comprehensive city-level analysis commissioned by the National Research Council (NRC) suggests that, consistent with the observations made by Zimring (2006) and Levitt (2004), rising incarceration rates during the 1990s were instrumental in driving crime rates down in America (Baumer 2008). This study also concludes that improving economic conditions played a significant role (consistent with Zimring, contrary to Levitt), as did a decline in "lagged" teen birth rates (consistent with Levitt, contrary to Zimring). Another series of studies focused on the role of policing shifts, especially in particular cities. In particular, much has been made about the New York experience during the 1990s, and in particular that the crime declines observed there were much greater than those observed elsewhere and that a shift in policing focus (most notably, a movement toward zero-tolerance, quality-of-life policing) was a strong reason why this was the case (Zimring 2006). While there is some empirical support for such claims, a growing body of empirical evidence casts doubt on whether New York patterns differed substantially from other cities and whether order maintenance policing was a major factor in the magnitude of the crime drop there (Rosenfeld, Fornango, and Baumer 2005; Messner et al. 2007; Rosenfeld, Fornango, and Rengifo 2007).

Two other themes that have emerged in recent studies highlight economic perceptions (Rosenfeld and Fornango 2007; Rosenfeld 2009) and early exposure to lead (Nevin 2007; Reyes 2007). Rosenfeld and Fornango's (2007) study suggests that previous assessments of the role of economic factors on crime trends, including the 1990s crime decline, may be incomplete because of an exclusive focus on "objective" economic conditions. They focus additionally on perceived economic conditions (i.e., the Index of Consumer Sentiment). Their region-level panel regression analysis indicates that increasing consumer sentiment (i.e., positive assessments about the current state and future expectations of personal finances and economic conditions) in the 1990s can account for about one-third of the reduction in rates of robbery and other property crimes. Rosenfeld and Fornango (2007) speculate that this occurred primarily because better perceived economic conditions reduce participation in illegal markets.

Other recent research has focused on a possible link between early lead exposure and contemporary crime rates (Nevin 2007; Reyes 2007). Following Donohue and Levitt (2001), these studies explore how the quality of early life experiences among contemporary cohorts in high-offending age groups (in this case, how much lead they were likely exposed to during childhood) might shape their current offending rates. Although there are significant challenges in assessing long-lagged relationships such as these, the results suggest a robust link between contemporary crime trends and the degree of exposure contemporary populations likely had to lead when they were young children. Further, although the methods used are subject to the normal cautions associated with establishing causation through nonexperimental methods, the magnitude of this association is nontrivial. Reyes (2007, 33) concludes from her analysis that reductions in lead exposure during the 1970s "predict a 56 percent decline in the per capita violent crime rate."

The latter two sets of studies—focusing on consumer sentiment and lead exposure—take on some added value because, unlike many of the other factors emphasized in the literature on the 1990s crime decline, there is some evidence that they are relevant not only to the observed American trends. Rosenfeld and Messner (2009) examine the effect of changing consumer economic sentiment on burglary rates for a sample of nations that includes America but also nine European nations. Their pooled cross-sectional, time-series analysis shows that, controlling for a wide variety of other factors, rising consumer sentiment helps to account for reductions in burglary in both the United States and Europe. Similarly, Nevin (2007) provides compelling evidence that lagged temporal patterns in lead exposure fit contemporary crime trends both in the United States and several other nations. While the methods applied in these studies do not clearly establish causal connections, they generate compelling empirical patterns that should stimulate additional research along the same lines.

Such patterns might appeal even to historians of crime trends; Eisner (2008) has expressed skepticism about many of the conventional explanations of the 1990s crime drop because they tend to be specific to the American experience. Still, aside from Rosenfeld and Messner (2009) and Nevin (2007), existing research on the

Great Transnational Crime Decline of the 1990s has not integrated data or insights from multiple societies to evaluate whether other factors, including broader cultural or structural forces, may have contributed to the observed patterns.

3. *Explaining the 2000s*

The first decade of the 2000s has been described as a particularly woeful one by some national commentators (e.g., Serwer 2009), and perhaps rightfully so. A brief recession in America early in the decade was overshadowed by a much longer, more severe, and more global recession during its last few years. From 2006 on, unemployment rates in some places in the United States have doubled, home foreclosures have increased substantially, and consumer confidence has plunged to record low levels. But crime rates in America remained relatively flat. There have been some notable short-term fluctuations, but the overall trend has been fairly stable since the early part of the decade, and there are no clear signs of a significant uptick (Rosenfeld and Oliver 2008). This appears to be the case as well in England and Wales (Walker et al. 2009) and the handful of European nations for which the relevant data are easily accessible (van Dijk, van Kesteren, and Smit 2007). Conditions in many of these nations seem ripe for a notable spike in crime rates, especially property crimes, but as of 2010 this has not happened. Or if it has, the research community has not yet detected it systematically.

III. CONCLUSION

In recent years, the literature on crime trends has flourished. Data archives on both historical and contemporary crime trends have grown and improved, and there is now a considerable active research aimed at describing and explaining crime trends. The study of crime trends could benefit from greater volume, but equally important, we need better research on crime trends. We need to monitor and track crime rates on a more consistent basis and in a more timely fashion, to share data more freely and develop some consensus on best methodological practices given existing data constraints, and to engage in an ongoing program of comprehensive research.

The absence of an ongoing, time-sensitive, crime monitoring program has long been an impediment to understanding current crime trends, accurately forecasting future crime, and accumulating knowledge in a timely fashion that could support the development of sound policy responses to significant shifts in crime. One highly disappointing feature of the history of research on the major crime shifts of the past half-century is that pertinent analyses and serious policy discussion of the corresponding crime trends and the settings and conditions that may have given rise to them occurred well *after the fact*, lagging significantly behind the points at which they might have generated useful information for policymakers and the public about the trends underway, the factors underlying them, and their likely future course.

Little attention was devoted before or during these periods of major crime swings to producing detailed and rigorous assessments of emerging crime patterns or short- and long-term forecasts of anticipated crime trends. It is uncertain whether more timely research would have made a significant difference in affecting what actually happened. But had a comprehensive, evidence-based, crime-trends monitoring program been in place during these three periods, it might have yielded information for policymakers that would have helped them better understand the direction and scope of the emerging trends.

The absence of rigorous crime-monitoring programs continues to limit assessments of current crime patterns in the United States and elsewhere. Final counts of crimes known to the police for a given year often are not released officially until several months into the following year. Victim-based survey data often lag behind even further. The absence of timely crime data and ongoing analysis hampers efforts to inform policymakers about current or emerging crime problems, and it weakens the foundation on which to develop criminal justice policy, spending, and research priorities.

It also would be useful to centralize existing data resources and to seek greater uniformity in the methodological approaches used to study crime trends in different contexts. Empirical specification and model choices tend to vary widely across crime trend studies (Baumer 2008). Research on recent crime trends has been conducted across multiple units of analysis, most often nations, states, counties, cities, neighborhoods, and police precincts. It is not necessarily important that a particular unit of analysis be identified, a priori, as superior for studying crime trends, but it would be useful to know the empirical implications of using different units of analysis, something that cannot be deciphered easily from existing research. There is usually some overlap, but the models typically estimated using different units (e.g., states vs. counties vs. cities) incorporate quite different sets of explanatory variables (cf. Ousey and Lee 2002; Moody and Marvell 2005; Kovandzic and Vieraitis 2006). There is also a lack of uniformity across studies of recent crime trends based on the same unit of analysis (cf. Donohue and Levitt 2001; Liedka, Piehl, and Useem 2006). Without some uniformity in model specification within and across units of analysis, it is very difficult to detect general emergent patterns and to draw definitive conclusions about the relevance of given factors. Thus, it would be useful not only to broaden the empirical scope of studies that employ each of the most common units of analysis significantly, but to estimate a common set of models across units to better document the implications of using different units of analysis.

Only time will tell what the implications of current economic adversities playing out in many parts of the globe are for future crime trends. We do very little forecasting of crime trends. Much of the research on crime trends is done well after the changes under study have occurred. It could be argued that describing and explaining crime trends has some intrinsic value for societies, as it can provide vital information about what has happened (and, if data are provided in an extremely timely manner, what is happening) and why it may have happened. These are useful things to know about, especially for periods when crime rates have taken a particularly sharp change in direction and the lessons learned might have value for subsequent happenings. But an equally important and fundamental reason to describe and explain crime trends is to facilitate the development of meaningful, empirically informed, forecasts of *future* crime trends (Goldberger and Rosenfeld 2008). Most societies routinely forecast economic output and performance, health outcomes, and the weather, presumably because doing so provides data to facilitate good planning for what might lie ahead. Information about anticipated crime rates seems useful too, both as something the public might wish to know so they can better understand the social context within which they are living and as something that policymakers could use with respect to decisions about police hires, prison populations, and budget cuts.

Unfortunately, we rarely engage in crime forecasting. A handful of scholars have done so (e.g., Sagi and Wellford 1968; Fox 1978; Cohen, Felson, and Land 1980; Cohen and Land 1987; Steffensmeier and Harer 1987; Fox 1997), but many of these pioneering efforts have been built on relatively simple forecasting approaches typically geared toward yielding single-point estimates. Such approaches are not well suited for forecasting behavior for which there is a good deal of uncertainty (Land and McCall 2001). This may be a significant reason why past efforts to forecast crime rates have yielded disappointing results. As Pepper states, "over the past three decades, a handful of criminologists have tried unsuccessfully to forecast aggregate crime rates. Long-run forecasts have been notoriously poor. Crime rates have risen when forecasted to fall (e.g., the mid-1980s) and have fallen when predicted to rise (e.g., the 1990s)" (Pepper 2008, 177). In theory, it should be possible to generate more accurate crime forecasts with existing data resources and state-of-the-art econometric methods. But, as Pepper (2008) recently concluded, "For further headway [on forecasting crime rates] to be made, a focused and sustained research effort is needed . . . [and] . . . to make notable advances, there would also need to be a sustained methodological research program aimed at developing and assessing the performance of different forecasting approaches."

I do not know whether crime rates in America (or elsewhere) will remain flat, increase, or decrease over the short or long term. However, I think it is quite within our reach to provide reasonably accurate assessments of this sort for the public and policymakers if we take crime forecasting seriously.

NOTES

1. The theoretical literature has produced an extensive list of possible explanations for recent crime trends, but the empirical literature generally has focused narrowly on a small subset of these factors, most typically police force size, drug arrest rates, and incarceration. For example, city- and county-level studies of recent crime trends (e.g., Levitt 1997; Baumer et al. 1998; Lott 1998; Ousey and Lee 2002; Gallup-Black 2005; Phillips 2006) often exclude time varying indicators of many relevant factors, including incarceration and jail confinement rates. Similarly, although the occasional study examines wages (Gould, Weinberg, and Mustard 2002), levels of "domesticity" (Dugan, Nagin, and Rosenfeld 1999), and indicators relevant to assessing the role of abortion law changes (Donohue and Levitt 2001, 2006), most studies do not consider these factors despite evidence suggesting that they may be important.

2. The regression models typically estimated using different units (e.g., states vs. counties vs. cities) incorporate quite different sets of explanatory variables (cf. Ousey and Lee 2002; Moody and Marvell 2005; Kovandzic and Vieraitis 2006). There is also a lack of uniformity across studies of recent crime trends based on the same unit of analysis (cf. Gould, Weinberg, and Mustard 2002; Phillips 2006; also, cf. Donohue and Levitt 2001; Liedka, Piehl, and Useem 2006). Additionally, a variety of different methods (e.g., growth curve regression models, econometric panel regressions, models with and without fixed effects to capture time-stable unmeasured factors and/or shared temporal shifts, outcomes measured in levels and/or differences) have been applied to estimate models of crime trends, and this may be one reason for the lack of consistency in findings (see also Phillips and Greenberg 2008; Spelman 2008).

REFERENCES

Adler, Jeffrey S. 2001. "Halting the Slaughter of the Innocents: The Civilizing Process and the Surge in Violence in Turn-of-the-Century Chicago." *Social Science History* 25:29–52.

Arvanites, Thomas M., and Robert H. Defina. 2006. "Business Cycles and Street Crime." *Criminology* 44:139–64.

Barclay, Gordon, and Cynthia Tavares. 2003. "International Comparisons of Criminal Justice Statistics 2001." Bulletin of statistical information on criminal justice from the Home Office and the Council of Europe 12:1–24.

Baumer, Eric P. 2008. "An Empirical Assessment of the Contemporary Crime Trends Puzzle: A Modest Step toward a More Comprehensive Research Agenda." In *Understanding Crime Trends*, ed. Arthur Goldberger and Richard Rosenfeld. Washington, DC: National Academies Press.

Baumer, Eric P., and Janet L. Lauritsen. 2010. "Reporting Crime to the Police, 1973–2005: A Multivariate Analysis of Long-Term Trends in the NCS and NCVS." *Criminology* 48:131–86.

Baumer, Eric P., Janet L. Lauritsen, Richard Rosenfeld, and Richard Wright. 1998. "The Influence of Crack Cocaine on Robbery, Burglary, and Homicide Rates: A Cross-City, Longitudinal Analysis." *Journal of Research in Crime and Delinquency* 35:316–40.

Blumstein, Alfred. 1995. "Youth Violence, Guns, and the Illicit-drug Industry." *Journal of Criminal Law and Criminology* 86:10–36.

Blumstein, Alfred, and Richard Rosenfeld. 1998. "Explaining Recent Trends in US Homicide Rates." *Journal of Criminal Law and Criminology* 88, no. 4: 1175–216.

Blumstein, Alfred, and Joel Wallman. 2006. *The Crime Drop in America*, rev. ed. New York: Cambridge University Press.

Bureau of Justice Statistics. 2010*a*. "Key Facts at a Glance." http://bjs.ojp.usdoj.gov/content/glance/tables/viortrdtab.cfm, and http://bjs.ojp.usdoj.gov/content/glance/tables/proptrdtab.cfm.

Bureau of Justice Statistics. 2010*b*. "State and National Level Crime Trend Estimates." http://bjs.ojp.usdoj.gov/dataonline/Search/Crime/State/StateCrime.cfm.

Cantor, David, and Kenneth C. Land. 1985. "Unemployment and Crime Rates in the Post-World War II United States: A Theoretical and Empirical Analysis." *American Sociological Review* 50:317–32.

Cohen, Lawrence E., and Marcus Felson. 1979. "Social Change and Crime Rate Trends: A Routine Activity Approach." *American Sociological Review* 44:588–608.

Cohen, Lawrence E., Marcus Felson, and Kenneth C. Land. 1980. "Property Crime Rates in the United States: A Macrodynamic Analysis, 1947–1974, with Ex Ante Forecasts for the Mid-1980s." *American Journal of Sociology* 86:90–118.

Cohen, Lawrence E., and Kenneth C. Land. 1987. "Age Structure and Crime: Symmetry vs. Asymmetry, and Projections of Crime Rates Through the 1990's." *American Sociological Review* 52:170–83.

Cook, Philip J., and Gary A. Zarkin. 1985. "Crime and the Business Cycle." *Journal of Legal Studies* 14:115–28.

Cork, Daniel. 1999. "Examining Space-Time Interaction in City-Level Homicide Data: Crack Markets and the Diffusion of Guns among Youth." *Journal of Quantitative Criminology* 15:379–406.

DiIulio, John J. 1996. "Fill Churches, Not Jails: Youth Crime and 'Superpredators.'" Senate Judiciary Committee, Subcommittee on Youth Violence. http://courses.missouristate.edu/KarlKunkel/SOC540/dilulio.pdf.

Donohue, John, and Steven D. Levitt. 2001. "The Impact of Legalized Abortion on Crime." *Quarterly Journal of Economics* 116:379–420.

Donohue, John, and Steven D. Levitt. 2006. "Measurement Error, Legalized Abortion, and the Decline in Crime: A Response to Foote and Goetz (2005)." NBER Working Paper No. 11987. Cambridge, MA: National Bureau of Economic Research.

Dugan, Laura, Daniel S. Nagin, and Richard Rosenfeld. 1999. "Explaining the Decline in Intimate Partner Homicide: The Effects of Changing Domesticity, Women's Status, and Domestic Violence Resources." *Homicide Studies* 3, no. 3: 197–214.

Eckberg, Douglas. 1995. "Estimates of Early Twentieth-Century U.S. Homicide Rates: An Econometric Forecasting Approach." *Demography* 32:1–16.

Eisner, Manuel. 2001. "Modernization, Self-Control and Lethal Violence: The Long-term Dynamics of European Homicide Rates in Theoretical Perspective." *British Journal of Criminology* 41:618–38.

Eisner, Manuel. 2003. "Long-Term Historical Trends in Violent Crime." In *Crime and Justice: A Review of Research*, vol. 30, edited by Michael Tonry. Chicago: University of Chicago Press.

Eisner, Manuel. 2008. "Modernity Strikes Back? A Historical Perspective on the Latest Increase in Interpersonal Violence (1960–1990)." *International Journal of Conflict and Violence* 2:268–316.

Elias, Norbert. 1978. *The Civilizing Process,* vols. 1–2. Oxford: Oxford University Press.

Finch, Andrew. 2001. "Homicide in Contemporary Japan." *British Journal of Criminology* 41:219–35.

Fox, James A. 1978. *Forecasting Crime Data: An Econometric Analysis.* Lexington, MA: Lexington Books.

———. 1996. *Trends in Juvenile Violence.* Washington, DC: Bureau of Justice Statistics.

———. 1997. *Update on Trends in Juvenile Violence: A Report to the United States Attorney General on Current and Future Rates of Juvenile Offending.* Washington, DC: Bureau of Justice Statistics.

Fryer, Roland, Paul Heaton, Steven D. Levitt, and Kevin Murphy. 2006. "Measuring the Impact of Crack Cocaine." NBER Working Paper No. 11318. Cambridge, MA: National Bureau of Economic Research.

Goldberger, Arthur S., and Richard Rosenfeld, eds. 2008. *Understanding Crime Trends.* Washington, DC: National Academies Press.

Gould, Eric D., Bruce A. Weinberg, and David B. Mustard. 2002. "Crime Rates and Local Labor Market Opportunities in the United States, 1979–1997." *Review of Economics and Statistics* 84:45–61.

Greenberg, David F. 1977. "Delinquency and the Age Structure of Society." *Contemporary Crises* 1:189–224.

Greenberg, David. 2001. "Time Series Analysis of Crime Rates." *Journal of Quantitative Criminology* 17: 291–327.

Grogger, Jeffrey, and Michael Willis. 2000. "The Emergence of Crack Cocaine and the Rise in Urban Crime Rates." *Review of Economics and Statistics* 82:519–29.

Gurr, Ted R. 1981. "Historical Trends in Violent Crime: A Critical Review of the Evidence." *Crime and Justice: An Annual Review of Research* 3:295–350.

Hicks, Joe, and Grahame Allen. 1999. "A Century of Change: Trends in UK Statistics Since 1900." Research Paper 99/111. House of Commons Library. http://www.parliament.uk/commons/lib/research/rp99/rp99-111.pdf.

Jencks, Christopher. 1991. "Behind the Numbers: Is Violent Crime Increasing?" *American Prospect* 8:98–109.

Johnson, David T. 2008. "The Homicide Drop in Postwar Japan." *Homicide Studies* 12:146–60.

Kovandzic, Tomislav, and Lynne M. Vieraitis. 2006. "The Effect of County-Level Prison Population Growth on Crime Rates." *Crime and Public Policy* 5:213–44.

LaFree, Gary. 1998. *Losing Legitimacy: Street Crime and the Decline of Institutions in America.* Boulder, CO: Westview.

———. 2005. "Evidence for Elite Convergence in Cross-National Homicide Victimization Trends, 1956 to 2000." *Sociological Quarterly* 46:191–211.

LaFree, Gary, and Kriss A. Drass. 1996. "The Effect of Changes in Intraracial Income Inequality and Educational Attainment on Changes in Arrest Rates for African Americans and Whites, 1957 to 1990." *American Sociological Review* 61, no. 4:614–34.

LaFree, Gary, and Kriss A. Drass. 2001. "Homicide Trends in Finland and 33 Other Nations since 1955: Is Finland Still Exceptional?" In *Homicide Trends in Finland*, ed. Tapio Lappi-Seppälä. Helsinki: National Research Institute of Legal Policy.

LaFree, Gary, and Kriss A. Drass. 2002. "Counting Crime Booms Among Nations: Evidence for Homicide Victimization Rates, 1956 to 1998." *Criminology* 40:769–99.

LaFree, Gary, and Andromachi Tseloni. 2006. "Democracy and Crime: A Multilevel Analysis of Homicide Trends in Forty-Four Counties, 1950–2000." *Annals of the American Academy of Political and Social Science* 605:25–49.

Land, Kenneth C., and Patricia L. McCall. 2001. "The Indeterminacy of Forecasts of Crime Rates and Juvenile Offenses." In *Juvenile Crime, Juvenile Justice*, ed. Joan McCord, Cathy S. Widom, and Nancy. A. Crowell. Washington, DC: National Academies Press.

Lane, Roger. 1997. *Murder in America: A History*. Columbus: Ohio State University Press.

Lane, Roger. 1979. *Violent Death in the City: Suicide, Accident, and Murder in Nineteenth-Century Philadelphia*. Cambridge, MA: Harvard University Press.

Lauritsen, Janet L., and Robin J. Schaum. 2005. "Crime and Victimization in the Three Largest Metropolitan Areas, 1980–1998." *NCJ* 208075. Washington, DC: US Department of Justice, Bureau of Justice Statistics.

Lehti, Martti, and Janne Kivivuori. 2005. "Rikollisuustilanne Suomessa." Oikeuspoliittinen tutkimuslaitos II.A.2:13–41.

Levitt, Steven D. 1997. "Using Electoral Cycles in Police Hiring to Estimate the Effect of Police on Crime." *American Economic Review* 8:280–90.

———. 1999. "The Limited Role of Changing Age Structure in Explaining Aggregate Crime Rates." *Criminology* 37, no. 3: 581–97.

———. 2004. "Understanding Why Crime Fell in the 1990s: Four Factors that Explain the Decline and Six that Do Not." *Journal of Economic Perspectives* 18:163–90.

Liedka, Raymond V., Anne M. Piehl, and Bert Useem. 2006. "The Crime Control Effect of Incarceration: Does Scale Matter?" *Criminology and Public Policy* 5:245–76.

Lott, John R., Jr. 1998. *More Guns, Less Crime*. Chicago: University of Chicago Press.

Maltz, Michael D. 1999. "Bridging Gaps in Police Crime Data." Report No. NCJ-1176365. Washington, DC: Bureau of Justice Statistics, Office of Justice Programs, US Department of Justice. http://www.ojp.usdoj.gov/bjs/pub/bgpcd.pdf.

Marshall, Ineke H., and Carolyn R. Block. 2004. "Maximizing the Availability of Cross-National Data on Homicide." *Homicide Studies* 8:267–310.

Marvell, Thomas B., and Carlisle E. Moody. 1991. "Age Structure and Crime Rates: The Conflicting Evidence." *Journal of Quantitative Criminology* 7, no. 3: 237–73.

———. 1994. "Prison Population Growth and Crime Reduction." *Journal of Quantitative Criminology* 10:109–40.

McAra, Lesley. 2008. "Crime, Criminology and Criminal Justice in Scotland." *European Journal of Criminology* 5:181–504.

McDowall, David, and Colin Loftin. 2005. "Are U.S. Crime Rate Trends Historically Contingent?" *Journal of Research in Crime and Delinquency* 42:359–83.

Messner, Steven F., Lawrence E. Raffalovich, and Richard McMillan. 2001. "Economic Deprivation and Changes in Homicide Arrest Rates for White and Black Youths, 1967–1998: A National Time-Series Analysis." *Criminology* 39:591–614.

Messner, Steven F., Sandro Galea, Kenneth J. Tardiff, Melissa Tracy, Angela Bucciarelli, Tinka Markham Piper, Victoria Frye, and David Vlahov. 2007. "Policing, Drugs, and the Homicide Decline in the 1990s." *Criminology* 45:385–414.

Monkkonon, Eric H. 2001a. *Murder in New York City.* Berkeley: University of California Press.

———. 2001b. *Homicides in New York City, 1797–1999* [And Various Historical Comparison Sites] [Computer file]. ICPSR03226-v1. Ann Arbor, MI: Inter-university Consortium for Political and Social Research.

———. 2005. "Homicide in Los Angeles, 1827–2002." *Journal of Interdisciplinary History* 36:167–83.

Moody, Carlisle E. and Thomas B. Marvell. 2005. "Guns and Crime." *Southern Economic Journal* 71:720–36.

Mouzos, Jenny. 2003. "Australian Homicide Rates: A Comparison of Three Data Sources." In *Trends and Issues in Crime and Criminal Justice No. 261.* Canberra: Australian Institute of Criminology.

Murray, Charles. 1994. *Underclass: The Crisis Deepens.* London: IEA Health and Welfare Unit.

Neapolitan, Jerome. 1997. *Cross-national Crime: A Research Review and Sourcebook.* Westport, CT: Greenwood Press.

Nevin, Rick. 2007. "Understanding International Crime Trends: The Legacy of Preschool Lead Exposure." *Environmental Research* 104:315–36.

O'Brien, Robert M. 1985. *Crime and Victimization.* Beverly Hills, CA: Sage.

———. 1996. "Police Productivity and Crime Rates: 1973–1992." *Criminology* 34:183–207.

———. 2003. "UCR Violent Crime Rates, 1958–2000: Recorded and Offender-Generated Trends." *Social Science Research* 32:499–518.

O'Brien, Robert M., Jean Stockard, and Lynne Isaacson. 1999. "The Enduring Effects of Cohort Characteristics on Age-Specific Homicide Rates, 1960–1995." *American Journal of Sociology* 104:1061–95.

O'Donnell, Ian. 2005. "Lethal Violence in Ireland, 1841 to 2003. Famine, Celibacy, and Parental Pacification." *British Journal of Criminology* 45:671–95.

Oestreich, Gerhard. 1968. "Strukturprobleme des europaischen Absolutismus." *Vierteljahreszeitschrift fur Sozial-and Wirtschaftsgeschichte* 55:329–47.

———. 1982. *Neostoicism and the Early Modern State.* Cambridge: Cambridge University Press.

Office of Management and the Budget (OMB). 1974. *Social Indicators 1973.* Washington, DC: USGPO.

Ousey, Graham C., and Matthew R. Lee. 2002. "Examining the Conditional Nature of the Illicit Drug Market-Homicide Relationship: A Partial Test of the Theory of Contingent Causation." *Criminology* 40:73–102.

———. 2004. "Investigating the Connections between Race, Illicit Drug Markets, and Lethal Violence, 1984–1997." *Journal of Research in Crime and Delinquency* 41:352–83.

Pepper, John V. 2008. Forecasting Crime: A City-Level Analysis. In *Understanding Crime Trends,* ed. Arthur S. Goldberger and Richard Rosenfeld. Washington, DC: National Academies Press.

Phillips, Julie A. 2006. "The Relationship between Age Structure and Homicide Rates in the United States, 1970–1999." *Journal of Research in Crime and Delinquency* 43:230–60.

Phillips, Julie A., and David F. Greenberg. 2008. "A Comparison of Methods for Analyzing Criminological Panel Data." *Journal of Quantitative Criminology* 24:51–72.

Police Executive Research Forum (PERF). 2006. *A Gathering Storm: Violent Crime in America.* Washington, DC: Police Executive Research Forum. http://www.policeforum.org./.

Police Executive Research Forum (PERF). 2007. *Violent Crime in America: 24 Months of Alarming Trends*. Washington, DC: Police Executive Research Forum. http://www.policeforum.org./.

Pridemore, William A., and Mitchell B. Chamlin. 2006. "A Time-Series Analysis of the Impact of Heavy Drinking on Homicide and Suicide Mortality in Russia, 1956–2002." *Addiction* 101, no. 12: 1719–29.

Rand, Michael R., James P. Lynch, and David Cantor. 1997. *Criminal Victimization, 1973–95*. Washington, DC: US Department of Justice, Bureau of Justice Statistics.

Reyes, Jessica Wolpaw. 2007. "Environmental Policy as Social Policy? The Impact of Childhood Lead Exposure on Crime." *B.E. Journal of Economic Analysis & Policy* 7:1–41.

Riedel, Marc. 1990. "Sources of Homicide Data: A Review and Comparison." In *Homicide: A Sourcebook of Social Research*, ed. M.D. Smith and M.A. Zahn. Thousand Oaks, CA: Sage.

Roberts, Aki, and Gary LaFree. 2005. "Explaining Japan's Postwar Violent Crime Trends." *Criminology* 42:179–209.

Rosenfeld, Richard. 2009. "Crime is the Problem: Homicide, Acquisitive Crime, and Economic Conditions." *Journal of Quantitative Criminology* 25:287–306.

Rosenfeld, Richard, and Robert Fornango. 2007. "The Impact of Economic Conditions on Robbery and Property Crime: The Role of Consumer Sentiment." *Criminology* 45:735–69.

Rosenfeld, Richard, Robert Fornango, and Eric P. Baumer. 2005. "Did Ceasefire, CompStat, and Exile Reduce Homicide?" *Criminology and Public Policy* 4:419–50.

Rosenfeld, Richard, Robert Fornango, and Andres F. Rengifo. 2007. "The Impact of Order-Maintenance Policing on New York City Homicide and Robbery Rates: 1988–2001." *Criminology* 45:355–84.

Rosenfeld, Richard, and Steven F. Messner. 2009. "The Crime Drop in Comparative Perspective: The Impact of the Economy and Imprisonment on American and European Burglary Rates." *British Journal of Sociology* 60, no. 3: 445–71.

Rosenfeld, Richard, and Brian E. Oliver. 2008. "Evaluating Recent Changes in Homicide and Robbery Rates." *Justice Research and Policy* 10:49–65.

Sagi, Phillip C., and Charles F. Wellford. 1968. "Age Composition and Patterns of Change in Criminal Statistics." *Journal of Criminal Law, Criminology, and Police Science* 59:29–36.

Savolainen, Jukka, Martti Lehti, and Janne Kivivuori. 2008. "Historical Origins of a Cross-National Puzzle." *Homicide Studies* 12:67–89.

Serwer, Andy. 2009. "The '00s: Goodbye (at Last) to the Decade from Hell." http://www.time.com/time/nation/article/0,8599,1942834,00.html.

Smith, Kevin, John Flatley, Kathryn Coleman, Sarah Osborne, Peter Kaiza, and Stephen Roe. 2010. *Homicides, Firearm Offences and Intimate Violence 2008/09*. London: Home Office Statistical Bulletin.

Spelman, William. 2006. "The Limited Importance of Prison Expansion." In *The Crime Drop in America*, rev. ed., ed. Alfred Blumstein and Joel Wallman. New York: Cambridge University Press.

Spelman, William. 2008. "Specifying the Relationship between Crime and Prisons." *Journal of Quantitative Criminology* 24:149–78.

Spierenburg, Pieter. 1996. "Long-Term Trends in Homicide: Theoretical Reflections and Dutch Evidence, Fifteenth to Twentieth Centuries." In *The Civilization of Crime:*

Violence in Town and Country since the Middle Ages, ed. Eric A. Johnson and Eric H. Monkkonen. Urbana: University of Illinois Press.

Stamatel, Janet P. 2006. "An Overview of Publicly Available Quantitative Cross-national Crime Data." *IASSIST Quarterly* 30:16–20.

Steffensmeier, Darrell, and Miles Harer. 1987. "Is the Crime Rate Really Falling? An 'Aging' U.S. Population and Its Impact on the Nation's Crime Rate, 1980–1984." *Journal of Research in Crime and Delinquency* 24:23–48.

Stemen, Donald. 2007. *Reconsidering Incarceration: New Directions for Reducing Crime.* New York: Vera Institute.

Thome, Helmut, and Christoph Birkel. 2007. *Sozialer Wandel und die Entwicklung der Gewaltkriminalität. Deutschland, England und Schweden im Vergleich, 1950 bis 2000.* Wiesbaden: VS Verlag für Sozialwissenschaften.

Travis, Jeremy. 1998. "Declining Crime and our National Research Agenda: A New Yorker's View." *Security Journal* 12:145–50.

Travis, Jeremy, and Michelle Waul. 2002. *Reflections on the Crime Decline in America: Lessons for the Future?* Washington, DC: Urban Institute Press.

van Dijk, Jan. 2007. "Mafia Markers: Assessing Organized Crime and Its Impact upon Societies." *Trends in Organized Crime* 10:39–56.

van Dijk, Jan, John van Kesteren, and Paul Smit. 2007. *Criminal Victimisation in International Perspective: Key Findings from the 2004–2005 ICVS and EU ICS.* The Hague: Boom Juridische uitgevers.

———. 2008. *Criminal Victimisation in International Perspective, Key findings from the 2004–2005 ICVS and EU ICS.* The Hague: Boom Juridische uitgevers.

van Kesteren, John. 2008. "Some Main Results on International Comparison and Trends: Results from the International Crime Victims Survey and the European Survey on Crime and Safety." The International Victimology Institute (INTERVICT), Tilburg University, The Netherlands.

Walker, Allison, John Flatley, Chris Kershaw, and Debbie Moon. 2009. *Crime in England and Wales 2008/09.* London: Home Office Statistical Bulletin.

Zimring, Frank E. 2006. *The Great American Crime Decline.* New York: Oxford University Press.

CHAPTER 3

......

EVIDENCE-BASED CRIME POLICY

......

BRANDON C. WELSH AND
DAVID P. FARRINGTON*

CRIME policy should be rational and based on the best possible research evidence. One might expect that decision-makers would take careful account of any available evidence on what works or what does not work. How can a program or policy that has produced no discernible evidence of effectiveness, as shown through numerous evaluations, be considered for wider public use? Unfortunately, this happens all the time. Consider the short-lived revival of the prison deterrence program (known as Scared Straight) despite past evaluations showing not only that it failed to deter juvenile delinquents from future criminal activity but that it actually made them worse (Petrosino, Turpin-Petrosino, and Buehler 2006). Consider also the long-standing and widely popular school-based substance abuse prevention program known as DARE (Drug Abuse Resistance Education) for which the accumulated evidence shows that it has a trivial effect on substance use and delinquency (U.S. General Accountability Office 2003; Gottfredson, Wilson, and Najaka 2006). Many other examples exist in the United States and elsewhere.

It is, of course, wholly naïve to think that the evidence base on the effectiveness of a particular program or strategy will be the sole influence on policy. There are many considerations involved in implementing new policies (as well as in expanding effective ones or putting an end to ineffective or harmful ones). For example, there may be different government priorities, such as military defense spending, environmental protection, or prescription drug benefits for seniors, which are competing for scarce public resources. National polls may show that the public is more concerned with issues other than crime and its control. Other factors include the worry by politicians that they may be perceived as soft on crime by supporting prevention instead of law and order measures (Gest 2001), as well as the short time-horizons of politicians (Tonry and Farrington 1995b), which makes programs that show results only in the longer term less appealing to those who come up for election every few years. Regrettably, evidence of what works best is rarely a factor in the development of crime policy. Political and other considerations drive much of the crime policy agenda.

While no laughing matter, a recent example from the United Kingdom illustrates how politics of the day can trump research evidence. In October 2009, Professor David Nutt became the first chairman of the British government's Advisory Council on the Misuse of Drugs to be fired in its thirty-eight-year history. In a paper, he had suggested that alcohol and tobacco were more harmful than many illegal drugs, including marijuana, LSD, and ecstasy, and said that politicians "distort" and "devalue" research evidence (Tran 2009).

An evidence-based approach attempts to avoid these mistakes by ensuring that the best available evidence is considered in any decision to implement a program or policy designed to reduce crime. "An evidence-based approach requires that the results of rigorous evaluation be rationally integrated into decisions about interventions by policymakers and practitioners alike" (Petrosino 2000, 635). An evidence-based approach is crucial to understanding where, when, and if different interventions reduce crime, as well as helping to establish why an intervention does or does not work.

The evidence-based approach has garnered much support in medicine (Millenson 1997; Halladay and Bero 2000). But even in medicine, a discipline noted for its adherence to scientific principles and high educational requirements, most practice is still "shaped by local custom, opinions, theories, and subjective impressions" (Sherman 1998, 6). Of course, making scientific evidence on what works best available to policymakers and practitioners (regardless of the discipline) and having them put it into practice are two entirely different matters.

Support for an evidence-based approach to crime policy is growing. This growth has been fostered by a number of recent developments, including a movement toward an evidence-based approach in other disciplines such as medicine (Millenson 1997), education (Mosteller and Boruch 2002), and the social sciences more generally (Sherman 2003); large-scale reviews of "what works" in crime prevention and criminal justice (Tonry and Farrington 1995a; Sherman et al. 1997; Nuttall, Goldblatt, and Lewis 1998; Skogan and Frydl 2004; MacKenzie 2006; Sherman et al. 2006; Farrington and Welsh 2007; Braga and Weisburd 2010); and, most recently, the establishment of the Campbell Collaboration and its Crime and Justice Group (Welsh and Farrington 2006a).

This chapter provides a comprehensive overview of research on and key issues facing the evidence-based movement as it applies to crime and justice. Several observations and conclusions emerge:

- An evidence-based approach relies on the most scientifically valid evaluation studies (i.e., experimental and high quality quasi-experimental designs) and the most rigorous review methods (i.e., systematic review and meta-analysis) to arrive at conclusions about what works.
- The evidence-based paradigm seeks to increase the influence of research on policy or, in a manner of speaking, put systematic research evidence at center stage in the policy-making process. The linkages between research and policy are sometimes less than clear, with evaluation influence on policy taking a number of different routes.
- There exists an institutional base to guide an evidence-based approach. For crime and justice this base is the Campbell Collaboration and its Crime and Justice Group. The Crime and Justice Group aims to prepare, maintain, and disseminate systematic reviews of research conducted across the world on what works to reduce crime and improve justice. As of this writing, they had published twenty-four systematic reviews, with more than a dozen others in progress.
- In recent years a number of key developments have advanced evidence-based crime policy in some Western nations. For example, in the United States, Colorado—through state law—implemented the evidence-based, early childhood home visiting program developed by David Olds. In the United Kingdom, the Ministry of Justice and the National Policing Improvement Agency have commissioned new systematic reviews to investigate the effectiveness of various criminal justice interventions. In Australia, systematic evidence has greatly influenced early childhood policies to reduce child abuse and neglect.
- The movement toward rational and evidence-based crime policy is here to stay. It does not appear to be yet another fad or fleeting idea in the annals of criminal justice policy making. While there remains much to be done to elevate systematic evidence into center stage in the policy-making process, the good news is that this work is well under way.

Section I describes the core elements of the evidence-based paradigm with its focus on the most scientifically valid evaluation studies and the most rigorous methods for assessing evidence. It also includes a discussion of economic analyses. Section II discusses crucial linkages that exist between research and policy processes, including research on the use of evaluations in public policy. Section III overviews the institutional base of the evidence-based approach, from its beginnings in medicine to social sciences more generally, including the development of the Campbell Collaboration and its Crime and Justice Group. Section IV reports on key developments that have advanced evidence-based crime policy in a number of leading Western countries, including the United States, the United Kingdom, and Australia. Section V outlines the main challenges that confront an evidence-based approach.

I. THE EVIDENCE-BASED MODEL

In characterizing the evidence-based model and its application to the prevention and control of crime, it is important to first define what is meant by "evidence." By evidence is meant scientific, not criminal, evidence (see Sherman 1998, 2n1). Evidence introduced in criminal court proceedings, while bound by laws and procedures, is altogether different from scientific evidence. The latter "refers to its common usage in science to distinguish data from theory, where evidence is defined as 'facts . . . in support of a conclusion, statement or belief'" (*Shorter Oxford English Dictionary* 2002, as cited in Sherman 2003, 7). This focus on the empirical dimension of evidence is not to suggest that systematic evidence can come only from empirical research. Indeed, there are many different sources of systematic evidence (Hood 2002; Tonry 2003; Tonry and Green 2003).

While it is acknowledged that evidence-based crime prevention can serve other useful purposes (e.g., improving police-training standards, improving community relations, and so on), the main outcome of interest or "bottom line" is the prevention of crime.[1] Indeed, this is the main reason why we use empirical research as our source of systematic evidence. The parallel is with evidence-based medicine's primary focus on saving lives or improving the quality of life of those suffering from terminal or chronic illnesses. For evidence-based crime prevention, the prevention of crime is a first tier or primary outcome.

At the heart of the evidence-based model is the notion that "we are all entitled to our own opinions, but not to our own facts" (Sherman 1998, 4). Use of opinions instead of facts to guide crime policy may cause harmful or iatrogenic effects (McCord 2003), may lead to the implementation of programs that do not work at all, may waste scarce public resources (Welsh and Farrington 2000), and may divert policy attention from the most important crime priorities of the day (Mears 2007). Moreover, within the evidence-based paradigm, drawing conclusions based on facts calls attention to two fundamental issues: the validity of the evidence, and the methods used to locate, appraise, and synthesize the evidence (Welsh and Farrington 2001).

A. Evaluating the Effects of Programs

According to Donald Campbell and his colleagues (Campbell and Stanley 1966; Cook and Campbell 1979; Shadish, Cook, and Campbell 2002), the methodological quality of evaluation studies depends on four criteria: statistical conclusion validity, internal validity, construct validity, and external validity.[2] "Validity refers to the correctness of inferences about cause and effect" (Shadish, Cook, and Campbell 2002, 34).

Statistical conclusion validity is concerned with whether the presumed cause (the intervention) and the presumed effect (the outcome) are related. The main threats to this form of validity are insufficient statistical power to detect the effect (e.g., because of small sample size) and the use of inappropriate statistical techniques.[3]

Internal validity refers to how well the study unambiguously demonstrates that an intervention (e.g., closed-circuit television [CCTV] surveillance cameras) had an effect on an outcome (e.g., crime). Here, some kind of control condition is necessary to estimate what would have happened to the experimental units (e.g., people or areas) if the intervention had not been applied to them—termed the "counterfactual inference." The main threats to internal validity are as follows (Shadish, Cook, and Campbell 2002, 55):

- Selection: the effect reflects preexisting differences between experimental and control conditions.
- History: the effect is caused by some event occurring at the same time as the intervention.
- Maturation: the effect reflects a continuation of preexisting trends, for example, in normal human development or in crime rates.
- Instrumentation: the effect is caused by a change in the method of measuring the outcome.
- Testing: the pretest measurement causes a change in the post-test measure.
- Regression to the mean: where an intervention is implemented on units with unusually high scores (e.g., people or areas with high crime rates), natural fluctuation will cause a decrease in these scores on the post-test, which may be mistakenly interpreted as an effect of the intervention. The opposite (an increase) can happen when the interventions are applied to low-crime areas or low-scoring people.[4]
- Differential attrition: the effect is caused by differential loss of units (e.g., people) from experimental compared to control conditions.
- Causal order: it is unclear whether the intervention preceded or followed the effect (e.g., a change in crime rates).

Construct validity refers to the adequacy of the operational definition and measurement of the theoretical constructs that underlie the intervention and the outcome. For example, if a CCTV project aims to investigate the effect of increased surveillance on offending, did CCTV really cause an increase in surveillance? The main threats to this form of validity rest on the extent to which the intervention succeeded in changing what it was intended to change (e.g., to what extent was there treatment fidelity or implementation failure) and on the validity and reliability of outcome measures (e.g., how adequately do police-recorded crime rates reflect true crime rates).

External validity refers to how well the effect of an intervention on an outcome is generalizable or replicable in different conditions: different operational definitions of the intervention and various outcomes, different persons, different environments, and so on. It is difficult to investigate this within one evaluation study. External validity can be established more convincingly in systematic reviews and meta-analyses of a number of evaluation studies. As noted by William Shadish and his colleagues (2002, 87), the main threats to this form of validity consist of interactions of causal relationships (effect sizes) with types of persons, settings, interventions, and outcomes. For example, an intervention designed to reduce crime may be effective with some types of people and in some types of places, but not in other cases. A key issue is whether the effect size varies according to the degree to which those who carried out the research had some kind of stake in the results (see Eisner 2009).

An evaluation of a crime-prevention program is considered to be high quality if it possesses a high degree of internal, construct, and statistical conclusion validity. Put another way, we can have a great deal of confidence in the observed effects of an intervention if it has been evaluated using a design that controls for the major threats to these three forms of validity. Experimental (randomized and nonrandomized) and quasi-experimental research designs are the types of evaluation designs that can best achieve this aim.

The randomized controlled experiment is considered the "gold standard" in evaluation research designs. It is the most convincing method of evaluating crime-prevention programs (Farrington 1983; Farrington and Welsh 2005; 2006a). The key feature of randomized experiments is that the random assignment equates the experimental and control groups before the experimental intervention on all possible extraneous variables that might influence the outcome (e.g., crime). Hence, any subsequent differences between the groups must be attributable to the intervention. Randomization is the only method of assignment that controls for unknown and unmeasured confounders as well as those that are known and measured (Weisburd, Lum, and Petrosino 2001). However, the randomized experiment is the most convincing method of evaluation only if it is implemented with full integrity. To the extent that there are implementation problems (problems of maintaining random assignment, differential attrition, crossover between control and experimental conditions), internal validity could be reduced.

Another important feature of the randomized experiment is that a sufficiently large number of units (people or areas) need to be randomly assigned to ensure that the treatment group is equivalent to the control group on all extraneous variables (within the limits of statistical fluctuation). As a rule of thumb, at least fifty units in each category are needed (Farrington 1997). This number is relatively easy to achieve with individuals but very difficult to achieve with larger units such as communities, schools, classrooms, or areas. There have been only a few experiments (e.g., on "hot spots" policing—see Farrington and Welsh 2005; 2006a) in which one hundred or more areas were randomly assigned to conditions. Another important limiting factor is the cost associated with the area-based evaluation design.

An evaluation design in which experimental and control units are matched or statistically equated (e.g., using a prediction score) prior to intervention—what is called a nonrandomized experiment—has lower internal validity than a randomized experiment. It is important to note, however, that statistical conclusion validity and construct validity may be just as high for a nonrandomized experiment as for a randomized experiment.

In area-based studies, the best and most feasible design usually involves before-and-after measures in experimental and comparable control conditions, together with statistical control of extraneous variables. This is an example of a quasi-experimental evaluation design. Even better, the effect of an intervention on crime can be investigated after controlling (e.g., in a regression equation) not only for prior crime but also for other factors that influence crime. Another possibility is to match two areas and then choose one at random to be the experimental area. Of course, several pairs of areas would be better than only one pair. These are the best ways of dealing with threats to internal validity when random assignment of a large number of units to experimental and control conditions cannot be achieved. Here again, statistical conclusion validity and construct validity may not be any lower than in a randomized experiment.

B. Assessing Research Evidence

Just as it is crucial to use the highest quality evaluation designs to generate evidence about the effects of crime prevention or criminal justice programs and policies, it is also important to use the most rigorous methods to assess the available research evidence. Efforts to assess if a particular prevention strategy (e.g., situational, community), intervention modality (e.g., CCTV, mentoring), or some other grouping of prevention programs is effective in preventing crime can take many different forms. The systematic review and the meta-analytic review (or meta-analysis) are the most rigorous methods for assessing effectiveness (Petticrew and Roberts 2006; Welsh and Farrington 2006b; Petrosino and Lavenberg 2007).[5]

1. *Systematic Review Method*

Systematic reviews "essentially take an epidemiological look at the methodology and results sections of a specific population of studies to reach a research-based consensus on a given study topic" (Johnson et al. 2000, 35). They use rigorous methods for locating, appraising, and synthesizing evidence from prior evaluation studies, and they are reported with the same level of detail that characterizes high-quality reports of original research. Key features of a systematic review include the following six.

First, the eligibility criteria are explicit. The reviewers specify in detail why they included certain studies and rejected others. What was the minimum level of methodological quality? Did they consider only a particular type of evaluation design, such as randomized experiments?[6] What types of interventions were included? What kinds of outcome data had to be reported in the studies? In the final report, the reviewers should explicitly present all the criteria or rules used in selecting eligible studies.

Second, the search for studies is designed to reduce potential bias. Because there are many possible ways that bias can compromise the results of a review, reviewers must explicitly state how they conducted their search of potentially relevant studies to reduce such bias. How did they try to locate studies reported outside scientific journals? How did they try to locate studies reported in foreign languages? All bibliographic databases that were searched should be made explicit so that potential gaps in coverage can be identified.

Third, each study is screened according to eligibility criteria, with exclusions justified. The searches will undoubtedly locate many citations and abstracts to potentially relevant studies. Each of the reports of these potentially relevant studies must be screened to determine if the study meets the eligibility criteria for the review. A full listing of all excluded studies and the justifications for exclusion should be made available to readers.

Fourth, the most complete data possible are assembled. The systematic reviewer will generally try to obtain all relevant evaluations meeting the eligibility criteria. In addition, all data relevant to the objectives of the review should be carefully extracted from each eligible report and coded and computerized. Sometimes, original study documents lack important information. When possible, the systematic reviewer will attempt to obtain these data from the authors of the original reports.

Fifth, quantitative techniques are used, when appropriate and possible, in analyzing results. A systematic review may or may not include a meta-analysis. The use of meta-analysis may not be appropriate because of a small number of studies, heterogeneity across studies, or different units of analysis of the studies (i.e., a mix of area- and individual-based studies). But when suitable, meta-analyses should be conducted as part of systematic reviews.

Sixth, the report is structured and detailed. The final report of a systematic review is structured and detailed so that the reader can understand each phase of the research, the decisions that were made, and the conclusions that were reached.

As noted by Anthony Petrosino and his colleagues (2001, 20), "the foremost advantage of systematic reviews is that when done well and with full integrity, they provide the most reliable and comprehensive statement about what works." Systematic reviews are not, however, without their limitations, although these limitations or challenges appear to be most closely linked with administrative and dissemination issues, such as getting them in the hands of decision-makers (see Petrosino et al. 2001). Some of the challenges involving the "substance" of systematic reviews include the transparency of the process (e.g., the need to present the reasons why studies were included or excluded) and the need to reconcile differences in coding of study characteristics and outcomes by multiple researchers (e.g., by measuring inter-rater reliability).

2. *Meta-Analytic Review Method*

A meta-analysis addresses the question: How well does the program work? It involves the statistical or quantitative analysis of the results of prior research studies (Lipsey and Wilson 2001). Since it involves the statistical summary of data (in particular, effect sizes), it requires a reasonable number of intervention studies that are sufficiently similar to be grouped together; there may be little point in reporting an average effect size based on a very small number of studies. Nevertheless, quantitative methods can be very important in helping the reviewer determine the average effect of a particular intervention.

One major product of a meta-analysis is a weighted average effect size. For example, the percentage reduction in offending would be one simple effect size. In calculating the average, each effect size is usually weighted according to the sample size on which it is based, with larger studies having greater weights. There is usually also an attempt to investigate factors (moderators) that predict larger or smaller effect sizes in different studies. This is to establish whether an intervention works better in certain contexts and which features of the intervention are most related to a successful outcome.

Some of the strengths of the meta-analytic review method include its transparent nature—the detailed specification of its methods and the studies involved—which makes it easily replicated by other researchers, its ability to handle a very large number of studies that may be overwhelming for other review methods, and the "statistical methods of meta-analysis help guard against interpreting the dispersion in results as meaningful when it can just as easily be explained as sampling error" (Wilson 2001, 84). Limitations of meta-analysis include, on a practical side, its time-consuming nature and its inability to synthesize "complex patterns of effects found in individual studies" (Wilson 2001, 84). Another problem concerns how to select effect sizes for analysis in studies that report many different outcomes.

3. *Assessing Value for Money*

Assessing the value for money of programs is closely linked to evidence-based crime prevention. A fair and reliable assessment of a program's efficiency is the purview of economic analysis. An economic analysis (e.g., cost-benefit analysis, cost-effectiveness analysis) can be described as a policy tool that allows choices to be made between alternative uses of resources or alternative distributions of services (Knapp 1997, 11). Many criteria are used in economic analysis. The most common is efficiency or value for money (achieving maximum outcomes from minimum inputs). However, the specific focus on economic efficiency is not meant to imply that programs should be continued only if their benefits outweigh their costs. There are many important noneconomic criteria on which these programs should be judged (e.g., equity in the distribution of services).

Of the two main techniques of economic analysis—cost-benefit and cost-effectiveness analysis—only cost-benefit analysis allows for an assessment of both costs and benefits. A cost-effectiveness analysis can be referred to as an incomplete cost-benefit analysis. This is because no attempt is made to estimate the monetary value of program effects (benefits or disbenefits), only resources used (costs). For example, a cost-effectiveness analysis might specify how many crimes were prevented per $1,000 spent on a program. Another way to think about how cost-benefit and cost-effectiveness analysis differ is that "cost-effectiveness analysis may help one decide among competing program models, but it cannot show that the total effect was worth the cost of the program" (Weinrott, Jones, and Howard 1982, 179), unlike cost-benefit analysis.

A cost-benefit analysis is a step-by-step process that follows a standard set of procedures. There are six main steps: (1) define the scope of the analysis; (2) obtain estimates of program effects; (3) estimate the monetary value of costs and benefits; (4) calculate present value and assess profitability; (5) describe the distribution of costs and benefits (an assessment of who gains and who loses, e.g., program participant, government/taxpayer, crime victim); and (5) conduct sensitivity analyses by varying the different assumptions made (Barnett 1993, 143–48).[7]

A major aim in a cost-benefit analysis is to produce a benefit-to-cost ratio for an intervention. For example, Lawrence Schweinhart, Helen Barnes, and David Weikart (1993) estimated that for every child who received the Perry Preschool Program, $7 were saved for every $1 expended, mainly because the program reduced the arrest rate by half. This kind of information often has a large influence on practitioners and policymakers, and can be crucial in encouraging them to implement programs.

Two other key features of economic analysis require brief mention. First, an economic analysis is an extension of an outcome or impact evaluation, and it is only as defensible as the evaluation on which it is based. David Weimer and Lee Friedman (1979, 264) recommended that economic analyses be limited to programs that have been evaluated with an "experimental or strong quasi-experimental design." As mentioned, the most convincing method of evaluating interventions is to conduct a randomized experiment.

Second, many perspectives can be taken in measuring program costs and benefits. Some cost-benefit analyses adopt a society-wide perspective that includes the major parties that can receive benefits or incur costs, such as the government or taxpayer, crime victim, and program participant. Other analyses may take a more narrow view, focusing only on one or two of these parties. The decision about which perspective to take has important implications for evaluating a program, particularly if it is being funded by public money. That is, if conclusions are to be drawn about the monetary benefits or costs of a program to the public, the benefits or costs must be those that the public will either receive or incur.

II. Policy Processes

The linkages between research and policy are sometimes less than clear, and some have posited that they constitute two different communities (Weiss et al. 2008; Kothari, MacLean, and Edwards 2009). By no means is this situation unique to crime and justice; it affects many disciplines in the social and behavioral sciences as well as the physical and medical sciences. Interestingly though, this was not always the case in crime and justice, with many landmark studies having a great influence on criminal justice policy of the day, including police deployment in cities, prosecution-led career criminal programs, and risk classification for inmates (see Petersilia 1987). It has really only been in the last couple of decades that research influence on crime policy has waned (Petersilia 1991; Blumstein and Petersilia 1995; Blumstein 1997).

The evidence-based paradigm seeks to increase the influence of research on policy or, in a manner of speaking, put systematic research evidence at center stage in the policy-making (and political) process. There are a growing number of examples that this is indeed happening in crime and justice, and this is the subject of section IV on international developments. Here, we discuss policy processes and the extent to which they are or can be evidence-based. We begin with a general overview of evaluation influence on policy and then take a more specific look at the research and policy connections in crime and justice.

Drawing upon a sizeable body of scholarship spanning the last four decades (see e.g., Weiss 1980; Shulha and Cousins 1997; Weiss 1998; Henry and Mark 2003), Weiss, Murphy-Graham, and Birkeland (2005) delineate four main ways that evaluation research can exert influence on policy decisions. One is *instrumental*, whereby evaluation results are used to provide direction to policy. This is the traditional approach that has come to define how many think about the processes leading to evidence-based policy. Weiss and her colleagues remind us that pure instrumental use is rare: "Decision makers pay attention to many things other than the evaluation of program effectiveness. They are interested in the desires of program participants and staff, the support of constituents, the claims of powerful people, the costs of change, the availability of staff with necessary capacities, and so on" (2005, 13).

Another well-known but often derided route to policy influence is *political* or symbolic. This type of use or influence of evaluation results provides legitimation—to "justify what decision makers want to do anyway" (Weiss et al. 2005, 13). Instead of policy flowing in a timely manner from the scientific research in the traditional sense, the research is picked up at a later time to support a policy position or course of action that is based on the intuition or self-interest of the advocate. For example, a local politician wishing to support the hiring of additional police officers for street patrols in order to reduce crime, despite his or her knowledge about what the research evidence says, will seek out studies that support the intended course of action. Of course, it is far more problematic when the research is purposely misused to support one's position.

A third type of influence is *conceptual*. Here, evaluation results are considered but not acted upon in any direct or immediate fashion. Instead, evaluation results find their way into policy discussions, sometimes becoming conventional wisdom. Weiss has referred to this as "enlightenment." This does not take place overnight, but rather in a slow, creeping fashion. Think of the Perry Preschool Project's substantial cost savings—a benefit-to-cost ratio of 7 to 1 at the age-twenty-seven follow-up—from reduced crime, less reliance on public services, and increased employment earnings (Schweinhart et al. 1993). The conceptual influence here was spurring interest in the monetary benefits that can be accrued from investing in early childhood prevention programs. Weiss, Murphy-Graham, and Birkeland (2005, 14) argue that this type of influence has been the "most important effect that research and evaluation have had on policy."

The fourth and newest way that evaluation results can have an influence on policy is what the authors refer to as *imposed use*. In this case, state or federal government agencies mandate that for any local program to receive funding it first needs to be evidence-based (Weiss et al. 2008). This usually comes in the form of a list of best practices that are put together and approved by the agency. One example is the "list of exemplary and promising prevention programs" of the U.S. Department of Education's Safe and Drug-Free Schools (SDFS) program. Programs not on this list are not eligible for government funding. Research by Weiss and her colleagues (2008) on the application of this list with respect to DARE and other school-based, substance-abuse prevention programs showed some advantages and shortcomings. In concluding that the imposed use of evaluation is in need of some tinkering, the researchers are clear in asserting that "giving evaluation more clout is a worthwhile way to increase the rationality of decision making" (Weiss et al. 2008, 29).

In the context of crime and justice, Michael Tonry and David Green (2003; see also Tonry 2009) identify four key filters that separate knowledge from policy. One has to do with *prevailing paradigms*. In the context of U.S. penal policy, they relate the following example:

> The individualized sentencing ethos of indeterminate sentencing was not sympathetic to research findings that "nothing works" (whether things worked or not), but the retributive ethos of determinate sentencing was. Scholars had raised empirical and normative questions about individualized sentencing for a quarter of a century before Martinson's famous article was published in 1974, but until paradigms shifted many people were not ready to pay attention. When a new determinate sentencing ethos predicated on retributive conceptions of justice took hold, people were ready to attend to the arguments in Martinson's article and acted on what they thought they learned. (Tonry and Green 2003, 487)

A second filter is *prevailing ideology*. Here, the beliefs held by elected officials and the public (or public views reinterpreted by politicians for their own gain, as in the "mythical" punitive public; see Listwan et al. 2008) shape the policy that comes to be adopted.

Another filter is *short-term political considerations*. This has everything to do with the worry by politicians that they may be perceived as soft on crime by supporting prevention or treatment instead of law and order measures, as well as the short time horizons of politicians, which favor quick fixes over longer-term strategies. Of course, this is not to suggest that only prevention or treatment measures are effective and research-based. But it remains all too common for short-term, untested law-and-order measures to be seen as the next panacea (Tonry 2003; Waller 2006).

The fourth filter is *short-term bureaucratic considerations and inertia*. Resistance to change and losing sight of the larger goals (e.g., crime reduction, improved health) are all-too-common reactions of some organizations dedicated to improving the human condition or serving the public.

In concluding their analysis of filters that have the effect of separating research knowledge from public policy, Tonry and Green (2003, 489) note that while real, they "do not mean that policy-making is impervious to influence from research findings and other systematic evidence. They do mean that influence is often indirect and partial." More recent writing on the topic by Michael Tonry (2009) perhaps best captures the elusive influence of research evidence on policy: "Some times on some subjects in some places policy makers and practitioners gratefully take account of evidence. Other times on other subjects in other places, they do not" (2).

How to overcome some of these realities as well as misconceived political barriers in order to get more scientific evidence about what works in preventing crime into policy and practice is by no means an easy task. Fortunately, this is receiving some attention in criminal justice (see Cullen 2002; Crime and Justice Institute 2004; Latessa 2004). For example, some research is looking at the transference of principles of effective treatment into secure correctional settings (Bourgon and Armstrong 2005).

The acceptance of decision-makers to make the use of systematic evidence a top priority may be facilitated by efforts that bring together the three main groups of researchers, policymakers, and practitioners. Mears (2007), building on the works of other scholars (Petersilia 1991; Blumstein 1997; Cullen 2005), proposes that individual states establish "criminal justice policy councils" that would serve both research and policy functions. He argues that these councils should be "autonomous, to the extent possible, and charged with conducting research and bringing together scholars, practitioners, and policymakers to discuss crime problems, proposed or existing solutions, and the research that should be undertaken" (679). Blumstein (1997) argues that these councils or "policy forums" must also play a role in educating the public about the complexities involved in the development of rational crime policy. Some of the thinking behind this collaborative approach is at the heart of the organizations that are leading the charge for evidence-based policy.

III. The Institutional Base

Efforts to use the best available evidence to inform policy, whether it is in early prevention or corrections, do not exist in a vacuum; rather, they are part of a larger movement or institutional base. This section overviews the institutional base of the evidence-based approach, from its beginnings in medicine to social sciences more generally, including the development of the Campbell Collaboration and its Crime and Justice Group.

A. From Cochrane to Campbell

In 1993 the Cochrane Collaboration, named after the renowned British epidemiologist Sir Archie Cochrane, was established to prepare, maintain, and make accessible systematic reviews of research on the effects of health care and medical interventions. The Cochrane Collaboration established collaborative review groups (CRGs) across the world to oversee the preparation and maintenance of systematic reviews on specific topics. For example, the Cochrane Injuries Group prepares systematic reviews relevant to the prevention, treatment, and rehabilitation of traumatic injury. All reviews produced by Cochrane CRGs follow a uniform structure. The same level of detail and consistency of reporting is found in each, and each review is made accessible through the *Cochrane Library*, a quarterly electronic publication.

In the United Kingdom, the National Institute for Health and Clinical Excellence (NICE) depends heavily on Cochrane reviews in deciding whether a treatment can be provided as part of the National Health Service (NHS): NICE operates as an independent organization to produce guidance in three areas of health: public health, health technologies, and clinical practice. It draws upon the expertise of the NHS and the wider health care community (e.g., healthcare professionals, medical researchers, patients, industry) in developing guidelines in these areas. To this end, it is committed to the use of the "best available evidence and involving all stakeholders in a transparent and collaborative manner" (National Institute for Health and Clinical Practice 2009).

The success of the Cochrane Collaboration in reviewing the effectiveness of medical and health care interventions stimulated international interest in establishing a similar infrastructure for conducting systematic reviews of research on the effects of interventions in the social sciences, including education, social work and social welfare, and crime and justice. In 2000 the Campbell Collaboration was established, named after the influential experimental psychologist Donald Campbell (see Campbell 1969). Funding for the Campbell Collaboration is provided by the Norwegian government.

Following the example of the Cochrane Collaboration, the Campbell Collaboration aims to prepare rigorous and systematic reviews of high-quality research evidence about what works. Recognizing that evidence is changing all the time, the Campbell Collaboration is also committed to updating reviews on a periodic basis. This is a particularly important feature of the registries of systematic reviews of both organizations. In medical science as well as the social sciences timely updates are crucial to accurately reflect the present state of scientific evidence, which in some cases can change rather dramatically with the addition of one large study, and to remain relevant to public policy. Lastly, through international networking, the Campbell Collaboration ensures that relevant evaluation studies conducted across the world are taken into account in its systematic reviews and that evidence from these reviews is made accessible globally through language translation and worldwide dissemination.

B. The Crime and Justice Group

To coordinate the work of the Crime and Justice Group, the Campbell Collaboration appointed a Crime and Justice Steering Committee (CJSC). The CJSC currently consists of eighteen members from eleven countries. The broad mission of the CJSC is to oversee the preparation and maintenance of systematic reviews of the highest-quality research on the effects of criminological interventions and to make them accessible electronically to practitioners, policymakers, scholars, and the general public. Reviews are focused on interventions designed to reduce delinquency or crime (presently the main focus of the CJSC), as well as those attempting to improve the management or operations of the criminal justice system. As of this writing, the Crime and Justice Group had twenty-four published systematic reviews, and a number of these have already been updated. As shown in table 3.1, the published reviews span a broad array of criminological domains, including families (parent training), place-based or situational prevention (improved street lighting, closed-circuit television surveillance), communities (neighborhood watch), policing (hot spots policing, problem-oriented policing), and courts and corrections (court-mandated batter treatment, boot camps, cognitive behavioral therapy for offenders).

All published reviews are available at the Crime and Justice Group website: www.campbellcollaboration.org/reviews_crime_justice/index.php. Another fifteen systematic reviews are in progress (see Farrington, Weisburd, and Gill 2011).

One of the problems that currently hinder the role of systematic reviews as an evidence-based resource in criminology and criminal justice is that they tend to be "one-off" exercises conducted as time, funding, and interest permit. Traditional print journals often lack the capacity for or interest in updating reviews once they have been published. As existing reviews become outdated, funding agencies usually pay for another set of researchers to start anew trying to locate, retrieve, code,

Table 3.1. Published Systematic Reviews by the Campbell Crime
and Justice Group

Type of Intervention	Lead Author
1. Scared straight	Anthony Petrosino
2. Boot camps	David Wilson
3. Counter-terrorism strategies	Cynthia Lum
4. Non-custodial employment programs for ex-offenders	Christy Visher
5. Incarceration-based drug treatment	Ojmarrh Mitchell
6. Custodial vs. non-custodial sentences	Martin Killias
7. Hot spots policing	Anthony Braga
8. Police-led drug enforcement strategies	Lorraine Mazerolle
9. Cognitive behavioral therapy for offenders	Mark Lipsey
10. Programs for serious juvenile offenders in secure corrections	Vicente Garrido
11. Cost-benefit and cost-effectiveness of sentencing	Cynthia McDougall
12. Early family/parent training	Alex Piquero
13. Court-mandated batterer treatment	Lynette Feder
14. Improved street lighting	Brandon Welsh
15. Problem-oriented policing	David Weisburd
16. Second responder programs for repeat incidents of family abuse	Robert Davis
17. Mentoring	Patrick Tolan
18. Closed-circuit television surveillance	Brandon Welsh
19. Neighborhood watch	Trevor Bennett
20. Parental imprisonment	Joseph Murray
21. Cyber abuse prevention	Faye Mishna
22. Drug substitution programs	Nicole Egli
23. School anti-bullying programs	David Farrington
24. Formal processing of juvenile offenders	Anthony Petrosino

Source: Crime and Justice Group, Campbell Collaboration. 2009. "Crime and Justice Reviews."
www.campbellcollaboration.org/reviews_crime_justice/index.php.

and analyze many of the same studies. Typically, previous researchers do not share their raw or coded data with a new researcher, which militates against the development of cumulative knowledge. Although the results of new reviews may not be duplicative, the resources and effort that go into them most certainly are.

The CJSC overcomes this state of affairs by having systematic reviews updated every three or four years (in accordance with the Campbell policy). These updates take account of new studies, cogent criticisms, and methodological advances. One of the ways that the CJSC helps to make sure that systematic reviews are maintained over time is that researchers, upon submitting a title to do a review, are asked to make a commitment to periodically update this review. Another way that the CJSC maintains systematic reviews is by establishing links between funding agencies and researchers; lack of funding is a major deterrent to updating reviews. Major funding for reviews in recent years has come from the US National Institute of Justice, the UK

National Policing Improvement Agency, Sweden's National Council for Crime Prevention, the Danish National Center for Social Research, and private foundations.

Like Cochrane's CRGs, Campbell's Crime and Justice Steering Committee acts as a vehicle for bringing to the attention of practitioners, policymakers, and others the most rigorous and up-to-date evidence on what works to prevent crime. At present, systematic reviews are disseminated or published in a wide range of outlets, such as government reports, academic journals, World Wide Web documents, and online publications. Each of these publication outlets has its own set of rules, structure, jargon and technical language, quality assurance methods, and capacity for detail and thoroughness.

Through the electronic publication of the Campbell Collaboration Library of Systematic Reviews, this archive will standardize the way systematic reviews are reported. Most importantly, systematic reviews will be more current and more easily accessible to those who need the evidence for their decision-making.

IV. INTERNATIONAL DEVELOPMENTS

In section II, we discussed key obstacles that impinge on the use of scientific evidence to inform public policy. In the previous section, we described the institutional base of the evidence-based approach, a base that is dedicated to the systematic development of scientific evidence and helping to overcome these obstacles. This section reports on key developments that have advanced evidence-based crime policy in a number of leading Western countries, including the United States, the United Kingdom, and Australia. Important to this accounting is a description of recent examples in which systematic evidence has influenced policy processes.

A. United States

The U.S. interest, as well as the interest of many other Western countries, in an evidence-based approach to crime policy may be said to have begun with the release of *Preventing Crime: What Works, What Doesn't, What's Promising*, by Lawrence Sherman and his colleagues (1997). This report was commissioned by the U.S. Congress as an independent, scientifically rigorous assessment of more than $4 billion worth of federally sponsored crime prevention programs. Using a scientific methods scale to rate program evaluations combined with a vote-counting review method (see n. 5), evidence-based conclusions were drawn about the effects of the full range of crime prevention measures, from early childhood programs to correctional treatment. The *New York Times* called the report "the most comprehensive study ever of crime prevention" (Butterfield 1997, A20).

Preceding the report by Sherman et al. (1997) was the federally funded Communities That Care (CTC) strategy, developed by David Hawkins and Richard Catalano (1992). This prevention strategy is based on a theory (the social development model) that organizes risk and protective factors. The intervention techniques are tailored to the needs of each particular community. The CTC strategy aims to reduce delinquency and other problem behaviors by implementing particular prevention programs that have demonstrated effectiveness in reducing risk factors or enhancing protective factors. It is modeled on large-scale, community-wide public health programs designed to reduce illnesses such as coronary heart disease by tackling key risk factors (Farquhar et al. 1985; Perry, Klepp, and Sillers 1989). As a risk-focused, evidence-based prevention model, CTC continues to be supported at the local level across the United States, at last count in several hundred communities (Harachi et al. 2003). It is also undergoing a large-scale randomized controlled trial in the United States (Hawkins, Brown, et al. 2008; Hawkins, Catalano, et al. 2008; Hawkins et al. 2009). It has also been implemented in more than twenty sites in England, Scotland, and Wales, and in Australia, Canada, and the Netherlands (Utting 1999; France and Crow 2001; Flynn 2008).

Funded by the U.S. Office of Juvenile Justice and Delinquency Prevention, Blueprints for Violence Prevention is another important federal initiative set up to help local jurisdictions use what works best to prevent violent crime and replicate these effective programs across the country. For programs to be labeled as effective, they must adhere to a set of strict scientific standards similar to those used by Sherman et al. (1997). The initiative has identified eleven model (proven effective) and twenty-three promising programs (Elliott and Mihalic 2004; Mihalic et al. 2004).

Two statewide initiatives—one in Colorado and the other in Washington State—provide clear-cut examples in which systematic evidence has influenced policy processes. In Colorado, the focus is on home visiting services to prevent child maltreatment by targeting poor, first-time mothers. This initiative, known as the Nurse Home Visitor Program (NHVP), was created by state law in 2000 and was based on the evidence-based early childhood home visiting program developed by David Olds (see Olds 2007). In a series of randomized trials, Olds's program has shown consistent desirable effects across a range of outcomes, including prenatal health behaviors, child abuse and neglect, and criminal involvement of the mothers and children. Importantly, NHVP is not funded as a one-off program or designed to be limited to the most at-risk families: "the intention of the legislation is that the program be expanded annually so that the services will be available for all eligible mothers who choose to participate in all parts of the state" (Calonge 2005, 5).

In 1997, the Washington State legislature commissioned the Washington State Institute for Public Policy to assess the effectiveness and economic efficiency of a range of crime prevention and criminal justice programs with the aim to "identify interventions that reduce crime and lower total costs to taxpayers and crime victims" (Aos, Barnoski, and Lieb 1998, 1). The researchers referred to their methodological approach as "bottom line" financial analysis, which they considered to parallel the approach used by investors who study rates of return on financial investments. The research began with a literature review of high-quality programs, carried out in conjunction with the University of Washington's Social Development Research Group. A five-step analytical model was used to describe the overall picture of each program's economic contribution.[8]

What started out as a highly rigorous yet fairly modest policy research initiative soon turned into the most comprehensive approach to develop evidence-based crime policy in the United States and one revered by other countries (Greenwood 2006; Aldhous 2007). Following the Institute's first set of reports (e.g., Aos et al. 1999), the legislature authorized a number of system-level randomized evaluations of the most effective and cost-beneficial juvenile and adult programs. The results of these trials helped to refine local practice and service delivery. By 2006, the Institute had systematically reviewed and analyzed 571 of the highest-quality evaluations of crime prevention and criminal justice programs, estimated the costs and benefits of effective programs, and "projected the degree to which alternative 'portfolios' of these programs could affect future prison construction needs, criminal justice costs, and crime rates in Washington" (Aos, Miller, and Drake 2006, 1). This work was commissioned by the legislature to address the projected need for two new state prisons by 2020 and possibly a third by 2030. Based on a moderate-to-aggressive portfolio of evidence-based programs ($63–$171 million expenditure in the first year), it was found that a significant amount of future prison construction costs could be avoided, about $2 billion saved by taxpayers, and crime rates lowered slightly (Aos, Miller, and Drake 2006, 16). The state legislature has since approved a version of this approach and abandoned plans to build one of the prisons.

B. United Kingdom

The benefits of systematic research evidence to inform crime policy has also received some interest in the United Kingdom in recent years. The British Government's Crime Reduction Programme (CRP), which ran between 1999 and 2002 and was funded to the tune of £400 million (approximately $640 million), was the central organizing body for evidence-led initiatives. The CRP grew out of a 1997 London conference and a subsequent report—modeled on the report by Sherman et al. (1997)—that assessed the research evidence on what is effective and cost-effective in preventing crime (Nuttall, Goldblatt, and Lewis 1998). Administered by the Home Office, the CRP's main goal was to "reduce crime and disorder through an evidence-led strategy of what works . . . with a special focus on promoting innovation, generating a significant improvement in knowledge about effectiveness and cost-effectiveness, and fostering progressive mainstreaming of emerging knowledge about good practice" (Dhiri et al. 2001, 179, 181).

Some of the initiatives under the CRP included the setting up and (independent) evaluation of numerous programs designed to reduce repeat residential burglary victimization, domestic violence and violence against women, and other priority crime problems; the establishment of the University of York's Centre for Criminal Justice Economics and Psychology (a program dedicated to advancing economic evaluation research in the area of crime and justice); the commission of research on the application of evidence-based principles (Tilley and Laycock 2002); the commission of systematic reviews on the effects of CCTV surveillance cameras and improved street lighting on crime (Farrington and Welsh 2002; Welsh and Farrington 2002; see also Welsh and Farrington 2009); funding of the Campbell Collaboration Crime and Justice Group; and the first randomized experiment in crime and justice in the country in twenty-five years (Farrington 2003a)—a multisite restorative justice program directed by Lawrence Sherman and Heather Strang (see Sherman 2003).

Despite these accomplishments (but in the face of many unmet objectives), the CRP was criticized for failing to deliver on its primary objective of using a "research-driven" approach to guide policy and practice on what works best to reduce crime (see e.g., Maguire 2004). Four main challenges faced the implementation of the CRP and ultimately lead to its demise: "(1) translating the evidence base into local practical programmes and projects; (2) managing programme implementation and coherence; (3) delivering financial and other resources; and (4) establishing effective processes for evaluation, learning and change" (Nutley and Homel 2006, 14).

Since the end of the CRP, an evidence-based approach has maintained a role in British crime policy. The promotion of the use of what works to prevent crime based on systematic research evidence (e.g., Hutchings, Gardner, and Lane 2004; Lösel 2007) has been embraced in some policy areas. For example, in September 2006, former British Prime Minister Tony Blair announced the creation of the Action Plan on Social Exclusion.[9] The action plan emphasizes early intervention, better coordination of agencies, and evidence-based practice to reduce physical aggression and the associated social problems that lead young people to become disconnected from society (Farrington and Sutton 2006). As part of this action plan, the British government, in April 2007, launched a ten-city pilot study to test the effectiveness of the evidence-based nurse-family partnership (NFP) program developed by David Olds (Rumbelow and Miles 2007). Additionally, the Ministry of Justice (formerly the crime section of the Home Office) and the National Policing Improvement Agency (through the Campbell Collaboration Crime and Justice Group) have commissioned new systematic reviews to investigate the effectiveness of various criminal justice interventions. Another important development has been the support for high-quality evaluations. According to Farrington (2003a, 163), "the Home Office seems more interested in using randomized experiments now than at any time in the past twenty-five years."

C. Australia

Set up in 1997, the Australian Government's National Crime Prevention Pro-gramme (NCP), while not established with the expressed intent of adhering to the evidence-based model, has seemingly embraced the notions of using research on what works best and contributing to the state of science in crime prevention and criminal justice through evaluation research, albeit of varying methodolog-ical quality. An independent review of the NCP in 2004 concluded that it "had made measurable contributions to both the evidence base and the national crime prevention infrastructure, particularly at the local level" (Australian Government Attorneys General's Department 2005). The Australian criminologist Peter Homel (2005) notes that an absence of commitment to a research and evaluation process greatly hampered national crime-prevention policy in the early years and is sorely needed in order to build up the evidence base from which policies can be formulated.

Like the UK, Australia has embraced the evidence-based nurse-family partner-ship (NFP) program developed by David Olds. At least two Australian states (New South Wales and South Australia) have implemented the NFP program as a central component of early childhood intervention to improve health and other life-course outcomes of newborns and their young parents. In South Australia, a mixed model of the program is offered: a universal home visit for all newborns and two years of home visits for targeted groups identified as having the greatest need. In New South Wales, a universal visit is provided to all newborns, and any subsequent visits are based on the discretion and resources of local health authorities (Bowen, Zwi, Sainsbury, and Whitehead 2009). This is one area in which it can be said that systematic evidence has influenced policy processes.

Other efforts that point to a growing interest in the promotion and use of evidence-based crime prevention in Australia include various government-sponsored publications such as *The Promise of Crime Prevention* (Gant and Grabosky 2000) and *Pathways to Prevention* (Homel et al. 1999), as well as the development, by the Australian Institute of Criminology (AIC) and the Attorney-General's Department of New South Wales, of an international conference on evidence-based crime prevention that took place in November 2005. Titled "Delivering Crime Prevention: Making the Evidence Work," the conference aimed to "critically exam-ine the role of evidence-based policy approaches in the development and delivery of crime prevention policies and programs in Australia today" (Australian Institute of Criminology 2005).

In recent years, there has also been a trend toward the use of higher-quality evaluation designs, including randomized experiments, to assess the impact of crime prevention and criminal justice programs. Perhaps the best known of these evaluations are the randomized experiments of restorative justice conferences by Strang and Sherman (2006). Other important Australian randomized experiments have focused on early parent training to prevent child behavior problems (Hiscock et al. 2008), including the Triple P—Positive Parenting Program developed by Sanders, Markie-Dadds, Tully, and Bor (2000).

V. Challenges and Future Directions

A movement toward evidence-based crime policy is not without its challenges. There are two key substantive and practical challenges that limit the capacity of the evidence-based model to deliver more efficacious crime reduction. One is implementation and the ability to tailor systematic evidence about what works best to local context and conditions. Another is the use of evidence-based programs by practitioners.

A. Implementation

The importance of implementation to the evidence-based model is perhaps best captured by the following two passages. The first comes from Lawrence Sherman's (1998) research on the application of the evidence-based model to policing: "Evidence-based policing assumes that experiments alone are not enough. Putting research into practice requires just as much attention to implementation as it does to controlled evaluations" (7). The second passage comes from Joan Petersilia's (2008) research and experience as an "embedded criminologist" in California's correctional system: "The current literature on 'what works' in rehabilitation programs is insufficient to guide policy without corresponding literature on program implementation" (349). "We need to begin developing a science around program implementation . . ." (350).

Successful implementation calls for taking account of local context and conditions. Some critics of the evidence-based paradigm (e.g., Lab 2003; Pawson 2006) claim that it fails adequately to account for local context and conditions in reaching conclusions about what works. The main thrust of this argument is that unless local context and conditions are investigated undue weight may be ascribed to any effects of the intervention on the outcome of interest.

Evidence-based crime prevention has in place the capacity to take account of these features. For example, those tasked with investigating the research evidence on the effectiveness of an intervention program to deal with a particular crime problem can question the original researchers or solicit unpublished reports to learn about how local context and conditions may have influenced the observed results. This information can then be integrated into the existing profile of the program.

Evidence-based crime prevention also has the capacity to tailor proven strategies or practices appropriately to the local setting. While perhaps obvious and supported in research on diffusion of knowledge and replication studies (e.g., Ekblom 2002; Liddle et al. 2002), not paying attention to this (and using the "one-size-fits-all" approach) can severely affect both the implementation and the overall effectiveness of the intervention. Hough and Tilley (1998, 28) make clear this point:

> Routinely-used techniques often cannot be taken off the shelf and applied
> mechanically with much real prospect of success. Standard, broad-brush,
> blockbuster approaches to problems tend to produce disappointing results.
> Where new approaches are adopted it is likely that adjustments will be needed in
> the light of early experience. All crime prevention measures work (or fail to do
> so) according to their appropriateness to the particular problem and its setting.

Detailed observational and other information on the crime problem that is the focus of attention, as well as the setting (urban density, unemployment rates), can be matched with the proven intervention program and modifications can then be made as needed.

B. Practitioner Use

There will always be barriers to getting some practitioners to use research evidence on what works best to reduce crime. Some of these barriers include administrative constraints (too few resources, need for training of personnel), philosophical differences, and institutional resistance to change. Overcoming the disconnection between research evidence and practice may best be achieved through the employment of a research scientist or manager. In the capacity of a research scientist this individual would be responsible for keeping current on the latest research findings and coming up with recommendations based on the accumulated research evidence. In the capacity of a manager this individual's role would be to monitor that crime prevention practices in the field adhere to recommendations based on research evidence. Importantly, their role would also be to "redirect practice through compliance rather than punishment" (Sherman 1998, 3).

The wider crime and justice community could learn from similar initiatives that have shown promise in the fields of medicine and agriculture. Some hospitals in the United States employ a medical researcher who is in charge of developing evidence-based guidelines for surgical procedures and patient care based on the most up-to-date scientific evidence (Millenson 1997). In the field of agriculture in the United States, the development of land-grant universities by the federal government brought science to local farmers to improve crop production. Land-grant universities, which exist throughout the country, "focused on practical problem-solving and gave farmers access to scientific knowledge" (MacKenzie 1998, 1). While somewhat different today, schools of agriculture in these universities still uphold the mission of aiding the farming community by making available scientific evidence on what works best.

It needs to be acknowledged that the majority of other, especially not-for-profit, organizations involved in preventing crime and improving justice will not have the resources to retain the in-house services of a research scientist or manager. But it may be feasible to pool resources among a number of like-minded organizations, such as in the form of a coalition, to have an individual serve in this capacity.

It will also be important to understand the specific needs of local practitioners and the relationships among the scientific community (and the research evidence produced), policymakers, and practitioners. What are the resource, service delivery, and training needs of practitioners with respect to an evidence-led approach? What systems do practitioners need for the adoption of new evidence as it becomes available? Should accountability and performance measures be adopted to ensure that the latest scientific findings are being used? These are just a few of the questions that must be addressed in the context of a wider program of research on incorporating scientific evidence into policy and practice.

The movement toward rational and evidence-based crime policy is here to stay. It does not appear to be yet another fad or fleeting idea in the annals of criminal justice policy making. While there remains much to be done to elevate systematic scientific research into center stage in the policy-making process, the good news is that this work is well under way. This is evidenced by a growing body of high-quality evaluations, including randomized experiments, of crime prevention and criminal justice programs and policies; continuing efforts by the Campbell Collaboration's Crime and Justice Group to prepare, maintain, and disseminate systematic reviews of research conducted across the world on what works to reduce crime and improve justice; emerging developments in the United States and other Western countries to make some crime policies more evidence-based; and some emerging research on the transference of knowledge. In the United States, this is taking place in the context of a renewed federal government commitment to science. This is a very welcome development indeed.

Almost a decade ago, we concluded one of our first articles on evidence-based crime policy (Welsh and Farrington 2001) with a quote from an important essay by Richard Rosenfeld (2000) on evaluation research on gun policy. The passage transcends the immediate subject matter and speaks to the critical dimensions of making crime policy more rational and evidence-based. It was fitting then and remains equally so today: "although political considerations will always play a prominent role in policy development, politics that has to contend with the results of good science should produce better policy than politics based on poor science or none at all" (Rosenfeld 2000, 616).

NOTES

*   We are grateful to Meghan Peel for timely research assistance and Michael Tonry and Christopher Sullivan for especially helpful comments.
1. We use the term "evidence-based crime prevention" to capture the full universe of programs and policies designed to reduce crime.

2. Descriptive validity, which refers to the adequacy of reporting of information, could be added as a fifth criterion of the methodological quality of evaluation research (Farrington 2003b; see also Lösel and Koferl 1989).

3. Statistical power refers to the probability of correctly detecting an effect; that is, of rejecting the null hypothesis (of no effect of the intervention) when it is false (i.e., when the intervention really has an effect on crime). Studies based on small numbers may not yield statistically significant results even when the intervention has a large effect on crime.

4. We estimated the importance of regression to the mean using recorded crime rates in police Basic Command Units in England and Wales in 2002–03 and 2003–04, and concluded that, in reasonable comparisons between areas with high and moderately high crime rates, this effect may cause a 4 percent decrease in crimes (Farrington and Welsh 2006b).

5. While not as rigorous as these two methods, another widely used and robust review method is vote-counting. It adds a quantitative element to the narrative review by counting the number of statistically significant and desirable results out of all findings (Farrington et al. 2006).

6. The criterion of methodological quality that is used for including (or excluding) studies is perhaps the "most important and controversial" issue in conducting systematic reviews (Farrington and Petrosino 2001, 42). How high to set the "bar" of methodological rigor as part of a review of the literature, systematic or other, is a question that all researchers face. For a brief discussion of this issue in the context of the vote-counting review method, see MacKenzie (2000).

7. It is beyond the scope of this chapter to discuss each step, but interested readers should consult the reviews of this methodology as applied in the context of crime prevention (see Welsh and Farrington 2000). In addition, for methodological features of cost-benefit analysis in general, see Layard and Glaister (1994) and Welsh, Farrington, and Sherman (2001).

8. The first step of the model involved estimating each program's "most likely practical application within the state's justice or early intervention systems" (Aos, Barnoski, and Lieb 1998, 8). Step 2 looked at whether program results could be replicated in the state. Step 3 involved an assessment of program costs, estimated on the basis of what it would cost the Washington State government to implement a similar program (if the program was not already operating in the state). Step 4 involved monetizing each program's effects on crime. Savings to the criminal justice system and crime victims were estimated. The final step involved calculating the economic contribution of the programs, expressed as benefit-to-cost ratios. From this, programs could then be judged on their independent and comparative monetary value.

9. Social exclusion is a general concept including antisocial behavior, teenage pregnancy, educational failure, and mental health problems (Cabinet Office 2006).

REFERENCES

Aldhous, Peter. 2007. "Applying Science to Prison Overcrowding." *New Scientist*, February 10, 2007. http://www.newscientist.com.

Aos, Steve, Robert Barnoski, and Roxanne Lieb. 1998. "Preventive Programs for Young Offenders: Effective and Cost-Effective." *Overcrowded Times* 9(2):1, 7–11.

Aos, Steve, Polly Phipps, Robert Barnoski, and Roxanne Lieb. 1999. *The Comparative Costs and Benefits of Programs to Reduce Crime: A Review of National Research Findings with Implications for Washington State*, version 3.0. Olympia: Washington State Institute for Public Policy.

Aos, Steve, Marna Miller, and Elizabeth Drake. 2006. *Evidence-Based Public Policy Options to Reduce Future Prison Construction, Criminal Justice Costs, and Crime Rates.* Olympia: Washington State Institute for Public Policy.

Australian Government Attorneys General's Department. 2005. The National Crime Prevention Programme. http://www.crimeprevention.gov.au/agd/WWW/ncphome. nsf/Page/National_Crime_Prevention_Programme.

Australian Institute of Criminology. 2005. Delivering Crime Prevention: Making the Evidence Work. http://www.aic.gov.au/conferences/2005-cp/.

Barnett, W. Steven. 1993. "Cost-Benefit Analysis." In *Significant Benefits: The High/Scope Perry Preschool Study Through Age 27*, Lawrence J. Schweinhart, Helen V. Barnes, and David P. Weikart. Ypsilanti, MI: High/Scope Press.

Blumstein, Alfred. 1997. "Interaction of Criminological Research and Public Policy." *Journal of Quantitative Criminology* 12:349–61.

Blumstein, Alfred, and Joan Petersilia. 1995. "Investing in Criminal Justice Research." In *Crime: Twenty-Eight Leading Experts Look at the Most Pressing Problem of Our Time*, edited by James Q. Wilson and Joan Petersilia. San Francisco, CA: Institute for Contemporary Studies Press.

Bourgon, Guy, and Barbara Armstrong. 2005. "Transferring the Principles of Effective Treatment into a 'Real World' Prison Setting." *Criminal Justice and Behavior* 32:3–25.

Bowen, Shelley, Anthony B. Zwi, Peter Sainsbury, and Margaret Whitehead. 2009. "Killer Facts, Politics and Other Influences: What Evidence Triggered Early Childhood Intervention Policies in Australia?" *Evidence and Policy* 5:5–32.

Braga, Anthony A., and David Weisburd. 2010. *Policing Problem Places: Crime Hot Spots and Effective Prevention.* New York: Oxford University Press.

Butterfield, Fox. 1997. "Most Efforts to Stop Crime Fall Short, Study Finds." *New York Times*, April 16, A20.

Cabinet Office. 2006. *Reaching Out: An Action Plan for Social Exclusion.* London: Cabinet Office.

Calonge, Ned. 2005. "Community Interventions to Prevent Violence: Translation into Public Health Practice." *American Journal of Preventive Medicine* 28(2S1): 4–5.

Campbell, Donald T. 1969. "Reforms as Experiments." *American Psychologist* 24:409–29.

Campbell, Donald T., and Julian C. Stanley. 1966. *Experimental and Quasi-Experimental Designs for Research.* Chicago: Rand McNally.

Cook, Thomas D., and Donald T. Campbell. 1979. *Quasi-Experimentation: Design and Analysis Issues for Field Settings.* Chicago: Rand McNally.

Cullen, Francis T. 2002. "Rehabilitation and Treatment Programs." In *Crime: Public Policies for Crime Control*, edited by James Q. Wilson and Joan Petersilia. San Francisco, CA.: Institute for Contemporary Studies Press.

———. 2005. "The Twelve People Who Saved Rehabilitation: How the Science of Criminology Made a Difference." *Criminology* 43:1–42.

Crime and Justice Group, Campbell Collaboration. 2009. "Crime and Justice Reviews." www.campbellcollaboration.org/reviews_crime_justice/index.php.

Crime and Justice Institute. 2004. *Implementing Evidence-based Principles in Community Corrections: Leading Organizational Change and Development*. Washington, DC: National Institute of Corrections, Community Corrections Division, U.S. Department of Justice.

Dhiri, Sanjay, Peter Goldblatt, Sam Brand, and Richard Price. 2001. "Evaluation of the United Kingdom's 'Crime Reduction Programme:' Analysis of Costs and Benefits." In *Costs and Benefits of Preventing Crime*, edited by Brandon C. Welsh, David P. Farrington, and Lawrence W. Sherman. Boulder, CO: Westview Press.

Eisner, Manuel. 2009. "No Effects in Independent Prevention Trials: Can We Reject the Cynical View?" *Journal of Experimental Criminology* 5:163–83.

Ekblom, Paul. 2002. "From the Source to the Mainstream Is Uphill: The Challenge of Transferring Knowledge of Crime Prevention Through Replication, Innovation and Anticipation." In *Analysis for Crime Prevention*, edited by Nick Tilley. Vol. 13 of *Crime Prevention Studies*, edited by Ronald V. Clarke. Monsey, NY: Criminal Justice Press.

Elliott, Delbert S., and Sharon F. Mihalic. 2004. "Issues in Disseminating and Replicating Effective Prevention Programs." *Prevention Science* 5:47–52.

Farquhar, John W., Stephen P. Fortmann, Nathan MacCoby, William L. Haskell, Paul T. Williams, June A. Flora, C. Barr Taylor, Byron W. Brown, Douglas S. Solomon, and Stephen B. Hulley. 1985. "The Stanford Five-City Project: Design and Methods." *American Journal of Epidemiology* 122:323–34.

Farrington, David P. 1983. "Randomized Experiments on Crime and Justice." In *Crime and Justice: An Annual Review of Research*, vol. 4, edited by Michael Tonry and Norval Morris. Chicago: University of Chicago Press.

Farrington, David P. 1997. "Evaluating a Community Crime Prevention Program." *Evaluation* 3:157–73.

———. 2003a. "British Randomized Experiments on Crime and Justice." *Annals of the American Academy of Political and Social Science* 589:150–67.

———. 2003b. "Methodological Quality Standards for Evaluation Research." *Annals of the American Academy of Political and Social Science* 587:49–68.

Farrington, David P., Denise C. Gottfredson, Lawrence W. Sherman, and Brandon C. Welsh. 2006. "The Maryland Scientific Methods Scale." In *Evidence-Based Crime Prevention*, rev. ed., edited by Lawrence W. Sherman, David P. Farrington, Brandon C. Welsh, and Doris Layton MacKenzie. New York: Routledge.

Farrington, David P., and Anthony Petrosino. 2001. "The Campbell Collaboration Crime and Justice Group." *Annals of the American Academy of Political and Social Science* 578:35–49.

Farrington, David P., and Carole Sutton. 2006. "The Prevention of Physical Aggression in the UK." Paper prepared for the Action Plan on Social Exclusion, Cabinet Office.

Farrington, David P., David Weisburd, and Charlotte E. Gill. 2011. "The Campbell Collaboration Crime and Justice Group: A Decade of Progress." In *Handbook of International Criminology*, edited by C.J. Smith, S. Zhang, and Rosemary Barberet. New York: Routledge.

Farrington, David P., and Brandon C. Welsh. 2002. Effects of Improved Street Lighting on Crime: A Systematic Review. Home Office Research Study 251. London: Home Office.

———. 2005. "Randomized Experiments in Criminology: What Have We Learned in the Last Two Decades?" *Journal of Experimental Criminology* 1:9–38.

————. 2006a. "A Half-Century of Randomized Experiments on Crime and Justice." In *Crime and Justice: A Review of Research*, vol. 34, edited by Michael Tonry. Chicago: University of Chicago Press.

————. 2006b. "How Important is 'Regression to the Mean' in Area-Based Crime Prevention Research?" *Crime Prevention and Community Safety* 8(1):50–60.

————. 2007. *Saving Children from a Life of Crime: Early Risk Factors and Effective Interventions*. New York: Oxford University Press.

Flynn, Robert J. 2008. "Communities That Care: A Comprehensive System for Youth Prevention and Promotion, and Canadian Applications to Date." In *Towards More Comprehensive Approaches to Prevention and Safety. IPC Review*, vol. 2, edited by Ross Hastings and Melanie Bania. Ottawa, Canada: Institute for the Prevention of Crime, University of Ottawa.

France, Alan, and Iain Crow. 2001. *CTC—The Story So Far: An Interim Evaluation of Communities That Care*. York, UK: Joseph Rowntree Foundation.

Gant, Frances, and Peter N. Grabosky. 2000. *The Promise of Crime Prevention*, 2nd ed. Canberra: Australian Institute of Criminology.

Gest, Ted. 2001. *Crime & Politics: Big Government's Erratic Campaign for Law and Order*. New York: Oxford University Press.

Gottfredson, Denise C., David B. Wilson, and Stacy Skroban Najaka. 2006. "School-Based Crime Prevention." In *Evidence-Based Crime Prevention*, rev. ed., edited by Lawrence W. Sherman, David P. Farrington, Brandon C. Welsh, and Doris Layton MacKenzie. New York: Routledge.

Greenwood, Peter W. 2006. *Changing Lives: Delinquency Prevention as Crime-Control Policy*. Chicago: University of Chicago Press.

Halladay, Mark, and Lisa Bero. 2000. "Implementing Evidence-Based Practice in Health Care." *Public Money and Management* 20:43–50.

Harachi, Tracy W., J. David Hawkins, Richard F. Catalano, Andrea M. Lafazia, Brian H. Smith, and Michael W. Arthur. 2003. "Evidence-Based Community Decision Making for Prevention: Two Case Studies of Communities That Care." *Japanese Journal of Sociological Criminology* 28:26–38.

Hawkins, J. David, Eric C. Brown, Sabrina Oesterle, Michael W. Arthur, Robert D. Abbott, and Richard F. Catalano. 2008. "Early Effects of Communities That Care on Targeted Risks and Initiation of Delinquent Behavior and Substance Abuse." *Journal of Adolescent Health* 43:15–22.

Hawkins, J. David, and Richard F. Catalano. 1992. *Communities That Care: Action for Drug Abuse Prevention*. San Francisco, CA: Jossey-Bass.

Hawkins, J. David, Richard F. Catalano, Michael W. Arthur, Elizabeth Egan, Eric C. Brown, Robert D. Abbott, and David M. Murray. 2008. "Testing Communities That Care: The Rationale, Design and Behavioral Baseline Equivalence of the Community Youth Development Study." *Prevention Science* 9:178–90.

Hawkins, J. David, Sabrina Oesterle, Eric C. Brown, Michael W. Arthur, Robert D. Abbott, Abigail A. Fagan, and Richard F. Catalano. 2009. "Results of a Type 2 Translational Research Trial to Prevent Adolescent Drug Use and Delinquency: A Test of Communities That Care." *Archives of Pediatrics and Adolescent Medicine* 163:789–98.

Henry, Gary T., and Melvin M. Mark. 2003. "Beyond Use: Understanding Evaluation's Influence on Attitudes and Action." *American Journal of Evaluation* 24:293–314.

Hiscock, Harriet, Jordana K. Bayer, Anna Price, Obioha C. Ukoumunne, Susan Rogers, and
    Melissa Wake. 2008. "Universal Parenting Programme to Prevent Early Childhood
    Behavioural Problems: Cluster Randomised Trial." *British Medical Journal*. www.bmj.com.
Homel, Peter. 2005. "A Short History of Crime Prevention in Australia." *Canadian Journal
    of Criminology and Criminal Justice* 47:355–68.
Homel, Ross, Judy Cashmore, L. Gilmore, Jacqui Goodnow, Alan Hayes, Janet Law-
    rence, Marie Leech, Ian O'Connor, Tony Vinson, J. Najman, and John Western.
    1999. *Pathways to Prevention: Developmental and Early Intervention Approaches to
    Crime in Australia*. Canberra, Australia: Commonwealth Attorney-General's
    Department.
Hood, Roger. 2002. "Criminology and Penal Policy: The Vital Role of Empirical Research." In
    Ideology, Crime and Criminal Justice: A Symposium in Honour of Sir Leon Radzinowicz,
    edited by Anthony Bottoms and Michael Tonry. Cullompton, Devon, UK: Willan.
Hough, Michael, and Nick Tilley. 1998. *Getting the Grease to the Squeak: Research Lessons
    for Crime Prevention*. Crime Detection and Prevention Series Paper 85. London: Home
    Office.
Hutchings, Judy, Frances Gardner, and Eleanor Lane. 2004. "Making Evidence-Based
    Interventions Work." In *Support from the Start: Working with Young Children and Their
    Families to Reduce the Risks of Crime and Anti-Social Behaviour*. Research Report 524,
    edited by Carole Sutton, David Utting, and David P. Farrington. London: Department
    for Education and Skills.
Johnson, Byron R., Spencer De Li, David B. Larson, and Michael McCullough. 2000. "A
    Systematic Review of the Religiosity and Delinquency Literature: A Research Note."
    Journal of Contemporary Criminal Justice 16:32–52.
Knapp, Martin. 1997. "Economic Evaluations and Interventions for Children and Adolescents
    with Mental Health Problems." *Journal of Child Psychology and Psychiatry* 38:3–25.
Kothari, Anita, Lynne MacLean, and Nancy Edwards. 2009. "Increasing Capacity for
    Knowledge Translation: Understanding How Some Researchers Engage Policy
    Makers." *Evidence and Policy* 5:33–51.
Lab, Steven P. 2003. "Let's Put It in Context." *Criminology and Public Policy* 3:39–44.
Latessa, Edward J. 2004. "The Challenge of Change: Correctional Programs and Evidence-
    Based Practices." *Criminology and Public Policy* 3:547–60.
Layard, Richard, and Stephen Glaister, eds. 1994. *Cost-Benefit Analysis*, 2nd ed. New York:
    Cambridge University Press.
Liddle, Howard A., Cynthia L. Rowe, Tanya J. Quille, Gayle A. Dakof, Dana Scott Mills, Eve
    Sakran, and Hector Biaggi. 2002. "Transporting a Research-Based Adolescent Drug
    Treatment into Practice." *Journal of Substance Abuse Treatment* 22:231–43.
Lipsey, Mark W., and David B. Wilson. 2001. *Practical Meta-Analysis*. Thousand Oaks, CA:
    Sage.
Listwan, Shelley J., Cheryl L. Jonson, Francis T. Cullen, and Edward J. Latessa. 2008.
    "Cracks in the Penal Harm Movement: Evidence from the Field." *Criminology and
    Public Policy* 7:423–65.
Lösel, Friedrich. 2007. "COUNTERBLAST: The Prison Overcrowding Crisis and Some
    Constructive Perspectives for Crime Policy." *Howard Journal of Criminal Justice*
    46:512–19.
Lösel, Friedrich, and Peter Koferl. 1989. "Evaluation Research on Correctional Treatment
    in West Germany: A Meta-Analysis." In *Criminal Behavior and the Justice System:*

Psychological Perspectives, edited by Hermann Wegener, Friedrich Lösel, and Jochen Haisch. New York: Springer-Verlag.

MacKenzie, Doris Layton. 1998. "Using the US Land-Grant University System as a Model to Attack this Nation's Crime Problem." *Criminologist* 23(2):1, 3–4.

———. 2000. "Evidence-Based Corrections: Identifying What Works." *Crime and Delinquency* 46:457–71.

———. 2006. *What Works in Corrections: Reducing the Criminal Activities of Offenders and Delinquents*. New York: Cambridge University Press.

Maguire, Mike. 2004. "The Crime Reduction Programme in England and Wales: Reflections on the Vision and the Reality." *Criminal Justice* 4:213–37.

McCord, Joan. 2003. "Cures That Harm: Unanticipated Outcomes of Crime Prevention Programs." *Annals of the American Academy of Political and Social Science* 587:16–30.

Mears, Daniel P. 2007. "Towards Rational and Evidence-Based Crime Policy." *Journal of Criminal Justice* 35:667–82.

Mihalic, Sharon F., Abigail Fagan, Katherine Irwin, Diane Ballard, and Delbert S. Elliott. 2004. *Blueprints for Violence Prevention*. Washington, DC: Office of Juvenile Justice and Delinquency Prevention, U.S. Department of Justice.

Millenson, Michael L. 1997. *Demanding Medical Excellence: Doctors and Accountability in the Information Age*. Chicago: University of Chicago Press.

Mosteller, Frederick, and Robert F. Boruch, eds. 2002. *Evidence Matters: Randomized Trials in Education Research*. Washington, DC: Brookings Institution Press.

National Institute for Health and Clinical Excellence. 2009. "About NICE: How We Work." http://www.nice.org.uk/aboutnice/howwework/how_we_work.jsp.

Nutley, Sandra, and Peter Homel. 2006. "Delivering Evidence-Based Policy and Practice: Lessons from the Implementation of the UK Crime Reduction Programme." *Evidence and Policy* 2:5–26.

Nuttall, Christopher, Peter Goldblatt, and Chris Lewis, eds. 1998. *Reducing Offending: An Assessment of Research Evidence on Ways of Dealing with Offending Behaviour*. Home Office Research Study 187. London: Home Office Research and Statistics Directorate.

Olds, David L. 2007. "Preventing Crime with Prenatal and Infancy Support to Parents: The Nurse-Family Partnership." *Victims and Offenders* 2:205–25.

Pawson, Ray. 2006. *Evidence-Based Policy: A Realist Perspective*. London: Sage.

Perry, Cheryl L., Knut-Inge Klepp, and Cynthia Sillers. 1989. "Community-Wide Strategies for Cardiovascular Health: The Minnesota Heart Health Program Youth Program." *Health Education Research* 4:87–101.

Petersilia, Joan. 1987. *The Influence of Criminal Justice Research*. Santa Monica, CA: RAND.

———. 1991. "Policy Relevance and the Future of Criminology." *Criminology* 29:1–15.

———. 2008. "Influencing Public Policy: An Embedded Criminologist Reflects on California Prison Reform." *Journal of Experimental Criminology* 4:335–56.

Petrosino, Anthony. 2000. "How Can We Respond Effectively to Juvenile Crime?" *Pediatrics* 105:635–37.

Petrosino, Anthony, Robert F. Boruch, Haluk Soydan, Lorna Duggan, and Julio Sanchez-Meca. 2001. "Meeting the Challenges of Evidence-Based Policy: The Campbell Collaboration." *Annals of the American Academy of Political and Social Science* 578:14–34.

Petrosino, Anthony, and Julia Lavenberg. 2007. "Systematic Reviews and Meta-Analyses: Best Evidence on 'What Works' for Criminal Justice Decision Makers." *Western Criminology Review* 8:1–15.

Petrosino, Anthony, and Carolyn Turpin-Petrosino, and John Buehler. 2006. "Scared Straight and Other Juvenile Awareness Programs." In *Preventing Crime: What Works for Children, Offenders, Victims, and Places*, edited by Brandon C. Welsh and David P. Farrington. New York: Springer.

Petticrew, Mark, and Helen Roberts. 2006. *Systematic Reviews in the Social Sciences: A Practical Guide*. Malden, MA: Blackwell.

Rosenfeld, Richard. 2000. "Tracing the Brady Act's Connection with Homicide and Suicide Trends." *Journal of the American Medical Association* 284:616–18.

Rumbelow, Helen, and Alice Miles. 2007. "How to Save this Child from a Life of Poverty, Violence and Despair." *The Times* (London), June 9. http://www.timesonline.co.uk.

Sanders, Matthew R., Carol Markie-Dadds, Lucy A. Tully, and William Bor. 2000. "The Triple P—Positive Parenting Program: A Comparison of Enhanced, Standard, and Self-Directed Behavioural Family Interventions for Parents of Children with Early Onset Conduct Problems." *Journal of Consulting and Clinical Psychology* 68:624–40.

Schweinhart, Lawrence J., Helen V. Barnes, and David P. Weikart. 1993. *Significant Benefits: The High/Scope Perry Preschool Study Through Age 27*. Ypsilanti, MI: High/Scope Press.

Shadish, William R., Thomas D. Cook, and Donald T. Campbell. 2002. *Experimental and Quasi-Experimental Designs for Generalized Causal Inference*. Boston: Houghton Mifflin.

Sherman, Lawrence W. 1998. *Evidence-Based Policing*. Washington, DC: Police Foundation.

———. 2003. "Misleading Evidence and Evidence-Led Policy: Making Social Science More Experimental." *Annals of the American Academy of Political and Social Science* 589:6–19.

Sherman, Lawrence W., David P. Farrington, Brandon C. Welsh, and Doris L. MacKenzie, eds. 2006. *Evidence-Based Crime Prevention*, rev. ed. New York: Routledge.

Sherman, Lawrence W., Denise C. Gottfredson, Doris Layton MacKenzie, John E. Eck, Peter Reuter, and Shawn D. Bushway. 1997. *Preventing Crime: What Works, What Doesn't, What's Promising*. Washington, DC: National Institute of Justice, U.S. Department of Justice.

Shulha, Lyn M., and J. Bradley Cousins. 1997. "Evaluation Use: Theory, Research, and Practice Since 1986." *Evaluation Practice* 18:195–208.

Skogan, Wesley G., and Kathleen Frydl, eds. 2004. *Fairness and Effectiveness in Policing: The Evidence*. Committee to Review Research on Police Policy and Practices. Washington, DC: National Academies Press.

Strang, Heather, and Lawrence W. Sherman. 2006. "Restorative Justice to Reduce Victimization." In *Preventing Crime: What Works for Children, Offenders, Victims, and Places*, edited by Brandon C. Welsh and David P. Farrington. New York: Springer.

Tilley, Nick, and Gloria Laycock. 2002. *Working out What to Do: Evidence-Based Crime Reduction*. Crime Reduction Research Series Paper 11. London: Home Office.

Tonry, Michael. 2003. "Evidence, Elections and Ideology in the Making of Criminal Justice Policy." In *Confronting Crime: Crime Control Policy Under New Labour*, edited by Michael Tonry. Portland, OR: Willan.

———. 2009. "Evidence-Based Penal Policies and Practices." Paper presented at Gunther Kaiser Memorial Conference, Freiburg, Germany.

Tonry, Michael, and David P. Farrington, eds. 1995a. *Building a Safer Society: Strategic Approaches to Crime Prevention*. Vol. 19 of *Crime and Justice: A Review of Research*, edited by Michael Tonry. Chicago: University of Chicago Press.

Tonry, Michael, and David P. Farrington. 1995*b*. "Strategic Approaches to Crime Prevention." In *Building a Safer Society: Strategic Approaches to Crime Prevention*, edited by Michael Tonry and David P. Farrington. Vol. 19 *Crime and Justice: A Review of Research*, edited by Michael Tonry. Chicago: University of Chicago Press.

Tonry, Michael, and David A. Green. 2003. "Criminology and Public Policy in the USA and UK." In *The Criminological Foundations of Penal Policy: Essays in Honour of Roger Hood*, ed. Lucia Zedner and Andrew Ashworth. New York: Oxford University Press.

Tran, Mark. 2009. "Government Drug Adviser David Nutt Sacked." *Guardian*, October 31. http://www.guardian.co.uk.

U.S. General Accountability Office. 2003. *Youth Illicit Drug Use Prevention: DARE Long-Term Evaluations and Federal Efforts to Identify Effective Programs*. Report GAO-03-172R. Washington, DC: General Accountability Office.

Utting, David, ed. 1999. *A Guide to Promising Approaches*. London: Communities That Care.

Waller, Irvin. 2006. *Less Law, More Order: The Truth about Reducing Crime*. Westport, CT: Praeger.

Weimer, David L., and Lee S. Friedman. 1979. "Efficiency Considerations in Criminal Rehabilitation Research: Costs and Consequences." In *The Rehabilitation of Criminal Offenders: Problems and Prospects*, edited by Lee Sechrest, Susan O. White, and Elizabeth D. Brown. Washington, DC: National Academy of Sciences.

Weinrott, Mark R., Richard R. Jones, and James R. Howard. 1982. "Cost-Effectiveness of Teaching Family Programs for Delinquents: Results of a National Evaluation." *Evaluation Review* 6:173–201.

Weisburd, David, Cynthia M. Lum, and Anthony Petrosino. 2001. "Does Research Design Affect Study Outcomes in Criminal Justice?" *Annals of the American Academy of Political and Social Science* 578:50–70.

Weiss, Carol H. 1980. *Social Science Research and Decision-Making*. New York: Columbia University Press.

———. 1998. "Have We Learned Anything New About the Use of Evaluation?" *American Journal of Evaluation* 19:21–33.

Weiss, Carol H., Erin Murphy-Graham, and Sarah Birkeland. 2005. "An Alternative Route to Policy Influence: How Evaluations Affect D.A.R.E." *American Journal of Evaluation* 26:12–30.

Weiss, Carol H., Erin Murphy-Graham, Anthony Petrosino, and Allison G. Gandhi. 2008. "The Fairy Godmother—and Her Warts: Making the Dream of Evidence-Based Policy Come True." *American Journal of Evaluation* 29:29–47.

Welsh, Brandon C., and David P. Farrington. 2000. "Monetary Costs and Benefits of Crime Prevention Programs." In *Crime and Justice: A Review of Research*, vol. 27, edited by Michael Tonry, Chicago: University of Chicago.

———. 2001. "Toward an Evidence-Based Approach to Preventing Crime." *Annals of the American Academy of Political and Social Science* 578:158–73.

———. 2002. *Crime Prevention Effects of Closed Circuit Television: A Systematic Review*. Home Office Research Study 252. London: Home Office.

———. 2006*a*. "Evidence-Based Crime Prevention." In *Preventing Crime: What Works for Children, Offenders, Victims, and Places*, edited by Brandon C. Welsh and David P. Farrington. New York: Springer.

———, eds. 2006*b*. *Preventing Crime: What Works for Children, Offenders, Victims, and Places*. New York: Springer.

————. 2009. *Making Public Places Safer: Surveillance and Crime Prevention*. New York: Oxford University Press.

Welsh, Brandon C., David P. Farrington, and Lawrence W. Sherman, eds. 2001. *Costs and Benefits of Preventing Crime*. Boulder, CO: Westview Press.

Wilson, David B. 2001. "Meta-Analytic Methods for Criminology." *Annals of the American Academy of Political and Social Science* 578:71–89.

PART I

PURPOSES AND FUNCTIONS

CHAPTER 4

....

PUNISHMENT

....

MICHAEL TONRY

We are not very good at talking about punishment of offenders. There are many different ways to talk about it and many different reasons to do so. Practitioners talk about it in relation to their ideas about appropriate outcomes of cases; policymakers in relation to public safety, public opinion, and political self-interest; philosophers in relation to abstract consideration of retributive and distributive justice; social scientists in relation to what happens in courts and prisons, and (so far as they can tell) why; and victims and offenders in relation to their personal experiences and senses of justice and injustice.

The people doing the talking seldom do it outside their own settings, or to people outside their own circles. American judges and lawyers want to make appropriate decisions about individual cases, but subject to practical constraints; most, for example, believe that case pressures require that they offer defendants inducements to plead guilty. Legislators usually want to enact sensible laws that are effective; many believe, however, that it is sometimes appropriate to authorize or mandate unusually harsh punishments because public opinion is more than usually concerned about crime or outraged about a recent case. Philosophers want decisions about punishment to result from rational and detached reflection on what justice requires in this case under these circumstances. Many victims want punishment to restore their losses and to vindicate their sense of grievance. Many offenders want it to take account of the circumstances of their lives and the immediate situations in which crimes occurred. Minority group advocates want punishment policies to take account of the implications of alternate approaches for the interests of members of groups they care about.

That diversity of interests and perspectives means that most people's views of the subject are partial and distorted, like those of the blind men who were each asked to touch a different part of an elephant's body, and then to describe what they thought an elephant looked like. One common depiction of the punishment elephant is that it is a rational if complex and flawed human process in which individuals attempt to make sensible decisions in light of what they believe to be applicable rules, relevant normative considerations, and limited resources. In dealing with individual cases, most people usually try to "do justice." In the narrowest traditional ways of thinking, "doing justice" involves careful assessment of a series of questions about offenders' culpability, the harm they caused or risked, and the likely consequences for society and offenders of possible alternative punishments that might be ordered. This is how judges and lawyers usually talk about it.

The description in the preceding paragraph is not incorrect, but it is incomplete. It does not take account of the aims of policymakers when they criminalize behavior or enact punishment laws. They tend not to focus on individual cases, or on how laws might affect individual cases but on other considerations. Sometimes they want to reduce victimization generally by deterring, incapacitating, and rehabilitating offenders. Sometimes they want to denounce and discourage particular troubling behaviors (new ones in recent years, for example, include Internet frauds and identity theft) by making them illegal and authorizing punishments for them. Sometimes they want to send moral messages (in recent years, for example, concerning the unacceptability of drug use and domestic violence), almost without regard to whether the law or punishment will reduce the incidence of the proscribed behaviors. Sometimes they want to enact expressive or symbolic legislation that responds to public anxieties, emotions, and fears, whether or not there are reasonable grounds for believing the new laws will have useful effects. Sometimes they want to make ideological statements about themselves and their political beliefs. Many laws enacted to serve purposes other than crime prevention or imposition of just punishments create arbitrary categories or rigid rules that result in punishments many practitioners consider inappropriate or unjust.

The traditional description of punishment does not take account of ideas that have emerged or reemerged in the past forty years. Adherents of restorative (e.g., Braithwaite 2001) and community justice (e.g., Clear and Karp 1999) believe that punishment policies and processes should serve primarily to resolve conflicts, solve problems, and strengthen communities, and that traditional criminal justice processes and ideas about punishment should be reserved for a residual category of cases for which newer approaches are not feasible. Adherents of therapeutic jurisprudence argue that practitioners in every case should take account of the therapeutic (and possible destructive) effects of every action they take and process in which they participate—in regard to offenders, victims, and practitioners themselves (Wexler and Winick 2003).

Nor does the narrow traditional description of punishment as "doing justice" take account of other institutions and processes that shape it and cause it to perform social functions that most analysts and courtroom officials do not recognize. These include such things as reinforcing social norms (e.g., Durkheim 1933

[1893]), protecting the interests of economically or politically powerful groups (e.g., Rusche and Kircheimer 1968 [1939]), maintaining existing patterns of racial, ethnic, and social hierarchy (e.g., Wacquant 2002a, 2002b), and shaping people to play roles required by the social and economic systems of their times (e.g., Foucault 1979). Punishment thus sometimes serves functional ends unrelated to its nominal purposes.

But it is still more complicated. Punishment laws, institutions, and practices are shaped by personal interests of individuals (for example, the prosecutor who wants to be re-elected and the assistant prosecutor who wants to be promoted; the legislator who wants to become governor; the legislative faction that agrees to vote in favor of a bill on one subject in exchange for another faction's agreement to vote in favor of a bill on some other subject). Punishment decisions are also shaped by the institutional interests of organizations (for example, most cases have to be dismissed or dealt with by plea bargains because there are not enough assistant prosecutors, courtrooms, and jail cells). They are influenced by professional social pressures; courtrooms are complex places, and they function better if people respect local expectations and conventions. They are also influenced by serendipity—the judge who is afraid of young black men, the prosecutor who is highly emotional about sex crimes against children, the probation officer with a Little Caesar complex.

Here are some of the different ways of thinking and talking about punishment:

- Some philosophers and legal theorists regard punishment policies and practices as systems for calibrating amounts of punishment to offenders' moral fault.
- Other philosophers and legal theorists regard punishment policies and practices as systems for maximizing happiness or preventing crime.
- Still other philosophers and legal theorists believe that punishment policies and practices should take account of both moral fault and crime prevention considerations.
- And others still believe that punishment policies and practices serve primarily to reinforce or undermine basic social norms.
- Some analysts believe that punishment policies and processes (usually operating under other names such as restorative justice, community justice, or therapeutic jurisprudence) should serve primarily to resolve conflicts, solve problems, and strengthen communities.
- Some social theorists explain punishment policies and decisions as devices for achieving functional goals only peripherally related to crime or punishment.
- Some analysts explain punishment policies and decisions as devices for realizing personal goals of officials or institutional goals of organizations that may or may not be closely related to crime and punishment.

- Some analysts explain punishment policies and decisions as primarily expressive, as forms of communication through which the state and state actors express solidarity with social values, acknowledge public fears and resentments, and respond to public concerns.

These different ways of talking about punishment come to a head in difficult cases and troubled times. Northern, personally abolitionist judges called upon to enforce "Fugitive Slave Laws" before the Civil War offer a classic example (Cover 1984). Was any option open to them other than to enforce the law or resign on principle? Should they have disregarded their moral beliefs about slavery or disregarded the law? Should they have refused to enforce the law because doing so would sustain slavery and further the interests of slave owners, or should they have enforced the law because not doing so would undermine rule-of-law ideas upon which democracies depend? Should they have hypocritically ducked the problem by looking for and finding technical reasons to dismiss the cases other than on the merits? Should they have taken into account the implications for their own careers or reputations of whatever choices they made? Should they have taken into account the complex political calculus that led to the federal Missouri Compromise provision that fugitive slave laws should be enforced in states that did not allow slavery under their own laws?

Non-Nazi professional judges in Nazi Germany are another classic example (Hart 1968). What should they have done when facing defendants charged, accurately, with violating a law that made it a crime to provide assistance to a Jew? Should they have refused to enforce the laws because they were immoral, or because their enforcement might undermine social norms calling for compassionate assistance to troubled people, or because their enforcement reinforced the legitimacy of the Nazi regime? Should they have taken into account dangers to themselves or their families if they did not enforce the laws? Were they entitled to take account of the implications of their choices for their own later careers?

United States federal district court judges offer a less obvious but more apt—because more familiar—example. When called upon by federal law to impose a mandatory minimum sentence of twenty years on a young first offender—the first college-attending member of a poor black family—who agreed for a few dollars to carry a briefcase containing 100 grams of crack from St. Louis to Minneapolis, what should a judge do? Should he or she take account of the defendant's personal background and sympathy for the plight of disadvantaged black Americans at this historical moment? Should the judge impose the sentence, and disregard his or her personal belief that the sentence is unjust because grotesquely severe? Should the judge defy the law and impose some other sentence (or figure out a disingenuous way to avoid doing so, as by refusing to accept a guilty plea and acquitting the obviously guilty defendant)? Should the judge be influenced by knowledge that alcohol, a substance commonly used by the middle and upper classes that causes much greater human suffering and economic loss than any other recreational substance, is legally available, while less dangerous substances like marijuana, cocaine, and heroin, more commonly used by poorer people, are illegal? Should the judge be influenced by knowledge that cocaine-offense defendants, mostly black, who sell crack are subject to much harsher penalties than those, mostly white, who sell powder? However polemically or neutrally the observation is made, it cannot be pure coincidence that the law more heavily punishes the misbehavior of the less well-off and the nonwhite. Should that matter when the judge sets a sentence or when observers try to understand what is going on?

These are, of course, extreme cases. Most criminal cases are more mundane. What these cases share with ordinary cases, however, is that much more was going on, and needs to be understood, than the simple mechanical (or the subtle, principled) application to individual cases of legal rules about punishment. The narrow traditional picture of punishment as "doing justice" shows only a small part of the story.

Different kinds of analysts ponder different facets of punishment. Philosophers try to clarify the relevant normative principles. Legal theorists try to relate principles to policies and practices. Social theorists try to understand why punishment takes the forms it does in particular places and times. Political scientists explain punishment as the product of political judgments shaped by the interests of groups in society and of individual politicians, or as the outcome of institutional considerations that constrain the choices of individuals operating in complex organizational settings. Most of these theorists do not talk to each other, or take account of one another's perspectives, insights, and writings. And few exponents of the diverse scholarly perspectives are very good at communicating with practitioners or public officials. All of the separate ways of thinking and talking about punishment are incomplete. Often they operate at cross-purposes.

The rest of this chapter more systematically discusses important ways of thinking about punishment. Section I discusses the history and recent past of work by philosophers and legal theorists. Section II surveys major works by social theorists, and section III sketches work by political scientists on the day-to-day workings of criminal courts. The conclusion discusses a number of difficult issues concerning punishment that implicate all of the different ways of thinking about it.

I. Philosophers and Legal Theorists

Consider capital punishment of murderers. Some people believe it is a Good Thing, because it deters would-be killers and thereby saves lives. Others believe it is a Bad Thing, because it does not deter would-be killers, and sacrifices the lives of murderers for no good purpose. Still others think disagreements about the practical effects of capital punishment are irrelevant. They believe that some murderers should be killed, because they deserve it, or that no murderers should be killed, because no one deserves *that*, irrespective of what the effects of the killings might be.

A. Philosophers

It is common to describe the arguments about good and bad effects as *consequentialist* (or *teleological*), and the arguments about moral prescription as *deontological*. Both are kinds of moral arguments, but they differ in what they mean by morality. Consequentialists believe that means must be justified by their ends. Murderers may be executed, if doing so on balance accomplishes something good. If killing murderers saves lives, or achieves other valid public purposes that outweigh offenders' losses of life, then that is fine. If it does not, then we can't do it. Jeremy Bentham (1970), the nineteenth-century English utilitarian theorist, was adamant that punishments could not properly be imposed if they were "inefficacious," by which he meant that their imposition would not make future offending less likely. He used the term *parsimony* as shorthand for the proposition that no pain should be imposed on wrongdoers in excess of that required to achieve valid social aims. If no such aims could be realized, then parsimony forbade infliction of any punishment at all.

Unfortunately, no term of art exists that satisfactorily categorizes people who subscribe to deontological (or nonconsequentialist) views. Few people write or talk about "deontologists," probably because the term is outside ordinary usage and sounds arcane or pretentious. "Nonconsequentialist" is unsatisfactory because it is a mouthful and is a definition by negation. It indicates nothing about what people believe. Sometimes the term *retributivist* is used in relation to punishment, but this does not work for capital punishment because some retributivists oppose it on moral grounds while others who oppose it on moral grounds also oppose retributivism. Those who support and oppose capital punishment on deontological grounds might be called moralists, but this too is unsatisfactory because it implies that consequentialist arguments are not also moral arguments. They are. Nonetheless, I follow common practice below and sometimes refer to deontological arguments as moral or moralistic ones.

People who subscribe to deontological theories believe that means must be justified per se, irrespective of ends. If morality requires that offenders be executed, then they should be. The German idealist philosopher Immanuel Kant (1965 [1787]) believed that the capacity for moral choice is what makes human beings human, and that failure to attach consequences to moral choices implies that the person who made them is not morally responsible and therefore not human. Respect for peoples' autonomy thus requires that their wrongdoing be punished in the appropriate way.

Kant described a hypothetical island society that was about to dissolve, with its members to disperse to the ends of the earth. Kant famously argued that the murderers in prison should be executed before the ships departed, even though no possible public benefit could be realized from their killings. His hypothetical was designed to isolate the moral case for capital punishment. If the island society was going to dissolve, deterrent and incapacitative considerations were irrelevant. No one would remain to be deterred or to benefit from reduced threats of future crime resulting from the killer's incapacitation. The sole question then became, Should the murderer be executed if there is no possible consequential benefit? Kant's answer was yes. Conversely, if morality forbids the taking of life by the state, then murderers should not be executed.

The "morality" referred to here is not like consequentialist morality, which in principle derives from knowledge of the world: capital punishment does or does not deter would-be murderers. When we are confident we know whether it does, we will know what consequentialist morality requires. For people who subscribe to deontological punishment beliefs, the sources of morality are a priori. Moral truths come from God or his agents on earth or are inferable from knowledge about the universe or are simply (alas) the unexamined, culturally transmitted, conventional wisdom of particular groups.

These two sets of views create the frameworks within which philosophers analyze punishment problems. Consequentialists and "retributivists" operate on different ground. The former do not acknowledge a priori moral claims; they want evidence. Retributivists and other "moralists" do not care about evidence; they want moral clarity. Concerning capital punishment, there are also irreconcilable differences among the "moralists." Some believe that a priori morality requires it, and others believe that a priori morality forbids it.

Thus there are at least three sets of irreconcilable views about capital punishment. This might raise skepticism about the value of philosophical analyses of punishment. If philosophers cannot agree among themselves or find ways to resolve irreconcilable differences among themselves, how can they help nonphilosophers gain increased understanding? The answer is that people other than philosophers also divide into those who instinctively subscribe to retributivist and consequentialist views, and if philosophers can help clarify and enrich understanding of each, that is a good thing. It will help the rest of us clarify our own views and be able more clearly to understand our differences with others. It may sometimes cause us to change our minds.

Some philosophers say that they work in the realm of "ideal theory" which is premised on the application of their ideas in an ideal, or just, world. If the world is not just, as almost every philosopher who writes about punishment acknowledges, ideal theories cannot tell us what to do (Murphy 1973; Duff 1986; Honderich 2006). They can, however, provide frames of reference for characterizing and criticizing imperfect institutions in an imperfect world, and thereby provide inspiration for (at least) incremental improvements.

Legal, social, and political theorists also have essential and fundamental insights to offer to thinking about punishment. In writing about their views, I shift from a focus on capital punishment to criminal punishment generally. Capital punishment nicely demonstrates differences between consequentialist and opposed moralistic views, but it is seldom imposed. Each year, however, millions of other criminal punishments are imposed in the United States (and equivalently large numbers in other countries). These range from minor fines to sentences of imprisonment for life without the possibility of parole. The stakes are lower than when death is not a possibility, but similar questions are raised about just punishments.

For punishment generally, "retributivist" is an adequate alternative to consequentialist because the opposed a priori moral views about capital punishment do not arise for other punishments. Although retributivists believe that offenders should be punished because they deserve it, just as some retributivists believe that some offenders should be executed because they deserve it, no one argues that punishments short of death should never be imposed (as moralistic death penalty opponents argue that death should never be imposed).[1] So from this point I no longer occasionally refer to moralistic but instead to retributive theories.[2]

It is commonly said that retributive and consequentialist positions are irreconcilable. Retributivists say that, in principle at least, no matter what happens in the real world, consequences do not matter. Consequentialists say that in principle any imposition of pain, including punishment of offenders, is a bad thing, and can be justified only by reference to more-than-offsetting good consequences. For a very long time, a shouting match resulted.

Retributivists argued that the logic of utilitarianism required that utilitarians (then the only category of consequentialists[3]) approve punishment of innocent offenders if sufficiently great beneficial consequences could be expected. A commonly used illustration was the prosecution (and potentially the execution) in the early twentieth-century American South of a black, alleged rapist who was known (only) by the judge to be innocent if that would prevent the lynchings of other innocent black men (e.g., McCloskey 1968). Retributivists charged that no morally acceptable theory of punishment could countenance such a result.

Utilitarians denied that attack. Usually they argued that such actions could never be kept secret and that the legal system's legitimacy would be undermined. Huge public insecurities would result if citizens knew that they could be "punished" even if they had committed no crimes. Those negative consequences of the punishment of innocents, utilitarians argued, would outweigh any possible gain. Sometimes they argued that the punishment-of-the-innocent problem is not a difficulty for utilitarian theories because criminal punishment presupposes that a crime has been committed and consequently, by definition, an innocent cannot be "punished."[4]

Moving from defense to offense, utilitarians argued that retributivism, whatever its claim to philosophical purity, was at base no more than the expression of vindictive and vengeful human instincts, which should not be given free rein. Retributivists, of course, denied this.

The philosophy of punishment was not a major specialty until the 1960s. Until then, philosophers worked within their own traditions and disagreed among themselves. It is only a small exaggeration to say that no one else much noticed or cared. Most criminal justice practitioners and legal theorists, while acknowledging that retributive instincts existed and had sometimes to be acknowledged, subscribed primarily to consequentialism (e.g., Michael and Adler 1933; Michael and Wechsler 1937; Henry Hart 1958; Allen 1959, 1964). Rehabilitative and incapacitative ideas were widespread. The *Model Penal Code* (American Law Institute 1962), the most influential criminal law document of the twentieth century, illustrates this. The *Code*, drafted in the 1950s, nowhere mentions "just deserts," "just punishment," "deserved punishment," or retribution as aims of sentencing or of the criminal law generally. Its punishment provisions aim to empower judges, parole boards, and probation officers to tailor punishments to individualized consideration of offenders' needs for rehabilitation or incapacitation (Tonry 2004, chaps. 6, 7).

The primacy of consequentialist ideas began to wane in the 1960s,[5] and by the 1970s a retributive resurgence occurred. There was renewed interest in the philosophy of punishment. The first few major works attempted to reconcile retributive and utilitarian theories. John Rawls (1955) and Edmond Pincoffs (1966) offered analyses that assigned different kinds of theories to different realms. Utilitarian considerations were said to pertain to general legislative consideration of criminal law doctrine and statutory frameworks for sentencing decisions. Retributive considerations were said to be germane to judges' decisions about punishment in individual cases. For a variety of reasons, that analysis persuaded few people.

A breakthrough occurred in *Punishment and Responsibility* (1968), a book by the Oxford philosopher H. L. A. Hart. Hart argued that the conflict between utilitarians and retributivists had been misconceived because it was based on the assumption that criminal punishment raised only one fundamental question: "How is punishment to be justified?" To the contrary, Hart argued, there are three separate important questions:

1. *General Justifying Aim*. How is the existence of a state institution of punishment to be justified?
2. *Liability*. Who may be punished?
3. *Amount*. How much punishment may be imposed?

Hart argued that a comprehensive theory of punishment might coherently provide different answers to those questions. His own, which he called a "middle way," was that prevention, a consequentialist idea, is the general justifying aim, that—possibly with some exceptions[6]—punishment should be imposed only on offenders, for offenses, and that both retributive and consequentialist considerations were relevant to the amount of punishment.

For some kinds of theories, for example, what might be called "thorough-going retributivism," Hart's three questions changed nothing. For a Kantian theorist who believed that moral principles require that offenders be punished (e.g., the island example), essentially the same answers would be given to all three questions. What is the general justifying aim of punishment? The imposition of morally deserved punishments. Who may be punished? Offenders, for offenses. How much? As much as is deserved.

For other theories, however, things did change. A consequentialist could neatly sidestep the punishment-of-the-innocent challenge. Crime prevention, or positive social utility, or happiness, or economic efficiency could be the justifying aim, and decisions about the amount of punishment could be predicated on maximizing it. Liability to punishment, however, could be based on retributive considerations.

I describe this as a breakthrough because it allowed a place for what have become known as mixed or hybrid theories (like Hart's own). Academic lawyers leaped into the opening Hart created.

B. Legal Theorists

Legal theorists try to devise punishment theories that take account of the world's imperfections and can inform real decisions in a real world. If perfect justice cannot be achieved, efforts to achieve justice in practice can at least be improved. Many people believe that punishment decisions should be related to offenders' moral responsibility and desert, and also that punishment decisions should take account of the likely crime-preventive effects of alternate punishment possibilities. Theorists have therefore tried to figure out ways to bridge gaps between what I described as irreconcilable views in philosophy. They might be thought of as applied philosophers. Typically they propose *hybrid theories*.

In 1975 utilitarian ideas had been predominant in the English-speaking countries for a century, and served as the theoretical rationale for what we now call *indeterminate sentencing*.[7] That system, which some American states today largely retain, gave officials broad discretion to individualize sentences to take account of individual offenders' circumstances. Legislatures defined crimes and set maximum authorized sentences. Judges could usually impose any sentence, ranging from unsupervised probation to the statutory maximum prison sentence. Prison officials could shorten prisoners' sentences to take account of good behavior, participation in treatment programs, and work, and could oppose or support prisoners' applications for parole release. Parole boards could release any prisoner who was eligible. In the most far-reaching indeterminate systems, in California and Washington State, judges sentenced offenders to the state prison system for a term from one year up to the statutory maximum; parole boards determined when they were released (Rothman 1971, 1980).

In the early 1970s, indeterminate sentencing fell out of favor. A number of things contributed to this. First, people inside and outside the legal system began to be concerned about the possibilities of biased and idiosyncratic decisions by officials accorded such broad discretion (Davis 1969). One influential critique concerned unwarranted sentencing disparities (Frankel 1972). Second, the civil rights and prisoners' rights movements focused attention on the disproportionate number of blacks in prison and on the possibility that indeterminate sentencing produced biased decisions that caused and worsened racial disparities (American Friends Service Committee 1971). Third, the U.S. Supreme Court in the 1960s issued a number of decisions—most notably *Goldberg v. Kelly*, 397 U.S. 254 (1970)—extending procedural rights to citizens in a wide range of their interactions with the state. People affected by government decisions were at minimum entitled to be told what rule they were accused of violating, to present evidence on their own behalf, to have the issues decided by an independent fact finder, and to appeal decisions adverse to their interests. Critics soon observed that by those standards prosecution and parole systems (Davis 1969) and sentencing (Frankel 1972) were essentially "lawless." There were no clear rules governing such decisions and possibilities of appeal were either nonexistent or erratic. This critique had particular relevance to a sentencing process that provided no guidance to judges about their decisions and afforded defendants no opportunities to appeal the sentences they received. Fourth, researchers evaluating the effectiveness of rehabilitative programs, which in large part gave indeterminate sentencing its rationale, concluded that few programs if any could be shown to reduce re-offending. The most famous synthesis of treatment effectiveness studies, "What Works? Questions and Answers about Prison Reform" (Martinson 1974), was generally interpreted to conclude that "Nothing Works" (it didn't really; its conclusions were much more qualified than that, but what it was perceived to conclude proved much more influential than what it did conclude).

This indictment that indeterminate sentencing caused unwarranted disparities, facilitated racially biased decision-making, lacked minimum procedural safeguards, and was based on assumptions about rehabilitative programs that were unwarranted was devastating. The results include the development of sentencing guidelines, "truth-in-sentencing," mandatory minimum sentence laws, three-strikes laws, and abolition of parole.[8] The indictment also left a void in normative thinking and writing. Few people had been writing about punishment based on retributive premises.

The obvious answer to the problems of indeterminate sentencing was to establish some form of rules to guide judicial and parole decision-making. Retributive ideas provided a ready rationale for rules. If a principal criterion of punishment is that it be morally deserved, attention is drawn almost inexorably to the seriousness of the crime as a measure of moral desert and to the idea of proportionality— harsher punishments for more serious crimes, comparable punishments for comparably serious crimes. From there the leap was easy to sentencing guidelines that ranked offenses in terms of severity and criminal records in terms of extensiveness, and directed judges to base their decisions on those factors.

Some philosophers, such as John Rawls (1955), Edmond Pincoffs (1966), and H. L. A. Hart (1968), had anticipated the change in direction, and a few philosophers began to take account of it in their writing (e.g., H. Morris 1966; Kleinig 1973), but legal theorists quickly staked out the territory. They had two comparative advantages. Many—notably Alan Dershowitz, Norval Morris, Andrew von Hirsch, Franklin Zimring, and the writer of this chapter—were involved in the sentencing reform movement as law reform activists and as scholars. This gave them familiarity with the real-world issues involved. In addition, most were primarily interested in normative analyses of sentencing (Hart's "How much?" question), unlike philosophers who had traditionally written about, in Hart's terms, the General Justifying Aim.

Most of the analyses offered by legal theorists were hybrid theories with significant retributive elements. Sentencing guidelines based on retributive ideas addressed all the major critiques of indeterminate sentencing: the absence of rules and resulting unwarranted disparities—guidelines for decisions; broad discretions facilitating racially biased decisions—narrowed discretion constrained by guidelines; lack of procedural fairness—published guidelines coupled with a right to appeal decisions inconsistent with them; ineffective treatment programs—don't allow judges to base sentences on treatment considerations.

The legal theorists rushed in (e.g., Frankel 1972; N. Morris 1974; Dershowitz 1976; von Hirsch 1976; Morris and Tonry 1978; Singer 1979). Two perspectives quickly became predominant. The first, called *desert* or *proportionality theories*, proposed that punishments be linked to scales of offense severity and that little latitude be accorded judges to take account of consequentialist concerns. The leading figure is Andrew von Hirsch of Cambridge (1976, 1985, 1993, 2005 [with Ashworth]). The second, called *limiting retributivist* theories, are most famously associated with the late Professor Norval Morris of the University of Chicago (1974, 1990 [with Tonry]). Limiting retributivist theories posit that there is a range of not-undeserved punishments and that, within that range and assuming other criteria are satisfied, judges may take consequentialist considerations into account. In the 1980s, desert theories were highly influential and government bodies as diverse as the Australian Law Reform Commission (1980), the Canadian Sentencing Commission (1987), the Minnesota Sentencing Guidelines Commission (1980), and the Home Office of England and Wales (1990) explicitly adopted desert theory as their guiding normative rationale. More recently, limiting retributivist theories have become more influential as evidenced by their adoption by the American Law Institute (2007; in the *Model Penal Code*, 2nd ed.) and a major English sentencing reform body (Home Office 2001) as guiding rationales.

C. The Return of the Philosophers

Interest in retributive punishment theories revived among philosophers at the same time as legal theorists argued among themselves. For the most part they focus primarily on Hart's first question. *Intuitionist* theorists argue that the widely shared intuition that people who commit serious crimes deserve to be punished provides an adequate and persuasive justification for retributive punishment (e.g., Moore 1993). *Benefits and burdens* or *equilibrium* theorists start from a social-contract premise by which citizens are deemed to have assented to rules and conventions that provide a sense of security, which enables each to plan and live the life they choose:[9] offenders benefit from other peoples' law-abiding ways and obtain an unfair advantage or benefit, which must be repaid, or a law-abiding equilibrium restored, when they offend against others (e.g., Murphy 1973). *Paternalist* theorists argue that the imposition of deserved punishments provides an occasion to teach offenders about right values in order to enable them later to live more satisfying, law-abiding lives (e.g., H. Morris 1981). *Censure* theorists argue that punishment is a blaming institution that appropriately censures offenders in proportion to the seriousness of their wrongdoing (e.g., von Hirsch 1993). *Communicative* theorists argue that imposition of deserved punishments provides a noncoercive occasion to help offenders and others understand why offenders deserve to be punished in order that they may come to share that understanding (e.g., Hampton 1984; Murphy and Hampton 1988). *Communitarian* theorists argue that punishment provides an occasion to help offenders understand and comply with the values of communities of which they are members and thereby enable them more fully to enjoy the benefits of membership in a socially organized community (e.g., Duff 2001).

Legal theorists and philosophers cannot tell us all that we need to know about punishment. They both start from the assumption that punishments result from rational processes in which individual judges and other practitioners make better or worse decisions about individual cases. Social theorists and political scientists instruct that that is an oversimplified view of the world.

II. Social Theories

Life, and punishment, are more complicated than philosophers and legal theorists usually want to acknowledge. Social theorists try to describe the functions punishment performs and to explain why it takes the forms that it does, rather than to justify it in normative terms. Social institutions and practices exist for reasons, and the reasons are not always obvious.

Social theorists often write about punishment's functions. By this they seldom mean, as lawyers and philosophers might, crime-preventive utilitarian functions (or purposes) such as rehabilitation, deterrence, and incapacitation. Instead they are interested in what broader social functions are served. Work by the sociologist Loïc Wacquant provides a good illustration (2002a, 2002b). In a series of articles published since 2000, he argues that modern American punishment policies and practices serve to maintain patterns of social, economic, and political hierarchy in which blacks as a group are kept subordinate to whites. Punishment, in this analysis, is the latest in a series of social and legal institutions that have in turn maintained a racial hierarchy in which whites dominate blacks. The earlier ones were slavery, the "Jim Crow laws" and social conventions that allowed explicit racial discrimination after the Civil War, and the urban ghettos of mid- and late twentieth century America. When one form of hierarchy maintenance became no longer possible or effective, another one came into being. Lincoln's Emancipation Proclamation ended slavery, but Jim Crow took its place. The civil rights movement of the 1950s and 1960s ended legal forms of racial discrimination, but the urban ghetto kept blacks in their marginalized place. As American cities revived late in the twentieth century, the law-and-order movement that began in the 1960s took hold and assured that the life chances of blacks, especially poor black males, remained inferior to those of whites. As a result, black men have a one-third chance of spending time in prison during their lives, compared with 11.3 percent of whites, and black men's imprisonment rates are six to seven times those of whites (Bureau of Justice Statistics 2003; Tonry 2011). Criminal justice policies and practices have the effect of assuring that blacks fare worse than whites by every measure of social and economic well-being (others have developed similar arguments: e.g., Loury 2007; Massey 2007).

Functionalist accounts are not conspiracy theories. Wacquant does not claim that a self-perpetuating cabal of racist whites has met regularly for two centuries and devised and implemented a succession of strategies for disempowering blacks and diminishing their chances of achieving satisfying lives. The argument instead is that whites *as a group* realize psychic and other benefits from their dominant economic, social, and political positions compared with blacks, and thus they develop institutions—often unconsciously and often rationalized in neutral, nonracial terms—that operate to maintain white dominance. Of course, there are always racists and bigots of other kinds, and they certainly played major roles in perpetuating slavery and Jim Crow. During the periods when the urban ghetto and law-and-order policies have damaged black interests, bigotry, however, has been much less evident and its presence has been vigorously denied. Policies on zoning, lending, and mortgage insurance that long limited blacks' housing opportunities, for example, were explained in terms of neighborhood ambience, protection of property values, and sound investment practices. They were never openly rationalized in terms of preferences for black exclusion from middle-class areas and concentration in disadvantaged areas, but that is what they accomplished (e.g., Massey and Denton 1993).

The best single piece of evidence for Wacquant's case in the criminal justice system is a federal law passed in 1986, the "100-to-1 rule" (in 2010 it was replaced by an "18-to-1 rule"). It punished crack cocaine offenses, for which most of those arrested are black, as severely as powder cocaine offenses 100 times larger (for which most of those arrested are white). That law quickly became the single largest cause of racial disparities in federal prisons (McDonald and Carlson 1993), and its 18-to-1 successor continues to have that effect. Crack and powder cocaine are pharmacologically indistinguishable, as state supreme courts have noted in striking down crack/powder sentencing differentials, and as the U.S. Sentencing Commission has reiterated (1995, 2007). More generally, the "War on Drugs" launched in the late 1980s disproportionately focuses on crack offenses and has long generated arrest rates for blacks for drug crimes generally that are three to six times those for whites (although blacks are less likely than whites to use illicit drugs). These laws are generally justified in terms of the immorality and dangers of drug use, and are never justified in terms of their effects on poor, black Americans. Yet they have powerful adverse effects in reducing poor, black (especially male) Americans' likelihood of achieving satisfying lives (through diverse mechanisms that include stigma, stereotyping, removal from the labor market, disqualification from many kinds of jobs, and disenfranchisement from voting). Policies adopted in the past twenty years to invest less in treatment programs, to make prisoners ineligible for federal Pell grants that fund poor peoples' college educations, and to deny ex-prisoners eligibility for a wide range of social service programs exacerbate the effects of criminal justice policies (e.g., Western 2006; Tonry and Melewski 2008).

Neither housing and mortgage lending practices nor criminal justice policies explicitly aim disproportionately to damage black Americans or to benefit whites. In both cases, that is indeed what they do, and what they could have been foreseen to do. Wacquant asks how and why those patterns came to be, and tries to show that the best and most plausible explanation is the one he offers.

The Scottish sociologist David Garland (2001) tells a different story but reaches a similar conclusion. His account is in some ways more damning than Wacquant's because it makes the causes of black overrepresentation in courts and prisons the products of deliberate eyes-open political decisions rather than of an invisible hand. Although recent American and English crime-control policies are often publicly rationalized in terms of deterrence and incapacitation, they are—Garland suggests—actually "expressive" efforts by governments to reassure anxious publics and gain or regain citizens' respect. Governments, he argues, recognize the modest limits of their capacities to affect crime rates and patterns, but want to be seen to be doing something, and loudly proclaim that what they do will work, whether they believe it or not. Expressive policies once adopted need to be implemented, and to be seen to be implemented, but it must be done in such a way that it does not undermine government's credibility and support among the broad electorate and opinion leaders. Targeting expressive policies on the crimes of the dispossessed and groups with little political power (Garland refers to "the criminology of the other") enables government to be seen to be tough without seriously undermining its broad political support. In the United States, the dispossessed and the politically powerless are disproportionately disadvantaged members of minority groups. In England they are the same groups and socially marginal members of the white, lower working class

(English Labour politicians like to denounce "yobs," "thugs," and "louts.") Though Garland travels a route different from Wacquant's, the destination is the same: an explanation for why in the United States black Americans disproportionately comprise criminal court dockets and occupy prison beds.

Social theorists have offered many kinds of functionalist arguments. I used Wacquant's illustratively because it is controversial, easy to understand, and speaks to developments of our time. The three most famous functionalist arguments relating to the criminal law are associated with the French theorist Emile Durkheim, the German theorist Karl Marx and some of his followers, and the French theorist Michele Foucault.

Durkheim (1933 [1893]) argued that law is primarily a mechanism for declaring, reinforcing, and changing basic social norms. The criminal law's ostensible functions of incapacitation, deterrence, and rehabilitation are not, he argued, very important (or especially effective). Criminal convictions and punishments serve instead to channel public dissatisfaction and indignation with wrongdoers and through those processes reaffirm the behavioral norms that were violated. Durkheimian ideas can also be expressed in terms of the law's dramaturgical effects. Criminal trials and punishments serve as morality plays that denounce wrong behaviors and validate good ones. Although practitioners and lawmakers may act and talk as if the criminal law affects behavior by changing or controlling peoples' behavior, Durkheim would say, they are mistaken. What they are doing, even if it is not what they think they are doing, is useful all the same.

Karl Marx might be expected to have written about the criminal law as an institution for furthering the interests of the dominant economic classes, but he wrote little on the subject (e.g., Marx 1853). Others did, however, most influentially the German scholars Georg Rusch and Otto Kirschheimer (1968 [1939]). They tried to show that the criminal law, and especially prisons and capital punishment, were best understood as mechanisms by which society adapted to changing labor market conditions. When economies are strong and labor is valuable and in demand, prison use and executions fall: able-bodied workers are too valuable to waste. When economies are weak and workers are idle and not economically valuable, prisons fill and executions rise ("life is cheaper"). Countless people have observed that the criminal law focuses much more on poor than on privileged peoples' crimes, prosecutes them much more often, and punishes them much more severely. As a functionalist matter, these things are probably not a coincidence.

Michele Foucault (1979) argued that punishment forms vary over time and serve different functions depending on historical circumstances. Before the Enlightenment, and before the development of modern bureaucratized police, court, and prison systems, punishments though rare were sometimes repulsively severe and served to emphasize and celebrate the power of the king. Beginning in the nineteenth century, the primary function of punishment (and of other mass institutions like schools, armies, industrial factories) became the socialization and reformation of people into conformity with the kinds of roles a mass and heavily bureaucratized society requires be played. Thus as the function of punishment changed from expressing and celebrating the authority of the king to socializing people into particular kinds of social and economic roles, the nature and forms of punishment changed. Corporal and capital punishment and banishment declined in use, and the nineteenth-century's rehabilitative and reformative correctional institutions came into being.

To describe an institution or process in terms of social functions does not mean that people are not sometimes consciously aware of those functions. Presumably some people recognize that mortgage-lending practices that redline minority neighborhoods do damage to black people, are happy about that, and regard that as a good reason to maintain the practice. Some people may feel that way about modern American drug policies.

Similarly, people may recognize functions of institutions and want to regularize them. Scandinavian judges and scholars, for example, subscribe to ideas akin to Durkheim's about law as a mechanism for reinforcing basic social norms (e.g., Andenaes 1974). They believe with Durkheim that incapacitation, deterrence, and rehabilitation have at best marginal influence on crime; except under extreme conditions, people do or do not commit crimes because they have or have not been socialized into values with which much criminality is incompatible. They also believe that law's role is collateral; families, schools, neighborhoods, churches, and other primary institutions do the heavy lifting in instilling and reinforcing social norms. But they believe it important that the law back up those norms. As a result, though criminal punishments in Finland are not severe by international standards, punishments are more likely to be imposed than elsewhere (so that bad behavior has consequences) and are highly proportionate (so that norms about the comparative seriousness of misconduct are not undermined). Finns refer to law's "moral-educative" or "general-preventive" effects as its most important ones (Lappi-Seppälä 2001).

In a somewhat different—but not completely unrelated—vein, English-language theorists have developed other ideas linked to socialization, norm reinforcement, and moral-educative effects. One of these is the development in philosophy over the past thirty years of what are called "communicative theories of punishment" (e.g., Hampton 1984; Duff 1986; Murphy and Hampton 1988). Such theories take diverse forms but at their core is the proposition that punishment as a process ought to be centrally concerned with communication with offenders, observers, or both, about good values.

A different, and more pernicious, development is the concept of "expressive" policies or punishments. In our time, many punishment policies, especially in the United States and England, are said primarily to be expressive (e.g., Garland 2001). This can mean as many things as there are speakers. In the narrowest sense, it can mean what Finns mean when they talk about moral education: the idea that criminal law and punishment endorse prevailing social norms and may reinforce them. Somewhat more broadly, it can mean denunciation of wrongful behavior and declaration that it is wrong. More broadly, and more commonly, it refers to the adoption of punitive laws that are meant in some general way to express solidarity with public opinion and reassure the public that its anxieties and fears have been taken into account and acted upon. Such things as three-strikes-and-you're-out laws, lengthy mandatory minimum sentence laws, and life-without-the-possibility-of-parole sentences are examples.[10] One characteristic of expressive policies is that most, for well-known reasons that have long been understood, cannot accomplish the goals set for them. For example, laws requiring judges and prosecutors to impose punishments they believe to be unconscionably severe are often circumvented, and are always inconsistently enforced. Many expressive laws make no sense in instrumental, effectiveness terms. They also make no sense in the terms in which philosophers and legal theorists, whether retributivists or consequentialists, talk about punishment.

III. Political Science Accounts

Expressive laws and policies do not necessarily, or even probably, have the socializing, norm-validating effects that Durkheim attributed to the criminal law. Those processes are natural, unselfconscious, and inexorable. Expressive laws and policies are more like judges' efforts to deter crime through the legal threats punishments express, a process about whose effectiveness Durkheim was skeptical. They are conscious efforts to harness the criminal law to achieve something that politicians or public officials want.

Politicians and officials dealing with punishment issues may be moved by a wide range of considerations. At their most benign, officials may be genuinely concerned to prevent crime, to calm an upset public, to reassure fearful people, and to enhance citizens' confidence in the state. At their most venal, officials may cynically manipulate public fears and anxieties—exacerbating fears in order to be seen to be trying to assuage them—to gain public support and win elections. No doubt in many cases motives are mixed.

What happens in criminal courts is powerfully shaped by political and managerial concerns. Political theory in its grand sense examines classical (e.g., Locke, Hobbes) and modern (e.g., Rawls 1971) notions about the properties, functions, and responsibilities of the state. Here I mean something much humbler: analysis of how personal and institutional interests shape punishment systems, policies, and practices. Promotion and adoption of expressive policies is an example.

Anyone who wants to understand punishment must try to understand how courts process cases.[11] At least in the United States, courts seldom operate as philosophers and legal theorists presuppose.[12] The model of punishment implicit in much normative writing is one in which defendants are charged with crimes that the prosecutor believes they committed and believes he or she has the evidence to prove, in which judges or juries consider the evidence and enter judgments of guilt when they believe the charges have been proven, and in which punishments are imposed based on the offenses committed and proven. That is seldom what happens.

Three interacting sets of personal and institutional interests shape what happens. First, for the vast majority of cases, resource constraints preclude the operation of the archetypal criminal process described in the preceding paragraph. Neither prosecutors' offices nor courts have sufficient resources to try every case. Only a tiny fraction goes to trial, and juries are involved only in a comparative handful. However, every case must be dealt with somehow. Methods must be devised for diverting many cases from the system altogether and persuading the vast majority of the defendants who remain to plead guilty. A whole series of policies and processes are implicated: prosecutorial charging standards; eligibility criteria for diversion to treatment, mediation, and other nonadjudicative dispositions; prosecution resource allocation policies on priority offenses; prosecution plea negotiation standards; eligibility criteria for judicial diversion programs; sentencing guidelines; and judicial authority to stay the entry of a judgment or the imposition or execution of a punishment. Among other consequences of these processes are that offenders are often not convicted of the crimes they committed. Many cases are resolved without convictions. Among those offenders who are convicted, most plead guilty on the inducement that the charges against them will be reduced in seriousness or number, or that an agreed sentence will be imposed.

Second, personal interests of judges and prosecutors influence their behavior. Elected chief prosecutors and elected or politically selected judges may want to be re-elected or re-appointed, or to be elected or appointed to a higher office. This at the very least creates risks that individuals' political or career ambitions will influence how cases are handled. In many jurisdictions, prosecutors run openly demagogic election campaigns meant to show that they are tougher than their opponents; this almost inevitably affects how their offices handle at least some categories of cases. Some assistant prosecutors also aspire to run for electoral office later or to be promoted within their offices and must be concerned to keep senior prosecutors happy and not to do things that might lessen their chances for electoral nomination or victory. Every elected prosecutor or judge must worry about cases in which a seemingly "lenient" sentence is imposed in a case that has attracted or may attract media attention. And it would be a foolhardy, dishonest, or self-deceiving judge or prosecutor who claimed that he or she always handles emotional, high-visibility cases exactly as any other case is handled.

Third, courts are complicated organizations and work most effectively when people get along and behave in ways that one another regard as reasonable. Research on "courtroom work groups" and "local legal cultures" shows that judges, prosecutors, defense lawyers, and probation officers often establish informal understandings about reasonable performance of their respective roles. These understandings, of course, vary over space and time, but in general they acknowledge that resources and time are limited and that most cases must be disposed of by mutual agreement. Courtroom practitioners learn that, to a considerable degree, in order to get along they must go along with existing ways of doing business including styles of plea negotiation and going rates for sentences. They also learn that mundane things matter: judges and other lawyers do not want hearings or trials to take too long, especially routine ones; they want to go to lunch on time, to go home early on Friday, and not to be required to do busywork caused by someone else's "unreasonable" behavior. At least in places where people are assigned for extended periods to work in particular courtrooms, people newly assigned are quickly socialized into work-group norms and expectations. Any actor is always free to defy existing norms, but only at the risk of being seen by others as unreasonable and undependable. There are also retaliatory risks that others will deny benefit of customary accommodations to the uncooperative lawyer and the benefit of plea negotiation conventions and sentencing going rates to his or her clients.

Considerations like those just described partly explain why many criminal laws and punishments are not applied as their proponents wished or intended or as the laws' plainest, most literal meanings might imply. Laws are not self-executing. Human beings must apply them. Whether and how they do that depends on whether they believe a particular law is reasonable, sensible, and just; whether punishments authorized or required are appropriate and consistent with prevailing local norms; and whether the law can be applied without unacceptable disruption to existing ways of doing business. Many expressive and other laws mandating severe penalties are routinely circumvented for these reasons. Even when such laws are applied to some cases, courtroom work groups generally devise ways to do so without disrupting court operations or mobilizing additional resources. Evaluators commonly report, for example, that offenders convicted of salient offenses receive harsher penalties, fewer people than before are convicted of those offenses (the others are convicted of less serious offenses not covered by the enhanced penalty), and overall, sometimes after a short period of perturbation, guilty plea and trial rates revert to traditional levels (Blumstein et al. 1983, chap. 3).

Thus ends this travelogue of institutional and disciplinary frameworks within which people make serious efforts to understand punishment. More could be visited. Psychologists, for example, offer instruction into ways human beings process information, including how we attribute characteristics to others, including offenders whom we may arrest, prosecute, or sentence (or in each case not), but those processes operate in many social settings. Evolutionary psychologists investigate hypotheses that human beings have been naturally selected for punitive responses to wrongdoing and that this shapes how we respond to criminals and think about punishment. Anthropologists can instruct on how different societies in different places deal with offenders, and historians can instruct on different times.

IV. Thinking about Punishment

Thinking about punishment needs to take account of the subjects discussed in this chapter separately and together. We can think only of one thing at a time. It is always necessary artificially to isolate aspects of a subject one by one if each is to be given its due. Philosophers' ideal theories of punishment attend to norms and values and cannot fairly be faulted for failing to integrate Foucauldian insights. Social theorists pondering punishment's functions should not be faulted for failing to examine normative analyses that may seem epiphenomenal to the operation of deeper social and economic forces. Political scientists studying courtroom work groups use a combination of qualitative and quantitative methods to study courts as complex systems and to study aggregate flows of cases through them. Normative analyses of dispositions of individual cases are not central to their subject.

One might argue, and some people do, that enrichment of knowledge for its own sake is a worthwhile activity. That may be so, but few philosophers, legal theorists, social theorists, or political scientists would describe their analyses and conclusions about punishment in that way. The imposition of pains or burdens on individuals because they are believed to have violated important behavioral norms is a rich, complex, human activity. Scholars of every stripe want to understand it better, usually with some thought that their efforts may contribute to doing less of it or doing it in ways that are more self-aware, just, or effective. Philosophers may not believe their ideal theories are realizable but may hope that their illumination of problems nudges practices and policies in more morally justifiable directions. Social theorists may not believe that their insights will lead to the dissolution or radical reconstitution of social institutions, but may hope that their analyses make people who exercise power more modest and self-aware. Political scientists may not expect their findings to lead to fundamental reorganization of court processes, but may hope that policies and practices will be improved because of their work.

That we can understand why the literatures about punishment are separate and distinct, and largely unaware of one another, does not mean that we can adequately understand punishment without taking account of all of them. The overriding rationale of this chapter is that we need to see as much of the elephant as we can if we are to hope to understand or control it. Without better questions, we are unlikely to settle on better answers. Here are a few:

1. *How can severe expressive punishment policies be justified?*

There may be ways, but reconciliation with any of the mainstream philosophies or legal theories of punishment will be hard. Consider California's three-strikes law requiring minimum twenty-five-year sentences for any third felony conviction including, famously, thefts of pizza slices on a playground and of four CDs from K-Mart. Every retributive, desert, and limiting retributivist theory would lead to condemnation of such penalties on proportionality grounds: the law mandates punishments for comparatively minor offenses that are much more severe than those imposed for many robberies, rapes, and homicides. Consequentialist theories would condemn such punishments for imposing pains that cannot be justified by larger offsetting gains and thereby violate parsimony constraints. Durkheimian analysts would point out that such penalties are no more likely than deterrent penalties to influence behavior and thereby reduce the incidence of crime, but to the contrary may undermine basic social norms through the exemplary imposition of punishments that are grossly disproportionate to the seriousness of the crimes that triggered them. Socialization is a gradual accretive process not a sudden pulverizing one; moral confusion and ambiguity results when punishments do not respect conventional ideas about what is more serious than what. Wacquant would point out that most who receive such extreme penalties are members of minority groups and ask whether we should not be deeply troubled by that. Rusche and Kirchheimer would point out that nearly all the people receiving such punishments are outside the regular labor force. Social scientists who study courts would point out that such laws often are circumvented by practitioners and always will be inconsistently applied.

The law-and-economics scholar Richard Posner (1977), assuming that deterrence is a—or the—primary purpose of sentencing, once argued that only a small number of guilty offenders should be imprisoned and that they should receive very long sentences. His starting point was the notion that the risk of punishment is the price an offender thinking of committing a crime must be prepared to pay. The threatened punishment "costs" must be such as to outweigh the expected gains. He then assumed that punishing one hundred offenders with one-year prison sentences would provide the optimal punishment costs for a particular kind of crime. He observed, however, that sentencing ten offenders to ten-year prison terms each would also provide the optimal punishment costs, but at less expense and with less human suffering. Either approach would impose the same number of years of imprisonment. Economists estimate the punishment costs of crime by calculating the statistical probability that an offense will result in a conviction and punishment, and then calculating the average punishment imposed per crime. It is important to note that the denominator in the punishment calculation is the number of crimes committed, not the number of convictions or punishments. The cost thus is the average amount of punishment expected to be incurred for each offense committed in the community.

What matters is not the number of offenders punished but the total amount of punishment imposed. By that calculus, ten prison terms of ten years each involves the same aggregate amount of punishment as one hundred terms of one year. Posner argues that the ten-year sentences would be preferable because they would cost less to administer. And, because people discount the future—the sixth year of imprisonment is not as painful as the first—the ten would experience less aggregate subjective suffering than would the hundred.

That's one argument, based on the economic model of amoral people who make decisions entirely on the basis of self-interested calculation, that could conceivably be stretched to justify California's three-strikes law. It is, however, based on assumptions of punishment's deterrent effects that Durkheim rejected a priori and that most social scientists (though not most economists) reject as unsound (e.g., Doob and Webster 2003; Pratt et al. 2006; Tonry 2008; cf. Levitt 2002). It gains its shock value from the way it contravenes the widely shared intuition that like offenders should be treated alike and for that reason, even were such a policy adopted, it would be unlikely often to be applied.

2. How can policies and practices that disproportionately affect members of disadvantaged groups be justified?

People who have not thought much about punishment may find this question glib in the extreme and observe that the criminal law applies to all people of all incomes and social classes: disproportionate numbers of poor people commit thefts, steal cars, and sell drugs, and accordingly disproportionate numbers are punished. The law in its majestic impartiality, Anatole France observed, equally forbids the rich and the poor to sleep beneath the bridges of Paris. That answer begs the questions of why those crimes are more likely to be prosecuted (compared with, for example, equally prevalent tax evasion and domestic violence) and to result in severe punishments. It also begs the questions as to why poorer peoples' deviance is more likely to be criminalized than richer peoples' deviance, or why alcohol is a licit substance and the less socially damaging marijuana, heroin, and cocaine are not.

Neither philosophers nor legal theorists are much help here either. As a practical matter, they ignore the problem.[13] Both discuss just punishments in individual cases (when they discuss individual cases at all) as they appear for sentencing in court following a conviction. Whether cases appear in court, however, as political scientists have shown, and for what offenses, is the outcome of a series of decisions shaped by influences that lie largely outside the reach of normative punishment theories.

Functionalist analyses could help explain why criminal law seems mostly directed at poorer peoples' deviance. It is relatively easy to imagine Marx's, Foucault's, and Wacquant's arguments elaborated in ways that do this. The usefulness of Durkheim's arguments is less clear: whether the dramaturgical effects of punishment of members of distinctly disadvantaged social classes is likely effectively to model good and bad behavior is at best an empirical question with no obvious answer.

3. Should normative theories of punishment take into account the findings of empirical studies of the operation of courts?

How might that be done? This would be hard, and almost no one has tried to do it.

Within a state, plea bargaining differences between counties (charge bargaining in some, sentence bargaining in others; bargaining over the number of counts in some, and over the most serious charge in others) mean that the people being sentenced for a particular crime, or set of crimes, in one county, may have engaged in very different behaviors than people being sentenced for the same crimes in a different county. Similar issues arise every day in most court systems when some defendants charged with robbery are allowed to plead guilty to theft and others are convicted of robbery. Yet sentencing guidelines systems,[14] and most philosophers and legal theorists, treat the offense of conviction as the measure of an offender's wrongdoing.

There is something awkward and, once brought into the light of day, unedifying about theories that elegantly argue for treating like offenders in like ways and different offenders differently, without taking into account the empirical reality that the offenses of which people are convicted and for which they are punished stand in at best uncertain relation to the crimes they are believed to have committed. In earlier times, during the heyday of indeterminate and individualized sentencing, punishing people in ways that were disproportionate to the seriousness of their crimes was not widely seen as a serious problem. Consequentialist strategies of deterrence, incapacitation, and rehabilitation could be invoked to justify widely divergent punishments suffered by like-situated offenders.

4. *Should normative theories of punishment take into account the insights of social theorists such as Durkheim, Marx, Foucault, and Wacquant, and how might that be done?*

Their point is that things are not what they appear to be, but are really something else. The drawing, quartering, and burning of a traitor is not a loathsome punishment but a validation of the king's power. The penitentiary is not, as some early reformers saw it, a place for penitence and revelation or, as some Progressive reformers saw it, a place to rehabilitate offenders into law-abiding ways, but an institution for converting pre–Industrial Revolution human beings into the shapes required for them to become factory workers, soldiers, and government bureaucrats. Contemporary crime control policies and the "experiment" with mass incarceration are not good-faith efforts to suppress crime and reassure citizens but devices for destabilizing and disempowering black communities. Or maybe they are devices for helping politicians get re-elected or for maintaining the legitimacy of government in citizens' eyes.

To some extent functionalist analyses are paradoxical. They are hypotheses that things are not as they seem. Many people, to the contrary, will say that things are exactly as they seem. Some will simply reject the hypothesis that contemporary American crime control policies operate to maintain existing patterns of racial hierarchy. A social theorist might well cite that denial as a form of false consciousness, as evidence in support of the hypothesis. Existing policies do, as an empirical matter, demonstrably disadvantage minority groups, and lessen the life chances of many of their members. People's inability to recognize that, or to be troubled by its implications, can be argued to show that the system is performing its hierarchy maintenance function: blacks are disadvantaged as the outcome of policy processes that whites control and honestly claim are not meant to be discriminatory. The politically dominant white majority has the satisfaction of believing it has acted in a principled, nondiscriminatory way while benefiting from an outcome that sustains its economic, social, and political advantages.

It is not, however, impossible to gain policy insights from functionalist analyses. The relationship between Durkheimian ideas about norm reinforcement and Scandinavian theories about the moral-educative effects of punishment provides an illustration. Some existing practices—for example, shortening prison terms of aboriginal prisoners in Canada and Australia because of their short life expectancies—can be described as efforts to address the implications of functionalist analyses of the law as a device for maintaining existing patterns of racial (Wacquant) or class (Marx) relations.

5. Should race, ethnicity, or nationality matter?

This, I think, is the hardest question of them all. What should a judge do who simultaneously subscribes to a principled theory of punishment and yet believes, with Wacquant, that the American history of race relations largely explains the 100-to-1 rule, the War on Drugs, and disproportionate black incarceration, or with Marxist analysts, that the explanations can be found in class-based functional analyses of the criminal law. The disproportionate black presence among American prison inmates mirrors comparably disproportionate presences of Moroccans in Dutch prisons, Algerians in French prisons, Turks in German ones, and foreigners in Swiss ones (Tonry 1997).

Insofar as minority disparities can be attributed to social and economic characteristics associated with elevated rates of criminality, minority disparities might be interpreted as another manifestation of a general social pattern that links disadvantage to crime and punishment. Higher rates of crime and imprisonment can be expected to decline as successive generations of immigrant groups become more fully assimilated. However, in some countries, notably those with aboriginal populations (e.g., Australia, Canada, New Zealand) and the United States in relation to black Americans, elevated levels of crime and imprisonment have endured for many generations. How, if at all, can the criminal law and punishment doctrine take account of that?

Related issues have arisen in other places. In countries with large aboriginal populations, should normal prison sentence lengths be discounted to take account of aboriginal citizens' shorter life expectancies? Appellate courts in Australia and Canada have explicitly discussed the question. If there are jurisprudential bases for such a discount, the same argument might apply in many countries to members of ethnic minority groups afflicted by significantly lower life expectancies than the majority population—for example, to blacks in the United States.

Should immigrants or visitors from countries with especially harsh legal systems be punished by different standards than a country's majority population? The issue usually arises in places like Germany or the Scandinavian countries with relatively mild punishment traditions. Should, for example, Turks convicted of drug trafficking be sentenced by Finnish standards (a few months or a year; seldom for many years) or according to the much more severe standards of Turkish courts and prisons (Andenaes 1974)? Concern for equality before the law leads many people to dismiss such a proposal out of hand. Its rejection, however, creates a perverse incentive for would-be offenders from harsher places to come to Scandinavia, for example, to market their drugs.

None of these questions has easy answers. There are no easy ways to integrate the insights about punishment of philosophers, legal theorists, social theorists, and political scientists. We will understand punishment better, however, if we try to answer such questions and to integrate diverse insights.

NOTES

1. In the 1970s and 1980s, "abolitionists" proposed the abolition of punishment, but what they meant in substance was major diminution in resort to the criminal justice system and development of other mechanisms operating under other names (for example, mental health or social welfare) for dealing with egregious offenses or dangerous people (Bianchi and van Swaaningen 1986). More recently, many people have urged a shift away from criminal justice toward restorative justice approaches, but almost invariably they allow for criminal justice handling of egregious cases and incorrigible offenders (e.g., Braithwaite 2001).

2. Some people who argue that corporal punishments should never be imposed, and U.S. courts agree (e.g., *Jackson v. Bishop*, 404 F.2d 571 [8th Cir., 1968]) but that is not an argument about punishment per se. It is a human rights argument akin to the argument that torture should never be used to obtain evidence from recalcitrant suspects or witnesses. In much of the developed world, capital punishment is not an authorized punishment on the basis of human rights arguments. The constitutional distinction between death and lesser forms of corporal punishment as authorized punishments is distinctively American.

3. Other modern consequentialist theories would weigh the effects of alternative choices on "dominion" (individuals' capacities and opportunities to live satisfying lives within organized communities; Braithwaite and Pettit 1990) or on the community (Lacey 1988).

4. H. L. A. Hart (1968, chap. 1) disparaged this as an illegitimate "definitional stop": an effort to evade the problem by defining it away.

5. The novelist and Christian apologist C. S. Lewis (1949) and the novelist Anthony Burgess (1962, 1986) earlier offered moral critiques of consequentialism, especially in its rehabilitative aspirations.

6. He had in mind strict liability crimes. Some like traffic offenses are administrative offenses that threaten only financial penalties (and sometimes loss of a driver's license).

Others are business regulatory offenses (such as violation of pure food and drug laws) in which the stakes are so high and proof of fault is so difficult that corporations and sometimes their executives are made strictly liable for their violation. The aim is to create powerful incentives to assure compliance with the law. Prison sentences are rarely if ever imposed for such crimes.

7. Utilitarian ideas were influential in all developed countries. Most countries developed treatment programs and institutions for offenders, and many developed formal systems of parole and probation. Retributive ideas however also remained influential in most countries. Only in the United States were the institutions of the criminal justice system radically transformed to reflect utilitarian ideas. Examples include the "inventions" of the reformatory, the juvenile court, probation, parole, and the indeterminate sentence. Other countries later adopted some of the American innovations but usually in less full-blown forms. None, for example, removed authority to set lengths of prison sentences from judges and gave it to parole boards.

8. In addition, between the mid-1970s and mid-1980s a number of states starting with California in 1976 enacted systems of "statutory determinate sentencing" that in fairly crude ways enacted statutory provisions which prescribed punishments for particular offenses. Statutory systems were quickly recognized to be less effective than sentencing guidelines at addressing the perceived weaknesses of indeterminate sentencing. After 1985 no more statutory systems were enacted (Blumstein et al. 1983).

9. Stated more fully: it is assumed that citizens, if rational, would, if given the opportunity, assent to be governed by a set of rules that forbids serious intrusions by others into their lives and by them into the lives of others. Acceptance of such a body of rules would allow each citizen to plan and conduct his life or her life in the way he or she wishes in the expectation that the rules will be observed by all. Accordingly, if those rules are violated, the violator has benefited from others' obedience to the rules has thereby obtained an unfair advantage.

10. A narrower example is provided by laws forbidding sex offenders to live within three miles of a school, a distance that in many towns effectively forbids any sex offender to live there. Other expressive laws mandate especially harsh punishments for drug sales within specified distances of a school; the distances often effectively mandate the harsher punishment for any drug sale in the town.

11. I discuss the issues raised in this section and provide references to the major literature, in an earlier article (Tonry 2006). The classic works by political scientists on the operation of criminal courts are Jacob and Eisenstein (1977), Eisenstein, Flemming, Nardulli (1988), and Nardulli, Eisenstein, and Flemming (1988).

12. The issues raised in this section though they probably arise in weaker forms in every court system in their strong forms are distinctively American. Punishment questions are universal even if their answers are inevitably local. With small and partial exceptions (most notably in Switzerland), however, in no developed country other than the United States are judges and prosecutors elected or openly selected on the basis of political criteria. And in no other country are most criminal cases and many sentences resolved by means of plea negotiations.

13. That's not quite true. It is more accurate to say that sometimes they recognize the problem (e.g., von Hirsch 1976, last chap.) and then step around it, and other times they acknowledge it as a reason why their ideal theories are unsuitable for implementation in the real world (Duff 1986).

14. The exception is the U.S. Sentencing Commission's "real offense" policy under which convicted offenders were sentenced for the "actual offense behavior" found by the judge to have occurred using a civil law burden of proof, irrespective of whether charges were not filed for part of that behavior, or been dismissed, or resulted in a not guilty verdict.

REFERENCES

Allen, Francis A. 1959. "Legal Values and the Rehabilitative Ideal." *Journal of Criminal Law, Criminology, and Police Science* 50:226–32.

———. 1964. *The Borderland of Criminal Justice: Essays in Law and Criminology*. Chicago: University of Chicago Press.

American Friends Service Committee. 1971. *Struggle for Justice: A Report on Crime and Punishment in America*. New York: Hill and Wang.

American Law Institute. 1962. *Model Penal Code* (Proposed Official Draft). Philadelphia: American Law Institute.

———. 2007. *Model Penal Code: Sentencing*. Tentative Draft no. 1 (April 9, 2007). Philadelphia: American Law Institute.

Andenaes, Johannes. 1974. *Punishment and Deterrence*. Ann Arbor: University of Michigan Press.

Australia Law Reform Commission. 1980. *Sentencing of Federal Offenders*. Canberra: Australian Government Publishing Service.

Bentham, Jeremy. 1970. "The Utilitarian Theory of Punishment." In *An Introduction to Principles of Morals and Legislation,* ed. Jeremy Bentham, J. H. Burns and H. L. A. Hart. London: Methuen.

Bianchi, Herman, and René van Swaaningen. 1986. *Abolitionism: Towards a Non-Repressive Approach to Crime*. Amsterdam: Free University Press.

Blumstein, Alfred, Jacqueline Cohen, Susan Martin, and Michael Tonry, eds. 1983. *Sentencing Research and the Search for Reform. Report of the National Academy of Sciences Panel on Sentencing Research*. Washington, DC: National Academies Press.

Braithwaite, John. 2001. *Restorative Justice and Responsive Regulation*. New York: Oxford University Press.

Braithwaite, John, and Philip Pettit. 1990. *Not Just Deserts: A Republican Theory of Criminal Justice*. New York: Oxford University Press.

Bureau of Justice Statistics. 2003. "Prevalence of Imprisonment in the U.S. Population, 1974–2001." Washington, DC: Bureau of Justice Statistics.

Burgess, Anthony. 1962. *A Clockwork Orange*. London: Heinemann.

———. 1986. "Introduction: A Clockwork Orange Resucked." *A Clockwork Orange*. New York: W. W. Norton.

Canadian Sentencing Commission. 1987. *Sentencing Reform: A Canadian Approach*. Ottawa: Canadian Government Publishing Centre.

Clear, Todd R., and David Karp. 1999. *Community Justice Ideal*. Denver: Westview Press.

Cover, Robert. 1984. *Justice Accused: Antislavery and the Judicial Process*. New Haven: Yale University Press.

Davis, Kenneth Culp. 1969. *Discretionary Justice: A Preliminary Inquiry*. Baton Rouge: Louisiana State University Press.

Dershowitz, Alan. 1976. *Fair and Certain Punishment*. New York: McGraw-Hill.

Doob, Anthony, and Cheryl Webster. 2003. "Sentence Severity and Crime: Accepting the Null Hypothesis." In *Crime and Justice: A Review of Research*, vol. 30, edited by Michael Tonry. Chicago: University of Chicago Press.

Duff, Antony. 1986. *Trials and Punishments*. Cambridge: Cambridge University Press.

———. 2001. *Punishment, Communication, and Community*. New York: Oxford University Press.

Durkheim, Emile. 1933 [1893]. *The Division of Labor in Society*. Trans. George Simpson. New York: Macmillan.

Eisenstein, James, Roy Flemming, and Peter Nardulli. 1988. *The Contours of Justice: Communities and Their Courts*. Boston: Little, Brown.

Foucault, Michel. 1979. *Discipline and Punish: The Birth of the Prison*. London: Penguin.

Frankel, Marvin. 1972. *Criminal Sentences—Law without Order*. New York: Hill and Wang.

Garland, David. 2001. *The Culture of Complaint*. Chicago: University of Chicago Press.

Hampton, Jean. 1984. "The Moral Education Theory of Punishment." *Philosophy and Public Affairs* 13(3):208–38.

Hart, Henry M. 1958. "The Aims of the Criminal Law." *Law and Contemporary Problems* 23:401–42.

Hart, H. L. A. 1968. *Punishment and Responsibility*. Oxford: Clarendon.

Home Office. 1990. *Crime, Justice, and Protecting the Public*. Cm 965. London: Her Majesty's Stationery Office.

———. 2001. The Halliday Report: "Making Punishments Work: A Review of the Sentencing Framework for England and Wales." http://www.homeoffice.gov.uk/documents/halliday-report-sppu/.

Honderich, Ted. 2006. *Punishment: The Supposed Justifications Revisited*. London: Pluto.

Jacob, Herbert, and James Eisenstein. 1977. *Felony Justice: An Organizational Analysis of Criminal Courts*. Boston: Little, Brown.

Kant, Immanuel. 1965 [1787]. "The Penal Law and the Law of Pardon." *The Metaphysical Elements of Justice*, trans. John Ladd. Indianapolis: Liberal Arts Press/Bobbs-Merrill.

Kleinig, John. 1973. *Punishment and Desert*. Dordrecht, Netherlands: Martinus Nijhoff.

Lacey, Nicola. 1988. *State Punishment: Political Principles and Community Values*. New York: Routledge.

Lappi-Seppälä. 2001. "Sentencing and Punishment in Finland: The Decline of the Repressive Ideal." In *Sentencing and Sanctions in Western Countries*, ed. Tonry and Richard S. Frase. New York: Oxford University Press.

Levitt, Steve. 2002. "Deterrence." In *Crime: Public Policies for Crime Control*, ed. James Q. Wilson and Joan Petersilia. Oakland, CA: Institute for Contemporary Studies Press.

Lewis, C. S. 1949. "The Humanitarian Theory of Punishment." *20th Century: An Australian Quarterly Review*. 3(3)3:5–12 (repr. in God in the Dock: Essays on Theology and Ethics, ed. Walter Hooper. Grand Rapids, MI: Eerdmans).

Loury, Glenn C. 2007. "Racial Stigma, Mass Incarceration and American Values." *The Tanner Lectures in Human Values delivered at Stanford University* on April 4 and 5, 2007. http://www.econ.brown.edu/fac/Glenn_Loury/louryhomepage/.

Martinson, Robert. 1974. "What Works? Questions and Answers about Prison Reform." *The Public Interest* 35(2):22–54.

Marx, Karl. 1853. "Capital Punishment—Mr. Cobden's Pamphlet's—Regulations of the Bank of England." *New York Tribune*, February 17, p. 3.

Massey, Douglas S. 2007. *Categorically Unequal*. New York: Russell Sage Foundation.

Massey, Douglas S., and Nancy Denton. 1993. *American Apartheid: Segregation and the Making of the Underclass*. Cambridge, MA: Harvard University Press.

McCloskey, H. J. 1968. "A Non-utilitarian Approach to Punishment." In *Contemporary Utilitarianism*, ed. Michael D. Bayles. New York: Doubleday.

McDonald, Douglas, C., and Kenneth E. Carlson. 1993. *Sentencing in the Federal Courts: Does Race Matter?* Washington, DC: U.S. Department of Justice, Bureau of Justice Statistics.

Michael, Jerome, and Mortimer Adler. 1933. *Crime, Law, and Social Science*. New York: Harcourt Brace.

Michael, Jerome, and Herbert Wechsler. 1937. "A Rationale of the Law of Homicide." *Columbia Law Review* 37:701–61(pt. 1), 1261–1335 (pt. 2).

Minnesota Sentencing Guidelines Commission. 1980. *Report to the Legislature*. St. Paul: Minnesota Sentencing Guidelines Commission.

Moore, Michael S. 1993. "Justifying Retributivism." *Israeli Law Review* 27:15–36.

Morris, Herbert. 1966. "Persons and Punishment." *Monist* 52:475–501.

———. 1981. "A Paternalist Theory of Punishment." *American Philosophical Quarterly* 18:263–71.

Morris, Norval. 1974. *The Future of Imprisonment*. Chicago: University of Chicago Press.

Morris, Norval, and Michael Tonry. 1978. "Sentencing Reform in America." In *Reshaping the Criminal Law—A Festschrift in Honor of Glanville Williams*, ed. Peter Glazebrook. London: Stevens.

———. 1990. *Between Prison and Probation: Intermediate Punishments in Rational Sentencing System*. New York: Oxford University Press.

Murphy, Jeffrie. 1973. "Marxism and Retribution." *Philosophy and Public Affairs* 2:217–43.

Murphy, Jeffrie G., and Jean Hampton. 1988. *Forgiveness and Mercy*. Cambridge: Cambridge University Press.

Nardulli, Peter, James Eisenstein, and Ron Flemming. 1988. *The Tenor of Justice: Criminal Courts and the Guilty Plea Process*. Champaign, IL: University of Illinois Press.

Pincoffs, Edmund. 1966. *The Rationale of Legal Punishment*. New York: Humanities Press.

Posner, Richard. 1977. *Economic Analyses of Law*. 2nd ed. Boston: Little, Brown.

Pratt, Travis C., Francis T. Cullen, Kristie R. Blevins, Leah H. Daigle, and Tamara D. Madensen. 2006. "The Empirical Status of Deterrence Theory: A Meta-Analysis." In *Taking Stock: The Status of Criminological Theory*, ed. Francis T. Cullen, John Paul Wright, and Kristie R. Blevins. New Brunswick, NJ: Transaction.

Rawls, John. 1955. "Two Concepts of Rules." *Philosophical Review* 64:3–32.

———. 1971. *A Theory of Justice*. Cambridge, MA: Harvard University Press.

Rothman, David J. 1971. *The Discovery of the Asylum: Social Order and Disorder in the New Republic*. Boston: Little, Brown.

———. 1980. *Conscience and Convenience*. Boston: Little, Brown.

Rusche, Georg, and Otto Kirchheimer 1968 [1939]. *Punishment and Social Structure*. New York: Russell and Russell. New York: Columbia University Press.)

Singer, Richard. 1979. *Just Deserts: Sentencing Based on Equality and Desert*. Cambridge, MA: Ballinger.

Tonry, Michael. 1997. "Ethnicity, Crime and Immigration." In *Ethnicity, Crime, and Immigration: Comparative and Cross-national Perspectives*, edited by Michael Tonry.

Vol. 21 of *Crime and Justice: A Review of Research,* edited by Michael Tonry. Chicago: University of Chicago Press.

——. 2004. *Thinking about Crime: Sense and Sensibility in American Penal Culture.* New York: Oxford University Press.

——. 2006. "Purposes and Functions of Sentencing." In *Crime and Justice: A Review of Research,* vol. 34, edited by Michael Tonry. Chicago: University of Chicago Press.

——. 2008. "Learning from the Limitations of Deterrence Research." In *Crime and Justice: A Review of Research*, vol. 37, edited by Michael Tonry. Chicago: University of Chicago Press.

——. 2011. *Punishing Race: An American Dilemma Continues.* New York: Oxford University Press.

Tonry, Michael, and Matthew Melewski. 2008. "The Malign Effects of Drug and Crime Control Policies on Black Americans." In *Crime and Justice: A Review of Research*, vol. 37, edited by Michael Tonry. Chicago: University of Chicago Press.

U.S. Sentencing Commission. 1995. *1995 Special Report to the Congress: Cocaine and Federal Sentencing Policy.* Washington, DC: U.S. Sentencing Commission.

——. 2007. *Cocaine and Federal Sentencing Policy.* Washington, DC: U.S. Sentencing Commission.

von Hirsch, Andrew. 1976. *Doing Justice: The Choice of Punishments.* New York: Hill and Wang.

——. 1985. *Past or Future Crimes: Dangerousness and Deservedness in the Sentencing of Criminals.* New Brunswick, NJ: Rutgers University Press.

——. 1993. *Censure and Sanctions.* Oxford: Clarendon.

von Hirsch, Andrew. and Andrew Ashworth. 2005. *Proportionate Sentencing: Exploring the Principles.* Oxford: Oxford University Press.

Wacquant, Loïc. 2002*a*. "From Slavery to Mass Incarceration." *New Left Review* 13 (January-February): 41–60.

——. 2002*b*. "Deadly Symbiosis: Rethinking Race and Imprisonment in Twenty-First-Century America." *Boston Review* 27(2):22–31.

Western, Bruce. 2006. *Punishment and Inequality in America.* New York: Russell Sage Foundation.

Wexler, David B., and Bruce Winick, eds. 2003. *Justice in a Therapeutic Key.* Durham, NC: Carolina Academic Press.

CHAPTER 5

CRIME PREVENTION

BRANDON C. WELSH

THE modern-day history of crime prevention in America is closely linked with a loss of faith in the criminal justice system, which occurred in the wake of the dramatic increase in crime rates in the 1960s. This loss of faith was due to a confluence of factors, including declining public support for the criminal justice system, increasing levels of fear of crime, and criminological research that demonstrated that many of the traditional modes of crime control were ineffective and inefficient in reducing crime and improving the safety of communities (Curtis 1987). For example, research studies on motorized preventive patrol, rapid response, and criminal investigations—the staples of law enforcement—showed that they had little to no effect on crime (Visher and Weisburd 1998). It was becoming readily apparent among researchers and public officials alike that a criminal justice response on its own was insufficient for the task of reducing crime. This was not limited to law enforcement but included the courts and prisons (Tonry and Farrington 1995b). Interestingly, this loss of faith in the justice system was not unique to the United States. Similar experiences were taking place in Canada, the United Kingdom, and other Western European countries, and for some of the same reasons (Waller 1990; Bennett 1998).

Writing in the mid-1980s, the observations of the American urban affairs scholar Paul Lavrakas perhaps best captures this need to move beyond a sole reliance on the criminal justice system:

> Until we change the emphasis of our public policies away from considering the police, courts, and prisons to be the primary mechanisms for reducing crime, I believe that we will continue to experience the tragic levels of victimization with which our citizens now live. These criminal justice agencies are our means of

reacting to crime—they should not be expected to *prevent* it by themselves. (Lavrakas 1985, 110, emphasis in original)

These events, coupled with recommendations of presidential crime commissions of the day—the President's Commission on Law Enforcement and Administration of Justice (1967), chaired by Nicholas deB. Katzenbach, and the National Commission on the Causes and Prevention of Violence (1969), chaired by Milton S. Eisenhower—ushered in an era of innovation of alternative approaches to addressing crime. A few years later, the National Advisory Commission on Criminal Justice Standards and Goals (1973) sought to reaffirm the role of the community in preventing crime. Operating outside of the purview of the justice system, crime prevention came to be defined as an alternative, noncriminal justice means to reducing crime.

A focus on neighborhood, family, and employment was at the heart of this new approach to addressing crime, with a special emphasis on the most impoverished inner-city communities. Nonprofit organizations were the main vehicle used to deliver programs in these substantive areas. A number of situational or opportunity-reducing measures were also implemented to ensure the immediate safety of residents. Some of these programs included neighborhood patrols, block watches, and escort services (Curtis 1987, 11). By some accounts, this urban crime prevention and reconstruction movement produced a number of models of success and many more promising programs (see Curtis 1985, 1987; Eisenhower Foundation 1990).

This mode of crime prevention also came to be known as community-based crime prevention, an amalgam of social and situational measures (see Rosenbaum 1986, 1988). This approach was popularized with a number of large-scale, multi-site programs referred to as "comprehensive community initiatives" (Hope 1995; Rosenbaum, Lurigio, and Davis 1998). Examples (always with catchy acronyms) included T-CAP (Texas City Action Plan to Prevent Crime) and PACT (Pulling America's Communities Together).

The roots of this comprehensive approach—on the social side at least—go as far back as the early 1930s, with Clifford Shaw and Henry McKay's Chicago Area Project (CAP; Shaw and McKay 1942). The CAP was designed to produce social change in communities that suffered from high delinquency rates and gang activity. Local civic leaders coordinated social service centers that promoted community solidarity and counteracted social disorganization, and developed other programs for youths, including school-related activities and recreation. Some evaluations indicated desirable results, but others showed that CAP efforts did little to reduce delinquency (Schlossman and Sedlak 1983).

The New York City–based Mobilization for Youth (MOBY) program of the 1960s is another example of this type of crime prevention initiative. Funded by more than $50 million, MOBY attempted an integrated approach to community development (Short 1974). Based on Richard Cloward and Lloyd Ohlin's (1960) concept of providing opportunities for legitimate success, MOBY created employment opportunities in the community, coordinated social services, and sponsored social action groups such as tenants' committees, legal action services, and voter registration. But the program ended for lack of funding amid questions about its utility and use of funds.

A newer generation of these programs, which includes the well-established Communities That Care (CTC) strategy developed by David Hawkins and Richard Catalano (1992), incorporates principles of public health and prevention science—identifying key risk factors for offending and implementing evidence-based prevention methods designed to counteract them. The CTC group has become the best developed and tested of these prevention systems. Findings from the first large-scale randomized controlled trial show that CTC reduces targeted risk factors and delinquent behavior community-wide (Hawkins, Oesterle, et al. 2008; Hawkins, Brown, et al. 2009).

By the early 1990s, crime prevention found itself in the national spotlight, although not all to the liking of its supporters. This came about during the lead-up to and subsequent passage of the federal crime bill of 1994—the most expensive in history (Donziger 1996). Known officially as the Violent Crime Control and Law Enforcement Act, it ultimately became famous for its authorization of funding to put 100,000 new police officers on the streets, as well as infamous for making sixty more federal crimes eligible for the death penalty and authorizing $10 billion for new prison construction. Crime prevention programs (in the broadest sense) were allocated a sizeable $7 billion, but most of this was used on existing federal programs like Head Start in order to keep them afloat (Gest 2001).

From the beginning of the bill's debate on Capitol Hill and across the country, crime prevention—especially programs for at-risk youth—was heavily criticized. The growing political thirst to get tough on juvenile and adult criminals alike with an array of punitive measures sought to paint prevention and its supporters as soft on crime. Midnight basketball became their scapegoat. Prevention was characterized as nothing more than pork, wasteful spending of tax-payer dollars. The end result of all of this was mixed: Crime prevention had received substantial funding, but it had been relegated to the margins in the public discourse on crime (Mendel 1995).

In more recent years, crime prevention has emerged as an important component of an overall strategy to reduce crime. One reason for this is the widely held view of the need to strike a greater balance between prevention and punishment (Waller 2006). Another key reason has to do with a growing body of scientific evidence that shows that many different types of crime prevention programs are effective (Sherman, Gottfredson, et al. 1997; Sherman, Farrington, et al. 2006; Welsh and Farrington 2006), and many of these programs save money (Welsh and Farrington 2000; Aos, Miller, and Drake 2006). Not surprisingly, the economic argument for prevention has attracted a great deal of interest from policymakers and political leaders (Greenwood 2006). The recent evidence-based movement has figured prominently in these developments in raising the profile of crime prevention.

This chapter provides a comprehensive overview of research on and key issues facing crime prevention. Several observations and conclusions emerge:

- Crime prevention is best viewed as an alternative approach to reducing crime, operating outside of the confines of the criminal justice system. Developmental, community, and situational strategies define its scope.
- Developmental prevention has emerged as an important strategy to improve children's life chances and prevent them from embarking on a life of crime.
- Community crime prevention seemingly holds much promise for preventing crime, but little is known about its effectiveness. Advancing knowledge on this front is a top priority.
- Situational crime prevention can boast a growing evidence base of effective programs and many more that are promising in reducing crime. Among these programs there is also evidence that crime displacement is a rare occurrence.
- Crime prevention is an important component of an overall strategy to reduce crime. Striking a greater balance between prevention and punishment will go a long way toward building a safer, more sustainable society for all.

The organization of this essay is as follows. Section I summarizes the main ways of classifying or organizing crime prevention programs. Sections II, III, and IV review, respectively, the research on the major crime-prevention strategies of developmental, community, and situational prevention. Here, primary emphasis is placed on research carried out in the last decade. An evidence-based approach is a major theme of these reviews. Section V discusses implications of the current knowledge base on crime prevention and outlines an agenda of highest-priority research for the next decade.

I. Classifying Crime Prevention

Crime prevention means many different things to many different people. Programs and policies designed to prevent crime can include the police making an arrest as part of an operation to deal with gang problems, a court sanction to a secure correctional facility, or, in the extreme case, a death penalty sentence. These measures are more correctly referred to as crime control or repression. More often, though, crime prevention refers to efforts to prevent crime or criminal offending in the first instance—before the act has been committed. Both forms of crime prevention share a common goal of trying to prevent the occurrence of a future criminal act, but what distinguishes crime prevention from crime control is that prevention typically does not involve the formal justice system. In this respect, prevention might be considered a fourth pillar of crime reduction, alongside the institutions of police, courts, and corrections (Waller 2006). This distinction draws attention to crime prevention as an alternative approach to these more traditional responses to crime.

There are many possible ways of classifying crime prevention programs. One of the first efforts drew upon the public health approach to preventing diseases and injuries (Brantingham and Faust 1976; see also Moore 1995). This divides crime prevention activities into three categories: primary, secondary, and tertiary. *Primary prevention* involves measures focused on improving the general well-being of individuals through such measures as access to health care services and general prevention education, and modifying conditions in the physical environment that are conducive to crime through such measures as removing abandoned vehicles and improving the appearance of buildings. *Secondary prevention* focuses on intervening with children and youth who are at risk for becoming offenders because of the presence of one or more risk factors as well as the provision of neighborhood programs to deter known criminal activity. *Tertiary prevention* involves measures targeted on offenders. Here, the goal is to reduce repeat offending or recidivism.

The Dutch criminologists Jan van Dijk and Jaap de Waard (1991) expanded on this classification system to include a second dimension: the target group or focus of crime prevention programs. Influenced by routine activity theory (Cohen and Felson 1979), this second dimension distinguished among offender-, situation-, and victim-oriented activities. This "two-dimensional" typology allowed for programs to be organized by the different stages of the development of criminal activity (primary, secondary, or tertiary) and the target group. In many respects, the key contribution of this new typology was to reaffirm that efforts to prevent crime must also consider the crime victim (or potential victim) alongside the more traditional targets of offender (or potential offender) and place.

Several years later, the British criminologist Paul Ekblom (1994) ventured into the crime prevention taxonomy debate with a highly detailed scheme that attempted to reconcile these earlier versions with the mechanism- and context-based evaluation approach advocated by Ray Pawson and Nick Tilley (1994; see also Pawson and Tilley 1997). Three characteristics of prevention programs were relevant: (1) its ultimate objective; (2) "final intermediate objectives" if multiple interventions were employed; and (3) the actual methods used, from development to intervention. Ekblom's approach was not meant as a "rigid 'take it or leave it' classification" but rather a "conceptual toolkit which can be realized in a number of ways in relation to both form and content according to a wide range of needs" (1994, 227).

Another classification scheme distinguishes four major prevention strategies (Tonry and Farrington 1995b). Developmental prevention refers to interventions designed to prevent the development of criminal potential in individuals, especially those targeting risk and protective factors discovered in studies of human development (Tremblay and Craig 1995; Farrington and Welsh 2007b). Community prevention refers to interventions designed to change the social conditions and institutions (e.g., families, peers, social norms, clubs, organizations) that influence offending in residential communities (Hope 1995). Situational prevention refers to interventions designed to prevent the occurrence of crimes by reducing opportunities and increasing the risk and difficulty of offending (Clarke 1995*b*; Cornish and Clarke 2003). Criminal justice prevention refers to traditional deterrent, incapacitative, and rehabilitative strategies operated by law enforcement and criminal justice system agencies (Blumstein, Cohen, and Nagin 1978; MacKenzie 2006).

In *Building a Safer Society: Strategic Approaches to Crime Prevention*, Michael Tonry and David Farrington (1995*a*) purposely did not address criminal justice prevention in any substantial fashion. This was because this strategy had been adequately addressed in many other scholarly books, and more importantly, there was a growing consensus about the limited effects of this approach and the need for governments to strike a greater balance between these emerging and promising alternative forms of crime prevention and the more traditional responses to crime. For some of these same reasons, a similar approach has been adopted here, as well as in *The Oxford Handbook of Crime Prevention* (Welsh and Farrington, forthcoming). Also important to the decision to focus exclusively on developmental, community, and situational crime prevention is their shared focus on addressing the underlying causes or motivations that lead to a criminal event or a life of crime. Crucially, each operate outside of the confines of the criminal justice system and, thus represent, as a collection of independent strategies, an alternative, perhaps even socially progressive, way to reduce crime.

Other classification schemes that are specific to one type of crime prevention or another have also been proposed. For example, in one that is largely drawn from psychology and focused on the individual, prevention methods can be viewed as universal, selected, or indicated (see Tremblay and Craig 1995; Wasserman and Miller 1998). A *universal program* is one applied to a complete population, as in primary prevention. A *selective program* is one applied to a high-risk subgroup of the population, as in secondary prevention. An *indicated program* is one applied to identified cases such as offenders. For situational crime-prevention programs, Derek Cornish and Ron Clarke (2003) have proposed a revised scheme that includes twenty-five different techniques divided into five main approaches (for earlier versions, see Clarke 1992; Clarke and Homel 1997). Tim Hope (1998) has done likewise for community crime prevention.

II. Developmental Crime Prevention

The developmental perspective postulates that criminal offending in adolescence and adulthood is influenced by "behavioral and attitudinal patterns that have been learned during an individual's development" (Tremblay and Craig 1995, 151). The early years of the life course are most influential in shaping later experiences. As Greg Duncan and Katherine Magnuson (2004, 101) note: "Principles of developmental science suggest that although beneficial changes are possible at any point in life, interventions early on may be more effective at promoting well-being and competencies compared with interventions undertaken later in life." They further state that "early childhood may provide an unusual window of opportunity for interventions because young children are uniquely receptive to enriching and supportive environments. . . . As individuals age, they gain the independence and ability to shape their environments, rendering intervention efforts more complicated and costly" (102–3).

Developmental prevention is informed generally by motivational or human development theories on criminal behavior, and specifically by longitudinal studies that follow samples of young persons from their early childhood experiences to the peak of their involvement with crime in their teens and twenties. It aims to influence the scientifically identified risk factors or "root causes" for delinquency and later criminal offending, and is often referred to as "risk focused prevention." Some of the most important risk factors include low intelligence and attainment, impulsiveness, criminal or antisocial parents, poor parental supervision, parental conflict, disrupted families, living in deprived areas, and growing up in a low socio-economic status household (Farrington and Welsh 2007*b*).

Richard Tremblay and Wendy Craig's (1995) classic, sweeping review of developmental crime prevention identified three key characteristics of effective programs in preventing delinquency and later offending: they lasted for a sufficient duration (at least one year); they were multimodal, meaning that multiple risk factors were targeted with different interventions; and they were implemented before adolescence. Since their review, many more have focused on specific types of early developmental prevention programs and a few have looked at the broader field, with the latter often dividing interventions into those focused on the individual and the family. Two main types of individual-based programs have been found to be effective in preventing delinquency or offending: preschool intellectual enrichment and child skills training. A similar number of family-based programs have been found to be effective in preventing delinquency or offending: general parent education (in the context of home visiting and parent education plus daycare services) and parent management training.

A. Preschool Intellectual Enrichment

Preschool intellectual enrichment programs are generally targeted on the risk factors of low intelligence and attainment. Improved cognitive skills, school readiness, and social and emotional development are the main goals (Currie 2001). Some of the key features of these programs include the provision of developmentally appropriate learning curricula, a wide array of cognitive-based enriching activities, and activities for parents, usually of a less intensive nature, so that they may be able to support the school experience at home (Duncan and Magnuson 2004, 105–6).

On the basis of four evaluations of preschool programs (three evaluated with randomized experimental designs), a meta-analysis found that this type of early developmental prevention produced a significant 12 percent reduction in delinquency and offending (e.g., from 50 percent in a control group to 38 percent in an experimental group) (Farrington and Welsh 2007b).

Duncan and Magnuson's (2004) review of preschool education programs distinguished between "intensive efficacy interventions" (or research and demonstration projects) and "more policy-relevant, less intensive interventions" (or routine practice). Their coverage of the former group of preschool intellectual enrichment programs is similar to those in the foregoing meta-analysis, and they, too, found that these programs have long-term beneficial effects on children's criminal behavior (as well as on other outcomes). On the matter of less intensive preschool education interventions like Head Start, the authors found that the evidence was less clear about the ability of these programs to produce results similar to the intensive efficacy ones. However, they concluded that, "the weight of the evidence to date indicates that these programs may also improve children's life courses" (105).

B. Child Skills Training

Interpersonal skills training or social competence programs for children are generally targeted on the risk factors of impulsivity, low empathy, and self-centeredness. As noted by Carolyn Webster-Stratton and Ted Taylor (2001, 178), this type of individual-based program is designed to "directly teach children social, emotional, and cognitive competence by addressing appropriate social skills, effective problem-solving, anger management, and emotion language." A typical program includes one or more of these elements and is highly structured with a limited number of sessions, thus lasting for a relatively short period of time (Lösel and Beelmann 2003).

The criminologists Friedrich Lösel and Andreas Beelmann (2006; see also Lösel and Beelmann 2003) carried out a systematic review and meta-analysis of the effects of child skills training on antisocial behavior (including delinquency). Four evaluations (all randomized controlled experiments) measured delinquency. Effects of the intervention on delinquency were consistent at two different follow-up periods. At immediate outcome or postintervention (defined as within two months after treatment) the meta-analysis yielded a significant 9 percent reduction in delinquency in an experimental group compared to a control group. At later follow-up (defined as three months or more after treatment), the average effect was slightly higher—a 10 percent reduction in delinquency (also a significant effect). The meta-analysis also found that the most effective skills-training programs used a cognitive-behavioral approach and were implemented with older children (thirteen years and over) and higher-risk groups who were already exhibiting some behavioral problems.

C. Parent Education

Home visiting with new parents, especially mothers, is a popular, although far from universal, method of delivering the family-based intervention known as general parent education. The main goals of home-visitation programs center around educating parents to improve the life chances of children from a very young age, often beginning at birth and sometimes in the final trimester of pregnancy. Some of the main goals include the prevention of preterm or low-weight births, the promotion of healthy child development or school readiness, and the prevention of child abuse and neglect (Gomby, Culross, and Behrman 1999, 4). Home visits very often also serve to improve parental well-being, linking parents to community resources to help with employment, education, or addiction recovery. Home visitors are usually nurses or other health professionals with a diverse array of skills in working with families.

In a meta-analysis that included four home-visitation programs (all randomized controlled experiments), it was found that this form of early intervention was effective in preventing antisocial behavior and delinquency, corresponding to a significant 12 percent reduction (e.g., from 50 percent in a control group to 38 percent in an experimental group) (Farrington and Welsh 2007b).

As part of the Task Force on Community Preventive Services, which receives support from the Centers for Disease Control and Prevention, Oleg Bilukha and his colleagues (2005) carried out a systematic review of the effectiveness of early childhood home visitation in preventing violence. Four studies were included that reported the effects on the visited children of home-visitation programs on violence. Mixed results were found for effects on criminal violence (in adolescence) and child externalizing behavior across the four programs: two reported desirable but nonsignificant effects; one reported a significant desirable effect; and one reported mixed results. On the basis of these results, the authors concluded that the "evidence is insufficient to determine the effectiveness of home visitation interventions in preventing child violence" (17).

This systematic review also assessed, using these and many other studies, the effectiveness of early childhood home visitation on parental violence, intimate partner violence, and child maltreatment. For the first two outcomes, there was also insufficient evidence to make a determination of effectiveness. Strong evidence of effectiveness was, however, found for home-visiting programs in preventing child abuse and neglect.

The best known home-visiting program (and the only one with a direct measure of delinquency) is the Nurse-Family Partnership (NFP) carried out in the semirural community of Elmira, New York, by David Olds and his colleagues (1998). The program enrolled four hundred women prior to their thirtieth week of pregnancy. Women were recruited if they had had no previous live births and had at least one of the following high-risk characteristics prone to health and developmental problems in infancy: under nineteen years of age, unmarried, or poor. The women were randomly assigned to receive home visits from nurses during pregnancy, or to receive visits both during pregnancy and during the first two years of life, or to a control group who received no visits. Each visit lasted about one and one-quarter hours, and the mothers were visited on average every two weeks. The home visitors gave advice about prenatal and postnatal care of the child, infant development, and the importance of proper nutrition and avoiding smoking and drinking during pregnancy.

The results showed that the postnatal home visits caused a significant decrease in recorded child physical abuse and neglect during the first two years of life, especially by poor, unmarried, teenage mothers (Olds et al. 1986), and in a fifteen-year follow-up, significantly fewer experimental compared to control group mothers were identified as perpetrators of child abuse and neglect (Olds et al. 1997). At the age of fifteen, children of the higher-risk mothers who received prenatal or postnatal home visits or both had incurred significantly fewer arrests than their control counterparts (twenty as opposed to forty-five per one hundred children; Olds et al. 1998). Several benefit-cost analyses show that the benefits of this program outweighed its costs for the higher-risk mothers (see Aos et al. 2004; Greenwood 2006).

A small number of parent education programs that include daycare services for the children of the participating parents have also measured delinquency (e.g., Johnson and Walker 1987; Lally, Mangione, and Honig 1988). Daycare programs are distinguished from preschool programs in that the former are not necessarily focused on the child's intellectual enrichment or on readying the child for kindergarten and elementary school, but serve largely as an organized form of child care to allow parents (especially mothers) to return to work. Daycare also provides children with a number of important benefits, including social interaction with other children and stimulation of their cognitive, sensory, and motor control skills.

In a meta-analysis of three daycare programs, it was found that this form of parent education resulted in a small but nonsignificant 7 percent reduction in antisocial behavior and delinquency (e.g., from 50 percent in a control group to 43 percent in an experimental group) (Farrington and Welsh 2007b).

D. Parent Management Training

Many different types of parent training have been used to prevent and treat child externalizing behavior problems and delinquency (Wasserman and Miller 1998). Parent management training refers to "treatment procedures in which parents are trained to alter their child's behavior at home" (Kazdin 1997, 1349). Gerald Patterson (1982) developed behavioral parent management training. His careful observations of parent-child interaction showed that parents of antisocial children were deficient in their methods of child rearing. These parents failed to tell their children how they were expected to behave, failed to monitor their behavior to ensure that it was desirable, and failed to enforce rules promptly and unambiguously with appropriate rewards and penalties. The parents of antisocial children used more punishment (such as scolding, shouting, or threatening), but failed to make it contingent on the child's behavior.

Patterson attempted to train these parents in effective child-rearing methods, namely, noticing what a child is doing, monitoring behavior over long periods, clearly stating house rules, making rewards and punishments contingent on behavior, and negotiating disagreements so that conflicts and crises did not escalate. His treatment was shown to be effective in reducing stealing and antisocial behavior over short periods in small-scale studies (Patterson, Chamberlain, and Reid 1982; Patterson, Reid, and Dishion 1992).

On the basis of ten, high-quality evaluations of parent management training programs, a meta-analysis found that this type of early intervention produced a significant 20 percent reduction in antisocial behavior and delinquency (e.g., from 50 percent in a control group to 30 percent in an experimental group) (Farrington and Welsh 2007b). Each of the ten parent management training programs included in this meta-analysis aimed to teach parents to use rewards and punishments consistently and contingently in child rearing. The programs were usually delivered in guided group meetings of parents, including role-playing and modeling exercises, and three of the programs were delivered by videotape. Just one of the ten programs combined parent management training with another intervention (child skills training).

Wendy Serketich and Jean Dumas (1996) carried out a meta-analysis of twenty-six controlled studies of behavioral parent training (also called parent management training) with young children up to age ten. Most were based on small numbers (average total sample size was twenty-nine), and most were randomized experiments. They concluded that parent management training was effective in reducing child antisocial behavior, especially for (relatively) older children.

Alex Piquero and his colleagues (2009) carried out a much broader systematic review and meta-analysis of parent training and found it to be effective in reducing child behavior problems, including antisocial behavior and delinquency. The review, which included fifty-five randomized controlled experiments, investigated the full range of early/family parent training programs for children up to age five years, including home visiting, parent education plus daycare, and parent management training. Significant differences were not detected across program type (traditional parent training versus home visiting) or outcome source (parent, teacher, or direct observer reports).

III. COMMUNITY CRIME PREVENTION

More often than not, community-based efforts to prevent crime are thought to be some combination of developmental prevention, with its focus on reducing the development or influence of early risk factors for offending, and situational prevention, with its focus on reducing opportunities for crime. Unlike these two crime prevention strategies, there is little agreement in the academic literature on the definition of community prevention and the types of programs that fall within it. This stems from its early conceptions, with one view focused on the social conditions of crime and the ability of the community to regulate them, and another that "it operates at the level of whole communities regardless of the types of mechanisms involved" (Bennett 1996, 169).

Hope's (1995) definition that community crime prevention involves actions designed to change the social conditions and institutions that influence offending in residential communities is by far the most informative. This is not just because it demarcates itself from developmental and situational prevention, but it also speaks to the strength of the community to address the sometimes intractable social problems that lead to crime and violence. This focus on the social leaves aside physical redesign concepts, including Oscar Newman's (1972) defensible space and C. Ray Jeffrey's (1977) crime prevention through environmental design. Ron Clarke (1992, 1995b) describes how these important concepts are more correctly viewed as contributing to the early development of situational crime prevention.

Numerous theories have been advanced over the years to explain the community level influence on crime and have come to form the basis of community crime-prevention programs (for excellent reviews, see Byrne and Sampson 1986; Reiss and Tonry 1986; Farrington 1993; Sampson and Lauritsen 1994; Wikström 1998). Community disorganization, community disorder, community empowerment, and community regeneration theories are among the most important (Bennett 1998). While there is a rich theoretical literature on communities and crime, less is known about the effectiveness of community crime-prevention programs.

Review after review on the effectiveness of community crime prevention—going back to Rosenbaum's (1988) and Hope's (1995) classics—have consistently reported two findings. First, there are a number of well-known program types or modalities that are of unknown effectiveness in preventing crime. These are interventions for which there is not an adequate body of evaluation research to make an assessment. One example is community mobilization. Comprehensive crime-prevention strategies frequently involve the mobilization of community members to participate actively in planning and implementing prevention activities. This includes the "creation of formal community development organizations to the mobilization of resources from outside the community to help solve local problems like crime and unemployment" (Sherman 1997, 3:9). In a review of community mobilization programs, Welsh and Hoshi (2006) concluded that this approach is of unknown effect in preventing crime. Only four programs had been evaluated, and the scientific rigor of the evaluations as a group was deemed very poor.

Second, up until recently, there were no program types of proven effectiveness in preventing crime. Importantly, this was not a claim that "nothing works" and that community crime prevention should be abandoned. Some program types were found to be promising in their ability to prevent crime.[1] The latest research on the effectiveness of community crime prevention finds that mentoring and neighbor-hood-watch programs are effective, and after-school programs are promising in preventing crime.

A. Mentoring

This type of program usually involves nonprofessional adult volunteers spending time with young people at risk for delinquency, dropping out of school, school fail-ure, and other social problems. Mentors behave in a "supportive, nonjudgmental manner while acting as role models" (Howell 1995, 90). In many cases, mentors work one-on-one with young people, often forming strong bonds. Care is taken in matching the mentor and the young person.

Darrick Jolliffe and David Farrington's (2008) systematic review and meta-analysis of eighteen mentoring programs found this to be an effective approach to preventing criminal offending. The average effect across the studies corresponded to a significant 10 percent reduction in offending. The authors found that mentoring was more effective in reducing offending when the average duration of each contact between mentor and mentee was greater, in smaller scale studies, and when men-toring was combined with other interventions.

B. Neighborhood Watch

This highly popular form of citizen surveillance has long been an important compo-nent of community crime prevention in the United States, United Kingdom, and other Western countries. Used mostly to prevent crimes at private residences, it is also known as block watch, home watch, and community watch. Many neighborhood-watch programs are carried out in partnership with police, with the police providing advice on needed security measures in the home, marking property, and educating the public about home break-ins and their prevention. A number of mechanisms have been proposed for how neighborhood-watch programs can reduce crime, in-cluding residents watching out for suspicious activities and reporting these to the police, reducing opportunities for crime by way of making the home looked lived in when residents are away, and improving informal social control and community co-hesion (Bennett, Holloway, and Farrington 2006).

A systematic review and meta-analysis of neighborhood watch, which included eighteen high quality studies, found that it was associated with a 16 percent reduc-tion in crime in communities where it was implemented compared to similar com-munities that did not receive it (Bennett, Holloway, and Farrington 2006). Further analyses showed that there was no difference in effectiveness between programs based on neighborhood watch alone and those that also included property marking and security surveys carried out by the police. Interestingly, no difference was found in the effectiveness of neighborhood-watch programs over time; that is, the first generation of programs evaluated in the 1970s and 1980s were just as effective as their more modern counterparts that were evaluated in the 1990s.

C. After-School Programs

This type of program is premised on the belief that providing prosocial opportunities for young people in the after-school hours can reduce their involvement in delinquent and criminal behavior in the community. After-school programs target a range of crime risk factors, including alienation and association with delinquent peers. There are many different types of these programs, including recreation-based, drop-in clubs, dance groups, and tutoring services.

Welsh and Hoshi (2006) identified three high-quality, after-school programs with an evaluated impact on delinquency or crime. Each program produced desirable effects on delinquency or crime, and one program also reported lower rates of drug activity for participants compared to controls. Welsh and Hoshi concluded that community-based after-school programs represent a promising approach to preventing juvenile offending, but this conclusion applies only to areas immediately around recreation centers.

Denise Gottfredson and her colleagues (2004), as part of a larger study to investigate the effects of after-school programs on delinquency in Maryland, reported on a brief review of the effectiveness of these programs. They concluded that there is insufficient evidence at present to support claims that after-school programs are effective in preventing delinquency or other problem behaviors. However, they noted that among a small number of experimental and quasi-experimental studies, after-school programs that "involve a heavy dose of social competency skill development . . . may reduce problem behavior" (256).

In Gottfredson et al.'s (2004) Maryland study, which used randomized experimental and quasi-experimental methods with statistical matching designs to evaluate the effects of fourteen after-school programs, it was found that participation in the programs reduced delinquent behavior among children in middle school but not elementary school. Increasing intentions not to use drugs and positive peer associations were identified as the mechanisms for the middle school programs' favorable effects on delinquency, while decreasing time spent unsupervised or increasing involvement in constructive activities played no significant role (263–64).

IV. Situational Crime Prevention

Situational prevention stands apart from the other crime prevention strategies by its singular focus on the setting or place in which criminal acts take place as well as its crime-specific focus. Related to this is the widely held finding that crime is not randomly distributed across a city or community, but is instead highly concentrated at certain places known as crime "hot spots" (Sherman, Gartin, and Buerger 1989). For example, it is estimated that across the United States 10 percent of the places are sites for around 60 percent of the crimes (Eck 2006, 242). In the same way that individuals can have criminal careers, there are also criminal careers of places (Sherman 1995).

Situational crime prevention is defined as "a preventive approach that relies, not upon improving society or its institutions, but simply upon reducing opportunities for crime" (Clarke 1992, 3). Reducing opportunities for crime is achieved essentially through some modification or manipulation of the physical environment in order directly to affect offenders' perceptions of increased risks and effort and decreased rewards, provocations, and excuses (Cornish and Clarke 2003). These different approaches serve as the basis of the highly detailed classification system of situational crime prevention, which can further be divided into twenty-five separate techniques each with any number of examples of programs (Cornish and Clarke 2003).

The theoretical origins of situational crime prevention are wide ranging (see Newman, Clarke, and Shoham 1997; Garland 2000), but it is largely informed by opportunity theory. This theory holds that the offender is "heavily influenced by environmental inducements and opportunities and as being highly adaptable to changes in the situation" (Clarke 1995a, 57). Opportunity theory includes several more specific theories. One of these is the rational choice perspective. This perspective appears to have had the greatest influence on the pragmatic orientation of situational crime prevention, as articulated by its chief architect, Ron Clarke (1995a, b, 1997).

The situational approach is also supported by theories that emphasize natural, informal surveillance as a key to crime prevention. For example, Jane Jacobs (1961) drew attention to the role of good visibility combined with natural surveillance as deterrents to crime. She emphasized the association between levels of crime and public street use, suggesting that less crime would be committed in areas with an abundance of potential witnesses.

Lighting improvements, for instance, may encourage increased street usage, which intensifies natural surveillance. The change in routine activity patterns works to reduce crime because it increases the flow of potentially capable guardians who can intervene to prevent crime (Cohen and Felson 1979). From the potential offender's perspective, the proximity of other pedestrians acts as a deterrent since the risks of being recognized or interrupted when attacking personal or property targets are increased. From the potential victim's perspective, the perceived risks and fears of crime are reduced.

Fairly or unfairly, situational crime prevention often raises concerns over the displacement of crime. This is the notion that offenders simply move around the corner or resort to different methods to commit crimes once a crime prevention project has been introduced.[2] Thirty years ago, Thomas Reppetto (1976) identified five different forms of displacement: *temporal* (change in time), *tactical* (change in method), *target* (change in victim), *territorial* (change in place), and *functional* (change in type of crime). Usually, displacement follows from target hardening (e.g., the installation of locks or physical barriers) and other situational measures that attempt to increase the perceived effort required to commit a crime.

What Clarke (1995*b*) and many others (Gabor 1990; Hesseling 1995) have found and rightly note is that displacement is never 100 percent. Furthermore, a growing body of research has shown that situational measures may instead result in a diffusion of crime prevention benefits or the "complete reverse" of displacement (Clarke and Weisburd 1994). Instead of a crime prevention project displacing crime, the project's crime-prevention benefits are diffused to the surrounding area, for example. Ron Clarke and David Weisburd (1994) contend that diffusion occurs in one of two ways: by affecting offenders' assessment of risk (deterrence), or by affecting offenders' assessment of effort and reward (discouragement).[3]

John Eck's (2006) review of situational crime-prevention programs is the most comprehensive that has been carried out thus far. It focused on the full range of situational measures implemented in both public and private settings, and included both published and unpublished studies. In keeping with its evidence-based approach (see Welsh and Farrington, this volume), it included only the highest-quality evaluations in arriving at conclusions about what works and what does not. This had the effect of excluding many situational measures with demonstrated preventive effects—including steering column locks, redesigned credit cards, and exact-change policies (see Clarke 1997). Some of these first-generation situational prevention measures employed weak evaluations that could not support the assertion that the program produced the reported effect. Since Eck's review, a number of others have been carried out to assess the effectiveness of specific situational interventions, and findings from these will be integrated here. Eck found that two types of programs were effective and another seven were promising in preventing crime. Nuisance abatement and improved street lighting were the effective ones.

A. Nuisance Abatement

Nuisance abatement involves the use of civil law to curtail drug dealing and related crime problems in private residential premises. It is considered a situational crime prevention measure because of its place-specific focus, as well as its use of the threat of civil action to curtail the problem. It would fall under the strategy of decreasing excuses for committing a crime in Cornish and Clarke's (2003) taxonomy of situational prevention. Four high-quality evaluations, including two randomized experiments, were identified, and each of the four showed evidence of reduced drug-related crime. In one of the randomized experiments, in Oakland, California, Lorraine Mazerolle and her colleagues (1998) compared the impact in controlling social disorder of civil remedies (police working with city agency representatives to inspect drug nuisance properties, coerce landlords to clean up blighted properties, post "no trespassing" signs, enforce civil law codes and municipal regulatory rules, and initiate court proceedings against property owners who failed to comply with civil law citations) versus traditional police tactics (surveillance, arrests, and field interrogations). Observations of street blocks showed that conditions improved in the experimental places compared with the control places. In the most direct measure of offending—observed drug selling—there was a significant reduction in prevalence in experimental blocks compared to control blocks.

B. Improved Street Lighting

With respect to improved street lighting, a more recent systematic review and meta-analysis (based on thirteen high-quality evaluations from the United States and the United Kingdom) confirmed Eck's finding that this form of situational prevention is effective. Welsh and Farrington (2009a; see also Farrington and Welsh 2007a) found that improved street lighting is effective in city and town centers, residential areas, and public housing communities, and is more effective in reducing property crimes than in reducing violent crimes. Interestingly, both nighttime and daytime crimes were measured in nine of the thirteen studies. These nine night/day studies also showed a significant desirable effect of improved lighting on crime, almost a one-third (30 percent) decrease in crimes in experimental areas compared with control areas. However, the studies that measured only nighttime crime showed no effect. These findings suggest that a theory of street lighting focusing on its role in increasing community pride and informal social control may be more plausible than a theory focusing on increased surveillance and increased deterrence.

C. Closed-Circuit Television (CCTV)

CCTV cameras have also been shown to be an effective form of situational prevention, but under certain conditions. In a systematic review of forty-four high-quality evaluations from the United States, the United Kingdom, and several other Western countries, it was found that CCTV is most effective in reducing crime in parking lots, is most effective in reducing vehicle crimes, and is more effective in reducing crime in the UK than in other countries (Welsh and Farrington 2009a; see also Welsh and Farrington 2009b). Other reviews by Jerry Ratcliffe (2006) and Dean Wilson and Adam Sutton (2003) also conclude that CCTV is effective under similar conditions.

The exact optimal circumstances for effective use of CCTV programs are not entirely clear at present, and this needs to be established by future evaluation research. It is interesting to note that the success of the CCTV programs in parking lots was mostly limited to a reduction in vehicle crimes (the only crime type measured in five of the six plans) and camera coverage was high for those evaluations that reported on it. In the national British evaluation of the effectiveness of CCTV, David Farrington, Martin Gill, Sam Waples, and Javier Argomaniz (2007) found that effectiveness was significantly correlated with the degree of coverage of the CCTV cameras, which was greatest in parking lots. Furthermore, all six parking lot plans included other interventions, such as improved lighting and security officers. It is plausible to suggest that CCTV programs with high coverage and other interventions, targeted on vehicle crimes, are effective.

The systematic review also found that CCTV is associated with a nonsignificant and rather small 7 percent reduction in crimes in city and town centers. This may raise particular interest among policymakers. This is because this is the most popular public setting for the implementation of CCTV systems in the United States and elsewhere (Savage 2007). There was no clear indication about what may work best in this setting, but lessons can be drawn from the effectiveness of CCTV in parking lots. For example, CCTV in city and town centers may be more effective if they are targeted on property crimes, targeted at specific places such as high-crime areas (as part of an effort to increase camera coverage), and combined with other surveillance measures. Regular crime analysis by the police, such as that used in CompStat (Computer Statistics), could be used to identify those places that are at greatest risk for property crimes, which, in turn, could be used to guide the implementation of video surveillance. The advent of mobile and redeployable CCTV cameras may make this a more feasible and perhaps less costly option (Waples and Gill 2006). This more targeted approach could also go some way toward reducing the pervasiveness of the threat to the general public's privacy and other civil liberties.

D. Preventing Repeat Residential Burglary Victimization

Situational measures figure prominently in efforts to prevent repeat victimization, a highly important component of crime. It is based on the voluminous body of literature showing that crime victims are at increased risk of further victimization (Farrell 1995). It is generally defined as the "repeated criminal victimization of a person, household, business, other place or target however defined" (Farrell and Pease 2006, 161). Following the success of a number of comprehensive crime prevention programs, most notably the British Kirkholt Burglary Prevention Project (Pease 1991), efforts to prevent repeat victimization have become an important component of crime prevention and policing policy, especially in the United Kingdom.

A systematic review of the prevention of repeat residential burglary victimization by the British criminologists Graham Farrell and Ken Pease (2006) found that the most effective schemes involve strong preventive mechanisms tailored to the local burglary problem in high burglary-rate areas, often combining multiple tactics usually including security upgrades. Furthermore, strong implementation is required, which is not easy to achieve, and reductions in repeat burglaries do not necessarily coincide with an overall reduction in burglary. In contrast, the authors found that the least effective schemes have weak preventive mechanisms (e.g., advice to victims that does not guarantee that preventive measures are taken) and poor implementation (e.g., failing to contact victims, lack of security equipment).

E. Other Programs

The programs that Eck (2006) found to be promising included the use of multiple clerks and store redesign at commercial stores; training for serving staff at bars and taverns; target hardening of public facilities; and street closures or barricades. The latter was recently the focus of a systematic review on the effects of defensible space—Oscar Newman's (1972) principle of changes to the built environment to maximize the natural surveillance of open spaces afforded by people going about their day-to-day activities—and was determined to be effective in reducing both property and violent crimes in inner-city neighborhoods (Welsh and Farrington 2009a; see also Welsh, Mudge, and Farrington 2010). Security guards operating in public places can also be added to the list of promising situational interventions. A systematic review found that security guards are promising when implemented in parking lots and targeted at vehicle crimes (Welsh and Farrington 2009a; see also Welsh, Mudge, and Farrington, 2010).

V. Conclusions and Directions for Policy and Research

Crime prevention has entered a new, more robust phase of research activity and holds greater relevance to policy and practice today than ever before. It stands as an important component of an overall strategy to reduce crime. These achievements are not just the cumulative effect of years of a slow, sometimes less than steady progress of a social movement; other developments figure more prominently. Perhaps most important is the recent movement toward rational and evidence-based crime policy. This has brought greater attention to the need for higher-quality evaluations of programs and policies as well as the need for more rigorous, systematic methods to synthesize the research evidence and examine policy implications. Related to this development is the growing evidence base of scientific knowledge on the effectiveness and economic benefits of a wide range of crime prevention modalities. Also of importance to crime prevention's standing is the widely held view of the need to strike a greater balance between prevention and punishment. This has become more urgent in recent years as many states across the country are faced with budget crises, compounded by years of punitive crime policies.

In their own way, the crime prevention strategies of developmental, community, and situational offer many important benefits as well as a number of challenges.

In the case of developmental prevention, there is a growing body of high-quality scientific evidence on the effectiveness of different programs, including preschool intellectual enrichment, child skills training, home visiting, and parent management training. This is a fairly new research development, and is one of many that have drawn increased attention of late to the importance of this approach in an effort to improve children's life chances and prevent them from embarking on a life of crime.

The effectiveness of developmental prevention programs is not limited to delinquency and offending outcomes. Results are highly favorable and robust for impacts on other important life-course outcomes, such as education, government assistance (e.g., welfare), employment, income, substance abuse, and family stability. This should not come as a surprise to many, given that the original impetus of the majority of these programs was to improve early childhood outcomes well before offending could be measured. Indeed, the desirable effects on offending outcomes could be considered spin-off benefits. These benefits are also apparent from cost-benefit analyses of many individual- and family-based programs (Aos et al. 2004; Karoly, Kilburn, and Cannon 2005).

Developmental prevention is by no means without its challenges. These range from ethical concerns over intervening with young children to improving access to families in need to maintaining high rates of family participation and retention. One challenge that has long confronted early prevention policy at both national and state levels in the United States, as well as in other Western countries, is the matter of "scaling-up" or "rolling-out" evidence-based programs for wider public use. The concern here is that program effects will attenuate once they are scaled up. Some of the main reasons for this include a reduced level of risk, a more heterogeneous population, insufficient service infrastructure, and loss of program fidelity (e.g., Karoly et al. 1998; Dodge 2001). If attenuation of program effects is not only possible but is highly probable, then the issue for researchers and policymakers should be how to preserve or even enhance effects in moving from efficacy trials to community effectiveness trials to broad-scale dissemination. This should be a top research priority.

Also needed is a program of evaluation research of new early developmental prevention programs incorporating high quality designs. These new programs should be selected to contribute to the knowledge base that is presently insufficient or as part of a program of replications to test effective practices with different populations and in different regions of the country.

Experiments and quasi-experiments should have large samples, long follow-up periods, and follow-up interviews. Long-term follow-ups are needed to establish the persistence of effects. This information may point to the need for booster sessions. Long follow-ups are unusual for criminological interventions and should be a top priority of funding agencies. Research is also needed to identify the active ingredients of successful programs. Many developmental programs are multimodal, which makes it difficult to isolate the independent or interactive effects of the different components. Future experiments are needed that attempt to disentangle the different elements of the most successful programs.

Community crime prevention seemingly holds much promise (and has done so for many years) for preventing crime. However, the fact that only two types of community-based programs can be said to be effective is cause for concern. Disappointingly, the words of Dennis Rosenbaum more than two decades ago still seem applicable today: "The primary reason we do not know 'what works' in community crime prevention is the quality of the evaluation research" (1988, 381). Some of the key methodological issues that hamper evaluations include mixed units of analysis, heterogeneity of effect across different populations, and systematic attrition, accretion, and ecological validity (Catalano et al. 1998, 278–80).

Random assignment is also problematic in the design of community-based programs. This difficulty stems from the need to randomize a large enough number of communities to "gain the benefits of randomization in equating experimental and control communities on all possible extraneous variables" (Farrington 1997, 160). As a rule of thumb, at least fifty units in each category are needed (Farrington and Welsh 2006). This number is relatively easy to achieve with individuals but very difficult to achieve with larger units such as communities. For larger units, the best and most feasible design usually involves before-and-after measures in experimental and control communities together with statistical control of extraneous variables.

One proposal for advancing knowledge about community crime prevention without unduly compromising methodological rigor, and thus the confidence that can be placed in the observed outcomes, is to define communities at the level of census tract, which could, for a large city, produce hundreds of units for assignment and analysis (Sherman 1997). Richard Catalano and his colleagues (1998, 279) report on a number of alternatives that can be adopted when resources do not allow for the minimum number of units to be randomly assigned, some of which include: "matching communities prior to randomization on variables related to the outcomes of interest," "randomized block and factorial designs to stratify communities by factors known to affect key outcomes," and "generalized estimating equations to estimate both the individual-and group-level components of variation."

Abraham Wandersman and Paul Florin (2003) also point to other key factors that may explain the lack of results from community-level interventions, including the complexities involved in the implementation process and the difficulties involved in developing and sustaining a coalition of agencies that are often involved in such programs.

Advancing knowledge about the effectiveness of community-based programs to prevent crime should begin with attention to these key issues, together with a rigorous program of replications and evaluations of the promising approach of after-school programs.

Like its developmental counterpart, situational crime prevention can boast a growing evidence base of effective programs and many more that are promising in reducing crime. Among these programs there is also evidence that the displacement of crime to other areas or targets is a rare occurrence; indeed, some produce a diffusion of crime prevention benefits. Situational prevention's highly specific nature does limit generalizations about the effectiveness of some programs. For example, CCTV has been found to be most effective when implemented in parking lots, targeted at vehicle crimes, and carried out in the United Kingdom. Other evidence suggests that its effectiveness in parking lots is also due to high camera coverage and the presence of other (secondary) interventions such as lighting and security guards. Information about the specific conditions under which situational measures are effective (or ineffective) is of course more helpful to practitioners and policymakers.

More so than developmental or community crime prevention, situational prevention is used in private settings. Convenience stores, banks, shopping malls, and homes are just a few of the private places where various situational measures are used. While programs in both public and private places present unique challenges, there is a paucity of evaluations of some forms of situational prevention in the private sector (e.g., formal and natural surveillance). One of the reasons for this is the private sector's resistance to independent evaluation of their practices and, equally important, making any evaluations (independent or otherwise) publicly available. There are some excellent evaluations of the application of situational measures in the private sector (see e.g., Hunter and Jeffrey 1997; Eck 2006), but until such time that the private sector embraces evaluation research more fully, it will be difficult to assess in any comprehensive way the effectiveness of certain situational practices in preventing crime in private places. Another reason for the poor state of evaluation research in the private sector may stem from biases of criminologists about what is interesting and useful research, and because governments have not fully understood that assisting private security benefits the public sector as much as the private.

Evaluating situational programs share a number of the same challenges that face community-based programs. Most situational evaluations are area-based. Advancing knowledge about the effectiveness of situational crime prevention should begin with attention to the methodological rigor of the evaluation designs. As noted with community programs, the best and most feasible design usually involves before and after measures of crime in experimental and comparable control conditions, together with statistical control of extraneous variables. It is desirable in future evaluations to compare several experimental areas with several comparable control areas. If the areas were relatively small, it might be possible to randomly allocate areas to experimental and control conditions or to have alternate periods with or without the intervention. In addition, future evaluations should include interviews with potential offenders and potential victims to find out what they know about the intervention and their views on associated social costs, to test hypotheses about mediators between the intervention and crime, and to have measures of crime other than those from official sources.

It would also be desirable to have a long time-series of crime rates in experimental and comparable control areas before and after the intervention to investigate the persistence of any effects on crime. In the situational crime prevention literature, brief follow-up periods are the norm, but "it is now recognized that more information is needed about the longer-term effects of situational prevention" (Clarke 2001, 29).

The time is ripe to invest in crime prevention. Governments need to take full advantage of the benefits that developmental, community, and situational prevention offer as part of an overall crime reduction strategy, and launch a program of high-quality research to confront the current challenges and expand the frontiers of prevention science, policy, and practice.

NOTES

1. Promising programs are those where the level of certainty from the available scientific evidence is too low to support generalizable conclusions, but where there is some empirical basis for predicting that further research could support such conclusions (Farrington et al. 2006).
2. For a discussion of "benign" or desirable effects of displacement, see Barr and Pease (1990).
3. Martha Smith, Ron Clarke, and Ken Pease (2002) argue that researchers should also investigate the closely related phenomenon of "anticipatory benefits," whereby crime reduction benefits occur earlier than anticipated. The authors note that there are many possible reasons for why this may occur, including publicity by the project organizers or media.

REFERENCES

Aos, Steve, Roxanne Lieb, Jim Mayfield, Marna Miller, and Annie Pennucci. 2004. *Benefits and Costs of Prevention and Early Intervention Programs for Youth*. Olympia: Washington State Institute for Public Policy.

Aos, Steve, Marna Miller, and Elizabeth Drake. 2006. *Evidence-Based Public Policy Options to Reduce Future Prison Construction, Criminal Justice Costs, and Crime Rates*. Olympia: Washington State Institute for Public Policy.

Barr, Robert, and Ken Pease. 1990. "Crime Placement, Displacement, and Deflection." In *Crime and Justice: A Review of Research*, vol. 12, edited by Michael Tonry and Norval Morris. Chicago: University of Chicago Press.

Bennett, Trevor H. 1996. "Community Crime Prevention in Britain." In *Kommunale Kriminalprävention: Paradigmenwechsel und Wiederentdeckung alter Weisheiten*, edited by Thomas Trenczek and Hartmut Pfeiffer. Bonn, Germany: Forum Verlag Godesberg.

Bennett, Trevor H. 1998. "Crime Prevention." In *The Handbook of Crime and Punishment*, edited by Michael Tonry. New York: Oxford University Press.

Bennett, Trevor H., Katy Holloway, and David P. Farrington. 2006. "Does Neighborhood Watch Reduce Crime? A Systematic Review and Meta-Analysis." *Journal of Experimental Criminology* 2:437–58.

Bilukha, Oleg, Robert A. Hahn, Alex Crosby, Mindy T. Fullilove, Akiva Liberman, Eve Moscicki, Susan Snyder, Farris Tuma, Phaedra Corso, Amanda Schofield, and Peter A. Briss. 2005. "The Effectiveness of Early Childhood Home Visitation in Preventing Violence: A Systematic Review." *American Journal of Preventive Medicine* 28(2S1): 11–39.

Blumstein, Alfred, Jacqueline Cohen, and Daniel S. Nagin, eds. 1978. *Deterrence and Incapacitation*. Washington, DC: National Academies Press.

Brantingham, Paul J., and Frederick L. Faust. 1976. "A Conceptual Model of Crime Prevention." *Crime and Delinquency* 22:284–96.

Byrne, James R., and Robert J. Sampson, eds. 1986. *The Social Ecology of Crime*. New York: Springer-Verlag.

Catalano, Richard F., Michael W. Arthur, J. David Hawkins, Lisa Berglund, and Jeffrey J. Olson. 1998. "Comprehensive Community-and School-Based Interventions to Prevent Antisocial Behavior." In *Serious and Violent Juvenile Offenders: Risk Factors and Successful Interventions*, edited by Rolf Loeber and David P. Farrington. Thousand Oaks, CA: Sage.

Clarke, Ronald V. 1992. "Introduction." In *Situational Crime Prevention: Successful Case Studies*, edited by Ronald V. Clarke. Albany, NY: Harrow and Heston.

———. 1995*a*. "Opportunity-Reducing Crime Prevention Strategies and the Role of Motivation." In *Integrating Crime Prevention Strategies: Propensity and Opportunity*, edited by Per-Olof H. Wikström, Ronald V. Clarke, and Joan McCord. Stockholm, Sweden: National Council for Crime Prevention.

———. 1995*b*. "Situational Crime Prevention." In *Building a Safer Society: Strategic Approaches to Crime Prevention*, edited by Michael Tonry and David P. Farrington. Volume 19 of *Crime and Justice: A Review of Research,* edited by Michael Tonry, Chicago: University of Chicago Press.

———, ed. 1997. *Situational Crime Prevention: Successful Case Studies*, 2nd ed. Guilderland, NY: Harrow and Heston.

———. 2001. "Effective Crime Prevention: Keeping Pace with New Developments." *Forum on Crime and Society* 1(1): 17–33.

Clarke, Ronald V., and Ross Homel. 1997. "A Revised Classification of Situational Crime Prevention Techniques." In *Crime Prevention at a Crossroads*, edited by Steven P. Lab. Cincinnati: Anderson.

Clarke, Ronald V., and David Weisburd. 1994. "Diffusion of Crime Control Benefits: Observations on the Reverse of Displacement." In *Crime Prevention Studies*, vol. 2, edited by Ronald V. Clarke. Monsey, NY: Criminal Justice Press.

Cloward, Richard, and Lloyd Ohlin. 1960. *Delinquency and Opportunity*. New York: Free Press.

Cohen, Lawrence E., and Marcus Felson. 1979. "Social Change and Crime Rate Trends: A Routine Activity Approach." *American Sociological Review* 44:588–608.

Cornish, Derek B., and Ronald V. Clarke. 2003. "Opportunities, Precipitators and Criminal Decisions: A Reply to Wortley's Critique of Situational Crime Prevention." In *Theory for Practice in Situational Crime Prevention*, edited by Martha J. Smith and Derek B. Cornish. Volume 16 *Crime Prevention Studies,* edited by Ronald V. Clarke. Monsey, NY: Criminal Justice Press.

Currie, Janet. 2001. "Early Childhood Education Programs." *Journal of Economic Perspectives* 15:213–38.

Curtis, Lynn A. 1985. "Neighborhood, Family, and Employment: Toward a New Public Policy against Violence." In *American Violence and Public Policy: An Update of the National Commission on the Causes and Prevention of Violence*, edited by Lynn A. Curtis. New Haven, CT: Yale University Press.

———. 1987. "Preface." Policies to Prevent Crime: Neighborhood, Family, and Employment Strategies, Lynn A. Curtis, ed. *Annals of the American Academy of Political and Social Science* 494:9–18.

Dodge, Kenneth A. 2001. "The Science of Youth Violence Prevention: Progressing from Developmental Epidemiology to Efficacy to Effectiveness to Public Policy." *American Journal of Preventive Medicine* 20(1S): 63–70.

Donziger, Steven R., ed. 1996. *The Real War on Crime: The Report of the National Criminal Justice Commission.* New York: HarperPerennial.

Duncan, Greg J., and Katherine Magnuson. 2004. "Individual and Parent-Based Intervention Strategies for Promoting Human Capital and Positive Behavior." In *Human Development Across Lives and Generations: The Potential for Change*, edited by P. Lindsay Chase-Lansdale, Kathleen Kiernan, and Ruth J. Friedman. New York: Cambridge University Press.

Eck, John E. 2006. "Preventing Crime at Places." In *Evidence-Based Crime Prevention*, rev. ed., edited by Lawrence W. Sherman, David P. Farrington, Brandon C. Welsh, and Doris L. MacKenzie. New York: Routledge.

Eisenhower Foundation. 1990. *Youth Investment and Community Reconstruction: Street Lessons on Drugs and Crime for the Nineties.* Washington, DC: Milton S. Eisenhower Foundation.

Ekblom, Paul. 1994. "Proximal Circumstances: A Mechanism-Based Classification of Crime Prevention." In *Crime Prevention Studies*, vol. 2, edited by Ronald V. Clarke. Monsey, NY: Criminal Justice Press.

Farrell, Graham. 1995. "Preventing Repeat Victimization." In *Building a Safer Society: Strategic Approaches to Crime Prevention*, edited by Michael Tonry and David P. Farrington. Volume 19 of *Crime and Justice: A Review of Research*, edited by Michael Tonry. Chicago: University of Chicago Press.

Farrell, Graham, and Ken Pease. 2006. "Preventing Repeat Residential Burglary Victimization." In *Preventing Crime: What Works for Children, Offenders, Victims, and Places*, edited Brandon C. Welsh and David P. Farrington. New York: Springer.

Farrington, David P. 1993. "Have Any Individual, Family or Neighbourhood Influences on Offending Been Demonstrated Conclusively?" In *Integrating Individual and Ecological Aspects of Crime*, edited by David P. Farrington, Robert J. Sampson, and Per-Olof H. Wikström. Stockholm, Sweden: National Council for Crime Prevention.

———. 1997. "Evaluating a Community Crime Prevention Program." *Evaluation* 3:157–73.

Farrington, David P., Martin Gill, Sam J. Waples, and Javier Argomaniz. 2007. "The Effects of Closed-Circuit Television on Crime: Meta-Analysis of an English National Quasi-Experimental Multi-Site Evaluation." *Journal of Experimental Criminology* 3:21–38.

Farrington, David P., Denise C. Gottfredson, Lawrence W. Sherman, and Brandon C. Welsh. 2006. "The Maryland Scientific Methods Scale." In *Evidence-Based Crime Prevention*, rev. ed., edited by Lawrence W. Sherman, David P. Farrington, Brandon C. Welsh, and Doris L. MacKenzie. New York: Routledge.

Farrington, David P., and Brandon C. Welsh. 2006. "A Half-Century of Randomized Experiments on Crime and Justice." In *Crime and Justice: A Review of Research*, vol. 34, edited by Michael Tonry. Chicago: University of Chicago Press.

Farrington, David P., and Brandon C. Welsh. 2007a. *Improved Street Lighting and Crime Prevention: A Systematic Review*. Stockholm, Sweden: National Council for Crime Prevention.

——. 2007b. *Saving Children from a Life of Crime: Early Risk Factors and Effective Interventions*. New York: Oxford University Press.

Gabor, Thomas. 1990. "Crime Displacement and Situational Prevention." *Canadian Journal of Criminology* 32:41–74.

Garland, David. 2000. "Ideas, Institutions and Situational Crime Prevention." In *Ethical and Social Perspectives on Situational Crime Prevention*, edited by Andrew von Hirsch, David Garland, and Alison Wakefield. Oxford: Hart.

Gest, Ted. 2001. *Crime and Politics: Big Government's Erratic Campaign for Law and Order*. New York: Oxford University Press.

Gomby, Deanna S., Patti L. Culross, and Richard E. Behrman. 1999. "Home Visiting: Recent Program Evaluations—Analysis and Recommendations." *Future of Children* 9(1): 4–26.

Gottfredson, Denise C., Stephanie A. Gerstenblith, David A. Soulé, Shannon C. Womer, and Shaoli Lu. 2004. "Do After School Programs Reduce Delinquency?" *Prevention Science* 5:253–66.

Greenwood, Peter W. 2006. *Changing Lives: Delinquency Prevention as Crime-Control Policy*. Chicago: University of Chicago Press.

Hawkins, J. David, and Richard F. Catalano. 1992. *Communities That Care: Action for Drug Abuse Prevention*. San Francisco, CA: Jossey-Bass.

Hawkins, J. David, Eric C. Brown, Sabrina Oesterle, Michael W. Arthur, Robert D. Abbott, and Richard F. Catalano. 2008. "Early Effects of Communities That Care on Targeted Risks and Initiation of Delinquent Behavior and Substance Abuse." *Journal of Adolescent Health* 43:15–22.

Hawkins, J. David, Sabrina Oesterle, Eric C. Brown, Michael W. Arthur, Robert D. Abbott, Abigail A. Fagan, and Richard F. Catalano. 2009. "Results of a Type 2 Translational Research Trial to Prevent Adolescent Drug Use and Delinquency: A Test of Communities That Care." *Archives of Pediatrics and Adolescent Medicine* 163:789–98.

Hesseling, René. 1995. "Theft From Cars: Reduced or Displaced?" *European Journal on Criminal Policy and Research* 3(3): 79–92.

Hope, Tim. 1995. "Community Crime Prevention." In *Building a Safer Society: Strategic Approaches to Crime Prevention*, edited by Michael Tonry and David P. Farrington. Volume 19 of *Crime and Justice: A Review of Research*, edited by Michael Tonry. Chicago: University of Chicago Press.

Hope, Tim. 1998. "Community Crime Prevention." In *Reducing Offending: An Assessment of Research Evidence on Ways of Dealing with Offending Behaviour*. Home Office Research Study 187, edited by Christopher Nuttall, Peter Goldblatt, and Chris Lewis. London: Home Office Research and Statistics Directorate.

Howell, James C., ed. 1995. *Guide for Implementing the Comprehensive Strategy for Serious, Violent, and Chronic Juvenile Offenders*. Washington, DC: U.S. Department of Justice, Office of Juvenile Justice and Delinquency Prevention.

Hunter, Ronald D., and C. Ray Jeffrey. 1997. "Preventing Convenience Store Robbery Through Environmental Design." In *Situational Crime Prevention: Successful Case Studies*, 2nd ed., edited by Ronald V. Clarke. Guilderland, NY: Harrow and Heston.

Jeffrey, C. Ray. 1977. *Crime Prevention Through Environmental Design*, 2nd ed. Beverly Hills, CA: Sage.

Jolliffe, Darrick, and David P. Farrington. 2008. *The Influence of Mentoring on Reoffending*. Stockholm, Sweden: National Council for Crime Prevention.

Johnson, Dale L., and Todd Walker. 1987. "Primary Prevention of Behavior Problems in Mexican-American Children." *American Journal of Community Psychology* 15:375–85.

Karoly, Lynn A., Peter W. Greenwood, Susan S. Everingham, Jill Houbé, M. Rebecca Kilburn, C. Peter Rydell, Matthew Sanders, and James Chiesa. 1998. *Investing in Our Children: What We Know and Don't Know About the Costs and Benefits of Early Childhood Interventions*. Santa Monica, CA: RAND.

Karoly, Lynn A., M. Rebecca Kilburn, and Jill S. Cannon. 2005. *Early Childhood Interventions: Proven Results, Future Promise*. Santa Monica, CA: RAND.

Kazdin, Alan E. 1997. "Parent Management Training: Evidence, Outcomes, and Issues." *Journal of the American Academy of Child and Adolescent Psychiatry* 36: 1349–56.

Lally, J. Ronald, Peter L. Mangione, and Alice S. Honig. 1988. "The Syracuse University Family Development Research Program: Long-Range Impact of an Early Intervention with Low-Income Children and their Families." In *Parent Education as Early Childhood Intervention: Emerging Directions in Theory, Research and Practice*, edited by D. R. Powell. Norwood, NJ: Ablex.

Lavrakas, Paul J. 1985. "Citizen Self-Help and Neighborhood Crime Prevention Policy." In *American Violence and Public Policy: An Update of the National Commission on the Causes and Prevention of Violence*, edited by Lynn A. Curtis. New Haven, CT: Yale University Press.

Lösel, Friedrich, and Andreas Beelmann. 2003. "Effects of Child Skills Training in Preventing Antisocial Behavior: A Systematic Review." *Annals of the American Academy of Political and Social Science* 587:84–109.

Lösel, Friedrich, and Andreas Beelmann. 2006. "Child Social Skills Training." In *Preventing Crime: What Works for Children, Offenders, Victims, and Places*, edited by Brandon C. Welsh and David P. Farrington. New York: Springer.

MacKenzie, Doris L. 2006. *What Works in Corrections: Reducing the Criminal Activities of Offenders and Delinquents*. New York: Cambridge University Press.

Mazerolle, Lorraine G., Jan Roehl, and Colleen Kadleck. 1998. "Controlling Social Disorder Using Civil Remedies: Results from a Randomized Field Experiment in Oakland, California." In *Civil Remedies and Crime Prevention*, edited by Lorraine G. Mazerolle and Jan Roehl. Volume 9 of *Crime Prevention Studies*, edited by Ronald V. Clarke. Monsey, NY: Criminal Justice Press.

Mendel, Richard A. 1995. *Prevention or Pork? A Hard-Headed Look at Youth-Oriented Anti-Crime Programs*. Washington, DC: American Youth Policy Forum.

Moore, Mark H. 1995. "Public Health and Criminal Justice Approaches to Prevention." In *Building a Safer Society: Strategies Approaches to Crime Prevention*, edited by Michael

Tonry and David P. Farrington. Volume 19 of *Crime and Justice: A Review of Research*, edited by Michael Tonry. Chicago: University of Chicago Press.

National Advisory Commission on Criminal Justice Standards and Goals. 1973. *Report on Community Crime Prevention*. Washington, DC: U.S. Government Printing Office.

National Commission on the Causes and Prevention of Violence. 1969. *To Establish Justice, To Insure Domestic Tranquility, Final Report*. Washington, DC: U.S. Government Printing Office.

Newman, Oscar. 1972. *Defensible Space: Crime Prevention Through Urban Design*. New York: Macmillan.

Newman, Graeme, Ronald V. Clarke, and Shlomo Giora Shoham, eds. 1997. *Rational Choice and Situational Crime Prevention: Theoretical Foundations*. Aldershot, UK: Ashgate/Dartmouth.

Olds, David L., Charles R. Henderson, Robert Chamberlin, and Robert Tatelbaum. 1986. "Preventing Child Abuse and Neglect: A Randomized Trial of Nurse Home Visitation." *Pediatrics* 78:65–78.

Olds, David L., John Eckenrode, Charles R. Henderson, Harriet Kitzman, Jane Powers, Robert Cole, Kimberly Sidora, Pamela Morris, Lisa M. Pettitt, and Dennis W. Luckey. 1997. "Long-Term Effects of Home Visitation on Maternal Life Course and Child Abuse and Neglect: Fifteen-Year Follow-Up of a Randomized Trial." *Journal of the American Medical Association* 278:637–43.

Olds, David L., Charles R. Henderson, Robert Cole, John Eckenrode, Harriet Kitzman, Dennis W. Luckey, Lisa M. Pettitt, Kimberly Sidora, Pamela Morris, and Jane Powers. 1998. "Long-Term Effects of Nurse Home Visitation on Children's Criminal and Antisocial Behavior: 15-Year Follow-Up of a Randomized Controlled Trial." *Journal of the American Medical Association* 280:1238–44.

Patterson, Gerald. 1982. *Coercive Family Process*. Eugene, OR: Castalia.

Patterson, Gerald, Patricia Chamberlain, and John B. Reid. 1982. "A Comparative Evaluation of a Parent Training Program." *Behavior Therapy* 13:638–50.

Patterson, Gerald, John B. Reid, and Thomas J. Dishion. 1992. *Antisocial Boys*. Eugene, OR: Castalia.

Pawson, Ray, and Nick Tilley. 1994. "What Works in Evaluation Research." *British Journal of Criminology* 34:291–306.

———. 1997. *Realistic Evaluation*. Thousand Oaks, CA: Sage.

Pease, Ken. 1991. "The Kirkholt Project: Preventing Burglary on a British Public Housing Estate." *Security Journal* 2:73–77.

Piquero, Alex R., David P. Farrington, Brandon C. Welsh, Richard E. Tremblay, and Wesley G. Jennings. 2009. "Effects of Early/Family Parent Training Programs on Antisocial Behavior and Delinquency." *Journal of Experimental Criminology* 5:83–120.

President's Commission on Law Enforcement and Administration of Justice. 1967. *The Challenge of Crime in a Free Society*. Washington, DC: U.S. Government Printing Office.

Ratcliffe, Jerry H. 2006. *Video Surveillance of Public Places*. Problem-Oriented Guides for Police Response Guides Series, no. 4. Washington, DC: Office of Community Oriented Policing Services, U.S. Department of Justice.

Reiss, Albert J., Jr., and Michael Tonry, eds. 1986. *Communities and Crime*. Volume 8 of *Crime and Justice: A Review of Research*, edited by Michael Tonry. Chicago: University of Chicago Press.

Reppetto, Thomas A. 1976. "Crime Prevention and the Displacement Phenomenon." *Crime and Delinquency* 22:166–77.

Rosenbaum, Dennis P., ed. 1986. *Community Crime Prevention: Does It Work?* Beverly Hills, CA: Sage.

———. 1988. "Community Crime Prevention: A Review and Synthesis of the Literature." *Justice Quarterly* 5:323–95.

Rosenbaum, Dennis P., Arthur J. Lurigio, and Robert C. Davis. 1998. *The Prevention of Crime: Social and Situational Strategies.* Belmont, CA: Wadsworth.

Sampson, Robert J., and Janet Lauritsen. 1994. "Violent Victimization and Offending: Individual-, Situational-, and Community-Level Risk Factors." In *Understanding and Preventing Violence. Social Influences*, vol. 3, edited by Albert J. Reiss, Jr. and Jeffrey A. Roth. Washington, DC: National Academies Press.

Savage, Charlie. 2007. "US Doles Out Millions for Street Cameras: Local Efforts Raise Privacy Concerns." *Boston Globe*, August 12, 2007. www.boston.com

Serketich, Wendy J., and Jean E. Dumas. 1996. "The Effectiveness of Behavioral Parent Training to Modify Antisocial Behavior in Children: A Meta-Analysis." *Behavior Therapy* 27:171–86.

Schlossman, Steven, and Michael Sedlak. 1983. "The Chicago Area Project Revisited." *Crime and Delinquency* 29:398–462.

Shaw, Clifford R., and Henry D. McKay. 1942. *Juvenile Delinquency and Urban Areas: A Study of Rates of Delinquents in Relation to Differential Characteristics of Local Communities in American Cities.* Chicago: University of Chicago Press.

Sherman, Lawrence W. 1995. "Hot Spots of Crime and Criminal Careers of Places." In *Crime and Place*, edited by John E. Eck and David Weisburd. Volume 4 of *Crime Prevention Studies*, edited by Ronald V. Clarke. Monsey, NY: Criminal Justice Press.

———. 1997. "Communities and Crime Prevention." In *Preventing Crime: What Works, What Doesn't, What's Promising*, by Lawrence W. Sherman, Denise C. Gottfredson, Doris L. MacKenzie, John E. Eck, Peter Reuter, and Shawn D. Bushway. Washington, DC: National Institute of Justice, U.S. Department of Justice.

Sherman, Lawrence W., David P. Farrington, Brandon C. Welsh, and Doris L. MacKenzie, eds. 2006. *Evidence-Based Crime Prevention*, rev. ed. New York: Routledge.

Sherman, Lawrence W., Patrick R. Gartin, and Michael E. Buerger. 1989. "Hot Spots of Predatory Crime: Routine Activities and the Criminology of Place." *Criminology* 27:27–55.

Sherman, Lawrence W., Denise C. Gottfredson, Doris L. MacKenzie, John E. Eck, Peter Reuter, and Shawn D. Bushway. 1997. *Preventing Crime: What Works, What Doesn't, What's Promising.* Washington, DC: National Institute of Justice, U.S. Department of Justice.

Short, James F. 1974. "The Natural History of an Applied Theory: Differential Opportunity and 'Mobilization for Youth.'" In *Social Policy and Sociology*, edited by Nicholas J. Demerath, Otto Larsen, and Karl F. Schuessler. New York: Seminar Press.

Smith, Martha J., Ronald V. Clarke, and Ken Pease. 2002. "Anticipatory Benefits in Crime Prevention." In *Analysis for Crime Prevention*, edited by Nick Tilley. Volume 13 of *Crime Prevention Studies*, edited by Ronald V. Clarke. Monsey, NY: Criminal Justice Press.

Tonry, Michael, and David P. Farrington, eds. 1995a. *Building a Safer Society: Strategic Approaches to Crime Prevention.* Volume 19 of *Crime and Justice: A Review of Research*, edited by Michael Tonry. Chicago: University of Chicago Press.

———. 1995b. "Strategic Approaches to Crime Prevention." In *Building a Safer Society: Strategic Approaches to Crime Prevention*, edited by Michael Tonry and David P.

Farrington. Volume 19 of *Crime and Justice: A Review of Research*, edited by Michael Tonry. Chicago: University of Chicago Press.

Tremblay, Richard E., and Wendy M. Craig. 1995. "Developmental Crime Prevention." In *Building a Safer Society: Strategic Approaches to Crime Prevention*, edited by Michael Tonry and David P. Farrington. Volume 19 of *Crime and Justice: A Review of Research*, edited by Michael Tonry. Chicago: University of Chicago Press.

van Dijk, Jan J. M., and Jaap de Waard. 1991. "A Two-Dimensional Typology of Crime Prevention Projects; with a Bibliography." *Criminal Justice Abstracts* 23:483–503.

Visher, Christy A., and David Weisburd. 1998. "Identifying What Works: Recent Trends in Crime Prevention Strategies." *Crime, Law and Social Change* 28:223–42.

Waller, Irvin. 1990. "With National Leadership Canada Could Turn the Tide on Crime." *Canadian Journal of Criminology* 32:185–90.

Waller, Irvin. 2006. *Less Law, More Order: The Truth about Reducing Crime*. Westport, CT: Praeger.

Wandersman, Abraham, and Paul Florin. 2003. "Community Interventions and Effective Prevention." *American Psychologist* 58:441–48.

Waples, Sam, and Martin Gill. 2006. "The Effectiveness of Redeployable CCTV." *Crime Prevention and Community Safety* 8(1): 1–16.

Wasserman, Gail A., and Laurie S. Miller. 1998. "The Prevention of Serious and Violent Juvenile Offending." In *Serious & Violent Juvenile Offenders: Risk Factors and Successful Interventions*, edited by Rolf Loeber and David P. Farrington. Thousand Oaks, CA: Sage.

Webster-Stratton, Carolyn, and Ted Taylor. 2001. "Nipping Early Risk Factors in the Bud: Preventing Substance Abuse, Delinquency, and Violence in Adolescence Through Interventions Targeted at Young Children (0–8 Years)." *Prevention Science* 2:165–92.

Welsh, Brandon C., and David P. Farrington, eds. Forthcoming. *The Oxford Handbook of Crime Prevention*. New York: Oxford University Press.

Welsh, Brandon C., and David P. Farrington. In this volume. "Evidence-Based Crime Policy."

———. 2000. "Monetary Costs and Benefits of Crime Prevention Programs." In *Crime and Justice: A Review of Research*, vol. 27, edited by Michael Tonry. Chicago: University of Chicago Press.

———, eds. 2006. *Preventing Crime: What Works for Children, Offenders, Victims, and Places*. New York: Springer.

———. 2009a. *Making Public Places Safer: Surveillance and Crime Prevention*. New York: Oxford University Press.

———. 2009b. "Public Area CCTV and Crime Prevention: An Updated Systematic Review and Meta-Analysis." *Justice Quarterly* 26: 716–45.

Welsh, Brandon C., and Akemi Hoshi. 2006. "Communities and Crime Prevention." In *Evidence-Based Crime Prevention*, rev. ed., edited by Lawrence W. Sherman, David P. Farrington, Brandon C. Welsh, and Doris L. MacKenzie. New York: Routledge.

Welsh, Brandon C., Mark E. Mudge, and David P. Farrington. 2010. "Reconceptualizing Public Area Surveillance and Crime Prevention: Security Guards, Place Managers, and Defensible Space." *Security Journal* 23:299–319.

Wikström, Per-Olof H. 1998. "Communities and Crime." In *The Handbook of Crime and Punishment*, edited by Michael Tonry. New York: Oxford University Press.

Wilson, Dean, and Adam Sutton. 2003. *Open-Street CCTV in Australia*. Trends and Issues in Crime and Criminal Justice, no. 271. Canberra: Australian Institute of Criminology.

CHAPTER 6

....

TREATMENT AND
REHABILITATION

....

FRANCIS T. CULLEN
AND PAULA SMITH

THE American correctional system is exceptional in its sheer size. On any given day in the United States, there are more than 2.2 million offenders under some form of incarceration and nearly 5 million others under supervision in the community (Glaze and Parks 2012). The reach of the correctional system is even more starkly evident when we realize that these numbers mean that at the dawn of each day, about one in every hundred Americans is behind bars and one in thirty-four is under some form of correctional supervision (Pew Center on the States 2008, 2009; Glaze and Parks 2012). Until recently, the growth in these populations has been seemingly intractable. Between 1982 and 2007, imprisoned offenders rose by nearly 1.7 million, whereas community supervisees increased by over 3.5 million (Pew Center on the States 2009). Further, issues of social justice are unavoidable when the differential involvement in the correctional system by race is unmasked. Among black adults, one in eleven is under correctional control at any given time, a rate four times higher than whites and two-and-a-half times higher than Hispanics (Pew Center on the States 2009; see also Clear 2007).

These numbers are repeated with such regularity that they risk inspiring banality rather than genuine concern. The annual announcement that correctional populations have increased yet again has created a sense of inevitability—the feeling that this expansion is akin to a natural disaster that is beyond human control. Underlying this collective fatalism is the assumption that the correctional system is the mere recipient of criminals. This observation rests on a kernel of truth, for as Tonry (2004, 28) notes, "more crime yields more arrests yields more convictions yields more prison sentences yields high prison populations and imprisonment rates." Still, we know that the length and harshness of criminal sanctions—especially the use of imprisonment—are only weakly tied to crime rates. Especially when examined cross-culturally, the data show that fluctuations in crime rates are not strong determinants of the size of prison populations (Tonry 2004, 2007). This stubborn reality means that the size of correctional populations is not a naturally occurring social phenomenon—like a perpetual tsunami that continues to wash over us—but rather is produced by policies and decisions. In a sense, the United States has the correctional system it has chosen to have.

These considerations lead to the broader issue of what we hope to accomplish by bringing this endless flow of offenders under the auspices of correctional control. Perhaps the principal goal is to ensure that just deserts are meted out. Most often, however, sanctions are levied not only to achieve justice—a balancing of the scales, harm to offenders for the harm they have caused—but also as a means of reducing crime. That is, we want sanctions to do justice *and* to serve the utilitarian end of protecting public safety. An enduring controversy is how best to achieve this utilitarian goal of crime control. Two distinct models or approaches—punishment and rehabilitation—propose opposite solutions to this puzzle (Cullen and Wright 1996).

The punishment model is based on two incompatible views of offenders. One view is that offenders—and those contemplating crime—make rational choices and thus can be deterred by experiencing, directly or vicariously, certain and harsh punishment, especially imprisonment. The other view is that offenders are incurably wicked and hence beyond redemption; thus, to ensure public safety, the state has no choice but to cage them for purposes of incapacitation. In either case, the punishment model favors getting tough, with the prison being the indispensable conduit for delivering pain sufficiently stinging to achieve deterrence and delivering constraint sufficiently secure to achieve incapacitation.

The rehabilitation model starts with the premise that criminal behavior, like any human conduct, is caused. These underlying causes will not vanish unless they are targeted for change and treated with an appropriate intervention. To assume offender rationality, when crime is caused by, for example, antisocial values and low self-control, is anti-scientific. Basing correctional interventions on the assumption of rationality simply compounds the difficulties. It means that offenders will, in effect, be given the wrong "medicine" to cure their behavior. Harsh punishment might have marginal effects, but this kind of sanction is incapable of reforming offenders. What is needed instead is rehabilitation, which is *a planned intervention that uses evidence-based treatment programs that can change the factors leading a person to offend* (Cullen and Gendreau 2000).

The legitimacy of the correctional system hinges on how fairly it exacts just deserts and on how effectively it advances public safety. When sanctions seem too harsh, too lenient, or too biased, then the system is seen as "unjust." When sanctions lead offenders to engage in more rather than in less crime—that is, when they do not "work"—then the system is seen as ineffective. Correctional models—whether punishment or rehabilitation—are ultimately judged on whether they advance justice and advance public safety.

In this context, we explore the role of rehabilitation as a core purpose of American corrections. This assessment is conveyed in six sections. Thus, section I argues that rehabilitation has been a fundamental sensibility of the correctional enterprise from its beginning stages. Despite the seeming hegemony of the punishment model for more than three decades, this abiding belief that the correctional system should not only punish but also "correct" remains strong. Section II traces the seeming collapse of the rehabilitation model in the 1970s. This attack on rehabilitation was initiated largely on grounds of justice, but eventually it was reframed as an issue of utility or effectiveness—that is, as a claim that "nothing works" to reform offenders. This section also proposes that the subsequent rise of a movement to revitalize rehabilitation was due in part to the failure of the punishment model to develop intervention programs that would curtail recidivism among offenders. In short, the label that "nothing works" was ironically applied to punishment-oriented programs. By contrast, empirical evidence emerged that showed that treatment programs overall reduce reoffending, sometimes substantially. Section III builds on these insights and presents what has become the dominant rehabilitation model, which is typically captured under the label of the *principles of effective correctional intervention*. This paradigm has three components: an underlying psychology of criminal conduct on which it is based; a set of principles that, if followed, produce effective interventions; and a technology that allows treatment programs to be delivered with integrity. This section also considers the challenges that must be addressed to achieve effective correctional rehabilitation in "real world" settings. Section IV concludes with a discussion of the future of rehabilitation as a core purpose of American corrections.

Our main conclusions are as follows:

- Rehabilitation is an American "habit of the heart"—a core cultural belief that has endured from the 1820s to the present day. Opinion polls reveal widespread public support for rehabilitation as an integral goal of corrections. Given decades of get-tough rhetoric, harsh sentencing policies, and mass incarceration, the public's continued endorsement of offender treatment is a remarkable criminological fact. Rehabilitation also must be seen as an invaluable cultural resource that can be used to justify effective and humane correctional policies.
- The attack on rehabilitation in the late 1960s and into the 1970s was mostly fueled by a concern that social welfare ideologies justified the use of state power to regulate, if not coerce, the behavior of poor and deviant

populations. When state officials—such as judges, corrections staff, and parole boards—exercised unfettered discretionary power, the argument went, they did so in discriminatory and punitive ways. Although these allegations had merit, critics did not appreciate the role played by the rehabilitative ideal in combating alternative ideologies that explicitly embraced inflicting pain on offenders. Today, our concern is not with too much social welfare for offenders and others but with too little.

- Martinson's (1974) essay claiming, in essence, that "nothing works" in rehabilitation to reduce recidivism deepened the legitimacy crisis for correctional treatment. However, his work also shifted the debate over offender rehabilitation away from the appropriate limits on state discretionary power and toward the empirical issue of whether programs "work." Two important insights resulted. First, subsequent evaluation research demonstrated that punitively oriented interventions do not reduce offender recidivism, thus casting suspicion on the wisdom of get-tough correctional practices. Second, this research also revitalized the reputation of correctional rehabilitation by revealing that, overall, rehabilitation programs reduce reoffending. In fact, some interventions were shown to achieve substantial reductions in recidivism.

- The variability in treatment effects is known as "heterogeneity." Canadian psychologists—most notably Don Andrews, James Bonta, and Paul Gendreau—have made a major contribution by offering a coherent paradigm that explains why some but not other treatment programs "work." Rooted in an empirically grounded theory of human conduct in general and of criminal conduct in particular, they have specified principles of effective correctional intervention and have developed the technology for delivering appropriate treatment services. Although not sacrosanct, their paradigm represents both a significant guide for correctional intervention and an exemplar to be modeled by those advancing alternative treatment strategies.

- The future of rehabilitation in America depends not only on its status as a "habit of the heart" but on the ability of its advocates to implement programs manifesting treatment integrity within the challenging constraints characterizing most correctional environments.

I. Habit of the Heart

In *Habits of the Heart*, Robert Bellah and his colleagues (1985) sought to demarcate the beliefs or sensibilities that are at the core of what it means to be an American. In so doing, they were attempting to update the work of Alexis de Tocqueville (1969, 287), who in *Democracy in America* (published in two parts in 1835 and 1840)

initially coined the concept of "habits of the heart" and probed the nation's character. Most often, commentators emphasize Americans' unique allegiance to two
values, which at times are incompatible: individualism and equality. To this we add
a third: a belief in offender rehabilitation (Cullen et al. 2007).

Claiming that rehabilitation is an American "habit of the heart" might seem, in
light of the times, farfetched. After all, what Todd Clear (1994) calls the "penal harm
movement" can be traced to the Nixon presidential "law and order" campaign of
1968 and certainly was under way by the mid-1970s (Cullen and Gilbert 1982). Since
that time, a number of commentators have documented the dominance of a harsh
"culture of control" or "penal culture" both produced by and conducive to a range of
get-tough policies (e.g., mandatory incarceration, truth-in-sentencing laws, three-
strikes-and-you're out laws) (see, e.g., Garland 2001; Tonry 2004; Simon 2007).
Indeed, virtually every elected official now claims to be tough on crime (Simon
2007). Still, Americans' support for offender reform remains strong. The persistence, even vitality, of the belief that rehabilitation should be an integral goal of
corrections in the face of an unprecedented punitive onslaught is a "remarkable
criminological fact" (Cullen 2006, 665). It points to rehabilitation being a habit of
the American heart.

It would require much hubris to claim that we know why this is so, but we propose that historically religion and science converged to make saving the criminally
wayward a core cultural habit. Thus, the American prison system, an invention of
the 1820s and 1830s, earned worldwide acclaim, so much so that de Tocqueville's
rationale for traveling to the United States was to report to the French government
on this invention. But why was there so much curiosity and excitement about such
institutions? In large part, the American prison experiment earned attention
because of the promise it held: its purpose was not simply to cage offenders but to
reform them.

It is instructive that these early prisons were not called justice or punishment
centers but rather "penitentiaries." As Rothman (1971) so eloquently described in
The Discovery of the Asylum, there was great faith that by carefully designing the
internal regimen of the prison, offenders could be transformed, gaining the moral
fiber to reenter society and resist its temptations. The principles of effective treatment were religion, daily labor, and separation from criminal influences. The
conundrum faced, however, was that placing offenders behind sturdy walls would
remove them from the criminogenic risks faced in their communities but only at
the expense of concentrating the wayward together. Much debate ensued over
whether insulation from fellow criminals, the prime potential source of bad influence in prison, was best achieved through solitary confinement, as was practiced
in Pennsylvania, or by enforced silence, as was practiced in New York. Regardless,
the important point is that the penitentiary's appeal rested in its founders' promise
that the institutional world they had created could transform law-breakers into
law-abiders. The American penitentiary was thus intended, from its inception, to

be rehabilitative. Indeed, from this point in American history, whether prisons reformed offenders would be integral to discussions on whether such institutions were fulfilling their mission.

By the post–Civil War era, it was apparent that as originally conceived, the penitentiary was a failure. Perpetual solitary confinement proved a warping experience, and overcrowding ended hopes of preventing inmates' interactions. Prisons also were now filled increasingly with impoverished immigrants who could be portrayed as part of the "dangerous class." Social Darwinist ideology grew stronger and argued that the wayward were intractably inferior and undeserving of government assistance that might extend their lives or allow them to reproduce (Werth 2009). In this context, it might have been expected that thoughts of rehabilitation would have receded, and the purpose of prisons redirected simply to incapacitating the dangerous for as long as possible.

But this embrace of merely caging or warehousing offenders did not occur. In 1870, a remarkable gathering of the nation's corrections experts, which drew participants from across the world, was held in Cincinnati. This National Congress on Penitentiary and Reformatory Discipline demarcated a "new penology" that would seek to overcome the failures of the penitentiary paradigm with a fresh prescription on how to reform offenders. Again, in bleak correctional times, rehabilitation showed itself as a habit of the heart. The congress affirmed that the "supreme aim of prison discipline is the reformation of criminals, not the infliction of vindictive suffering" (Wines 1871, 541).

As Christians, the congress's members placed religious training at the core the reformatory process, thus revealing the role of spiritual belief in calling them to save the wayward and to reject any notion that the wicked were beyond redemption. "Of all reformative agencies," they observed, "religion is first in importance, because [it is] most potent in its action upon the human heart and life" (Wines 1871, 542). The remainder of the principles promulgated by the congress, however, might be mistaken for a twenty-first-century blueprint for prison reform. Thus, the new penology called for expanded education and industrial training. Inmates should not be mixed together but carefully classified by degree of criminality, gender, and age. The congress favored restorative approaches—"a prisoner's self-respect should be cultivated" and "every effort made to give back to him his manhood"—and decried the use of "degradation as a part of punishment" (542). Offenders' behavior should be shaped "by a well-devised and skillfully-applied system of rewards for good conduct, industry and attention to learning" (541). "Rewards," they added, "more than punishments, are essential to every good prison system." Further, the "reformatory officer" should receive "special training" and possess the "serious conviction" that inmates "are capable of being reformed" (542). Reentry into the community was also a concern. "More systematic and comprehensive methods should be adopted to save discharged prisoners," they asserted, "by providing them with work and encouraging them to redeem their character and regain their lost position in society" (545). And "since hope is a more potent agent than fear," the congress concluded, "it should be made an ever-present force in the minds of prisoners" (541).

Not long thereafter—in the first two decades of the 1900s—the new penology paradigm was infused with positivism—the scientific study of offenders—to yield the model of "individualized treatment" and the outlines of the modern correctional system (Rothman 1980). Each offender, this approach asserted, enters crime due a unique set of causal factors. Only by studying individuals is it thus possible to diagnose why offending occurred. In turn, to cure an individual, that person must receive treatment tailored to his or her criminogenic needs. To accomplish such individualized treatment, corrections officials—much as do doctors attempting to cure their patients—required the discretion to deliver the appropriate intervention to each person. Given the unique needs of juveniles, a separate court system would have to be developed. When offenders came before a judge, they would be accompanied by a pre-sentence report spelling out the details of their lives, their prospects for success, and a sentencing recommendation. Probation officers were invented to undertake this task and to watch and help offenders placed on "probation" in the community. Those sent to prison would serve indeterminate sentences and would be allowed to reenter society only when rehabilitated. Parole boards would be needed to determine who should be released and parole officers would be needed to help reintegrate offenders returning to society. By the mid-1920s, most states had built court and corrections systems shaped by this model. Rehabilitation, in short, was institutionalized into a set of policies, practices, and organizations that persist to this day (Rothman 1980; Cullen and Gilbert 1982).

In subsequent decades, rehabilitation was increasingly entrenched as the model guiding offender sanctioning. In the context of modernization, prisons became secular rather than religious institutions, although the presence of chaplains allowed religion to sustain a healthy foothold inside facilities (Sundt and Cullen 1998). Beyond education and work, offenders now were exposed to counseling, group therapy, behavior modification, token economies, and therapeutic communities. Most instructive, in 1954, the American Prison Association changed its name to the American Correctional Association. Prisons became known as "correctional institutions," and probation and parole were subsumed under the umbrella of "community corrections." Much like "penitentiary," the embrace of the term "corrections" captured the persistence of rehabilitation as an American habit of the heart (Cullen and Gendreau 2000). Indeed, by the 1960s it was largely assumed, including by most criminologists, that rehabilitation represented forward-looking thinking and that punishment was "a vestigial carryover of a barbaric past and will disappear as humanitarianism and rationality spread" (Toby 1964, 332).

The hegemony of the individual treatment model was soon shattered and, as noted, the United States entered a period of unprecedented punitiveness. Some commentators have viewed these punitive policies and, especially, mass imprisonment as a reflection of the public will—a case of democracy at work. These claims rest on a shaky foundation because it seems that this is a case of the tail wagging the dog. Thus, rather than moving elected officials to act, public support for such policies was often incited by opportunistic politicians (Beckett 1997; Tonry 2004). But however punitive public opinion became, this did not mean that Americans forfeited their support for rehabilitation (Cullen, Fisher, and Applegate 2002; Tonry 2004). A 2001 national poll illustrates this point. When asked what should be the "main emphasis" of prisons, 55 percent selected the goal of rehabilitation versus 25 percent who chose "protect society" and 14 percent who chose "punishment" (6 percent were not sure). Further, 87 percent stated that rehabilitation was an important correctional goal, and 92 percent agreed that "it is a good idea to provide treatment for offenders who are in prison" (Cullen, Pealer, et al. 2002, 136–37). Public support for saving juveniles is even more pronounced (Cullen et al. 2007; Piquero et al. 2010). In short, for a period now spanning nearly two hundred years, the hope of reforming offenders has been integral to our cultural conception of the purpose of the correctional enterprise. It remains, again, a habit of the heart.

II. The Fall and Rise of Rehabilitation

From the middle part of the 1960s into the 1970s, a confluence of events caused Americans to doubt the legitimacy of state power—a shift in public opinion called the "confidence gap" by Lipset and Schneider (1983). The roster of challenging and/or disquieting occurrences included: the civil rights, women's, and countercultural movements; widespread protests against the Viet Nam War, including students shot down at Kent State University; urban insurgencies that left cities burning; and revelations of government lies, abuse of power, and corruption, culminating in the Watergate scandal. These events created a context in which traditional worldviews were questioned and often abandoned. Rehabilitation, which trusted the state to act in good faith toward offenders, was one of those ways of thinking that came under intense scrutiny (Cullen and Gilbert 1982).

A. The Fall of Rehabilitation

For conservatives, 1960s America initiated a period of inexcusable disorder. The state was seen as weak, giving welfare to the lazy and coddling those who wantonly victimized innocent citizens. In their view, the government needed to be tougher. Rehabilitation came under attack because it was seen as welfare for criminals. Offenders did not need to be given services and treated, they claimed, but rather held responsible for their law-breaking and shown that crime did not pay. They deserved and would learn from harsh sanctions, especially from a lengthy stay in prison stripped of the normal amenities of life. More generally, conservatives asserted, America required a large dose of law and order (Cullen and Gilbert 1982).

More surprising, the traditional advocates of rehabilitation—liberals—also called for the elimination of individualized treatment in corrections. As Rothman (1980) noted, rehabilitation was a benevolent "conscience" or theory of how to respond to offenders. In reality, however, it was corrupted by "convenience" or by the political and bureaucratic interests of those administering treatment. The culprit was the unfettered discretion given to judges, corrections officials, and parole boards, which created what Frankel (1972) called a system of "law without order."

Similar to the medical model through which physicians healed patients, the individualized-treatment model gave officials the discretionary freedom to diagnose what was wrong with offenders, to retain them in the community or send them to prison, to keep them incarcerated until cured, and to return them to prison if they proved a recidivist. But what if this discretion was not based on sound science and used for these purposes? It could be that liberals' trust in the state to act in good faith was misplaced. Thus, what if judges' personal biases caused them not to individualize treatments but to incarcerate the poor and minorities disproportionately? What if release from prison was not based on being rehabilitated but on an inmates' strict obedience to guards' coercive demands? What if politics rather than criminological knowledge shaped who parole boards returned to the community? If so, then the discretionary powers given to the state were not used to treat but to victimize offenders—to expose them to discrimination, coercion while imprisoned, and incompetent decision-making. In short, said liberals, rehabilitation was responsible for the injustices that permeated the correctional system (Cullen and Gilbert 1982).

For liberals, the solution was to constrain state power by extending due process rights to offenders. Various versions of this "justice model" were proposed, but they shared similar recommendations: limit judges' discretion through sentencing guidelines; the use of determinate sentences so that offenders' stay in prison would be known at the time of sentencing; the elimination of mandatory rehabilitation and the use of treatment progress as a criterion of release from prison; and the elimination of parole (American Friends Service Committee 1971; von Hirsch 1971; Morris 1974; Fogel 1979). In essence, the goal would be to penalize the crime—with short sentences written into law—and not to penalize the person as had been the premise of individualized treatment. In this way, there would be equality before the law.

These reforms were implemented in various pieces and in various ways in a number of states. This is not the place to evaluate what transpired, but we will note that the justice model, as the rehabilitation model before it, was substantially corrupted by political and bureaucratic interests (for assessments, see Griset 1991; Tonry 1996). Most troubling, this model transferred power from judges and corrections officials to legislators and prosecutors. With judges' sentencing decisions

constrained by the penalties stipulated in the criminal law and with parole eliminated, legislators now regulated which punishment attached to which crimes. Prosecutors controlled what crime an offender would be charged with and what plea
bargain would be allowed; increasingly they decided who would go to prison and
for how long. Discretion was not eliminated but merely moved to the front of the
justice system. Further, in the conservative get-tough era that emerged, concerns
about justice receded and politicians increasingly engaged in "eraser justice," repeatedly rewriting laws so that they mandated lengthier prison terms. In short, the justice model was in large part transformed into the punishment model.

The key point here is that the liberal abandonment of individualized treatment
began largely as a criticism of discretionary justice and of the inequities that made
the criminal justice system unfair generally and, in particular, biased toward the
disadvantaged and racial minorities. Commentators worried that however benevolent its intentions, the discretion inherent in the administration of offender rehabilitation within the justice system would inevitably be misused and undermine the
goal of treatment. Implicit in this critique was that correctional rehabilitation
programs would not be effective. Even so, this was a secondary consideration—
something that was seen as the inevitable outcome of an unjust system.

B. The Rise of Rehabilitation

In 1974 Robert Martinson published his classic article in the quarterly *The Public
Interest*, "What Works? Questions and Answers about Prison Reform." Martinson
was reporting on an extensive review of evaluations of correctional treatment
programs. After examining 231 studies, he observed that "with few and isolated
exceptions, the rehabilitative efforts that have been reported so far have had no
appreciable effect on recidivism" (1974, 25). This technical-sounding conclusion
prompted him to ask a more fundamental question with disturbing implications:
Does "nothing work" to reform offenders? Martinson stopped short of giving an
affirmative answer, but the tenor of his article—and his statements thereafter—
made it clear that he doubted that the correctional system could ever rehabilitate
(Cullen and Gendreau 2000).

In a very real way, Martinson's study was the final nail in rehabilitation's coffin.
The "nothing works doctrine" became accepted wisdom in the ivory-tower halls of
academic criminology and in the grimier halls of correctional institutions. Importantly, it is not so much that Martinson's work changed the minds of critics—they
had already lost their faith in treatment—but rather that it gave them another means
to discredit correctional rehabilitation. In any debate, they merely had to repeat that
"nothing works"; science indeed appeared to be on their side.

Importantly, however, Martinson's research reframed the debate over rehabilitation, switching it from a criticism of the correctional system (Was a discretionary
system based on the rehabilitative ideal just?) to the empirical issue of *program*

effectiveness (Do treatment programs work?). The future of rehabilitation now hinged on the science of correctional intervention: Was it really the case that offenders were beyond change? Palmer (1975) quickly pointed out that 48 percent of the studies in Martinson's report showed reductions in recidivism. Not long thereafter, Gendreau and Ross (1979) offered "bibliotherapy for cynics" by discussing the positive effects of numerous treatment programs. The technique of meta-analysis, which is similar to taking a batting average of whether treatment works across all evaluation studies, subsequently proved particularly influential. Meta-analyses by Andrews and his colleagues (1990) and by Lipsey (1992), among others, revealed that the overall effect of rehabilitation programs was to reduce recidivism (see also Lipsey and Cullen 2007). In the face of these findings, it became increasingly difficult to argue that "nothing works" to save the criminally wayward. As the 1990s progressed and as the twenty-first century dawned, the case for rehabilitation grew increasingly stronger.

Reframing the debate had another salient consequence—it brought punishment-oriented programs under empirical scrutiny. The shoe, in effect, was now on the other foot: Does correctional punishment work? The central premise of these interventions is that offenders will be specifically deterred if they receive harsher rather than more lenient sanctions. Based on the rational choice model, this approach implicitly argues that all other known risk factors associated with recidivism are irrelevant or cannot be changed. Instead, it is proposed that offenders are sufficiently rational to curb their criminal behavior if they experience the sting of painful sanctions or face the realistic threat of a punitive sanction should they misbehave. When the costs rise and outstrip the benefits, they will calculate that it is prudent to refrain from offending.

Although some dispute exists, there is evidence that, on a macro-level, punishment-oriented policies are associated with general deterrent and incapacitation effects that diminish crime rates. Setting these issues aside, however, studies reveal little evidence that punishment-oriented correctional interventions that seek to specifically deter individuals reduce reoffending (Cullen, Wright, and Applegate 1996; Cullen, Pratt, et al. 2002; MacKenzie 2006). Intensive supervision programs, electronic monitoring/home incarceration, boot camps, and scared straight programs, for example, have limited and, at times, criminogenic effects. Further, while the evidence is restricted, research fails to confirm the punishment model's thesis that recidivism is lower among those who receive imprisonment over probation, serve a longer rather than a shorter sentence, or live in a harsher rather than a nicer prison setting (Gendreau, Goggin, and Cullen 1999; Chen and Shapiro 2007; Nagin, Cullen, and Jonson 2009).

Taken together, these empirical findings showing the effectiveness of treatment programs and the ineffectiveness of punishment programs have made it increasingly difficult to dismiss rehabilitation as an integral goal of the correctional system (Cullen 2005). Ironically, Martinson's insistence that corrections be evidence-based, in effect undermined rehabilitation in the short term but created an empirical contest that in the long term revitalized it. Still, as evidence favorable to treatment appeared, important issues remained to be addressed. A central finding of the meta-analyses was that correctional interventions' effects on recidivism are not homogeneous—the same across all programs—but rather are *heterogeneous*. That is, some treatment programs have null or criminogenic effects, some have modest effects, and others have substantial effects. Why is this so?

III. THE PARADIGM OF EFFECTIVE CORRECTIONAL TREATMENT

Traditionally, advocates of rehabilitation focused on the effectiveness of specific treatment modalities, such as job training, GED or college degree programs, substance abuse programs, psychodynamic treatment, or group therapy (for a summary of much of this research, see MacKenzie 2006; Lipsey and Cullen 2007). Martinson's (1974) original critique argued that within each modality, it seemed that some programs worked but others did not. No treatment modality could be counted on to reduce reoffending consistently. As a result, Martinson concluded that it was not possible to give clear-cut advice on how to reform offenders and, in that sense, "nothing works" (Cullen and Gendreau 2000). Martinson did have a point. The treatment literature was largely atheoretical. It was more similar to a cafeteria where corrections officials would select a little bit of this program and a little bit of that program. These interventions yielded only modest benefits, because they were often implemented without care or integrity.

   As an alternative, a group of Canadian psychologists—led most prominently by Don Andrews, James Bonta, and Paul Gendreau—proposed a coherent paradigm for correctional interventions. We use the term "paradigm" to mean a coherent approach to rehabilitation that is not rooted in a specific treatment modality. Rather, this paradigm integrates theory, empirical evidence, and the tools for delivering treatment into an organized method for correctional intervention. Specifically, it includes three key components: (1) an empirically based theory of offending on which treatment is based; (2) a set of principles for effective treatment; and (3) technology for assessing offenders and agencies to ensure that treatment integrity is achieved. Further, this paradigm accounts for treatment heterogeneity: rehabilitation programs that conform to the paradigm's principles, and thus are "appropriate," produce large reductions in recidivism, whereas as "inappropriate" interventions have small or criminogenic effects. Importantly, this paradigm has emerged as the leading offender rehabilitation approach and increasingly is guiding the delivery of treatment services in North America and beyond. Accordingly, it merits close consideration.

A. The Psychology of Criminal Conduct

The psychology of criminal conduct is based on general principles of human behavior rooted in the interrelated perspectives of behavioral (operant conditioning), social learning, and cognitive psychology. These perspectives have received experimental and other empirical support from literally thousands of studies. They provide the theoretical grounding for interventions that emphasize the use of various types behavioral therapy. As Spiegler and Guevremont (1998, 491) observe, across a variety of conduct difficulties, "behavior therapy arguably has the broadest and strongest empirical base of any form of psychotherapy." Notably, this approach rejects psychodynamic (e.g., Freudian) theories and the intervention strategies they suggest. It also asserts that atheoretical programs that are not rooted in empirically established behavioral and cognitive principles will use inappropriate interventions, which target factors unrelated or only weakly related to the conduct that is to be changed. As a result, such programs will be ineffective.

The psychology of criminal conduct thus argues that, while illegal behavior may have unique features, it occurs largely by the same processes as do other forms of human conduct, whether antisocial or prosocial. In a sense, this theory argues that behavior is, in the end, behavior, and that it is altered—including criminal behavior—by standard rather than by exotic means. In this context, the psychology of criminal conduct contends that most antisocial and criminal behaviors develop, are maintained, and can be changed primarily through learning. Interventions based on this approach focus on creating learning experiences for offenders in which new (prosocial) cognitions and behaviors replace old (antisocial) ones. Three interrelated strategies are used in this regard.

First, most behavioral treatments with offenders are based on the principle of operant conditioning, whereby positive reinforcers are used to increase prosocial behavior and antisocial behavior is punished or ignored. This is often referred to as "contingency management" in corrections. Second, social learning programs rely extensively on modeling prosocial behaviors so that offenders can learn through observation and practice. Planned modeling activities often involve teaching the individual skill steps associated with a behavior, demonstrating the behavior in a role play, and then having the offender engage in behavioral rehearsal to practice the skill and receive feedback. Third, cognitive approaches target antisocial attitudes and values through cognitive restructuring. These theories also underscore the need to teach certain cognitive skills such as problem solving and moral reasoning.

The psychology of criminal conduct as a general theoretical approach has received consistent empirical support in the treatment of criminal behaviors. In fact, a recent assessment of treatment modalities in the area of corrections reported that sixteen of twenty-two meta-analyses (72.7 percent) on the effectiveness of cognitive-behavioral approaches yielded estimates greater than $r = .15$ (Smith, Gendreau, and Swartz 2009). In concrete terms, this means that offenders receiving this treatment would have a recidivism rate that was 15 percentage points lower than those in the control group. As noted in section B to follow, within correctional settings, interventions based on this approach have been most effective when they have targeted the criminogenic needs (i.e., attitudes, behaviors, personality factors, and life circumstances that contribute to criminality) of higher-risk offenders (Gendreau, French, and Gionet 2004). In contrast, "other" treatment modalities (i.e., nonbehavioral) were associated with much smaller average reductions in recidivism.

B. Principles of Effective Intervention

A key empirical finding is that some programs are far more effective than others (Andrews et al. 1990). This finding of heterogeneity of effects helped to prompt the Canadian psychologists to explore which factors distinguish programs that work from those that do not. Equipped with their views on the psychology of criminal conduct, they thus developed principles of effective intervention, arguing that programs that conformed to these principles would reduce recidivism whereas "inappropriate" programs would have null or iatrogenic effects. In turn, these scholars sought to assess empirically whether their principles could predict the effectiveness of correctional interventions (Andrews et al. 1990; Andrews and Bonta 2006).

In this context, more than forty meta-analyses have been published in the field of corrections (for a review, see Smith, Gendreau, and Swartz 2009). The results of these meta-analyses have been replicated with remarkable consistency, and it is now widely recognized that three conditions must be met in order for correctional rehabilitation to be effective. First, treatment programs must be delivered to higher-risk offenders; this is termed the *risk principle*. Second, programs must target criminogenic needs; this is the *need principle*. Third, programs must use cognitive-behavioral approaches (e.g., behavioral, social learning, cognitive) while making adjustments to the mode and style of service delivery in order to accommodate certain offender characteristics; this is the *responsivity principle*. Taken together, these three conditions constitute the core of the principles of effective correctional intervention (Andrews and Bonta 2006; Gendreau, Smith, and French 2006), and thus they merit detailed discussion below.

1. *The Risk Principle*

The results of meta-analytic reviews of the literature have found that there are two types of risk factors that predict offender recidivism: static and dynamic. Static factors are offender characteristics that cannot be changed, such as a person's criminal history. Dynamic risk factors earn their name because these are offender characteristic that lead to recidivism and are malleable, such as having attitudes that encourage crime. Dynamic risk factors are also commonly referred to as *criminogenic needs*. The existence of dynamic risk factors is critical because "something" must be targeted and changed if a treatment intervention is going to be effective. This is why having a sound empirical understanding of the sources of recidivism underlies efficacious intervention (see Gendreau, Little, and Goggin 1996; Andrews and Bonta 2006).

Meta-analyses that quantitatively synthesize the existing studies show that the most robust dynamic risk factors include antisocial attitudes and values, antisocial peer associations, personality factors (e.g., lack of self-control and self-management skills, aggression, impulsivity), dysfunctional family/marital relationships, substance abuse, lack of education and employment skills, and poor use of leisure time. In contrast, other factors that were once thought to be important—such as low self-esteem and fear of official punishment—have not been found to be related to recidivism (see Gendreau, Little, and Goggin 1996; Bonta, Law, and Hanson 1998; Dowden and Andrews 1999; Andrews and Bonta 2006).

The risk principle also states that the most intensive interventions should be reserved for higher-risk offenders because they pose more risk to the public and require a greater "dosage" of treatment. In contrast, lower-risk offenders require much less intervention due to the fact that they have fewer criminogenic needs— that is, fewer "things" about them that would lead them back into crime. Previous studies have demonstrated that lower-risk offenders can be adversely affected by participating in treatment (e.g., Andrews, Bonta, and Hoge 1990; Lowenkamp and Latessa 2005; Smith and Gendreau 2007). This is likely because participation in treatment can both disrupt protective factors and often forces lower-risk offenders to socialize with their higher-risk counterparts.

To use the risk principle efficaciously, the Canadian psychologists designed relevant technology. Based on existing knowledge, they argued that offenders should be assessed not through clinical judgments but with an actuarial risk instrument. This instrument, they reasoned, should include both static and dynamic factors so as to have adequate predictive validity (Andrews and Bonta 2006). In this regard, they developed the Level of Service Inventory (LSI) for the purposes of assessing the level of the risks manifested by offenders. Studies have demonstrated that the LSI is useful in assessing offender risk and in predicting recidivism (Gendreau, Goggin, and Smith 2002; Campbell, French, and Gendreau 2007; Vose, Cullen, and Smith 2008; Smith, Cullen, and Latessa 2009; Vose et al. 2009).

2. *The Need Principle*

The need principle follows from the risk principle in that the most effective (or "appropriate") treatment programs target dynamic risk factors for change in order to reduce recidivism. The need principle underscores the importance of using an actuarial risk assessment that includes dynamic risk factors, given that this information should be employed to guide security classification and transfer decisions, determine suitability for parole and the parameters for community supervision, and identify pre-treatment criminogenic needs. Furthermore, criminogenic needs should be routinely reassessed over time (i.e., every six to twelve months) in order to monitor changes in risk/need levels and to make adjustments to treatment if necessary (Andrews and Bonta 2006).

3. *The Responsivity Principle*

The responsivity principle is subdivided into two parts. First, the *general responsivity principle* states that the most effective interventions are based on cognitive, behavioral, and social learning theories. This is because these programs are based in the psychology of criminal conduct and are capable of changing—that is, they are "responsive to"—the factors that cause recidivism (e.g., antisocial attitudes). Specifically, treatment programs should employ behavioral strategies such as operant conditioning in which positive reinforcers are administered to increase prosocial behaviors and punishers are used to suppress antisocial behaviors. There are five basic types of positive reinforcers that are commonly used in correctional programs: tangible (e.g., food, books, clothes), activities (e.g., recreation), token (e.g., money or points), social (e.g., attention, praise, acknowledgement, approval), and covert (e.g., thoughts, self-evaluation). The most effective correctional treatment programs also incorporate social learning techniques such as modeling, shaping, and behavioral rehearsal to enhance prosocial skills and competencies. Finally, cognitive restructuring should be integrated into treatment packages in an attempt to restructure distorted or maladaptive antisocial cognitions.

Second, while the general responsivity principle identifies the cognitive-behavioral treatment model as the most effective for the vast majority of offenders, the *specific responsivity principle* supports the practice of matching styles and modes of treatment service to the learning styles and personal characteristics of offenders (Andrews and Bonta 2006). Some factors that should be taken into consideration include motivation to participate in the program, feelings of anxiety or depression, and cognitive functioning. To illustrate, an offender with a low IQ would respond more favorably to an instructional format that requires less verbal and written fluency and that uses more concrete examples. In addition, they would likely benefit from a more extensive use of positive reinforcers and from repeated, graduated behavioral rehearsal (Cullen et al. 1997).

C. The Importance of Treatment Integrity

Some critics of the "what works" movement in corrections have argued that "successful" treatment programs are often utopian demonstration projects and do not represent the reality of "routine practice" programs (e.g., Lab and Whitehead 1990).

These demonstration projects often involve interventions with considerable *therapeutic integrity* that have been implemented and monitored by academic researchers and clinicians with substantial resources. As such, therapists are more likely to have been adequately trained and supervised in these settings, and are often assessed for core correctional competencies (e.g., relationship skills, effective reinforcement and disapproval, structuring skills, effective modeling, structured skill learning, problem solving, and effective use of authority) (Gendreau, et al. 2006). The effectiveness of "routine" programs, on the other hand, is often compromised by staff turnover, organizational resistance, and a variety of other social and political contextual factors (see Hamm and Schrink 1989; Hollin 1995; Gendreau, Goggin, and Smith 1999). The widespread lack of therapeutic integrity continues to be a major area of concern in the field of corrections (Lowenkamp, Latessa, and Smith 2006).

The Correctional Program Assessment Inventory (CPAI-2000) was developed by Don Andrews and Paul Gendreau for the purposes of assessing the integrity of correctional programs (Gendreau and Andrews 2001). The instrument uses the principles of effective correctional treatment as a template for the "ideal" program and then measures how closely the program under review is to this ideal (Gendreau and Andrews 2001; Andrews and Bonta 2006). Perhaps one of the most important advantages of the CPAI-2000 is that it is based on empirical research and operationalizes the principles of effective correctional treatment. Given the applicability of the principles of effective intervention to various subgroups of offender populations (see Andrews and Bonta 2006; Gendreau, Smith, and French 2006; Smith, Cullen, and Latessa 2009), the CPAI-2000 has become accepted as a tool to evaluate virtually all types of correctional interventions aimed at reducing recidivism, regardless of the client group or the type of program under review. It has been applied to hundreds of correctional programs in Canada and the United States (Gendreau et al. 2006; Lowenkamp, Latessa, and Smith 2006).

The instrument contains a total of 131 scored items across eight domains: organizational culture, program implementation and maintenance, management and staff characteristics, client risk and need practices, program characteristics, core correctional practices, interagency communication, and evaluation (Gendreau and Andrews 2001). Each domain is scored and rated as "Very Satisfactory" (70 percent and above), "Satisfactory" (50–69 percent), or "Unsatisfactory" (49 percent and below). The overall score is then calculated and rated using the same cutoffs.

Unfortunately, the vast majority of correctional programs (approximately 60 percent) that have been assessed with the CPAI-2000 did not receive a passing grade, with only 6 percent of programs receiving a rating of "Very Satisfactory." Several authors have argued that this is indicative of the fact that "routine programs" in corrections must deal with many barriers to successful implementation (Gendreau, Goggin, and Smith 1999; Lowenkamp, Latessa, and Smith 2006). It also underscores the need to measure treatment integrity, especially when one considers that total scores on the instrument have been found to correlate with offender outcomes (Nesovic 2003; Lowenkamp, Latessa, and Smith 2006).

Thus, Nesovic (2003) gathered 173 primary studies of correctional treatment and calculated 266 effect sizes between program quality (using the CPAI-2000) and recidivism. Notably, correctional treatments that were classified as having high scores on the measure of program quality were associated with a 20 percent reduction in recidivism, whereas programs that were classified as having medium or low scores were associated with an 11 percent and 1 percent reduction in recidivism, respectively. Similarly, Lowenkamp, Latessa, and Smith (2006) conducted thirty-eight reviews of correctional treatment programs that included direct comparisons of treatment and matched comparison groups (i.e., gender, race, actuarial risk measure score). Reincarceration was used as the outcome measure. Despite the fact that many of the programs were ineffective—it was not uncommon to find *higher* recidivism rates among the treatment group—the CPAI total score was strongly correlated with outcome ($r = .41$). In practical terms, this means that there was a 41 percent difference in the recidivism rates (or treatment effects) for programs that scored high on the instrument versus ones that scored low.

On a more encouraging note, we are aware that some states—such as Indiana, Ohio, and Oklahoma—have demonstrated a commitment to evidence-based approaches and are presently engaged in establishing rigorous treatment program accreditation standards based on best practices. Further, some exemplary individual programs have been assessed more than once with the CPAI-2000 and have shown improvement over time.

IV. Conclusion

The punishment model that has dominated American corrections for four decades appears to have exhausted itself. This is not to say that get-tough rhetoric will vanish or that an era of leniency is on the horizon. But it does mean that the economic and human costs of a system of mass incarceration have grown so transparent that space exists to consider whether there is a better way of doing things. In this context, we propose that rehabilitation is re-emerging as an important source of progressive reform in corrections (Listwan et al. 2008).

Rehabilitation has gained legitimacy not only from the failures of punishment-oriented policies and programs but also from the hard work of scholars who compiled evidence demonstrating treatment effectiveness and who have detailed specifically "what works" to change offenders (Cullen 2005). Still, openness to the treatment enterprise is also possible because, as argued in section I, rehabilitation remains for Americans a habit of the heart. Although often portrayed as punitive and vengeful, this characterization of the public is only partially accurate. As Wuthnow (1991, 10) notes, Americans have long manifested a "spirit of caring" and engaged in "acts of compassion." Three-fourths of the public, his survey data show, believe that it is important to help those in need. Offenders comprise a less attractive object of caring, but it is clear that the willingness to assist them persists (Moon, Cullen, and Wright 2003). Americans are believers in giving the wayward second chances, and their religious inclinations foster an optimism that few among us are beyond redemption.

Even so, the challenge for those arguing that rehabilitation should be reaffirmed as a core purpose of corrections is to show that, within the context of real-world settings buffeted by limited resources, political interests, and organizational inertia and resistance, it is possible to reduce recidivism. In so doing, it will be necessary to avoid the hubris of earlier reformers who assumed that the penitentiary and the model of individualized treatment would lead ineluctably to a humane and efficacious correctional system. Changing offenders entrapped on a criminal life course is a daunting task. It will take more than good faith; it will require rigorous science to produce sound knowledge about effective treatment strategies and considerable effort to translate that research into viable correctional interventions.

REFERENCES

American Friends Service Committee. 1971. *Struggle for Justice.* New York: Hill and Wang.

Andrews, D. A., and James Bonta. 2006. *The Psychology of Criminal Conduct*, 4th ed. Cincinnati, OH: Anderson.

Andrews, D. A., James Bonta, and Robert D. Hoge. 1990. "Classification for Effective Rehabilitation: Rediscovering Psychology." *Criminal Justice and Behavior* 17:19–22.

Andrews, D. A., Ivan Zinger, Robert D. Hoge, James Bonta, Paul Gendreau, and Francis T. Cullen. 1990. "Does Correctional Treatment Work? A Clinically Relevant and Psychologically Informed Meta-Analysis." *Criminology* 28:369–404.

Beckett, Katherine. 1997. *Making Crime Pay: Law and Order in Contemporary American Politics.* New York: Oxford University Press.

Bellah, Robert N., Richard Madsen, William M. Sullivan, Ann Swidler, and Steven M. Tipton. 1985. *Habits of the Heart: Individualism and Commitment in American Life.* Berkeley: University of California Press.

Bonta, James, Moira Law, and R. Karl Hanson. 1998. "The Prediction of Criminal and Violent Recidivism Among Mentally Disordered Offenders: A Meta-Analysis." *Psychological Bulletin* 123:123–42.

Campbell, Mary Ann, Sheila French, and Paul Gendreau. 2007. *Assessing the Utility of Risk Assessment Tools and Personality Measures in the Prediction of Violent Recidivism for Adult Offenders* (Research Report 2007–04). Ottawa: Public Safety Canada.

Chen, M. Keith, and Jesse M. Shapiro. 2007. "Do Harsher Prison Conditions Reduce Recidivism? A Discontinuity-Based Approach." *American Law and Economic Review* 9:1–19.

Clear, Todd R. 1994. *Harm in American Penology: Offenders, Victims, and Their Communities*. Albany: State University of New York Press.

———. 2007. *Imprisoning Communities: How Mass Incarceration Makes Disadvantaged Neighborhoods Worse*. New York: Oxford University Press.

Cullen, Francis T. 2005. "The Twelve People Who Save Rehabilitation: How the Science of Criminology Made a Difference—The American Society of Criminology 2004 Presidential Address." *Criminology* 43:1–42.

———. 2006. "It's Time to Reaffirm Rehabilitation." *Criminology and Public Policy* 5:665–72.

Cullen, Francis T., Bonnie S. Fisher, and Brandon K. Applegate. 2002. "Public Opinion About Punishment and Corrections." In *Crime and Justice: A Review of Research*, vol. 14, edited by Michael Tonry. Chicago: University of Chicago Press.

Cullen, Francis T., and Paul Gendreau. 2000. "Assessing Correctional Rehabilitation: Policy, Practice, and Prospects." In *Policies, Processes, and Decisions of the Criminal Justice System*, edited by Julie Horney, vol. 3 of *Criminal Justice 2000*. Washington, DC: US Department of Justice, National Institute of Justice.

Cullen, Francis T., Paul Gendreau, G. Roger Jarjoura, and John Paul Wright. 1997. "Crime and the Bell Curve: Lessons from Intelligent Criminology." *Crime and Delinquency* 43:387–411.

Cullen, Francis T., and Karen E. Gilbert. 1982. *Reaffirming Rehabilitation*. Cincinnati, OH: Anderson.

Cullen, Francis T., Jennifer A. Pealer, Bonnie S. Fisher, Brandon K. Applegate, and Shannon A. Santana. 2002. "Public Support for Correctional Rehabilitation in America: Change or Consistency?" In *Changing Attitudes to Punishment: Public Opinion, Crime and Justice*, edited by Julian V. Roberts and Michael Hough. Devon, UK: Willan.

Cullen, Francis T., Travis C. Pratt, Sharon Levrant Miceli, and Melissa M. Moon. 2002. "Dangerous Liaison? Rational Choice Theory as the Basis for Correctional Intervention." In *Rational Choice and Criminal Behavior: Recent Research and Future Challenge*, edited by Alex R. Piquero and Stephen G. Tibbetts. New York: Routledge.

Cullen, Francis T., Brenda A. Vose, Cheryl Lero Jonson, and James D. Unnever. 2007. "Public Support for Early Intervention: Is Child Saving a 'Habit of the Heart'?" *Victims and Offenders* 2:109–24.

Cullen, Francis T., and John Paul Wright. 1996. "Two Futures of American Corrections." In *The Past, Present, and Future of American Corrections*, edited by Brendan Maguire and Polly Radosh. New York: General Hall.

Cullen, Francis T., John Paul Wright, and Brandon K. Applegate. 1996. "Control in the Community: The Limits of Reform?" In *Choosing Correctional Interventions That Work: Defining the Demand and Evaluating the Supply*, edited by Alan Harland. Thousand Oaks, CA: Sage.

Dowden, Craig, and D. A. Andrews. 1999. "What Works in Young Offender Treatment: A Meta-Analysis." *Forum on Corrections Research* 11, no. 2:21–24.

Fogel, David. 1979. *We Are the Living Proof: The Justice Model for Corrections*, 2nd ed. Cincinnati, OH: Anderson.

Frankel, Marvin E. 1972. *Criminal Sentences: Law Without Order*. New York: Hill and Wang.

Garland, David. 2001. *The Culture of Control: Crime and Social Order in Contemporary Society*. Chicago: University of Chicago Press.

Gendreau, Paul, and D. A. Andrews. 2001. *Correctional Program Assessment Inventory* (CPAI-2000). Saint John, Canada: University of New Brunswick.

Gendreau, Paul, Sheila French, and Angela Gionet. 2004. "What Works (What Doesn't Work): The Principles of Effective Correctional Treatment." *Journal of Community Corrections* 13:4–6, 27–30.

Gendreau, Paul, Claire Goggin, and Francis T. Cullen. 1999. *The Effects of Prison Sentences on Recidivism.* Ottawa: Solicitor General of Canada.

Gendreau, Paul, Claire Goggin, Sheila French, and Paula Smith. 2006. "Practicing Psychology in Correctional Settings: 'What Works' in Reducing Criminal Behavior." In *The Handbook of Forensic Psychology*, 3rd ed., edited by A. K. Hess and I. B. Weiner. New York: John Wiley.

Gendreau, Paul, Claire Goggin, and Paula Smith. 1999. "The Forgotten Issue in Effective Correctional Treatment: Program Implementation." *International Journal of Offender Therapy and Comparative Criminology* 43:180–87.

Gendreau, Paul, Claire Goggin, and Paula Smith. 2002. "Is the PCL-R Really the 'Unparalleled' Measure of Offender Risk?" *Criminal Justice and Behavior* 29:397–426.

Gendreau, Paul, Tracy Little, and Claire Goggin. 1996. "A Meta-Analysis of the Predictors of Adult Offender Recidivism: What Works!" *Criminology* 34:575–607.

Gendreau, Paul, and Robert R. Ross. 1979. "Effective Correctional Treatment: Bibliotherapy for Cynics." *Crime and Delinquency* 25:463–89.

Gendreau, Paul, Paula Smith, and Sheila French. 2006. "The Theory of Effective Correctional Intervention: Empirical Status and Future Directions." In *Taking Stock: The Status of Criminological Theory*, edited by Francis T. Cullen, John Paul Wright, and Kristie R. Blevins, vol. 15 of Advances in Criminological Theory. New Brunswick, NJ: Transaction.

Glaze, Lauren E., and Erica Parks. 2012. *Correctional Populations in the United States, 2011.* Washington, DC: US Department of Justice, Bureau of Justice Statistics.

Griset, Pamala L. 1991. *Determinate Sentencing: The Promise and the Reality of Retributive Justice.* Albany: State University of New York Press.

Hamm, Mark L., and Jeffrey L. Schrink. 1989. "The Conditions of Effective Implementation: A Guide to Accomplishing Rehabilitation Objectives in Corrections." *Criminal Justice and Behavior* 16:166–82.

Hollin, Clive R. 1995. "The Meaning and Implications of Programme Integrity." In *What Works: Reducing Reoffending: Guidelines from Research and Practice*, edited by James McGuire. New York: John Wiley and Sons.

Lab, Steven P., and John T. Whitehead. 1990. "From 'Nothing Works' to 'the Appropriate Works': The Latest Stop on the Search for the Secular Grail." *Criminology* 28:405–17.

Lipset, Seymour Martin, and William Schneider. 1983. *The Confidence Gap: Business, Labor, and Government in the Public Mind.* New York: Free Press.

Lipsey, Mark W. 1992. "Juvenile Delinquent Treatment: A Meta-Analytic Treatment Inquiry into the Variability of Effects." In *Meta-Analysis for Explanation: A Casebook*, edited by Thomas D. Cook, Harris Cooper, David S. Cordray, Heidi Hartmann, Larry V. Hedges, Richard J. Light, Thomas A. Lewis, and Frederick Mosteller. New York: Russell Sage Foundation.

Lipsey, Mark W., and Francis T. Cullen. 2007. "The Effectiveness of Correctional Rehabilitation: A Review of Systematic Reviews." *Annual Review of Law and Social Science* 3:297–320.

Listwan, Shelley Johnson, Cheryl Lero Jonson, Francis T. Cullen, and Edward J. Latessa 2008. "Cracks in the Penal Harm Movement: Evidence from the Field." *Criminology and Public Policy* 7:423–65.

Lowenkamp, Christopher T., and Edward J. Latessa. 2005. "Increasing the Effectiveness of Correctional Programming through the Risk Principle: Identifying Offenders for Residential Placement." *Criminology and Public Policy* 4:263–89.

Lowenkamp, Christopher T., Edward J. Latessa, and Paula Smith. 2006. "Does Correctional Program Quality Really Matter? The Importance of Adhering to the Principles of Effective Intervention." *Criminology and Public Policy* 5:201–20.

MacKenzie, Doris Layton. 2006. *What Works in Corrections: Reducing the Criminal Activities of Offenders and Delinquents*. New York: Cambridge University Press.

Martinson, Robert. 1974. "What Works?—Questions and Answers About Prison Reform." *Public Interest* 35, Spring:22–54.

Moon, Melissa M., Francis T. Cullen, and John Paul Wright. 2003. "It Takes a Village: Public Willingness to Help Wayward Youths." *Youth Violence and Juvenile Justice* 1:32–45.

Morris, Norval. 1974. *The Future of Imprisonment*. Chicago: University of Chicago Press.

Nagin, Daniel S., Francis T. Cullen, and Cheryl Lero Jonson. 2009. "Imprisonment and Reoffending." In *Crime and Justice: A Review of Research*, vol. 38, edited by Michael Tonry. Chicago: University of Chicago Press.

Nesovic, Aleksandra. 2003. "Psychometric Evaluation of the Correctional Program Assessment Inventory (CPAI)." Unpublished PhD diss., Carleton University, Department of Psychology, Ottawa.

Palmer, Ted. 1975. "Martinson Revisited." *Journal of Research in Crime and Delinquency*. 12:133–52.

Pew Center on the States. 2008. *One in 100: Behind Bars in America 2008*. Washington, DC: Pew Charitable Trusts.

———. 2009. *One in 31: The Long Reach of American Corrections*. Washington, DC: Pew Charitable Trusts.

Piquero, Alex R., Francis T. Cullen, James D. Unnever, Nicole Leeper Piquero, and Jill Gordon. 2010. "Never Too Late: Public Opinion About Juvenile Rehabilitation." *Punishment and Society* 12:187–207.

Rothman, David J. 1971. *The Discovery of the Asylum: Social Order and Disorder in the New Republic*. Boston: Little, Brown.

———. 1980. *Conscience and Convenience: The Asylum and Its Alternatives in Progressive America*. Boston: Little, Brown.

Simon, Jonathan. 2007. *Governing Through Crime: How the War on Crime Transformed American Democracy and Created a Culture of Fear*. New York: Oxford University Press.

Smith, Paula, Francis T. Cullen, and Edward J. Latessa. 2009. "Can 14,737 Women Be Wrong? A Meta-Analysis of the LSI-R and Recidivism." *Criminology and Public Policy* 8:183–208.

Smith, Paula, and Paul Gendreau. 2007. "The Relationship between Program Participation, Institutional Misconduct and Recidivism among Federally Sentenced Adult Male Offenders." *Forum on Corrections Research* 19:6–10.

Smith, Paula, Paul Gendreau, and Kristin Swartz. 2009. "Validating the Principles of Effective Intervention: A Systematic Review of the Contributions of Meta-Analysis in the Field of Corrections." *Victims and Offenders* 4:148–69.

Spiegler, Michael D., and David C. Guevremont. 1998. *Contemporary Behavior Therapy*, 3rd ed. Pacific Grove, CA: Brooks/Cole.

Sundt, Jody L., and Francis T. Cullen. 1998. "The Role of the Contemporary Prison Chaplain." *Prison Journal* 23:272–98.

Toby, Jackson. 1964. "Is Punishment Necessary?" *Journal of Criminal Law, Criminology, and Police Science* 55:332–37.

Tocqueville, Alexis de. 1969. *Democracy in America*. Ed. J. P. Meyer. Trans. George Lawrence. New York: Harper and Row. (Originally published in 1835 and 1840.)

Tonry, Michael. 1996. *Sentencing Matters*. New York: Oxford University Press.

———. 2004. *Thinking About Crime: Sense and Sensibility in American Penal Culture*. New York: Oxford University Press.

———. 2007. "Determinants of Penal Policies." In *Crime, Punishment, and Politics in Comparative Perspective*, edited by Michael Tonry. Vol. 36 of *Crime and Justice: A Review of Research*, edited by Michael Tonry. Chicago: University of Chicago Press.

von Hirsch, Andrew. 1971. *Doing Justice: The Choice of Punishments*. New York: Hill and Wang.

Vose, Brenda, Francis T. Cullen, and Paula Smith. 2008. "The Empirical Status of the Level of Service Inventory." *Federal Probation* 72, no. 3:22–29.

Vose, Brenda, Christopher T. Lowenkamp, Paula Smith, and Francis T. Cullen. 2009. "Gender and Predictive Validity of the LSI-R: A Study of Parolees and Probationers." *Journal of Contemporary Criminal Justice* 25:459–71.

Werth, Barry. 2009. *Banquet at Delmonico's: Great Minds, the Gilded Age, and the Triumph of Evolution in America*. New York: Random House.

Wines, E. C., ed. 1871. "Declaration of Principles Adopted and Promulgated by the Congress." In *Transactions of the National Congress on Penitentiary and Reformatory Discipline*. Albany, NY: Wee Parsons and Company.

Wuthnow, Robert. 1991. *Acts of Compassion: Caring for Others and Helping Ourselves* Princeton, NJ: Princeton University Press.

CHAPTER 7

....

GENERAL DETERRENCE

....

ROBERT APEL AND
DANIEL S. NAGIN

THE criminal justice system (CJS) dispenses justice by apprehending, prosecuting, and punishing individuals who break the law. These activities may also prevent crime by three distinct mechanisms—incapacitation, specific deterrence, and general deterrence. Convicted offenders are often punished with imprisonment. Incapacitation refers to the crimes averted by their physical isolation during the period of their incarceration. Specific and general deterrence involve possible behavioral responses. Specific deterrence refers to the reduction in re-offending that is presumed to follow from the *experience* of actually being punished. We note, however, that there are many sound reasons for suspecting that the experience of punishment might instead increase re-offending. The *threat* of punishment might also discourage potential and actual criminals in the general public from committing crime. This effect is known as general deterrence and is the subject of this chapter. For a review of the evidence on the effect of the experience of punishment on reoffending see Nagin, Cullen, and Jonson (2009) and for a review of the evidence on incapacitation effects see Spelman (1994) or Zimring and Hawkins (1995).

Going back to the Enlightenment-era legal philosophers Cesare Beccaria (1764) and Jeremy Bentham (1789), scholars have speculated on the general deterrent effect of official sanctions, but sustained efforts to verify their effects empirically did not begin until the 1960s. This review is not intended to be encyclopedic of the ensuing research findings; its objective is to highlight key findings and conclusions. Because evidence through the late 1990s has been well summarized elsewhere (Zimring and Hawkins 1973; Andenaes 1974; Gibbs 1975; Blumstein, Cohen, and Nagin 1978; Cook 1980; Nagin 1998), our focus is primarily on research in the past decade, but important findings from the older literature are also discussed.

We find overwhelming evidence of a substantial general deterrent effect. Therefore, a well-balanced crime-control portfolio must necessarily include deterrence-based policies. Yet this general deterrent effect is far from uniform, as it appears to vary according to sanction type, crime type, jurisdiction, and the targeted individuals. Questions concerning general deterrence are best posed in terms of whether incremental (i.e., "marginal") increases in sanction threats deter crime, and if they do, whether the benefits of crime reduction outweigh the social and economic costs of imposing the sanction. The basic arguments here are three:

- There is substantial evidence from a diverse literature that increases in the certainty of punishment substantially deters criminal behavior. Certainty-based deterrence measures include the use of imprisonment threats to enforce court-ordered fine payments as well as increasing the visibility of the police by hiring more officers or re-allocating existing officers in ways that materially heighten the risk of apprehension (e.g., "hot spots" policing).
- There is little evidence that increases in the severity of punishment yield general deterrent effects that are sufficiently large to justify their social and economic costs. Severity-based deterrence measures include "Three Strikes and You're Out" and the death penalty. One notable exception to this claim may be targeted efforts to increase punishment severity among known felony offenders, such as violent gang members (e.g., Operation Ceasefire [Kennedy et al. 2001]).
- Research on perceptual deterrence suggests that while external or contextual sources of information about punishment risk are only weakly correlated with sanction risk perceptions, people's own experiences with crime and punishment are quite salient determinants of their risk perceptions, and therefore their behavior.

In reviewing the evidence, we begin in section I with discussion of key concepts. In section II we turn to empirical research on general deterrence. We begin with the deterrent effect of the penultimate and ultimate legally prescribed sanctions, imprisonment and execution. In section III, we discuss the deterrent effect of police, and review studies of aggregate police presence in addition to police deployment strategies. In section IV, we evaluate the strength of the evidence for perceptual deterrence, and the interplay of sanctions, perceptions, and behavior among individuals. We conclude with some general remarks, a cautionary message about the limits of deterrence as a crime-control policy, and recommendations concerning future deterrence-based inquiry.

I. Key Concepts of Deterrence

Deterrence is a theory of choice in which would-be offenders balance the benefits and costs of crime. Benefits may be pecuniary in the case of property crime but may also involve intangibles such as defending one's honor, expressing outrage, demonstrating dominance, cementing a reputation, or seeking a thrill. The potential costs of crime are comparably varied. Crime can entail personal risk if the victim resists (Cook 1986). It may also invoke pangs of conscience or shame (Braithwaite 1989). Here, we are concerned mainly with offender response to the costs that attend the imposition of official sanctions for crime such as arrest, imprisonment, execution, fines, and other restrictions on freedom and liberty (e.g., mandated drug testing, electronic monitoring).

An example of a deterrence-based sanction policy is the "Three Strikes and You're Out" law, which mandates a lengthy minimum sentence (e.g., twenty-five years in California) following a third conviction for a "strikeable" offense, often a type of felony. Another example is the widespread requirement for a mandatory sentence enhancement if a firearm is used in the commission of another felony such as robbery or rape. More generally, any sanction policy that increases sentence length or mandates the imposition of a more onerous sanction (e.g., imprisonment rather than probation) is an example of a policy that may have a deterrence-based rationale.

The theory of deterrence is predicated on the idea that if state-imposed sanction costs are sufficiently severe, criminal activity will be discouraged, at least for some. Thus, one of the key concepts is the severity of punishment. Our review of severity effects focuses on research findings concerning the penultimate and ultimate sanctions, imprisonment and capital punishment, respectively.

Severity alone, however, cannot deter. There must also be some possibility that the sanction will be incurred if the crime is committed. For that to happen, the offender must be apprehended, usually by the police. He must next be charged and successfully prosecuted, and finally sentenced by the judiciary. None of these successive stages is certain. Thus, another key concept in deterrence theory is the certainty of punishment. In this regard the most important set of actors are the police—absent detection and apprehension, there is no possibility of conviction or punishment. For this reason we discuss separately what is known about the deterrent effect of police.

One of the key conclusions that emerged from the 1960s- and 1970s-era deterrence literature was that the certainty of punishment was a more powerful deterrent than the severity of punishment. The analyses of this era generally used cross-sectional data on states and involved testing the effects on the statewide crime rate of the certainty and severity of punishment, along with other demographic and socio-economic control variables. (The statistical method is called regression analysis.) The certainty of punishment was measured by the ratio of prison admissions to the number of reported crimes, while the severity of punishment was measured by median time served of recent prison releases. The basis for the "certainty not severity" deterrence conclusion was that punishment certainty was consistently found to have a negative and significant association with the crime rate, whereas punishment severity generally had no significant association.

This conclusion at the time was probably based on faulty statistical inference. Two primary criticisms were leveled. The first was that the negative association between the certainty measure and crime rate was an artifact of the number of crimes appearing in the denominator of the certainty measure and the numerator of the crime rate. It can be mathematically demonstrated that errors in the measurement of the number of crimes, of which there are many, will force a negative, deterrent-like association between the crime rate and certainty even if, in fact, the certainty of punishment had no deterrent effect on crime. The second involved the use of theoretically indefensible statistical methods for parsing out the cause-effect relationship between sanction levels and the crime rate. After all, sanctions may deter crime, but crime may also affect sanction levels (Nagin 1978). For example, overcrowded prisons might reduce the chances of newly caught offenders going to prison. However, subsequent findings from the so-called perceptual deterrence literature, and economic studies of the effects of contact with the criminal justice system on access to legal labor markets, provide a far firmer empirical and theoretical basis for the "certainty" contention. The perceptual deterrence literature examines the relationships of perceived sanction risks to either self-reported offending or intentions to do so, and was spawned by researchers interested in probing the perceptual underpinnings of the deterrence process. We review the contributions of research on perceptual deterrence as well.

II. THE DETERRENT EFFECT OF CRIMINAL PUNISHMENT

The latest research on the deterrent effect of punishment is composed of two types of studies. One focuses on the deterrent effect of the imprisonment rate, typically measured as the number of inmates per capita in state and federal prisons on December 31 of any given year. The other focuses on the deterrent effect of capital punishment, measured as the number of executions per capita or the probability of execution conditional on receiving a death sentence. We review both types of studies below.

A. Imprisonment and Crime

There have been two distinct waves of studies of the deterrent effect of imprisonment. Studies in the 1960s and 1970s examined the relationship of the crime rate to the certainty of punishment, measured by the ratio of prison admissions to reported crimes, and the severity of punishment as measured by median time served. These studies suffered from a number of serious statistical flaws that are detailed in Blumstein, Cohen, and Nagin (1978). In response to these deficiencies, a second generation of studies emerged in the 1990s. Unlike the first-generation studies that primarily involved cross-sectional analyses of states, second-generation studies had a longitudinal component in which data were analyzed not only across states but also over time. Another important difference is that the second-generation studies did not attempt to estimate certainty and severity effects separately. Instead they examined the relationship between the crime rate and rate of imprisonment as measured by prisoners per capita.

A review by Donohue (2007) identifies six such studies. All find statistically significant negative associations between imprisonment rates and crimes rates, implying a crime-prevention effect of imprisonment. However, the magnitude of the estimate varied widely; from nil for a study that allowed for the possibility of diminishing returns (Liedka, Piehl, and Useem 2006), to an elasticity of -0.4 (Spelman 2000). (By an elasticity of -0.4, we mean that 10 percent growth in the imprisonment rate reduced the crime rate by 4 percent.) It is important to note that these studies are actually measuring a combination of deterrent and incapacitation effects. Thus, it is impossible to decipher the degree to which crime prevention is occurring because of a behavioral response by the population at large or because of the physical isolation of crime-prone people.

Donohue (2007) shows that the small elasticity estimates imply that the current imprisonment rate is too large, while the high-end estimates imply the rate is too small. He lists a variety of technical shortcomings of these studies that, in our view, make it impossible to distinguish among the widely varying effect size estimates. The most important is the degree to which the studies were successful in separating cause from effect. While imprisonment prevents crime through a combination of deterrence and incapacitation, crime also generates the prison population. This is an example of what is called the "simultaneity problem," whereby we want to ascertain the effect of one variable (the imprisonment rate) on another variable (the crime rate) in a circumstance where we know or suspect that reverse causation is also present, namely that the crime rate simultaneously affects the imprisonment rate. Thus, statistical isolation of the crime-prevention effect requires properly accounting for the effect of crime on imprisonment. The Levitt (1996) study is arguably the most successful in this regard. It uses court-ordered prison releases as an instrument for untangling the cause-and-effect relationship. However, even the Levitt analysis suffers from many of the technical limitations detailed by Donohue.

More fundamentally, this literature suffers from more than just technical short-comings that future research might strive to correct. It also suffers from important conceptual flaws that limit its usefulness in devising crime-control policy. Prison population is not a policy variable; rather, it is an outcome of sanction policies dictating who goes to prison and for how long, namely the certainty and severity of punishment. In all incentive-based theories of criminal behavior, the deterrence response to sanction threats is posed in terms of the certainty and severity of punishment, not in terms of the imprisonment rate. Therefore, to predict how changes in certainty and severity might affect the crime rate requires knowledge of the relationship of the crime rate to certainty and severity as separate entities, which is not provided by the literature that analyzes the relationship of the crime rate to the imprisonment rate. The studies are also conducted at too global a level. There are good reasons for predicting differences in the crime reduction effects of different types of sanctions (e.g., mandatory minimums for repeat offenders versus prison diversion programs for first-time offenders). Obvious sources of heterogeneity in offender response include factors such as prior contact with the criminal justice system, demographic characteristics, and the mechanism by which sanction threats are communicated to their intended audience.

Three studies nicely illustrate heterogeneity in the deterrence response to the threat of imprisonment: the Weisburd, Einat, and Kowalski (2008) study on the use of imprisonment to enforce fine payment finds a substantial deterrent effect; the Helland and Tabarrok (2007) analysis of the deterrent effect of California's third-strike provision finds only a modest deterrent effect; and the Lee and McCrary (2009) examination of the heightened threat of imprisonment that attends coming under the jurisdiction of the adult courts at the age of majority finds no deterrent effect.

Weisburd, Einat, and Kowalski (2008) report on a randomized field trial of alternative strategies for incentivizing the payment of court-ordered fines. The most salient finding involves the "miracle of the cells," namely, that the imminent threat of incarceration is a powerful incentive for paying delinquent fines. The miracle of the cells, we believe, provides a valuable vantage point for considering the oft repeated conclusion from the deterrence literature that the certainty rather the severity of punishment is the more powerful deterrent. Consistent with the "certainty principle," the common feature of treatment conditions involving incarceration was a high certainty of imprisonment for failure to pay the fine. However, that Weisburd and colleagues label the response the "miracle of the cells" and not the "miracle of certainty" is telling. Their choice of label is a reminder that certainty must result in a distasteful consequence, namely incarceration in this experiment, in order for it to be a deterrent. The consequences need not be draconian, just sufficiently costly to deter proscribed behavior.

Helland and Tabarrok (2007) examine whether California's "Three Strikes and You're Out" law deters offending among individuals previously convicted of strike-eligible offenses. The future offending of individuals convicted of two previous strikeable offenses was compared with that of individuals who had been convicted of only one strikeable offense but who, in addition, had been tried for a second strikeable offense but were ultimately convicted of a nonstrikeable offense. The study demonstrates that these two groups of individuals were comparable on many characteristics such as age, race, and time in prison. Even so, it finds that arrest rates were about 20 percent lower for the group with convictions for two strikeable offenses. The authors attribute this reduction to the greatly enhanced sentence that would have accompanied conviction for a third strikeable offense.

For most crimes, the certainty and severity of punishment increases discontinuously upon reaching the age of majority, when jurisdiction for criminal wrongdoing shifts from the juvenile to the adult court. In an extraordinarily careful analysis of individual-level crime histories from Florida, Lee and McCrary (2009) attempt to identify a discontinuous decline in the hazard of offending at age eighteen, the age of majority in Florida. Their point estimate of the discontinuous change is negative as predicted, but minute in magnitude and not even remotely close to achieving statistical significance.

In combination, these three studies nicely illustrate that the deterrent effect of the threat of punishment is context specific and that debates about whether deterrence works are ill posed. Instead the discussion should be in terms of whether the specific sanction deters, and if it does, whether the benefits of crime reduction are sufficient to justify the costs of imposing the sanction. To illustrate, while Helland and Tabarrok (2007) conclude that the third-strike effect in California is a deterrent, they also conclude, based on a cost-benefit analysis, that the crime-saving benefits are likely far smaller than the increased costs of incarceration. The Helland and Taborrok study is an exemplar of the approach that should be taken in evaluating different sanctioning regimes.

B. Capital Punishment and Crime

Like research on the deterrent effect of imprisonment, research on the deterrent effect of capital punishment has come in waves. The latest wave of research on capital punishment and deterrence is based on the data that have become available following the reintroduction of the death penalty in different states beginning in 1976, after a four-year moratorium on death sentences and executions resulting from the U.S. Supreme Court decision in *Furman v. Georgia* (408 U.S. 238 [1972]). Not all states reintroduced capital punishment at the same time when the decision in *Gregg v. Georgia* (428 U.S. 153 [1976]) lifted the constitutional barrier; they acted at different times to restore capital punishment and used it at widely varying rates. The resulting natural variation in execution rates across states and over time forms the empirical basis for the new wave of studies.

This new body of work has failed to produce a consensus on whether deterrent effects are present. Dezhbakhsh, Rubin, and Shepherd (2003), Dezhbakhsh and Shepherd (2006) and Mocan and Gittings (2003) find strong deterrent effects from the death penalty. Yet their claims have been challenged by Donohue and Wolfers (2005), Berk (2005), Fagan (2006), and Cohen-Cole et al. (2009), who argue that the evidence that has been adduced in favor of strong deterrent effects is fragile, in that they may be reversed by small changes in model specification. Other studies have argued that more substantive differences in the formulation of the deterrence mechanism lead to different results. Katz, Levitt, and Shustorovich (2003), focusing on the fact that executions are relatively infrequent, argue that prison mortality rates represent a deterrent to serious crime, whereas capital punishment does not. Other studies find that deterrent effects are heterogeneous, so that important properties are masked by imposing a single measure on the statistical analysis. Shepherd (2005) draws mixed conclusions, suggesting that capital punishment will raise murder rates when the number of executions is small, producing what she calls a "brutalization effect." However, the brutalization effect is overcome by the deterrent effect when the number of executions exceeds some empirically identified threshold. Hjalmarsson (2009) explores whether executions have short-run local deterrent effects by studying city-level, high-frequency (daily) data. Focusing on Texas, she finds little evidence of deterrence.

III. The Deterrent Effect of Police

The police may prevent crime through many possible mechanisms. Apprehension of active offenders is a necessary first step for their conviction and punishment. If the sanction involves imprisonment, crime may be prevented by the incapacitation of the apprehended offender. The apprehension of active offenders may, also, deter would-be criminals by increasing their perception of the risk of apprehension and thereby the certainty of punishment. Many police tactics such as rapid response to calls for service at crime scenes or post-crime investigation are intended not only to capture the offender but to deter others by projecting a tangible threat of apprehension. Police may, however, deter without actually apprehending criminals because their very presence projects a threat of apprehension if a crime were to be committed. Indeed, some of the most compelling evidence of deterrence involve instances where there is complete or near complete collapse of police presence. In September 1944, German soldiers occupying Denmark arrested the entire Danish police force. According to an account by Andeneas (1974), crime rates rose immediately but not uniformly. The frequency of street crimes like robbery, whose control depends heavily upon visible police presence, rose sharply. By contrast, crimes like fraud were less affected. See Sherman and Eck (2002) for other examples of crime increases following a collapse of police presence.

The Andenaes anecdote illustrates two important points. First, sanction threats (or the absence thereof) may not uniformly affect all types of crime and more generally all types of people. Second, it draws attention to the difference between absolute and marginal deterrence. Absolute deterrence refers to the difference in the crime rate between the status quo level of sanction threat and a complete (or near) absence of sanction threat. The Andenaes anecdote is a compelling demonstration that the absolute deterrent effect is large. However, from a policy perspective, the important question is whether, on the margin, crime deterrence can be affected by incrementally manipulating sanction threats.

Research on the marginal deterrent effect of police has evolved in two distinct literatures. One has focused on the deterrent effect of the aggregate police presence measured, for example, by the relationship between police per capita and crime rates. The other has focused on the crime prevention effectiveness of different strategies for deploying police. We review these two literatures separately.

A. Aggregate Police Presence and Crime

Studies of police hiring and crime rates have been plagued by a number of impediments to causal inference. Among these are cross-jurisdictional differences in the recording of crime, feedback effects from crime rates to police hiring, the confounding of deterrence with incapacitation, and aggregation of police manpower effects across heterogeneous units, among others (see Nagin 1978, 1998). Yet the challenge that has received the most attention in empirical applications is the simultaneity problem, or the feedback from crime rates to police hiring. Simultaneity describes a situation in which two variables mutually influence one another in such a way that it is impossible, in the absence of exogenous variation or restrictive assumptions, to untangle the unique influence of one variable on the other in a cross section.

Two studies of police manpower by Marvell and Moody (1996) and Levitt (1997) are notable for their identification strategies as well as for the consistency of their findings. The Marvell and Moody (1996) study is based on an analysis of two panel datasets, one composed of forty-nine states for the years 1968–93 and the other of fifty-six large cities for the years 1971–92. To untangle the causality problem they regress the current crime rate on lags of the crime rate as well as lags of police manpower. If the lagged police measures are jointly significant, they are said to "Granger cause" crime. The strongest evidence for an effect of police hiring on total crime rates comes from the city-level analysis, with an estimated elasticity of -0.3, meaning that a 10 percent growth in police manpower produces a 3 percent decline in the crime rate the following year. In the spirit of Marvell and Moody's multiple time series analysis, Corman and Mocan (2000) conduct tests of Granger causality using a single, high-frequency (monthly) time series of crime in New

York City (January 1970–December 1996). They find that the number of police officers is negatively correlated with some crimes (robbery, burglary) but not with others. In addition, the number of felony arrests is a robust predictor of several kinds of crime (murder, robbery, burglary, vehicle theft). They conclude that policymakers can deter serious crimes by adding more police officers, but also by allocating existing police resources to aggressive felony enforcement (see also Corman and Mocan 2005).

Levitt (1997) performs an instrumental variables (IV) analysis from a panel of fifty-nine large cities for the years 1970–92. Reasoning that political incumbents have incentives to devote resources to increasing the size of the police force in anticipation of upcoming elections, he uses election cycles to help untangle the cause-effect relationship between crime rates and police manpower. Levitt's model produces elasticities of about -1.0 for the violent crime rate and -0.3 for the property crime rate (but see McCrary 2002 for correction of a technical problem in Levitt's analysis, as well as a reply and new analysis by Levitt 2002). Following Levitt's use of the electoral cycle as an instrument for the number of sworn police officers, other studies have employed the number of firefighters and civil service workers (Levitt 2002), as well as federal subsidies disbursed through the Office of Community Oriented Policing Services for the hiring of new police officers (Evans and Owens 2007). These studies reach conclusions that are very similar to Levitt; for example, the elasticities estimated by Evans and Owens (2007) are -0.99 for violent crime and -0.26 for property crime.

In recent years, a number of more targeted tests of the police-crime relationship have appeared. These studies are important because they provide a more transparent test of the effect of police presence on crime and are less subject to biases that may attend analyzing data across a highly heterogeneous set of cities. Several of these targeted studies investigate the effect on the crime rate of reductions in police presence and productivity as a result of massive budget cuts or lawsuits following racial profiling scandals. Such studies have examined the Cincinnati Police Department (Shi 2009), the New Jersey State Police (Heaton 2010), and the Oregon State Police (DeAngelo and Hansen 2008). Each of these studies concludes that increases (or decreases) in police presence and activity substantially decrease (or increase) crime. By way of example, Shi (2009) studies the fallout from an incident in Cincinnati in which a white police officer shot and killed an unarmed African American suspect. The incident was followed by three days of rioting, heavy media attention, the filing of a class action lawsuit, a federal civil rights investigation, and the indictment of the officer in question. These events created an unofficial incentive for officers from the Cincinnati Police Department to curtail their use of arrest for misdemeanor crimes, especially in communities with higher proportional representation of African Americans out of concern for allegations of racial profiling. Shi demonstrates measurable declines in police productivity in the aftermath of the riot and also documents a substantial increase in criminal activity. The estimated elasticities of crime to policing based on her approach were -0.5 for violent crime and -0.3 for property crime.

The ongoing threat of terrorism has also provided a number of unique opportunities to study the effect of police resource allocation in cities around the world, including the District of Columbia (Klick and Tabarrok 2005), Buenos Aires (Di Tella and Schargrodsky 2004), Stockholm (Poutvaara and Priks 2006), and London (Draca, Machin, and Witt 2008). The Klick and Tabarrok (2005) study examines the effect on crime of the color-coded alert system devised by the U.S. Department of Homeland Security in the aftermath of the September 11, 2001, terrorist attack to denote the terrorism threat level. Its purpose was to signal federal, state, and local law enforcement agencies to occasions when it might be prudent to divert resources to sensitive locations. Klick and Tabarrok (2005) use daily police reports of crime (collected by the District's Metropolitan Police Department) for the period March 2002–July 2003, during which time the terrorism alert level rose from "elevated" (yellow) to "high" (orange) and back down to "elevated" on four occasions. During high alerts, anecdotal evidence suggested that police presence increased by 50 percent. Their estimate of the elasticity of total crime to changes in police presence as the alert level rose and fell was -0.3.

To summarize, aggregate studies of police presence conducted since the mid-1990s consistently find that putting more police officers on the street—either by hiring new officers or by allocating existing officers in ways that put them on the street in larger numbers or for longer periods of time—has a substantial deterrent effect on serious crime. There is also consistency with respect to the size of the effect. Most estimates reveal that a 10 percent increase in police presence yields a reduction in total crime in the neighborhood of 3 percent. Yet these police manpower studies speak only to the number and allocation of police officers and not to what police officers actually do on the street beyond making arrests. The next section reviews recent evaluations of deployment strategies used by police departments in order to control crime.

B. Police Deployment and Crime

Much research has examined the crime prevention effectiveness of alternative strategies for deploying police resources. This research has largely been conducted by criminologists and sociologists. Among this group of researchers, the preferred research designs are quasi-experiments involving before-and-after studies of the effect of targeted interventions as well as true randomized experiments. The discussion that follows draws heavily upon two excellent reviews of this research by Weisburd and Eck (2004) and Braga (2008). Here, we draw the theoretical link between police deployment, and the certainty and severity of punishment. For the most part, deployment strategies affect the certainty of punishment through its impact on the probability of apprehension. There are, however, notable examples where severity may also be affected.

One way to increase apprehension risk is to mobilize police in a fashion that increases the probability that an offender is arrested after committing a crime.

Strong evidence of a deterrent as opposed to an incapacitation effect resulting from the apprehension of criminals is limited. Studies of the effect of rapid response to calls for service (Kansas City Police Department 1977; Spelman and Brown 1981) find no evidence of a crime prevention effect, but this may be because most calls for service occur well after the crime event with the result that the perpetrator has fled the scene. Thus, it is doubtful that rapid response materially affects apprehension risk. Similarly, because most arrests result from the presence of witnesses or physical evidence, improved investigations are not likely to yield material deterrent effects because, again, apprehension risk is not likely to be affected.

A series of randomized experiments were conducted to test the deterrent effect of mandatory arrest for domestic violence. The initial experiment conducted in Minneapolis by Sherman and Berk (1984) found that mandatory arrest was effective in reducing domestic violence reoffending. Findings from follow-up replication studies (as part of the Spouse Assault Replication Program, or SARP) were inconsistent. Experiments in two cities found a deterrent effect, but no such effect was found in three other cities (Maxwell, Garner, and Fagan 2002). Berk et al. (1992) found that the response to arrest in the SARP data depended upon social background. Higher-status individuals seemed to be deterred by arrest, but the assaultive behavior of lower-status individuals seemed to be aggravated. The heterogeneity in response is important because it illustrates a more general point—the response to sanction threats need not be uniform in the population. Sherman and Smith (1992) propose a theory to explain the status-based heterogeneity in response to mandatory arrest.

The second source of deterrence from police activities involves averting crime in the first place. In this circumstance, there is no apprehension because there was no offense. In our view this is the primary source of deterrence from the presence of police. If an occupied police car is parked outside a liquor store, a would-be robber of the store will likely be deterred because apprehension is all but certain. Thus, measures of apprehension risk based only on enforcement actions and crimes that actually occur, such as arrests per reported crime, are seriously incomplete because such measures do not capture the apprehension risk that attends criminal opportunities, which were not acted upon by potential offenders, because the risk was deemed too high.

Two examples of police deployment strategies that have been shown to be effective in averting crime in the first place are "hot spots" policing and problem-oriented policing. Weisburd and Eck (2004) propose a two-dimensional taxonomy of policing strategies. One dimension is "Level of Focus" and the other is "Diversity of Focus." Level of focus represents the degree to which police activities are targeted. Targeting can occur in variety of ways, but Weisburd and Eck give special attention to policing strategies, which target police resources in small geographic areas (e.g., blocks or specific addresses) that have very high levels of criminal activity, so-called crime hot spots.

The idea of hot spots policing stems from a striking empirical regularity uncovered by Sherman and colleagues. Sherman, Gartin, and Buerger (1989) found that only 3 percent of addresses and intersections ("places," as they were called) in Minneapolis produced 50 percent of all calls to the police. Weisburd and Green (1995) found that 20 percent of all disorder crime and 14 percent of crimes against persons in Jersey City, New Jersey, arose from fifty-six drug-related crime hot spots. Fifteen years later in a study in Seattle, Washington, Weisburd et al. (2004) report that between 4 and 5 percent of street segments in the city accounted for 50 percent of crime incidents for each year over a fourteen-year period. Other more recent studies finding comparable crime concentrations include Brantingham and Brantingham (1999), Eck, Gersh, and Taylor (2000), and Roncek (2000). Just as in the liquor store example, the rationale for concentrating police in crime hot spots is to create a prohibitively high risk of apprehension and thereby deter crime at the hot spot in the first place.

The first test of the efficacy of concentrating police resources on crime hot spots was conducted by Sherman and Weisburd (1995). In this randomized experiment, hot spots in the experimental group were subjected to, on average, a doubling of police patrol intensity compared to hot spots in the control group. Declines in total crime calls ranged from 6 to 13 percent. In another randomized experiment, Weisburd and Green (1995) found that hot spots policing was similarly effective in suppressing drug markets.

Braga's (2008) informative review of hot spots policing summarizes the findings from nine experimental or quasi-experimental evaluations. The studies were conducted in five large U.S. cities and one Australian suburb. Crime-incident reports and citizen calls for service were used to evaluate impacts in and around the geographic area of the crime hot spot. The targets of the police actions varied. Some hot spots were generally high-crime locations whereas others were characterized by specific crime problems like drug trafficking. All but two of the studies found evidence of significant reductions in crime. Further, no evidence was found of material crime displacement to immediately surrounding locations. On the contrary, some studies found evidence of crime reductions, not increases, in the surrounding locations—a "diffusion of crime-control benefits" to nontargeted locales. We also note that the findings from the previously described econometric studies of focused police actions, for example in response to terror alert level, buttress the conclusion from the hot spots literature that the strategic targeting of police resources can be very effective in reducing crime.

The second dimension of the Weisburd and Eck taxonomy is diversity of approaches. This dimension concerns the variety of approaches that police use to impact public safety. Low diversity is associated with reliance on time-honored law enforcement strategies for affecting the threat of apprehension, for example, by dramatically increasing police presence. High diversity involves expanding beyond conventional practice to prevent crime. One example of a high-diversity approach is problem-oriented policing. Problem-oriented policy comes in so many different forms that it is regrettably hard to define.

One of the most visible examples of problem-oriented policing is Boston's Operation Ceasefire (Kennedy et al. 2001). The objective of the collaborative operation was to prevent inter-gang gun violence using two deterrence-based strategies. One was to target enforcement against weapons traffickers who were supplying weapons to Boston's violent youth gangs. The second involved a more innovative use of deterrence. The youth gangs themselves were assembled (and reassembled) to send the message that the response to any instance of serious violence would be "pulling every lever" legally available to punish gang members collectively. This included a salient severity-related dimension—vigorous prosecution for unrelated, nonviolent crimes such as drug dealing. Thus, the aim of Operation Ceasefire was to deter violent crime by increasing the certainty and severity of punishment but only in targeted circumstances, namely, if the gang members were perpetrators of a violent crime. While there have been challenges as to whether the decline in violence that accompanied Operation Ceasefire was attributable to the program, we concur with the judgment of Cook and Ludwig (2006) that Ceasefire seemed to play a role. Just as importantly, Operation Ceasefire illustrates the potential for combining elements of certainty and severity enhancement to generate a targeted deterrent effect. Further evaluations of the efficacy of this strategy should be a high priority.

IV. SANCTION RISK PERCEPTIONS

Deterrence is, fundamentally, a process of information transmission intended to discourage law violation (Geerken and Gove 1975). It entails communicating to a collection of individuals the sanctions that will potentially ensue if they fail to conform to proscribed behavior. Discourse about deterrence theory therefore acknowledges that risk perceptions are an important intermediate link between sanctions and behavior (Waldo and Chiricos 1972). But in order for a sanction policy to influence behavior, individual perceptions of the certainty and severity of sanctions must have some grounding in reality. Indeed, Nagin (1998, 18) observes that "behavior is immune to policy manipulation" to the degree that there is no link between policy and perceptions.

There are three distinct research traditions that examine the interrelationship between criminal sanctions, risk perceptions, and criminal behavior (referred to as studies of the contextual effect of sanctions, studies of the deterrent effect of risk perceptions, and studies of the experiential effect of behavior). Each is described in more detail.

A. The Contextual Effect of Sanctions on Risk Perceptions

One major research tradition in the study of perceptual deterrence entails estimating the degree of correspondence between area-level measures (usually the county) of criminal punishment and individual perceptions of sanction risk. This interest follows from studies that have identified a modest, inverse correlation between aggregate sanctions and individual delinquent and criminal behavior (Viscusi 1986; Mocan and Rees 2005). If these correlations reflect perceptual deterrence, at least in part, there should be a positive correlation between aggregate sanctions and individual perceptions of sanction risk—a contextual effect of sanctions on risk perceptions.

Recent studies of the contextual effects of sanctions on risk perceptions have revealed a generally weak and oftentimes negligible correlation. For example, Kleck et al. (2005) conducted a telephone survey of adults residing in fifty-four large urban counties, inquiring about estimates of the certainty, severity, and celerity of punishment pertaining to a variety of criminal offenses (homicide, robbery, burglary, aggravated assault). Their measures of actual and perceived punishments were generally uncorrelated. Lochner (2007) reports, in a nationally representative sample of youth, a positive and significant correlation between the county arrest clearance rate for auto theft and young males' estimates of the likelihood that they would be arrested if they stole a car. The correlation, however, did not withstand inclusion of basic demographic (age, race/ethnicity) and contextual (metropolitan area residence) control variables. MacCoun et al. (2009) use data from a nationally representative sample of adults to study the relationship between prevailing state punishments and individual perceptions of the maximum penalty for first-time marijuana possession. Residents of states that decriminalized marijuana possession, compared to states in which marijuana possession was still criminalized, did indeed report more lenient sanctions for violation, but the actual differences were surprisingly modest in substantive terms. Moreover, almost one-third of the sample reported not knowing the maximum penalty for marijuana possession.

The recent research on perception formation that considers the contextual effects of sanctions has therefore yielded only modest correlations, at best, between area-level punishments and individual risk perceptions. At first glance, these results are discouraging for perceptual deterrence. If people are only vaguely aware of the criminal punishments in their state or county, then the deterrence rationale of punishment is seriously undermined. However, there are a number of important limitations in this research relating to measurement, sampling, and contingencies.

First, articulations of risk perceptions in survey instruments are likely subject to a large degree of measurement error that will attenuate the strength of the correlation between perceptions and actual punishment risk. Measurement error may be large if people form punishment judgments in a fairly abstract way. Rather than forming crime-specific estimates of the certainty, severity, and celerity of punishment, the average individual (but not necessarily the average offender) might instead rely on an omnibus assessment or some generalized conception of punishment risk. Furthermore, individual risk perceptions are subject to well-known distortions and biases (see Pogarsky, forthcoming, for a review and discussion of research on crime decision-making). Considered as a whole, these observations imply that researchers should place a premium on the refinement and validation of measures of sanction risk perceptions.

Second, a sizable proportion of the population is not "in the market" for law-violating behavior—they are committed law abiders. For committed law abiders, there is no reason to invest effort in forming accurate assessments of sanction risk because criminal activity is not an option that they consider. By the same token, another portion of the population is probably not "in the market" for law-abiding behavior—they are committed law violators. It might only be individuals in the middle of the criminal propensity continuum that are truly "deterrable" (Pogarsky 2002). It is these individuals who have an incentive to invest in forming accurate sanction risk perceptions. Population-based studies are likely to be composed largely of committed law abiders, especially when serious crimes are under consideration. Consequently the relationship between sanctions and perceptions in these studies will be modest at best.

Third, there are likely contingencies for perception formation whereby contextual factors moderate the strength of the correlation between sanctions and perceptions. A study by Apel, Pogarsky, and Bates (2009) considers this possibility in the school context. Using a nationally representative school-based survey, they find that the correlation between the prevailing sanctions in a school and student perceptions of rule strictness is strongest in schools that are the smallest and the least disordered. In the largest and most disordered schools, by contrast, student perceptions are largely unrelated to changes in school sanctions. They conclude that large school size and disorder are contextual contingencies that impede the flow of information from school authorities to students and therefore dilute deterrence messages. Their findings might help to explain the weak correlation between sanctions measured at a highly aggregated level, such as the county or state, and individual-level risk perceptions.

B. The Deterrent Effect of Risk Perceptions on Behavior

Research on the deterrent effects of perceptions on behavior has proceeded along three distinctive methodological lines: cross-sectional surveys, panel studies, and vignette research. Cross-sectional surveys inquire about individuals' current perceptions of sanction risks (certainty, severity) and either their behavior within some reference period prior to the interview or their *behavioral intentions* to commit crime in the future. Cross-sectional surveys consistently show that risk perceptions are inversely correlated with both measures of offending behavior (see Paternoster 1987). Panel studies are designed to untangle temporal priority for the perceptions-behavior link that vexes cross-sectional research by relating perceptions in period t to actual behavior in period $t + 1$ (as opposed to intended future behavior in period t). Findings from panel studies tend to show that the actual perceptions-behavior correlation is smaller than that estimated from cross-sectional surveys and often diminishes to nonsignificance with the inclusion of control variables (see Paternoster 1987). But there are notable exceptions. A recent example of this approach is provided by Wright et al. (2004), who find long-term perceptual deterrent effects on behavior in a cohort of New Zealand youth. They find that the perceived risk of getting caught for criminal behavior in late adolescence is inversely and significantly correlated with criminal behavior at age twenty-six.

Vignette research provides respondents with a detailed, hypothetical crime scenario and then asks them about their perceptions of the certainty and severity of punishment for the crime, as well as their own behavior if they found themselves in the same situation. A unique feature of this design is that situational characteristics can be experimentally manipulated in order to study how subjects respond to a variety of incentives, disincentives, and opportunity structures. A growing number of vignette designs in perceptual deterrence research have been employed in recent years (Nagin and Pogarsky 2001; Piquero and Pogarsky 2002; Pogarsky 2002, 2004; Pogarsky and Piquero 2003). To consider one example in detail, Nagin and Pogarsky (2001) issued to university students a scenario describing an incident of drunk driving in which they experimentally manipulated the severity and celerity of punishment. Respondents given a scenario with a longer length of license suspension upon conviction for drunk driving (higher severity) reported a significantly lower likelihood of driving drunk, although this effect appeared to be diminished among individuals who were more present-oriented or impulsive (i.e., those with a higher "discount rate"). However, a shorter delay between conviction and the suspension period (higher celerity) was unrelated to drunk driving intentions. When the authors inquired about subjects' own estimated likelihood of being apprehended and convicted for drunk driving (a measure of certainty) under the conditions described in the scenario, they found that it was a robust predictor of intentions to drive drunk.

Research on the perceptual deterrent effects of punishment has produced two other sets of findings that are important to understanding the sources of deterrence. The first concerns the comparative deterrent effects of the certainty and severity of punishment. Like the literature on the preventive effects of police and imprisonment, the perceptual deterrence literature finds more consistent evidence of the certainty of punishment as a crime deterrent relative to the severity of punishment. The second concerns the role of informal sanctions in the deterrence process. Zimring and Hawkins (1973, 174) observe that formal punishment may best deter when it sets off informal sanctions: "Official actions can set off societal reactions that may provide potential offenders with more reason to avoid conviction than the officially imposed unpleasantness of punishment." Andenaes (1974) makes the same argument. Much perceptual deterrence confirms this linkage. This research has consistently found that individuals who report higher stakes in conventionality are more strongly deterred by their perceived risk of punishment for law breaking.

A salient example of research supporting the "certainty principle" as well as untangling the link between formal and informal sanctions concerns tax evasion. In the United States, civil enforcement actions by tax authorities are a private matter unless the taxpayer appeals the action. Because tax authorities are scrupulous about maintaining the confidentially of tax return information, for civil enforcement actions noncompliers are gambling only with their money and not their personal reputations. In Klepper and Nagin (1989), a sample of generally middle-class adults were posed a series of tax noncompliance scenarios. The scenarios laid out the essential features of a tax report—income from different sources, number of exemptions, and various deductions. They then experimentally varied the amount and type of noncompliance (e.g., overstating charitable deductions or understating business income) across tax-return line items and found that a majority of respondents reported a non-zero probability of taking advantage of the noncompliance opportunity described in the scenario. Plainly, the respondents were generally willing to consider tax noncompliance when only their money was at risk. They also seemed to be calculating: the attractiveness of the tax noncompliance gamble was inversely related to the perceived risk of civil enforcement.

The one exception to the rule of confidentially of enforcement interventions is criminal prosecution. As with all criminal cases, criminal prosecutions for tax evasion are a matter of public record. Here Klepper and Nagin found evidence of a different decision calculus—seemingly all that was necessary to deter evasion was the perception of a non-zero chance of criminal prosecution. Stated differently, if the evasion gamble also involved putting reputation and community standing at risk, the middle-class respondents were seemingly unwilling to consider taking the noncompliance gamble.

This finding helps explain why the certainty of punishment may be a greater deterrent than severity. If the social and economic costs of punishment are strictly proportional to the punishment received, for example, if the cost to the individual of a two-year prison term is twice that of a one-year sentence, certainty and severity will equally affect expected cost. This is because expected cost is simply the product of certainty, P, and severity, S. The value of the product, $P*S$, is equally affected by proportional changes in P or S. For example, the impact on expected cost of a 50-percent increase in P is the same as a 50 percent increase in S. The Klepper and Nagin study suggests that people do *not* perceive that costs are proportional to potential punishment. Instead they perceive that there is fixed cost associated with merely being convicted or even apprehended if it is in the public record.

While Klepper and Nagin (1989) did not pin down the specific sources of these costs, other research on the impact of a criminal record on access to the legal labor market suggests a very real basis for the fear of stigmatization. For example, Freeman (1995) estimates that a prison record depresses the probability of employment by 15–30 percent and Waldfogel (1994) estimates that conviction for fraud reduces income by as much as 40 percent. More recent studies reinforce these earlier findings. Western (2002) estimates the wage reduction effect of incarceration to be about 16 percent. He also finds that incarceration deflects individuals onto a flatter wage trajectory in which wage growth is slowed by 31 percent relative to comparably high-risk men who were not incarcerated. Pager (2003) reports that employers advertising entry-level job openings were less than half as likely to call back applicants who reported a criminal history (a felony cocaine trafficking conviction with eighteen months prison time). She concludes that "criminal records close doors in employment situations" (956).

C. The Experiential Effect of Behavior on Risk Perceptions

An early conclusion of perceptual deterrence researchers was that people's own experiences with crime and punishment were more salient determinants of their risk perceptions than external sources of information about sanction risk (Parker and Grasmick 1979). Perceptual deterrence research also found that those individuals who have experience as criminal offenders tended to have substantially lower risk perceptions and therefore *more accurate risk perceptions* compared to individuals who lack such experience (Scheider 2001; Lochner 2007; MacCoun et al. 2009).

This raises the question of whether offenders' lower risk perceptions might be a consequence of their criminal behavior as well as a cause. Panel studies of the deterrent effect of perceptions are well positioned to speak to this question. The first wave of such studies indicated that there is a pronounced experiential effect of delinquent or criminal behavior on risk perceptions (e.g., Paternoster et al. 1982; Saltzman et al. 1982). Furthermore, among active offenders, the experience of being sanctioned (and sanctioned more severely) itself contributes to an increase in risk perceptions (Apospori and Alpert 1993). There are also compelling reasons to believe that individuals change their risk perceptions, in part, on the basis of the crime and punishment experiences of their friends and family members. Stafford and Warr (1993) refer to such effects as indirect or *vicarious* experiences (see also Paternoster and Piquero 1995).

Yet an equally important determinant of risk perceptions in addition to personal and vicarious *punishment experience*, according to Stafford and Warr (1993), is personal and vicarious *punishment avoidance*. There is evidence from a number of studies that, other things equal, a higher level of unsanctioned offending lowers one's perceptions of formal sanction risk (e.g., Bridges and Stone 1986; Piliavin et al.

1986; Horney and Marshall 1992; Paternoster and Piquero 1995; Piquero and Paternoster 1998). For example, in the study by Horney and Marshall (1992), offenders with higher "arrest ratios" (i.e., more reported arrests per reported offenses) had higher perceptions of the risk of detection. Stated differently, offenders with more unsanctioned offenses—that is, more successful criminal careers, with success defined as avoidance of arrest—had lower and more realistic risk perceptions.

These findings on the experiential effects of punishment and behavior on risk perceptions have led to an emerging, second-generation literature concerned with the development and testing of formal models of within-individual change in risk perceptions as a consequence of personal and vicarious experiences with, and avoidances of, arrest and punishment (Pogarsky and Piquero 2003; Pogarsky, Piquero, and Paternoster 2004; Pogarsky, Kim, and Paternoster 2005; Matsueda, Kreager, and Huizinga 2006; Lochner 2007; Hjalmarsson 2008; Anwar and Loughran 2009). Many of these studies appeal to a Bayesian model of learning. A Bayesian model of risk perceptions and criminal behavior begins with an individual's initial assessment of the likelihood of apprehension for criminal conduct. This is known as the *prior probability* of the risk of arrest (among other sanctions). The perceptual deterrence literature strongly suggests that the prior probability estimates of individuals without offending experience systematically and often substantially overstate the true risk of apprehension. Over time, the individual will accumulate personal or vicarious experiences, or both, as a successful or unsuccessful criminal offender. Note the parallel with Stafford and Warr's (1993) conceptualization of personal and vicarious punishment experience and punishment avoidance. The expectation is that the individual will then *update* his or her assessment of the risk of apprehension based on these experiences. The resulting *posterior probability* of the risk of arrest is a weighted sum of the individual's prior probability and the new information.

As an example of the Bayesian empirical approach, Hjalmarsson (2008) takes advantage of cross-state variation in the age of criminal majority and finds that individual perceptions of the risk of jail following an arrest (for auto theft) increase discontinuously when youth become adults in the eyes of the law. Lochner (2007) also finds evidence for updating of risk perceptions in the same dataset but with a different analytical focus. His results indicate that risk perceptions increase in response to arrest in the previous year, decrease in response to criminal behavior in the previous year (which, by controlling for arrest, signifies successful or unsanctioned offending), and decrease in response to sibling criminal behavior in the previous year as reported by siblings themselves, although the latter result is somewhat fragile.

Anwar and Loughran (2009) have significantly advanced empirical testing of the Bayesian updating model by looking for more fine-grained predictions of it. First, they observe that the effect of arrest within a reference window should depend on the number of crimes committed during that period. For example, being arrested once should matter more for an offender who committed only one crime as opposed to an offender who committed ten crimes. In the case of the former, the "experienced arrest certainty" (a term employed by Matsueda, Kreager, and Huizinga 2006) is 100 percent, while in the case of the latter it is only 10 percent. Second, Anwar and Loughran observe that the effect of arrest should diminish as individuals gain more offending experience. In other words, since posterior risk perceptions are a function of prior risk perceptions and new information in the form of their arrest ratio (what they refer to as a "signal"), experienced offenders should place more weight on their prior risk perceptions in the sense that they should "update less" in response to new information simply because they have more experience upon which to draw. Inexperienced offenders, by contrast, should "update more" to bring their risk perceptions closer in line with their actual punishment risk. Third, Anwar and Loughran observe that the effect of arrest should be crime-specific, or at least specific within a class of criminal behaviors. That is, an arrest for a violent crime should influence risk perceptions of violent crime only, and not risk perceptions of property crime. All three of these predictions were tested and supported from a sample of serious juvenile offenders.

V. Conclusions

This chapter examines the evidence on the general deterrent effect of sanctions. Evidence of a substantial effect is overwhelming. Just as important is the evidence that the effect is not uniform across different sanctions, different jurisdictions, different criminal offenses, and different groups of individuals. Both conclusions are important to devising crime-control policies that make effective use of sanctions to prevent crime. The first conclusion implies that a well-balanced portfolio of strategies and programs to prevent crime must necessarily include deterrence-based policies. The second conclusion implies that not all deterrence policies will be effective in reducing crime or, if effective, that the crime-reduction benefits may fall short of the social and economic costs of the sanction. In this regard our conclusions echo issues raised in two other recent reviews of the deterrence literature by Doob and Webster (2003) and Tonry (2008).

The evidence does not allow for bold pronouncements about policy, but it does support two generalizations with important policy implications. There is little evidence that increases in the severity of punishment yield large deterrent effects. By contrast, there is substantial evidence that the strategic deployment of police can deter crime (e.g., hot spots policing). In some circumstances, implementation of such strategies may require a greater resource commitment to policing, but in other circumstances the deterrent gains may well be achievable by the re-deployment of existing resources.

Future research on sanction effects will be most useful for policy evaluation if it moves closer to a medical model. Medical research is not organized around the theme of whether medical care cures diseases, the analog to the question of whether sanctions prevent crime. Instead, medical researchers address far more specific questions. Is a specific drug or procedure effective in treating a specific disease? Does the drug or procedure have adverse side effects for certain types of people? Furthermore, most such research is comparative—is the specific drug or procedure more effective than the status quo alternative? The analogous questions for deterrence research are whether and in what circumstances are sanction threats effective, and which threats are more effective and in what circumstances. There are many examples of "medical-model" type research in the policing literature on the effectiveness of alternative strategies for deploying police resources. Other examples outside of the policing literature include the Helland and Tabarrok (2007) study of the California's Three Strikes law and the Lee and McCrary (2009) study of the deterrent effect of aging out of the jurisdiction of the juvenile court and into the jurisdiction of the adult court.

Devising sensible deterrence-based crime policies also requires much better knowledge of the determinants of sanction risk perceptions. In recent years, greater attention has been devoted to analyzing the linkage of sanction risk perceptions to policy and to personal and vicarious experiences with the criminal justice enforcement apparatus. The Bayesian learning model provides a valuable theoretical structure for organizing and building on this research. Continued testing and extension of this model should be given a high priority in deterrence research.

REFERENCES

Andenaes, Johannes. 1974. *Punishment and Deterrence*. Ann Arbor, MI: University of Michigan Press.

Anwar, Shamena, and Thomas A. Loughran. 2009. "Testing a Bayesian Learning Theory of Deterrence among Serious Juvenile Offenders." Unpublished manuscript. School of Public Policy and Management, Carnegie Mellon University, Pittsburgh, PA.

Apel, Robert, Greg Pogarsky, and Leigh Bates. 2009. "The Sanctions-Perceptions Link in a Model of School-Based Deterrence." *Journal of Quantitative Criminology* 25:201–26.

Apospori, Eleni, and Geoffrey Alpert. 1993. "Research Note: The Role of Differential Experience with the Criminal Justice System in Changes in Perceptions of Severity of Legal Sanctions over Time." *Journal of Research in Crime and Delinquency* 39:184–94.

Beccaria, Cesare. 1963 [1764]. *On Crimes and Punishments*. Translated by Henry Paolucci. New York: Macmillan.

Bentham, Jeremy. 1988 [1789]. *The Principles of Morals and Legislation*. Amherst, NY: Prometheus Books.

Berk, Richard. 2005. "New Claims about Executions and General Deterrence: Déjà Vu All Over Again?" *Journal of Empirical Legal Studies* 2:303–30.

Berk, Richard A., Alec Campbell, Ruth Klap, and Bruce Western. 1992. "The Deterrent Effect of Arrest in Incidents of Domestic Violence: A Bayesian Analysis of Four Field Experiments." *American Sociological Review* 57:698–708.

Blumstein, Alfred, Jacqueline Cohen, and Daniel Nagin. 1978. *Deterrence and Incapacitation: Estimating the Effects of Criminal Sanctions on Crime Rates*. Washington, DC: National Academies Press.

Braga, Anthony A. 2008. *Police Enforcement Strategies to Prevent Crime in Hot Spot Areas*. Crime Prevention Research Review (No. 2). Washington, DC: Office of Community Oriented Policing, U.S. Department of Justice.

Braithwaite, John. 1989. *Crime, Shame, and Reintegration*. New York: Cambridge University Press.

Brantingham, Patricia L., and Paul J. Brantingham. 1999. "Theoretical Model of Crime Hot Spot Generation." *Studies on Crime and Crime Prevention* 8:7–26.

Bridges, George S., and James A. Stone. 1986. "Effects of Criminal Punishment on Perceived Threat of Punishment: Toward an Understanding of Specific Deterrence." *Journal of Research in Crime and Delinquency* 23:207–39.

Cohen-Cole, Ethan, Steven Durlauf, Jeffrey Fagan, and Daniel Nagin. 2009. "Model Uncertainty and the Deterrent Effect of Capital Punishment." *American Law and Economics Review*. 11:335–69.

Cook, Philip J. 1980. "Research in Criminal Deterrence: Laying the Groundwork for the Second Decade." In *Crime and Justice: An Annual Review of Research*, vol. 2, edited by Norval Morris and Michael Tonry. Chicago: University of Chicago Press.

———. 1986. "The Relationship between Victim Resistance and Injury in Noncommercial Robbery." *Journal of Legal Studies* 15:405–16.

Cook Philip J., and Jens Ludwig. 2006. "Aiming for Evidenced-Based Gun Policy." *Journal of Policy Analysis and Management* 25:691–735.

Corman, Hope, and H. Naci Mocan. 2000. "A Time-Series Analysis of Crime, Deterrence, and Drug Abuse in New York City." *American Economic Review* 90:584–604.

———. 2005. "Carrots, Sticks, and Broken Windows." *Journal of Law and Economics* 48:235–66.

DeAngelo, Greg, and Benjamin Hansen. 2008. "Life and Death in the Fast Lane: Police Enforcement and Roadway Safety." Unpublished manuscript. Department of Economics, University of California, Santa Barbara.

Dezhbakhsh, Hashem, Paul H. Rubin, and Joanna M. Shepherd. 2003. "Does Capital Punishment Have a Deterrent Effect? New Evidence from Postmoratorium Panel Data." *American Law and Economics Review* 5:344–76.

Dezhbakhsh, Hashem, and Joanna M. Shepherd, 2006. "The Deterrent Effect of Capital Punishment: Evidence from a 'Judicial Experiment.'" *Economic Inquiry* 44:512–35.

Di Tella, Rafael, and Ernesto Schargrodsky. 2004. "Do Police Reduce Crime? Estimates Using the Allocation of Police Forces after a Terrorist Attack." *American Economic Review* 94:115–33.

Donohue, John J., and Justin Wolfers. 2005. "Uses and Abuses of Empirical Evidence in the Death Penalty Debate." *Stanford Law Review* 58:791–846.

Donohue, John. 2007. "Assessing the Relative Benefits of Incarceration: The Overall Change over the Previous Decades and the Benefits on the Margin." Working paper. Yale Law School, New Haven, CT.

Doob, Anthony, and Cheryl Webster. 2003. "Sentence Severity and Crime: Accepting the Null Hypothesis." In *Crime and Justice: A Review of Research*, vol. 30, edited by Michael Tonry. Chicago: University of Chicago Press.

Draca, Mirko, Stephen Machin, and Robert Witt. 2008. *Panic on the Streets of London: Police, Crime and the July 2005 Terror Attacks.* IZA Discussion Paper no. 3410. Bonn, Germany: Institute for the Study of Labor.

Eck, John E., Jeffrey S. Gersh, and Charlene Taylor. 2000. "Finding Crime Hot Spots through Repeat Address Mapping." In *Analyzing Crime Patterns: Frontiers of Practice*, edited by Victor Goldsmith, Philip G. McGuire, John H. Mollenkopf, and Timothy A. Ross. Thousand Oaks, CA: Sage Publications.

Evans, William N., and Emily G. Owens. 2007. "COPS and Crime." *Journal of Public Economics* 91:181–201.

Fagan, Jeffrey. 2006. "Death and Deterrence Redux: Science, Law and Causal Reasoning on Capital Punishment." *Ohio State Journal of Criminal Law* 4:255–319.

Freeman, Richard B. 1995. "Why Do So Many Young American Men Commit Crimes and What Might We Do About It?" *Journal of Economic Perspectives* 10:25–42.

Geerken, Michael R., and Walter R. Gove. 1975. "Deterrence: Some Theoretical Considerations." *Law and Society Review* 9:497–513.

Gibbs, Jack P. 1975. *Crime, Punishment, and Deterrence.* New York: Elsevier.

Hjalmarsson, Randi. 2009. "Does Capital Punishment Have a 'Local' Deterrent Effect on Homicides?" *American Law and Economics Review* 11:310–34.

Hjalmarsson, Randi. 2008. "Crime and Expected Punishment: Changes in Perceptions at the Age of Criminal Majority." Unpublished manuscript. School of Public Policy, University of Maryland, College Park.

Heaton, Paul. 2010. "Understanding the Effects of Anti-Profiling Policies." *Journal of Law and Economics* 53:29–64.

Helland, Eric, and Alexander Tabarrok. 2007. "Does Three Strikes Deter? A Nonparametric Estimation." *Journal of Human Resources* 42:309–30.

Horney, Julie, and Ineke Haen Marshall. 1992. "Risk Perceptions among Serious Offenders: The Role of Crime and Punishment." *Criminology* 30:575–93.

Kansas City Police Department. 1977. *Response Time Analysis.* Kansas City, MO: Kansas City Police Department.

Katz, Lawrence, Steven D. Levitt, and Ellen Shustorovich. 2003. "Prison Conditions, Capital Punishment, and Deterrence." *American Law and Economics Review* 5:318–43.

Kennedy, David M., Anthony A. Braga, Anne Morrison Piehl, and Elin J. Waring. 2001. *Reducing Gun Violence: The Boston Gun Project's Operation Ceasefire.* Washington, DC: National Institute of Justice.

Kleck, Gary, Brion Sever, Spencer Li, and Marc Gertz. 2005. "The Missing Link in General Deterrence Research." *Criminology* 43:623–59.

Klepper, Steven, and Daniel Nagin. 1989. "The Deterrent Effect of Perceived Certainty and Severity Revisited." *Criminology* 27:721–46.

Klick, Jonathan, and Alexander Tabarrok. 2005. "Using Terror Alert Levels to Estimate the Effect of Police on Crime." *Journal of Law and Economics* 48:267–79.

Lee, David S., and Justin McCrary. 2009. "The Deterrent Effect of Prison: Dynamic Theory and Evidence." Unpublished manuscript. Industrial Relations Section, Princeton University, New Jersey.

Levitt, Steven D. 1996. "The Effect of Prison Population Size on Crime Rates: Evidence from Prison Overcrowding Legislation." *Quarterly Journal of Economics* 111:319–52.

———. 1997. "Using Electoral Cycles in Police Hiring to Estimate the Effect of Police on Crime." *American Economic Review* 87:270–90.

———. 2002. "Using Electoral Cycles in Police Hiring to Estimate the Effect of Police on Crime: Reply." *American Economic Review* 92:1244–50.

Liedka, Raymond V., Anne Morrison Piehl, and Bert Useem. 2006. "The Crime-Control Effect of Incarceration: Does Scale Matter?" *Criminology and Public Policy* 5:245–76.

Lochner, Lance, 2007. "Individual Perceptions of the Criminal Justice System." *American Economic Review* 97:444–60.

MacCoun, Robert, Rosalie Liccardo Pacula, Jamie Chriqui, Katherine Harris, and Peter Reuter. 2009. "Do Citizens Know Whether Their State Has Decriminalized Marijuana? Assessing the Perceptual Component of Deterrence Theory." *Review of Law and Economics* 5:347–71.

Marvell, Thomas, and Carlisle Moody. 1996. "Specification Problems, Police Levels, and Crime Rates." *Criminology* 34:609–46.

Matsueda, Ross L., Derek A. Kreager, and David Huizinga. 2006. "Deterring Delinquents: A Rational Choice Model of Theft and Violence." *American Sociological Review* 71:95–122.

Maxwell, Christopher D., Joel H. Garner, and Jeffrey A. Fagan. 2002. "The Preventive Effects of Arrest on Intimate Partner Violence: Research, Policy and Theory." *Criminology and Public Policy* 2:51–80.

McCrary, Justin. 2002. "Using Electoral Cycles in Police Hiring to Estimate the Effect of Police on Crime: Comment." *American Economic Review* 92:1236–43.

Mocan, H. Naci, and R. Kaj Gittings. 2003. "Getting Off Death Row: Commuted Sentences and the Deterrent Effect of Capital Punishment." *Journal of Law and Economics* 46:453–78.

Mocan, H. Naci, and Daniel I. Rees. 2005. "Economic Conditions, Deterrence and Juvenile Crime: Evidence from Micro Data." *American Law and Economics Review* 7:319–49.

Nagin, Daniel. 1978. "General Deterrence: A Review of the Empirical Evidence." In *Deterrence and Incapacitation: Estimating the Effects of Criminal Sanctions on Crime Rates*, edited by Alfred Blumstein, Jacqueline Cohen, and Daniel Nagin. Washington, DC: National Academies Press.

———. 1998. "Criminal Deterrence Research at the Outset of the Twenty-First Century." In *Crime and Justice: A Review of Research*, vol. 23, edited by Michael Tonry. Chicago: University of Chicago Press.

Nagin, Daniel S., Francis T. Cullen, and Cheryl Lero Jonson. 2009. "Imprisonment and Re-Offending." In *Crime and Justice: A Review of Research*, vol. 38, edited by Michael Tonry. Chicago: University of Chicago Press.

Nagin, Daniel S., and Greg Pogarsky. 2001. "Integrating Celerity, Impulsivity, and Extralegal Sanction Threats into a Model of General Deterrence: Theory and Evidence." *Criminology* 39:865–91.

Pager, Devah. 2003. "The Mark of a Criminal Record." *American Journal of Sociology* 108:937–75.

Parker, Jerry, and Harold G. Grasmick. 1979. "Linking Actual and Perceived Certainty of Punishment: An Exploratory Study of an Untested Proposition in Deterrence Theory." *Criminology* 17:366–79.

Paternoster, Raymond. 1987. "The Deterrent Effect of the Perceived Certainty and Severity of Punishment: A Review of the Evidence and Issues." *Justice Quarterly* 4:173–217.

Paternoster, Raymond, and Alex Piquero. 1995. "Reconceptualizing Deterrence: An Empirical Test of Personal and Vicarious Experiences." *Journal of Research in Crime and Delinquency* 32:251–86.

Paternoster, Raymond, Linda E. Saltzman, Theodore G. Chiricos, and Gordon P. Waldo. 1982. "Perceived Risk and Deterrence: Methodological Artifacts in Perceptual Deterrence Research." *Journal of Criminal Law and Criminology* 73:1238–58.

Piliavin, Irving, Craig Thornton, Rosemary Gartner, and Ross L. Matsueda. 1986. "Crime, Deterrence, and Rational Choice." *American Sociological Review* 51:101–19.

Piquero, Alex, and Raymond Paternoster. 1998. "An Application of Stafford and Warr's Reconceptualization of Deterrence to Drinking and Driving." *Journal of Research in Crime and Delinquency* 35:3–39.

Piquero, Alex R., and Greg Pogarsky. 2002. "Beyond Stafford and Warr's Reconceptualization of Deterrence: Personal and Vicarious Experiences, Impulsivity, and Offending Behavior." *Journal of Research in Crime and Delinquency* 39:153–86.

Pogarsky, Greg. 2002. "Identifying 'Deterrable' Offenders: Implications for Research on Deterrence." *Justice Quarterly* 19:431–52.

———. 2004. "Projected Offending and Contemporaneous Rule-Violation: Implications for Heterotypic Continuity." *Criminology* 42:111–35.

———. Forthcoming. "Deterrence and Decision-Making: Research Questions and Theoretical Refinements." In *Handbook on Crime and Deviance*, edited by Marvin D. Krohn, Alan J. Lizotte, and Gina P. Hall. New York: Springer.

Pogarsky, Greg, KiDeuk Kim, and Ray Paternoster. 2005. "Perceptual Change in the National Youth Survey: Lessons for Deterrence Theory and Offender Decision-Making." *Justice Quarterly* 22:1–29.

Pogarsky, Greg, and Alex R. Piquero. 2003. "Can Punishment Encourage Offending? Investigating the 'Resetting' Effect." *Journal of Research in Crime and Delinquency* 40:95–120.

Pogarsky, Greg, Alex R. Piquero, and Ray Paternoster. 2004. "Modeling Change in Perceptions about Sanction Threats: The Neglected Linkage in Deterrence Theory." *Journal of Quantitative Criminology* 20:343–69.

Poutvaara, Panu, and Mikael Priks. 2006. "Hooliganism in the Shadow of a Terrorist Attack and the Tsunami: Do Police Reduce Group Violence?" Unpublished manuscript. Department of Economics, University of Helsinki, Finland.

Roncek, Dennis W. 2000. "Schools and Crime." In *Analyzing Crime Patterns: Frontiers of Practice*, edited by Victor Goldsmith, Philip G. McGuire, John H. Mollenkopf, and Timothy A. Ross. Thousand Oaks, CA: Sage Publications.

Saltzman, Linda E., Raymond Paternoster, Gordon P. Waldo, and Theodore G. Chiricos. 1982. "Deterrent and Experiential Effects: The Problem of Causal Order in Perceptual Deterrence Research." *Journal of Research in Crime and Delinquency* 19:172–89.

Scheider, Matthew C. 2001. "Deterrence and the Base Rate Fallacy: An Examination of Perceived Certainty." *Justice Quarterly* 18:63–86.

Shepherd, Joanna M. 2005. "Deterrence versus Brutalization: Capital Punishment's Differing Impacts among States." *Michigan Law Review* 104:203–55.

Sherman, Lawrence and David Weisburd. 1995. "General Deterrent Effects of Police Patrol in Crime 'Hot Spots': A Randomized Study." *Justice Quarterly* 12:625–48.

Sherman, Lawrence W., and Richard A. Berk. 1984. "The Specific Deterrent Effects of Arrest for Domestic Assault." *American Sociological Review* 49:261–72.

Sherman, Lawrence W. and Douglas A. Smith. 1992. "Crime, Punishment, and Stake in Conformity: Legal and Informal Control of Domestic Violence." *American Sociological Review* 57:680–90.

Sherman, Lawrence W., and John E. Eck. 2002. "Policing for Prevention." In *Evidence Based Crime Prevention*, edited by Lawrence W. Sherman, David Farrington, and Brandon Welsh. New York: Routledge.

Sherman, Lawrence W., Patrick Gartin, and Michael Buerger, E. 1989. "Hot Spots of Predatory Crime: Routine Activities and the Criminology of Place." *Criminology* 27:27–55.

Shi, Lan. 2009. "The Limits of Oversight in Policing: Evidence from the 2001 Cincinnati Riot." *Journal of Public Economics* 93:99–113.

Spelman, William. 1994. *Criminal Incapacitation*. New York: Plenum Press.

———. 2000. "What Recent Studies Do (and Don't) Tell Us about Imprisonment and Crime." In *Crime and Justice: A Review of Research*, vol. 27, edited by Michael Tonry. Chicago: University of Chicago Press.

Spelman, William, and Dale K. Brown. 1981. *Calling the Police: A Replication of the Citizen Reporting Component of the Kansas City Response Time Analysis*. Washington, DC: Police Executive Research Forum.

Stafford, Mark C., and Mark Warr. 1993. "A Reconceptualization of General and Specific Deterrence." *Journal of Research in Crime and Delinquency* 30:123–35.

Tonry, Michael. 2008. "Learning from the Limitations of Deterrence Research." In *Crime and Justice: A Review of Research*, vol. 37, edited by Michael Tonry. Chicago: University of Chicago Press.

Viscusi, W. Kip. 1986. "The Risks and Rewards of Criminal Activity: A Comprehensive Test of Criminal Deterrence." *Journal of Labor Economics* 4:317–40.

Waldfogel, Joel. 1994. "The Effect of Criminal Conviction on Income and the Trust 'Reposed in the Workmen'." *Journal of Human Resources* 29:62–81.

Waldo, Gordon P., and Theodore G. Chiricos. 1972. "Perceived Penal Sanction and Self-Reported Criminality: A Neglected Approach to Deterrence Research." *Social Problems* 19:522–40.

Weisburd, David, Shawn Bushway, Cynthia Lum, and Su-Ming Yang. 2004. "Trajectories of Crime at Places: A Longitudinal Study of Street Segments in the City of Seattle." *Criminology* 42:283–320.

Weisburd, David, and John Eck. 2004. "What Can Police Do to Reduce Crime, Disorder, and Fear?" *Annals of the American Academy of Political and Social Science* 593:42–65.

Weisburd, David, Tomar Einat, and Matt Kowalski. 2008. "The Miracle of the Cells: An Experimental Study of Interventions to Increase Payment of Court-Ordered Financial Obligations." *Criminology and Public Policy* 7:9–36.

Weisburd, David and Lorraine Green. 1995. "Policing Drug Hot Spots: The Jersey City Drug Market Analysis Experiment." *Justice Quarterly* 12:711–35.

Western, Bruce. 2002. "The Impact of Incarceration on Wage Mobility and Inequality." *American Sociological Review* 67:526–46.

Wright, Bradley R.E., Avshalom Caspi, Terrie E. Moffitt, and Ray Paternoster. 2004. "Does the Perceived Risk of Punishment Deter Criminally Prone Individuals? Rational Choice, Self-Control, and Crime." *Journal of Research in Crime and Delinquency* 41:180–213.

Zimring, Franklin E., and Gordon J. Hawkins. 1973. *Deterrence: The Legal Threat in Crime Control.* Chicago: University of Chicago Press.

Zimring, Franklin E., and Gordon Hawkins. 1995. *Incapacitation: Penal Confinement and the Restraint of Crime.* New York: Oxford University Press.

CHAPTER 8

REPARATION AND RESTORATION

KATHLEEN DALY AND
GITANA PROIETTI-SCIFONI

REPARATION is a recent addition to domestic criminal justice in common law countries, although it has been a principle of domestic and international law for many centuries. *Restoration* is a recent addition to domestic criminal justice, international law, and transitional justice, having emerged as part of restorative justice in the 1980s. Both concepts are defined and used differently, depending on a writer's domestic or international law frame of reference and theoretical position. Empirical research on reparation and restoration ranges from case studies of countries' truth and reconciliation commissions to randomized field experiments with hundreds of people assigned to "treatment" and "control" groups.

Restoration emerged with advocacy, theory, and research associated with restorative justice, beginning in the mid 1980s. Today, restoration and restorative justice are largely confined to domestic criminal justice, although this is changing. For example, restoration now appears in international human rights instruments as an element of restitution,[1] and restorative justice is associated with truth commissions (Roche 2003; Brahm 2004), one mechanism for countries in transitions to democracy and peace. In general, reparation is more often associated with international human rights and humanitarian law and justice mechanisms in connection with war, internal conflict, and states' wrongful acts against other states or against individuals.

Reparation and restoration are *nouns*, but they have cognate meanings and uses *as adjectives*, when referencing types of justice, e.g., reparative and restorative justice.

This introduces more definitional variety and imprecision. Furthermore, whether used as nouns or adjectives, the terms are jumping across the literatures on domestic and international criminal law and justice. The terms are not only defined and used differently, they may be used to contrast different modes of justice.

A domestic example can be seen in Howard Zehr (1985 [2003]), whose early work identified "two lenses" of retributive and restorative justice, with the latter focused on "restoration, making things right . . . on repair of social injury" (80–81). Subsequent discussions of restorative justice in domestic settings refer not only to repairing harms, but also to "reparative" outcomes (see, e.g., Bottoms 2003; Dignan 2005) and to reparation, which Roche (2003, 27) says is regarded by many "as an alternative to punishment." In international settings, REDRESS, a nongovernment organization for torture victims, describes reparation as "refocusing on the restorative in addition to the retributive" (REDRESS, "What is Reparation," undated, 1). Here, the likely allusion is to mechanisms of "access to justice" *and* "reparation" (the latter including restitution, compensation, among other items), which together form remedies for violations of human rights and humanitarian law in the UN Resolution (2006). By contrast, Kiss (2005), who writes from an international law perspective, contrasts "two visions of transitional justice," retributive and restorative.

Anyone new to the field would be completely lost. Why are key terms being used in different ways? What do reparation, restoration, retributive justice, and restorative justice mean, exactly? What do they include and exclude? Dictionaries do not offer clear guidance, even the specialized ones in criminology and law. This chapter aims to bring a semblance of order to a new and popular field of knowledge that often appears to be chaotic and incoherent.

In section I, we give an overview of the varied meanings of reparation, restoration, and restorative justice, as they are applied in domestic and international contexts of law and criminal justice. We also consider why these terms have become popular in recent decades. Sections II and III explore the history, etymology, and uses of the terms reparation, restoration, and restorative justice, and their links to retribution, restitution, and punishment. Section IV reviews a selected set of practices in domestic and international criminal justice, and transitional justice. The practices associated with reparation and restoration came first, and theories of their social mechanisms came later. Section V describes a selected set of theories, with a focus on behavior, speech, and interaction; and the conclusion considers several key points.

We give attention in this chapter to developments in international law and criminal justice, but our focus is on domestic criminal justice. Here are the main points:

- Reparation, restoration, and restorative justice contain new roles for victims, offenders, and other participants; and new ideas about what should occur. These center on a more informal, dialogic process, which may provide openings for offender remorse and victim validation; active participation by lay actors; and sanctions that are linked in a meaningful way to offenses.

- Writers attribute different meanings to reparation and restoration, depending on their idiosyncratic frame of reference and affiliation with domestic or international criminal justice.
- Etymologically and historically, reparation and restoration developed from similar roots, but they evolved differently in international and domestic criminal justice.
- The international criminal justice field bifurcates "justice" and "reparation," with the former focused on standard modes of adjudicating and punishing offenders, and the latter, on modes of redress for victims, typically as collectivities. Reparation is an umbrella term that includes restitution, compensation, rehabilitation, satisfaction, and guarantees of nonrepetition.
- The domestic criminal justice field aims to supplement, infuse, or transform conventional criminal justice with ideals and practices of restoration, reparation, and restorative justice. It does not separate "justice" from "reparation" or "restoration."
- Within international criminal justice, there is a selective, often caricatured, incorporation of ideas about restorative justice.
- Within domestic criminal justice, reparation and restoration are defined and used differently, as are associated terms of restitution and compensation.
- Within domestic criminal justice, there is confusion and debate over the relationship of retribution to restoration and restorative justice, and the relationship of punishment to restorative justice.
- Restorative justice is a contested concept, with different political agendas; it can be misused to refer to any response that involves a community-based penalty; and it has increasingly become an idea without boundaries or limits. The restorative justice field is dynamic, evolving, and extraordinarily varied.

I. Meanings and Popularity

Analysts of restorative justice, international criminal justice, and transitional justice say there is a lack of consensus on, common misperceptions about, and contested uses of key concepts (see, e.g., Zehr and Toews 2005, chs. 1–3; van Ness and Strong 2006, 22–23; Bradley 2006, 2–3). In part, this has occurred because restorative justice rose to immense global popularity, and in part, because key terms are moving across domestic and international contexts of law and criminal justice.

A. No Settled Definitions

The problem of definition is most acutely felt by those working within the restorative justice field.[2] By comparison, international law and transitional justice scholars may selectively draw from the literature a particular meaning of restorative justice that suits their analysis. These selected meanings may be caricatured and in error, and this introduces further problems in defining terms.

Five major reasons can be given for a lack of a settled definition of restorative justice and its key terms. First, as van Ness and Strong (2006, 23, 33–35) note, restorative justice "has developed in a piecemeal fashion," with significant temporal and national variation across the world and with distinct "stages of growth." Early practices included victim-offender reconciliation, community justice, and mediation and reparation projects in Canada, the United States, Norway, Finland, and England in the mid-1970s to mid-1980s. In the 1990s significant growth and expansion occurred, with widely varying models and programs increasingly branded as "restorative justice," both within and outside the criminal justice system. In 2002 the United Nations Economic and Social Council endorsed the use of restorative justice in criminal matters, encouraging member states to reform their domestic criminal justice systems. In that Resolution (2002), the definitions of "restorative process" and "restorative outcome" include activities at all stages of the criminal justice process (see van Ness and Strong 2006, 207–13). A significant limitation, which advocates rarely note, is that restorative justice is not a system of justice. Specifically, it has no fact-finding mechanism, at least not yet; its focus is on the penalty and post-penalty phase of the criminal process.

Second, is the popularity of the idea of restorative justice.[3] It rode on the waves of its predecessors in domestic criminal justice in the 1970s and 1980s—a range of restitution, reparation, reconciliation, and informal justice projects—and its momentum picked up any justice activity, which remotely seemed alternative, in its path. As Davis, Boucherat, and Watson (1988, 127) observe with respect to the "mild splutter of interest in the concept of 'reparation' from offender to victim" during the mid-1980s, reparation was "another of those abstract ideas, lacking precise definition, which can, for a while, appeal to everyone." So too for restorative justice. A decade later Marshall (1997, 2) said that many names were given to new justice ideas that had been proposed in the previous decade or so. Among them were communitarian, neighborhood, progressive, reparative, holistic, real, negotiated, balanced, restitutive, relational, community, alternative, participatory, and transformative justice. "Whatever the term," he said, "the tendency is to bring in everything." So too for restorative justice. By the mid- to late 1990s, it emerged as the victor among many competitors in the "new justice" race.[4] Inclusive, capacious, and aspirational, restorative justice seemed to offer something for everyone. Its immense popularity attracted more recruits and advocates (along with a few critics and skeptics), not only in academia but also in government and practice sectors.

With so many people involved, often with a partial view of the burgeoning literature, discussion and critique flew in many directions, unfettered by concepts that had fixed meanings or referents. The term was applied to many different types of activities within criminal justice, some of which were only distantly related or not related at all. The term was also applied to noncriminal justice contexts, for example, to child welfare cases, schools, and other workplace organizations. Its popularity reached into many humanities and social science disciplines, including law, criminology and criminal justice, linguistics, politics, sociology, psychology, and international relations, among others. Thus, discussions of meanings, practices, and effects took widely different forms, depending on a writer's disciplinary lens, and academic, policy, or practice location.

Third, the major theorists of and contributors to the restorative justice field have divergent views on what it is and what it includes. This point is developed more below, but several examples suffice for now. Although his ideas have evolved and continue to change, Braithwaite (2002a, 2002b) applies his "republican normative theory" or "civic republican perspective" to identify a mix of restorative justice values and processes. Drawing from several UN human rights declarations, Braithwaite (2002b, 2003) identifies more than twenty values (or standards) that should inform restorative justice practice. His conception of restorative justice is not limited to crime and criminal justice, but construed broadly in normative and transformative terms: it is "about struggling against injustice in the most restorative way we can imagine" (Braithwaite 2003, 1). He argues for applying restorative justice not just to youth offenders but also to adult offenders, war crime, corporate crime, world peacemaking, and sustainable development. Other well-known figures in the restorative justice field (e.g., Zehr 1990, 2002; van Ness and Strong 2006) restrict their analyses to domestic crime and criminal justice, or at times, to community conflicts. A second area of debate is what concepts or theories are part of restorative justice. Some of us argue that retribution and punishment can be coherently related to restorative justice (e.g., Daly 2001, 2002; Duff 2002); others disagree (e.g., Braithwaite 2002b, 2003; Walgrave 2003, 2004, 2008).

Fourth, in the late 1990s, the idea of restorative justice was adopted by transitional justice analysts, initially with regard to South Africa's Truth and Reconciliation Commission and local courts in postconflict Rwanda (Minow 1998; Drumbl 2000). A jumping across the domestic and international criminal justice literatures has occurred without a full appreciation that such terms as "restoration" and "reparation" mean different things when applied to common crime in domestic criminal justice in affluent nations, compared to human rights abuses and violations of humanitarian law in poorer, nondemocratic, and war-torn nations. For the former, the focus is typically on processes and outcomes that "repair the harm" (and for some, address the wrong) for an individual victim of a common crime carried out by another individual in a democratic society at peace. For the latter, the focus is on redressing victimization and death arising from state terror, abuses of power by security and political officials, and confiscation of property and displacement resulting from internal conflicts and war. In this latter context, restorative justice and restoration are concerned not only with individuals but also collectivities, and with regime change and state building. International human rights and transitional justice writers have selectively incorporated elements of, or redefined, "restorative justice" and "restoration" to suit their specific frame of reference. Thus, key terms have come to signify differing meanings and aspirations in the domestic criminal justice, transitional justice, and international criminal justice literatures.

Fifth, and related, in the international law and transitional justice literatures, we find better guidance for defining some key terms. For example, reparation was first defined explicitly in international law in a 1928 case heard in the Permanent Court of International Justice, although there is considerable debate as to whether the principles in that case are applicable to all breaches of international law (Gray 1999, 418, discussing the *Chorzow Factory* case). In 1996 the United Nations International Law Commission released Draft Articles concerning "the rights of the injured state and obligations of the state which has committed an internationally wrongful act," which defined key terms such as reparation, restitution, and compensation (1996, 134). About a decade later, in March 2006, the United Nations finalized these articles. The UN Resolution (2006)[5] set out three major rights for victims of international human rights and humanitarian law: access to justice, adequate reparation, and access to information. Further, it identified five major forms that reparation may take: restitution, compensation, rehabilitation, satisfaction, and guarantees of nonrepetition. Transitional justice scholars are reflecting and building upon these principles and guidelines, and identifying the ways that they may be put into practice (de Greiff 2006b; Verdeja 2006; Magarrell 2009). Increasing attention has been paid to women, gender, and reparation (Rubio-Marín 2006, 2009; Bell and O'Rourke 2007; Rubio-Marín and de Greiff 2007). The Nairobi Declaration on the Rights of Women and Girls to a Remedy and Reparation, drafted in March 2006, is premised on taking a more explicit victims' perspective to gendered violence, and on redefining reparation to include a transformative and participatory process (Couillard 2007). The UN Resolution and the Nairobi Declaration were constructed with particular justice contexts in mind, i.e., human rights abuses (including gendered-based violence) during war, internal conflicts, and repressive political regimes; but there is a degree of cross-over in the international and domestic criminal justice literatures when scholars and activists consider the "symbolic" and "material" forms that reparation and restoration take.

B. Immense Popularity

Domestic criminal justice uses of restorative justice, social movements to "end impunity" in international criminal justice, and sustained efforts to effect democracy in transitional justice, have all enjoyed immense popularity and tremendous growth since the late 1980s. Why has this occurred? Although we can recognize that there are widely different justice contexts, there are three points of common concern.

First, all identify the need for justice mechanisms for victims, not just offenders. This is a recent development for domestic criminal justice, international criminal justice, and transitional justice, although it was set in motion with different types of rights claims (i.e., victims' rights and human rights). Second, all recognize the limits of conventional methods of prosecution and trial. In domestic criminal justice, the failure of the criminal justice system to deter offenders and aid or "heal" victims is emphasized by all restorative justice advocates. In international criminal justice, the costs of prosecuting individuals for gross human rights violations and crimes against humanity are prohibitive. Combs (2007, 2) notes that "genocide trials are not cheap. . . . [The tribunals for the former Yugoslavia and Rwanda] spend more than $200 million per year to prosecute perhaps a dozen people." For transitional justice, commentators suggest the need for "several measures that complement one another," and they note that "without any truth-telling or reparation efforts, punishing a small number of perpetrators can be viewed as a form of political revenge" (International Center for Transitional Justice 2008, 2; see also Minow 1998). Third, reparation and restoration are new types of aims and purposes for criminal justice. They may sit in an uncertain relationship to other aims and purposes that are expressly about establishing guilt and punishing individual offenders. They contain new, more active roles for victims, offenders, and other participants; and new ideas about what can occur in justice activities. These new roles, activities, and outcomes are attractive to many people; they spark excitement about more meaningful and effective ways of doing justice.

II. HISTORY AND DEVELOPMENT OF KEY TERMS

The development of reparation and restoration in international law and domestic criminal justice has proceeded on separate tracks until recently. Today, in international law, reparation is the overarching concept, with restorative justice or restoration as secondary terms. In domestic criminal justice, restorative justice is the overarching concept, with reparation or restoration as secondary terms. There are some exceptions. Case and country examples of transitional justice show that international or domestic criminal prosecutions may be combined with reparation and with approaches that are now termed restorative justice. Restorative justice has also been brought into international criminal justice as a proposed procedural mechanism in prosecuting war crime and genocide (Combs 2007).

A. Etymological Mingling

One dictionary shows that from the late fourteenth century, reparation was associated with repairing and restoration, and then later, with compensation for war damages:

> c. 1384, from LL. reparationem (nom. reparatio) "act of repairing, restoration," from L. reparatus, pp. of reparare "restore" (see repair (1)). Meaning "act of repairing or mending" is attested from c. 1400. Reparations "compensation for war damages owed by an aggressor" is attested from 1921, from Fr. réparations (1991). (Harper 2001, 1)

Etymologically, reparation includes repairing, setting right, and making amends, and also to restore to good condition. Drawing from *Webster's Third International Dictionary* (1923, 1936, unabridged 1966), Jacob (1970) notes that reparation is a broad concept that includes restitution, although each of these concepts refers to payment from an offender to a victim, and as an "act of restoring." Likewise, Nehusi (2000, 31) suggests there are "a number of meanings or shades of meanings" of reparation, including "to restore, . . . to set right, or make amends."

One point raised by several observers (e.g., Ashworth and von Hirsch 1993, 11; Daly and Immarigeon 1998, 40n17) is the "mnemonic attractiveness" and frequency of "R words" in discussions of restorative justice. They include recognition, redistribution, repair, remedy, rehabilitation, reconciliation, reintegration, restitution, restore and restoration, redeem, redress, and retribution. Why is this the case? When examining the etymology of "re," its Latin source refers to "back" or "backwards," although the precise sense of "re" is not necessarily fixed in Latin usage, and secondary meanings can emerge. Etymologically and in contemporary thinking, reparation and restoration are associated with addressing past damages and wrongs. In this light, retribution, which is associated with addressing past crime would seem to be logically related to reparation and restoration. This point has recently been acknowledged by well-known restorative justice advocates (e.g., Zehr 2002; Walgrave 2004).

B. Reparation and Restoration in Domestic and International Law and Criminal Justice

There are significant differences in how key terms such as reparation, restitution, and restoration are defined and used in the domestic and international criminal justice literatures. In the domestic literature, one often sees a contrast drawn between the aims and elements of conventional criminal justice and those of restorative justice, the latter depicted as the superior justice form. In the international domain, restorative justice is proposed as a parallel process that works alongside or is part of, but not constitutive of, criminal justice.

1. *Domestic Law*

For the uses of reparation in domestic law, there are several historical accounts of Anglo-Saxon law, but we draw authority from Schafer (1968). During the tenth century, the principles of compensation (wer, bot, and wite)[6] replaced earlier group- and individual-based forms of retaliation and revenge. Increasing centralization of the state and sovereign replaced the authority of smaller family or kin groups in criminal matters. During the twelfth and thirteenth centuries, the state (represented by the king) assumed the role of offended party. Crimes (public wrongs or breaches of the "King's Peace") began to be differentiated from private wrongs; and offenders were required to pay fines to the state, rather than direct compensation to a victim. From the sixteenth to the nineteenth century, various figures, including Sir Thomas Moore, Jeremy Bentham, and Herbert Spencer, suggested elements of reparation be used in criminal justice. They proposed, respectively, that offenders perform community work and restitution to a victim, pay compensation to a victim or restitution in kind, and pay income from prison work as compensation to a victim.

In the 1950s, interest in reparation to victims was reawakened with the work of penal reformer Margaret Fry. Fry initially argued that offenders should pay damages to victims, emphasizing its potential for rehabilitation: "repayment is the best first step towards reformation that a dishonest person can take" (Fry 1951, 126). However, she subsequently proposed that the state should assume responsibility for offender rehabilitation *and* victim compensation through social welfare (Fry 1959). Schafer (1968) reported findings from a survey of reparation in twenty-nine countries and concluded that "restitution or compensation to victims of crime is restricted to payment of civil damages, and its inclusion in criminal law would be regarded as an achievement" (109).

In the 1960s, state compensation to crime victims emerged in New Zealand, Great Britain, and the United States (see Jacob 1970).[7] Such programs have since expanded worldwide; they vary in scope, operation, amounts of compensation, and eligibility (see Goodey 2003; Miers 2007), all of which are beyond the scope of this chapter. During the 1970s and 1980s, victim compensation as part of the sentencing process came to be associated with "restitution" (Barnett 1977) and "reparation" (Campbell 1984). Divergent views soon became apparent: Barnett wanted to remove a punitive intent from compensation, whereas Campbell argued that compensation should be viewed as a type of punishment, drawing from Schafer (1960). By the 1990s, with increased attention to how restitution or compensation related to criminal justice, reparation was associated with a wider set of aims. Lucia Zedner's (1994, 234) discussion of the key concepts in "reparative justice" notes that

> Compensation suggests a civil purpose . . . which misses the penal character, . . . restitution seems too narrow a term, suggesting little more than the returning of property or its financial equivalent . . . Reparation is not synonymous with

restitution, still less does it suggest a straightforward importation of civil into
criminal law. . . . [It] should connote a wider set of aims.

She suggests that the wider aims would include not only " 'making good' the damage
[but also] . . . recognition of the harm done to the social relationship between victim
and offender" (234). On this view, we would infer that reparative justice, which soon
was re-branded as restorative justice, should include notions of addressing the
"harm" (damages) and the "wrong" (crime) (see also Watson, Boucherat, and Davis
1989). However, many in the restorative justice field resist the idea that reparation or
restoration should have a punitive quality or elements of punishment.

2. *International Law*

In international law, reparation is used in two ways. Drawing from the *Encyclopedia
of Public International Law*, vol. 4 (Bernhardt and MacAlister 1992, 178), the earliest
use, dating from the mid-sixteenth century was a victor's entitlement to a "tribute
on the vanquished . . . for internationally wrongful acts," which served not only as
"reparation. . . . [but] also as punishment and atonement." Such tributes or "war
indemnities" became a common feature of a victor's claim to cover war costs, from
the end of the eighteenth century on. After World War I, reparation replaced the
term "war indemnities," and that term was used in treaties of peace after the war.
Today, reparation refers generally to a state's entitlement against another state to
seek redress for "internationally wrongful acts," not just those related to war.

A second use of the term evolved from a series of international instruments on
human rights, beginning post–World War II with *The Universal Declaration of
Human Rights* (1948). These center on an individual's rights as a subject in international law to pursue violations of human rights and humanitarian law. Section VII of
the UN Resolution (2006) identifies three rights for victims: ". . . access to justice, . . .
reparation for harm suffered, [and] access to relevant information concerning violations and reparation mechanisms" (A/RES/60/147, 6). In section IX, reparation is
defined as taking these forms: restitution, compensation, rehabilitation, satisfaction,
and guarantees of nonrepetition.[8] Because this UN Resolution (2006) now stands as
the key document in defining rights, remedies, and reparation for victims in international human rights and humanitarian law, we briefly compare its terms and definitions with those used in the restorative justice field, in five areas.[9]

First, the definition of restitution in the UN Resolution (2006) is to restore a
person to their original position, with an emphasis on *restoration* of human rights
and lost property and employment. By comparison, in domestic contexts, restitution
normally refers to the return of lost property, e.g., the return of a stolen bicycle in the
same condition before it was stolen. In section III, the matter is further complicated
by the fact that there is no consistent use of key terms by those in the restorative
justice field. For example, monetary or material forms of recompense are variably
referred to as compensation, reparation, restitution, and so forth; and emotional

(or nonmaterial) restoration is defined in different ways. Varied uses of terms in international and domestic criminal justice settings arise, in part, because violations of human rights and humanitarian law have both a collective and individual component, whereas violations of criminal law are largely individual. For example, writing from an international law context, Atuahene (2007, 31–32) conceives of restoration as *a people's* reconnection to society as valued and active citizens. By contrast, in domestic settings, the referent is to restoring an *individual's* security or the bonds between individuals.

Second, compensation generally has a similar meaning across international and domestic legal settings: it is an economic means by which physical harms and damages are calculated and money paid to victims. However, in the classic early writings that came to be associated with restorative justice in domestic settings by Eglash (e.g., 1957–58a, 1977) and Barnett (1977) (discussed in section III), *restitution* was the term used to refer to money or labor, given in lieu of money payments, to a victim.[10] In contrast, Campbell (1984, 339) defined *reparation* as criminal justice schemes for victim compensation, when an offender takes an active role, differentiating these from welfare schemes and state-based compensation. Today, in restorative justice texts, restitution and reparation are both used to refer to financial or labor modes of "making amends" or recompensing a victim; compensation is sometimes used in its more restrictive sense, or used interchangeably with restitution.

Third, the UN Resolution (2006) defines satisfaction to encompass varied actions that constitute nonmaterial or symbolic forms of reparation. Apologies, commemorations and memorials, and official pronouncements are all ways that wrongs suffered by victims can be recognized and validated. In domestic contexts of restorative justice, the "core sequence" of genuine shame and remorse expressed by an offender and some steps toward forgiveness by a victim is termed symbolic reparation (Retzigner and Scheff 1996), although some suggest that an apology alone is symbolic reparation (Strang 2001, 185). Other related outcomes in domestic settings are noted, such as handshakes, smiles, or other gestures of conciliation and friendship.[11]

Fourth, in the UN Resolution (2006), reparation is one of three rights victims have. Another is access to justice, which includes administrative, civil, or criminal actions and remedies for individuals. Thus, in the international context, "justice" and "reparation" are distinct remedies.[12] However, in domestic contexts of restorative justice, the terms are collapsed. In part, this is because the focus is on processes and outcomes post-plea,[13] and in part, it reflects a desire by many restorative justice advocates to replace penal sanctions and punishment ("justice") with a new justice form ("reparation" or "restoration").

Finally, there are key differences in international and domestic instruments concerning reparation and restorative justice. This is evident when comparing the UN Resolution (2006), which focuses on international criminal justice, and the UN's Economic and Social Council Resolution (2002), which focuses on restorative justice in domestic criminal justice. In the latter, restorative justice is defined as "an evolving response to crime that respects the dignity and equality of each person, builds understanding, and promotes social harmony through the healing of victims, offenders, and communities" (Annex). Restoration is never mentioned in the text; rather, the closest terms used are addressing participants' "needs" and achieving "reintegration." Nor are reparation and restitution defined. By comparison to the UN Resolution (2006), which stipulates that victims have rights of redress in the absence of the identification, arrest, or conviction of a perpetrator, the UN's Council Resolution (2002) sees restorative justice as an activity running parallel to a criminal justice process. In general, the latter sets forth guidelines for restorative justice as a legal process (having elements of a mediated civil hearing, it appears), but not a fully criminal justice process.[14]

C. Retribution and Punishment: Are They Related to Restoration or Are They "Dirty Words"?

There is debate and confusion about the relationship of retribution and what is termed "retributive justice" to restoration and restorative justice, and the relationship of punishment to restorative justice. This state of affairs can be traced to two impulses.

First, when proponents introduce new ideas into the justice field, they use strong contrasts or dualisms to bring into dramatic relief the failure of the "older" justice and the benefits of and the need for a new justice form. This discursive frame is evident in Mead's (1917–18, repr. 1998) paper on "The Psychology of Punitive Justice,"[15] where he contrasted two methods of responding to crime, one using an "attitude of hostility toward the lawbreaker" and the other, a "reconstructive attitude." Whereas the former "brings with it the attitudes of retribution, repression, and exclusion" (47–48), the latter tries to "understand the causes of social and individual breakdown, to mend . . . the defective situation. . . . not to place punishment but to obtain future results" (52). When arguing for a new justice form, proponents caricature elements in the older form. They do not present a true comparison, but rather a simple dichotomy, using comparison terms that have a nice ring to them. This is what Zehr (1985) did in comparing the two lenses of retributive and restorative justice to contrast, respectively, conventional criminal justice with a proposed new justice form. In his comparison, "retributive justice" in fact refers to elements in conventional criminal justice that had to be replaced, although at the time, Zehr did not see it this way. Words such as "retribution," "retributive," or "retributive justice," which are on the negative side of the dualism,[16] refer to what is wrong or has failed with conventional justice system practices.

Second, as evidenced in Mead in the early twentieth century and the work of Barnett (1977),[17] is a distaste for "punishment" and a desire for a more enlightened response to crime. Barnett argues that the "paradigm of punishment . . . [has] lost 'its moral legitimacy and its practical efficacy'" (285). In its place, he proposes a restitutional system, which, he concedes at the end of his paper, collapses the distinction between crime and tort (299). Barnett's position is an early argument for the "civiliza-tion thesis" in two meanings of that word: to bring offenders under civil, not criminal law; and to have a more enlightened response to acts called "crime" (300).[18] He equates punishment with "retributive justice," and calls for nonpunitive forms of restitution ("pure restitution," 288). His ideas raise questions for how elements of civil law could be incorporated within restorative justice in domestic settings (see Johnstone 2003, 8–14). Like Barnett, some restorative justice advocates say they are against punish-ment or punitive modes of intervention; they believe that because the "intention of the punisher" in a restorative justice process is a constructive one, the outcome is not punishment (Walgrave 2004, 48–49). Others argue that despite the benevolent inten-tions of advocates, the criminal justice process is coercive and can impose burdens on offenders; consequently, restorative justice sanctions (or outcomes) are, and will be experienced as, punishment to offenders (Daly 2000, 2002; Crawford and Newburn 2003, 46–47; see also Levrant et al. 1999).

What explains the aversion by some to punishment? Drawing from Garland (1990, discussing Elias, ch. 10), it likely reflects changing sensibilities about what are "civilized" methods of responding to crime.[19] Punishment conjures a variety of im-ages in people's heads, but for many in the restorative justice field, it is frequently equated with prison and other forms of unacceptable ("uncivilized") pain infliction. What is believed to be more acceptable are constructive efforts by an offender to do something for a victim ("to mend the situation"), whether by working for a victim or paying back money or property in some way. However, as Johnstone (2003, 22) sug-gests, such outcomes are punitive because they are coerced or imposed as a burden.

How restorative justice practices should relate to punishment is keenly con-tested. Some argue that incarceration and fines are punishments because they are *intended deprivations*, whereas probation or what are termed "reparative measures" (such as doing work for a crime victim) are not punishment because they are *intended to be constructive* (Wright 1991). Others define punishment more broadly to include anything that is unpleasant, a burden, or an imposition; the intentions of a decision-maker are less significant (Davis 1992; Duff 2001). Barnett's (1977) con-trast of *punitive* and *pure* restitution illustrates the fine line that is often drawn between "punishment" and "non-punishment." In punitive restitution, an offender is forced to compensate a victim; in pure restitution, an offender returns stolen goods or money, (or "makes good" in some way), but the aim is not that the offender should suffer but that a victim "desires compensation" (Barnett 1977, 289).

Related to debates about punishment is the role of retribution in restorative practices. According to Cottingham (1979), philosophers have put forward at least nine theories of retribution to justify punishment, although he believes that there is a "basic sense" of what the term means: repayment (238). Although he argues that the relationship between repayment and "inflicting suffering" (i.e., punishment) is "left unexplained," it is "both ancient and widely held" (238). For this reason, he says that the "repayment sense" of retribution should be viewed as a metaphor more than a theory of punishment. Cottingham's observations help us to see why there are varied meanings of retribution in the restorative justice field. Some use the term to describe a *desert justification* for punishment (e.g., intended to be in proportion to the harm caused; see Walgrave and Aertsen 1996), whereas others use it to describe a *form* of punishment. For the latter, some use retribution in a *neutral* way to refer to a censuring of harms (e.g., Duff 1996), whereas most use the term to connote a *punitive* response, which is associated with the intention to inflict pain (Wright 1991).

In the early years of restorative justice, the strong contrast drawn between retributive justice and restorative justice may have been an "elegant and catchy exposition" (Roche 2007, 87), but it is now seen as a caricature, with little foundation. We can observe, for example, that in the last century and a half, criminal justice has wavered between desires to treat some and punish others; and there are multiple, often contrary, aims, purposes, and practices of criminal justice. For some writers, it was clear early on that apparently contrary principles of retribution and reparation (or restoration) were not antithetical, but complementary or dependent upon one another (see, e.g., Duff 1992, 1996, 2001; Hampton 1992, 1998; Zedner 1994; Bottoms 1998; Daly 2000). More recently, Zehr (2002), Walgrave (2004), and van Ness and Strong (2006) have conceded that the better comparison is between conventional criminal justice and restorative justice, and that retribution does have a place in restorative processes.

Any comparison of conventional criminal justice with proposed newer forms (e.g., restorative or reparative justice) must acknowledge that the new forms deal only with the *post-plea* or *penalty phase* of the criminal process. There is as yet no "restorative" or "reparative" mechanism of adjudication; and thus, no justice system is based on these ideas. Often we hear that restorative justice differs from established criminal justice in being participatory and consensually based, not adversarial. This may sound pleasing, but it is misleading. Established criminal justice is adversarial because adjudicating crime rests on a right of those accused to defend themselves against the state's allegations of wrong-doing.[20] There may, of course, be better ways to adjudicate; but no one believes we should dispense with the right of citizens to defend themselves against the state's power to prosecute and punish alleged crime. Thus, whether we call it restorative, reparative, or restitutive justice, none can yet replace conventional criminal justice unless mechanisms for fact-finding are identified. It is striking how often the domestic restorative justice literature overlooks this fact.

III. Restorative Justice

Challenges to conventional criminal justice emerged, in part, from civil rights and women's movements of the 1960s, which identified race- and gender-based mistreatment of offenders and victims in the criminal justice process (Daly and Immarigeon

1998). Practices that would become associated with restorative justice grew out of activities and programs developed in the 1970s and 1980s, including alternatives to prisons, community boards and neighborhood justice centers, victim-offender mediation, reparation projects, and post-sentence victim-offender reconciliation. Paralleling these activities were academic research and theories emerging in the 1970s and 1980s on informal justice, abolitionism, restitution, and reintegrative shaming.

A. Early Ideas

Four influential thinkers are associated with the development of restorative justice: Albert Eglash, Randy Barnett, Howard Zehr, and Nils Christie. All say that conventional criminal justice is inadequate and accomplishes little for victims or offenders.

1. Eglash

The introduction of the term "restorative justice" is credited to Albert Eglash. An academic psychologist based in the Midwest and then in Maryland, Eglash was actively involved in programs for youth offenders and adult prisoners. He drew from these experiences in outlining a "creative" meaning of restitution, comparing it to a conventional meaning, in several articles written in the late 1950s (Eglash 1957–58a, 1957–58b, 1959–60) (see table 8.1).

Creative restitution aims to be constructive, varied depending on context, offender self-determined but guided, and related to constructive acts for a victim or others (Eglash 1957–58a). Eglash distinguished the "first mile" of the return of

Table 8.1. Conventional and Creative Restitution (from Eglash 1957–58a)

Element	Conventional Restitution	Creative Restitution
Restitution defined	Synonym for reparations or indemnity	Distinguished from reparations or indemnity
Four elements compared	Financial obligation	Constructive act
	Extent is limited	Creative and unlimited
	Court-determined	Guided, self-determined behavior
	Individual act	Can have a group basis
Relationship of restitution to punishment	Individual pays debt to society: financial only	Individual carries out "constructive, redeeming act" to the victim or others
	Determined by legal officials, "first mile" is punishment	Offender participates, goes a "second mile" beyond what the court requires or others expect
	Individual only: "in punishment, a man stands alone"	Group of offenders can discuss and participate in restitutional acts

property under court order or by the expectations of friends and family from the "second mile" of restitution "in its broad meaning of a complete restoration of goodwill and harmony. Creative restitution requires that a situation be left better than before an offense was committed" (620). Eglash also assumed that restitution should be "life long" and a "form of psychological exercise" (622) that would encourage human growth and "ease stigma" (621). At the article's close, Eglash (1957–58*a*, 621) reflects on whether restitution is the correct term, when "restoration, redeeming, or redemption" may be preferable. He elects to "use restitution in [the] broader sense," and to "use reparations or indemnity for the narrower term of mandatory financial settlement." Restorative justice does not appear in this article or the two others produced at this time (1957–58*b*, 1959–60).

Nearly two decades later Eglash (1977) explicitly used the term restorative justice.[21] He defined it as the "technique of [creative] restitution" (Eglash 1977, 91), contrasting it to retributive and distributive justice, which use techniques of punishment and treatment, respectively. Creative restitution is also called "guided restitution," in which an offender is required to make amends for an offense, "but is free to determine what form this amends will take" (Eglash 1977, 93). The elements of the "restitutional act" are an "active, effortful role," which is "constructive [and] directed toward the victim, and related to the damage or harm resulting from the offense." That relationship is seen as "reparative of the damage done to a person or property" (94). Eglash again includes "the second mile" by saying that creative restitution goes "beyond coercion into a creative act" by leaving a situation better than before (95). He says that creative or guided restitution "fits best as a requirement of probation," but gives no indication of how it relates to other sentence elements. He concludes by saying he is "offender oriented," "seldom thinks about the victim," has "never visited any victims," and it never occurred to him to ask victims what they thought of creative restitution. Rather, his proposal is concerned with offenders, and "any benefit to victims is a bonus, gravy" (99).

Restorative justice, as Eglash (1977) defines it, is some distance from principles and practices associated with it today. However, some similarities can be discerned: a strong contrast between the failure of old, and the superiority of a new, justice form; relating an offender's "effortful role" to the damage and harm caused by an offense; and an overly optimistic view of offenders' abilities and interests to want to go "the second mile."

2. Barnett

Randy Barnett's (1977) proposal for "a new paradigm" of restitutional justice has elements that are more directly traceable to emerging ideas of restorative justice in domestic settings. This is because he defines crime as an offense of one person against another (rather than against the state), defines justice as a "culpable offender making good the loss" caused, and says that he is "against" punishment. In its place he proposes "pure restitution" (rather then "punitive restitution," which is forced compensation or imposed fines). The goal is "reparations paid to the victim" (289), which would be ordered, when an offender is "sentenced to make restitution to the victim" (289). In Barnett's analysis, reparations (he uses the plural) and restitution refer to the same thing: financial payments. He considers a variety of ways of "re-paying the victim" (289–91) and addresses potential objections of his proposal. Johnstone (2003, 21–22, 26n4) suggests that Barnett does not satisfactorily explain why "we are not entitled to impose punishment upon offenders but are entitled to *force* them to pay restitution" (emphasis in original). For example, Barnett argues for "pure restitution," but says that this is accomplished by sentencing an offender to make restitution. It is difficult to see how this differs from sentencing an offender to pay compensation.[22]

3. *Zehr*

Howard Zehr's (1985, repr. 2003, 69–82) contrast of retributive and restorative jus-tice tracks Barnett's argument closely in several ways, but departs from it in others. Zehr also argues for a new paradigm, but he calls it restorative justice. Like Barnett, he redefines crime (an offense between two individuals), but has many more terms associated with justice, including restoration, reconciliation, the process of making things right, right relationships measured by the outcome, repair of social injury, and healing. Like Barnett, his preferred response is restitution, which he sees "as a means of restoring *both* parties" (81, emphasis in original), not as a type of punish-ment. Zehr is also concerned with addressing conflict between individuals: he calls for offenders and victims "to see one another as persons, to establish or re-establish a relationship" (79). Compared to Barnett, who draws mainly from legal authority, Zehr draws from religious history and Judeo-Christian ideals. His work with the Victim-Offender Reconciliation Project, a Mennonite-based program that facili-tated meetings between victims and imprisoned offenders, informed a good deal of his early thinking about restorative justice.

4. *Christie*

Of the four writers, Nils Christie (1977, repr. 2003, 57–68) focuses more on the pro-cesses and procedures of optimal justice activities than sanctions alone. His article opens by taking us to a small village in Tanzania, where there is a conflict about prop-erty after a marital engagement broke off. He approves of the way the dispute (a civil matter) is settled: the protagonists are at the center of attention, with family members and other villagers participating. They are the experts, not the judges.[23] Christie puts forward two related points. First, professionals, especially lawyers "are particularly good at stealing conflicts" (59) between individuals. Second, these conflicts should be seen "as property" because they have great value. They offer a chance for people to participate in society, they provide "opportunities for norm clarification," and they help protagonists to meet and get to know each other (61). These interactions and "personalized encounters" (62) bring victims more fully into the criminal process and invite reflection by an offender about "how he can make good again" (62). His ideas for a model court go further than others in suggesting how civil and criminal processes might be blended.

His proposed court is victim-centered and lay-oriented, and has four stages. The first is to establish that a law has been broken and the right person is identified. The second is to focus attention on the victim's situation and what can be done to address it, "first and foremost by the offender" (63), then the local neighborhood, and then the state. Christie has in mind repairing windows and locks, offenders paying compensation with money or by performing labor for a victim, and in other ways, "restoring the victim's situation" (64). After all of this occurs, the third stage is a judicial officer deciding if further punishment is required, "in addition to those unintended constructive sufferings the offender would go through in his restitutive actions [for] the victim" (64). The last stage, which is post-sentence, is service to an offender. This would include addressing his or her social, medical, and educational needs.

Several observations can be drawn from the early works that are now linked to restorative justice. First, the authors all believe that conventional criminal justice is a failure, and they propose different models of criminal justice. Second, they argue that convicted defendants should have a more direct and constructive role in "repaying" victims for crime. This role is variably termed creative restitution, pure restitution, restorative justice, or restoring the victim's situation. The authors refer to the consequences of this new offender role as restoration, making reparations, healing, among other terms; and they have different ideas about its impact on offenders. Eglash believed that the new role might change an offender in positive ways, whereas Christie did not expect or care if face-to-face meetings led to reductions in reoffending. Third, all the authors struggle in imagining how this new role for offenders relates to conventional criminal justice. For all (except perhaps Christie), there is a rejection of punishment and the "retributive paradigm," and a desire to identify "nonpunitive," more constructive responses. Finally, for some (Zehr and Christie), there is also a new role for victims and others, who should be able to speak and participate in decisions about responding to crime.

B. Later Ideas

Restorative justice became more complex from the mid-1990s on. By 1996 Braithwaite (1996, repr. 2003, nn9–29,94–95) could itemize over twenty books, articles, and conference papers having "restorative justice" in the title. As ideas and arguments were put forward, several types of criminal justice activities then in place (e.g., prisoner-victim reconciliation in North America, youth justice conferences in New Zealand and Australia, victim-offender mediation in North America and Europe) were being re-branded as "restorative justice." Meanwhile, Braithwaite's

(1989) concept of "re-integrative shaming" (described in section V) began to be applied in the early 1990s as the theory guiding "community conferencing" and then, restorative justice.[24] Community conferences are meetings between an admitted offender, victim, and their supporters and other relevant participants, guided by a facilitator (a police officer or other professional) with the aims of encouraging offender accountability, victim voice, mutual understanding, and group decision-making on fashioning an outcome.

In this section, we consider selected conceptual developments as restorative justice evolved, with a focus on key terms of reparation, restoration, and restitution, and related understandings of what constitutes reparative and restorative processes and outcomes. Four points are clear. First, there is inconsistent use of key terms. Second, there is no single definition of restorative justice: advocates, critics, and researchers conceptualize and want to apply the idea in different ways. Third, as ideas of reparative and restorative processes and outcomes gained in popularity, particularly with governments, they were mislabeled and misused. Fourth, restorative justice has become unleashed from criminal justice and is increasingly difficult to characterize.

1. *Inconsistent Use of Key Terms*

Articles in an early edited collection by Galaway and Hudson (1996) exemplify what is and continues to be an inconsistent use of key terms. The contributing authors use the terms "reparation" and "restitution," either together or separately, to refer to outcomes, typically financial or labor (e.g., community service), that may come from restorative justice (see, e.g., Jervis 1996; Lee 1996; Wemmers 1996). "Reconciliation" is rarely defined although it is often named as a goal of restorative justice. Contributors write from their own frames of reference as each attempts to understand and come to terms with the idea of restorative justice, and there is little reflection on the disparate use of terms. One exception is the last chapter by Harland (1996), who says the field should "define and clarify the most essential aims and related mechanisms, beginning with restoration itself [but also] reconciliation, reparation to the community, mediation . . . and so on" (507).

A significant theoretical contribution to the volume is Retzinger and Scheff (1996), who consider the social-psychological mechanisms in the community conferences they observed in Australia.[25] They distinguish "material" and "symbolic reparation" processes. The former leads to a specific outcome, what an offender agrees to do (or, as they say, "restitution or compensation for damage done, and some form of community service," 316). This is the visible and "largely unambiguous" part of the process. Less visible and more complex is an ideal outcome of "symbolic reparation," which has two steps in the "core sequence." First, the offender "clearly expresses genuine shame and remorse over his/her actions," and next, "in response, the victim takes a first step toward forgiving the offender for the trespass"

(316). This core sequence "generates repair and restoration of the bond between victim and offender [which was] severed by the offender's crime" (316). Further, they say that the repair of this bond (that is, between the dyad) "symbolizes a more extensive restoration that is to take place between the offender and other participants." The core sequence may "only [be] a few seconds," but it is "the key to reconciliation, victim satisfaction, and decreasing recidivism" (316). Without the core sequence, they argue that the "path toward settlement is strewn with impediments" (317). They view symbolic reparation as unique to community conferences compared to any other type of justice system response. Importantly, they discovered that symbolic reparation did not occur in the formal phase of *any* of the nine conferences they observed. This was because offenders did not "clearly express genuine shame and remorse" (321). Such expression, or what may be termed a "sincere apology," is "a difficult and delicate undertaking even when the transgression is minor" (Tavuchis 1991, 22), and this is further complicated by the presence of third parties, as occurs in the conference process (see Hayes 2006).

Strang (2001) also considers the "emotional dimensions" of victimization, emphasizing that victims see "emotional restoration as far more important than material or financial reparation" (184; see also Strang 2002, 18).[26] Drawing on Marshall and Merry's (1990) review, she says that "often what victims want most [is] not substantial reparation but rather symbolic reparation, primarily an apology" (Strang 2001, 185). In both publications, Strang depicts the material forms of recompense with a plethora of terms (variably as restitution, material restitution, material restoration, material reparation, material compensation, substantial reparation, financial reparation), a not atypical pattern in the field. However, what may be queried is equating "symbolic reparation" with "an apology." This is because Retzinger and Scheff (1996) point out that the core sequence involves not only an offender expressing genuine remorse but also a readiness and ability of a victim to respond. In other words, "symbolic reparation" is not something a victim can "want." Although an apology is the first step in the core sequence, a victim has an equally important role in deciding to acknowledge and respond to it. Further, as Retzinger and Scheff (1996, 317) suggest, symbolic reparation "depends entirely upon the play of emotions and social relationships during the conference."[27]

By contrast, Duff (2002, 84–85) defines restoration as the reinstatement of a victim to an "original favorable condition," whereas "reparation and compensation . . . make up for the loss of what cannot be restored . . . and are the means to restoration." He then asks, "what can repair the wrong that was done?" His answer, an apology, which includes elements of "recognition, repentance, and reconciliation" (87). To give added "forceful expression" to an apology, Duff identifies the following as examples of "moral reparation: . . . undertaking some service for the victim, buying a gift, contributing time or money to a charity" (90).[28] Sharpe (2007, 29) picks up on Duff's point but refers to his cited examples of moral reparation as types of symbolic reparation (which, she says, are sometimes also called partial restitution). Still other writers do not distinguish material and symbolic reparation. For example, while recognizing that victim-offender meetings aim to address "victims' emotional needs as well as their material ones," Marshall (1998, repr. 2003, 32) itemizes the following simply as forms of reparation: money payments, work for a victim or community case, undergoing counseling, or a combination of these. Zedner (1994, 238) discusses the material and symbolic (which she also terms "psychological") forms of reparation but notes that in practice the differences between them are not clear-cut: "sums paid in compensation seldom approach the actual value of the loss suffered, and the significance of the payment may often be largely symbolic."

This is but a small sampling from the literature to make a general point. Currently there is no authoritative glossary of terms to which people can refer when discussing reparation, restoration, restitution, and how these relate to restorative justice and its goals in domestic criminal justice settings.[29] People use different terms to refer to the same thing, or the same term to refer to different things. Optimistically, we may say that the restorative justice field is evolving and dynamic; more critically, that it is chaotic and incoherent. We suggest a way through the chaos at the end of this section.

Restoration, as a concept, faces another critique. Most people assume or claim that the goal of restorative justice is restoration or "to restore" a victim[30] (Walgrave 1995; Braithwaite 2002b, respectively). In other words, it is understood *literally* to mean a justice activity that aims to restore a person to their original position. Others suggest that restorative justice should be viewed as a *nominal concept*, standing for a set of justice activities; and it should not be narrowly construed as restoring people, property, or social relations (Curtis-Fawley and Daly 2005, 605). One reason for taking the latter view is that it addresses some critics, in particular, those who consider the appropriateness of restorative justice for gendered violence, who say that "the concept of restoration suggests that a prior state existed in which [a domestic violence] victim experienced significant liberty and the offender was integrated into the community [when] neither may be true" (Coker 2002, 143; see also Cossins 2008 on child sexual abuse). Other critics say that the point is not restoration to a status quo or what existed before, but rather a transformation of social relations and society (Sullivan and Tifft 2005).[31]

2. Conceptions, Definitions, and Agendas of Restorative Justice

Johnstone and van Ness (2007a, 6) argue that restorative justice is not only a "persistently vague concept, it is in fact a deeply *contested* concept" (emphasis in original). There is no one definition, nor should this be expected because, they say, the character of the restorative justice movement is not coherent or unified. They identify three conceptions, although these can overlap in practice: *encounter* (a focus on the processes of face-to-face meetings and decision-making); *reparative* (a focus on outcomes that "repair the harm," including those decided by criminal justice professionals); and *transformative* (a focus on transformations of self and society). Some writers emphasize the process; others the outcome; and others still focus on the *values* associated with it. Not surprisingly, the list of values varies, depending on the writer. For example, van Ness (2002, 11) identifies four values of encounter, amends, reintegration, and inclusion, which are then linked to a set of activities or outcomes that should be in a "fully restorative response." Braithwaite (2002*b*) has a far more elaborated structure of twenty-four values.

Johnstone (2008) identifies five agendas of restorative justice to distinguish the different political directions the field is taking. Agenda one, the most familiar, is concerned with changing the response to crime; two, with changing the way in which "crime" and "justice" are defined; three, with widening the uses of restorative justice to other organizational settings (e.g., schools, prisons, workplaces); four, with "projects of political reconciliation" (e.g., applications postconflict societies, among others); and five, with transforming social organization and "personal life-style" (72). Although these agendas may overlap and are themselves "internally complex," the point is that people are seeking to achieve different aims under the rubric of restorative justice.

3. *Popular Uses and Misuses*

An enduring problem for any new justice idea is truth in labeling. This occurred more than two decades ago when so-called reparation schemes were introduced in England. As Davis, Boucherat, and Watson (1988, 128) point out, these were "misde-scribed" because their main aims were not "reparative justice," but diversion from court or mitigation of sentence. The authors were critical of these "half-baked" attempts "to promote 'reparation,'" all of which were "disappointing." We see the same problem today for restorative justice. It is often used to refer to any response to crime that does not involve a prison sentence or that is "nonpunitive." For instance, Pennsylvania sentencing guidelines identify "restorative sanction pro-grams" as "least restrictive, non-confinement intermediate punishments" (sec. 303.12 (a) (5)). Roberts and Stalans (2004, 325–26) contrast "punitive" and "restor-ative" sanctions, the latter including anything that is a community or noncustodial penalty. Aware of the "McDonaldization of justice" problem, when the label of restorative justice is wrongly applied to a justice activity, restorative justice propo-nents have created continua that identify practices ranging near and far from the restorative ideal (see, e.g., Umbreit 1999; McCold 2000; van Ness 2002).

4. *Restorative Justice Unleashed*

Reflecting, in part, the different agendas of restorative justice, two types of conceptual expansion have occurred. First, the well-known restorative justice advocate and theo-rist John Braithwaite has created a far larger, more encompassing project, based on a transformative agenda. His work evolved from more modest beginnings, applications to youth crime in the early and mid-1990s (e.g., Braithwaite and Daly 1994, Braithwaite 1996); but expanded at the turn of the twenty-first century to include broader mechanisms of regulation and societal transformation (Braithwaite 1999, 2002a, 2003). Indicative of his vision of "holistic restorative justice," Braithwaite argues that it is not just about "reforming the criminal justice system, [but] a way of transforming our entire legal system, our family lives, our conduct in the workplace, our practice of politics" (Braithwaite 2003, 1). He continues by saying that restorative justice is

> about struggling against injustice in the most restorative way we can manage. . . . It targets injustice reduction [not merely crime reduction]. It aspires to offer practical guidance on how we can lead the good life as democratic citizens by struggling against injustice. It says we must conduct that struggle while seeking to dissuade hasty resort to punitive rectification or other forms of stigmatising response. (1)

Like others, but in a more sophisticated fashion, Braithwaite (2002b) takes a values orientation to restorative justice. He identifies twenty-four values of three types: *constraining* (specifying rights and limits), *maximizing* (specifying sites and types of restoration), and *emergent* (properties such as remorse, apology, and forgiveness that emerge when restorative justice succeeds, but which cannot be expected to occur). The maximizing values include not only emotional restoration but also restoration of human dignity, property loss, safety or health, damaged human relationships, communities, the environment, freedom, compassion or caring, peace, and sense of duty as a citizen. This list is more extensive than any other in the field today, which normally includes restoration of property loss, of damaged human relations, and a victim's emotional restoration. Braithwaite's vision for restorative justice is a "radical redesign of legal institutions" and "regulating injustice restoratively" (Braithwaite 2003, 18–19).

Conceptual expansion takes another form. Some commentators use restorative justice as *the single term* to encapsulate emergent, and quite varied, justice forms and practices. This is exemplified in a review essay by Menkel-Meadow (2007), in which restorative justice is used as an umbrella concept to refer not only to mediated meetings between victims and offenders (and others) but also to contemporary forms of Indigenous sentencing practices and problem-solving courts (e.g., drug courts). She also claims that restorative justice "helped form a new field of international law and political structure: transitional justice" (164). How did it come to be that varied and disparate justice activities have been categorized as types of "restorative justice?"

Menkel-Meadow begins by saying that practices associated with restorative justice ideally have "four R's [of] repair, restore, reconcile, and reintegrate" (162). Later she says that these elements are seen in problem-solving courts, which use "restorative principles," "more reparative sentences" (168), and are "specialized reparative courts" (177). This is inaccurate. There are some affinities between restorative justice, Indigenous sentencing courts, and therapeutic jurisprudence (the last being associated with problem-solving courts). However, they are distinctive, and merging them as one type of justice creates confusion and incoherence (see, e.g., Daly, Hayes, and Marchetti 2006; Marchetti and Daly 2007). Likewise, truth commissions are just one activity in a transitional justice process; some but not all truth commissions adopt approaches that have restorative justice elements. It is inaccurate to say that transitional justice was formed from restorative justice principles, as Menkel-Meadow suggests (2007, 164). Better to use "innovative justice" as the umbrella concept,[32] within which a variety of justice activities, with different aims, practices, and socio-political contexts, can be documented and understood. Why, then, do some commentators use restorative justice as an umbrella concept? It may stem from a lack of familiarity about the justice practices themselves, or it may reflect a desire to generate enthusiasm that something large and important is happening.

C. Cutting through the Chaos?

There may be a way to make sense of analysts' varied uses of key terms in domestic contexts of restorative justice by observing that their start points differ. Some identify *reparation* as the master term; others, *restoration*; others, *making amends*; and still others, a combination of these. Further, the terms can be used in different ways, depending on whether the author explicitly considers their relationship to conventional criminal justice.

For Sharpe (2007), *reparation* is the master term, within which there is material reparation and symbolic reparation, which may overlap. Material reparation generally addresses "the *specific harms* . . . while symbolic reparation speaks to the *wrongness of the act*" (27, emphasis added). The former includes restitution (the broader term referring to return of property whether by payment or by service) and compensation (monetary payment in lieu of return or repair of property, or acknowledging a "fundamental loss"). Symbolic reparation refers mainly to an apology, but as Sharpe understands the term, it is also "expressed" by buying a gift, doing community service, or entering a treatment program. Others such as Marshall (1998) use reparation as the master concept, but without drawing distinctions among terms such as compensation or community service.

Restoration is the master term for Braithwaite (2002b), Duff (2002), Walgrave (2002), and Strang (2002), among others, but the scope and elements of restoration vary, and except for Duff, the elements are not clearly specified. With restoration as the master term, Duff views reparation and compensation as subsidiary activities that may assist in moving a victim to an initial state before the crime; a sincere apology may address the "wrong," but can be given added force with other actions. Other writers, such as Strang (2002), focus mainly on an apology as a source of emotional restoration.

Making amends is the master term for von Hirsch, Ashworth, and Shearing (2003), who focus on a "negotiated process between offender and victim" (also termed a "moral dialogue"), which leads to the offender's "acknowledgment of fault and the undertaking of a reparative task" (26). The reparative task should recognize the victim's status as a wronged individual and express a "regretful stance" (32). The model assumes an *imposition* on an offender, which includes "adverse judgments" and loss of property or time by paying compensation or undertaking a task. An amends model is also used by van Ness and Strong (2006), but they focus on the harm caused by crime, more so than a victim's status as a wronged individual.

Dignan (2003) uses a combination of master terms in identifying restorative justice as a "replacement discourse" in his systemic model of criminal justice, conceptualized as an enforcement pyramid, building on Braithwaite (1999). At the base are minor property or assault offenses, and their handling is similar to von Hirsh, Ashworth, and Shearing's (2003) making amends model: reparative undertakings are agreed to in an informal restorative justice process, which demonstrate "respect for the rights of others." The next level in the pyramid addresses cases that go to court because victims do not want to participate, suspects deny guilt, and the parties cannot agree on reparation outcomes. Court sentencing would be limited to imposing a "restoration order" (147), which may be compensation, reparation for the victim, or community service. The next two levels up the pyramid involve more serious cases and repeat offenders; these would attract court sentences of "restorative" punishment, and ultimately, incapacitation.[33]

Identifying these conceptual starting points is one way to cut through the chaos. However, there remain profound problems in establishing an agreed-upon set of aims and mechanisms of restorative justice: the field lacks definitional discipline, and analysts are divided over whether and in what ways retribution and punishment should have a role in restorative practices.

IV. Selected Applications of Reparation, Restoration, and Restorative Justice

We provide a sampling of applications of these ideas in international and domestic criminal justice contexts. Edited collections by Sullivan and Tifft (2006) and Johnstone and van Ness (2007*b*) contain articles and examples that are relevant here and in section V.

A. Reparation and Restoration in International Criminal Law and Justice

Reparation, restoration, and restorative justice are terms used in transitional justice and international criminal justice. Here is a brief review of how they are understood and used.

1. *Transitional Justice*

Transitional justice is "a framework for confronting past abuse as a component of a major political transformation" (Bickford, *Encyclopedia of Genocide and Crimes against Humanity* 2004, 1045). It is not a type of justice but rather a *context* of justice for societies undergoing transformation, which may occur quickly or take many decades. From the International Center for Transitional Justice (hereafter termed the ICTJ) (2008, 1), transitional justice "emerged in the late 1980s and early 1990s, mainly in response to political change in Latin America and Eastern Europe and to demands in these regions for justice." At the time, commentators argued that a state's uses of violence and terror toward citizens had to be addressed, but without undermining the potential for a state to shift to democracy. Such shifts were initially termed "transitions to democracy," but in time the field was called "transitional justice" (ICTJ 2008, 1). Its legal basis is, in part, an Inter-American Court of Human Rights decision in 1988, stipulating that states had "four fundamental obligations in the area of human rights: . . . to prevent human rights violations, to conduct . . . investigations of [them], to impose sanctions on those responsible . . ., and to ensure reparation for the victims" (ICTJ 2008, 1).

ICTJ says a "holistic approach" (2) is necessary. The complexity and scale of abuse and victimization, coupled with the costs of legal redress and the likelihood of continuing political and judicial corruption, render standard approaches of prosecution and trial not feasible or practical. Further, there are pressing needs to reintroduce social organization and cohesion in a society, which could be thwarted by prosecution alone. Thus, a variety of approaches is recommended. In addition to criminal prosecutions, these include truth commissions, reparation programs, changes to a state's security system (including the police, military, and judiciary), and memorial activities. Starting about 2005, scholars and activists began to systematically consider women and gender differences in transitional justice. They identified the gender specificity of victimization, urged greater awareness of women as victims, and called for appropriate mechanisms of redress for women (Rubio-Marín 2006, 2009; Bell and O'Rourke 2007; Couillard 2007; Rubio-Marín and de Greiff 2007).

2. *Truth Commissions*

Truth commissions are one mechanism of transitional justice, although they have also been used to address political conflicts in countries at peace (e.g., the Greensboro Truth and Reconciliation Commission in the United States, 2004–06).[34] Brahm (2004) says that twenty-seven commissions established since 1974 were characterized by diverse goals, ways of operating, and outcomes. He suggests that one claimed benefit of truth commissions is "delivering . . . restorative justice," which he defines as "trauma healing [and] . . . restor[ing] dignity to victims" (6).

This may result from victims telling their story of what occurred and listening to the accounts of perpetrators and other victims. He notes, however, that these "therapeutic benefits" have not been established empirically. Likewise, Erin Daly (2008, 24) suggests that "insufficient attention has been paid to the hazards of truth-seeking and truth-revealing."

How did restorative justice come to be linked to truth commissions? The connection was first made when (then) Archbishop Desmond Tutu framed the establishment of South Africa's Truth and Reconciliation Commission in 1995 (hereafter termed the TRC). As chairperson of the commission, Tutu (1999) embraced the idea of restorative justice, associating it with traditional African jurisprudence (*ubuntu*) and reconciliation. He said that rather than having mass prosecutions for state violence and human rights abuses that had occurred under the apartheid regime, the decision taken was to use a restorative approach. The framing of the 1995 TRC legislation drew a contrast between restorative justice and vengeance (the latter associated with retributive justice): "there is a need for understanding but not for vengeance, a need for reparation but not for retaliation, a need for *ubuntu* [humanity to others] but not for victimization" (cited in Roche 2007, 78). As Roche points out, this false opposition between the restorative ("African") and a vengeance-defined retributive ("Western") justice left little role for formal prosecution and punishment; and as Wilson (2001, 11) says, there was no "space to discuss fully the middle position: the pursuit of legal retribution as a possible route to reconciliation itself."

We cannot examine the TRC in any depth. Rather, we make several observations on how international legal analysts have come to associate its practices with restorative justice. Minow (1998, 91) suggests that the focus of the TRC "moved away from prosecutions toward an ideal of restorative justice," which, she says

> seeks to repair the injustice, to make up for it, and to effect corrective changes. . . . Offenders have responsibility in the resolution. The harmful act, rather than the offender, is to be renounced. Repentance and forgiveness are encouraged (91).

She believes that this ideal is "unlike punishment, which imposes a penalty or injury for a violation," and is unlike "retributive approaches, which may reinforce anger. . . . The TRC emphasizes truth-telling, public acknowledgment, and actual reparations as crucial elements for restoration of justice and community" (91–92). Thus, Minow's early and widely cited work recapitulates the contrast between "restorative justice" and "retributive approaches," creating a false opposition, as noted by Roche and Wilson above. This is a typical practice in the international criminal justice and transitional justice literatures, as analysts have selectively adopted ideas from the restorative justice field. In general, and except for Combs (2007), restorative justice is used to refer to a parallel set of justice activities, with different aims and purposes than conventional mechanisms of prosecution and trial.

3. *Other Reparation Mechanisms*

In addition to truth commissions, other reparation mechanisms are used, although they are typically not termed restorative justice. de Greiff (2006a) summarizes eleven cases in the post–World War II period: four in postwar contexts; six in postconflict societies; and one in the aftermath of the September 11 attacks in the United States. In most contexts, individual victims were political prisoners and torture victims. Forms of reparation were made through legislative measures, truth commission recommendations, treaties, and the establishment of national and United Nations bodies to allocate funds to claimants. Among the types of reparation were restitution (e.g., reinstating citizenship and being released from wrongful detention), compensation (e.g., money and pensions), rehabilitation (e.g., education support and health assistance), and satisfaction (e.g., identifying the remains of family members and creating sites of memory).

Reparation can also be established in less formalized ways by, for example, community groups. Nikolic-Ristanovic (2005) identifies community-based initiatives (which she calls restorative justice), such as "storytelling workshops, days of reflection, and permanent living memorial museums" (280). These can be used to fill a gap in responding to war-related sexual violence that is not addressed by any legal system.

4. *Restorative Justice in International Criminal Justice*

One novel approach extends the idea of truth commissions. It recognizes that efforts to bring to trial all (or even many) of those accused of war-related crime are impossible and prohibitively expensive. Combs (2007) proposes an aggressive policy of plea bargaining, carried out with a credible threat of prosecution, along with the "restorative justice guilty plea," which contains elements that make the guilty plea hearing more meaningful. These include truth-telling by a defendant, describing what was done in detail; and victim participation, including voicing the effects of crimes and asking questions (e.g., about the location of bodies).

B. Restorative Justice in Domestic Criminal Justice and in Addressing Wider Political Conflict

In domestic criminal justice, the most frequent form that restorative justice takes is facilitated meetings between victims, offenders, and others. These occur only after an admission or plea, and they are termed victim-offender mediation and conferencing. The differences between the two are not as sharp as they once were (when mediation referred to just a victim and offender meeting), and some countries may use the terms mediation or conferencing to refer to similar processes.

1. *Victim-Offender Mediation*

Victim-offender mediation (VOM)[35] is the term frequently used in North America, England and Wales, and European countries to refer to post-plea meetings between adult offenders and victims, facilitated by a trained person. These can occur at different stages of the criminal process, with different sources of referral, and they may be run by volunteer groups or state agencies. The general idea is that there is an exchange of information and expression of feelings between the protagonists, and an outcome determined. Early texts include Marshall and Merry (1990) and Davis (1992) on reparation and mediation in England and Wales, and Umbreit (1994) on mediation in the United States.

2. *Youth Justice Conferences*

These began in 1989 with family group conferences in New Zealand, and from the early 1990s on, community conferences, and then youth justice conferences in Australia. The police-led conferencing model was exported to North America and England in the mid 1990s. Compared to earlier forms of victim-offender mediation, conferences normally have a larger number of participants, and in New Zealand and Australia they are statutorily based. The aim is for offenders, victims, their supporters, and other relevant people to discuss the offense and its impact, and to consider a suitable undertaking or outcome. They are typically used as diversion from court, but are also used as pre-sentence advice, depending on the jurisdiction. Key empirical works include Maxwell and Morris (1993) for New Zealand; Strang et al. (1999) and Strang (2002) on the Re-Integrative Shaming Experiments (RISE) in Canberra; Daly (2001, 2002, 2003) on the South Australia Juvenile Justice Conferencing; and Hoyle, Young, and Hill (2002) on Thames Valley restorative cautioning.

3. *Adult Pre-Sentence Conferences*

Compared to VOMs, conferences are less frequently used in adult cases. Pre-sentence (post-plea) adult conferencing was introduced in four New Zealand jurisdictions in 2001 (Morris et al. 2005), expanding to a wider number of jurisdictions in 2005. Pre-sentence conferencing was also introduced in England in several jurisdictions during the early 2000s with RISE-UK (Sherman et al. 2005; see also Shapland et al. 2007). In both jurisdictions, cases do not go forward unless first victims, and then offenders, agree to participate. The London site for RISE-UK utilizes an experimental design, in which cases are randomly assigned to a conference (or not). In both jurisdictions, the conference is viewed as supplemental or providing advice to the sentencing: a report describing the conference and outcome is provided to the sentencing judge, who may take into account what occurred in fashioning a sentence.

4. *Post-Sentence and Prison Pre-Release*

The uses of restorative justice, broadly defined, in prison contexts varies greatly (see Liebmann and Braithwaite 1999 for an inventory). van Ness (2005) sketches five applications, ordered from least to most ambitious. First, is developing prisoner awareness and empathy, using educational projects; second is identifying the mechanisms by which prisoners can make amends to victims or communities (including monetary recompense or community service); third is facilitated dialogue between prisoners, family members, and victims; fourth is developing ties between prisoners and those who live in the surrounding area; and fifth is addressing conflicts in prison (among prisoners, among staff and management, and between both groups). As might be expected, compared to youth and adult conferencing, more serious offenses are addressed in facilitated dialogue between prisoners and others. Umbreit et al. (2003) describe serious violence cases (mainly homicide, but also rape and robbery) with prisoners, family members, and victims in Texas and Ohio; and Gustafson (2005) review similar developments that began in British Columbia in the late 1980s, but have since expanded throughout other Canadian provinces. In many prison-based contexts of restorative justice, the activity is carried out by voluntary groups and is outside the criminal justice system. For example, facilitated dialogue (application three) is not supposed to have any bearing on parole decisions.

5. *Wider Political Conflict*

Restorative justice processes are used to address wider political conflicts, which, depending on the writer or specific case, may also be viewed as an instance of transitional justice. Community-based restorative justice was introduced in 1997 to address Republican and Loyalist paramilitary violence in Northern Ireland and to facilitate the peace process (McEvoy and Mika 2002). Disputes involved individuals, families, and groups of households; they included both antisocial behavior and crime, ranging from relatively minor matters (property damage or noise) to more severe (paramilitary threat). If shuttling between disputants did not address a problem, a mediation or conference was held.

Restorative justice forums have been used to address various manifestations of hate crime in the United States (see Coates, Umbreit, and Vos 2006). The authors present case studies of racial conflict in a school and community, the impact of the murder of a transgendered Navajo youth, and the impact of threats made to an Islamic Cultural Center after the September 11 attacks. Each case has a unique configuration of elements, but they typically involve large community meetings, where protagonists discuss and address offenses committed, fears about safety, and sources of animosity and prejudice, as initial steps toward developing more cohesive relations.

V. THEORIES RELATED TO REPARATION, RESTORATION, AND RESTORATIVE JUSTICE

In domestic and international criminal justice settings, reparation, restoration, and restorative justice contain new roles for victims, offenders, and other participants; and new ideas about what should occur. These center on a more informal, dialogic process, although one circumscribed by law and legal limits; rights of participation to speak and contribute to decisions on outcomes by victims, offenders, and relevant others; processes that provide openings for offender remorse and victim validation; and sanctions that are linked in a meaningful way to offenses. We consider a small set of theories, those focusing on social interaction and behavior, mainly in domestic criminal justice contexts. However, there are many normative theories and legal arguments, including Braithwaite and Pettit (1992), Duff (2001), Hudson (2003) for domestic criminal justice settings; and Tomuschat (2002), Verdeja (2006), and Magarrell (2009) for international settings. We point to empirical work associated with the theories, but space limitations preclude a distillation of empirical findings.

A. Reintegrative Shaming

Braithwaite introduced the term reintegrative shaming in 1989, and he refined it further as conferencing developed in the Antipodes (Braithwaite and Daly 1994; Braithwaite and Mugford 1994; Braithwaite 1995, 1996). The key elements are encapsulated in his 1995 publication, from which we draw. Shaming (defined as "all social processes of expressing disapproval that have the intention or the effect of involving remorse in the person being shamed or condemnation by others," 191) is a more effective deterrent to crime than formal punishment. It accomplishes "moral education" about what is right and wrong, setting in motion processes of both self and social disapproval; and it involves active citizen discussion and participation in disapproving certain acts. There are two types of shaming: stigmatizing and reintegrative. The former communicates disrespectful disapproval, humiliation, labeling both the person and the deed as bad, and offering only "ceremonies to certify deviance." The latter communicates respectful disapproval, labeling the person as good but the act as bad, and "ceremonies to certify deviance" followed by those that decertify it (194). Braithwaite argues that community conferencing (as practiced in New Zealand and Australia with large numbers of people), rather than victim-offender mediation (as normally having just a facilitator and victim-offender dyad), exemplifies a "micro form of communitarianism" (198), which structures both shame and reintegration into the justice activity. Although his theory has mainly been applied in studies of re-offending, Braithwaite argues that the process has a "victim-centered agenda that conduces to a sequence of confrontation-remorse-apology-forgiveness-help" (199).

Braithwaite's re-integrative shaming contains ideas that had been developing for some time: a preference for informal processes, where "citizens talk about crime" (192) and professionals are sidelined, and outcomes involve "the payment of restitution" (199). However, Braithwaite's theory caught on rapidly because "shaming" and "re-integration" had great popular appeal, and the theory was amenable to studies of re-offending. Hayes (2005, 2007) provides a review of the re-offending literature; and Dignan (2005, 102–3, 116–18), an analysis of re-integrative shaming.

B. Procedural Justice

As developed by Tyler (1990, 2006 2nd ed.), procedural justice aimed to de-couple citizens' assessments of procedural fairness from the favorability (or not) of outcomes received. Contrary to caricatured versions of a more complex argument, Tyler did not say that outcomes did not matter, nor that process was more important than outcomes. Rather, he said that procedural fairness (termed process control) and outcome favorability (termed outcome control) were "distinct, but not independent" (92). The "markers" of process control are trust (an authority is benevolent or caring), neutrality, voice (being able to state one's case), and standing (being treated with dignity and respect). Tyler (1990) noted that because informal legal procedures had more opportunities for citizen participation and allowed a greater degree of decision-maker flexibility, they "may correspond more closely than trials to people's intuitions about what is a fair procedure" (155).[36] And why do citizens' judgments matter? If procedures are judged to be fair, this reinforces a view that authorities are legitimate; and such legitimacy "promotes compliance with the law" (170). Tyler's ideas were explicitly featured in early research on restorative justice and conferencing in Australia (see, e.g., Daly et al. 1998, 2001; Strang et al. 1999), which focused on participants' perceptions of the fairness of the process and outcome, whether there were higher levels of perceived procedural justice in conference than court settings, and whether the conference experience generated increased levels of legitimacy and respect toward the police, law, and courts. Selected findings are available in Strang et al. (1999) and Daly (2001). One finding from Daly (2001) that is relevant to the next section is very high levels of procedural fairness are registered by offenders, and to a lesser degree victims, but there is relatively less evidence of "restorativeness" (defined as positive movement or mutual understanding of victims, offenders, or supporters) during the conference process.

C. Remorse, Contrition, and Apology

All analysts recognize the unique capacity of informal justice processes to provide openings for the expression of an offender's remorse, contrition, and sincere apology. If perceived as sincere or genuine by a victim, there is potential for accepting the apology or forgiving an offender. With some exceptions (e.g., Retzinger and Scheff 1996; Bottoms 2003; Daly 2003; Hayes 2006; Dignan 2007), few in the restorative justice field have called attention to the fragile quality of the apology process and why sincere apologies are difficult to achieve. Tavuchis's (1991) comprehensive sociological analysis of apology and reconciliation shows why. An apology "consists of a genuine display of regret and sorrow," and "in its purest expression, . . . [it] clearly announces that 'I have no excuses for what I did or did not do or say. I am sorry and regretful. I care. Forgive me'" (19). Following the apology itself is the "response of the injured party: whether to accept . . . by forgiving, to refuse and reject the offender, or to acknowledge [but defer] a decision" (23). If all of this is carried off successfully, an apology "is a decisive moment in a complex restorative project" (45), although "there are . . . overwhelming odds against its success" (46). Many things get in the way of success, but two are important in a criminal justice context: offenders may offer "accounts" (explanations or excuses) rather than apologies, and the presence of third parties, who introduce new, potentially negative dynamics in what is optimally a dyadic, private activity (Tavuchis 1991). For these reasons, it is not surprising to learn that the "core sequence" of apology and steps toward forgiveness was not observed by Retzinger and Scheff (1996) in the youth justice conferences they observed, and that just 27 percent and 41 percent, respectively, of victims interviewed in the South Australia Juvenile Justice (SAJJ) and RISE projects believed an offender's apology was sincere (Daly 2006, 139–40; see also Hayes 2006).

D. Theories Regarding Victims

Some authors call attention to the claimed, but poorly theorized or empirically demonstrated, benefits of informal justice processes for victims. Questions are rightly raised about the superficiality of "satisfaction" as a measure of victims' judgments of their involvement, and more generally, of the lack of using relevant psychological theories in assessing the ability of victims to recover from crime (Pemberton, Winkel, and Groenhuijsen 2007, 4). Critiques are rightly lodged of the "profoundly ambivalent . . . attitudes toward victims" evident in the theories underpinning restorative justice (Dignan 2007, 312; see also Dignan 2005, ch. 4). Several types of theoretical arguments are now emerging. Pemberton, Winkel, and Groenhuijsen (2007) consider psychological theories related to anxiety (control and attributions of the causes of victimization) and anger (rumination, forgiveness, and apologies); they call for more careful attention to the "intra-psychic" dimensions to victims' experiences in restorative justice and how this varies, depending on the severity of offenses to victims. In addition to Tavuchis (1991) on apologies, Dignan (2007, 314–16) identifies "narrative theory," with its emphasis on storytelling and the ability to reframe events, and cognitive behavioral theory, which may "neutralize trauma" and "desensitize victims to the emotional trauma" caused by an offense.[37] In understanding the specific experiences of domestic and sexual violence victims, Herman (2005) emphasizes their need for validation, vindication, and integration, not from an offender but from "the community," saying that victims seek "the restoration of their own honor and the re-establishment of their own connections with the community" (585). She challenges the offender-centered assumptions of reintegrative shaming, which are more relevant for nonviolent property crime than domestic and sexual violence, by suggesting that "the person who needs to be welcomed back into the community, first and foremost, is the victim" (598). All those who are concerned with victims' experiences raise questions about the value of apologies, how they are made and received, and the potential for revictimization when apologies are insincere.

VI. Conclusion

Reparation and restoration emerged as criminal justice aims in the last half century, mushrooming to global prominence during the 1990s in domestic and international criminal justice settings. Many people, who are working in varied academic disciplines and analyzing crime in developed, developing, and postconflict societies, have been inspired to reflect upon, critique, and conduct research on how these terms relate to the ideal and actual practices of "doing justice." The newness of the ideas and excitement they have generated, the large numbers of people involved, the range of disciplinary and practice contexts, and movement across domestic and international criminal justice contexts—all of this has contributed to a huge field of knowledge that is not easily depicted.

In general, international criminal justice bifurcates "justice" and "reparation." The former centers on modes of adjudicating and punishing offenders, and the latter, on modes of redress for victims, typically as collectivities. In international contexts, reparation is also concerned with state building and developing new citizen-state relationships. By comparison, when restorative justice was introduced in domestic settings, many believed that it offered an alternative to standard modes of punishing offenders, with its objectives of restoration and reparation. (It is important to remember that restorative justice has no mechanism of adjudication.) What "restoration" and "reparative outcomes" for an individual offender and victim would actually mean in a criminal justice activity was (and is) less clear.

In domestic contexts, some argue that censure and punishment are integral to restoration and reparation, whereas others say that restoration or reparation are "nonpunitive" or "nonpunishment" responses. Thus, there is a significant divide between those who wish to build a new model of criminal justice that retains retribution and punishment, but in a new form (e.g., Duff 2001, 2003; Dignan 2003); and those who eschew these ideas and advocate a new type of legal and justice order that is built primarily on restorative values (e.g., Braithwaite 2003). This schism will not go away any time soon because it is profoundly political and ideological.

Those new to the field face significant hurdles in grasping key concepts, which are defined differently, depending on the author. The restorative justice field would have greater presence and stature with more definitional discipline. At a minimum, it would help to have one set of definitions for restitution, compensation, reparative outcomes, symbolic reparation, among many other terms. Although it may not be possible to fully define restorative justice (not unlike the problems that philosophers have had in discussing retribution as a theory of punishment), a glossary of key terms, which explicates and harmonizes the different ways they have been used, would be a good start. It is also important to move beyond the simple oppositional contrast of retributive and restorative justice. Although as Roche (2007, 87) suggests, it served its purpose as a "catchy exposition" in the early years, it now confuses more than enlightens.

Despite the ideological differences and definitional problems, it is possible to describe what sets restorative justice, and associated ideas of reparation and restoration, apart from other theories or practices of criminal justice in domestic settings. The distinctive elements are a dual focus on victims and offenders as active participants and subjects of justice mechanisms; and an interest to address crime directly by the actions, words, or burdens imposed on offenders directly to victims, and where relevant, to a wider social group. No other criminal justice theory has an explicit place for victims, nor an emphasis on interactions between them, admitted offenders, and relevant others in coming to terms with crime. Formal legality has an important role in checking informal processes like restorative justice (Braithwaite 1996), holding decision-makers accountable (Roche 2003), and striking a balance between victim and offender interests, which are often in conflict (Dignan 2005, 179–87). A significant challenge, however, lies with "ordinary citizens," upon whom the "whole operation" of criminal justice has long relied (Lacey 1994, 8). We are called upon to play an even greater role in criminal justice, with more generous, empathetic, and supportive orientations; and abilities to engage with others, to speak and listen well, and to negotiate novel and meaningful outcomes. Ideally, our orientations, words, and ideas are to have as much or more weight than those of legal actors in "doing justice."

NOTES

1. *Basic Principles and Guidelines on the Right to a Remedy and Reparation for Victims of Gross Violations of International Human Rights Law and Serious Violations of International Humanitarian Law* (Resolution adopted by the United Nations in March 2006), where section IX, no. 19 states that "restitution includes as appropriate: restoration of liberty, enjoyment of human rights, identity." Hereafter, we refer to this as the UN Resolution (2006).

2. Hereafter, when referring to "the restorative justice field," we mean those who consider its application mainly in domestic contexts, and particularly in criminal justice.

3. See Bottoms (2003) for a more detailed analysis of why and where restorative justice has been popular.

4. Although restorative and reparative justice connote different meanings, it may be an accident of history that restorative, not reparative justice was the victor.

5. In the transitional justice literature, this Resolution is referred to as the Basic Principles, the shorthand for *Basic Principles and Guidelines on the Right to a Remedy and Reparation for Victims of Gross Violations of International Human Rights Law and Serious Violations of International Humanitarian Law.*

6. The wer was a "payment to a family for the death of one of its members; the bot . . . a family payment for injuries less than death; and the wite, a sum of money paid to the lords to cover the cost of over-seeing the system of compensation" (Hudson and Galaway 1975, xix; see also Schafer 1968).

7. Jacob (1970) uses the term "Great Britain." Throughout this chapter, we preserve the geographical names of places that authors themselves cite.

8. de Greiff (2006b), among others, refers to these as reparation*s* (see 452–53 for the distinction he draws between reparation and reparation*s*). In the literature, analysts have other views and variably use the singular or plural form. Here, we preserve their original language; however, we refer to reparation in the singular.

9. We consider only those terms relevant to restorative justice in domestic settings, i.e., restitution, compensation, and satisfaction. Rehabilitation for victims is not part of domestic criminal justice, although some believe that it should be (Coker 2000, 2002); and except for assurances of a victim's safety, the guarantees of nonrepetition are not apt. One important difference between the UN Resolution (2006) and domestic criminal justice codes is that the Resolution recognizes that a person can be a "victim regardless of whether the perpetrator . . . is identified, apprehended, prosecuted, or convicted." (6). In domestic contexts, this is applicable in some state compensation programs.

10. Roberts (2009, 163) says that financial recompense to a victim is referred to as *compensatory* in the United Kingdom and *restitutive* in the United States. Writing from a British context, Ashworth (1986) says that compensation refers to both individual and state payments to a victim, whereas in the United States, it usually refers only to state payments to victims.

11. These are viewed as indicators of "restorativeness" between victims, offenders, and/or their supporters (Daly 2001, 2003), "reintegration" (Roche 2003, 30, drawing from Braithwaite 1989), or the second step in Retzinger and Scheff's (1996) core sequence.

12. This distinction is challenged by the Nairobi Declaration (2007), which seeks "comprehensive reparations for victims of sexual violence and reaffirms the need for both restorative and retributive justice" (Couillard 2007, p. 447).

13. There can be exceptions to this, of course; for example, restorative justice processes could occur in the absence of offenders or admissions to offending (Coates, Umbreit, and Vos 2006).

14. Many justice activities that are now called restorative justice (e.g., youth diversionary and pre-sentence conferences in Australia, New Zealand, and elsewhere) do not fully accord with the elements set forth in the Resolution (2002). For example, conferences are part of the criminal justice process, they operate under police and court discretionary criteria, and outcomes are recorded in offenders' criminal histories.

15. Mead was making this argument to defend the merits of an emerging juvenile court.

16. Or, as Roche (2007, 78) suggests, "'retributive justice' is [considered] a dirty word, not a theory of punishment." See Roche (2007) and Crawford and Newburn (2003, 45–46) for good summaries of the relationship of retribution and punishment to restorative justice.

17. In fact, Zehr's (1985) argument draws a good deal more from Barnett's (1977) formulation than is often credited. Barnett developed the idea of a Kuhnian paradigm "shift of world view" (287) from punishment to restitution; and the definition of crime as an offense against an individual, not society (or the state).

18. See Bottoms (2003) for discussion of the "civilization thesis" and the problems it raises for restorative justice.

19. This connection to Elias was also made by Walgrave (2004, 24), who says that "maybe the next step in civilization is to reduce state violence itself by not taking for granted pain infliction after a crime."

20. Although the term "adversarial" is associated with specific mechanisms by which "truth" is discerned in common law adjudication, the presumption of innocence and right to defend oneself against the state's allegations is, of course, also part of inquisitorial adjudication in civil law countries.

21. The story is a bit more complicated. In Eglash (1957–58b), he says "the relationship between offense and restitution is reparative, restorative" (20). In Eglash (1959–60, 116), the term "restorative justice" appears, but it is indented in the text as "condensed" from Schrey, Whitehouse, and Walz (1955), which is an English translation of a German text, *The Biblical Doctrine of Justice and Law*. Skelton's LLD (2005, 84–89) research discovered that the third author, the Reverend Whitehouse, carried out a translation and adaptation of the original text; and he created the term "restorative justice" from the German expression "*heilende Gerechtigkeit*" ("healing justice"). It was argued that restorative justice added a "fourth dimension" to justice and differed from secular forms of retributive, commutative, and distributive justice in that it "can heal the . . . wound of sin" (Skelton 2005, 88).

22. This is Campbell's (1984) argument: reparation (which he defines as criminal justice schemes for victim compensation) is a "form of punishment" (347), not in opposition to it. Thus, "the idea of compensation as punishment is in general a restoration of the moral breach between victim and offender created by the offence" (346). Ashworth (1986) argues that the state should punish an "offender's mental attitude . . . so as to restore the order of justice in the community which was disrupted by the crime" (97), and this should be distinguished from a victim's right to also receive compensation. At the same time, he viewed the (then) new British compensation order as an appropriate sentence outcome.

23. See Bottoms (2003) for an analysis and critique of Christie's romantic view of dispute resolution.

24. See Daly (2001, 63–65) for a summary of the serendipitous connection that was made between re-integrative shaming and New Zealand family group conferencing in 1990 by an Australian police officer, which was then applied to a *police-led* youth cautioning program in New South Wales in 1991, and subsequently to other Australian jurisdictions. Police-led conferencing, which was exported to North America and England in the mid 1990s, differs from what is termed "New Zealand style" conferencing, which is not facilitated by a police officer and does not rely exclusively or mainly on the theory of re-integrative shaming.

25. We do not consider their analysis of "shame as a master emotion" (318) and how this may (or may not) relate to re-integration. For them, community conferences were one site to observe their theorizations on shame, emotions, and micro interactions.

26. However, in Strang (2002, 18), the wording changes slightly: "victims see emotional *reconciliation* to be far more important than material or financial reparation" (emphasis added).

27. Strang (2001) is principally interested to show the benefits of conferences over court processes for victims' emotional restoration: apologies are more often given in conferences than in court, and victims' emotional restoration (on various measures) is higher. Despite this, victims do distinguish between sincere and insincere apologies, as discussed in section 5.

28. Both Duff (2002) and Sharpe (2007) are concerned with addressing the *wrong* of crime by an apology, whereas others such as Strang are concerned with addressing the "emotional harm" a victim may have suffered. The two are not the same.

29. Dignan (2005, 196–200) provides a glossary of terms, with reference mainly to England and Wales; it could be a good base to build a larger, more authoritative analysis of terms.

30. Depending on the writer, the goal may also be restoration of an offender and "the community." Zedner (1994, 235) suggests that the goal of reparative justice is "reintegration [of the offender] and restoration simultaneously."

31. Braithwaite (2002*b*, 570) attempts to address this problem by adding a maximizing value of "providing support to develop human capabilities to the full" so that restorative justice is not "used to restore an unjust status quo." The aspiration to transform, rather than to restore to a status quo, is at the heart of the Nairobi Declaration (2007) (see Couillard 2007, 450–51).

32. Some authors (e.g., King et al. 2009) use the term "non-adversarial justice" as the umbrella concept to include restorative justice, therapeutic jurisprudence, alternative dispute resolution, problem-oriented courts, Indigenous sentencing courts, preventive law, holistic approaches to law, among other areas.

33. This model builds on Cavadino and Dignan's (1997, 248n1) earlier work where they contrast two meanings of reparation: in a narrow sense, it refers to offenders making amends to individual victims (with "restitution as a near synonym"); but in a wider sense, it refers to measures that "recompense the community as a whole" (including community service or paying fines), with "restoration" as the term closest in meaning. This distinction in the meanings of reparation does not appear in Dignan's (2005) glossary of terms, however.

34. This truth commission examined events in November 1979 in Greensboro, North Carolina, when five African American protesters were killed in a union demonstration; all of those accused were acquitted (see Brown et al. 2006; Androff 2008).

35. Victim-Offender Reconciliation Projects (VORPs), first used in North America in the mid 1970s, preceded VOMs. As the idea expanded from its Mennonite religious base, van Ness and Strong (2006, 28) say that the "terms "mediation" or "dialogue" [were used] instead of "reconciliation" because . . . the latter term sounded too religious."

36. It is odd that he chose the term "trial" here; his Chicago study surveyed people by phone, asking them about their experiences with the police and courts; for the latter, it appears that most surveyed experiences were not of criminal matters (see 89), but Tyler is not explicit on this point.

37. Dignan (2007) briefly considers Collins' (2004) analysis of restorative justice as "interaction ritual." However, when reading the single paragraph that Collins devotes to restorative justice (111) in a book of over four hundred pages, we find that he has a misinformed view of the routine practices of restorative justice: he assumes a highly romanticized and atypical "nirvana story" (Daly 2002).

REFERENCES

Androff, David. 2009. "Community Reconciliation and Welfare: Victims' Perspectives on the Greensboro Truth & Reconciliation Commission." Paper presented at the National Conference on Restorative Justice, San Antonio, TX, May 13–15.

Ashworth, Andrew. 1986. "Punishment and Compensation: Victims, Offenders and the State." *Oxford Journal of Legal Studies* 6(1): 86–122.

Ashworth, Andrew, and Andrew von Hirsh. 1993. "Desert and the Three Rs." *Current Issues in Criminal Justice* 5(1): 9–12.

Atuahene, Bernadette. 2007. "From Reparation to Restoration: Moving Beyond Restoring Property Rights to Restoring Political and Economical Visibility." *Southern Methodist University Law Review* 60(4): 1419–70.

Barnett, Randall. 1977. "Restitution: A New Paradigm of Criminal Justice." *Ethics* 87: 279–301.

Bell, Christine, and Catherine O'Rourke. 2007. "Does Feminism Need a Theory of Transitional Justice? An Introductory Essay." *The International Journal of Transitional Justice* 1(1): 23–44.

Bernhardt, Rudolf, and Peter MacAlister-Smith, eds. 1992. *Encyclopedia of Public International Law*, vol. 4. Amsterdam: North-Holland Publishing Company.

Bickford, Louis. 2004. "Transitional Justice." In *Encyclopedia of Genocide and Crimes against Humanity*, vol. 3, edited by Dinah Shelton, Howard Adelman, Frank Chalk, Alexandre Kiss, and William A. Schabas. Detroit: Macmillan Reference.

Bottoms, Anthony E. 1998. "Five Puzzles in von Hirsch's Theory of Punishment." In *Fundamentals of Sentencing Theory: Essays in Honour of Andrew von Hirsch*, edited by Andrew Ashworth and Martin Wasik. Oxford: Clarendon Press.

———. 2003. "Some Sociological Reflections on Restorative Justice." In *Restorative Justice and Criminal Justice: Competing or Reconcilable Paradigms?*, edited by Andrew von Hirsch, Julian Roberts, Anthony E. Bottoms, Kent Roach., and Mara Schiff. Oxford: Hart Publishing.

Bradley, Megan. 2006. *FMO Research Guide: Reparations, Reconciliation and Forced Migration*. Oxford: Refugee Studies Centre. http://repository.forcedmigration.org/show_metadata.jsp?pid=fmo:5155

Brahm, Eric. 2004. "Truth Commissions." In *Beyond Intractability*, edited Guy Burgess and Heidi Burgess. Boulder, CO: Conflict Research Consortium, University of Colorado.

Braithwaite, John. 1989. *Crime, Shame and Reintegration*. Cambridge: Cambridge University Press.

———. 1995. "Reintegrative Shaming, Republicanism, and Policy." In *Crime and Public Policy: Putting Theory to Work*, edited by Hugh D. Barlow. Boulder, CO: Westview Press.

———. 1996. "Restorative Justice and a Better Future." *Dalhousie Review* 76(1): 9–32. Reprinted in *A Restorative Justice Reader*, edited by Gerry Johnstone. 2003. Cullompton: Willan Publishing.

———. 1999. "Restorative Justice: Assessing Optimistic and Pessimistic Accounts." In *Crime and Justice: A Review of Research*, vol. 25, edited by Michael Tonry. Chicago: University of Chicago.

———. 2002a. *Restorative Justice and Response Regulation*. Oxford: Oxford University Press.

———. 2002b. "Setting Standards for Restorative Justice." *British Journal of Criminology* 42(3): 563–77.

———. 2003. "Principles of Restorative Justice." In *Restorative Justice and Criminal Justice: Competing or Reconcilable Paradigms?*, edited by Andrew von Hirsch, Julian Roberts, Anthony E. Bottoms, Kent Roach, and Mara Schiff. Oxford: Hart Publishing.

Braithwaite, John, and Kathleen Daly. 1994. "Masculinities, Violence and Communitarian Control." In *Men, Masculinities and Crime. Just Boys Doing Business?*, edited by Tim Newburn and Elizabeth A. Stanko. New York: Routledge.

Braithwaite, John, and Philip Pettit. 1992. *Not Just Deserts: A Republican Theory of Criminal Justice*. Oxford: Oxford University Press.

Braithwaite, John, and Stephen Mugford. 1994. "Conditions of Successful Reintegration Ceremonies." *British Journal of Criminology* 34(2): 139–71.

Brown, Cynthia, Patricia Clark, Muktha Jost, Angela Lawrence, Robert Peters, Mark Sills, and Barbara Walker. 2006. *Greensboro Truth and Reconciliation Commission Report*. http://www.greensborotrc.org/

Campbell, Tom. 1984. "Compensation as Punishment." *University of New South Wales Law Journal* 7(2): 338–61.

Cavadino, Michael, and James Dignan. 1997. "Reparation, Retribution and Rights." *International Review of Victimology* 4(4): 233–53.

Christie, Nils. 1977. "Conflicts as Property." *British Journal of Criminology* 17(1): 1–5. Reprinted in *A Restorative Justice Reader*, edited by Gerry Johnstone. 2003. Cullompton: Willan Publishing.

Coates, Robert, Mark Umbreit, and Betty Vos. 2006. "Responding to Hate Crimes through Restorative Justice Dialogues." *Contemporary Justice Review* 9(1): 7–21.

Coker, Donna. 2000. "Shifting Power for Battered Women: Law, Material Resources, and Poor Women of Color." *U.C. Davis Law Review* 33: 1009–55.

———. 2002. "Transformative Justice: Anti Subordination Processes in Cases of Domestic Violence." In *Restorative Justice and Family Violence*, edited by Heather Strang and John Braithwaite. Cambridge: Cambridge University Press.

Collins, Randall. 2004. *Interaction Ritual Chains*. Princeton, NJ: Princeton University Press.

Combs, Nancy. 2007. *Guilty Pleas in International Criminal Law: Constructing a Restorative Justice Approach*. Stanford, CA: Stanford University Press.

Cossins, Annie. 2008. "Restorative Justice and Child Sex Offences." *British Journal of Criminology* 48: 557–66.

Cottingham, John. 1979. "Varieties of Retribution." *Philosophical Quarterly* 29(116): 238–46.

Couillard, Valérie. 2007. "The Nairobi Declaration: Redefining Reparations for Women Victims of Sexual Violence." *The International Journal of Transitional Justice, Special Issue: Gender and Transitional Justice* 1(3): 444–53.

Crawford, Adam, and Tim Newburn. 2003. *Youth Offending and Restorative Justice* Cullompton: Willan Publishing.

Curtis-Fawley, Sarah, and Kathleen Daly. 2005. "Gendered Violence and Restorative
    Justice. The Views of Victim Advocates." *Violence Against Women* 11(5): 603–38.
Daly, Erin. 2008. "Truth Skepticism: An Inquiry into the Value of Truth in Times of
    Transition." *The International Journal of Transitional Justice* 2(1): 23–41.
Daly, Kathleen. 2000. "Revisiting the Relationship between Retributive and Restorative
    Justice." In *Restorative Justice: Philosophy to Practice*, edited by Heather Strang and
    John Braithwaite. Aldershot: Dartmouth/Ashgate.
———. 2001. "Conferencing in Australia and New Zealand: Variations, Research Findings,
    and Prospects." In *Restorative Justice for Juveniles: Conferencing, Mediation and Circles*,
    edited by Allison Morris and Gabrielle Maxwell. Oxford: Hart Publishing.
———. 2002. "Restorative Justice: The Real Story." *Punishment and Society* 4(1): 55–79.
———. 2003. "Mind the Gap: Restorative Justice in Theory and Practice." In *Restorative
    Justice and Criminal Justice: Competing or Reconcilable Paradigms?*, edited by Andrew
    von Hirsch, Julian Roberts, Anthony E. Bottoms, Kent Roach, and Mara Schiff.
    Oxford: Hart Publishing.
———. 2006. "Limits of Restorative Justice." In *Handbook of Restorative Justice: A Global
    Perspective*, edited by Dennis Sullivan and Larry Tifft. New York: Routledge.
Daly, Kathleen, Hennessey Hayes, and Elena Marchetti. 2006. "New Visions of Justice." In
    Crime and Justice: A Guide to Criminology, edited by Andrew Goldsmith, Mark Israel,
    and Kathleen Daly. Sydney: Lawbook.
Daly, Kathleen, with the assistance of Michele Venables, Mary McKenna, Liz Mumford,
    and Jane Christie-Johnston. 1998. *South Australia Juvenile Justice Technical Report No.
    1: Project Overview and Research Instruments*. Brisbane: School of Criminology and
    Criminal Justice, Griffith University.
Daly, Kathleen, and Russ Immarigeon. 1998. "The Past, Present and Future of Restorative
    Justice: Some Critical Reflections." *Contemporary Justice Review* 1(1): 21–45.
Davis, Gwynn. 1992. *Making Amends: Mediation and Reparation in Criminal Justice*.
    London: Routledge.
Davis, Gwynn, Jacky Boucherat, and David Watson. 1988. "Reparation in the Service of
    Diversion: The Subordination of a Good Idea." *Howard Journal of Criminal Justice*
    27(2): 127–34.
de Greiff, Pablo. 2006*a*. "Introduction. Repairing the Past: Compensation for Victims of
    Human Rights Violations." In *The Handbook of Reparations*, edited by Pablo de Greiff.
    Oxford: Oxford University Press.
———. 2006*b*. "Justice and Reparations." In *The Handbook of Reparations*, edited by Paolo
    de Greiff. Oxford: Oxford University Press.
Dignan, James. 2003. "Towards a Systemic Model of Restorative Justice: Reflections on the
    Concept, its Context and the Need for Clear Constraints." In *Restorative Justice and
    Criminal Justice: Competing or Reconcilable Paradigms?*, edited by Andrew von Hirsch,
    Julian Roberts, Anthony E. Bottoms, Kent Roach., and Mara Schiff. Oxford: Hart
    Publishing.
———. 2005. *Understanding Victims and Restorative Justice*. Berkshire, Eng.: Open Univer-
    sity Press.
———. 2007. "The Victim in Restorative Justice." In *Handbook of Victims and Victimology*,
    edited by Sandra Walklate. Cullompton: Willan Publishing.
Drumbl, Mark A. 2000. "Retributive Justice and the Rwandan Genocide." *Punishment and
    Society* 2(3): 287–308.

Duff, R. Antony. 1992. "Alternatives to Punishment—or Alternative Punishments?" In *Retributivism and Its Critics*, edited by Wesley Cragg. Stuttgart: Franz Steiner.

———. 1996. "Penal Communications: Recent Work in the Philosophy of Punishment." In *Crime and Justice: A Review of Research*, vol. 20, edited by Michael Tonry. Chicago: University of Chicago Press.

———. 2001. *Punishment, Communication, and Community*. New York: Oxford University Press.

———. 2002. "Restorative Punishment and Punitive Restoration." In *Restorative Justice and the Law*, edited by Lode Walgrave. Cullompton: Willan Publishing.

———. 2003. "Restoration and Retribution." In *Restorative Justice and Criminal Justice: Competing or Reconcilable Paradigms?*, edited by Andrew von Hirsch, Julian Roberts, Anthony E. Bottoms, Kent Roach, and Mara Schiff. Oxford: Hart Publishing.

Eglash, Albert. 1957–58*a*. "Creative Restitution: A Broader Meaning for an Old Term." *Journal of Criminology and Police Science* 48(6): 619–22

———. 1957–58*b*. "Creative Restitution: Some Suggestions for Prison Rehabilitation Programs." *American Journal of Corrections* 20: 20–34.

———. 1959–60. "Creative Restitution: Its Roots in Psychiatry, Religion and Law." *British Journal of Delinquency* 10: 114–19.

———. 1977. "Beyond Restitution: Creative Restitution." In *Restitution in Criminal Justice*, edited by Joe Hudson and Burt Galaway. Lexington, MA: D. C. Heath and Company.

Fry, Margaret. 1951. *Arms of the Law*. London: Victor Gollancz.

———. 1959. "Justice for Victims." *Journal of Public Law* 8: 191–94.

Galaway, Burt, and Joe Hudson. 1996. *Restorative Justice: International Perspectives*. Monsey, NY: Criminal Justice Press.

Garland, David. 1990. *Punishment and Modern Society*. Oxford: Oxford University Press.

Goodey, Jo. 2003. *Compensating Victims of Violent Crime in the European Union with a Special Focus on Victims of Terrorism*. Vienna: The National Centre for Victim of Crime.

Gray, Christine. 1999. "The Choice between Restitution and Compensation." *European Journal of International Law* 10(2): 413–23.

Gustafson, David L. 2005. "Exploring Treatment and Trauma Recovery Implications of Facilitating Victim-Offender Encounters in Crimes of Severe Violence: Lessons from the Canadian Experience." In *New Directions in Restorative Justice: Issues, Practice, Evaluation*, edited by Elizabeth Elliott and Robert M. Gordon. Cullompton: Willan.

Hampton, Jean. 1992. "Correcting Harms versus Righting Wrongs: The Goal of Retribution." *UCLA Law Review* 39(6): 1659–1702.

———. 1998. "Punishment, Feminism, and Political Identity: A Case Study in the Expressive Meaning of the Law." *Canadian Journal of Law and Jurisprudence* 11(1): 23–45.

Harland, Alan. 1996. "Towards a Restorative Justice Future." In *Restorative Justice: International Perspectives*, edited by Burt Galaway and Joe Hudson. Monsey, N.Y.: Criminal Justice Press.

Harper, Douglas. 2001. "Reparation." *Online Etymological Dictionary*. http://www.etymonline.com/

Hayes, Hennessey. 2005. "Assessing Re-offending in Restorative Justice Conferences." *Australian and New Zealand Journal of Criminology* 38(1): 77–101.

———. 2006. "Apologies and Accounts in Youth Justice Conferencing: Reinterpreting Research Outcomes." *Contemporary Justice Review* 9(4): 369–85.

———. 2007. "Reoffending and Restorative Justice." In *Handbook of Restorative Justice*, edited by Daniel van Ness and Gerry Johnstone. Cullompton: Willan Publishing.

Herman, Judith. 2005. "Justice from the Victim's Perspective." *Violence Against Women* 11(5): 571–602.

Hoyle, Carolyn, Richard Young, and Roderick Hill. 2002. *Proceed with Caution: An Evaluation of the Thames Valley Police Initiative in Restorative Cautioning*. York: Joseph Rowntree Foundation.

Hudson, Joe and Burt Galaway, eds. 1975. *Considering the Victim: Readings in Restitution and Victim Compensation*. Springfield, IL: Charles C. Thomas.

Hudson, Barbara. 2003. *Justice and the Risk Society: Challenging and Re-Affirming Justice in Late Modernity*. London: Sage Publications.

International Center of Transitional Justice. 2008. "What is Transitional Justice?" http://www.ictj.org/en/tj/

Jacob, Bruce R. 1970. "Reparation or Restitution by the Criminal Offender to His Victim: Applicability of an Ancient Concept in the Modern Correctional Process." *Journal of Criminal Law, Criminology and Police Science* 61(2): 152–67.

Jervis, Bernard. 1996. "Developing Reparation Plans through Victim-Offender Mediation by New Zealand Probation Officers." In *Restorative Justice: International Perspectives*, edited by Burt Galaway and Joe Hudson. Monsey, N.Y.: Criminal Justice Press.

Johnstone, Gerry, ed. 2003. *A Restorative Justice Reader*. Cullompton: Willan Publishing.

Johnstone, Gerry. 2008. "The Agendas of the Restorative Justice Movement." In *Restorative Justice: From Theory to Practice*, edited by Holly Ventura Miller. Bingley: Emerald Group.

Johnstone, Gerry, and Daniel van Ness. 2007a. "The Meaning of Restorative Justice." In *Handbook of Restorative Justice,* edited by Gerry Johnstone and Daniel van Ness. Cullompton: Willan Publishing.

———, eds. 2007b. *Handbook of Restorative Justice*. Cullompton: Willan Publishing.

King, Michael, Arie Freibreg, Becky Batagol, and Ross Hyams. 2009. *Non-Adversarial Justice*. Sydney: Federation Press.

Kiss, Elizabeth E. 2005. "Righting Wrongs: Two Visions of Transitional Justice." Paper presented at the Association for Social, Political, and Legal Philosophy APSA Conference, Washington, DC, September 3.

Lacey, Nicola. 1994. "Introduction." In *A Reader on Criminal Justice*, edited by Nicola Lacey. Oxford: Oxford University Press.

Lee, Angela. 1996. "Public Attitudes towards Restorative Justice." In *Restorative Justice: International Perspectives*, edited by Burt Galaway and Joe Hudson. Monsey, N.Y.: Criminal Justice Press.

Levrant, Sharon, Francis Cullen, Betsy Fulton, and John Wozniak. 1999. "Reconsidering Restorative Justice: The Corruption of Benevolence Revisited?" *Crime and Delinquency* 45(1): 3–27.

Liebmann, Marian, and Stephanie Braithwaite. 1999. *Restorative Justice in Custodial Settings: Report for the Restorative Justice Working Group in Northern Ireland*. Belfast: Restorative Justice Ireland Network.

Magarrell, Lisa. 2009. "Reparations in Theory and Practice." Reparative Justice Series 1: 1–16. International Center for Transitional Justice.

Marchetti, Elena, and Kathleen Daly. 2007. "Indigenous Sentencing Courts: Towards a Theoretical and Jurisprudential Model." *Sydney Law Review* 29: 415–43.

Marshall, Tony. 1997. "Seeking the Whole Justice." Paper presented at the Repairing the Damage: Restorative Justice in Action Conference, Institute for the Study and Treatment of Delinquency, London, March 20.

———. 1998. "Restorative Justice: An Overview." Repr. in *A Restorative Justice Reader*, edited by Gerry Johnstone. 2003. Cullompton: Willan Publishing.

Marshall, Tony, and Sally Merry. 1990. *Crime and Accountability: Victim Offender Mediation in Practice*. London: Home Office.

Maxwell, Gabrielle, and Allison Morris. 1993. *Family, Victims and Culture: Youth Justice in New Zealand*. Wellington: Social Policy Agency and Institute of Criminology, Victoria University of Wellington.

McCold, Paul. 2000. "Toward a Holistic Vision of Restorative Juvenile Justice: A Reply to the Maximalist Model." *Contemporary Justice Review, Special Issue: Symposium on Restorative Justice* 3(4): 357–414.

McEvoy, Kieran, and Harry Mika. 2002. "Restorative Justice and the Critique of Informalism in Northern Ireland." *British Journal of Criminology* 43(30): 534–63.

Mead, George H. 1917–1918. "The Psychology of Punitive Justice." *American Journal of Sociology* 23: 577–602. Repr. in *The Sociology of Punishment: Socio-Structural Perspectives*, edited by Dario Melossi. 1998. Aldershot: Ashgate/Dartmouth.

Menkel-Meadow, Carrie. 2007. "Restorative Justice: What Is It and Does It Work?" *Annual Review of Law and Social Science* 3: 161–87.

Miers, David. 2007. "Looking Beyond Great Britain: The Development of Criminal Injuries Compensation." In *Handbook of Victims and Victimology*, edited by Sandra Walklate. Cullompton: Willan Publishing.

Minow, Martha. 1998. *Between Vengeance and Forgiveness*. Boston: Beacon Press.

Morris, Allison, Venezia Kingi, Elisabeth Poppelwell, and Sue Triggs. 2005. *New Zealand Court-Referred Restorative Justice Pilot: Evaluation*. Wellington: Ministry of Justice.

Nehusi, Kimani. 2000. "The Meaning of Reparation." *Caribnet* 3: 31–39.

Nikolic-Ristanovic, Vesna. 2005. "Sexual Violence, International Law and Restorative Justice." In *International Law: Modern Feminist Approaches*, edited by Doris Buss and Ambreena Manji. Oxford: Hart Publishing.

Pemberton, Antony, Frans W. Winkel, and Marc S. Groenhuijsen. 2007. "Taking Victims Seriously in Restorative Justice." *International Perspectives in Victimology* 3(1): 4–13.

The Pennsylvania Code. 1982. § 303.12. *Guideline Sentence Recommendations: Sentencing Programs*. http://www.pacode.com/secure/data/204/chapter303/s303.12.html

REDRESS. undated. "What is Reparation?" *Reparation for Victims of Genocide, Hate Crimes, and Crimes against Humanity*. http://www.redress.org/what_is_reparation.html

Retzinger, Suzanne M., and Thomas J. Scheff. 1996. "Strategy for Community Conferences: Emotions and Social Bonds." In *Restorative Justice: International Perspectives*, edited by Burt Galaway and Joe Hudson. Monsey, N.Y.: Criminal Justice Press.

Roberts, Julian. 2009. "Introduction to chapter 5 on Restorative Justice." In *Principled Sentencing: Readings on Theory and Policy*, edited by Andrew Ashworth, Andrew von Hirsch, and Julian Roberts. Oxford: Hart Publishing.

Roberts, Julian V. and Loretta J. Stalans. 2004. "Restorative Sentencing: Exploring the Views of the Public." *Social Justice Research* 17(3): 315–34.

Roche, Declan. 2003. *Accountability in Restorative Justice*. Oxford: Oxford University Press.

———. 2007. "Retribution and Restorative Justice." In *Handbook of Restorative Justice*, edited by Gerry Johnstone and Daniel van Ness. Cullompton: Willan Publishing

Rubio-Marín, Ruth, ed. 2006. *What Happened to the Women? Gender and Reparations for Human Rights Violations*. New York: Social Science Research Council.

Rubio-Marín, Ruth, ed. 2009. *The Gender of Reparations: Unsettling Sexual Hierarchies While Redressing Human Rights Violations*. Cambridge: Cambridge University Press.

Rubio-Marín, Ruth and Pablo de Greiff. 2007. "Women and Reparations." *The International Journal of Transitional Justice, Special Issue: Gender and Transitional Justice* 1(3): 318–37.

Schafer, Stephen. 1960. *Restitution to Victims of Crime*. Chicago: Quadrangle Books Inc.

———. 1968. *The Victim and His Criminal*. New York: Random House.

Schrey, Heinz Horst, Hans Hermann Walz, and W.A. Whitehouse. 1955. *The Biblical Doctrine of Justice and Law*. London: SCM Press, World Council of Churches.

Shapland, Joanna, Anne Atkinson, Helen Atkinson, Becca Chapman, James Dignan, Marie Howes, Jennifer Johnstone, Gwen Robinson, and Angela Sorsby. 2007. *Restorative Justice: The Views of Victims and Offenders. The Third Report from the Evaluation of Three Schemes*. London: Ministry of Justice.

Sharpe, Susan. 2007. "The Idea of Reparation." In *Handbook of Restorative Justice*, edited by Gerry Johnstone and Daniel van Ness. Cullompton: Willan Publishing.

Sherman, Lawrence W., Heather Strang, Caroline Angel, Daniel Woods, Geoffrey C. Barnes, Sarah Bennet, and Nova Inkpen. 2005. "Effects of Face-to-Face Restorative Justice on Victims of Crime in Four Randomized, Controlled Trials." *Journal of Experimental Criminology* 1(3): 367–95.

Skelton, Ann. 2005. "The Influence of the Theory and Practice of Restorative Justice in South Africa with Special Reference to Child Justice." LLD thesis, University of Pretoria, Faculty of Law.

Strang, Heather. 2001. "Justice for Victims of Young Offenders: The Centrality of Emotional Harm and Restoration." In *Restorative Justice for Juveniles: Conferencing, Mediation and Circles*, edited by Allison Morris and Gabrielle Maxwell. Oxford: Hart Publishing.

———. 2002. *Repair or Revenge: Victims and Restorative Justice*. Oxford: Oxford University Press.

Strang, Heather, Lawrence W. Sherman, Geoffrey C. Barnes, and John Braithwaite. 1999. *Experiments in Restorative Policing: A Progress Report to the National Police Research Unit on the Canberra Reintegrative Shaming Experiments (RISE)*. Canberra: Australian Federal Police and Australian National University.

Sullivan, Dennis, and Larry Tifft. 2005. *Restorative Justice: Healing the Foundations of Our Everyday Lives*, 2nd ed. Monsey, NY: Willow Tree Press.

Sullivan, Dennis and Larry Tifft, eds. 2006. *Handbook of Restorative Justice*. New York: Routledge.

Tavuchis, Nicholas. 1991. *Mea Culpa: A Sociology of Apology and Reconciliation*. Stanford, Calif.: Stanford University Press.

Tomuschat, Christian. 2002. "Reparation for Victims of Grave Human Rights Violations." *Tulane Journal of International and Compensatory Law* 10: 157–84.

Tyler, Tom R. 1990. *Why People Obey the Law: Procedural Justice, Legitimacy, and Compliance*. New Haven, Conn.: Yale University Press. 2nd ed. 2006. Princeton, NJ: Princeton University Press.

Tutu, Desmond. 1999. *No Future without Forgiveness*. London: Rider Books.

Umbreit, Mark. 1994. *Victim Meets Offender: The Impact of Restorative Justice and Mediation*. Monsey, NY: Criminal Justice Press.

———. 1999. "Avoiding the Marginalization and 'McDonaldization' of Victim-Offender Mediation: A Case Study in moving Toward the Mainstream." In *Restorative Juvenile Justice: Repairing the Harm of Youth Crime*, edited by Gordon Bazemore and Lode Walgrave. Monsey, NY: Criminal Justice Press.

Umbreit, Mark S., Betty Vos, Robert B. Coates, and Katherine A. Brown. 2003. *Facing Violence: The Path of Restorative Justice and Dialogue*. Monsey, NY: Criminal Justice Press.

United Nations High Commissioner for Human Rights. 1948. *The Universal Declaration of Human Rights*. New York: United Nations Department of Public Information. http://www.ohchr.org/EN/UDHR/Documents/UDHR_Translations/eng.pdf.

United Nations General Assembly. 2006. *Basic Principles and Guidelines on the Right to a Remedy and Reparation for Victims of Gross Violations of International Human Rights Law and Serious Violations of International Humanitarian Law: Resolution/adopted by the General Assembly*, 21 March A/RES/60/147. http://www.unhcr.org/refworld/docid/4721cb942.html.

United Nations High Commissioner for Human Rights. 2002. *Resolutions and Decisions Adopted by the Economic and Social Council at its Substantive Session of 2002*. http://www.unhcr.ch/Huridocda/Huridoca.nsf/e06a5300f90fa0238025668700518ca4/45d44fb49cdeea43c1256c7f00543573/$FILE/N0252842.pdf.

United Nations International Law Commission. 1996. "Yearbook of the International Law Commission. Vol. 1. Summary records of the meetings of the forty-eighth session." http://untreaty.un.org/ilc/publications/yearbooks/Ybkvolumes(e)/ILC_1996_v1_e.pdf.

van Ness, Daniel. 2002. "The Shape of Things to Come: A Framework for Thinking about a Restorative Justice System." In *Restorative Justice: Theoretical Foundations*, edited by Elmar Weitekamp and Hans-Jürgen Kerner. Cullompton: Willan Publishing.

———. 2005. "Restorative Justice in Prisons." Paper presented at the Symposium on Restorative Justice and Peace in Colombia, Cali, Colombia, February 9–12.

van Ness, Daniel, and Karen H. Strong. 2006. *Restoring Justice: An Introduction to Restorative Justice*, 3rd ed. Cincinnati: Anderson Publishing.

Verdeja, Ernesto. 2006. "A Normative Theory of Reparations in Transitional Democracies." *Metaphilosophy* 37(3–4): 449–68.

von Hirsch, Andrew, Andrew Ashworth, and Clifford Shearing. 2003. "Specifying Aims and Limits for Restorative Justice: A 'Making Amends' Model." In *Restorative Justice and Criminal Justice: Competing or Reconcilable Paradigms?*, edited by Andrew von Hirsch, Julian Roberts, Anthony E. Bottoms, Kent Roach, and Mara Schiff. Oxford: Hart Publishing.

Walgrave, Lode. 1995. "Restorative Justice for Juveniles: Just a Technique or a Fully Fledged Alternative?" *Howard Journal of Criminal Justice* 34: 228–49.

———. 2002. "Restorative Justice and the Law: Socio-Ethical and Juridical Foundations for a Systemic Approach." In *Restorative Justice and the Law,* edited by Lode Walgrave. Cullompton: Willan Publishing.

———. 2003. "Imposing Restoration Instead of Inflicting Pain." In *Restorative Justice and Criminal Justice: Competing or Reconcilable Paradigms?*, edited by Andrew von Hirsch, Julian Roberts, Anthony E. Bottoms, Kent Roach, and Mara Schiff. Oxford: Hart Publishing.

———. 2004. "Has Restorative Justice Appropriately Responded to Retribution Theory and Impulses?" In *Critical Issues in Restorative Justice*, edited by Howard Zehr and Barb Toews. Monsey, NY: Criminal Justice Press.

————. 2008. *Restorative Justice, Self Interest and Responsible Citizenship.* Cullompton: Willan Publishing.

Walgrave, Lode, and Ivo Aertsen. 1996. "Reintegrative Shaming and Restorative Justice: Interchangeable, Complementary or Different?" *European Journal on Criminal Policy and Research* 4: 67–85.

Watson, David, Jacky Boucherat, and Gwynn Davis. 1989. "Reparation for Retributivists." In *Mediation and Criminal Justice*, edited by Martin Wright and Burt Galaway. London: Sage Publications.

Wemmers, Jo-Anne M. 1996. "Restitution and Conflict Resolution in The Netherlands." In *Restorative Justice: International Perspectives*, edited by Burt Galaway and Joe Hudson. Monsey, N.Y.: Criminal Justice Press.

Wilson, Richard. 2001. *The Politics of Truth and Reconciliation in South Africa: Legitimizing the Post-Apartheid State.* Cambridge: Cambridge University Press.

Wright, Martin. 1991. *Justice for Victims and Offenders.* Philadelphia: Open University Press.

Zedner, Lucia. 1994. "Reparation and Retribution: Are They Reconcilable?" *Modern Law Review* 57(2): 28–50.

Zehr, Howard. 1985. "Retributive Justice, Restorative Justice." Repr. in *A Restorative Justice Reader,* edited by Gerry Johnstone. 2003. Cullompton: Willan Publishing.

————. 1990. *Changing Lenses: A New Focus for Crime and Justice.* Scottdale, PA.: Herald Press.

————. 2002. *The Little Book of Restorative Justice.* Intercourse, PA: Good Books.

Zehr, Howard, and Barbara Toews, eds. 2004. *Critical Issues in Restorative Justice.* Monsey, NY: Criminal Justice Press.

....

CHAPTER 9

REASSURANCE, REINFORCEMENT, AND LEGITIMACY

....

MATT MATRAVERS*

POLITICAL, legal, and penal philosophers often focus on substantive questions in the criminal law and on justifications of punishment. Disciplinary boundaries and the particular analytic techniques of philosophy lend themselves to the maintenance of this focus. Yet, the system of criminal justice is embedded in society, and its effects go far beyond those achieved by the threat or imposition of punishments. This chapter is concerned with precisely those other effects. Here, we are concerned with the ways in which the criminal law shapes the behavior of citizens other than by fear of punishment. This issue, in turn, opens up questions of the appropriate relationship of the state to its citizens and of what the state might legitimately do to try to secure the obedience of its citizens.

To address these questions, section I briefly considers the purpose of the criminal law and the broader system of criminal justice. In part, of course, their purpose is to reduce and to respond to criminal wrongdoing. It is easy to think of this in terms of the deterrence effects of threatened hard treatment, and of the infliction of that hard treatment as punishment. However, compliance with the law is not primarily achieved by either of these things, but rather depends on wider socialization. Criminal law and criminal justice do not stand apart from that wider process but are part of it, which is precisely why the focus on the non-threat elements is so important.

To argue that the system of criminal justice contributes to socialization and to compliance is one thing, but it leaves unaddressed how it does this and the issue of what constraints there should be on the process (how, normatively, it ought to do it). In the main sections of the chapter, these questions are taken up through a discussion of Durkheim, the "moral educative" effects of the criminal law, the evidence we have concerning why people obey the law, and, finally, the recent punitive turn in parts of the developed world.

Section II examines Émile Durkheim's argument that the relationship between a society's system of criminal justice and its moral order is reciprocal. That is, the criminal law gives expression to deep and important social and moral norms. Crimes violate these norms, and the response of the criminal law to such violations is to reassert and reinforce those norms. In closing this section, some pressure is put on this account both in terms of whether it is necessarily the case that crimes, the criminal law, and the moral order are so benignly connected, and whether any such connection—even were it to hold—could provide an appropriate model for contemporary, pluralistic, societies.

Section III turns to a more recent attempt to analyze the criminal law in broadly Durkheimian ways, but without the support of Durkheim's byzantine conceptual scaffolding. This is the (largely German and Swedish) development of the idea that the criminal law has "moral educative" effects that are critical in shaping behavior. Although plausible, the evidence for this claim is shaky. Moreover, as is admitted by its proponents, the looser connection between the law and morality and between the state and its citizens—looser, that is, than in Durkheim's model—means that there is no guarantee that the law will reinforce rather than undermine compliance or that behavior will be effected in desirable ways. A bad law may undermine faith in the law or (perhaps, worse) contribute to the corruption of the morality of the citizens by being effective.

The absence of firm evidence for, and the conceptual dead end of, the Durkheimian model prompts a different way of looking at the question. Instead of focusing on the direct effects of the criminal on the behavior of citizens, section IV asks why people obey the law and what we can learn from that. Using Tom Tyler's work as the focus, the argument follows the claim that compliance is best achieved in circumstances of procedural justice and where the law broadly reflects the preexisting values of the citizen body. There is a great deal to learn from this, but there is also a great deal to fear. Procedural justice is important, but it can easily mask power and substantive injustice. Similarly, the state has a legitimate interest in creating and nurturing moral values in its citizens, but we also have a critical duty to examine and to scrutinize those values.

Finally, in section V the chapter turns to a conundrum. The evidence points to the fact that the fear and infliction of punishment, just by themselves, make a negligible difference to the overall existence of crime. Yet, in recent decades, parts of the developed world—and, in particular, the United States and the United

Kingdom—have pursued increasingly punitive criminal justice policies. We consider here the argument that this is so because of the felt need of politicians to assert their sovereign power and to try to shore up their legitimacy in the eyes of their citizens. Thus, in a sense, the chapter comes full circle with a return to the Durkheimian theme of reaffirmation.

The overall claims of the chapter do not include that the various authors considered were all asking the same questions or addressing the issues in precisely the same ways. Nor is there an attempt to offer a comprehensive survey of the field. Rather, the chapter is informed by the thought that the most important effects of criminal justice do not result only from its involving the threat and imposition of punishment. Moreover, these effects are intimately tied to the idea of legitimacy, and in evaluating them, we cannot but help ask normative questions about the proper relation of the state to its citizens. By placing in juxtaposition authors as different as Durkheim, Andenaes, Tyler, and Garland, the hope is to bring out some of these issues in ways that are mutually illuminating.

This chapter thus:

- Considers the point of systems of criminal justice.
- Reviews Durkheim's theory and its application to contemporary societies.
- Reviews the evidence concerning the ways in which the criminal law can shape behavior other than by threat or imposition of punishment.
- Examines the evidence for why people obey the law and the significance of the state's claim to legitimacy.
- Discusses the explosion of punishment in the United States and the United Kingdom, and analyses this as an expressive, Durkheimian attempt to shore up both the state's claim to legitimate sovereignty and the moral order of society.

I. INTRODUCTION

The criminal justice system in its entirety is vast and costly. It is (as far as we can tell) a necessary component of social life. Like death and taxes, criminal justice will always be with us. However, it is not at all obvious what criminal justice is for. In a sister volume to this one, Michael Tonry makes the straightforward claim that "criminal law enforcement is what the criminal justice system does" (Tonry 2009, 7). Interpreted narrowly—as the claim that the only function of the criminal justice system is the direct enforcement of the criminal law—this is clearly too restrictive. However, that is not how Tonry intends his claim to be read. Rather, the context makes clear that he means something much more broad; that what the criminal justice system is about is reducing infringements of the criminal law (which, for example, could be achieved by a criminal justice system that somehow ensured that no one was ever tempted to violate the law) as well as—and in part by—responding to those infringements when they occur. This is to stretch the word "enforcement." Even so, it may still be thought to be too restrictive an account of the criminal justice system, for example, by those who think that one role for that system is to ensure that culpable wrong doers get what they deserve.

If we accept that (at least *one*) role of the criminal justice system is to reduce infringements of the criminal law, then the question arises as to how it does that. Tonry offers "through deterrence, incapacitation, rehabilitation, and moral education" (Tonry 2009, 7). This chapter is not concerned with the first three of those, nor only with the last. It is more generally concerned with the ways in which the criminal justice system influences (or fails to influence) people's behavior other than by the threat or effects of punishment. This question is critical: no complex society could sustain order and ensure appropriate behavior only through punishment. Rather, society depends on "mainstream processes of socialization," glossed by David Garland as "internalized morality and the sense of duty, the informal inducements and rewards of conformity, the practical and cultural networks of mutual expectation and interdependence, etc." (Garland 1990, 288–89).

As the quotation from Garland makes clear, much of what we depend upon is not itself part of the criminal justice system. As even Hobbes recognized, men "need to be diligently, and truly taught; because [civil society] cannot be maintained by . . . terrour of legal punishment" (Hobbes 1991, pt. ii, ch. 30, 337).[1] Nevertheless, the criminal justice system may contribute to this broader agenda both positively and negatively. Positively, by reinforcing moral and social norms; negatively, by undermining them.

It is worth noting that even those whose accounts of punishment are most (notoriously) instrumental—who conceive of the justification and purpose of punishment as resting primarily on its ability to deter—allow for this wider norm-affecting function. On the positive side, Jeremy Bentham argued that a punishment could "answer the purpose of a moral lesson" by inspiring "the public with sentiments of aversion towards those pernicious habits and dispositions with which the offence appears to be connected; and thereby to inculcate the opposite beneficial habits and dispositions" (Bentham 1970, 171). On the negative, the committed consequentialist theorist Cesare Beccaria argued the flip side of Bentham's point:

> [I]f humiliating punishments are given for crimes that are not held to be dishonorable [Beccaria is discussing smuggling], then the feeling of disgrace aroused by those that really are so diminishes. One who sees the same punishment . . . for the killer of a pheasant as for the killer of a man or for the forger of an important document, cannot see any difference among these crimes. In this way the moral sentiments are destroyed. (Beccaria 1995, 87)

That said, neither Bentham nor Beccaria thought the moral educative, and wider sociological, effects of punishment were at the heart of the matter. For that position, it is necessary to turn to a very different theorist: Émile Durkheim (for example, in Durkheim 1973, 1983, 1984).

II. Durkheim: Reassurance and Reinforcement[2]

For Durkheim, the relationship of criminal justice and society's moral order is reciprocal. Punishment not only reflects and represents the moral order, but also sustains it. This follows in part from Durkheim's understanding of crime. For Durkheim, crimes violate the moral order of society; an order that is reflected in the moral views of each citizen. The response of punishment has three interlinked functions: it gives expression to the adverse reaction of both the society and the citizens of that society, and it reinforces the moral order that holds the society together. In more Durkheimian language, the citizens of a given society share a set of beliefs and sentiments that together constitute the "*conscience collective*" (Durkheim 1984, 79). The state guards the *conscience collective* without which the moral and social order of the society could not be sustained. Crimes violate the *conscience collective* either directly or in virtue of being offences against the state. This in turn calls forth punishment because of the outrage felt by the citizenry who demand vengeance. It is this—the peculiar authority of the norms violated that arises from the significance of those norms and the resulting anger and indignation at their violation—that explains the necessarily punitive response to which crime gives rise.

This explains how punishment reflects and represents the moral and social order, but it also sustains that order. How so? The answer is by reinforcement and reassurance. The best summary of this from a sympathetic, if critical, stance is given by David Garland. "When crimes occur which violate the norms of social life," he writes,

> these norms are weakened and shown to be less universal in their binding force. The effect, however, of the upswelling of a collective passionate reaction to such crimes is to give a powerful demonstration of the real force which supports the norms, and thereby reaffirm them in the consciousness of individual members. This functional outcome effectively completes a virtuous circle set off by crime. . . . Crime and punishment, for Durkheim, are important in so far as they set this moral circuitry in motion. (Garland 1990, 33)

Durkheim went on to develop a more *communicative* account of punishment (in particular in Durkheim 1973) that emphasized the need to uphold the moral order by censuring the criminal. However, the essence of his account remains in the claim that the function of punishment is to reinforce the moral and social order of society and to reassure the society's citizens of the solidity of that order.

For Durkheim, then, it is clear that society's moral and social order cannot depend on the "terrour of legal punishment" alone, but equally that punishment and socialization do not run in parallel. Rather, punishment is one mechanism of socialization; it channels, reinforces, and reasserts the sentiments and values at the heart of that order. For that reason, the account invites (at least) two sets of questions; one regarding the plausibility of the account itself, the other with a focus on the applicability of the account to modern pluralist societies. These questions turn out to be interconnected and, at their heart, is the notion of a *conscience collective*.

As we have seen, Durkheim defines the *conscience collective* as consisting in a set of values and norms whose authority rests on their being held by the citizen body in a certain sort of way. In a much criticized historical account, Durkheim argues that for primitive societies the *conscience collective* was roughly "the sacred" and that the reverence and awe with which these norms continue to be held in modern societies has equivalent status. The breakdown of the *conscience collective*, or the alienation of an individual from it, is thus traumatic (hence Durkheim's justly famous inquiries into anomie and suicide). Punishment both channels the violent reaction of citizens to the violation of these fundamental norms (equivalent to the outrage earlier persons felt in response to blasphemy), and, as we have seen, in doing so reasserts the status of those norms.

Whatever the historical accuracy of Durkheim's account, his rich description of the *conscience collective* renders the theory strange to contemporary liberal ears. Of course, all societies need some set of shared commitments to sustain themselves, but modern liberal theory broadly eschews reference to substantive conceptions of the public *good*, preferring instead to think in terms of the *rights* that structure the interactions of citizens among themselves and with the state (Barry 1995; Rawls 1971, 2005). The reason for prioritizing the right over the good being that modern liberal (and other) societies are characterized by pluralism; by the presence of many conflicting conceptions of the good.

Even without this general skepticism about the availability of a common good, there is something too benign about Durkheim's conception of the *conscience collective*. Durkheim presents us with a model of a set of authoritative norms and values that arises organically in a society and that is reflected neatly in the norms and values of each "healthy" individual in that society. But, authoritative public norms are established in competition and their place is contested. They are, in short, the outcome of power struggles between classes and groups whose place in the heart of each citizen will vary over time and between persons. What this means, of course, is that the "virtuous circle" set off by the crime may not be completed. Instead, for some citizens, there is the chance that punishment will reinforce their belief that the regime is illegitimate (as, for example, happens when the Burmese government tried and punished the opposition leader Aung San Suu Kyi). For others, the match between the judicial system of punishment and their moral beliefs will simply be loose (as, for example, in the case of those who line up to scream abuse at particular classes of offenders on their way to trial and who believe that these offenders—often child killers and pedophiles—are never sufficiently punished by the system).

In sum, Durkheim may be right that punishment attempts to reassert the authority of an existing moral and social order, but whether it succeeds depends on the nature of that order. Where public norms are contested—which is, contemporary liberal claims, more or less everywhere—the impact of punishment will be to some degree unpredictable (this is, of course, a point that Michel Foucault makes a great deal of in Foucault 1977). Punishment "works," in Durkheimian terms, only where there is an already existing *conscience collective* of the kind he describes. But, if the critics of Durkheim's historical analysis are to be believed, even simple primitive societies were not characterized by any such *conscience*, and if contemporary liberals are right there is no place for such a notion in the study of modern punishment.

III. Variations on Durkheimian Themes

As with any account that aspires to be both descriptive and normative, there are two possible responses to this critique of the Durkheimian position. One is to reject it as descriptively inaccurate, the other is to ask whether it is normatively valid. That is, one might argue that criminal justice and punishment is legitimate and/or justified only against the background of a *conscience collective* or something like it. Consider, for example, the sophisticated communicative theory developed by Antony Duff (Duff 1986, 2001, 2007). For Duff, the criminal trial aspires to be a communicative exercise in which the offender (if guilty) is confronted with his crime and called to account for it. His punishment aims to express the appropriate degree of censure for his moral and legal wrongdoing and to invoke in him a kind of "penitential" response. Although eager to stress that his account is both liberal and communitarian (Duff 2001, chap. 2), it is clear that for Duff, as for Durkheim, punishment is a moral exercise, albeit one that is aimed in Duff's theory primarily at the wrongdoing of the offender (and only secondarily at reasserting the public value of the violated norm). Insofar as real-world conditions do not allow such an account of punishment—perhaps because of the absence of any moral consensus—then the account does not hold. This, though, is not a problem for the account of punishment but rather for the society. Similarly, one response to the absence of the *conscience collective* could be to argue that it is precisely this absence that is problematic; that as contemporary liberals we are at sea without any moral anchor to hold us and our societies together other than perhaps the endless seeking of utilitarian pleasures (MacIntyre 1984, 1988, 1990), although few people have found that claim compelling (Barry 1995, chap. 5; Horton and Mendus 1994; Nagel 1988).

A different response to the critique of the *conscience collective* might be to grant that such a rich, moralized notion does not belong in contemporary reflections on crime and criminal justice, but then resist the thought that this shows that the instrumental goal of deterrence or enforcement of the criminal law (narrowly understood) is all that there is to punishment. In his *Punishment and Deterrence*, Johannes Andenaes cites a modern German and Swedish theoretical movement that is concerned with the "moral-educative" effects, or the "reinforcement of social values," as the main goals of the criminal law (Andenaes 1974, 114). Andenaes himself offers five ways in which the existence of the criminal law can shape behavior: (1) that persons obey the law just because it is the law and, as such, merits respect; (2) that the fact of something being criminal(ized) makes citizens more aware of its harmful character; (3) that punishment in expressing social disapproval can alter behavior in the long term; (4) that offenses that go unpunished provide "bad examples" and encourage copycat offenses; and (5) that the system of criminal justice is part of the general background against which other forms of socialization occur (Andenaes 1974, 114–25). Although Andenaes is committed to the claim that the "law, and not least the criminal law" is a "fundamental socializing influence," he admits that the evidence for each of the five categories of influence is difficult to determine. That is not, in his view, to say that it is not there, but that because the law's "influences permeate society in so many ways," the evidence is "difficult to isolate and measure" (Andenaes 1974, 126).

Andenaes's arguments seem to have led to something of a dead end. It seems likely—it is surely plausible—that the existence of the criminal law, and the whole edifice of the system of criminal justice—has *some* effect in some circumstances on the behavior of citizens other than by direct threat, or application, of punishment. Under some circumstances, the law will help to shape norms and behaviors and thus to sustain a social order that cannot be maintained by "terrour" alone. In other circumstances, a miscalculated or misapplied law will shape norms and behaviors in ways that undermine that order. However, the variables are too many and the counterfactual too difficult (in the absence of the law what would this person have thought about this form of behavior?) for us to be able to say anything very meaningful about these effects. If so, then to get further we need to proceed from another angle; to ask different questions. Not, "when and to what magnitude does the law shape behavior?," but perhaps "why do people obey the law?," and "how do people respond to the law?" Progress in answering those questions may allow us to reflect on the nature of the relationship between the law and behavior and the conditions and circumstances that enable, or disable, the law's shaping of citizens' attitudes, norms, and behaviors.

IV. LEGITIMACY

In a series of works, the psychologist Tom Tyler has investigated why people obey the law; he led an assault on the instrumental account that has it that they do so because the existence of a sanction alters the payoffs of the choice not to do so in ways that deter (Tyler's pioneering work is presented in Tyler 1990; for a recent statement of his position, see Tyler 2009). In *Why People Obey the Law*, Tyler presented evidence that congruence between the law and the person's own moral beliefs, and the person's belief that the law is legitimate, played the most significant roles in compliance (Tyler 1990, 64).[3] As Tyler puts it in the later presentation of his findings:

> First, values shape rule-following. In particular, values lead to voluntary behavior, including both voluntary decision acceptance and cooperation with legal authorities. Second, procedural justice shapes values. If authority is exercised fairly, the law and legal authorities are viewed as legitimate and seen as entitled to be obeyed. (Tyler 2009, 326)

It is important to note that Tyler is asking a different question to, for example, Andenaes. He is not asking what effects the law has on the values and behavior of persons, but rather *why* persons obey the law. The fact that the evidence Tyler produces shows that people are more likely to comply with the law when it accords with their values entails some connection between the law and values, but the direction of fit is important: the evidence supports the claim that "values shape rule-following," not the other way around (although that of course is not ruled out). What does shape values is "procedural justice" and it is important to understand this claim.

Tyler's argument is not that "procedural justice" affects persons' substantive moral beliefs (say, about the rightness or wrongness of private property ownership, market speculation, or abortion), but that the willingness of persons to comply with the law is, in important part, a function of the degree to which they regard that law—and the legal authority from which it emanated—as "legitimate." Legitimacy is defined as "the property that a rule or an authority has when others feel obligated to voluntarily defer to that rule or authority. In other words, a legitimate authority is one that is regarded by people as entitled to have its decisions and rules accepted and followed by others" (Tyler 2009, 313; Tyler attributes this definition to Skogan and Frydl 2003, 297). In turn, legitimacy is secured in large part by the perception of *procedural* (which Tyler somewhat confusingly contrasts with *distributive*) justice. That is, people's perceptions of the legitimacy of a given authority depend on whether they think the procedures followed by that authority are fair (do they take everyone's view into account, are they impartial, etc.) more than they do on the whether the outcomes decided by that authority are favorable ("distributive justice" is a matter of outcomes; of the distribution of the benefits and burdens that follow from some rule or decision of the authority). As Tyler puts it elsewhere:

> [T]he key aspect of authorities and institutions that shapes their legitimacy and, through it, the willingness of people to defer to the decisions of authorities and to the rules created by institutions is the fairness of the procedures through which institutions and authorities exercise authority. This procedural justice effect on legitimacy is found to be widespread and robust and occurs in legal, political, and managerial settings. (Tyler 2006, 382. See also Tyler 2000; 2001).

Thus, the overall argument is simple, and since it is intuitively plausible, it is encouraging that there is hard evidence in its support. It is this: people's compliance is positively influenced where they are convinced of the legitimacy of the authority from which some decision or rule has emerged, and this is reinforced—and compliance more likely—where the content of the decision or rule is in accordance with their moral beliefs. What follows if Tyler's evidence is sound and our intuition vindicated?

According to Tyler, what follows are some fairly specific policy implications, and by considering these we can return to some of the themes from the discussion of Durkheim and his successors. Before that, however, it is worth concentrating on one aspect of Tyler's findings that speaks more directly the influence—all be it, negative—that the law can have on people's attitudes and behavior. Tyler argues that "the deterrence approach"—that is, a criminal justice system driven by punishment designed to deter—has two negative consequences: first, it "define[s] people's relationship to law and legal authorities as one of risk and punishment. This lessens people's focus on other aspects of their connection to society, such as shared values and concerns, and encourages people to act in ways that are linked to personal gains and losses." Second, "because people associate law and legal authorities with punishment, the instrumental relationship between the public and the legal system is antagonistic." This in turn means that "people become more likely to resist and avoid legal authorities and less likely to cooperate with them" (Tyler 2009, 310; see also Tyler 2013). This is something to which we will return when considering both the instrumentalist response to noninstrumentalist attacks and the punitive turn that has taken place in recent years particularly in the United States and the United Kingdom.

Tyler's policy recommendations follow fairly straightforwardly from the evidence he presents. If the deterrence approach not only fails but undermines compliance, and compliance is best ensured by engaging people's values, then it makes sense to develop and engage people's values and to ensure the procedural justice (and so legitimacy) of the legal authority. More specifically, Tyler argues that we should make "value creation a priority" ideally by making sure that the right values are developed "early in people's lives as part of the general socialization process," which will "lead to rule-following as part of a general lifestyle." Second, we should "evaluate legal policies in terms of their impact upon values." Third, we should

"institutionalize mechanisms for evaluating legal authorities in terms of their legitimacy as well as their consistency of theory policies and practices with the principles of procedural justice" (Tyler 2009, 331–34).

These policy goals have much to recommend them. To give some examples,
they suggest that police interactions with citizens (and in particular with adolescent
citizens) should be procedurally just and scrupulously fair even when that sacrifices
efficiency (for example, by ruling out racial profiling when using stop and search
powers); that punishment practices should have "restorative" foci (on restorative
justice, see Braithwaite 1989, 2002) as well as being procedurally just; that participants in court should have things explained to them and the chance to express
themselves as appropriate; and that the trust and confidence of citizens in the criminal justice system should be thought to be important by legislators and others (for
a fuller account of these policy suggestions, and citations of additional evidence, see
Tyler 2009, 331–34).

At the same time, there is something worrying about the emphasis on "value
creation" and "procedural justice." In the case of the former, one might hesitate for
two reasons. First, although of course a state can have a legitimate interest in
instilling the right values in its young citizens in the expectation that this will lead
to compliant rule-following, there is the danger of suppressing legitimate criticism
and conflict. Indeed, the whole language of instilling values and compliance is likely
to make liberals wary.

Second, and interconnected, the state of course has an interest in instilling *its*
values. Tyler's account is structural, and as he recognizes, it thus hangs free of any
particular content those values might have (Tyler 2009, 330). This is an issue that
Andenaes confronts directly. He writes (somewhat surprisingly) that "no value
judgment is implied" when he speaks of "moral or educative influence." Rather, he
thinks of himself as simply referring to "the attitude-shaping influence of criminal
law," which can result just as much from "bad" as from "good" laws (Andenaes 1974,
112–13). Tyler is less clear and the tone of his work is much more suggestive of an
evangelical proponent of value creation whose confidence in the efficacy of his
methods has left him desensitized to their potential dangers.

When it comes to the emphasis on procedural justice, a similar worry arises
about *content*. In this case, the worry is not that there might be the wrong content—
bad laws or immoral norms—but that the account disregards the justice of the content in favor of the fairness of the procedures. "The law" as Anatole France famously
put it, "in its majestic equality, forbids rich and poor alike to sleep under bridges,
beg in the streets or steal bread" (France 1921, chap. 7). One need not be a critical
legal studies theorist, Foucauldian, or Marxist to perceive the danger (although, of
course, it helps. For an extensive critical review of Tyler's book from a broadly Critical Legal Studies perspective, see Sarat 1993).

Tyler's case, then, is not that the law and legal norms shape our behavior in ways
other than by fear, but that the empirical evidence shows that our response to the

law is driven not so much by fear as by values and by our perception of the law as having arisen in a way that is procedurally fair. The conclusions he draws from this are worthy of serious consideration, but the evidence also points to dangers inherent in any socializing program and in any politics that hides substantive injustices behind a cloak of procedural fairness.

While the evidence for the direct moral educative effects of the law is suspect, and punishment's role as the glue that holds us together at best unproven, what all the theorists discussed earlier agree on is that the straightforward use of fear of punishment is, at best, fairly ineffective and, at worst, positively undermining of compliance (and not just these theorists; see Doob and Webster 2003; Western 2006, chap. 6; Young 1999, chap. 5; Zimring and Hawkins 1995). Yet, the recent history of much of the developed world—and in particular of the United States and the United Kingdom—is precisely a history of increased punitiveness and rising prison populations (although one should be careful not to overstate the similarities between countries. See Cavadino and Dignan 2006; Tonry 2007). What explains this is, of course, highly contested. But the fact that these developments have gained—and sometimes been driven by—popular support raises a new set of interesting issues about the relationship between the criminal justice system and the citizens it governs.

V. The Expressive Power of Policy

So far, we have mainly been considering the ways in which the criminal law, and the criminal justice system more widely, effects the behavior of people other than by threat or implementation of punishment. There is a broader question that concerns not just how the existence of the criminal law contributes to socialization and rule-following, but how the fact of crime *together with* our response to it shapes our moral and social worlds. This is a question that takes on particular significance given the rise in crime rates since the Second World War. In thinking about the criminal justice system and its effects, then, we must consider "crime and punishment as part of the same process" (Young 2003, 231).

For David Garland, crime and our adaptations in response to it, characterize, create (and so define) late modernity. As he puts it, "crime control today does more than simply manage problems of crime and insecurity." In addition,

> it also institutionalizes a set of responses to these problems that are themselves consequential in their social impact. In America and Britain today, 'late modernity' is lived—not just by offenders but by all of us—in a mode that is more than ever defined by institutions of policing, penality, and prevention. (Garland 2001, 194).

Garland's book covers a great deal of territory and has generated a considerable debate (see, e.g., the essays in Matravers 2004; Young 2003; Zedner 2002). Much of it considers the attempt to control and regulate behavior by direct means: by threat of increased punishment, CCTV cameras, private security firms, and so on. What is of interest here is Garland's analysis of both why crime has become so central to our lives and how that fact, and the responses to it, have made criminal justice such a dominant part of (as Andenaes put it) "the general background against which other forms of socialization occur."

In part, crime is more visible because there is more of it. However, it is also— as we have seen—ineffectively controlled by threat of punishment. In short, the U.S. and UK governments can do little about crime just as, in the modern globalized world, they can do little about their economies, the rates at which their currencies trade, and so on. Against a background of reduced sovereignty and loss of power, the

> perception of high crime rates as a normal social fact, together with the widely acknowledged limitations of the criminal justice system, had the effect of eroding one of the foundational myths of modern society: the myth that the sovereign state is capable of delivering "law and order" and controlling crime within its territorial boundaries. (Garland 2001, 109)

This, as Garland puts it, leads to a "predicament" for government. Those who vie to run the state know that they cannot deliver what is required by the "myth," yet they also know the "political costs" of admitting the same. The result is "a remarkably volatile and ambivalent pattern of policy development" (Garland 2001, 110) that revolves around two poles. On the one hand, there is the presentation of criminality and criminals as an ordinary part of everyday life; responsive to rational (dis)incentives and posing a risk that needs to be managed (like any other risk). On the other, there is the need to demonize offenders, to give voice to popular outrage and resentments, and to assert sovereignty by ever-increasing expressive responses to serious crimes. Both responses, of course, put crime and criminality at the heart of political and social life. The one by asserting that crime is "always and everywhere" and needs (risk) management by both the state and by individuals; the other by cranking up the significance of crime as a threat from the dangerous outsider, and asserting the claim of political elites to be effective (and so electable) in response to this. Both also contrast with a past, more optimistic "penal welfarism" in which crime was thought to be manageable through the manipulation of its social causes (poverty, disadvantage, etc.) and rehabilitation of offenders.

Garland's analysis—and in particular the degree to which he generalizes to "late modernity" from the cases of the United States and the United Kingdom—has proved controversial (see Lacey 2008, chap. 1; Zedner 2002), and it is certainly the case that not all developed countries have followed the United States and the United Kingdom by massively increasing punishments. Nevertheless, his analysis of the

way in which crime has moved center stage, both politically and socially, is compelling. In the light of the above analysis, what sense can be made of this development?

   If Tyler, and many others, are right then the one explanation that seems unlikely
is that increased punishments are a simple, deliberate, and instrumental attempt to
reduce crime. Put bluntly, "criminal justice policy is largely irrelevant as a means of
reducing crime" (Garside 2006, quoted in Lacey (2008), 17). Indeed, it is not in the
interests of the politicians who propose increased punishments to make much of
punishment's instrumental effectiveness given that if the policy were to be judged
by that thesis, it would be shown to be a manifest failure. Garland himself connects
the rhetoric—and results—of the policymakers to two different aspects of legitimacy building. In virile expressions of criminal justice policy, the politician tries to
firm up the foundational myth of sovereignty. He also, in Durkheimian fashion,
reasserts and reaffirms the "correct" values—values shared by "normal" upright citizens and disregarded by offenders who thus put themselves outside civil society—
at a time of increasing (and frightening) value pluralism (cf. Lacey 2008, who offers
a more structural explanation of the behavior of politicians; for more radical interpretations of the US situation, see Simon 2007; Wacquant 2009). Thus, in addition,
the politician seeks to blunt the negative effects of an instrumental, antagonistic
approach to criminal justice predicted by Tyler. If society divides into "us" and
"them" then "our" relationship with the state is one based on right values and compliance. "Theirs," of course, is different, but that reaffirms the need for criminal
justice and unites "us" in our values.

VI. Concluding Thoughts

If it is true that criminal justice is destined to be always with us, one other certainty
is that criminal justice policies and their effects are complex, multifaceted, and
impossible to reduce to simple, still less single, explanations. It is striking that
despite widespread skepticism about the effects of punitive policies, many countries
have proceeded recently down a distinctly punitive path. Moreover, that has not
happened in the teeth of popular resistance. Rather, "criminal justice policy has
been driven in [this] direction with—perhaps even because of—popular, and hence
literally democratic support" (Lacey 2008, 8).[4] It does not strike me as sensible, or
even possible, to conjecture about the precise mental states of the policymakers who
have led the way. Perhaps some think of themselves as Machiavellian master politicians who are cynically trying to position themselves for reelection or to pull the
wool over the eyes of the electorate. But, it is equally likely that some are genuine,
well-meaning individuals who believe that they are doing what they can in responding to the fears and circumstances of their citizens.

It is important to recognize that policy in this area has consequences far beyond whatever deterrence effects may be achieved. The law gives expression to values, and best invokes in citizens compliance when it is transparently and fairly constructed and when the values to which it gives expression are consonant with the moral beliefs of those it seeks to govern. This is a dangerous power, however. In times of uncertainty, and in multicultural conditions in which public values can exclude as well as bond, the expressive use of criminal justice may be appealing, but of course it has consequences for the growth of actual punishments. Moreover, it has the potential to alienate and to divide in particular where the background conditions are of distributive *in*justice (as they are throughout the world). Nevertheless, as Foucault famously reminded us, that something is dangerous "is not exactly the same as bad. If everything is dangerous, then we always have something to do. So my position leads not to apathy but to hyper- and pessimistic-activism" (Dreyfus and Rabinow 1982, 231–32) We cannot give up on the expressive power of the criminal law—condemning is, after all, what it does[5]—but then we cannot give up either on its critique.

NOTES

* I am grateful to Michael Tonry for advice on this chapter and, as ever, to my colleagues and students at the University of York.

1. Of course, the thought that successful societies are held together by more than force has a long history. It appears, for example, in Aristotle's account of unstable constitutions and in Spinoza's recommendations about the use of narratives. See Sinclair and Saunders 1981; Spinoza in Curley forthcoming.

2. Despite the title of this subsection, the aim is not to give an account of Durkheim's theory, still less a comprehensive analysis of it. Rather, the aim is to pick out some central themes in Durkheim's work relating to the question of how the existence of the criminal justice system affects persons' behavior other than through the instrumental effects of the threat (or application) of punishment. See, for a fuller account of Durkheim's position, Lukes and Scull (1983).

3. Interestingly, a significant majority of those Tyler surveyed (82 percent) also reported that they believed "people should obey the law even if it goes against what they think is right" (Tyler 1990, 45), although, like Andenaes, he seems skeptical about the actual role of such "respect for the formal law" in explaining compliance. See Andenaes 1974, 114–16).

4. Or, as Young puts it, "populist and sometimes punitive approaches to the law and order are popular because they resonate with opinions and anxieties widely held within the population" (Young 2003, 230). That said, both Young and Lacey are aware of difficulties of interpretation here. See Lacey 2008, chaps 3 and 4); Roberts and Hough, 2002).

5. It may also be that in responding to wrongs, the criminal justice system gives expression to a psychological reaction we have to rule breakers (Tyler et al. 1997)

REFERENCES

Andenaes, Johannes. 1974. *Punishment and Deterrence.* Ann Arbor: University of Michigan Press

Aristotle. 1981. *The Politics.* Trans. Thomas Alan Sinclair and Trevor J. Saunders Rev. ed. by Trevor J. Saunders. Harmondsworth: Penguin.

Barry, Brian M. 1995. *Justice as Impartiality.* Vol. 2 of *A Treatise on Social Justice.* Oxford: Clarendon Press.

Beccaria, Cesare. 1995. *Beccaria: "On Crimes and Punishments" and Other Writings.* Edited. Richard Bellamy. Trans. Richard Davies. Cambridge: Cambridge University Press.

Bentham, Jeremy. 1970. *An Introduction to the Principles of Morals and Legislation.* The Collected Works of Jeremy Bentham, edited Fred Rosen and Philip Schofield. Oxford: Oxford University Press.

Braithwaite, John. 1989. *Crime, Shame and Reintegration.* Cambridge: Cambridge University Press.

———. 2002. *Restorative Justice and Responsive Regulation.* Oxford: Oxford University Press.

Cavadino, Michael, and James Dignan. 2006. *Penal Systems: A Comparative Approach.* London: SAGE.

Doob, Anthony N., and Cheryl M. Webster. 2003. "Sentence Severity and Crime: Accepting the Null Hypothesis." In *Crime and Justice:A Review of Research*, vol. 30. edited Michael Tonry. Chicago: University of Chicago Press.

Dreyfus, Hubert L., and Paul Rabinow. 1982. *Michel Foucault: Beyond Structuralism and Hermeneutics.* Brighton: Harvester.

Duff, R. Antony. 1986. *Trials and Punishments.* Cambridge: Cambridge University Press.

———. 2001. *Punishment, Communication, and Community.* Oxford: Oxford University Press.

———. 2007. *Answering for Crime: Responsibility and Liability in the Criminal Law.* Oxford: Hart Publishing.

Durkheim, Émile. 1973. *Moral Education.* New York: Macmillan.

———. 1983. "The Evolution of Punishment." In *Durkheim and the Law,* edited Steven Lukes and Andrew Scull. Oxford: Oxford University Press.

———. 1984. *The Division Of Labour in Society,* trans. W. D. Halls. London: Macmillan.

Foucault, Michel. 1977. *Discipline and Punish: The Birth of the Prison,* trans. Alan Sheridan. London: Allen Lane.

France, Anatole. 1921. *The Red Lily. A Translation by Winifred Stephens.* (The Works of Anatole France in an English Translation. London: J. Lane.

Garland, David. 1990. *Punishment and Modern Society: A Study in Social Theory.* Oxford: Clarendon.

———. 2001. *The Culture of Control: Crime and Social Order in Contemporary Society.* Oxford: Oxford University Press.

Garside, Richard. 2006. *Right for the Wrong Reasons: Making Sense of Criminal Justice Failure.* London: Crime and Society Foundation.

Hobbes, Thomas. 1991. *Leviathan.* Tuck edition. Cambridge: Cambridge University Press.

Horton, John, and Susan Mendus. 1994. *After MacIntyre: Critical Perspectives on the Work of Alasdair MacIntyre.* Cambridge: Polity.

Lacey, Nicola. 2008. *The Prisoners' Dilemma: Political Economy and Punishment in Contemporary Democracies.* The Hamlyn Lectures 2007. Cambridge: Cambridge University Press.

Lukes, Steven, and Andrew Scull, eds. 1983. *Durkheim and the Law.* Oxford: Oxford University Press.

MacIntyre, Alasdair. 1984. *After Virtue: A Study in Moral Theory,* 2nd ed. Notre Dame, IN: University of Notre Dame Press.

———. 1988. *Whose Justice? Which Rationality?.* Notre Dame, IN: University of Notre Dame Press.

———. 1990. *Three Rival Versions of Moral Enquiry.* Notre Dame, IN: University of Notre Dame Press.

Matravers, Matt. 2004. *Managing Modernity: Politics and the Culture of Control.* London: Routledge.

Nagel, Thomas. 1988. "MacIntyre Versus the Enlightenment," *Times Literary Supplement,* July 8–14.

Rawls, John. 1971. *A Theory of Justice.* Cambridge, MA: Harvard University Press.

———. 2005, *Political Liberalism.* Exp. ed. New York: Columbia University Press.

Roberts, Julian V., and Michael J. Hough. 2002. *Changing Attitudes to Punishment: Public Opinion, Crime and Justice.* Cullompton: Willan.

Sarat, Austin. 1993. "Review: Authority, Anxiety, and Procedural Justice: Moving from Scientific Detachment to Critical Engagement," *Law and Society Review* 27(3):647–71.

Simon, Jonathan. 2007. *Governing Through Crime: How the War on Crime Transformed American Democracy and Created a Culture of Fear.* New York: Oxford University Press.

Spinoza de Benedictus. Forthcoming. Tractatus Theologico-Politicus. In *The Collected Works of Spinoza,* edited by E. M. Curley. Princeton, NJ: Princeton University Press.

Tonry, Michael. 2007. "Determinants of Penal Policies." In *Crime, Punishment, and Politics in Comparative Perspective,* edited by Michael Tonry. Vol. 36 of *Crime and Justice: A Review of Research,* edited by Michael Tonry. Chicago: University of Chicago Press.

———. 2009. "Crime and Public Policy." In *The Oxford Handbook of Crime and Public Policy,* edited by Michael Tonry. New York: Oxford University Press.

Tyler, Tom R. 1990. *Why People Obey the Law.* New Haven: Yale University Press.

———. 2000. "Social Justice: Outcome and Procedure." *International Journal of Psychology* 35:117–25.

———. 2001. "Public Trust and Confidence in Legal Authorities: What Do Majority and Minority Group Members Want from the Law and Legal Authorities?" *Behavioral Science and Law* 19:215–35.

———. 2006. "Psychological Perspectives on Legitimacy and Legitimation." *Annual Review of Psychology* 57(1):375–400.

———. 2009. "Legitimacy and Criminal Justice: The Benefits of Self-Regulation." *Ohio State Journal of Criminal Law* 7(307):307–59.

———. 2013. *Why People Cooperate.* Princeton, NJ: Princeton University Press.

Tyler, Tom R., Robert J. Boeckmann, Heather J. Smith, and Yuen J. Huo. 1997. *Social Justice in a Diverse Society.* Boulder, CO: Westview Press.

Wacquant, Loïc J. D. 2009. *Punishing the Poor: The Neoliberal Government of Social Insecurity.* Durham, NC: Duke University Press.

Western, Bruce. 2006. *Punishment and Inequality in America.* New York: Russell Sage.

Young, Jock. 1999. *The Exclusive Society: Social Exclusion, Crime and Difference in Late Modernity.* London: Sage.

———. 2003. "Searching for a New Criminology of Everyday Life: A Review of *The Culture of Control* by David Garland. *British Journal of Criminology* 43(1):228–43.

Zedner, Lucia. 2002. "Dangers of Dystopias in Penal Theory." *Oxford Journal of Legal Studies* 22(2):341–66.

Zimring, Franklin E., and Gordon Hawkins. 1995. *Incapacitation: Penal Confinement and the Restraint of Crime.* New York: Oxford University Press.

PART II

PROBLEMS AND PRIORITIES

CHAPTER 10

....

DRUGS AND CRIME

....

JONATHAN P. CAULKINS AND
MARK A. R. KLEIMAN

Two things most people agree on are that drugs and crime are inextricably linked and that someone ought to do something about it.

Two things few people agree on are *how* exactly drugs and crime are linked or *what* should be done about it.

This article does not solve the puzzle of how much crime is caused by drugs and how much by drug-control policies; the answer depends both on the drug and the context. Nevertheless, we do explain why various policies are or are not likely to reduce the amount of crime that is associated with drugs, by marrying a simple typology of the types of drug-related crime with analysis of how different interventions affect drug markets and drug use.

This approach is motivated by simultaneous respect for and disappointment with the extant literature on drugs-crime connections. Part of that ambivalence is a comment on quality. The literature is enormous, and some of it is solid: e.g., Chaiken and Chaiken, 1990; Roth, 1994; Kleiman, 1993; Boyum and Kleiman 2001; Boyum and Reuter 2005; Bennett and Holloway 2005. Yet much does not stand up under careful scrutiny.

The other source of disappointment is that even the better studies do not offer much in the way of solutions. One strand in the literature strives for dispassionate investigation of the tangled causal linkages connecting drugs and crime. That is indeed a fascinating scientific puzzle; the statistical challenges raised by endogeneity and simultaneity among the interrelated conceptual constructs has entertained social scientists for decades, and probably will for years to come. Meanwhile, people are dying every day.

Fortunately, although the science of the drugs-crime relationship may remain eternally mysterious, the engineering need not be. The more policy-analytic strand of the literature starts with a list of policy choices and examines each from a crime-control perspective. This is more likely to be useful to policymakers, but the standard menu of policy choices offers little promise of greatly improving the situation. Aggressive supply control is often counterproductive, whereas treatment and prevention efforts, which look better in theory, tend to stumble in practice.

The good news is that the list of genuinely promising interventions is much more impressive now than it was five years ago. We examine the literature on the standard drug-policy repertoire somewhat summarily, devoting more attention to recent innovations.

Section I addresses the science half of the literature but forgoes the usual detailed review of the empirical evidence. Its goal is to protect readers against commonly offered but fallacious claims rooted in selective quotation from that evidence. We also draw attention to the indirect (and therefore non-obvious) effects of drugs and drug policies on crime, which may be as important as the direct effects (such as theft by drug users to feed their habits), but are often neglected because they are harder to study.

Much confusion and disagreement over how drug policies affect crime comes not from disagreement about the drugs-crime connection but rather from confusion about how policies affect drug markets. Hence, Section II lays down principles for thinking about the impact of drug-control interventions on drug production, distribution, and use.

Section III sketches the main effects one can expect from various alternatives that figure prominently in policy discussions, plus some others that are less discussed but perhaps more promising.

The principal conclusions can be briefly stated:

- Most crime associated with illegal drugs is caused by illicit commerce and the enforcement that tries to control it, rather than by drug use; the reverse is true for alcohol.
- Alcohol causes more violence than all other drugs combined.
- The preponderance of crime associated with illegal drugs relates to cocaine (including crack), heroin, and methamphetamine. Marijuana plays a minor role, so changing marijuana policy will have very minor direct effects on drug-related crime.
- Legalization would all but eliminate the crime now associated with illegal markets, but at a large, uncertain, and substantially irreversible cost in terms of increased use and use-related problems.
- Decriminalization would be as likely to exacerbate as to ameliorate drug-related crime; in either case, the effect would be slight.

- Likewise, expanding conventional supply-control programs is as likely as not to exacerbate drug-related crime; reducing use by driving up prices can have ambiguous effects on market-related crime.
- Conventional demand reduction programs are helpful but limited. Prevention is cost-effective because it is cheap, not because it is highly effective; treatment has more to offer those dependent on opiates (roughly 10 percent of the illicit-drug problem) than those dependent on cocaine or other stimulants (75+ percent of the problem).
- Drug testing coupled with certain and immediate, but mild, sanctions can successfully coerce abstinence among the majority of substance abusers, thus shrinking the market and reducing those users' non-drug criminal activity. Testing-and-sanctions also help focus scarce treatment resources on the smaller numbers who cannot abstain without professional help even in an environment designed to promote abstinence.
- Flagrant drug markets generate crime and disorder, and focused enforcement can force them underground, with substantial neighborhood benefit. Those benefits remain even when, as is usually the case, the volume of drugs sold is not much reduced. High-deterrence, low-arrest strategies can substitute for massive crackdowns in breaking up flagrant markets.
- Two-tiered sanctions that punish the most violent (or otherwise destructive) dealers much more severely than run-of-the-mill dealers offer hope for managing the collateral damage caused by drug dealing.
- Raising alcohol excise taxes is the simplest way to materially reduce drug-related crime and violence.

I. TRADITIONAL THEMES AND TYPOLOGIES

A substantial literature tries to understand how and how much drugs cause crime, crime causes drug use, and other things cause, or result from, both.

A. Goldstein's Tripartite Framework

Goldstein (1985) suggested a three-way categorization of drug-related crime and violence (other than the drug-defined crimes of possession and sale) that remains the essential point of departure for understanding drugs-crime linkages. He distinguished among: psychopharmacological crime driven by drug intoxication or withdrawal; economic-compulsive crime committed by users to finance their drug habits; and systemic crime related to markets. Economic-compulsive crime includes not only property crime but also prostitution. The stereotypical systemic offense is fighting for drug-selling turf, but disputes between transaction partners over money (people given drugs on advance not paying up) or work performance (punishing workers who appear to shirk, cheat, or backstab) or to suppress testimony may be as important as turf battles, sometimes even more so. Systemic crime also includes money laundering and corruption.

Goldstein's categories are not mutually exclusive; for example, withdrawal might incite a dependent user to rob a dealer; that crime would fit all three definitions. They are also not collectively exhaustive; one of us once read a transcript describing a man who beat up the dealer he blamed for getting his baby sister hooked on heroin.

For policy purposes, though, a key insight from Goldstein's framework is distinguishing crime and violence caused directly by use (psychopharmacological) from crime and violence driven by money. Economic-compulsive crime is clearly driven by money; that is its definition. So is systemic crime, since people produce and distribute drugs for profit, not fun, and the disputes would lose their urgency if the stakes were pennies not dollars.

In the late 1980s and early 1990s efforts were made to count how many drug-related incidents belonged to each category (e.g., Goldstein et al. 1990). Caulkins et al. (1997) summarize this literature as suggesting that five-sixths of cocaine-related crime in the United States was economic-compulsive or systemic versus only one-sixth that was driven directly by cocaine use.

That proportion surely varies by drug and time, as well as across societies. The overall tenor of the literature, though, is that whatever the particular split between economic-compulsive and systemic, the sum of those two is much greater than the share that is psychopharmacological. That is, more drug-related crime is related to drug markets and drug spending than to drug use per se.

This stands in marked contrast to the situation with legally distributed alcohol. Companies selling legal goods compete fiercely but rarely with guns or knives. And alcohol is so cheap that impoverished alcoholics can finance their habit for a modest fraction of what daily cocaine and heroin abusers spend. Nevertheless, more crime and violence is alcohol-related than is related to all of the illegal drugs combined (Fagan 1990; Lipsey et al. 1997; Parker 2004). Under current conditions and policies, alcohol is a powerful promoter of psychopharmacological crime.

One reason alcohol use generates so much psychopharmacological crime is simply that so many people use alcohol so often. The sheer number of hours of alcohol intoxication is greater than it is for all the illegal drugs combined. But alcohol also ranks high—surely higher than cannabis, the most prevalent illicit drug—in terms of violent acts per hour of intoxication.

If this seems counterintuitive, it is partly because alcohol is so familiar; most Americans drink, and most of the people we know drink, without turning into

Mr. Hyde. Crack and heroin seem to be more addictive, and it is tempting to conclude that these must also be stronger promoters of psychopharmacological crime.

However, the majority of episodes of intoxication do not lead to any crime, regardless of the substance, and there is no necessary correlation between addictiveness and tendency to promote crime. By some metrics, nicotine is the most addictive of the commonly abused substances, but for all intents and purposes there is no tobacco-crime link except where heavy taxation has created an illicit tobacco trade.

B. Quantifying the Magnitude of Drugs-Crime Connections: Tilting at Windmills

It seems a bit unsatisfying to fill in the entries in table 10.1 below with words rather than numbers, but further precision is neither possible nor necessary to reach policy conclusions.

The precise magnitudes vary by drug, time, and context. Here we address a different source of imprecision; muddied causal linkages. If the relationship were simply that drugs cause crime, it would be relatively straightforward to tote up what proportion of crimes had some drug-relatedness.

However, not only do drugs cause crime, but crime causes drug use, and third factors cause both. Crime leads to drug use by generating funds that enable purchase; evidence that money constitutes a risk factor for drug abuse abounds, from the old phenomenon of weekly binge drinking on payday to more modern studies of transfer-payment checks (Satel 1995; Dobkin and Puller 2007).

It is possible to systematically describe these various pathways and to assemble evidence concerning each; Bennett and Holloway (2005) do an excellent job of this. In light of the multiple pathways and their feedbacks, lags, and other complications, no experiment or statistical analysis can determine with any precision how much crime is caused by each pathway at the national or global level. So rather than undertaking the Quixotic task of providing the "right" quantification, a more fruitful objective is to highlight the main themes.

Table 10.1. Relative Magnitude of Different Categories of
            Drug-Related Crime

	Legal Alcohol	All Illegal Drugs Collectively
Crime driven by use (Psychopharmacological)	Huge	Modest
Crime driven by spending (Economic-compulsive and Systemic)	Minimal	Important

1. *Point: Drug Involvement is Pervasive among Criminals*

Since criminals are deeply involved with drugs, aggressive drug control seems at first blush an obvious approach to controlling drug-related crime.

An astonishing proportion of street criminals are involved with drugs. Arrestees test positive at very high rates not only for marijuana but also for drugs such as cocaine and heroin, even though these are retained in the body for a relatively brief time. In many US cities more than half of those arrested for property offenses test positive for a substance other than marijuana (ONDCP 2009), and similar results have been observed by the NEW-ADAM survey in England and Wales and by DUMA in Australia (Holloway and Bennett 2004; Schulte, Mouzos, and Makkai 2005).

Inmate interviews also point to high rates of drug use. Two-thirds of US jail inmates reported using an illegal drug regularly, half reported symptoms of drug dependence or abuse in the year before incarceration, and two-thirds of them had received drug treatment at some time in the past, (Karberg and James 2005). Dependence rates were particularly high for property offenders, reaching 74 percent for burglars.

If drug users finance even a modest share of drug purchases through property crime, then much property crime is economic-compulsive. Reuter (1984) illustrates the logic of the analysis, while highlighting the frailty of the numbers. Drug users in the United States spend about $50 billion per year on the expensive illicit drugs: cocaine/crack, heroin, and methamphetamine (ONDCP 2001), more than three times the estimated total "take" from all property crime (FBI 1996; Rand 2009). Most illicit-drug expenditures are due to approximately 4 million dependent people who spend about $10,000 per year each. If even a quarter of their $40 billion in annual spending were financed by property crime, that $10 billion would account for two-thirds of the estimated revenues from property crime.

Drug users commit crime at much higher rates than do non-users. For example, the Office of National Drug Control Policy notes that past-year drug users are about ten times more likely to report being arrested for committing various non-drug crimes (ONDCP 2000). Furthermore, one can see a "dose-response" relationship; the more intensive the drug use, the greater the self-reported participation in non-drug crime. A dose-response relationship also shows with respect to the number of different illegal substances used (Bennett and Holloway 2005).

2. *Counter-Point: Not All drug-related Crime Is Caused by Drugs*

Of course correlation alone does not imply a cause-and-effect relationship. People prone to deviance may manifest that tendency through both crime and substance use (Reuter and Stevens 2007). Evidence suggests that not all of the crime by drug users is due to their drug use.

Perhaps the least intensive category of illicit drug users are those who have used nothing in the last thirty days and nothing except marijuana in the past year. Even they are several times more likely to report being arrested for property crimes than are abstainers.[1] That suggests that some of the observed correlation between drug use and elevated offending is spurious.

However, it is easy to overinterpret the finding that drug-using offenders usually commit their first non-drug crime before they start using drugs (Farabee, Joshi, and Anglin 2001; Pudney 2002). True, drug use rarely causes the "transition" from non-offender to offender. But even if drugs played no role at all in initiation into crime, they could still cause a very large proportion of offending by influencing escalation, persistence, and (absence of) desistance (Chaiken and Chaiken 1990). Most crimes are committed by a relatively small number of high-rate offenders who persist in offending for some time (Chaiken and Chaiken 1982; Blumstein, Canelo-Cacho, and Cohen 1993; Moffitt 1993), and their offense rates go up and down in synch with periods of greater or lesser drug use. While a very high proportion of males commit at least one crime at some point in their lives (Elliott et al. 1983), those who merely dabble in crime account for a tiny share of all crime.

Only a minority of offenders report having used an illegal drug at the time of their offense. For example, Karberg and James (2005) report a figure of 30 percent for convicted US jail inmates (lower, 20 percent, for assault and homicide; higher, 40 percent, for robbery and burglary). However, that finding places an upper bound only on the amount of psychopharmacological crime; it says nothing about crime committed for money to buy drugs or crimes by, among, and against drug sellers.

It is also true that only a minority of incarcerated offenders self-report having committed their crime to finance a drug purchase. For convicted US jail inmates the figures are 27 percent for property offenders and 25 percent for drug offenders (Karberg and James 2005). However, even leaving aside potential under-reporting, there is an ambiguity in fund accounting. Karberg and James (2005) also report that 53 percent met criteria for drug abuse or dependence, a figure which grows to 68 percent when alcohol abuse and dependence are included. When a person dependent on expensive illegal drugs steals money to pay for room and board, one can still consider whether that person's drug dependence contributes to the resort to crime. If drug use blocks employment and crime substitutes to pay (non-drug) bills, then those property crimes are caused by drug use even if they are not "drug-related" in the narrow sense.

3. *Orthogonal Point: Drug Laws Cause Drug-related Crime*

Drugs are the proximate cause of much crime in large part because the drugs are illegal. The drug molecules might be blamed for the minority of drug-related crime that is psychopharmacological, but it is the production, distribution, and use of an illegal product that links with economic-compulsive and systemic crime. These problems would decrease if the drugs were legal, even as total consumption rose.

We return to the merits and limitations of legalization below, but note here that it is an excellent example of the principle that there is no fixed relationship between the amount of drug use and the amount of non-drug crime. The context, including the legal context, matters.

4. *Moving On*

The debate about drugs and crime is a part of the larger "culture war," which is largely a dialogue of the deaf. Those who want to "win the drug war" as part of a larger project of defending what they take to be traditional values against what they see as deviant practices perceive the problem as drugs causing non-drug crime along with many other ills; those who want to "end prohibition" as part of a larger project of challenging what they see as unjust repression of diverse lifestyle choices view the problem as laws against "victimless crimes."

Neither side has had much success converting the other. Stubbornness may play a role, as do data limitations, but more fundamentally there is truth to both sets of claims: drugs and drug policies both cause crime, to an extent that varies by type of drug, stage of epidemic, aspects of the larger social context, and the policies themselves.

Much effort has been invested in attempting to determine the social costs of the illicit drug problem, but it is unclear how achieving greater precision would affect policy. Cost-of-illness (COI) studies find that crime-related outcomes account for a large share of the estimated $180 billion per year in social costs associated with illegal drugs (ONDCP 2004). If new scholarship revised the estimate of how much crime is drug-related up or down by 25 percent, then that would push the COI totals up or down. Yet Reuter (1999) has observed that few policy decisions hinge on specific estimates. Rather, they depend only on the general perception that drug-related crime is a big part of why we are troubled by drug abuse and that the absolute magnitude of the social cost of drug-related crime is large.

C. Overlooked Point: Drugs Cause Crimes that Are Not "Drug-related"

The standard academic criticism of Goldstein's framework is that not all drug-related crimes are caused by drugs. But, as noted earlier, it is also true that drugs cause crimes that the Goldstein analysis does not identify as "drug-related."

Goldstein's framework is useful when confronting a crime that is clearly drug-related, and the task is to figure out which causal mechanism was most pertinent: psychopharmacological, economic-compulsive, or systemic. To identify crime not directly linked to drugs requires counterfactual reasoning: we need to imagine how an individual's life course might have played out had there been no drug involvement. Sometimes even occasional drug use can have lasting ramifications: for example, when casual use leads to a drug conviction and the consequences of conviction snowball, via the effects of labeling, denial of benefits such as scholarship support and public housing, incarceration with hardened criminals, and acquiring a criminal record.

Nevertheless, it is dependence—as opposed to casual use—that is more likely to have long-term effects. Drug use is believed to adversely affect school performance (Engberg and Morral 2006; van Ours and Williams 2008, but see Bachman et al. 2008, for an opposing view), and low educational attainment has been linked to a broad array of adverse outcomes, including greater participation in crime. Likewise, periods of prolonged, uncontrolled dependence as an adult can wreak havoc on a career, with effects that can last well into recovery.

Long-term use of stimulants can lead to psychosis, which in some forms can increase criminality. There is now some (not uncontroversial) evidentiary basis (Arseneault et al. 2004) for the claim that cannabis use is a risk factor for psychosis, though not (or at least not yet) for the claim that the hypothesized cannabis-linked psychoses lead to crime. Other studies find steroid use associated with elevated rates of violence (e.g., Stretesky 2009).

These long-term effects complicate the interpretation of data about rates of intoxication among offenders, if substance abuse sometimes triggers mental health problems that later lead to offenses not committed under the influence.

Similarly, drug dealing can exacerbate violence other than by generating illicit-market business disputes. Blumstein and Cork (1996) argue that drug selling gives youth the means and the incentive to acquire firearms, and that their gun possession can trigger an arms race among youth in the community. Once armed, disputes over perceived slights, romantic triangles, and a host of other things that have nothing to do with drugs are more likely to be lethal.

Drugs can even cause crimes by people who never used drugs. Brazen drug markets can drive legitimate businesses to relocate, creating a spatial mismatch between where people live and the location of (legitimate) jobs. That contributes to urban poverty, unemployment, and a range of social ills linked to increased criminal involvement (Kain 1992).

Enforcement associated with drug markets can also aggravate racial tensions and damage police-community relations, which in turn can make it harder for police to solve non-drug crimes (Goldstein 1990).

Drug markets can swamp the capacity of both law enforcement and informal social controls to maintain order (Kleiman 1993), and the resulting disorder may be criminogenic (Kelling and Coles 1996; Keizer, Lindenberg, and Steg 2008). Filling cells with drug offenders can reduce the incarceration of non-drug offenders, thus sacrificing both deterrence and incapacitation against non-drug crime (Benson et al. 1992). There can be similar effects upstream in production and transshipment countries.

On the order of two million children in the United States live with one or more parents who are dependent on or who abuse illegal drugs (SAMHSA 2008). Others suffer from the absence of one or both parents from drug-related causes. At one time, concerns about the impact of drug use on children focused on physiological effects *in utero*. The "crack babies" panic proved to be overblown, but Pollack (2000) argues that, from a child's perspective, drug abuse is largely a pediatric rather than obstetric problem. Drug dependence is a risk factor for child abuse, neglect, and general bad parenting, any of which can adversely affect children's school performance, mental health, relationship skills, labor market performance, and life course more generally, including criminality.

It is easy to identify many ways drugs cause crime indirectly, and indirect effects are even harder to quantify than direct ones. The mainstream academic perspective that downplays the drugs-crime connection tends to overconcentrate on the more easily measurable direct effects.

D. Drug Type and Other Contextual Factors that Interact with Typology

The precise relationship between drugs and crime depends on both the drug and on the social context of its sale and use (Fagan 1990), including price and other conditions of availability.

1. *Drug Type*

Drug policy discussions often assume that if something is true for one illegal drug, it must also be true for another, but lumping cannabis and crack together makes about as much sense as classing tigers with tabby cats. There are too many substances to consider them all separately, but one should at least distinguish among diverted pharmaceuticals, the major "expensive" illegal drugs (cocaine/crack, heroin, and methamphetamine), cannabis, and all the minor illegal drugs (PCP, GHB, LSD, etc.). Of course when thinking about crime, alcohol represents a fifth, and arguably most important category.

Diverted pharmaceuticals—particularly opioid analgesics—account for an astonishing share of drug-related overdoses (Compton and Volkow 2006). The Drug Abuse Warning Network (DAWN) estimates that in 2006 about 750,000 emergency department visits involved nonmedical use of prescription and over the counter pharmaceuticals and dietary supplements, more than cocaine (550,000), marijuana (290,000), heroin (190,000), or stimulants (110,000) (SAMHSA 2008). However, diverted pharmaceuticals are not associated with much street crime.

The market value of all the minor drugs combined is still very small compared to the four major drugs; ONDCP (2001) estimates a $2.4 billion market value out of a $64 billion total, or less than 4 percent. Even if the minor drugs generated crime at the same rate per million dollars spent or per dependent user, they would still account for a small proportion of drug-related crime.

Marijuana dominates US drug use in terms of the prevalence of past-year use. It also—surprisingly to many—looms large in terms of the population in need of treatment by clinical criteria. Of the estimated 7 million Americans estimated to be clinically dependent on or abusing illegal drugs in 2008, 4.2 million were dependent on or abused marijuana or hashish (SAMHSA 2009b).[2] The cannabis market accounts for between one-sixth and one-fourth of total US black-market drug revenues (ONDCP 2001). However, marijuana's direct role in drug-related crime in the United States is minor. The drug seems to generate little psychopharmacological crime. Most retail distribution is embedded in social networks and is therefore discreet rather than flagrant; retail cannabis dealers do not typically stand on street corners. This limits systemic crime, though there is violence around marijuana farms that need to be defended from "patch pirates" and considerable violence among high-level trafficking organizations in northern Mexico. Economic-compulsive crime is rare because even most dependent users remain functional, able to retain employment, and because marijuana is cheap: even daily use can be sustained for $1,000 per year.

There is enormous debate about whether marijuana serves as a "gateway" to other drugs. To the extent that it does, then marijuana might indirectly be associated with considerably more drug-related crime than it is associated with directly. While it is clear that marijuana use typically predates use of other substances in the normal sequence of substances (CASA 1994), and that the association holds up even after controlling for standard covariates (Merrill et al. 1999), and while there is even some evidence from controlled laboratory studies that marijuana use can cause users to self-administer heroin at higher rates (Ellgren, Spano, and Hurd 2007), much of the association may be statistical rather than causal (Morral, McCaffrey, and Paddock 2002). For example, people who are novelty-seeking may be more prone to use both marijuana and other drugs, with the marijuana use coming earlier just because it is more readily available at younger ages.

The vast majority of drug-related crime in the United States is related to the three expensive major illicit drugs: heroin, cocaine (including crack), and methamphetamine. These three drugs collectively account for about 80 percent of black-market revenues; to criminals involved in those markets, that $50 billion is worth fighting over. Also, compulsive use is expensive, and most dependent users have limited legitimate income. So the vast majority of drug-related crime that is proximately caused by illegal drugs is associated with heroin, cocaine/crack, and methamphetamine.

Other substances may indirectly play a larger role. If the root cause of someone's criminal career lies in a poor or chaotic home life as a child, it might make little difference whether the parent lost his or her job due to dependence on heroin or on oxycodone.

However, an argument that an intervention pertaining to an illegal drug other than heroin, cocaine/crack, or methamphetamine is going to have a material effect on drug-related crime would require evidence of important indirect effects. That holds for arguments made by both drug warriors and drug reformers. Neither cracking down on marijuana nor legalizing it would have much direct effect on drug-related crime.

2. *Price*

As the example of cannabis indicates, prices of drugs matter; a drug that is cheap to use will not generate much economic-compulsive crime, and a drug that generates only small illicit revenues is not likely to generate much systemic crime. But there is no simple relationship between the price of a drug and its criminogenic effects; that, too, is context-dependent, depending also on the pharmacology of the drug.

Socially, the composition of the user base matters; a drug whose users are prosperous will generate less street crime than one used by the poor. If high prices keep the market for a drug exclusive, that will tend to make use of the drug less criminogenic.

The key pharmacological variables driving the drugs-crime relationship are the strength of the desire to use and the extent to which it creates what pharmacologists call "tolerance": the tendency, common to many drugs, to require larger and larger doses to maintain its original efficacy as a user becomes inured to its effects.

Drugs such as nicotine, cannabis, and alcohol are so inexpensive under current US conditions that even very heavy users need not resort to crime: $10 per day would support very heavy daily use of those drugs (two packs of cigarettes, ten drinks, about four "joints" assuming that the cannabis is bought at bulk rather than retail prices). While all of those drugs generate tolerance, few users stabilize at levels very much higher than those. In the case of alcohol, consuming much more than twenty drinks at a time risks death, even for someone who has been drinking heavily for a long time; thus a very heavy user with advanced tolerance might consume ten times as much alcohol at a sitting as would be enough to intoxicate a naïve user, but not much more than that.

The tolerance to heroin can build up to much higher levels. A naïve user of heroin would probably find 5 milligrams to be an effective dose, and 50 milligrams might well be fatal. By contrast, experienced users in Swiss heroin-maintenance programs typically consume almost 500 milligrams per day if taken intravenously and 1,000 milligrams per day if smoked (Gschwend et al. 2004), or roughly 100 times the consumption of a new user.

That means that heroin (and other opiates) provides an expensive habit at almost any price encountered in practice; the size of a habit is determined by how much money a user is able to scrape together, and $30–$50 per day, or something more than $10,000 per year, seems to be typical of advanced addiction: a number that has not changed very much even as heroin prices have plunged 90 percent in inflation-adjusted terms.

The same seems to be true of cocaine, especially in smoked form (freebase or crack). Indeed, as a matter of history, cocaine generated more crime among its users after cocaine prices fell in the early to mid-1980s than it had before. Expensive cocaine (generally snorted as powder) was largely a plaything of the affluent and therefore a source of crime among dealers but not so much by users. When the decline in cocaine prices and the introduction of crack—which lowered both the effective dose and the duration of the "high"—made cocaine available to poorer (and younger) people, who rapidly formed tolerance and thus expensive habits, cocaine use began to generate more crime than before.

3. Search Time and Other Conditions of Availability

Drug price is not the only market condition that influences consumption. Consumers of illicit drugs face discouragements other than financial ones. They risk arrest, robbery, and being sold diluted drugs that have less effect than they bargained for or adulterated drugs that may be damaging. In many cases, even an experienced buyer cannot easily or quickly find a seller who has the drug the buyer wants and has enough confidence that the buyer is not an undercover police officer to be willing to sell. Often drug dealing is concentrated in areas that some buyers prefer to avoid. Since dealing areas are by no means ubiquitous, buyers may have to travel substantial distances even to start the process of searching for a seller. One study of long-term heroin users found that the median time between having money in hand with the intention to buy drugs and the actual purchase was forty-five minutes, and that in some cities buyers reported occasions when an attempt to buy did not succeed in the course of a day (Rocheleau and Boyum 1994).

The effort, inconvenience, risk, and time required to purchase a drug constitutes a sort of second "price." As with the dollar price, we would expect some elasticity of demand: as drugs get harder to find, fewer people buy them. Mark Moore (1973), who pioneered this line of analysis, summarized all of the factors that go into this "second price" as "search time," and pointed out that retail enforcement strategies can influence it substantially: the more vigorous the police effort against retail dealing, the higher the search time.

Unlike enforcement effort aimed at increasing money price, whose effect on crime is ambiguous as to direction, anything that increases search time shrinks volume without increasing the money price, thus unambiguously reducing both drug consumption and the revenues of drug dealers. Thus increases in search time are crime-reducing. That effect will be accentuated when the increase in search time results from the adoption of less flagrant styles of dealing—e.g., home delivery as opposed to street sales or drug houses—which translate into less disorder and less crime against dealers and users.

4. *Epidemic Stage*

At the societal level, patterns of illegal drug use follow a predictable sequence. From originally low levels of population use, something triggers a period of very rapid growth with initiation rising to a peak and then ebbing (Caulkins 2005). Total past-year prevalence peaks soon after, because the modal length of a drug-using career is short, but levels of dependent use and associated problems can continue to grow as it takes time for dependence to develop.

It is common to refer to this trajectory as an "epidemic" of drug use because the explosive spread of initiation is thought to occur primarily from interpersonal contact between recent initiates and susceptible users. There is of course no pathogen, so it is not a literal epidemic. The process is rather one of word-of-mouth diffusion (Ferrence 2001), just as in "epidemic" models of new product adoption (Bass 1969).

An important consequence is that the mix of user types varies dramatically over the epidemic. Early in the epidemic most users will be relatively recent initiates, few of whom are dependent. Later, in the endemic stage, the proportion of users who are dependent becomes much larger. Furthermore, since dependent users consume so much more of a drug per capita than do non-dependent users, consumption is dominated by dependent users later in the epidemic (Caulkins et al. 2004).

Inasmuch as non-dependent or light users are less likely to be involved in crime than heavy users, the extent of the association between a drug and crime can change dramatically over time, even if there is no change in policy.

5. *Other Contextual Factors*

Any number of societal factors can mediate the nature of a drugs-crime linkage. An important example is the overall level of violence in society. In the 1980s, street markets in the United States were extremely violent. The same volume of sales in a country where possession of firearms is rare might have led to just as many assaults but fewer homicides if the fighting was with knives instead of guns. Conversely, the death toll might have been even higher if the medical system had been less skilled at saving people with potentially fatal penetrating wounds.

Geography can also matter. Two countries with similar rates of drug use might have very different rates of drug-related violence if one's location makes it a convenient transshipment point for drugs destined for some other, larger country.

Access to legal income might also matter. It has been theorized that one way to control economic-compulsive crime would be to offer dependent users government income support sufficient to preclude their needing to commit crime to support their habit (Reuter and MacCoun 1996).

Given all the ways in which the nature and strength of the drugs-crime nexus depends on the context, it should come as no surprise that most sweeping generalizations about drugs and crime fail to survive close scrutiny.

II. Policy Analysis: General Principles

Sensible analysis of proposals for reducing drug-related crime has to recognize four general principles. We set them out as a separate section here because they are relevant to several different policy interventions.

A. Drug Consumption Follows a Pareto Law

Many phenomena, such as people's height, have a bell-shaped (Gaussian or "normal") distribution: the mean equals the median, most observations cluster around that typical value, and roughly equal numbers are found, symmetrically distributed, above and below it. However, other phenomena, including drug consumption, are better described by distributions where large deviations are much more common. In both log-normal and power-law distributions, the mean is much larger than the median; that is, the average behavior is more extreme than the behavior of the typical user. When some quantity (income, wealth, airplane miles travelled, drug consumption) follows a power-law or log-normal distribution, the behavior of the small number of cases at the top of the distribution dominates the total. This effect was first observed by Pareto (1896–97) with respect to the ownership of land: the top quintile (20 percent) of Italian landowners held 80 percent of the land. Although those precise figures do not inevitably result from such skewed distributions, the management theorist Joseph Juran generalized the 80/20 claim under the name Pareto's Law, also sometimes called "the law of the vital few and the trivial many."

Pareto distributions show up in diverse facets of human behavior, including the use of habit-forming drugs. Cook (2007) elaborates on the evidence concerning alcohol: the top decile of drinkers consume 50 percent of all alcohol, and the top 20 percent consume 80 percent. ONDCP (2001) estimates that the minority of cocaine and heroin users who are "hardcore" account for 84 percent and 93 percent of total drug spending on those drugs, respectively. Among household respondents, 20 percent of past-year marijuana users account for two-thirds of the reported days of use; they likely also consume more marijuana per day of use, so these heavy users probably account for well more than two-thirds of the total volume consumed.

A related principle applies at the other end of the consumption distribution. Many past-year users are not just light users but "very light" users. The bottom third of past-year marijuana users accounted for just 1 percent of the days of use.[3] Hence, statistics on past-year users can be utterly uninformative for purposes of understanding drug-related crime; there is no reason to think that the small subset of users who account for most of the drug-related crime need look anything like the typical past-year user, or that their numbers will go up and down in tandem. Insofar as systemic crime results from the money that flows through the illicit markets, the vast bulk of that money comes from the small minority of heavy users rather than the large majority of light users. Thus the claim that most drug users are neither unemployed nor poor, while accurate, does not imply that middle-class, employed drug users are responsible for the bulk of drug-related crime.

B. Drug Demand is Not Perfectly Inelastic, and Not All Drugs are Substitutes for Each Other

When drug prices go up, people use less. When prices go down, people use more. The price responsiveness is greater than the myth of the drug addict with a fixed habit size would allow.

Users' response to price in no way implies their consumption is rational in the sense of Becker and Murphy (1988). It just means users respond to incentives. (Even plants do that, in a sense, when they grow toward the light.) So rejection of rational addiction theory does not require rejecting the belief that drug users respond to price changes.

Economists define "elasticity of demand" as the percentage change in consumption caused by a 1 percent increase in price. For example, if consumption drops by 5 percent when prices go up by 10 percent, the elasticity of demand is -0.5.

The overall price elasticity of demand is the sum of the "participation elasticity," the percentage change in number of users per 1 percent increase in price, and the "conditional elasticity" the percentage change in consumption per person who uses.

It was once thought that a drug addict would do anything to "get his fix." On that theory, if prices went up addicts would just commit more crime in order to generate more money to buy the same amount of drug. The idea that drug demand is perfectly inelastic has now been thoroughly discredited by a very large literature, reviewed by Grossman (2005) and, more recently, Babor et al. (2009).

Almost every serious estimate of the elasticity of demand finds some price-responsiveness, but estimates of the degree of responsiveness vary by substance, population, time period, legal status, and by elasticity type (short- or long-term elasticity, total, conditional, or participation), etc. If one had to pick a single short-term elasticity estimate most consistent with the literature, -0.75 might be a good guess, meaning that a 10 percent increase in price would lead to a 7.5 percent total reduction in quantity consumed. (If some users have malleable but slow-to-change habits—for example, cigarette smokers who decide to quit in the face of higher prices but do so only after several unsuccessful attempts—then demand will be more elastic in the long run than it is in the short run.)

It is crucial to recognize that the empirical evidence comes from changes in price that are close to today's prices. There is danger in extrapolating elasticity estimates beyond the range of the data It is easy to show how alternative assumptions about the shape of the demand curve away from the current price—each equally consistent with the available empirical evidence—could produce wildly different predictions about how large changes in price would affect use (Caulkins 2001; Kilmer et al., 2010). For example, even if a 10 percent decrease in price would lead to a 7.5 percent increase in use, that does not imply that a 100 percent decrease in price (making the drugs free) would lead to only a 75 percent increase in consumption, a claim favorable to the case for legalization. (Of course legalization would change more than price: drugs would be easier to find and the mix of messages about them would tilt in a more favorable direction.)

Changes in the price of one item can affect consumption of another item through substitution or complementarity. If steak becomes more expensive, people might eat more of substitutes such as chicken or fish, and buy fewer complements such as steak sauce or steak knives. Jofre-Bonet and Petry (2008) review the growing literature that tries to determine which pairs of drugs are complements and which are substitutes. Unfortunately, estimating cross-elasticities is harder than estimating own price elasticity, and the literature is less decisive.

Pharmacology provides some hints. The more closely the effects of two drugs resemble one another, the more likely they are to be substitutes. Clearly, two different brands of beer or two different brands of wine are competitors, that is to say substitutes. Indeed, that seems to be true for all alcoholic drinks: beer and wine substitute for one another, and for distilled spirits. The same is probably true of other drugs that, like alcohol, act as central-nervous-system depressants: the opiates and the barbiturates, for example. (Only "probably" because even different drugs in the same general class can "potentiate" one another—strengthen one another's effects— as they interact with the nervous system, as alcohol tends to do with the opiates.)

The same may be true among stimulants; different amphetamines compete with one another, and probably with cocaine.

But stimulants and depressants are likely to be complements, with the stimulants allowing users of depressants to consume more before passing out and depressants helping stimulant users calm down and, eventually, go to sleep. Café royale and rum-and-cola illustrate the complementarity between the depressant alcohol and the stimulant caffeine; the heroin-and-cocaine mixture known as a "speedball" illustrates the same principle. The combination use of stimulants and depressants ("uppers and downers," in drug-user slang) is considered a particular risk factor for progression to drug abuse and dependence. In the specific case of alcohol and cocaine, the mixture has a special risk in the form of the cocaethylene molecule that forms in users' bloodstreams; cocaethylene, unlike cocaine itself, is a potent generator of aggressive behavior.

Some pairs of drugs may be substitutes in the short run, with users switching from one drug to another in response to availability, yet become complements in the long run if price declines of one drug increase escalation of use to dependence on both leading to eventual polydrug use.

All these speculations are plausible and not inconsistent with the empirical evidence (Jofre-Bonet and Petry 2008). However, in ten years we will likely know quite a bit more about the extent of substitution and complementarity, and some of what we guessed now might look naively wrong upon retrospect.

What is certain is that the notion that all pairs of drugs are substitutes—as if there were a fixed number of intoxicated hours with which different drugs compete for market share—is unsound. One of the most potent arguments for the legalization of cannabis is that, since the drug is on balance less dangerous than alcohol, legalizing cannabis would create benefits by reducing alcohol consumption. Alas, the empirical evidence on that point is decidedly mixed; some studies show complementarity, some substitution, and some complementarity among some user groups and substitution among others.

C. Drug Markets are Markets

Drugs are produced, distributed, and retailed primarily through markets. Marijuana users who grow their own supply and backyard gardeners who make their own wine are the exceptions. Likewise, retail distribution is often embedded within a friendship network (Caulkins and Pacula 2006). The distribution chain may have as many as eight to ten transactions between a farmer who grows poppy or coca and the user, and only the final transaction is likely to be a social interaction among friends; the rest is business, done for profit and not for amusement or self-expression. Thus economic analysis applies to these transactions.

The drug-distribution system adapts to interventions, as legal markets do. This point is most easily made with respect to seizures. The "physical flow" model of drug distribution assumes that seizing a kilogram of drugs reduces the quantity available for consumption by one kilogram. But suppliers can respond to ongoing seizures by producing more.

The physical-flow model has largely disappeared from informed discussion of drug policy. Unfortunately, an equally naïve model persists, one that is as overly pessimistic as the physical flow model was overly optimistic. Drug sellers are not indifferent about whether their drugs are seized because it costs them something to replace lost or stolen drugs. Since dealers are in business for profit, they pass those costs along to users in the form of higher prices. Those higher prices reduce consumption. Seizure of drugs presumably reduces drug use, but the reduction is much less than one for one. The amount of reduction per kilogram seized depends on where the drug is seized (farther down the distribution chain means higher replacement costs) and how responsive drug use is to price increase.

Reuter and Kleiman (1986) provide a framework to estimate by how much seizures and other enforcement outcomes affect price, production, and consumption. To illustrate this thinking, suppose all of the roughly 100 metric tons of cocaine seized in or en route to the United States was seized at a market level where the replacement cost is $10,000 per kilogram. Since total US consumption is about 250 metric tons, that means suppliers at that market level would need to receive $14,000 per kilogram for each of the 250 metric tons sent farther down the distribution chain to cover their costs of obtaining 350 metric tons at $10,000 per kilogram, since 250,000 times $14,000 = 350,000 times $10,000.

There is debate about how that seizure-induced $4,000 markup from $10,000 to $14,000 per kilogram would affect the retail price. The so-called additive model says it is passed through on a one-for-one basis, increasing retail prices by $4 per gram or roughly 4 percent, from $100 to $104 per gram. If the elasticity of demand is -0.75, that implies a reduction in consumption of 3 percent from 257.5 to 250 metric tons. In other words, seizing 100 metric tons reduces consumption by 7.5 metric tons.

The multiplicative model of price transmission is more optimistic. It assumes price increases are passed along on a percentage basis. If in the absence of seizures the price at the interdicted level would have been only $10,000 instead of $14,000, then the retail price would be only $10,000/$14,000 = 5/7 as great. Using the same price elasticity of demand, that implies consumption would have been $(5/7)^{-0.75}$ = 29% higher. So, according to the multiplicative model, seizing 100 metric tons on an ongoing basis is reducing consumption by 0.29 times 250 or roughly 70 metric tons.

The true price transmission model is probably somewhere between the pure additive and pure multiplicative models (Boyum 1992; Caulkins 1994). The true effect of seizing 100 metric tons in the hypothesized manner would probably avert somewhere between 7 and 70 metric tons of consumption. The range can be narrowed by making the calculations more precise; this numerical example is only meant to illustrate the general principle that seized drugs are replaced, but not one for one.

Similar logic holds for seized assets, disrupted connections, and all the other products of supply-side enforcement, including incarceration; incarcerated sellers are replaced, but not necessarily one-for-one.

D. Drug Markets Have Multiple Equilibria

Many models of drug markets have at least two stable equilibria, one at very low levels of use and one at high levels of use (Kleiman 1988, 1993; Baveja et al. 1993; Caulkins 1993; Tragler, Caulkins, and Feichtinger 2001).

Tipping points are balance points between two stable equilibria (Grass et al. 2008). If the system is a little below the tipping point, then the system will tend to fall naturally into the low-level equilibrium; if it starts a little above the tipping point, the system will tend to grow toward the high-level equilibrium. If the system happens to be near the tipping point, then a small shove could tip the system into approaching an equilibrium very different than what would otherwise have happened. Conversely, if the system is in the high-level equilibrium then interventions that knock the market away from the equilibrium, but not past the tipping point, will produce only temporary success.

Thus effects of interventions can depend enormously on the state of the system. Starting from modest levels of current use, then enforcement can maintain the market at such *de minimus* levels relatively easily and, hence, prevent a surge in drug-related crime. However, once the genie is out of the bottle, it is very difficult for law enforcement to restore the original state.

These observations imply that lessons from alcohol prohibition are of limited relevance to evaluating heroin prohibition. Alcohol prohibition was an attempt to suppress a market that was already established at a high-level equilibrium; heroin prohibition is an attempt to maintain a relatively low-level equilibrium. Even if heroin and alcohol were entirely similar in their addictive potential and criminogenic effects, heroin prohibition might still be a good policy even though alcohol prohibition was a flop; an intervention that fares badly when applied to an established mass market might be successful applied to a drug whose sale and use remain relatively rare.

Dual-equilibirum models also apply to retail markets, with respect to the level of indiscreet or "flagrant" selling. At the low-level equilibrium, drugs are still sold and used, but in surreptitious ways, such as transactions arranged by cell phones, rather than through anonymous open transactions in public places or through single-use drug-selling locations such as crack houses.

When there is little or no flagrant selling, an individual dealer who sells flagrantly stands out from the background and is likely to be arrested. However, in a flagrant market large enough to swamp law enforcement capacity (Kleiman 1993), open selling carries a much lower risk of arrest. Even if the police make many arrests rather than giving up in despair, the risk of arrest per dealer may still be low enough that advantages of selling flagrantly in the form of visibility to potential customers outweigh the risks in the dealer's calculation.

Flagrant selling generates much more crime and disorder per kilogram sold than does surreptitious selling. Tipping local markets from high to low flagrancy is, therefore, no less relevant to crime control than tipping national markets from high to low levels of aggregate use. If the goal is to reduce drug use, then pushing a market underground has only modest benefits. If the goal is to reduce drug-related crime and disorder, then pushing a flagrant market toward discreet conduct while leaving its volume unchanged might be more valuable than cutting its size in half while leaving it flagrant.

III. POLICY ANALYSIS

These principles support assessment of the primary drug control strategies from the perspective of their potential for controlling drug-related crime.

A. Legalization

Superficially, legalization might seem like a painless way to cut the Gordian knot of substance abuse problems; reflection suggests more complexity. But its one undeniable benefit would be a great reduction in drug-related crime.

The decision to ban a substance is essentially a decision to tolerate increased drug-related crime for the sake of reduced drug use. Choosing the legal status of a substance lets society choose the kind of drug problem it faces, but there is no way to choose not to have a problem (Kleiman 1992). When substances are legal (alcohol, tobacco) the problem is high rates of use and use-related harms. When substances are illegal, use is much lower, but prohibition engenders black markets and black-market associated crime. The way this general principle plays out in practice varies by substance.

Legalizing marijuana would do little directly to reduce drug-related crime in final market countries for the simple reason that marijuana markets do not generate a lot of crime. There might be indirect effects, but one of the most commonly cited effects—freeing up enforcement resources for other purposes—would not be large (Kilmer et al., 2010). Marijuana offenders generate many arrests, but it is incarceration that is most costly, and marijuana offenders account for less than 10 percent of imprisoned drug law violators (Sevigny and Caulkins 2004). Perhaps the biggest indirect effect would be from alcohol use. If marijuana substituted for alcohol use, marijuana legalization might reduce alcohol-related crime; if increased marijuana dependence led to greater alcohol abuse, crime might go up.[4] (As mentioned earlier, the empirical literature on this is mixed; see Boyum, Caulkins, and Kleiman [2010] for a review.)

In stark contrast, the direct effects of legalization of the three major expensive illegal drugs make it a very high stakes choice. If these substances were legalized, then prices could fall to 1–5 percent of current retail prices in the developed world. Cocaine now sells for only $1,500 per kilogram ($1.50 per gram) in Colombia even though it costs $100+ per gram at retail ($100,000+ per kilogram) in final market countries, and legalization would presumably lower not raise production costs (Babor et al. 2009). It costs less than $50 to overnight express a (legal) one kilogram package from South America to the United States or Europe. Legal distribution costs in the final market country would be minimal because the product is already in final form, ready to consume. So the legalized, untaxed retail price would be a few dollars per pure gram versus $100+ today (Fries et al. 2008). The economics of heroin are similar, but with prices being roughly a factor of two higher.[5]

Since consumption responds to price, the best guess is that legalization would lead to large increases in use, dependence, and psychopharmacological crime. More precise statements are not possible because no modern industrialized country has ever legalized any of the expensive illegal drugs. The conditions are outside the support of any available data, either quantitative or qualitative (cf., Kilmer et al.,

2010; Caulkins and Reuter, 2010).[6] Whether this trade-off is appealing depends both upon value judgments—how to weight crime, incarceration, and the loss of personal liberty against the health, economic, psychological, and social damage from increased addiction—and upon the size of the post-legalization increase in the number of problem users. To some extent, those effects could be buffered by regulations: for example, by making the production and distribution of legalized psychoactives a state monopoly, at prices much higher than market prices, though below current illicit prices and without marketing. But the tighter the regulation and the higher the legal price, the more room such a model would create for a new illicit market (Kleiman 1992b). The massive drug-legalization literature, rich in polemic against the current drug control regime, is poor in detailed designs for "after the revolution."

As with marijuana, the above outcomes also depend on imperfectly-understood relationships of substitution and complementarity among drugs. Post-legalization, would the currently illicit drugs substitute for alcohol? If it were the case that a certain proportion of the population is born with an addictive personality, and will end up dependent on some addictive substances regardless, it would follow that increased dependence on cocaine or heroin would be offset by reduced alcohol use. But if variety in consumers' choices increases total consumption, the result might be otherwise. Legalizing the expensive drugs is not only high-stakes with respect to unanticipated affects on use. It is also an irreversible experiment. If legalization turned out badly, in the sense that use and dependence went up more than expected, re-imposing prohibition would not restore the status quo *ex ante*. The additional people who became dependent when prices were low would not magically cease being dependent when the laws were changed back. Prohibition re-imposed after a failed legalization would face a much larger black market that it faces today.

B. Regulation

Legalized products can be regulated stringently (e.g., explosives) or not (e.g., handicrafts). It is sometimes imagined that stringent regulation can offset the use-promoting effects of legalization, but this is not realistic for the expensive drugs that drive most drug-related crime.

For example, the idea that excise taxes could keep legal prices near current levels is patently unrealistic. The required tax rate would be on the order of 10,000 percent. When Canada raised excise taxes on tobacco in the early 1990s, tax-evading smugglers quickly began to supply a large proportion of the market giving rise to flagrant selling of untaxed cigarettes, so the tax had to be repealed (Galbraith and Kaiserman 1997). That tax varied by province and over time but appears to have been at most 500 percent of the legal price, or just one-twentieth of what would be needed to keep the expensive illegal drugs at their current prices if they were legalized. The situation is even worse in terms of tax per unit weight. A $30 tax on a

300-gram carton of cigarettes is only $0.10 per gram. If a $0.10 per gram tax generates prohibitive amounts of tax-evading smuggling, a $100 or even a $10 per gram tax on legalized cocaine seems implausible. Again, a state-monopoly system might avoid some of this problem, but would require very tight internal controls to prevent diversion.

It is not even clear the situation is materially better with relatively cheaper marijuana (Kilmer et al., 2010). Caputo and Ostrom (1994) sought to estimate potential tax revenues from legalizing marijuana. Based on tobacco data, they estimated production costs for legal marijuana of only about $1 per pound and argued that almost the entire markup between that and the $1,800–$3,000 per pound paid by consumers could be captured as tax revenue. Tea selling for $5 per ounce ($80 per pound) may be a better analog than tobacco, but replacing the $1 per pound by $80 per pound does not change the basic insight; current marijuana prices are extraordinarily high for an agricultural product. Where we diverge from Caputo and Ostrom is in skepticism that this price gap can be converted into tax revenue. Even a $1,000 per pound tax is over $2 per gram, or more than twenty times the tax rate that was unsustainable for cigarettes in Canada.

Controlled provision for use exclusively on regulated premises is a different matter, because it uses physical controls to prevent diversion or resale. The heroin maintenance trials suggest this is possible for opiates, although that is probably more usefully thought of as liberalization of treatment rather than as a form of regulated legalization. It is less clear the concept applies to stimulants.

C. Decriminalization

Many people think of decriminalization as being a sort of legalization-lite, but the direct effects of decriminalization on crime are almost the opposite of those of legalization.

Decriminalization means reducing or eliminating criminal penalties for possession of modest amounts of a substance. Decriminalization *per se* should have little direct effect on enforcement risk to producers and suppliers. (Jurisdictions that decriminalize often do so as part of a general backing away from tough enforcement. We consider changes in enforcement intensity below. For now, we focus on decriminalization itself, not a package of conceptually distinct changes that happen often to be implemented in tandem.)

Decriminalization does reduce some risk to users. All other things being equal, reducing the risk of doing something tends to increase participation in that activity. This has been observed for a range of activities, such as rock climbing and sky diving (Wilde 1994).[7]

If decriminalization increases drug demand and does nothing to change supply, then the result will be both greater consumption and higher prices, and thus greater spending. In other words, decriminalization will tend to increase all three of

Goldstein's direct causes of drug-related crime. The general experience with decriminalization is that increases in use and, hence, black-market spending, are not large (MacCoun and Reuter 2001). However, while the direct effects on crime may be modest, they are still in the wrong direction.

If decriminalization is expected to reduce drug-related crime, it has to be through indirect mechanisms. For example, decriminalization might save law enforcement resources, although even in the United States imprisonment is almost exclusively reserved for people with some (perhaps minor) involvement in drug distribution rather than consumption (Sevigny and Caulkins 2004). More plausibly, decriminalization might improve the attitudes toward police of those who use illicit drugs but do not commit other crimes. Moreover, while possession arrests rarely lead to incarceration, they can still be damaging to those arrested, perhaps in ways that make them more likely to be involved in crime in the future. There is simply not sufficient evidence to conclude one way or another how decriminalization might affect drug-related crime through indirect mechanisms. But the central point is that if decriminalization has any important beneficial effects on reducing drug-related crime, it has to be through indirect channels; the direct effects are all perverse.

D. Effects on Crime of Changes in Supply and Demand

Drug-related crime is caused both by drug use and by drug spending. Reducing supply reduces use but may increase spending. Reducing demand shrinks both. Therefore, while successful demand-reduction efforts necessarily reduce drug-related crime, the effects on crime of successful supply reduction efforts are ambiguous. Thus, ironically, the supply-reduction efforts run by police agencies will benefit health but may actually increase crime, while the drug-treatment programs run by health departments have unambiguous crime-control benefits.

For example, suppose that the elasticity of demand is -0.75 and that one-quarter of drug-related crime (in total, counting direct and indirect effects) is pharmacological and the other three-quarters economic-compulsive (driven by drug spending by users) or systemic (driven by the revenues of drug dealers). Suppose also that those components of drug-related crime are proportional to drug use and drug spending, respectively. If increased supply control drove up retail prices by 10 percent, then, drug use would decrease by -7.5 percent. In contrast, with consumption declining by less than price increased, spending would go up, in this case by 2.5 percent. So we expect a 7.5 percent reduction in the quarter of crime that is driven by use and a 2.5 percent increase in the three-quarters of crime that is driven by spending. Those effects would exactly cancel, leaving no net effect on drug-related crime.

The numerical example can be generalized, yielding the following rule of thumb.[8] Supply control reduces crime if the elasticity of demand, η, is greater in absolute value than the proportion of drug-related crime that is driven by spending, as opposed to use. If demand is elastic, meaning $|\eta| > 1$, then tighter supply control will necessarily reduce crime. But if drug demand is less price-responsive and most drug-related crime is economic-compulsive or systemic, then even successful drug supply-control efforts could be counterproductive in terms of crime. There is no such ambiguity for demand reduction.

Those conclusions come from what economists call "comparative-statics analysis," which examines the effects of a change once the rest of the system has adjusted to a "shock" in supply. (It is generally not possible to "shock" demand because most demand stems from heavy or dependent users whose demand changes slowly.) The results may be different during the period of adjustment. Most drug markets spend most of their time in equilibrium, but supply of every major drug has been disrupted at one time or another in the United States and other countries (Caulkins and Reuter 2010). The effects of temporary supply disruption on drug-related crime are subject to a similar analysis but with less favorable results in terms of reduced crime, because the (absolute value of the) elasticity of demand is smaller in the short run than in the long run.[9] So generally we would not expect transitory supply disruptions to reduce drug-related crime.

To the extent that one drug substitutes for another, some of the benefit of driving up the price of one drug will be offset by increased use of other drugs, including alcohol. Treatment, by contrast, is likely to reduce demand for all drugs at once.

Insofar as conventional supply-control efforts are typified by law enforcement and demand-control efforts by prevention and treatment, the side-effects of supply control (arrest and incarceration) are mostly damaging to the subjects while the side-effects of treatment are mostly helpful; for example, incarceration tends to reduce employability while prevention and treatment enhance it. Employment is a strong correlate of staying out of crime in the first place and of desisting from a criminal career (Fagan and Freeman 1999).

Thus in terms of reducing drug-related crime, the deck is clearly stacked against supply control. But the temptation to overgeneralize should be resisted. A treatment program that fails to reduce drug use is still a waste of money, while a highly effective supply-control effort can do enormous good at modest cost. For example, if the significant reduction in heroin availability in Australia that began in 2001 was brought about by police effort (as argued by Degenhardt et al. 2005 but denied by Wodak 2008), then that effort reduced crime far more cost-effectively than police efforts devoted to arresting non-drug criminals.

E. Traditional Supply and Demand Control Programs

Drug control interventions are traditionally categorized into treatment, prevention, and enforcement or supply control programs, although there are many reasons to be dissatisfied with such a partition (Kleiman 1992). For example, if supply control drives up prices, that might both prevent some initiation and induce some current users to seek treatment. None of those categories, as conventionally understood, seems to hold out much promise of substantially reducing drug-related crime.

1. *Standard Treatment*

The mantra in the literature is "treatment works." Many studies have found that treatment has benefits that exceed its costs (Gerstein et al. 1994; Rajkumar and French 1997; Cartwright 2000; Harwood et al. 2002; Belenko, Patapsis, and French 2005).

This is not because treatment is highly effective. Relapse rates are very high, and many users continue to use even while in standard treatment (e.g., Iguchi et al. 1997). However, the modest cost of most treatment compared to the high social cost per crime means that treatment more than pays for itself. For example, offenders who commit even one acquisitive crime per week can easily generate $50,000 in direct costs and $100,000 in total social costs per year, even when the mix is skewed toward larceny and away from robbery (Miller, Cohen, and Wiersema 1996). Even if post-treatment relapse were instantaneous and certain, one would still be willing to spend $10,000 per year for a treatment program that reduced current offending by just 10 percent, or $20,000 per year for a program that reduced current offending by 20 percent.[10] Hence, the bar is set fairly low when treating dependent users who regularly commit crimes. Even a small amount of effectiveness makes the effort cost-justified.

This claim requires some qualification. To reduce crime, treatment has to target the drugs and drug users that generate crime. Between 1992 and 2007 the annual number of treatment episodes in the United States expanded by more than 250,000, but 75 percent of that expansion came from treating people whose primary substance of abuse was marijuana.[11] That might have been a great crime-control investment if those individuals were saved from escalating to dependent use of one of the expensive drugs, but the direct effects on crime from reduced cannabis demand are modest.

Second, not all treatment clients are street criminals, and the distribution of offense rates among offenders is highly skewed (Blumstein, Canelo-Cacho, and Cohen 1993), so a small subset of users are responsible for a grossly disproportionate proportion of all drug-related offending. No matter how successful the treatment, no economic-compulsive or psychopharmacological crimes are averted by treating people who were not going to commit any crimes in the first place (There presumably would still be a beneficial effect on systemic crimes by reducing overall drug demand).

Third, among the expensive illegal drugs, the strongest evidence for treatment efficacy pertains to opiate substitution therapies to treat heroin dependence (methadone, buprinorphine, LAAM [Leva-Alpha Acetyl Methadol], even heroin itself in

Switzerland and the Netherlands). Despite considerable research investment, no comparable pharmacotherapies exist for stimulants, and Manski, Pepper, and Petrie (2001) were sharply negative concerning the lack of rigorous evidence for existing stimulant therapies. That does not matter much where heroin is the primary illicit-drug problem, as tends to be true in Europe and Asia; it is of much greater importance in the Western Hemisphere. Stimulants account for at least three-quarters of the social costs of illegal drug use in the United States (Caulkins et al. 2002).

Fourth, most criminally active drug users do not want to quit drug use enough to enter and stay in treatment. Expanding treatment supply will be ineffective in the face of inadequate treatment demand.

2. *Coerced Treatment: Diversion Programs and Drug Courts*

Treatment demand can be created by making treatment the alternative to incarceration. That approach also focuses treatment attention on the criminally active population. Such is the logic of diversion programs and drug courts.

Drug-diversion programs, under a variety of labels including Treatment Alternatives to Street Crime (TASC) and the California Substance Abuse Control and Crime Prevention Act (SACPA, more commonly referred to as Proposition 36) involve offering drug users arrested either for drug possession or sale or for non-drug crimes the opportunity to avoid a jail or prison sentence in return for agreeing to enter, and remain in, drug treatment. Each offender is given a formal "needs assessment" and then assigned a specific treatment plan. Successful treatment completion (which need not involve actual desistance from drug use) can lead to "expungement" of the official record of the offense. Failure to attend treatment can be punished as a violation of probation.

Unfortunately, neither the promise of expungement nor the threat of probation sanctions has proven an especially potent incentive for treatment completion. Probation officers only know about missed treatment appointments if informed by the treatment providers, who have no strong reason to make such reports. Even if a report is made, a busy probation officer may take no action beyond a verbal reprimand when the alternative is reporting the violation to the court, and asking for probation to be revoked and the offender sent to jail or prison; this seems a disproportionate response to many probation officers and judges. As a result, nominally mandatory drug treatment in diversion programs is in fact largely voluntary, sacrificing the opportunity to use the leverage provided by criminal-justice supervision to potentiate treatment (Mitchell and Harrell 2006; Skodbo et al. 2007).

Of offenders who accept the California Proposition 36 treatment-in-lieu-of-incarceration deal, one in four never appears for even one treatment session, and three-quarters of those who start treatment end it prematurely; thus fewer than one in four Proposition 36 clients completes the assigned course of treatment

(Urada et al. 2008). That is a worse-than-typical record among diversion programs, in part because the only sanction available to a judge for the first two instances of reported noncompliance is re-referral to treatment, but noncompletion rates of 50 percent are typical. Diversion may still represent a less socially costly option than incarceration, although follow-up studies of Proposition 36 strongly suggest that diversion programs may postpone more incarceration than they prevent.

Because diversion programs are designed to handle large numbers of offenders, and because they require all of their clients to attend treatment, budget and capacity limitations force most diversion programs to assign most of their clients to low-intensity outpatient drug-free counseling. That is true even for opiate addicts, who demonstrably have far better outcomes if assigned to substitution therapies such as methadone. These low-intensity programs often also have low efficacy; Proposition 36 treatment completers are only slightly less criminally active than dropouts, and only slightly less active than otherwise-similar offenders not subject to mandatory drug treatment; compared to routine handling, Proposition 36 does not reduce criminal activity among its client base as a whole. A small minority (less than 2 percent) of offenders with very high rates of pre-admission arrests (five or more arrests in the thirty months before the arrest leading to Proposition 36 placement) account for a large proportion of new crimes by Proposition 36 clients.

Where diversion programs are used for offenders with little or no non-drug criminal activity—for example, people arrested for simple possession of cannabis—they can actually reduce the social value that can be extracted from a given pool of treatment resources by forcing people to be treated for an illness they do not have. An arrest is not a diagnosis. (Some diversion programs are better than others at selecting out low-needs clients for very-low-intensity treatment.)

Drug courts attempt to solve the problem of noncompliance with mandated treatment by keeping the judge actively involved in monitoring the treatment process. Many drug-court judges hold hearings every two weeks at which the participant, probation officer, and treatment provider discuss the participant's progress, and the judge offers praise for good behavior and, in some drug courts, sanctions including jail time for misbehavior. As a result, drug courts are far more expensive on a per-participant basis than diversion programs, though still much less expensive than incarceration. They also tend to achieve much higher rates of treatment completion, and most evaluations show reductions in criminal activity among drug-court participants and net cost savings compared to routine criminal-justice processing (Belenko 2001; Shanahan et al. 2004; US GAO 2005).

But the resource-intensity of drug courts—not only their rather profligate use of treatment capacity but also the typical judge-to-offender ratios of 50 or 75 to 1—limit the scope of the intervention. After twenty years and despite broad political support, drug courts across the United States serve fewer than 80,000 clients:

less than 2 percent of the probation population (Bhati, Roman, and Chalfin 2008). Expansion to truly mass scale seems impracticable; assigning all drug-involved probationers and parolees to drug court—even if they were all willing to participate and all met the sometimes rigorous selection criteria—would require the assignment to drug court of every felony trial court judge in the United States. Moreover, drug courts tend to be selective about admitting clients; many still reject any offender with a history of violence. This improves measured success rates while limiting the capacity of drug courts to reduce drug-related violent crime. Even among those eligible for drug-court participation, participation is voluntary; offenders can, and some do, reject the offer of supervised mandatory treatment in favor of routine criminal-justice processing, either gambling on a probation sentence or preferring a relatively short jail stay to the treatment effort and sanctions risks that form part of the drug-court bargain.

In sum, then, diversion programs are generally not very effective, and drug courts are, and will likely remain, a "boutique" program operating at a scale too small to noticeably dent either drug abuse or crime.

3. *Prevention*

Properly speaking, "prevention" names a goal—preventing initiation and escalation of drug use—rather than a set of programs. But it is conventional to refer to efforts in schools and in the mass media to persuade people not to use drugs as "prevention."

The literature on the effectiveness of such drug-abuse prevention efforts is disappointing. Many of the evaluations do not meet rigorous standards. Stringent evaluations often show no effect on drug use; such negative findings are typical of DARE (Drug Abuse Resistance Education) evaluations (Kanof 2003), and DARE remains the dominant school-based model. Even for the few model programs that have been shown clearly to affect drug use, the effects on lifetime prevalence decay within a few years (Babor et al. 2009): that is, the programs seem to delay initiation more than to prevent it outright. Furthermore, follow-up data are usually limited to a few years, and those who become high-rate dependent users usually do not escalate until later. Hence, extrapolation from observed effects on initiation during the follow-up window to lifetime effects on criminal offending requires heroic assumptions and extrapolation.

Prevention programs are inexpensive, particularly with respect to direct budgetary costs (as opposed, for example, to the opportunity costs of classroom time spent on drug prevention rather than reading, math, science, history, or art) and may bring a wide range of non-crime benefits—such as reduced smoking. So prevention may still be a good social investment despite its modest effects on lifetime consumption (Caulkins et al. 2002.) However, traditional drug prevention programs simply cannot be expected to play a decisive role in controlling drug-related crime.

4. *Supply Control*

The majority of drug control spending goes towards supply control, even in countries such as Australia and the Netherlands that officially embrace harm reduction (Moore 2008; Rigter 2006). A variety of studies have attempted to assess the relative cost-effectiveness of constraining supply at different levels, from source countries all the way down the distribution chain to the street level (Rydell and Everingham 1994; Rydell, Caulkins, and Everingham 1996; Caulkins et al. 1997).

The general finding of models that implement Reuter and Kleiman's (1986) risks and prices theory is that enforcement is most cost-effective (where effectiveness is measured in terms of increasing price and reducing volume) when directed at the higher distribution layers within the final market country (importers and high-level wholesalers). Lower-level dealers are easy to replace (Kleiman 1997*b*); so are drugs seized in transit or destroyed in the farmer's field (Reuter 1988). Yet even domestic enforcement is not predicted to be an especially cost-effective way to drive up price once the markets are large and well-established (Rydell, Caulkins, and Everingham 1996; Caulkins et al. 1997). Unlike the incarceration of a burglar, which tends to reduce the number of burglaries at least by preventing that burglar from breaking into homes while locked up, the incarceration of a drug dealer generally creates a niche for another dealer to enter the trade. The key observation is that while burglars do not have to compete for places to break into, thus making the number of willing burglars the determining factor in the rate of burglary, dealers have to compete for customers, thus making the demand side of the market the determining factor in drug volume.

The empirical evidence supports these gloomy views. A series of measures designed to restrict access to precursor chemicals used in methamphetamine production have created substantial spikes in purity-adjusted US methamphetamine prices (Cunningham and Liu 2003, 2005), but the market adapts and then prices return to baseline within a year or two (Dobkin and Nicosia 2009).

Despite very considerable efforts, most notably in the United States, the prices of cocaine and heroin fell substantially in the 1980s and 1990s, both in Europe (Farrell, Mansur, Tullis 1996; UNODC 2009) and in the United States (Fries et al. 2008). Kuziemko and Levitt (2004) argue that the contemporaneous massive expansion in incarceration of drug law violators in the United States helped avert an even sharper price decline. However, even if their estimates are correct, they imply a lower cost-effectiveness than the modeling analyses predicted (Babor et al. 2009). Recent reviews of progress over the last ten years are also pessimistic (Reuter 2009). The long-term effects of enforcement can be perverse. One theory of the dramatic decline in wages at the bottom of the crack cocaine trade, and therefore in crack prices, experienced over the 1990s is that the large number of crack dealers imprisoned earlier and then released with poor prospects in the licit job market were in effect "trapped" into continued crack dealing. That excess supply of dealing labor could push down dealers' wages and, hence, drug prices.

To summarize: suppressing supply in established markets is extraordinarily difficult. For supply control to reduce drug-related crime, two conditions need to be true. First, it has to be possible to drive up prices by restricting supply. Second, the elasticity of demand has to be large, in absolute value. Thirty years ago there was optimism about the ability to drive up prices but pessimism about the elasticity of demand. Today, we know that the elasticity of demand is higher than previously thought, but it turns out to be harder than expected to raise prices.

F. More Promising Approaches to Control Drug Related Crime

Thus, except for opiate substitution therapies, conventional drug control strategies do not seem to hold much promise of reducing drug-related crime. Fortunately, there are now more promising alternatives. In one way or another, most try to "Get Deterrence Right" by applying punishment systematically and sparingly (Kennedy 1997, 2008; Kleiman 1997a, 2009), thus constituting a middle way between undifferentiated toughness and laissez-faire. These new approaches recognize that incapacitation is an expensive way to reduce crime; at best it substitutes one bad (incarceration) for another (crime). By contrast, successful deterrence suppresses crime by threatening incarceration rather than actually locking people up.

Estimates of the deterrent effect of incremental changes in conventional sanctions do not find powerful results (Nagin 1998; Apel and Nagin, 2010). A popular but old-fashioned reaction has been calls for ever tougher sentences. In the classic framing of Becker (1968), anything that increases the expected cost of committing a crime should be a deterrent: make the sanction harsh enough, and it becomes unprofitable to commit crimes, so rational actors will not offend.

Over the last twenty-five years, behavioral decision theorists have repeatedly vindicated the commonsense notion that people do not always act in ways that maximize their expected utility, even in relatively simple laboratory settings. In a world of limited cognitive and information-gathering capacity, the use of decision heuristics is inevitable, but will lead to bad results in situations for which the heuristics are a bad match. Laboratory subjects systematically misjudge probabilities (Kahneman, Slovic, Tversky 1982), discount future events "too heavily" (Laibson 1997), become distracted by less relevant information, or fail to imagine accurately how happy or unhappy they will feel if they actually find themselves in a different state (Loewenstein, O'Donoghue, and Rabin 2003). These frailties are particularly likely to manifest when balancing immediate gains against distant, probabilistic consequences and can be exacerbated by cravings brought on by withdrawal, both strongly present in drug-associated decisions (Badger et al. 2007).

The "Getting Deterrence Right" approach attempts to create effective disincentives for imperfectly rational potential offenders. A key principle stresses certainty and celerity (swiftness) over severity (Beccaria 1764/2008).

1. *Coerced or Mandated Abstinence*

An alternative to the diversion-program or drug-court approach of mandating treatment participation is a mandate to desist from drug use. Adherence with such a mandate can be monitored by chemical testing. This approach, once called "coerced abstinence" (Kleiman 1997*a*) but now more commonly referred to as HOPE (after its best-known successful implementation, Hawaii's Opportunity Program with Enforcement) economizes on treatment capacity because treatment is mandated only for the minority of offenders who repeatedly violate the rules. Angela Hawken (2010) has called this approach "behavioral triage" because it substitutes observed behavior for expert assessment in determining what treatment is appropriate. It is not easy for even skilled clinicians to determine whether a drug-involved offender really needs treatment; one can view coerced abstinence as a first-pass filter, dividing drug-using offenders into those who can achieve abstinence through frequent testing alone and those who cannot and reserving treatment mandates for the latter group. A smaller number of people in formal treatment allows for the use of more intensive treatment in place of the weekly outpatient counseling which is the standard in many diversion programs.

The HOPE approach involves frequent drug testing (to start with, either random testing six times per month or scheduled testing twice per week); a guaranteed sanction for each missed or "dirty" test, with sanctions starting relatively mild (days rather than weeks of incarceration) but increasing with repeated violations; minimal delays between violation and sanction (nearly immediate except when that would interfere with work); and rapid arrest of those who fail to appear. The results are impressive, including an 80 percent decline in failed or missed tests relative to regular probation and reductions of more than half in both new arrests and days behind bars (Hawken and Kleiman 2007).

South Dakota's 24/7 Sobriety program offers what is essentially a pure implementation of frequent testing backed by immediate and mild sanctions. In its original form, it required repeat DUI offenders awaiting trial to submit to *twice daily* alcohol testing. Blowing "hot" led to immediate confinement. The guilty party was literally escorted across the hall and deposited in a cell for a twenty-four-hour stay, even before the tester went on to test the next person waiting in line. The program has been expanded beyond DUI to cover illegal drugs as well as alcohol, and can be applied to any offender on pretrial release, probation, parole, or with a suspended sentence. It can even be used as a condition for abused or neglected children to be returned to their parents (Long 2009; Caulkins and DuPont 2010). Frequent testing with certain, immediate consequence has also been used to successfully prevent relapse from abstinence-oriented treatment programs (DuPont et al. 2009).

The modest cost of mandated-desistance programs makes them appropriate for mass application. With proper implementation—not easy to achieve because these programs require coordinated efforts among the courts, probation offices, prosecutors, defense counsel, police, jails, and treatment providers—frequent testing with immediate and certain sanction shows promise of dramatic change in the behavior of the majority of drug-involved offenders.

2. Crackdowns on Flagrant Retail Drug Markets

Flagrant drug dealing (that is, dealing in public places such as street corners or parks and dealing from dedicated drug locations such as crack houses) generates greater harm to society per kilogram sold than does more discreet activity: selling within social networks, in multi-use indoor locales such as bars, or in private locations at times prearranged by cell phone. Flagrant markets have been a traditional target of police efforts, both because of the level of damage they cause and because they are easy to observe (and generate demands from neighbors that the police "do something"). Routine enforcement, including occasional "street sweeps," may satisfy neighborhood demands for visible action and provide the police with a satisfactory quota of arrests, but retail dealers are readily replaced, greatly limiting if not eliminating the benefits of such efforts in terms of reduced dealing, disorder, and crime (Kleiman 1997a).

An alternative to routine enforcement is the focused "crackdown." (Kleiman 1988) which tries to move flagrant dealing in the target area from a high-activity to a low-activity equilibrium. Flagrant markets tend to have a minimum economic size, both because they are maintained by the confidence of buyers that they will be able to find sellers (and vice versa) and because of the reduced risk of arrest (due to enforcement swamping [Kleiman 1993]) created by high rates of activity. Below some critical rate of activity, the market cannot sustain itself; the purpose of a crackdown is to move the market below that "tipping point" for long enough so that it will not bounce back when enforcement pressure is relaxed (Caulkins, 1993). Kleiman (1988) and Caulkins, Larson, and Rich (1993) describe case studies in Lynn, Massachusetts, and Hartford, Connecticut, respectively. Operation Pressure Point in New York City is the best-known example; its success was spectacular, but its profligate use of police, prosecutorial, and court capacity (Press 1987) made it impossible to repeat.

The expense of a crackdown depends on how long it takes for dealers to adjust to the new level of enforcement. That suggests the value of explicit warnings; if a warning alone is sufficient to scare away a large share of the dealers, the cost of arresting the remainder will be proportionately lower.

That frugal form of crackdown seems to have been achieved in the West End of High Point, North Carolina (Kidd 2006; Schoofs 2006; Kennedy 2008). Police identified all of the active dealers in a flagrant market and gathered evidence sufficient to sustain a felony case against each of them. Instead of prosecuting those cases, they then issued a warning (via a meeting to which all of the dealers were invited) that any dealer who did not stop forthwith and permanently would face prison. Because that threat was so convincing—at the meeting, police showed a montage of video footage of the undercover "buys"—that only a few dealers ignored it, and those skeptics (along with three dealers who were also violent offenders whom the police and prosecutors wanted to imprison) were easily dealt with. Removing all the dealers at once had a far more profound effect than making a similar number of arrests spread out in time; the one new dealer who tried to take advantage of the disappearance of the rest was quickly apprehended and imprisoned. Once the dealers stopped coming, so did the users. That approach (replicated with similarly satisfactory effects in East Hempstead, Long Island, and several other locations, including Seattle) did not eliminate drug dealing in High Point, but it did largely eliminate flagrant drug dealing. Crack is still sold, but in strip clubs rather than on street corners, with great benefits in the form of reduced disorder and crime.

3. *Two-Tiered Toughness*

Not all dealers of a given drug in a given location are equally noxious. In addition to the distinction between flagrant and discreet dealing, some dealers are more prone than others to use violence, to employ juvenile apprentices, and to attempt to corrupt law enforcement.

Consider the arithmetic of dealing-related violence. Approximately one million people sell cocaine in the United States in any given twelve-month period (Caulkins 2000; Caulkins and Reuter 2009), but the 1 million commit no more than 5,000 homicides per year, and probably far fewer. If law enforcement were able to identify and eliminate the small proportion at greatest risk of committing a homicide, then that might greatly reduce the worst form of drug-related crime (Caulkins 2002).

This suggests the possible value of a targeting algorithm that attempts to focus arrests and long sentences on the worst dealers. This will incapacitate and deter noxious conduct, even if it fails to suppress drug dealing (Caulkins and Reuter 2009).

Canty, Sutton, and James (2000) (following Moore 1977) describe this as a market regulation model of enforcement. It is a natural extension of Goldstein's (1990) model of problem-oriented policing that recognizes that there are important drug-related problems besides drug use or dealing per se. Enhanced sentencing for dealing near schools turns out to be a poor implementation of this idea, because the 1,000-foot radius that defines a "drug-free school zone" defines too large an area to actually pick out dealers whose activities disrupt schooling (Brownsberger 2001).

4. *Alcohol-control Policies*

Since alcohol contributes more to violent crime than all the illicit drugs combined, no discussion of drug policy for crime control would be complete without some discussion of how to reduce that contribution.

The simplest approach would be to raise alcohol taxes. Alcohol use responds to prices, and inflation has dramatically eroded the real value of alcohol excise taxes in the United States (Cook 2007). The current tax averages approximately ten cents per drink (can of beer, glass of wine, or shot of whisky, with wine taxed less and whisky more). That in turn makes up about 10% of the price of a drink purchased at a package-goods store. Adjusting alcohol taxes for inflation to restore them to the real-dollar levels of 1950 would make a substantial contribution to controlling drug-related crime without costing casual drinkers very much (Cook 2008). Even doubling the tax to twenty cents per drink—a much smaller adjustment—would be expected to raise the price of alcohol by about 10 percent and thus reduce the homicide and motor-vehicle fatality rates by a few percent each, which is to say it would be expected to save hundreds of lives per year.

A more complicated approach would be to make it harder for those who commit crimes under the influence of alcohol to drink. This would require that sellers of alcohol check the identity of every buyer, not only those who look as if they might be too young to drink, and a modification of the driver's license of those who have been convicted of alcohol-related violence (or drunken driving). Perfect compliance could not be achieved, but the concentration of alcohol-related violence among a small group of drinkers means that even imperfect compliance might make a significant dent in the overall statistics (Kleiman 1992, ch. 8).

Unlike many ideas with much less prospect of reducing drug-related crime, neither of these ideas commands any substantial political support.

IV. Conclusions

Across-the-board tough enforcement against suppliers is not a promising way to reduce drug-related crime.

Drug law reform does not offer a viable "quick fix" to drug-related crime. Legalization of the expensive illicit drugs (cocaine/crack, heroin, and meth) would dramatically reduce drug-related crime but has very little political support, and the consequences in terms of increased drug abuse could be profound. Legalization of marijuana is a more plausible idea, but it would not avert much drug-related crime for the simple reason that there is not much crime related to marijuana markets. Decriminalization of any substance would be as likely to exacerbate drug-related crime as to ameliorate it, by reducing the non-dollar costs of use while keeping dollar prices high and the black market intact.

Three options offer hope for substantially reducing drug-related crime:

Raising alcohol excise taxes and making it harder for mean drunks to drink, especially in public. These two ideas are both potentially very valuable and operationally feasible, but neither is feasible politically under current conditions in the United States.

Requiring drug-involved offenders living in the community on bail, probation, or parole to desist from illicit drug use by making them subject to frequent testing and quick sanctions. These individuals commit a substantial proportion of all drug-related crime. Forcing them to remain abstinent through frequent testing backed by immediate but modest sanctions would eliminate most of that crime. Coerced or mandated abstinence works for most offenders. A secondary benefit is narrowing the user population down to those unable to achieve abstinence despite close supervision, which can triage treatment to those whose need is greatest. It is also viable politically. The great challenges to this strategy are administrative and bureaucratic.

Focusing drug law enforcement on flagrant markets and on especially noxious dealers. This would create a two-tiered system that imposes routine sanctions for routine drug selling (in order to preserve the benefits of prohibition) and severe sanctions for those selling in ways particularly corrosive to the community. Notable, attainable targets might be those using violence or selling flagrantly. The goal is market jujitsu—making it unprofitable for drug businesses to operate in ways that promote violence (Dorn and South, 1990).

Two-tiered toughness is not easy to sell politically. It requires making distinctions between behaviors that are bad and those that are very bad. It also requires entrusting the criminal justice system to make discretionary judgments, a power that could be abused, for example to discriminate against minorities. However, the current one-tiered toughness imposes so disproportionate a burden on minority communities that the bar for improvement is not set very high.

These three ideas are not in competition; indeed, they nicely complement each other. Two-tiered toughness targets systemic crime directly. The HOPE approach—mandated desistance for drug-using offenders—targets economic-compulsive crime and the portion of psychopharmacological crime committed by criminally involved offenders, while also shrinking the markets and thus attacking systemic crime indirectly. Higher alcohol excise taxes and a selective prohibition aimed at convicted offenders whose crimes were committed under the influence of alcohol would help across the board, including psychopharmacological crime committed by people who are not otherwise heavily involved in crime (e.g., domestic violence and barroom brawling).

In summary, there are ways to substantially reduce drug-related crime, but they are not the ways currently receiving the most attention in political and mass-media discussions. It is not hard to imagine these three ideas producing crime reductions comparable in scale to the dramatic declines in crime rates between 1994 and 2004. Yet, while such reductions are not hard to imagine, they are hard to achieve. Serious progress will take a convergence of policy entrepreneurship and determined leadership from public officials who can break down bureaucratic silos and communicate to the public ideas longer than a sound bite or tweet.

NOTES

1. Authors' calculations using the Substance Abuse and Mental Health Data Archive (SAMHDA) site for online analysis of the National Survey of Drug Abuse and Health (NSDUH), http://www.icpsr.umich.edu/cocoon/SAMHDA/DAS3/00064.xml.

2. These official estimates are based on the household survey, so they likely underestimate dependence on other drugs, but even estimates that synthesize data from other, complementary sources do not conclude that there are as many as 4.2 million people dependent on cocaine, crack, heroin, and methamphetamine (ONDCP 2001).

3. Authors calculations using the SAMHDA site for online analysis of the National Survey of Drug Abuse and Health (NSDUH).

4. Hall and Pacula (2003) assess the social costs and benefits of marijuana regime change.

5. Note that comparisons with other crop-based consumer goods with high mark-ups from farm-gate to retail are misleading (cf. Miron, 2003). While it is true that the farm-gate price of corn is a very small portion of the retail price of cornflakes, farm-gate corn is an entirely different commodity than cornflakes. What sells for about $1,500 per kilogram in Colombia is not coca leaves but cocaine powder that is ready to use. International transportation costs are driven by weight, and the value per weight ratio is enormous for the expensive illegal drugs, and would remain very high even after legalization. Shipping corn for $50 per kilogram makes no sense. Even the box of cornflakes retails for about $5 per kilogram. In contrast, a $50 per kilogram distribution cost would add only $0.05 per gram of cocaine or heroin, a negligible fraction of a $2–$3/gram legalized retail price. There is no legal commodity with such a high value-to-weight ratio whose price increases by a dramatic percentage when moving through the distribution chain in final product form, and there is no reason to think legalized drugs would be any different.

6. The Netherlands has a unique policy toward cannabis that might be described as legalization of the lower market levels, but even the Netherlands has not in any way legalized the expensive illegal drugs. The Netherlands approach to prohibition places greater emphasis on treatment and harm reduction, and less on aggressive enforcement. However, the expensive illegal drugs are still illegal. Indeed, convictions per capita are within a factor of three of those in the United States even though the US has generally higher rates of drug use (Babor et al. 2009). Given the US's massive expansion in drug-related incarceration over the last twenty-five years, by some measures the Netherlands might enforce a tougher prohibition of the expensive drugs today than the United States did under the Reagan administration.

7. One can tell stories about a "forbidden-fruits effect," and speculate that removing sanctions might undermine the symbolic protest value of using a substance. So in a theoretical sense the affect of decriminalization on demand is ambiguous (MacCoun 1993). We proceed, however, on the assumption that the direct effects of reduced risk swamp any forbidden-fruits effect; it should be clear how the analysis plays out differently for readers who believe that that effect is the more powerful force.

8. If the components of drug-related crime are proportional to use and to spending then a simple formula applies. Percent change in crime per 1 percent increase in price $= \eta$ $(1-f) + (1 + \eta)f = \eta + f$ where $\eta < 0$ is the elasticity of demand, f is the proportion of drug-related crime that is driven by spending, and $1-f$ is the proportion driven by use.

Eliminating the proportionality assumption complicates the notation without changing the basic insight.

9. Dave (2008) estimated a long-run elasticity for heroin that was almost twice the short-run elasticity. Saffer and Chaloupka (1999) and Becker, Grossman, and Murphy (1994) obtained similar results for cocaine and cigarettes. Historical studies, although perhaps less relevant to the modern era, point to similar results. Using records from the pre–World War II Dutch East Indies Opium Regie, Van Ours (1995) estimated the short- and long-run elasticity for opium to be -0.70 and close to -1, respectively. Liu et al.'s (1999) parallel estimates for opium use in Taiwan between 1895 and 1945 were -0.48 and -1.38, respectively.

10. If treatment changed long-term behavior, the cost-effectiveness could be even better. Long-term abstinence can be achieved (e.g., DuPont et al. 2009), but many treatment professionals do not like to evaluate programs in terms of permanent abstinence. They stress that dependence is a chronic relapsing condition, and one should think of managing that condition—not curing it—so most of the benefits accrue while the client is in treatment and not subsequent to treatment (McLellan et al. 2005).

11. Author's analysis of TEDS data available on line through SAMHDA (http://www.icpsr.umich.edu/SAMHDA/using-data/sda.html).

REFERENCES

Apel, Robert, and Daniel S. Nagin. 2010. "General Deterrence: A Review of Recent Evidence." In *Crime and Public Policy*, ed. James Q. Wilson and Joan Petersilia, Oxford: Oxford University Press.

Arseneault, Louise, Mary Cannon, John Witten, and Murray Robin M. 2004. "Causal Association between Cannabis and Psychosis: Examination of the Evidence." *British Journal of Psychiatry* 184:110–17.

Babor, Thomas, Jonathan Caulkins, Griffith Edwards, David Foxcroft, Keith Humphreys, Maria Medina Mora, Isidore Obot, Jurgen Rehm, Peter Reuter, Robin Room, Ingeborg Rossow, and John Strang. 2009. *Drug Policy and the Public Good*. New York: Oxford University Press.

Bachman, Jerald G., Patrick M. O'Malley, John E. Schulenberg, Lloyd D. Johnston, Peter Freedman-Doan, and Emily E. Messersmith 2008. *The Education-Drug Use Connection: How Successes and Failures in School Relate to Adolescent Smoking, Drinking, Drug Use, and Delinquency*. New York: Lawrence Erlbaum Associates/Taylor and Francis.

Badger, Gary J., Warren K. Bickel, Louis A. Giordano, Eric A. Jacobs, and George Loewenstein. 2007. "Altered States: The Impact of Immediate Craving on the Valuation of Current and Future Opioids." *Journal of Health Economics* 26, no. 5: 865–76.

Bass, Frank M. 1969. "A New Product Growth Model for Consumer Durables." *Management Science* 15, no. 5: 215–27.

Baveja, Alok, Rajan Batta, Jonathan P. Caulkins, and Mark H. Karwan. 1993. "Modeling the Response of Illicit Drug Markets to Local Enforcement." *Socio-Economic Planning Sciences* 27, no. 2: 73–89.

Beccaria, Caesar. 1764/2008. *"Dei delitti e delle pene"* ("Of Crimes and Punishments"). In *On Crimes and Punishments and Other Writings,* ed., trans. Thomas Aaron Beccaria, and trans. Jeremy Parzen. (Toronto: University of Toronto Press.)

Becker, Gary 1968. "Crime and Punishment: An Economic Approach." *Quarterly Journal of Economics* 76:169–217.

Becker, Gary S., Michael Grossman, and Kevin M. Murphy. 1994. "An Empirical Analysis of Cigarette Addiction." *American Economic Review* 84:397–418.

Becker, Gary, and Kevin Murphy. 1988. "A Theory of Rational Addiction" *Journal of Political Economy* 96:675–700.

Belenko, Steven R. 2001. *Research on Drug Courts: A Critical Review: 2001 Update.* New York: National Center on Addiction and Substance Abuse at Columbia University.

Belenko, Steven, Nicholas Patapsis, and Michael T. French, eds. 2005. *Economic Benefits of Drug Treatment: A Critical Review of the Evidence for Policy Makers.* http://www.nsula.edu/laattc/documents/EconomicBenefits_2005Feb.pdf.

Bennett, Trevor, and Katy Holloway. 2005. *Understanding, Drugs, Alcohol, and Crime.* Berkshire, UK: Open University Press.

Benson, Bruce L., Iljoong Kim, David W. Rasmussen, and Thomas W. Zuehlke. 1992. "Is Property Crime Caused by Drug Use or Drug Enforcement Policy?" *Applied Economics* 24:679–92.

Bhati, Avinash, John Roman, and Aaron Chalfin. 2008. *To Treat or Not To Treat: Evidence on the Prospects of Expanding Treatment to Drug-Involved Offenders.* Washington, DC: The Urban Institute.

Blumstein, Alfred, and Daniel Cork. 1996. "Linking Gun Availability to Youth Gun Violence." *Law and Contemporary Problems* 59, no. 1: 5–24.

Blumstein, Alfred, Canela-Cacho, Jose, and Jacqueline Cohen. 1993. "Filtered Sampling from Populations with Heterogeneous Event Frequencies." *Management Science* 39, no. 7: 886–99.

Boyum, David. 1992. Reflections on Economic Theory and Drug Enforcement, PhD diss., Harvard University, Department of Public Policy.

Boyum, David, and Peter Reuter. 2005. *An Analytic Assessment of US Drug Policy.* Washington, DC: AEI Press.

Boyum, David, Jonathan P. Caulkins, and Mark A. R. Kleiman. Forthcoming. "Drugs, Crime, and Public Policy." In *Crime and Public Policy,* ed. James Q. Wilson and Joan Petersilia, Oxford: Oxford University Press.

Boyum, David, and Mark A. R. Kleiman. 2001. "Substance Abuse Policy from a Crime Control Perspective." In Wilson and Petersilia, *Crime,* 2nd ed., Oakland, CA: Institute for Contemporary Studies.

Brownsberger, William. 2001. "An Empirical Study of the School Zone Law in Three Massachusetts Cities" http://www.jointogether.org/resources/pdf/school_zone.pdf.

Canty, Chris, Adam Sutton, and Steve James. 2000. "Models of Community-Based Drug Law Enforcement." *Police Practice and Research* 2:171–87.

Caputo, Michael R., and Brian J. Ostrom. 1994. "Potential Tax Revenue from a Regulated Marijuana Market: A Meaningful Revenue Source." *American Journal of Economics and Sociology,* 53, no. 4: 475–90.

Cartwright, William S. 2000. "Cost-Benefit Analysis of Drug Treatment Services: A Review of the Literature." *Journal of Mental Health Policy Economics* 3:11–26.

Caulkins, Jonathan P. 1993. "Local Drug Markets' Response to Focused Police Enforcement." *Operations Research* 41, no. 5: 848–63.

———. 1994. *Evaluating the Effectiveness of Interdiction and Source Country Control.* Santa Monica, CA: RAND.

———. 2000. *Do Drug Prohibition and Enforcement Work?* White paper published in the "What Works?" series. Lexington Institute, Arlington, VA.

———. 2001. "When Parametric Sensitivity Analysis Isn't Enough." *INFORMS Transactions on Education* 1, no. 3: 88–101. http://ite.informs.org/Vol1No3/caulkins/caulkins.html.

———. 2002. *Law Enforcement's Role in a Harm Reduction Regime.* Crime and Justice Bulletin no. 64. Sydney: New South Wales Bureau of Crime and Justice Research.

———. 2005. "Models Pertaining to How Drug Policy Should Vary Over the Course of an Epidemic Cycle." In *Substance Use: Individual Behavior, Social Interactions, Markets, and Politics,* Advances in Health Economics and Health Services Research, ed. Bjorn Lindgren and Michael Grossman. Amsterdam: Elsevier.

Caulkins, Jonathan P., and Robert L. DuPont. 2010. "Is 24/7 Sobriety a Good Goal for Repeat DUI Offenders?" *Addiction* 105:575–77.

Caulkins, Jonathan P., Richard C. Larson, and Thomas F. Rich. 1993. "Geography's Impact on the Success of Focused Local Drug Enforcement Operations." *Socio-Economic Planning Sciences* 27, no. 1: 119–30.

Caulkins, Jonathan P., and Rosalie Pacula. 2006. "Marijuana Markets: Inferences from Reports by the Household Population." *Journal of Drug Issues* 36, no. 1: 173–200.

Caulkins, Jonathan P., Rosalie Pacula, Susan Paddock, and James Chiesa. 2002. *School-Based Drug Prevention: What Kind of Drug Use Does it Prevent?* Santa Monica, CA: RAND

Caulkins, Jonathan P., and Peter Reuter. 2009. "Toward a Harm Reduction Approach to Enforcement." *Safer Communities* 8, no. 1: 9–23.

———. 2010. "How Drug Enforcement Affects Drug Prices." In *Crime and Justice: A Review of Research,* vol. 39, edited by Michael Tonry. Chicago: University of Chicago Press.

Caulkins, Jonathan P., Doris A. Behrens, Claudia Knoll, Gernot Tragler, and Doris Zuba. 2004. "Markov Chain Modeling of Initiation and Demand: The Case of the US Cocaine Epidemic." *Health Care Management Science* 7, no. 4: 319–29. DOI:10.1007/s10729-004-7540-4.

Caulkins, Jonathan P., C. Peter Rydell, W. L. Schwabe, and James Chiesa. 1997. *Mandatory Minimum Drug Sentences: Throwing Away the Key or the Taxpayers' Money?* Santa Monica, CA: RAND.

Center on Addiction and Substance Abuse. 1994. *Cigarettes, Alcohol, Marijuana: Gateways to Illicit Drug Use. White Paper.* New York: Columbia University.

Chaiken, Jan, and Marcia Chaiken. 1982. *The Varieties of Criminal Behavior.* Santa Monica, CA: RAND.

———. 1990. "Drugs and Predatory Crime." In *Drugs and Crime,* ed. Michael Tonry and James Q. Wilson. Chicago: University of Chicago Press.

Compton, Wilson M., and Nora D. Volkow. 2006. "Major Increases in Opioid Analgesic Abuse in the United States: Concerns and Strategies." *Drug and Alcohol Dependence* 81:103–7.

Cook, Philip J. 2007. *Paying the Tab: The Economics of Alcohol Policy.* Princeton, NJ: Princeton University Press.

Cook Philip J. 2008 "A Free Lunch." *Journal of Drug Policy Analysis,* http://www.bepress.com/jdpa/vol1/iss1/art2.

Cunningham, James K., and Lon-Mu Liu. 2003. "Impacts of Federal Ephedrine and Pseudoephedrine Regulations on Methamphetamine-Related Hospital Admissions." *Addiction* 98:1229–37.

———. 2005. "Impacts of Federal Precursor Chemical Regulations on Methamphetamine Arrests." *Addiction* 100, no. 4: 479–88.

Dave, Dhaval. 2008. "Illicit Drug Use among Arrestees, Prices and Policy." *Journal of Urban Economics* 63:694–714.

Degenhardt, Louisa, Peter Reuter, Linette Collins, and Wayne Hall. 2005. "Evaluating Explanations of the Australian Heroin Drought." *Addiction* 100:459–69.

Dobkin, Carlos, and Nancy Nicosia. 2009. "The War on Drugs: Methamphetamine, Public Health, and Crime." *American Economic Review* 99:324–49.

Dobkin Carlos, and Steven Puller. 2007. "The Effects of Government Transfers on Monthly Cycles in Drug Abuse, Hospitalization and Mortality." *Journal of Public Economics* 91:2137–57.

Dorn, Nicholas, and Nigel South. 1990. "Drug Markets and Law Enforcement." *British Journal of Criminology* 30:171–88.

DuPont, Robert L., A. Thomas McLellan, William L. White, Lisa J. Merlo, Mark S. Gold. 2009. "Setting the Standard for Recovery: Physicians' Health Programs." *Journal of Substance Abuse Treatment* 36:159–71.

Ellgren Maria, Sabrina M. Spano, and Yasmin L. Hurd. 2007. "Adolescent Cannabis Exposure Alters Opiate Intake and Opioid Limbic Neuronal Populations in Adult Rats." *Neuropsychopharmacology*. 32, no. 3: 607–15.

Elliott, Delbert S., Suzanne S. Ageton, David Huizinga, Brian A. Knowles, and Rachel J. Canter. 1983. *The Prevalence and Incidence of Delinquent Behavior: 1976–1980*. National Youth Survey Report no. 26. Boulder, CO: Behavioral Research Institute.

Engberg, John, Andrew R. Morral. 2006. "Reducing Substance Use Improves Adolescents' School Attendance." *Addiction* 101:1741–51.

Fagan, Jeffrey. 1990. "Intoxication and Aggression." In *Drugs and Crime*, edited by Michael Tonry and James Q. Wilson. Vol. 13 of *Crime and Justice: A Review of Research*, edited by Michael Tonry. Chicago: University of Chicago Press.

Fagan, Jeffrey, and Richard B. Freeman. 1999. "Crime and Work." In *Crime and Justice: A Review of Research*, vol. 25, edited by Michael Tonry. Chicago: University of Chicago Press.

Farabee, David, Vandana Joshi, and M. Douglas Anglin. 2001. "Addiction Careers and Criminal Specialization." *Crime and Delinquency*. 47, no. 2: 196–220.

Farrell, Graham, Kashfia Mansur, and Melissa Tullis. 1996. "Cocaine and Heroin in Europe 1983–1993: A Cross-national Comparison of Trafficking and Prices." *British Journal of Criminology* 36:255–81.

Ferrence, Roberta. 2001. "Diffusion Theory and Drug Use." *Addiction* 96:165–73.

FBI. 1996. *Uniform Crime Report 95*. Washington, DC: FBI National press Office. http://www.fbi.gov/ucr/ucr95prs.htm.

Fries, Arthur, Robert W. Anthony, Andrew Cseko Jr., Carl C. Gaither, and Eric Schulman. 2008. *The Price and Purity of Illicit Drugs: 1981–2007*. Alexandria, VA: Institute for Defense Analysis.

Galbraith, John W., and Murray Kaiserman. 1997. "Taxation, Smuggling, and Demand for Cigarettes in Canada: Evidence from Time-Series Data." *Journal of Health Economics* 16:287–301.

Gerstein, Dean R., Robert A. Johnson, Henrick Harwood, Douglas Fontain, Natalie Suter, and Kay Malloy. 1994. *Evaluating Recovery Services: The California Drug and Alcohol Treatment Assessment*. Chicago: National Opinion Research Center.

Goldstein, Herman. 1990. *Problem-Oriented Policing*. New York: McGraw Hill.

Goldstein, Paul J. 1985. "The Drugs/Violence Nexus: A Tripartite Conceptual Framework." *Journal of Drug Issues* 15, no. 4: 493–506.

Goldstein, Paul J., Henry H. Brownstein, Patrick J. Ryan, and Patricia A. Bellucci. 1990. "Crack and Homicide in New York City, 1988: A Conceptually Based Event Analysis." *Contemporary Drug Problems* 16, no. 4: 651–87.

Grass, Dieter, Jonathan P. Caulkins, Gustav Feichtinger, Gernot Tragler, and Doris Behrens. 2008. *Optimal Control of Nonlinear Processes: With Applications in Drugs, Corruption, and Terror*. Berlin, Heidelberg: Springer.

Grossman, Michael. 2005. "Individual Behaviours and Substance Use: The Role of Price." In *Substance Use: Individual Behaviour, Social Interactions, Markets, and Politics, Advances in Health Economics and Health Services Research*, vol. 16, ed. B. Lindgren and M. Grossman. Amsterdam: Elsevier.

Gschwend Patrick, Jürgen Rehm, Richard Blättler, Thomas Steffen, André Seidenberg, Stephan Christen, Christoph Bürki, and Felix Gutzwiller. 2004. "Dosage Regimes in the Prescription of Heroin and Other Narcotics to Chronic Opioid Addicts in Switzerland–Swiss National Cohort Study." *European Addiction Research* 10, no. 1: 41–48.

Hall, Wayne, and Rosalie L. Pacula, 2003. *Cannabis Use and Dependence: Public Health and Public Policy*. Melbourne, Australia: Cambridge University Press.

Harwood, Henrick J., Deepti Malhrota, Christel Villarivera, Connie Liu, Umi Chong, and Jawaria Gilani. 2002. *Cost Effectiveness and Cost Benefit Analysis of Substance Abuse Treatment: A Literature Review*. Washington, DC: US Department of Health and Human Services.

Hawken Angela. 2010. "A Behavioral Triage Model for Identifying and Treating Substance-Abusing Offenders." *Journal of Drug Policy Analysis,* 3(1). http://www.bepress.com/jdpa/vol3/iss1/art1/.

Hawken, Angela, and Mark Kleiman. 2007. "H.O.P.E. for Reform: What a Novel Probation Program in Hawaii Might Teach Other States." *American Prospect Online* (April 10), http://www.prospect.org/cs/articles?article=hope_for_reform.

Holloway, Katy, and Trevor Bennett. 2004. *The Results of the First Two Years of the NEW-ADAM Programme*, Home Office Online Report 19/04, London: Home Office.

Iguchi, Martin Y., Mark A. Belding, Andrew R. Morral, Richard J. Lamb, and Stephen D. Husband. 1997. "Reinforcing Operants Other Than Abstinence in Drug Abuse Treatment: An Effective Alternative for Reducing Drug Use." *Journal of Consulting and Clinical Psychology* 65, no. 3: 421–28.

Jofre-Bonet, Mireia, and Nancy M. Petry. 2008. "Trading Apples for Oranges? Results of an Experiment on the Effects of Heroin and Cocaine Price Changes on Addicts' Polydrug Use." *Journal of Economic Behavior and Organization* 66:281–311.

Kahneman, Daniel, Paul Slovic, and Amos Tversky, eds. 1982. *Judgment Under Uncertainty: Heuristics and Biases*. New York: Cambridge University Press.

Kain, John F. 1992. "The Spatial Mismatch Hypothesis: Three Decades Later." *Housing Policy Debate* 3, no. 2: 371–460.

Kanof, Marjorie E. to Senator R. Durbin. US General Accounting Office. 2003. *Youth Illicit Drug Use Prevention: DARE Long-Term Evaluations and Federal Efforts to Identify Effective Programs*, GAO-03-172R. Washington, DC: General Accounting Office.

Karberg, Jennifer C., and Doris J. James. 2005. *Substance Abuse, Dependence, and Treatment of Jail Inmates, 2002*. Washington, DC: US Bureau of Justice Statistics, NCJ 209588.

Keizer, Kees, Siegwart Lindenberg, and Linda Steg. 2008. "The Spreading of Disorder." *Science* 322, no. 5908: 1681–85.

Kelling, George L., and Catherine M. Coles. 1996. *Fixing Broken Windows: Restoring Order and Reducing Crime in Our Communities*. New York: Free Press.

Kennedy, David M. 1997. "Pulling Levers: Chronic Offenders, High-Crime Settings, and a Theory of Prevention." *Valparaiso University Law Review* 31, no. 2: 449–84.

———. 2008. *Deterrence and Crime Prevention: Reconsidering the Prospect of Sanction*. Abingdon, UK: Routledge.

Kidd, Don. 2006. "The High Point West End Initiative: A New Strategy to Reduce Drug-Related Crime." *Criminal Justice Institute's Management Quarterly* (Fall), http://www.cji.edu/Files/MQ2006Fall.pdf.

Kilmer, Beau, Jonathan P. Caulkins, Rosalie Liccardo Pacula, Robert MacCoun, Peter Reuter. 2010. *Altered State? Assessing How Marijuana Legalization in California Could Influence Marijuana Consumption and Public Budgets*. Santa Monica, CA: RAND.

Kleiman, Mark A. R. 1988. "Crackdowns: The Effects of Intensive Enforcement on Retail Heroin Dealing." In *Street-Level Drug Enforcement: Examining the Issues*, ed. Marcia R. Chaiken. Washington, DC: National Institute of Justice.

———. 1992a. *Against Excess: Drug Policy for Results*. New York: Basic Books.

———. 1992b "Neither Prohibition Nor Legalization: Grudging Toleration in Drug Control Policy." *Daedalus* 121 (Summer): 53–83.

———. 1993. "Enforcement Swamping: A Positive-Feedback Mechanism in Rates of Illicit Activity." *Mathematical and Computer Modeling* 17:65–75.

———. 1997a. "Coerced Abstinence: A Neo-Paternalistic Drug Policy Initiative." In *The New Paternalism*, ed. Lawrence M. Mead, 182–219. Washington, DC: Brookings Institution Press.

———. 1997b. "The Problem of Replacement and the Logic of Drug Law Enforcement." *Drug Policy Analysis Bulletin* 3:8–10.

———. 2009. *When Brute Force Fails: Strategy for Crime Control*. Princeton, NJ: Princeton University Press.

Kuziemko, Ilyana, and Steven D. Levitt. 2004. "An Empirical Analysis of Imprisoning Drug Offenders." *Journal of Public Economics* 88:2043–66.

Laibson, David. 1997. "Golden Eggs and Hyperbolic Discounting." *Quarterly Journal of Economics* 112:443–77.

Lipsey Mark W., David B. Wilson, Mark A. Cohen, and James H. Derzon. 1997. "Is There a Causal Relationship between Alcohol Use and Violence? A Synthesis of Evidence." *Recent Developments in Alcoholism* 13:245–82.

Liu, Jin-Long, Jin-Tan Liu, James K. Hammitt, and Shin-Yi Chou. 1999. "The Price Elasticity of Opium in Taiwan, 1914–1942." *Journal of Health Economics* 18:795–810.

Loewenstein, George, Ted O'Donoghue, and Matthew Rabin. 2003. "Projection Bias in Predicting Future Utility." *Quarterly Journal of Economics* 118:1209–11.

Long, Larry. 2009. "The 24/7 Sobriety Project." *Public Lawyer* 17, no. 2: 2–5.

MacCoun, Robert J. 1993. "Drugs and the Law: A Psychological Analysis of Drug Prohibition." *Psychological Bulletin* 113:497–512.

MacCoun, Robert J., and Peter Reuter. 2001. *Drug War Heresies.* New York: Cambridge University Press.

Manski, Charles F., John V. Pepper, and Carole V. Petrie. 2001. *Informing America's Policy on Illegal Drugs: What We Don't Know Keeps Hurting Us.* Washington, DC: National Academies Press.

McLellan, A. Thomas, James R. McKay, Robert Forman, John Cacciola, and Jack Kemp. 2005. "Reconsidering the Evaluation of Addiction Treatment: From Retrospective Follow-up to Concurrent Recovery Monitoring." *Addiction* 100:447–58.

Merrill, Jeffrey C., Herbert D. Kleber, Michael Shwartz, Hong Liu, and Susan R. Lewis. 1999. "Cigarettes, Alcohol, Marijuana, Other Risk Behaviors, and American Youth." *Drug and Alcohol Dependence* 56, no. 3: 205–12.

Miller, Ted R., Mark A. Cohen, and Brian Wiersema. 1996. *Victim Costs and Consequences: A New Look.* Washington, DC: National Institute of Justice Report.

Miron, Jeffrey A. 2003. "The Effect of Drug Prohibition on Drug Prices: Evidence from the Markets for Cocaine and Heroin." *Review of Economics and Statistics* 85, no. 3: 522–30.

Mitchell, Ojmarrh, and Adele V. Harrell. 2006. "Evaluation of the Breaking the Cycle Demonstration Project: Jacksonville, FL and Tacoma, WA." *Journal of Drug Issues* 36:97–118.

Moffitt, Terrie E. 1993. "Adolescence-Limited and Life-Course-Persistent Antisocial Behavior: A Developmental Taxonomy." *Psychological Review* 100, no. 4: 674–701.

Moore, Mark H. 1977 *Buy and Bust: The Effective Regulation of an Illicit Market in Heroin.* Lexington, MA: Lexington Books.

———. 1973. "Policies to Achieve Discrimination on the Effective Price of Heroin." *American Economic Review* 63, no. 2: 270–77.

Moore, Timothy J. 2008. "The Size and Mix of Government Spending on Illicit Drug Policy in Australia." *Drug and Alcohol Review* 27:404–13.

Morral, Andrew R., Daniel F. McCaffrey, and Susan M. Paddock. 2002. "Reassessing the Marijuana Gateway Effect." *Addiction* 97, no. 12: 1493–504.

Nagin, Daniel S. 1998. "Deterrence and Incapacitation." In *The Handbook of Crime and Punishment,* ed. Michael Tonry. New York: Oxford University Press.

Office of National Drug Control Policy. 2000. Drug-Related Crime. NCJ-181056 (March), http://www.whitehousedrugpolicy.gov/publications/pdf/ncj181056.pdf.

———. 2001. *What America's Users Spend on Illegal Drugs.* Washington, DC: The White House.

———. 2004. *The Economic Costs of Drug Abuse in the United States, 1992–2002.* Washington, DC: Executive Office of the President.

———. 2009. *ADAM II 2008 Annual Report.* Washington, DC: Executive Office of the President.

Pareto, Vilfredo. 1896–97. *Cours d'économie politique professé à l'Université de Lausanne.* Lausanne: Rouge.

Parker, Robert N. 2004. "Alcohol and Violence: Connections, Evidence and Possibilities for Prevention." *Journal of Psychoactive Drugs* 2:157–63.

Pollack, Harold A. 2000. "When Pregnant Women Use Crack." *FAS Drug Policy Analysis Bulletin,* no. 8 (February), http://www.fas.org/drugs/issue8.htm.

Press, Aric. 1987. *Piecing Together the System: The Response to Crack.* New York: Bar Association.

Pudney, Stephen. 2002. *The Road to Ruin? Sequences of Initiation into Drug Use and Offending by Young People in Britain*. London: Home Office.

Rajkumar, Andrew S., and Michael T. French. 1997. "Drug Abuse, Crime Costs, and the Economic Benefits of Treatment." *Journal of Quantitative Criminology* 13:291–323.

Rand, Michael R. 2009. *Criminal Victimization, 2008*. Washington, DC: US Bureau of Justice Statistics, NCJ 227777.

Reuter, Peter. 1984. "The (Continued) Vitality of Mythical Numbers." *Public Interest* 75:135–47.

———. 1988. "Quantity Illusion and Paradoxes of Drug Interdiction: Federal Intervention into Vice Policy." *Law and Contemporary Problems* 51, no. 1: 233–52.

———. 1999. "Are Calculations of the Economic Costs of Drug Abuse Either Possible or Useful?" *Addiction* 94:635–38.

———. "Report for the European Commission. 2009. Assessing Changes in Global Drug Problems." In *A Report on Global Drug Markets 1998–2007*, ed. Peter Reuter, and Franz Trautmann. Brussels, Netherlands: European Communities. http://ec.europa.eu/justice_home/doc_centre/drugs/studies/doc/report_10_03_09_en.pdf.

Reuter, Peter, and Mark Kleiman. 1986. "Risks and Prices: An Economic Analysis of Drug Enforcement." In *Crime and Justice: A Review of Research*, vol. 7, edited by. Michael Tonry and Norval Morris. Chicago: University of Chicago Press.

Reuter, Peter, and Robert J. MacCoun. 1996. "Harm Reduction and Social Policy: Should Addicts be Paid?" *Drug and Alcohol Review* 15, no. 3: 225–30.

Reuter, Peter, and Alex Stevens. 2007. *An Analysis of UK Drug Policy*. London: UK Drug Policy Commission.

Rigter, Henk. 2006. "What Drug Policies Cost. Drug Policy Spending in the Netherlands in 2003." *Addiction* 101:323–29.

Rocheleau, Ann M., and David Boyum. 1994. *Measuring Heroin Availability in Three Cities*. Washington, DC: Office of National Drug Control Policy.

Roth, Jeffrey A. 1994. *Psychoactive Substances and Violence. National Institute of Justice, Research in Brief*. Washington, DC: US Department of Justice.

Rydell, C. Peter, and Susan S. Everingham. 1994. *Controlling Cocaine. Supply versus Demand Programs*. Santa Monica, CA: RAND.

Rydell, C. Peter, Jonathan P. Caulkins, and Susan Everingham. 1996. "Enforcement or Treatment: Modeling the Relative Efficacy of Alternatives for Controlling Cocaine." *Operations Research* 44, no. 5: 687–95.

Saffer, Henry, and Frank Chaloupka. 1999. "Demographic Differentials in the Demand for Alcohol and Illicit Drugs." In *The Economic Analysis of Substance Use and Abuse: An Integration of Econometric and Behavioral Economic Research*, ed. Frank J. Chaloupka, Michael Grossman, Warren K. Bickel, and Henry Saffer. Chicago: University of Chicago Press for the National Bureau of Economic Research.

Satel, Sally. 1995. "When Disability Benefits Make Patients Sicker." *New England Journal of Medicine* 333:794–96.

Schoofs, Mark. 2006. "Novel Police Tactic Puts Drug Markets Out of Business Confronted by the Evidence, Dealers in High Point, N.C., Succumb to Pressure Some Dubbed It Hug-a-Thug." *Wall Street Journal,* September 27, p. A1.

Schulte, Carmen, Jenny Mouzos, and Toni Makkai. 2005. *Drug Use Monitoring in Australia: 2004 Annual Report on Drug Use among Police Detainees*. Canberra: Australian Institute of Criminology.

Sevigny, Eric, and Jonathan P. Caulkins. 2004. "Kingpins or Mules? An Analysis of Drug Offenders Incarcerated in Federal and State Prisons." *Criminology and Public Policy* 3, no. 3: 401–34.

Shanahan, Marian, Emily Lanscar, Marion Haas, Bronwyn Lind, Don Weatherburn, and Shuling Chen. 2004. "Cost-Effectiveness Analysis of the New South Wales Adult Drug Court Program." *Evaluation Review* 28:3–27.

Skodbo, Sara, Geraldine Brown, Sarah Deacon, Alisha Cooper, Alan Hall, Tim Millar, Jonathan Smith, and Karen Whitham. 2007. *The Drug Intervention Programme (DIP): Addressing Drug Use and Offending Through "Tough Choices."* London: Home Office.

Stretesky, Paul B. 2009. "National Case-Control Study of Homicide Offending and Methamphetamine Use." *Journal of Interpersonal Violence* 24, no. 6: 911–24.

Substance Abuse and Mental Health Services Administration, Office of Applied Studies. 2008. *Drug Abuse Warning Network, 2006: National Estimates of Drug-Related Emergency Department Visits.* Rockville, MD.

———. 2009a. *The NSDUH Report: Children Living with Substance-Dependent or Substance-Abusing Parents: 2002 to 2007.* Rockville, MD

———. 2009b. *Results from the 2008 National Survey on Drug Use and Health: National Findings.* Rockville, MD

Tragler, Gernot, Jonathan P. Caulkins, and Gustav Feichtinger. 2001. "Optimal Dynamic Allocation of Treatment and Enforcement in Illicit Drug Control." *Operations Research* 49, no. 3: 352–62.

United Nations Office on Drugs and Crime (UNODC). 2009. *2008 World Drug Report.* New York: Oxford University Press.

US Government Accountability Office. 2005. *Adult Drug Courts: Evidence Indicates Recidivism Reductions and Mixed Results for Other Outcomes.* Washington, DC.

Urada, Darren, Andrea Hawken, Bradley Conner, Elizabeth Evans, M. Douglas Anglin, Joy Yang, Cheryl Teruya, Diane Herbeck, Jia Fan, Beth Ruthkowski, Rachel Gonzales, Richard Rawson, Christine Grella, Michael Prendergast, Yih-Ing Hser, Jeremy Hunter, and Annie Poe. 2008. *Evaluation of Proposition 36: The Substance Abuse and Crime Prevention Act of 2000.* Los Angeles, CA: UCLA.

Van Ours, Jan C. 1995. "The Price Elasticity of Hard Drugs: The Case of Opium in the Dutch East Indies, 1923–1938." *Journal of Political Economy* 103:261–79.

Van Ours, Jan C., and Jenny Williams. 2008. "Why Parents Worry: Initiation Into Cannabis Use By Youth and Their Educational Attainment." *Journal of Health Economics* 28, no. 1: 132–42.

Wilde, Gerald J. S. 1994. *Target Risk.* PDE Publications. http://psyc.queensu.ca/target/index.html.

Wodak, Alex. 2008. "What Caused the Recent Reduction in Heroin Supply in Australia?" *International Journal of Drug Policy* 19, no. 4: 279–86.

CHAPTER 11

RACE, ETHNICITY, AND CRIME

CASSIA SPOHN

IN 1918, the Bureau of the Census published a report on the "Negro Population" in which the authors noted that in 1910 blacks made up only 11 percent of the population but constituted 22 percent of the inmates of prisons, penitentiaries, jails, reform schools, and workhouses. They then posed a question that would generate controversy and spark debate throughout the twentieth century:

> While these figures . . . will probably be generally accepted as indicating that there is more criminality and lawbreaking among Negroes than among whites and while that conclusion is probably justified by the facts . . . it is a question whether the difference . . . may not be to some extent the result of discrimination in the treatment of white and Negro offenders on the part of the community and the courts. (US Department of Commerce 1918, 438)

The authors speculated that the racial differences in incarceration rates might be because crimes committed by blacks, and especially crimes committed by blacks against whites, were more likely to be punished than crimes committed by whites, and that blacks might be less able than whites to pay fines in lieu of incarceration. The authors also posited that black defendants might be more likely than white defendants to appear in court without attorneys to defend them. They pointed out that it was important to consider these possibilities "before accepting the record of prison commitments as an accurate measure of the differences between the two races in respect to criminality" (438).

The question posed by the Bureau of the Census is still being asked today. As the proportion of the prison population that is black (38 percent) or Hispanic

(21 percent) approaches 60 percent (Bureau of Justice Statistics 2008), social scientists and legal scholars continue to ask whether and to what extent discrimination infects the criminal justice system. Those on one side of the debate contend that the overrepresentation of blacks in arrest and imprisonment statistics reflects systematic racial discrimination within the criminal justice system (Mann 1993). Those on the other side assert that these results can be attributed primarily to the disproportionate involvement of blacks in serious criminal activity (Blumstein 1982; 1993) and argue that the idea of systematic discrimination within the criminal justice system is a "myth" (Wilbanks 1985). Others take more moderate positions. Some scholars contend that the disparities in incarceration result "to some extent" from differential treatment but acknowledge that they result to a large extent from differential involvement in crimes that merit imprisonment (Walker, Spohn, and DeLone 2007). Others suggest that the disparities reflect deliberate policy decisions made by officials waging the war on crime—and particularly the war on drugs—decisions that "caused the ever harsher treatment of blacks by the criminal justice system" (Tonry 1995, 52; see also Mauer 2006; Provine 2007; Tonry and Melewski 2008).

The purpose of this article is to survey research findings on racial and ethnic differences in offending, victimization, and justice system processing. Section I focuses on racial and ethnic disparities in victimization and offending, as well as the causal explanations that have been proffered to explain these disparities. There is compelling evidence that racial minorities are overrepresented as victims of household and personal crime, and among those arrested for violent, property, and drug offenses. Although there is less evidence regarding the causal factors that produce these patterns, research on young offenders highlights the importance of individual, family, and community-level factors, with some studies finding that racial and ethnic differences in the likelihood of victimization and arrest disappear once these factors are taken into account.

Section II reviews historical and contemporary research exploring the effects of race and ethnicity on justice system processing, with a focus on police decision making and noncapital and capital sentencing decisions. Reforms mandated by the US Supreme Court or adopted voluntarily by the states have eliminated much of the blatant or overt racism directed against blacks and Hispanics who find themselves in the arms of the law, but inequities persist at all stages of the criminal justice system. There is historical evidence that blacks and Hispanics were more likely than whites to be victimized by excessive physical force—including deadly force—by the police, and contemporary evidence that racial profiling by the police is widespread. There also is evidence of differential treatment during court processing and sentencing, with particularly compelling evidence of disparity in the application of the death penalty.

Section III discusses the policy implications of the research conducted thus far and suggests directions for future research.

A number of conclusions can be drawn:

- The disproportionate number of blacks and Hispanics locked up in our nation's prisons raises questions about the fairness of the criminal justice system and calls into question the policies pursued during the Wars on Crime and Drugs.
- There is clear and convincing evidence that blacks and Hispanics are overrepresented in crime statistics; they are more likely than whites to be victimized by crime and they are arrested at a disproportionately high rate, especially for violent crimes such as murder and robbery.
- These patterns, especially for young offenders, can be attributed in part to differences in offenders' background characteristics, family situations, and community contexts.
- Racial minorities who find themselves in the arms of the law are treated more harshly than similarly situated whites.
- Differences in treatment, which are found to some extent at all stages of the criminal justice system, are particularly pronounced with respect to police use of excessive and deadly force, profiling by the police, and capital sentencing.
- Racial discrimination in noncapital sentencing has not been eliminated; there is substantial evidence of racial disparity in sentencing of drug offenders and there also is evidence that young, black, and Hispanic males pay an "imprisonment penalty."
- Considered together, the evidence of racial disparities in criminal justice case processing decisions suggests that "racial profiling" is an institutional practice that is deeply embedded in the agencies of the criminal justice system and that therefore will be difficult to eradicate. This is especially so given recent court decisions that allow the use of race in decision making provided that it is only one of several factors taken into account.
- Although we have learned much from the research conducted to date, there is a need for additional research designed to pinpoint more accurately where discrimination occurs and to identify the mechanisms that produce discriminatory outcomes.

I. RACIAL DISPARITIES IN VICTIMIZATION AND OFFENDING

There is clear and convincing evidence that blacks and Hispanics are overrepresented in official crime statistics; they are more likely than whites to be victimized by household and personal crime, and they are arrested at a disproportionately high rate, especially for violent crimes such as murder and robbery (Walker et al. 2007).[1] These patterns are applicable to youth as well as adults (Hawkins et al. 2000; Lauritsen 2003; Sampson, Morenoff, and Raudenbush 2005; Haynie and Payne 2006) and to both women and men (Lauritsen and White 2001; Dugan and Apel, 2003). Moreover, the racial disparities in victimization and offending are remarkably stable over time (Walker, et al., 2007).[2]

The largest and most striking racial differences in victimization are for the crime of homicide (Bureau of Justice Statistics 2007). Data from the Supplemental Homicide Reports (SHR) submitted by law enforcement agencies to the US Federal Bureau of Investigation (FBI) as part of the Uniform Crime Reports (UCR) Program reveal that blacks face a substantially greater risk of death by homicide than do whites. For example, in 2005 the homicide rate for blacks (20.6/100,000) was more than six times higher than the rate for whites (3.3/100.000). Figure 11.1 shows that there are even more striking differences when considering rates for race, sex, and age groups. Among males aged 18 to 24, the rate for blacks (102/100,000) was nearly nine times higher than the rate for whites (12.2/100,000). The rate for black females (11.3) was substantially higher than the rate for white females (2.5); in fact, the rate for black females was only slightly lower than the rate for white males (Bureau of Justice Statistics 2007).

In terms of offending, the largest racial disparities in arrest rates are found for violent crimes, especially murder and robbery (see table 11.1). In 2007 whites made up approximately 83 percent of the US population, and blacks comprised approximately 13 percent. That same year, whites comprised 59 percent and blacks

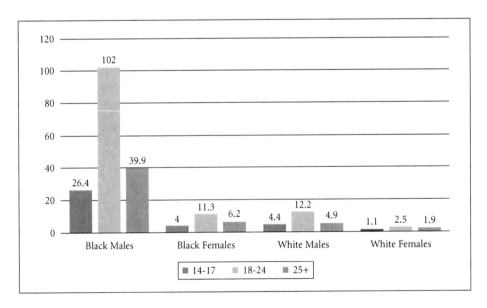

Figure 11.1. Homicide Victimization Rates, 2005
Source: Homicide Trends in the US, (Bureau of Justice Statistics 2007).

Table 11.1. Race of Suspects Arrested

	Percent Distribution	
	Black	White
VIOLENT CRIME	39.0	58.9
Murder and Non-negligent Manslaughter	50.4	47.6
Forcible Rape	33.5	64.4
Robbery	56.7	42.0
Aggravated Assault	33.7	64.0
PROPERTY CRIME	29.8	67.9
Burglary	29.8	68.5
Larceny-Theft	29.3	68.3
Motor Vehicle Theft	35.8	62.2
Arson	23.4	74.6
DRUG ABUSE VIOLATIONS	35.1	63.7
WEAPONS OFFENSES	40.6	57.8

Source: Federal Bureau of Investigation, n.d., table 43.

comprised 39 percent of all persons arrested for violent crimes; for robbery, the figures were 42 percent (whites) and 57 percent (blacks) and for murder and non-negligent homicide they were 48 percent (whites) and 50 percent (blacks). Blacks also were overrepresented in arrests for drug offenses, weapons offenses, and most other violent and property crimes (FBI, n.d., table 43). As is the case with victimization, these patterns are found for youth as well as adults (Walker, Spohn, and DeLone 2007, table 10.4).

It is clear from these official data sources that racial minorities are overrepresented as victims of household and personal crime, and among those arrested for violent, property, and drug offenses. These data, however, are not sufficient for drawing conclusions about causality; the data tell us that the victimization and arrest rates for blacks (and Hispanics in the case of victimization) are substantially higher than those for whites, but they do not tell us why this is so.

A. Causal Explanations

Much of the research addressing causal explanations for racial and ethnic disparities in victimization and offending focuses on adolescent or youthful offenders. Although a detailed discussion of this body of research is beyond the scope of this chapter, the studies generally investigate the effects of community-level social disorganization (Shaw and McKay 1942; Sampson and Wilson 1995; Anderson 1999; Cobbina, Miller, and Brunson 2008), individual and family-level risk factors (Gottfredson and Hirschi 1985; Massey and Denton 1993), weakened family attachments and weak bonds to school and work (Hirschi 1969; Cernkovich and Giordano 1992), and involvement with delinquent peers and gangs (Akers 1994; Haynie and Payne 2006).

The findings produced by this body of research notwithstanding, explanations of the association between race/ethnicity, victimization, and crime "remain controversial and unresolved" (Haynie and Payne 2006, 776). Most studies examine the effects of *either* individual and family influences or community-level risk factors such as social disorganization. There are relatively few studies that examine the causes of victimization and crime across levels of analysis (for exceptions see Lauritsen 2003; McNulty and Bellair 2003; Parker and Reckdenwald 2008), but those that do tend to find that the racial/ethnic differences in victimization and offending are reduced substantially once controls for individual and community-level factors are taken into consideration. Lauritsen (2003), for example, used 1995 data from the National Crime Victimization Survey (NCVS) to explore the effects of individual, family, and community characteristics on the risk for nonlethal violence among youth. She found that the racial and ethnic differences in risk for violent victimization disappeared when the characteristics of the youth's family and community were included in the analysis. Black and Hispanic youth had greater risks for violent victimization than white youth because they were more likely than white youth to spend time away from home, to live in single-parent families, to have less stable living arrangements, and to live in disadvantaged communities, all strong predictors of violent victimization. As Lauritsen (2003, 9) noted, "the sources of risk are similar for all adolescents, regardless of their race or ethnicity."

McNulty and Bellair's (2003) analysis of violent offending produced similar results. They found that Asians were significantly less likely than whites to engage in serious violent behavior and that Native Americans, Hispanics, and blacks were more likely than whites to report that they had committed violent acts. To explain these differences, McNulty and Bellair controlled for individual factors, family characteristics, social bonds indicators, involvement in gangs, exposure to violence, and community characteristics. They found that the racial/ethnic differences in violent behavior disappeared when they took these explanatory factors into account. This led them to conclude that "statistical differences between whites and minority groups are explained by variation in community disadvantage (for blacks), involvement in gangs (for Hispanics), social bonds (for Native Americans), and situational variables (for Asians)" (McNulty and Bellair 2003, 709).

The results of these (and other) studies, then, suggest that racial and ethnic differences in victimization and offending rates can be attributed in large part to individual, family, and community characteristics. The sources of risk of victimization and offending are similar for all racial/ethnic groups, but the likelihood of experiencing these risk factors is higher for people of color than for whites. As Sampson and Wilson so eloquently put it, "macrosocial patterns of residential inequality give rise to the social isolation and ecological concentration of the truly disadvantaged, which in turn leads to structural barriers and cultural adaptations that undermine social organization and hence the control of crime" (Sampson and Wilson 1995, 127).

II. Race, Ethnicity and Justice System Processing

In 2004, the United States celebrated the fiftieth anniversary of *Brown v. Board of Education,* the landmark Supreme Court case that ordered desegregation of public schools. Also in 2004, the Sentencing Project issued a report "Schools and Prisons: Fifty Years after *Brown v. Board of Education*" (The Sentencing Project 2004). The report noted that, whereas many institutions in society had become more diverse and more responsive to the needs of people of color in the wake of the *Brown* decision, the American criminal justice system had taken "a giant step backward" (5). To illustrate this, the report pointed out that in 2004 there were *nine times* as many African Americans in prison or jail as on the day the *Brown* decision was handed down—the number had increased from 98,000 to 884,500. The report also noted that one of every three African American males and one of every eighteen African American females born today could expect to be imprisoned at some point in his or her lifetime. The authors of the report concluded that "such an outcome should be shocking to all Americans" (5).

Differential treatment of racial minorities by the American criminal justice system is not confined to sentencing and corrections. Members of racial minorities are arrested, stopped and questioned, and shot and killed by the police out of all proportion to their representation in the population. Racial minorities, and particularly those charged with crimes against whites, also are the victims of unequal justice in the courts. Although reforms mandated by the Supreme Court or adopted voluntarily by the states have eliminated much of the blatant racism directed against racial minorities who find themselves in the arms of the law, inequities persist in decisions regarding bail, charging, plea bargaining, sentencing, and the death penalty.

Criminologists and legal scholars use several complementary theoretical perspectives to explain differential treatment of whites and racial minorities. Critical race theorists contend that racism (and sexism) are ubiquitous and deeply embedded in laws and criminal justice policies, and that the criminal justice system is an institution that reinforces hierarchies in society based on race, class, gender, and other sociodemographic characteristics (Crenshaw et al. 1995; Delgado and Stefancic 2001). Similarly, conflict theorists (Turk 1969; Quinney 1970; Chambliss and Seidman 1971) argue that the administration of criminal justice reflects the unequal distribution of power in society, and contend that the more powerful groups (i.e., whites) use the criminal justice system to maintain their dominant position and to repress groups or social movements that threaten it. Other theoretical perspectives, such as attribution theory (Bridges and Steen 1998) or the focal concerns perspective (Steffensmeier, Ulmer, and Kramer 1998), focus on the role that race-linked stereotypes or attributions of dangerousness and threat play in criminal justice decision making. According to the focal concerns perspective, the decisions of criminal justice officials reflect their assessments of the blameworthiness or culpability of offenders, as well as their desire to protect the community by incapacitating dangerous offenders or deterring potential offenders. Because officials rarely have enough information to determine a defendant's dangerousness or threat accurately, they develop a "perceptual shorthand" based on stereotypes and attributions that are themselves linked to offender characteristics such as race, gender, and age (Hawkins 1981, 280). Thus, the offender's race, age, and gender will interact to influence decision making as a result of "images or attributions relating these statuses to membership in social groups thought to be dangerous and crime prone" (Steffensmeier, Ulmer, and Kramer 1998, 768).

The following sections review the empirical evidence regarding racial disparities in criminal justice outcomes. The first section examines evidence regarding differential treatment by police, with a focus on racial profiling and use of force by the police. The next section reviews evidence regarding the treatment of racial minorities in court. Here the focus is on sentencing decisions and the application of the death penalty.

A. Race, Ethnicity and Policing: Differential Enforcement of the Law?

In January 2009, Oakland, California was the scene of an urban riot sparked by the death of Oscar Grant, an unarmed twenty-two-year-old black man who was shot in the back by a Bay Area Rapid Transit (BART) police officer while lying face down in a train station. Eight years earlier riots had erupted in Cincinnati, Ohio, after a white police officer shot and killed Timothy Thomas, an unarmed black teenager who became the fifteenth black man killed by Cincinnati police since 1996. The four-day riot that ensued was the most prolonged urban disorder since the 1992 Los Angeles riots that followed the acquittal of four white Los Angeles Police Department officers charged in the videotaped beating of Rodney King, a black man stopped for a traffic violation.

As these incidents illustrate, tension between the police and minority communities is not a thing of the past. Although changes in police procedures and policies—for example, the elimination of the so-called "fleeing felon rule," the establishment of police-community relations programs, and the employment of greater numbers of black and Hispanic officers—have improved the situation, significant problems persist. Research has documented that racial and ethnic minorities have higher levels of dissatisfaction with the police and lower levels of trust in the police than do whites (Huang and Vaughn 1996; Weitzer 2000, 2002; Skogan 2005; Carr, Napolitano, and Keating 2007), and there is a growing body of research suggesting that these negative attitudes reflect at least in part respondents' perceptions of their *treatment* by the police (Smith and Hawkins 1973; Skogan 2005; Brunson and Miller 2006).

1. *Differential Enforcement of the Law*

There also is evidence of differential enforcement of the law by police and other law enforcement officials. The evidence is most compelling with respect to police use of force, especially deadly force. Blacks and Hispanics are more likely than whites to be victimized by excessive physical force at the hands of the police (Bureau of Justice Statistics 2001; Weitzer and Tuch 2004; for contrary results, see Reiss 1971); blacks and Hispanics also are more likely than whites to be shot at and to be killed by the police (Fyfe 1982; Sparger and Giacopassi 1992; Sorensen, Marquart, and Brock 1993). Eliminating the fleeing felon rule in favor of the defense-of-life rule[3] reduced, but did not eliminate, the racial disparity in police use of deadly force; nationally, the disparity between blacks and whites declined from 8:1 in the 1970s to 4:1 by 1998 (Bureau of Justice Statistics 2001). Nonetheless, a 1998 report by Human Rights Watch concluded that "race continues to play a central role in police brutality in the United States" (1998, 39).

The evidence regarding the effects of race and ethnicity on the likelihood of arrest is mixed. Some studies find that the race of the suspect has no effect once crime seriousness and the suspect's demeanor is taken into account (Black 1980; for a different interpretation, see Klinger 1994). Other studies conclude that black suspects are significantly more likely than white suspects to be arrested, especially if the victim of the crime is white (Smith, Visher, and Davidson 1984), or that the police arrest blacks and Hispanics on less stringent evidentiary criteria than whites (Petersilia 1983). Moreover, recent research reveals that blacks and Hispanics are heavily overrepresented among those arrested for drug offenses (Beckett, Nyrop, and Pfingst 2006; Western 2006; Provine 2007; Tonry and Melewski 2008), gang-related crimes (Leyton 2003; Zatz and Krecker 2003), and misdemeanor and ordinance violations in the context of zero-tolerance policing (Greene 1999; McArdle and Erzen 2001; Rosenfeld, Fornango, and Rengifo 2007).

2. *Racial Profiling*

Racial profiling has generated a substantial amount of research. Kennedy defines it as the "use of race as a proxy for an increased likelihood of criminal misconduct" (1997, 137). Walker and his colleagues contend racial profiling has been "the major controversy surrounding police practices in recent years" (2007, 123). Applied to the police, racial profiling generally refers to the use of a driver's race or ethnicity in deciding whether to make a traffic stop and, having made the stop, whether to conduct a search; it also refers to the use of an individual's race/ethnicity in deciding whether to stop citizens who appear to be "out of place," whether to stop, question, and frisk citizens encountered in high-crime neighborhoods or areas where drug dealing is common, and whether to make an arrest. Although stopping someone solely because of race or ethnicity is clearly an illegal form of discrimination, most courts that have addressed the issue have ruled that police can use race/ethnicity in making decisions about whether to stop, detain, or search persons so long as doing so is reasonably related to more efficient law enforcement and so long as race/ethnicity is one of several factors taken into account (see, for example, *State v. Dean*, 543 P.2d 425, 427 [Arizona 1975] and *State v. Martinez-Fuerte*, 428 U.S.543 [1976]).

Public opinion data (Harris 2002) and studies of attitudes toward the police (Weitzer 2000, 2002; W. R. Smith et al. 2003) reveal that both whites and racial minorities believe that racial profiling by the police is widespread. These views are substantiated by a growing body of empirical research, which generally provides evidence in support of racial profiling in the context of traffic stops (Browning et al. 1994; Lundman and Kaufmann 2003; Warren et al. 2006; for a review of this research see Withrow 2006). Although questions have been raised about methodological issues that plague racial profiling research (Engel, Calnon, and Bernard 2002), studies using official police data, observational data, and interview data consistently conclude that racial minorities, particularly blacks, are more likely than whites to be stopped by the police and, if stopped, are more likely to be searched. Among those searched, on the other hand, the "hit rates"—that is, the rates at which police find illegal drugs or weapons or other contraband—either do not differ for racial minorities and whites (Harris 2002; Lamberth 2003) or are significantly lower for blacks and Hispanics than for whites (W. R. Smith et al. 2003).

Critics of racial profiling claim not only that it is not an effective law enforcement tool, but that the costs and collateral consequences of profiling—for example, large numbers of innocent persons stopped, detained, and searched (many more than once) and more negative attitudes toward and less trust in the police on the part of racial minorities—are unreasonably high (Kennedy 1997; Harris 2002). As Kennedy put it, racial profiling negates the idea that "individuals should be judged on the basis of their own, particular conduct and not on the basis—not even partly on the basis—of racial generalizations" (1997, 157) and "nourishes powerful feelings of racial grievance against law enforcement authorities that are prevalent in every strata of black communities" (1997, 151).

It is clear that the relationship between the police and racial minorities has improved since the mid-1960s, when cities throughout the United States exploded in riots sparked in many cases by allegations of police brutality. Nonetheless, significant problems persist. Blacks and Hispanics have more negative attitudes toward the police than do whites, and both racial minorities and whites believe that the police engage in racial profiling. These beliefs are substantiated by empirical research, which reveals that there are racial disparities in police use of excessive or deadly force and that racial minorities are more likely than whites to be arrested, especially for drug offenses, gang-related crimes, and ordinance violations. Policy changes and legal reforms notwithstanding, racial minorities continue to suffer discrimination at the hands of the police.

B. Race, Ethnicity and the Court System

Gunnar Myrdal, a Swedish social scientist and the author of *An American Dilemma*, a book examining the "Negro Problem" in the United States in the late 1930s and early 1940s, concluded his chapter on "Courts, Sentences, and Prisons" by noting that "the whole judicial system of courts, sentences, and prisons in the South is overripe for fundamental reforms" (Myrdal 1944, 555). Relying primarily on anecdotal evidence of differential treatment of blacks and whites in southern court systems, Myrdal documented widespread discrimination in assignment of counsel, bail setting, jury selection, court processing, and sentencing. Myrdal noted that although the danger of discrimination was greatest in lower state courts, where judges with limited education were more susceptible to the pressures of public opinion, it was found to some extent in all state courts in the South. He observed, "In a court system of this structure, operating within a deeply prejudiced region, discrimination is to be expected" (Myrdal 1944, 550).

Although Myrdal clearly was dismayed by the racial inequities he observed, he was optimistic that southern courts would become more impartial. He saw numerous signs of change. He observed that the US Supreme Court and lower federal courts were increasingly willing to censure state courts for violating the rights of criminal defendants and that it was becoming easier for black defendants to obtain the services of competent attorneys. He also predicted that socioeconomic changes in the South, coupled with the growing activism of civil rights groups and the increasingly important black vote, would lead to reform.

Some observers might contend that Myrdal's predictions were overly optimistic and that the reforms he envisioned have not produced the results he anticipated. It is certainly true that the past six decades have witnessed significant changes. The Supreme Court has handed down decisions designed to protect the rights of criminal defendants and to prohibit racial discrimination in the selection of the jury pool, the use of peremptory challenges, and the imposition of the death penalty. States likewise have enacted legislation and adopted policies designed to decrease the likelihood of overt class- and race-based discrimination in the processing and sentencing of criminal defendants.

Despite these reforms, inequalities persist. Racial and ethnic minorities who are arrested by the police continue to suffer direct and indirect discrimination in decisions regarding bail (Chiricos and Bales 1991; Demuth and Steffensmeier 2004), charging (Spohn, Gruhl, and Welch 1987; Crutchfield et al. 1995; Sorensen and Wallace 1999), plea bargaining (Maxfield and Kramer 1998; for contrary results, see Nardulli, Eisenstein, and Flemming 1988), jury selection (Kennedy 1997; Turner et al. 1986), and sentencing (for reviews, see Spohn 2000; Mitchell 2005). As Marc Mauer of the Sentencing Project concluded, "the extended reach of the criminal justice system has been far from uniform in its effects upon different segments of the population . . . as has been true historically, but even more so now, the criminal justice system disproportionately engages minorities and the poor" (Mauer 1990, 1).

1. *Racial Disproportionality in Incarceration Rates*

Although charges of racial discrimination have been leveled at all aspects of the criminal court system, the harshest criticism has focused on the sentencing process. Citing statistics showing that racial minorities constitute more than half of the US prison population, critics charge that black and Hispanic offenders are more likely to be incarcerated, and are incarcerated for longer periods of time, than are white offenders.

There is clear and convincing evidence that black and Hispanic men face higher odds of incarceration than white men (Bureau of Justice Statistics 2008, table 6). As shown in figure 11.2, in 2007 the incarceration rate for black men (3,138/100,000) was six and a half times greater than the rate for white men (481/100,000); the rate for Hispanic men (1,261) was less than half the rate for black men but two and a half times greater than the rate for white men. Among females, blacks were three times as likely as whites to be incarcerated, and the incarceration rate for Hispanics was somewhat higher than the rate for whites.

The question, of course, is whether these racial and ethnic disparities reflect the disproportionate involvement of blacks and Hispanics in serious criminal activity, discrimination against blacks and Hispanics by prosecutors and judges, or some combination of these two possibilities. Researchers have used a variety of strategies to resolve this issue and to untangle the complex relationship between race and sentence severity. One approach compares the racial disparity in arrest rates for serious crimes with the racial disparity in incarceration rates for these crimes. According to

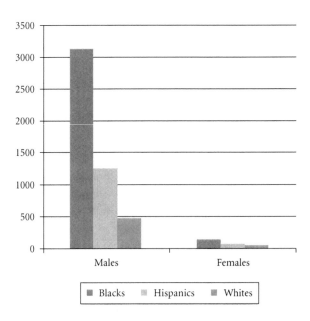

Figure 11.2. Imprisonment Rates for Sentenced Prisoners, by Race and Sex: 2007.

Source: Bureau of Justice Statistics 2008, table 6.

the author of the most frequently cited work using this approach, if there is no discrimination after arrest, then "one would expect to find the racial distribution of prisoners who were sentenced for any particular crime to be the same as the racial distribution of persons arrested for that crime" (Blumstein 1982, 1264).

To determine the overall portion of the racial disproportionality in prison populations that could be attributed to differential involvement in crime, Blumstein calculated the proportion of the prison population that, based on arrest rates, was expected to be black for twelve separate violent, property, and drug offenses. He then compared these expected rates with the actual rates of incarceration for blacks. Using 1979 data, he found that 80 percent of the racial disproportionality in incarceration rates could be attributed to racial differences in arrest rates (Blumstein 1982, 1267). He reached a similar conclusion when he replicated the analysis using 1991 data; 76 percent of the disproportionality in incarceration rates could be attributed to racial differences in arrest rates (Blumstein 1993, 751). However, Blumstein stressed that these results did not mean that racial discrimination did not exist. As he noted, "there are too many anecdotal reports of such discrimination to dismiss that possibility." Rather, his findings implied that "the bulk of the racial disproportionality in prison is attributable to differential involvement in arrest, and probably in crime, in those most serious offenses that tend to lead to imprisonment" (Blumstein 1993, 750).

Blumstein's estimate that 80 percent (76 percent in 1991) of the racial disproportionality in imprisonment could be explained by racial differences in arrest rates, which did not go unchallenged (Hawkins and Hardy 1987; Sabol 1989; Crutchfield, Bridges, and Pitchford 1994; Mauer 2006; Keen and Jacobs 2009), did not apply to each of the crimes he examined. For some crimes (e.g., murder) arrest explained more than 80 percent of the disparity, but for others (e.g., burglary and drug offenses), arrest accounted for substantially less than 80 percent. Most notably, racial differences in arrest rates for drug offenses explained only half of the racial disproportionality in imprisonment for drug offenses, a finding exacerbated by the fact that racial minorities face higher odds of arrest for drug offenses than do whites (Tonry 1995). As Blumstein himself pointed out, "arrests for drug offenses are far less likely to be a good proxy for offending patterns than they are for aggravated assault, murder, and robbery" and the black arrest rate for drug offenses grew "dramatically in the late 1980s" (Blumstein 1993, 752). In other words, the fact that drug offenders make up an increasing share of the prison population coupled with the fact that blacks are increasingly likely to be arrested for drug offenses means that "a declining proportion of the prison population can be explained by higher rates of crime" (Mauer 2006, 128).

2. Race/Ethnicity and Sentencing Decisions

Considering the evidence produced by Blumstein and others, it seems reasonable to conclude that the racial disproportionality in the prison population results to a large extent from racial disparities in criminal involvement but to some extent from racial discrimination at various stages in the criminal justice process, including sentencing. This is confirmed by empirical research on examining the effect of race on judges' sentencing. Social scientists and legal scholars have conducted dozens of studies designed to determine whether blacks and Hispanics are sentenced more harshly than whites. In fact, as Zatz noted, this issue "may well have been the major research inquiry for studies of sentencing in the 1970s and early 1980s" (1987, 69). The studies that have been conducted vary enormously in theoretical and methodological sophistication; their findings and the conclusions drawn by their authors also vary.

Studies conducted from the 1930s through the 1960s generally concluded that racial disparities in sentencing reflected overt racial discrimination. For example, the author of one of the earliest sentencing studies, published in 1935, claimed that "equality before the law is a social fiction" (Sellin 1935, 217). Reviews of these early studies, however, found that most of them were methodologically flawed (Hagan 1974; Kleck 1981). They typically used simple bivariate statistical techniques, and they failed to control adequately for crime seriousness and prior criminal record.

The conclusions of these early reviews coupled with the findings of its own review of sentencing research led the National Research Council Panel on Sentencing Research to state (in 1983) that the sentencing process was not characterized by "a widespread systematic pattern of discrimination" (Hagan and Bumiller 1983). Rather, "some pockets of discrimination are found for particular judges, particular crime types, and in particular settings" (Blumstein et al. 1983, 93). Marjorie Zatz (1987), who reviewed the results of four waves of race and sentencing research conducted from the 1930s through the early 1980s, reached a somewhat different conclusion. Although she acknowledged that "it would be misleading to suggest that race/ethnicity is *the* major determinant of sanctioning," Zatz nonetheless asserted that "race/ethnicity is *a* determinant of sanctioning, and a potent one at that" (1987, 87).

The three most recent reviews of research on race and sentencing confirm Zatz's assertion (Chiricos and Crawford 1995; Spohn 2000; Mitchell 2005). Spohn (2000), for example, reviewed thirty-two studies of state-level sentencing decisions and eight studies of sentencing at the federal level. Consistent with the earlier conclusions of Chiricos and Crawford (1995), Spohn reported that many of these studies found a *main effect* for race, ethnicity, or both (2000, exhibit 1). At both the state and federal levels, there was evidence that blacks and Hispanics were more likely than whites to be sentenced to prison (e.g., United States Sentencing Commission 1995; Albonetti 1997; Steffensmeier, Ulmer, and Kramer 1998;Everett and Nienstedt 1999). At the federal level, there was also evidence that blacks received longer sentences than whites (McDonald and Carlson 1993; B. L. Smith and Damphouse 1996; Albonetti 1997; Maxfield and Kramer 1998). Noting that "evidence concerning direct racial effects . . . provides few clues to the circumstances under which race matters," Spohn also evaluated the forty studies included in her review for evidence of indirect or contextual discrimination; she concluded that the studies revealed four "themes" or "patterns" of contextual effects (2000, 458).

The first theme was that the combination of race or ethnicity and other legally irrelevant offender characteristics produces greater sentence disparity than race or ethnicity alone (Spohn 2000, 460–61). That is, the studies demonstrated that certain minorities—males, the young, the unemployed, the less educated—were singled out for harsher treatment (e.g., Steffensmeier et al., 1998; Wooldredge 1998; Spohn and Holleran 2000;for more recent research, see Steen, Engen, and Gainey 2005; Steffensmeier and Demuth 2006; Kramer and Ulmer 2009; Spohn and Sample, forthcoming). Some studies found that each of these offender characteristics, including race or ethnicity, had a direct effect on sentence outcomes, but the combination of race or ethnicity and one or more of the other characteristics was a more powerful predictor of sentence severity than any characteristic individually. Other studies found that race or ethnicity had an effect only when the offender was male, young, or unemployed.

The second pattern of indirect or interaction effects, according to Spohn, was that a number of process-related factors conditioned the effect of race/ethnicity on sentence severity (2000, 455–67). Some of the studies revealed, for example, that pleading guilty (Albonetti 1997), hiring a private attorney (Holmes et al. 1996), or providing evidence or testimony in other cases (Albonetti 1997; for more recent research, see Hartley, Madden, and Spohn 2007; Johnson, Ulmer, and Kramer 2008) resulted in greater sentence discounts for white offenders than for black or Hispanic offenders. Other studies showed that members of racial minorities paid a higher penalty—received harsher sentences—for being detained prior to trial (Chiricos and Bales 1991; Crew 1991; for more recent research, see Demuth and Steffensmeier 2004 and Spohn 2009), having serious prior criminal records (Zatz 1984; McDonald and Carlson 1993; Ulmer and Kramer 1996), or refusing to plead guilty (Zatz 1984; Crew 1991; Ulmer 1997). As Spohn noted, these results demonstrate that race and ethnicity influence sentence outcomes through their relationships with earlier decisions and suggest that these process-related determinants of sentence outcomes do not operate in the same way for racial minorities and whites.

The third theme or pattern revealed by the studies included in Spohn's review concerned an interaction between the race of the offender and the race of the victim. Consistent with research on the death penalty and earlier research on sexual assault case outcomes, two studies found that blacks who sexually assaulted whites were sentenced more harshly than other offenders (Walsh 1987; Spohn and Spears 1996). Thus, "punishment is contingent on the race of the victim as well as the race of the offender" (Spohn 2000, 469). The final pattern of indirect or interaction effects, which Spohn admitted was "less obvious" than the other three, was that the effect of race or ethnicity was conditioned by the nature of the crime (2000, 461). Some studies found that racial discrimination was confined to less serious, and thus more discretionary, crimes (Crawford, Chiricos, and Kleck 1998). Other studies revealed that racial discrimination was most pronounced for drug offenses or, alternatively, that harsher sentencing of racial minorities was found only for the most serious drug offenses (Albonetti 1997; Crawford, Chiricos, and Kleck 1998; Spohn and Spears 2003).

The most recent review of research on race and sentencing is Mitchell's (2005) meta-analysis of published and unpublished studies that included controls for offense seriousness and prior criminal record. Mitchell's quantitative analysis focused on the direction and size of the effect (the "effect size") of race on sentencing. His analysis revealed that 76 percent of the effect sizes from the non-federal studies and 73 percent of the effect sizes from the federal studies indicated that blacks were sentenced more harshly than whites, especially for drug offenses and especially for imprisonment decisions. The effect sizes were smaller in studies that used more precise controls for offense seriousness and criminal history; they were larger in jurisdictions that did not use structured sentencing guidelines. Moreover, the analysis revealed that the amount of unwarranted disparity in sentencing had not changed appreciably since the 1970s. Mitchell concluded that his findings "undermine the so-called 'no discrimination thesis,'" given that "independent of other measured factors, on average African Americans were sentenced more harshly than whites" (2005, 462).

That a majority of the studies reviewed by Spohn (2000), and Mitchell (2005) found that African Americans and (in the case of Spohn's review) Hispanics were more likely than whites to be sentenced to prison, even after taking crime seriousness and prior criminal record into account, suggests that racial discrimination in sentencing has not been eliminated. These findings also provide additional evidence that the disproportionate number of racial minorities incarcerated in state and federal prisons reflects "to some extent" racial discrimination within the criminal justice system.

3. *Race, Ethnicity, and the Death Penalty*

In 1987, the US Supreme Court rejected Warren McCleskey's claim that the Georgia capital sentencing process was administered in a racially discriminatory manner (*McCleskey v. Kemp*, 481 U.S. 279 [1987]). McCleskey, an African American who was convicted of killing a white police officer during the course of an armed robbery, claimed that those who killed whites—particularly blacks who killed whites—were substantially more likely to be sentenced to death than those who killed blacks. In support of his claim, McCleskey offered the results of a study conducted by David Baldus and his colleagues (Baldus, Woodworth, and Pulaski 1990). The "Baldus study," which is widely regarded as the most comprehensive and sophisticated analysis of death penalty decisions to date, concluded that the race of the victim was "a potent influence in the system" and that the state of Georgia was operating a "dual system" for prosecuting homicide cases (Baldus, Woodworth, and Pulaski 1990, 185).

Although the majority accepted the validity of the Baldus study, the Supreme Court nonetheless refused to accept McCleskey's argument that the disparities documented by the study signaled the presence of intentional racial discrimination. Writing for the majority, Justice Powell asserted that the disparities were "unexplained" and stated that "at most, the Baldus study indicates a discrepancy that appears to correlate with race" (*McCleskey* at 312). The Court concluded that the Baldus study was "clearly insufficient to support an inference that any of the decisionmakers in McCleskey's case acted with discriminatory purpose" (*McCleskey* at 298).

The four dissenting justices were outraged. Justice Brennan, who was joined in dissent by Justices Blackmun, Marshall, and Stevens, wrote, "The Court today finds that Warren McCleskey's sentence was constitutionally imposed. It finds no fault with a system in which lawyers must tell their clients that race casts a large shadow on the capital sentencing process." (*McCleskey* at 315 [Brennan, J., dissenting]). The analysis of legal scholars was similarly harsh. They characterized the decision as a "badge of shame upon America's system of justice" (Bright 1995, 947) and concluded that "the central message of the McCleskey case is all too plain: de facto racial discrimination in capital sentencing is legal in the United States" (Gross and Mauro 1989, 212).

Justice Powell's assertion that the Baldus study revealed no more than "a discrepancy that appears to correlate with race" is challenged by the weight of the evidence documenting racial disparity in the capital sentencing process. Studies conducted prior to 1972 (the date of the Supreme Court decision (*Furman v. Georgia*, 409 U.S. 238 [1972]) that ruled that the death penalty was unconstitutional as it was being administered under existing statutes), revealed that blacks, particularly blacks who were convicted of murdering or raping whites, were sentenced to death and executed at disproportionately high rates during the pre-*Furman* era (e.g., Mangum 1940; Johnson 1941; Garfinkel 1949; Wolfgang and Riedel 1973). These studies revealed that the death penalty "was largely used for punishing blacks who had raped whites," and that blacks who killed whites were substantially more likely than any other race-of-offender and race-of-victim group to be sentenced to death and executed (Kleck 1981, 788).

More recent research reaches similar conclusions. Studies conducted since 1976 (the date of Supreme Court decisions (*Gregg v. Georgia*, 428 U.S. 153 [1976], *Proffitt v. Florida*, 428 U.S. 242 [1976], and *Jurek v. Texas*, 428 U.S. 262 [1976]) upholding newly enacted guided discretion death penalty statutes) document substantial discrimination in the application of the death penalty (see, for example, Radelet 1981; Paternoster 1984; Gross and Mauro 1989; Baldus, Woodworth, and Pulaski 1990; Keil and Vito 1990). A report by the General Accounting Office (1990), which reviewed twenty-eight post-*Gregg* studies, noted that the race of the *victim* had a significant effect in all but five studies. Those who murdered whites were more likely to be charged with capital murder and to be sentenced to death than those who murdered blacks. Moreover, these differences could not be attributed to differences in the defendant's prior criminal record, the seriousness of the crime, or other legally relevant factors. The GAO also pointed out that although the evidence regarding the race of the *defendant* was "equivocal," about half of the studies did find that blacks were more likely than whites to be charged with capital crimes and to be sentenced to death (GAO 1990, 6). The overall conclusion proffered by the GAO was that there was "a pattern of evidence indicating racial disparities in the charging, sentencing, and imposition of the death penalty after the *Furman* decision" (1990 5).

The findings of research conducted since the publication of the GAO report are consistent with this conclusion. Research in Maryland (Paternoster and Brame 2008), North Carolina (Unah and Boger 2001), Virginia (American Civil Liberties Union 2003), Ohio (Welsh-Huggins 2005), and California (Pierce and Radelet 2005) provides strong evidence of racial disparities in the capital sentencing process in the 1990s and early 2000s in both southern and non-southern jurisdictions. For example, research conducted in California, which had the largest death row population in the United States in 2005, found that offenders who killed whites were 3.7 times more likely to be sentenced to death than offenders who killed blacks; those who killed whites were 4.7 times more likely to be sentenced to death than those who killed Hispanics (Pierce and Radelet 2005). The fact that these differences did not disappear when they controlled for the number of aggravating circumstances that the crime involved, and for the population density and racial makeup of the county where the crime occurred, led the authors of the study to conclude that "the data clearly show that the race and ethnicity of homicide victims is associated with the imposition of the death penalty (Pierce and Radelet 2005, table 4).

In short, there is both historical and contemporary evidence of racial discrimination in the capital sentencing process. There is irrefutable evidence that the death penalty for rape was reserved primarily for black men who raped white women, and there is strong evidence that those who kill whites have been and continue to be sentenced to death and executed at a disproportionately high rate. Although evidence about discrimination based on the race of the offender is, as the GAO report noted, "equivocal," most studies reveal that blacks accused of murdering whites are substantially more likely than any other race-of-victim and race-of-offender category to be charged with a capital crime and sentenced to death.

Most commentators assumed that the Supreme Court's opinion in *McCleskey* delivered a fatal blow to attempts to strike down the death penalty. They based this conclusion on the fact that the Court found the statistical evidence of victim-based discrimination documented in the Baldus study to be unpersuasive. Recent publicity about continuing race and class inequities inherent in the capital sentencing process—coupled with calls for death penalty moratoriums at both the state and federal level—suggests that the issue has not been laid to rest.

III. POLICY IMPLICATIONS AND RESEARCH AGENDA

The criminal justice system that Myrdal (1944) wrote about no longer exists, in the South or elsewhere. Reforms mandated by Supreme Court decisions or adopted voluntarily by the states have tempered the blatant racism directed against racial minorities by criminal justice officials. It is no longer true that whites who commit crimes against blacks are beyond the reach of the criminal justice system, that blacks suspected of crimes against whites receive justice at the hands of white lynch mobs, or that black defendants are routinely tried by all-white juries without attorneys to defend them. Nonetheless, racial inequities persist. Persuasive evidence exists that racial minorities suffer discrimination at the hands of the police: they are subject to racial profiling, and they are more likely than whites to be shot and killed, arrested, and victimized by excessive physical force. Compelling evidence also points to the persistence of discrimination within the court system. Supreme Court decisions and statutory reforms have not eliminated racial bias in decisions regarding bail, charging, plea bargaining, jury selection, sentencing, and juvenile justice processing.

The fact that racial and ethnic discrimination persists in the face of concerted efforts to eradicate it suggests that racial profiling is not confined to policing, but infects all stages of the criminal justice system. It also suggests that racial profiling, whether on the streets or in the courtroom, does not result simply from the prejudice of individual police officers, prosecutors, or judges. Rather, it is an institutional practice deeply embedded in the agencies of the criminal justice system and which is widely regarded as a legitimate and effective weapon in the war on crime. It is a practice that labels blacks and Hispanics—particularly young black and Hispanic men—potential criminals and likely recidivists, without regard for the presumption of innocence or for the notion that individuals should be judged on the basis of their own conduct and not on the basis of racial and ethnic stereotypes. It is a practice that "does great damage to individuals, to the social fabric of our country, to the rule of law, and to the entire legal and criminal justice system" (Harris 2002, 241).

The difficulties inherent in making informed, rational, and appropriate decisions about individuals who commit crimes, coupled with the pervasiveness of stereotypes of danger, threat, and criminality that are linked to race and ethnicity, lead to the conclusion that eliminating racial profiling from the criminal justice system will not be easy. The situation is further complicated by state and federal court decisions that rather than condemning the practice of racial profiling as a violation of the Equal Protection Clause of the Fourteenth Amendment, place a stamp of approval—albeit a limited one—on its use in the context of law enforcement. As discussed earlier, courts have ruled that the Fourteenth Amendment is not violated if race is only one of several factors taken into account or if race is not the dominant factor used in determining suspiciousness. These rulings, according to Kennedy are "profoundly wrong . . . even if race is only one of several factors behind a decision, tolerating it at all means tolerating it as potentially the *decisive* factor" (Kennedy 1997, 148). David Harris's critique is even more pointed. He argues that using skin color as evidence of criminal involvement "means, in clear and unequivocal terms, that *skin color itself has been criminalized*" (Harris 2002, 242).

The task of eliminating racial disparities from the American criminal justice system is made even more difficult by crime control policies implemented at both the state and federal levels over the past several decades: crackdowns on quality-of-life offenses, three-strikes laws that require life sentences for habitual offenders, mandatory minimum sentences for drug and gun offenses, disparity in sentences imposed for drug offenses involving crack and powder cocaine, and sentence enhancements for gang-involved offenses. As numerous studies have shown, racial minorities—particularly young black and Hispanic men—have borne the brunt of these policies. Until these policies, which as Tonry and Melewski have pointed out "were adopted primarily for symbolic or expressive purposes rather than with any basis for believing that they would significantly affect crime rates," are modified or repealed, it will be difficult, if not impossible, to achieve a racially equitable criminal justice system (Tonry and Melewski 2008, 37).

The research conducted by social scientists and legal scholars provides at least a partial answer to the question posed by the Bureau of the Census in 1918. The weight of the evidence leads inevitably to a conclusion that racial and ethnic disproportionality in the prison population reflects "to some extent" discrimination against racial minorities. This conclusion notwithstanding, there is a need for additional research designed to pinpoint the stages of the criminal justice system where discrimination is most likely to occur and to determine whether racial minorities suffer from cumulative disadvantage as they proceed through the criminal justice process. Research is also needed on the mechanisms that produce discriminatory outcomes; we know very little about the processes that link attributions of dangerousness and threat to race and ethnicity in the minds of criminal justice officials or the ways in which these attributions affect decision making. There also is a need for additional research examining the causes of victimization and offending across levels of analysis. Most of the extant research examines the influence of either individual, family, or community factors; moreover, the limited research incorporating factors at each level of analysis focuses primarily on violent victimization and offending among youth. We do not know if the patterns of results found for youth are applicable to adults or if the factors that explain violent victimization and offending are applicable to other types of offenses.

NOTES

1. Criminal justice data on victimization, offending, and justice system processing have a number of limitations. One problem is that criminal justice agencies do not always use the same racial and ethnic categories. This is particularly true with respect to Hispanic Americans. Some agencies, including the FBI, use the racial categories identified by the Bureau of the Census; in these data, then, there is no separate category for ethnicity, and Hispanics are

most likely counted as whites. Although the NCVS and the BJS National Prisoner Statistics program do report data on whites, blacks, and Hispanics, many local jurisdictions use "white" and "nonwhite" categories that aggregate all racial minorities as "nonwhites."

2. There is limited data on groups other than whites, blacks, and Hispanics. The NCVS provides victimization rates for "other" racial groups (and, more recently, for persons reporting two or more races), but does not separate out Asian Americans or Native Americans. Arrest data is provided for whites, blacks, Native Americans, and Asian Americans. These data reveal that Native Americans are overrepresented for some types of crimes, e.g., vandalism, liquor law violations, and drunkenness) and that Asian Americans are underrepresented for all crimes except gambling (Walker et al., 2007).

3. The fleeing felon rule authorizes police use of fatal force to prevent the flight of anyone police reasonably believe to be a fleeing felon. The defense-of-life rule allows fatal force only when the felon is reasonably believed to have committed a violent felony or to pose a threat of violence.

REFERENCES

Akers, Ronald L. 1994. *Social Learning and Social Structure: A General Theory of Crime and Deviance*. Boston, MA: Northeastern University Press.

Albonetti, Celesta A. 1997. "Sentencing under the Federal Sentencing Guidelines: Effects of Defendant Characteristics, Guilty Pleas, and Departures on Sentencing Outcomes for Drug Offenses, 1991–1992." *Law and Society Review* 31:789–822.

American Civil Liberties Union. 2003. "Broken Justice: The Death Penalty in Virginia." http://www.aclu.org/DeathPenalty/DeathPenalty.cfm?ID=14388&c=17.

Anderson, Elijah. 1999. *Code of the Street: Decency, Violence, and the Moral Life of the Inner City*. New York: Norton.

Baldus, David C., George G. Woodworth, and Charles A. Pulaski Jr. 1990. *Equal Justice and the Death Penalty: A Legal and Empirical Analysis*. Boston, MA: Northeastern University Press.

Beckett, Katherine, Kris Nyrop, and Lori Pfingst. 2006. "Race, Drugs and Policing: Understanding Disparities in Drug Delivery Arrests." *Criminology* 44:105–37.

Black, Donald. 1980. *The Manners and Customs of the Police*. New York: Academic Press.

Blumstein, Alfred. 1982. "On the Racial Disproportionality of United States Prison Populations." *Journal of Criminal Law and Criminology* 73:1259–81.

———. 1993. "Racial Disproportionality of US Prison Populations Revisited." *University of Colorado Law Review* 64:743–60.

Blumstein, Alfred, Jacqueline Cohen, Susan E. Martin, and Michael H. Tonry, eds. 1983. *Research on Sentencing: The Search for Reform*, vol. 2. Washington, DC: National Academies Press.

Bridges, George S., and Sara Steen. 1998. "Racial Disparities in Official Assessments of Juvenile Offending: Attributional Stereotypes as Mediating Mechanisms." *American Sociological Review* 65:554–70.

Bright, Stephen B. 1995. "Discrimination, Death and Denial: The Tolerance of Racial Discrimination in the Infliction of the Death Penalty." *Santa Clara Law Review* 35:901–50.

Browning, Sandra. L., Francis T. Cullen, Liqun Cao, Renee Kopache, R., and Thomas J. Stevenson. 1994. "Race and Getting Hassled by the Police: A Research Note." *Police Studies* 17:1–11.

Brunson, Rod K., and Jody Miller. 2006. "Young Black Men and Urban Policing in the United States." *British Journal of Criminology*: 46:613–40.

Bureau of Justice Statistics. 2001. *Policing and Homicide, 1976–98.* Washington, DC: US Department of Justice.

———. 2007. *Homicide Trends in the US* Washington, DC: US Department of Justice.

———. 2008. *Prisoners in 2007.* Washington, DC: US Department of Justice.

Carr, Patrick J., Laura Napolitano, and Jessica Keating. 2007. "We Never Call the Cops and Here Is Why: A Qualitative Examination of Legal Cynicism in Three Philadelphia Neighborhoods." *Criminology* 45:445–80.

Cernkovich, Stephen A., and Peggy C. Giordano. 1992. "School Bonding, Race, and Delinquency." *Criminology* 30:261–91.

Chambliss, William J., and Robert B. Seidman. 1971. *Law, Order and Power.* Reading, MA: Addison-Wesley.

Chiricos, Theodore G., and William D. Bales. 1991. "Unemployment and Punishment: An Empirical Assessment." *Criminology* 29:701–24.

Chiricos, Theordore G., and Charles Crawford. 1995. "Race and Imprisonment: A Contextual Assessment of the Evidence." In *Ethnicity, Race and Crime*, ed. Darnell F. Hawkins. Albany, NY: State University of New York Press.

Cobbina, Jennifer E., Jody Miller, and Rod K. Brunson. 2008. "Gender, Neighborhood Danger, and Risk-Avoidance Strategies Among Urban African-American Youths." *Criminology* 46:673–709.

Crawford, Charles, Theodore Chiricos, and Gary Kleck. 1998. "Race, Racial Threat, and Sentencing of Habitual Offenders." *Criminology* 36:481–511.

Crenshaw, Kimberle, Neil T. Gotanda, Garry Peller, and Kendall Thomas. 1995. *Critical Race Theory: The Key Writings that Formed the Movement.* New York: New Press.

Crew, Keith B. 1991. "Sex Differences in Criminal Sentencing: Chivalry or Patriarchy?" *Justice Quarterly* 8:59–84.

Crutchfield, Robert D., George S. Bridges, and Susan R. Pitchford. 1994. "Analytical and Aggregation Biases in Analyses of Imprisonment: Reconciling Discrepancies in Studies of Racial Disparity." *Journal of Research in Crime and Delinquency* 31:166–82.

Crutchfield, Robert D., Joseph G. Weis, Rodney L. Engen, and Randy R. Gainey. 1995. *Racial and Ethnic Disparities in the Prosecution of Felony Cases in King County.* Olympia, WA: Washington State Minority and Justice Commission.

Delgado, Richard, and Jean Stefancic. 2001. *Critical Race Theory: An Introduction.* New York: New York University Press.

Demuth, Stephen, and Darrell Steffensmeier. 2004. "The Impact of Gender and Race-Ethnicity in the Pretrial Release Process." *Social Problems* 51:222–42.

Dugan, Laura, and Robert Apel. 2003. "An Exploratory Study of the Violent Victimization of Women: Race/Ethnicity and Situational Context." *Criminology* 41:959–77.

Engel, Robin S., Jennifer M. Calnon, and Thomas J. Bernard. 2002. "Theory and Racial Profiling: Shortcomings and Future Directions in Research." *Justice Quarterly* 19:249–73.

Everett, Ronald S., and Barbara C. Nienstedt. 1999. "Race, Remorse, and Sentence Reduction: Is Saying You're Sorry Enough?" *Justice Quarterly* 16:99–122.

Federal Bureau of Investigation. N.d. Crime in the United States, 2007. http://www.fbi.gov/ucr/cius2007/data/index.html.

Fyfe, James J. 1982. "Blind Justice: Police Shootings in Memphis." *Journal of Criminal Law and Criminology* 73:707–22.

Garfinkel, Harold. 1949. "Research Note on Inter- and Intra-Racial Homicides." *Social Forces* 27:369–81.

Gottfredson, Michael R., and Travis Hirschi. 1985. *A General Theory of Crime.* Stanford, CA: Stanford University Press.

Greene, Jack A. 1999. "Zero Tolerance: A Case Study of Police Policies and Practices in New York City." *Crime and Delinquency* 45:171–87.

Gross, Samuel R., and Robert Mauro. 1989. *Death & Discrimination: Racial Disparities in Capital Sentencing.* Boston, MA: Northeastern University Press.

Hagan, John. 1974. "Extra-Legal Attributes and Criminal Sentencing: An Assessment of a Sociological Viewpoint." *Law and Society Review* 8:357–83.

Hagan, John, and Kristin Bumiller. 1983. "Making Sense of Sentencing: A Review and Critique of Sentencing Research." In *Research on Sentencing: The Search for Reform,* vol.2, ed. Alfred Blumstein, Jacqueline Cohen, Susan E. Martin, and Michael H. Tonry. Washington, DC: National Academies Press.

Harris. David A. 2002. *Profiles in Injustice: Why Racial Profiling Cannot Work.* New York: New Press.

Hartley, Richard, Sean Madden, and Cassia Spohn. 2007. "Prosecutorial Discretion: An Examination of Substantial Assistance Departures in Federal Crack-Cocaine and Powder-Cocaine Cases." *Justice Quarterly* 24:382–407.

Hawkins, Darnell. 1981. "Causal Attribution and Punishment for Crime." *Deviant Behavior* 1:191–215.

Hawkins, Darnell F., and Kenneth A. Hardy. 1987. "Black-White Imprisonment Rate: A State-by-State Analysis." *Social Justice* 16:75–94.

Hawkins, Darnell F., John H. Laub, Janet L. Lauritsen, and Lynn Cothern. 2000. *Race, Ethnicity and Serious and Violent Juvenile Offending.* Washington, DC: US Department of Justice, Office of Justice Programs, Office of Juvenile Justice and Delinquency Prevention.

Haynie, Dana L., and Danielle C. Payne. 2006. "Race, Friendship Networks, and Violent Delinquency." *Criminology* 44:775–805.

Hirschi, Travis. 1969. *Causes of Delinquency.* Berkeley: University of California Press.

Holmes, Malcolm D., Harmon M. Hosch, Howard C. Daudistel, Dolores A. Perez, and Joseph B. Graves. 1996. "Ethnicity, Legal Resources, and Felony Dispositions in Two Southwestern Jurisdictions." *Justice Quarterly* 13:11–30.

Huang. W. S. Wilson, and Michael S. Vaughn. 1996. "Support and Confidence: Public Attitudes toward the Police." In *Americans View Crime and Justice: A National Public Opinion Survey,* ed. Timothy J. Flanagan and Dennis R. Longmire. Thousand Oaks, CA: Sage.

Human Rights Watch. 1998. *Shielded From Justice: Police Brutality and Accountability in the United States.* New York: Human Rights Watch.

Johnson, Brian E., Jeffery T. Ulmer, and John H. Kramer. 2008. "The Social Context of Guidelines Circumvention: The Case of Federal District Courts." *Criminology* 46:737–83.

Johnson, Guy. 1941. "The Negro and Crime." *Annals of the American Academy* 217:93–104.

Keen, Bradley, and David Jacobs. 2009. "Racial Threat, Partisan Politics, and Racial Disparities in Prison Admissions: A Panel Analysis." *Criminology* 47:209–38.

Keil Thomas, and Gennaro Vito. 1990. "Race and the Death Penalty in Kentucky Murder Trials: An Analysis of Post- *Gregg* Outcomes." *Justice Quarterly* 7:189–207.

Kennedy, Randall. 1997. *Race, Crime, and the Law.* New York: Vintage Books.

Kleck, Gary. 1981. "Racial Discrimination in Sentencing: A Critical Evaluation of the Evidence with Additional Evidence on the Death Penalty." *American Sociological Review* 43:783–805.

Klinger, David. 1994. "Demeanor or Crime: Why 'Hostile' Citizens Are Most Likely To Be Arrested." *Criminology* 32:475–93.

Kramer, John H., and Jeffery T. Ulmer. 2009. *Sentencing Guidelines: Lessons from Pennsylvania.* Boulder, CO: Lynne Rienner Publishers.

Lamberth, John. 2003. *Racial Profiling Data Analysis: Final Report for the San Antonio Police Department.* Chadds Ford, PA: Lamberth Consulting.

Lauritsen, Janet L. 2003. "How Families and Communities Influence Youth Victimization." *OJJDP Juvenile Justice Bulletin.* Washington, DC: US Department of Justice.

Lauritsen, Janet L., and Norman A. White. 2001. "Putting Violence in its Place: The Influence of Race, Ethnicity, Gender and Place on the Risk for Violence." *Criminology and Public Policy* 1:37–59.

Leyton, Stacey. 2003. "The New Blacklists: The Threat to Civil Liberties Posed by Gang Databases." In *Crime Control and Social Justice: The Delicate Balance*, ed. Darnell F. Hawkins, Samuel L. Meyers Jr., and Randolph N. Stone. Westport, CT: Greenwood.

Lundman, Richard J., and Robert L. Kaufman. 2003. "Driving While Black and Male: Effects of Race, Ethnicity, and Gender on Citizen Self-Reports of Traffic Stops and Police Actions." *Criminology* 41:195–220.

Mangum, Charles S., Jr. 1940. *The Legal Status of the Negro.* Chapel Hill, NC: North Carolina Press.

Mann, Coramae R. 1993. *Unequal Justice: A Question of Color.* Bloomington: Indiana University Press.

Massey, Douglas S., and Nancy A. Denton. 1993. *American Apartheid: Segregation and the Making of the Underclass.* Cambridge, MA: Harvard University Press.

Mauer, Marc. 1990. *Young Black Men and the Criminal Justice System: A Growing National Problem.* Washington, DC: The Sentencing Project.

———. 2006. *Race To Incarcerate.* 2nd ed. New York: New Press.

Maxfield, Linda D., and John H. Kramer. 1998. *Substantial Assistance: An Empirical Yardstick Gauging Equity in Current Federal Policy and Practices.* Washington, DC: United States Sentencing Commission.

McArdle, Andrea, and Tanya Erzen. 2001. *Zero Tolerance: Quality of Life and the New Police Brutality in New York City.* New York: New York University Press.

McDonald, Douglas C., and Kenneth E. Carlson. 1993. Sentencing in the Federal Courts: Does Race Matter? The Transition to Sentencing Guidelines, 1986–90. Washington, DC: US Department of Justice, Bureau of Justice Statistics. NCJ 145–328.

McNulty, Thomas, and Paul E. Bellair. 2003. "Explaining Racial and Ethnic Differences in Serious Adolescent Violent Behavior." *Criminology* 41:709–48.

Mitchell, Ojmarrh. 2005. "A Meta-Analysis of Race and Sentencing Research: Explaining the Inconsistencies." *Journal of Quantitative Criminology* 21:439–66.

Myrdal, Gunnar. 1944. *An American Dilemma: The Negro Problem and Modern Democracy.* New York: Harper and Brothers.

Nardulli, Peter F., James Eisenstein, and Roy B. Flemming. 1988. *The Tenor of Justice; Criminal Courts and the Guilty Plea Process.* Chicago: University of Chicago Press.

Parker, Karen F., and Amy Reckdenwald. 2008. "Concentrated Disadvantage, Traditional Male Role Models, and African-American Juvenile Violence." *Criminology* 46:711–33.

Paternoster, Raymond. 1984. "Prosecutorial Discretion in Requesting the Death Penalty: A Case of Victim-Based Discrimination." *Law and Society Review* 18:437–78.

Paternoster, Raymond, and Robert Brame. 2008. "Reassessing Race Disparities in Maryland Capital Cases." *Criminology* 46:971–1008.

Petersilia, Joan. 1983. *Racial Disparities in the Criminal Justice System.* Santa Monica, CA: Rand.

Pierce, Glenn L., and Michael Radelet. 2005. "The Impact of Legally Inappropriate Factors on Death Sentencing for California Homicides, 1990–1999." *Santa Clara Law Review* 46:1–47.

Provine, Doris M. 2007. *Unequal Under Law; Race in the War on Drugs.* Chicago: University of Chicago Press.

Quinney, Richard. 1970. *The Society Reality of Crime.* Boston: Little, Brown.

Radelet, Michael. 1981. "Racial Characteristics and the Imposition of the Death Penalty." *American Sociological Review* 46:918–27.

Reiss, Albert J. 1971. *The Police and the Public.* New Haven: Yale University Press.

Rosenfeld, Richard, Robert Fornango, and Andres F. Rengifo. 2007. "The Impact of Order-Maintenance Policing on New York City Homicide and Robbery Rates, 1998–2001." *Criminology* 45:355–84.

Sabol, William J. 1989. "Racially Disproportionate Prison Populations in the United States: An Overview of Historical Patterns and Review of Contemporary Issues." *Contemporary Crises* 13:405–32.

Sampson, Robert J., Jeffrey D. Morenoff, and Stephen Raudenbush. 2005. "Social Anatomy of Racial and Ethnic Disparities in Violence." *American Journal of Public Health* 95:224–32.

Sampson, Robert J., and William J. Wilson. 1995. "Toward a Theory of Race, Crime, and Urban Inequality." In *Crime and Inequality*, ed. John Hagan and Ruth D. Peterson. Stanford, CA: Stanford University Press.

Sellin, Thorsten. 1935. "Race Prejudice in the Administration of Justice." *American Journal of Sociology* 41:212–17.

Shaw, Clifford R., and Henry D. McKay. 1942. *Juvenile Delinquency and Urban Areas.* Chicago: University of Chicago Press.

Skogan, Wesley G. 2005. "Citizen Satisfaction with Police Encounters." *Police Quarterly* 8:298–321.

Smith, Brent L., and Kelly R. Damphouse. 1996. "Punishing Political Offenders: The Effect of Political Motive on Federal Sentencing Decisions." *Criminology* 34:289–321.

Smith, Douglas A., Christy Visher, and Laura A. Davidson. 1984. "Equity and Discretionary Justice: The Influence of Race on Police Arrest Decisions." *Journal of Criminal Law and Criminology* 75:234–49.

Smith, Paul E., and Richard O. Hawkins. 1973. "Victimization, Types of Citizen-Police Contacts, and Attitudes toward Police." *Law and Society Review* 8:135–52.

Smith, William R., Donald Tomaskovic-Devey, Matthew Zingraff, H. Marcinda Mason, Patricia Y. Warren, Cynthia P. Wright, Harvey McMurray, and C. Robert Fenlon. 2003. *The North Carolina Highway Traffic Study: Final Report to the National Institute of Justice.* Washington, DC: US Department of Justice.

Sorensen, Jonathan R., James W. Marquart, and Deon E. Brock. 1993. "Factors Related to Killings of Felons by Police Officers: A Test of the Community Violence and Conflict Hypotheses." *Justice Quarterly* 10:417–40.

Sorensen, Jonathan, and Donald H. Wallace. 1999. "Prosecutorial Discretion in Seeking Death: An Analysis of Racial Disparity in the Pretrial Stages of Case Processing in a Midwestern County. *Justice Quarterly* 16:559–78.

Sparger, Jerry R. and David Giacopassi. 1992. "Memphis Revisited: A Reexamination of Police Shootings after the *Garner* decision." *Justice Quarterly* 9:211–25.

Spohn, Cassia. 2000. "Thirty Years of Sentencing Reform: The Quest for a Racially-Neutral Sentencing Process. In *Policies, Processes, and Decisions of the Criminal Justice System*, vol. 3, ed. Julie Horney. Washington, DC: National Institute of Justice.

———. 2009. "Race, Sex and Pretrial Detention in Federal Court: Indirect Effects and Cumulative Disadvantage." *University of Kansas Law Review* 57:879–901.

Spohn, Cassia, John Gruhl, and Susan Welch. 1987. "The Impact of the Ethnicity and Gender of Defendants on the Decision To Reject or Dismiss Felony Charges." *Criminology* 25:175–91.

Spohn Cassia, and David Holleran. 2000. "The Imprisonment Penalty Paid by Young, Unemployed Black and Hispanic Male Offenders." *Criminology* 38:281–306.

Spohn, Cassia, and Lisa L. Sample. Forthcoming. "The Dangerous Drug Offender in Federal Court: Intersections of Race, Ethnicity, and Culpability." *Crime and Delinquency*.

Spohn, Cassia, and Jeffrey Spears. 1996. "The Effect of Offender and Victim Characteristics on Sexual Assault Case Processing Decisions." *Justice Quarterly* 13:649–79.

———. 2003. "Sentencing of Drug Offenders in Three Cities: Does Race/Ethnicity Make a Difference?" In *Crime Control and Social Justice: The Delicate Balance*, ed. Darnell F. Hawkins, Samuel L. Myers Jr., and Randolph N. Stone. Westport, CT: Greenwood.

Steen, Sara, Rodney L. Engen, and Randy R. Gainey. 2005. "Images of Danger and Culpability: Racial Stereotyping, Case Processing, and Criminal Sentencing." *Criminology* 43:435–68.

Steffensmeier, Darrell, and Stephen Demuth. 2006. "Does Gender Modify the Effects of Race-Ethnicity on Criminal Sanctioning? Sentences for Male and Female White, Black, and Hispanic Defendants." *Journal of Quantitative Criminology* 22:241–61.

Steffensmeier, Darrell, Jeffery T. Ulmer, and John H. Kramer. 1998. "The Interaction of Race, Gender, and Age in Criminal Sentencing: The Punishment Cost of Being Young, Black, and Male." *Criminology* 36:763–98.

The Sentencing Project. 2004. *Schools and Prisons: Fifty Years after Brown v. Board of Education*. Washington, DC: The Sentencing Project.

Tonry, Michael. 1995. *Malign Neglect: Race, Crime and Punishment in America*. New York: Oxford University Press.

Tonry, Michael, and Matthew Melewski. 2008. "The Malign Effects of Drug and Crime Control Policies on Black Americans." In *Crime and Justice: A Review of Research*, vol. 37, edited by Michael Tonry. Chicago: University of Chicago Press.

Turk, Austin. 1969. *Criminality and Legal Order*. Chicago: Rand McNally.

Turner, Billie M., Rickie D. Lovell, John C. Young, and William F. Denny. 1986. Race and Peremptory Challenges during Voir Dire: Do Prosecution and Defense Agree?" *Journal of Criminal Justice* 14:61–69.

Ulmer, Jeffery T. 1997. *Social Worlds of Sentencing: Court Communities under Sentencing Guidelines*. Albany, NY: SUNY Press.

Ulmer, Jeffery T., and John H. Kramer. 1996. "Court Communities under Sentencing Guidelines: Dilemmas of Formal Rationality and Sentencing Disparity." *Criminology* 34, no. 3: 383–408.

Unah, Isaac, and Jack Boger. 2001. "Race and the Death Penalty in North Carolina: An Empirical Analysis, 1993–1997." http://www.common-sense.org/pdfs/NCDeath-PenaltyReport2001.pdf.

United States Department of Commerce, Bureau of the Census. 1918. *Negro Population: 1790–1915*. Washington, DC: US Government Printing Office.

United States General Accounting Office. 1990. *Death Penalty Sentencing: Research Indicates Pattern of Racial Disparities.* Washington, DC: US General Accounting Office.

United States Sentencing Commission. 1995. *Substantial Assistance Departures in the United States.* Washington, DC: US Sentencing Commission.

Walker, Samuel, Cassia Spohn, and Miriam DeLone. 2007. *The Color of Justice: Race, Ethnicity and Crime in America.* Belmont, CA: Thomson/Wadsworth.

Walsh, Anthony. 1987. "The Sexual Stratification Hypothesis and Sexual Assault in Light of the Changing Conceptions of Race." *Criminal Justice and Behavior* 12:289–303.

Warren, Patricia, Donald Tomaskovic-Devey, William Smith, Matthew Zingraff, and H. Marcinda Mason. 2006. "Driving While Black: Bias Processes and Racial Disparity in Police Stops." *Criminology* 44:709–38.

Weitzer, Ronald. 2000. "Racialized Policing: Residents' Perceptions in Three Neighborhoods." *Law and Society Review* 34:129–55.

———. 2002. "Incidents of Police Misconduct and Public Opinion." *Journal of Criminal Justice* 30:397–408.

Weitzer, Ronald, and Steven Tuch. 2004. "Race and Perceptions of Police Misconduct." *Social Problems* 51:305–25.

Welsh-Huggins, Andrew. 2005. "Death Penalty Unequal." *Cincinnati Enquirer,* May 7, 51.

Western, Bruce. 2006. *Punishment and Inequality in America.* New York: Russell Sage.

Wilbanks. William. 1985. *The Myth of a Racist Criminal Justice System.* Monterey, CA: Brooks/Cole.

Withrow, Brian L. 2006. *Racial Profiling: From Rhetoric to Reason.* Upper Saddle River, NJ: Pearson.

Wolfgang, Marvin E., and Marc Riedel. 1973. "Race, Judicial Discretion, and the Death Penalty." *Annals of the American Academy of Political and Social Science* 407:119–33.

Wooldredge, John. 1998. "Analytical Rigor in Studies of Disparities in Criminal Case Processing." *Journal of Quantitative Criminology* 14:155–79.

Zatz, Marjorie . 1984. "Race, Ethnicity, and Determinate Sentencing: A New Dimension to an Old Controversy." *Criminology* 22:147–71.

———. 1987. "The Changing Forms of Racial/Ethnic Biases in Sentencing." *Journal of Research in Crime and Delinquency* 24:69–92.

Zatz, Marjorie S., and Richard P. Krecker Jr. 2003. "Anti-Gang Initiative as Racialized Policy." In *Crime Control and Social Justice: The Delicate Balance*, ed. Darnell F. Hawkins, Samuel L. Myers Jr., and Randolph N. Stone. Westport, CT: Greenwood.

CHAPTER 12

SEX, GENDER, AND CRIME

ROSEMARY GARTNER

ASK people to imagine a criminal and most will see a male, probably young and possibly nonwhite. Ask them to visualize a crime victim and many will picture a female, perhaps a small child or an elderly woman, a teenaged girl or a young wife. Ask them whether men and women are treated differently by the police or the courts and many will say women often receive sympathy, understanding, or a "slap on the wrist" for behaviors that men are convicted and imprisoned for.

In ways they have not in the past, scholars now recognize that notions about masculinity and femininity are embedded in, and influence criminal behaviors and the operation of, the criminal justice system. The term "gender"—a socially constructed characteristic of individuals, as well as social relations, interactions, and institutions—regularly appears in current research and policy about crime and criminal justice. In contrast, the term "sex," where it refers to the categorization of people as biologically female or male[1], has been relegated to the sidelines. Consider the number of surveys that ask people to identify not their "sex" but their "gender," as either "male" or "female." This shift in terminology has opened up new avenues for thinking about crime, but it also has important limitations. Offenders experience their crimes through both sexed and gendered bodies, and they target victims with sexed and gendered bodies. Furthermore, the criminal justice system—police, courts, jails, and prisons—acts on sexed and gendered bodies.[2]

For these and other reasons, this article includes "sex" in its title. Sex deserves attention because official organizations and surveys provide data not on gender but on sex. For example, the FBI, in its Uniform Crime Reports (UCR), categorizes arrestees not as "masculine" or "feminine" but as "male" or "female." As a legal category, sex also plays a role in the definition of some criminal acts. Only females can commit the crime of infanticide in legal systems that define this as a separate category of homicide.[3] Furthermore, sex is important to several explanations of criminal behavior including developmental, socio-biological, and psycho-physiological perspectives. This article, then, assumes that both sex and gender are reflected in criminal behavior, criminal justice institutions, and the criminal law.

Those who work on issues related to sex, gender, and crime do so for different reasons. Some, particularly criminologists, are interested in understanding and developing explanations for people's criminal behavior. Because sex and gender are strongly associated with crime, they are expected to offer insights into its causes. Other scholars—especially historians and feminists—study sex, gender, and crime as a way to explore gender relations, social norms and cultural ideologies about masculinity and femininity, and gendered sources of inequality. They seek to identify the ways legal institutions, criminal justice practices, and criminal behavior reflect and reinforce a society's gender order.[4] Developing appropriate interventions, services, and resources for women and men who come into contact with the criminal justice system, as victims or offenders, motivates the work of many criminal justice scholars and professionals. Finally, legal scholars, philosophers, and political scientists, among others, explore topics related to sex, gender, and crime out of an interest in concepts such as justice, equality, and discrimination. The first and second types of work are the focus of this article.

Section I describes sex-specific patterns of offending and discusses explanations for sex similarities and differences in criminal behavior. Section II focuses on sex-specific patterns of victimization, and follows the same organization as the previous section. Section III reviews data and research on how sex and gender influence criminalization, and outlines explanations for these influences. Section IV offers a brief discussion of the policy implications of current knowledge about sex, gender, and crime and priorities for future research.

Among the article's major findings:

- Males outnumber females as criminal offenders in all societies and time periods for which records are available. The more serious the crime, the more males outnumber females. Males are more criminally active than females because of the ways in which sex differences in neuro-cognitive functioning and in socialization interact with gendered social practices and inequalities.
- Although female and male offenders engage in somewhat different types of crime and commit crimes in distinctive ways, they have much in common. Their early lives, personal characteristics, and motivations appear to be more similar than different. Furthermore, the social environments that increase their risks of offending are similar.
- Males also outnumber females as victims of crime, but to a lesser extent and with some exceptions. In particular, females outnumber males as victims of serious intimate partner violence. However, most violent crime is between males and is motivated by what antagonists see as challenges to their masculinity. In times and places where masculinity is primarily defined in

terms of dominance, aggression, and willingness to take risks, violence is more common and more male-dominated.

- Rates of female and male offending and victimization, on the whole, have been declining in the United States since the early to mid-1990s. Sex-specific rates of many types of violent crime have reached their lowest levels in more than thirty years. In other words, both sexes have contributed to the "great American crime decline" (Zimring 2007).
- Women's involvement in violence, as both victims and offenders, appears to be less concentrated in the home and among family members and intimate partners than it has been in the past. This is due in part to a greater drop in "domestic violence" than other forms of violence in recent years.
- Male offenders are treated more punitively by the criminal justice system than female offenders, even when legal factors such as prior record and seriousness of the crime are taken into account. The comparative lenience toward females has been linked to chivalry, paternalism, and pragmatism. Lawyers, judges, and juries have at times seen women as less responsible for their crimes, more sinned against than sinning, or in need of protection rather than punishment.
- There is some evidence that the disparity in the treatment of females and males by the criminal justice system is diminishing. For example, growing intolerance for minor forms of violence has increased the likelihood that violence by women and girls will be criminalized.

Criminal offending and victimization are largely a "man's game." Variations over time and across societies in crime, especially violent crime, are driven primarily by men's behavior. Where and when violent crime is more common, it is also more male-dominated. Despite this, the causes and consequences of both offending and victimization probably are less distinctive between the sexes than is often believed. One of the reasons for this belief is that gender shapes our understanding of crime and our assumptions about criminals and victims. This is as true of scholars as it is of anyone else. As a consequence, the ways society responds to crime and the ways scholars study crime almost inevitably reflect assumptions about sex and gender, men and women. These are some of the reasons that the topic of sex, gender, and crime is such an important and enduring area of inquiry.

I. Sex, Gender, and Offending

Probably the questions most often asked about sex, gender, and crime are how and why females and males differ in their criminal behavior, particularly their violent offending. In this section, I review evidence from the contemporary United States and from other countries and time periods that shows remarkable consistency in sex differences in violent offending. By comparison, the relationship between sex and nonviolent crime varies somewhat more over time and place.

Explanations of offending by females and males have focused on both similarities and differences between the sexes in their criminal behavior, and on both sex and gender as the sources of the differences.

A. Research on the Gender Gap in Crime

A good deal of research on sex, gender, and offending[5] has looked at what is called "the gender gap in crime"—or the disparity between males and females in the prevalence of offending. The questions typically posed are: "Has the gender gap narrowed over time?" and "Are women becoming 'more like men' in their criminal behavior?" For over a century, scholars have predicted that the gap would become smaller as gender inequality diminished but have found little support for this prediction. Nevertheless, the debate over whether the gender gap in crime has narrowed is as strong as ever and is fueled by disagreements over how to measure the gap, how to explain trends in it, and what constitutes stability vs. change (see, e.g., Heimer, Lauritsen, and Lynch 2009; Lauritsen, Heimer, and Lynch 2009; Schwartz et al. 2009). With each passing year there are more data to analyze and more sophisticated methods with which to analyze them, thus there is unlikely to be a natural end to the debate.

Research on the gender gap in crime is not without its critics. Some object to what they see as the implicit assumption that female crime is of interest largely in terms of how it compares to male crime (Heidensohn and Gelsthorpe 2007). Another limitation is that many studies report trends only in the gender gap but not in the separate male and female rates that constitute it, making it impossible to determine whose rates have changed and how. For example, the gender gap in offending could narrow because female and male crime rates both decrease, but the latter decreases more; female rates increase while male rates decrease or remain stable; female and male rates both increase, but the former increases more. Interpreting a narrowing of the gender gap in crime depends on which of these trends is responsible for it. Explaining a decrease in the gender gap by focusing on changes in women's lives could be misguided if changes in men's offending are largely responsible for it. For these and other reasons, I do not discuss findings from research specifically about trends in the gender gap in crime.

B. Sex-specific Levels and Trends in Offending

For more than one hundred years, scholars from different disciplines have documented, analyzed, and attempted to explain similarities and differences between female and male offenders. Cesare Lombroso (1893) and Willem Bonger (1916) did so in the late nineteenth and early twentieth centuries; W. I. Thomas (1923) and Sheldon and Eleanor Glueck (1934) followed in the 1920s and 1930s; Otto Pollak (1951) and Gisela Konopka (1966) contributed to this work in the 1950s and 1960s; and in the 1970s feminist perspectives on women and crime emerged (Klein 1973; Smart 1976). Much of the work prior to the 1970s has been roundly criticized and relegated to footnotes in criminology texts. This is unfortunate because early scholarship provides important historical data on the ways crime has been patterned by sex, along with revealing earlier taken-for-granted notions about sex, gender, and crime.[6] I draw on some of these data below but first present more recent evidence about sex and offending.

Criminal behaviors of females and males can be described using official arrest statistics, crime victims' descriptions of their assailants, and self-reports of offending. Each source tells the same story: Males commit more crime than females. This sex difference varies, however, by the type of crime, characteristics of the offenders, and social context.

1. *Violent Offending in the United States*

Data on arrests for criminal homicide provide one of the most accurate pictures of sex differences in violent offending. Males greatly outnumber females among those arrested for homicide in the United States, according to the FBI's Uniform Crime Reports (UCR).[7] In 2007, for example, males accounted for 90 percent of all people arrested for homicide. Despite this difference in magnitude, male and female homicide arrest rates share many of the same structural correlates[8] and follow similar trends over time (Steffensmeier and Haynie 2000; Schwartz 2006). At the beginning of the twenty-first century, homicide arrest rates for both sexes reached their lowest points since the 1960s.

The size of the sex difference in homicide varies by other characteristics of offenders. For example, arrest rates for black males aged eighteen to twenty-four are about seventeen times larger than rates for black females in the same age group, whereas arrest rates for white males aged eighteen to twenty-four are about eleven times larger than rates for white females in the same age group. In other words, homicides by blacks are more male-dominated than homicides by whites. Similarly, homicides by those under eighteen are more male-dominated than homicides by those eighteen and older.

Women and men differ in whom they kill. Males are most likely to kill what police term "acquaintances"[9] (55 percent of homicides by males); strangers make up the next largest proportion of male killers' victims (25 percent). Intimate partners account for only about 10 percent of the victims of male killers. By contrast, female killers are most likely to target their intimate partners (37 percent of homicides by females) or their children (10 percent). Less than 10 percent of female killers target strangers. The proportion of victims of female homicides who are family members or intimate partners has decreased somewhat over time (Zahn and McCall 1999). This shift is due partly to a dramatic drop in killings of males by their female intimate partners since the early 1990s (Rosenfeld 2009).

Sex differences in nonlethal violence can be measured with both UCR arrest data and data from the National Crime Victimization Survey (NCVS)[10], which asks victims of violence about the sex of their victimizers. According to both data sources, the sex difference in offending is not as large for nonlethal violence as it is for homicide, although males still commit about 80 percent of all nonlethal violent crime (table 12.1). In general, the more serious the violence, the more males predominate among offenders.

The "crime drop" that began in the early to mid-1990s in the United States is a consequence of reductions in violent offending by both sexes. Robbery and aggravated and simple assault rates decreased for females and males, and were lower in the first years of the twenty-first century than in the previous three decades, according to the NCVS (Lauritsen, Heimer, and Lynch 2009); UCR arrest data largely, but not completely, parallel these findings. Arrests of females and males for robbery and aggravated assault have dropped since at least the mid-1990s. Despite this decline, arrests of females for aggravated assault are still substantially higher now than in the 1980s (Schwartz, Steffensmeier, and Feldmeyer 2009). Two interpretations of the relatively high arrest rates of females for assault early in the twenty-first century have been offered. They could reflect a real change in women's violence. Alternatively, they could reflect changes in police responses, such that women's violence is more likely to be criminalized now than in the past. There is support for both interpretations and, of course, both could be correct. Nonetheless, the weight of the evidence indicates that both men and women contributed to the 1990s crime drop in the United States by reducing their violent behavior.

Sex differences in the relationships between offenders and their victims are less dramatic for nonlethal violence than for lethal violence. For example, intimate partners account for a similar and relatively small percentage (approximately 10 percent) of the victims of both female and male violent offenders. Female violent offenders,

Table 12.1. Percentage of violent crimes committed by males, according to official statistics and reports from crime victims

	FBI UCR	NCVS
% of offenders who were male		
Robbery	88%	88%
Aggravated assaults	79%	81%
Simple/other assaults	75%	75%

Sources: *Uniform Crime Reports,* Federal Bureau of Investigation, 2007; *National Crime Victimization Survey,* Bureau of Justice Statistics, 2006.

however, are much more likely to know their victims than are male violent offenders. Since about 1994, arrests of males and females for nonlethal violence against all types of victims have dropped, with one exception. The exception is arrests of women for nonlethal intimate partner violence, which—in contrast to intimate partner homicide by women—have not declined since the early 1990s. This may reflect real stability in intimate partner violence by females; or it may reflect greater willingness of males to report violence by their female partners, greater willingness of police to arrest women for intimate partner violence, or both (Chesney-Lind 2002; Miller 2005; Henning, Renauer, and Holdford 2006).

2. Violent Offending in Other Countries

The overrepresentative of males among homicide offenders extends to other countries. For example, in Canada, Australia, Hong Kong, England and Wales, and most European countries males account for between 87 percent and 92 percent of homicide offenders (Broadhurst 1999; Aebi et al. 2006; Li 2008; Australian Institute of Criminology 2009; Povey et al. 2009).[11] Sex-specific trends in homicide arrest rates track each other relatively closely over time in other Western countries, as they do in the United States. There is another important similarity between trends in homicide in the United States and trends elsewhere: Homicides by women have been shifting away from the home and the family in recent decades. In Canada, for example, about 80 percent of female killers targeted family members or intimate partners in the 1960s compared to only 50 percent in recent years (Gartner 1995; Dauvergne 2005).

Nonlethal violence in other countries appears to be even more male-dominated than in the United States. In countries reporting data to the European Sourcebook of Crime and Criminal Justice Statistics (ESCCJ), males accounted for an average of 91 percent of arrests for assault, 93 percent of arrests for robbery, and 99 percent of arrests for rape (Aebi et al. 2006). Victimization and self-report offending data replicate these patterns (van Kesteren, Mayhew, and Nieuwbeerta 2004; Budd, Sharp, and Mayhew 2005; Hansen 2006; van Dijk, van Kesteren, and Smit 2007).

3. Nonviolent Offending in the United States

Compared to violent crimes, nonviolent crimes in the United States are less male-dominated, and in a few cases not male-dominated at all. Although males accounted for 66 percent of all property crime arrests in the United States in 2007, females were more likely than males to be arrested for embezzlement, prostitution, and running away. The last two offenses have historically been thought of as "female crimes." That females continue to outnumber males in arrests for prostitution and running away—which are profoundly influenced by discretionary enforcement practices and decisions—indicates that the US criminal justice system remains gendered in important respects.

Sex-specific trends in nonviolent crimes have been documented using unpublished sources and data sets. Heimer (2000) did so and found that between the mid- to late 1980s and 1997, male arrest rates for a range of property crimes declined. The picture for females is more complicated. While arrests of females for larceny, motor vehicle theft, and burglary declined (albeit negligibly in some cases), arrests of females for forgery and embezzlement increased.

4. *Nonviolent Offending in Other Countries*

Nonviolent crimes are also largely the province of males in other countries. In Canada and England and Wales, for example, males accounted for (respectively) 76 percent and 69 percent of arrests for property crimes, a slightly larger percentage than in the United States (Kong and AuCoin 2008; Ministry of Justice 2009). In most European countries males account for an average of 85 percent of arrests for theft and drug offenses (Aebi et al. 2006), meaning that nonviolent crimes may be more male-dominated in other countries than in the United States. However, similar to the United States, in other countries females consistently outnumber males in arrests for prostitution-related offenses.

5. *Offending by Young People in the United States*

Arrest data from the UCR, self-report offending data and victimization reports from the NCVS all show that male youths are more likely to engage in crime, especially violent crime, than female youths. The proportions of juvenile arrests accounted for by males are remarkably similar to the proportions of adult arrests accounted for by males: 82 percent of juveniles arrested for violent crime and 66 percent of juveniles arrested for property crime were male. Crime victims similarly report that about 85 percent of the juveniles who victimized them were males. Self-reports from high school students collected annually from 1991 for the Monitoring the Future (MTF) project show males outnumbered females in each of the thirteen different violent and property crimes measured in the survey; this sex difference tended to be largest for the most serious crimes (Johnston, Bachman, and O'Malley various years).

Violence by girls and boys has—depending on the data source—either been stable or decreased since the early 1990s, with one exception. After the mid-1990s arrests of girls for simple assaults increased, whereas arrests of boys decreased. Net-widening practices by schools and criminal justice institutions—such as zero tolerance and mandatory arrest policies—appear to be responsible for much if not all of this increase (Steffensmeier et al. 2005; Chesney-Lind and Irwin 2008; Goodkind et al. 2009). Consequently, popular concerns about a rise in violence by young females are very likely misplaced.

6. *Offending by Young People in Other Countries*

The sex distribution of offending by young people in other countries largely parallels that in the United States. In the International Self-Reported Delinquency Study, boys reported much greater involvement than girls in serious and violent offending in each of the ten European countries participating in the survey. In contrast, girls and boys reported similar levels of truancy and running away, and only small differences (with higher rates for boys) in property offending and vandalism (Junger-Tas, Marshall, and Ribeaud 2003). These patterns are consistent with official statistics and other self-report surveys in these and other countries. Girls outnumber boys only in prostitution-related arrests and—in some cases—in self-reported shoplifting (Wikstrom and Butterworth 2007; Sprott and Doob 2009). In the United Kingdom and Canada, as in the United States, arrests of girls for less serious assaults have increased. This too appears to reflect not so much a change in girls' violence as a change in official responses to it (Carrington 2006; Heidensohn and Gelsthorpe 2007; Sprott and Doob 2009).

7. *Offending Over the Centuries*

Historical research in various jurisdictions shows that men have outnumbered women among serious and violent offenders in virtually all societies and eras for which information is available. In their summaries of dozens of studies in Europe from the thirteenth century on, both Eisner (2003) and Gurr (1989) concluded that males consistently accounted for between about 85 percent and 95 percent of serious violent offenses. Bonger (1916) reported a similar sex distribution in violent offending in late nineteenth-century Germany, Italy, France, the Netherlands, and England.

Similarly, in North America from colonial times to the nineteenth century, about 90 percent of serious violent offenses were committed by males (Lane 1997; Bellesiles 1999), with a few notable but unsurprising exceptions. In some frontier areas and early settlements dominated by the military, males were responsible for more than 95 percent of serious violent crimes. This was a consequence of both highly skewed sex ratios and the cultures of violence that often develop in places with many young, unattached males (Courtwright 1996; May and Phillips 2001; Peterson del Mar 2002). Another exception is the southern United States, where historically serious violence has been unusually male-dominated (Vandal 2000). These are places and times in which homicide rates were quite high, suggesting that where serious violence is more prevalent, it is also more male-dominated—a pattern that occurs in victimization as well. By the late nineteenth and early twentieth centuries, the sex distribution of homicide offending in major North American cities looked much as it did over the rest of the twentieth century, with males on average accounting for between 85 percent to 90 percent of killers (Lane 1997; Monkkonen 2001; Adler 2006).

The conclusion that historically homicide offending has been an overwhelmingly male phenomenon can be challenged in one important respect. Discarded and badly buried bodies of newborns and infants who showed signs of violence were discovered with considerable frequency in Europe and America from at least the sixteenth century to the early twentieth century. Certainly many more infants' bodies were never found, and those that were often did not receive serious investigation (Jackson 2002; Adler 2006; Gartner and McCarthy 2006). If infanticides could be accurately counted and included in homicide rates, women may well have outnumbered men as killers in some times and places.

There is substantial consensus that serious interpersonal violence in the Western world decreased from the sixteenth century on (Gurr 1989; Eisner 2003). This appears to have been driven by a drop in brawls, duels, knife fights, and other types of violence typically engaged in by young males in public places (Spierenburg 1998; Shoemaker 2002; Kaspersson 2003). While some have explained this by reference to an apparently gender-neutral "civilizing process," others argue that changing notions of masculinity were deeply implicated in this long-term decline in violence. In the early modern period, ideal masculinity was defined in terms of a passionate and impulsive willingness to use violence to defend one's honor, one's family, and one's possessions. By the late eighteenth and early nineteenth centuries, a new form of masculinity—one that emphasized self-restraint, control, rationality, and notions of fairness—began to emerge, particularly in England and later in North America (Wiener 2004; Emsley 2005). Of course, this ideal masculinity was just that and not the only form of masculinity available. Many men still engaged in public displays of violence as well as violence behind closed doors. Importantly, however, the law became less tolerant of male violence over time, wherever it occurred, reflecting and reinforcing a new version of masculinity.

While reliable data on property crimes by women and men over the centuries are not available, it is possible to get a general sense of sex differences in property offending from the historical record. Most types of property crime had much smaller sex differences than violent crimes. In fact, at times women apparently were as likely or even slightly more likely than males to engage in thefts, frauds, and other property offenses. Just over half of those charged with property crimes at the Old Bailey between 1690 and 1713 were female (Beattie 2001), a proportion similar to that in Amsterdam and other northern European cities in the seventeenth and eighteenth centuries (Eisner 2003). The particularly harsh economic climate faced by women who migrated to cities from rural areas was partly responsible for their relatively high rates of property crime. In addition, women's participation in the preindustrial mercantile economy provided them many opportunities to engage in economic crimes. As production moved from the home to the factory in the eighteenth century, women's share of property offending dropped (Feeley and Little 1991). By the late nineteenth century, women accounted for about 20 percent of those charged with and convicted of thefts and frauds in England, Austria, Italy,

France, and the Netherlands[12](Bonger 1916)—a smaller proportion than in these countries currently. This may represent a real reduction in women's property crimes; or perhaps the new form of masculinity that emerged in the nineteenth century encouraged greater lenience in legal responses to women's property crimes.

C. Characteristics of Female and Male Offenders

In the United States and elsewhere, males and females who engage in crime have much in common. They tend to be young, undereducated and underemployed, economically disadvantaged, and not married. Often they abuse drugs and/or alcohol. Dysfunctional family backgrounds, histories of physical abuse, sexual abuse, and mental health problems also characterize the childhood and adolescence of many offenders, both male and female (Lanctôt and LeBlanc 2002; Farrington and Painter 2004; Junger-Tas, Ribeaud, and Cruyff 2004). The types of childhood conduct problems that predict violence in adulthood, including violence against intimate partners, are the same for females and males (Moffitt et al. 2001; Henning, Jones, and Holdford 2003). Furthermore, the developmental patterns, pathways to serious offending by adolescents, and linkages between adolescent and adult offending are also similar for the two sexes (Lanctôt and LeBlanc 2002; Odgers et al. 2008; Johansson and Kempf-Leonard 2009), as are the processes of desistance from crime (Giordano, Cernkovich, and Rudolph 2002). Thus, while there are sex differences in the trajectories into and out of offending—for example, females' involvement in crime tends to begin, peak, and end earlier—these are differences more of degree than kind.

There has been and continues to be considerable debate over whether females' and males' motivations for crime are distinctly different. Research suggests that on the whole they are not. Women and men, now and in the past, engage in property crimes for a diverse but common array of reasons—economic need, peer pressure, greed, alcohol and drug habits, excitement, and impulse (Maher 1997; Walker 2003; Palk 2006). In contrast to violence by men, violence by women conventionally is viewed as a response to victimization, a consequence of mental disorder, or a desperate, impulsive loss of control. This is a narrow reading of women's violence. Preservation of honor, reputation and respect, retaliation, jealousy, self-help, and illicit gain all emerge as motivations for violence for both sexes, in contemporary times and in the past (Kruttschnitt and Carbone-Lopez 2006; Miller and Mullins 2006; Spierenburg 2008.) Violence by females, similar to violence by males, is often the intentional behavior of a self-conscious agent, albeit one whose "choice is not completely free in a world of intersubjective construction and power disparity" (Sjoberg and Gentry 2007, 17; see also Morrissey 2003; Murphy and Whitty 2006).[13] None of this is to deny that the ways and situations in which females and males commit crimes are distinctive in some respects. For example, men are much more likely to use firearms when committing violent crimes and to engage in "overkill" in intimate partner homicides; women's violence is more likely to take place in private locations and is probably motivated by self-preservation more often than men's. Nevertheless, the sexes are much more distinctive in the *extent* of their involvement in crime than in the *reasons* for that involvement.

Many scholars have explored the generality of theories of crime for females and males and asked if similar characteristics are associated with their criminal behaviors. In general, the answer is yes. For example, delinquent or criminal peers; absence of informal social controls from family and school; limited attachment to parents and teachers; and harsh and erratic parental discipline all predict involvement in crime for adolescent females and males (Meadows 2007; Wikstrom and Butterworth 2007; Bell 2009). Similarly, although the concept of "blurred boundaries" between victimization (as a child or an adult) and subsequent offending was initially applied to women's offending (Daly 1992), offenders of both sexes tend to have extensive histories of victimization in their early lives (Belknap and Holsinger 2006; Daigle, Cullen, and Wright 2007; Cernkovich, Lanctôt, and Giordano 2008). Living in unsafe neighborhoods, attending poorly resourced and dangerous schools, belonging to ethnic/cultural/racialized groups that are disadvantaged and discriminated against—all of these raise the risks of criminal behavior for both males and females. In multivariate analyses, the effects of some explanatory variables are sometimes stronger for one sex than the other; the sex differences in these effects are not consistent across studies and therefore do not make a strong case for sex- or gender-specific theories of crime.

D. Explanations of Sex Differences in Offending

If the sexes are more alike than different in the nature of their criminal behavior and the factors associated with it, why are they so different in the levels of their offending? One important reason is sex differences in socialization practices and family supervision that encourage conventional behavior among girls and risk-taking behavior among boys (Hagan 1988). Girls are less likely to engage in delinquent acts because they are socialized to fear risky behaviors, to develop empathy for others, to value close personal and family relationships, and to avoid aggression; and because they are likely to spend more time with family members and other girls who reinforce conventional behavior. In contrast, boys are typically encouraged to value risk-taking, to associate masculinity with physical power and control, and to prize autonomy and independence; and they are likely to spend their time with male peers who reinforce these characteristics. Delinquent activities for boys then tend to be more rewarding and more affirming of their identities. These tendencies are reinforced as boys and girls move into adolescence and early adulthood, when women's criminal opportunities are more limited than men's, and women's family responsibilities make the costs of crime greater for them (Steffensmeier and Allan 1996).

There is widespread agreement that these differences in gender socialization are an important source of sex differences in crime generally, as well as the larger sex difference in violent crime. There are, however, other approaches to understanding sex differences in criminal behavior: while they do not fundamentally challenge this explanation, they frame it differently. Some approaches do so by emphasizing sex, others do so by emphasizing gender as a social institution and a social practice.

Biological sex is key to developmental approaches that focus on differences between males and females in neuro-cognitive functioning and deficits (Moffitt et al. 2001).[14] Males are more likely than females to experience poor impulse control, hyperactivity, and difficult temperaments. Females tend to acquire social information processing skills earlier in life, which allow them to develop empathy and anticipate the consequences of their actions (Bennett, Farrington, and Huesmann 2005). As a consequence of these differences, boys are more vulnerable than girls to stressful life events and to risk factors—particularly delinquent peers and poor parental supervision—associated with problem behavior and crime. In general, males and females are endowed with some sex-specific biological and genetic factors that shape how they understand, interact with, and are affected by their environments from a very early age.

An alternative way to frame the socialization explanation of sex differences in crime emphasizes gender, not sex. Here gender is a characteristic not only of individuals, but also a feature of social relations and interactions, power arrangements, and institutional processes. Many gender-based perspectives argue that sex differences in socialization, supervision, family attachments, and peer networks are all a function of and exist within a broader set of patriarchal arrangements (Giordano, Deines, and Cernkovich 2006). Parents do not "naturally" choose to socialize girls to spend more time with their families, avoid risky activities and deviant peers, or define crime as a male activity. Nor do parents "naturally" socialize boys so that they spend less time with their families and more time in unsupervised activities with male peers, seek excitement through risk-taking, and find criminal behavior rewarding. Rather, these are gendered social practices (Bottcher 2001\) that reflect and reinforce modern Western society's gender order and the inequalities that accompany it. One of the consequences of these practices is the sex difference in crime.

One criticism of all of these approaches is that they depict females and males as essentially passive beings whose behaviors are determined by socialization, brain functioning, and/or patriarchal structures. To counterbalance this tendency, some work has treated gender as an emergent property of social relations and interactions, not a fixed role or trait. Because gender is accomplished, not given, and because it is highly flexible, females and males are active participants in creating it and make choices about how to enact it. Committing crimes that are risky, violent, and allow one to dominate others is a way for men and boys to accomplish a certain type of masculinity. For women and girls, these sorts of crimes are unlikely to be resources for accomplishing femininity in most contexts (Messerschmidt 2004; Hobbs, O'Brien, and Westmarland 2007).

Each of these accounts contributes to our understanding of why males are more likely to engage in crime than females. The factors and processes identified in these accounts almost certainly interact with each other, altering their role in criminal behavior in complex ways. More research is needed that integrates concepts and findings from the extensive research on sex and gender differences in crime and that avoids treating these as competing ways of understanding the criminal behavior of females and males.

II. Sex, Gender, and Victimization

Compared to research on offending, research on how victimization is shaped by sex and gender is of more contemporary origin. In the 1970s, feminist criminologists generated a variety of theoretical frameworks that encouraged and informed work on the victimization of women. In addition, the development and growth of large-scale victimization surveys in the 1970s and 1980s provided greater opportunities for research on sex differences in victimization.

A. Sex-specific Levels and Trends in Violent Victimization

Sex-specific patterns of violent victimization can be documented from official statistics on homicide and from victimization surveys on other types of violence. According to evidence from the United States and other countries, while males outnumber females among victims of violence, sex differences in victimization are much smaller than sex differences in offending. This section reviews data on lethal and nonlethal victimization, in general, and then turns to intimate partner victimization. It concludes with a brief discussion of explanations for sex differences in victimization.

1. Violent Victimization in the United States

The more serious the violence, the greater the sex differences in victimization. Currently in the United States almost 80 percent of homicide victims are male. Even so, trends in female and male homicide victimization rates—as with homicide offending rates—track each other closely over time (Marvel and Moody 1999) and are associated with similar social characteristics (Batton 2004). In 2007 rates for both sexes reached their lowest point since the mid-1960s, having dropped steadily from about 1993 (fig. 12.1).

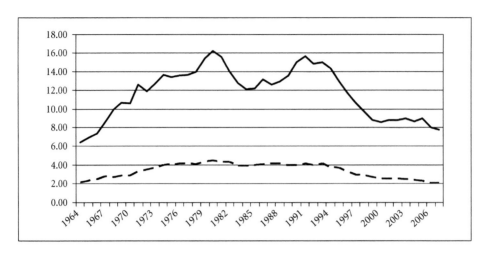

Figure 12.1. Male and Female Homicide Victimization Rates, United States, 1964–2007
Note: The male victimization rate is indicated by the solid line; the female rate is indicated by the dashed line. *Source: Uniform Crime Reports,* Federal Bureau of Investigation, various years.

The association between sex and homicide victimization is conditioned by other factors. In particular, race differences in homicide victimization can cancel out or even reverse sex differences. For example, in 2007, the victimization rate for black females (5.8 per 100,000 black females) was higher than the rate for white males (4.6 per 100,000 white males). Furthermore, the size of the sex difference also varies by race. Black males were six times more likely to be victims of homicide than black females, whereas white males were only about two-and-one-half times more likely to be victims of homicide than white females in 2007. Race is not the only characteristic that can shape victimization risks more strongly than sex. Age is another: the homicide victimization rate for females aged twenty to twenty-four is greater than the rate for males aged sixty-five to sixty-nine.

Currently in the United States, both females and males are more likely to be killed by an acquaintance than by a family member, intimate partner, or stranger. For males, this has been consistently the case over time; until recently, however, females were more likely to be killed by family members or intimate partners than by acquaintances or strangers. The shift away from "domestic" homicides of females is due in part to a steady drop in family and intimate partner killings of both sexes since the early 1990s (Rosenfeld 2009).

Sex differences in nonlethal victimization are not as large as sex differences in homicide. According to the NCVS, only slightly more than half (53 percent) of the more than 5 million victims of violent crime in 2007 were males (Rand 2008). Males outnumbered females as victims of robbery, aggravated assault, and simple assault, whereas females outnumbered males as victims of sexual assault/rape (table 12.2). As with homicide, race conditions the relationship between sex and victimization. For example, black females have higher victimization rates than white males.

Table 12.2. **Annual victimization rates for males and females (per 100,000 male or female population aged 12 and older) in the United States**

	Males	Females
Robbery	3.4	1.4
Aggravated assault	4.5	2.4
Simple assault	14.5	13.2
Sexual assault	0.1	1.8

Source: National Crime Victimization Survey, Bureau of Justice Statistics, 2006.

Females and males are victimized by different types of people. In 2007 half of male victimizations were by strangers, whereas only 3 percent were by intimate partners. In contrast, strangers accounted for 28 percent of female victimizations whereas intimate partners accounted for fully 23 percent. Similar percentages (44–46 percent) of female and male victims were harmed by acquaintances and family members. Overall, then, males have more distant (if any) relationships with their victimizers compared to females. Indeed, much of the sex difference in victimization is due to the higher rates at which men are attacked by strangers (Lauritsen and Heimer 2008). Describing sex-specific trends in victimization is complicated because of design changes to the NCVS. After correcting for these, Lauritsen and Heimer (2008) found the risks of robbery, aggravated assault, and simple assault declined for both males and females from the mid-1990s through 2007.

2. *Violent Victimization in Other Countries*

Sex differences in homicide vary greatly cross-nationally. In some European nations, where homicide rates are low, males are only slightly more likely than females to be victims (LaFree and Hunnicutt 2006).[15] In Great Britain and its ex-colonies, Canada and Australia, between 60 percent and 65 percent of homicide victims are male. Compared to the United States, then, homicide victimization is not nearly as male dominated in other Western industrialized countries. However, in countries with very high homicide rates—such as Venezuela, Mexico, and Puerto Rico—males account for more than 90 percent of victims. This suggests that where homicide is more common, the population of victims is likely to be more male-dominated. National context can override the rule that males almost universally are at greater risk of homicide than females. For example, between 1950 and 2000, females in Canada, on average, were more likely to be killed than males in Ireland. One pattern consistent across different countries is that females are much more likely to be killed by family members or intimate partners than are males; and males are more likely to be killed by strangers and acquaintances than are females.

For other types of violent victimization, estimates of sex differences vary widely because of differences among countries in victimization survey designs. For example, the British Crime Survey (BCS) and the Personal Safety Survey in Australia find that males are almost twice as likely to be victims of nonlethal violence as females (Kershaw, Nicholas, and Walker 2008; Australian Bureau of Statistics 2005). However, Canada's General Social Survey (GSS) finds little or no sex difference in victimization (Gannon and Mihorean 2005).[16] The International Crime Victim Survey (ICVS) uses the same methodology in participating countries to minimize the effects of design differences. According to the ICVS, male victimization rates are consistently higher than female rates in Europe and North America. In contrast, in Africa, South and Central America, and Asia, women report being victims of nonlethal violence much more often than men (van Kesteren, Mayhew, and Nieuwbeerta 2004; van Dijk 2008).[17]

3. *Intimate Partner Violence in the United States*

Women are between three and four times more likely than men to be killed by their intimate partners in the United States. As with total homicide, the sex difference in intimate partner homicide varies by race: white female victims of intimate partner homicide outnumber white male victims by more than four times, whereas black female victims outnumber black male victims by about two-and-one-half times. Since the mid-1970s, the risks of intimate partner homicide have decreased for both women and men (Rosenfeld 2009), although the drop has been greater for male victims. Overall homicide rates for both sexes have declined over time, so it is unclear how much of the drop in intimate partner homicide is attributable to a more general downturn in violence and how much is due to changes specific to intimate partner homicide. At least some of decline in intimate partner homicides is a consequence of the expansion of domestic violence services and legal reforms. These changes, however, have had the unexpected effect of reducing intimate partner killings of men, but not of women (Dugan, Nagin, and Rosenfeld 2003).

While there is no dispute that women are more likely than men to be killed by an intimate partner, there is considerable debate over whether women are also more likely to be victims of nonlethal partner violence.[18] The debate is fueled by differences across data sources in estimates of partner violence and differences in ideology (Hines 2009).[19] According to the NCVS and the National Violence Against Women Survey (NVAWS)[20], women's risks of nonlethal partner violence are greater than men's (Tjaden and Thoennes 2000). According to the National Family Violence Surveys,[21] a slightly larger proportion of men are victims of nonlethal intimate partner violence (Straus 2004). In general, surveys that capture less severe forms of violence are more likely to find similar or somewhat higher rates of male victimization. Conversely, surveys that capture more serious and more frequent violence find a larger proportion of female victims (Dobash and Dobash 2004). Nonlethal intimate partner violence, like intimate partner homicide, has declined since the mid-1970s, but unlike intimate partner homicide, this is largely due to a drop in female victimization.

4. Intimate Partner Violence in Other Countries

Females outnumber males as victims of intimate partner homicide around the world. However, as with homicide generally, in countries where rates of intimate partner homicide are very high, males account for a particularly large proportion of the killers (WHO 2005). Intimate partner homicide rates have declined over the last several years in some countries—such as Canada and Australia—but not in others—such as England and Wales (Coleman, Hird, and Povey 2006). Estimates of nonlethal partner violence vary greatly cross-nationally, in part because of differences in the way national surveys define and measure it. For example, estimates of the annual prevalence of nonlethal partner violence against women in different countries range between 2 percent and 52 percent (United Nations 2006). The best evidence suggests that in Western countries women are only somewhat more likely than men to be victims of less serious forms of intimate partner violence. In contrast, in less developed countries, female victims greatly outnumber male victims (WHO 2005; Johnson, Öllus, and Nevala 2008; Muratore and Corazziari 2008). In all countries, however, women are much more likely than men to be victims of serious forms of intimate partner violence, especially homicide.

5. Victimization of Young People in the United States

Similar to patterns for adults, teenaged males are more likely than teenaged females to be victims of violence. Victimization rates for male youth are about 40 percent higher than those for female youth, according to the NCVS. Male high school seniors in the Monitoring the Future project also report higher rates of both violent and property victimization than female seniors. As with adults, race alters the relationship between sex and victimization. African American girls face much higher risks of victimization compared to girls from all other racial groups and compared to boys from some other racial groups (Lauritsen 2003; Miller 2008). The victimization risks for male and female youths of all races have decreased since the mid-1990s, according to the NCVS and the MTF survey.

6. Victimization of Young People in Other Countries

Boys and young males are at particularly high risk of victimization not just in the United States but in other countries as well. Their rates exceed rates for girls and young women by a substantial amount, when excluding nonsexual and intimate partner violence (van Dijk 2008). In Great Britain and Canada, nonlethal victimization rates for young males and females, and the differences between them, are similar to those in the United States (e.g., Tanner and Wortley 2002; Wikstrom and Butterworth 2007).

7. Victimization over the Centuries

Sex differences in violent victimization have varied more than sex differences in violent offending over the centuries. In pre-modern Europe, when homicide rates were particularly high, the proportion of male victims (about 93 percent) was much greater than in Europe today (Eisner 2003). As homicide rates declined, victimization became less male-dominated. Males accounted for about 85–90 percent of homicide victims in the seventeenth century, but only about 75 percent in the eighteenth century. By the nineteenth century in many cities in Britain and northern Europe, the proportion of male homicide victims had dropped to 65 percent (Johnson and Monkkonen 1996; Spierenburg 2008). In contrast, in major cities in the United States in the nineteenth and early twentieth centuries, where homicide rates were higher than in their European counterparts, the percentage of homicide victims who were male remained relatively high, at between 75–85 percent (Lane 1997; Monkkonen 2001; Adler 2006).

These patterns are consistent with those noted earlier and with the conclusions of other scholars: Where and when homicide rates are higher, the proportion of victims who are male is greater (Verkko 1951; Eisner 2003; Spierenburg 2008). Changes in total homicide rates, then, are largely driven by changes in male victimization. Conversely, female homicide victimization rates are more stable over time and place. The long-term decline in lethal violence in the Western world, as noted earlier, primarily resulted from a drop in serious male-on-male violence.[22]

B. Characteristics of Female and Male Victims

Victims of violence are similar in many respects to violent offenders. Regardless of their sex, those who are young, economically disadvantaged, not married, members of marginalized racial and ethnic groups, unemployed, and who frequent bars and clubs are at much greater risk of victimization (Kershaw, Nicholas, and Walker 2008; van Dijk 2008; Australian Institute of Criminology 2009; Rosenfeld 2009). Furthermore, victims of violence, especially male victims, often have histories of violent offending. For some types of victimization, risk factors differ between the sexes. For example, women who are separated from their intimate partners are at much higher risk of being killed by them than are women living with their partners. Separation does not, however, appear to raise men's risks of intimate partner homicide. Nevertheless, overall male and female victims appear to be more like each other and more similar to male and female offenders than is often assumed.

Given these commonalities, it is not surprising that the same types of social and cultural characteristics are associated with high rates of violent victimization for both sexes. Societies with extreme levels of economic and gender inequality tend to be more dangerous for females and males (Verweij and Nieuwbeerta 2001; Ghanim 2009). In a number of Middle Eastern, Latin and South American, Asian, and African countries, gender relations are strongly patriarchal and the distribution of income and wealth is highly skewed. In many of these countries, both females and males face high risks of violent victimization (Manderson and Bennett 2003; WHO 2005; Johnson, Öllus, and Nevala 2008).

C. Explanations of Sex Differences in Victimization

Males outnumber females among both victims and perpetrators of serious violence, but the sex difference in victimization is smaller than the sex difference in offending. For example, in the United States, females account for 10 percent of homicide offenders but about 20 percent of homicide victims; and they account for about 15–20 percent of other serious violent offenders but about 45 percent of the victims of serious violence. In other words, when females are involved in violence, they are more likely to be victims than offenders. Conversely, when males are involved in violence, they are more likely to be offenders than victims.

Many explanations of sex differences in victimization point to differences in risk-taking, routine daily activities, and informal controls—the same factors associated with sex differences in offending. Given that females are relatively more likely to be victims than offenders, though, these explanations do not go far enough. What is needed, according to many scholars, is more attention to gender inequalities and the ways in which men use violence against women as an expression of patriarchal control (Renzetti, Edleson, and Bergen 2001; Bahun-Radunović and Rujan 2008). Women live under conditions of unequal personal and systemic power that affect all aspects of their lives, including their risks of violence. Within this context, men feel freer to use violence and coercive behaviors as one means to maintain power and control over women. This "gender inequality" model of violence against women predicts that where the economic, political, and social disadvantages women face are greater, their risks of victimization will also be greater. As suggested earlier, cross-national research has consistently confirmed this prediction; research conducted within the United States, however, has found at best mixed support for it (Verweij and Nieubeerta 2001; Kruttschnitt, Gartner, and Ferraro 2002; Johnson, Öllus, and Nevala 2008).

III. Sex, Gender, and Criminalization

Processes of criminalization are inevitably shaped by sex and gender because the criminal justice system has been and continues to be dominated by males who focus their attention on the actions of other males. However, these institutions are gendered for reasons not solely due to the sex of the individuals populating them. Policing is considered a masculinist institution because of its hierarchical, authoritarian structure and the value it places on action, excitement, physical toughness, and violence (Fielding 1994; Waddington 1999). The law is considered gendered because it has conceptualized legal subjects based on characteristics culturally associated with the masculine (Lacey 2002; Naffine 2002). Thus, cultural notions about gender are deeply embedded within the criminal justice system.

Most research on sex, gender, and criminalization focuses on whether females and males are dealt with differently by the criminal justice system. Decisions by police about whom to arrest and with what to charge them determine subsequent patterns in criminal justice processing. Because this is one of the least visible points of decision making in the criminal justice process, we have only limited evidence about whether men and women are treated differently by police. We know a great deal more about sex disparities after the arrest stage, particularly in sentencing and imprisonment, from research analyzing quantitative data from historical and contemporary sources. In addition, some scholars have used qualitative approaches to explore the ways in which female and male defendants and victims are constructed in the courtroom, the ways in which the courtroom serves as an arena for performing gender, and how these influence criminal justice outcomes.

A. Sex, Gender, and Criminalization: Quantitative Evidence

There is substantial consensus that the recent increase in arrests of women and girls for assault in the United States (and elsewhere) is due more to changes in how police and other authorities respond to violence by females than to changes in females' violent behaviors. In other words, violent behavior by women and girls appears to have been increasingly criminalized over the past several years. Consistent with this is evidence suggesting that mandatory charging policies have had a disproportionate effect on women's arrest rates for domestic violence (Chesney-Lind 2002). Thus, some behaviors by females that previously may *not* have led to a formal response are now resulting in arrests and criminal charges. This means that a person's sex may now have less influence on arrest and charging decisions than in the past.[23]

1. *Sex, Gender, and Criminalization in the Contemporary United States*

Once charged with a crime, a defendant's sex matters to different degrees at different stages of the criminal justice process. According to data from the Bureau of Justice Statistics, conviction rates in American state courts vary little, if at all, by sex. For example, males constituted 82 percent of all felony defendants and 82 percent of all felony convictions in 2004. For violent crimes there was a small disparity: males accounted for 86 percent of those charged with, but 90 percent of those convicted of violent crimes (US Department of Justice 2008*a*). In other words, among those charged with violent crimes, females were slightly less likely than males to be convicted.

In contrast to conviction decisions, decisions about incarceration and sentence length consistently show substantial sex disparities. In 2004 in both state and federal courts, convicted males were more likely to be incarcerated than convicted females. At the federal level, for example, 83 percent of convicted males and 58 percent of convicted females were sentenced to incarceration. Sex disparities exist across all crime types, but are smaller for more serious crimes. Among those sentenced to prison, males also receive substantially longer sentences. Of those sentenced to prison for violent offenses in 2004 the average sentence lengths for males and females were, respectively, one hundred months and seventy-seven months (US Department of Justice 2008*b*).[24] These patterns have changed little over time.

Sex differences in incarceration and sentence length could be due to differences in the characteristics of male and female defendants or to differences in the nature of their crimes. Males are more likely to have criminal records and commit more serious crimes, factors that judges are expected to consider in sentencing. When studies take these into account, by controlling for legally relevant variables, they find that a defendant's sex, alone or in combination with other characteristics, still influences sentencing decisions. While the strength of this effect appears to have diminished over time, studies done before and after the introduction of sentencing reforms and guidelines in the 1990s find that women were and still are less likely to be incarcerated if convicted, especially if they are mothers of dependent children, married, or white (Daly and Tonry 1997). Women, particularly those convicted of property or drug offenses, also tend to receive shorter sentences than males (Koons-Witt 2002; Griffin and Wooldredge 2006; Rodriguez, Curry, and Lee 2006; Johnson, Ulmer, and Kramer 2008). Conversely, some studies find that young black males receive longer sentences than any other sex/race/age group (Steffensmeier, Ulmer, and Kramer 1998; Mustard 2001).

The sex of a defendant's victim can also influence court decision making. According to some studies, those charged with victimizing women are more likely to be convicted and to receive longer sentences, especially if the defendant is male and the victim is white (Glaeser and Sacerdote 2000; Curry, Lee, and Rodriguez 2004).

2. *Sex, Gender, and Criminalization in Other Countries*

In other Western countries, men's crimes also are responded to more severely than women's crimes. England and Wales is one of the few countries to publish data on police decision making. There, men and boys are less likely to be cautioned (i.e., reprimanded or warned) and more likely to be formally proceeded against than women and girls, a difference that exists across all crime types and is especially large for adults. In other words, females are diverted from prosecution more often than males in England and Wales. When proceeded against, however, women and men are about as likely to be released on bail and to be found guilty (Steward 2006). For decisions about imprisonment and sentence length, sex disparities in favor of women reappear. Convicted males are more likely to be given prison sentences and sentences of greater length than convicted women, who are more likely to receive fines as sentences (Ministry of Justice 2009).

While data on sex differences in criminalization from other countries are limited, they show that in most European countries and Canada, women also are less likely to be convicted, if arrested, than males (Aebi et al. 2006; Kong and AuCoin 2008). Convicted males also receive longer sentences than convicted females in some countries, including Canada and New Zealand (Jeffries 2001). One notable departure from this pattern of harsher treatment of men regards drug crimes. In England and other European countries there is typically little or no sex difference in imprisonment decisions for drug offenses; and in Canada among those convicted of drug crimes, women are somewhat *more* likely to be imprisoned than men (Kong and AuCoin 2008).

3. *Historical Patterns in Sex, Gender, and Criminalization*

The best historical evidence about sex disparities in the criminal process comes from records of the Old Bailey in London. Based on these historical records, it appears that from the late sixteenth to at least the late nineteenth centuries female defendants were more likely to have their charges reduced, were less likely to be found guilty, and received less severe sentences than male defendants (Beattie 2001; Wiener 2004; Hurl-Eamons 2005; King 2006). In other times and places, however, there were sometimes no differences in the treatment of male and female offenders, and where differences existed, which sex was the beneficiary varied by place, type of crime, and type of court (Phillips and May 2002; Walker 2003; Martin 2008). In general, however, historically females tend to have been treated less harshly by the courts, whether because of chivalry, paternalism, pragmatic reasons, or other factors.

B. Sex, Gender, and Criminalization: Qualitative Evidence

Because courtroom proceedings and the documents produced by and for them often are public, there is a good deal of qualitative evidence about how sex and gender have influenced the trial stage of the criminalization process. Historical work documents the complex and at times surprising ways in which notions about femininity and masculinity, especially as these have been influenced by race and class, have infused legal proceedings and outcomes. Judicial paternalism toward women at times has depended on whether defendants demonstrate appropriate feminine characteristics, such as deference, vulnerability, and sobriety (Rublack 1999; Palk 2006). A defendant's social class, race, or ethnicity in combination with her or his sex also can shape legal responses to crime. Working class, immigrant, and non-Caucasian males in many instances have received harsher treatment than their more well-to-do white brethren charged with similar crimes (Peterson del Mar 1996; Emsley 2005). To the extent the formers' criminal behavior was targeted at similar others and coincided with notions about what "those types of men" were like, it could go relatively unpunished (Adler 2006). Poor, minority, and immigrant women, even when they committed homicide, also have been beneficiaries of stereotypes about feminine defenselessness, emotionality, and weakness (Strange 1992; Conley 2007); but when such women engaged in sex freely or got drunk in public places they often were dealt with more harshly than their male counterparts.

Responses to female and male offenders have also varied because of different cultural tolerances for certain crimes or cultural anxieties about changing gender and family relations. Attitudes toward male violence, particularly violence toward wives, hardened in England in the nineteenth century leading to more severe punishments for violent males (Wiener 2004; Wood 2004; Conley 2007). In Germany and elsewhere, how rigorously women were prosecuted for killing their newborns and infants varied greatly between the seventeenth and the nineteenth centuries (Hoffer and Hull 1981; Rublack 1999).

Gender also has played a role in courtroom dramas through the construction of victims and the performance of lawyers. This is well documented for rape victims, whose claims to respectable femininity have often been challenged in court to the benefit of defendants. But defense lawyers also have attempted to construct males, both victims and offenders, as not appropriately masculine, cowardly, conniving, or debauched and thus less deserving of sympathy (Phillips and Gartner 2003; Strange 2003). The courtroom itself is a sort of stage on which male lawyers have performed masculinity in various ways: as chivalrous toward women on the stand, as aggressive toward each other and toward male defendants, and as upholders of the law more generally.

While much of the qualitative evidence about sex, gender, and criminalization comes from historical research, there is evidence that the criminal process continues to be influenced by notions about gender although in less obvious ways than in the past. Since Allen (1987) showed how women, even those who commit horrendous crimes, can be constructed by medical and legal experts as not truly responsible for their acts and therefore as in need of help not punishment, others have noted how notions about femininity and masculinity still shape legal decision making (Kilty and Frigon 2006; Baker 2008).

C. Explanations of Sex Differences in Criminalization

Explanations of sex differences in criminalization typically focus on what is seen as the lenience afforded women by the criminal justice system and the concepts of chivalry and paternalism, which imply somewhat different reasons for treating women less severely than men. Women can be said to be beneficiaries of chivalric justice to the extent that male lawyers, judges, and juries are inclined to respect womanhood, to see women as the upholders of morality and to behave toward them with gentleness and graciousness. While examples of chivalric justice exist, paternalistic justice appears to be more common. Paternalistic justice assumes that women are the weaker sex, in need of protection from themselves as well as others, and not fully responsible for their actions. Sometimes this has lead to imprisonment and longer sentences for women, but more often it has resulted in less severe outcomes compared to men (Morash 2006).

According to this approach to sex differences in criminalization, women's treatment by the criminal justice system is gendered because it departs from the standard set by the treatment of men. This ignores the possibility that men's treatment by the criminal justice system is also gendered, in other words, based on hierarchies of and notions about masculinity (Strange 2003). To the extent that some types of masculinity are associated with dangerousness, aggression, and defiance of authority, men who are seen to embody these characteristics may be targets of highly punitive responses by the male-dominated criminal justice system. What links male punitiveness toward some male defendants—especially those who are poor and nonwhite—to male mercifulness toward some female defendants is a version of masculinity embraced by courtroom actors.

Another perspective on sex differences in criminalization points to the pragmatic concerns of judges. Sentencing women who have children to prison places a burden on others or the state to assume care of the children; since men are much less likely to be the sole caregivers of their children, the same concern rarely arises for male defendants (Daly and Tonry 1997). As a consequence, women are sometimes sentenced to community alternatives instead of incarceration as a way to preserve the family and reduce costs to society.

II. Implications for Policy and Future Research

The evidence discussed in this chapter suggests that programs designed to prevent, reduce, or respond to crime are likely to be similarly effective (or ineffective) for both sexes. This is because female and male offenders share many characteristics and environments; and their rates of offending and victimization follow similar trends and are affected by similar individual and contextual characteristics. Programs found to be effective for both sexes—such as home visiting nurses and preschool enrichment programs for children, and drug treatment and prison vocational education programs for adult offenders (MacKenzie 2006; Olds 2007)—should therefore have higher priority than sex-specific policies and programs. Unfortunately, many correctional and community programs have been evaluated for their effects on men only. Despite the commonalities between female and male offenders, we cannot assume these programs will affect women in similar ways. Often correctional policies and practices developed with male offenders in mind—such as risk assessment tools—are applied to female offenders with little or no evidence of their usefulness for either sex or much thought about differential effects on females and males.

One of the most important implications for social policy is that both sexes will be less inclined to crime and safer if their social environments—families, schools, neighborhoods, and cities—provide them with a sense that they are connected to and valued by others. Conversely, and at a broader level, in societies that send many of their members the opposite message, we can expect both sexes to have high rates of offending and victimization. One way to send such a message is by criminalizing an ever-increasing portion of the population. Doing so may have a greater effect on women and girls than on men and boys; as the criminal justice net widens, it pulls in a larger proportion of those who commit less serious crimes. And, as we have already seen, females make up a relatively large proportion of those arrested for less serious crimes.

For decades, scholars studying the relationships among sex, gender, and crime tended to focus either explicitly on women or implicitly on men. Those whose work focused on women typically treated their findings as specific to women. Those who studied men's criminal behavior typically implied their findings were applicable generally to all criminals. In a major advance in the field, scholars have started to integrate work on both sexes, attending not just to what is similar and different between them but also to what makes crime a gendered activity and victimization a gendered experience. The next step is to integrate work across disciplinary boundaries and understandings of sex, gender, and crime, rather than treating these as in competition with each other.

We now know a good deal about sex, gender, and crime, but most of what we know is from the Western world. The ways in which sex, gender, and crime are related elsewhere may be very different, not least because gender relations, ideologies, and inequalities—as well as definitions of crime—vary so much around the world. Important efforts have been made to gather information on crime from other countries, particularly through victimization surveys. However, such surveys, which were initially developed in the West, may not adequately capture women's and men's experiences of crime and victimization elsewhere—especially in highly authoritarian and highly patriarchal countries. Yet it is precisely such countries in which crime and violence may have particularly profound effects on the lives of women and men (Ghanim 2009). In countries riven by warfare, violence is not limited to battlefields but is a daily reality for everyone. A decade of investigations by international bodies has shown how states and armies use rape as a weapon of war and an instrument of terror; and how genocides are accomplished through sexual violence, which is often targeted at certain racial and ethnic groups (Hagan and Rymond-Richmond 2009). Sexual violence puts gender inequalities into stark relief, especially when it is state supported. Research on how sex and gender shape violence in such contexts requires attention to how states and collectivities are organized to exploit and reinforce gender inequalities in a number of spheres of life—with harmful outcomes for both women and men. Focusing on these aspects of sex, gender, and crime is important as a way to advance knowledge, pursue justice, and improve people's lives.

NOTES

....

    1. Sex, like gender, can be seen as socially constructed. Typically, however, sex is used to refer to a biologically determined characteristic that is dualistic.

    2. The conventional distinction between gender as socially constructed and sex as biologically given is contested by some scholars. They argue that this distinction creates a false duality between the biological (sex/body) and the cultural (gender/mind); and that in practice sex and gender incorporate each other (Harrison 2006; Merry 2009).

    3. For example, according to the Canadian Criminal Code (R.S., c. C-34, s.216), "a female person commits infanticide when by a willful act or omission she causes the death of her newly born child, if at the time of the act or omission she is not fully recovered from the effects of giving birth to the child and by reason thereof or of the effect of lactation consequent on the birth of the child her mind is then disturbed."

    4. Gender order refers to patterns of power relations between masculinities and femininities that are widespread throughout society.

    5. This applies to research on victimization, though to a lesser extent.

    6. Scholars are beginning to resurrect some of this work so that its contributions can be more adequately assessed (see, e.g., Rafter and Gibson 2004).

    7. References to arrest rates in the United States here and throughout the remainder of this chapter are based on the FBI's Uniform Crime Reports for 2007. See "Crime Data Sources" after the references for links to this and other data sources used in this chapter.

    8. Sex-specific robbery and assault rates also share similar correlates.

    9. The acquaintance category includes a wide range of relationships, from friends and neighbors to gang members who know each other by sight or reputation.

    10. The National Crime Victimization Survey, the most extensive victimization data source in the world, has been conducted on a continuous basis in the United States since 1972. Reference to NCVS data here and throughout the remainder of this chapter is based on the 2007 survey, unless otherwise noted.

    11. There is some year-to-year variation outside of this range because of the small number of homicides in some countries. However, the range applies, on average, to most European countries.

    12. Only in late nineteenth-century Germany did women account for a substantial proportion (40 percent) of those charged with theft.

    13. There is an ongoing debate, particularly among feminist criminologists, over how to understand serious violence by women. Some scholars argue that women's violence is largely a consequence of and determined by the patriarchal structure of society. From this perspective, such violence is self-defensive, due to male coercion, and/ or committed by women who are accomplices to males. Others argue that this portrayal denies women agency and infantilizes them, and that it is not supported by the evidence. The latter perspective, which is represented by the quotation in the text by Sjoberg and Gentry (2007), acknowledges that gender inequalities disadvantage women in many

ways, but do not take away their ability to make choices within the constraints of these inequalities.

14. Sex is also key to other perspectives on the sex difference in crime, such as evolutionary psychology. In addition, "sexed bodies" and "sexed subjectivities" are at least as important as gender in some theorizing on crime (Collier 1998).

15. Among the thirty-five countries in LaFree and Hunnicutt's (2006) analysis, there is a strong positive correlation (.84) between the size of the homicide rate and the percentage of male victims.

16. Surveys that ask more detailed questions about sexual assault and intimate partner violence tend to find little or no sex difference in victimization.

17. Despite the efforts of the ICVS designers and administrators, estimates of the prevalence of some types of victimization in some countries are highly questionable. For example, the ICVS found one-year prevalence rates of sexual assault of o in Egypt, Zimbabwe, and Mexico (van Dijk, van Kesteren, and Smit 2007).

18. Same-sex partners account for about 4 percent of female intimate partner victimizations and about 18 percent of male intimate partner victimizations, according to the NCVS.

19. Differences in estimates are due to variation across the surveys in their framing, definitions of violence, and data collection instruments.

20. The National Violence Against Women Survey was a nationwide survey conducted in 1995 and 1996. Nearly 12,000 women and men were interviewed about their experiences of violence, including intimate partner violence. For more information, see Tjaden and Thoennes (2000).

21. Three National Family Violence Surveys were conducted in 1975, 1985, and 1992 and were designed to provide a comprehensive examination of violence arising from conflicts within the family, including spouse abuse.

22. Nevertheless, it is still the case that long-term trends in male and female homicide victimization are very similar (Eisner 2003).

23. As noted earlier, for some behaviors—such as minor sexual misdemeanors, running away, and prostitution—women and, in particular, girls are still more likely than males to be dealt with formally. However, this sex disparity also appears to have decreased somewhat over time.

24. Race conditions this sex effect. Black males and females are sentenced to an average of twelve more months of prison if convicted of a violent offense, compared to white males and females convicted of a violent offense.

REFERENCES

Adler, Jeffrey S. 2006. *First in Violence, Deepest in Dirt: Homicide in Chicago, 1875–1920.* Cambridge, MA: Harvard University Press.

Aebi, Marceki F., Kauko Aromaa, Bruno Aubusson de Cavarlay, Gordon Barclay, Beata Gruszczyñska, Hanns von Hofer, Vasilika Hysi, Jörg-Martin Jehle, Martin Killias, Paul Smit, and Cynthia Tavares. 2006. *European Sourcebook of Crime and Criminal Justice Statistics—2006.* The Hague: Minister of Justice, the Netherlands.

Allen, Hilary. 1987. *Justice Unbalanced: Gender, Psychiatry, and Judicial Decisions.* Milton Keynes, UK: Open University Press.

Australian Bureau of Statistics. 2005. *Personal Safety Survey.* Canberra: Australian Bureau of Statistics.

Australian Institute of Criminology. 2009. *Homicide Offender Statistics.* Canberra: Australian Institute of Criminology. http://www.aic.gov.au/research/homicide/stats/html.

Bahun-Radunović, Sanja, and V. G. Julie Rujan, eds. 2008. *Violence and Gender in the Globalized World: The Intimate and the Extimate.* Burlington, VT: Ashgate.

Baker, Helen. 2008. "Constructing Women Who Experience Male Violence: Criminal Legal Discourse and Individual Experiences." *Liverpool Law Review* 29:123–42.

Batton, Candice. 2004. "Gender Differences in Lethal Violence: Historical Trends in the Relationship Between Homicide and Suicide Rates." *Justice Quarterly* 21:423–62.

Beattie, John M. 2001. *Policing and Punishment in London, 1600–1750.* Oxford: Oxford University Press.

Belknap, Joanne, and Kristi Holsinger. 2006. "The Gendered Nature of Risk Factors for Delinquency." *Feminist Criminology* 1:48–71.

Bell, Kerryn E. 2009. "Gender and Gangs: A Quantitative Comparison." *Crime and Delinquency* 55:363–87.

Bellesiles, Michael A., ed. 1999. *Lethal Imagination: Violence and Brutality in American History.* New York: New York University Press.

Bennett, Sara, David P. Farrington, and L. Rowell Huesmann. 2005. "Explaining Gender Differences in Crime and Violence: The Importance of Social Cognitive Skills." *Aggression and Violent Behavior* 10:263–88.

Bonger, Willem. 1916. *Criminality and Economic Conditions.* New York: Little, Brown.

Bottcher, Jean. 2001. "Social Practices of Gender: How Gender Relates to Delinquency in the Lives of High-risk Youths." *Criminology* 39:893–931.

Broadhurst, Roderic. 1999. "Homicide in Hong Kong: The Homicide Monitoring Data Base, 1989–1997." Paper presented at the Hong Kong Sociological Association, December 10. University of Hong Kong.

Budd, Tracey, Clare Sharp, and Pat Mayhew. 2005. *Offending in England and Wales: First Results from the 2003 Crime and Justice Survey.* London: Home Office Research, Development and Statistics Directorate.

Carrington, Kerry. 2006. "Does Feminism Spoil Girls? Explanations for Official Rises in Female Delinquency." *Australia and New Zealand Journal of Criminology* 39:34–53.

Cernkovich, Stephen A., Nadine Lanctôt, and Peggy C. Giordano. 2008. "Predicting Adolescent and Adult Antisocial Behavior among Adjudicated Delinquent Females." *Crime and Delinquency* 54:3–33.

Chesney-Lind, Meda. 2002. "Criminalizing Victimization: The Unintended Consequences of Pro-arrest Policies for Girls and Women." *Crime and Public Policy* 2:81–90.

Chesney-Lind, Meda, and Katherine Irwin. 2008. *Beyond Bad Girls: Gender, Violence and Hype.* New York: Routledge.

Coleman, Kathryn, Celia Hird, and David Povey. 2006. *Violent Crime Overview, Homicide and Gun Crime 2004/2005.* Home Office Research, Development and Statistics Directorate. http://www.homeoffice.gov.uk/rds/pdfs06/hosb0206.pdf.

Collier, Richard. 1998. *Masculinities, Crime and Criminology: Men, Heterosexuality and the Criminal(ised) Other.* London: Sage.

Conley, Carolyn A. 2007. *Certain Other Countries: Homicide, Gender and National Identity in Late 19th Century England, Ireland, Scotland and Wales.* Columbus: Ohio State University Press.

Courtwright, David T. 1996. *Violent Land: Single Men and Social Disorder from the Frontier to the Inner City.* Cambridge, MA: Harvard University Press, 1996.

Curry, Theodore, Gang Lee, and S. Fernando Rodriguez. 2004. "Does Victim Gender Increase Sentencing Severity? Further Explorations of Gender Dynamics and Sentencing Outcomes." *Crime and Delinquency* 50:319–43.

Daigle, Leah E., Francis T. Cullen, and John Paul Wright. 2007. "Gender Differences in the Predictors of Juvenile Delinquency: Assessing the Generality-specificity Debate." *Youth Violence and Juvenile Justice* 5:254–86.

Daly, Kathleen. 1992. "Women's Pathways to Felony Court: Feminist Theories of Lawbreaking and Problems of Representation." *Southern California Review of Law and Women's Studies* 2:11–52.

Daly, Kathleen, and Michael Tonry. 1997. "Gender, Race, and Sentencing." In *Crime and Justice: A Review of Research*, vol. 22, edited by Michael Tonry. Chicago: University of Chicago Press.

Dauvergne, Mia. 2005. "Homicide in Canada, 2004." *Juristat* 25:1–27.

Dobash, Russell P., and R. Emerson Dobash. 2004. "Women's Violence to Men in Intimate Relationships: Working on a Puzzle." *British Journal of Criminology* 44:324–49.

Dugan, Laura, Daniel Nagin, and Richard Rosenfeld. 2003. "Exposure Reduction or Retaliation? The Effects of Domestic Violence Resources on Intimate Partner Homicide." *Law and Society Review* 37:169–98.

Eisner, Manuel. 2003. "Long-term Historical Trends in Violent Crime." In *Crime and Justice: A Review of Research*, vol. 30, edited by Michael Tonry. Chicago: University of Chicago Press.

Emsley, Clive. 2005. *Hard Men: Violence in England Since 1750.* London: Hambledon and London.

Farrington, David P., and Kate A. Painter. 2004. *Gender Differences in Offending: Implications for Risk-Focused Prevention.* Home Office OnLine Report 09/04. London: Home Office.

Feeley, Malcolm, and Deborah L. Little. 1991. "The Vanishing Female: The Decline of Women in the Criminal Process, 1687–1912." *Law and Society Review* 25:719–57.

Fielding, Nigel. 1994. "Cop Canteen Culture." In *Just Boys Doing Business: Men, Masculinity and Crime*, ed. Tim Newburn and Elizabeth Stanko. London: Routledge.

Gannon, Maire, and Karen Mihorean. 2005. "Criminal Victimization in Canada, 2004." *Juristat* 25:1–25.

Gartner, Rosemary. 1995. "Homicide in Canada." In *Violence in Canada: Socio-political Perspectives*, ed. Jeffrey I. Ross. Don Mills, ON: Oxford University Press.

Gartner, Rosemary, and Bill McCarthy. 2006. "Killing One's Children: Maternal Infanticide and the Dark Figure of Homicide." In *Gender and Crime: Patterns of Victimization and Offending*, ed. Karen Heimer and Candace Kruttschnitt. New York: New York University Press.

Ghanim, David. 2009. *Gender and Violence in the Middle East.* Westport, CT: Praeger.

Giordano, Peggy, Stephen Cernkovich, and Jennifer L. Rudolph. 2002. "Gender, Crime, and Desistance: Toward a Theory of Cognitive Transformation." *American Journal of Sociology* 4:990–1064.

Giordano, Peggy, Jill Deines, and Stephen Cernkovich. 2006. "In and Out of Crime: A Life Course Perspective on Girls' Delinquency." In *Gender and Crime:Patterns in Victimization and Offending*, edited by Karen Heimer and Candace Kruttschnitt. New York: New York University Press.

Glaeser, Edward L., and Bruce Sacerdote. 2000. "The Determinants of Punishment: Deterrence, Incapacitation and Vengeance." *Harvard Institute of Economic Research*. Cambridge, MA: National Bureau of Economic Research.

Glueck, Sheldon, and Eleanor Glueck. 1934. *Five Hundred Delinquent Women*. New York: Knopf.

Goodkind, S., J. Wallace, J. Shook, Jerald Bachman, and Patrick M. O'Malley. 2009 "Are Girls Really Becoming More Delinquent? Testing the Gender Convergence Hypothesis by Race and Ethnicity, 1976–2005." *Children and Youth Services Review* 31:885–95.

Griffin, Timothy, and John Wooldredge. 2006. "Sex-based Disparities in Felony Dispositions Before Versus After Sentencing Reform in Ohio." *Criminology* 44:893–924.

Gurr, Ted R. 1989. "Historical Trends in Violent Crime: Europe and the United States." In *The History of Crime*, vol. 1, *Violence in America*, ed. Ted R. Gurr. Newbury Park, CA: Sage.

Hagan, John. 1988. *Structural Criminology*. Cambridge: Polity Press.

Hagan, John, and Winona Rymond-Richmond. 2009. *Darfur and the Crime of Genocide*. New York: Cambridge University Press.

Hansen, Kirstine. 2006. "Gender Differences in Self-reported Offending." In *Gender and Justice: New Concepts and Approaches*, ed. Frances Heidensohn. Cullompton, UK: Willan.

Harrison, Wendy. 2006. "The Shadow and the Substance: The Sex/Gender Debate." In *Handbook of Gender and Women's Studies*, ed. Kathy Davis, Mary Evans, and Judith Lorber. London: Sage.

Heidensohn, Frances, and Lorraine Gelsthorpe. 2007. "Gender and Crime." In *Oxford Handbook of Criminology*, 4th ed., ed. Mike Maguire, Rod Morgan and Robert Reiner. Oxford: Oxford University Press.

Heimer, Karen. 2000. "Changes in the Gender Gap in Crime and Women's Economic Marginalization." In *The Nature of Crime: Continuity and Change, Criminal Justice 2000*, vol. 1, ed. Gary LaFree. Washington, DC: National Institute of Justice.

Heimer, Karen, Janet L. Lauritsen, and James P. Lynch. 2009. "The National Crime Victimization Survey and the Gender Gap in Offending: Redux." *Criminology* 47:427–38.

Henning, Kris, Angela Jones, and Robert Holdford. 2003. "Treatment Needs of Women Arrested for Domestic Violence: A Comparison with Male Offenders." *Journal of Interpersonal Violence* 18:839–56.

Henning, Kris, Brian Renauer, and Robert Holdford. 2006. "Victim or Offender: Heterogeneity Among Women Arrested for Intimate Partner Violence." *Journal of Family Violence* 21:351–68.

Hobbs, Dick, Kate O'Brien, and Louise Westmarland. 2007. "Connecting the Gendered Door: Women, Violence and Doorwork." *British Journal of Sociology* 58: 21–38.

Hines, Denise A. 2009. "Domestic Violence." In *The Oxford Handbook of Crime and Public Policy*, ed. Michael Tonry. New York: Oxford University Press.

Hoffer, Peter C., and N. E. H. Hull. 1981. *Murdering Mothers: Infanticide in England and New England, 1558–1803*. New York: New York University Press.

Hurl-Eamons, Jennine. 2005. Gender and Petty Violence in London, 1680–1720. Columbus: Ohio State University Press.

Jackson, Mark, ed. 2002. *Infanticide: Historical Perspectives on Child Murder and Concealment, 1550–2000.* Aldershot, UK: Ashgate.

Jeffries, Samantha. 2001. "Gender Judgments: An Investigation of Sentencing and Remand in New Zealand." Paper presented at the 2001 Australian Sociological Association Annual Conference, Sydney.

Johansson, Pernilla, and Kimberly Kempf-Leonard. 2009. "A Gender-specific Pathway to Serious, Violent, and Chronic Offending? Exploring Howell's Risk Factors for Serious Delinquency." *Crime and Delinquency* 55:216–40.

Johnson, Brian, Jeffrey Ulmer, and John H. Kramer. 2008. "The Social Context of Circumvention: The Case of Federal District Courts." *Criminology* 46:737–83.

Johnson, Eric A., and Eric H. Monkkonen, eds. 1996. *The Civilization of Crime: Violence in Town and Country since the Middle Ages.* Urbana: University of Illinois Press.

Johnson, Holly, Natalia Öllus, and Sami Nevala. 2008. *Violence Against Women: An International Comparison.* New York: Springer.

Johnston, Lloyd D., Jerald Bachman, and Patrick M. O'Malley. *Various years. Monitoring the Future Project.* Ann Arbor: Institute for Social Research, University of Michigan.

Junger-Tas, Josine, Ineke Haen Marshall, and J. Denis Ribeaud. 2003. *Delinquency in International Perspective: The International Self-Reported Delinquency Study.* Monsey, NY: Criminal Justice Press.

Junger-Tas, Josine, J. Denis Ribeaud, and Maarten J.L.F. Cruyff. 2004. "Juvenile Delinquency and Gender." *European Journal of Criminology* 1:333–75.

Kaspersson, Maria. 2003. "'The Great Murder Mystery' or Explaining Declining Homicide Rates." In *Comparative Histories of Crime*, ed. Barry S. Godfrey, Clive Emsley, and Graeme Dunstall. Portland, OR: Willan.

Kershaw, Chris, Sian Nicholas, and Alison Walker. 2008. *Crime in England and Wales 2007–2008: Findings from the British Crime Survey and Police Recorded Crime.* London: Home Office Research, Development and Statistics Directorate.

Kilty, Jennifer M., and Sylvie Frigon. 2006. "Karla Homolka: From a Woman in Danger to a Dangerous Woman: Chronicling the Shifts." *Women and Criminal Justice* 17:37–61.

King, Peter. 2006. *Crime and Law in England, 1750–1840: Remaking Justice from the Margins.* Cambridge: Cambridge University Press.

Klein, Dorie. 1973. "The Etiology of Women's Crime: A Review of the Literature." *Issues in Criminology* 8:3–30.

Kong, Rebecca, and Kathy AuCoin. 2008. "Female Offenders in Canada." *Juristat* 28:1–22.

Konopka, Gisela. 1966. *The Adolescent Girl in Conflict.* Englewood Cliffs, NJ: Prentice Hall.

Koons-Witt, Barbara. 2002. "The Effect of Gender on the Decision to Incarcerate Before and After the Introduction of Sentencing Guidelines." *Criminology* 40:297–327.

Kruttschnitt, Candace, and Kristin Carbone-Lopez. 2006. "Moving Beyond the Stereotypes: Women's Subjective Accounts of Their Violent Crime." *Criminology* 44:321–52.

Kruttschnitt, Candace, Rosemary Gartner, and Kathleen Ferraro. 2002. "Women's Involvement in Serious Interpersonal Violence." *Aggression and Violent Behavior* 7:529–65.

Lacey, Nicola. 2002. "Violence, Ethics and Law: Feminist Reflections on a Familiar Dilemma." In *Visible Women: Essays on Feminist Legal Theory and Political Philosophy*, ed. Susan James and Stephanie Palmer. Oxford: Hart.

LaFree, Gary, and Gwen Hunnicutt. 2006. "Female and Male Homicide Victimization Trends: A Cross-national Context." In *Crime and Gender: Patterns in Victimization and Offending*, ed. Karen Heimer and Candace Kruttschnitt. New York: New York University Press.

Lanctôt, Nadine, and Mare LeBlanc. 2002. "Explaining Deviance by Adolescent Females." In *Crime and Justice: A Review of Research*, vol. 29, edited by Michael Tonry. Chicago: University of Chicago Press.

Lane, Roger. 1997. *Murder in America: A History*. Columbus: Ohio State University Press.

Lauritsen, Janet. 2003. *How Families and Communities Influence Youth Victimization*. Juvenile Justice Bulletin. Washington, DC: US Department of Justice.

Lauritsen, Janet, and Karen Heimer. 2008. "The Gender Gap in Victimization, 1973–2004." *Journal of Quantitative Criminology* 24:125–47.

Lauritsen, Janet, Karen Heimer, and James P. Lynch. 2009. "Trends in the Gender Gap in Violent Offending: New Evidence from the National Crime Victimization Survey." *Criminology* 47:361–99.

Li, Geoffrey. 2008. "Homicide in Canada, 2007." *Juristat* 28:1–26.

Lombroso, Cesare, and Guglielmo Ferrero. 1893. *La donna delinquente, la prostituta e la donna normale*. Turin: Roux.

MacKenzie, Doris L. 2006. *What Works in Corrections: Reducing the Criminal Activities of Offenders and Delinquents*. New York: Cambridge University Press.

Maher, Lisa. 1997. *Sexed Work: Gender, Race and Resistance in a Brooklyn Drug Market*. Oxford: Clarendon Press.

Manderson, Lenore, and Linda Rae Bennett, eds. 2003. *Violence Against Women in Asian Societies*. New York: Routledge.

Marvel, Thomas B., and Carlisle Moody. 1999. "Female and Male Homicide Victimization Rates: Comparing Trends and Regressors." *Criminology* 37:879–902.

Martin, Randall. 2008. *Women, Murder and Equity in Early Modern England*. Abingdon, UK: Routledge.

May, Allyson N., and Jim Phillips. 2001. "Homicide in Nova Scotia, 1749–1815." *Canadian Historical Review* 82:625–61.

Meadows, Sarah O. 2007. "Evidence of Parallel Pathways: Gender Similarity in the Impact of Social Support on Adolescent Depression and Delinquency." *Social Forces* 85:1143–67.

Merry, Sally E. 2009. *Gender Violence: A Cultural Perspective*. Malden, MA: Wiley Blackwell.

Messerschmidt, James W. 2004. *Flesh and Blood: Adolescent Gender Diversity and Violence*. Lanham, MD: Rowman and Littlefield.

Miller, Jody. 2008. *Getting Played: African American Girls, Urban Inequality and Gendered Violence*. New York: New York University Press.

Miller, Jody, and Christopher Mullins. 2006. "Stuck Up, Telling Lies, and Talking Too Much: The Gendered Contexts of Young Women's Violence." In *Gender and Crime: Patterns of Victimization and Offending*, ed. Karen Heimer and Candace Kruttschnitt. New York: New York University Press.

Miller, Susan L. 2005. *Victims as Offenders: The Paradox of Women's Violence in Relationships*. New Brunswick, NJ: Rutgers University Press.

Ministry of Justice. 2009. *Statistics on Women and the Criminal Justice System*. London: The Institute for Criminal Policy Research, School of Law, King's College.

Moffitt, Terrie E., Avshalom Caspi, Michael Rutter, and Phil Silva. 2001. *Sex Differences in Anti-Social Behavior: Conduct Disorder, Delinquency, and Violence in the Dunedin Longitudinal Study*. New York: Cambridge University Press.

Monkkonen, Eric H. 2001. *Murder in New York City*. Berkeley: University of California Press.

Morash, Merry. 2006. *Understanding Gender, Crime and Justice*. Thousand Oaks, CA: Sage.

Morrissey, Belinda. 2003. *When Women Kill: Questions of Agency and Subjectivity*. London: Routledge.

Muratore, Maria G., and Isabella Corazziari. 2008. "The New Italian Violence Against Women Survey." In *Victimisation Surveys in International Perspective*, ed. Kauko Aromaa and Marku Heiskanen. Helsinki: European Institute for Crime Prevention and Control.

Murphy, Thérèsa, and Noel Whitty. 2006. "The Question of Evil and Feminist Legal Scholarship." *Feminist Legal Studies* 14:1–26.

Mustard, David B. 2001. "Racial, Ethnic and Gender Disparities in Sentencing: Evidence from the US Federal Courts." *Journal of Law and Economics* 44:285–314.

Naffine, Ngaire, ed. 2002. *Gender and Justice*. Aldershot, UK: Dartmouth.

Odgers, Candice L., Terrie E. Moffitt, Jonathan M. Broadbent, Nigel Dickson, Robert J. Hancox, Honalee Harrington, Richie Poulton, Malcolm Sears, W. Murray Thomson, and Avshalom Caspi. 2008. "Female and Male Antisocial Trajectories: From Childhood Origins to Adult Outcomes." *Development and Psychopathology* 20:673–716.

Olds, David L. 2007. "Home Visiting Nurses? Preventing Crime by Improving Pre-natal and Infant Health and Development." *Criminal Justice Matters* 69:4–5.

Palk, Diedre. 2006. *Gender, Crime and Judicial Discretion, 1780–1830*. Woodbridge, UK: Boydell Press.

Peterson del Mar, David. 1996. *What Trouble I Have Seen: A History of Violence Against Wives*. Cambridge, MA: Harvard University Press.

———. 2002. *Beaten Down: A History of Interpersonal Violence in the West*. Seattle: University of Washington Press.

Phillips, Jim, and Allyson N. May. 2002. "Female Criminality in 18th-Century Halifax." *Acadiensis* 31:71–97.

Phillips, Jim, and Rosemary Gartner. 2003. *Murdering Holiness: The Trials of Franz Creffield and George Mitchell*. Vancouver: University of British Columbia Press.

Pollak, Otto. 1951. *The Criminality of Women*. New York: Barnes.

Povey, David, Kathryn Coleman, Peter Kaiza, and Stephen Roe. 2009. *Homicides, Firearm Offenses and Intimate Violence 2007/08*. London: Home Office Research, Development and Statistics Directorate.

Rafter, Nicole Hahn, and Mary Gibson. 2004. Translation of and introduction to *Criminal Woman, the Prostitute, and the Normal Woman*, by Cesare Lombroso and Guglielmo Ferraro. Durham, NC: Duke University Press.

Rand, Michael R. 2008. *Criminal Victimization, 2007*. NJC 224390. Washington, DC: Bureau of Justice Statistics.

Renzetti, Claire M., Jeffrey L. Edleson, and Raquel Kennedy Bergen, eds. 2001. *Sourcebook on Violence Against Women*. Thousand Oaks. CA: Sage.

Rodriguez, S. Fernando, Theodore Curry, and Gang Lee. 2006. "Gender Differences in Criminal Sentencing: Do Effects Vary Across Violent, Property and Drug Offenses?" *Social Science Quarterly* 87:318–39.

Rosenfeld, Richard. 2009. "Homicide and Serious Assaults." In *The Oxford Handbook of Crime and Public Policy*, ed. Michael Tonry. New York: Oxford University Press.

Rublack, Ulinka. 1999. *The Crimes of Women in Early Modern Germany*. Oxford: Clarendon Press.

Schwartz, Jennifer. 2006. "Effects of Diverse Forms of Family Structure on Female and Male Homicide." *Journal of Marriage and the Family* 68:1291–312.

Schwartz, Jennifer, Darrell Steffensmeier, and Ben Feldmeyer. 2009. "Assessing Trends in Women's Violence via Data Triangulation: Arrests, Convictions, Incarcerations, and Victim Reports." *Social Problems* 56:494–525.

Schwartz, Jennifer, Darrell J. Steffensmeier, Hua Zhong, and Jeff Ackerman. 2009. "Trends in the Gender Gap in Violence: Reevaluating NCVS and Other Evidence." *Criminology* 47:401–26.

Shoemaker, Robert. 2002. "The Taming of the Duel: Masculinity, Honour and Ritual in London, 1660–1800." *Historical Journal* 45:525–45.

Sjoberg, Laura, and Caron E. Gentry. 2007. *Mothers, Monsters, Whores: Women's Violence in Global Politics*. London: Zed Books.

Smart, Carol. 1976. *Women, Crime and Criminology: A Feminist Critique*. London: Routledge and Kegan Paul.

Spierenburg, Pieter, ed. 1998. *Men and Violence: Gender, Honor and Rituals in Modern Europe and America*. Columbus: Ohio State University Press.

———. 2008. *A History of Murder: Personal Violence in Europe from the Middle Ages to the Present*. Cambridge, MA: Polity Press.

Sprott, Jane B., and Anthony N. Doob. 2009. *Justice for Girls? Stability and Change in the Youth Justice Systems of the United States and Canada*. Chicago: University of Chicago Press.

Steffensmeier, Darrell, and Emilie Allan. 1996. "Gender and Crime: Toward a Gendered Theory of Crime." *Annual Review of Sociology* 22:459–87.

Steffensmeier, Darrell, and Dana Haynie. 2000. "Gender, Structural Disadvantage, and Urban Crime: Do Macrosocial Variables Explain Female Offending Rates?" *Criminology* 38:403–39.

Steffensmeier, Darrell, Jennifer Schwartz, Hua Zhong, and Jeff Ackerman 2005. "An Assessment of Recent Trends in Girls' Violence Using Diverse Longitudinal Sources: Is the Gender Gap Closing?" *Criminology* 43:355–405.

Steffensmeier, Darrell, Jeffrey Ulmer, and John H. Kramer. 1998. "The Interaction of Race, Gender and Age in Criminal Sentencing: The Punishment Cost of Being Young, Black and Male." *Criminology* 36:763–87.

Steward, Kate. 2006. "Gender Considerations in Remand Decision-making." In *Gender and Justice: New Concepts and Approaches*, ed. Frances Heidensohn. Cullompton, UK: Willan.

Strange, Carolyn. 1992. "Wounded Womanhood and Dead Men: Chivalry and the Trials of Clara Ford and Carrie Davies." In *Gender Conflicts*, ed. Franca Iacovetta and Mariana Valverde. Toronto: University of Toronto Press.

———. 2003. "Masculinities, Intimate Femicide and the Death Penalty in Australia, 1890–1920." *British Journal of Criminology* 43:310–39.

Straus, Murray. 2004. "Women's Violence Toward Men is a Serious Social Problem." In *Current Controversies on Family Violence*, ed. Donileen R. Loseke, Richard J. Gelles, and Mary M. Cavanaugh. Thousand Oaks, CA: Sage.

Tanner, Julian, and Scot Wortley. 2002. *The Toronto Youth Crime and Victimization Survey: Overview Report.* Toronto: Centre of Criminology.

Thomas, William I. 1923. *The Unadjusted Girl.* Boston: Little Brown.

Tjaden, Patricia, and Nancy Thoennes. 2000. Extent, Nature, and Consequences of Intimate Partner Violence: Findings from the National Violence Against Women Survey. http://www.ojp.usdoj.gov/nih/victdocs.htm#2000.

United Nations. 2006. *In-Depth Study of All Forms of Violence Against Women. Report of the Secretary General.* New York: United Nations.

US Department of Justice. 2008a. Felony Defendants in Large Urban Counties, 2004 Statistical Tables. http:///www.ojp.usdog.gov/bjs.put/html/fdluc/2004/tables/fdluc04sto2.htm

———. 2008b. State Court Sentencing of Convicted Felons, 2004 Statistical Tables. http:///www.ojp.usdog.gov/bjs.put/html/scscf04/tqbles/scso4206tab.htm

Vandal, Giles. 2000. *Rethinking Southern Violence: Homicide in Post-Civil War Louisiana, 1866–1884.* Columbus: Ohio State University Press.

van Dijk, Jan. 2008. *World Crime: Breaking the Silence on Problems of Security, Justice and Devlopment Across the World.* Los Angeles, CA: Sage.

van Dijk, Jan, John van Kesteren, and Paul Smit. 2007. *Criminal Victimization in International Perspective: Key Findings from the 2004–2005 ICVS and EU ICS.* Den Haag: Boom Juridische uitgevers.

van Kesteren, John, Pat Mayhew, and Paul Nieuwbeerta. 2004. *Criminal Victimization in Seventeen Industrialized Countries: Key Findings from the 2000 International Crime Victims Survey.* Den Haag: Boom Juridische uitgevers.

Verkko, Veli. 1951. "Are There Regular Sequences in Crime Against Life Which Can Be Formulated as Laws?" *Homicides and Suicides in Finland and Their Dependence on National Character. Scandinavian Studies in Sociology*, 3:50–57. Copenhagen: Gads Forlag.

Verweij, Antonia, and Paul Nieuwbeerta. 2001. "Gender Differences in Violent Victimization in 18 Industrialized Countries: The Role of Emancipation." In *International Comparison of Crime and Victimization: The International Crime Victimization Survey*, ed. Helmut Kury. Willowdale, ON: de Sitter.

Waddington, P. A. J. 1999. "Police (Canteen) Subculture: An Appreciation." *British Journal of Criminology* 39:287–309.

Walker, Garthine. 2003. *Crime, Gender and Social Order in Early Modern England.* New York: Cambridge University Press.

Wiener, Martin J. 2004. *Men of Blood: Violence, Manliness and Criminal Justice in Victorian England.* New York: Cambridge University Press.

Wikstrom, Per-Olof H., and David Butterworth. 2007. *Adolescent Crime: Individual Differences and Lifestyles.* Cullompton, UK: Willan.

Wood, J. Carter. 2004. *Violence and Crime in 19th-Century England: The Shadow of Our Refinement.* London: Routledge.

World Health Organization. 2005. *WHO Multi-Country Study on Women's Health and Domestic Violence Against Women: Summary Report of Initial Results on Prevalence, Health Outcomes and Women's Responses.* Geneva: WHO.

Zahn, Margaret A., and Patricia L. McCall. 1999. "Homicide in the 20th-Century United States." In *Studying and Preventing Homicide*, ed. M. Dwayne Smith and Margaret A. Zahn. Thousand Oaks, CA: Sage.

Zimring, Franklin E. 2007. *The Great American Crime Decline*. New York: Oxford University Press.

Crime Data Sources

2005 Australian Personal Safety Survey. http://www.abs.gov.au/AUSSTATS/abs@.nsf/DetailsPage/4906.02005.

British Crime and Justice Survey. http://www.data-archive.ac.uk/FindingData/snDescription.asp?sn=5258.

British Crime Survey. http://www.homeoffice.gov.uk/rds/crimeew0709.html.

European Sourcebook of Criminal Justice Statistics. http://www.europeansourcebook.org/index_e3doc.html.

Canadian General Social Survey. http://www.statcan.gc.ca/dli-ild/data-donnees/ftp/gss-eng-end.htm.

International Crime Victimization Survey. http://ruljis.leidenuniv.nl/group/jfcr/sss/icvs/.

National Crime Victimization Survey. http://www.ojp.usdog.gov/bjs/.

National Family Violence Survey http://www.socio.com/srch/summary/afda/fam32.htm.

National Violence Against Women Survey. http://www.ojp.usdoj.gov/nih/victdocs.htm#2000.

Uniform Crime Reports. http://www.fbi.gov/ucr/ucr.htm.

CHAPTER 13

IMMIGRANTS AND CRIME

SANDRA M. BUCERIUS

BOTH the general public and policymakers have often seen immigration and crime as inextricably connected. While questions about the relationship between immigration and crime are widely discussed, clear answers have not yet been found. Whether speaking of an immigration and crime nexus means that immigrants are thought to be more criminal *before* they migrate (i.e., criminal members of the sending society tend to migrate more often than noncriminal members), whether they turn to a criminal lifestyle *after* settling in the new country (i.e., due to social, political, or economical exclusion), or whether they become criminal *through the process* of immigration itself (i.e., immigration *causes* immigrants, non-immigrants, or both to engage in crime), seems unclear.

Data show that "members of *some* disadvantaged minority groups in every Western country are disproportionately likely to be arrested, convicted, and imprisoned for violent, property, and drug crimes" (Tonry 1997, 1). This applies not only to recent or fairly recent immigrants and their children, such as Moroccans in the Netherlands, Finns in Sweden, or Turks in Germany, but to visible "racial" minorities as well, such as African Americans in the United States or Afro-Caribbeans in England. This trend also applies to groups that are long established in a country, such as aboriginal populations in Canada or Australia. One has to keep in mind though, that all minority groups with higher incarceration or crime rates experience some form of social, political, or economic disadvantage. However, not *all* disadvantaged immigrant groups have higher crime rates than the native-born population. In fact, most have lower crime rates. In addition, disadvantaged immigrant groups who are disproportionately represented in crime statistics in one country do not necessarily have high crime rates in another, despite having similar socioeconomic backgrounds and migration histories.

Research findings on the criminal involvement of second-generation immigrants show a different picture than for the first generation. Second-generation immigrants typically have higher crime rates than first-generation immigrants. In the US context, however, most second-generation immigrant groups continue to enjoy *lower* crime rates than the native-born population. In stark contrast, research findings in European countries indicate that some second-generation immigrant groups have crime rates that drastically *exceed* those of the native-born population.

While the specifics vary from country to country, Western societies are especially concerned about immigration and crime. Public opinion has frequently linked trends in immigration to social problems in the country, and members of these countries have been particularly concerned about a possible relationship between rising numbers of immigrants and levels of crime and violence. Data collected for the recent General Social Survey indicate that almost three-quarters of Americans believe that a rise in immigrant numbers causes higher crime rates (cited in Rumbaut and Ewing 2007; Feldmeyer 2009, 718).

These worries are usually initiated when crime rates increase (or are thought to be rising, even if they are not), during times of an immigration influx, or after exceptional circumstances, such as the attacks of September 11, 2001. In the context of the 9/11 terrorist attacks, an automatic association has developed between the words "immigration" and "terrorism" (Portes 2003; Ismaili, forthcoming). Although none of the terrorists involved in the 9/11 attacks were recent immigrants to the United States, and the majority of the US population was (at various points in time) in favor of immigration before 9/11, surveys have shown that this positive attitude toward immigrants changed dramatically after 9/11 (Kohut et al. 2006).[1]

Along these lines, the most important conclusions of this chapter can be summarized as follows:

- Popular opinion and theoretical assumptions notwithstanding, first-generation immigrants do not typically have higher crime involvement than the native-born. This finding does not only hold true in the US context but also in most other Western countries.
- Similarly to individual level studies, research on the macro level shows that immigration does not increase crime. Some research suggests that immigration may decrease crime and has had an influence on the overall crime drop in the United States. Macro-level research particularly shows that the percentage of immigrant populations in a given geographical area is not positively associated with violent crime rates. If there is an association, it tends to be a negative one.
- For reasons that are still up for debate, most second-generation immigrant groups experience higher crime levels than the first generation. However, despite having higher crime rates than the parent generation,

second-generation immigrants in the United States and Canada typically continue to have lower (or similar) criminal involvement than the native-born.

- In contrast to the findings in the United States and Canada, the crime rates of some second-generation immigrant groups in the European context drastically exceed the crime rates of the native-born population.

- Sociological research suggests that the quality of reception and the extent of social, economic, and political inclusion or exclusion and other contextual factors in the receiving country are crucial factors for social integration. Weak social integration may be an important contributing factor to criminal involvement. Thus, the crime rates of immigrants seem not only to be influenced by their generational status but also by the reception and the specific opportunity structures they and their particular immigrant group face.

- Generally speaking, most studies on immigration and crime draw on aggregate level data and do not take the heterogeneity of the immigrant population into account. Future research clearly has to pay attention to group differences based on generational status, legal status, reasons behind immigration, characteristics of the ethnic or national culture, assimilation, and social welfare policies of the receiving country.

- Immigration research beyond criminology also stresses that we must emphasize the heterogeneity of *both* immigrant and non-immigrant populations in order to draw insightful comparisons. Building on this research, future research (quantitative and qualitative) on the immigration and crime nexus—though always subject to limits on available data—ought to take race, national origin, and ethnicity into account wherever possible.

- Numerous studies have shown that second- and third-generation immigrants perceive social exclusion to a much higher degree than the first generation. As crime rates also exceed for this group, effective policy recommendations should focus on reducing social, economic, and political exclusion of the second and third generation.

This chapter presents an overview of the literature on immigration and crime. Section I discusses a number of considerations that need to be kept in mind when talking about a link between immigration and crime. Section II provides an overview of the research and data examining crimes committed *by* immigrants, including a historical framework, an overview of the research findings on the individual and the macro level—including a separate section on the criminal involvement of second generation immigrants—and a discussion of undocumented immigrants. In section III, research and data on crimes committed *against* immigrants are presented. Particular attention is paid to measurement difficulties in research on immigrant victimization, research findings on immigrant victimization, and the social control of immigrants post-9/11. Section IV assesses comparative and international studies on immigration and crime. Section V concludes with an outline of important areas for future research and provides suggestions for public policy.

I. The Immigration and Crime Nexus

The relationship between immigration and crime is highly complex, and it is difficult to answer or even comment on the question of whether there is an immigration and crime nexus. Although there is a large American and international literature on the topics of immigration and ethnicity (including work on race and minorities), surprisingly few criminologists have examined the relationship between immigration and crime. Recently, academics have become increasingly interested in the immigration and crime nexus, but published studies remain scarce. There are not enough data sources available to disprove *any* positive correlation between immigration and crime, even though historical and contemporary studies have consistently found that immigrants are, on average, *less* criminal than the native-born population and that immigration may even *decrease* crime rates. To complicate matters further, there is no consensus on what is meant by the immigration and crime nexus that is so readily talked about in both the academic and the public sphere (for a detailed overview, see Mears 2001).

When an immigration and crime nexus is discussed, most people automatically assume that it describes immigrants' involvement in crime or the macro-level influence of immigration on crime. If this connection exists, a rise in immigration should demonstrably lead to an increase in crime rates at the national level. Countries with higher immigration rates should consequently experience elevated levels of crime, and cities like Toronto, San Diego, and New York, which have large immigrant populations, should be among the cities with the highest national crime rates. Ultimately, this assumption requires research to demonstrate that immigrants commit more crimes than native-born individuals, independent of their social, political, and economic conditions.

Even though many people readily assume that the relationship between immigration and crime relates to crimes committed by immigrants, we must look at the issue from several different angles. First, we must determine whether an immigration and crime nexus reflects immigrants' or non-immigrants' involvement in crime. Increasing immigration rates may have an interruptive influence in certain areas; non-immigrants (and not just immigrants) living in these areas may become more easily engaged in criminal activity. Furthermore, as incidents of discrimination and hate crimes illustrate, non-immigrants' engagement in crime may be linked to immigration.[2] Last, an examination of the immigration and crime nexus should also consider the extent to which immigrants will be victimized by both hate crimes and other incidents.

When considering an immigration and crime nexus, clear distinctions should be made between legal and illegal immigrants. It is possible that there are differences in the offenses (and victimization) of legal and illegal immigrants. Most studies cannot account for legal status, and accurate and reliable estimates of the number of undocumented immigrants are not yet available; in the United States, estimates of the number of undocumented immigrants in the country differ on a scale of millions. Hence, very little can be said about the different offending patterns. It can be argued that undocumented immigrants are more likely to engage in criminal behavior because this may be the only way to earn a living. Given their vulnerable situation and illegal status, the exact opposite can also be argued: undocumented immigrants will do everything they can to comply with the law and to avoid contact with law enforcement officials.

Age groups and gender should also be considered. Research suggests that being male and young is closely associated with increased criminal behavior (Waters 1999). Because recent immigrants are disproportionately young and male, this group is more prone to criminal activity.

Additionally, there are significant differences between various immigrant generations. Almost all studies in Western countries show that first-generation immigrants have much lower crime rates than subsequent generations, independent of cultural background. Crime rates increase over time and with later generations, although there are some exceptions (e.g., first-generation Antilleans in the Netherlands; Engbersen van der Leun, and de Boom 2007).

Ethnic and socioeconomic background must also be considered when determining whether there is an immigration and crime nexus. Many studies merely look at the relationship between immigration and crime, assuming that recent immigrants are a homogeneous group. While this was the case during periods of high European immigration in the early twentieth century, immigrants today represent a very heterogeneous group.

In addition to different ethnic origins and socioeconomic backgrounds, individuals' reasons for immigrating also vary and need to be properly assessed. The immigration and crime nexus may look very different for labor migrants as compared to asylum seekers or those who migrated to reunite with their families.

It is also important to distinguish between different types of crime. To date, most studies of immigration and crime look at the relationship between immigration and violence (Hagan and Palloni 1998; Martinez and Lee, 2000; Lee and Martinez 2002; Martinez 2002; Lee 2003; Feldmeyer 2009; Stowell et al. 2009), mostly neglecting other types of crime. Because anti-immigrant sentiments typically arise in times of economic downturn and scarce employment opportunities (Yeager 2002), it is important to remember that white-collar crimes and corporate crimes, which often influence employment situations when they are discovered, are usually not committed by immigrants.

The quality of reception in the host country is also a crucial factor (see Reitz 2003 and Reitz et al. 2008); the extent of social, economic, and political inclusion or exclusion and other contextual factors in the receiving country are very important. Turks in Germany, for example, not only experience social and economic disadvantages but the vast majority has also been politically excluded by not qualifying for German citizenship for many decades. On the contrary, Eastern Europeans who are ethnically German (*Aussiedler*) but whose families have not lived in Germany for centuries automatically receive citizenship and the rights that come with it upon their arrival.[3]

Taken together, the immigration and crime nexus reflects a number of issues and cannot be examined by measuring only whether immigrants commit more crimes than non-immigrants. However, most policymakers, members of the general public, and even academics[4] have a very one-dimensional view of the immigration and crime nexus. Not surprisingly, the largest body of research concentrates on the question of whether and to what extent immigrants are involved in crime on the individual level and whether immigration increases crime as a macro-level process.

II. Crimes Committed by Immigrants in the United States

In many ways, Edwin Sutherland can be seen as the pioneer of criminological research on immigration and crime. In 1924 he suggested that immigrants are generally more law-abiding than their native-born counterparts and that it is acculturation to the United States that escalates criminal involvement among immigrants and their children (Sutherland 1924). To prove this point, Sutherland provided evidence showing that first-generation immigrants had lower crime rates than second-generation immigrants and that people living in their country of origin had lower crime rates than immigrants from those countries residing in the United States. Furthermore, immigrants who came to the United States as children were more likely to be incarcerated than immigrants who came to the United States as adults. Thus, Sutherland concluded that criminal involvement increases over time and with later generations. While his argument is nearly a century old, Sutherland's findings are still supported by a great deal of evidence today.

Interestingly (and despite Sutherland's early findings), not only popular opinion but also many theoretical approaches suggest that immigrants are more prone to criminal behavior than non-immigrants due to various cultural or structural barriers that they tend to face. Given the existing theoretical explanations, it is surprising that various studies have shown immigrants to be less involved in crime than native-born citizens. Contemporary theories focus on social-psychological factors (e.g., strain and tension from the acculturation process) or sociological variables (e.g., neighborhood and community disorganization) to explain a link between immigration and crime. Both perspectives are helpful in trying to understand immigrant criminality, yet they cannot explain why the majority of immigrants do not commit crime at a higher level than the native-born population.

While popular belief and major theoretical explanations suggest otherwise, most studies at the individual and macro levels have shown that "in many cases, compared with native groups, immigrants seem better able to withstand crime-facilitating conditions than native groups" in the United States (Martinez and Lee 2000, 486). This pattern generally holds true when looking at aggregate data. However, there are important differences between immigrant groups and generations. Hence, when looking at disaggregated data, immigrants seem to have both higher and lower crime rates depending on their generational status and the specific opportunity structures they and their particular immigrant group face in society (see also Engbersen, van der Leun, and de Boom 2007).

A. Historical Framework

The idea of an immigration and crime nexus is not new. Historically speaking, some early academics argued that there is a biological explanation for immigrant crime (see, for example, Henderson 1901, 247; Laughlin 1939). Following that line of thought, these researchers believed that immigrants were biologically inferior to non-immigrants (Martinez and Lee 2000, 488). Today, genetic explanations have been strongly discredited by the academic community as overtly racist in nature and are seen to have no empirical or theoretical value (Gabor and Roberts 1990; Wortley 2003).

Similarly to biological explanations, some researchers emphasized the importance of cultural differences in explaining crime rates across different ethnic and racial groups. According to this perspective, culture, cultural traditions, or culture conflicts, rather than socioeconomic characteristics, account for ethnic and racial differences in crime rates (Taft 1933; Sellin 1938; Curtis 1975; Hawkins 1994, 102; Erlanger 1995). For example, Italians were reported to have high rates of conviction for homicide in 1920s America, possibly because they used to conduct a certain degree of self-justice regarding honor-related incidents (Sutherland and Cressey 1960). Likewise, Lind (1930) conducted research among Chinese immigrants in Hawaii and found them particularly prone to certain types of gambling and grafting, which resemble Chinese traditions. Again, these approaches have been widely discredited among academics as they fail to explain immigrant involvement in crime that is perpetuated by or mirrors that of non-immigrant groups (e.g., gambling among black Americans).[5]

Other historical work on immigration and crime found that some immigrant populations slightly increase the American crime problem, yet stated that this is largely due to "difficulties of adjustment" and that immigrants are neither "inherently worse" nor in any sense "to blame" (Taft 1933, 77). Tony Waters' (1999) work on the history of the relationship between immigration and crime in the United States demonstrated that in the rare cases when immigrants appeared to be more engaged in criminal activity than the native-born population, large immigration waves had resulted in disproportionately high numbers of young males in the country; being male and being young both positively correlate with criminal behavior (and victimization).

In 1901 the Industrial Commission issued a "Special Report on General Statistics of Immigration and the Foreign-Born," noting that foreign-born whites were committing fewer crimes than native-born whites (Industrial Commission 1901). Another federal panel, the Immigration Commission, released its own study a decade later, stating that there was no satisfactory evidence showing immigrants to be disproportionately engaged in criminal activity (Dillingham 1911). Rather, immigration was believed to suppress crime rates. It was claimed, however, that southern Europeans in general and Italians in particular were more prone to personal violence, especially homicide; however, the data underlying these assumptions did not show this effect.

In 1931, yet another study conducted by the National Commission on Law Observance and Enforcement (known as the Wickersham report) concluded that, on average, immigrants did not have elevated crime levels.[6] However, the report found that some immigrant groups were disproportionately engaged in specific types of crime (National Commission on Law Observance and Enforcement 1931).

B. Research on the Link between Immigration and Crime

Both individual-level and macro-level research clearly suggest that at least first-generation immigrants have *lower* crime rates than the native-born population. Crime rates are increasing for the second generation in comparison to the first; however, some research demonstrates that the second generation continues to have lower crime rates than the native-born population.

1. *Individual Level*

Taken together, contemporary research at the individual level finds that immigrants are less prone to criminal activity than other populations. Numerous studies clearly indicate that on an average and on the individual level, immigrants have lower offense, arrest, or incarceration rates than the native-born population (though very little is known about the mechanisms that keep crime rates among immigrants at a low level).

However, research in this area is limited by the lack of relevant available data. Most individual jurisdictions do not collect any data on ethnic group differences, nationality, or immigration status but focus solely on racial indicators. Hence, incarceration data are the only official national data available that mention immigration status (McDonald 1997). Because research conducted by Hagan and Palloni (1999) indicated that immigrants (especially undocumented immigrants) face a higher risk of being incarcerated than native-born individuals, using incarceration data as an indicator to examine the immigration and crime nexus poses methodological problems.

Despite the fact that immigrants are more likely to be incarcerated, research has shown that immigrants tend to be less frequently imprisoned than their native-born counterparts (Butcher and Piehl 1998b, 2006; Hagan and Palloni 1999). Butcher and Piehl (2006) used 1980, 1990, and 2000 US Census data to show that immigrants are institutionalized at one-fifth the rate of the native-born population. Furthermore, recent immigrants were less likely to be institutionalized than immigrants who had been in the country for a while; this finding resonates with Sutherland's point that incarceration rates increase with time spent in the United States. The gap in the incarceration rate between the immigrant and native-born populations increased between 1980 and 2000. Butcher and Piehl concluded that the process of immigration itself self-selects immigrants who are more responsive to deterrence than native-born individuals.

Comparisons of criminal justice data between non-border and border cities showed that border cities actually have lower crime rates (Hagan and Palloni 1999). Furthermore, neighborhood research in El Paso, San Diego, and Miami examined the link between immigration and homicide and showed that immigration is not associated with higher levels of homicide (Lee, Martinez, and Rosenfeld 2001). Specifically, Martinez (2002) found immigration to have either no effect or a negative effect on most types of Latino homicide.

Other individual-level research using a nationally representative sample also found that immigrants were less engaged in crime, including property crime (Butcher and Piehl 1998b). Sampson, Raudenbush, and Earl's work (1997) on "collective efficacy" pointed out that Latinos are more likely to intervene to stop criminal activity than non-Latinos.

2. *Second-Generation Immigrants*

An important observation for individual-level studies is that crime rates seem to increase with later generations and time spent in the United States; Tonry (1997) called this the "not the foreign born but their children" phenomenon. Some researchers suggest that the increase in crime rates among subsequent generations can be explained by the role of assimilation in enhancing criminal involvement (Sutherland 1924). In that sense, the more American the subsequent generations become, the more do their crime rates approach the levels of the native-born population.

Alternatively, the increase in crime rates among subsequent generations might be explained by the group's lack of an actively chosen and consciously decided immigration experience. Thus, the first generation may interpret experiences of "othering" and exclusion in the receiving country as actions of a few rude individuals as opposed to systematic discrimination (Viruell-Fuentes 2007). In sharp contrast, second- and third-generation immigrants seem to be more receptive to systematic "othering" experiences and are less likely to interpret them as isolated incidents. Instead, they tend to view them as processes of discrimination, marginalization, disempowerment, and social exclusion (Waldinger and Feliciano 2004; Viruell-Fuentes 2007; Bucerius 2008, 2009a, 2009b). For later-generation immigrants to become Americans (or Europeans), they must contend with and place themselves in the country's racial stratification system; often, they are relegated to a disadvantaged minority status and therefore face higher risks of engaging in crime.

Another explanation could be that second-generation immigrants refer to a different comparison group when they evaluate their situation in the new country. Members of the first generation most likely compare their situation to the living conditions in the country of origin. Additionally, they are willing to defer immediate gratification in the interest of longer-term advancement for themselves and their children. In contrast to that, members of the second generation refer to the native population as their comparison group and soon realize that they are worse off than the native born.

Theoretically speaking, one could argue that the second generation shares the same cultural goals (e.g., a middle-class lifestyle and the American dream) as the native-born population, yet suffers more than the first generation from the fact that opportunities (such as education, jobs, etc.) are not equally distributed in society (Merton 1938).[7] Consequently, they may innovate alternative ways to achieve success and take advantage of the illegitimate opportunities available to them (Merton 1938).[8]

Neither of these perspectives can explain why some second-generation immigrants continue to have lower crime rates (Kasinitz et al. 2008). Obviously, the specific opportunity structures they and their particular immigrant group face in society (Engbersen, van der Leun, and de Boom 2007), the parental human capital, the modes of incorporation, family structure (Portes and Zhou 1993; Portes and Rumbaut 2001), and the neighborhood in which they live may play a role as well (Shaw and McKay 1969).

Independent of the open question as to why the crime rates among second- and subsequent-generation immigrants increase in most cases, several studies could demonstrate that they actually do increase. For example, Sampson, Morenoff, and Raudenbush's (2005) self-report study on violence in Chicago found that first-generation immigrants were half as likely to have committed a violent crime as third-generation immigrants; the odds for second-generation immigrants were about 75 percent of those of the third generation. Morenoff and Astor (2006) similarly used a self-report study and found a linear increase in the level of violence for their participants across generations. Likewise, relying on data collected among Vietnamese youth, Zhou and Bankston's (2006) study indicated that crime rates are higher among those who have been born in the United States. Rumbaut's longitudinal data on arrest and incarceration rates demonstrated significant differences between second-generation immigrants and foreign-born youths in San Diego; the foreign-born had lower rates of both arrest and incarceration.

Tonry (1997) showed that these patterns appear not only in the United States but resonate internationally (with some variations depending on ethnic group, cause of migration, immigration policies in the respective receiving country, and generational status). It is important to note, though, that research in the United States demonstrates that second-generation immigrants continue to be less prone to criminal activity when compared to native-born groups (Sampson, Morenoff, and Gannon-Rowley 2002; for similar findings in Canada see Hagan, Levi, and Dinovitzer 2007).

3. Macro level

Research showing the influence of immigration on crime at the macro level is scarce, and longitudinal research is almost entirely absent. This is particularly interesting because immigration is a macro-level process that unfolds over time. Large immigrant populations enter preexisting local structures and can either contribute to "structural factors conducive to crime" (and therefore increase crime rates) or "rejuvenate economically stagnant metropolitan areas" (and therefore lessen crime rates) (Reid et al. 2005, 758). As Ousey and Kubrin (2009, 465) point out, "virtually all empirical findings" to date "are based on cross-sectional analyses that do not measure over-time change in immigration, crime, or other relevant social factors."

Various studies that have been conducted on the effects of macro-level aspects of immigration on aggregate criminal offenses (Butcher and Piehl 1998a, Hagan and Palloni 1999; Lee, Martinez, and Rosenfeld 2001; Martinez 2002; Reid et al. 2005; Ousey and Kubrin 2009; Stowell et al. 2009) support the argument that immigration does not increase violent crime rates and may even reduce violent crime rates.

Butcher and Piehl (1998a) analyzed the relationship between immigration and crime in several dozen US metropolitan areas. Although cities with large immigrant populations had higher crime rates than those with lower immigrant populations, when they controlled for other factors that may influence crime levels, Butcher and Piehl found no significant relationship between immigration and crime.

By combining 2000 US Census data and 2000 Uniform Crime Report data, Reid et al. (2005) looked at violent crime and property offenses and found that in some aspects (namely, recent immigration and Asian immigration) immigration actually lowers rates of homicide and theft in metropolitan areas. Additionally, after controlling for a series of demographic and economic characteristics, immigration was not found to increase crime levels in any aspect.

Ousey and Kubrin (2009) and Stowell et al. (2009) offer the only analyses that evaluate *longitudinal* macro-level data and assess various factors subject to change over time such as police force capacity, economic deprivation, demographic structure, family structure, illegal drug markets, and labor markets. It was concluded that increased immigration has a decreasing effect on the violence rate in cities. As in individual-level studies, their longitudinal analyses from 1980 to 2000 (Ousey and Kubrin) and from 1994 to 2004 (Stowell et al.) indicate that the macro-level process of immigration itself may buffer against crime and violence.

Sampson and his colleagues (2005) take this conclusion a step further and argue that the macro-level process of immigration may decrease crime rates and therefore be a key factor contributing to the overall crime drop in the United States in the 1990s (see also Reid et al. 2005; Rumbaut and Ewing 2007; Ousey and Kubrin 2009). This finding resonates with research conducted in the areas of education, health, and risk-taking behavior (Palloni and Morenoff 2001; Portes and Rumbaut 2001; Bui and Thingniramol 2005). As David Brooks (2006, A25) put it, "immigrants themselves are like a booster shot of traditional morality injected into the body." According to this view, their high morals and work ethic contribute to an overall decrease in crime rates; for example, the relatively high marriage rates among Hispanics may lead to less family disruption and hence lower crime rates (Sampson, Morenoff, and Raudenbush 2005). Moreover, there is some evidence that immigration bolsters two-parent family structures by lowering divorce rates in US cities; lower divorce rates are, in turn, negatively related to crime rates (Ousey and Kubrin 2009).

C. Undocumented Immigrants

In contrast to the immigrant population in US state prisons, undocumented immigrants (or illegal immigrants) seem to be disproportionately represented in the federal prison system; they accounted for nearly 27 percent of federal inmates in 2004 (Government Accountability Office 2005, 2). However, the federal prison population accounts for only 8 percent of the total prison population (Sabol, Minton, Harrison 2007, 3).

Unauthorized entry into the United States is a crime; hence, undocumented immigrants are automatically prosecuted under the federal system for committing immigration offenses should they be arrested. Imprisoned immigrants in the federal system, therefore, may additionally have committed a criminal offense or they may be incarcerated just because of their immigration status. Most immigrants in the federal system are imprisoned because of immigration violations, not, as is widely assumed, because of other criminal acts (Immigration Policy Center 2008, 2).

It is obviously very difficult to make accurate statements about the crime rates of undocumented immigrants. Many studies do not clearly distinguish between legal and illegal immigrants, and estimates of the number of undocumented immigrants currently residing in the Unites States vary by millions.[9] What is known, however, is that the number of undocumented immigrants roughly doubled between 1994 and 2004 and now ranges around 12 million (Immigration Policy Center 2008, 1). Border cities and other large cities with presumably large numbers of undocumented people (such as San Diego, Los Angeles, Miami, or New York) experienced a decline in crime rates during that period of time. According to Zimring, in the case of New York, the decline was double that of the rest of the country (Zimring 2007, 140). This decline, then, not only appeared nationwide but also in cities where the presence of large numbers of immigrants might be expected to increase crime rates.[10]

Hagan and Palloni (1999) examined Hispanic undocumented immigrants and noted multiple problems with using incarceration data to draw comparisons between illegal immigrants and the native-born population. Undocumented immigrants who have been accused of a crime are more likely to face pretrial detention because of the assumption that they may leave the country before being sentenced. Being on pretrial detention, however, generally increases the risk of conviction. The study revealed that depending on the national origin of the accused, incarceration rates are three to seven times higher than the crime rates of undocumented immigrants relative to citizens. However, once specific measures like age and gender are taken into account, Hispanic undocumented immigrants are less likely to be incarcerated than native-born individuals (Hagan and Palloni 1999).

Some researchers suggest that the reason underlying the unauthorized immigration should be considered when the criminal behavior of undocumented immigrants is examined (Gottfredson 2004, 7). While some people illegally enter the country because of better legal economic opportunities, others enter seeking greater opportunities for theft or drug sales; these reasons play a significant role in determining whether undocumented immigrants are more or less likely to be involved in crime. However, research in border cities indicates that crime rates are lower in these geographical areas than in other cities in the country; these findings suggest that the number of people who circulate between the borders to commit crimes in the United States is not significant (Hagan and Palloni 1999).[11]

III. Crimes Committed against Immigrants in the United States

Crimes like sex trafficking, child labor, assault, robberies, hate crimes, homicides, and slave-like labor conditions have significant effects on victims. Criminological research, therefore, does not only focus on crimes committed *by* immigrants, but also on crimes committed *against* immigrants. Studies of immigrants as victims are scarce. Most existing literature focuses on ethnic or racial factors, yet few studies have examined the link between immigrant status and victimization.

A. Data Collection

Collecting data on crime against immigrants is difficult because immigrants may be afraid to talk to law enforcement officials and report incidents of victimization. Research has shown that even though immigrants have a more positive view of the police than do native-born individuals, they are significantly less likely to contact the police for assistance or to report a crime (Davis and Hendricks 2007).

Fear of contacting the police is probably intensified if victims do not have a legal status in the country and have to fear deportation when notifying the police. Although intensified community policing has helped to overcome this problem, with the recent decline of community policing in the aftermath of 9/11 (Arnold 2007), trust in the police is most likely going to subside. Under recently created memorandums of agreement, trained state and local law enforcement authorities are now permitted to "question and detain undocumented immigrants suspected of committing a state crime" (Ismaili, forthcoming). The likelihood that officers will stop immigrants in order to check their immigration status is therefore significantly increased, even though law enforcement officials are not officially authorized to execute random street-checks. It has been argued that this sends a very negative signal to immigrant communities; the police can make a community safe and counteract victimization only when they work with its residents and not against them (Harris 2006, 7).

B. Studies on Immigrant Victimization

The victimization of—especially—undocumented immigrants is probably not of primary relevance for most state officials, who are mainly concerned with prosecution, deportation, and security. Research has shown, for example, that neither of the two central approaches to combating human trafficking has adequately addressed immigration options in the protection of the victim. Neither the "incarcerating the offender" nor the "protecting the victim" model protects the victim of deportation. As a result, if victims comply with the law and provide stronger evidence with which their traffickers can be prosecuted, their own status in the country is at risk (Haynes 2004).

Other research on immigrant victimization examines the relationship between homicide and immigrant victimization in specific cities and across certain populations (Martinez 1997, 2002). Latinos in Miami with its large Latino population are found to face a victimization rate that is approximately half of that expected, given the population size (Martinez 1997). Lee, Martinez, and Rodriguez's (2000) comparative study of Latino homicide victimization in Miami and El Paso found that Latinos were even less likely to be victimized in El Paso.

Some data on Muslim immigrants, however, reveal that discrimination against and violent victimization of immigrant youth is associated with the way immigrants feel they are portrayed in the media. Those who reported that the American media propagates negative and prejudiced representations of Arab people were more attuned to personal experiences of prejudice and victimization based on their ethnic identity (Wray-Lake, Syvertsen, and Flanagan 2008).

Research has also examined the mistreatment of barrio residents by state authorities (Goldsmith et al. 2009), finding that people who appear Mexican are more likely than the general US population to experience mistreatment. Additionally, the study showed that being a second-generation immigrant, a naturalized immigrant, or well-educated does not offer protection from mistreatment by authorities. This finding suggests that mistreatment is rooted in institutional racism rather than dependent on immigration status.

A body of literature on fear of crime among immigrant populations suggests that this fear does not decrease over time spent in the United States (e.g., Sundeen 1984; Ackah 2000; Lee and Ulmer 2000; Menjivar and Bejarano 2004). Most importantly, immigrants' former experiences with crime and the justice system in their countries of origin, their contacts with US immigration officials, and the social networks through which they learn about the US police, crime, and criminals influence their fear of crime (Menjivar and Bejarano 2004). However, research on the fear of crime among immigrants lacks a native comparison group. Although these studies can make some statements about the fear of crime among certain immigrant populations at a given time, they cannot show whether the fear of crime in that population is higher or lower than that of other populations, particularly non-immigrants, living in similar neighborhoods.

Despite criminal victimization, immigrants face various forms of marginalization and discrimination on social, political, and economic levels. Naber (2006) describes the increasing difficulties immigrants have finding or keeping jobs, and the lack of security in their communities and urban spaces due to threats or hate crimes. Various studies show how particular groups of immigrants experience significant disadvantages in the school system and on the job market. Those facing disadvantages are not randomly distributed across nationalities but disproportionately originate from Mexico, Latin American, and Caribbean countries, including El Salvador, Guatemala, Haiti, the Dominican Republic, and the West Indies (Portes and Rumbaut 2001; Farley and Alba 2002; Kasinitz et al. 2008; Portes and Fernandez-Kelly 2008; Rumbaut 2008; Telles and Oritz 2008; Zhou et al. 2008).

C. The Social Control of Immigrants since 9/11

Social exclusion, marginalization, and discrimination are not limited to educational institutions or the housing market but also occur in immigration policy. In the aftermath of 9/11, domestic US immigration policy has been increasingly intertwined with, if not substantially subsumed under, terrorism policy (Tumlin 2004). Reshaping immigration policy in the name of the "war on terror" is not only administratively significant, it also produces the notion that immigrants are suspects first and welcome newcomers second (if at all).

The US government launched several programs and initiatives[12] in the name of the "war on terrorism" (for a detailed overview see Ismaili, forthcoming) that mainly target non-citizens (undocumented immigrants as well as permanent residents, green card holders, etc.). Most of these initiatives have a significant influence on ordinary non-citizens who now tend to face an emerging securitization in their everyday lives (Rodriguez 2008). Leading academics have come to think of this development as a "war on immigrants" (Kanstroom 2005; Ismaili, forthcoming).

Some researchers have argued that the definition of a suspected terrorist in the Patriot Act is so broad and ambiguous that virtually every immigrant, involved in no crime at all or involved in the violation of a minor immigration policy, may be detained (Cole 2002).

September 11 also precipitated a practice of racial profiling that legitimizes a presumptive suspicion against Middle Eastern, South Asian, and Muslim individuals living in the United States. In sweeps following 9/11, more than 1,200 persons of presumed Middle Eastern origin were detained without charges or even links to the terrorist attacks (Volpp 2002; Tumlin 2004).

In addition to the increasing forms of securitization performed by state actors, the fear of terrorism among the general public has also led to increased surveillance of immigrants by non-state actors such as neighbors, public transport workers, co-workers, teachers, and classmates. Through these practices of everyday surveillance, the social marginalization of immigrants and their exclusion from mainstream US society has increased rapidly (Rodriguez 2008).

Scholars who examine the historical dialectic between immigrant detention and the racialized othering of non-citizens argue that contemporary policies following the 9/11 terrorist attacks are not new or anomalous but emerge out of the historic relationship between the United States and non-citizens (Miller 2002;

Naber 2006; Hernandez 2007). Recognizing these various forms of marginalization, discrimination, and social exclusion is important because the quality of the reception of immigrants in the host country is one of the main indicators of successful integration into mainstream society (Reitz 2003; Peek 2005; Portes and Fernandez-Kelly 2008; Reitz et al. 2008). Associating immigrants with terrorism and therefore viewing them with suspicion may, in fact, contribute to weak social integration.[13]

IV. COMPARATIVE RESEARCH

Immigration is a macro-level process that evolves over time. Its outcomes very much depend on the particular political, economic, and social circumstances of the receiving society and the characteristics of the particular immigrant group. Thus, it is not surprising that the immigration and crime nexus takes on different forms in various countries.

A. Limitations to Rigorous Comparisons

When studies on immigrants and crime from different countries are compared, various contextual differences arise and need to be taken into account. An initial problem is terminological. Each country uses different definitions of who is to be called an "immigrant" and who is "native-born." This question in itself already causes confusion in immigrant nations like Canada and the United States. Naturally, nearly everyone is a descendent of an immigrant, and members of the second generation (or any subsequent generation) could be called either "native-born" or a "second-generation immigrant."

In other countries, however, terminology varies to an even greater extent. For example, like other official statistics on Germany's population, Germany's official crime statistics (namely the *polizeiliche Kriminalitätsstatistiken*) only distinguish between Germans (meaning citizens) and foreigners (meaning non-citizens). Hence, non-citizens are lumped together into one category regardless of their ethnic backgrounds and length of time in the country. Consequently, even second- or third-generation immigrants may appear under the category "foreigners" as long as they do not have German citizenship, whereas recent immigrants who can successfully claim citizenship status before immigrating fall under the category of "Germans." Statistical comparisons between the United States and Germany (and other countries) are therefore difficult, if not impossible.

Moreover, countries have very different citizenship policies, influencing whether and how quickly an immigrant can potentially become a citizen. In other words, in some countries like Germany, the majority of immigrants will most likely always fall in the category of "foreigners" (non-citizens) in official crime statistics due to citizenship policies that make naturalization difficult. In other countries like Canada, the majority of immigrants will become citizens relatively quickly. Cross-national comparisons between citizens and non-citizens in various countries may therefore look at very different groups.

Due to limited data sources, countries like Germany can only compare the crime rates of foreigners and citizens. This in itself is highly problematic and tends to overstress the criminal involvement of immigrants (Drewniak 2004; Bucerius 2009b). The official crime statistics report as "crimes by foreigners" not only those crimes committed by non-citizens living in the country but also crimes committed by tourists or transients (who naturally do not appear in the population census data). Moreover, some criminal offenses can be committed only by immigrants who lack citizenship, and offenses against immigration law appear in the German crime statistics.

German research has also shown that victims' willingness to report a crime is significantly higher if the perpetrator was perceived to be an immigrant or a group of immigrants (Wilmers et al. 2002; Mansel 2003). Additionally, labeling theories suggest that the chances of criminalizing an actual perpetrator are two to three times as high when the perpetrator is non-German (Mansel and Albrecht 2003). Naturally, ethnic profiling and intensified police stops in immigrant communities also increase the likelihood that immigrants are overrepresented in the crime statistics of any country. Moreover, similarly to findings in the United States, German research has also shown that convicted immigrants face more severe sanctions than their German counterparts (Pfeiffer, Kleimann, and Peterson 2005, 77ff.).[14]

B. Comparative Data on Ethnicity, Crime, and Immigration

Despite these limitations to rigorous comparison, a group of researchers started to gather comparative data on ethnicity, crime, and immigration in the late 1990s (Tonry 1997). One of the major difficulties that arose was that most countries do not collect ethnic identifiers for their official data systems. Some collect data on national origin, but these data often obscure important ethnic differences within a national-origin category. Therefore, cross-national comparisons of crime rates for different ethnic groups cannot be made. More importantly, comparisons of specific ethnic groups within one country cannot be made either, and research has to rely on self-report studies. As Tonry's effort shows, European countries are particularly hesitant to collect ethnicity-related statistics, and the legacy of Nazi Germany has left most countries with an aversion against collecting such information. However, officially refusing to record ethnic identifiers does not keep police from collecting other euphemistic data that help to identify certain populations (Albrecht 1997).

Despite having had limited resources to compare national data on ethnicity, crime, and immigration, Tonry (1997, 12) concluded that the findings "are so robust and so consistent across national boundaries" that five meaningful generalizations could be presented. First, he concluded that for each of the nine countries, crime and incarceration rates for members of some minority groups were greatly elevated and exceeded those of the native population. Second, every minority group that was characterized by higher levels of crime or imprisonment simultaneously experienced some form of social and economic disadvantage. Third, in the countries that could provide such data, individual biases could not explain racial or ethnic differences in crime and incarceration rates. In fact, group disparities in offense rates seem to be the primary explanation. Fourth, although procedures and practices in the criminal justice system should theoretically be neutral, they worked to the systematic disadvantage of minority groups. Fifth, contacts with the criminal justice system were influenced by subcultural behaviors and stereotyping that worked to the disadvantage of minority group members.

Moreover, drawing on European research, the researchers working with Tonry came to the conclusion that the multigenerational crime model (i.e., the idea that crime rates increase with generations) is simplistic and only partially true for self-selected economic migrants (Tonry 1997, 22). Self-selected economic migrants from many Asian cultures continue to have lower crime rates even in subsequent generations. This finding resonates with sociological research in the United States, which shows that many second-generation Asian immigrants perform significantly better (in terms of education and economic employment) than their native-born counterparts (Kasinitz et al. 2008). The assumption that lower crime rates are found in Asians as they are less discriminated against was shown to be erroneous (Smith 2005).

Moreover, cultural differences between immigrant populations that seem to be in a similar structural situation can result in different crime patterns. In the Netherlands, for example, Turks and Moroccans arrived around the same time and in approximately the same numbers. Despite comparable migration experiences and histories and similar socioeconomic backgrounds (both groups are comparably disadvantaged socially and economically), Moroccans are disproportionately more likely to be incarcerated. Incarceration rates for Turks are not much higher than for the Dutch native population (Junger-Tas 1997; van Gemert 1998; Engbersen van der Leun, and de Boom 2007). This is particularly interesting, as incarceration rates for Turks in Germany are much higher than for the native population even though Dutch-Turks and German-Turks come from similar socioeconomic backgrounds and share similar migration histories (Koopmans 2003). This suggests that the quality of reception and the perception of certain immigrant groups in the receiving country affect an immigrant's integration into mainstream society and identification with the receiving country (Portes and Rumbaut 1990; Portes and Fernandez-Kelly 2008; Bucerius 2009a).

Tonry (1997) also argues that, all else being equal, the incorporation policies of some countries foster integration in a way that reduces crime rates among subsequent generations. Most importantly, Sweden's immigration policies have been known to significantly reduce the "second-generation effect"; research shows that second-generation immigrants in Sweden show less criminal activity than non-immigrant Swedes (Ahlberg 1996).

Though unique in the European context, these findings resonate with Canadian research. Recent studies conducted by Hagan, Levi, and Dinovitzer (2007) and Dinovitzer, Hagan, and Levi (2009) looked at two different cohorts of youth living in a city just outside of Toronto with a large immigrant population; this setting provided the opportunity for a cross-generational analysis of immigration and delinquency. Very similar to the findings of US studies, the Canadian analyses found that first-, one-and-a-half-, or second-generation immigrant youth were not more likely to commit offenses than their native-born counterparts. In fact, the results showed that immigrants become more akin to the native-born youth across time and generations; however, even second-generation immigrant youth are still less likely to commit offenses than their Canadian counterparts. Following Tonry's argument, this may be a result of Canada's incorporation policies that foster integration in a way that decreases crime rates among second-generation immigrants.

Along those lines, Germany can serve as a counterexample, showing how a lack of timely integration policies can influence crime levels among the second and third generation.[15] In the postwar period, Germany recruited millions of guest workers for its flourishing economy. As neither the guest workers nor Germany had intended for this relationship to be a long-term commitment, Germany did not create appropriate integration policies or many programs to assist its guest workers' integration. While the majority of guest workers eventually left the country, a great number stayed and are now living in Germany with their children and grandchildren. Until recently, however, Germany has denied that it is an immigrant country at all.

The former guest workers and their families have faced various modes of social, political, and economic exclusion over the past several decades in Germany,[16] making the informal economy attractive, especially to second- and third- generation immigrants (Chapin 1997; Shapland et al. 2003; Bucerius 2007, 2009a). While details vary from country to country, immigrants in other European countries with guest-worker histories like the Netherlands, Great Britain, and France face similar or even greater difficulties, resulting in elevated crime rates among the second generation that—for some groups—drastically exceed the crime levels of the native-born population (Smith 2005; Engbersen, van der Leun, and de Boom 2007).

Tonry's comparative project also notes that the reasons for migration powerfully shape assimilation and criminality. Research on former Yugoslavian immigrants to Germany demonstrated that guest workers recruited in the 1960s and 1970s had lower crime rates than the native-born population. In comparison, recent research has shown that crime rates among war refugees from the same geographical area are much higher (Wetzels et al. 2001; Goldberg 2006; for examples in Sweden see Martens 1997).

Finally, Tonry notes that there are many immigrants who are not captured by any of the categories discussed in immigration and crime research. Academics from various countries have had a long history of taking jobs in the US academic job market (Welch and Zhen 2008; Hunter, Oswald, and Charlton 2009). Their economic, social, and cultural position does not pose any particular risk for criminal activity,[17] and the crime rates of these immigrants (and their children) can be expected to be lower than the rates among the native population.

V. Implications

Although several significant studies have explored whether immigrants are more prone to criminal activity than non-immigrants, there is still much to be learned about immigration and crime. Some of these questions are addressed in the following section that outlines future research areas and policy recommendations. I make no claim that this section is complete.

A. Future Research Areas

First, there is a very basic need for future studies to clearly indicate whether the immigrants included are legal or illegal, first, second, or third generation, and economic migrants or asylum seekers. These factors are important in the development of knowledge about different ethnic populations and in understanding the immigration and crime nexus. Most importantly, future studies must move beyond the questions of whether and to what degree immigration and crime are linked.

Although previous studies looking at the relationship between immigration and crime controlled for factors such as socioeconomic status, unemployment, deprivation, some important factors have been overlooked in most existing studies. Because many families in various immigrant communities come from very traditional backgrounds, the divorce rate among their population is expected to be lower than among the native-born population. When we look at crime rates of children and young adults, however, they are higher among children from single-parent households. Therefore, controlling for family composition in future studies would help to explain whether immigrants are truly less involved in crime (if immigrants from two-parent households are solely compared with native-born individuals from two-parent households) or whether their advantageous family composition serves as a buffer.[18] To fully understand crime buffers, it would be equally important to distinguish between single-parent households run by a mother and single-parent households run by a father. Moreover, controlling for religious involvement, extended family ties, and community-level collective efficacy in quantitative analyses may help us understand why some immigrant groups—despite their disadvantaged positions in society—seem to be resilient to criminal involvement.

Building on non-criminological immigration research that recognizes the importance of the heterogeneity of today's immigrant and non-immigrant population, future research (quantitative and qualitative) on the immigration and crime nexus has to take race, national origin, and ethnicity into account wherever possible in order to draw insightful comparisons (see Lee 2003, 132). Because not all Western countries collect data on race, ethnicity, and national origin, neighborhood-level studies and ethnographic insights may be particularly helpful for understanding the constraints and dynamics of different groups.

Previous research has consistently shown that immigrants, on average, are not more involved in criminal activities than non-immigrants. Although this is a powerful and very important political message, it would be helpful if future research moved away from simply reproducing this message in various localities. Instead, there is a lack of knowledge about why certain ethnic populations are involved in crime at higher levels than the native-born population and why others are involved at lower levels.[19] A number of studies have shown that certain populations are more easily socially and economically integrated than others with the same socioeconomic background. At the same time, research has shown that certain populations seem to resist criminal activity and experience much lower levels of criminal involvement despite having socioeconomic characteristics that are similar to those of at-risk populations (see, for example, Tonry's (1997) discussion of Asian groups).

Future research needs to focus on micro-level studies and examine populations with high and low levels of crime in order to understand why certain populations are more resistant to high crime levels than others. The strength of inter- and intraethnic social networks, health status, the existence of or changes in community organizations and resources, the degree of resident involvement in neighborhood life, and the extent to which ethnic codes that tolerate or condemn crime may operate to shape the population's involvement in crime all need to be taken into account. Qualitative analyses may serve best as a means to examine what factors are at play when similar disadvantaged groups have different crime levels. Additionally, qualitative research may help understand the "second-generation effect."

Ecological factors may also play a significant role. Thus, neighborhood-level studies need to explore the micro-level processes that may serve as a buffer in certain immigrant neighborhoods and prevent high levels of crime. The literature has shown that inner-city neighborhoods in the United States with certain structural characteristics (including demographic, socioeconomic, and housing features) experience higher levels of violent crime (Krivo and Peterson 2000; Sampson, Morenoff, and Gannon-Rowley 2002).[20] Because immigrants have been shown to commit higher levels of violent crime than other types of crime, this finding seems especially relevant to the study of immigration and crime. Future research needs to focus on the processes that may buffer immigrant neighborhoods from high levels of violent crime despite their structural similarities to high-crime neighborhoods.

Studies using longitudinal data are scarce, and research on immigration and crime is limited because it has mostly looked at cross-sectional data in restricted geographical areas. Stowell et al. (2009) are an exception and have estimated pooled cross-sectional time series data looking at various metropolitan areas over a period of ten years. Future research looking at longitudinal data to investigate the immigration and crime relationship could be helpful for understanding the overall drop in crime rates in recent years.

Future research should also examine the effects of changes in immigration on other forms of criminal offenses. To date, most scholars have looked at the direct and indirect effects of immigration on violent offenses and have generally neglected other types of crimes (e.g., Martinez 1997, 2002; Lee, Martinez, and Rodriguez 2000, 2001; Stowell 2007; Martinez, Rosenfeld, and Mares 2008; Feldmeyer 2009; Stowell et al. 2009). The primary focus should move beyond levels of violence to examine the influence of immigration on other types of crime.

In order to understand fully the complexity of the relationship between immigration and crime, studies must also examine factors beyond the individual level. Contextual factors must be taken into account, especially when the situation of immigrants is compared across different cities and nations. To date, no study has attempted to capture these factors (e.g., the influences of the quality of schools, community resources, and local drug trafficking).

Currently, we know very little about the experiences and contacts of immigrants with law enforcement officials or courts. Additionally, our knowledge about immigrants' experience as victims of crime is negligible. There is a great need for research that examines immigrants' experiences with the criminal justice system.

Certain politically sensitive issues such as trafficking or prostitution (for a more detailed discussion see Chapkis 2003) require particular attention and need to be studied in their full complexities. Research on these issues has to challenge the distinctions between "innocence and knowing, between mere exploitation and severe abuse" (Chapkis 2003, 935) and needs to acknowledge that immigrant women can consent to economically motivated migration and sex.

One area that seems to be particularly understudied is so-called honor-related violence among certain immigrant populations. Given the sensitivity of the subject matter[21] and the political implications that may follow, social scientists have been hesitant to look at honor-related incidents more closely. However, distinctions meant for analytic purposes as opposed to legal purposes may prove to be helpful to understand the phenomenon and to develop adequate services for people who are at risk. It is interesting that honor-related violence seems to be higher in European countries than in the United States or Canada. It is an open question as to whether the long history of immigration to the United States and Canada and their friendlier attitudes toward immigrants contribute to this or whether honor-related violence is not reported as such in these countries.

Another phenomenon that is equally understudied (yet also politically sensitive) relates to the very low crime rates of Turkish and Moroccan women in European countries. Popular wisdom among the German and Dutch population, for example, assumes that ethnic differences in gender roles (urging females to stay at home) contribute to the finding that Turkish and Moroccan females seem to have crime rates that are close to zero. However, systematic studies that can explain this phenomenon are lacking.

Lastly, research on immigration and crime completely overlooks the relationship between immigrants and the many organizations and institutions (despite immigration officials and law enforcement) that may shape their view of the particular host society (e.g., child welfare offices, schools, local government, day cares, and fiscal authorities). Future research in this area needs to determine whether there is a connection between the different immigrant groups' perceptions of and interactions and experiences with these institutions and organizations and group differences in criminal involvement.

B. Policy Implications

Numerous studies have shown that second- and third-generation immigrants perceive social exclusion to a much higher degree than the first generation. As pointed out earlier, crime rates increase for second- and third-generation immigrants (in some countries even exceeding the crime rates of the native born). Although—on average—the subsequent generations in the United States continue to commit crimes at a lower level than native-born youths, they are (at the average rate) significantly more likely to engage in risk behaviors such as delinquency, violence, and substance abuse than their parent generation (Harris 1999; Bui and Thingniramol 2005). Hence, the main focus of policies regarding immigration and crime should lie on this population.

Tackling social, political, and economical exclusion of immigrants should be the highest goal of policies in every Western country. Naturally, priorities need to be different. While some European countries still have not granted citizenship rights to second- and third-generation immigrants and continue to exclude them politically, certain immigrant populations in the United States go to the most ill-funded schools in the country. Since the increase of crime rates among subsequent generations can be understood in the context of their perceived exclusion, promising policies will have to focus on reducing social, political, and economic exclusion and discrimination of second- and third-generation immigrants.

Numerous studies have shown that one key area in which second-generation immigrants experience disadvantages and exclusion is the educational system.

Although the majority of second-generation immigrant youth are making educational and occupational progress, a significant minority are being left behind (Portes and Rumbaut 2001; Farley and Alba 2002; Kasinitz et al. 2008; Portes and Fernandez-Kelly 2008; Rumbaut 2008; Zhou et al. 2008). It is this minority (though significant) that policies need to draw their attention to. As Telles and Oritz (2008) have demonstrated in great detail, Mexican immigrants especially have been systematically excluded for multiple generations, thus suggesting that their situation in the United States deserves particular attention.

Policies that help educational attainment and improve the occupational situation of second- and third-generation immigrants must be a high priority. As research by Dinovitzer, Hagan, and Levi (2009) pointed out, strong educational ties may be the most important factor why certain immigrant groups have lower crime levels than native-born groups. In order to counteract exclusion in the educational system, research has shown that thriving and accepted programs for disadvantaged immigrants that strengthen ethnic networks and actively connect parents, schools, and community centers are needed (Henderson and Mapp 2002; Harris, Jamison, and Trujillo 2008; Portes and Fernandez-Kelly 2008, Bucerius 2009a). Bringing parents, schools, and community together is a means to significantly counteract social exclusion by enhancing family and co-ethnic social networks and thus, foster academic success.

Western countries in general and European countries in particular also need to rethink their strategy of policing undocumented immigrants. In the United States, prosecuting undocumented immigrants under federal law has an immense criminalizing effect on this population. Expanding temporary and permanent labor programs would not only reduce the criminalizing effect but also serve those sectors of the economy that are dependent on the presence of these laborers. Naturally, it would also help the undocumented workers to reside and work legally in the country.

NOTES

1. Several studies have shown that the public perception of Muslim immigrants especially has changed drastically (Gerstle 2003; Naber 2006; Hernandez 2007; Wray-Lake, Syvertsen, and Flanagan 2008).

2. This seems to be even truer for the European context than for the United States. Due to different citizenship policies, hate crimes in Germany, for example, are almost always directed toward immigrants who do not have German citizenship, whereas hate crimes in the United States or Canada can be racially motivated and targeted against citizens of different color (e.g., African Americans).

3. In contrast to the former guest workers living in Germany, *Aussiedler* are descendents of German emigrants who "migrated long before the creation of a German nation

state (in the case of the Siebenbürger Sachsen from Transylvania as much as 800 years ago) to areas which have never been part of Germany" (Koopmans 1999, 631). Therefore, according to German citizenship law, which is mostly based on blood relations, they qualify for German citizenship.

4. Academics probably focus on finding evidence of whether immigrants are more or less criminal than their native counterparts because of the highly loaded political message of the topic.

5. However, some new discussion about the role of ethnicity and culture is emerging in European countries that face disproportionately high rates of criminality among certain ethnic groups of second-generation immigrants (see van Gemert 1998 for a discussion on the role of Moroccan culture in explaining crime rates of the second generation).

6. The report compared the population over the age of fifteen and found immigrants to be half as likely to be incarcerated as native-born individuals. However, aggregation bias may underlie this comparison. Since the immigrant population was, at that time, older than the native-born population, the age difference between immigrants and native-born individuals may have significantly contributed to the finding that immigrants appeared to be less likely to be incarcerated.

7. Somewhat similar to Merton's ideas of blocked opportunities, Max Weber (1956) introduced the concept of social closures (more commonly known as the concept of social exclusion). He stated that a dominant group (e.g., the white majority) safeguards its position and privileges itself by monopolizing and restricting resources and opportunities for its own group while denying access to outsiders (e.g., immigrants). According to Weber, this entails singling out certain social or physical attributes as a basis to justify exclusion. Its purpose is always the closure of social and economic opportunities to outsiders.

8. Cloward and Ohlin (1960) developed Merton's idea further, stating that access to illegitimate opportunities may be distributed just as unequally as access to legitimate opportunities. They agreed with Merton's assumption that the deprivation of legitimate means produces a push toward delinquent activities, especially among boys from racial and ethnic minority groups. However, they stressed that the types of criminal subculture that flourish (if any) and the illegitimate opportunities depend on the opportunities available in the specific community (i.e., criminal role models, etc.).

9. Additionally, "crime" is also difficult to measure since, just as with "illegal status," most criminal offenses remain unsolved.

10. Data from the Bureau of Justice Statistics (Rand 2007) as well as the FBI (2008) show that the violent crime rate increased for two consecutive years after 2004 and started falling again in 2007. Because rates of both violent and property crimes fell significantly during the 1990s while immigrant numbers consistently increased, it is unlikely that the rising crime numbers between 2004 and 2006 were related to immigration.

11. Additionally, criminological research shows that offenders typically do not travel to unfamiliar areas to commit crimes (Gottfredson and Hirschi 1990).

12. Three examples include: The Penttbom investigation allowed federal officers to detain immigrants suspected of having ties to terrorism on the basis of immigration law. As a result, 762 non-citizens were held in detention facilities by August 6, 2002; none had any ties to the 9/11 events (Miller 2005). The USA Patriot Act (HR 3162), enacted six weeks after the attacks, allowed officials to hold immigrants indefinitely and with no access to lawyers should they represent a reasonable threat to national security (Byng 2008; Ismaili, forthcoming). A third initiative, the National Security Entry Exit Registration System

(NSEERS), was used as a tracking device for male Arab or Muslim visitors between the ages of sixteen and sixty-five from twenty-five different nations.

13. This seems particularly important because weak social integration may represent a risk factor for criminal activities (Gartner 1990; Junger-Tas 2001).

14. Taking all these data limitations into account does not diminish the fact that crime statistics are significantly higher for second- and third-generation immigrants compared to the German native population (Walter and Trautmann 2003). Self-report studies among high school students are in agreement with the official crime statistics and show that immigrant students report a higher level of involvement in crime in general, and for specific offenses in particular (Mansel and Hurrelmann 1998; Oberwittler 2003; Fuchs et al. 2005). Goldberg (2006) and Wetzels et al. (2001) have been able to collect data on different ethnic populations and found that violent offenses are by far more likely to be reported by immigrant students of Turkish background (not accounting for generational status), followed by those of former Yugoslavian background, southern European background, and German background.

15. Germany has recently changed its official rhetoric—now accepting the fact that the country has become an "immigration country" and trying to make integration a new priority (Geißler 2007).

16. The great majority of second- and third-generation immigrants still lack citizenship, for example. Several OECD studies have also indicated that the gap in school performance between native-born individuals and second-generation immigrants is greatest in Germany; immigrant students are, on average, two school years behind their German counterparts (Bucerius 2008).

17. These groups may, however, have a greater risk to be involved in white-collar crimes. Traditionally, these types of offenses have been ignored in immigration and crime research.

18. Some researchers suggest that childbirth among unmarried couples will very soon become normative for younger Americanized immigrants. Therefore, pro-family arguments will fade with generations, leaving behind a generation of immigrants more likely to live in poverty and be single-parents (Oropesa and Gorman 2000).

19. Similarly, disaggregated crime rates of the native-born population (and not only the immigrant population) might offer new insights on why immigrants—on average—have lower crime rates than the native-born population.

20. Social disorganization theories suggest that in highly disorganized inner-city areas, where high resident turnover and population heterogeneity are typical, residents are not able to develop common goals and values or solutions to problems experienced by the community (Thomas and Znaniecki 1918–1920). Instead, conflicting and competing values develop very easily, and delinquency becomes a powerful means of gaining economic satisfaction and earning prestige. According to this view, immigrants are often sorted into these resource-poor, disorganized neighborhoods because they arrive without the qualifications needed to compete successfully for occupational and residential opportunities. Instead of viewing immigration as the cause of disorganization, this theory acknowledges that immigration and crime are interlinked through the social structural characteristics of the neighborhoods in which immigrants tend to settle (Shaw and McKay 1969).

21. There are two main concerns about using the term "honor": it may easily be used to legitimize violence that would otherwise be treated as domestic violence; and particular cultures may be stigmatized and linked to this type of violence.

REFERENCES

Ackah, Yaw. 2000. "Fear of Crime among an Immigrant Population in Washington, DC Metropolitan Area." *Journal of Black Studies* 30:553–74.

Ahlberg, Jan. 1996. *Criminality among Immigrants and Their Children: A Statistical Analysis*. BRA-Report. Stockholm, Sweden: Fritzes.

Albrecht, Hans-Jörg. 1997. "Ethnic Minorities, Crime, and Criminal Justice in Germany." In *Ethnicity, Crime, and Immigration: Comparative and Cross-national Perspectives*, edited by Michael Tonry. Vol. 21 of *Crime and Justice: A Review of Research*, edited by Michael Tonry. Chicago: University of Chicago Press.

Arnold, Carrie. 2007. "Racial Profiling in Immigration Enforcement: State and Local Agreements to Enforce Federal Immigration Law." *Arizona Law Review* 49:113–37.

Brooks, David. 2006. "Immigrants To Be Proud of." *New York Times*, March 30. http://select.nytimes.com/2006/03/30/opinion/30brooks.html.

Bucerius, Sandra. 2007. "What Else Should I Do—Cultural Influences on the Drug Trade of Young Migrants in Germany." *Journal of Drug Issues* 37:673–98.

———. 2008. "Drug Dealers between Islamic Values, Everyday Life in Germany and Criminal Activity." *Zeitschrift für Soziologie* 3:246–65.

———. 2009a. "Fostering Academic Opportunities to Counteract Social Exclusion." In *Contemporary Issues in Criminal Justice Policy: Policy Proposals From the American Society of Criminology Conference*, ed. Natasha A. Frost, Joshua D. Freilich, and Todd R. Clear. Belmont, CA: Cengage/Wadsworth.

———. 2009b. *Migration, soziale Exklusion und informelle Ökonomie*. PhD diss. Frankfurt: Universität Frankfurt, Graduate School of Humanities and Social Sciences.

Bui, Hoan, and Ornuma Thingniramol. 2005. "Immigration and Self-Reported Delinquency: The Interplay of Immigrant Generations, Gender, Race, and Ethnicity." *Journal of Crime and Justice* 28:79–100.

Butcher, Kristin, and Anne Morrison Piehl. 1998a. "Cross-city Evidence on the Relationship between Immigration and Crime." *Journal of Policy Analysis and Management* 17:457–93.

———. 1998b. "Recent Immigrants: Unexpected Implications for Crime and Incarceration." *Industrial and Labor Relations Review* 51:654–79.

———. 2006. "Why Are Immigrants' Incarceration Rates So Low?" Rutgers University Economics Department working paper 05. Rutgers University, Newark, NJ.

Byng, Michelle. 2008. "Complex Inequalities." *American Behavioral Scientist* 51:659–74.

Chapin, Wesley. 1997. "Auslander raus? The Empirical Relationship between Immigration and Crime in Germany." *Social Science Quarterly* 78:543–58.

Chapkis, Wendy. 2003. "Trafficking, Migration, and the Law: Protecting Innocents, Punishing Immigrants." *Gender and Society* 17:923–37.

Cloward, Richard, and Lloyd Ohlin. 1960. *Delinquency and Opportunity: A Theory of Delinquent Gangs*. New York: Free Press.

Cole, David. 2002. "Terrorizing Immigrants in the Name of Fighting Terrorism." *Human Rights* 29:11–13.

Curtis, Lynn A. 1975. *Violence, Race, and Culture*. Lexington, MA: Lexington Books.

Davis, Robert C., and Nicole J. Hendricks. 2007. "Immigrants and Law Enforcement: A Comparison of Native-Born and Foreign-Born Americans' Opinions of the Polices." *International Review of Victimology* 14:81–94.

Dillingham, William. 1911. *Report of the Immigration Commission*. Washington, DC: US Government Printing Office.

Dinovitzer, Ronit, John Hagan, and Ron Levi 2009. "Immigration and Youthful Illegalities in a Global Edge City." *Social Forces* 88:337–72.

Drewniak, Regine. 2004. "Ausländerkriminalität zwischen 'kriminologischen Binsen-weisheiten' und 'ideologischem Minenfeld.'" *Zeitschrift für Jugendkriminalrecht und Jugendhilfe* 15:372–78.

Engbersen, Godfried, Joanne van der Leun, and Jan de Boom. 2007. "Fragmentation of Migration and Crime in the Netherlands." In *Crime and Justice in the Netherlands*, edited by Michael Tonry and Catrien Bijleveld. Vol. 35 of *Crime and Justice: A Review of Research,* edited by Michael Tonry. Chicago: University of Chicago Press.

Erlanger, Howard S. 1995. "Estrangement, Machismo, and Gang Violence." In *Latinos in the United States. Criminal Justice and Latino Communities*, ed. Antoinette Lopez. New York: Garland.

Farley, Reynolds, and Richard Alba. 2002. "The New Second Generation in the United States." *International Migration Review* 36:669–701.

Federal Bureau of Investigation. 2008. *Preliminary Annual Uniform Crime Report, January-December 2007.* Washington, DC: Federal Bureau of Investigation.

Feldmeyer, Ben. 2009. "Immigration and Violence: The Offsetting Effects of Immigrant Concentration on Latino Violence." *Social Science Research* 38:717–31.

Fuchs, Marek, Siegfried Lamnek, Jens Luedtke, and Nina Baur. 2005. *Gewalt an Schulen 1994-1999-2004.* Wiesbaden, Germany: Verlag für Sozialwissenschaften.

Gabor, Thomas, and Julian Roberts. 1990. "Rushton on Race and Crime: The Evidence Remains Unconvincing" *Canadian Journal of Criminology* 32:335–43.

Gartner, Rosemary. 1990. "The Victims of Homicide: A Temporal and Cross-National Comparison." *American Sociological Review* 55:92–106.

Geißler, Rainer. 2007. "Einwanderungsland Deutschland—Herausforderungen an die Massenmedien." *Journalistik Journal* 10:11–13.

Gerstle, Gary. 2003. "Pluralism and the War on Terror." *Dissent* 50:31–38.

Goldberg, Brigitta. 2006. "Freizeit und Kriminalität bei Achtklässlern mit und ohne Migrationshintergrund." In *Kriminalpolitik und ihre wissenschaftliche Grundlagen*, ed. Thomas Feltes, Christian Pfeiffer, and Gernot Steinhilper. Heidelberg, Germany: Müller Verlag.

Goldsmith, Pat, Mary Romero, Raquel Rubio-Goldsmith, Miguel Escobedo, and Laura Khoury. 2009. "Ethno-racial Profiling and State Violence in a Southwest Barrio." *Aztlan* 34:93–123.

Gottfredson, Michael. 2004. *Crime, Immigration and Public Policy*. Report for the Merage Foundation for the American Dream, Newport Beach, CA.

Gottfredson, Michael, and Travis Hirschi. 1990. *A General Theory of Crime*. Stanford, CA: Stanford University Press.

Government Accountability Office. 2005. *Information on Criminal Aliens Incarcerated in Federal and State Prisons and Local Jails*. Washington, DC: US Government Accountability Office.

Hagan, John, Ron Levi, and Ronit Dinovitzer. 2007. "The Symbolic Violence of the Crime-Immigration Nexus: Migrant Mythologies in the Americas." *Criminology and Public Policy* 7:801–18.

Hagan, John, and Alberto Palloni. 1998. "Immigration and Crime in the United States." In *The Immigration Debate*, ed. James P. Smith and Barry Edmonston. Washington, DC: National Academies Press.

——. 1999. "Sociological Criminology and the Mythology of Hispanic Immigration and Crime." *Social Problems* 46:617–32.

Harris, Angel L., Kenneth Jamison, and Monica H. Trujillo. 2008. "Disparities in the Educational Success of Immigrants: An Assessment of the Immigrant Effect for Asians and Latinos." *Annals of the American Academy of Political and Social Science* 620:90–114.

Harris, David. 2006. "The War on Terror, Local Police, and Immigration Enforcement: A Curious Tale of Police Power in Post 9/11 America." *Rutgers Law Journal* 38:1–60.

Harris, Kathleen. 1999. "The Health Status and Risk Behavior of Adolescents in Immigrant Families." In *Children of Immigrants: Health, Adjustment, and Public Assistance*, ed. Donald Hernandez. Washington, DC: National Academy of Sciences Press.

Hawkins, Darnell. 1994. "Ethnicity: The Forgotten Dimension of American Social Control." In *Inequality, Crime, and Social Control*, ed. George Bridges and Martha Myers. Boulder, CO: Westview.

Haynes, Dina. 2004. "Used, Abused, Arrested and Deported: Extending Immigration Benefits to Protect the Victims of Trafficking and to Secure the Prosecution of Traffickers." *Human Rights Quarterly* 26:221–71.

Henderson, Anne, and Karen Mapp. 2002. *A New Wave of Evidence: The Impact of School, Parent, and Community Connections on Student Achievement*. Austin, TX: Southwest Educational Development Laboratory.

Henderson, Charles. 1901. *Introduction of the Study of Dependent, Defective, and Delinquent Classes*. Boston, MA: D. C. Heath.

Hernandez, David. 2007 "Undue Process: Racial Genealogies of Immigrant Detention." In *Constructing Borders/Crossing Boundaries: Race, Ethnicity, and Immigration*, ed. Caroline Brettell. Lanham, MD: Lexington Books.

Hunter, Rosalind, Andrew Oswald, and Bruce Charlton. 2009. "The Elite Brain Drain." *Economic Journal* 119:231–51.

Immigration Policy Center. 2008. *From Anecdotes to Evidence: Setting the Record Straight on Immigrants and Crime*. Washington, DC: The Immigration Policy Center.

Industrial Commission. 1901. *Special Report on General Statistics of Immigration and the Foreign Born Population*. Washington, DC: US Government Printing Office.

Ismaili, Karim. Forthcoming. "Surveying the Many Fronts of War on Immigrants in Post-9/11 U.S. Society." *Contemporary Justice Review*.

Junger-Tas, Josine. 1997. "Ethnic Minorities and Criminal Justice in the Netherlands." In *Ethnicity, Crime, and Immigration: Comparative and Cross-national Perspectives*, edited by Michael Tonry. Vol. 21 of *Crime and Justice: A Review of Research*, edited by Michael Tonry. Chicago: University of Chicago Press.

——. 2001. "Ethnic Minorities, Social Integration and Crime." *European Journal on Criminal Policy and Research* 9:5–29.

Kanstroom, Daniel. 2005. "Immigration Law as Social Control: How Many Without Rights Does Take It To Make You Feel Secure?" In *Civil Penalties, Social Consequences*, ed. Christopher Mele, and Teresa Miller. New York: Routledge.

Kasinitz, Philip, John Mollenkopf, Mary Waters, and Jennifer Holdaway. 2008. *Inheriting the City: The Children of Immigrants Come of Age*. Cambridge, MA: Harvard University Press.

Kohut, Andrew, Scott Keeter; Carroll Doherty, and Roberto Suro. 2006. *America's Immigration Quandary*. Washington, DC: Pew Research for the People and the Press and Pew Hispanic Center.

Koopmans, Ruud. 1999. "Germany and Its Immigrants: An Ambivalent Relationship." *Journal of Ethnic and Migration Studies* 25:627–47.

———. 2003. "Good Intentions Sometimes Make Bad Policy: A Comparison of Dutch and German Integration Policies." In *The Challenge of Diversity: European Social Democracy Facing Migration, Integration, and Multiculturalism*, ed. René Cuperus, Karl Duffek, and Johannes Kandel. Innsbruck, Austria: Studienverlag.

Krivo, Lauren, and Ruth Peterson. 2000. "The Structural Context of Homicide: Accounting for Racial Differences in Process." *American Sociological Review* 65:547–59.

Laughlin, Harry, 1939. *Immigration and Conquest*. Report to the Special Committee on Immigration and Naturalization of the Chamber of Commerce of the State of New York.

Lee, Matthew. 2003. *Crime on the Border: Immigration and Homicide in Urban Communities*. New York: LFB Scholarly Publishing.

Lee, Matthew, and Ramiro Martinez Jr. 2002. "Social Disorganization Revisited: Mapping the Recent Immigration and Black Homicide Relationship in Northern Miami." *Sociological Focus* 35:365–82.

Lee, Matthew, Ramiro Martinez Jr., and Fernando Rodriguez. 2000. "Contrasting Latinos in Homicide Research: The Victim and Offender Relationship in El Paso and Miami." *Social Science Quarterly* 14:375–88.

Lee, Matthew, Ramiro Martinez Jr., and Richard Rosenfeld. 2001. "Does Immigration Increase Homicide? Negative Evidence from Three Border Cities" *Sociological Quarterly* 42:559–80.

Lee, Min, and Jeffrey Ulmer. 2000. "Fear of Crime among Korean Americans in Chicago Communities." *Criminology* 38:1173–206.

Lind, Andrew. 1930. "The Ghetto and the Slum." *Social Forces* 9:206–15.

Mansel, Jürgen. 2003. "Konfliktregulierung bei Straftaten—Variation des Anzeigeverhaltens nach Ethnie des Täters." In *Die Ethnisierung von Alltagskonflikten*, ed. Axel Groenemeyerand and Jürgen Mansel. Opladen, Germany: Leske und Budrich.

Mansel, Jürgen, and Hans-Jörg Albrecht. 2003. "Migration und das kriminalpolitische Handeln staatlicher Strafverfolgungsorgane. Ausländer als polizeilich Tatverdächtige und gerichtlich Abgeurteilte." *Kölner Zeitschrift für Soziologie und Sozialpsychologie* 55:679–715.

Mansel, Jürgen, and Klaus Hurrelmann. 1998. "Aggressives und delinquentes Verhalten Jugendlicher im Zeitvergleich. Befunde der Dunkelfeldforschung aus den Jahren 1988, 1990 und 1996. " *Kölner Zeitschrift für Soziologie und Sozialpsychologie* 50: 78–109.

Martens, Peter. 1997. "Immigrants, Crime, and Criminal Justice in Sweden." In *Ethnicity, Crime, and Immigration: Comparative and Cross-national Perspectives*, edited by Michael Tonry. Vol. 21 of *Crime and Justice: A Review of Research*, edited by Michael Tonry. Chicago: University of Chicago Press.

Martinez, Ramiro, Jr. 1997. "Homicide among Miami's ethnic groups: Anglos, Blacks and Latinos in the 1990s." *Homicide Studies* 1: 17–34.

———. 2002. *Latino Homicide: Immigration, Violence, and Community*. New York: Routledge Press.

Martinez, Ramiro, Jr., and Matthew Lee. 2000. "On Immigration and Crime." In *Criminal Justice 2000: The Changing Nature of Crime*, vol. 1, ed. Gary LaFree and Robert Bursik. Washington, DC: National Institute of Justice.

Martinez, Ramiro, Jr., Richard Rosenfeld, and Dennis Mares. 2008. "Social Disorganization, Drug Market Activity, and Neighborhood Violent Crime." *Urban Affairs Review* 43:846–74.

McDonald, William. 1997. "Crime and Illegal Immigration: Emerging Local, State and Federal Partnerships." *National Institute of Justice Journal* 232:2–10.

Mears, Daniel. 2001. "The Immigration-Crime Nexus: Toward an Analytic Framework for Assessing and Guiding Theory, Research, and Policy." *Sociological Perspectives* 44:1–19.

Menjívar, Cecilia, and Cynthia Bejarano. 2004. "Latino Immigrants' Perceptions of Crime and of Police Authorities: A Case Study from the Phoenix Metropolitan Area." *Ethnic and Racial Studies* 27:120–48.

Merton, Robert. 1938. "Social Structure and Anomie." *American Sociological Review* 3:672–82.

Miller, Teresa. 2002. "The Impact of Mass Incarceration in Immigration Policy. " In *Invisible Punishment: The Collateral Consequences of Mass Incarceration*, ed. Marc Mauer and Meda Chesney-Lind. New York: Free Press.

———. 2005. "Blurring the Boundaries between Immigration and Crime Control after September 11th." *Boston College Third World Law Journal* 25:81–123.

Morenoff, Jeffrey, and Avraham Astor. 2006. "Immigrant Assimilation and Crime: Generational Differences in Youth Violence in Chicago." In *Immigration and Crime: Race, Ethnicity, and Violence*, ed. Ramiro Martinez Jr. and Abel Valenzuela Jr. New York: New York University Press.

Naber, Nadine. 2006. "The Rules of Forced Engagement: Race, Gender, and the Culture of Fear among Arab Immigrants in San Francisco Post-9/11." *Cultural Dynamics* 18:235–67.

National Commission on Law Observance and Enforcement. 1931. *Report on Crime and the Foreign Born*. Washington, DC: US Government Printing Office.

Oberwittler, Dietrich 2003. "Geschlecht, Ethnizität und sozialräumliche Benachteiligung. Überraschende Interaktionen bei sozialen Bedingungsfaktoren von Gewalt und schwerer Eigentumsdelinquenz von Jugendlichen." In *Geschlecht- und Gewaltgesellschaft*, ed. Siegfried Lamnek. Opladen, Germany: Leske und Budrich.

Oropesa, R. S. (Sal), and Bridget Gorman 2000. "Ethnicity, Immigration and Beliefs about Marriage as Ties that Bind." In *The Ties that Bind*, ed. Linda Waite. Hawthorne, CA: Aldine de Gruyter.

Ousey, Graham, and Charis Kubrin. 2009. "Exploring the Connection between Immigration and Violent Crime Rates in U.S. Cities 1980–2000." *Social Problems* 56:447–73.

Palloni, Alberto, and Jeffrey Morenoff. 2001. "Interpreting the Paradoxical in the Hispanic Paradox: Demographic and Epidemiological Approaches." *Annals of the New York Academy of Sciences* 954:140–74.

Peek, Lori. 2005. "Becoming Muslim: The Development of a Religious Identity." *Sociology of Religion* 66:215–42.

Pfeiffer, Christian, Matthias Kleimann, and Sven Petersen. 2005. *Migration und Kriminalität. Ein Gutachten für den Zuwanderungsbeirat der Bundesregierung*. Baden-Baden, Germany: Nomos.

Portes, Alejandro. 2003. "Ethnicities: Children of Immigrants in America." *Development* 46:42–52.

Portes, Alejandro, and Patricia Fernandez-Kelly. 2008. "No Margin for Error: Educational and Occupational Achievement among Disadvantaged Children of Immigrants." *Annals of the American Academy of Political and Social Science* 620:12–36.

Portes, Alejandro, and Ruben Rumbaut. 1990. *Immigrant America: A Portrait.* Berkeley: University of California Press.

———. 2001. *Legacies: The Story of the Immigrant Second Generation.* Berkeley: University of California Press.

Portes, Alejandro, and Min Zhou. 1993. "The New Second Generation: Segmented Assimilation and Its Variants." *Annals of the American Academy of Political and Social Science* 530:74–96.

Rand, Michael. 2007. *Criminal Victimization 2007.* Washington, DC: US Department of Justice.

Reid, Lesley, Harald Weiss, Robert Adelman, and Charles Jaret. 2005. "The Immigration-crime Relationship: Evidence across US Metropolitan Areas." *Social Science Research* 34:757–80.

Reitz, Jeffrey. 2003. *Host Societies and the Reception of Immigrants.* San Diego: University of California, Center for Comparative Immigration Studies.

Reitz, Jeffrey, Rupa Banerjee, Mai Phan, and Jordan Thompson. 2008. "Race, Religion, and the Social Integration of New Immigrant Minorities in Canada." http://www.utoronto.ca/ethnicstudies/RaceReligion.pdf.

Rodriguez, Robyn. 2008. "(Dis)unity and Diversity in Post 9/11 America." *Sociological Forum* 23:379–89.

Rumbaut, Ruben. 2008. "The Coming of the Second Generation: Immigration and Ethnic Mobility in Southern California." *Annals of the American Academy of Political and Social Science* 620:196–236.

Rumbaut, Ruben, and Walter Ewing. 2007. *"The Myth of Immigrant Criminality and the Paradox of Assimilation." Immigration Policy Center Special Report.* Washington, DC: American Immigration Law Foundation.

Sabol, William, Todd Minton, and Paige Harrison. 2007. *Prison and Jail Inmates at Midyear 2006.* Washington, DC: US Department of Justice

Sampson, Robert J., Jeffrey Morenoff, and Thomas Gannon-Rowley. 2002. "Assessing 'Neighborhood Effects': Social Processes and New Directions in Research." *Annual Review of Sociology* 28:443–78.

Sampson, Robert J., Jeffrey Morenoff, and Stephen Raudenbush. 2005. "Social Anatomy of Racial and Ethnic Disparities in Violence." *American Journal of Public Health* 95:224–32.

Sampson, Robert J., Stephen Raudenbusch, and Felton Earls. 1997. "Neighborhoods and Violent Crime: A Multilevel Study of Collective Efficacy." *Science* 277:918–24.

Sellin, Thorsten. 1938. *Cultural Conflict and Crime.* New York: Social Science Research Council.

Shapland, Joanna, Hans-Jörg Albrecht; Jason Ditton; Thierry Godefroy. 2003. *The Informal Economy: Threat or Opportunity in the City.* Freiburg im Breisgau, Germany: Edition Iuscrim.

Shaw, Clifford, and Henry McKay. 1969. *Juvenile Delinquency and Urban Areas.* Chicago: University of Chicago Press.

Smith, Daniel. 2005. "Ethnic Differences in Intergenerational Crime Patterns." In *Crime and Justice: A Review of Research*, vol. 32, edited by Michael Tonry. Chicago: University of Chicago Press.

Stowell, Jacob. 2007. *Immigration and Crime. The Effects of Immigration on Criminal Behavior*. New York: LFB Publishing.

Stowell, Jacob, Steven Messner, Kelly McGeever. and Lawrence Raffalovich. 2009. "Immigration and the Recent Violent Crime Drops in the U.S.: A Pooled, Cross-sectional Time-series Analysis of Metropolitan Areas." *Criminology* 47: 889–928.

Sundeen, Richard. 1984. "Explaining the Fear of Crime among International Students from Developing Countries: A Revised Model." *Criminal Justice Review* 2:7–13.

Sutherland, Edwin. 1924. *Criminology*. Philadelphia: Lippincott.

Sutherland, Edwin, and Donald Cressey. 1960. *Principles of Criminology*. New York: Lippincott.

Taft, Donald. 1933. "Does Immigration Increase Crime?" *Social Forces* 12:69–77.

Telles, Edward, and Vilma Oritz. 2008. *Generations of Exclusion*. New York: Russell Sage Foundation.

Thomas, William, and Florian Znaniecki. 1918–1920. *The Polish Peasant in Europe and America: A Monograph of an Immigrant Group*. Boston: R. G. Badger.

Tonry, Michael. 1997. "Ethnicity, Crime, and Immigration." In *Ethnicity, Crime, and Immigration: Comparative and Cross-national Perspectives*, edited by Michael Tonry. Vol. 21 of *Crime and Justice: A Review of Research*, edited by Michael Tonry. Chicago: University of Chicago Press.

Tumlin, Karen. 2004. "Suspect First: How Terrorism Policy Is Reshaping Immigration Policy." *California Law Review* 92:1173–239.

Van Gemert, Frank. 1998. *Ieder voor zich: Kansen, cultuur en criminaliteit van Marokkaanse jongen*. Amsterdam: Het Spinhuis.

Viruell-Fuentes, Edna. 2007. "Beyond Acculturation: Immigration, Discrimination, and Health Research among Mexicans in the United States." *Social Science and Medicine* 65:1524–35.

Volpp, Leti. 2002. "The Citizen and the Terrorist." *UCLA Law Review* 49:1575–600.

Waldinger, Roger, and Cynthia Feliciano. 2004. "Will the New Second Generation Experience 'Downward Assimilation'? Segmented Assimilation Re-Assessed." *Ethnic and Racial Studies* 27:376–402.

Walter, Michael, and Sebastian Trautmann. 2003. "Kriminalität junger Migranten—Strafrecht und gesellschaftliche (Des)-Integration." In *Kriminalität und Gewalt im Jugendalter: Hell- und Dunkelfeldberichte im Vergleich*, ed. Jürgen Raithel and Jürgen Mansel. Weinheim, Germany: Juventa.

Waters, Tony. 1999. *Crime and Immigrant Youth*. Thousand Oaks, CA: Russell Sage.

Weber, Max. 1956. *Wirtschaft und Gesellschaft—Grundriss der verstehenden Soziologie. Studienausgabe von Johannes Winckelmann*. Berlin, Germany: Kiepenheuer and Witsch.

Welch, Anthony, and Zhang Zhen. 2008. "Higher Education and Global Talent Flows: Brain Drain, Overseas Chinese Intellectuals, and Diasporic Knowledge Networks." *Higher Education Policy* 25:519–37.

Wetzels, Peter, Dirk Enzmann, Eberhard Mecklenburg, and Christian Pfeiffer. 2001. *Jugendliche und Gewalt—eine repräsentative Dunkelfeldanalyse in München und acht anderen deutschen Städten*. Baden-Baden: Nomos.

Wilmers, Nicola, Dirk Enzmann; Dagmar Schaefer; Karin Herbers, Werner Greve, and Peter Wetzels. 2002. *Jugendliche in Deutschland zur Jahrtausendwende: Gefährlich oder gefährdet?* Baden-Baden: Nomos.

Wortley, Scot. 2003. "Hidden Intersections: Research on Race, Crime, and Criminal Justice in Canada." *Canadian Ethnic Studies* 35:99–117.

Wray-Lake, Laura, Amy Syvertsen, and Constance Flanagan. 2008. "Contested Citizenship and Social Exclusion: Adolescent Arab American Immigrants' Views of the Social Contract." *Applied Developmental Science* 12:84–92.

Yeager Matthew. 2002. "Rehabilitating the Criminality of Immigrants under Section 19 of the Canadian Immigration Act." *International Migration Review* 36:178–92.

Zhou, Min, and Carl L. Bankston. 2006. "Delinquency and Acculturation in the Twenty-First Century: A Decade's Change in a Vietnamese-American Community." In *Immigration and Crime: Ethnicity, Race, and Violence*, ed. Ramiro Martinez Jr. and Abel Valenzuala Jr. New York: New York University Press.

Zhou, Min, Jennifer Lee, Jody Agius Vallejo, Rosaura Tafoya-Estrada, and Yang Sao Xiong. 2008. "Success Attained, Deterred, and Denied: Divergent Pathways to Social Mobility in Los Angeles's New Second Generation." *Annals of the American Academy of Political and Social Science* 620:37–61.

Zimring, Frank. 2007. *The Great American Crime Decline.* New York: Oxford University Press.

CHAPTER 14

····································

GUNS AND CRIME

····································

CHARLES F. WELLFORD

ONE characteristic that sets the United States of America apart from the other industrialized democracies is the extent to which private ownership of guns is established in the most basic legal documents of the country. The Second Amendment to the United States Constitution provides "A well regulated Militia, being necessary to the security of a free State, the right of the people to keep and bear Arms, shall not be infringed." Immediately after freedom of expression, the press, religion, and assembly, which are guaranteed in the First Amendment, the founding fathers established the right of every citizen to bear arms. No other industrialized democracy has this right in its basic legal documents. As a result no other country for which data are available has a higher rate of households with firearms[1] (40 percent in the United States; 32 percent in Norway, the next closest country), and no industrialized democracy has a rate of firearm homicides that approximates the rate in the United States (7 per 100,000 in the United States in 2008 compared to rates of less than 1 per 100,000 in other industrialized democracies).[2]

For the first 150 years after the founding of the United States, there was almost no regulation of gun ownership and lawful use. Some states sought to ban guns early in that history; after the Civil War, gun laws were enacted with a purpose of denying gun rights to former slaves; and even today some local ordinances limit the possession and use of guns. However, the country and the legal system did not seek or approve efforts to limit the citizens' right to bear arms materially. Guns could be purchased without registration of any kind. They could be purchased through the mail.

Gradually, beginning in the late 1920s federal legislation emerged to place some limits on the right to bear arms. In 1927 the U.S. Congress banned the sending through the mail of weapons that could be concealed on the person (essentially handguns). Seven years later Congress prohibited the sale and possession of fully automatic weapons (e.g., the Thompson submachine gun) when it enacted the National Firearms Act of 1934. These early national efforts at gun control were aimed, primarily, at organized gangs and criminal enterprises that developed during the time when national Prohibition banned alcoholic beverages and when the Great Depression of the 1930s prompted a series of well-known gangs of bank robbers. There was no thought of restricting law-abiding citizens in their access to and use of guns. When the 1934 law was challenged in court, the Supreme Court eventually found it constitutional (*United States v. Miller,* 307 U.S. 174 [1939]). Still, these and other federal laws applied only to the actions of the federal government and were not binding on the states. It would take rising concern with crime; widespread urban riots; the assassinations of President John F. Kennedy, the Reverend Martin Luther King Jr., and Robert Kennedy; and the attempted assassination of President Ronald Reagan to mobilize efforts to further control guns.

In 1968 Congress sought to prohibit the sale of guns to those "not legally entitled to possess them because of age, criminal background, or incompetence." To accomplish this Congress sought to also eliminate the importation of certain guns (inexpensive handguns often referred to as "Saturday night specials") and to expand the record-keeping function of those federally licensed to sell guns (a position created in 1938 by congressional actions). Over the next twenty-six years efforts would be made to further restrict access to guns by criminals and those judged to be incompetent, and the courts would be called upon to determine if such restrictions were constitutional. In each case that came to the U.S. Supreme Court, the Court found the laws constitutional, although in each case the Court also noted that limits on the Second Amendment needed to be carefully tailored.[3]

In 1994 Congress passed the Brady Handgun Violence Prevention Act requiring background checks on all purchasers, and when an "instant" check could not be made, a five-day waiting period to complete the purchase. In separate legislation Congress also banned the sale of assault weapons (high-powered, multishot rifles that could easily be converted to from semi to fully automatic weapons). Again these efforts were aimed at denying access to guns by those who since 1968 were unable legally to own or possess them. Although, again, groups mounted legal challenges to these efforts, the courts consistently upheld these limits on the Second Amendment. Although the assault weapon ban has expired, these federal laws seeking to limit access to guns have been in operation for more than forty years. Three major questions remain: Do these laws achieve their stated purposes? Should they apply to the states as well as the federal government (the question of incorporation)?[4] and Is the Second Amendment a collective right (to form a militia) or is it an individual right?

Throughout the nineteenth and twentieth centuries the Second Amendment was most widely interpreted as a collective right. That is, the focus was on the creation of a militia and the need of citizens to have guns so that they could partic-ipate in the collective protection of the state. It was not until 2001 that a federal appellate court held that the Second Amendment guaranteed to individuals a right to bear arms (although that right could also be limited). The Fifth Circuit Court of Appeals considered an appeal of a case (*United States v. Emerson*, 270 F.3d 203 [5th Cir. 2001]) in which an individual had been convicted of violating a federal statute that prohibited anyone who was the object of a protective order from possessing a gun. The appellant claimed this was an infringement of his Second Amendment right to posses a weapon. In the Emerson decision, the court noted:

> Although, as we have held, the Second Amendment does protect individual
> rights, that does not mean those rights may never be made subject to any limited,
> narrowly tailored specific exceptions or restrictions.

The contention that the Second Amendment conveyed an individual right was growing in academic and political circles (Gast 2005) but this was the first time the courts accepted this interpretation.

In 1977 the District of Columbia adopted local legislation to ban all handguns and require registration of rifles and shotguns. On June 26, 2008, the Supreme Court in a 5-to-4 decision affirmed the decision of the court of appeals striking down the DC law (*District of Columbia v. Heller*, 128 S.Ct.645). In doing so the Court noted its determination that the Second Amendment conferred an indi-vidual right but that the right to bear arms was not absolute and was subject to reasonable limitations (see *UCLA Law Review 2009* for an analysis and discussion of this case). The Supreme Court did not rule on the incorporation of this right, leaving unsettled the applicability of this decision (and other federal statutes) to the states. Now that the Second Amendment is an individual right, the federal government, and perhaps soon the states, will be held to a much higher standard when the courts determine if a restriction on that right is constitutional. However, as the majority noted in Heller, properly tailored restrictions may be placed on the Second Amendment.

In the remainder of this chapter I explore the role that guns play in American society and especially in crime. Section I discusses the possession and use of firearms. Sections II and III examine guns as deterrents to crime including how carrying guns might affect crime levels. Section IV discusses how gun markets are regulated and operated, and section V examines what we know about effective gun crime prevention and control. The chapter concludes with a discussion of the policy implications of current knowledge and sketch a research agenda to advance our understanding the role guns play in crime.

A number of conclusions can be drawn:

- Between 300 and 350 million firearms are in circulation in the United States. Firearms can be found in nearly 40 percent of U.S. households.

- Firearms play a major role in violent deaths. There are nearly seven homicides involving firearms per 100,000 U.S. population, compared with an average of one per 100,000 in other developed countries.
- Sixty-eight percent of U.S. homicides are caused by firearms as are 36 percent of suicides.
- Firearms are used for self-defense, but there are major disagreements among researchers as to how often their use prevents crime.
- No conclusions can be drawn as to whether permitting private citizens to carry concealed weapons decreases crime rates.
- Convincing evidence does not exist that state-level restrictions on gun sales, gun costs, or mandatory sentences for gun crimes reduces crime rates.
- There is no convincing evidence that gun-safety training or technological methods to limit unauthorized users' access to guns reduces crime rates.
- Various police efforts have reduced gun use in violent crime.

I. The Possession and Use of Firearms In the United States

The vast majority of firearm owners possesses and uses them legally. They are used for recreational, hunting, defensive, and collecting purposes that are consistent with any interpretation of the Second Amendment. However, firearms are also used to kill and injure thousands of Americans every year. The widespread availability of firearms is a correlate of these negative effects and may be a direct cause. This availability is a large part of the explanation of how so many who are not legally allowed to possess firearms do, in fact, possess them and why so many of the intentional deaths and injuries that occur every year involve guns.

There are between 300,000,000 and 350,000,000 firearms in the United States, of which approximately one third are handguns.[5] Approximately 40 percent of all households own a firearm, with an average of more than three guns per possessing household.[6] It is estimated that each year about 600,000 handguns are stolen and not retrieved by their owners. This stock and illegal circulation of firearms must be remembered as one considers any attempts to reduce the extent to which those who should not have firearms have access to them. The stock of firearms has doubled in the last thirty years (see data from Legault and Lizotte, forthcoming, in appendix 2 for details on gun stock and its growth).

The benefits of having firearms are easily identified but hard to quantify. The pleasure gun owners get from target firing, hunting, and participation in related recreational activities is clear but difficult to measure. Firearms are also used to prevent the occurrence of crime. Later in this chapter I consider what we have learned about the extent of defensive gun uses and the relationship between carrying guns and crime. Those concerned with the harms associated with the availability of guns sometimes ignore these substantial benefits.

Of course the harms associated with the availability of firearms are substantial. In 2007 there were 15,707 homicides, 68 percent of which were committed with a firearm. The proportion of homicides committed with a gun has remained at approximately two-thirds of all homicides for the past thirty years (Uniform Crime Reports 2008—see appendix 3 for data since 2000). In 2008 there were also 34,000 suicides of which 36 percent were committed with a firearm (Ajdacic-Gross et. al. 2008). While firearms are not as involved in nonfatal injuries, they do play a substantial role (20 percent of all nonfatal intentional injuries involved the use of a firearm). Since 2001 more than 35,000 people have been murdered with a firearm—ten times the number killed in the terrorist attacks on the World Trade Center.

The incidence of firearm homicides is not randomly distributed throughout the population. Males have rates of firearm-related homicide five times greater than do females. Young adults and adolescents have much higher rates than do older people. According to the National Vital Statistics System (2007), rates for blacks (15 per 100,000) are much greater than they are for whites (2 per 100,000) and Hispanics (6 per 100,000). For young black males, homicide is the leading cause of death.

How do those who use guns illegally acquire them? Our knowledge of gun markets, primary and secondary, is limited by the limits of survey data[7] and restrictions placed on federal[8] and state data that could be used to describe the flow of guns from the manufacturer to criminal and noncriminal users. Our best available data indicate guns used criminally are acquired (in descending order of importance) by theft; informal transfers (e.g., buying from friends, "renting," illegal dealers, and unregulated sales at gun shows); diversion of guns in the legal market (e.g., lying and buying and straw sales [buying guns in bulk, selling to those unable to pass background checks]); and purchases from legal sellers. With 350,000,000 guns in circulation, theft and informal transfers are difficult to control without substantial changes in how guns are kept legally (e.g., locking them up at home and work, more effective trigger locks, and the development of personalized weapons [weapons that will only fire after a biometric key unlocks the weapon]). The economics of the gun industry suggests that these changes will not come without government intervention, but mandating any of these options may run afoul of the newly established individual right to possess arms.

Efforts to ban guns (e.g., the DC ban that was overthrown by the Heller decision and the assault weapons ban) have not demonstrated an ability significantly to reduce gun-related crimes and harm (Wellford, Pepper, and Petrie 2005, 98). While some early research (Loftin et.al. 1991) indicated the ban reduced handgun-related homicides, more recent work (Britt, Kleck, and Bordua 1996) has shown that these results are sensitive to sampling years and other model choices. There is no conclusive evidence that supports a finding that gun bans in one jurisdiction surrounded by jurisdictions without gun bans reduced gun-related violent crime. Efforts to buy back guns to reduce the stock of available weapons have not been effective (Wellford, Pepper, and Petrie 2005, 96). Typically, the guns turned in are old or of limited use. Replacement guns are so easily available that someone turning in a gun can easily replace it with a more effective weapon. Research on gun violence before and after buy backs (Rosenfeld 1996) finds no effects of the program. Limiting the number of guns that can be purchased in a period of time has shown limited success, partly because of the ability to move purchases to states that do not impose such regulations (Wellford, Pepper, and Petrie 2005, 93). Weil and Knox (1996) show that a law limiting sales in Virginia reduced the number of weapons seized in New York that had been purchased in Virginia but also showed that the proportion of guns seized that had been purchased in other states had increased. Finally, although the Brady Act has resulted in hundreds of thousands of gun applicants being rejected and therefore denied access to guns in the legal market, research to date demonstrates no effect of the law on homicides (Ludwig and Cook 2000). They suggest that the effectiveness of the act may have been reduced because those who were prohibited from purchasing guns under the Brady Act moved to unregulated secondary markets to make their purchases.

In short, given the stock of weapons, our limited knowledge of gun markets, the failure of many different types of efforts to reduce access to guns for criminal purposes, and the limitations that government faces when trying to restrict access to guns by those legally able to possess them, those who want a gun for a criminal purpose will have minimal difficulty acquiring one (or more).

II. The Defensive Use of Guns

Every day there are substantial numbers of instances where firearms are used to defend against crime. Two issues dominate the research literature on such defensive use: Can we translate the term "substantial" into a numerical estimate, and when guns are used for defense, do they reduce the harm associated with the crime being perpetrated? The answer to the first question is, unfortunately, it depends. The answer to the second is yes, harm is reduced—both physical harm and monetary loss.

The primary problem in determining how many defensive gun uses occur in any time period is what we mean by a defensive use of a gun. Lower estimates occur when the researcher defines a defensive use as occurring only after a criminal attack is imminent. For example, someone is trying to break in your home, and you confront the burglar with a gun and she retreats. Other researchers count as a defensive use a response to a perceived or imminent threat of criminal attack. For example, someone responds with their gun to a noise that they think is a burglar, but it turns out to be the neighbor's dog. Definitional differences produce dramatic differences in the estimates of the extent of defensive gun use.

Gary Kleck (Kleck and Gertz 1995; Kleck 2001a), the most influential researcher on this topic, estimates there are at least 2,500,000 instances of defensive gun use each year. This estimate comes from a survey conducted by Kleck in which a representative national sample of adults were interviewed by phone and asked:

> Within the past five years, have you yourself or another member of your household used a handgun, even if it was not fired, for self-protection or for the protection of property at home, work or elsewhere? Please do not include military service, police work, or work as a security guard.
> If the respondent said yes; they were asked: Did this incident (any of these incidents) happen in the past twelve months?

The two-part structure of the question is to minimize the extent to which respondents move events from the past to the time frame of inference ("telescoping"). The logic of the question is that a defensive use occurs whenever a respondent perceives that they have engaged in a self-protective act using a gun. For Kleck, a defensive use can occur in response to a perceived threat or a realized threat. Using this approach Kleck and Gertz (1995) estimated that there were 2,549,862 instance of defensive use of guns annually or on average of 7,000 per day.

David McDowall and his associates (McDowall and Wiersman 1994; McDowall, Loftin, and Wiersman 1998; McDowall, Loftin, and Presser 2000) estimate that there are slightly more than 100,000 defensive gun uses each year. This estimate comes from the use of the National Crime Victimization Survey.[9] In this survey respondents are asked a series of carefully developed questions that allow one to determine if there has been a sexual assault, assault, burglary, personal or household larceny, or car theft of any member of the household fourteen years of age or older. If there was a household crime, the respondent is asked:

> Was there anything you did or tried to do about the incident while it was going on? And,
> Did you do anything (else) with the idea of protecting yourself or your property while the incident was going on?

One of the categories of response to these questions is whether the respondent attacked or threatened the offender with a gun. Using this approach these researchers estimate there are 116,398 annual incidents of defensive gun use or an average of 319 per day—or less than 5 percent of the number estimated by Kleck.

What is the right number? It depends. Which operationalization do you think best captures what we mean by defensive gun use? Which data collection system will give the most accurate measure? How can survey respondents answer our questions if we do not know what we are talking about and leave it up to them to decide if what they did was self-protection? Setting aside the many methodological issues in this area of research (for a full discussion of these see Wellford, Pepper, and Petrie [2005]), the question is: Are perceived threats real and does the use of a gun in response to them qualify as a defensive gun use? For example, is every time a person walks in a large city in a high-crime neighborhood and carries a gun for protection a defensive gun use? They perceived they were at risk and carried the gun for protection. What if you see someone you do not know coming up your sidewalk with a gun, and you get your gun but do not use it . . . but the person knowing you are there and may have a gun then leaves? What if someone says they are going to rape you, but you produce a gun and the potential assailant leaves? Few would doubt the last is an example of a defensive use. Few would think the first example is a defensive use. I believe most people would classify the response to the potential burglar or assaulter as a defensive gun use, but it would not be counted as such in the McDowall approach to defensive gun measurement.

In addition to the definitional ambiguities and the methodological problems associated with surveys of sensitive topics, the higher estimates of the extent of defensive gun use have been challenged on the basis of weak external validity. Cook and Ludwig (1998) and Hemenway (1997) demonstrated that the upper estimates are inconsistent with other data on gun crimes that are thought to be more accurately measured. For example, they point out that the Kleck (1997) estimates would mean that defensive uses must occur in every home burglary and 60 percent of rapes. The over 200,000 offenders reported as injured by defensive gun use in the surveys dwarf the actual number of admissions to emergency rooms for nonfatal firearm injuries. While troubling, these external validity issues are not totally convincing as a means to validate any estimates of defensive gun use. The measurement problems in the surveys, the small numbers of cases in some of the subestimates, and that there is error in the data used for external validation mean that these issues are really another indicator that we do not know the true extent of defensive gun use.

In addition to the issue of how often defensive gun use occurs, a smaller body of research has considered the effectiveness of using a gun in response to a crime. This research relies almost exclusively on the NCVS and thus the lower number of these incidents. In these data it is quite clear that defensively using a gun reduces the harm and loss to the victim. Kleck (2001b), Kleck and Delone (1993), Kleck and Sayles (1990), and Lizotte (1986) report a series of studies assessing the outcome of violent crimes reported in the NCVS. They demonstrate in these data that defensive gun use is correlated with less injury and monetary loss compared with other forms of defense or passive acceptance of the crime. For the case of rape, those who use guns to defend themselves are less likely to report a completed act. While we do not know if these results exist in the larger set of defensive gun uses that are identified in other surveys, and we do not know if these are just correlations or if defensive gun use is a causal factor in the explanation of the crime outcomes, we do know that when a potential crime is eminent, the use of a gun to defend oneself reduces harm and loss for the victim.

The use of guns in self-defense, especially in one's home, is one of the most fundamental justifications for seeking a minimally fettered application of the Second Amendment to gun possession. Until we have much better measures of the extent and consequences of defensive gun use, we will not be able to inform this aspect of the gun issue in our society. Until then we will continue to debate the extent of use with inadequate data, and we will limit our understanding of the efficacy of defensive gun use to the most extreme situations in which guns are used for self protection.

III. The Effect of Right-to-Carry Laws on Crime

If guns are effectively used defensively, would it not make sense to allow legal gun possessors the right to carry a gun with them wherever (or almost wherever[10]) they go? This is the logic behind state permitting procedures that allow someone to carry a concealed weapon with them. Until quite recently, in almost all states the granting of a permit was based on a demonstrated need (e.g., high-risk occupation or documented threat). More recently states have enacted legislation that requires local officials to issue a carry permit to any qualified adult.[11] Currently, forty states have enacted some form of right-to-carry laws to make it easier to receive a permit to carry a weapon. Deterrence is the theory underlying this development in the law. The expectation is that potential offenders, fearing that a potential victim may have a gun with them, will be less likely to commit the crime. In addition, the availability of the gun increases the likelihood of an effective defensive gun use if the crime occurs. More important than the theory of deterrence to the spread of these laws has been the research of John Lott (1999, 2000) and his associate (Lott and Mustard 1997) that purport to demonstrate that these laws substantially reduce violent crimes. In part because Lott has been so willing to share his data and analysis with others, there have been many other analyses that have supported and challenged his conclusions. In part as a response to the controversy around the differing estimates of the impact of the effects of shall-carry laws, in 2002 the National Academy of Sciences established a panel to consider the role of firearms in crime and suicide and especially the impact of shall-carry laws.

The research on shall-carry laws demonstrates all of the major difficulties facing those who do research on various aspects of guns and crime. The research relies on observational data making causal interpretations very difficult. It requires estimates of gun possession and use, especially defensive use, with all of the problems noted earlier that such measurements entail. The absence of strong theories to guide the research results in the use of controls of unknown completeness and relevance. The NAS panel that reviewed this research area in particular concluded: "[I]f further headway is to be made . . . new analytic approaches and data are needed" (Wellford, Pepper, and Petrie 2005, 7).

Using county-level panel data including crime rates, potentially explanatory and confounding control variables, and an indicator of when the shall-carry laws became effective, Lott and associates consider the effect of the law (dichotomized as before and after adoption) on crime rates controlling for a large number of controls—these models give estimates of the effects of a one-time shift in crime rates following adoption. They also estimate trend models to measure the effects of the laws over time relative to the date of adoption using controls and trends in national crime rates. Lott and others find for the period 1977–92 that the adoption of shall-carry laws is associated with a 5 percent decrease in violent crime (murder 8 percent, rape 5 percent, aggravated assault 7 percent, and robbery 2 percent) and a 3 percent increase in property crimes (7 percent increase for auto theft, .5 percent increase in burglary, and a 3 percent increase in larceny). The trend analysis found decreases for all crime types and categories analyzed although the effects were generally smaller (1–3 percent decreases). The conclusion from Lott, one that has been cited in almost all states that have adopted shall-carry laws, is that making it easier to acquire a permit to carry a firearm is associated with decreases in crime, especially violent crime.

The NAS panel that considered this literature concluded that "with the current evidence it is not possible to determine that there is a causal link between the passage of right-to-carry laws and crime rates" (Wellford, Pepper, and Petrie 2005, 150). The panel reached this conclusion for the following reasons. There is no relationship between the adoption of right-to-carry laws and crime when none of the controls are included in the models. That is, the zero-order relationship is not significantly different from zero. Only when the controls are added to the models does the relationship emerge. Ordinarily, the introduction of controls is to see if an observed relationship might be the result of the relationships between the independent and dependent variables and the controls. In this case, the relationship is not observable until the controls are included. While this could suggest a suppressor effect of one or more of the controls, it does draw attention, in the absence of strong theory, to the effect of control selection. Duggan (2001) found that dropping the controls and including only fixed county effects led to conclusions that were the opposite of those reached by Lott. Similar results were reported by Black and Nagin (1998) and Ayres and Donohue (2003). In addition, these researchers demonstrated that the results were highly sensitive to the states included in the models. In summary, the research literature examining the Lott results, using the same data and analytic techniques, finds that the estimate of the effect of right-to-carry laws depends on the crimes, controls, and states included in the models. The NAS panel reached this same conclusion.

The NAS committee also observed that the time frame for the data included in the analysis can affect the estimates of the impact of right-to-carry laws. The committee, using Lott's data as a base and adding eight additional years of data (i.e., 1977–2000), and using the same controls Lott used, found the results to be quite different.[12] Recall that a positive effect means that crime increased after the legal change, and a negative effect means crime decreased. The extended data results yielded estimates in which the sign changed for total violent crime and aggravated assault (both positive in the extended models). For all property crimes the sign remained positive, but the coefficients increased in size. For murder and rape the signs remained negative, but the coefficients decreased (only slightly for murder [-9 for the original period Lott used and -8 for the extended period], but more substantially for rape [from -6 to -.16]). While those who are committed to the Lott's findings will dwell on the fact that the coefficient for murder was not substantially changed, the committee and objective observers would note the highly sensitive nature of these results raises several questions about the findings overall.[13]

Note also that the basic independent variable in all of this work is whether a state has adopted a right-to-carry law. In one state after adoption, let us imagine that every eligible citizen took advantage of the law to acquire a permit, had or purchased a firearm, carried it with him at all times, and was fully prepared to use it. Now imagine a state that adopts the legislation but in which no one seeks a permit and no one owns or carries a firearm. Undoubtedly we would predict different outcomes for crime in these states, assuming we accepted the deterrence model that underlies all of this research. To really estimate the impact of the law we need to know how many permits are issued, to whom, and if those people actually carry a weapon and use it defensively in crime situations. We also need to know what those contemplating committing crime in each state know or believe about the law and its use. The research question is not how states or counties "act" but how these laws change behavior at the level at which crime occurs—the individual offender and victim. Absent such data, we are unlikely ever to know the true effect of these laws.

While the right-to-carry issue has generated substantial research and controversy, in the end it has not done much more than demonstrate the problems of doing research on firearms and crime. The research clearly does not establish that right-to-carry laws decrease crime, even murder. It does not prove the laws do not have an effect. As the NAS committee stated:

[I]t is not possible to reach any scientifically supported conclusions because of (a) the sensitivity of the empirical results to seemingly minor changes in model specification, (b) a lack of robustness of the results to the inclusion of more recent years of data (during which there were many more law changes that in the earlier period), and (c) the statistical imprecision of the results. (Wellford, Pepper, and Petrie 2005, 7)

This conclusion has not stopped legislatures from adopting such laws or prompted those that have to rescind them.

IV. Reducing Gun Crime: The Role of the Criminal Justice System

Illegal possession and use of firearms are among the most important activities addressed by the criminal justice system. The criminal justice system addresses these crimes before and after the crimes occur. The goal is to reduce the number of the crimes through use of the legal system to control offenders. For gun crimes these efforts can include disrupting the supply of guns to those who plan to use them to commit crimes, specialized courts devoted to gun crimes, enhanced sentencing for those who use guns during the commission of a crime, and gun crime–focused policing. To date, the scientific evidence suggests that only the last has had the effect of reducing gun related crime.

A. Disrupting Gun Markets

In 1938 Congress passed legislation requiring that anyone selling a gun must be a Federal Firearm Licensee (FFL), licensed by the federal government. In the beginning, a license cost one dollar and there were no real restrictions on who could get one. In 1972 the Bureau of Alcohol, Tobacco, and Firearms (BATF) was created, in part to oversee those with licenses to sell guns. Today, FFLs are required to see identification of the buyer, have the buyer sign a form saying they are not prohibited from purchasing a weapon, do a background check, maintain a record of the transaction, report multiple sales and stolen guns, and, if the sellers go out of business, send all records to the BATF. The data supplied by FFLs to the BATF allow that agency to trace guns that have been used in crimes and that are confiscated back to the original sale. These trace data have proven useful to law enforcement and researchers, although the Tiahart amendment discussed earlier has limited the effectiveness of the data for both groups.

Until the 1990s, the oversight of FFLs was not as effective as it should have been. In 1992 legislation was passed increasing the requirements for FFLs. As a result, some 180,000 FFLs declined to renew their licenses. With fewer FFLs (about 103,000 in 1995) the BATF was able to do more effective oversight. In addition, the BATF conducted an analysis of all of its investigations from 1996 to 1998. This study (BATF 2000) demonstrated that a very small number of FFLs (9 percent) accounted for more than half of the illegally diverted guns.

Today, the BATF and local and state law enforcement agencies are working closely together to attack gun markets. However, the size of the stock of guns, the availability of the unregulated secondary market (e.g., private sales, including at gun shows), and the ease of criminals penetrating the legal market severely limit the effectiveness of the criminal justice system to significantly disrupt the gun market.

B. Gun Courts

The popularity of drug courts has suggested the use of that model for those first-time offenders (usually juveniles) who used a gun in the commission of their crime but where the victim was not injured. The idea is to use the court to focus increased supervision and services on the offender, which will result in reduced gun crime recidivism. The treatment services can include specialized residential facilities. To date there have not been any scientifically valid evaluations of these efforts, although they are growing in number, especially in large urban areas with high rates of juvenile crime.

C. Enhanced Sentencing

Criminal sentences can be increased above the sentence for the underlying offense if a gun is used in the commission of the crime. There are also mandatory sentence laws that require minimum prison sentences following conviction of illegal possession of a gun whether *or not* it is used in the commission of a crime. Evaluating the effect of these laws raises many of the same concerns as those noted in the discussion of right-to-carry laws—weak data, sensitivity to controls and time frames, and difficulties of statistical inference.

The Bartley-Fox law in Massachusetts mandated a one-year prison sentence for unlawful carrying of a gun and a two-year mandatory sentence for crimes committed while in possession of a gun. That the law contained both of these elements has made it difficult to estimate the effects of either, apart from the joint influence of both. Some researchers have found decreases in gun assaults and robberies after the passage of Bartley-Fox but not decreases in gun homicides (Deutsch and Alt 1977; Berk et al. 1979); while other researchers found little if any reductions in gun assaults and armed robberies (Pierce and Bowers 1981; Hay and McCleary 1979). The conflicting results demonstrate the fragility and sensitivity of results to model specifications and analytic choices. Also, the absence of information on changes in carrying and illegal use at the individual level requires the researcher to make largely untestable assumptions about the effect of the law. Finally, some evidence suggests that the effect of the law was reduced by the unwillingness of some criminal justice actors to take full advantage of it (i.e., thinking the punishment too harsh, different charges being imposed at arrest or indictment to avoid the mandatory penalty) (Carlson 1982). A recent analysis of the effects of mandatory sentences more generally further demonstrates how the system modifies legislatively mandated penalties (Tonry 2009). In any case, the effectiveness of mandatory sentences has been questioned, especially as state and local budgets have been stressed by large prison and jail populations (Pew 2008).

Many other jurisdictions have adopted sentencing enhancements for the use of a gun with a crime. Kessler and Levitt (1999) concluded that sentence enhancements are associated with crime reductions, although the literature on sentencing enhancements on gun crime does not consistently find a negative effect on gun crime (e.g., see Webster, Doob, and Zimring 2006). In a comprehensive assessment across all states and a number of years, Marvel and Moody (1995) find no evidence that the adoption of mandatory sentence laws have any impact on crime rates or firearms use. With the exception of some smaller studies (McPheters, Mann, and Schlagenhauf 1984), the overwhelming body of research on this topic finds little if any effect of mandatory gun–sentencing laws on crime and gun crimes. While this research suffers from the methodological and data problems noted earlier, the consistency of the findings suggests this is not an effective way to use the resources of the criminal justice system to reduce gun crime.

D. Focused Policing and "Pulling Levers"

Beginning with the Kansas City Gun Project (Sherman and Rogan 1995), a series of well-designed studies have demonstrated that the policing of areas with concentrations of gun crime can reduce gun crimes without displacing the crimes to other areas. This is especially true in the experience of New York City and other large police departments where, following aggressive enforcement of gun statutes, there were dramatic decreases in homicides and nonfatal shootings (Wellford, Pepper, and Petrie 2005, 233). Given the consistency of these findings with similar results from experimental tests of place-based policing, we can have high confidence that police targeting of gun crimes can affect their occurrence.

Similarly there are encouraging results from studies assessing the effects of a police focus on violent gun offenders, especially when that focus includes other criminal justice agencies and a mobilized community. The Boston Gun Project (subsequently referred to as Operation Ceasefire) is the most successful and best known of these efforts. Beginning as a focus on youth homicides and shootings, the effort identified youth groups and conflict between them as a focus. Using prosecutors, probation officers, and community leaders the project sought to exercise every legally available "lever" to change the behaviors of youths involved in these groups and in gun crimes (for a full description see Kennedy 1997). The evaluations of this project by Braga et al. (2001) and Winship (2002), while not strong enough to demonstrate how the effort affected crime, leave no doubt that this is an approach worth replicating with stronger evaluation designs. This effort also included steps to disrupt gun markets that also appear to have been effective (Braga and Pierce 2005). Later work by Kennedy (1997) in a number of cities using the same approach has also been well-received by police officials and community members, and has been successful as measured by before-after designs without controls. The success of the Boston project (and an effort in Richmond that gained considerable attention but less supportive evaluation results, see Raphael and Ludwig [2003] and Levitt [2003]) prompted the establishment of Project Safe Neighborhoods in an attempt to replicate this effort nationally. An evaluation has not yet been completed. Ludwig has urged these efforts to place greater emphasis on the demand for guns by those with known criminal records (2005).

V. Preventing Firearm Injuries

There are two broad approaches to preventing injuries and deaths associated with guns: educational programs, especially for children, and technologies to limit the use of a gun. Neither has proven effective at reducing gun crimes and injuries. Advances are most likely to come from the development of prevention programs based on sound behavioral theories similar to those that have been found to work in the areas of smoking and drug abuse prevention (Najaka et al. 2001).

Prevention programs developed by the National Rifle Association (Eddie Eagle) and the Brady Center to Prevent Gun Violence (Straight Talk About Risks or STAR) seek to educate youth about guns and the danger of their misuse, and to encourage them to avoid mishandling guns. Hardy (2002) using a randomized prospective design found both programs to be ineffective in changing attitudes or behavior. While other studies with much weaker designs have found some positive effects, the NAS panel, after considering more than eighty studies evaluating prevention programs (Wellford, Pepper, and Petrie 2005, 214), found no evidence to support a conclusion that these approaches are effective at preventing firearm injuries.

Locking technologies include trigger locks and "personalized weapons." Some states have mandated that all guns sold must come with a trigger lock, and some have mandated that the purchaser be offered such technology. The theory is that by keeping the gun locked, it cannot be used by an unauthorized user. This is thought to be particularly helpful in preventing access to weapons by children and thus a means to reduce accidental deaths and injuries, and the possibility that they could get access to weapons for use in crimes. We know that many gun owners do not use trigger locks and do not use other forms of safe storage. There are no studies of the effects of using this type of technology although conceptual models suggest they should be effective when used (e.g., Cook and Leitzel 2002). Getting data on how individuals keep and store there guns has proven difficult.

Beginning with Florida in 1989, seventeen states have adopted legislation making owners liable if a child uses an unlocked firearm. These child access prevention laws have been reviewed by Lott and Whitley (2002) using the same approach and basic data as Lott (1999, 2000) used in the right-to-carry research. They found no effects on juvenile gun accidents or suicides and an increase in violent and property crime. Cummings et al. (1997) found that the laws reduced juvenile gun injuries, suicides, and homicides. Again the differences in results appear to be a result of different models and statistical techniques.

Finally, research has been undertaken on whether personalized weapons may be developed. These are guns that can be operated only by the person whose biometrics matches those in the gun (e.g., a fingerprint reader on the gun that has to have a match with a specific fingerprint to operate) or who possesses a key (e.g., an RFID transmitter emitting a frequency that allows the gun to operate). While these technologies have proven to be possible (National Academy of Engineering 2003), early work suggests they are not acceptable for law enforcement purposes and may have higher failure rates than current models, thereby creating civil liabilities for manufacturers. Currently, there is not a program of personalized gun research being supported by federal, state, or local justice agencies.

In summary, to date no prevention programs or technologies have been identified in which we can have confidence. These programs and technologies may have other effects (e.g., reductions in firearm suicides) but they do not prevent gun crime.

VI. Future Research and Policy

Substantial data issues must be overcome before gun crime research can better address many of the issues discussed in this chapter. However, some research topics can be addressed while data improvements are being made. Fortunately, we know what we have to do to improve data and to undertake immediately needed research.

Two primary types of data are needed: on the acquisition, possession, and use of firearms; and on the incidents of death and injury associated with firearms. The primary obstacles are political and financial. Data are being collected on first purchases of firearms from licensed dealers and on those screened for purchasing firearms. However, access to these data is severely restricted. Groups supporting the fewest possible restrictions on guns have organized politically to minimize the data that government has on gun ownership, in part because they feel that such knowledge could be used by government to confiscate all weapons. Similarly, even though these groups have fought efforts to fund research, we know that survey methods can be developed to collect information while protecting the confidentiality of records (illegal drug use, for example, has a long history of methodological work to improve measurement). Reducing the barriers to current data on gun acquisition, improving those data to include transfers after initial purchase, and developing scientifically sound survey methods on use of firearms would greatly improve our understanding of the gun/crime nexus. To improve data on deaths and injuries associated with firearms, we need fully to fund the National Violent Death Reporting System (NVDRS), and include better firearms data in injury surveillance systems. The NVDRS is now operating in seventeen states. For each violent death in those states, data are collected from a variety of sources (e.g., coroner, police, child welfare) to provide as complete a picture of violent deaths as official records can provide. The system is fully developed and tested; it only needs funding to implement it in the remaining states. This would materially improve our ability to identify gun deaths and to understand better how they occur and the roles guns play. The case of injury data is more complicated. The Centers for Disease Control report that forty-four different federal data systems operated by sixteen different agencies and three private injury registry systems provide nationwide injury-related data. None reports detailed data on firearm-involved injuries. However, this type of information could be added to any or all of these systems and provide a comprehensive picture of gun-related injuries.

While these improvements are being made in data systems, research should be conducted on a number of substantive issues. Everyone agrees that the best approach to minimizing the deaths and injuries in which guns are involved is prevention. We also know that no prevention programs have proven effective. The federal government should undertake a research program to develop prevention programs based on what we have learned about the prevention of other high-risk behaviors and on basic behavioral theory and rigorously test them. If this were done we would, in two to five years, have the beginnings of sound gun-death and injury-prevention programs. Everyone also agrees that criminals, juveniles, and the mentally risky should not have access to guns. Targeted, micro-area policing has proven effective, but we do not fully understand why or how effectively to replicate and extend these efforts. A research program devoted to this offers the best hope for more effectively deterring criminals from getting and using guns.

While it is relatively easy to identify data improvements and research needs, predicting the future of gun policy is much more difficult. The weak research base makes it difficult to make recommendations that have a scientific foundation. We know that no sound evidence supports the effectiveness of right-to-carry laws. We know that market restrictions that vary by state do not work. We know that the harms associated with firearm use are substantial and need to be reduced. The policy need is for a more rational, consistent, and effective set of gun regulations and enforcement strategies. These could include (1) a decision by the Supreme Court applying federal law to the states, (2) closing all secondary gun markets so that all transactions would be reported and follow the gun, (3) removing legislative restrictions on access to and research use of BATF and Brady background check data, and (4) including real-time mental health and drug-use checks in the background checks for gun purchases.

APPENDIX

Table 14.1. Appendix A: Comparative Data

Country	Firearm Homicide Rate	Firearm Suicide Rate	% Households with Firearms
United States	7	6	39
Finland	.9	6	25
Portugal	1.3	1.3	N/A
Israel	.7	2	N/A
Italy	1.7	1.1	16
Scotland	.2	.3	5
Canada	.8	4	24
Australia	.4	2.4	15
South Korea	.04	.02	N/A
Belgium	.6	2.6	17
Switzerland	.6	5.6	27
Sweden	.2	2	15
Denmark	.2	2.3	N/A
Germany	.2	1.2	9
France	.4	5	23
Norway	.3	4	32
Japan	.02	.04	.6
England and Wales	.07	.33	5

Taken from Wellford, Pepper and Petrie, 2005. Source Krug, et.al. 1998; United Nations, 2000.

Table 14. 2.   Appendix B Civilian Firearm Stock and Population Estimates (in thousands) United States, 1970–2006[1]

	Resident	Firearm			Cumulative
Year	US Population	Total Firearm[2]	Handguns	Long Guns	Gun Stock[3]
1970	203,302	4,287	1,533	2,754	104,401
1971	206,827	4,703	1,640	3,063	109,103
1972	209,284	5,283	2,071	3,212	114,386
1973	211,357	5,422	1,887	3,535	119,808
1974	213,342	6,399	2,023	4,376	126,207
1975	215,465	6,117	2,163	3,954	132,324
1976	217,563	5,718	1,976	3,742	138,042
1977	219,760	5,233	1,925	3,308	143,275
1978	222,095	5,360	1,903	3,457	148,635
1979	224,567	5,691	2,171	3,520	154,326
1980	226,546	5,882	2,449	3,432	160,208
1981	229,466	5,475	2,591	2,886	165,682
1982	231,664	5,349	2,708	2,642	171,031
1983	233,792	4,581	2,219	2,353	175,612
1984	235,825	4,411	1,905	2,507	180,023
1985	237,924	3,974	1,684	2,290	183,997
1986	240,133	3,524	1,538	1,986	187,521
1987	242,289	4,345	1,842	2,503	191,866
1988	244,499	4,840	2,236	2,605	196,706
1989	246,819	5,123	2,353	2,769	201,829
1990	249,464	4,334	2,110	2,225	206,163
1991	252,153	3,873	1,941	1,929	210,035
1992	255,030	6,479	2,803	3,676	216,514
1993	257,783	7,759	3,881	3,879	224,273
1994	260,327	6,641	3,324	3,316	230,914
1995	262,803	4,911	2,199	2,713	235,825
1996	265,229	4,391	1,821	2,569	240,216
1997	267,784	4,242	1,773	2,469	244,458
1998	270,248	4,445	1,727	2,717	248,903
1999	272,691	4,693	1,565	3,128	253,596
2000	282,194	4,969	1,918	3,051	258,565
2001	285,112	4,211	1,593	2,618	262,775
2002	287,888	5,152	2,003	3,149	267,927
2003	290,448	4,944	1,841	3,103	272,871
2004	293,192	4,793	1,826	2,970	277,664
2005	295,896	4,923	1,907	3,016	282,587
2006	298,755	5,587	2,395	3,192	288,174

[1]Data obtained from Legault, Richard L. and Alan J. Lizotte (forthcoming).

[2]According to Legault and Lizotte (forthcoming), total firearms in the US was calculated by estimating numbers of privately held firearms in the US by starting with ATF numbers on firearms produced per year, adding imports, and subtracting exports from the Dept of Commerce with a yearly attrition rate of 1 percent. Totals do not include firearms produced or imported for the US Military.

[3]Cumulative gun stock calculated as all firearms produced and not exported, plus imports, minus 10 percent of the total per year to account for attrition.

Table 14.3. Appendix C: Homicide data in the United States by firearm type (percentage) 2000–2008[1]

Year	Total[2] Murder	Total firearm (%)	Handguns (%)	Rifles (%)	Shotguns (%)	Other Guns (%)	Firearm type unknown (%)
2000	13,230	8661 (65.46)	6778 (51.23)	411 (3.11)	485 (3.67)	53 (0.40)	934 (7.06)
2001	14,061	8890 (63.22)	6931 (49.29)	386 (2.75)	511 (3.63)	59 (0.42)	1003 (7.13)
2002	14,263	9528 (66.80)	7294 (51.14)	488 (3.42)	486 (3.41)	75 (0.53)	1185 (8.31)
2003	14,465	9659 (66.77)	7745 (53.54)	392 (2.71)	454 (3.14)	76 (0.53)	992 (6.86)
2004	14,210	9385 (66.05)	7286 (51.27)	403 (2.84)	507 (3.57)	117 (0.82)	1072 (7.54)
2005	14,965	10158 (67.88)	7565 (50.55)	445 (2.97)	522 (3.49)	138 (0.92)	1488 (9.94)
2006	15,087	10225 (67.77)	7836 (51.94)	438 (2.90)	490 (3.25)	107 (0.71)	1354 (8.97)
2007	14,916	10129 (67.91)	7398 (49.60)	453 (3.04)	457 (3.06)	116 (0.78)	11705 (1.43)
2008	14,180	9484 (66.88)	6755 (47.64)	375 (2.64)	444 (3.13)	79 (0.56)	11831 (2.91)

[1]*Source*: FBI's Uniformed Crime Report (2000–2008). http://www.fbi.gov/ucr/ucr.htm.

[2]Total Murder figures were obtained from Expanded Homicide Data Tables. Figures might appear different from what is presented in the trend data on www.fbi.gov/ucr. Trend data was not available prior to 2006. The data for 2000–2003 were taken from CIUS 2004 pp.19; table 2.9. The data for 2004–2006 were taken from CIUS 2007 Expanded Homicide Data Table 7. The data for 2007–2008 was taken from CIUS 2008 Expanded Homicide Data Table 8.

NOTES

1. While I will occasionally consider data and research from outside the United States, such comparisons are very difficult due to the vast differences in laws and gun use in crime. In addition, the data and research on guns and crime is overwhelmingly based in and on the United States.

2. For a detailed comparison see the data from Wellford, Pepper, and Petrie (2005) in this chapter.

3. For a discussion of these cases and a review of the development of the Second Amendment, see Gast (2005).

4. This refers to whether the Supreme Court would rule that the laws enacted by Congress would apply to the states. To date, the court has not determined that the Second Amendment is such a basic right of individuals that it should apply to all state laws and actions (Gast 2005).

5. Data on firearm possession and use, especially criminal possession and use, are not well developed. While I do not discuss these methodological weaknesses in this chapter, the reader should be aware that all estimates are approximations, usually with unknown error terms. Only when it is critical to understanding the issue at hand do I discuss measurement problems. For a full discussion of this issue see Wellford, Pepper, and Petrie (2005, 19–52).

6. In 1950 it is estimated that there were 60,000,000 firearms in the United States (a rate of 381 per 1,000 persons), Kleck 1997. Today the estimate is more than 300,000,000 or a rate of over one per adult person (Legault and Lizotte, forthcoming).

7. There is no national survey dedicated to understanding gun possession and use. Nor is there a program of research to improve our ability to use survey methods in this

area. This was identified by the National Academy of Sciences panel as one of the major impediments to improving research on firearms and crime (Wellford, Pepper, and Petrie 2005, 3–5).

8. Beginning in 2003, Congress has adopted limits on the use of federal gun data. Known as the Tiahart amendments in recognition of the key role of Rep. Todd Tiahart played in their adoption, they limit BATF sharing of trace data with police officials and researchers, and limit the FBI's retention of record check information. Both of these actions limit the ability to use the data for research and enforcement efforts.

9. The NCVS is an ongoing national survey of households that measures victim reported instances of crime victimization (for full discussion see Groves and Cork 2009). The survey has numerous methodological strengths that cannot be found in one-time surveys like the one used by Kleck.

10. Common exceptions are bars, government buildings, and schools. For a fuller discussion of carry permit laws see *UCLA Law Review (2009)*.

11. The definition of qualified varies but usually includes a citizen of the state, who is an adult, has no criminal record, is mentally competent, and does not have a record of drug arrests.

12. Lott and others have also reported estimates based on additional years, but these models also included different control variables.

13. There are also statistical issues identified by the NAS committee that raise concerns about the Lott approach. For a discussion of these see Horowitz (2005).

REFERENCES

Adjacic-Gross, Vladeta, Mitchell G. Weiss, Mariann Ring, Urs Hepp, Matthias Bopp, Felix Gutzwiller, and Wulf Rossler. 2008. "Methods of Suicide: International Suicide Patterns Derived from the WHO Mortality Database." *Bulletin of the World Health Organization* 86:9.

Ayres, Ian, and John J. Donohue III. 2003. "The Latest Misfires In Support of the 'More Guns Less Crime' Hypothesis." *Stanford Law Review* 55:1371–98.

Berk, Richard A., Donnie M. Hoffman, Judith Maki, David Rauma, and Herbert Wong. 1979. "Estimated Procedures For Pooled Cross-Sectional and Time Series Data." *Evaluation Quarterly* 3, (2): 385–411.

Black, Dan A., and Daniel S. Nagin. 1998. "Do Right-To-Carry Laws Deter Violent Crime?" *Journal of Legal Studies* 27:209–19.

Braga, Anthony A., D. M. Kennedy, A. M. Piehl, and E. J. Waring. 2001. "Measuring the Impact of Operation Ceasefire." In *Reducing Gun Violence: The Boston Gun Project's Operation Ceasefire. National Institute of Justice Research Report, National Institute of Justice.* Washington, DC: U.S. Department of Justice.

Braga, Anthony A., and Glenn L. Pierce. 2005. "Disrupting Illegal Firearm Markets in Boston." *Criminology and Public Policy* 4(4):717–48.

Britt, Chester, III, Gary Kleck, and David J. Bordua. 1996. "A Reassessment of the DC Gun Law: Some Cautionary Notes on the Use of Interrupted Time Series Design for Policy Impact Assessment." *Law and Society Review* 30:361–80.

Bureau of Alcohol, Tobacco, and Firearms (BATF). 2000. *ATF Regulatory Actions.* Washington, DC: U.S. Department of the Treasury.

Carlson, Kenneth. 1982. *Mandatory Sentencing: The Experience of Two States. National Institute of Justice*, Washington, DC: U.S. Department of Justice.

Cook, Phillip J., and Jens Ludwig. 1998. Defensive Gun Uses. *Journal of Quantitative Criminology* 14(2):111–13.

Cook, Phillip J., and James A. Leitzel. 2002. "'Smart' Guns: A Technological Fix for Regulating Secondary Market." *Contemporary Economic Policy* 20(1):38–49.

Cummings, Peter, David C. Grossman, Frederick P. Rivara, and Thomas D. Koepsell. 1997. "State Gun Safe Storage Laws and Child Mortality Due To Firearms." *Journal of the American Medical Association* 278:1084–86.

Deutsch, Stephen J., and Francis B. Alt. 1977. "The Effect of the Massachusetts' Gun Control Law on Gun-Related Crimes in the City of Boston." *Evaluation Quarterly* 1:543–68.

Duggan, Mark. 2001. "More Guns More Crime." *Journal of Political Economy* 109(4): 1086–114.

Gast, Scott. 2005. "Judicial Scrutiny of Challenged Gun Control Regulations." In *Firearms and Violence*, ed. C. Wellford, J. Pepper, and C. Petrie. Washington, DC: NAS Press.

Groves, Robert M., and Daniel L. Cork. 2009. *Ensuring the Quality, Credibility, and Relevance of US Justice Statistics.* Washington, DC: NAS Press.

Hardy, Marjorie S. 2002. "Teaching Firearm Safety to Children: Failure of a Program." *Journal of Developmental and Behavioral Pediatrics* 23(2):71–76.

Hay, Richard A., and Richard McCleary. 1979. "Box-tiao Time Series Models for Impact Assessment: A Comment of Deutsch and Alt." *Evaluation Quarterly* 3:277–314.

Hemenway, David. 1997. "Survey Research and Self-Defense Gun Use: An Explanation of Extreme Overestimates." *Journal of Criminal Law and Criminology* 87(4):1430–45.

Horowitz, Joel L. 2005. "Statistical Issues in the Evaluation of the Effects of Right-To-Carry Laws." In *Firearms and Violence,* edited by C. Wellford, C. Pepper, and C. Petrie. Washington, DC: NAS Press.

Kennedy, David. M. 1997. "Pulling Levers: Chronic Offenders, High-Crime Settings, and a Theory of Prevention." *Valparaiso University Law Review* 31(2): 449. http://www.saf.org/LawReviews/KennedyD1.htm.

Kessler, Daniel, and Stephen D. Levitt. 1999. "Using Sentence Enhancements to Distinguish between Deterrence and Incapacitation." *Journal of Law and Economics* 42:343–63.

Kleck, Gary. 1997. *Targeting Guns.* New York: Aldine de Gruyter.

———. 2001a. "The Frequency of Defensive Gun Use." In *Armed: New Perspectives on Gun Control*, edited by G. Kleck and D. Kates. New York: Prometheus Books.

———. 2001b "The Nature and Effectiveness of Owning and Carrying and Using Guns for Self-protection." In *Armed: New Perspectives on Gun Control,* edited by G. Kleck and D. Kates,.

Kleck, Gary, and Mariam A. Delone. 1993. "Victim Resistance and Offender Weapon Effects in Robbery." *Journal of Quantitative Criminology* 9(1):55–81.

Kleck, Gary, and Marc Gertz. 1995. "Armed Resistance to Crime: The Prevalence and Nature of Self Defense with a Gun." *Journal of Criminal Law and Criminology* 86(1): 150–87.

Kleck, Gary, and Susan Sayles. 1990. Rape and Resistance. *Social Problems* 37:149–62.

Krug, E. G., K. E. Powell, and L. Dahlberg. 1998. "Firearm Related Deaths in the United States and 35 Other High and Upper Middle Income Countries." *International Journal of Epidemiology* 7:214–21.

Legault, Richard L., and Alan J. Lizotte. Forthcoming. "Caught in a Crossfire: Legal and Illegal Firearms Ownership in America." In *Handbook on Crime and Deviance*, ed. Marvin D. Krohn, Alan J. Lizotte, and Gina P. Hall. New York: Springer Science and Business Media.

Levitt, Stephen. 2003. "Commentary of Raphael and Ludwig." In *Evaluating Gun Policy: Effects on Crime and Violence*, edited by J. Ludwig and P. Cook. Washington, DC: Brookings Institution Press.

Lizotte, Alan. 1986. "Determinants of Completing Rape and Assault." *Journal of Quantitative Criminology* 2:203–17.

Loftin, Colin, David McDowall, Brian Weirsma, and Talbert J. Cottey. 1991. "Effects of Restrictive Licensing of Handguns on Homicide and Suicide in the District of Columbia." *New England Journal of Medicine* 325(23):1615–20.

Lott, John R. 1999. "More Guns, Less Crime." Working paper 247. Program for studies in law, economics, and public policy, Yale Law School. Boston, MA.

———. 2000. *More Guns, Less Crime*. Chicago: Chicago University Press.

Lott, John R., and David B. Mustard. 1997. "Crime, Deterrence, and Right to Carry Concealed Handguns." *Journal of Legal Studies* 26(1):1–68.

Lott, John R., and John E. Whitley. 2002. "A Note of the Use of County Level UCR Data." Working paper. American Enterprise Institute: Working Paper Series. Available at Available at SSRN: http://ssrn.com/abstract=320102 or doi:10.2139/ssrn.320102

Ludwig, Jens. 2005. "Better Gun Enforcement, Less Crime." *Criminology and Public Policy* 4(1): 677–716.

Ludwig, Jens, and Phillip.J. Cook. 2000. "Homicide and Suicide Rates Associated with the Implementation of the Brady Handgun Violence Prevention Act." *Journal of the American Medical Association* 284:585–91.

Marvell, Thomas B., and Carlisle E. Moody. 1995. "The Impact of Enhanced Prison Terms for Felonies Committed with Guns." *Criminology* 33(1): 247–81.

McDowell, David, and Brian Wiersma. 1994. "The Incidence of Defensive Firearm Use by US Crime Victims: 1987 through 1990." *American Journal of Public Health* 84(12): 1982–84.

McDowall, David, Colin Loftin, and Brian Wiersma. 1998. "Estimates of the Frequency of Firearm Self Defense from the Redesigned National Crime Victimization Survey." Violence Research Group Discussion Paper 20. College Park, University of Maryland, Department of Criminology and Criminal Justice.

McDowall, David, Colin Loftin, and Stanley Presser. 2000. "Measuring Civilian Defensive Firearm Use: A Methodological Experiment." *Journal of Quantitative Criminology* 16(2): 1–19.

McPheters, Lee R., Robert Mann, and Dann Schlagenhauf. 1984. "Economic Response to a Crime Deterrence Program: Mandatory Sentencing for Robbery with a Firearm." *Economic Inquiry* 22(2): 550–70.

Najaka, Stacy. S., Denise C.Gottfredson, and David B. Wilson. 2001. "A Meta-analytic Inquiry into the Relationship between Selected Risk Factors and Problem Behavior." *Prevention Science* 2(4): 257–71.

National Academy of Engineering. 2003. *Owner Authorized Handguns.* Washington DC: National Academies Press.

National Violent Death Reporting System (NVDRS). 2009. http://www.cdc.gov/NCIPC/profiles/nvdrs/default.htm

Pew Sentencing and Corrections Program. 2008. http://www.pewcenteronthestates.org/initiatives

Pierce, Glenn L., and William J. Bowers. 1981. "The Bartley-Fox Gun Laws Short Term Impact Of Crime In Boston." *Annals of the American Academy of Political and Social Sciences* 455:120–37.

Raphael, Steven, and Jens Ludwig. 2003."Prison Sentence Enhancements: The Case of Project Exile." In *Evaluating Gun Policy: Effects on Crime and Violence,* edited by J. Ludwig and P. Cook. Washington D.C.: Brookings Institution Press.

Rosenfeld, Richard. 1996. "Gun Buy-Backs: Crime Control or Community Mobilization?" In *Under Fire: Gun Buy-Backs, Exchanges and Amnesty Programs.* Washington, DC: Police Executive Research Forum.

Sherman, Lawrence W., and Dennis P. Rogan. 1995. "Effects of Guns Seizures on Gun Violence: 'Hot Spots' Patrol in Kansas City." *Justice Quarterly* 12(4): 673–94.

Tonry, Michael. 2009. "Mandatory Penalties." In *Crime and Justice: A Review of Research,* edited by Michael Tonry, vol. 38. Chicago: University of Chicago Press.

UCLA Law Review. 2009. Symposium: The Second Amendment and the Right to Bear Arms After D.C. v. *Heller.* 56, no. 5. http://uclalawreview.org/?p=84&side=symposia.

United Nations. 2000. Study of Firearm Regulations. www.ifs.unive.ac.at/~uncjin/firearms.

Webster, Cheryl Marie, Anthony N. Doob, and Franklin E. Zimring. 2006. "Proposition 8 and Crime Rates in California: The Case for the Disappearing Deterrent." *Criminology and Public Policy* 5:417–48.

Weil, Douglas S., and Rebecca C. Knox. 1996. "Effects of Limiting Handgun Purchases on Interstate Transfer of Firearms." *Journal of the American Medical Association* 275:1759–61.

Wellford Charles F., John V. Pepper, and Carol V. Petrie, eds. 2005. *Firearms and Violence: A Critical Review.* Washington, DC. National Academies Press.

Winship, Christopher. 2002. "Reducing Youth Violence in Boston." In *Why Must We Fight,* edited by.William Ury. Boston: Jossey-Bass.

CHAPTER 15

WORK AND CRIME

AARON CHALFIN AND
STEVEN RAPHAEL

SEVERAL empirical regularities suggest that access to well-paying legitimate employment opportunities is an important determinant of whether one engages in
crime. For example, most crime is committed by relatively young, less-educated
men, precisely those with the lowest potential earnings and weakest prospects for
stable employment. Most of these young men age out of criminal participation, with
the decline in criminal activity corresponding with improvement in their labor
market prospects (Grogger 1998). Moreover, in the United States members of racial
minority groups that have traditionally experienced weak employment prospects
and labor market discrimination offend at a disproportionately high rate (Raphael
and Sills 2005).

An additional empirical trend suggestive of a link between work and crime
concerns the more than fourfold increase in the U.S. incarceration rate occurring
since the late 1970s. The increase in U.S. incarceration rates coincides with profound
changes in the distribution of earnings and income. Beginning in the mid-1970s,
wage inequality increased greatly, with real absolute declines in the earnings of the
least skilled workers and stagnating wages for workers at the center of the wage
distribution (Katz and Murphy 1992; Freeman 1996; Autor and Katz 1999). Coinci-
dent with these changes were pronounced declines in the labor force participation
rates of less-skilled men (Juhn and Potter 2006). In particular, the labor force participation and employment rates of relatively less-educated, black men have dropped
precipitously (Raphael 2005), precisely those men who experienced the largest
increases in incarceration.

Finally, crime rates tend to be lowest in communities where wages are high and unemployment rates are low, suggesting that there is a spatial relationship between economic conditions and crime. For example, inner-city neighborhoods characterized by concentrated poverty as well as rural areas with high unemployment tend to have higher localized crime rates. Though each of these empirical regularities has obvious alternative explanations, the fact that a relationship between employment and crime is seen over time, across space, and in the cross-section is compelling.

The relationship between work and crime is complex, likely to vary from person to person, and involves causal forces operating in both directions. Beginning with the effect of employment prospects on crime, the responsiveness of one's propensity to engage in criminal activity to changes in economic incentives is likely to vary greatly from individual to individual. In particular, most people are likely to be "infra-marginal" in the sense that whether they engage in criminal activity is independent of the legitimate labor market opportunities available to them. In other words, there might be many who never engage in criminal activity and never would, while there might also be a few who actively commit crime and whose criminal offending is insensitive to changes in legitimate employment prospects. Those individuals who fit into neither of these categories are those on the margin between offending and not offending, and whose choices may be influenced by the availability of legitimate employment opportunities. This degree of responsiveness and how it varies across the population is an important factor in determining the success of policy interventions designed to reduce crime through workforce development. For example, programs targeted toward high-risk youth, such as the U.S. Job Corps program, or interventions designed to provide transitional employment to former prison inmates, will reduce crime insofar as the criminal activity of program participants is responsive to such treatment interventions.

In addition to heterogeneity of this relationship across individuals it is also likely that the crime-employment relationship varies by type of crime. In particular, the theoretical arguments offered to support a link between work and crime are perhaps more applicable to property crime and violent crimes that are derivative of criminal activity that is motivated by economic gain.

Beyond the contemporaneous relationship between work and crime, current participation in criminal activity may have delayed effects on future employment prospects, especially if one's criminal activity leads to official involvement with the criminal justice system. A felony conviction is likely to limit one's future employment prospects as employers are wary of those with official criminal history records and often act on this wariness through informal and formal screening practices. For those who serve time, the failure to accumulate legitimate work experience as well as further enculturation into criminally active social networks may retard progress in the legitimate labor market through much of adult life. In addition, crime may also lead to fewer and less attractive employment opportunities at the aggregate level. High crime rates may discourage private investment in local businesses, which has the effect of lowering both the quantity and quality of available employment in an urban area (Skogan 1986; Schwartz, Susin, and Voicu 2003). Moreover, high crime rates may induce geographically mobile, higher wage earners to leave an urban area for outlying areas with lower crime rates (Cullen and Levitt 1999). Finally, higher crime rates may destroy the social fabric of communities, diminishing investments in human capital and producing a self-perpetuating social and economic malaise (Sampson and Groves 1989).

In this article, we review these connections between work and crime. We begin in section I with a discussion of a simple microeconomic model of criminal participation. The particular theoretical framework models criminal participation in terms of the traditional time-use allocation model that forms the bedrock of the economic analysis of labor supply. While simplistic, this theoretical construct offers straightforward, intuitive, and precise predictions regarding the relationship between legitimate economic opportunity and crime.

To assess the extent to which the model is supported by existing empirical research, section II reviews three bodies of literature: research by economists on the relationship between incentives and participation in crime measured at the individual level, experimental evaluations of labor market interventions targeted at former prison inmates, and research analyzing the aggregate relationship between crime and measures of macroeconomic conditions. While the demonstrated responsiveness of criminal activity to economic incentives differs across these three research literatures (with greater responsiveness demonstrated in the first and last categories, and limited responsiveness associated with the program interventions), we believe that these findings can be reconciled by heterogeneity in the populations effectively treated by the variation in incentives studied.

Section III analyzes the effects of past criminal activity on future employment prospects operating through the effects of having served time. We present a theoretical discussion highlighting the causal channels linking time in prison to post-release employment prospects. We then review the most recent body of empirical evidence evaluating whether serving time affects an individual's future legitimate labor market trajectory. Section IV offers some conclusions.

Our main conclusions can be summarized as follows.

- The relationship between work and crime is complex, likely to be bi-directional and likely to vary from person to person. There are many for whom an increase or decrease in their legitimate wages will not induce them to participate in criminal activity and a few for whom the returns to crime always exceed the returns to legitimate employment. Such "infra-marginal" individuals are generally insensitive to changes in incentives to participate in crime. Those on the margin—those for whom small changes in the returns to crime or the returns to legitimate work may alter their criminal behavior—are individuals with wages that are generally comparable to the marginal financial returns to criminal activity. Such individuals are likely to be young, less educated, and in the U.S. context, members of racial and ethnic minorities.

- Observational microdata research clearly reveals higher offending during unemployment spells and a higher propensity to offend among those with lower potential legitimate wages. While this literature is subject to criticism regarding selection bias and unobserved omitted factors that may explain the observed empirical relationship, the empirical connection between employment prospects and crime is fairly robust.

- Experimental interventions that increase the incomes or employment prospects of high-risk individuals yield mixed results in terms of their effects on subsequent criminal activity. Most such interventions find some evidence of an effect of providing income support, a transitional job, or job training on criminal activity. However, not all individuals are affected equally, and the significant effects that are uncovered tend to be small.

- Studies that analyze aggregate data, such as state-level panel studies in the United States, tend to find significant positive effects of unemployment on property crime, but no effects (or sometimes negative effects) of unemployment on violent crime.

- Aggregate-level studies of the relationship between regional wages and crime find fairly consistent and robust evidence that decreases in regional wages tend to be associated with increases in crime. Those studies that employ wage measures for low-skilled workers tend to find the strongest aggregate relationship. Similar to the results from the research analyzing the effects of unemployment, the largest effects are observed for property crime.

- Prior criminal activity is likely to affect future employment prospects through a number of channels, especially if an individual is apprehended and convicted. Many who serve time fail to accumulate work experience during key periods of their lives. Once parole violations and time between prison spells are taken into account, it has been shown that prison inmates spent large portions of their twenties and thirties cycling in and out of many institutions. Moreover, prior convictions tend to carry a stigma with employers and hamper job searches.

- Analysis of longitudinal household surveys consistently finds negative effects of having served time in the past on earnings and employment. Analysis of administrative records for released inmates tends to find more mixed results. However, this latter body of research is plagued by methodological problems pertaining to measurement of employment status and the identification of the proper counterfactual for released prison inmates.

I. The Opportunity Cost of Crime: The Effect of Legitimate Employment Prospects

There are many personal and ecological determinants of participation in criminal activity. Age, gender, degree of material poverty, characteristics of one's childhood and upbringing, level of cognitive ability, and many other personal and institutional factors all exert influences on one's behavior. In light of this complexity, economic forces necessarily play a limited partial role in explaining who offends and how much. Nonetheless, the basic microeconomic model of crime provides a framework for thinking about how the commission of a crime may at times reflect a rational considered decision-making process in which the potential offender weighs the costs and benefits of specific actions and behaves accordingly. The reasoning underlying the economic theory regarding the effect of employment on crime is no different than that underlying the argument for criminal deterrence.

The microeconomic theory of criminal participation often models crime as a time-allocation decision, in which individuals allocate efforts among legitimate labor market activity, the criminal labor market, or other uses. The wage that an individual's time can command in the legitimate labor market represents the "opportunity cost" of allocating time toward other uses, such as participating in crime, taking leisure, and engaging in home production. In other words, when someone chooses to devote time to something other than work, the implicit cost of doing so is the value of the wages foregone. The standard neoclassical model of crime posits that the supply of criminal offending is a function of three factors: (1) the probability of capture conditional on offending, (2) the severity of the sanction if captured, and (3) the expected profit above the opportunity cost of a criminal transaction. In this framework, the conditional probability of capture refers to the likelihood of arrest and conviction, the severity of the sanction refers to the amount of unhappiness created by the sanction in the event that one is caught and convicted (determined by the amount time to serve or the size of the fine to pay), while net profits refer to the payoff to the crime less what would have been earned had the time and effort been devoted to legitimate activity. From this reasoning, it follows that increases in the probability of arrest or increases in the severity of criminal sanctions should reduce the supply of crimes. Likewise, the lower one's potential earnings, the more attractive are criminal opportunities with income generating potential.

The model presented by Grogger (1998) provides an excellent illustration of the economic approach to crime. Grogger adopts the perspective of an amoral consumer who faces a constant market wage and diminishing marginal returns to participation in crime.[1] This consumer maximizes a utility function that increases (at a decreasing rate) in both leisure (L) and consumption (c), where consumption is financed by time spent engaged in either legitimate employment (given by h_m) at a market wage (denoted by w) or time spent in crime (denoted by h_c). The individual's constrained optimization problem is to maximize the utility function, U(c,L), subject to the consumption and time constraints:

$$c = wh_m + r(h_c) + I$$

$$L = T - h_m - h_c$$

where T is the individual's time endowment and I represents non-labor income (income that is independent of labor supply or level or criminal activity).

Grogger assumes that the returns to crime diminish as the amount of time devoted to criminal activity increases—i.e., the function $r(\bullet)$ that translates hours spent participating in crime into income is concave. Diminishing returns implies that those engaging in criminal activity first commit crimes with the highest expected payoffs (lowest probability of getting caught and highest stakes) before exploring less lucrative opportunities. The function $r(\bullet)$ also reflects incidental costs of committing crime—including search costs and ability to identify suitable victims—as well as the risk of capture and the expected criminal sanction if captured. In other words, $r(\bullet)$ can be thought of as the wage rate of crime, net of the expected costs associated with capture. In this way, criminal sanctions drive a wedge between the consumer's productivity in offending and his market wage, in turn, incentivizing market work over crime.

The model yields quite plausible predictions regarding who will participate in crime and how much crime one will commit. In order for an individual to commit any crime at all, there are two necessary and sufficient conditions. First, the marginal return to the first instant of time supplied to crime must exceed the individual's valuation of time (in terms of how much consumption the person would be willing to forego for more time) when all time is devoted to non-market, non-crime activities. Second, the marginal return to crime for the first crime committed must exceed the individual's market wage. Thus, those who can command high wages or those who place very high value on time devoted to non-market/non-criminal uses will be the least likely to engage in criminal activity.

The model also implies that some individuals will simultaneously engage in income-generating criminal activity and work. In this instance, the individual will participate in crime up until the point where the marginal return to crime equals the market wage—i.e., when $r'(h_c) = w$. To finance consumption beyond the amount afforded by non-labor income and this threshold level of criminal activity, the person will supply labor to the legitimate labor market where the marginal compensation is higher. Of course, for individuals with very low market wages, it may be the case that r'(h$_c$) > w for all possible values of h$_c$. Such individuals will only commit crime and will not work.

This optimization problem can be illustrated graphically. Figures 15.1A and 15.1B depict the implicit budget constraints and the optimization problem faced by two different individuals. The budget constraint in each graph shows the trade-off between income and non-market time. In figure 15.1A, the individual has discretion over T hours of time and non-labor income equal to the vertical distance I. The function r(•) is depicted by the curved line segment ABC. This function is drawn in such a way that the marginal return to the first instance of time devoted to crime exceeds the market wage. The individual supplies time to the legitimate labor market only after higher-paying criminal opportunities have been fully exploited. This occurs at the point D where the person has allocated *T-to* time to crime and where the marginal return to crime equals potential wages. Beyond point B, wages exceed the returns to criminal activity (as is evident by the steeper slope of the budget constraint segment BE).

Figure 15.1A also presents two indifference curves mapping the individual's preferences. Each indifference curve charts out a set of income/non-market time pairs between which the individual is indifferent (in terms of our utility function, the indifference curves are defined implicitly by the equation U(c,L) = Ū, where Ū gives a constant level of utility). The negative slope indicates that both income and non-market time are valued, and that if one is diminished the other must be increased in order to maintain the welfare level of our decision maker. Of course, the individual will prefer to be on the highest indifference curve possible, with movements to the upper righthand corner improving welfare. In figure 15.1A, utility

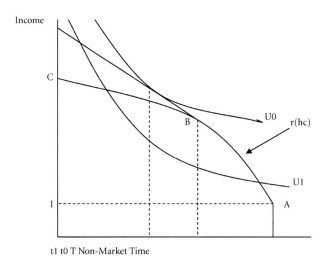

Figure 15.1A

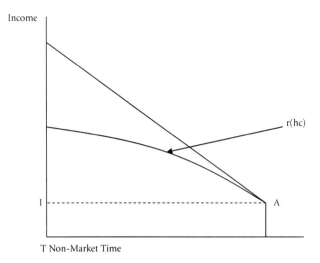

Figure 15.1B

is maximized when *T-to* time is allocated to criminal activity, *to-t1* time is supplied to the labor market, and the remaining *t1* hours are allocated to other activities.

This graphical analysis can be used to analyze how a change in wages will affect one's degree of criminal participation. Suppose that this individual's wages now increase to the point at which the returns to crime never exceed the returns to legitimate employment. This case is depicted in figure 15.1B. Here, the marginal income generated by criminal activity (given by the curve BD) is always less than the income generated by an additional hour of legitimate work (line BC). Hence, there is no point of crossover, and the individual will not commit crime.

Similarly, a reduction in potential market wages increases the threshold value of criminal activity beyond which the returns to crime fall short of the returns to legitimate work. A higher threshold indicates a larger amount of time allocated to criminal activity. While we have not included a graph for this particular comparative static exercise, one can easily envision the impact of a decline in wages by imagining a movement to the left of the point *to* in figure 15.1A.

This simple model can also be used to highlight those likely to be influenced by a small change in incentives and those who are not. In figure 15.1B, any further increases in wages have absolutely no effect on an individual's criminal activity, as the person with the budget constraint depicted would not be allocating time to crime in the first place. Moreover, it is possible to choose a sufficiently small decline in wages that the returns to crime still never exceed the returns to the first hour of legitimate work. Such individuals are infra-marginal in the sense that small changes in incentives do not affect whether they commit crimes or how much crime they commit. One might speculate that the returns to such crimes as armed robbery, burglary, or auto theft are not likely to co-vary with one's legitimate wages. This implies that the disparity between the returns to crime and the returns to work will be greatest for those with high earnings potential and the smallest for those who command relatively low wages.

Infra-marginal criminals can also be imagined. In particular, it is possible that for some individuals the returns to crime always exceed the returns to legitimate labor market activity. This could be due to the person being particular skilled at committing crime, the person's particularly bleak legitimate labor market prospects, or some combination of the two. In terms of the model presented in figure 15.1A, the slope of the curve ABC (the rate at which the person converts time into money through income-generating crime) would always exceed this person's legitimate potential wage. Hence, the person would generate income through crime only and would not supply any time to the legitimate labor market.

Economists often distinguish between variation occurring at the extensive and intensive margins. In this model, those who cross over into criminal participation due to a decline in wages (or perhaps a marginal increase in the returns to crime) represent expansions along the extensive margin, as a general reduction in wages would increase the proportion of adults engaging in any crime. However, the wage-induced increase in time devoted to criminal activity among those who are already criminally active represents an increase in the intensity of such activity among the already initiated.

II. Economic Conditions, Labor Market Incentives, and Crime: Empirical Evidence

The empirical literature examining the links among employment, wages, and crime can be loosely divided into two strains of research. The first examines the relationship between employment opportunities and crime using individual-level microdata. This literature addresses questions such as whether individuals who experience changes in their labor market opportunities are more likely to engage in crime or whether individuals are more likely to participate in crime while involuntarily unemployed. Likewise, it includes a large and growing experimental literature that evaluates how at-risk individuals have responded to the provision of job coaching, employment counseling, career placement, and other employment-based services.

The second body of research examines the relationship between employment conditions and crime at an aggregate level, generally using city, regional, or state-level panel data that spans both time and place. To address the simultaneity between employment and crime, the most recent literature generally relies on an instrumental variable (or, in a few cases, an explicit policy change) to identify a causal effect. We examine each of these bodies of research in turn.

A. Individual-level Studies

The most direct approach to estimating the contribution of labor market conditions to crime rates is to examine how individuals respond to various types of economic shocks. There are several advantages to microdata analyses. First, analysis with microdata often permits controlling for a host of personal characteristics and life experiences that are theoretically related to both labor market outcomes and participation in crime. Second, individual-level studies allow researchers to consider more nuanced explanatory variables that are typically unavailable at higher levels of aggregation—e.g., the effect of job stability, job satisfaction, or the length of unemployment spells. Finally, individual-level data are more conducive to uncovering heterogeneity in the effects of labor market conditions on participation in crime. For example, separate estimates can be tabulated for any characteristics observed in the microdata, such as race, education, or gender (sample size permitting).

There are also several disadvantages of using individual-level data. First, offending cannot be measured with a great deal of precision in these studies. Microdata analyses typically rely on self-reported offending or on arrest records. Self-reported criminal activity suffers from obvious problems associated with reporting bias, while the incidence of official arrests underestimates criminal activity, since only a fraction of offenses result in an arrest.

Second, much of the research on the individual determinants of criminal activity consists of either non-experimental or experimental interventions applied to fairly narrow sub-populations. As with all observational studies, individual-level analyses need to contend with likely omitted variables bias and the simultaneous determination of criminal activity and employment status in order to infer the true causal effects of labor market opportunity on criminal behavior. Experimental interventions must contend with substitution bias among the non-treated and the often weak incremental services delivered to treated participants. In both types of studies, external validity concerns abound, especially in light of theoretical arguments that suggest that the relationship between marginal changes in economic incentives and criminal activity is likely to exhibit great heterogeneity. With these considerations in mind, we review this body of empirical evidence.

Perhaps the most straightforward method of determining the extent of a labor market-crime link is simply to ask offenders whether their employment status or labor market prospects were in any way related to their offending. Sviridoff and Thompson (1983) interviewed adult male offenders recently released from New York City's Rikers Island correctional facility and determined that unemployment did not play an important role in the typical offender's decision to offend.[2]

The drawback of this approach lies in the lack of a counterfactual group of non-offenders with similar personal characteristics against whom one could compare the employment prospects of the offenders. Moreover, there is reason to be concerned about the reliability of self-reported data and about the external validity of the result given the characteristics of the interview sample.

A number of studies use longitudinal data to examine the temporal relationship between labor market shocks, typically measured by periods of involuntary unemployment, and offending. Farrington et al. (1986) report the results of a longitudinal study of 411 London males followed from age eight until age eighteen. The authors demonstrate a higher propensity to offend during periods of unemployment, in particular, for crimes with a pecuniary motive. In a similar study, Thornberry and Christensen (1984) analyze longitudinal data for 9,500 individuals born in Philadelphia in 1945. The authors find no association between unemployment spells and arrest between the ages of eighteen and thirty. In an analysis of data from the 1979 National Longitudinal Survey of Youth (NLSY79) Crutchfield and Pitchford (1997) find that individuals are more likely to engage in crime when they are out of the labor force and when they expect their current job to be of short duration.

While the results from this research are generally consistent with an effect of labor market conditions on crime, it is possible that a change in an important unobserved factor may be driving both spells out of work and criminal activity. For example, illegal drug use may simultaneously cause both an unemployment spell and participation in crime. Alternatively, other life stresses—such as problems with personal relationships or mental health problems—may cause the simultaneous co-occurrence of unemployment (or underemployment) and criminal activity. To be sure, such issues of causal identification pose a challenge in all micro-level social science research using observational data. Nonetheless, absent a clear source of exogenous variation in employment status or employment prospects, cross-sectional and longitudinal estimates should probably considered as providing upper bounds of the likely effect sizes.

A related body of research considers the effect of job quality, measured by either self-reported satisfaction or the consistency and quantity of work hours, on offending. Although the standard neoclassical labor supply model says little about non-pecuniary aspects of employment, the model could easily be extended to accommodate job quality or satisfaction by adding this variable to the utility function or by thinking of the wage as incorporating both the tangible and intangible benefits of work. To the extent that criminal activity precludes employment in a satisfying job (or affects the future probability of acquiring a satisfying job), there might be a trade-off between job satisfaction and offending. More importantly, for an individual in an unsatisfying job for reasons beyond his or her control, the theory would likely predict an effect on the likelihood of engaging in income-generating crime.

Allan and Steffensmeier (1984) examine the relationship between employment conditions and juvenile arrests for property crimes using age-specific profiles from

1977 to 1980. They find that low-quality jobs with low hours are associated with higher arrest rates for young adults. In contrast, later work has established a positive relationship between hours worked and delinquent behavior among juveniles (Mortimer et al 1996; Wright, Cullen, and Williams 1997; National Research Council 1998; McMorris and Uggen 2000). However, Steinberg, Fegley, and Dornbusch (1993) have noted that juveniles who worked the greatest number of hours enter the labor market with less completed schooling, a third factor that may explain the association between hours and crime. Reasoning along similar lines, Newcomb and Bentler (1989) argue that the precocious desire to engage in adult behaviors such as work at a young age may correlate with preferences toward criminal activity, a factor that would create a spurious correlation between hours and delinquency.

More recent research has hypothesized more complex relationships between working conditions and crime, permitting greater heterogeneity and more nuanced analysis. In an analysis of delinquent behavior among high school seniors, Staff and Uggen (2003) find that youth working at jobs that were supportive of the youth's academic responsibilities had the lowest rates of school behavioral problems, alcohol use, and arrest. In contrast, many qualities of work considered desirable for adults such as autonomy, social status, and wages appear to increase delinquency in adolescence. Apel et al. (2006) note that "a job isn't a job" and, using the National Longitudinal Survey of Youth (NLSY), find that employment in informal jobs is more likely to lead to delinquency than employment in formal jobs. Likewise, Wright and Cullen (2004) use data from the National Youth Survey and find that prosocial coworkers disrupt previously established delinquent peer networks and are associated with reductions in adult criminal behavior. Addressing the effect of job quality for adult offenders, Uggen (1999) uses data from the National Supported Work Demonstration to construct a job satisfaction scale and, after correcting for selection into employment, finds that higher job satisfaction reduces the propensity to engage in all forms of criminal activity. Similarly, Sampson and Laub (2005) find that job stability is significantly related to adult crime over the life course even after conditioning on a variety of demographic characteristics.

The model of crime and labor market participation presented above placed great emphasis on the key effect of one's earnings potential in determining the likelihood of committing crime. The theory predicts that those with higher potential wages should be less likely to offend and, conditional on offending at all, should offend less. Despite the centrality of wage potential to this theoretical argument, there have been only a few attempts to estimate this relationship structurally. Grogger (1998), using data from the NLSY79, estimates the structural parameters of the model presented in the theoretical section above and uses the model to estimate the sensitivity of criminal participation to changes in potential earnings for youth in the sample. The calibrated model predicts that a 10 percent increase in wages decreases the likelihood of participating in income-generating criminal activity by roughly 2.5 percentage points. He argues that much of the observed decline in criminal activity as the cohort ages may be attributable to the improved labor market prospects associated with aging and maturity.

One of the key methodological challenges to studying the effect of wage potential on offending is the likely endogeneity of wages with criminal behavior. In other words, those with low earnings potential are more likely to offend than those with higher earnings potential for reasons that have little to do with labor market prospects. To address this issue of causal identification, Gould, Weinberg, and Mustard (2002) study the relationship between geographic variation in the wages of low-skilled men and self-reported criminal activity among NLSY79 youth. If one were to assume that the NLSY79 youth are randomly distributed across geographic regions, then this particular source of wage variation would be exogenous. They find that lower wages are associated with higher rates of property crime but not robbery.

In a similar analysis, Kallem (2004) analyzes the NLSY97 and estimates a fixed effects regression of participation in crime on the minimum wage in the state of residence. The inclusion of individual fixed effects implies that Kallem is relying on variation in the minimum wage occurring within the state to identify the effects of wage potential on the probability of offending. He finds no effect of the minimum wage though the ratio of the minimum wage to the average wage is positively related to larceny in some specifications.

Finally, a number of papers have studied whether local economic conditions and labor market outcomes affect recidivism rates among recent arrestees or recently paroled, former prison inmates. It is often noted that stable employment is one of the best predictors of post-release success (Sampson and Laub 1997; Visher, Winterfield, and Coggeshall 2005). Whether stable employment is a cause of success or an indicator of a determined individual is less well understood. Within this line of research, there are two types of studies. The first examines the effect of labor market conditions or employment experiences on recidivism or re-incarceration. The second consists primarily of experimental research of a variety of interventions designed to improve the employability of returning offenders.

In a study of prison releases in North Carolina, Witte (1980) finds little evidence of an effect of local wage levels on the likelihood of recidivism. In contrast, Myers (1983) finds that favorable labor market conditions lower recidivism rates among a sample of ex-prisoners in Maryland. In an analysis of California arrestees for the period 1984 through 1986, Grogger (1991) finds no relationship between employment status and subsequent arrest. However, higher income individuals are significantly less likely to be re-arrested. A more recent analysis of California data by Raphael and Weiman (2007) examines the relationship between local economic conditions (measured by monthly county unemployment rates) and the likelihood that a released prison inmate is returned to custody. A very small average effect of local economic conditions on the return-to-custody rate is found, though the effect for relatively low-risk offenders is fairly large and significant.

The experimental evaluations focus on programs that provide income, employment-based services, or skills-building social services. There are more than a dozen experimental evaluations of such efforts in the United States in which treatment group members are randomly assigned. A key advantage of these studies is that the treatment is clearly exogenous, and thus any observed effects represent true causal effects. Moreover, since these studies evaluate programs that are in operation, the findings can have a significant effect on the design of public policies that address public safety. Thus, the results are of interest both for answering the theoretical questions and for informing policymakers.

However, care is required in interpreting results. Many members of the randomized control group may receive similar services elsewhere, and thus it is not always self-evident that the intervention has a large marginal effect on service delivery. Furthermore, those most likely to benefit from employment and workforce development services are likely to seek out and procure such services whether they are assigned to the treatment or control group. Thus, the intervention will often affect service delivery for those who are the least motivated or stand to benefit the least, likely understating the average effect on the targeted population. Finally, most interventions are targeted at particular groups with offense histories that cross fairly stringent severity levels (former prisoners, for example), meaning individuals who may not be particularly responsive to positive incentives.

Community-based employment interventions became popular in the United States beginning in the 1970s. Under authority of the 1962 Manpower Development and Training Act, the U.S. Department of Labor launched a number of programs aimed at former prisoners beginning with the Living Insurance for Ex-Prisoners (LIFE) program, which provided a living stipend and job-placement assistance to prisoners returning to Baltimore between 1972 and 1974, and the Transitional Aid Research Project (TARP), which provided various combinations of cash assistance and job-placement services to five different experimental groups of ex-offenders in Georgia and Texas. The LIFE evaluation found significant effects of the income-support program, with considerably lower offending rates among the treatment group (Mallar and Thorton 1978). However, the evaluation of the larger scale TARP program found little effect (Rossi, Berk, and Lenihan 1980). The latter evaluation also found a large negative effect of the transitional cash assistance on the labor supply of released inmates. Rossi, Berk, and Lenihan (1980) speculate that the lack of an overall effect on recidivism reflected the offsetting effects of the reduction in recidivism due to the cash assistance and the increased criminal activity associated with being idle.

There have been several high-quality evaluations of the effects of providing transitional employment to former inmates. The National Supported Work Program (NSW) (re-analyzed by Uggen [2000]) and the New York Center for Employment Opportunities (CEO) currently under evaluation by MDRC (Bloom et al. 2007) find some evidence that providing prison releasees with transitional employment forestalls recidivism during the two years after release. However, these programs found considerable heterogeneity in program effects with the NSW finding significant effects for older releases and the CEO evaluation reporting significant effects for only those most recently released.

More recent models have been built around the idea that successfully reintegrating former inmates requires wraparound services that begin while the individual is incarcerated and continue well into the parole terms and if needed, beyond. The programs funded under the Serious and Violent Offender Reentry Initiative (SVORI) serve as examples (Lattimore, Visher, and Steffey 2008). SVORI is a U.S. multi-agency federal initiative providing grants to localities to provide holistic, complete, and coordinated reentry services that begin pre-release and continue through the parole terms of releases. While each locality was permitted the leeway to design its own programs, the grants are conditional on certain service elements, including pre-release assessment, the use of reentry plans, the use of transition teams that coordinate release and reentry, efforts to connect reentering men to community resources, and the use of graduated levels of supervision and sanctions. While the evaluation of this effort is still in progress, many believe that this coordinated continuous process of service deliver, commencing prior to release, is the key to avoiding quick reentry failures.

What then do these individual level studies reveal about the effects of employment prospects on criminal activity? The non-experimental microdata analysis clearly reveals higher offending during unemployment spells and a higher propensity to offend among those with lower potential legitimate wages. While this body of literature is subject to criticism regarding selection bias and unobserved omitted factors that may explain the observed empirical relationship, the empirical connection between employment prospects and crime is fairly robust. The evidence from the experimental program evaluations is a bit less supportive of these observations. In particular, the relatively small effects on the recidivism rates of released prison inmates of providing transitional employment suggest that offending among this particular population is overwhelmingly determined by causes other than not being able to find a job.

While it may seem that these bodies of literature are at odds, the differential findings are reconcilable with heterogeneity in responsiveness to economic incentives. To use the language of our neoclassical model, the individuals studied in the experimental program evaluations are perhaps infra-marginal while the (mostly) young men studied in the longitudinal studies are on the margin and can be influenced.

B. Aggregate-level Studies

A second approach to evaluating the degree to which employment conditions affect crime has been to use aggregate data to determine if macroeconomic conditions and crime rates are related across time and place. This approach offers several advantages. First, with aggregate analysis, one is better able to capture general equilibrium effects of changes in labor market conditions that may be missed at the individual level. For example, an individual-level study might find that individuals participate in crime more often while unemployed. However, a broad increase in unemployment may result in a smaller change in crime, as fewer employed people may translate into limited criminal opportunities. Second, aggregate-level studies allow the researcher to control explicitly for time- and place-invariant fixed effects that may affect both economic conditions and crime rates. Third, because aggregate studies are based on data generated across different times and places, such studies offer a greater sense of external validity than the typical individual-level study which may involve only a particular cross-section of individuals followed generally for only a short length of time.

The literature that uses aggregate data to disentangle the effect of economic conditions on crime presents a mixed picture. The results are sensitive to the period studied, the population under consideration, the measure of work employed, and the criminal offenses analyzed. In general, these aggregate-level studies have examined two primary explanatory variables—unemployment and wages.

1. *Unemployment*

Periods of unemployment are thought to generate incentives to engage in criminal activity either as a means of income supplementation or consumption smoothing or, more generally, due to the effect of psychological strain. In examining the relationship between work and crime, unemployment rates have been a popular choice among researchers and, as a result, there is a rich literature from which to draw inferences. The literature has produced mixed and frequently contradictory results leading Chiricos (1987) to characterize scholarly opinion on the topic as a "consensus of doubt." In particular, the older literature produces little consensus. Reviewing sixty-eight studies relating unemployment and crime, Chiricos (1987), found that fewer than half find positive significant effects of aggregate unemployment rates on crime rates. Likewise, a number of studies find a significant, negative relationship between unemployment and certain crime, violent crime in particular (Cook and Zarkin 1985; Chiricos 1987).

Nonetheless, Chiricos' review also found that the unemployment-crime relationship was three times more likely to be positive than negative, and fifteen times more likely to be positive and significant than negative and significant. The results were especially strong for property crimes; in particular for larceny and burglary, which together comprise approximately 80 percent of property crimes in the United States.

Chiricos suggests that research results are generally consistent by level of aggregation though they tend to be more consistently positive and significant at lower levels of aggregation. Consequently, he hypothesizes that the national-level analysis may cancel out the substantial heterogeneity in unemployment rates and crime rates that exists across regions, cities, and neighborhoods. Levitt (2001) likewise argues that national-level time-series analyses obscure the unemployment-crime relationship by failing to account for rich variation across space.

A number of studies have been published since Chiricos's 1987 review. The newer ones have benefited from several methodological advances; in particular the use of panel data as opposed to a cross-sectional or time-series data, and the use of instrumental variables to break the endogeneity between unemployment and crime. In addition, the newer studies have typically used data spanning a longer period of time, with the advantage that there is greater variation in both unemployment and crime rates upon which to base inferences. Papps and Winkelmann (1998) use a panel of regions from New Zealand and find that unemployment does not have an effect on the total crime rate, but positively (albeit modestly) affects the incidence of property crimes. Entorf and Spengler (2000), using a state panel for Germany find ambiguous unemployment effects. In contrast, a panel design using Swedish data spanning 1988–99 and using county fixed effects and a linear and quadratic time trend reveals strong evidence that unemployment rates are positively related to burglary, car theft, and bicycle theft (Edmark 2005).

For the United States, Raphael and Winter-Ebmer (2001) use a state-level panel data set covering 1979–98 to study the effect of unemployment rates on various types of crime. To address the potential simultaneous determination of unemployment and crime, they employ two instruments for the unemployment rate—the value of military contracts with the federal government accruing during a particular state-year, along with the regional effect of shocks to the price of oil. For property crime rates, the results consistently indicate that unemployment increases crime. For violent crime, however, the results are mixed, with some evidence of positive unemployment effects on robbery and assault and negative unemployment effects for murder and rape.

On the whole, the preponderance of the evidence suggests that there is a relationship between unemployment rates and property crime but little effect on violent crime. The relationship between unemployment and property crime is found regardless of the level of aggregation and the relationship appears to remain after making considerable effort to address omitted variable bias and simultaneity. Nevertheless, the relationship between unemployment and property crime is not empirically large, and the estimates are sensitive to the time period studied.

2. *Wages*

There are several recent aggregate analyses that explore the effects of wage levels on crime rates. The neoclassical model predicts that a decrease in the market wage will alter the consumer's decision calculus, inducing him to spend a greater amount of time participating in crime. Indeed, Freeman (1996) has argued that deteriorating real wages for unskilled men during the 1980s may be linked to increases in crime during this period. In particular, it has been proposed that since criminal participation is associated with a set of fixed costs, crime may well be more responsive to long-term labor market measures such as levels of human capital or wages than to unemployment spells, which are typically ephemeral (Gould, Weinberg, and Mustard 2002). Moreover, the number of individuals employed in low-wage jobs vastly outnumbers the number of unemployed at any time, and as a result, wages for unskilled men may play a proportionally greater role than unemployment in encouraging crime (Hansen and Machin, forthcoming). Among individuals who reported engaging in crime during the past year, a large majority reported wage earnings (Grogger 1998) and three quarters were employed at the time of their arrest (Lynch and Sabol 2001), indicating that the behavior of a majority of offenders should be sensitive to changes in the wage.

The literature linking wages to crime has generated far more consensus than the unemployment literature. Cornwell and Trumbull (1994) used a panel of ninety counties over seven years in North Carolina to study the effect of sectoral wages on the total crime rates. Across all sectors, only manufacturing wages were associated with crime rates. However, the authors study only the effect on overall crime. Thus, the design may obscure a relationship between wages in low-skilled sectors and property crime. Doyle, Ahmed, and Horn (1999) analyzed a state-level panel for 1984–93 and find that higher average wages reduce both property and violent crime. They further demonstrate that the reduction in crime associated with higher average wages is greatest in sectors with a higher concentration of low-skilled workers.

Of course, average wages may not be the most relevant point along the wage distribution when considering individuals who have a proclivity toward criminal activity. Based on this insight, Gould, Weinberg, and Mustard (2002) restrict their analysis to the wages of relatively low-skilled men. In addition, they make a key methodological improvement to the existing literature, accounting for the fact that specific types of workers or employers may migrate in response to increasing crime, thus confounding estimates of the relationship between local labor market conditions and crime. To address this, they use several instruments—the industrial composition of the local area, aggregate industrial trends, and demographic changes within industries. They find, using a county-level panel spanning 1979–97, that the falling wages of unskilled men in this period led to an 18 percent increase in robbery, a 14 percent increase in burglary, a 9 percent increase in aggravated assault, and a 7 percent increase in larceny. These findings are striking in that they indicate that wage trends explain more than half of the increase in both violent and property crimes over the entire period. In a similar analysis for the United Kingdom, Machin and Meghir (2004) examined changes in regional crime rates in relation to changes in the tenth and twenty-fifth percentile of the region's wage distribution and focus on the retail sector, an industry where low-skilled workers have the ability to manipulate their hours of work. They find that crime rates are higher in areas where the bottom of the wage distribution is low.

III. How Does Serving Time Affect Employment Prospects?

Thus far we have explored the potential causal effect of variation in employment prospects on propensities to commit crime. The source of this variation may be macroeconomic, structural disparities (for example, persistent racial discrimination in labor markets), or personal deficiencies in skills valued by employers. It is also possible that participation in criminal activity may have reciprocal dynamic effects on future employment prospects. In particular, when criminal activity results in an apprehension, conviction, or incarceration spell, the effect of this official record and interaction with the criminal justice system is something that the offending individual may need to address for the remainder of his or her work life.

What causal pathways might link prior criminality with concurrent and future employment prospects? First, for the incarcerated, there is a simple contemporaneous mechanical incapacitation effect of incarceration, in that institutionalized men cannot be employed in a conventional manner. To be sure, those admitted to prison are less likely to be employed anyway. Nonetheless, increases in incarceration will mechanically reduce the employment rate for those affected to the extent that some of the newly admitted inmates were employed at the time of arrest.

Beyond this contemporaneous effect, however, conviction and incarceration are also likely to have a dynamic lagged impact on the employment prospects for the convicted, as well as a contemporaneous effect on the employment outcomes of men who have not been to prison yet who come from demographic sub-groups with high incarceration rates. The dynamic effects are derived from the failure to accumulate human capital while incarcerated as well as the stigmatizing effects (sometimes exacerbated by state and federal policy) associated with a prior felony conviction and incarceration. The alternative contemporaneous effect results from employers engaging in statistical discrimination against men from high incarceration demographic groups in an attempt to avoid hiring ex-offenders. All of these pathways are likely to suppress the current and future employment and earnings of men from demographic groups with high incarceration rates. This adversely affects the material well-being of those men and those intimates and children whose welfare is determined interdependently.

A. Incarceration and the Accumulation of Work Experience

Serving time interrupts the work career. The extent of this interruption depends on both the expected amount of time served on a typical term as well as the likelihood of serving subsequent prison terms. The average prisoner admitted during the late 1990s on a new commitment faced a maximum sentence of three years and a minimum of one year (with many serving time closer to the minimum) (Raphael and Stoll 2005). If this were the only time served for most, then the time interruption of prison would not be that substantial.

However, many people serve multiple terms in prison, either due to the commission of new felonies or due to violation of parole conditions. A large body of criminological research consistently finds that nearly two-thirds of ex-inmates are re-arrested within a few years of release from prison (Petersilia 2003). Moreover, a sizable majority of the re-arrested will serve subsequent prison terms. Thus, for many offenders, the typical experience between the ages of eighteen and thirty is characterized by multiple short prison spells with intermittent, and relatively short, spells outside of prison.

In longitudinal research on young offenders entering the California state prison system, Raphael (2005) documents the degree to which prison interrupts the early potential work careers of young men. The author follows a cohort of young men entering the state prison system in 1990 and gauged the amount of time served over the subsequent decade. This analysis found that the median inmate served 2.8 years during the 1990s, with the median white inmate (3.09 years) and median black inmate (3.53 years) serving more time and the median Hispanic inmate (2.23 years) serving less time. Roughly 25 percent served at least 5 years during the 1990s while another 25 percent served less than 1.5 years.

However, as an indicator of the extent of the temporal interruption, these figures are misleading. Cumulative time served does not account for the short periods of time between prison spells when inmates may find employment, yet are not able to solidify the employment match with any measurable amount of job tenure. A more appropriate measure of the degree to which incarceration impedes experience accumulation would be the time between the date of admission to prison for the first term served and the date of release from the last term.

Using time lapsed between first admission and final release during the 1990s, Raphael (2005) found that five years elapses between the first date of admission and the last date of release for the median inmate. For median white, black, and Hispanic inmates, the figures are 6.2, 6.5, and 3.2 years, respectively. For approximately one quarter of inmates, nine years pass between their initial admission to prison and their last release. In other words, one quarter of these inmates spend almost the entire decade cycling in and out of prison. These figures for California are comparable to the characteristics of parolees receiving employment services from the New York–based Center for Employment Opportunities (CEO) whose transitional employment program is currently being evaluated by Bloom et al. (2007). Among participant parolees in the recent experimental evaluation of CEO, Bloom et al. (2007) document an average age of 33.7, and an average lifetime cumulative time served in state prison of nearly five years.

Spending five or more years of early life cycling in and out of institutions must affect an individual's earnings prospects. Clearly, incarceration spells in conjunction with a series of short spans of time outside of prison prohibit the accumulation of human capital during a period of life when the returns to experience are the greatest.

B. Does Having Been in Prison Stigmatize Ex-Offenders?

The potential effect of serving time on future labor market prospects extends beyond the failure to accumulate work experience. Employers are averse to hiring former prison inmates and often use formal and informal screening tools to weed ex-offenders out of the applicant pool. Given the high proportion of low-skilled men with prison time on their criminal history records, such employer sentiments and screening practices represent an increasingly important employment barrier, especially for low-skilled African American men.

Employers consider criminal history records when screening job applicants for a number of reasons. First, certain occupations are closed to felons under local, state, and, in some instances, federal law (Hahn 1991). Second, in many states employers can be held liable for the criminal actions of their employees. Under the theory of negligent hiring, employers can be required to pay punitive damages as well as damages for loss, pain, and suffering for acts committed by an employee on the job (Craig 1987). Finally, employers looking to fill jobs where employee monitoring is imperfect may place a premium on trustworthiness and screen accordingly.

In all known employer surveys in which employers are asked about their willingness to hire ex-offenders, employer responses reveal a strong aversion to hiring applicants with criminal history records (Pager 2003; Holzer, Raphael, and Stoll 2006, 2007). For example, more than 60 percent of employers surveyed in the Multi-City Study of Urban Inequality indicated that they would "probably not" or "definitely not" hire applicants with criminal history records, with "probably not" being the modal response. By contrast, only 8 percent responded similarly when queried about their willingness to hire current and former welfare recipients.

The ability of employers to act on an aversion to ex-offenders, and the nature of the action in terms of hiring and screening behavior, will depend on employer access to criminal history record information. If an employer can and does check criminal history records, the employer may simply screen out applicants based on their arrest and conviction records. In the absence of a formal background check, an employer may act on their aversion to hiring ex-offenders using perceived corre-lates of previous incarceration, such as age, race, or level of educational attainment. In other words, employers may statistically profile applicants and avoid hiring those from demographic groups with high rates of involvement in the criminal justice system.

The propensity to discriminate statistically is evident in the interaction effect of employers' stated preference regarding their willingness to hire ex-offenders, their screening behavior on this dimension, and their propensity to hire workers from high incarceration rate groups. In particular, Holzer, Raphael, and Stoll (2007) find that employers with a stated aversion to hiring convicted felons but who do not perform formal criminal history record reviews are the least likely to hire African American men. They are also the least likely to indicate a willingness to hire applicants with gaps in their employment histories. These findings suggest that in the absence of a formal screen for criminal histories, employers instead use perceived correlates of prior criminality, thus likely discriminating against some with clean histories.

With regard to the direct effect of stigma on former inmates themselves, an audit study by Pager (2003) offers the clearest evidence of employer aversion to ex-offenders and the stigma associated with having served time in prison. The study uses male auditors matched on observable characteristics including age, education, general appearance, demeanor, and race to assess the effects of prior prison experi-ence on the likelihood that each auditor is called back for an interview. Consistently sizable negative effects of prior prison experience were found on the likelihood of being called back by the employer, with callback rates for the auditor with prior prison time one half that of the matched co-auditor.

C. Existing Research on the Employment Consequences of Incarceration

In conjunction, the effects of stigma combined with the effect of incarceration on human capital accumulation, and perhaps depreciation, suggest that serving time is likely to adversely affect employment prospects. Moreover, for men from high incarceration sub-groups, the high rate of involvement with the criminal justice system may have a negative spillover effect to the extent that employers wish to screen out ex-offenders and do so using informal perceived signals of criminality such as race, or gaps in one's employment history.

A growing body of empirical research investigates the effects of being convicted and serving time on post-release employment and earnings. In nearly all of these studies, researchers analyze the pre/post incarceration path of earnings and em-ployment of those who serve time. To be sure, the principal empirical challenge is to define the counterfactual path of earnings and employment for those who go to prison. Defining such a counterfactual path is difficult considering that men tend to go prison during a time in their lives (early to mid-twenties) when labor force attachment and earnings are changing rapidly, and those who serve time are quite different from those who do not, both on observable and unobservable dimensions.

The challenges to this line of research are illustrated in figures 15.2 and 15.3. To construct these figures, we identified all young men in the NLSY79 who were interviewed while incarcerated (the principal gauge of serving time in these data) for the first time at the age of twenty-three or later. We then matched each of these youth to one non-incarcerated male in the sample, defined as youth who never do time during the period covered by the NLSY79. In choosing matches, we identified all never-incarcerated youth who match each incarcerated youth exactly on age, region of residence in the country, and education at twenty-two years of age. From these exact matches, we then chose either the match with the closest Armed Forced Qualifying Test (AFQT) score when the AFQT was available for the incarcerated youth, or a random match (among those who exact matched on observable dimensions) for incarcerated youth with no AFQT score. Each figure presents the mean of an outcome for the group of incarcerated youth or the never-incarcerated youth for years relative to the year of first incarceration (t=0). The figure compares outcomes for the five years preceding incarceration as well as the subsequent eight-year period.

Figure 15.2 compares annual weeks worked. During the pre-incarceration period, average weeks worked among future inmates and the never incarcerated both increased (by 5.5 weeks among future inmates and by 8 weeks among the comparison youth). At the point of first incarceration, however, the two series diverge sharply. Among the never incarcerated, average weeks worked continues to increase from approximately 33 weeks at year zero to 40 weeks at year five (followed by a decline in employment corresponding to the early '90s recession). Among the incarcerated, there is a sharp drop in weeks worked in the first survey year following the year of first observed incarceration (to 11 weeks). The pre-incarceration peak of 22 weeks is recovered five years post-incarceration, but does not rise above the pre-incarceration level during the latter eight-year period. The departure between the incarcerated and comparison groups is illustrated by the difference in mean weeks worked during the pre-incarceration period and the post incarceration period. For the five pre-incarceration years, the never-incarcerated work roughly 9.5 more weeks per year than the group of future inmates. In the eight post-incarceration years, this average difference increases to 17.4 weeks. Figure 15.3 shows similar patterns for average annual earnings. During the pre-incarceration period, the ratio of annual earnings for the comparison sample to the incarcerated sample is roughly 1.5. During the post-incarceration period, this ratio increases to an average of 2.6.

These two figures illustrate the difficulties faced by research on this topic. As is evident from the employment and earnings path of the treatment group, incarceration occurs at a point in the age-earnings profile of young men where labor force

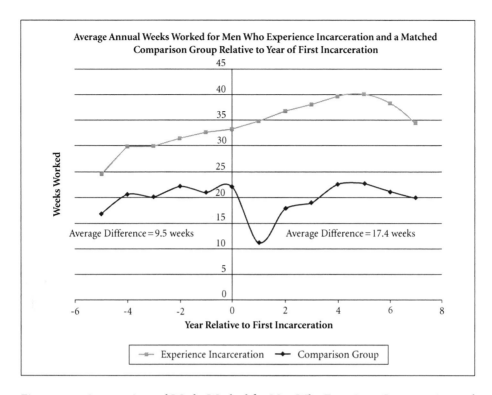

Figure 15.2. Average Annual Weeks Worked for Men Who Experience Incarceration and a Matched Comparison Group Relative to Year of First Incarceration.

attachment is strengthening and annual earnings are increasing. Simple before/after comparisons of earnings and employment among those who experience incarceration will underestimate the true consequences of having served time to the extent that earnings and employment would have grown through this period in the absence of an incarceration spell.

The figure also reveals the large baseline disparities between those who eventually serve time and those who do not, even after having matched on a number of demographic and human capital dimensions. The comparison sample works nine additional weeks and earns 50 percent more than the sample of future inmates even before the first incarcerated spell. Thus, while pre-incarceration employment and earnings dynamics are similar, the large pre-treatment disparity in average outcomes raises questions about whether the post-incarceration employment and earnings paths of non-inmates provide accurate counterfactuals for those who serve time.

Several researchers using diverse strategies have addressed these methodological challenges using data from the NLS79. Western (2002) compares the earnings trajectories of NLSY79 youth who serve time to high-risk youth who do not and finds a sizable relative decline in the hourly wages of the formerly incarcerated.

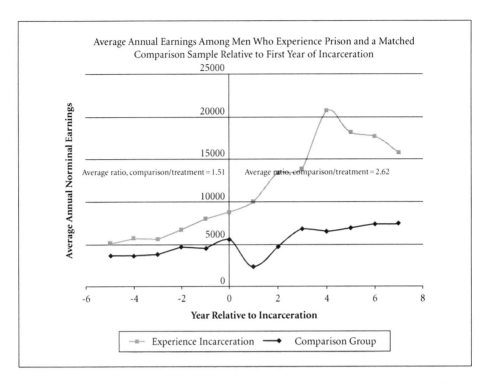

Figure 15.3. Average Annual Earnings Among Men Who Experience Prison and a Matched Comparison Sample Relative to First Year of Incarceration.

Raphael (2007) compares the employment outcomes of NLSY79 youth who serve time early in their lives to those who serve time later in life. He finds a significant and substantial negative effect of prior incarceration on annual weeks worked that corresponds in time with one's first incarceration spell. Using the more recent NLSY97 data, Sweeten and Apel (2007) estimate the effects of a prior incarceration spell on various employment, educational, and criminal justice outcomes after matching youth who serve time to those who do not along a large number of observable variables. They find sizable effects of a previous incarceration spell on the probability of employment five years later. They also find some evidence that a prior incarceration spell predicts future criminal activity and poorer educational outcomes.

A number of studies have used administrative data on arrest and incarceration matched to administrative earnings records. Waldfogel (1994) and Grogger (1995) were among the first to pursue this research strategy. Waldfogel uses data on individuals convicted in federal court and compares pre- and post-conviction employment outcomes culled from federal parole records. He finds the largest earnings penalties for those who serve time and those convicted of a "breach" crime. Grogger (1995) uses California administrative data to study the distributed lagged effect of arrest, conviction, probation, being sentenced to jail, and being sentenced to prison on subsequent earnings and employment; he finds that arrest has a short-lived negative effect on earnings, while serving a prison sentence has a more pronounced and longer-lasting negative effect on earnings.

A number of recent studies have used state and federal prison administrative records combined with ES-202 earnings records to analyze the pre- and post-employment and earnings patterns of prison inmates. Kling (2006) analyzes data for federal prisoners in California and state prisoners in Florida, Jung (2007) and Cho and Lalonde (2005) analyze data for state prisoners in Illinois, Pettit and Lyons (2007) analyze data for prisoners in Washington state, while Sabol (2007) analyzes data for prisoners in Ohio. While these studies differ from one another along a number of dimensions, there are several consistent findings. First, the ES-202 records measure very low employment and earnings among state-prison inmates prior to incarceration (with roughly one-third showing positive quarterly earnings in any given quarter for the two years period preceding incarceration). While this is partially explained by the incompleteness of administrative data,[3] these findings also suggest low labor force participation rates among soon-to-be inmates.

Second, nearly all of the studies find that employment increases above pre-incarceration levels immediately following release and then declines to pre-incarceration levels or falls below pre-incarceration levels within a couple of years. The small post-release employment increase is likely because most released prisoners are conditionally released to parole authorities and must meet certain obligations, including employment search or even formal employment requirements (perhaps entailing a job more likely to be captured in ES-202 records), to remain in the community.

Third, several studies find that the post-release increase in employment is larger for inmates who serve longer terms (Cho and Lalonde 2005; Kling 2006; Jung 2007). However, Kling (2006) shows that this disparity does not survive controlling for differences in inmate characteristics and program participation between inmates serving shorter and longer terms (of particular importance is the difference in participation in work release programs).

While these studies suggest a positive effect of conditional release on employment, they are generally unable to identify the effects of incarceration on the age-earnings and age-employment profiles of those who serve time. The reliance on quarterly unemployment insurance records renders these results particularly sensitive to any factors that are likely to affect the probability of working for an employer that complies with labor market regulations. If employers who participate in work-release programs or who have working relationships with labor market intermediaries that place former inmates have a high degree of compliance, pre- and post-incarceration employment outcomes as measured by unemployment insurance earnings records may not be comparable.[4]

In addition, these studies do not identify a comparison group of individuals who do not serve time to whom we could compare the average earnings and employment paths of those who do. Failing to account for the slope of the age-earning profile at the time of incarceration seriously distorts inferences regarding the ultimate impacts of incarceration.

A final group of studies uses data from the U.S. census to estimate the partial correlation between the proportion of a given demographic group that is incarcerated and the average employment outcomes of the non-incarcerated among the corresponding group (Raphael 2005, Raphael and Ronconi 2006). These studies show that those demographic sub-groups that experience the largest increase in incarceration rates also experience the largest decreases in employment among the non-incarcerated.

IV. Conclusion

The reciprocal relationship between work and crime is an important topic for theory and policy. To the extent that the choice to refrain or desist from criminal activity is somewhat responsive to positive incentives, our conceptualization of crime and how to control crime should be altered. Clearly, preventing criminal activity through a series of policy carrots and sticks is a more proactive strategy than punishment and incapacitation. Given the high costs of victimization and the private costs of crime prevention, effective preventative strategies based on transitional employment, skills building, and job-search assistance, or any such workforce development efforts targeted at those likely to offend would certainly generate significant social savings. The responsiveness of potential criminals to positive incentives is quite similar theoretically to responsiveness to more punitive incentives. The underlying models are essentially the same, yet crime preventing strategies framed by the need to deter with punishment attract more support than strategies of deterrence through reward.

There is much we do not know. While there are many studies on this topic, the likely diversity in the responsiveness of potential offenders renders most research efforts somewhat specialized with limited external validity. More effort should be devoted to fleshing out this diversity in behavioral responsiveness to positive and negative incentives. In particular, understanding differential responsiveness based on age, prior criminal history, extensiveness of past interaction with law enforcement, and number of past prison terms served would permit better targeting of policy efforts designed to reduce crime through positive incentives.

One line of inquiry that has received less explicit attention concerns the differential effect of temporary as opposed to permanent variation in earnings and employment. For example, do we really expect those with strong employment prospects to turn to crime due to a recession-induced employment shock? Alternatively stated, does an increased employment rate for the least-skilled and lowest-earning workers during boom times really alter their life chances in a manner that fundamentally affects the mental calculus behind whether they will engage in crime? Some measure of permanent earnings potential may be the most relevant predictor of the relative returns to crime. However, permanent earnings are so closely tied with human capital accumulation, social class, and race and ethnicity, all factors that are likely to influence criminal involvement independently of employment prospects. A fruitful line for future research would search for independent shifts in human capital (such as schooling) and attempt to assess the effect on crime (if any) and the extent to which wage increases mediate such effects. While research to date has focused on regional and temporal variation in aggregate unemployment and wages largely due to the availability of such data, a deepening of our understanding of the crime-work relationship rests on developing better measures of permanent earnings potential.

Moreover, the most recent research on the relationship between employment prospects and crime and prior criminality and future employment prospects has focused considerable effort on the clear identification challenges faced by non-experimental research designs. This focus is clearly merited. More such efforts to devise creative strategies for disentangling causal relationships represents a fruitful direction for further research.

NOTES

1. The following discussion does assume some familiarity with microeconomic modeling. However, much of the intuition of this more formal analysis has already been articulated in the introductory paragraphs to this section. For readers less interested in formal modeling, one can skip directly to section 3.

2. Among their findings were that a majority of offenders, primarily convicted of misdemeanor offenses, were employed and engaged in crime as a means of supplementing their legitimate earnings. Note that this is consistent with the model presented. Other respondents engaged in crime exclusively though few respondents claimed that an involuntary unemployment spell was the cause of their offending.

3. Kling (2006) is the only study that compares employment as measured by quarterly earnings records to inmate self-reported employment at the time of arrest. The author reports that while only 33 percent of inmates have positive earnings in the typical pre-incarceration quarter, nearly 65 percent report being employed at the time of arrest. Based on analysis of Current Population Survey (CPS) data for comparable men, Kling concludes that most of this disparity reflects that inmates are employed in informal jobs where employers are not paying social security taxes or paying into the unemployment insurance system.

4. Kornfeld and Bloom (1999) provide a detailed comparison of earnings as measured by quarterly unemployment insurance records to survey data earnings as measured in the Job Training Partnership Act (JTPA) training experiments and provide estimated program effects using the two sources of data. The authors show that earnings from the unemployment insurance data are systematically lower than earnings from the survey records. However, relative program effects are similar in magnitude using the two sources of information. The one exception to this rule, however, is for young men with criminal records. The unemployment insurance data yield larger program-effect estimates than the survey records, suggesting that for this particular group, program participation is increasing the likelihood of working for an employer that complies with reporting and tax requirements.

REFERENCES

Allan, Emelie, and Darrell J. Steffensmeier. 1984. "Youth Underemployment, and Property Crime: Differential Effects of Job Availability and Job Quality on Juvenile and Young Adult Arrest Rates." *American Sociological Review* 54, no. 1: 107–23.

Apel, Robert, Raymond Paternoster, Shawn D. Bushway, and Robert Brame. 2006. "A Job Isn't Just a Job: The Differential Impact of Formal Versus Informal Work on Adolescent Problem Behavior." *Crime & Delinquency* 52, no. 2: 333–69.

Autor, David H., and Lawrence F. Katz. 1999. "Changes in the Wage Structure and Earnings Inequality." In *Handbook of Labor Economics*, ed. Orley Ashenfelter and David Card. Amsterdam: Elsevier.

Bloom, Dan, Cindy Redcross, Janine Zweig, and Gilda Azurdia. 2007. "Transitional Jobs for Ex-Prisoners: Early Impacts from a Random Assignment Evaluation of the Center for Employment Opportunities Prisoner Reentry Program." Working Paper. New York: MDRC.

Chiricos, Theodor. 1987. "Rates of Crime and Unemployment: An Analysis of Aggregate Research Evidence." *Social Problems* 34, no. 2: 187–211.

Cho, Rosa, and Robert Lalonde. 2005. "The Impact of Incarceration in State Prison on the Employment Prospects of Women." Harris School Working Paper #5–10, University of Chicago, Chicago, IL.

Cook, Philip J., and Gary A. Zarkin. 1985. "Crime and the Business Cycle." *Journal of Legal Studies* 14, no. 1: 115–28.

Cornwell, Christopher, and William N. Trumbull. 1994. "Estimating the Economic Model of Crime with Panel Data." *Review of Economics and Statistics* 76, no. 2: 360–66.

Craig, Scott R. 1987. "Negligent Hiring: Guilt By Association." *Personnel Administrator* October: 32–34.

Crutchfield, Robert D., and Susan R. Pitchford. 1997. "Work and Crime: The Effects of Labor Stratification." *Social Forces* 76, no. 1: 93–118.

Cullen, Julie B., and Steven D. Levitt. 1999. "Crime, Urban Flight, and the Consequences for Cities." *Review of Economics and Statistics* 81, no. 2:159–69.

Doyle, Joanne M., Ehsan Ahmed, and Robert N. Horn. 1999. "The Effects of Labor Markets and Income Inequality on Crime: Evidence from Panel Data." *Southern Economic Journal* 65:717–31.

Edmark, Karin. 2005. "Unemployment and Crime: Is There a Connection?" *Scandinavian Journal of Economics* 107, no. 2: 353–73.

Entorf, Horst, and Hannes Spengler. 2000. "Criminality, social cohesion and economic performance." Wurzburg Economic Papers No. 22. Department of Economics, University of Wurzburg, Wurzburg, Germany.

Farrington, David, Bernard Gallagher, Lynda Morley, Raymond J. St. Ledger, and Donald J. West. 1986. "Unemployment, School Leaving, and Crime." *British Journal of Criminology* 26:335–56.

Freeman, Richard B. 1996. "Why Do So Many Young Americans Commit Crimes and What Might We Do About It?" *Journal of Economic Perspectives* 10, no. 1: 25–42.

Gould, Eric D., Weinberg, Bruce A., and David B. Mustard. 2002. "Crime Rates and Local Labor Market Opportunities in the United States: 1979–1997." *Review of Economics and Statistics* 84, no. 1: 45–61.

Grogger, Jeffrey. 1991. "Certainty vs. Severity in Punishment." *Economic Inquiry* 29, no. 2: 297–309.

———. 1995. "The Effect of Arrest on the Employment and Earnings of Young Men." *Quarterly Journal of Economics* 110, no. 1: 51–71.

———. 1998. "Market Wages and Youth Crime." *Journal of Labor Economics* 16, no. 4: 756–91.

Hahn, J. M. 1991. "Pre-Employment Information Services: Employers Beware." *Employee Relations Law Journal* 17, no. 1: 45–69.

Hansen, Kirstine, and Stephen Machin. Forthcoming. "Crime and the Minimum Wage." *Journal of Quantitative Criminology*.

Holzer, Harry J., Steven Raphael, and Michael A. Stoll. 2006. "Perceived Criminality, Criminal Background Checks and the Racial Hiring Practices of Employers." *Journal of Law and Economics* 49, no. 2: 451–80.

———. 2007. "The Effect of an Applicant's Criminal History on Employer Hiring Decisions and Screening Practices: Evidence from Los Angeles." In *Barriers to Reentry? The Labor Market for Released Prisoners in Post-Industrial America*, ed. Shawn Bushway, Michael Stoll, and David Weiman. New York: Russell Sage Foundation.

Juhn, Chinhui, and Simon Potter. 2006. "Changes in Labor Force Participation in the United States." *Journal of Economic Perspectives* 20, no. 3: 27–46.

Jung, Haeil. 2007. "The Effects of First Incarceration on Male Ex-Offenders' Employment and Earnings." Working Paper, University of Chicago. Harris School of Public Policy, University of Chicago, Chicago, IL

Kallem, Andrew. 2004. "Youth Crime and the Minimum Wage." SSRN Working Paper No. 545382. Department of Economics, Harvard University, Cambridge, MA.

Katz, Lawrence F., and Kevin M. Murphy. 1992. "Changes In Relative Wages, 1963–1987: Supply And Demand Factors." *Quarterly Journal of Economics* 107, no. 1: 35–78.

Kornfeld, Robert, and Howard Bloom. 1999. "Measuring Program Impacts on Earnings and Employment: Do Unemployment Insurance Wage Records Agree with Survey Reports of Individuals?" *Journal of Labor Economics* 17, no. 1: 168–97.

Kling, Jeffrey R. 2006. "Incarceration Length, Employment, and Earnings." *American Economic Review* 96, no. 3: 863–76.

Lattimore, Pamela K., Christy A. Visher, and Danielle M. Steffey. 2008. *Pre-Release Characteristics and Service Receipt Among Adult Male Participants in the SVORI Multi-Site Evaluation*. Washington, DC: Urban Institute.

Levitt, Steven D. 2001. "Alternative Strategies for Identifying the Link Between Unemployment and Crime." *Journal of Quantitative Criminology* 17, no. 4: 377.

Lynch, James P., and William J. Sabol. 2001. "Prisoner Reentry in Perspective." Urban Institute Crime Policy Report. Washington, DC: Urban Institute.

Machin, Stephen, and Costas Meghir. 2004. "Crime and Economic Incentives." *Journal of Human Resources* 39. no. 4: 958–79.

Mallar, Charles D., and Craig V. D. Thornton. 1978. "Transitional Aid for Released Prisoners: Evidence from the Life Experiment." *Journal of Human Resources* 13, no. 2: 208–36.

McMorris, Barbara, and Christopher Uggen. 2000. "Alcohol and Employment in the Transition to Adulthood." *Journal of Health and Social Behavior* 41:276–94.

Myers, Samuel L. 1983. "Estimating the Economic Model of Crime: Employment Versus Punishment Effects." *Quarterly Journal of Economics* 98, no. 1: 157–66.

Mortimer, Jeylan T., Ellen Efron Pimentel, Seongryeol Ryu, Katherine Nash, and Chaimun Lee. 1996. "Part-Time Work and Occupational Value Formation in Adolescence." *Social Forces* 74:1405–18.

National Research Council. 1998. Protecting Youth at Work: Health, Ssafety, and Development of Working Children and Adolescents in the United States. Washington, DC: National Academies Press.

Newcomb, M. D., and P. M. Bentler. 1989. "Substance Use and Abuse among Children and Teenagers." *American Psychologist* 44, no. 2: 242–48.

Pager, Devah. 2003. "The Mark of a Criminal Record." *American Journal of Sociology* 108, no. 5: 937–75.

Papps, Kerry, and Rainer Winkelman. 1998. "Unemployment and Crime: New Answers to an Old Question." Unpublished manuscript, Department of Economics, University of Canterbury, New Zealand.

Petersilia, Joan. 2003. *When Prisoners Come Home*. Oxford: Oxford University Press.

Pettit, Becky, and Christopher Lyons. 2007."Status and the Stigma of Incarceration: The Labor Market Effects of Incarceration by Race, Class, and Criminal Involvement." In *Barriers to Reentry? The Labor Market for Released Prisoners in Post-Industrial America*, ed. Shawn Bushway, Michael Stoll, and David Weiman. New York: Russell Sage Foundation.

Raphael, Steven. 2005. "The Socioeconomic Status of Black Males: The Increasing Importance of Incarceration." In *Poverty, the Distribution of Income, and Public Policy*, ed. Alan Auerbach, David Card, and John Quigley. New York: Russell Sage Foundation.

———. 2007. "Early Incarceration Spells and the Transition to Adulthood." In *The Price of Independence*, ed. Sheldon Danziger and Cecilia Rouse. New York: Russell Sage Foundation.

Raphael, Steven, and Lucas Ronconi. 2006. "Reconciling National and Regional Estimates of the Effects of Immigration on the U.S. Labor Market: The Confounding Effects of Native Male Incarceration Trends." Working Paper, University of California, Berkeley. Goldman School of Public Policy, University of California, Berkeley, CA.

Raphael, Steven, and Melissa Sills. 2005. "Urban Crime in the United States." In *A Companion to Urban Economics*, ed. Richard Arnott and Dan McMillen. Malden, MA: Blackwell Publishing.

Raphael, Steven, and Michael Stoll. 2005. "The Effect of Prison Releases on Regional Crime Rates." In *The Brookings-Wharton Papers on Urban Economic Affairs*, vol. 5, ed. William G. Gale and Janet Rothenberg Pack. Washington, DC: Brookings Institution.

Raphael, Steven, and David Weiman. 2007. "The Impact of Local Labor Market Conditions on the Likelihood that Parolees are Returned to Custody." In *Barriers to Reentry? The Labor Market for Released Prisoners in Post-Industrial America*, ed. Shawn Bushway, Michael Stoll, and David Weiman. New York: Russell Sage Foundation.

Raphael, Steven, and Rudolf Winter-Ebmer. 2001. "Identifying the Effect of Unemployment on Crime," *Journal of Law and Economics* 44, no. 1: 259–84.

Rossi, Peter, Berk, Richard A., and Kenneth J Lenihan. 1980. *Money, Work, and Crime: Experimental Evidence: Quantitative Studies in Social Relations.* New York: Academic Press.

Sabol, William J. 2007. "Local Labor-Market Conditions and Post-Prison Employment Experiences of Offenders Released from Ohio State Prisons." In *Barriers to Reentry? The Labor Market for Released Prisoners in Post-Industrial America*, ed. Shawn Bushway, Michael Stoll, and David Weiman. New York: Russell Sage Foundation.

Sampson, Robert J., and W. B. Groves. 1989. "Community Structure and Social Disorganization." *American Journal of Sociology* 94, no. 4: 774–802.

Sampson, Robert J., and John H. Laub. 1997. "A Life Course Theory of Cumulative Disadvantage and the Stability of Delinquency." In *Developmental Theories of Crime and Delinquency*, ed. Terence Thornberry. New Brunswick, NJ: Transaction Publishers.

———. 2005. "A Life-Course View of the Development of Crime." In *Developmental Criminology and Its Discontents: Trajectory of Crime from Adulthood to Old Age*, ed. Sampson, Robert J. and John H. Laub. Vol. 602 of *Annals of the American Academy of Political and Social Sciences*. Thousand Oaks, CA: Sage Publications.

Schwartz, Amy Ellen, Scott Susin, and Ioan Voicu. 2003. "Has Falling Crime Driven New York City's Real Estate Boom?" *Journal of Housing Research* 14, no. 1: 101–36.

Skogan, Wesley G. 1986. "Fear of Crime and Neighborhood Change." In *Communities and Crime*, edited by Albert J. Reiss Jr. and Michael Tonry. Vol. 8 of *Crime and Justice: A Review of Research*, edited by Michael Tonry and Norval Morris. Chicago: University of Chicago Press.

Staff, Jeremy, and Christopher Uggen. 2003. "The Fruits Of Good Work: Early Work Experiences and Adolescent Deviance." *Journal of Research in Crime and Delinquency* 40, no. 3: 263–90.

Steinberg, Laurence, Suzanne Fegley, and Sanford M. Dornbusch. 1993. "Negative Impact of Part-Time Work on Adolescent Adjustment: Evidence from a Longitudinal Study." *Developmental Psychology* 29:171–80.

Sviridoff, Michelle, and James W. Thompson. 1983. "Links between Employment and Crime: A Qualitative Study of Rikers Island Prisoners." *Crime and Delinquency* 29, no. 2: 195–212.

Sweeten, Gary, and Robert Apel. 2007. "Incarceration and the Transition to Adulthood." Working Paper, Arizona State University. School of Criminology and Criminal Justice, Arizona State University.

Thornberry, T. P., and R. L. Christensen. 1984. "Unemployment and Criminal Involvement: An Investigation of Reciprocal Causal Structures." *American Sociological Review* 49:398–411.

Christopher Uggen. 1999. "Ex-Offenders and the Conformist Alternative: A Job Quality Model of Work and Crime." *Social Problems* 46:127–51.

———. 2000. "Work as a Turning Point in the Life Course of Criminals: A Duration Model of Age, Employment, and Recidivism." *American Sociological Review* 67:529–46.

Visher, Christy A., Laura Winterfield, and Mark B. Coggeshall. 2005. "Ex-Offender Employment Programs and Recidivism: A Meta-Analysis." *Journal of Experimental Criminology* 1:295–315.

Waldfogel, Joel. 1994. "The Effect of Criminal Convictions on Income and the Trust 'Reposed in the Workmen.'" *Journal of Human Resources* 29, no. 1: 62–81.

Western, Bruce. 2002. "The Impact of Incarceration on Wage Mobility and Inequality." *American Sociological Review* 67, no. 4: 526–46.

Witte, Ann Dryden. 1980. "Estimating the Economic Model of Crime with Individual Data." *Quarterly Journal of Economics* 94, no. 1: 57–84.

Wright, John P., and Francis T. Cullen. 2004. "Employment, Peers and Life-course Transitions." *Justice Quarterly* 21, no. 1: 183–205.

Wright, John P., Francis T. Cullen, and Nicholas Williams. 1997. "Working While in School and Delinquent Involvement: Implications for Social Policy." *Crime and Delinquency* 43:203–21.

PART III

POLICE AND POLICING

CHAPTER 16

....

POLICE ORGANIZATION

....

STEPHEN D. MASTROFSKI AND
JAMES J. WILLIS[*]

NEARLY two decades ago, Albert J. Reiss Jr. (1992) tracked the major features of American police organization continuity and change in the twentieth century, indicating that some aspects of policing had changed little, while others had changed much. Policing occurs in a dynamic environment, and so a decade into the twenty-first century is an appropriate time to reflect on what has become of American local police organizations and the forces that shape them, and to note opportunities for future research.

American policing demonstrates both continuity and change as it completes the first decade of the twenty-first century. A high degree of industry decentralization persists, as do bureaucratic structures of larger police agencies. The structures and practices of the nation's numerous small agencies remain underexamined. The potential growth of professional structures inside and outside the police organization is largely unexplored. The core police patrol technology has remained essentially unchanged for decades, and early police adaptations to the information technology revolution have not yet profoundly altered policing structures and processes in easily observable ways. Yet the increasing centrality of police as "information workers" bears close watching. The demography and education levels of police workers are changing, but the consequences are unclear. Police culture has been under siege since the 1960s. Currently, powerful reforms attempt to reduce the occupation's isolation from the communities they serve and the scientific community that presumably serves them. Mechanisms and styles for governing police retain considerable variation, but the growing role of grassroots community groups remains underexplored. The complexity of the dynamics of change manifests itself in the reaction of American police organizations to one of the most consequential reform movements of the twenty-first century thus far: terrorist-oriented policing. American police agencies have shown a remarkable capacity to absorb these reforms while buffering core structures and practices from change. However, profound changes may take more time than a couple of decades, so observers should take care to attend to incremental change over longer periods.

The chapter is organized as follows. Section I discusses the structure of the American policing industry. Section II examines the internal structure of American police agencies. Section III looks at changes in police technology. Section IV discusses the people serving in police organizations, and section V reviews the organizational culture of police. Section VI discusses external governance of police. Section VII surveys forces of stability and change.

A number of conclusions emerge:

- Compared with police in other countries, policing in America is highly fragmented.
- Routine and reactive patrolling remain the staple activities of American police, even though several decades of research concludes that patrolling is ineffective as a crime reduction measure.
- Community- and problem-oriented policing techniques have been adopted in many—especially larger—forces but have not fundamentally re-oriented police.
- New technologies have been adopted widely but have not fundamentally altered police activities or priorities.
- Police forces have in the last thirty years become much more diverse in terms of race, ethnicity, and gender, but evidence about effects on police culture and activity does not demonstrate major effects.
- Although serious efforts have been made to integrate local police into anti-terrorist activities, except for activities of a few large urban departments, local police activities and priorities do not appear to have been much affected.
- Conceptions of police culture are influential, but little is known about how "police culture" differs from other professional cultures and what the effects of those differences might be.

I. The Structure of America's Policing Industry

America is the most fragmented, decentralized system for delivering public policing services in the industrialized world (Bayley 1985; 1992; Skogan and Frydl 2004, 48). A 2004 census showed 12,766 local police agencies, 3,067 sheriff's departments, and 1,481 special jurisdiction agencies operating in the United States (Bureau of Justice Statistics 2007, 2). No other nation matches the United States in the number of agencies embedded in different levels of government and the complexity of inter-agency arrangements (Bayley 1992; Skogan and Frydl 2004, 48).

A. Character of Industry Fragmentation

The fragmentation of American policing appears to be associated with a fondness for decentralized democratic governance (Geller and Morris 1992, 233), but it is unclear whether these democratic predilections fostered a fragmented structure of policing, or whether the latter made the former possible. Regardless, the degree of fragmentation may be declining, albeit at a glacial pace. A study of Ohio found an 11 percent reduction in the number of departments from the 1970s through the 1990s (Maguire and King 2007, 340). The research also found a net increase in number of agencies in two other states with high population growth in the 1990s. The overall national picture is uncertain, but were the pattern to continue nationwide at the rate observed in Ohio, the high degree of police industry defragmentation in the United States would continue far into the future.

Counts of police agencies do not show the complete picture. The 2004 census of state and local law enforcement agencies showed that the largest 6 percent of state and local agencies (100 or more full-time sworn) accounted for 64 percent of all sworn personnel, while the 74 percent of the nation's departments with fewer than twenty-five officers accounted for only 14 percent (Reaves 2007, 2). Although these statistics reflect a still impressive level of multiplicity within the police industry, they show that America's policing industry is more concentrated than a mere tally of agencies suggests.

Further, the high degree of police service fragmentation is concentrated in patrol services. The provision of many specialized services (including criminal investigations, training, and crime labs) is more centralized, often provided to smaller departments by larger nearby municipal, county, or state agencies, or regional facilities (Ostrom et al. 1978; Parks 2009). Observers often suggest that the American system is rife with overlapping jurisdictions and sporadic coordination of agencies (President's Commission 1967, 301; Reiss 1992, 65; Manning 2006, 118) but there is some evidence suggesting the overlap (though real) is not characterized by conflict but is largely managed through a web of arrangements that is *cooperative* and institutionalized (McDavid 1977; Ostrom et al. 1978, 301–16; Parks 2009).

B. Police Consolidation Movement

The desire to consolidate small American police agencies first surfaced as a reform in the 1930s and then again in the late 1960s and 1970s (Altshuler 1970, 38; Douthit 1975; Murphy and Plate 1977; Walker 1977, 141–46; Parks 2009). The principal objective of the consolidation advocates, merging the nation's many small agencies into much larger entities, has never gathered much steam. Their arguments are that new police technologies cost more than most small departments can afford, large departments make cost-efficient the hiring of specialist experts that small departments cannot afford, small communities cannot afford to deal with the increasing litigation or threat of litigation against the police, larger departments can afford to hire better qualified personnel and give them more training, larger departments can provide more and better service by achieving economies of scale, and larger agencies are better equipped to adapt to the changing nature of crime (e.g., cybercrime) (Tully 2002).

The ability of so many policing "Lilliputs" (Ostrom and Smith 1976) to withstand these criticisms comes from several sources. First, there are explanations deriving from technical performance. Small agencies have dealt with the challenges of cost-efficiency and economies of scale by seeking consolidated assistance for the specialist functions expected of contemporary police, while continuing to deliver more basic patrol service. This patrol efficiency appears especially easy for small agencies because as they grow in size, they seem to require disproportionately more administrative, supervisory, and support staff (Ostrom et al. 1978, 85–91; Langworthy and Hindelang 1983; Scott 1998; Klinger 2004, 132). Other sources of small-department efficiency undoubtedly derive from the lower salary and benefits offered, and lower investment in training (Weisheit and Hawkins 1997; Weisheit 2005). If the cost of policing is directly related to its quality, smaller and rural departments should be in trouble, but at least one standard indicator of performance suggests that they tend to outperform large agencies in clearance rates for major offenses (Cordner 1989; Falcone, Wells, and Weisheit 2002).

Second, the people served by small departments may place a premium on certain things that they deliver with greater ease, but which large departments struggle to produce: accessibility and interpersonal familiarity with the community and law enforcement that is customized to the preferences of a smaller community (Wilson 1968, 211–15; Crank and Wells 1991; Mastrofski and Ritti 1996; Maguire 2003; Weisheit and Wells 1999; Schafer, Burruss, and Giblin 2009). This may be reflected in the often higher levels of satisfaction with police reported by residents of smaller communities, thus undermining claims that big city police service is *necessarily* better than that of small towns (Mastrofski 1981, ch. 3; Skogan and Frydl 2004; Parks 2009).

Finally, there is an array of political and historical forces at work (Reiss 1992, 63–68): the enduring American fondness for using *local* government to deliver key services, a community environment conducive to the explosive growth of suburbs, and the absence of a cohesive constituency, including police leadership, to support consolidation (Mastrofski 1989). If "autopsies" were routinely held for disestablished small police organizations (King 2009, 228), a useful hypothesis would be that the more frequent cause of death was failure to be able to secure financial resources, not public dissatisfaction with performance.

C. Private Security

The efflorescence of private security and private policing in the United States adds to the fragmentation of the policing industry (Cunningham, Strauchs, and Van Meter 1991; Reiss 1992, 65; Bayley and Shearing 1996; Jones and Newburn 1998; Loader 1999). To the extent that public and private police compete in the same market place, it seems clear that in the latter half of the twentieth century private policing considerably expanded its share of the market, with private security officers outnumbering sworn public officers by a factor of four by 1995 (Maguire and King 2004, 20; Forst 2005, 363). Yet, it is not clear that private security is moving American police out of their traditional niche; rather, it may be expanding much more aggressively into rapidly growing sectors of the market place for policing services, for example, mass private space (Shearing and Stenning 1981). Indeed, the public side of the American policing industry increased employment in the 1990s and early 2000s (Reaves 2007), a time when crime was declining nationally (Blumstein and Wallman 2006). What may have changed is the appetite for public policing services desired by communities and their ability to pay for them in an expanding national economy. Take, for example, the public's growing desire for a more community-oriented style of policing (Mastrofski 2006, 45) coupled with the emergence in 1994 of a federal program to add 100,000 officers nationally to engage in this practice (Roth 2000).

The implications of private policing's excrescence in the market place may not be obvious. First, off-duty public police are one source of labor for private policing (Reiss 1988). Second, there are at least two alternatives to a zero-sum competitive market model that have been noted abroad (Crawford 2003, 157): one in which the public police serve in a "steering capacity" to accredit and govern private policing, and another in which public and private police are coordinated in a loose network rather than in a hierarchical relationship. Adding to this complexity is the emergence in the late twentieth century of many authorizing entities other than the state (private corporations and not-for-profit groups, for example) (Shearing 1992). It remains unclear who governs the domains of private policing and to what effect. A useful line of research would establish more clearly the presence of each model and its implications for policing.

II. The Internal Structure of American Police Organizations

Organizational structure is the "internal differentiation and patterning of relationships among an organization's components" (Thompson 1967, 51). We attend to a police organization's structure because of the belief that structure plays an important role in its effectiveness. Presumably, some structures are better than others in mediating between an organization's technologies and task environment, which is characterized as those parts of an organization's surroundings or context that are "relevant or potentially relevant to goal setting and goal attainment" (Dill 1958, quoted in Thompson 1967, 27).

A. An Overview of Historical Trends

The dominant structural trend in American police agencies from the late nineteenth to the late twentieth century is "bureaucratization" (Reiss 1992, 69): more hierarchy, specialization, and formalization (specific rules/policies and documentation of adherence to them). The social, economic, and cultural forces driving this trend were manifested in various police reform waves (Fogelson 1977; Walker 1977) that appeared almost as soon as American policing shifted from avocational and entrepreneurial modes to vocational ones embedded in municipal and county organizations (Klockars 1985, chs. 2–3). Both the law and the military served as models for reform (Fogelson 1977; Klockars 1988), first creating "politicized bureaucracies" and later weakening local political influences with the introduction of civil service reforms (Reiss 1992, 69–72). The consequences for the structure of American police organizations, especially visible among medium-size and large departments, were much greater relevance of internal decision processes as political penetration declined, the elaboration of an internal command and control hierarchy designed to centralize the power of top department officials, and increased complexity in the form of the division of labor among growing numbers of specialist units. In 2010 American police organizations are still well characterized as bureaucratic, although perhaps more for larger than smaller ones in at least some ways, since most of what we know about police organization structure comes from studying departments with one hundred or more officers (Langworthy 1986; Mastrofski, Ritti, and Hoffmaster 1987; Hassell, Zhao, and Maguire 2003; Maguire 2003; Maguire et al. 2003).

B. Measuring Dimensions of Organizational Structure and Structural Change

Police organization researchers, drawing on Blau (1970) and others, have identified many dimensions of organizational structure that subsume the three described in the previous paragraph (Langworthy 1985; Maguire et al. 2003; Wilson 2003; 2006). One group pertains to how the organization's work can be divided: *functionally* (across different department units), *occupationally* (different occupations), *vertically* (hierarchical differentiation), and *spatially* (geographical dispersion). In addition, there are structural elements associated with control and coordination of the organization's work: *centralization* (the concentration of decision making), *formalization* (rules and procedures), and *administrative intensity* (resources committed to administration or support).

How much do American police agencies vary structurally, and how, if at all, is this pattern changing? Students of American police typically characterize the structure of local agencies in the United States as highly variable, yet it is not so clear just how much variation there is. This is due in large part to the difficulties in acquiring comparable data for a fully representative sample of local police agencies. Even when looking just at the fewer large agencies, the pattern of structural variability does not conform to expectations. For example, one study of large departments found impressive levels of variation on spatial differentiation, but much less variation on other forms of differentiation and control, such as formalization (Wilson 2003). One might expect even less variation among smaller agencies especially, those with fewer than twenty-five officers, because of the constraints placed by small size on the number of beats, hierarchy, functional specialization, and administrative staff (Falcone, Wells, and Weisheit 2002, 374).

How much the internal structure of police organizations has changed depends on the time frame. Recently researchers have tried to track longitudinal change from surveys of large numbers of police agencies conducted at more or less regular intervals. They have found some changes over six to eight years, but the trends are not always consistent and the changes quite modest (Maguire 1997; Maguire et al. 2003). Further, the reliability of some measures is a concern, and perhaps even more telling, so is the validity of measures derived from institutional surveys requiring a single respondent to make broad generalizations about the organization's structures (Weiss 1997; Maguire and Mastrofski 2000; Wilson 2006). Measurement reliability and validity aside, what these studies appear to show is that in the 1990s there was no dramatic change in the forms of bureaucratic structure noted by Reiss early in the decade.

C. Consequences of Structure for Organization Success

We face many challenges in learning the influence of structure on police organization performance. First is the challenge of defining and measuring success (Moore and Braga 2004). The most frequently used measures of police organization success focus on crime and disorder control and law enforcement, yet these indicators present a limited picture of what police organizations are expected to accomplish (Skogan and Frydl 2004, chs. 5–6). Less frequent are measures of citizen satisfaction or the special concerns of democratic societies, such as the abuse of police powers (use-of-force, complaints against police) (Gallagher et al. 2001; Mastrofski 2006, 58).

Second, the research on the effects of police organization structure is captive to the limitations of readily available data sets (often large surveys and censuses of American police departments and the communities they serve). The empirical analysis is impoverished by its limited capacity to test interesting theoretical propositions. Professionalism has long been a goal of American police reform (and is a key element of community- and problem-oriented policing), but studies of police organization structure virtually ignore the measurement of structural elements that might promote it (e.g., education requirements for entry and promotion, the quality of training, professional autonomy in review of police practices and citizen complaints).

Another limitation of this research is the focus on police organization structures at a given time. Longitudinal data cover a few years, but it is unrealistic to expect most trends to be distinguishable except over much longer time periods. Cross-sectional data sets make causal inference challenging, and it is very difficult to gather reliable, theoretically useful data across large numbers of agencies, not only on performance measures but to control for other influences that might mask or reveal as spurious the effects of structure on performance.

Finally, with rare exceptions American police research has avoided studying rural and small town policing, despite what appear to be profound differences from larger departments in terms of structure. The nation's major engines of police reform gear their recommendations to larger agencies, yet there is very little evidence of the value of these reforms for smaller departments. In the absence of such research, we are left to ask what works for the distinctly less-bureaucratic departments that are small and rural. In the face of all the above hurdles, it is not surprising that the National Research Council panel on policing concluded that relatively little can be said about the effects of police organization structure on actual police practice (Skogan and Frydl 2004, 173–85).

III. POLICE TECHNOLOGY

The structure of police organizations is widely thought to be influenced by and to influence technologies that police adopt. "A *technology* is a design for instrumental action that reduces the uncertainty in the cause-effect relationships involved in achieving a desired outcome" (Rogers 2003, 13–14). Technologies can have a number of components: *material* (physical), *logical* (processes that transform inputs into work products), and *social* (who does what and in what manner) (Mastrofski and Ritti 2000).

Technologies employed by the police are numerous and support diverse functions (Manning 1992, 351): *coercion* (weapons and martial arts), *mobility* (transportation vehicles), *detection* (forensics methods, such as DNA analysis), *surveillance* (closed-circuit television), and *analysis* (data mining software). Technologies may also coalesce to perform some function (Rogers 2003, 14), such as those involved in crime prevention and problem solving (Eck 2006). Some technologies have been slow to change (e.g., the basic elements of standard police patrol), while others (e.g., communications and surveillance technologies) have changed considerably, vastly increasing the accessibility of information to law enforcement officials (Haggerty and Ericson 1999). We focus on patrol and information because they afford opportunities for insights on technologies' stability and changeability.

A. Police Patrol Technology

Preventive patrol has been used by police as early as in thirteenth century Hangchow (Kelling et al. 1974), and for at least seventy years it has been the central strategy employed by American police. The technology consists of making uniformed police visible on the streets and in other public areas to create a sense of police presence sufficient to deter potential wrongdoers, and to enable them to respond quickly to developing problems and crimes in progress. The boon companion of preventive patrol is "reactive patrol," which requires the patrol officer to interrupt preventive patrol to respond to requests for intervention. Presumably, a rapid response enables the police to deal with problems before they can escalate further, catch criminals, or at least gather information and evidence that will facilitate apprehension of the offender (Spelman and Brown 1981). Together these techniques have been termed the "standard" model of police crime and disorder control because they rely heavily on interventions that are reactive and one-size-fits all, as opposed to targeted and customized (Skogan and Frydl 2004, 223).

Research conducted in the 1970s and 1980s largely discredited these standard model technologies, failing to find crime-control effects (Kelling et al. 1974; Spelman and Brown 1981), and nowadays police researchers regard these approaches as ineffective and inefficient (Sherman et al. 1997; Weisburd and Eck 2004). In the wake of these revelations, other patrol techniques have been developed and tested: disorder (broken windows) policing, police crackdowns, hot spots policing, repeat offenders policing, and community and problem-oriented policing (Bayley 2008). The evaluations of most of these approaches have produced small or no effects, mixed results, been subject to few tests, or used weak evaluation designs. The striking exception is hot spots policing, which has repeatedly yielded positive results using rigorous evaluation designs (Braga and Weisburd, 2010).

We do not have studies drawing on a representative cross-section of departments that tell us the extent to which the standard patrol model has been displaced by alternative approaches. However, some case studies of a few progressive agencies committed to community and problem-oriented policing suggest that departments implementing these reforms worked hard to maintain their commitment to standard patrol technology while creating smaller groups of patrol officers who were given time to engage in community and problem-oriented policing (Skogan 2006b, 59–64, and personal communication). Systematic observation of similar efforts in other cities has shown that although community policing specialists do spend significantly more time on nontraditional methods, traditional patrol and engaging the public in face-to-face service contacts tend to dominate the work of community policing specialists, as well as traditional patrol officers (Parks et al. 1999; Smith, Novak, and Frank 2001). Thus, while the last three decades have witnessed police agencies' experimenting with new methods for patrol officers, they do not appear yet to have supplanted the primary resource commitment of American police to continue standard preventive/reactive patrol in the traditional fashion (Lum 2009).

What could account for the persistence of a largely discredited patrol technology? One possibility is that American police are simply too invested in the structures and practices of the standard patrol technology. Another is that scientific evaluations of the standard model have not measured the performance indicators that exert the greatest influence on police policies and practices. The public still appears to place a high value on what the standard model promises to deliver: high visibility and responsiveness to individual calls for service (Jones, Newburn, and Smith 1994, 185–86; Gallagher et al. 2001; Skogan and Frydl 2004, ch. 8; Skogan 2005; 2006a; Dukes, Portillos, and Miles 2009). And it may be the very *nonstrategic* nature of the standard model that appeals to the public, as it requires less selectivity in determining who gets served, hence enhancing the view of police as equitable in the distribution of their services (Skogan and Frydl 2004, 315).

B. Information Technology

We focus our discussion of information technology (IT) on how much innovations in IT alter police structures and practices. Optimists find that technological advances improve efficiency and performance by requiring and stimulating changes in the structures, culture, and practices of policing. Skeptics find that new technologies have few effects on these aspects of policing or that they have perverse consequences (Chan 2003).

The growth in personal computers and more integrated data systems has exploded since the 1990s, and new approaches to surveillance strategies have grown rapidly as well (Allen, McGowan, and Mastrofski 1983; Haggerty and Ericson 1999; Hickman and Reaves 2006). Meanwhile, analytic technologies, though growing more slowly, also consumed more department resources (Maguire 2003, 126; O'Shea and Nicholls 2003). The impact of these ITs is variable by type of technology and police organization. For example, the widespread use of surveillance devices (e.g., CCTV) in the United Kingdom (Goold 2004) presumably frees officers from routine patrol to perform other duties. Evidence of CCTV's crime-control effectiveness is mixed (though generally positive), and is heavily contingent on the type of offense and spatial context in which the technology is used (Ratcliffe 2006, 20).

Ericson and Haggerty (1997) see the proliferation of such devices as key to facilitating the growth of police work as "information work." They and others (Chan et al. 2001) note that much of the patrol officer's time is spent acquiring, recording, and using information from records, and that this far exceeds the amount of time consumed in law enforcement activities. It is difficult to know how much time was spent on information work before the IT revolution, but we can be fairly confident that police now rely more heavily on certain IT-based forms of surveillance, for example "database policing," where officers use computers to "patrol" massive data files looking for "hits" on information they possess on suspects (Haggerty and Ericson 1999, 240; Meehan and Ponder 2002; Chan 2003, 659). Yet the technology may be less useful for other functions, such as problem-oriented policing, which require an analytic capacity to detect *patterns* in events (Nunn and Quinet 2002).

Systematic observation of police can tell us the extent to which street-level officers are investing more time in their computer screens and less in face-to-face contact with people. Perhaps more importantly, these studies can tell us how such a trend is affecting the way that the police and public conceive the police mission and how decision making is altered. Finally, the new IT may be altering police work by providing a system to structure and monitor, not only information gathering, but decision making about how to handle situations. Computerized reporting requirements essentially structure decision protocols about how to deal with situations (Ericson and Haggerty 1997), and the transparency of the officer's work is facilitated by the ready availability of this information to supervisors and even the public (Chan 2001; 2003).

What seems clear is that rapidly emerging technologies for surveillance and analysis present tremendous possibilities for radical transformation of policing. This includes the use of portable video headgear that records police-citizen interactions (Noguchi 2009) and "predictive policing," which links cutting-edge surveillance technologies with predictive analytics to anticipate and prevent problems before they occur (Bratton, Morgan, and Malinowski 2009). Little is known about the effects of such technologies, although they could profoundly reshape how police organizations control their workers as well as how the police engage and understand their work environment.

From a skeptic's perspective, the potential effects of new IT on the police organization and police work have not been realized. Much of the available evidence suggests that early experiences with technological advancements have had modest effect, have been perverted or undermined by police users, or have had unanticipated and undesirable consequences. Peter Manning (1992; 2003; 2005), one of the main proponents of this perspective, has argued that the rank-and-file workers resist using or actively undermine many of the innovative ITs. When used, they tend to be employed in support of traditional practices and structures (Weisburd et al. 2003; Willis, Mastrofski, and Weisburd 2007), or these technologies may be poorly adapted to police uses. Based on his own research and that of others, Manning concluded, "There is little evidence thirty years of funding technological innovations has produced much change in police practice or effectiveness" (Manning 2003, 136), and that the principal function of most of the new police IT has been to serve as "icons of science" that legitimate the police (Manning 2005, 243).

While Manning's skepticism may be justified, we can think of several reasons to expect that the impact of IT innovations in the first thirty years would be substantially less than what we can anticipate in the next thirty. First, technological innovations, most of them originating in other industries (Haggerty and Ericson 1999), require time to be adapted for police use. Second, many technologies require major changes in the skill set and culture of the police that can only be realized over the course of turnover of a generation or two of police workers. And third, it takes time and energy to know what structures work best for a given technology and then to adjust those well-embedded structures. Some of these new technologies may *eventually* have profound effects on police, but those who expect them early and without peripatetic trial and error will often be disappointed.

IV. The People Doing Policing

The people brought into police organizations should influence how police work is done and how successfully. From the mid-nineteenth century until well into the twentieth century, American police drew heavily on certain European immigrant groups who found police work to be a ladder for upward mobility. But other groups, such as women and blacks, were largely excluded until civil rights reforms took hold in the latter part of the twentieth century (Fogelson 1977; Walker 1977). The representation of previously excluded racial minorities has continued to increase into the twenty-first century, although in most jurisdictions it still has not achieved parity with their presence in the community (Williams and Murphy 1990; Sklansky 2006). The same can be said for women in policing (Sklansky 2006). Those brought into policing have received more formal education and training than ever before (Reaves and Hickman 2002, 3; Mastrofski 2005).

The changes in the demographic profile of American police are readily attributable to equal employment and affirmative action changes in hiring laws and court and administrative rulings, which had been stimulated by the civil rights and women's rights movements and litigation (Skogan and Frydl 2004, 79–81; Sklansky 2006; Zhao, He, and Lovrich 2006). The increasing presence of more formal education and training (Weisburd et al. 2001, 11) emerges from a more diffuse set of forces but was undoubtedly given focus since the 1970s by reformers, police leaders, and professional associations wishing to raise policing's occupational status and improve performance (Skogan and Frydl 2004, 139–42). So the profile of American police is changing, but with what consequence?

There is insufficient evidence to answer with confidence, and much of what does exist is contradictory (Sklansky 2006). A few studies document a difference between black and white officers' beliefs and attitudes, but most studies of actual behavior fail to find a difference in such things as arrest, use of force, demeanor, methods of restoring order, and engaging in community policing (Skogan and Frydl 2004, 148–49). The National Academies of Sciences panel on policing concluded that the small body of available research provided "no credible evidence that officers of different racial or ethnic backgrounds perform differently during interactions with citizens simply because of race or ethnicity" (Skogan and Frydl 2004, 148). When considering the effects of the officer's sex on police behavior and the impact of increased formal education and training on police practice, they found the amount of research too small and results too variable to offer conclusions (Skogan and Frydl 2004, 139–47, 151).

Some suspect that the changing demography of American police organizations is profoundly affecting organizational dynamics—that by having to work closely with persons of a different race, sex, or sexual orientation, the culture of policing is changing (Sklansky 2006, 1229–34). Evidence here is scant, although the emergence of "rival trade groups" of minority officers who are willing to challenge the traditional perspective of other police fraternal and bargaining units raises the possibility that these new groups encourage and sustain a more fragmented culture. It would be useful to learn the effects of different levels of minority presence on police forces by comparing the culture and practices of police in departments with different levels of minority presence.

Despite the lack of evidence on the consequences of the trend toward more demographic diversity and education/training in American police agencies, there is considerable public approval of these change trajectories, but less so on how they should be achieved and used. For example, overwhelming majorities of the American public support the principle that a community's police should reflect the racial composition of the city. Half or more (depending on race) say that more minority officers should serve more minority neighborhoods (Weitzer and Tuch 2006, 139–44). Where consensus breaks down is whether this diversity should be achieved with racially preferential hiring practices; minority citizens approve at more than twice the rate of whites. The high support for the abstract principle of police force diversification undoubtedly derives from the general support in the American populace for the desirability of representative democracy (Krislov and Rosenbloom 1981).

V. POLICE CULTURE

What changes, if any, have occurred in the things that police believe and value? For many contemporary reformers, changing the culture of police is the key to reform. We use the term "culture" for the set of understandings and interpretations that are shared within a group, that create meanings for the significant events and challenges the group experiences, that guide how members of the group deal with each other and those outside the group, that assist them in managing the strains of their shared tasks, and that distinguish the group and its members from outsiders (Skogan and Frydl 2004, 131).

A. Types of Police Culture

There are three ways in which the quality of "culture" has been ascribed to police (Paoline 2001, ch. 1). First, *occupational* culture captures those value and belief orientations that are presumed to differentiate police as an occupation from all others and the general public. Second, *organizational* culture has made possible the observation that culture may vary from one police organization to another. Third, *subculture* has introduced the proposition that across the occupation and within organizations, it is possible to distinguish distinctly different beliefs, values, and perceptions that police employ in their daily work. We draw on Paoline's (2001) review of this literature in characterizing each.

When social scientists began ethnographic studies of police, they looked for and found a number of features of contemporary police work that illuminated a monolithic occupational culture. Hypersensitivity to threats of physical danger and their special authority to coerce in fact reinforced the value of suspicion and reaction to anything that seems to undermine their authority, resulting in a sense of isolation from the general public and loyalty to fellow officers (Skolnick 1966; Westley 1970). Because police work is laden with uncertainty about what is really going on and because of the pressure to act authoritatively, officers develop very different tolerances for error than characterize people without police experience, and they resist after-the-fact judgments made with the benefit of information gathered outside the pressures of the actual decision-making environment (Bittner 1967; Muir 1977, ch. 10). Further, there may be uncertainty about what the organization hierarchy will, after the fact, judge to be the order of priorities, as well as a strong suspicion that the consequences will depend largely on matters beyond the decision maker's control (Reuss-Ianni and Ianni 1983). The pervasive threats of a punitive response from the organization encourage a lay-low-and-play-it-safe attitude toward unnecessary risk, while clinging to the ideal of the crime-fighter image.

This view of policing as a more-or-less uniform and distinct occupation has influenced scholars, policymakers, and the police themselves, but the evidence on the explanatory power of police culture as a determinant of police practice is virtually nonexistent (Skogan and Frydl 2004, 130). Researchers have not demonstrated the extent to which these features of the police culture distinguish it from other occupational groups. The ubiquity of these cultural values is undercut by research of the last four decades that shows considerable variation in how officers adhere to a common set of perspectives. We turn next to the possibility of police culture as something that varies with the organization.

Wilson's *Varieties of Police Behavior* (1968) proposed that officers' policing styles are patterned by features of police organizations (especially the chief's priorities and methods), which in turn are shaped by the political culture of their communities. His much-cited depiction of watchman, legalistic, and service style departments sought validation in field research coupled with an examination of patterns in arrest rates for various offenses. Although researchers have attempted to test various aspects of Wilson's framework (Wilson 2003), we lack a comprehensive assessment of the extent to which different organizational cultures, as reflected in the attitudes and beliefs of officers, actually distinguish police organizations and with what impact. A few studies have explored in limited terms the variation in police culture that may be attributable to police organization characteristics, examining differences in integrity standards about corruption and abuse (Klockars et al. 2000; Klockars, Ivkovic, and Haberfeld 2004, 2006) and law enforcement tendencies (Brown 1981; Mastrofski, Ritti, and Hoffmaster 1987; Terrill and Mastrofski 2004). Is there enough cultural coherence *within* police organizations to speak meaningfully about police organization culture and its consequences for practice? Researchers have simply not explored this issue in enough places to answer with confidence.

The most examined aspect of police culture has been how much it may be fragmented into subcultures within police departments. A number of studies have identified different styles of policing, some looking for distinct differences between management and street officers (Reuss-Ianni and Ianni 1983; Paoline 2001), but most focusing on the rank and file only (Broderick 1972; Muir 1977; Brown 1981; Paoline 2001; Mastrofski, Willis, and Snipes 2002; Wood, Davis, and Rouse 2004). Most of these studies highlight to what degree officers, even within the same department, exhibit different cultural orientations toward a wide range of issues. Although there are some similarities among some of the studies in the attitudes, beliefs, and perceptions that are considered, measures and methods of observation vary, especially between the studies that explore each of the three general approaches to defining police culture. Thus, while it is tempting to accept these findings as undermining the occupational and organizational cultural theses, they constitute only a fuzzy test. Careful attention to using common measures and methods across multiple jurisdictions would enable researchers to say more conclusively whether and how culture varies at all three levels.

B. Changes in Police Culture

We now turn to the question of whether police culture has changed or is changing. The answer depends upon what type of culture we are considering. If there are some aspects of police culture that bridge all American police, then by virtue of the size and complexity of the American policing industry, this would be the slowest to change and the most difficult to detect. One might do so by tracking representative samples of American police officers, conducting a survey every several years. This has not been done, but the Police Foundation conducted a single such national survey (Weisburd et al. 2001). The authors found that certain police attitudes differed substantially from the traditional characterization of the occupational culture as isolated, defensive, and hostile to legal constraints. The problem, of course, is the difficulty in assessing the validity of the studies used as a baseline to compare to this study's formulation of the "traditional view," especially if we take seriously the criticism that the earlier research was not structured to capture and measure variation (Paoline 2001).

We may also draw on case studies of police organizations that track the change in police attitudes over time. An interesting study used a variety of measures to assess whether the police culture changed over six years in two Illinois police departments that were trying to implement community policing (Rosenbaum and Wilkinson 2004). Although some changes were observed, there was backsliding, causing the researchers to conclude that the officers' orientations had not changed for the most part. While one might attribute some of this to limitations in the departments' efforts, we think it more likely represents a much broader challenge. Police organizations try to control the transmission of culture through formal mechanisms, such as selection, training, supervision, and exhortation by top leaders (Muir 1977, ch. 12), but police agencies, like many other organizations, transmit their culture largely through *informal* mechanisms over which police leaders simply have little direct control, at least in the short run. Changing fundamental police values and beliefs rarely happens as a Pentecost or revelation (Buerger 1998), but rather can be expected to evolve only as the "old hands" depart, leaving more of the new ones, who may have been selected with a particular new orientation or at least be more open to accepting new ways.

This is not to say that short-term behavioral change is impossible. There are a variety of ways to structure work to achieve compliance with expectations. Commissioner William Bratton (1998) reported "turning around" the New York City Police Department, moving it away from its lassitude about enforcing minor quality-of-life violations, but we doubt that much of the impressive increase in citations and arrests was accomplished by changing the police culture. Rather, it was by changing the supervisory and incentive/disincentive systems that harnessed existing cultural values to the leader's goals. But we hypothesize that widespread internalization of a remarkably different set of beliefs and priorities simply takes sustained effort over the course of at least a couple of generations of workers to accomplish.

VI. Governance of the Police

American democratic principles prescribe that the police be subject to the governance of other institutions in all three branches of government. The key issues here are what forms this governance takes, how much direction and oversight they impose, and with what consequence for police practice.

A. Historical Trends in Police Governance

American police governance began as a system in which police were at the center of partisan politics, but good government and professional reform waves of the first quarter of the twentieth century set in motion a series of changes (Fogelson 1977; Walker 1977; Kelling and Moore 1988). These changes shaped many police forces with the result that by mid-century they were buffered from local politicians' ability to manipulate the particulars of policing, relegating their influence primarily to selecting the chief, approving the police budget, and passing local ordinances for police to enforce.

Wilson (1968) traced a relationship between the political structure of a city (traditional and unreformed at one extreme, and reformed at the other), its structures and modes of operation, and ultimately the style of policing its officers tended to employ. The local political culture influenced police operations by establishing the boundaries within which the police could operate without concern for external interference. The key mechanism for this was the determination of who would be the police chief, not direct issue-specific intervention by elected officials. This is not inconsequential, of course, since the selection or removal of a chief can powerfully signal to his or her successor the consequences of pleasing or failing to please officials with responsibility for police governance (Reiss and Bordua 1967).

Nonetheless, these earlier reforms had clearly given police considerable freedom from everyday political intervention, but by the late 1960s they received intense public criticism for becoming too removed from the community they served, especially from ethnic minorities and the poor who lacked political power. The emergence of community policing in the 1980s is directly attributable to a desire among reformers to rebuild police legitimacy and strengthen effectiveness by establishing a bond with the community, one that had strong elements of participatory and deliberative democracy.

Police governance practices have proven not to conform so readily to sweeping historical generalizations. In the late 1970s, research showed that among a sample of twenty-four municipalities and counties, American communities still displayed considerable variety in the structures and practices of governance, some exhibiting the sort of police autonomy expected, but others retaining the artifacts of the "political" era—an active level of involvement in directing policing by local elected officials (Mastrofski 1988). A review of research on police governance showed that little research (mostly case studies) had been conducted, showing that local officials governed by shaping who sat in the chief's chair (Skogan and Frydl 2004, 196). Some of the studies suggested that the involvement of political officials in policing matters falls safely within the bounds of democratic accountability, but others found evidence of inappropriate or negative interventions (Skogan and Frydl 2004, 198–202).

Besides these case studies, most scholarship that concerns itself with the effects of governing structures on policing examines cross-sectional variation in the structures, not processes, of governance in large numbers of communities. Hence, beginning with Wilson's work, a few researchers have used cross-sectional data to assess the effects of reformed versus unreformed local political systems on staffing levels, internal organization structure, and patterns of law enforcement, but they have generally failed to replicate his findings, at least with regard to explaining variation in internal organization structure (Liederbach 2008). But, considering a broader historical perspective, this line of inquiry may be barking up the wrong governance tree. The overarching effect of decades of professional reform may well have been to move formal governing officials in many cities further to the periphery of police governance, but other entities may be filling the void. We consider one possibility, local community organizations.

B. Grassroots Governance

Inasmuch as community policing has been the most visible banner of recent progressive reform, it may be especially important to know to what extent the participatory and deliberative democracy goals for the governance of America's local police have been realized. Community policing promises to reestablish a link between the police and members of the community, but one that focuses not on promoting the political prospects of partisan interests but on improving the quality of life in neighborhoods. By encouraging residents and businesses to participate in associations that frequently and actively engage the police in public meetings, the police themselves become directly involved with them in a grassroots politics of municipal service delivery. In theory, the direct engagement of police and public in grassroots politics should have profound consequences for who gets what from the police (Thacher 2001).

Evidence on the effects of community policing on governance is mixed. For example, Chicago developed a vibrant citywide program promoting citizen participation in community groups who work with the police to identify and solve neighborhood problems (Skogan 2006b, chs. 4–5). The police and an array of other municipal services were responsive to the residents' priorities and meeting attendance rates (Skogan 2006b, 208). By contrast, Seattle's experience with police-neighborhood partnerships in the 1990s produced a very different result (Lyons 1999). Some early advances in participatory and deliberative democracy were achieved (in terms of police-public engagement, problem-solving, and accountability), but these withered, leaving the researcher to judge that they had become less a two-way communications mechanism than a means for police to garner community acquiescence to police priorities.

These experiences hardly constitute a sufficient sample from which to generalize, but the striking difference between them suggests that those wishing to understand the governance of police and its consequences during the community policing era would do well to pay at least as much attention to variations *within* jurisdictions as to variations between them. Where police have established vital grassroots linkages, there may well be developing a form of governance that renders even less relevant the traditional electoral mechanisms for influencing who gets what in the community.

VII. Stability and Change in American Policing

A leitmotif of this chapter has been the tension between the temptation to overstate the capacity of American police to resist change (Guyot 1979; Manning 2006, 104) and the temptation to overstate their susceptibility to change (Zhao 1996). In this section we consider one of the most highly visible movements to have emerged in the twenty-first century: terrorist-oriented policing. Our purpose is to use this single case (recognizing that it cannot represent all movements for change) to illuminate some of the relevant issues surrounding organizational innovation, including its origins, characteristics, and implementation. In doing so, we highlight how the scope and direction of reform may be heavily influenced by police efforts to protect the core service-oriented structures and operations that have long sustained American police. To the extent that these preservationist efforts reflect conscious leadership choices, we suspect that the motivation is primarily one of not putting at risk whatever the public currently values most.

A. Terrorist-oriented Policing as Innovation

Just as one must acknowledge the crisis mentality that spawned community policing, we are struck by the similar sense of urgency that propels the movement to involve state and local police in countering terrorism in the United States in the decade following the terrorist attacks of September 11, 2001. These events reshaped national policy and also focused attention on the role of local police in combating the threat of terrorism (Greene, 2011; Maguire and King, 2011). Unlike other recent "big reforms" such as community policing (Bayley 2008), few local police have been in the vanguard of this movement. It arguably has been led by national leaders who have urged federal law enforcement and homeland security agencies to recruit local law enforcement into this role.

Given the far greater number of state and local police officers compared with federal law enforcement agents, reformers envision a substantial counterterrorism role for local agencies. In addition to the response and recovery operations, local police are expected to be on the lookout for likely suspects or people with useful information about terrorism, to pass potentially useful information along to federal agencies, to investigate terrorists on their own, and, by collaborating with other agencies in special multi-agency Joint Terrorism Task Forces, to participate in the interrogation of suspects and witnesses, to collaborate in the disruption of terrorist plans, to perform risk analyses and target hardening recommendations, and to mobilize the community for prevention and detection (Kelling and Bratton 2006; Bayley and Weisburd 2009, 87; Greene and Herzog 2009; Maguire and King, 2011). Local police are encouraged to acquire and use special technologies to combat terrorism, to acquire special training in the use of these technologies as well as intelligence gathering, and to increase security and surveillance efforts (Lum et al. 2009).

Given the many changes called for by the movement toward terrorist-oriented policing, it represents the confluence of a large number of innovations brought to bear on local departments. Organizational focus runs the gamut from highly technical (the application of security and surveillance technologies) to administrative (extensive interagency collaboration and information sharing). It is expected to alter what all police officers look for and report in the way of suspicious persons and activities, so some of its features are central and pervasive. Yet the need for limiting the dissemination of sensitive information also demands confining information to a few people, thereby driving certain activities to the organization's peripheral, specialized units. Some demands of counterterrorism require radical changes in policing strategies (giving priority to gathering intelligence over gathering and acting on criminal evidence), but others require little or no change (making routine traffic stops and reporting them). And to the extent that reformers call for local involvement in intelligence gathering and clandestine terrorism disruption measures (called "high policing"), one can anticipate both police and public resistance to a method that is incompatible with the historical preference for a more visible, transparent, and reassuring approach (Brodeur 1983; Bayley and Weisburd 2009). Thus, even more than with community policing, we might expect to see a very mixed pattern in the willingness of local police to adopt and implement certain features of counterterrorism.

Some dramatic changes have been reported in agencies that responded to the 9/11 attacks (Holden et al. 2009), but the limited evidence available suggests that most American police agencies have been slow to adopt many of the new structures and practices of terrorist-oriented policing (Bayley and Weisburd 2009). Although a few (mostly) larger departments, such as New York City and Los Angeles, have committed significant resources to the development of terrorism intelligence units with full-time personnel (some even deployed overseas), the vast majority had not done so by 2003 (Lum et al. 2009; Schafer, Burruss, and Giblin 2009).

Thus, in the decade following the 9/11 attacks, local American police, even in most large organizations, appear to have assigned counterterrorism to the periphery of their operations, at least those parts that they are willing to report to researchers. While local law enforcement agency leaders clearly are concerned about the threat of terrorism, as judged by actions taken by agencies to plan for dealing with future attacks following 9/11 (Davis et al. 2004; International Association of Chiefs of Police 2005; Bureau of Justice Statistics 2006), there appears to be considerable ambivalence about what the role of local law enforcement should be. Most American police leaders appear reluctant to reallocate substantial resources used for dealing with the "ordinary" crime, disorder, and service needs of their communities. The "high policing" aspects of counterterrorist policing are neither visible nor tangible in the ways that routine police activities are, thus undermining a powerful source of community legitimacy and support, especially important among the segments of society most at risk for police counterterrorist attention (Bayley and Weisburd 2009, 94).

Just because counterterrorism appears not to have significantly displaced routine policing structures and practices of the local police does not mean that new developments are insignificant. One predictable consequence of the movement toward involving local police in counterterrorism is an industry that is less loosely coupled, where once impermeable information membranes between local and federal agencies (Geller and Morris 1992) are increasingly permeable. Networks designed for one purpose may be exploited for others, so America's complex police industry structure may be becoming more tightly connected by "information highways" created to combat terrorism. However, we have not observed a systemwide centralization of policing structures that several observers have associated with an increased focus on combating terror on domestic soil (Bayley and Weisburd 2009; Feucht et al. 2009; Greene and Herzog 2009).

Thus, even while the threat of terrorism remains a daily news topic, American police remain heavily focused on the same local problems, using essentially the same structures and systems that preceded 9/11. This is not to dismiss the peripheral changes (especially in specialist units) but to note that they operate largely independent from the core policing operation. Of course, this could change if the United States were subjected to a much greater frequency of terrorist attacks, such as those experienced by Israel.

VIII. Conclusion

This chapter has addressed several aspects of police organization in the twenty-first century. We have found that the American policing industry remains highly decentralized and has strong prospects for continuing to do so. This has many implications for how and how well American police do their work and with what success, but it is difficult to test propositions without meaningful cross-national comparisons to systems less fragmented than the American case.

Studies of the internal structure of American police confirm the persistence of its bureaucratic character, finding little change over short time periods. However, most of this research ignores the effects of professional structures, and hence is unable to tell us how much competing frameworks for organizational control may be developing.

We have described how some policing technologies have changed little over many decades, while recent years have observed a large number of important changes in others. There are a number of rational explanations for the persistence of standard patrol technologies in the face of scientific evidence that discredits their effectiveness. We have also indicated that although the capacity of police organizations to resist and pervert the use of new IT is great in the short run, there is evidence to suggest that profound long-term effects into the future are possible.

There are distinct trends in *who* does police work, as the numbers of racial minorities, women, and college-educated and better-trained personnel continue to grow. Although there are theories that predict that these personnel trends will have profound consequences for the practice of policing, thus far the evidence of those effects has been modest and mixed.

Police culture can assume several meanings. There is not much evidence testing the notion that policing is culturally distinct from other occupations. Relatively few studies exist that demonstrate how police *organization culture* differs and with what effects. And although there is a growing body of studies that finds diversity in the outlook of police on a number of dimensions, it is not yet obvious how influential that diversity is for the actual practice of policing.

Despite the importance of external governance to the preservation of democratic policing, this topic remains underdeveloped. Even many decades after the triumph of good-government reform, America's local governments exhibit variation in the ways that they govern their police. Case studies have tended to focus on the role of political officials. The roles of grassroots community organizations are largely unexamined, although there is reason to expect that they may be having increasing influence.

American police agencies today, as in the nineteenth century, are the target of change, often from forces outside their boundaries (Bayley 2008), but we should not underestimate the capacity of those who are members of the organization to resist (Skogan 2008), and to channel these pressures to change. Indeed, what we may have witnessed in the last few decades of the twentieth century, was an increasing capacity of police leaders to appropriate and engineer reforms that were originally powered by external pressure. Community policing, problem-oriented policing, broken-windows policing, and pulling-levers policing (Weisburd and Braga 2006) can all be understood in that way, while CompStat and the just-emerged predictive policing are the progeny of the police themselves. That does not mean that police leaders are becoming masters of the industry's destiny, but it does suggest that in our efforts to discern and predict the trajectory of police organization stability and change, we need to attend closely to the inclinations and capacities of the police themselves to shape it.

NOTES

* The authors are grateful to Roger B. Parks, who made many useful comments on an earlier draft of this manuscript. This chapter is based on a longer treatment of the topic (Mastrofski and Willis 2010) "Police Organization Continuity and Change: Into the Twenty-first Century." In *Crime and Justice: A Review of Research*, vol. 39, edited by Michael Tonry. Chicago: University of Chicago Press.

REFERENCES

Allen, David N., Robert P. McGowan, and Stephen D. Mastrofski. 1983. "Analytic Reports and Computerized Information Processing in Medium and Large Police Agencies." *Computers, Environment, and Urban Systems* 8, no. 3: 175–86.

Altshuler, A. A. 1970. *Community Control*. New York,: Bobbs-Merrill Co.

Bayley, David H. 1985. *Patterns of Policing: A Comparative Analysis*. New Brunswick, NJ: Rutgers University Press.

———. 1992. "Comparative Organization of the Police in English-Speaking Countries." In *Modern Policing*, edited by Michael Tonry and Norval Morris. Vol. 15 of *Crime and Justice: A Review of Research,* edited by Michael Tonry. Chicago: University of Chicago Press.

———. 2008. "Police Reform: Who Done it?" *Policing and Society* 18, no. 1: 7–17.

Bayley, David H., and Clifford D. Shearing. 1996. "The Future of Policing." *Law and Society Review* 30, no. 3: 585–606.

Bayley, David H., and David Weisburd. 2009. "Cops and Spooks: The Role of the Police in Counterterrorism." In *To Protect and To Serve: Policing in an Age of Terrorism*, ed. David Weisburd, Thomas E. Feucht, Idit Hakimi, Lois Felson Mock, and Simon Perry. New York: Springer.

Bittner, Egon. 1967. "The Police on Skid-Row: A Study of Peace Keeping." *American Sociological Review* 32:699–715.

Blau, Peter M. 1970. "A Formal Theory of Differentiation in Organizations." *American Sociological Review* 35:201–18.

Blumstein, Alfred, and Joel Wallman, eds. 2006. *The Crime Drop in America*. Cambridge: Cambridge University Press.

Braga, Anthony A., and David L. Weisburd. 2010. *Policing Problem Places: Crime Hot Spots and Effective Prevention*. New York: Oxford University Press.

Bratton William, with Peter Knobler. 1998. *Turnaround: How America's Top Cop Reversed the Crime Epidemic*. New York: Random House.

Bratton, William, John Morgan, and Sean Malinowski. 2009. "Fighting Crime in the Information Age: The Promise of Predictive Policing." Paper presented at the annual meeting of the American Society of Criminology. Philadelphia, PA.

Broderick, John J. 1972. *Police in a Time of Change*. Morristown, NJ: General Learning Press.

Brodeur, Jean-Paul. 1983. "High and Low Policing: Remarks about the Policing of Political Activities." *Social Problems* 39, no. 5: 507–20.

Brown, Michael K. 1981. *Working the Street: Police Discretion and the Dilemmas of Reform.* New York: Russell Sage Foundation.

Buerger, Michael. 1998. "*Police* Training as a *Pentecost*: Using Tools Singularly Ill-Suited to the Purpose of Reform." *Police Quarterly* 1:27–63.

Bureau of Justice Statistics. 2006. *Law Enforcement Management and Administrative Statistics LEMAS:2003 Sample Survey of Law Enforcement Agencies.* Washington, DC: US Department of Justice.

———. 2007. *Census of State and Local Law Enforcement Agencies, 2004.* Bulletin NCJ 212749. Washington, DC: US Department of Justice.

Chan, Janet. 2001. "The Technological Game: How Information Technology is Transforming Police Practice." *Criminal Justice* 1, no. 2: 139–59.

———. 2003. "Police and New Technologies." In *Handbook of Policing*, ed. Tim Newburn. Portland, OR: Willan Publishing.

Chan, Janet, D. Brereton, M. Legosz, and S. Doran. 2001. *E-policing: The Impact of Information Technology on Police Practices.* Brisbane: Criminal Justice Commission.

Cordner, Gary W. 1989. "Police Agency Size and Investigative Effectiveness." *Journal of Criminal Justice* 17, no. 3: 145–55.

Crank, John P., and L. E. Wells. 1991. "The Effects of Size and Urbanism on Structure Among Illinois Police Departments." *Justice Quarterly* 8:169–82.

Crawford, Adam. 2003. "The Pattern of Policing in the UK: Policing beyond the Police." In *Handbook of Policing*, ed. Tim Newburn. Portland, OR: Willan.

Cunningham, W. C., J. Strauchs, and C. Van Meter. 1991. *Private Security: Patterns and Trends.* Washington, DC: National Institute of Justice.

Davis, L. M., J. K. Riley, G. Ridgeway, J. E. Pace, S. K. Cotton, P. Steinberg, K. Damphousse, and B. L. Smith. 2004. *When Terrorism Hits Home: How Prepared are State and Local Law Enforcement?* Santa Monica, CA: RAND Corporation.

Dill, William R. 1958. "Environment as an Influence on Managerial Autonomy." *Administrative Science Quarterly* 2:409–43.

Douthit, Nathan. 1975. "August Vollmer, Berkeley's First Chief of Police, and the Emergence of Police Professionalism." *California Historical Quarterly* 54(Spring): 101–24.

Dukes, Richard L., Edwardo Portillos, and Molly Miles. 2009. "Models of Satisfaction with Police Service." *Policing: An International Journal of Police Strategies and Management* 32, no. 2: 297–318.

Eck, John E. 2006. "Science, Values, and Problem-oriented Policing: Why Problem-oriented Policing?" In *Police Innovation: Contrasting Perspectives*, ed. David Weisburd and Anthony A. Braga. New York: Cambridge University Press.

Ericson, Richard V., and Kevin D. Haggerty. 1997. *Policing the Risk Society.* Toronto: University of Toronto Press.

Falcone, David N., L. Edward Wells, and Ralph A. Weisheit. 2002. "The Small-town Police Department." *Policing: An International Journal of Police Strategies and Management* 25, no. 2: 371–84.

Feucht, Thomas E., David Weisburd, Simon Perry, Lois Felson Mock, and Idit Hakimi. 2009. In *To Protect and To Serve: Policing in an Age of Terrorism*, ed. David Weisburd, Thomas E. Feucht, Idit Hakimi, Lois Felson Mock, and Simon Perry. New York: Springer.

Fogelson, Robert M. 1977. *Big City Police.* Cambridge, MA: Harvard University Press.

Forst, Brian. 2005. "Private Policing." In *Encyclopedia of Law Enforcement*, vol. 1: *State and Local*, ed. Larry E. Sullivan and Marie Simonetti Rosen. Thousand Oaks, CA: Sage Publications.

Gallagher, Catherine, Edward Maguire, Stephen D. Mastrofski, and Michael Reisig. 2001. *The Public Image of the Police: Final Report to the International Association of Chiefs of Police.* Manassas, VA: George Mason University, Administration of Justice Program. http://marcpi.jhu.edu/marcpi/Ethics/ethics_toolkit/public_image.htm.

Geller, William A., and Norval Morris. 1992. "Relations between Federal and Local Police." In *Modern Policing*, edited by Michael Tonry and Norval Morris. Vol. 15 of *Crime and Justice: A Review of Research,* edited by Michael Tonry. Chicago: University of Chicago Press.

Goold, Benjamin. 2004. *CCTV and Policing: Public Area Surveillance and Police Practices in Britain.* Oxford: Oxford University Press.

Greene, Jack R. 2011. "Community Policing and Terrorism: Problems and Prospects for Local Community Security." In *Criminologists on Terrorism and Homeland Security*, ed. Brian Forst, Jack Greene, and James Lynch. Cambridge: Cambridge University Press.

Greene, Jack R., and Sergio Herzog. 2009. "The Implications of Terrorism on the Formal and Social Organization of Policing in the US and Israel: Some Concerns and Opportunities." In *To Protect and To Serve: Policing in an Age of Terrorism*, ed. David Weisburd, Thomas E. Feucht, Idit Hakimi, Lois Felson Mock, and Simon Perry. New York: Springer.

Guyot, Dorothy. 1979. "Bending Granite: Attempts to Change the Rank Structure of American Police Departments." *Journal of Police Science and Administration* 7, no. 3: 253–84.

Haggerty, Kevin D., and Richard V. Ericson. 1999. "The Militarization of Policing in the Information Age." *Journal of Political and Military Sociology* 27, no. 2: 233–55.

Hassell, Kimberly D., Jihong "Solomon" Zhao, and Edward R. Maguire. 2003. "Structural Arrangements in Large Municipal Police Organizations: Revisiting Wilson's Theory of Local Political Culture." *Policing: An International Journal of Police Strategies and Management* 26, no. 2: 231–50.

Hickman, Matthew J., and Brian A. Reaves. 2006. *Local Police Departments, 2003.* Washington, DC: Bureau of Justice Statistics.

Holden, Gwen, Gerard Murphy, Corina Solé Brito, and Joshua Ederheimer. 2009. *Learning from 9/11: Organizational Change in the New York City and Arlington County, VA., Police Departments.* NCJ 2273456. Washington, DC: National Institute of Justice.

International Association of Chiefs of Police. 2005. *Post 9–11 Policing: The Crime-control-homeland Security Paradigm—Taking Command of New Realities.* Alexandria, VA: International Association of Chiefs of Police.

Jones, Trevor, and Timothy Newburn. 1998. *Private Security and Public Policing.* Oxford: Clarendon Press.

Jones, Trevor, Tim Newburn, and D. J. Smith. 1994. "Policing and the Idea of Democracy." *British Journal of Criminology* 36, no. 2: 182–98.

Kelling, George L., and William J. Bratton. 2006. *Policing Terrorism.* New York: Manhattan Institute. http://www.manhattan-institute.org/html/cb_43.htm.

Kelling, George L., and Mark H. Moore. 1988. "From Political to Reform to Community: The Evolving Strategy of Police." In *Community Policing: Rhetoric or Reality*, ed. Jack R. Greene and Stephen D. Mastrofski. New York: Praeger.

Kelling, George L., Tony Pate, Duane Dieckman, and Charles E. Brown. 1974. *The Kansas City Preventive Patrol Experiment: A Summary Report.* Washington, DC: Police Foundation.

King, William R. 2009. "Toward a Life-Course Perspective of Police Organizations." *Journal of Research in Crime and Delinquency* 346, no. 2: 213–44.

Klinger, David A. 2004. "Environment and Organization: Reviving a Perspective on the Police." *Annals of the American Academy of Political and Social Science* 593 (May): 119–36.

Klockars, Carl B. 1985. *The Idea of Police*. Beverly Hills, CA: Sage Publications.

———. 1988. "The Rhetoric of Community Policing." In *Community Policing: Rhetoric or Reality*, ed. Jack R. Greene and Stephen D. Mastrofski. New York: Praeger.

Klockars, Carl B., Sanja Kutnjak Ivkovich, William E. Harver, and Maria R. Haberfeld. 2000. *The Measurement of Police Integrity*. Research in Brief. Washington, DC: National Institute of Justice.

Klockars, Carl B., Sanja Kutnjak Ivkovic, and Maria R. Haberfeld. 2004. *The Contours of Police Integrity*. Thousand Oaks, CA: Sage.

———. 2006. *Enhancing Police Integrity*. Dordrecht, Netherlands: Springer.

Krislov, Samuel, and David H. Rosenbloom. 1981. *Representative Bureaucracy and the American Political System*. New York: Praeger.

Langworthy, Robert H. 1985. "Police Department Size and Agency Structure." *Journal of Criminal Justice* 13:15–27

———. 1986. *The Structure of Police Organizations*. Westport, CT: Praeger.

Langworthy, Robert H., and Michael J. Hindelang. 1983. "Effects of Police Agency Size on the Use of Police Employees: A Reexamination of Ostrom, Parks, and Whitaker." *Police Studies* 5:11–19.

Liederbach, John. 2008. "Wilson Redux: Another Look at Varieties of Police Behavior." *Police Quarterly* 11, no. 4: 447–67.

Loader, Ian. 1999. "Consumer Culture and the Commodification of Policing and Security." *Sociology* 33, no. 2: 373–92.

Lum, Cynthia 2009. *Translating Police Research into Practice*. Ideas in American Policing, Washington, DC: The Police Foundation.

Lum, Cynthia, Maria Maki Haberfeld, George Fachner, and Charles Lieberman. 2009. "Police Activities to Counter Terrorism: What We Know and What We Need to Know." In *To Protect and To Serve: Policing in an Age of Terrorism*, ed. David Weisburd, Thomas E. Feucht, Idit Hakimi, Lois Felson Mock, and Simon Perry. New York: Springer.

Lyons, William. 1999. *The Politics of Community Policing: Rearranging the Power to Punish*. Ann Arbor: University of Michigan Press.

Maguire, Edward R. 1997. "Structural Change in Large Municipal Police Organizations during the Community Policing Era." *Justice Quarterly* 14, no. 3: 547–76.

———. 2003. *Organizational Structure in American Police Agencies: Context, Complexity, and Control*. Albany: State University of New York Press.

Maguire, Edward R., and William R. King. 2004. "Trends in the Policing Industry." *Annals of the American Academy of Political and Social Science* 593:15–41.

———. 2007. "The Changing Landscape of American Police Organizations." In *Policing 2020: Exploring the Future of Crime, Communities, and Policing*, ed. Joseph A. Schafer. Washington, DC: Federal Bureau of Investigation.

———. 2011. "Federal-Local Coordination in Homeland Security." In *Criminologists on Terrorism and Homeland Security*, ed. Brian Forst, Jack Greene, and James Lynch. Cambridge: Cambridge University Press.

Maguire, Edward R., and Stephen D. Mastrofski. 2000. "Patterns of Community Policing in the United States." *Police Quarterly* 3, no. 1: 4–45.

Maguire, Edward R., Yeunhee Shin, Jihong "Solomon" Zhao, and Kimberly D. Hassell. 2003. "Structural Change in Large Police Agencies during the 1990s." *Policing: An International Journal of Police Strategies and Management* 26, no. 2: 251–75.

Manning, Peter K. 1992. "Information Technologies and the Police." In *Modern Policing*, edited by Michael Tonry and Norval Morris. Vol. 15 of *Crime and Justice: A Review of Research,* edited by Michael Tonry. Chicago: University of Chicago Press.

———. 2003. *Policing Contingencies.* Chicago, IL: University of Chicago Press.

———. 2005. "Information Technologies." In *Encyclopedia of Law Enforcement*, vol. 1: *State and Local*, ed. Larry E. Sullivan and Marie Simonetti Rosen. Thousand Oaks, CA: Sage Publications.

———. 2006. "The United States of America." In *Plural Policing: A Comparative Perspective*, ed. Trevor Jones and Tim Newburn. London: Routledge.

Mastrofski, Stephen D. 1981. "Reforming Police: The Impact of Patrol Assignment Patterns on Officer Behavior in Urban Residential Neighborhoods." PhD diss., University of North Carolina.

———. 1988. "Varieties of Police Governance in Metropolitan America." *Politics and Policy* 8:12–31.

———. 1989. "Police Agency Consolidation: Lessons from a Case Study." In *Police Management Today*, ed. James J. Fyfe. Washington, DC: International City Management Association.

———. 2005. "Education of Police." In *Encyclopedia of Law Enforcement*, vol. 1: *State and Local*, ed. Larry E. Sullivan and Marie Simonetti Rosen. Thousand Oaks, CA: Sage Publications.

———. 2006. "Community Policing: A Skeptical View." In *Police Innovation: Contrasting Perspectives*, ed. David Weisburd and Anthony A. Braga. New York: Cambridge University Press.

Mastrofski, Stephen D., and R. Richard Ritti. 1996. "Police Training and the Effects of Organization on Drunk Driving Enforcement." *Justice Quarterly* 13:291–320.

———. 2000. Making Sense of Community Policing: A Theoretical Perspective. *Police Practice and Research Journal* 1, no. 2: 183–210.

Mastrofski, Stephen D., R. Richard Ritti, and Debra Hoffmaster. 1987. "Organizational Determinants of Police Discretion: The Case of Drinking-Driving." *Journal of Criminal Justice* 15:387–402.

Mastrofski, Stephen D., and James J. Willis. 2010. "Police Organization Continuity and Change: Into the Twenty-first Century." In *Crime and Justice: A Review of Research*, vol. 39, edited by Michael Tonry. Chicago: University of Chicago Press

Mastrofski, Stephen D., James J. Willis, and Jeffrey B. Snipes. 2002. "Styles of Patrol in a Community Policing Context." In *The Move to Community Policing: Making Change Happen*, ed. Merry Morash and J. K. Ford. Thousand Oaks, CA: Sage.

McDavid, James. 1977. "The Effects of Interjurisdictional Cooperation on Police Performance in the St. Louis Metropolitan Area." *Publius* 7, no. 2: 3–30.

Meehan, Albert J., and Michael Ponder. 2002. "Race and Place: The Ecology of Racial Profiling African American Motorists." *Justice Quarterly* 19, no. 3: 401–32.

Moore, Mark, and Anthony Braga. 2004. "Police Performance Measurement: A Normative Framework." *Criminal Justice Ethics* 23:3–19.

Muir, William Ker, Jr. 1977. *Police: Streetcorner Politicians.* Chicago: University of Chicago Press.

Murphy, Patrick, and T. Plate. 1977. *Commissioner: A View from the Top.* New York: Simon and Schuster.

Noguchi, Sharon. 2009. "San Jose Police Test Head-Mounted Cameras for Officers." http://www.mercurynews.com/ci_14030412?source=most_viewed.

Nunn, Sam, and Kenna Quinet. 2002. "Evaluating the Effects of Information Technology on Problem-oriented Policing: If It Doesn't Fit, Must We Quit?" *Evaluation Review* 26, no. 1: 81–108.

O'Shea, Timothy C., and Keith Nicholls. 2003. "Police Crime Analysis: A Survey of US Police Departments with 100 or More Sworn Personnel." *Police Practice and Research* 4, no. 3: 233–50.

Ostrom, Elinor, Roger B. Parks, and Gordon P. Whitaker. 1978. *Patterns of Metropolitan Policing.* Cambridge, MA: Ballinger.

Ostrom, Elinor, and Dennis C. Smith. 1976. "On the Fate of 'Lilliputs' in Metropolitan Policing." *Public Administration Review* 36, no. 2: 192–200.

Paoline, Eugene A., III. 2001. *Rethinking Police Culture: Officers' Occupational Attitudes.* New York: LFB Scholarly Publishing.

Parks, Roger B. 2009. "Metropolitan Organization and Police." In *The Practice of Constitutional Development*, ed. Filippo Sabetti, Barbara Allen, and Mark Sproule-Jones. Lanham, MD: Lexington Books.

Parks, Roger B., Stephen D. Mastrofski, Christina DeJong, and M. Kevin Gray. 1999. "How Officers Spend Their Time with the Community." *Justice Quarterly* 16: 483–518.

President's Commission on Law Enforcement and Administration of Justice. 1967. *The Challenge of Crime in a Free Society.* Washington, DC: US Government Printing Office.

Ratcliffe, Jerry. 2006. *Video Surveillance of Public Places.* Washington, DC: Office of Community Oriented Policing Services.

Reaves, Brian A. 2007. *Census of State and Local Law Enforcement Agencies, 2004.* Washington, DC: Bureau of Justice Statistics.

Reaves, Brian A., and Matthew J. Hickman. 2002. *Police Departments in Large Cities, 1990–2000.* Washington, DC: Bureau of Justice Statistics.

Reiss, Albert J., Jr. 1988. *Private Employment of Public Police.* Washington, DC: National Institute of Justice.

———. 1992. "Police Organization in the Twentieth Century." In *Modern Policing*, edited by Michael Tonry and Norval Morris. Vol. 15 of *Crime and Justice: A Review of Research*, edited by Michael Tonry. Chicago: University of Chicago Press.

Reiss, Albert J. Jr., and David J. Bordua. 1967. "Environment and Organization: A Perspective on the Police." In *The Police: Six Sociological Essays,* ed. David J. Bordua. New York: John Wiley and Sons.

Reuss-Ianni, Elizabeth, and F. A. J. Ianni. 1983. "Street Cops and Management Cops: The Two Cultures of Policing." In *Control in the Police Organization*, ed. Maurice Punch, 251–74. Cambridge, MA: MIT Press.

Rogers, Everett. 2003. *Diffusion of Innovations.* 5th ed. New York: The Free Press.

Rosenbaum, Dennis P., and Deanna L. Wilkinson. 2004. "Can Police Adapt? Tracking the Effects of Organizational Reform over Six Years." In *Community Policing: Can It Work*, ed. Wesley G. Skogan. Belmont, CA: Wadsworth.

Roth, Jeffrey A., ed. 2000. *National Evaluation of the COPS Program—Title I of the 1994 Crime Act*. Washington, DC: National Institute of Justice.

Schafer, Joseph A., George W. Burruss, Jr., and Matthew J. Giblin. 2009. "Measuring Homeland Security Innovation in Small Municipal Agencies: Policing in a Post–9/11 World." *Police Quarterly* 12, no. 3: 263–88.

Scott, W. Richard. 1998. *Organizations: Rational, Natural, and Open Systems*. 4th ed. Upper Saddle River, NJ: Prentice Hall.

Shearing, Clifford D. 1992. "The Relation between Public and Private Policing." In *Modern Policing*, edited by Michael Tonry and Norval Morris. Vol. 15 of *Crime and Justice: A Review of Research*, edited by Michael Tonry. Chicago: University of Chicago Press.

Shearing, Clifford D., and Philip C. Stenning. 1981. "Modern Private Security: Its Growth and Implications." In *Crime and Justice: A Review of Research*, vol. 3, edited by Michael Tonry and Norval Morris. Chicago: University of Chicago Press.

Sherman, Lawrence, Denise Gottfredson, Doris Mackenzie, John Eck, Peter Reuter, and Shawn Bushway. 1997. *Preventing Crime: What Works, What Doesn't, What's Promising*. Washington, DC: National Institute of Justice, US Department of Justice.

Sklansky, David Alan. 2006. "Not Your Father's Police Department: Making Sense of the New Demographics of Law Enforcement." *Journal of Criminal Law and Criminology* 96, no. 3: 1209–44.

Skogan, Wesley G. 2005. "Citizen Satisfaction with Police Encounters." *Police Quarterly* 8, no. 3: 298–301.

———. 2006a. "Asymmetry in the Impact of Encounters with Police." *Policing and Society* 16, no. 2: 99–126.

———. 2006b. *Police and Community in Chicago: A Tale of Three Cities*. New York: Oxford University Press.

———. 2008. "Why Reforms Fail." *Policing and Society* 18, no. 1: 23–34.

Skogan, Wesley, and Kathleen Frydl, eds. 2004. *Fairness and Effectiveness in Policing: The Evidence*. Washington, DC: National Academies Press.

Skolnick, Jerome H. 1966. *Justice without Trial: Law Enforcement in Democratic Society*. New York: Wiley.

Smith, Brad W., Kenneth J. Novak, and James Frank. 2001. "Community Policing and the Work Routines of Street-Level Officers." *Criminal Justice Review* 26, no. 1: 17–37.

Spelman, William G., and Dale K. Brown. 1981. *Calling the Police: A Replication of the Citizen Reporting Component of the Kansas City Response Time Analysis*. Washington, DC: Police Executive Research Forum.

Terrill, William, and Stephen D. Mastrofski. 2004. "Toward a Better Understanding of Police Use of Nonlethal Force." In *Police Integrity and Ethics*, ed. Alex Piquero, Matthew Hickman, and Jack R. Greene. Belmont, CA: Wadsworth.

Thacher, David. 2001. "Equity and Community Policing: A New View of Community Partnerships." *Criminal Justice Ethics* (Winter/Spring): 3–16.

Thompson, James D. 1967. *Organizations in Action: Social Science Bases of Administrative Theory*. New York: McGraw-Hill.

Tully, Edward J. 2002. "Regionalization or Consolidation of Law Enforcement Services in the United States." National Executive Institute Associates, Major Chiefs Association and Major County Sheriff's Association. http://www.neiassociatews.org/regionalization.htm.

Walker, Samuel. 1977. *A Critical History of Police Reform: The Emergence of Professionalism*. Lexington, MA: Heath and Company.

Weisburd, David, and Anthony A. Braga. 2006. "Introduction: Understanding Police
    Innovation." In *Police Innovation: Contrasting Perspectives*, ed. David Weisburd and
    Anthony A. Braga. New York: Cambridge University Press.
Weisburd, David, and John E. Eck. 2004. "What Can Police Do to Reduce Crime, Disorder,
    and Fear?" *Annals of the American Academy of Political and Social Science* 593 (May):
    42–65.
Weisburd, David, Rosann Greenspan, Edwin E. Hamilton, Kellie A. Bryant, and Hubert
    Williams. 2001. *The Abuse of Police Authority: A National Survey of Police Officers'
    Attitudes*. Washington, DC: Police Foundation.
Weisburd, David, Stephen D. Mastrofski, Anne-Marie McNally, Rosann Greenspan, and
    James J. Willis. 2003. "Reforming to Preserve: CompStat and Strategic Problem-
    Solving in American Policing." *Criminology and Public Policy* 2:421–56.
Weisheit, Ralph A. 2005. "Rural Police." In *Encyclopedia of Law Enforcement*, vol. 1: *State
    and Local*, ed. Larry E. Sullivan and Marie Simonetti Rosen. Thousand Oaks, CA: Sage
    Publications.
Weisheit, Ralph A., and Carl W. Hawkins Jr. 1997. "The State of Community Policing in
    Small Towns and Rural Areas." In *Community Policing in a Rural Setting*, ed. Quint C.
    Thurman and Edmund F. McGarrell. Cincinnati, OH: Anderson Publishing Co.
Weisheit, Ralph A., and L. E. Wells. 1999. *Crime and Policing in Rural and Small-town
    America*, 2nd ed. Pospect Heights, IL: Waveland.
Weiss, Alexander. 1997. "The Communication of Innovation in American Policing."
    Policing: An International Journal of Police Strategies and Management 29, no. 2:
    292–310.
Weitzer, Ronald, and Steven A. Tuch. 2006. *Race and Policing in America: Conflict and
    Reform*. New York: Cambridge University Press.
Westley, William A. 1970. *Violence and the Police: A Sociological Study of Law, Custom, and
    Morality*. Cambridge, MA: MIT Press.
Williams, Hubert, and Patrick Murphy. 1990. "Evolving Strategy of Police: A Minority
    View." Report to the National Institute of Justice. Washington, DC: National Institute
    of Justice.
Willis, James J., Stephen D. Mastrofski, and David Weisburd. 2007. "Making Sense of
    CompStat: A Theory-based Analysis of Organizational Change in Three Police
    Departments." *Law and Society Review* 41: 147–88.
Wilson, James Q. 1968. *Varieties of Police Behavior: The Management of Law and Order in
    Eight Communities*. Cambridge, MA: Harvard University Press.
Wilson, Jeremy M. 2003. "*Measurement and Association in the Structure of Municipal Police
    Organizations*" 26, no. 2: 276–97.
———. 2006. *Community Policing in America*. New York: Routledge.
Wood, Richard L., Mariah Davis, and Amelia Rouse. 2004. "Diving into Quicksand:
    Program Implementation and Police Subcultures." In *Community Policing: Can it
    Work*, edited by Wesley G. Skogan. Belmont, CA: Wadsworth.
Zhao, Jihong. 1996. *Why Police Organizations Change: A Study of Community-Oriented
    Policing*. Washington, DC: Police Executive Research Forum.
Zhao, Jihong "Solomon," Ni He, and Nicholas P. Lovrich. 2006. "Pursuing Gender Diversity
    in Police Organizations in the 1990s: A Longitudinal Analysis of Factors Associated
    with the Hiring of Female Officers." *Police Quarterly* 9: 463–85.

CHAPTER 17

....

POLICE AND CRIME CONTROL

....

LAWRENCE W. SHERMAN[*]

THE democratic police institution can do more about crime today than at any previous time in its history. The growth of rigorous evidence about what works in policing has substantially expanded police knowledge about more effective ways to control crime. Yet the result is a paradox: the more we learn from research, the bigger the gap becomes between knowledge and practice. Police today may actually do *less* than they *can* do, or what scientific knowledge *suggests* can be done, than at any other time in police history. This growing gap means that

- Police do not do many things that could enhance the prevention and detection of crime, which research finds to be cost-effective.
- Police invest substantially in practices that increase crime, such as making misdemeanor arrests of juveniles and domestic violence offenders.
- Police invest far more time in the "standard model" of policing than in the cost-effective "customized policing" approach that research has identified.
- Police—like doctors—often reject research evidence that could enhance public safety, without citing good logical or factual basis for their views.
- Police-led science may be the necessary condition for a major change to science-led policing.

This paradox of growing knowledge afflicts many aspects of government in an evidence-based society: *the more evidence we have about what can be done, the greater the potential failure to do it.* Only a relentless institutional commitment to digesting and applying the latest research evidence on policing can reduce, if not resolve, this paradox. That commitment, in turn, depends upon the police institution's recognition of a growing knowledge base and the value of that knowledge for continuous improvement in police practices.

This chapter examines the growing gap between evidence and practice in democratic policing, primarily in the English-speaking nations (especially the United States, the United Kingdom, and Australia). Section I describes the framework for evidence-based knowledge about policing for crime control, with recent advances in some of the tools for generating such knowledge. It considers four kinds of evidence that can enhance police effectiveness. The first is reliable measurement and classification, which still plagues crime statistics from London to New Delhi. The second, with enormous potential, is the prediction of crime, or "predictive policing" as it has recently been labeled. Predictions can help to allocate resources to prevent the greatest harms to society, with a triage letting some problems get less attention because they are predicted to be less harmful than certain people or crimes. A third kind of evidence is about theories of causation, which are central to policing but rarely given healthy debate. Section I concludes by analyzing how we know the most fundamental knowledge about evidence-based practice: what works, what doesn't, and the comparative cost effectiveness of different practices.

Section II describes our knowledge about the effectiveness of two very different approaches to policing: the traditional "standard model," and the newly emergent "customized policing" model. Each part of this analysis considers two questions in sequence: what does research show, and what do police generally do? The research shows that the speed of police responses to calls for service make little difference in the protection of crime victims or the arrest of an offender, but many police agencies still invest substantial resources in rapid response. The research shows that detectives could use tools to predict which cases they are most likely to solve, but many police agencies invest equal resources in crimes that are solvable and crimes that are not. The research shows that collecting more DNA evidence at burglary scenes could lead to the arrest of many more burglars, but police generally do not collect such evidence. The research shows that customized policing of "hot spots," repeat offenders, and continuing problems (or patterns) of crime and disorder reported to police are all effective strategies, but police rarely invest as much in them as in the "standard model." Finally, the research shows that making arrests in certain kinds of cases merely causes more crime, but police continue to do so for reasons of public expectation.

In summary, section II reviews the police activities about which the most is known, and where the gap between knowledge and practice is greatest. Yet it also shows how much has been learned, and how complex the knowledge requirements for *optimal* policing have become. This leads to the final question that the chapter can only briefly address: the question of "GRIP."

In section III, "Police Demand for Knowledge," the brief discussion of GRIP concludes the chapter with two specific issues in the future of policing: what can be done to close the gap between research evidence and police practice, and how can that strategy be accomplished? The answers offered are informed by two examples of how knowledge revolutions have transformed major institutions: agriculture and medicine. While neither of those examples shows a complete closing of the gap between knowledge and practice, they both show substantial progress at what this chapter calls a "GRIP": getting research into practice. The evidence suggests that the best prospects of GRIP lie in efforts to increase the demand for knowledge by police leaders. Graduate programs customized for police leadership, fed by political pressure on police to improve their performance, may also play an important role. As the political environment of policing changes, that could lead in turn to police-led science. And that, in turn, could foster science-led policing.

I. Evidence and Crime Control: A Framework

Any reading of a series of reviews of what is known about police and crime control, now spanning four decades (Sherman 1974, 1983, 1986, 1990, 1992*a*, 1995, 1997*a*, 1998*a*, 2001, 2011), must note the growth of evidence on key questions. The key questions are about (1) how much crime, of what type, is occurring over time and across space, (2) how can we best predict where, when, by and against whom crime will occur in the immediate future, (3) what theories may best explain why and how to make better predictions of criminal events, and (4) how cost-effective are various police practices designed to control crime.

It is important to establish the idea of evidence-based practice as encompassing *all* of these questions, not just the cost-effectiveness question of "what works." Answers to "what works?" depend upon answers to the other key questions of measurement, theories, and prediction. The same policy or practice may cause very different results with different classifications of crimes, victims or criminals, places or neighborhoods, cultures or ethnic groups. The evidence needed for policing is far broader than the results of a series of experiments, or what we know about cost-effectiveness.

Many dimensions of each of these questions have enjoyed substantial advances in knowledge since the 1970s. What follows here is a selective review of the advances in evidence that have been of particular relevance to policing.

A. Measurement and Classification

Police measurement and classification of crime cannot be taken for granted. It is still absent in many parts of the world. Even in the United States, many cities only attained reasonably reliable crime measurement in the 1990s (Sherman 1997a). Debates still rage over whether statistics are reliable (e.g., Rashbaum 2010). Given the crucial role of crime rates as evidence of police performance, the lack of evidence about crime measurement remains a core issue for evidence-based policing (Sherman 1998b). While some police agencies claim to have extensive internal auditing of crime reporting, the data are not made public, nor are they subjected to independent scrutiny. Absent transparency about how we measure the reliability of crime data, the idea that police can control crime at all is subject to distrust and debate.

Even in the United Kingdom, which has among the most reliable crime reporting in the world, controversy plagues the reliability of crime statistics. As recently as 2010, the UK Statistics Commissioner reprimanded a major political leader for misusing crime trend data (McSmith 2010). At the same time, however, the multiple institutions established there to audit police practice make for greater levels of evidence about how police classify and count crime. Whether or not these audits increase trust and confidence in police, they at least provide an evidence base for crime data to which the rest of the world can aspire.

Whatever their flaws, crime data are now being put to broader and more precise use than ever before. Two developments helped to put crime stats to work. One was the revolution of information technology, converting police records from paper to electronic files. The other was the performance revolution, which used the newly digitized records to manage police actions in relation to short-term trends and differences in crime rates. These two changes are most famously reflected in "CompStat," a management-by-crime-statistics strategy developed in New York City in 1993 that soon spread across the world (Sherman 1997a; Bratton 1998). The CompStat, or "comparative statistics" method of managing police agencies, broke down crude totals of crime into specific crime patterns that could be targeted by police operations.

Computerized evidence about crime patterns is now far more precise and useful than ever. In keeping with the premises of problem-oriented policing (Goldstein 1979, 1990), police can mine their data for patterns as specific as "home invasion robberies of Puerto Rican grocery store owners in the Bronx who keep cash under their mattresses." Identification of such patterns clearly helps to investigate the offenses and arrest the offenders. It also helps police to *prevent* such crimes, by such problem-solving methods as visiting the kinds of people who have been victimized, encouraging them to keep their cash in a bank.

Such precise analysis of crime, however, is missing from many police agencies. Undigested statistics, rather than nuanced crime patterns, is all these agencies draw from their massive investment in crime measurement. In Philadelphia, for example, a full-time officer in each police district audited the classification of each reported crime for many years after a scandal over crime reporting in the late 1990s. But only with the appointment of a new police commissioner in 2008 did Philadelphia apparently use those data to assign patrol operations in a highly focused way. In the United Kingdom, where more than one thousand crime analysts support the fifty-four police agencies, few holders of these posts truly analyze crime. Most are assigned to produce routine crime counts and trends, without searching each week or month for unique or novel features in the types of crime or criminals causing harm in the jurisdiction.

Thus in crime measurement and classification, as in all police practice, there is a gap between what *can* be done with the evidence, and how much evidence is actually employed. The better the available methods of analysis get, the bigger the gap between potential and performance.

B. Prediction

The most useful product of measurement evidence is the predictions they make possible about where and when crime will occur. One key example is the extreme concentration of violent crime on weekend evenings near premises serving alcohol. The analysis of such distributions is the primary basis for predicting where and when serious crimes will occur, with what likelihood, across each address in a city. The discovery that 3 percent of all street addresses produced more than half of the crime in Minneapolis (Sherman, Gartner, and Buerger 1989) and other cities (Braga and Weisburd 2010) led to greater awareness of crime "hot spots." These places are often defined as clusters of addresses on street corners (Sherman and Weisburd 1995) or street segments (Weisburd et al. 2004) that have predictably elevated risks of crime—especially those involving interpersonal encounters. Hot spots of property crime (Weisburd, Maher, and Sherman 1993) can also be identified in these analyses, as can hot spots of specific kinds of crime, such as auto theft (Eck and Spelman 1987) and gun crime (Sherman and Rogan 1995). But as Weisburd (2008) recently concluded, most police agencies do not even identify micro-level hot spot crime clusters, let alone organize their preventive patrol operations around them.

A similar fate befell a British initiative in the 1990s to focus police more on repeat victims. Identifying high concentrations of crime against the same people, especially in residential addresses, became a widely discussed idea in the United Kingdom (Farrell 1995). Yet as of early 2010, very few UK agencies even compiled lists of the phone numbers most frequently reporting crimes to the police, even after a tragic suicide by a victim who did not receive the help she asked police for in combating ongoing harassment from neighborhood youth (Bird 2009).

A much more recent prediction tool now offers police, like probation and parole agencies, a way to forecast the individual known offenders most likely to be charged with murder. Using a data-mining method known as "random forests" modeling, Richard Berk and his colleagues (2009) correctly identified (in advance) about 93 percent of a sample of some thirty thousand Philadelphian offenders under community supervision who would be either charged or not charged with homicide or attempted homicide over the next two years. While previous police efforts to predict the most dangerous criminals at large had correctly found high levels of criminal activity (Martin and Sherman 1986; Abrahamse et al. 1991), the subjective methods they employed limited their accuracy of prediction. More important, these methods limited the extent to which the forecast can identify the most *serious* crimes (such as murder), rather than just *any* kind of repeat offending (such as shoplifting or burglary).

Quantitative, actuarial tools for forecasting behavior have proven more accurate in virtually every comparison with qualitative, clinical methods for more than fifty years (Meehl 1954). Yet skepticism about individual offending forecasts remains widespread. As one prosecutor asked about the Berk team's research "What can it tell me that I don't already know by looking at a rap sheet [a criminal history of convictions]?" According to the Philadelphia adult probation agency, their answer is "a lot." Since 2005 the adult probation agency has gradually re-allocated its priorities to focus far more resources on preventing serious crime by the most dangerous offenders identified by the random forests models (Sherman 2007). Police agencies could do, but have not yet done, much the same.

The use of the term "forecasting" suggests the example of weather forecasts, which have recently become far more accurate in the United States as more data have been included in the prediction models. Again, police could do, but have not yet done, far more workload-planning using weather forecasts. If labor union contracts allowed it, call-takers and dispatchers could be called in or asked to stay home on twenty-four- to forty-eight-hour notice. The same is possible for officers. If "a good rain is worth a thousand police officers," as a veteran New York police sergeant said to me in 1971, then police time could be conserved for the weather patterns most predictably increasing violence and disorder on certain days of the week—such as low pressure, high humidity weather fronts with high temperatures during summer weekends (see LeBeau and Corcoran 1990; Cohn and Rotton 2000).

C. Theories of Causation

One of the central benefits of more accurate prediction is the development of more accurate theories that explain *why* the predictions are correct. Such explanations are central to the police task of crime prevention, especially the disruption of ongoing crime patterns. Problem-oriented policing (Goldstein 1990) implicitly depends on having a theory of what causes the crime pattern "problem." Routine activities theory (Cohen and Felson 1979) could suggest that substantial cash on hand attracts robbery of commercial premises and may suggest that limiting accessible cash to

$25 would reduce robberies (see Reiss and Roth 1993). If such a theory accurately points to a form of intervention that would remove one or more of the causes, then nothing else is as practical as a good theory.

Conversely, nothing may be as dangerous as a bad theory. The theory of "displacement," for example, says that whenever crime is prevented in a certain location, there is little reduction in total crime in a city. Instead, the theory goes, the same crimes will still happen, only now at different locations. This theory has been falsified in recent years by substantial evidence (Weisburd et al. 2006; Guerette and Bowers 2009). Yet it is still widely held in policing, and may explain the gap between evidence and practice in focusing police patrols at high-crime hot spots.

Similarly, the theory of deterrence may be vastly overgeneralized in policing, especially when aimed at individuals rather than places. The simple idea that more arrests mean less crime is clearly too crude to manage resources wisely—especially when it takes many hours of police time to process an arrest. Traditional police interventions in bar fights and other conflicts tended to de-emphasize arrest and prosecution in favor of separating the parties, on a theory that peacekeeping worked better with less involvement of the courts (Wilson 1968). More recently, the broken windows theory (Wilson and Kelling 1982) suggested that increases in misdemeanor arrests would reduce disorder, and thereby reduce serious crime. While there is good evidence that disorder fosters disorder (Keizer, Lindenberg, and Steg 2008) and perhaps even robbery (Sampson and Raudenbush 1999), the evidence on arrests, disorder, and homicide is far less clear.

Policing can, but has generally not yet, put these and other theories to work in controlling crime. Even without explicit use of theories, however, they can control crime by making better use of the growing volume of cost-effectiveness evaluations of crime control strategies.

D. What Works: Cost-Effectiveness of Crime Control

The cost-effectiveness of policing practices can be learned best by controlled experiments, or at least close approximations of that kind of research design (Zimring and Hawkins 1973). The growth of such experiments is the most important area in which knowledge about crime control has increased. The results of such experiments, however, have yet to be widely applied. Thus they also constitute the largest part of the gap between research and practice.

1. *RCTs*

A randomized controlled trial (RCT) is a test of the hypothesis that one policy or practice causes a different result than another policy or practice for dealing with the same units of analysis (Sherman 2010*a*, 2010*b*). This definition applies to many fields of research, from medicine to agriculture. In policing, the units are typically high in volume of police activity, such as victims, offenders, locations, or criminal investigations. The RCT design requires that a large sample of such units be split into two or more groups by subjecting each case in the sample to a kind of lottery that uses what statisticians call "random numbers" (Sherman 2010*b*). This method is actually a highly complicated computerized lottery that places each case into a particular group with an equal probability for all of the (two or more) groups in the study. Once the entire sample is divided in this way, any *bias* of placing different kinds of people (or places, or other units) into different treatments is generally eliminated. That means that if the groups differ in their outcome, the only reasonable cause of that difference is the difference in how the groups of cases were dealt with.

If, for example, police double patrols at fifty crime hot spots, but not at fifty others, then the extra patrol can be credited with any difference in average crime rates in the fifty locations that received extra patrol compared to the fifty that did not (Sherman and Weisburd 1995). That not only shows that patrol "works" in the hot spots (setting aside the displacement question) but also shows the exact number of minutes of police patrol required to make that much difference. In this example, a difference of police patrol presence at 7 percent of the time in one group and 15 percent of the time in the other group reduced crime in the target locations by about half. Using the known costs of police salaries, this formula can be applied to show the cost of patrol in relation to the number of crimes prevented.

While few if any evaluations of police practices actually compute cost-effectiveness data, such evidence is highly relevant to the ongoing debate about police budgets. Researchers (including this author) have been remiss in not drawing out more explicit cost-benefit calculations, with the benefits expressed in term of each additional police officer used in this way. The increasing volume of controlled experiments and systematic reviews of police practice presently allow economists or other scholars to produce more cost-effectiveness comparisons than are presently available. If they did, it could increase the demand for more RCTs to evaluate police practices.

2. *QEDs*

Even when large-sample controlled experiments are not possible, there is still much that can be learned by small-sample comparisons of different police practices before and after they are introduced. Such studies are called "quasi-experimental designs," or QEDs, as long as they offer a comparison between two different conditions. With repeated tests using a QED, consistent results can provide a good indication of what might be found with an RCT design. Even with repeated tests, however, the results of RCTs tend to differ from those of QEDs (Weisburd, Lum, and Petrosino 2001), and may generally be less favorable toward the policy evaluated than the results of QEDs.

3. *Meta-Analyses*

From medicine to policing, one of the most important new tools in evidence-based practice is research synthesis: drawing overall conclusions from repeated tests of the same practices. Conclusions about the exact "bottom line" of multiple tests of a single policy are derived from what are called *meta-analyses*, or studies of studies, using a method that combines the results of multiple tests of the same hypotheses. The method of identifying all relevant studies is called a *systematic review*. Regardless of whether all relevant studies have been included, any mathematical combination of the results of studies constitutes a meta-analysis.

There are two basic ways in which meta-analyses are done. One is called a *multivariate* analysis. The other is a geometric graph called a *forest plot*. The multivariate approach can look at all the factors that could modify a policy's effects, such as the age of juvenile delinquents being prosecuted or diverted. This approach is merely correlational, like a QED, and cannot isolate cause and effect with the same precision that an RCT is able to.

The forest plot is arguably a more reliable approach to meta-analysis. Forest plots are limited to just one question: What is the average effect of the same policy across all available tests? That average is computed from a picture like figure 17.1. There is some debate about whether such graphs should be plotted with QED results. But there is strong consensus that they can be used for RCT results (Berk 2007). Then the entire "plot" of the evidence that allows readers to "see the forest from the trees" can ask whether the bottom-line conclusion would likely have been obtained by chance. In other words, the bottom line of a forest plot is whether the "findings" of all independent tests of the same hypothesis reveal a statistically significant *pattern*.

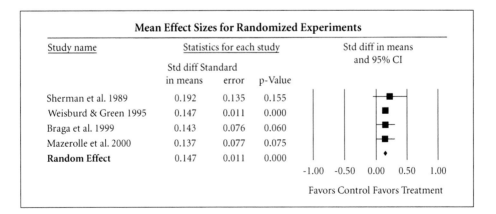

Mean Effect Sizes for Randomized Experiments				
Study name	Statistics for each study			Std diff in means and 95% CI
	Std diff in means	Standard error	p-Value	
Sherman et al. 1989	0.192	0.135	0.155	
Weisburd & Green 1995	0.147	0.011	0.000	
Braga et al. 1999	0.143	0.076	0.060	
Mazerolle et al. 2000	0.137	0.077	0.075	
Random Effect	0.147	0.011	0.000	

-1.00   -0.50   0.00   0.50   1.00

Favors Control Favors Treatment

Figure 17.1. A Forest Plot Showing the Effects of Problem-Oriented Policing on Crime or Disorder (Reprinted from Weisburd et al. 2008, 61).

As figure 17.1 shows, a forest plot displays a series of horizontal lines against a single vertical line. Each horizontal line has a square box in the middle representing the "finding" of one experiment. The farther away from the vertical line an experiment's finding may fall—in either direction—the bigger the difference in outcome there is between the two groups compared. Thus the vertical line represents the point of *no difference* between the outcomes of one group and another.

But why do the horizontal lines vary in length? The answer is that shorter lines are "better" than longer ones. A short line means that the study's conclusion was more "certain" because it had a smaller range of error than if the line were longer. The line shows how wide the "confidence intervals" of error are around the main finding. That finding, called a "point estimate," is shown at the square in the middle of each line. That midpoint—the finding—is each experiment's best estimate of the magnitude and direction (better or worse) of the difference in the outcomes between two groups (on crime, death, or anything being measured).

To read a forest graph, keep your eye on the *vertical* line, especially whether the horizontal lines are touching or crossing that line. If any part of the horizontal line touches the vertical line, it shows that the difference between the two groups is likely to have been due to chance (i.e., the difference was not "statistically significant" at a certain arbitrary threshold of likelihood, such as 1 percent or 5 percent).

To cut right to the conclusion, look down to the diamond shape at the bottom. This diamond represents the average effect across all of the RCTs. The average effect can be significant even when all of the horizontal lines touch the vertical line. The diamond shows whether the *pattern* of the lines, as represented by the average effect of all the tests, touches the vertical line. If it does not, then the diamond shows that the bottom line passes the threshold set for statistical significance.

Using these rules to interpret the evidence, figure 17.1 shows that on average, problem-oriented policing strategies tested in four independent RCTs have had a small but clear effect in reducing crime or disorder. It shows that the *pattern* of results is statistically significant—even though three out of the four tests failed, on their own, to show statistical significance. The additional confidence in the pattern is gained by the synthesis of repeated testing. That is one reason that it is important to combine these findings, where possible, into a meta-analysis that sees beyond one "tree" at a time to view the entire "forest" of results.

This tool will soon prove to be indispensable to policing—or at least to evidence-based policing. The scales of justice could even be replaced by a forest plot as a symbol of "weighing" the evidence—for or against a policy, if not for individual guilt.

4. *Systematic Reviews*

In contrast to a meta-analysis, a systematic review identifies as many published and unpublished tests of a hypothesis as possible. Many systematic reviews will analyze their results with a meta-analysis. But many meta-analyses are conducted without systematic reviews. Thus not all meta-analyses use systematic search methods, and not all systematic reviews use meta-analytic methods. Whether or not the results of multiple studies are combined into a meta-analysis, they can all be examined for their relevance to policing in any given community.

In its ideal form, evidence-based policing should consider all of the evidence about any given police practice or policy (Sherman 1998b). The methods for identifying all of that evidence are complicated and labor intensive. But they are well worth the investment. Selective analysis of evidence on a particular question always raises the potential for bias—even in the present chapter. The growth of this idea substantially raises the bar for science, and may soon render obsolete the less systematic ways of writing reviews on almost any empirical question.

The added value of a systematic review, with periodic updates, is so great that many national governments have joined together to support and communicate such reviews. The organization doing this work in medicine, created in the early 1990s, has now published more than four thousand systematic reviews of the effects of medical treatment on health (see www.cochrane.org). The Campbell Collaboration is the organization doing this work in education, criminal justice, and social services, with support from the Norwegian government (see www.campbellcollaboration.org). Founded in 2000, Campbell has not yet produced as many systematic reviews as Cochrane, partly because there is less primary evidence to review in these fields. But the number of reviews on police policies has grown rapidly in recent years.

What follows is a discussion of both systematic and non-systematic reviews of RCT and QED evidence on the effectiveness of police practices, as well as the actual and potential effect of that evidence on police success in controlling crime.

III. Evaluating Police Practices

The report by the U.S. National Research Council (NRC) report on *Fairness and Effectiveness in Policing: The Evidence* (Skogan and Frydl 2004) described what it called the "standard model" of policing in the United States and abroad. This model has three key elements: (1) random preventive patrol in cars, (2) rapid response to telephoned requests for emergency police services, and (3) criminal investigation by detectives to make as many arrests as possible. The model is widely seen as a "one-size-fits-all" strategy for cities large and small, with all kinds of crime problems and widely varying crime rates. The NRC report challenged that model as out of date and largely inconsistent with the evidence.

In place of the standard model, the NRC report suggested, police could achieve better crime control by developing more "focused" strategies against crimes. I prefer to call these strategies "customized policing," since they are unified by a departure from the idea that the *same* police strategy should work for all problems in all communities. The use of evidence is especially helpful to any effort that tries to tailor police work to the specific facts of the offenders, victims, crimes, or communities. What works depends on the question of "what for?" or "for whom" or "where" or "when." Customizing policing to these differences opens the door to clarifying the vast complexity of crime and disorder problems that police must address. It is arguably only with a model that presumes customization that policing can achieve better crime control.

But what is the evidence? The NRC panel's theory is not completely supported by direct tests of its hypotheses. In general, research does suggest the standard model to be less effective than strategies more focused on specific targets and goals (Sherman 1997*b*; Skogan and Frydl 2004). But that conclusion is not based on direct comparisons of the standard model to customized policing (see also Sherman 1997*b*). Few such comparisons have been done. Until they are, readers must be cautious in interpreting the separate tests of the two models *as if* they were direct comparisons. They are not. Rather, they are inferences from research about each approach separately. Until an experiment compares the two different models for all aspects of policing a given city or neighborhood, the cost-effectiveness of the two approaches cannot be compared with precision.

This section presents what research has discovered about each approach, starting with the standard model and some recent evidence on its successes and possible enhancements. It then examines the tests of customized policing strategies in a range of specific settings and targets. Taken together, research on the two models forms the core knowledge for evidence-based policing (Sherman 1998*b*).

A. The Standard Model

The evidence for the effectiveness of the standard model has used a wide range of research methods, including experiments and detailed descriptive analysis. This evidence embraces thousands of police dispatches and investigations, all of which have tested key assumptions of the standard model. In general, the model fails the tests. On the other hand, many more tests could still be conducted, including the idea of random patrol over a wide area, not concentrated in hot spots. The standard model is wounded by the evidence, but the wounds are not yet fatal.

1. *Preventive Patrol*

The bedrock strategy of the standard model is visible police presence on patrol in uniform. Various QED studies have shown that more patrol presence tends to reduce crime, at least in the short run (Sherman 1990). Police strikes, in particular, produce powerful evidence that violent crime increases substantially when patrol is suddenly restricted (Sherman 1992*a*). But whether *marginal* differences in police patrol visibility matter to crime is less easily demonstrated (Apel and Nagin 2010). The first controlled experiment in police patrol rejected that hypothesis (Kelling et al. 1974), but subsequent reviews by numerous independent analysts rejected the study's conclusions as invalid (see Sherman 1986). No further controlled experiments have attempted to answer that question by direct manipulation of patrol numbers in similar areas.

The question of marginal differences in patrol strength is probably less fundamental than the question of *where* and *when* patrols are performed. The cost-effectiveness of *random* patrol across an entire city has never been compared directly to an alternative way of allocating patrol, such as concentrating it in high-crime locations. For this reason, the available evidence on policing selective kinds of locations, such as crime hot spots, remains contested. For example, there have been no experiments comparing one hundred police beats with random patrol to one hundred police beats with patrols limited to hot spots. Until such evidence compares entire police areas with random versus focused patrol allocation, there remains a reasonable argument to be made for either strategy. What may not be reasonable is for police to use a very expensive strategy that could be highly wasteful, without generating the evidence needed to test that hypothesis.

2. *Rapid Response to Most Calls*

Perhaps the most important research on the standard model was the Kansas City (MO) Police (1977) analysis of how long it takes victims and witnesses to call police in the aftermath of crimes. By dividing emergency calls into crime in which victims had direct "contact" with offenders, and those in which victims made a "discovery" of a crime hours or days after it occurred, the KCPD showed how few emergency calls were about contact crimes. Once the time taken to report contact crime to police is acknowledged (an average of forty-one minutes), it is clearly impossible for police to arrive within five minutes or so of most reported crimes. Accordingly, well under 1 percent of all rapid responses resulted in an arrest in Kansas City. Even among the rare calls about serious crime, only 4 percent resulted in an arrest at the scene.

The Police Executive Forum quickly replicated the citizen delay time findings in four other U.S. cities (Spelman and Brown 1981). The conclusion that citizen delay neutralizes the value of most rapid response has yet to be challenged in the United States or abroad. Yet three decades after this knowledge was generated, there is little sign that police agencies have abandoned their traditional "rapid response" strategy. Elected officials, journalists, and the general public often imply that good policing requires it every time someone calls, without considering appropriate ways to allocate this expensive investment of police time.

Two indirect strategies, however, have started to put the response time research evidence into practice. One is the growing use of a three-digit non-emergency police number, such as "311," which may reduce the number of calls that might otherwise receive a rapid police response (Mazerolle et al. 2005). This phone number is generally answered by trained civilian responders who assist citizens by discussing the reason for their calls over the phone. In this strategy, police educate members of the public to divert their calls from rapid police response by their own discretion *not* to call 911 (or 999 in the United Kingdom).

The other indirect application of the response time evidence is called "Differential Police Response," or DPR. In this strategy, police themselves divert calls that do not require emergency response to other alternatives. This evidence-based strategy was tested in the 1980s in several RCTs (McEwen, Conners, and Cohen 1984) that randomly assigned callers with certain kinds of requests (such as non-contact burglary) either to immediate dispatch of a police officer, or to some other alternative. For example, a citizen might be offered an appointment to have a police officer come to their address the next day or next week, rather than waiting indefinitely on a busy night. Other options might be an immediate transfer to a telephone clerk, or a walk-in service at a designated location). Like the 311 responders, the clerks can take a crime report over the telephone—one that is valid and accessible for insurance purposes.

The findings of the three field tests showed that rapid response could be substantially reduced without any reduction in citizen satisfaction (Sherman 1986, 361). They also showed that citizens generally were happiest when the police delivered exactly what they promised, and the promise was as clear as possible. For example, if a police car was promised to be sent to the scene between 10 and 11 a.m. the next week, and then appeared as scheduled, the caller was usually satisfied. But if the citizen was promised an immediate response "as soon as possible" or "right away," yet police did not appear for several hours, citizens were far less satisfied.

Any police agency wishing to improve public satisfaction with police services would be well advised to look at this evidence. The DPR strategy could not only free resources for more effective strategies against crime, it could also raise public trust and confidence in the police. Failure to use DPR may create more than an evidence gap. It could also undermine trust and confidence in the police.

3. *Criminal Investigation by Detectives*

One of the oldest elements of the standard model is the investigation of reported crimes by detectives paid by tax revenues. Established in London in 1751 (Fielding 1755), paid detectives have been so visibly successful in highly publicized cases that they are a cultural icon of effectiveness. Yet the persistently low overall rates of solution of crimes has left the standard model vulnerable to criticism. British politicians often treat such low detection rates as a recent phenomenon. Yet there is no evidence that detectives could ever solve anywhere near a majority of all reported crimes.

Predictive research in the early 1970s showed that when detection succeeds, crucial information was already provided to police by victims, witnesses, or physical traces (Greenwood and Petersilia 1975). The main reason investigations fail, according to the same studies, is that insufficient information, or clues, is provided to detectives at the outset of the case. The research suggested that putting more time into each case would not alter the likely outcome based on initially available information. The clear implication is that, absent some way to focus cases likely to be solvable, most detective time is wasted on cases that will never be solved.

This waste of detective time in pursuing unsolvable cases has been avoidable since solvability factors were first established in 1979 by John Eck, who was then a criminologist at the Police Executive Research Forum. Working with a statistical model first developed at the Stanford Research Institute, Eck showed that detectives could predict with 85 percent accuracy whether or not the case is likely to be solved. These predictions worked in over twelve thousand cases across twenty-six police agencies. The predictions were based on a checklist of six statistically identified factors, which is easy and simple to use in operational settings. The checklist produced more accurate predictions of whether cases were solvable than traditional subjective assessments of the cases by experienced detectives.

Based on this research, many police agencies have adopted the checklist—but many others still have not. Some agencies have limited their workload by simply refusing to do investigations at all for large categories of crimes. These categories are not defined by solvability but solely on grounds of the cost of each crime (e.g., "we investigate no theft of under $1500 in value"). The cost and solvability methods of "rationing" investigations are easily confused; resistance to the checklist is often fueled by moral objections to the cost-cutoff approach. Yet they have opposite implications for crime control.

Declaring a category of crime unworthy of investigation is, theoretically, the opposite of deterrence: an open invitation to commit crimes with impunity. Declaring some crimes in every category subject to investigation, in contrast, maintains a clear deterrent threat, on a theory of random or unpredictable enforcement (Sherman 1990). Solvability-factors rationing also leaves open the possibility of improving detection rates if the structure of information-generation can be improved. The evidence suggests that the more evidence (of certain kinds) that is present at the outset of an investigation, the more likely the investigation is to identify a suspect and make an arrest. Thus providing more information could eventually raise detection rates overall, and make more cases pass a solvability test at the outset.

No better example of the latter possibility can be cited than the recent Urban Institute experiments in enhancing *DNA Collection at Burglary Crime Scenes* (Roman et al. 2008, 3). This study concluded that "cases where DNA evidence is processed have more than twice as many suspects identified, twice as many suspects arrested, and more than twice as many cases accepted for prosecution compared with traditional investigation." This National Institute of Justice–funded RCT design was undertaken in five communities (Orange County and Los Angeles, California; Topeka, Kansas; Denver, Colorado; and Phoenix, Arizona), with up to five hundred cases in each site in which biological evidence was collected. Cases in which it was demonstrably possible to collect such evidence were then randomly assigned to have the evidence processed in a forensic laboratory—or not. The design insured that the kinds of cases in each of the two groups were otherwise similar, and that there was no difference in the availability of biological evidence.

The research question was whether using such evidence would make a difference in the investigative results. The answer was it clearly did. The sample assigned to processing the DNA evidence led to arrests in 16 percent of cases, compared to just 8 percent of cases where no DNA evidence was analyzed.

The RCT evidence also identified the cost-effectiveness of identifying each additional suspect at $4,502, and a cost per additional arrest of $14,169. How any community interprets that finding for its own priorities may vary widely, depending on the total crime problem and costs of investigations. But it is at least an evidence-based enhancement of the standard model, one that police agencies may be happy to embrace if the public funding to do so is available.

The same cannot be said for another evidence-based enhancement of investigations, in the identification of suspects by *eyewitness lineups* (Sherman 2006). Substantial laboratory evidence that showing people a batch of photos simultaneously produces more identification errors than showing people one photo at a time. Yet American police have been reluctant to abandon the error-prone "batch" approach, including lineups. In principle, a lineup of suspects (even of similar height and build) is a like a batch of photos; victims may feel a social expectation to pick the "right" one, even if the true offender is not included in the lineup. Thus the laboratory evidence of error would seem to be highly applicable to field investigations.

Yet police in Illinois chose to do their own field test, allegedly using an RCT design, that gained front page coverage in the *New York Times* (Zernike 2006). This test claimed that batch lineups were more accurate than sequential presentation of one photo at a time. Unfortunately, the actual research report showed that there was no random assignment at all, and the lawyer who led and wrote up the study clearly did not understand what random assignment meant. The results of this invalid study have, sadly, strengthened police resistance to reducing eyewitness error by adopting sequential lineups, with almost certain tragic consequences of more wrongful conviction of innocent people.

4. *Arrests*

Perhaps the most surprising weakness of the standard model is the evidence that arrests often cause crime rather than preventing it. Throwing "the book" of criminal prosecution at offenders often causes more crime rather than less. A systematic review (Petrosino, Turpin-Petrosino, and Guckenberg) of twenty-nine studies with

7,300 juveniles has shown, for example, that most juvenile offenders become *more* criminal (not less) if they are arrested and prosecuted in court than if they are diverted to a nonlegalistic response. Serious violent offenders with early onset of crime, however, would likely be a notable exception.

Experiments have also shown that arrest causes crime in the case of domestic violence (Sherman 1992b). The arrest of minor domestic offenders has been found to increase, rather than decrease, repeat offending against victims among *unemployed* suspects. Arrests of *employed* suspects, in contrast, make them less likely to reoffend than if they are warned (Berk et al. 1992; Pate and Hamilton 1992; Sherman and Smith 1992). Both the domestic violence and the juvenile crime findings are consistent with the long tradition of labeling (Lemert 1951) and defiance theories (Sherman 1993), which offer exactly the opposite predictions as deterrence theory— but under well-specified conditions.

This research illustrates one of the challenges of the standard model: how to use it sometimes but not others. Police discretion has always raised issues of fairness, but on a case-by-case basis. Once the research is used to create categorical policies for arresting or not, there is a potential loss of *general* deterrence. The evidence on juvenile and domestic violence arrests is about *specific* deterrence, or the individual-level effects of arrest on future crime. It does not address the question of general deterrence, which might well be the opposite of the specific deterrent effects of arrest. It is possible that a visible, transparent policy of not arresting under widely known conditions could lead to more offenders committing the offenses covered by the policy. The only way to find the least harmful solution may be to examine the effects of arrest policies with RCTs of entire communities, and not just individuals.

B. The "Customized" Policing Model

Customized policing can be seen as a *supplement* to the standard model, not a complete *substitute*. The core elements of policing need not change in order to (1) use those elements in a more focused way, and (2) introduce additional elements that may work better than the standard model for controlling certain kinds of crimes. The practical difference, then, is between using *only* the standard model or supplementing that model with evidence-based customized strategies.

The importance of building evidence into the very definition of "customized" policing is illustrated by one of the oldest and most "focused" of supplements to the standard model: the DARE Program (Drug Abuse Resistance Education). For three decades, this focused police strategy has commanded hundreds of millions of dollars in local and federal U.S. funding. The program assigns uniformed police officers—who could otherwise be patrolling the streets or investigating crimes—to go to primary school classrooms to talk about resisting pressures to use illegal drugs. Despite consistent evidence that this program has no effect on crime or drug abuse (West and O'Neal 2004), both police and community supporters have resisted termination of the program. After Mayor Rocky Anderson of Salt Lake City eliminated police funding for the program in 2000 (Jensen 2000), he was subjected to intense political attacks by police and program advocates. But he was vindicated after a further investment of millions of dollars by major foundations to undertake a long-term RCT of an enhanced DARE program ("Take Charge of Your Life") in eighty-two school clusters (forty-one with and forty-one without the program). The results showed that the program not only failed to reduce drug use but actually increased teen smoking and alcohol use (Sloboda et al. 2009).

Getting research into practice requires more leaders to do what Mayor Anderson did: to stop doing what doesn't work and start doing what does. Just because an agency focuses on one crime at a time does not mean that its methods will work. But while DARE has failed, the much more flexible strategy of POP, or Problem-Oriented Policing (Goldstein 1979), has succeeded. Unlike DARE, POP can now be seen as an evidence-based policy that has withstood a series of RCTs.

1. *Problem-Oriented Policing*

The basic idea of POP is to identify and better manage specific patterns of crime and disorder. This is to be done not just by legal categories, but by the elements the incidents share in common: individual offenders or victims, locations of occurrence, times of day or social contexts. These elements may often help develop a theory of what causes the incidents, and how those causes might be counteracted.

Sometimes identifying causes of a disorder pattern can be a difficult process, with little help from criminological theory. Goldstein (1990) cites a Philadelphia case of a woman calling police hundreds of times about noise from a tavern next door to her home. But rapid police response to these calls rarely found loud noise in the tavern. One officer even used a sound meter to measure the decibel levels, which were within legal limits. Only when a persistent problem-solving officer sat with the complainant in her living room did he understand the true cause of the complaint: the small china statuettes and plates on a bureau rattling from vibrations of the wall abutting the tavern. The officer went right over to the tavern to discover that someone had just turned on the juke box; the vibrations had come from the bass sounds in the speakers. The officer asked the tavern owner to move the juke box to an outside wall. And that was that: no more calls to police.

On the clarity and force of such examples, POP has thrived. But so have many quack medicines. What now makes POP different from many other police innovations is a substantial body of RCT and QED tests of its effectiveness. Figure 17.1 shows a meta-analysis of the four RCTs of POP reviewed by Weisburd and his colleagues (2008). Their peer-reviewed, Campbell Collaboration systematic review also reports on six QED tests of POP strategies. Contrary to the usual pattern of QED studies showing stronger effects than RCTs (Weisburd, Lum, and Petrosino

2001), in this case the experiments showed better results for crime control than the quasi-experiments. The pattern for the QED evaluations was not even statistically significant. Only the most rigorous test design, the RCT, pulled the entire review into a significant pattern of crime and disorder control.

But what does that mean? Were the effects of problem-solving in general actually due to the specific tactics evaluated for use on a few specific problems? In the four RCTs synthesized by Weisburd and his colleagues (2008, 2010), for example, two were about drug-dealing locations, and two were about high-crime hot spots in Jersey City. If that were the only evidence, POP could be said to have no support beyond drugs and hot spots.

Yet there are at least two reasons to interpret the systematic review evidence as supporting a more general conclusion about the POP strategy as a kind of "new standard model": an approach that can be used, with appropriate focus, across a wide range of incident patterns. One reason for reading the evidence this way is in figure 17.1 itself. The largest *main effect* among the four RCTs was not in any of the narrowly focused samples but rather in the highly diverse Minneapolis Repeat Call Address Policing Program experiment (see Sherman 1992a), with some five hundred residential and commercial locations selected on the basis of high volumes of calls for police service. Moreover, the largest sample size in the forest plot comes from the RECAP experiment, which then drives the overall pattern of statistical significance for the four studies together.

Finally, a subsequent RCT of problem solving by Braga and Bond (2008) in hot spots of very diverse problems also found significant reductions in calls for service about assault, robbery, burglary, and disorder. This result, which was too late for inclusion in the Weisburd et al. (2008) Campbell review, also suggested the best effects came from situational crime prevention strategies (what many police think of as true POP tactics) as distinct from arrests or other standard model strategies.

2. *Hot Spots Policing*

If POP is a new standard model, then its toolkit could arguably include what Braga (2007) defines, generally, as hot spots policing. Wherever there is a pattern of crime in a single public location, one POP response could be assigning extra police officers to do something—or anything—in that location. The focus of hot spots policing is microplaces that Sherman, Gartin, and Buerger (1989) defined as small enough to be seen by the naked eye in a single location, and which have extremely high densities of crime and disorder incidents per square foot (e.g., Sherman and Weisburd 1995; Weisburd and Mazerolle 1995). Further measurement and classification evidence would help to standardize the use of the term "hot spot," which is highly variable. Some usage of the term denotes far larger areas, or even entire cities. The evidence in Braga's Campbell Collaboration review is generally limited to smaller microplaces, or at the most, single patrol beats.

The evidence shows that within samples of hot spots, applying additional police resources almost always reduces crime—when compared to similar hot spots where extra resources are not applied. The extra police resources can include routine uniformed patrol, intensive stop-and-search tactics, knock-down-the-door police raids to serve search warrants, or even situational crime prevention problem solving. This encouraging evidence is often rebuffed, however, by police who claim that crime reductions in hot spots will be nullified by displacement of an equal number of crimes to other locations not included in the study sample.

The evidence on *displacement* of crime from hot spots to other locations tends to refute that critique, although it is not as definitive as many would still like. One analysis in Jersey City, for example, found that in both prostitution and drug dealing areas, crackdowns that reduced crime and disorder caused no increases in those outcomes in the "catchment" or buffer zone surrounding the target areas (Weisburd et al. 2006). Another analysis of Seattle over fifteen years showed that when crime declined on the highest crime street segments, crime declined citywide, with most of the decline attributable to the drop in the hottest hot spots (Weisburd et al. 2004). Across a wide range of 102 crime prevention evaluations, Guerette and Bowers (2009) reported that displacement was only reported in 26 percent of the observations, with a further 27 percent reporting that crime *declined* in the surrounding buffer zones. In a smaller sample of more complete studies, they found that even when displacement did occur, the amount of crime displaced was less than the amount prevented.

The problem with the displacement critique is that it goes way beyond nearby locations. Offenders or offenses could, in theory, move almost anywhere. That possibility makes it almost impossible to test the displacement hypothesis thoroughly. One major addition, however, would be the tracking of individual offenders to other possible locations after they stop getting arrested in a target hot spot. When such a study was done of prostitutes after a hot spot crackdown in London, for example, there was no record of them being arrested in any other part of the metropolitan area (see Sherman 1990). Such evidence provides double support to a study showing no local buffer area displacement.

Until further experiments can be done showing that across an entire RCT no displacement of either spatial or offender-specific character undermines the reductions of crime observed in hot spots, police may resist a more radical implication of this evidence. That implication is to focus patrols very heavily on hot spots, and less so on beats, since most parts of most beats almost never have any crime (Sherman, Gartner, and Buerger 1989). This idea may be opposed on the grounds that police have many other tasks besides controlling crime (Skogan, personal communication, 2009). But it could still be applied to whatever proportion of police resources is deemed appropriate to the prevention of crime in public places.

3. *Police Crackdowns*

Another tool in the POP "new standard model" kit of customized policing is the short-term intensification of police surveillance and arrests. This strategy has emerged in the post-1960s crime wave as a focused response of generally limited duration, often in response to a sudden increase or "spike" in problems ranging from drunk driving to gun violence. Sherman's (1990) review of the QED evidence then available showed that such methods as roadblocks, stop-and-search, and sudden massive increases in police patrols generally had an immediate effect on reducing crime. The effect tended to dissipate or "decay" over time, with crime gradually rising to pre-crackdown levels. But where crackdowns were terminated fairly soon after they were initiated, the crime reduction usually continued for some time after police resources were removed. This "free bonus" of "residual deterrence" was also found in Koper's (1995) QED analysis of thousands of observed police arrivals and departures from Minneapolis hot spots. He found that the maximum residual deterrence was associated with patrols of ten to fifteen minutes, with shorter crime-free periods post-police-departure after less than ten minutes of patrol, and diminishing returns from more than fifteen minutes of patrol. Such evidence can help guide customized policing for not just large-scale operations but also for daily patrols.

4. *Policing Repeat Offenders*

Another tool for customized policing is to focus on either high-frequency or high-seriousness offenders. Most police agencies can identify their high-frequency offenders, some of whom are the subjects of police-probation partnerships. Few if any police agencies have the statistical capacity to identify their highest-seriousness potential offenders (see Berk et al. 2009). Since the two experiments testing focused interventions on high-frequency (or moderately high-seriousness) offenders were both successful (Martin and Sherman 1986; Abrahamse et al. 1991), a similar approach may also work for high-seriousness offenders.

5. *Restorative Policing*

Using a theory of rehabilitation, rather than deterrence or incapacitation, police have also accumulated substantial evidence that they can reduce repeat offending with restorative justice conferences (Sherman and Strang 2007; Strang et al. 2009). In twelve RCTs, on three continents, of a method taught to police by the same restorative justice trainer (John McDonald of Australia), police achieved a statistically significant pattern of modest reductions in the two-year frequency of repeat convictions. Among the seven UK trials led by Sherman and Strang that were independently evaluated by Joanna Shapland and her colleagues (2008), the pooled reduction in the frequency of repeat convictions was 27 percent over two years. The Shapland et al. cost-benefit analysis showed £8 in cost of crime prevented for every one pound invested in restorative justice.

While there are many approaches to restorative justice (Braithwaite 2002), the restorative justice conference (RJC) is the only one that requires an offender to meet with the personal victim of that offender, along with their respective families or friends. An RJC has three phases of discussion, in which all parties are equally entitled to speak while a trained police officer (in most of the RCTs) facilitates the discussion. The first phase established the facts of the crime, with the offenders asked to state exactly what they did. The second phase is a much longer discussion of how the crime affected the victim and everyone else in the room. The third phase discusses what the offenders can do to try to repair the damage the crime caused and to insure that they do not repeat their crimes.

Lasting from one to three hours, an RJC can create a fairly traumatic experience for an offender (Peter Woolf, personal communication, 2008). Offenders have later suffered racing thoughts or nightmares for years after the event. Not that the purpose of an RJC is to inflict retribution on the offender, but it is consistent with what is generally known about empathy among primates in general. As the primatologist Frans de Waal (2009, 75) says of his extensive research with chimpanzees and humans, "It's just awful to watch others in pain, which is, of course, the whole point of empathy." Despite years of appearing in court to be sentenced, some offenders in these experiments had never before heard victims discuss the pain they had suffered. Some of the offenders were devastated, many cried, and most wanted the RJC to be over much sooner than it was. All of this helps to answer Francis Cullen's (personal communication, 1996) question to me of "why would a short meeting like that be expected to change a lifetime pattern of offending?" Many people's lives can change drastically in a few moments, especially where a trauma occurs. Thus it is not implausible that police can engineer a turning point in offenders' lives in this way. Even if the offenders continue to commit crimes, any reduction in the frequency or cost of those crimes would contribute to the police mission for crime control.

6. *CompStat*

There are many more focused methods of policing for crime control, but only one widely known strategy for coordinating those methods. Introduced in the New York City Transit Police in the early 1990s (Bratton 1998), the CompStat strategy for managing police resources is a hallmark of focus. The discussions of crime patterns and responses in New York, at least, have been extremely focused. Not content with the standard model, CompStat is a leadership tool for insuring as much customized response as possible.

Whether CompStat is the best method for driving police resources is a question on which there is no evidence, so far. In theory, a variety of strategies would be possible for managing collective discussions by senior police officials. One very different model would be to introduce reviews of the research evidence, rather than just discussing crime patterns and trends. With advance notice, a quick review of the literature could be provided for each discussion of a particular crime problem. The basic approach of such reviews is to combine them with the local evidence of the crime patterns (Sherman 1998b). But the problem getting research into practice may be best solved in ways keeping with the prevailing management culture of the agency. Such cultures of management vary widely from Los Angeles to Atlanta, from Hong Kong to Sydney. Further ethnographic research on any efforts to bring research to the table would be helpful to all those engaged in creating and applying that research.

III. POLICE DEMAND FOR KNOWLEDGE

The question of knowledge revolutions has been a mainstay of the history and sociology of science. That interest is justified by what can be matters of life and death: how people do research, and how research influences the practices of professions, industries, and even child-rearing. Two different models of professions transformed by research can be seen in two famous examples. One model is science-led practice. The other model is practice-led science. The past century of agriculture is a good example of science-led practice. The past century of medicine, in contrast, has been dominated by practice-led science. Comparing these two cases suggests that policing has been in a state of science-led evidence for almost half a century. But if citizens are to benefit from that evidence, it may only happen by creating a culture of policing-led science (Neyroud 2009).

A. Science-Led Policing

Police research is now done much like research is done in agriculture. A stand-alone group of scientists, funded by government and foundations, sets the research agenda and publishes their results. Talking mostly to each other, the academics focus on the science and let others "translate" the research into practice. Police, like farmers, rarely set the research agenda with their own questions. The major difference between policing and agriculture is that universities have their own "field stations" for agricultural research, so they rarely need to persuade farmers to lend them their fields or livestock. Police researchers, of course, need to persuade police agencies to grant them "access."

The science-led practice model has worked very well in agriculture (Gawande 2009). In its first century, science-led agriculture has massively reduced the cost of food and the amount of labor needed to produce it. More than thirty thousand extension agents are employed in speaking one-on-one to individual farmers about more cost-effective farming techniques, and farmers often heed their advice. The agents also bring questions from the farmers back to the academics, which keeps their work informed by current field conditions. In principle, similar methods might work well with police, especially the one-on-one translation of research by extension agents (who might even be retired police officers, specially trained in applying research).

Yet farmers have a major incentive that police officers (fortunately) lack: the profit motive. An extension agent's advice could help a farmer make more money. So why shouldn't he take that advice? A veteran police professional, in contrast, cannot help a patrol officer get anything in particular out of taking advice. They get paid just the same whether crime goes up or down.

The same, with some differences, might be said of medicine. Doctors have been well paid regardless of whether their treatments cured or killed. But doctors do have something more important than profit to drive them: they have honor. Glory, reputation, admiration, and even fame—these can all reward a successful physician. That may explain, then, why doctors have followed the opposite path of practice-led science. Many doctors have themselves been scientists, conducting their own research.

Farmers have not generally done their own research. But police officers might.

B. Policing-Led Science

Medicine thus provides a possible solution to the evidence gap. It shows how police research could be done. Police officers trained to do research, like doctors, could work in collaboration with criminology programs and statisticians in universities. Inventive officers could come up with new techniques. Just as a policeman invented the Breathalyzer™ (Martin 2002), others could invent (and test!) new ways to prevent domestic violence. Just as surgeons develop (and test) new techniques for minimizing death due to blood loss, police could develop (and test) new methods for reducing burglary. Journals could be devoted to good research on these applied questions, just as medical journals are.

If prestige comparable to medical honors could be given to police leaders for leading research, such a world might be possible. By requiring evidence-based demonstrations (rather than blustery claims) of success in reducing crime, police research could become a case of practice-led science. How this might be achieved is beyond the scope of this chapter, but it is not by any means impossible. There could be many ways to restructure the incentive systems of policing around the advancement of knowledge, as well as of justice and safety. Salary incentives, research grants to officer-academic teams, even large cash prizes. One need only to imagine this to consider the potential culture change: a Nobel Prize in Policing.

Admittedly, the Nobel Prize in Medicine has failed to get doctors to wash their hands. The gap between evidence and practice is alive and well in medicine. But it is also under intensive research. The evidence gap is not an insuperable obstacle to evidence-based practice, neither in medicine nor policing. It is merely a problem like any other, awaiting new ideas and research evidence to discover a solution.

NOTE

* Research leading to the conclusions reported in this chapter was conducted while the author was a visiting scholar at the Regulatory Institutions Network (RegNet) of the Australian National University and the Australian Research Council Centre of Excellence in Policing and Security (CEPS).

REFERENCES

Abrahamse, Allan F., Patricia A. Ebener, Peter W. Greenwood, Nora Fitzgerald, and Thomas E. Kosin. 1991. "An Experimental Evaluation of the Phoenix Repeat Offender Program." *Justice Quarterly* 8: 141–68.

Apel, Robert J., and Daniel Nagin. 2009. "Deterrence." In *Crime and Public Policy*, edited by James Q. Wilson and Joan Petersilia. New York: Oxford University Press.

Berk, Richard. 2007. "Statistical Inference and Meta-Analysis." *Journal of Experimental Criminology* 3: 247–70.

Berk, Richard, Alec Campbell, Ruth Klap, and Bruce Western. 1992. "The Deterrent Effect of Arrest in Incidents of Domestic Violence: A Bayesian Analysis of Four Field Experiments." *American Sociological Review* 57: 698–708.

Berk, Richard, Lawrence Sherman, Geoffrey Barnes, Ellen Kurtz, and Lindsay Ahlman. 2009. "Forecasting Murder within a Population of Probationers and Parolees: A High Stakes Application of Statistical Learning." *Journal of the Royal Statistical Society. Series A. Statistics in Society* 172: 191–211.

Bird, Steve. 2009. "Family behind Fiona Pilkington Bullying 'Still Causing Problems.'" *Times* (London) (September 23), http://www.timesonline.co.uk/tol/news/uk/article6844380.ece.

Braga, Anthony. 2007. "The Effects of Hot Spots Policing on Crime." A Campbell Collaboration Systematic Review. http://www.campbellcollaboration.org/library.php.

Braga, Anthony, and Brenda J. Bond. 2008. "Policing Crime and Disorder in Hot Spots: A Randomized, Controlled Trial." *Criminology* 46: 577–607.

Braga, Anthony, and David Weisburd. 2010. *Putting Crime in Its Place*. New York: Oxford University Press.

Braithwaite, John. 2002. *Restorative Justice and Responsive Regulation*. New York: Oxford University Press.

Bratton, William. 1998. *Turnaround: How America's Top Cop Reversed the Crime Epidemic*. New York: Random House.

Cohen, Lawrence, and Marcus Felson. 1979. "Social Change and Crime Rate Trends: A Routine Activity Approach." *American Sociological Review* 44: 588–608.

Cohn, Ellen G., and James Rotton. 2000 "Weather, Seasonal Trends And Property Crimes In Minneapolis, 1987–1988: A Moderator-Variable Time-Series Analysis Of Routine Activities." *Journal of Environmental Psychology* 20: 257–72.

Cullen, Francis. 1996. Personal communication [n.d.] during a lecture at the University of Cincinnati.

De Waal, Frans. 2009. *The Age of Empathy*. New York: Random House.

Eck, John E. 1979. *Managing Case Assignments—The Burglary Investigation Decision Model Replication*. Washington, DC: Police Executive Research Forum.

Eck, John, and William Spelman. 1987. *Problem-Solving: Problem-Oriented Policing in Newport News*. Washington, DC: Police Executive Research Forum.

Farrell, Graham. 1995. "Preventing Repeat Victimization." *Strategic Approaches to Crime Prevention*, edited by Michael Tonry and David Farrington. Vol. 19 of *Crime and Justice: A Review of Research*, edited by Michael Tonry. Chicago: University of Chicago Press.

Fielding, Henry. 1755. *Journal of a Voyage to Lisbon*. London. http://ebooks.adelaide.edu. au/f/fielding/henry/lisbon/introduction2.html.

Gawande, Atul. 2009. "Testing, Testing." *New Yorker* (December), 14, 34–41.

Goldstein, Herman. 1979. "Improving Policing: A Problem-Oriented Approach." *Crime and Delinquency* 25:236–58.

———. 1990. *Problem-Oriented Policing*. New York: McGraw-Hill.

Greenwood, Peter, and Joan R. Petersilia. 1975. The Criminal Investigation Process. Vol. 1, *Summary and Policy Implications*. Santa Monica, CA: RAND.

Guerette, Rob T., and Kate Bowers. 2009. "Assessing the Extent of Crime Displacement and Diffusion of Benefits: A Review of Situational Crime Prevention Evaluations." *Criminology* 47: 1331–68.

Jensen, Derek. 2000. "Rocky Decks DARE Program in S.L. Schools." *Deseret News* (July 12), A1, A6.

Keizer, Kees, Siegwart Lindenberg, and Linda Steg. 2008. "The Spreading of Disorder." *Science* (December 12):1681–85.

Kelling, George L., Tony Pate, Duane Dieckman, and Charles Brown. 1974. *The Kansas City Preventive Patrol Experiment: Executive Summary*. Washington, DC: The Police Foundation.

Koper, Christopher. 1995. "Just Enough Police Presence: Reducing Crime and Disorderly Behavior By Optimizing Patrol Time In Crime Hot Spots." *Justice Quarterly* 12: 649–72.

LeBeau, James, and William Corcoran. 1990. "Changes in Calls for Police Service with Changes in Routine Activities and the Arrival and Passage of Weather Fronts." *Journal of Quantitative Criminology* 6: 269–91.

Lemert, Edwin. 1951. *Social Pathology: A Systematic Approach to the Theory of Sociopathic Behavior*. New York: McGraw-Hill.

Martin, Douglas. 2002. "Obituary: Robert F. Borkenstein, 89, Inventor of the Breathalyzer." *New York Times* (August 17). http://www.nytimes.com/2002/08/17/us/robert-f-borkenstein-89-inventor-of-the-breathalyzer.html.

Martin, Susan, and Lawrence Sherman. 1986. "Selective Apprehension: A Police Strategy for Repeat Offenders." *Criminology* 24: 55–72.

Mazerolle, Lorraine, Dennis Rogan, James Frank, Christine Famega, and John E. Eck. 2005. "*Managing Calls to the Police With 911/311 Systems*." Washington, DC: National Institute of Justice. http://www.ncjrs.gov/pdffiles1/nij/206256.pdf.

McEwen, J. Thomas, Edward F. Conners, and Marcia Cohen. 1984. *Evaluation of the Differential Police Response Field Test: Executive Summary*. Washington, DC: National Criminal Justice Reference Service.

McSmith, Andy. 2010. "Lies, Damn Lies and Tory Crime Statistics: Shadow Home Secretary is Accused of Using Figures 'Likely to Mislead the Public.'" *Independent*

(February 5). http://www.independent.co.uk/news/uk/politics/lies-damn-lies-and-tory-crime-statistics-1889927.html.

Meehl, Paul. 1954. *Clinical vs. Statistical Prediction: A Theoretical Analysis and a Review of the Evidence.* Minneapolis: University of Minnesota Press.

Neyroud, Peter. 2009. "Squaring the Circles: Research, Evidence, Policy-Making, and Police Improvement in England and Wales." *Police Practice and Research* 10: 437–49.

Pate, Antony, and Edwin E. Hamilton. 1992. "Formal and Informal Deterrents to Domestic Violence: The Dade County Spouse Assault Experiment." *American Sociological Review* 57: 691–98.

Petrosino, Anthony, Carolyn Turpin-Petrosino, and Sarah Guckenberg. 2010 "Formal System Processing of Juveniles: Effects on Delinquency." Campbell Collaboration Review. http://www.campbellcollaboration.org/library.php.

Rashbaum, William K. 2010. "Retired Officers Raise Questions on Crime Data." *New York Times* (February 6). http://www.nytimes.com/2010/02/07/nyregion/07crime.html.

Reiss, Albert J., and Jeffrey A. Roth. 1993. *Understanding and Preventing Violence.* Washington, DC: National Academy of Science.

Roman, John K., Shannon Reid, Jay Reid, Aaron Chalfin, William Adams, and Carly Knight. 2008. *The DNA Field Experiment: Cost-Effectiveness Analysis of the Use of DNA in the Investigation of High-Volume Crimes.* Washington, DC: Urban Institute.

Sampson, Robert J., and Stephen W. Raudenbush. 1999. "Systematic Social Observation of Public Spaces: A New Look at Disorder in Urban Neighborhoods." *American Journal of Sociology* 105: 603–51.

Shapland, Joanna, Anne Atkinson, Helen Atkinson, James Dignan, Lucy Edwards, Jeremy Hibbert, Marie Howes, Jennifer Johnstone, Gwen Robinson, and Angela Sorsby. 2008. *Does Restorative Justice Affect Reconviction? The Fourth Report from the Evaluation of Three Schemes.* London: Ministry of Justice.

Sherman, Lawrence W. 1974. "The Sociology and the Social Reform of the American Police: 1950–73." *Journal of Police Science and Administration* 3 (September 2): 255–63.

———. 1983. "Patrol Strategies for Police." In *Crime and Public Policy,* edited by James Q. Wilson. San Francisco: ICS Press/Transaction Books.

———. 1986. "Policing Communities: What Works?" In *Communities and Crime,* edited by Albert J. Reiss, Jr. and Michael Tonry. Volume 8 of *Crime and Justice: A Review of Research,* edited by Michael Tonry. Chicago: University of Chicago Press.

———. 1990. "Police Crackdowns: Initial and Residual Deterrence." In *Crime and Justice: A Review of Research*, vol. 12, edited by Michael Tonry and Norval Morris. Chicago: University of Chicago Press.

———. 1992a. "Attacking Crime: Police and Crime Control." In *Modern Policing,* edited by Norval Morris and Michael Tonry. Volume 15 of *Crime and Justice: A Review of Research,* edited by Michael Tonry. Chicago: University of Chicago Press.

———. 1992b. *Policing Domestic Violence: Experiments and Dilemmas.* New York: Free Press.

———. 1993. "Defiance, Deterrence and Irrelevance: A Theory of the Criminal Sanction." *Journal of Research in Crime and Delinquency* 30: 445–73.

———. 1995. "The Police." In *Crime,* edited James Q. Wilson and Joan Petersilia. San Francisco: Institute for Contemporary Studies.

———. 1997a. "A Bottom Line for Crime." *Wall Street Journal* (August 6), 20.

———. 1997b. "Thinking about Crime Prevention." In *Preventing Crime: What Works, What Doesn't, What's Promising,* edited by Lawrence W. Sherman, Denise Gottfredson, Doris MacKenzie, John Eck, Peter Reuter, and Shawn D. Bushway. Washington, DC: U.S. Department of Justice http://www.ncjrs.gov/works/.

———. 1998a. "American Policing." In *The Handbook of Crime and Punishment,* edited by Michael Tonry. New York: Oxford University Press.

——— 1998b. *Evidence-Based Policing.* Washington, DC: Police Foundation.

———. 2001. "Fair and Effective Policing." In *Crime: Public Policies for Crime Control,* edited by James Q. Wilson and Joan Petersilia. San Francisco: ICS Press.

———. 2006. "'To Develop and Test:' The Inventive Difference between Evaluation and Experimentation." *Journal of Experimental Criminology* 2: 393–406.

———. 2007. "Preventing Murder With Special Units in Probation and Parole Agencies." *Criminology and Public Policy* 6: 843–49.

———. 2010a. *Experimental Criminology.* London: Sage.

———. 2010b. "An Introduction to Experimental Criminology." In *Handbook of Quantitative Criminology,* ed. Alex Piquero and David Weisburd. New York: Springer.

———. 2011. "Democratic Policing on the Evidence." In *Crime and Public Policy,* edited by James Q. Wilson and Joan Petersilia. New York: Oxford University Press.

Sherman, Lawrence W., Patrick R. Gartin, and Michael E. Buerger 1989. "'Hot Spots' of Predatory Crime: Routine Activities and the Criminology of Place." *Criminology* 27(1): 27–55.

Sherman, Lawrence, and Dennis P. Rogan. 1995. "Deterrent Effects of Police Raids on Crack Houses: A Randomized, Controlled Experiment." *Justice Quarterly* 12: 755–81.

Sherman, Lawrence, and Douglas A. Smith. 1992. "Crime, Punishment and Stake in Conformity: Legal and Informal Control of Domestic Violence." *American Sociological Review* 57(5): 680–90.

Sherman, Lawrence, and Heather Strang. 2007. *Restorative Justice: The Evidence.* London: Smith Institute.

Sherman, Lawrence, and David Weisburd. 1995. "General Deterrent Effects of Police Patrol in Crime Hot Spots: A Randomized, Controlled Trial." *Justice Quarterly* 12(4): 635–48.

Skogan, Wesley G. 2009. Personal communication, November 4.

Skogan, Wesley G., and Kathleen Frydl, eds. 2004. *Fairness and Effectiveness in Policing: The Evidence.* Washington, DC: National Academies Press.

Sloboda, Zili, Richard C. Stephens, Peggy C. Stephens, Scott F. Grey, Brent Teasdale, Richard D. Hawthorne, Joseph Williams, and Jesse F. Marquette. 2009. "The Adolescent Substance Abuse Prevention Study: A Randomized Field Trial of a Universal Substance Abuse Prevention Program." *Drug and Alcohol Dependence* 102: 1–10.

Spelman, William, and Dale K. Brown. 1981. *Calling the Police: Citizen Reporting of Serious Crime.* Washington, DC: Police Executive Research Forum.

Strang, Heather, Lawrence Sherman, Daniel Woods, and Evan Mayo-Wilson. 2009. "Effects of Restorative Justice Conferencing on Victims and Offenders: A Systematic Review." Draft Review for the Campbell Collaboration. Cambridge University, Institute of Criminology, Jerry Lee Centre of Experimental Criminology.

Weisburd, David. 2008. "Place-Based Policing." *Ideas in American Policing Series.* Washington, DC: Police Foundation. http://www.policefoundation.org/pdf/placebasedpolicing.pdf.

Weisburd, David, Shawn Bushway, Cynthia Lum, and Sue-Ming Yang. 2004. "Trajectories of Crime at Places: A Longitudinal Study of Street Segments in the City of Seattle." *Criminology* 42: 283–322.

Weisburd, David, Cynthia Lum, and Anthony Petrosino. 2001. "Does Research Design Affect Study Outcomes in Criminal Justice?" *Annals of the American Academy of Political and Social Science* 578: 50–70.

Weisburd, David, Lisa Maher, and Lawrence W. Sherman. 1993. "Contrasting Crime-Specific and Crime-General Theory: Hot Spots of Predatory Crime." In *Advances in Criminological Theory*, vol. 4, edited by Freda Adler and William S. Laufer. New Brunswick, NJ: Transaction.

Weisburd, David, and Lorraine Mazerolle. 1995. "Policing Drug Hot Spots: the Jersey City DMA Experiment." *Justice Quarterly* 12: 711–36.

Weisburd, David, Cody W. Telep, Joshua C. Hinkle, and John E. Eck. 2008. "The Effects of Problem-Oriented Policing on Crime and Disorder." A Campbell Collaboration Systemaic Review. http://www.campbellcollaboration.org/library.php.

———. 2010. "Is Problem-Oriented Policing Effective in Reducing Crime and Disorder? Findings from a Campbell Systematic Review." *Criminology and Public Policy* 9: 139–72.

Weisburd, David, Laura Wyckoff, Justin Ready, John E. Eck, Joshua C. Hinkle, and Frank Gajewski. 2006 "Does Crime Just Move Around the Corner?: A Controlled Study of Spatial Displacement and Diffusion of Crime Control Benefits." *Criminology* 443: 549–91.

West, Steven L., and Keri K. O'Neal. 2004. " Project D.A.R.E. Outcome Effectiveness Revisited." *American Journal of Public Health* 94: 1027–29.

Wilson, James Q. 1968. *Varieties of Police Behavior: The Management of Law and Order in Eight Communities*. Cambridge, MA: Harvard University Press.

Wilson, James Q., and George L. Kelling. 1982. "Broken Windows: The Police and Neighborhood Safety." *Atlantic Monthly*, March, 29–38.

Woolf, Peter. 2008. Personal communication, February [n.d.].

Zernike, Kate. 2006. "Questions Raised Over New Trend In Police Lineups." *New York Times* (April 19), 1.

Zimring, Franklin H. and Gordon Hawkins. 1973. *Deterrence: The Legal Threat in Crime Control*. Chicago: University of Chicago Press.

CHAPTER 18

....

COMMUNITY AND PROBLEM-ORIENTED POLICING

....

MICHAEL D. REISIG*

FOR the better part of the twentieth century, police departments throughout the United States directed their efforts toward suppressing crime. In the 1960s, however, critics charged that the crime-attack model was too aggressive, often resulting in high levels of citizen disaffection with local police, especially in inner-city African American neighborhoods. In the 1970s, several high-profile studies called into question the effectiveness of crime-control policing strategies, such as the use of routine motorized patrols to deter crime. Two reform initiatives—community and problem-oriented policing—emerged in the late 1970s and early 1980s, sparking a lively debate on the role of American police that has continued for three decades.

Community policing is an organizational strategy in which police activities are geared toward addressing the conditions that give rise to public safety concerns, including crime, disorder, and fear of crime. Two community policing archetypes can be identified. One approach, which is rooted in "broken windows" theory, emphasizes the use of disorder-reduction police strategies (e.g., misdemeanor arrests, situational prevention, and citizen involvement) to reduce neighborhood crime. The second, which is guided by the basic tenets of social disorganization theory, focuses on bolstering local community social processes that mediate the adverse impact of structural constraints (e.g., poverty) on crime, disorder, and analogous outcomes. Although these two approaches rest on different assumptions about the disorder-crime connection, they employ a variety of common strategies and tactics to improve neighborhood quality of life.

Problem-oriented policing is an analytic framework used by police to identify and solve troubles that prompt citizens' calls for service. Such concerns may be large or small, cross police districts or be contained to a single street corner, or be directly related to crime or not. Although specific strategies often vary from one problem to the next, a common approach to addressing crime and disorder involves reducing opportunities for disorderly and criminal behavior by manipulating environmental conditions.

The literature on these subjects supports a number of conclusions:

- Community policing is a multidimensional concept. Its elements can be grouped into four key dimensions—philosophical, strategic, tactical, and organizational.
- Problem-oriented policing is a flexible analytic framework that police departments can use to address a wide variety of crime and non-crime problems.
- From 1995 to 2008, the Community Oriented Policing Services (COPS) program distributed approximately 13.6 billion nominal dollars in funding to law enforcement agencies throughout the United States. The research evidence addressing whether the COPS program has reduced crime is inconclusive.
- Studies using various methodological designs have shown that broken windows policing tactics (e.g., misdemeanor arrests) have a modest impact on crime and disorder.
- The crime-disorder nexus remains a topic of controversy. While some studies find support, other researchers report evidence that the effect of disorder on crime is spurious once neighborhood-level social processes are accounted for.
- Neighborhood-level research on the effects of formal/informal social control linkages on crime and crime-related outcomes is limited. Available research does indicate, however, that police-community collaboration mediates the adverse effect of structural disadvantage on perceived safety and incivilities.
- Despite the growing number of important empirical contributions to the community and problem-oriented policing literatures, gaps and limitations remain. Future research needs to develop more complete measures of order-maintenance policing, evaluate the potential intervening role of collective efficacy on the effect of misdemeanor arrests on violent crime, and assess whether community policing practices (e.g., beat meetings) promote levels of collective efficacy.

This chapter is divided into five sections. Section I provides an overview of community and problem-oriented policing, highlighting the key of elements of the two approaches. Section II discusses the history of the American police, with an emphasis on the antecedents and outcomes associated with prior reform efforts. In section III, the federal government's involvement in community and problem-oriented policing via the COPS program is described, and the research assessing the impact of the program on crime rates is reviewed. Section IV focuses on the theoretical frameworks that guide community and problem-oriented policing interventions, and extant empirical research. Community policing is rooted in two theories of neighborhood crime (i.e., broken windows and social disorganization), whereas problem-oriented policing is often couched in theories of criminal opportunity (i.e., rational choice and routine activity). Section V concludes with a discussion specifying priorities for future research.

I. An Overview

Community and problem-oriented policing are distinct concepts, yet in practice they are often used in tandem. Both concepts are quite expansive in nature. Community policing, for example, is sometimes framed as an amorphous philosophy that permeates every aspect of a police department. While this conceptualization may be partially correct, individuals have used this view to mislabel traditional law enforcement tactics, such as exploratory traffic stops, as community policing. Others view community policing as limited to specific police activities, such as school-based drug prevention programs and foot patrols. In practice, community policing often includes specific operational programs and tactics, but it encompasses much more.

Community and problem-oriented policing are sometimes conceptualized as "organizational strategies." Moore (1992), for example, argues that both concepts are best understood as strategic attempts to redefine the traditional functions of the police, to modify key programs, tactics, and technologies upon which the police rely, and to redefine sources of police legitimacy. This approach is helpful. If properly implemented, community and problem-oriented policing entail changing the way in which police work has been conducted for much of the twentieth century.

Community policing is a multidimensional concept. Cordner (1999) groups the many elements of community policing into four key dimensions—philosophical, strategic, tactical, and organizational. The *philosophical dimension* includes the core ideas and beliefs about what the police should do. For example, community policing values and promotes the active solicitation of input from neighborhood residents and civic organizations, especially with regards to decisions and policies that affect local residents. Citizens often want the police to address a variety of problems, such as maintaining social order and providing non-emergency assistance to area citizens, which go beyond the traditional police mandate (Trojanowicz and Buc-queroux 1990; Skogan 2008*b*). Community policing also involves the adoption of a personal service orientation to police work, which requires that local norms and values are taken into consideration, along with organizational, professional, and legal factors, during decision making at all levels of the police organization.

When the philosophical elements of community policing are translated into police action, Cordner (1999) contends, the focus shifts to the *strategic dimension*. From an operational standpoint, community policing requires police officers regularly to seek out face-to-face interactions with the general public. Two strategic elements aid officers in this. First, police officers spend less time in their squad cars by adopting alternative patrol strategies (e.g., foot and bike patrol). Second, police officers are assigned to specific beats for extended time periods. These two elements not only help officers develop positive relationships with local residents but also familiarize them with neighborhood concerns. Breaking down the social distance between the police and public can pay off in the form of increased levels of public trust and support.

Specific police practices and behaviors are included in the *tactical dimension* (Cordner 1999). One of the key tactical elements of community policing is problem solving. Following the four-step, problem-solving process established by Goldstein (1979, 1990), police officers are encouraged to investigate and develop an under-standing of local problems and tailor community-specific solutions to address them (Goldstein 1987). Police-community partnerships to solve local problems lie at the heart of community policing. The ability of police officers to build meaningful partnerships with local residents hinges to a great extent on how officers conduct themselves during everyday, routine interactions with the public. Officers who treat citizens respectfully, take time to listen to their concerns, and inquire about local problems on a regular basis are better able to cultivate active participation among residents in collaborative problem-solving projects, which also helps to ensure that police services are consistent with citizens' expectations.

The *organizational dimension* concerns altering traditional structural arrange-ments within police departments to support community policing activities (Cordner 1999). The paramilitary organizational structure that dominated American policing during the mid-twentieth century is not conducive to collaborative problem-solving practices (Greene 2000). Instead, community policing requires flattening the orga-nizational hierarchy (i.e., reducing the number of ranks), and increasing the formal authority and responsibility of low-ranking officers. Rules and supervisory practices are loosened to allow beat officers to use their creativity to solve local problems (Kelling and Moore 1988). Finally, community policing requires police departments to be systematic information seekers. Programs are evaluated, crime patterns are analyzed, and information is shared within the organization, with other municipal agencies, and with the community. In this way, police departments become catalysts for community change.

Over the past two decades, American police departments have adopted and implemented different community policing elements. The result has been a hodge-podge of organizational arrangements, strategies, and tactics, which varies from one city to the next. Different forms of community policing can also be observed within cities across beats. This is to be expected. After all, neighborhood problems and resources (both financial and social) vary both qualitatively and quantitatively between and within cities (Skogan 2008b). Despite widespread variation in the practice of community policing, an overarching conceptual definition has been advanced: "Community policing is a philosophy that promotes organizational strategies, which support the systematic use of partnerships and problem-solving techniques, to proactively address the immediate conditions that give rise to public safety issues such as crime, social disorder, and fear of crime" (U.S. Department of Justice 2009a, 3).

Problem-oriented policing entails identifying and solving the broad range of troubles that prompt citizens to call on the police for service and assistance. In his influential article, Goldstein (1979) provides the basic structure of problem-oriented policing. First, the police work to define a problem. To successfully accomplish this task, the police should avoid broad classifications based on criminal codes (e.g., robbery, assault, burglary). Broad labels, according to Goldstein, are problematic because they are too heterogeneous. Instead, Goldstein insists that the police develop highly nuanced and precise problem definitions. At the second step, the police work to understand the magnitude and nature of the problem. Successfully doing so requires information. The police should not simply rely on traditional information sources (e.g., crime records), but should take advantage of the information that is available from other agencies and community residents, among other sources. Next, the police need to search for possible solutions. Here, Goldstein (1979, 250) advises the police to engage in an "uninhibited search for alternative responses that might be an improvement over what is currently being done." The solution may involve traditional law enforcement tactics (e.g., arrests and citations), or it may call for mobilizing local residents to collaborate with police in the problem-solving process. Finally, the police need to assess whether their solution worked. Sherman (1991) urges police officials to employ basic principles of evaluation research when assessing the results of problem-solving interventions (e.g., history, testing, instability, and instrumentation). This four-step, problem-solving process is incorporated in the well-known SARA model (i.e., scanning, analysis, response, and assessment) (Eck and Spelman 1987).

As an analytic framework, problem-oriented policing is quite versatile. For example, the police may focus on problems that occur in contained spaces, such as a street corners and alleyways. Problems may also be identified that take place throughout large portions of a city, such as a rash of convenience store robberies. Not only can the scope of the problems vary but so too can the potential solutions. During the response stage, police may determine that traditional law enforcement tactics provide the greatest likelihood of success. In other instances, nontraditional approaches may seem more promising, such as mobilizing local residents. Community involvement in the problem-solving process is not a requisite. The police may identify problems on their own, or problems may be nominated by community members. Similarly, the process of solving problems may entail the police working with local residents, but it may also be that the responsibility of enacting problem-solving measures falls squarely on the shoulders of the police.

The history of American policing is littered with strategies and tactics that initially were received with great enthusiasm but eventually were discarded when believed to be ineffective. The cycle of adopting and replacing policing models has continued for more than a century. It was through this evolutionary development of American policing that community and problem-oriented policing emerged onto the scene.

II. Historical Development

The historical development of the American police can be grouped into three stages: early uniformed police, bureaucratic policing, and community and problem-oriented policing.

A. First Stage: Early Uniformed Police

Early policing in the United States was greatly influenced by the English experience. The first modern police force, the London Metropolitan Police, was established in 1829. The Home Secretary, Sir Robert Peel, and his commissioners sought to establish a police force that did not resemble a standing army, and where officers (or "bobbies") maintained a healthy level of social distance from community members (Monkkonen 1981). The latter was thought to contribute to an impartial, impersonal police image rooted not in community norms and values but in the English Constitution (Miller 1977). To help achieve this objective, officials regularly recruited new officers from rural areas outside of London. Peel's commissioners insisted that their officers exercise restraint and display a polite demeanor while on patrol (Lane 1980). Such interpersonal treatment, it was believed, helped "compensate for distance from local residents" and would even "win respect" among area residents (Miller 1977, 38). The legitimacy of the London police was based on the rule of law, which was thought to translate into more consistent, less discretionary policing across locales. London officers were closely monitored, and those who abused their authority were reprimanded by supervisors (Lane 1980).

The establishment of formal, unified police departments in New York, Chicago, and other major American cities was motivated by two factors. First, there were growing concerns that informal neighborhood social controls were rapidly deteriorating as urban populations grew larger and as more affluent citizens self segregated into local communities away from the lower classes (Miller 1977). At the time, collective disorders (e.g., food riots and wage protests), crime, and disorder were increasingly disruptive (Uchida 2005). The introduction of more effective and efficient formal social controls, such as uniformed police forces, was viewed as one way to help alleviate the social problems in urban areas. Second, the spread of formal, semi-bureaucratic police organizations in the United States occurred during a time when a broader movement to establish rational municipal governmental services was taking place (e.g., fire, health, and sewage) (Monkkonen 1981).

Some early police reformers in the United States regarded the London model as exemplar. Individuals holding this view argued that adopting the London model would be a significant improvement over the traditional constable-watch system, which was increasingly viewed as ineffective at dealing with and preventing urban crime and disorder. Opponents argued, however, that the London model encroached on civil liberties, would prove too costly, and resembled a military presence (Monkkonen 1981). Throughout the mid-1800s many American cities established new police departments (Haller 1975). Like their English counterparts, the American police donned uniforms (albeit reluctantly in many cases). On the whole, however, reformers selectively adopted certain aspects of the London model. What emerged in practice was a style of policing that was uniquely American.

The primary objective of the new American police was the prevention of crime and disorder (Miller 1977). Lane (1980) notes, however, that American foot-patrol officers went about their jobs differently than their London counterparts. Because of public concerns of government tyranny, American police officers were granted less formal legal authority. Instead, police officers exercised broad discretionary powers. Officers were expected to use their discretion in a manner consistent with informal community expectations, local norms, and values, as opposed to bureaucratic ideals and the rule of law (Miller 1977). Extralegal methods, such as physical force and verbal intimidation, were commonly employed. Indeed, foot-patrol officers were expected to physically dominate their beats, and use violence as opposed to arrest to handle disorderly individuals and petty criminals (Haller 1975). Individualized street justice was largely condoned by police supervisors (unless directed at respectable citizens) and members of the community, especially among middle- and upper-class residents who expected the police to control members of the "dangerous class" (i.e., tramps, foreign-born, out-of-towners, unemployed young men) who were thought to be more prone to criminal and disorderly behavior (Haller 1975; Miller 1977; Lane 1980). But the police did not only rely on coercive tactics to achieve class control. A number of social service mechanisms were also used, such as providing indigents with night lodging (Monkkonen 1981).

Policing scholars sometimes refer to this period as the "political era" because of the intimate connection that existed between the police and political actors (Kelling and Moore 1988). Local political agents exerted tremendous power. They appointed police captains in their districts, and used the force to provide patronage jobs to party loyalists (Haller 1975; Lane 1980). The police were also used to influence the outcomes of local elections (e.g., ballot rigging and voter intimidation) and to regulate vice (e.g., gambling and liquor). For example, local political concerns influenced how existing liquor laws were enforced. In some police districts liquor laws were enforced strictly, in others loosely, in still others not at all (Lane 1980). The regulation of vice provided the police opportunities to receive bribes, collect protection money, and to engage in extortive practices. Along with a portion of their salaries, officers regularly "contributed" shares of their ill-gotten gains to dominate political parties (Monkkonen 1981).

B. Second Stage: Bureaucratic Policing

As the nineteenth century drew to a close, many municipal agencies, not just the police, were criticized by Progressive Era reformers as inefficient, corrupt, and discriminatory. Political influences were viewed as a primary culprit. Progressive Era reformers argued that politics should set the objectives for administration and administration should carry out the policies in the absence of political meandering (Wilson 1887; Goodnow 1900; White 1926). This view is often referred to as the "politics-administration dichotomy" model. Applied to municipal government, the model holds that local politicians should stay out of the administrative affairs of local agencies (e.g., hiring and firing decisions in local police departments); agency managers should not get involved in shaping government policies; and the role of agency managers is that of a politically neutral expert who strives to effectively and efficiently carrying out the policies developed through political processes (Svara 1998). One result of this reform movement was the enactment of civil service laws that helped insulate municipal agencies from local political influences, especially with regards to employee selection and promotion. But such changes did not occur overnight but rather took several decades. The extent to which such laws influenced police officer behavior on the beat was probably modest (Haller 1975).

Progressive reformers also called on public agencies to employ management practices consistent with classical organization theory, which at the time were quite popular in the private sector (see, e.g., Taylor 1911; Fayol 1949 [1916]). The basic themes included: organizations and members behave rationally, organization strive to be efficient, efficiency is achieved through specialization and the division of labor, and efficiency is maximized through scientific inquiry (Shafritz and Ott 1996, 29–31). The ideas espoused by progressive activists were closely aligned with the objectives of several early police reformers (see, e.g., Smith 1940; Wilson 1950; Fosdick 1969

[1915]; Vollmer 1971 [1936]). August Vollmer, for example, advocated for a professional police force that was "an efficient, nonpartisan agency committed to the highest standards of public service" (Walker 1980, 134). This new approach to policing, which came to be known as the "professional model," featured a narrowing of the police mandate—no longer did the police employ a variety of tactics to control the dangerous class but instead focused specifically on crime control. Applying the basic themes from classical organization theory, the professional police department was characterized by a centralization of command and standardization of procedure, division of labor and task specialization, improved standards of recruiting and training, and the use of scientific methods to investigate crimes (Goldstein 1990, 6–8). Other reforms and innovations, including preventive motorized patrols, rapid response, systematic recording of crime data, and the use of two-way radios were geared toward accomplishing three objectives—enhancing organizational efficiency, reducing crime, and increasing control over patrol officers.

The professional model was the dominant organizational design in American policing for much of the mid-twentieth century. Police officers in large cities maintained a presence through motorized patrols, racing from one call to the next. The image they portrayed was that of a crime fighter. Over time, however, the professional model began to falter. In the 1960s, for example, crime was on the rise, and the inability of the police to reverse crime trends called into question their crime fighter image. Several televised civil rights marches showed African American demonstrators being beaten, water hosed by police, and attacked by dogs, leading many to view the police as the "symbol of a society that denied blacks equal justice under the law" (Uchida 2005, 33). In some cities, such as Detroit and Newark, police actions (e.g., raids and shootings) were perceived as the cause of urban riots. An investigation by the National Advisory Commission on Civil Disorders (1968) concluded the police represent "white power, white racism, and white repression" among black ghetto dwellers (5). Among other things, the commission recommended that the police "eliminate abrasive practices" in inner-city neighborhoods, and implement "innovate programs to insure widespread community support for law enforcement" (8).

A number of research studies conducted in the 1970s challenged key aspects of the professional model. For example, the Kansas City Preventive Patrol Experiment showed that not only do routine motorized patrols not deter crime but also have little effect on citizens' fear of crime (Kelling et al. 1974). Another influential study, conducted by researchers at the Rand Corporation, reported that variation in investigative training, staff, workload, and procedures had no meaningful effect on crime, arrest, and clearance rates. In addition, the Rand researchers found that over one-half of serious felonies (e.g., homicide and rape) reported to the police received only "superficial attention" by investigative staff (Greenwood and Petersilia 1975, vii). A study conducted by researchers at the Police Executive Research Forum (PERF) found that efforts to reduce police response time had no effect on arrest rates. The

PERF researchers discovered that other factors, such as citizen-reporting time, played a more important role (Spelman and Brown 1984). These studies provided evidence that caused many observers to question the merits of the professional model of policing.

C. Third Stage: Community and Problem-Oriented Policing

During the 1970s and 1980s, various attempts to improve policing practices were underway (see Moore 1992, 131–38; Skogan 2008b). One example, community crime prevention, sought to build collaborative partnerships between criminal justice agencies and community organizations to address crime and related problems. This approach rested on the assumption that crime-ridden, disorderly neighborhoods lacked the informal social controls necessary to regulate the behavior of residents and visitors (Hope 1995). Many crime prevention programs attempted to address the problem by organizing community members. Not only were residents encouraged to harden their domiciles to prevent break-ins but also to work collectively by communicating suspicious activity to neighbors, form civilian patrols to roam the neighborhood, call on and assist the police when crime happened, and engage in other collective anti-crime activities. However, participation in such programs proved difficult to sustain (Rosenbaum 1988). Based on his comprehensive review of the research literature, Skogan (1988) noted that community organizations were much more likely to arise and flourish in more affluent areas, and that program awareness and participation tended to be dominated by residents from higher socio-economic backgrounds (also see Rosenbaum, Lurigio and Davis 1998, 22–27).

Team policing was another attempt to move beyond the professional model. This police innovation called for establishing teams of officers in various beats throughout cities, and holding them accountable for local conditions (Bloch and Specht 1973). Traditional car patrols remained in use, but routine calls for service were first given to team officers in the area in which they originated. Evaluation research studies generally reported positive findings (see, e.g., Sherman, Milton, and Kelly 1973). However, the ability to strike a proper balance between a traditional crime fighting force and a second patrol force consisting of area teams that were more responsive to local community needs proved difficult. Team officers were expected to respond to calls for service and foster community involvement. The more citizen involvement officers were able to stimulate, the less time they were available to respond to calls. Given the traditional crime-fighter values that dominated police organizations, it was only a matter of time until team officers morphed back into traditional patrol officers (Sparrow, Moore, and Kennedy 1990).

A third set of reforms involved the re-emergence of foot patrols in a number of American cities (e.g., Houston, Boston, and Baltimore). Initiated because of growing concerns over the effectiveness of car patrols, investigators sought to determine whether foot patrols could reduce levels of perceived disorder (e.g., loitering and drug use), reduce perceived crime, improve perceptions of safety and citizen evaluations of police service, and reduce actual crime and victimization (see Pate 1986). In Flint, Michigan, Trojanowicz (1986) found that citizens residing in foot patrol areas reported higher levels of satisfaction with police services and that they felt safer. Crime rates also went down in the study areas, except for robbery and burglary. Trojanowicz notes, however, that these serious crimes were considerably higher in other areas of the city that did not receive foot patrols (also see Trojanowicz 1982). A second study, conducted in Newark, New Jersey, reported positive findings of foot patrols in terms of influencing individual perceptions of safety, perceptions of crime problems, perceptions of disorder problems, and ratings of police service. The researchers in Newark did not find any effect of foot patrols on reported crime levels (Pate 1986). Many police reformers interpreted these findings as showing that foot patrols could have positive effects.

Police reform in the United States gained momentum after the publication of two influential articles authored by prominent policing scholars. The first, Wilson and Kelling's (1982) "Broken Windows" article, used the Newark foot patrol experiments as a point of departure to support their reform agenda. The authors noted that Newark foot patrol officers became intimately familiar with their beats, and were quite effective at upholding local community standards, such as making sure "disreputable regulars" kept their alcoholic beverages in paper bags and did not lie down for sidewalk naps. Sometimes the police used their powers of arrest to remove disorderly people from the streets, at other times less formal (even extralegal) tactics were used. The authors likened this form of policing to the style observed in earlier periods of American history. Wilson and Kelling cautioned that some informal tactics employed by officers "probably would not withstand legal challenge" (31) and that they are not "easily reconciled with any conception of due process or fair treatment" (35). But, the authors argued, the rules were well understood by area residents who condoned informal and extralegal police tactics. According to Wilson and Kelling, citizens were pleased that the police were doing something about disorderly behavior.

Wilson and Kelling's paper sparked considerable debate on the topic of police reform. Focusing specifically on Wilson and Kelling's work, Walker (1984) rejected the notion that the police in the nineteenth century enjoyed high levels of legitimacy. As evidence, Walker pointed to the many political battles over the enforcement of drinking laws that undermined public support. Walker also claimed that Wilson and Kelling portrayed a highly romanticized view of early American policing. In actuality, Walker argued, early foot patrols were plagued by corruption and were terribly inefficient. Others focused their criticisms on the methodological limitations of the foot patrol experiments cited by Wilson and Kelling. For example, Greene and Taylor (1988) pointed out that none of the foot patrol experiments at the time, including the Newark study, actually used "ecologically valid neighborhood units" (217). Failing to do so meant that foot patrol officers toured several local communities, which made it incredibly difficult (if not impossible) to learn the specific local norms.

Other critics took aim at the order-maintenance function of policing more generally. Manning (1988, 44) argued, for example, that the police cannot "coerce, enforce, punish, and maintain formal social control" and expect to maintain high levels of support in all segments of the general population. But not everyone objected to the notion of police officers sometimes resorting to aggressive forms of order maintenance. Sykes (1986) argued that maintaining order was not inherently repressive, but instead actually provided protection and regulation that are necessary for a free, well-functioning community. Mastrofski (1988, 60) points out, however, that relaxing bureaucratic and legal constraints on police behavior can potentially increase "police misbehavior, abuse of authority, and bad judgment."

The second important article, authored by Herman Goldstein (1979), also directed criticism toward the professional model of policing. Goldstein argued that police professionals in the United States suffered from the "means-over-ends syndrome" (238). Put simply, too much emphasis had been placed on formalizing police processes. Goldstein conceded that the establishment of businesslike procedures was appropriate when Progressive Era reformers began their work. After all, at that time the police were horribly inefficient, poorly trained, and supervision was lax. But improvements to police efficiency came at a significant cost—police officials no longer concerned themselves with the objectives of preventing and controlling crime and related problems. Goldstein advocated that the police focus their attention on the problems that result in calls for service as opposed to the calls themselves.

Much of the early research in support of problem-oriented policing relied on case study methodologies, which provided detailed contextual assessment of problem-oriented policing interventions in departments throughout the United States. In his highly acclaimed book, *Problem-Oriented Policing* (1990), Goldstein presents a case study that he says is a classic example of problem-oriented policing at work. The case involved an increase in convenience store robberies in Gainesville, Florida. After carefully studying the problem, which included an independent assessment conducted by a university-based researcher, the police concluded that the robbers were targeting stores staffed by a single clerk during the night shift. At the urging of the police, the city council passed an ordinance requiring convenience stores to have two clerks on duty at specific times. Shortly after the ordinance passed, convenience store robberies dropped by 65 percent.

Although the Gainesville case is straightforward and, at first glance, appears to demonstrate to merits of problem-oriented policing, some observers argue that the findings are largely anecdotal. For example, Sherman (1991, 700–701) asks the following: Did the number of convenience stores decline after the new ordinance passed requiring more clerks be employed? Were known convenience store robbers apprehended about the same time the new law went into effect? In addition,

Sherman notes that clerks who worked alone at night could simply have pocketed money from the cash register and reported that they were robbed to the police to cover up the embezzlement. Once a second clerk was placed in the store, the scheme would require a co-conspirator, potentially making reported robberies less common. The Gainesville case study did not address these questions, nor did it adequately rule out potential rival explanations. Much like the criticisms directed at the early foot patrol experiments, police scholars in the early years of problem-oriented policing called for more systematic and exhaustive assessments of policing interventions that employed more scientifically-rigorous methodologies, such as experimental and quasi-experimental designs, to evaluate the impact of police interventions.

As the 1980s drew to a close, few could have predicted the rate at which the police reform movement would sweep across the country in the coming decade. Interest in community and problem-oriented policing among law enforcement agencies in big cities, rural counties, affluent suburban communities, and college towns grew by leaps and bounds in 1990s. At about the same time, approximately two years after William Jefferson Clinton was elected president, the federal government enacted legislation providing unprecedented levels of financial support to assist police departments move to community policing.

III. THE COPS PROGRAM

In the 1990s, the federal government became involved in the police reform movement with the passage of the Violent Crime Control and Law Enforcement Act of 1994 (Crime Act). Between fiscal years 1995 and 2000, the Crime Act authorized the appropriation of $8.8 billion in grants to support local law enforcement agencies' community policing efforts. The Community Oriented Policing Services (COPS) program was established by the Department of Justice to award a variety of different grants to law enforcement agencies to accomplish four goals: increase the number of police officers, foster police-community interaction and problem solving, encourage police innovation, and develop new police technologies to reduce crime (Roth and Ryan 2000). In 2005 the COPS program was reauthorized by Congress.

By 2000, the COPS program reportedly funded more than 100,000 police officers.[1] This was accomplished through the use of three-year hiring grants that paid up to 75 percent of the cost of hiring new officers. Agencies receiving these awards were required to hire police officers who would engage in community policing activities (Roth and Ryan 2000). The COPS grants were also used to acquire crime-fighting technology, fund innovative police programs, and establish a nationwide network of Regional Community Policing Institutes (RCPI). The RCPI network was set up to provide training and technical assistance to law

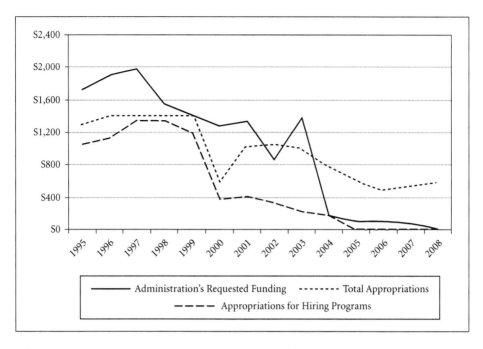

Figure 18.1. Funding Requests and Appropriations for the COPS Program, 1995–2008 (in millions of nominal dollars)

Source: James 2008, p. 11.

enforcement agencies (U.S. Department of Justice 2006). As of mid-year 2009, the RCPIs had trained more than 600,000 police officers, government officials, and community members (U.S. Department of Justice 2009*b*).

The amount of money appropriated to the COPS program from 1995 to 2008 was substantial (approximately 13.6 billion in nominal dollars). As figure 18.1 shows, a large percentage of the appropriations to the COPS program between 1995 and 1999 (approximately 86.7 percent) went to hiring programs. Federal appropriations for the COPS program remained fairly stable from 1995 to 1999 (average of about $1.4 billion per year), but declined thereafter. In 2000 appropriations were reduced by 57.5 percent (an $835 million reduction). Appropriations increased after that point for several years, even exceeding funding requests by the Bush administration. In 2008 the COPS program was appropriated $587 billion (James 2008).

A. COPS and Community Policing

The adoption of community and problem-oriented policing practices expanded following the passage of the Crime Act of 1994. Using multiple waves of survey data collected in 1996, 1998, and 2000 and site visits to police agencies, Roth,

Roehl, and Johnson (2004) tracked the adoption of four police reforms—tactics for building partnerships, problem solving, crime prevention, and supportive organizational changes—from 1995 to 2000. Roth and his colleagues found that the implementation of partnership building tactics increased significantly between 1995 and 1998 among large agencies. No change was observed between 1998 and 2000. From their site visits, Roth et al. found that partnerships usually took two forms: problem solving partnerships formed with other service providers, and community partnerships with neighborhood residents, groups, and businesses.

The adoption of problem-solving and crime prevention tactics followed patterns similar to partnership building—significantly increasing from 1995 to 1998 and observing no change between 1998 and 2000. The authors' fieldwork uncovered problems with police adoption of crime prevention. More specifically, Roth and his associates report that police officials usually pointed to existing programs (e.g., Drug Abuse Resistance Education [DARE] and Neighborhood Watch) rather than new initiatives, and seldom were able to "articulate any philosophy of prevention, logical productions of collaboration with communities and problem solving focused on underlying causes" (16). By comparison, the most modest community policing reforms adopted by large police departments were in the area of supportive organizational changes. When the specific elements were assessed separately, the findings showed that nearly 80 percent of large police departments reportedly established neighborhood patrol boundaries by 1998, and that beat integrity had exceeded 60 percent that same year (Roth, Roehl, and Johnson 2004).

More recent trends in the adoption of community policing practices can be traced using reports published by the Bureau of Justice Statistics (2000, 2006). Figure 18.2 provides a look at community policing practices in local police departments of all sizes at 1997 and 2003. The data show that training citizens in community policing, conducting citizen surveys, geographic assignment of patrol officers, and training new recruits in community policing were more common in 1997. Little change was observed in developing a written community policing plan and encouraging officers to engage in problem-solving activities. The percentage of departments with full-time, sworn community policing officers grew rather rapidly between the two observation periods.

The data presented in figure 18.2 provide some indication as to the popularity of community policing practices in American police departments. However, some caution must be exercised when interpreting these data. Perhaps most importantly is the dosage issue. Maguire and Mastrofski (2000) have pointed out that these data simply reflect whether departments reportedly adopted various community policing elements. They tell us little (if anything) about the extent to which agencies actually engage in specific activities.

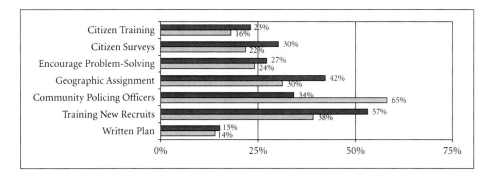

Figure 18.2. Community Policing in Local Police Departments (all sizes), 1997 & 2003.
Sources: Bureau of Justice Statistics, 2000, 2006.

B. COPS and Crime Research

Research investigating the effect of COPS grants on crime has been at the center of a fair amount of controversy. Some of it stems from the numerous methodological challenges confronting researchers who attempt to tackle the question (see Worrall 2010, 42–44), and some is probably associated with deep-seated political views regarding the proper role of the federal government. Zhao, Scheider, and Thurman (2002) were the first to evaluate the impact of COPS funding on crime rates. Using panel data (1995–99) from 6,100 cities, Zhao and his associates showed that two COPS programs (i.e., hiring and innovative grants) significantly reduced violent and property crime rates in cities with populations exceeding 10,000. Although they did not find similar effects in smaller cities and towns, Zhao et al. concluded that COPS grants appeared to be an effective way to reduce crime in the United States (also see Zhao, Scheider, and Thurman 2003).

The Zhao et al. (2002) study was the focus of considerable criticism. For example, Muhlhausen (2002, 8) argued that Zhao and associates' study was "critically flawed" because it failed to account for a variety of factors known to influence crime rates and control for local law enforcement efforts, among other shortcomings. Muhlhausen (2001) attempted to replicate Zhao et al.'s findings using panel data (1995–98) from 752 counties. Muhlhausen found that hiring grants and grants for purchasing new technology had no appreciable impact on violent crime.

Three additional studies followed soon thereafter. The Government Accountability Office (GAO) attempted to address criticisms of the Zhao et al. study, such as variable omission bias. For example, the GAO study included controls for other types of federal funding. Based of their analysis, the GAO concluded that "COPS grant expenditures did reduce crime during the 1990s" (GAO 2005, 17). Evans and Owens (2007) used panel data (1990–2001) from 2074 cities and towns to assess the impact of COPS funding. They found that four types of crime (i.e., auto theft, burglary, robbery, and aggravated assault) dropped in the years following the receipt of COPS hiring grants. That same year, however, a second study was published that arrived at a different conclusion. Worrall and Kovandzic (2007) assessed panel data (1990–2000) from 189 large cities. The authors included non-COPS police expenditures in their analysis, thus addressing criticism directed at the Zhao et al. study. After evaluating the impact of COPS funding on seven types of serious crime, the authors concluded that "COPS grants had no discernible effect on serious crime during the period covered by our analysis" (170).

The research evidence addressing whether the COPS program has reduced crime is mixed. While some observers conclude that investments made in policing to expand the number of police officers contributed to the crime drop in the 1990s (see, e.g., Levitt 2004), others remain steadfast in their position that COPS hiring grants failed to reduce crime (Muhlhausen and Walsh 2008).

IV. THEORY AND RESEARCH

Academic discussions of community policing are generally rooted in two neighborhood theories of crime—broken windows and social disorganization theory. Given its flexibility, a variety of theoretical frameworks (e.g., routine activity theory) can be used to guide problem-oriented policing interventions.

A. Broken Windows Theory

Broken windows theory posits that neighborhood disorder indirectly causes crime through a cascading sequence of events (see figure 18.3). Disorder is typically conceptualized as a two-dimensional concept. One dimension, social disorder, is defined as "boorish and threatening behavior" that disrupts urban life (Kelling and Coles 1996, 16). Examples include aggressive panhandling, street prostitution, public drinking and drug use, and urinating in public spaces. Albert J. Reiss Jr. (1985) referred to these behaviors as "soft crimes"—while technically crimes (usually misdemeanors or petty offenses), such behaviors are traditionally not a high police priority. The second dimension, physical disorder, refers to "visual signs of negligence and unchecked decay" in neighborhood settings (Skogan 1990, 4). Broken streetlights and windows, vacant lots filled with garbage, abandoned or burned-out buildings and cars, and gang graffiti are common examples of physical disorder. Importantly, broken windows theory posits that observable signs of disorder (or "incivilities"), when left unchecked, elevate levels of fear among area residents (Wilson and Kelling 1982). Fearful citizens take steps to reduce their perceived victimization risk. For example, some residents move to less disorderly (and presumably safer) neighborhoods. Those who are unable to relocate minimize their potential exposure to victimization by altering their daily routines (e.g., avoiding local markets, finding alternatives to public transportation, and spending more time indoors).

Fear-induced physical and social withdrawal has detrimental effects on the ability of local communities to regulate the behavior of residents and visitors. Citizens are more reluctant to intervene on behalf of the public (e.g., break up fights between children), less willing to participate in local civic organizations, and neglect their social ties with neighbors. In short, informal social controls break down as social isolation sets in (Kelling and Coles 1996, 20). In the absence of effective social controls, neighborhood conditions become increasingly criminogenic, and disorder becomes more pervasive and intense (e.g., panhandlers are more menacing, rowdy teens are emboldened, and gang graffiti accumulates), all of which signals miscreants that "no one cares" and thus the neighborhood is ripe for "criminal invasion" (Wilson and Kelling 1982, 31–32). In turn, open-air drug markets become larger and busier, street prostitutes increase in number, muggings become more frequent, and other forms of street violence happen with greater regularity. Over time, neighborhoods that reach the bottom of the spiraling cycle of decline "may no longer be recognized as neighborhoods" (Skogan 1990, 14).

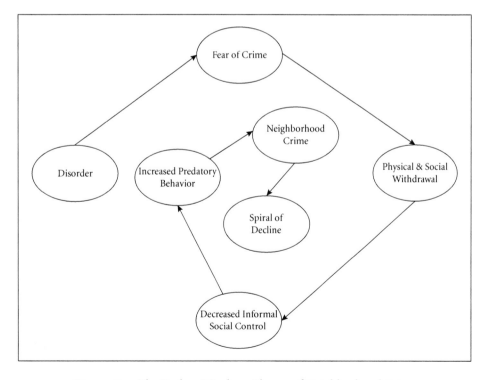

Figure 18.3. The Broken Windows Theory of Neighborhood Crime
Source: Adapted from Kelling and Bratton, 1998, p. 1219.

Broken windows theory has received a fair amount of empirical attention. Harcourt and Ludwig (2006) group broken windows research studies into two categories: those that assess the impact of broken windows policing, and those that test hypotheses derived from broken windows theory.

1. *Research on the Effect of Broken Windows Policing*

Broken windows theory is widely considered the guiding force behind order-maintenance policing (also termed "broken windows policing"). The idea is pretty straightforward: given the series of harmful effects that flow from neighborhood disorder, order-maintenance policing requires police officers to address disorder problems on a routine basis. Two important questions arise. First, when do disorder-related problems warrant police intervention? Kelling and Coles (1996) contend that police officers must determine the seriousness of the offense in context. For example, a group of intoxicated men consuming alcohol on a busy street corner during the day necessitates intervention more so than a single person drinking a beer in a paper sack in an alleyway at night. A teenager urinating on a car in a busy parking lot in broad daylight requires police intervention more so than a teen doing the same thing behind a dumpster after midnight. Police officers, according to Kelling and Coles, must also evaluate the harm done to the victim and impact on the community. Returning to the examples, the group of male drunkards will adversely impact the ability of nearby shop owners to conduct business. An elderly neighborhood resident walking by the parking lot will be disturbed by the sight of a teenager urinating in plain sight. In situations where the seriousness and harm of disorderly acts is not so clear cut, the police must rely on their training and departmental policy to determine whether intervention is warranted.

The second question concerns how police officers should handle encounters with disorderly individuals. In theory, order-maintenance policing calls on the police to exhaust non-arrest approaches, such as persuasion, counseling, and ordering, to resolve the disorder problems they encounter. If such attempts fail, then making an arrest for a misdemeanor offense is appropriate (Kelling and Coles 1996, 23). Research addressing the impact of broken windows policing has adopted two different strategies: assessments of department-wide, order-maintenance strategies across police precincts and targeted interventions focusing on specific urban locations.

A growing body of research has attempted to determine the effect broken windows policing had (if any) on the declining crime rate in New York City (NYC). The NYC crime drop has attracted the attention of researchers for several reasons. For example, NYC experienced dramatic decreases in rates of violent and property crime during the 1990s (56 percent and 65 percent, respectively). What is more, during the 1990s NYC officials, including Mayor Rudolph Giuliani and Police Commissioner William Bratton, implemented their version of order-maintenance policing, which resulted in an explosion of misdemeanor arrests. Reflecting on the NYC crime drop, Kelling and Bratton (1998, 1217) commented that the "police played an important, even central, role in getting people to stop committing crime in New York City." Some observers, however, contend that the contributions of policing strategies on NYC's declining crime rates are "exaggerated" (Levitt 2004, 173).

Kelling and Sousa's (2001) study was one of the first sophisticated attempts to investigate the impact of order-maintenance policing on NYC crime rates in the 1990s. Using police precincts as their unit of analysis, Kelling and Sousa operationalized order-maintenance policing as arrests for misdemeanor offenses. After regressing violent crime (murder, rape, robbery, and felonious assault) onto misdemeanor arrests and statistical control variables, the authors observed that order-maintenance policing contributed to the NYC crime drop. Specifically, Kelling and Sousa reported that for every twenty-eight misdemeanor arrests, one violent crime was prevented. The authors estimated that from 1989 to 1998, more than 60,000 violent crimes were prevented, which corresponds to a 5 percent reduction in violent crime (Kelling and Sousa 2001, 10). A second study, which used monthly time-series data over a twenty-five-year period (1974–99), arrived at a similar conclusion (Corman and Mocan 2005). Like Kelling and Sousa, the authors operationalized order-maintenance policing as misdemeanor arrests. However, Corman and Mocan assess the impact of misdemeanor arrests on specific types of crime (e.g., murder, robbery, motor vehicle theft, and grand larceny). Evidence in support of broken windows policing was observed: a 10 percent increase in misdemeanor arrests was associated with a 2.5–3.2 percent decline in robbery, a 1.6–2.1 percent decrease in motor vehicle theft, and a 0.5–0.6 percent decline in grand larceny (255). The authors report, however, that the effect of order-maintenance policing on the other types of crimes included in the study was null.

The Kelling and Sousa and Corman and Mocan studies were not met with universal praise. Harcourt and Ludwig (2006) took issue with several technical aspects of these two studies. For example, the Kelling and Sousa study, according to Harcourt and Ludwig, failed to account for a variety of important control variables and adjust their multivariate models to account for "mean reversion." Regarding the latter, Harcourt and Ludwig argued that those NYC precincts that received the most intense order-maintenance policing also experienced the largest increases in crime during the 1980s. Harcourt and Ludwig contend that areas where crime rates go up the most are usually the places where they decline the most. Their reassessment of the impact of misdemeanor arrests on violent crime, which included measures of police manpower, age composition, and structural disadvantage, showed that misdemeanor arrests had no significant impact violent crime in NYC between 1989 and 1999 (also see Harcourt and Ludwig 2007).

Other recent studies throw additional light on the effect of broken windows policing in NYC. Rosenfeld, Fornango, and Rengifo (2007) assessed the impact of order maintenance policing (operationalized as misdemeanor *and* ordinance violation arrests) on two types of violent crime—robbery and homicide—at the precinct level from 1988 to 2001. After controlling for a variety of factors hypothesized to influence violent crime rates (e.g., felony arrests and drug markets), Rosenfeld et al. found that order-maintenance policing resulted in declines in both robbery (about a 1–5 percent decline) and homicide (about a 7–12 percent decline) during the 1990s (377). Adopting a slightly different focus, Messner et al. (2007) assessed the effect of misdemeanor arrests on three measures of homicide (gun-related, non-gun related, and total homicides) and robbery across NYC precincts from 1990 to 1999. Like Rosenfeld et al., Messner and colleagues' analysis controlled for other factors hypothesized to influence aggregate crime rates, such as felony arrest rates, cocaine use, and neighborhood characteristics. Their findings revealed that misdemeanor arrests were associated with reductions in robbery, gun-related homicide, and total homicide. Messner and associates estimate that an increase of 833 misdemeanor arrests result in one less homicide for a precinct of 100,000 population (400) (also see Cerdá et al. 2009).

On balance, the research on the effect of policing strategies on the NYC crime drop indicates that order-maintenance policing had a modest impact on certain types of crime, especially robbery and gun-related homicide. Although informative, these studies employ a narrow operational definition of order-maintenance policing (e.g., misdemeanor arrests). As Thacher (2004, 393) notes, "simply equating order maintenance policing with misdemeanor arrests is clearly too simple" (also see Braga and Bond 2008, 581). Whether more nuanced order-maintenance measures that capture instances of police dealing with disorderly behavior by way of persuasion, warnings, and reminders in the absence of formal sanction also impacted crime rates across NYC precincts during the 1990s remains an open empirical question.

While a number of studies have sought to assess the impact of broken windows policing strategies and tactics on specific urban locations, three well-crafted studies are discussed here. Perhaps the most sustained, comprehensive, and methodologically rigorous evaluation of community policing is Wesley Skogan's work on the Chicago Alternative Policing Strategy (CAPS). Chicago-style community policing is based on broken windows theory. However, unlike the approach adopted in NYC, CAPS does not address "community problems by making tens of thousands of arrests for minor offenses," but in Chicago the "solution for broken windows is to fix them" (Skogan 2006, 179). The CAPS program incorporated several community policing characteristics, including officers assigned to specific beats, training officers in problem-solving, emphasis placed on community involvement, and crime analysis. When comparing research beats (i.e., those targeted for CAPS interventions) to comparison beats, Skogan and Hartnett (1997) found that citizens residing in disadvantaged areas reported that neighborhood conditions, such as drug sales and abandoned buildings, improved significantly following police intervention. In more affluent areas, however, improvements were also observed but it was not clear as to whether they were attributable to police interventions (i.e., conditions in comparison beats also improved). In short, Chicago's broken windows approach to community policing produced positive outcomes in distressed residential settings, but in areas where neighborhood problems were low to begin with, gains following police intervention were comparatively modest.

Operation Restoration, a policing program in Chandler, Arizona, emphasized order maintenance and zoning ordinance enforcement to address disorder problems (Katz, Webb, and Schaefer 2001). The police department targeted four intervention zones. At the beginning stages of the program, Chandler police actively sought community input by conducting community surveys and holding meetings with local residents and stakeholders. Citizen input showed that disorder-related problems were prevalent in a number of different residential communities. After selecting specific areas for intervention, the police held community meetings to educate residents about the operation and ask them to tell others about Operation Restoration. Katz and his colleagues tracked the number of calls for service over a 1,245-day period (from pre- to post-intervention). Their analyses revealed that the number of calls for service pertaining to public morals offenses, such as street prostitution and public drinking, decreased significantly. In sum, Operation Restoration proved successful in reducing community-nominated problems.

More recently, Braga and Bond (2008) evaluated the effect of broken windows policing on a variety of outcomes, such as citizen calls for service and pre- and post-intervention levels of physical and social disorder. The authors employed a randomized block field experimental design. The police intervention involved various broken windows policing tactics, including situational prevention, social service, and misdemeanor arrest. Braga and Bond found that the total number of calls, robbery and non-domestic assault calls, and disorder and burglary calls were all significantly reduced in the treatment areas. The authors were able to determine which police strategies had the largest effect on calls for service. The number of different situational prevention strategies proved most salient, followed by misdemeanor arrests. The effect of social service strategies on calls for service was null. Regarding pre- and post-intervention levels of disorder, Braga and Bond report that social (e.g., loiters, public drinkers, and the homeless) and physical disorder (trash, graffiti, and abandoned cars) were significantly reduced in the treatment areas. Summing up the implications of their study, the authors note that "a sole commitment to increasing misdemeanor arrests is not the most powerful approach" (600).

Broken windows policing is the subject of considerable debate. Critics argue that narrowly conceived order-maintenance strategies, which focus solely on making misdemeanor arrests, walk a fine line between keeping streets safer and harassing local citizens (see Kubrin 2008). A focus of attacking crime by aggressively cracking down on public order offenses via arrest is referred to as "zero-tolerance policing" (Greene 2000). Some claim that the broken windows policing strategy developed in NYC under William Bratton was more closely aligned with zero-tolerance policing than a community collaboration approach (Greene 1999; Skogan 2006: 179; cf.

Kelling and Coles 1996, 160). Arguably, zero-tolerance policing can result in both positive and negative outcomes.

Conventional wisdom states that police-community collaboration is exceedingly difficult to nurture and sustain in high-crime, minority neighborhoods where informal social controls are deteriorating, trust among neighbors is lacking, the police are viewed negatively, and social institutions are weak. Therefore, some might conclude that adopting a community policing approach that relies on citizen input to identify neighborhood problems, and involvement in crime reduction and prevention strategies, will be doomed to failure. Under such conditions, the argument follows, that a zero-tolerance policing approach geared toward eradicating crime in the short run will give local communities an opportunity to organize and develop the social controls necessary to regulate the behavior of residents and visitors, thus preventing crime in the long run (see Meares 1998).

Opponents of zero-tolerance policing take issue with this position. Neighborhood policing research consistently shows that police officers exercise a higher level of coercive authority in poverty-stricken, socially distressed residential settings (Smith 1986; Fagan and Davies 2000; Mastrofski, Reisig, and McCluskey 2002; Terrill and Reisig 2003; Ingram 2007), that inhabitants of these neighborhoods perceive the police to be more abusive (Weitzer 1999), and that disadvantaged citizens are not terribly receptive to such police tactics (Skogan 1990; Piquero et al. 2000; Stoutland 2001). Implementing police crackdowns on public order offenses in these communities can further alienate residents who already distrust and question the legitimacy of the police (Meares 1998; Greene 2000; Thacher 2001a).

2. *Research Testing Broken Windows Hypotheses*

Several studies have tested hypotheses derived from broken windows theory. The preponderance of research in this particular area has focused on two specific relationships: the disorder and crime nexus, and the connection between disorder and fear of crime.

Establishing the empirical relationship between disorder and crime is a salient undertaking for order-maintenance policing advocates. If it exists, it provides support for policing disorder. Skogan's (1990) early work appeared promising. After combing data from several research sites, Skogan assessed the impact of disorder on neighborhood robbery rates. He found that neighborhood characteristics (poverty and instability) and racial composition influenced crime rates, but Skogan argued that the empirical link between neighborhood features and robbery was largely mediated by disorder. Kelling and Coles (1996, 25–26) interpreted Skogan's finding as providing "empirical proof to confirm Wilson and Kelling's hypothesis."

Harcourt's (1998) reassessment of Skogan's data casts doubt on the disorder-crime link. Evaluating the scope of the connection between disorder and crime, Harcourt found that neighborhood disorder was not significantly related to two types of crime (i.e., purse snatching and sexual assault), and that the relationship between disorder and two other crime types (i.e., physical assault and burglary) was attenuated when poverty, stability, and racial composition were accounted for. Harcourt also found that the impact of disorder on robbery appeared to be highly situational. Specifically, he found that the relationship reported by Skogan was dependent on a select group of neighborhoods from a single research site (Newark).[2] Taylor's (2001) study also called into question the disorder-crime connection. His evaluation focused the effects of three different neighborhood disorder measures on changes in homicide, rape, robbery, and aggravated assault using longitudinal data. The results from his analyses failed to support the argument that disorder causes crime.

In 1999 an article published in the *American Journal of Sociology* challenged broken windows theory by proposing and testing an alternative explanation for the understanding of disorder and crime. The authors argued that disorder and crime reflect opposite ends of a seriousness continuum, and share the same structural and social origins (Sampson and Raudenbush 1999). At the bivariate level, Sampson and Raudenbush observed a significant correlation between disorder and three types of crime (i.e., homicide, robbery, and burglary). However, when more stringent tests were conducted, which controlled for concentrated disadvantage (a measure of racially segregated, economic deprivation), collective efficacy (a measure reflecting levels of trust among neighbors and informal social controls), and prior crime rates, the effect of disorder on crime was null. These results supported the authors' theoretical argument.[3] As for police policy and practice, Sampson and Raudenbush (1999, 638) concluded that attacking disorder via aggressive tactics represented a "weak strategy" because it fails to address the common origins of disorder and crime.

Some of the controversy surrounding research on the disorder-crime nexus focuses on the measurement of disorder. Systematic social observation (SSO) measures and neighborhood residents' subjective assessments both have strengths and weaknesses. SSO measures are constructed using physical and social inventory data collected by trained researchers, which may be viewed as more objective relative to perceptual indicators. However, observations may be restricted to daytime hours, which some argue overlooks "bar closings, early-morning drug sales, prostitution, and other forms of disorder that take place between dusk and dawn" (Bratton and Kelling 2006). Subjective disorder measures reflect local residents' perceptions. Comparing SSO to citizens' assessments, Skogan (2008a, 197) notes, "I am not sure why we should think that pairs of students who come in for an hour or so are more accurate raters of local conditions than many pairs of people who live there." Not all subjective measures are created equal, however. Thacher (2004, 396) argues that subjective measures that reflect context-specific forms of disorder, such as "lying down on public steps" and "flagrant public urination in a highly visible location" are preferred over broadly worded item (e.g., "panhandling" and "youth parties").[4] It is doubtful that the debate over SSO versus perceptual disorder measures will be resolved any time soon. For now, it may be sufficient to note that the evidence shows that measures derived from both sources are strongly correlated with one another at the neighborhood level (Raudenbush and Sampson 1999, 31; Sampson and Raudenbush 1999, 625).

Research on the empirical connection between neighborhood disorder and fear of crime has been frustrated by a lack of theoretical clarity and measurement ambiguity. Regarding the latter, fear of crime is measured in a variety of ways. Some researchers use survey-based measures that reflect cognitive judgments of victimization risk and safety. Others prefer survey measures that reflect affective emotions tapping into the anxiety about crime and crime-related symbols (Ferraro 1995). At the individual level, these different fear variables are empirically distinct. When aggregated to the neighborhood level, however, these items are highly correlated and tend to behave similarly with regards to their relationship with other known correlates of fear (see Markowitz et al. 2001). Three rigorous neighborhood-level studies show consistent findings. Reisig and Parks (2004) found that their neighborhood incivilities measure was significantly correlated with cognitive judgments of safety across fifty-nine neighborhoods in Indianapolis, Indiana, and St. Petersburg, Florida. Rountree and Land (1996) observed that neighborhood incivilities was associated with perceptions of crime/victimization risk (or cognitive judgments of safety) and burglary-specific fear (a measure reflecting affective emotions). Both of these studies are limited by the fact that they rely on cross-sectional designs. Using information from three waves of the British Crime Survey, Markowitz and company (2001) found support for the causal connection between disorder and fear (a composite measure consisting of both cognitive judgments and affective emotions). Which type of fear is most consistent with broken windows theory? A clear explanation remains elusive. To some observers, this represents a theoretical shortcoming in that those evaluating whether community policing can decrease fear among citizens fail to articulate whether effects should vary from one dimension of fear to the next, or whether the effects should be uniform (Greene and Taylor 1988, 205–6).

B. Social Disorganization Theory

Community policing can be conceptualized using variant forms of social disorganization theory. The use of social disorganization theory in the field of policing can be traced back to the community crime-prevention movement. During this time it was argued that the police should work with community organizations to alter neighborhood-level social conditions that give rise to crime (Hope 1995; Greene 2000). This view was influenced greatly by the pioneering work of the Chicago School of Sociology, especially the research of Shaw and McKay (1942). Early disorganization theorists posited that impoverished neighborhoods inhabited by racially and ethnically heterogeneous populations that experience high levels of residential instability were less likely to exhibit high levels of social organization. Socially disorganized local communities, according to Kornhauser (1978), share two common characteristics: a lack of value consensus among residents, and an inability to maintain effective social controls. According to this perspective, disorganized neighborhoods will experience higher rates of crime and delinquency. Although highly influential in the field of criminology, Shaw and McKay's theory is relatively limited in providing insights into how the police can improve criminogenic neighborhood conditions.

A more meaningful approach to situating the police within a social disorganization framework is provided by the systemic model, which focuses on the effects of social controls exerted from relational and social networks said to mediate the adverse effects of structural constraints (e.g., concentrated poverty and residential instability). Such networks vary both qualitatively and in terms of their ability to regulate the behavior of local residents and visitors. Specifically, Hunter (1985) identified three social orders, listed here in descending order of affect: *private* (e.g., close friends and family), *parochial* (neighbors and civic organizations), and *public* (e.g., the police) (also see Bursik and Grasmick 1993, 24–59). Since the informal social controls that flow from private and parochial networks have been shown to reduce neighborhood crime (see, e.g., Sampson and Groves 1989), scholars argue that the police should work with residents to develop stronger regulative mechanisms (Kubrin and Weitzer 2003). Hunter (1985), for example, notes that parochial networks are effective at surveillance, a facet of social control that the police are inadequately staffed to provide via patrol. By reaching out to neighborhood organizations and working with community residents, the argument follows, the police can help bolster informal social controls and, in turn, reduce neighborhood crime and improve residents' quality of life (e.g., increase perceptions of safety, reduce visible signs of disorder, and develop trust among neighbors).

Neighborhood-level research on the effects of formal/informal social control linkages on crime and crime-related outcomes is scant. Reisig and Parks' (2004) multilevel study of the impact of community policing on neighborhood quality of life sheds some light on the topic. Using data from the Project on Policing Neighborhoods, Reisig and Parks tested whether their measure of community policing—"police-community collaboration" (operationalized using information from citizen and police surveys aggregated to the neighborhood level)—mediated the effect of concentrated disadvantage on perceived incivility (visible signs of physical and social disorder) and perceived safety (cognitive judgments), net of violent crime rates and a host of individual-level statistical controls. Consistent with their expectations, Reisig and Parks found that police-community collaboration fully mediated the adverse effects of structural disadvantage, leading them to conclude that the "[p]olice should work to address crime and disorder by establishing mutual levels of trust, building working relationships with citizens, and strengthening both informal and formal social controls" (Reisig and Parks 2004, 163–64).

Yet another branch of social disorganization theory, one that features the concept of collective efficacy, has also been used in discussions of community policing. Collective efficacy is conceptualized as consisting to two key elements—social cohesion and informal social control. According to this perspective, neighborhood social controls are most effective when trust among area residents is high (Sampson 2004). Extant research has shown that collective efficacy is a strong predictor of neighborhood crime (Sampson, Raudenbush, and Earls 1997), delinquency (Simons et al. 2005), and disorder (Sampson and Raudenbush 1999; Reisig and Cancino 2004). However, collective efficacy is not restricted to indigenous neighborhood resources, but also draws on services and assistance from public agencies, such as the police, to achieve and maintain social order. As Skogan (2008*b*, 48) recently noted, however, the direct effects of community policing on collective efficacy are "undocumented."

How can community policing promote neighborhood collective efficacy? Broadly speaking, the police need to employ innovative strategies that enhance their legitimacy and promote procedurally just partnerships, which in turn encourage residents to take responsibility for public spaces and activate local social controls (Sampson 2004). Perhaps the most useful community policing tactic to achieving this objective is the "beat meeting." Bringing residents together in a forum that encourages interaction and dialogue, and the facilitation of collaborative efforts to improve neighborhood conditions (e.g., reduce disorder) may enhance levels of collective efficacy, and reduce crime in long run (Sampson and Raudenbush 2001; Sampson 2004).

Stimulating healthy levels of beat meeting participation can be a daunting task for the police. Whether residents decide to get involved is influenced by a number of factors. Local citizens may get involved because they are concerned about neighborhood conditions and want to do their part to improve things. However, participants may distrust their neighbors and get involved only to maintain a watchful eye on the interests that are being advanced (St. Jean 2007). Known justifications for nonparticipation are numerous, including fear of retaliation from individuals who become police targets, concern that friends and family will become targets of the police, a high level of distrust in the police, and a lack of free time. All of these factors shape beat meeting attendance, which is rarely representative of the community. In Chicago beat meetings, Skogan (2004) found evidence of a middle-class participation bias. More specifically, homeowners and individuals with higher levels of education were significantly more likely to turn out. Minority citizens, especially Latinos, were much less likely to get involved. Skogan found that participants' concerns with disorder-related problems (drugs, gangs, and physical decay) were generally reflective of the concerns expressed by the broader community; however, their views on crime problems, such as burglary, were less representative. The potential problem that emerges is that police responsiveness to the concerns expressed during beat meetings may conflict with the equally important value of equity, which necessitates that police services be provided fairly across all segments of the community (Thacher 2001b). For beat meetings to be successful, the police must not simply be reactive to concerns expressed by involved citizens, but rather engage participants in problem-solving activities that are consistent with the well-being of the community as a whole. Doing so may require that the police provide evidence (e.g., crime statistics, calls for service data, and results from officer investigations) to dispel local myths and correct misperceptions, and educate participants about legal constraints.

Based on his fieldwork, Thacher (2001a) cautions that value conflicts often surface when the police work to develop community partnerships. One area of contention concerns the goal of public safety. Thacher observed that residents who attended beat meetings were primarily concerned with disorder problems, whereas the police tended to focus on more serious crimes. Interestingly, broken windows theory helped provide common ground. Citizens' disorder concerns were addressed by the police who believed that doing so would reduce more serious crime. The second type of conflict, according to Thacher, concerns the proper use of legal authority. Thacher (2001a, 788) argues that sustaining community partnerships requires "greater attention to parsimonious and fair use of authority." Research supports Thacher's observations. Residents who perceive that police exercise their authority in a procedurally-just manner are more likely to view the police as legitimate, cooperate with the police, and express a willingness to participate in police programs (Sunshine and Tyler 2003; Tyler 2003; Reisig 2007; Reisig, Bratton, and Gertz 2007).

C. Problem-Oriented Policing: Theory and Research

The problem-oriented policing process can be demanding. It entails intensive scanning of the environment for recurring problems, the analysis of data from a variety of sources to better understand the underlying causes of problems, the development of creative responses to solve problems, and the rigorous assessment of the impact of interventions (Eck and Spelman 1987; Goldstein 1987). The actual framework of problem-oriented policing is quite flexible, however. The SARA model can be applied to a variety of crime and non-crime–related problems. The manner in which the police go about addressing any particular problem can take a variety of forms, including the use of traditional law enforcement tactics (e.g., directed patrol and crackdowns) and community policing tactics (e.g., neighborhood clean-up programs). Given this flexibility, a variety of theoretical perspectives can be used to guide problem-oriented policing interventions (see Braga 2008, 46–55).

One approach to problem-oriented policing involves reducing opportunities for crime by manipulating local environments. The opportunity-reduction approach to problem-oriented policing is similar to the concept of situational crime prevention (Clarke 1992). Braga (2008, 4) notes, the police "are best positioned to prevent crimes by focusing on the situational opportunities for offenders rather than to manipulate socio-economic conditions that are the subjects of much criminological theory." Two theories offer guidance with regard to limiting criminal opportunity. Rational choice theory, for example, posits that offenders weigh the potential risks, rewards, and effort involved prior to committing a crime. This perspective suggests that the police should work to change conditions in a way that causes potential criminals to re-evaluate their decisions. A host of tactics can be used to accomplish this goal. Police officials may opt for traditional law enforcement tactics, such as directed patrols, crackdowns, and stop-and-frisk interrogations, to elevate the risk of apprehension that potential offenders face when contemplating the commission of a crime.

A second approach, routine activity theory, posits that criminal incidents occur when three elements are present: suitable targets, absence of capable guardians, and motivated offenders (Cohen and Felson 1979). Police officials who adopt this perspective are aided by an important tool, the "crime triangle" (Hough and Tilley 1998; Clarke and Eck 2005; see Braga 2008, 28). The crime triangle was designed to help the police identify the elements of crime problems (i.e., victim, offender, and location) and develop effective interventions. According to routine activity theory, all three elements are necessary for crime to occur. The job of the police is to determine which of the three is most salient in a particular situation, and develop a strategy for reducing its influence. For example, the police may determine that criminal opportunities need to be reduced at a particular location, and work to change site features by asking other government agencies to add street lights and board up abandoned buildings (Braga 2008, 63).

Few police innovations have enjoyed as much empirical attention as problem-oriented policing (see Scott 2000, for a review). One line of research has focused on the effectiveness of problem-oriented policing in combating crime and disorder. The scientific rigor of research in this area varies widely, however. A recent meta-analysis, conducted by David Weisburd and his colleagues (2008), identified only ten studies (both published and unpublished) that evaluated the impact of problem-oriented policing on crime and disorder using either experimental or quasi-experimental designs (with comparison groups). Of the ten studies, eight reported favorable results. When grouped together, however, the magnitude of the treatment effect (i.e., problem-oriented policing interventions) was fairly modest (Cohen's d =.125; Weisburd et al. 2008, 25). The authors also looked at less methodologically rigorous studies (i.e., pre/post tests). Among this grouping, the impact of problem-solving policing was overwhelmingly positive (forty-three of the forty-five studies reported a decline in disorder or crime). Overall, the research literature is generally supportive of problem-oriented policing interventions, though the level of support appears to vary inversely with the level of scientific rigor characterizing the research designs employed.

A second empirical question has to do with how problem-oriented policing is actually practiced on the streets. Cordner and Biebel's (2005) study of the San Diego Police Department addressed this question. Using the SARA model to guide their assessment, the authors found that officers were fairly passive in the scanning stage. Personal observations and complaints were most frequently used to initiate the process. The analysis stage was largely informal. Officers generally depended on their own observations to frame problems. Cordner and Biebel found that traditional police tactics, such as targeted enforcement, directed patrol, and the like, were among the most common responses. Finally, the assessment stage was usually limited in scope, restricted largely to officers' personal observations. To some observers, these findings may simply reflect the use of problem-oriented policing jargon to legitimize traditional policing tactics. But Cordner and Biebel point out that the officers included in their study were regularly involved in problem-solving activities, even though the problems were of relatively small in scale and the process that was followed much less formal than prescribed by the SARA model.

V. Discussion

Community and problem-oriented policing have probably done more to shape the debate over the role of the American police than anything since the introduction of the patrol car and two-way radio. Indeed, many police departments nationwide have abandoned their strict reliance on reactive police patrols and have implemented community and problem-oriented policing tactics to reduce crime and disorder and improve citizens' quality of life. However, the extent to which such reforms have been adopted is uneven. Only time will tell whether community and problem-oriented policing will continue to influence debate over the proper role of the police. To do so, questions regarding the fair application of legal authority, and the development of meaningful training curricula will have to be addressed.

The research on community and problem-oriented policing is encouraging. Not only are such studies becoming increasingly sophisticated in terms of theoretical application and methodological rigor, but many of the questions regarding the utility of community and problem-oriented policing appear to have been answered. For example, the weight of the evidence suggests that community and problem-solving policing tactics can reduce crime, albeit modestly, and improve citizens' perceptions of neighborhood conditions. Echoing this conclusion, Harcourt and Ludwig (2006, 314–15) recently noted that "[o]utside of perhaps a few remaining university sociology departments and some Berkeley coffee shops, the notion that 'police matter' is (or at least should be) widely accepted." Yet, many gaps in the understanding of police strategies and tactics remain unanswered. Accordingly, three areas are ripe for empirical investigation.

Much of the broken windows policing research has assessed the impact of misdemeanor arrests on precinct-level crime rates. While informative, some observers have noted that focusing solely on misdemeanor arrests is only part of the picture. Future research that employs more complete order-maintenance variables, including a variety of tactics, would certainly be viewed as an important contribution. However, achieving such a feat could prove difficult. As Thacher (2004, 391) has noted, "one of the most serious gaps" in the policing literature are studies detailing "what exactly order maintenance policing activities involve—what behaviors they target in which contexts, and what actions police take to control them." Book-length ethnographic studies of policing were once quite common but are now rarely published. Qualitative accounts that discuss the ways in which police officers familiarize themselves with local norms and customs, the tactics they use to resolve encounters with disorderly individuals on the streets, and the ways in which the use of order-maintenance tactics varies across urban neighborhoods would assist macro-level researchers in their pursuit to operationalize more exhaustive order-maintenance policing measures.

To date, studies on the effect of policing strategies on aggregated crime rates have neglected the potential influence of social processes, such as collective efficacy. Accordingly, the possibility of variable omission bias cannot yet be ruled out. Cerdá et al. (2009, 540) identify two potential effects of collective efficacy. First, collective efficacy may mediate the effect of misdemeanor arrests on homicide because residents in more cohesive neighborhoods are more successful at securing vigorous police services. Second, it may be that the effect of misdemeanor policing on crime operates through collective efficacy. In other words, misdemeanor arrests increase the collective capacity of neighborhood residents to work together toward the common good. At this point in time, however, neither hypothesized effect has been subjected to empirical scrutiny.

Another issue in need of investigation is what effect (if any) do community policing practices, such as beat meetings and other social organizing activities, have on collective efficacy, and whether observed change in levels of neighborhood collective efficacy influence crime and disorder. Sampson (2004) has posited that beat meetings may promote collective efficacy. Unfortunately, very little is known about this causal connection at the present time (Skogan 2008b). A variety of research designs could be employed to address this issue. For example, evaluation research, employing pre- and post-tests (with matched comparison groups) could help determine whether community policing interventions facilitate collective engagement among residents and, in turn, improve neighborhood conditions.

Not only has community and problem-oriented policing transformed the ongoing debate on police policy and practice, but the two models have also been the impetus for a series of important research projects that have produced some of the most scientifically-rigorous studies published in the social sciences (see, e.g., Skogan 2006; Braga and Bond 2008). Contemporary policing scholars have raised the bar. To advance the field, future researchers must rise to the challenge and construct informative theoretical frameworks to guide their work, design thoughtful experiments and longitudinal studies, and develop reliable measures.

NOTES

* An expanded version of this essay appeared in *Crime and Justice: A Review of Research*, vol. 39, edited by Michael Tonry. Chicago: University of Chicago Press.

1. The actual number of new police officers hired using COPS grants is disputed (see, e.g., Davis et al. 2000). A study published by the Urban Institute estimates that COPS funding resulted in the hiring of between 69,100 and 92,200 police officers (Koper, Moore, and Roth 2002).

2. Various technical aspects of Harcourt's replication study have been criticized (see Xu, Fiedler, and Flaming 2005).

3. Research conducted in nonmetropolitan communities has also shown that the relationship between disorder and crime is mediated by aggregate-level social processes (Reisig and Cancino 2004).

4. For a list of disorder measures that have been used previously, see Ross and Mirowsky (1999, 427–29).

REFERENCES

Bloch, Peter B., and David Specht. 1973. *Neighborhood Team Policing: Prescriptive Package.* Washington, DC: U.S. Department of Justice, Law Enforcement Assistance Administration, National Institute of Law Enforcement and Criminal Justice.

Braga, Anthony A. 2008. *Problem-Oriented Policing and Crime Prevention*, 2nd ed. Monsey, NY: Criminal Justice Press.

Braga, Anthony A., and Brenda J. Bond. 2008. "Policing Crime and Disorder Hot Spots: A Randomized Controlled Trial." *Criminology* 46: 577–607.

Bratton, William, and George Kelling. 2006. "There are No Cracks in the Broken Windows." *National Review On-line*, February 28. http://www.nationalreview.com/comment/bratton_kelling200602281015.

Bureau of Justice Statistics. 2000. *Local Police Departments, 1997*. Washington, DC: U.S. Government Printing Office.

———. 2006. *Local Police Departments, 2003*. Washington, DC: U.S. Government Printing Office.

Bursik, Robert J., Jr., and Harold G. Grasmick. 1993. *Neighborhoods and Crime: The Dimensions of Effective Community Control*. Lanham, MD: Lexington.

Cerdá, Magdalena, Melissa Tracy, Steven F. Messner, David Vlahov, Kenneth Tardiff, and Sandro Galea. 2009. "Misdemeanor Policing, Physical Disorder, and Gun-Related Homicide: A Spatial Analytic Test of 'Broken-Windows' Theory." *Epidemiology* 20: 533–41.

Clarke, Ronald V. 1992. *Situational Crime Prevention: Successful Case Studies*. Albany, NY: Harrow and Heston.

Clarke, Ronald V., and John Eck. 2005. *Crime Analysis for Problem Solvers in 60 Small Steps*. Washington, DC: U.S. Department of Justice, Office of Community Oriented Policing Services.

Cohen, Lawrence E., and Marcus Felson. 1979. "Social Change and Crime Rate Trends: A Routine Activity Approach." *American Sociological Review* 44: 588–608.

Cordner, Gary. 1999. "Elements of Community Policing." In *Policing Perspectives: An Anthology*, edited by Larry K. Gaines and Gary W. Cordner. Los Angeles: Roxbury.

Cordner, Gary, and Elizabeth Perkins Biebel. 2005. "Problem-Oriented Policing in Practice." *Criminology and Public Policy* 4: 155–80.

Corman, Hope, and Naci Mocan. 2005. "Carrots, Sticks, and Broken Windows." *Journal of Law and Economics* 48: 235–66.

Davis, Gareth, David B. Muhlhausen, Dexter Ingram, and Ralph A. Rector. 2000. The Facts About COPS: A Performance Overview of the Community Oriented Policing Services Program. Center for Data Analysis Report no. 00–10. Washington, DC: The Heritage Foundation.

Eck, John E., and William Spelman. 1987. *Problem-Solving: Problem-Oriented Policing in Newport News*. Washington, DC: Police Executive Research Forum.

Evans, William N., and Emily G. Owens. 2007. "COPS and Crime." *Journal of Public Economics* 91: 181–201.

Fagan, Jeffrey A., and Garth Davies. 2000. "Street Stops and Broken Windows: *Terry*, Race, and Disorder in New York City." *Fordham Urban Law Journal* 28: 457–504.

Fayol, Henri. 1949 [1916]. *General and Industrial Management*. London: Pitman.

Ferraro, Kenneth F. 1995. *Fear of Crime: Interpreting Victimization Risk*. Albany, NY: SUNY Press.

Fosdick, Raymond B. 1969 [1915]. *European Police Systems*. Montclair, NJ: Patterson Smith.

Goldstein, Herman. 1979. "Improving Policing: A Problem-Solving Approach." *Crime and Delinquency* 25: 236–58.

———. 1987. "Toward Community-Oriented Policing: Potential, Basic Requirements, and Threshold Questions." *Crime and Delinquency* 33:6–30.

———. 1990. *Problem-Oriented Policing*. New York: McGraw-Hill.

Goodnow, Frank J. 1900. *Politics and Administration: A Study in Government*. New York: Russell and Russell.

Government Accountability Office. 2005. *Community Policing Grants: COPS Grants Were a Modest Contributor to Declines in Crime in the 1990s* (#GAO-06–104). Washington, DC: Government Accountability Office.

Greene, Jack R. 2000. "Community Policing in America: Changing the Nature, Structure, and Function of the Police." In *Criminal Justice 2000*, vol. 3, edited by Julie Horney. Washington, DC: U.S. Department of Justice, National Institute of Justice.

Greene, Jack R., and Ralph B. Taylor. 1988. "Community-Based Policing and Foot Patrol: Issues in Theory and Evaluation." In *Community Policing: Rhetoric or Reality*, edited by Jack R. Greene and Stephen D. Mastrofski. New York: Praeger.

Greene, Judith A. 1999. "Zero Tolerance: A Case Study of Police Policies and Practices in New York City." *Crime and Delinquency* 45: 171–87.

Greenwood, Peter W., and Joan Petersilia. 1975. *The Criminal Investigation Process* Vol. 1, *Summary and Policy Implications*. Santa Monica, CA: Rand Corporation.

Haller, Mark H. 1975. "Historical Roots of Police Behavior: Chicago, 1890–1925." *Law and Society Review* 10: 303–23.

Harcourt, Bernard E. 1998. "Reflecting on the Subject: A Critique of the Social Influence Conception of Deterrence, the Broken Windows Theory, and Order-Maintenance Policing New York Style." *Michigan Law Review* 97: 291–389.

Harcourt, Bernard E., and Jens Ludwig. 2006. "Broken Windows: New Evidence from New York City and a Five-City Social Experiment." *University of Chicago Law Review* 73:271–320.

———. 2007. "Refer Madness: Broken Windows Policing and Misdemeanor Marijuana Arrests in New York City, 1989–2000." *Criminology and Public Policy* 6: 165–82.

Hope, Tim. 1995. "Community Crime Prevention." In *Building a Safer Society*, edited by Michael Tonry and David P. Farrington. Vol. 19 of *Crime and Justice: A Review of Research*, edited by Michael Tonry. Chicago: University of Chicago Press.

Hough, Michael, and Nick Tilley. 1998. *Getting the Grease to Squeak: Research Lessons for Crime Prevention*. Crime Detection and Prevention Series no. 85. London: Home Office.

Hunter, Albert. 1985. "Private, Parochial, and Public Social Orders: The Problem of Crime and Incivility in Urban Communities." In *The Challenge of Social Control: Citizenship and Institution Building*, edited by Gerald D. Suttles and Mayer N. Zald. Norwood, NJ: Ablex.

Ingram, Jason R. 2007. "The Effect of Neighborhood Characteristics on Traffic Citation Practices of the Police." *Police Quarterly* 10:371–93.

James, Nathan. 2008. *Community Oriented Policing Services (COPS): Background, Legislation, and Issues*. CRS Report for Congress. Washington, DC: Congressional Research Service.

Katz, Charles M., Vincent J. Webb, and David R. Schaefer. 2001. "An Assessment of the Impact of Quality-of-Life Policing on Crime and Disorder." *Justice Quarterly* 18: 825–76.

Kelling, George L., and William J. Bratton. 1998. "Declining Crime Rates: Insiders' Views of the New York City Story." *Journal of Criminal Law and Criminology* 88: 1217–31.

Kelling, George L., and Catherine M. Coles. 1996. *Fixing Broken Windows: Restoring Order and Reducing Crime in Our Communities*. New York: Free Press.

Kelling, George L., and Mark H. Moore. 1988. "From Political to Reform to Community: The Evolving Strategy of Police." In *Community Policing: Rhetoric or Reality*, edited by Jack R. Greene and Stephen Mastrofski. New York: Praeger.

Kelling, George L., Tony Pate, Duane Dieckman, and Charles E. Brown. 1974. *The Kansas City Preventive Patrol Experiment: A Summary Report*. Washington, DC: Police Foundation.

Kelling, George L., and William H. Sousa Jr. 2001. *Do Police Matter?: An Analysis of the Impact of New York City's Police Reforms*. New York: Center for Civic Innovation at the Manhattan Institute.

Koper, Chris S., Gretchen E. Moore, and Jeffrey A. Roth. 2002. *Putting 100,000 Officers on the Street: A Survey-Based Assessment of the Federal COPS Program*. Washington, DC: Urban Institute.

Kornhauser, Ruth R. 1978. *Social Sources of Delinquency: An Appraisal of Analytic Models.* Chicago: University of Chicago Press.

Kubrin, Charis E. 2008. "Making Order of Disorder: A Call for Conceptual Clarity." *Criminology and Public Policy* 7: 203–14.

Kubrin, Charis E., and Ronald Weitzer. 2003. "New Directions in Social Disorganization Theory." *Journal of Research in Crime and Delinquency* 40: 374–402.

Lane, Roger. 1980. "Urban Police and Crime in Nineteenth-Century America." In *Crime and Justice: A Review of Research*, vol. 2, edited by Norval Morris and Michael Tonry. Chicago: University of Chicago Press.

Levitt, Steven D. 2004. "Understanding Why Crime Fell in the 1990s: Four Factors that Explain the Decline and Six that Do Not." *Journal of Economic Perspectives* 18: 163–90.

Maguire, Edward R., and Stephen D. Mastrofski. 2000. "Patterns of Community Policing in the United States." *Police Quarterly* 3: 4–45.

Manning, Peter K. 1988. "Community Policing as a Drama of Control." In *Community Policing: Rhetoric or Reality*, edited by Jack R. Greene and Stephen D. Mastrofski. New York: Praeger.

Markowitz, Fred E., Paul E. Bellair, Allen E. Liska, and Jianhong Liu. 2001. "Extending Social Disorganization Theory: Modeling the Relationships between Cohesion, Disorder, and Fear." *Criminology* 39: 293–320.

Mastrofski, Stephen D. 1988. "Community Policing as Reform: A Cautionary Tale." In *Community Policing: Rhetoric or Reality*, edited by Jack R. Greene and Stephen D. Mastrofski. New York: Praeger.

Mastrofski, Stephen D., Michael D. Reisig, and John D. McCluskey. 2002. "Police Disrespect toward the Public: An Encounter-Based Analysis." *Criminology* 40: 519–51.

Meares, Tracey L. 1998. "Place and Crime." *Chicago Kent Law Review* 73: 669–705.

Messner, Steven F., Sandro Galea, Kenneth J. Tardiff, Melissa Tracy, Angela Bucciarelli, Tinka Markham Piper, Victoria Frye, and David Vlahov. 2007. "Policing, Drugs, and the Homicide Decline in New York City in the 1990s." *Criminology* 45: 385–414.

Miller, Wilbur R. 1977. *Cops and Bobbies: Police Authority in New York and London, 1830–1870*. Chicago: University of Chicago Press.

Monkkonen, Eric H. 1981. *Police in Urban America, 1860–1920*. Cambridge: Cambridge University Press.

Moore, Mark H. 1992. "Problem-Solving and Community Policing." In *Modern Policing*, edited by Michael Tonry and Norval Morris. Volume 15 of *Crime and Justice: A Review of Research*, edited by Michael Tonry. Chicago: University of Chicago Press.

Muhlhausen, David B. 2001. *Do Community Oriented Policing Services Grants Affect Violent Crime Rates?* Center for Data Analysis Report no. CDA01-05. Washington, DC: Heritage Foundation.

———. 2002. *Research Challenges Claim of COPS Effectiveness.* A Report of the Heritage Center for Data Analysis no. CDA02-02. Washington, DC: Heritage Foundation.

Muhlhausen, David B., and Brian W. Walsh. 2008. "COPS Reform: Why Congress Can't Make the COPS Program Work," *Backgrounder* (Executive Summary #2188). Washington, DC: Heritage Foundation.

National Advisory Commission on Civil Disorders. 1968. *Report of the National Advisory Commission on Civil Disorders.* Washington, DC: U.S. Government Printing Office.

Pate, Anthony M. 1986. "Experimenting with Foot Patrol: The Newark Experience." In *Community Crime Prevention: Does it Work?*, edited by Dennis Rosenbaum. Beverly Hills, CA: Sage.

Piquero, Alex, Jack Greene, James Fyfe, Robert J. Kane, and Patricia Collins. 2000. "Implementing Community Policing in Public Housing Developments in Philadelphia: Some Early Results." In *Community Policing: Contemporary Readings*, 2nd ed., edited by Geoffrey P. Alpert and Alex Piquero. Prospect Heights, IL: Waveland.

Raudenbush, Stephen W., and Robert J. Sampson. 1999. "Ecometrics: Toward a Science of Assessing Ecological Settings, with Application to the Systematic Social Observation of Neighborhoods." *Sociological Methodology* 29: 1–41.

Reisig, Michael D. 2007. "Procedural Justice and Community Policing: What Shapes Residents' Willingness to Participate in Crime Prevention Programs?" *Policing: A Journal of Policy and Practice* 1:356–69.

Reisig, Michael D., Jason Bratton, and Marc Gertz. 2007. "The Construct Validity and Refinement of Process-Based Policing Measures." *Criminal Justice and Behavior* 34:1005–28.

Reisig, Michael D., and Jeffrey Michael Cancino. 2004. "Incivilities in Nonmetropolitan Communities: The Effects of Structural Constraints, Social Conditions, and Crime." *Journal of Criminal Justice* 32: 15–29.

Reisig, Michael D., and Roger B. Parks. 2004. "Can Community Policing Help The Truly Disadvantaged?" *Crime and Delinquency* 50: 139–67.

Reiss, Albert J., Jr. 1985. *Policing a City's Central District: The Oakland Story*. Washington, DC: U.S. Department of Justice, National Institute of Justice.

Rosenbaum, Dennis P. 1988. "Community Crime Prevention: A Review and Synthesis of the Literature." *Justice Quarterly* 5: 323–95.

Rosenbaum, Dennis P., Arthur J. Lurigio, and Robert C. Davis. 1998. *The Prevention of Crime: Social and Situation Strategies*. Belmont, CA: Wadsworth.

Rosenfeld, Richard, Robert Fornango, and Andres F. Rengifo. 2007. "The Impact of Order-Maintenance Policing on New York City Homicide and Robbery Rates: 1988–2001." *Criminology* 45: 355–84.

Ross, Catherine E., and John Mirowsky. 1999. "Disorder and Decay: The Concept and Measurement of Perceived Neighborhood Disorder." *Urban Affairs Quarterly* 34: 412–32.

Roth, Jeffrey A., and Joseph F. Ryan. 2000. *The COPS Program After 4 Years: National Evaluation*. Washington, DC: National Institute of Justice.

Roth, Jeffrey A., Jan Roehl, and Calvin C. Johnson. 2004. "Trends in the Adoption of Community Policing." In *Community Policing: Can it Work?*, edited by Wesley G. Skogan. Belmont, CA: Wadsworth.

Rountree, Pamela Wilcox, and Kenneth C. Land. 1996. "Perceived Risk versus Fear of Crime: Empirical Evidence of Conceptually Distinct Reactions in Survey Data." *Social Forces* 74: 1353–76.

Sampson, Robert. 2004. "Neighborhood and Community: Collective Efficacy and Community Safety." *New Economy* 11:106–13.

Sampson, Robert J., and W. Byron Groves. 1989. "Community Structure and Crime: Testing Social-Disorganization Theory." *American Journal of Sociology* 94: 774–802.

Sampson, Robert J., and Stephen W. Raudenbush. 1999. "Systematic Social Observation of Public Spaces: A New Look at Disorder in Urban Neighborhoods." *American Journal of Sociology* 105: 603–51.

———. 2001. *Disorder in Urban Neighborhoods—Does It Lead to Crime?* Research in Brief. Washington, DC: U.S. Department of Justice, National Institute of Justice.

Sampson, Robert J., Stephen W. Raudenbush, and Felton Earls. 1997. "Neighborhoods and Violent Crime: A Multilevel Study of Collective Efficacy." *Science* 277: 918–24.

Scott, Michael S. 2000. *Problem-Oriented Policing: Reflections on the First 20 Years.* Washington, DC: U.S. Department of Justice, Office of Community Oriented Policing Services.

Shafritz, Jay M., and J. Steven Ott. 1996. *Classics of Organization Theory*, 4th ed. Fort Worth, TX: Harcourt Brace.

Shaw, Clifford R., and Henry D. McKay. 1942. *Juvenile Delinquency and Urban Crime.* Chicago: University of Chicago Press.

Sherman, Lawrence W. 1991. "Problem-Oriented Policing by Herman Goldstein." *Journal of Criminal Law and Criminology* 82: 690–707.

Sherman, Lawrence W., Catherine H. Milton, and Thomas V. Kelly. 1973. *Team Policing: Seven Case Studies.* Washington, DC: Police Foundation.

Simons, Ronald L., Leslie Simons, Callie Burt, Gene Brody, and Carolyn Cutrona. 2005. "Collective Efficacy, Authoritative Parenting and Delinquency: A Longitudinal Test of a Model Integrating Community-and Family-Level Processes." *Criminology* 43: 989–1029.

Skogan, Wesley G. 1988. "Community Organizations and Crime." In *Crime and Justice: A Review of Research*, vol. 10, edited by Michael Tonry and Norval Morris. Chicago: University of Chicago Press.

———. 1990. *Disorder and Decline: Crime and the Spiral Decay in American Neighborhoods.* Berkeley: University of California Press.

———. 2004. "Representing the Community in Community Policing." In *Community Policing: Can it Work?*, edited by Wesley G. Skogan. Belmont, CA: Wadsworth.

———. 2006. *Police and Community in Chicago: A Tale of Three Cities.* New York: Oxford University Press.

———. 2008a. "Broken Windows: Why—and How—We Should Take Them Seriously." *Criminology and Public Policy* 7: 195–202.

———. 2008b. "An Overview of Community Policing: Origins, Concepts and Implementation." In *The Handbook of Knowledge-Based Policing: Current Concepts and Future Directions*, edited by Tom Williamson. New York: John Wiley.

Skogan, Wesley G., and Susan M. Hartnett. 1997. *Community Policing, Chicago Style.* New York: Oxford University Press.

Smith, Bruce. 1940. *Police Systems in the United States.* New York: Harper and Row.

Smith, Douglas A. 1986. "The Neighborhood Context of Police Behavior." In *Communities and Crime,* edited by Albert J. Reiss, Jr. and Michael Tonry. Volume 8 of *Crime and Justice: A Review of Research*, edited by Michael Tonry and Norval Morris. Chicago: University of Chicago Press.

Sparrow, Malcolm K., Mark H. Moore, and David M. Kennedy. 1990. *Beyond 911: A New Era for Policing.* New York: Basic Books.

Spelman, William, and Dale K. Brown. 1984. *Calling the Police: Citizen Reporting of Serious Crime.* Washington, DC: U.S. Government Printing Office.

St. Jean, Peter K.B. 2007. *Pockets of Crime: Broken Windows, Collective Efficacy, and the Criminal Point of View.* Chicago: University of Chicago Press.

Stoutland, Sara E. 2001. "The Multiple Dimensions of Trust in Resident/Police Relations in Boston." *Journal of Research in Crime and Delinquency* 38: 226–56.

Sunshine, Jason, and Tom R. Tyler. 2003. "The Role of Procedural Justice and Legitimacy in Shaping Public Support for the Police." *Law and Society Review* 37: 513–48.

Svara, James H. 1998. "The Politics-Administration Dichotomy Model as Aberration." *Public Administration Review* 58: 51–58.

Sykes, Gary W. 1986. "Street Justice: A Moral Defense of Order Maintenance Policing." *Justice Quarterly* 3:497–512.

Taylor, Frederick W. 1911. *The Principles of Scientific Management.* New York: Norton.

Taylor, Ralph B. 2001. *Breaking Away from Broken Windows: Baltimore Neighborhoods and the Nationwide Fight against Crime, Grime, Fear, and Decline.* Boulder, CO: Westview.

Terrill, William, and Michael D. Reisig. 2003. "Neighborhood Context and Police Use of Force." *Journal of Research in Crime and Delinquency* 40: 291–321.

Thacher, David. 2001a. "Conflicting Values in Community Policing." *Law and Society Review* 35: 765–98.

———. 2001b. "Equity and Community Policing: A New View of Community Partnerships." *Criminal Justice Ethics* 20: 3–16.

———. 2004. "Order Maintenance Reconsidered: Moving Beyond Strong Causal Reasoning." *Journal of Criminal Law and Criminology* 94: 381–414.

Trojanowicz, Robert. 1982. *An Evaluation of the Neighborhood Foot Patrol Program in Flint, Michigan.* East Lansing, MI.: National Neighborhood Foot Patrol Center, Michigan State University.

———. 1986. "Evaluating a Neighborhood Foot Patrol Program: The Flint, Michigan, Project. In *Community Crime Prevention: Does it Work?*, edited by Dennis Rosenbaum. Beverly Hills, CA: Sage.

Trojanowicz, Robert, and Bonnie Bucqueroux. 1990. *Community Policing: A Contemporary Perspective.* Cincinnati, OH: Anderson.

Tyler, Tom R. 2003. Procedural Justice, Legitimacy, and the Effectiveness of Rule of Law. In *Crime and Justice: A Review of Research*, vol. 30, edited by Michael Tonry. Chicago: University of Chicago Press.

Uchida, Craig D. 2005. "The Development of the American Police: An Historical Overview." In *Critical Issues in Policing: Contemporary Readings*, 5th ed., edited by Roger G. Dunham and Geoffrey P. Alpert. Long Grove, IL: Waveland.

U.S. Department of Justice. 2006. *Regional Community Policing Institutes: Training Network.* Washington, DC: U.S. Department of Justice.

———. 2009a. *Community Policing Defined.* Washington, DC: U.S. Department of Justice, Office of Community Oriented Policing Services.

———. 2009b. "Regional Community Policing Institutes." http://www.cops.usdoj.gov/Default.asp?Item=115.

Vollmer, August. 1971 [1936]. *The Police in Modern Society.* Monclair, NJ: Patterson Smith.

Walker, Samuel. 1980. *Popular Justice: A History of American Criminal Justice.* New York: Oxford University Press.

———. 1984. "Broken Windows and Fractured History: The Use and Misuse of History in Recent Police Patrol Analysis." *Justice Quarterly* 1: 75–90.

Weisburd, David, Cody W. Telep, Josua C. Hinkle, and John E. Eck. 2008. *The Effects of Problem-Oriented Policing on Crime and Disorder*. Campbell Systematic Reviews no. 2008-14. Oslo: The Campbell Collaboration.

Weitzer, Ronald. 1999. "Citizens' Perceptions of Police Misconduct: Race and Neighborhood Context." *Justice Quarterly* 16: 819–46.

White, Leonard D. 1926. *Introduction to the Study of Public Administration*. New York: MacMillan.

Wilson, James Q., and George L. Kelling. 1982. "Broken Windows: The Police and Neighborhood Safety." *Atlantic Monthly* 249: 29–38.

Wilson, O. W. 1950. *Police Administration*. New York: McGraw-Hill.

Wilson, Woodrow. 1887. "The Study of Administration." *Political Science Quarterly* 2: 197–222.

Worrall, John L. 2010. "The Effects of Policing on Crime: What Have We Learned?," In *Critical Issues in Policing: Contemporary Readings*, 6th ed., edited by Roger G. Dunham and Geoffrey P. Alpert. Long Grove, Ill.: Waveland.

Worrall, John L., and Tomislav V. Kovandzic. 2007. "COPS Grants and Crime Revisited." *Criminology* 45: 159–90.

Xu, Yili, Mora L. Fiedler, and Karl H. Flaming. 2005. "Discovering the Impact of Community Policing: The Broken Windows Thesis, Collective Efficacy, and Citizens' Judgment." *Journal of Research in Crime and Delinquency* 42: 147–86.

Zhao, Jihong, Matthew C. Scheider, and Quint Thurman. 2002. "Funding Community Policing to Reduce Crime: Have COPS Grants Made a Difference?" *Criminology and Public Policy* 2: 7–32.

———. 2003. "A National Evaluation of the Effect of COPS Grants on Police Productivity (Arrests) 1995–1999." *Police Quarterly* 6: 387–409.

CHAPTER 19

LEGITIMACY AND LAWFUL POLICING

SANJA KUTNJAK IVKOVIĆ

POLICING carries with it the legitimate right to use coercive force (Klockars 1985, 12). At the same time, it is a highly discretionary activity, routinely performed outside of the supervisor's site, before witnesses who would lack credibility in court, or before credible witnesses unwilling to talk. Thus, policing is rife with opportunities for unlawful conduct. Traditionally, the lawfulness of police actions is evaluated against legal rules, be they constitutional rules (e.g., Fourth Amendment to the US Constitution), laws (e.g., Section 1983 lawsuits, 1983 42 U.S.C. §1983 [1871]), or decisions by the highest court of the land (e.g., *Miranda v. Arizona*, 384 U.S. 436 [1966]), as well as against administrative standards (e.g., Standard Operating Procedures, Rules of Conduct) established by the society at large and by individual police departments. Various mechanisms of control and accountability have been put in place to evaluate whether, and to what extent, police officers cross the line. At the same time, ultimately, it is the public that evaluates police officer conduct. Compared to judgments about legality of police actions, public perceptions about the legitimacy of the police and their actions are subjective in nature; they truly lie in the hearts and minds of the public (National Research Council 2004, 291).

This article addresses a wide range of related literatures, from which a number of important generalizations can be distilled:

- Personal moral values influence whether people will obey the law and the instructions provided by the authority. Empirical research shows that people's views about the legitimacy strongly influence their willingness to obey the law. Well-publicized critical incidents of police misconduct have both short- and long-term effects on several measures of legitimacy (citizens' level of confidence in the police; citizens' willingness to obey the law). The effects of these critical incidents are not uniformly distributed across all racial and ethnic groups.

- Perceptions of police legitimacy are not static. They are influenced by personal experiences with the police. Personal experience, in turn, is evaluated through the general views about police legitimacy. Research indicates that citizens expect the police to treat them fairly, both in terms of the outcomes and, even more importantly, the procedures, particularly when the nature of the contact with the police is negative.

- Numerous studies have shown that African American citizens are less supportive of the police than white citizens are. African Americans are more likely to evaluate their contact with the police negatively and experience less satisfactory treatment. Research has documented that race and personal experience are the strongest predictors of negative attitudes toward the police.

- Although various legal rules and norms regulate police work, policing as an occupation requires a substantial degree of discretion, which creates opportunities for the police to engage in various forms of misconduct, ranging from the use of excessive force to police corruption. For a host of reasons, current measures of prevalence of police misconduct may be regarded, at best, as crude estimates of the actual prevalence of police misconduct.

- Societal reaction to police misconduct relies on various types of mechanisms of police control and accountability, from the internal ones (e.g., administrative rules, internal investigations), to the external ones (e.g., criminal courts, independent commissions), as well as mixed mechanisms (e.g., citizen reviews, accreditation). Research emphasizes that each of these mechanisms plays a critical role but, at the same time, points out certain problems associated with the application of these mechanisms toward effective control of misconduct and enhancement of accountability. Although largely understudied, the most promising novel mechanisms of control and accountability include the CompStat, early warning systems, police monitors, and pattern-and-practice lawsuits.

This chapter is organized as follows. Section I focuses on the concept of police legitimacy, explores it from the police agency perspective (i.e., why people obey the authority), and presents the empirical findings on legitimacy. The section proceeds with an analysis of legitimacy from the public's perspective, reviews empirical studies concerning the effect of the actual experience with the police, and analyzes the related racial differences. Section II discusses what happens when police officers cross the line that separates legitimate and illegitimate conduct. It describes police corruption, use of excessive force, and racial profiling, with a particular emphasis on the potential causes of such behavior and the results of empirical studies seeking to measure their prevalence. Section III analyzes traditional and novel responses to the situations in which policing went wrong, including internal mechanisms (e.g., internal affairs, early warning systems), external mechanisms (e.g., criminal courts, independent commissions), and mixed mechanisms of control and accountability (e.g., accreditation, citizen reviews). Section IV reflects on the key issues and provides ideas for future research.

I. Police Legitimacy

The National Research Council (2004, 291) defines police legitimacy as "the judgments that ordinary citizens make about the rightfulness of police conduct and the organizations that employ and supervise them." Literature on legitimacy (e.g., Tyler 1990; Tyler and Darley 2000; Tyler and Huo 2002) discusses three models of motivation for people to obey the law.

The first is the *deterrence* model or the *instrumental* model (Tyler 1990; Tyler and Darley 2000). This model postulates that individuals calculate potential gains and losses before they decide whether they will obey or violate the law. This model of human motivation, viewed as the rational-choice theory (e.g., Blumstein, Cohen, and Nagin 1978; Paternoster 1989) or social control model or deterrence (e.g., Zimring and Hawkins 1973; Paternoster and Iovanni 1986; Paternoster 1989; Nagin and Paternoster 1991), is the one guiding the American legal system (Tyler and Darley 2000, 712). Although the deterrence model has been supported by a number of empirical studies (e.g., Paternoster and Iovanni 1986; Paternoster 1989; Nagin and Paternoster 1991), the deterrent effect is not strong. For example, MacCoun (1993, 501) reports that the perceived severity of punishment explains only 5 percent of the variance in drug-use behavior. On the other hand, research reports that certainty of punishment has more deterrent potential (e.g., Paternoster and Iovanni 1986; Paternoster 1989; Nagin and Paternoster 1991).

The second model of human motivation to obey the law relies on *personal moral values* about appropriate or ethic conduct that rest on "the belief that following the rules is the morally appropriate thing to do" (e.g., Tyler and Darley 2000, 714). When the laws or decisions by the authority correspond with the moral beliefs held by the individuals, these individuals will voluntarily obey the law and respect the decisions because they share the belief that this is a morally right thing to do. Research suggests that the degree to which the individuals assess that the law overlaps with their own moral values directly affects whether they obey the law (e.g., Tyler 1990; Robinson and Darley 1995; Tyler and Darley 2000; Sunshine and

Tyler 2003). In reality, congruence between the legal norms and the moral values of various groups of citizens is not perfect, at least for some laws (e.g., laws prohibiting prostitution, euthanasia drug laws) and some decisions (e.g., *Roe v. Wade* 410 U.S. 113 [1973], declaring the right to abortion; *Brown v. Board of Education of Topeka*, 347 U.S. 483 [1954], ordering desegregation). In such instances, when citizens feel that the laws are morally unjust, their own moral values could lead them to disobey the law. Thus, as Tyler and Darley (2000) argue, the reliance on moral values could result in either the promotion or undermining of the rule of law.

The third model is the *social-psychological* model. It relies on the belief that authorities are viewed as legitimate and thus should be obeyed (e.g., Tyler and Darley 2000). Individuals who obey the law do so not because they think that the laws are morally right but because they believe that the authorities who enacted the laws or made such decisions were legitimate and thus should be obeyed (Tyler 1990, 4; Tyler and Darley 2000, 716).

When a citizen faces a dilemma and decides whether to engage in a behavior that is acceptable by his or her own moral norms but is prohibited by the law, there are two possible outcomes. If the citizen decides not to engage in the behavior because it violates the citizen's own moral norms, the decision is primarily influenced by personal morality. On the other hand, if the citizen decides not to engage in the behavior because the law that prohibits it was enacted by the authority and should be obeyed, the decision is primarily influenced by legitimacy of the authority (see, e.g., Tyler 1990, 25). When authorities need to make potentially unpopular decisions, they rely on the fact that authority is viewed as legitimate and that it ought to be obeyed. Tyler and Darley (2000, 722) give the example of the *Roe v. Wade* decision (410 U.S. 113 [1973]), in which the Supreme Court declared abortion to be a legal right. Although many citizens viewed this decision as morally wrong, they still obeyed the decision "[b]ecause they view the Supreme Court as a legitimate social institution whose decisions ought to be obeyed." Research (e.g., Tyler 1990; Tyler and Huo 2002) shows very clearly that legitimacy—independently of other motivations—strongly influences peoples' willingness to obey the law.

Tyler (1990, 45) measures legitimacy in two ways: as the perceived obligation to obey the law and as support for legal authorities. In two waves of his survey, Tyler (1990, 45) finds that the degree to which the respondents supported this obligation is "striking." In fact, more than 80 percent of the respondents in both waves of the survey agreed with the following two statements: "People should obey the law even if it goes against what they think is right" and "I always try to follow the law even if I think that it is wrong" (Tyler 1990, 45). When asked specific questions about the support for the police, the respondents still showed a substantial degree of support for the police in general (e.g., more than 75 percent agreed that "I feel that I should support the Chicago police" and that "I have a great deal of respect for the Chicago police"), but indicated that they were more skeptical about the honesty of the police (e.g., around 60 percent agreed that "On the whole Chicago police officers are honest"; Tyler 1990, 48). Measures of obligation to obey and support are only moderately strongly correlated, suggesting that the types of the questions asked and the way they are phrased affects the results and thus the results could differ substantially across empirical studies.

A. Data on Legitimacy

The annual Gallup Poll asks a nationwide sample of citizens about their confidence in various social institutions, including the police (Gallup 2010). The data covering the period of sixteen years (1993–2009) show that the majority of the citizens show "a great deal" or "quite a lot" of confidence in the police. These confidence rates vary from as low as 52 percent in 1993 to as high as 64 percent in 2004 (Gallup 2010). A more direct measure of legitimacy considers the perceived duty to obey the law, even when the authorities' decision or conduct violates one's own moral norms. The National Opinion Research Center (NORC) General Social Survey (reported in Tuch and Weitzer 1997) explores the respondents' level of approval of a police officer potential misconduct (hitting a male adult citizen). Starting from 1973, the rate of approval has been high, with about 70 percent of the respondents approving such behavior from year to year, with the lowest approval in 1991 (65 percent; Tuch and Weitzer 1997), the year of the Rodney King beating.

   A limited number of studies explore the influence of a critical police incident— like the Rodney King incident—on the level of public support for the police (e.g., Tuch and Weitzer 1997; Kaminski and Jefferis 1998). The results of Kaminski and Jefferis's study (1998) show that a televised use-of-force arrest had no efffect on any measure of the Cincinnati respondents' overall support; its effect was limited to just one aspect of specific support (the perceptions of the police use of excessive force) and to a nonwhite subset of their Cincinnati sample (Kaminski and Jefferis 1998).

   Tuch and Weitzer (1997) analyze the influence of two such high-profile incidents. In 1979 a black woman, Eulia Love, was shot and killed by two LAPD officers; the majority of the citizens (51 percent of whites, 66 percent of Latinos, and 81 percent of blacks; Tuch and Weitzer 1997, 642) evaluated the incident as a case of police brutality. According to the *Los Angeles Times* 1977 poll, the percentage of citizens who approved of the way the LAPD was doing its job declined in 1979 by 13 percent overall, but the effect was much stronger for minorities than it was for whites (10 percent decline for whites, 20 percent for Latinos, and 23 percent for blacks).

   The Rodney King beating on March 3, 1991, videotaped and broadcast across the globe, was another such critical incident. It had a devastating effect on the citizens' view of the LAPD. Compared to the overall approval of the way the LAPD was doing its job in 1988 (74 percent approval; Tuch and Weitzer 1997), the approval dropped to 46 percent immediately after the incident (March 7–8) and even lower, to its rock bottom of 34 percent, two weeks later (March 20–21). As was the case with Eulia Love in 1979, the Rodney King incident did not affect all racial/ethnic groups to the same extent. LAPD approval dropped in mid-May 1991 from the pre–Rodney King approval ratings by 33 percent for whites (from 74 percent in 1988 to 41 percent in mid-March of 1991), 49 percent for Latinos (from 80 percent to 31 percent), and 50 percent for blacks (from 64 percent to 14 percent; see Table 1, Tuch and Weitzer 1997). The overall approval approached the pre–Rodney King levels only four years later, in 1995 (Tuch and Weitzer 1997). Thus, it seems that the incidents of police misconduct publicized by the media have not only direct, short-term effects on public support for the police, but also sizeable long-term effects. In their subsequent study, Weitzer and Tuch (2006) report that serial or ongoing exposure to negative media reporting on the police was one of the most consistent factors related to public support for the police.

B. Procedural Justice

Tyler (1990, 71) argues that legitimacy should not only be explored from the perspective of legal authority but also from the public's perspective. The traditional view—the instrumental perspective—was to assume that people evaluate the authority based on the favorability of the outcomes (Tyler 1990, 71); those individuals who receive a more favorable outcome are more likely to evaluate the authority positively (see Tyler 1990 for the overview of the studies). Whereas this perspective argues that citizens are concerned only with securing favorable outcomes for themselves (see Tyler 1990, 2000, 2001), the normative perspective of justice is based on the citizens' perceptions of fairness and equity (see Tyler 1990, 2001). Tyler (1990, 2000) suggests that citizens' views of justice are primarily based on the notion of fairness, both distributive justice (fairness of outcomes) and procedural justice (fairness of the procedures).

Thibaut and Walker (1975) argue that people would be more likely to accept the outcomes if they were obtained through fair procedures. The results of their study and subsequent studies (Lind and Tyler 1988; Tyler 1990; Tyler and Huo 2002) strongly confirm this notion. Although the fairness of outcomes is important, fairness of procedures is even more important. In fact, Tyler (1990, 80) reports that fairness of the procedure is the only factor that has a significant influence "on generalizations from experiences to attitudes toward legal authorities, law, and government."

Tyler (2000, 121) elaborates on the theory of procedural justice, analyzes the data (e.g., Tyler 1990, 141), and proposes that four elements (participation, neutrality, trustworthiness of authorities, and treatment with dignity and respect) are the key factors affecting evaluations of procedural fairness. However, his analyses show that these elements are complex and that they may not matter equally for all legal settings (e.g., Tyler 1990, 142, 144–45). *Participation* (Tyler

2000, 121), or representation (Leventhal 1976, 1980), refers to the extent to which the parties believe that they have control over the process, not necessarily in terms of determining the outcome of the dispute, but in terms of being given opportunities to present their side of the story to the decision makers. Research shows that "having a voice" resonated quite positively in diverse settings, from plea bargaining (Houlden 1980) and sentencing hearings (Heinz and Kerstetter 1979) to mediation (Kitzmann and Emery 1993; MacCoun et al. 1988; Shapiro and Brett 1993), especially if the parties had the impression that their statements had a direct effect on the outcome of the case (see, e.g., Shapiro and Brett 1993). *Neutrality* (Tyler and Lind 1992; Tyler 2000, 122), or impartiality (Paternoster et al. 1997, 168), occurs when the decision makers do not allow personal characteristics of the parties or favoritism of one party to influence the decision and treatment during the process. Simply put, neutrality involves honesty and lack of bias (Tyler and Lind 1992, 141). *Trustworthiness of authorities* (Tyler 2000, 122) refers to the degree to which the decision maker can be trusted to behave fairly. *Treatment with dignity and respect* (Tyler 2000, 122), status recognition (Tyler and Lind 1992), or ethicality (Paternoster et al. 1997, 168), imply that evaluations of procedural fairness will be affected by views as to whether the decision makers treat the participants with dignity and with respect for their rights. Based on their empirical tests of the key elements, Tyler and Huo (2002, 195) conclude that "[p]eople's judgments about their trust in the legal authority with whom they dealt were influenced by respect, voice, and neutrality. When people knew their outcome, they relied on respect, voice, and neutrality. When they did not know their outcome, they relied primarily on respect."

C. Personal Experience with the Police and Police Legitimacy

Tyler (1990, 26) argues that legitimate authorities have discretion to perform their tasks and that "[the scope of legitimate authority] rests on a conception of obligation to obey any commands an authority issues so long as that authority is acting within appropriate limits." When citizens feel that the authority is overstepping its boundaries, the level of legitimacy will decrease. In the context of policing, police agencies and individual police officers—both of whom could be characterized as having legitimacy (see, e.g., Tyler 1990, 29)—exercise discretion as a regular part of their jobs (e.g., Davis 1969). Indeed, when a police agency decides to enforce the DUI laws more aggressively or when a police officer stops a motorist for speeding, both of these situations have the potential to affect their legitimacy.

As Tyler and Darley (2000, 718) emphasize, although the roots of law-abiding culture are planted in childhood, people are also influenced in their views of authorities by adult experiences with the authorities, be they in the form of suspects, victims, or third parties. Tyler summarizes the findings about the influence of experience on the perceptions of legitimacy (1990, 94):

> These findings confirm that personal experience with police officers or court officials affects general views about the legitimacy of these authorities and the quality of their job performance. The data also suggest that the effect of experience on performance evaluations is much stronger than its effect on legitimacy. People's views about the legitimacy of legal authorities are more strongly insulated than performance evaluations are from the influence of a good or bad experience with police officers or a judge.

Tyler (1990, 95) further emphasizes that the effect of personal experience on the general views about legitimacy is strong and that it persists even after controlling for prior views. However, how people will evaluate their own personal experience with the police depends on what they thought about the police *before* the experience (Tyler 1990, 95). In that sense, general views about legitimacy lead people to attribute more positive evaluations of the actual experience, which in turn affects their general views of legitimacy. In their subsequent work, Tyler and Huo (2002) find that people who evaluate police officers as legitimate are more likely to obey their orders. At the same time, the behavior of specific police officers influences the overall level of legitimacy toward the police.

Sunshine and Tyler (2003) report that general views about the police are primarily influenced by the procedural justice variables. Whereas people base their evaluations partly on the perceptions of fairness of outcomes, unfair or disrespectful treatment by particular police officers carries substantial weight (Tyler 1990; Tyler and Huo 2002) and influences how likely both the individual who went through the experience and other people who learned about the experience are to obey the law in the future. Regardless of how trivial the reason for the interaction between the police and citizens, people generalize from their own experiences with the police and from the experiences of their friends and relatives. Unfair or disrespectful treatment leads toward less obedience (see, e.g., Tyler 1990; Paternoster et al. 1997; Tyler and Smith 1997) and more resistance (e.g., White et al. 1994; Mastrofski et al. 1996), which makes the police job more difficult in the future. Reiss's empirical study (1971) shows that when people, both suspects and third parties, attach low legitimacy to the police, the police officers responding to calls for service are more likely to use force and the encounters are more likely to end with severe injuries to both citizens and officers.

On the other hand, Tyler and Huo (2002) point out that one encounter evaluated as unfair or disrespectful will lead citizens in the future to put more emphasis on the quality of the treatment by the authorities and less on their general views of the authority (see, also Tyler 1990, 172). Thus, experiencing unfair treatment sensitizes individuals more toward such issues, shifts the focus away from legitimacy of legal authorities to the fairness of the specific experience, and effectively undermines legitimacy (Tyler 1990, 172). Furthermore, Tyler and Huo (2002, 185) argue and confirm through their empirical research that the subsequent general evaluations of the authorities are more influenced by the perceptions of the quality of treatment than by their judgments about the outcomes.

Other empirical studies explored the influence of various types of contacts with the police (e.g., involuntary contacts, contacts initiated by the police, such as being arrested or receiving a traffic ticket; voluntary contacts, contacts initiated by the citizens, such as requesting police service or reporting victimization on the confidence in the police [see Decker 1981 on public evaluations of the police]). Some studies (e.g., Winfree and Griffiths 1977) suggest that involuntary contacts have a stronger effect on the public opinion about the police than voluntary contacts do. Tyler and Folger (1980) report that procedural justice is more important for the evaluation of the encounter when the contact is involuntary (i.e., being stopped by the police) than when it is voluntary (i.e., called the police for help). Moreover, whereas involuntary contacts erode the individual's opinion about the police, voluntary contacts do not substantially improve it (Jacob 1971). Other studies (see, e.g., Carter 1985) find that, *regardless* of the nature of contacts (i.e., voluntary or involuntary), as the number of contacts with the police increases, the level of satisfaction decreases. Thus, it is quite possible that the nature of the contact may not have as much effect on the level of public opinion about the police as the satisfaction with, or perceived fairness of, the treatment does. Indeed, several studies confirm this conclusion (see, e.g., Correia et al. 1996; Reisig and Parks 2000). Thus, although certain types of contacts are more likely than others to generate dissatisfaction (see, e.g., Southgate and Eklbom 1984; Skogan 1996), it seems that, on average, having *any* contact with the police results in more negative attitudes toward the police (Yeo and Budd 2000; see also Dean 1980) because contact with the police likely will be perceived as unfair, disrespectful, or antagonistic.

The most frequently studied type of voluntary contact occurs when a person becomes a crime victim and decides to report the victimization to the police. Studies show that reporting the victimization to the police further erodes the overall satisfaction with the police (e.g., Homant et al. 1984; Kutnjak Ivković 2008). Similarly, Shapland et al. (1985, 85) report that the victims' "lack of knowledge of what was happening to the case and, for a few, the consequent feeling that the police did not care and were not doing anything" are detrimental for the victims' opinions about the police. Just like Tyler and Huo (2002) find that both quality of treatment and outcome favorability matter (although quality of treatment has a stronger effect), other prior studies exploring public evaluations of the police have shown that both the treatment and the outcome matter. Poister and McDavid (1978) report that the victims' overall satisfaction with the police is related to both procedural variables (e.g., satisfaction with the response time, satisfaction with the initial investigation) and outcome variables (e.g., whether the investigation was initiated, quality of the investigation, likelihood of an arrest). The 1996 International Crime Victimization

Survey results demonstrate that the respondents from a number of European and North American countries who were victimized and were dissatisfied with their reporting experiences attributed the reasons for their dissatisfaction to both procedural-justice issues (e.g., lack of interest in pursuing the case, impoliteness, slow to arrive) and substantive-justice issues (e.g., the offender was not caught, the property was not recovered; van Dijk 1999, 39). The results of the 1998 British Crime Survey support the same argument: Yeo and Budd (2000, 3) find that the "police received higher ratings when they: recovered all or some of the victim's property (77 percent), charged the offender (73 percent), [and] had face-to-face contact with the victim (66 percent)."

D. Minority Views and Experiences

Since the President's Commission on Law Enforcement and Administration of Justice (1967a) and the Kerner Commission (National Advisory Commission 1968), research studies have found that race unequivocally matters in the context of analyzing public opinion about the police: African American respondents seem less satisfied with, and less confident in, the local police than white respondents are[1] (e.g., Jacob 1971; Walker et al. 1973; Hadar and Snortum 1975; Albrecht and Green 1977; Garofalo 1977; Scaglion and Condon 1980; Peek et al. 1981; Jesilow et al. 1995; Webb and Marshall 1995; Cao et al, 1996; Correia et al. 1996; Flanagan and Vaughn 1996; Huang and Vaughn 1996; Tuch and Weitzer 1997; Kaminski and Jefferis 1998; Sampson and Bartusch 1998; Weitzer and Tuch 1999, 2002; Reisig and Parks 2000, 2002).[2]

Divergent opinions between African American and white respondents stem from different experiences and cultural norms and expectations. The police may treat minority citizens differently, including more frequent searches (but not more frequent questioning or chasing, according to Erez 1984; Bureau of Justice Statistics 2006), stops (e.g., Weitzer and Tuch 2002), tickets (e.g., Bureau of Justice Statistics 2006), and arrests (e.g., Harris 1997; Tuch and Weitzer 1997; Bureau of Justice Statistics 2006, 2007a), all of which might induce perceptions of injustice and differential treatment. Weitzer and Tuch (2002) point out that only 5 percent of white respondents reported being stopped exclusively because of their race or ethnic background, yet the same is true for about 40 percent of black respondents, particularly young, black men. The Bureau of Justice survey of citizens stopped by the police in 2002 (Bureau of Justice Statistics 2006) shows that white and black drivers were stopped at similar rates (compared to their proportion in the US population of drivers), but black drivers, particularly young, black men, were more likely to say that the police did not give them the reason for the stop and were less likely to evaluate the stop as legitimate. They were also less likely to estimate that they were stopped for speeding, but more likely to be ticketed, to be physically searched, to have their vehicles searched (Bureau of Justice Statistics 2006), or to be arrested (Bureau of Justice

Statistics 2007a, 6). Among the residents who had any contact with the police (not just a traffic stop), black residents were more likely to say that the police used force or threatened to use force (Bureau of Justice Statistics 2006, 9; Bureau of Justice Statistics 2007a, 8), but there were no differences in the percentages of black and white respondents who evaluated the force as excessive (Bureau of Justice Statistics 2007a, 8). Research further suggests that African Americans are more likely to see traffic stops as unjustified (Wortley et al. 1997; Bureau of Justice Statistics 2001) and to say that they are at risk of unfair treatment by the police (Huang and Vaughn 1996, 39). African American respondents typically are more likely to say that the police "are allowed to use too much force" than whites report (60 percent and 33 percent, respectively; Huang and Vaughn 1996, 40), and that they have been victims of racial profiling (Weitzer and Tuch 2002).

Respondents who perceive the police to engage in misconduct more frequently, as African American respondents do (e.g., Flanagan and Vaughn 1996; Weitzer and Tuch 2002), are also less likely to express strong support for the police (see, e.g., Smith and Hawkins 1973; Dean 1980; Benson 1981; Soo Son et al. 1997; Tuch and Weitzer 1997; Weitzer and Tuch 2002). Weitzer and Tuch (2002) identify race and personal experience with police racial profiling are *the* strongest predictors of attitudes toward the police.

II. POLICE MISCONDUCT

Police agencies and police officers enjoy substantial discretion in the performance of their duties (Davis 1969). In addition to the federal and state statutes, the US Constitution serves as the springboard to evaluate the legality of police actions and the way they exercise discretion. Police officer discretion is also channeled by court cases, both criminal and civil, as well as the police agency's administrative rules. Still, some police officers cross the line, violate the rules, and engage in police misconduct. Legitimacy is a characteristic of both police agencies and individual police officers, and they can enhance it or undermine it. One way of undermining is to engage in police misconduct (line officers) or to allow misconduct to flourish in the police agency (supervisors).

A. Police Corruption

Police corruption is a form of police misconduct typically defined through the motivation to achieve personal gain (e.g., Sherman 1974; Goldstein 1975; Barker and Carter 1986; Klockars et al. 2000). It may involve a violation of the laws, police agency's internal administrative rules, and/or the codes of ethics.

In their joint work Barker and Roebuck (Barker and Roebuck 1973; Roebuck and Barker 1974) point out that corruption takes many forms. Based on several dimensions (e.g., acts and actors involved, norms violated, support from peer group, organizational degree, police department's reaction), they specify eight types of corruption: corruption of authority (which incorporates the acceptance of gratuities), kickbacks, opportunistic thefts, shakedowns, protection of illegal activity, the fix, illegal criminal activity, and internal payoffs. Punch (1985) added "flaking" or "padding" of evidence as the ninth type of corruption, which, according to Punch, typically is evident in drug-related cases. In a nationwide study of more than 3,000 police officers from thirty diverse US police agencies, Klockars et al. (2000) find that shakedowns and opportunistic thefts were evaluated to be the most serious types of corruption in all thirty agencies, while the acceptance of gratuities—be it on a regular basis or only for the holidays—was viewed as the least serious form of corruption in all thirty agencies, with the cases of internal corruption and kickbacks lying somewhere between these two extremes. These results are very consistent with results of surveys of police officers from thirteen other countries as diverse as Croatia, Finland, Japan, Pakistan, and South Africa (Klockars, Kutnjak Ivković, and Haberfeld 2004).

1. *Causes of Police Corruption*

The National Research Council (2004, 271) points out that "[t]he research literature [on causes of police corruption] is long on theory and short on evidence about what causes police corruption." Existing literature on causes of corruption could be classified into several categories.

First, some studies explore individual police officers and their characteristics (e.g., Muir 1977) or the "rotten apples" (Knapp Commission 1972). The literature tries to establish which features make police officers particularly prone to corruption (e.g., prior criminal record, weak moral values) but, at the same time, indicates that psychological screening tests are not accurate predictors of future behavior (e.g., Malouff and Schutte 1986; Talley and Hinz 1990).

Second, the literature focuses on the opportunities for corruption. Policing as an occupation is rife with opportunities for corruption (Klockars et al. 2000), with differential opportunities across various assignments, ranks, and laws that the police enforce. Detectives, particularly those assigned to narcotic units, have especially extensive opportunities for corruption (General Accounting Office 1998), as do police officers in charge of laws without moral consensus and vaguely defined laws (Knapp Commission 1972).

Third, a strand of the literature focuses on the police agency itself ("rotten barrels" or "rotten orchards," Punch 2003) and what the police agency does to influence the contours of corruption within the agency. The effect of the police agency on corruption within the agency is multifaceted. The police chief plays one of the dominant roles (e.g., Knapp Commission 1972; Pennsylvania Crime Commission 1974; Goldstein 1975; Weisburd and Greenspan 2000; Kutnjak Ivković 2005), as do first-line supervisors (e.g., Knapp Commission 1972; Burns and Sechrest 1992; Mollen Commission 1994; Weisburd and Greenspan 2000) and peers (e.g., McNamara 1967; Stoddard 1974; Klitgaard 1988; Sparrow et al. 1990; Weisburd and Greenspan 2000; Chen 2003; Kutnjak Ivković 2005). In a nutshell, police agencies play crucial roles by creating systems that establish rules, enforce rules, detect corruption, and control the code of silence (e.g., Sherman 1974, 1978; Klockars et al. 2000; Kutnjak Ivković 2005;).

Fourth, some studies examine the role of the broader environment and the influence it has on the level of corruption in the police agency. By criminalizing or by failing to criminalize certain behaviors, the society at large—through its legislative branch of government—sends the message about the standards of appropriate behavior and regulates the demand for corruption (Walker 1999). By enacting the laws prohibiting corruption, but by not enforcing them or enforcing them only sporadically, the society at large communicates a relaxed view of corruption and its seriousness (Kutnjak Ivković 2005). Public expectations of the appropriate ethical behavior by all governmental employees, including police officers, guide police agencies and police officers in their conduct (e.g., Goldstein 1975; Sherman 1977; Klockars 2003). These expectations are generated as part of the local political culture; as Sherman (1977) argues, communities differ greatly in their expectations, from "communities with a more public-regarding ethos" (like Charlotte, North Carolina; Kansas City, Missouri; and Portland, Oregon) to communities with more "private-regarding" (like New York City and New Orleans). Kutnjak Ivković's (2003, 612) study of International Crime Victim Surveys reveals that "the countries with the reputation in the international business community of being more corrupt, as indicated by a low score on the 1999 Corruption Perception Index (CPI) . . ., appear also to have a higher percentage of the respondents who said that they had been asked to pay a bribe to a police officer last year."

2. Data on Police Corruption

Obtaining accurate data on police corruption is very challenging. First, in most countries legal statutes do not feature a crime specifically titled "corruption" (instead, criminal statutes prohibit behaviors such as "bribery," "extortion," and "theft"). The same applies to police agencies; precisely what corrupt behaviors are prohibited by internal agency rules varies from agency to agency and across time within the same agency. Second, for various reasons, neither police officers nor citizens (participants or potential witnesses) have motives to report a corrupt transaction; in fact, they have motives *not* to report it (e.g., Stoddard 1974; Klockars 1999; Klockars et al. 2000; Kutnjak Ivković 2003, 2005;).

Surveys of citizens and police officers alike are burdened with these problems and are not reliable sources of data on corruption (see, e.g., Kutnjak Ivković 2003; National Research Council 2004, 269). In addition, most of the existing surveys focus on one country and are conducted locally, usually with the purpose of surveying the population of a particular city. The results of citizen surveys provide quite a divergent picture about police corruption, from fewer than 2 percent of Caucasian respondents nationwide who perceived in the 1960s that most of the police were corrupt (President's Commission on Law Enforcement and Administration of Justice 1967*b*) to 93 percent of New Yorkers in the 1990s who perceived corruption to be widespread (Kraus 1994). On the comparative front, the Gallup International 50th Anniversary Survey (1996) reports that approximately one-third of the respondents in the West European countries and Israel, and more than two-thirds of the respondents in the East European countries, the Far Eastern countries, and the Central and South American countries assessed that police corruption was widespread in their countries. Among the respondents in the International Crime Victimization Survey, about 1 percent of the respondents or fewer from Western democracies reported paying a bribe to the police, while the corresponding percentages were dramatically higher (between 10 percent and 20 percent) in some East European, Asian, and Latin American countries (Kutnjak Ivković 2003).

The official data, be they arrest rates or complaint rates within a police agency, at best reveal only the tip of the iceberg. At the federal level, there were between 83 and 150 officers convicted annually in the period from 1993 to 1997 (General Accounting Office 1998, 11). For a country with more than 600,000 officers (Bureau of Justice Statistics 2007*b*), focusing on these miniscule conviction rates would suggest naïvely that corruption is a minor issue. On the other hand, the Knapp Commission (1972) reports finding widespread corruption in the NYPD (the largest police agency in the country) in the 1970s. At the same time, the prosecutors filed about thirty cases of corruption annually (Kutnjak Ivković 2003), with about one-third of the police officers charged with corruption-related crimes not being convicted and, among those convicted, only one out of five receiving a prison sentence of a year or longer (Kutnjak Ivković 2003).

Similar problems could be encountered regarding the police agency's complaint data, if they are available at all, and compared with other sources of data about corruption. Reports by independent commissions (e.g., Mollen Commission 1994; Royal Commission 1997) and the results of victimization surveys across the world (Kutnjak Ivković 2003) suggest that citizens rarely report corruption to the police, and the official agency data are severe underestimates of the extent of corruption. For example, at the time the Knapp Commission (1972) reported widespread corruption in the NYPD, the complaint rate was less than 1 per 100 officers (Cohen 1972).

The best, most detailed and accurate data come from independent commissions, but they pertain only to a specific agency, time period, and are bound by the resources and powers granted to the commission. The Knapp Commission (1972), the Pennsylvania Crime Commission (1974), the Christopher Commission (1991), the Mollen Commission (1994), and the Royal Commission (1997) are examples of the best-known recent commissions. Their findings illustrate the evolving and dynamic nature of police corruption. Both the Knapp Commission and the Pennsylvania Crime Commission found widespread corruption in the NYPD and Philadelphia Police Department, respectively, along with the presence of a strong code of silence. In contrast, the Mollen Commission reported that most police officers in the NYPD were honest but still found pockets of police officers aggressively seeking opportunities to obtain money and drugs.

A novel approach toward collecting data about police corruption incorporates the approach developed by Klockars and Kutnjak Ivković (2003), in which the authors measure the level of police integrity and thus alleviate the methodological problems associated with the direct measurement of police corruption. A study of thirty police agencies (Klockars et al. 2000) revealed that police agencies varied considerably in the contours of their police integrity.

B. Use of (Excessive) Force

The right to use coercive force is a defining feature of policing (see, e.g., Bittner 1970; Klockars 1985). The police use of force has been studied extensively since the 1960s, when the President's Commission for Law Enforcement and Administration of Justice (1967a) confirmed that the allegations of use of excessive force, which ignited riots across the US cities, were legitimate. Despite intensive research activity, there is no clear consensus on what constitutes the use of force and, particularly, the use of excessive force. Typically, use of force is explored through the continuum of force (see, e.g., Desmedt and Marsh 1990), but the items on the matrix differ from one police agency to another (see, e.g., National Institute of Justice 1999).

Drawing a line between the appropriate and excessive force is even more challenging. The CALEA accreditation standards require that police officers "will use only the force necessary to accomplish lawful objectives." Klockars (1995) argues that the line between the legitimate force and excessive force can be drawn across several standards—excessive force creates criminal responsibility, civil liability, and/or a scandal. However, Klockars (1995, 17) further points out that these standards are necessary but not sufficient to define excessive force, and that the definition should be related to the skilled police officer standard ("the use of any more force than a highly skilled police officer would find necessary to use in a particular situation"). This approach fits with the US Supreme Court standard of a "reasonable police officer" decided in *Graham v. Connor* (490 U.S. 386 [1989]).

A particular kind of the use of force—the use of deadly or lethal force—is more regulated. The Supreme Court held in *Tennessee v. Garner* (471 U.S. 1 [1985]) that the fleeing-felon rule, which authorized police officers to use "all the means necessary to effect an arrest," was unconstitutional. Instead, the guidelines issued by the Court suggest that police officers are allowed to legitimately use deadly force only in the situations in which the suspect presents clear and present danger to himself or others ("deadly force ... may not be used unless necessary to prevent the escape and the officer has probable cause to believe that the suspect poses a significant threat of death or serious physical injury to the officer or others").

1. *Causes of Use of (Excessive) Force*

Unlike the study of corruption, the study of the use of force has been mostly atheoretical. In general, empirical research has sought to explore which variables are related to the use of (excessive) force (e.g., Riksheim and Chermak 1993; Terrill 2001). The issue is further complicated by the fact that this literature is situated within the broader topic of police behavior and discretion. Based on the nature of the variables explored, four dominant strands of the literature have emerged.

First, some studies focus on individual police officers and their characteristics (e.g., Muir 1977). Early research in the 1960s and 1970s (e.g., Balch 1972) sought to distinguish the degree to which police officers exhibit characteristics of an authoritarian personality, which would predispose them to use (excessive) force. Although Scrivner (1994) reports finding some evidence of those characteristics among the group of police officers referred to him for their use of excessive force, the jury is still out on whether police officers indeed generally are more likely to have these characteristics and, if they do, whether they are related to the use of excessive force. Another avenue of research explored police officer value or belief system and encountered two serious problems: first, the difficulty of separating the effects of contextual and organizational variables from the attitudes and, second, respondents' low attitude-behavior consistency. The few empirical tests conducted found very limited support for the role of individual characteristics (e.g., Worden 1995; Terrill and Mastrofski 2002). Worden (1995) reports that police officer use of force and excessive force is related to their views about citizens, but not to their views of the police role.

Second, the literature focuses on the dynamics of police-citizen encounters. Following Donald Black's theory of law (1976), the predictions are that the police will be more likely to use (excessive) force in the encounters with citizens who have a lower status, such as minorities and the poor (see, e.g., Terrill 2001, 14). The existing research (e.g., Reiss 1967; Friedrich 1980; Worden 1995; Terrill 2001) documents that police officers are more likely to use force (and use of excessive force when included in the studies) when citizens are defiant and antagonistic (recent evidence is somewhat less supportive; e.g., Terrill and Mastrofski 2002 *v.* Garner et al. 2002), lower-class (e.g., Terrill and Mastrofski 2002), intoxicated (e.g., Terrill 2001), male (e.g., Mastrofski et al., 1995; Worden 1995; Terrill 2001; Terrill and Mastrofski 2002), and black/nonwhite (recent evidence is more mixed; e.g., Alpert 1989; Garner et al. 1995, 2002; Engel et al. 2000 *v.* Fyfe 1982; Worden 1995; Terrill and Mastrofski 2002). In fact, situational factors seem to be *more* relevant than individual police officer or organizational characteristics (see, e.g., Worden 1989; Riksheim and Chermak 1993 for reviews).

Third, a strand of the literature focuses on the police agency. Wilson's organizational theory (1968) emphasizes the importance of the police agency's hierarchical structure and the larger social and political environment in which the police agency operates. By establishing administrative rules, the police agency creates a certain organizational culture or common vision about how policing should be done. However, establishing the official policies is a necessary but not sufficient step. Studies exploring individual police agencies show support for this idea, particularly in the case of deadly force. Fyfe (1979) analyzes the effect of the newly implemented policy on the use of firearms in the NYPD in 1972 and shows a decrease of about 30 percent in the number of police firearm discharges. At the same time, Fyfe (1982) compares the shooting rates in Memphis and the NYPD, and explains the difference between the two cities through the differences in the extent of official rules and the activity of the internal control mechanisms. The second subset of the literature focuses on police culture and its effect on the use of (excessive) force. Police culture (see, e.g., Bittner 1970; Stoddard 1974; Van Maanen 1974; Reuss-Ianni 1983; Sparrow et al. 1990) emphasizes danger, social isolation, group loyalty, and solidarity. Although the debate is centered on whether the increased diversity and the introduction of the community policing may challenge traditional views about the police culture, there are few studies that explored the influence of police culture on the use of (excessive) force. Researchers typically assumed that the police culture includes a predetermined set of values relatively static in nature (see, e.g., National Research Council 2004, 132). Worden (1995) compares the formal effects of the organizational structure (e.g., degree of bureaucratization, emphasis on crime-fighting activities) and the informal culture on the use of force and concludes that, of these three variables, only the degree of bureaucratization is related to the use of force.

Fourth, the literature focuses on the society at large and its effects on the use of (excessive) force. The "racial threat" hypothesis proposes that, once the percentage of minorities reaches a certain proportion of the population (e.g., Liska et al., 1985), they will be perceived as a threat to the existing order and, as such, will receive a harsher treatment by the police. At the neighborhood level, research suggests that the police officers are more likely to use force in the disadvantaged neighborhoods (e.g., Reisig and Parks 2000). At the state level, research suggests that police were more likely to use deadly force in the states with higher levels of income inequality (e.g., Jacobs and Britt 1979).

2. *Data on the Use of (Excessive) Force*

The lack of the common definitions of the use of force and, particularly, the use of excessive force is a serious problem in the collection of data as well. Consequently, there is no nationwide data source about the extent and nature of the use of force.

The key sources of data on the use of (excessive) force have been observational studies, surveys, police officer use of force reports, and citizen complaints, each of which features serious shortcomings.

Research indicates that the police use force rarely (e.g., McLaughlin 1992; Klinger 1995; Garner et al. 1996) and that, when police officers do use force, they typically rely on the less severe items on the use of force continuum, such as issuing verbal commands or grabbing the citizen (e.g., Klinger 1995; Garner and Maxwell 1999; Terrill 2001). Observational studies from the 1960s and 1970s (Reiss 1967; Friedrich 1977; Worden 1995) suggest that police officers had used force in fewer than 5 percent of the police-citizen contacts and had used excessive force even less frequently, in fewer than 3 percent of the contacts. More recent studies (e.g., Klinger 1995) incorporate verbal commands into the use of force as well, and find force to be used more frequently (17 percent of the time), with verbal commands accounting for more than one-third of the events.

The findings of the Bureau of Justice Statistics nationwide survey (Bureau of Justice Statistics 2001) of police-public contacts are consistent with the results of observational studies. Based on the survey of more than 80,000 people in 1999, the police officers used force, or threatened to use force, in fewer than 1 percent of the encounters with the citizens. The 2005 sweep of the survey shows that about 1.6 percent of the citizens experienced police using force or were threatened with the use of force (Bureau of Justice Statistics 2007a, 1). In about one-half of the incidents, 55 percent, the police used physical force (as opposed to verbal commands or threats to use force); when they used physical force, the police tended to use the least serious forms of physical force (they pushed or grabbed the person). The overwhelming majority of the citizens who said that they were either threatened with the use of force or actually experienced force claimed that the force was excessive (75 percent in 1999 and 83 percent in 2005).

Pate and Fridell (1993, 48) surveyed more than 1,000 police agencies, including sheriff's departments, country police departments, city police departments, and state agencies, and asked them to provide information about the use of force reports, citizen complaints, and the litigation concerning allegations of excessive force. Whereas their findings show substantial variation over different types of police agencies, the common feature is that police officers from all police agencies tended to use less serious forms of force more frequently. For example, among the city police agencies, police officers used handcuffs at the rate of 490 per 1,000, bodily force at the rate of 272, and weapons being drawn at the rate of 130 per 1,000 sworn officers (Pate and Fridell 1993, 74). On the other hand, police officers shot at civilians at the rate of less than 5 per 1,000, used electrical devices at the rate of 5 per 1,000, and used neck restraints at the rate of 1 per 1,000 sworn officers (Pate and Fridell 1993, 74). Pate and Fridell (1993, 107) document the rates of use-of-force citizen complaints per 1,000 sworn offices and report that these rates varied from 16 percent for the state agencies to 48 percent for the city police agencies. Fewer than

15 percent of all these complaints were sustained by the agencies (Pate and Fridell 1993, 114).

3. *Data on the Use of Deadly Force*

Although it is rare, the use of deadly force nevertheless is an important and sensitive topic; the disparity in the fatal shootings of African Americans and whites in the 1960s, sometimes to the extent of 6 or 8 to 1 (Robin 1963; Walker and Katz 2008, 404), sparked riots in the 1960s. The change occurred in the 1980s after the *Garner* decision (*Tennessee v. Garner*, 471 U.S. 1 [1985]), when the old fleeing-felon rule was reversed. Research suggests that the Garner decision was not as effective in changing state laws (Cassell and Hayman 1998) as it was effective in changing the police agencies' internal administrative rules (e.g., Skolnick and Fyfe 1993). Fyfe (1979) analyzed the NYPD data and reported that the number of shots fired was reduced by 30 percent, particularly in the area of fleeing-felon situations. In the end, the estimates are that the decision seemed to reduce the number of fatal police shootings nationwide by about 60 incidents annually (e.g., Tennenbaum 1994) or from 400 in 1983 to 300 in 1987 (Geller and Scott 1992) and that the ratio of African Americans and whites shot and killed dropped from 8 to 1 in the 1960s to 4 to 1 in the 1980s (Geller and Scott 1992).

Obtaining accurate data on the police use of deadly force or fatal shootings is challenging (National Research Council 2004, 259). The existing studies on lethal force show substantial variation across jurisdictions. Milton et al. (1977) analyze the rates of shootings in seven large US cities in the period 1973–74 and note that the rates of shooting varied from 1.6 to 8.5 shootings per 100,000 citizens (or by a factor of five). Fyfe's analyses (2002) of the fatal shootings in fifty-one municipal, county, and sheriff's departments in the period 1990–2000 also detect extensive variation across the agencies. The rate of shooting differential between the lowest and the highest varied by a factor of fourteen in county police agencies, a factor of eight within city agencies, and a factor of six among the sheriff's agencies.

C. Racial Profiling

The issue of racial profiling quickly grabbed the attention of the public in the mid-1990s, in the aftermath of two lawsuits that alleged racial profiling by state police agencies in Maryland and New Jersey (*New Jersey v. Soto*, 734 A.2d 350, Superior Court of New Jersey [1996]; *Wilkins v. Maryland State Police*, No. CCB-93-468 [D. Md. 1993], filed November 14, 1996). Despite the importance of the issue, there is no common definition of what constitutes unlawful racial profiling (Northeastern University Data Collection Resource Center 2010). Racial profiling is typically referred to as the use of race as a key or *the* key variable in the police practice of stopping, searching, arresting, and ticketing citizens (see, e.g., Weitzer and Tuch 2002, 435; Walker and Katz 2008, 415.

Whereas more than 60 percent of the police chiefs participating in a recent survey (Fridell et al. 2001) thought that racial profiling was not a problem in their jurisdiction, the overwhelming majority of citizens (black citizens in particular) believed that racial profiling indeed was widespread (Weitzer and Tuch 2002, 442). Black respondents—especially young, black men—were substantially more likely to say that they experienced racial profiling than white respondents were (Weitzer and Tuch 2002). Based on multivariate analyses, Weitzer and Tuch (2002, 446) conclude that race and personal experience with profiling were the strongest predictors of citizens' attitudes toward the police.

1. *Data on Racial Profiling*

The difficulty in data collection involves several different dimensions. First, racial profiling is a highly political issue. Second, the debate among criminologists on how to measure racial profiling correctly has not been resolved and "no industry standard exists for measuring racial or gender profiling" (Northeastern University Data Collection Resource Center 2010). Third, there is no established rule that would unequivocally determine when racial disparity becomes racial discrimination. In measuring racial profiling, the first step is to determine the number of persons stopped, arrested, searched, and/or ticked ("the numerator"). The second step is to compare their racial distribution with the racial distribution of the benchmark ("the denominator"). Determining the denominator, particularly for traffic and other moving violations, is particularly challenging. The last step in the process is to explore the size of the differences detected through the analyses and conclude whether the differences point toward racial disparity or racial discrimination.

As part of his expert testimony in *New Jersey v. Soto* (734 A.2d 350, Superior Court of New Jersey [1996]), John Lamberth undertook the first thorough effort to measure racial profiling. Lamberth and his team measured the speed of passing traffic on the New Jersey Turnpike and compared the racial distribution of drivers speeding with the racial distribution of the drivers stopped and ticketed by the New Jersey State Police. His analyses show that African Americans constituted 13.5 percent of drivers, 15 percent of drivers speeding, 35 percent of drivers stopped, and 73.2 percent of drivers arrested. In the Maryland case (*Wilkins v. Maryland State Police*, No. CCB-93-468 [D. Md. 1993], filed November 14, 1996; Consent Decree, US District Court for the District of Maryland), Lamberth showed that African Americans constituted 17.5 percent of the drivers speeding, 28.8 percent of the drivers stopped, and 71.3 percent of the drivers whose cars were searched. Matt Zingraff's team (2000) studied the North Carolina Highway Patrol and improved the benchmark by measuring not only whether the drivers were speeding but also the rate at which they were speeding (which indicates the severity of the violation).

The collection of official data on racial profiling is spurred by the Violent Crime Control and Law Enforcement Act of 1994 and by individual lawsuits. The act authorizes the attorney general to investigate any "pattern or practice of conduct by law enforcement officers . . . that deprives persons of rights, privileges, or immunities secured or protected by the Constitution or the laws of the United States." The threat of the lawsuit, the consent decree between the Department of Justice (DOJ) and a police agency, as well as the push from the civil liberties groups, have had two effects: (1) the sudden increase in the number of police departments collecting the data on racial profiling (more than 400 by 2003; McMahon et al. 2003) and (2) the enactment of state laws requiring racial profiling policies (see, e.g., Northeastern University Data Collection Resource Center 2010). According to that document, "more than twenty states have passed legislation prohibiting racial profiling and/or requiring jurisdictions within the state to collect the data on law enforcement stops and searches" and additional five have the legislation pending. With few exceptions (e.g., San Jose Police Department 1999), the police efforts in data collection were primarily focused on the numerator (see, e.g., National Research Council 2004, 321).

III. Responses to Police Misconduct

Reactions to the instances of police misconduct are far from uniform. On the one hand, instances could go completely unnoticed; on the other hand, they have the potential to create a scandal, ignite riots, lead toward the establishment of an independent commission or an citizen review board, result in convictions of police officers and their dismissal from the police agency, firing of the police chief, and the decline of police legitimacy. The extent and nature of the reaction depend on many factors including, for example, the nature of the legal rules violated, severity of misconduct, form of misconduct, level of organization, seriousness of consequences, and characteristics of the victims.

Control mechanisms have traditionally been divided into external ones (those housed outside of the police agency) and internal ones (those housed within the police agency). In addition, there are a few mixed mechanisms of accountability that have elements of both internal and external mechanisms (those housed outside of the police agency but potentially having police officers as members).

A. Internal Mechanisms of Control and Accountability

The police agency itself has one of the crucial roles in achieving accountability and controlling misconduct. What the agency does or does not do to control misconduct varies greatly: "[i]t starts with the recruitment and selection process and continues with training and supervision, incorporating various aspects of rule establishment, communication, and enforcement that stimulate, allow, or prevent police officers from turning their propensity toward corruption into actual corrupt behavior" (Kutnjak Ivković 2005, 68).

1. *Administrative Rules*

Administrative rules channel the use of discretion, describe appropriate conduct of police officers, and prohibit inappropriate conduct. These rules, typically made either by the police chief or the police chief and the mayor (see, e.g., Mastrofski 1988), seek to prescribe the use of discretion in critical incidents (e.g., arrest, use of force, use of deadly force, high-speed pursuits, domestic violence), instruct officers to complete written reports after each such incident, and require supervisory oversight (see, e.g., National Research Council 2004; Walker and Katz 2008). The content and nature of the rules vary substantially across police agencies; these official administrative rules, codified in the standard operating procedure manuals (SOP), could be several hundred pages long and typically put more emphasis on trivial issues (see, e.g., Bittner 1970; Walker and Katz 2008).

Even in the agencies with extensive rules, the rules could open the doors to misconduct by being ambiguous or by failing to regulate certain aspects. Fishman (1978) reports that police officers in the police agencies characterized as corrupt were more likely to say that the rules were not clear than did the police officers in the police agencies that were relatively free of corruption. Furthermore, multiple commission reports (e.g., Knapp Commission 1972; Pennsylvania Crime Commission 1974; Mollen Commission 1994;) document many instances in which police administrators, particularly the police chief, created unofficial rules that, in reality, trumped the official ones (Kutnjak Ivković 2005).

Official administrative rules have been used to characterize the use of deadly force, use of force, high-speed pursuits, and domestic violence. Studies exploring the effect of the administrative rules on the use of deadly force reported positive changes (Fyfe 1979; Geller and Scott 1992). For example, Fyfe's study of the NYPD restrictive policy on deadly force (1979) finds that the number of shots fired was reduced by 30 percent. Similarly, the regulation of the high-speed pursuits via administrative rulemaking seem to be successful (e.g., Alpert 1997). In his study of high-speed pursuits, Alpert (1997) finds strong evidence that official policies affect such pursuits. Alpert's results (1997) indicate that, when one of the agencies (Metro-Dade Police Department) implemented a more restricted policy of high-speed pursuits, the number of pursuits decreased dramatically the next year (82 percent). On the other hand, when another agency (Omaha Police Department) relaxed its rules regarding the high-speed pursuits, the number of pursuits increased by 600 percent the following year (Alpert 1997). The effect of administrative rulemaking on misconduct has been explored in several other areas (e.g., use of force, domestic violence); the evidence is more limited and shows less success (National Research Council 2004, 285).

2. *Police Chief and Administration*

Police chief and the top leadership in the police agency play one of the critical roles. Kutnjak Ivković (2005, 70) describes their role:

> Although the powers of police chiefs are either explicitly or implicitly limited by the mayor, politicians, public, media, civil service rules, police unions, existing laws, and court cases, police chiefs and the administration determine "the rules of the game" within the police agency. They may exert a substantial influence on the recruitment standards, training in ethics, leadership and management style, supervisory accountability and standards, internal control mechanisms, discipline, and rewards.

The importance of this role is recognized by police officers as well; in a nationwide sample of police officers (Weisburd and Greenspan 2000, 6), the majority agreed that "a chief's strong position against the abuse of authority can make a big difference in deterring officers from abusing their authority." The chief may himself behave ethically (see examples to the contrary in Kutnjak Ivković 2005, 74) but fail to perform the traditional managerial functions—planning, organizing, coordinating, and controlling (Moore and Stephens 1991)— that he is expected to perform as part of his role. Finding examples of such failures is not difficult.

Terrill's study (2001) of the police use of force shows that the official position of the police chief and his administration on the "style of policing practiced" had a direct influence on how police officers used force; in Indianapolis, where the top police administration emphasized the "get tough" approach, police officers were more likely to use higher levels of force than police officers in St. Petersburg, where the top administration emphasized a problem-solving model.

Both the Knapp Commission (1972) and the Pennsylvania Crime Commission (1974) enumerate many examples of police chiefs adhering to the "rotten apple" approach, turning a blind eye to corruption, and thus allowing it to flourish. The discrepancy between the official stance and the police chief's actual behavior has substantial influence on police officers' behavior (see, e.g., Knapp Commission 1972, 170–71).

3. *Supervisors*

Another layer of control and accountability in a police agency consists of supervisors. In a recent nationwide survey of police officers (Weisburd and Greenspan 2000, 6), the overwhelming majority of police officers (90 percent) viewed the supervisors' role in preventing misconduct as critical. Indeed, supervisors are expected to monitor police officers under their command, review their reports (e.g., use of force, arrest), advise police officers when their performance is less than satisfactory (e.g., annual performance evaluations), and file a report when they are aware that police officers violated the rules (Walker and Katz 2008, 482).

Supervisors can either actively take part in misconduct, as the Knapp Commission (1972) and the Pennsylvania Crime Commission (1974) find regarding supervisors in the NYPD and the Philadelphia Police Department, or may fail to take a stance on misconduct and enforce the official rules, as the Mollen Commission (1994) and the Christopher Commission (1991) document for the NYPD and the LAPD. Supervisors who reported misconduct in the NYPD in the 1990s were not rewarded for it; in fact, they suffered informal punishment for doing so (Mollen Commission 1994, 13). Overall, many reports by independent commissions suggest that supervisors in troubled agencies were not held accountable for behavior of their subordinates (e.g., Christopher Commission 1991; Los Angeles Police Department 2000; Knapp Commission 1972; Mollen Commission 1994).

The Christopher Commission (1991) reports that the supervisors, expected to monitor the discussion on the mobile digital terminal (MDT) communications (which contained numerous examples of racist language), failed to do so. The Mollen Commission (1994) points out that supervisors failed to review the reports and question subordinates who were falsifying search and arrest forms (29) or overtime payment forms (39). The LAPD's Board of Inquiry (Los Angeles Police Department 2000, 61) writes about the examples of poor supervision in the Rampart area, characterized by both corruption and use of excessive force; "the practice of officers printing or signing a sergeant's name to booking approvals and arrest reports was a particularly glaring illustration of poor CRASH [Community Resources Against Street Hoodlums] supervision."

The scandal that led toward the establishment of the Mollen Commission in July 1994 was ignited with the arrest of Michael Dowd and five other NYPD officers in May 1994. Dowd did not just accept bribes, he actually became a drug dealer himself, helped operate large drug rings (Mollen Commission 1994, 17), and was subsequently convicted to a fourteen-year sentence (Treaser 1994). His supervisors did not report his evident misconduct (which gave the impression to Dowd that he could do anything; Mollen Commission 1994, 82) and, in fact, gave Dowd glowing performance evaluations, citing him as "a role model" (Mollen Commission 1994, 118). The Christopher Commission (1991, ix), investigating the allegations of racism, sexism, and use of excessive force, heard the testimony from the Assistant Chief Dotson who said that "we [the top administration] have failed miserably" to hold supervisors accountable for excessive force by officers under their command.

In 1994 Bill Bratton and other top administrators in the NYPD developed CompStat, a new mechanisms to reduce crime and enhance accountability of the administrators and managers (see, e.g., McDonald et al. 2001). CompStat's purposes are achieved through the meetings in which the top administrators require of middle managers to discuss crime problems in their areas and hold them accountable. After the initial debut in New York, CompStat became popular and widespread; in 1999, one-quarter of the sample of police agencies with one hundred or more employees reported implementing CompStat, while an additional one-third of the sample was planning to do so (Weisburd et al. 2003). Research evaluating CompStat across both dimensions is scant; Silverman (1999) gave an excellent grade to the NYPD's CompStat, while Willis and colleagues (2003) expressed a more skeptical view of the CompStat in Lowell, Massachusetts; Newark, New Jersey; and Minneapolis. Research suggests that CompStat may be working as an accountability mechanism at the middle-manager level (existing studies conclude that middle managers experience more pressure to know about, and react to, crime in their areas). However, the accountability did not incorporate the middle managers' subordinates—these middle managers did not hold the CompStat meetings with their subordinates (National Research Council 2004, 188). Furthermore, accountability, as achieved through the CompStat meetings, extends to the crime level in the area but does not incorporate accountability for the level of integrity and control of rule-violating behavior by middle managers' subordinates.

4. *Internal System of Control*

The internal systems of control typically rely on separate units within the police agency (i.e., internal affairs units) to receive complaints, investigate them, and forward the case to the decision-making structures (e.g., police chief, chain of command). The overwhelming majority of these systems are exclusively internal (see, e.g., Perez 1994). Whereas the work of internal mechanisms could be both reactive (e.g., investigating a complaint) and proactive (e.g., integrity tests, conducted by a few agencies, Baueris 1977; Giuliani and Bratton 1995), proactive investigations are more an exception than the rule (Kutnjak Ivković 2005).

The internal system of control is typically initiated with the complained filed by citizens or police officers, or reports generated by police supervisors. As the existing research reports, whether citizens will choose to file a complaint depends on many issues. Citizens may be unfamiliar with the system (e.g., Russell 1978), required to sign, swear, or have their complaints notarized (e.g., Pate and Fridell 1993), or otherwise be asked to go through substantial hurdles to file the complaint, be threatened with criminal charges for false reports (e.g., President's Commission on Law Enforcement and Administration of Justice 1967b), fear that the police would retaliate (e.g., Guerrero-Daley 2000), be discouraged by the police to file a complaint (e.g., Walker and Bumphus 1992), distrust the police or think that the police will not investigate the complaint (e.g., Walker and Bumphus 1992). An in-depth study of citizen complaints by Klockars, Kutnjak Ivković, and Haberfeld (2006) illustrates the nature of the problems associated with the comparison of citizen complaints in three US police agencies. Rates of complaints vary greatly across cities, suggesting that more than just the level of misconduct influences them (e.g., West 1988). For example, a nationwide survey of police agencies by Pate and Fridell (1993) suggests that the rate of use of force complaints per 1,000 officers varies widely across agency types (20.7 percent for sheriff's departments, 33.8 percent for county agencies, 47.5

percent for municipal agencies, and 15.7 percent for state agencies), as well as across agency sizes within the same type. Pate and Hamilton's study (1991, 144) of the largest six police departments reports that the rate of complaints per 100 sworn officers ranged from 5.5 in Philadelphia, 10.5 in Los Angeles, 13.8 in Detroit, and 19.5 in New York, to 27.1 in Chicago and 36.9 in Houston.

Matters are even more complex in the context of complaint resolution; typically, police agencies sustain between 0 and 25 percent of all complaints (Pate and Fridell 1993, 42; Dugan and Breda 1991; Perez 1994), with 10 percent being typical (e.g., Pate and Fridell, 1993; Wagner 1980). However, the key issue is that the rate of complaints and the rate with which complaints are sustained are influenced by so many factors other than the actual rate of misconduct that these rates likely can tell more about the agency's openness to complaints, the ease with which citizens could file complaints, and the level of legitimacy of the police, than about the actual level of misconduct (see, e.g., Adams 1999; Walker 2001). Pate and Hamilton (1991, 142) conclude in their seminal research that "methods of filing and investigating complaints vary notably across departments. As a result, data concerning the disposition of complaints are not comparable."

The idea of the police policing themselves seems appealing in theory. The reality, however, is that these systems have failed, resulting in some cases with most severe violations of official rules going unprocessed. Findings by a few research studies (e.g., Sherman 1978) and reports by independent commissions, the best source of information on the topic, provide numerous examples of such failures (e.g., Knapp Commission 1972; Pennsylvania Crime Commission 1974; Christopher Commission 1991; Mollen Commission 1994). They can affect, and may be noticed in, many aspects of the system, from not establishing written guidelines and providing resources and manpower to the internal affairs units, to failing to investigate complaints, ignoring information, and openly hiding complaints (see, e.g., Knapp Commission 1972; Pennsylvania Crime Commission 1974; Christopher Commission 1991; Mollen Commission 1994;). The Mollen Commission (1994, 78) finds that the message from the top administrators not only failed to encourage reporting and investigation of corruption but actually condemned discovery of corruption and evaluated it as a "management failure."

The most recent addition to the arsenal of internal system of control or the internal accountability system, regarded as the "best practice" by the Department of Justice "Principles for Promoting Police Integrity," is the early warning systems. Although the US Commission on Civil Rights (1981) recommended the implementation of early warning systems in the 1980s, the idea did not gain popularity until the 1990s, with a few exceptions (e.g., Miami-Dade Police Department). The underlying philosophy of early warning systems complements and advances the earlier findings that, typically, a small group of police officers within the agency—as identified in the NYPD by the Mollen Commission (1994) and in the LAPD by the Christopher Commission (1991)—is responsible for a disproportionately large percentage of complaints. Before the early warning systems, typically nothing was done with such problem police officers (Walker 2001, 110). These systems, exclusively proactive in nature, operate under the assumption that, if potential problems are spotted and addressed early, they would not become serious problems later. Although the extent and nature of the information input in the early warning system varies, it typically includes use of force reports, accident reports, complaints, financial records, and other information sometimes routinely collected by the police agency (see, e.g., Walker, Alpert, and Kenney 2000; Walker and Katz 2008). Once red flags are raised, the process proceeds into intervention (typically informal counseling by the supervisor or retraining) and post-intervention (monitoring for a certain period of time; Walker, Alpert, and Kenney 2000). A 1998 nationwide survey of municipal police agencies reveals that about one-third of them either have already implemented or are developing their early warning systems (Walker, Alpert, and Kenney 2000). Additional systems are being developed as a consequence of the decrees between the Department of Justice and several police agencies (Walker and Katz, 2008, 489). Presently, the research evaluating the effectiveness of early warning systems is limited (e.g., Vera Institute of Justice 1999; Walker, Alpert, and Kenney 2000). The findings largely suggest that these early warning systems seem to be effective with respect to the reduction in the number of use of force reports and citizen complaints by the officers subject to early warning systems.

B. External Mechanisms of Control and Accountability

Aside from the police agency itself, various institutions and organizations play important roles in control of police misconduct and enhancement of police accountability. Their effects may potentially be limited to mostly the case at hand (e.g., prosecutions and convictions of police officers who used excessive force) or they may be far reaching (e.g., the US Supreme Court precedents), affecting policies and the practice of policing for decades.

1. *The Supreme Court*

The Supreme Court decided a number of cases relevant for policing in the 1960s, using the Fourteenth Amendment to expand the application of many federally established standards to the state and local police.

One of the key cases is *Mapp v. Ohio* (367 U.S. 643 [1961]), in which the Supreme Court decided that the evidence against Dolree Mapp was obtained illegally and concluded that illegally obtained evidence is inadmissible in a state court. Through the application of the Fourteenth Amendment, the Supreme Court extended the application of the exclusionary rule—which already existed at the federal level—to the state and local police agencies. Studies (e.g., Controller General of the United States 1979; Krantz et al. 1979) report that the exclusionary rule applies directly to a very small percentage of cases; the motion to suppress evidence (i.e., the exercise of the exclusionary rule) is filed in a relatively small percentage of cases (below 15 percent), and when the motion is filed, it is granted infrequently (about 20 percent of the motions). Thus, the overall "rate of success" of the motion to suppress evidence is under 3 percent.

Earlier studies exploring the effects of the Mapp decision on the police behavior (e.g., Skolnick 1966; Oaks 1970; Canon 1974) diverge in their assessments regarding whether the decision had a positive effect on police officer behavior during search and seizure. More recent studies (e.g., Orfield 1987; Cannon 1991) focus either on the effect of the Mapp decision or on the severity and nature of the search and seizure violations. Based on his interviews with twenty-six narcotics officers in Chicago, Orfield reports positive effects of the exclusionary rule at the institutional level among the police, prosecutors, and judges. On the individual level, Orfield reports that the detectives typically said during the interviews that they adhered to the constitutional standards of search and seizure when their conduct was motivated primarily by the potential prosecution of the offender. The exclusionary rule seems to have been less effective when other motives were dominant (confiscation of contraband, Ofield 1987; disruption of illicit networks or assertion of police powers, LaFave 1965; LaFave and Remington 1965).

The second critical Supreme Court decision is *Miranda v. Arizona* (372 U.S. 436 [1966]). The Miranda warnings have become part of the American popular culture (see, e.g., *Dickerson v. United States,* 530 U.S. 428 [2000]). In a nutshell, the Supreme Court held in Miranda that a confession obtained during custodial police interrogation constitutes a violation of the Fifth Amendment right against self-incrimination, unless the police provide specific warnings to the persons that they have the right to remain silent, that anything they say could be used against them, and that they have the right to counsel.

The early empirical studies, conducted immediately after the decision, were concerned with the effect these new Miranda warnings would have on the police ability to investigate crimes. They find that the Miranda warnings had only minimal effects (see, e.g., Black and Reiss 1967; Wald et al. 1967; Schaefer 1971). In fact, Black and Reiss (1967) find that there is plenty of other evidence available in the felony cases that the police could use instead of relying on the confession. Later studies suggest that the effect of the warning, measured as the reduction in confessions, resulted in a 4–16 percent decrease in the number of confessions, depending on the study (see, e.g., Wald et al. 1967; Stephens et al. 1972; Witt 1973; Neubauer 1974). Evidence further suggests that, even when the Miranda warnings were issued, they did not have a lot of weight on the outcome of the case because in most cases suspects—84 percent of suspects in Cassell and Hayman's study (1998) and 78 percent in Leo's study (1998)—voluntarily waived their Miranda rights.

The early study by Black and Reiss (1967), already in progress when the Miranda decision was made, suggests that police officers rarely gave the Miranda warnings.

Later studies (Leiken 1971; Baum 1979; Leo 1998) show that the warning is issued routinely, although the style in which the warning is issued tends to be superficial. The most recent study (Leo 1998), relying on direct observation, confirms that the police issued the Miranda warnings in about 96 percent of the cases and thus shows that the Miranda decision had a long-term effect on the police behavior (Leo and Thomas 1998).

2. *Criminal Courts*

Like any other citizens, police officers can be prosecuted, tried, and convicted for a broad range of crimes (e.g., robbery, assault). Unlike other citizens, they can also be prosecuted, tried, and convicted for crimes that require that the person who committed the crime is a public employee (e.g., extortion, 18 U.S.C. 1951; criminal liability for deprivation of civil rights, 18 U.S.C. 242). Despite the potential for general deterrence these convictions could bring, the reality is that, because of the very limited number of cases, their primary focus is more on specific deterrence and retribution.

Both state and federal prosecution for the use of *excessive force* cases are rare (e.g., Adams 1995; Cheh 1995, 241; Human Rights Watch 1998) and the rate of conviction is low. Out of about eight thousand police misconduct complaints that the Department of Justice receives annually (Cheh 1995, 241), about three thousand are investigated and only fifty presented to the grand jury. Thus, researchers have concluded that, because the chances of arrest and conviction are so low, criminal convictions for the use of force are not an effective deterrent mechanism (Skolnick and Fyfe 1993; Cheh 1995).

Similarly, in the period from 1992 to 1998, there were fewer than fifty convictions each year for federal law enforcement *corruption* (Kutnjak Ivković 2005, 59). At the state level, the convictions are almost equally sparse. At the time the Knapp Commission (1972) found corruption to be widespread in the NYPD, prosecutors initiated only about thirty cases per year, and, even then, only one out of five police officers prosecuted, tried, and convicted received a prison sentence of more than a year (Knapp Commission 1972, 252). Similarly, the Pennsylvania Crime Commission (1974), which investigated the extent and nature of corruption in the Philadelphia Police Department and found widespread corruption in the agency, reports that there were on average only seven arrest per year for corruption (Pennsylvania Crime Commission 1974, 446).

3. *Civil Courts*

Citizens who want to sue police agencies for violation of their civil rights can do so by relying on the state law or on the federal law. The payments resulting from the civil lawsuits vary from an average of 1.6 million annually in Cincinnati to an average of 35.8 million annually in Los Angeles (Kappeler 2006, 10). Civil lawsuits cover only a small segment of the overall number of contacts between the police and citizens—"one-tenth of 1 percent of all encounters between police and persons suspected of committing a crime could result in civil litigation" (Novak, Smith, and Frank 2003, 355).

At the federal level, citizens could file Section 1983 lawsuits (42 U.S.C. 1983), viewed as the most powerful of lawsuits. The power of the Section 1983 lawsuits is grounded on two Supreme Court decisions. In *Monroe v. Pape* (365 U.S. 167 [1961]), the Supreme Court determined that police officers could be held liable for deprivation of the Fourth Amendment rights under the civil rights statute. In *Monell v. Department of Social Services* (436 U.S. 658 [1978]), the Supreme Court established that municipalities could be held liable for police misconduct if it was pursuant to the agency's policy or custom. As these Supreme Court decisions opened the doors for citizens to sue police officers and police agencies, the estimates are (there is no systematic nationwide data) that the number of the Section 1983 lawsuits increased dramatically since the 1960s (Cheh 1995, 250).

The effect of Section 1983 for citizens as plaintiffs is limited to compensatory and punitive damages (Cheh 1995, 255); the Supreme Court in Lyons (*City of Los Angeles v. Lyons,* 461 U.S. 95 [1983]) set up a practically unattainable threshold and thus implicitly eliminated the possibility of injunctive relief for individual citizens. Some studies suggest that police officers are bothered by the idea that they could be sued (e.g., Kappeler 1997, 6), but the reality is that police officers face no financial incentives to change their behavior as a consequence of these lawsuits. The compensatory damages (and sometimes punitive damages) resulting from the lawsuit are paid by the city government, not by individual police officers or the police agency. Police officers in some jurisdictions are protected by law from paying legal fees and damages, and city attorneys represent the officers in the lawsuits (e.g., Patton 1993). Furthermore, even when police officers had lost the lawsuits, their careers as police officers were not affected; Chevigny (1995, 102) reports that, out of 185 officers involved in civil lawsuits, only eight were disciplined and fourteen were actually promoted.

The effect of civil suits on the police agencies is no stronger. Several studies that focus on specific cities (e.g., Yale Law Journal 1979; Littlejohn 1981) report that police misconduct suits have had very limited effect on the police agencies. Neither New York nor Los Angeles implemented any resulting changes (see Chevigny 1995). One police agency, concerned with the rising costs of lawsuits (e.g., Los Angeles County Sheriff's Department), took proactive steps to address the issue of civil lawsuits. In 1993 the Office of the Special Counsel was established to investigate problems, recommend reforms, and reduce the costs of litigation (Special Counsel to the Los Angeles County Sheriff's Department 1996). The reports issued by the Special Counsel (a form of citizen review) suggest positive changes (Special Counsel to the Los Angeles County Sheriff's Department 1999, 2002).

As authorized by the 1994 Violent Crime Control Act (42 U.S.C. 14141, 1994), the Department of Justice could act as a plaintiff and sue a police department when there is "a pattern or practice of conduct by law enforcement officers . . . that deprives persons of rights, privileges, or immunities secured or protected by the Constitution." The most recent data available from the Department of Justice (January 31, 2003) indicate that the investigation of fourteen police agencies is ongoing, that out of the ten lawsuits, four ended with consent decrees and six with out-of-court settlements (Department of Justice 2010). Each consent decree or memorandum of agreement required police agencies to conduct extensive reforms that, typically, would include revising the use of force reporting system, establishing the early warning system, revising the complaint procedures, and improving training (Walker and Katz 2008, 502). To ensure that the police agencies are implementing the required changes, all consent decrees and memoranda of agreement contain a provision of a court-appointed monitor. Walker and Katz (2008, 503) report that the 2005 conference on the pattern-and-practice lawsuits suggests that this litigation could be an effective tool in enhancing police accountability, particularly in the agencies in which the standards of accountability are low. However, systematic empirical evidence on the effects of these lawsuits does not exist. The Vera Institute, serving as a monitor for the Pittsburgh Police Department, generally reports that the police are on track with the required changes (Vera Institute of Justice 2002). On the other hand, the reports concerning police agencies in Los Angeles and Washington, DC indicate that they failed to meet some of the deadlines (Walker and Katz 2008, 503).

4. *Independent Commissions*

Independent commissions typically are established in the wake of scandals. Political pressure is generated and demands are made on the political leadership to establish an independent commission to investigate the extent and nature of misconduct and recommend changes. For example, the Christopher Commission (1991) was established *after* the Rodney King video circled the globe. The Mollen Commission (1994) was established *after* the arrest of Michael Dowd and five other police officers made front-page news. Other prominent examples of independent commissions include the Wickersham Commission (National Commission on Law Observance and Enforcement 1931), the President's Crime Commission (1967), and the Kerner Commission (National Advisory Commission on Civil Disorders 1968), Knapp Commission (1972), and Pennsylvania Crime Commission (1974).

A key advantage of the independent commissions, composed of prominent community members and experts on policing, is that they set the standards that could affect the way policing is done across the country (see, e.g., National Research Council 2004; Walker and Katz 2008). On the other side of the spectrum, the work of independent commissions could be troubled by the lack of political independence (e.g., Pennsylvania Crime Commission 1974), insufficient legal authority (e.g., Knapp Commission 1972, 44), or inadequate resources (e.g., Pennsylvania Crime Commission 1974, 762).

The most serious challenge related to independent commissions is their temporary nature (e.g., Kutnjak Ivković 2005; National Research Council 2004; Walker and Katz 2008). Even when the commission engages in a thorough investigation and proposes a set of recommendations, the quality work done by the commission would be largely wasted if nobody were to implement them. Illustrative of this point is the example of the aftermath of the Christopher Commission (1991). It recommended the establishment of the Office of Inspector General who would be in charge of auditing, investigating, and overseeing the LAPD's efforts to handle complaints, and the establishment of the early intervention system. A decade after the recommendation, the LAPD still did not have the early warning system (Walker 2005, 179). The establishment of the Office of Inspector General was postponed until 1995, and Katherine Mader, the inspector general, started performing her role in mid-1996. The opposition from the police administration and the police commission made the job impossible to perform and Mader resigned in 1998, after further attempts by the chairman of the police commission to restrict her authority (Walker 2001, 39).

C. Mixed Mechanisms of Control and Accountability

Finally, the last group incorporates mechanisms of control or accountability that may have police officers participating in them but which are housed outside the police agency.

1. Citizen Reviews

The idea of an independent agency entrusted to review citizen complaints had existed since the 1960s, yet citizen reviews gained popularity only in the last two decades (e.g., Walker 1995; Walker 2005). By 2005, scholars estimated that almost all large municipal agencies have some form of citizen review (e.g., Walker 2005, 37). However, the classification of citizen reviews as a mixed mechanism of control rests on the results of a survey conducted by Walker and Kreisel (2001), according to which about 23 percent (15 out of 65) of citizen reviews have police officers as members.

The idea behind citizen reviews is to establish a review of citizen complaints independent of the police agency itself. However, the only survey of citizen reviews (Class I citizen review; Walker 2001) suggests that citizens conduct the initial fact-finding completely independently from the police in only 34 percent of the reviews; they provide input in police processes in an additional 46 percent of the reviews (Class II citizen input; Walker 2001; Walker and Kreisel 2001). Class III citizen reviews ("citizen monitors") serve as appellate reviews once the investigation by the police agency is completed. Unless entrusted to do policy reviews as well, the focus of these three classes of citizen reviews is on individual cases; they try to ensure that justice is done in these cases and probably enhance the confidence in the complaint process (but not necessarily in the police!). Even when entrusted with the policy review, the scope of their investigation is limited to the issues raised in the complaints and is unlikely to explore some of the critical issues (e.g., failure to hold supervisors accountable).

The number of studies exploring the effect of these citizen reviews is very limited. One of the problems is associated with the accurate assessment of the citizen review effectiveness is that of finding matching cases investigated by the citizen reviews and internal affairs units; Hudson's comparative study (1972) uncovers that the citizen review ("Police Advisory Board") sustained a *lower* percentage of complaints than the internal affairs unit did, which may be explained by different nature of the cases handled by each unit. Kerstetter and Rasinski (1994) report that the level of public confidence in the complaint process increases after the establishment of a citizen review. On the other hand, Sviridoff and McElroy (1989) report that *both* citizens and the police officers evaluated the New York City Civilian Review Board to be biased against them.

Class IV citizen reviews ("citizen auditors") "do not investigate individual complaints, but are authorized to review, monitor, or audit the police department's complaint process" (Walker 2001, 62). Auditors constitute a small percentage of the overall number of citizen reviews (3 percent in the 1990s survey, Walker and Kreisel 2001; a total of twelve reviews as of 2005, Walker 2005, 136). These citizen reviews have the greatest potential to provide feedback relevant for the improvement of the overall complaint system and the operation of the police agency. The San Jose Independent Police Auditor, an example of a successful citizen auditor, used the information contained in the complaints to expand the inquiry into other elements of the system. The auditor, established in 1993, made over ninety policy recommendations by 2005, only seven of which were not accepted by the San Jose Police Department (Walker 2005, 156). Walker describes another successful auditor (Special Counsel to the Los Angeles County Sheriff's Department), but also lists examples of unsuccessful auditors (e.g., Seattle Police Auditor, Albuquerque Independent Counsel; Walker 2005, 165–66). Indeed, whereas this form of citizen review has the greatest potential of having a long-lasting and continuous effect on the police agency, "the police auditor concept does not automatically translate into success" (Walker 2005, 167). Indeed, citizen auditors may suffer from the failures in vision and direction, lack of cooperation, and political opposition. Systematic research into the effect of this and other types of citizen reviews is limited at best (see, e.g., Walker 2005).

2. *Accreditation*

The Commission on Accreditation for Law Enforcement Agencies (CALEA), established in 1979, is the primary source of self-regulation by the police profession. Since 1983 CALEA has been publishing standards, partly required and partly only recommended for the police agencies that seek accreditation. As of September 2009, CALEA has 463 standards (CALEA 2010). An agency that plans to become accredited typically has to undergo extensive organizational changes to comply with the CALEA standards. Walker and Katz (2008, 492) estimate that more than five hundred police agencies have been accredited at the time of publication of their book.

CALEA lists benefits to accreditation, which, among others, include enhanced internal accountability and reduced risk of civil lawsuits (CALEA 2010). Walker and Katz (2008, 493) provide examples of how accreditation reduced insurance costs, improved the use of force reporting, and improved procedures for juveniles in several agencies. Participation in the CALEA accreditation program is voluntary, however. Agencies characterized by widespread misconduct, those in the greatest need of control, are the least likely to go through the lengths to get accredited. Furthermore, while CALEA standards try to capture relevant innovations, a number of them are not required. In fact, they provide only the minimum standards and do not even try to assess the optimal or ideal standards (Walker and Katz 2008, 494).

IV. Challenges and Future Directions

More than four decades ago, the President's Commission on Law Enforcement and the Administration of Justice (1967a, 144) emphasized the importance of strong public support for the police as a necessary prerequisite for effective policing:

> Poor police-community relations adversely affect the ability of the police to prevent crime and apprehend criminals. People hostile to the police are not so likely to report violations of the law, even when they are the victims. They are even less likely to report suspicious persons or incidents, to testify as witnesses voluntarily, or to come forward and provide information. . . . Yet, citizen assistance is crucial to law enforcement agencies if the police are to solve an appreciable portion of the crimes that are committed.

Since Sir Robert Peel's times, legitimacy of the police has been an important requirement for successful democratic policing. Empirical assessments of the public support for the police show that public support varies over time (e.g., Tuch and Weitzer 1997) and is affected—both short- and long-term—by publicized critical incidents of police misconduct and personal experience with the authorities. Incidents like the Rodney King beating have an effect on how the public perceives the police and how the police subsequently behave. Research regarding the effects of these critical incidents on the legitimacy of the police is quite limited; the extant studies indicate that such incidents may exert differential influence on the views held by various racial/ethnic groups. Future research could carry out in-depth explorations of the effects of such critical incidents, the reasons why some groups tend to experience deeper decreases in confidence in the police as a consequence of these incidents, and why the recovery process varies across all groups. Furthermore, it is not clear how publicized incidents, personal experience, and race interact in shaping views about police legitimacy.

Although research has identified that the perceived procedural fairness is important and that unfair treatment by the police directly leads toward reduced legitimacy and less obedience, empirical research has only begun to explore the importance of procedural justice compared to distributive justice in police-citizen encounters. We also do not know whether all of the elements of procedural justice (participation, neutrality, trustworthiness, and treatment with dignity and respect) have to be activated and, if so, whether some of them carry more weight than others. Tyler and Huo (2002) seem to indicate that this may be the case. However, Leventhal's work (1976) and Tyler's work (1990; 2000) suggest that more than only four elements could be at play, but research on how they—individually or in some logical clusters—affect perceptions of police-citizen encounters is yet to be done.

Prior research did not provide in-depth assessment of how the perceptions of police legitimacy and the elements of procedural justice are associated with, and shaped by, different types of contacts with the police (e.g., voluntary, involuntary; Decker 1981). Do people who distrust the police evaluate all contacts equally, regardless of whether they or the police have initiated the contact? How low would the level of legitimacy have to be so that a pleasant and fair encounter with the police does not count and, if it does count, to what extent could it improve general views of legitimacy? How many unpleasant encounters with the police (and of what nature) can a citizen who supports the police have before his level of confidence in the police decreases? Are the pathways of assessment different for a victim who reported a crime to the police from those a person caught speeding faces when a police officer stops him? To what degree are those assessments affected by the characteristics of individual officers and police agencies, as opposed to the characteristics of citizens, neighborhoods, and cities in which they live? Tyler (2000, 123) argues that cultural backgrounds may affect the factors that individuals use to define fairness. To what degree do these diverse cultural backgrounds exert influence on the general assessments of police legitimacy and assessments of each individual encounter with the police? Current research also seems to indicate that what matters is not only personal experience but also vicarious experience (i.e., experience of other family members and friends). To what degree does personal experience—both positive and negative—carry more weight on the assessments of legitimacy than a vicarious experience?

Although the American society has made substantial strides toward equality of white and minority citizens since *Brown v. Board of Education*, the relationship between the police and the minority communities is far from ideal; research studies show that minorities are more likely to perceive the contact with the police as unfair than whites are, and are more likely, at least occasionally, to receive unfair treatment from the police, from more frequent stops and searches to more frequent tickets and arrests. Current research tends to indicate that, when they perceive that the police had mistreated them, people are more likely to disobey police commands in their subsequent encounters and evaluate further contacts primarily in terms of their procedural fairness. Research further shows that police officers are more likely to use force toward disrespectful and disobedient citizens, which in turn increases the risk of injury to both citizens and police officers and, at the same time, undermines citizens' views of police legitimacy. However, the extant research addressing a number of these issues is primarily focused on a small number of jurisdictions surveyed at a particular point in time. How race and ethnicity affect police-citizen interaction nationwide and how the nature and quality of this relationship could be enhanced (e.g., the role that community policing could play in enhancing legitimacy of the police) is far from clear; these pivotal issues crave further research.

It is equally crucial to get a firmer grasp on the actual extent of police misconduct. If citizens perceive that the police are treating them unfairly, do their perceptions match reality? Empirical research into the prevalence and nature of police misconduct did not reach the point at which reliable and systematic nationwide statistics on police corruption, use of excessive force, racial profiling, or other forms of police violation of constitutional, legal, and administrative rules are available. We have bits and pieces of information, obtained using various research methods, typically focusing on one police agency, but, in all honesty, we do not know what the prevalence and nature of police misconduct is. Problems associated with successful measurement are numerous and quite heterogeneous (see, e.g., Kutnjak Ivković 2005), ranging from building a common definition, designing research methodology, and obtaining funding, to convincing citizens and police officers alike to share their experiences as victims and witnesses with researchers and authorities. The Bureau of Justice Statistics police-citizen survey (Bureau of Justice Statistics 2007*a*), for example, is a promising step in the right direction.

At the outset, lack of reliable and systematic nationwide data on police misconduct implies problems with the mechanisms of control and accountability. Indeed, if we are struggling to measure the prevalence of the problem, we will not be able to assess the success in controlling misconduct and enhancing accountability. Faced with the reality of limited resources, how far do we want to go to push for control and accountability? What is the right balance in which we are able to control misconduct, but are not constraining discretion and creating unnecessary hurdles that undermine the efficiency of the fulfillment of the police role (see, e.g., Anechiarico and Jacobs 1996)?

Although the system of control and accountability incorporates many agencies and institutions (see, e.g., Kutnjak Ivković 2005), the reality is that most of these agencies and institutions do not operate proactively but reactively. The reports provided by independent commissions (e.g., Knapp Commission 1972; Christopher Commission 1991; Mollen Commission 1994) are the best illustrations of how low these mechanisms could sink in and around the agencies in the greatest need of successful control and accountability. With a few exceptions (e.g., Sherman 1974; Walker 2001; Klockars, Kutnjak Ivković, and Haberfeld 2006), research on the effect of these mechanisms of control and accountability is mostly limited to a single police agency and, thus, there cannot be any variation in a number of potentially crucial issues (e.g., level of police misconduct, administrative rules, internal system, larger social and political environment). Nevertheless, several promising mechanisms of control and accountability have surfaced, typically those that can have long-lasting, continuous, and proactive effect on police behavior—administrative rules, pattern-and-practice lawsuits, early warning systems, CompStat, and police auditors. Systematic and thorough evaluations of these mechanisms either do not exist or are just starting (e.g., Walker, Alpert, and Kenney 2000; Walker 2001). Further research could try to develop measures of success, design criteria to recognize successful mechanisms, explore how effective they are both short- and long-term, detect the obstacles they face, and identify conditions that could make them more successful. Indeed, although this topic has been studied for some time, a plethora of new, exciting, and undiscovered material awaits to be explored.

NOTES

1. The only exception is the study by Frank et al. 1996.
2. Some studies report that the race effect disappears or weakens substantially once various neighborhood characteristics, such as fear of crime, perceptions of disorder, and informal collective security, are taken into consideration (see, e.g., Cao et al. 1996; Sampson and Bartsuch 1998; Reisig and Parks 2002).

REFERENCES

Adams, Keith. 1995. "Measuring the Prevalence of Police Abuse of Force." In *And Justice for All*, ed. William A. Geller and Hans Toch. Washington, DC: Police Executive Research Forum.

——. 1999. "What We Know about Police Use of Force." In *Use of Force by Police: Overview of National and Local Data*. Washington, DC: Office of Justice Programs.

Albrecht, Stan L., and Miles Green. 1977. "Attitudes toward the Police and the Larger Attitude Complex." *Criminology* 15: 67–86.

Alpert, Geoffrey P. 1989. "Police Use of Deadly Force: The Miami Experience." In *Critical Issues in Policing: Contemporary Readings*, ed. Robert Dunham and Geoffrey P. Alpert. Prospect Heights, IL: Waveland Press.

——. 1997. *Pursuit Policies and Training*. Washington, DC: Government Printing Office.

Anechiarico, Frank, and James B. Jacobs. 1996. *The Pursuit of Absolute Integrity*. Chicago: University of Chicago Press.

Balch, Robert W. 1972. "Police Personality: Fact or Fiction?" *Journal of Criminal Law, Criminology and Police Science* 63: 106–19.

Barker, Thomas, and David L. Carter. 1986. "A Typology of Police Deviance." In *Police Deviance*, ed. Thomas Barker and David L. Carter. 3rd ed. Cincinnati, OH: Anderson Publishing.

Barker, Thomas, and Julian Roebuck. 1973. *An Empirical Typology of Police Corruption*. Springfield, IL: Charles C. Thomas Publisher.

Baueris, Vic. 1977. New York Police Department: Preventing Crime and Corruption. http://www.icac.nsw.gov.au/frame_pub.htm.

Baum, Lawrence. 1979. "Impact of Court Decisions on Police Practices." In *Determinants of Law Enforcement Policies*, ed. Fred A. Meyer and Ralph Baker. Lanham, MD: Lexington Books.

Benson, Paul R. 1981. "Political Alienation and Public Satisfaction with Police Services." *Pacific Sociological Review* 24: 45–64.

Bittner, Egon. 1970. Functions of the Police in Modern Society. Washington, DC: National Institute of Mental Health, *Center for Studies of Crime and Delinquency*.

Black, Donald. 1976. *The Behavior of Law*. New York: Academic Press.

Black, Donald, and Albert J. Reiss. 1967. "Patterns of Behavior in Citizen and Police Transactions." In *Studies of Crime and Law Enforcement in Major Metropolitan Areas, Field Surveys III*. Vol. 2, *President's Commission on Law Enforcement and the Administration of Justice*. Washington, DC: US Government Printing Office.

Blumstein, A., J. Cohen, and D. Nagin. 1978. *Deterrence and Incapacitation: Estimating the Effects of Criminal Sanctions on Crime Rates*. Washington, DC National Academy of Sciences.

Bureau of Justice Statistics. 2001. *Contacts between Police and the Public: Findings from the 1999 National Survey*. Washington, DC: US Department of Justice. http://bjs.ojp.usdoj.gov/content/pub/pdf/cpp99.pdf.

——. 2006. *Characteristics of Drives Stopped by Police, 2002*. Bureau of Justice Statistics, Special Report. http://bjs.ojp.usdoj.gov/content/pub/pdf/cdsp02.pdf.

——. 2007a. *Contacts between Police and the Public, 2005*. Washington, DC: US Department of Justice. http://bjs.ojp.usdoj.gov/content/pub/pdf/cpp05.pdf.

——. 2007b. *Census of State and Local Law Enforcement Agencies, 2004*. Washington, DC: US Department of Justice. http://bjs.ojp.usdoj.gov/content/pub/pdf/csllea04.pdf.

Burns, Pamela, and Dale K. Sechrest. 1992. "Police Corruption: The Miami Case." *Criminal Justice and Behavior* 19(3): 294–313.

[CALEA] Commission on Accreditation of Law Enforcement Agencies. 2010. *Law Enforcement Accreditation*. http://www.calea.org/Online/CALEAPrograms/LawEnforcement/lawenfbenefits.htm.

Canon, Bradley C. 1974. "Is the Exclusionary Rule in Failing Health? Some New Data and a Plea against a Precipitous Conclusion." *Kentucky Law Journal* 62: 681–730.

———. 1991. "Courts and Policy: Compliance, Implementation, and Impact." In *American Courts: A Critical Assessment*, ed. John B. Gates and Charles A. Johnson. Washington, DC: Congressional Quarterly Press.

Cao, Liqun, James Frank, and Francis T. Cullen. 1996. "Race, Community Context and Confidence in the Police." *American Journal of Police* 15: 3–22.

Carter, David L. 1985. "Hispanic Perception of Police Performance: An Empirical Assessment." *Journal of Criminal Justice* 13: 487–500.

Cassell, Paul G., and Brett S. Hayman. 1998. "Police Interrogation in the 1990s: An Empirical Study of the Effects of Miranda." In *The Miranda Debate: Law, Justice, and Policing*, ed. Richard A. Leo and George C. Thomas III. Boston, MA: Northeastern University Press.

Cheh, Mary M. 1995. "Are Law Suits an Answer to Police Brutality?" In *And Justice for All*, ed. William A. Geller and Hans Toch. Washington, DC: Police Executive Research Forum.

Chen, Janet B. L., with Chris Devery and Sally Doran. 2003. *Fair Cop: Learning the Art of Policing.* Toronto: University of Toronto Press.

Chevigny, Paul. 1995. *Edge of the Knife: Police Violence in the Americas.* New York: New Press.

[Christopher Commission]. Independent Commission on the Los Angeles Police Department. 1991. *Report of the Independent Commission on the Los Angeles Police Department.* Los Angeles: Independent Commission on the Los Angeles Police Department.

Cohen, Bernard. 1972. "The Police Internal System of Justice in New York City." *Journal of Criminal Law, Criminology, and Police Science* 63(1):54–67.

Controller General of the United States. 1979. *Impact of the Exclusionary Rule on Federal Criminal Prosecutions.* Report #GGD-79-45.

Correia, Mark E., Michael D. Reisig, and Nicolas P. Lovrich. 1996. "Public Perceptions of State Police: An Analysis of Individual-level and Contextual Variables." *Journal of Criminal Justice* 24: 17–28.

Davis, Kenneth Culp. 1969. *Discretionary Justice: A Preliminary Inquiry*, Baton Rouge, LA: Louisiana State University Press.

Dean, Debby. 1980. "Citizen Ratings of the Police: The Difference Contact Makes." *Law and Policy Quarterly* 2: 445–71.

Decker, Scott H. 1981. "Citizen Attitudes toward the Police: A Review of Past Findings and Suggestions for Future Policy." *Journal of Police Science and Administration* 9: 80–87.

Department of Justice. 2010. *FAQ.* http://www.justice.gov/crt/split/faq.php#primsource.

Desmedt, James, F., and John C. Marsh. 1990. "The Use of Force Paradigm for Law Enforcement and Corrections." Bureau of Justice Statistics. http://www.cops.usdoj.gov/files/ric/Publications/hampton.txt.

Dugan, John R., and Daniel R. Breda. 1991. "Complaints about Police Officers: A Comparison among Types and Agencies." *Journal of Criminal Justice* 19(2): 165–72.

Engel, Robin S., J. Sobol, and Robert E. Wordon. 2000. "Further Exploration of the Demeanor Hypothesis: The Interaction Effects of Suspects' Characteristics and Demeanor on Police Behavior." *Justice Quarterly* 17: 235–58.

Erez, Edna. 1984. "Self-defined 'Desert' and Citizens' Assessment of the Police." *Journal of Criminal Law and Criminology* 75: 1276–99.

Fishman, Janet E. 1978. *Measuring Police Corruption.* New York: John Jay College of Criminal Justice.

Flanagan, Timothy, and Michael Vaughn. 1996. "Public Opinion about Police Abuse and Force." In *Police Violence*, ed. William Geller and Hans Toch. New Haven, CT: Yale University Press.

Frank, James, Steven G. Brandl, Francis T. Cullen, and Amy Stichman. 1996. "Reassessing the Impact of Race on Citizens' Attitudes toward the Police: A Research Note." *Justice Quarterly* 13: 321–34.

Fridell, Lorie, Robert Lunney, Drew Diamond, and Bruce Kubu. 2001. *Racially Based Policing: A Principled Response.* Washington, DC: Police Executive Research Forum.

Friedrich, Robert J. 1977. "The Impact of Organizational, Individual, and Situational Factors on Police Behavior." Unpublished PhD Dissertation. University of Michigan.

———. 1980. "Police Use of Force: Individuals, Situations, and Organizations." *Annals of the American Academy of Political and Social Science* 452: 82–97.

Fyfe, James J. 1979. "Administrative Interventions on Police Shooting Discretion: An Empirical Examination." *Journal of Criminal Justice* 7: 303–23.

———. 1982. "Blind Justice: Police Shootings in Memphis." *Journal of Criminal Law and Criminology* 73: 707–22.

———. 2002. *Too Many Missing Cases: Holes in Our Knowledge about Police Use of Force.* Washington, DC: US Department of Justice.

Gallup International. 1996. *Gallup International 50th Anniversary Survey.* Unpublished manuscript. On file with the author.

Gallup Poll. 2010. "Confidence in Institutions." http://www.gallup.com/poll/1597/confidence-institutions.aspx?version=print.

Garner, Joel H., John Buchanan, Tom Schade, and John Hepburn. 1996. *Understanding the Use of Force By and Against the Police.* Washington, DC: National Institute of Justice.

Garner, Joel H., and Christopher D. Maxwell, 1999. "Measuring the Amount of Force Used By and Against the Police in Six Jurisdictions." In *Use of Force by Police: Overview of National and Local Data.* Washington, DC: National Institute of Justice.

Garner, Joel H., Christopher D. Maxwell, and Cedric G. Heraux. 2002. "Characteristics Associated with the Prevalence and Severity of Force Used by the Police." *Justice Quarterly* 19: 705–46.

Garner, Joel H., Thomas Schade, John Hepburn, and John Buchanan. 1995. "Measuring the Continuum of Force Used By and Against the Police." *Criminal Justice Review* 20: 146–698.

General Accounting Office. 1998. *Law Enforcement: Information on Drug-Related Police Corruption.* Washington, DC: General Accounting Office.

Goldstein, Herman. 1975. *Police Corruption: A Perspective on Its Nature and Control.* Washington, DC: The Police Foundation.

Garofalo, James. 1977. *Public Opinion about Crime: The Attitudes of Victims and Nonvictims in Selected Cities.* Washington, DC: US Government Printing Office.

Geller, William A., and Michael S. Scott. 1992. *Deadly Force: What We Know: A Practitioner's Desk Reference on Police-Involved Shootings.* Washington, DC: Police Executive Research Forum.

Giuliani, Rudolph W., and William J. Bratton. 1995. Police Strategy No. 7: Rooting Out Corruption. *Building Organizational Integrity in the New York Police Department.* New York: New York Police Department.

Guerrero-Daley, Teresa. 2000. *2000 Year-End Report*. San Jose, CA: Office of the Independent Police Auditor. http://www.sanjoseca.gov/ipa/2000%20YER.html.

Hadar, Ilana, and John R. Snortum. 1975. "The Eye of the Beholder: Differential Perceptions of Police by the Police and the Public." *Criminal Justice and Behavior* 2: 37–54.

Harris, David A. 1997. "'Driving While Black' and All Other Traffic Offenses: The Supreme Court and Pretextual Traffic Stops." *Journal of Criminal Law and Criminology* 87:544–82.

Heinz, Anne M., and Wayne A. Kerstetter. 1979. "Pretrial Settlement Conference: Evaluation of a Reform in Plea Bargaining." *Law and Society Review* 13: 349–66.

Homant, Robert J., Daniel B. Kennedy, and Roger M. Fleming. 1984. "The Effect of Victimization and the Police Response on Citizens' Attitudes toward Police." *Journal of Police Science and Administration* 12: 323–32.

Houlden, P. 1980. "The Impact of Procedural Modifications on Evaluations of Plea Bargaining." *Law and Society Review* 15: 267–92.

Huang, W. S. Wilson, and Michael S. Vaughn. 1996. "Support and Confidence: Public Attitudes toward the Police." In *American View Crime and Justice: National Public Opinion Survey*, ed. Timony J. Flanagan and Dennis R. Longmire. Thousand Oaks, CA: Sage Publications.

Hudson, James R. 1972. "Organizational Aspects of Internal and External Review of the Police." *Journal of Criminal Law, Criminology and Police Science* 63: 427–33.

Human Rights Watch. 1998. *Shielded from Justice: Police Brutality and Accountability in the United States*. New York: Human Rights Watch.

Jacob, Herbert. 1971. "Black and White Perceptions of Justice in the City." *Law and Society Review* 6:69–89.

Jacobs, David, and David Britt. 1979. "Inequality and Police Use of Deadly Force: An Empirical Assessment of a Conflict Hypothesis. *Social Problems* 26: 404–12.

Jesilow, Paul, J'ona Meyer, and Nazi Namazzi. 1995. "Public Attitudes toward the Police." *American Journal of Police* 14: 67–88.

Kaminski, Robert J., and Eric S. Jefferis. 1998. "The Effect of a Violent Televised Arrest on Public Perceptions of the Police: A Partial Test of Easton's Theoretical Framework." *Policing: An International Journal of Police Strategies and Management* 21(4): 683–706.

Kappeler, Victor E. 1997. *Critical Issues in Police Civil Liability*. 2nd edition. Prospect Heights, IL: Waveland Press.

———. 2006. *Police Civil Liability. 2nd edition*. Long Grove, IL: Waveland Press.

Kerstetter, Wayne A., and Kenneth A. Rasinski. 1994. "Opening a Window into Police Internal Affairs: Impact of Procedural Justice Reform on Thirt-Party Attitudes." *Social Justice Research* 7(2): 107–27.

Kitzman, Katharine M., and Robert E. Emery. 1993. "Procedural Justice and Parents' Satisfaction in a Field Study of Child Custody Dispute Resolution." *Law and Human Behavior* 17: 553–67.

Klinger, David A. 1995. "Policing Spousal Assault." *Journal of Research on Crime and Delinquency* 32: 308–24.

Klitgaard, Robert. 1988. *Controlling Corruption*. Berkeley, CA: University of California Press.

Klockars, Carl B. 1985. *The Idea of Police*. Newbury Park, CA: Sage.

———. 1995. "A Theory of Excessive Force and Its Control." In *And Justice for All: Understanding and Controlling Police Abuse of Force*, edited William A. Geller and Hans Toch. Washington, DC: Police Executive Research Forum.

———. 1999. "Some Really Cheap Ways of Measuring What Really Matters." In *Measuring What Matters: Proceedings from the Policing Institute Research Meetings*, ed. Robert H. Langworthy. Washington, DC: National Institute of Justice.

———. 2003. "The Virtues of Integrity." In *Police Corruption: Paradigms, Models and Concepts—Challenges for Developing Countries*, ed. Stanley Einstein and Menachem Amir. Huntsville, TX: Office of International Criminal Justice.

Klockars, Carl B., and Sanja Kutnjak Ivković. 2003. "Measuring Police Integrity." In *Police Integrity and Ethics*. ed. Matthew J. Hickman, Alex R. Piquero, and Jack R. Greene. Belmont, CA: Wadsworth Publishing.

Klockars, Carl B., Sanja Kutnjak Ivković, and Maria R. Haberfeld. 2006. *Enhancing Police Integrity.* Dordrecht, The Netherlands: Springer.

Klockars, Carl B., Sanja Kutnjak Ivković., William E. Harver, and Maria R. Haberfeld. 2000. *The Measurement of Police Integrity*. Research in Brief. US Department of Justice, Office of Justice Programs, National Institute of Justice: Washington, DC: Government Printing Office.

[Knapp Commission]. Commission to Investigate Allegations of Police Corruption and the City's Anti-Corruption Procedures. 1972. *Report on Police Corruption*. New York: G. Braziller.

Krantz, Sheldon, B. Gilman, C. G. Benda, C. R. Hallstrom, and E. J. Nadworny. 1979. *Police Policymaking*. Lexington, MA: Lexington Books.

Kutnjak Ivković, Sanja. 2003. "To Serve and Collect: Measuring Police Corruption." *Journal of Criminal Law and Criminology* 93(2–3): 593–649.

———. 2005. *Fallen Blue Knights: Controlling Police Corruption*. New York: Oxford University Press.

———. 2008. "A Comparative Study of Public Support for the Police." *International Criminal Justice Review*, 18(4): 406–34.

LaFave, Wayne. 1965. *Arrest-The Decision to Take a Suspect into Custody*. Boston: Little, Brown and Co.

LaFave, Wayne, and Frank J. Remington. 1965. "Controlling the Police: The Judge's Role in Making and Reviewing Law Enforcement Decisions." *Michigan Law Review* 63: 987–1005.

Leiken, Lawrence S. 1971. "Police Interrogation in Colorado: The Implementation of Miranda." *Denver Law Journal* 47: 1–53.

Leventhal, Gerald S. 1976. "Fairness in Social Relationships." In *Contemporary Topics in Social Psychology*, ed. John W. Thibaut, Janet T. Spense, Robert C. Carson, and Jack Williams Brehm. Morristown, NJ: General Learning Press.

———. 1980. "What Should be Done with Equity Theory." In *Social Exchange: Advances in Theory and Research*, ed. Kenneth J. Gergen, Martin S. Greenberg, and Richard Hartley Weiss. New York: Plenum.

Leo, Richard A. 1998. "The Impact of Miranda Revisited." In *The Miranda Debate: Law, Justice, and Policing*, ed. Richard A. Leo and George C. Thomas. Boston: Northeastern University Press.

Leo, Richard A., and George C. Thomas. 1998. *The Miranda Debate: Law, Justice, and Policing*. Boston: Northeastern University Press.

Lind, E. Allan, and Tom R. Tyler. 1988. *The Social Psychology of Procedural Justice*. New York: Plenum.

Liska, Allen E., Mitchell B. Chamlin, and Mark D. Reed. 1985. "Testing the Economic Production and Conflict Models of Crime Control." *Social Forces* 64: 119–38.

Littlejohn, Edward J. 1981. "Civil Liability and the Police Officer: The Need for New Deterrents of Police Misconduct." *University of Detroit Journal of Urban Law* 58: 365–431.

Los Angeles Police Department. 2000. Board of Inquiry into the Rampart Area Corruption Incident: Executive Summary. http://www.lapdonline.org.

MacCoun, Robert J. 1993. "Drugs and the Law: A Psychological Analysis of Drug Prohibition." *Psychological Bulletin* 113: 497–512.

MacCoun, Robert J., Lind Edgar, Deborah R. Hensler, David L. Bryant, and Patricia A. Ebener. 1988. *Alternative Adjudication: An Evaluation of the New Jersey Automobile Arbitration Program.* Santa Monica, CA: Rand.

Malouff, John M., and Nicole S. Schutte. 1986. "Using Biographical Information to Hire the Best New Police Officers: Research Findings." *Journal of Police Science and Administration* 14(3): 175–77.

Mastrofski, Stephen D. 1988. "Varieties of Police Governance in Metropolitan America." *Politics and Policy* 8: 12–31.

Mastrofski, Stephen D., Robert Wordon, and Jeffrey B. Snipes. 1995. "Law Enforcement in a Time of Community Policing." *Criminology* 33: 539–63.

Mastrofski, Stephen D., Jeffrey B. Snipes, and Anne E. Supina. 1996. "Compliance on Demand: The Public's Response to Specific Police Requests." *Journal of Research in Crime and Delinquency* 33: 269–305.

McDonald, Phyllis Parshall, Sheldon Greenberg, and William J. Bratton. 2001. *Managing Police Operations: Implementing the NYPD Crime Control Model Using COMPSTAT.* Belmont, CA: Wadsworth Publishing Co.

McLaughlin, Vance. 1992. *Police and the Use of Force: The Savannah Study.* Westport, CT: Praeger.

McMahon, Joyce, Joel Garner, Captain Ronald Davis, and Amanda Kraus. 2003. *How to Correctly Collect and Analyze Racial Profiling Data: Your Reputation Depends on It!* Washington, DC: US Department of Justice. http://ncjrs.org.

McNamara, John H. 1967. "Uncertainties in Police Work: The Relevance of Police Recruits' Background and Training." In *The Police: Six Sociological Essays*, ed. David J. Bordua. New York: Wiley.

Milton, Catherine H., Jenne Wahl Halleck, James Lerner, and Gary L. Abrecht. 1977. *Police Use of Deadly Force.* Washington, DC: Police Foundation.

[Mollen Commission] New York City Commission to Investigate Allegations of Police Corruption and the Anti-Corruption Procedures of the Police Department. 1994. *Commission Report.* New York: New York City Commission to Investigate Allegations of Police Corruption and the Anti-Corruption Procedures of the Police Department.

Moore, Michael H., and Daniel W. Stephens. 1991. "Organization and Management." In *Local Government Police Management*, ed. William A. Geller. Washington, DC: International City Management Association.

Muir, William K. 1977. *Police: Street Corner Politicians.* Chicago, IL: University of Chicago Press.

Nagin, Daniel, and Raymond Paternoster. 1991. "The Preventive Effects of the Perceived Risk of Arrest: Testing an Expanded Conception of the Deterrence Doctrine." *Criminology* 29: 561–88.

National Advisory Commission on Civil Disorders (Kerner Commission). 1968. *Report.* Washington, DC: Government Printing Office.

National Institute of Justice. 1999. *Use of Force by Police.* Washington, DC: Government Printing Office. http://www.ncjrs.gov/pdffiles1/nij/176330-1.pdf.

National Research Council. 2004. *Fairness and Effectiveness in Policing: The Evidence.* Committee to Review Research on Police Policy and Practices. Wesley Skogan and Kathleen Frydl, eds. Committee on Law and Justice, Division of Behavioral and Social Sciences and Education. Washington, DC: National Academies Press.

Neubauer, David W. 1974. "Confessions in Prairie City: Some Causes and Effects." *Journal of Criminal Law and Criminology* 65:103–12.

Northeastern University Data Collection Resource Center. 2010. Racial Profiling Data Collection Resource Collection. http://www.racialprofilinganalysis.neu.edu.

Novak, Kenneth J., Brad W. Smith, and James Frank. 2003. "Strange Bedfellows: Civil Liability and Aggressive Policing." *Policing: An International Journal of Police Strategies and Management,* 26(2): 352–68.

Oaks, Dallin H. 1970. "Studying the Exclusionary Rule in Search and Seizure." *University of Chicago School Law Review* 37: 655–757.

Orfield, Myron W., Jr. 1987. "The Exclusionary Rule and Deterrence: An Empirical Study of Chicago Narcotics Officers." *University of Chicago Law School Review* 54: 1016–69.

Pate, Anthony, and Lorie Fridell. 1993. *Police Use of Force: Official Reports, Citizen Complaints, and Legal Consequences.* Washington, DC: Police Foundation.

Pate, Anthony, and Edwin E. Hamilton. 1991. *The Big Six: Policing America's Largest Cities.* Washington, DC: Police Foundation.

Paternoster, Raymond. 1989. "Decisions to Participate in and Desist from Four Types of Common Delinquency: Deterrence and the Rational Choice Perspective." *Law and Society Review* 23(1): 7–40.

Paternoster, Raymond, and LeeAnn Iovanni. 1986. "The Deterrent Effect of Perceived Severity: A Reexamination." *Social Forces* 64: 751–77.

Paternoster, Raymond, Robert Brame, Ronet Bachman, and Lawrence W. Sherman. 1997. "Do Fair Procedures Matter? The Effect of Procedural Justice on Spouse Assault." *Law and Society Review* 31: 163–204.

Patton, Alison L. 1993. "The Endless Cycle of Abuse: Why 42 U.S.C. §1983 is Ineffective in Deterring Police Brutality." *Hastings Law Journal* 44: 753–808.

Peek, Charles W., George D. Lowe, and Jon P. Alston. 1981. "Race and Attitudes toward Local Police." *Journal of Black Studies* 11: 361–74.

Pennsylvania Crime Commission. 1974. Report on Police Corruption and the Quality of Law Enforcement in Philadelphia. Saint Davids, PA: Pennsylvania Crime Commission.

Perez, Douglas W. 1994. *Common Sense about Police Review.* Temple University Press.

Poister, Theodore H., and James C. McDavid. 1977. "Victims' Evaluations of Police Performance." *Journal of Criminal Justice* 6: 133–49.

———. 1978. "Victims' Evaluations of Police Performance." *Journal of Criminal Justice* 6: 133–49.

President's Commission on Law Enforcement and Administration of Justice. 1967a. *A National Survey of Police-Community Relations: Field Surveys V.* Washington, DC: Government Printing Office.

———. 1967b. *Task Force Report: The Police.* Washington, DC: Government Printing Office.

Punch, Maurice. 1985. *Conduct Unbecoming.* London: Tavistock.

———. 2003. "From 'Rotten Apple' to 'Rotten Orchards.'" In *Police Corruption,* ed. Amire Menachem and Stanley Einstein. Huntsville, TX: OICJ.

Reisig, Michael D., and Roger B. Parks. 2000. "Experience, Quality of Life, and Neighborhood Context: A Hierarchical Analysis of Satisfaction with Police." *Justice Quarterly* 17: 607–29.

———. 2002. *Satisfaction with Police—What Matters?* National Institute of Justice, Washington, DC. Available at http://www.ojp.usdoj.gov/nij.

Reiss, Albert J., Jr. 1967. *Studies in Crime and Law Enforcement in Major Metropolitan Areas*: Vol. 1 (President's Commission on Law Enforcement and Administration of Justice). Washington, DC: Government Printing Office.

———. 1971. *Police and the Public.* New Haven, CT: Yale University Press.

Reuss-Ianni, Elizabeth. 1983. *Two Cultures of Policing: Street Cops and Management.* New Brunswick, NJ: Transaction Pulishers.

Riksheim, Eric C., and Steven M. Chermak. 1993. "Causes of Police Behavior Revisited." *Journal of Criminal Justice,* 21(4): 353–82.

Robin, Gerald D. 1963. "Justifiable Homicide By the Police." *Journal of Criminal Law, Criminology, and Police Science* 54:225–31.

Robinson, Paul, and John M. Darley. 1995. *Justice, Liability, and Blame: Community Views and the Criminal Law.* Boulder, CO: Westview Press.

Roebuck, Julian B., and Thomas Barker. 1974. "A Typology of Police Corruption." *Social Problems* 21: 423–37.

Royal Commission into the New South Wales Police Service. 1997. *Final Report.* Sydney, Australia: NSW Police Integrity Commission.

Russell, K. V. 1978. "Complaints Against the Police: An International Perspective." *Police Journal* 51: 34–44.

Sampson, Robert J., and Dawn Jeglum Bertusch. 1998. "Legal Cynicism and (Subcultural?) Tolerance of Deviance: The Neighborhood Context of Racial Differences." *Law and Society Review* 32: 777–804.

San Jose Police Department. 1999. *Vehicle Stop Demographic Study: First Report.* San Jose, CA, December.

Scaglion, Richard, and Richard G. Condon. 1980. "Determinants of Attitudes toward City Police." *Criminology* 17: 485–94.

Schaefer, Roger C. 1971. "Patrolman Perspectives on Miranda." *Law and Social Order* 81–101.

Scrivner, Ellen M. 1994. *Controlling Police Use of Excessive Force: The Role of the Police Psychologist.* Washington, DC: National Institute of Justice.

Shapiro, D. L., and J. M. Brett. 1993. "Comparing Three Processes Underlying Judgments of Procedural Justice: A Field Study of Mediation and Arbitration." *Journal of Personality and Social Psychology* 65: 1167–77.

Shapland, Joanna, Jon Willmore, and Peter Duff. 1985. *Victims in the Criminal Justice System.* Aldershot, England: Gower Publishing Company.

Sherman, Lawrence L. 1974. "Becoming Bent: Moral Careers of Corrupt Policemen." In *Police Corruption*, ed. Lawrence Sherman. Garden City, NY: Anchor Press.

———. 1977. "Police Corruption Control." In *Police and Society*, ed. David Bayley. Thousand Oaks, CA: Sage.

———. 1978. *Scandal and Reform.* Berkeley: University of California Press.

Silverman, Eli B. 1999. *NYPD Battles Crime: Innovative Strategies in Policing.* Boston: Northeastern University Press.

Skogan, Wesley G. 1996. "The Police and Public Opinion in Britain." *American Behavioral Scientist* 39: 421–32.

Skolnick, Jerome H. 1966. *Justice without Trial.* New York: John Wiley and Sons, Inc.

Skolnick, Jerome H., and James J. Fyfe. 1993. *Above the Law: Police and the Excessive Use of Force.* New York: Free Press.

Smith, Paul E., and Richard O. Hawkins. 1973. "Victimization, Types of Citizen-police Contacts, and Attitudes toward the Police." *Law and Society* 8: 135–52.

Soo Son, In, Chiu-Wai Tsang, Dennis M. Rome, and Mark S. Davis. 1997. "Citizens' Observations of Police Use of Excessive Force and Their Evaluation of Police Performance." *Policing: An International Journal of Police Strategy and Management* 20: 149–59.

Southgate, Peter, and Paul Ekblom. 1984. *Contacts between Police and Public.* (Home Office Research Study No. 77). London: Her Majesty's Stationary Office.

Sparrow, Malcom K., Mark H. Moore, and David M. Kennedy. 1990. *Beyond 911: A New Era for Policing.* New York: Basic Books.

Special Counsel to the Los Angeles County Sheriff's Department. 1999. *11th Semiannual Report.* Los Angeles: Los Angeles County.

———. 2002. *15th Semiannual Report.* Los Angeles: Los Angeles County.

Stephens, Otis, Robert L. Flanders, and J. Lewis Cannon. 1972. "Law Enforcement and the Supreme Court: Police Perceptions of the Miranda Requirements." *Tennessee Law Review* 39: 407–32.

Stoddard, Edwin R. 1974. "A Group Approach to Blue-Coat Crime." In *Police Corruption: A Sociological Perspective*, ed. Lawrence W. Sherman. Garden City, NY: Anchor Press.

Sunshine, Jason, and Tom R. Tyler. 2003. "The Role of Procedural Justice and Legitimacy in Shaping Public Support for Policing." *Law and Society Review* 37: 555–89.

Sviridoff, Michele, and James E. McElro. 1989. *Processing Complaints against Police in New York City.* New York: Vera Institute of Justice.

Talley, Joseph E., and Lisa D. Hinz. 1990. *Performance Prediction of Public Safety and Law Enforcement Personnel: A Study in Race and Gender Differences and MMPI Subscales.* Springfield, IL: Charles C. Thomas.

Tennenbaum, Abraham N. 1994. "The Influence of the Garner Decision on Police Use of Deadly Force." *Journal of Criminal Law and Criminology* 85: 241–60.

Terrill, William. 2001. *Police Coercion: Application of the Force Continuum.* New York: LFB Scholarly Publishing.

Terrill, William, and Stephen Mastrofski. 2002. "Reassessing Situational and Office Based Determination of Police Coercion." *Justice Quarterly* 19: 215–48.

Thibaut, John W., and Laurens Walker. 1975. *Procedural Justice: A Psychological Analysis.* Hillsdale, NJ: Erlbaum.

Treaser, Joseph B. 1994. "Convicted Police Officer Receives A Sentence of at Least 11 Years." *New York Times,* July 12. http://nytimes.com.

Tuch, Steven A., and Ronald Weitzer. 1997. "Racial Differences in Attitudes toward the Police." *Public Opinion Quarterly* 61: 642–64.

Tyler, Tom R. 1990. *Why People Obey the Law.* New Haven, CT: Yale University Press.

———. 2000. "Social Justice: Outcome and Procedure." *International Journal of Psychology* 35(2): 117–25.

———. 2001. "Public Trust and Confidence in Legal Authorities: What do Majority and Minority Group Members Want from the Law and Legal Institutions." *Behavioral Sciences and the Law* 19: 215–35.

Tyler, Tom R., and John M. Darley. 2000. "Building a Law-abiding Society: Taking Public Views Abuot Morality and the Legitimacy of Legal Authorities into Account When Formulating Substantive Law." *Hofstra Law Review* 28: 707–39.

Tyler, Tom R., and Robert Folger. 1980. "Distributional and Procedural Aspects of Satisfaction with Citizen-Police Encounters." *Basic and Applied Social Psychology* 1: 281–92.

Tyler, Tom R., and Heather J. Smith. 1997. "Social Justice and Social Movements." In *Handbook of Social Psychology*, ed. Daniel T. Gilbert, Susan T. Fiske, and Gardner Lindzey, 4th ed. New York: McGraw-Hill.

Tyler, Tom R., and Yuen J. Huo. 2002. *Trust in the Law*. New York: Russell Sage Foundation.

Tyler, Tom R., and E. Allan Lind. 1992. "A Relation Model of Authority in Groups." *Advances in Experimental Social Psychology* 25: 115–91.

US Commission on Civil Rights. 1981. *Who is Guarding the Guardians?* Washington, DC: Government Printing Office.

Van Dijk, Jan J. M. 1999. "The Experience of Crime and Justice." In *Global Report on Crime and Justice*, ed. Graeme Newman. New York: Oxford University Press.

Van Maanen, John. 1974. "Working the Street: A Developmental View of Police Behavior." In *The Potential for Reform of Criminal Justice*, ed. Herbert Jacob. Thousand Oaks, CA: Sage.

Wagner, Allen E. 1980. "Citizen Complaints against the Police: The Complainant." *Journal of Police Science and Administration* 8(4): 373–77.

Vera Institute of Justice. 1999. *Respectful and Effective Policing: Two Examples in the South Bronx*. New York: Author.

———. 2002. "Pittsburgh's Experience with Police Monitoring." http://www.vera.org/project/project1_1asp?section_id=2&proejct_id=13.

Wald, Michael S., Richard Ayres, David W. Hess, Mark Schantz, and C. Whitebread. 1967. "Interrogations in New Haven: The Impact of Miranda." *Yale Law Journal* 76: 1519–648.

Walker, Darlene, Richard J. Richardson, Oliver Williams, Thomas Denyer, and Skip McGaughey. 1973. "Contact and Support: An Empirical Assessment of Public Attitudes toward the Police and the Courts." *North Carolina Law Review* 51: 43–79.

Walker, Samuel. 1995. *Citizen Review Resource Manual*. Washington, DC: Police Executive Research Forum.

———. 1999. *The Police in America: An Introduction*. 3rd ed. Boston: McGraw-Hill.

———. 2001. *Police Accountability: The Role of Citizen Oversight*. Belmont, CA: Wadsworth Publishing Company.

———. 2005. *The New World of Police Accountability*. Newbury Park, CA: Sage Publications.

Walker, Samuel, Geoffrey Alpert, and Dennis Kenney. 2000. *Responding to the Problem Officer: A National Evaluation of Early Warning Systems*. Washington, DC: National Institute of Justice.

Walker, Samuel, and Vic W. Bumphus. 1992. "The Effectiveness of Civilian Review: Observations on Recent Trends and New Issues Regarding the Civilian Review of Police." *American Journal of Police* 11: 1–26.

Walker, Samuel, and Charles M. Katz. 2008. *The Police in America: An Introduction*. 6th ed. Boston: McGraw-Hill.

Walker, Samuel, and Betsy Wright Kreisel. 2001. "Varieties of Citizen Review." In *Critical Issues in Policing*, ed. Roger G. Dunham and Geoffrey Alpert. 4th ed. Prospect Heights, IL: Waveland Press.

Webb, Vincent J., and Chris E. Marshall. 1995. "The Relative Importance of Race and Ethnicity on Citizen Attitudes toward the Police." *American Journal of Police* 14: 45–66.

Weisburd, David, and Rosann Greenspan, with Edwin E. Hamilton, Hubert Williams, and Kellie A. Bryant. 2000. *Police Attitudes toward Abuse of Authority: Findings from a National Survey*. Washington, DC: United States Department of Justice, National Institute of Justice, Research in Brief. http://www.ncjrs.gov/pdffiles1/nij/181312.pdf.

Weisburd, David, Stephen D. Mastrofski, Ann Marie McNally, Rosann Greenspan, and James J. Willis. 2003. "Reforming to Preserve: Compstat and Strategic Problem-solving in American Policing." *Criminology and Public Policy* 2: 421–56.

Weitzer, Ronald, and Steven A. Tuch. 1999. "Race, Class, and Perceptions of Discrimination by the Police." *Crime and Delinquency* 45: 494–507.

———. 2002. "Perceptions of Racial Profiling: Race, Class, and Personal Experience." *Criminology* 40: 435–56.

———. 2006. *Race and Policing in America: Conflict and Reform*. Cambridge: Cambridge University Press.

West, Paul. 1988. "Investigation of Complaints against the Police: Summary Report of a National Survey." *American Journal of Police* 7(2): 101–21.

White, Mervin F., Terry C. Cox, and Jack Basehart. 1994. In *Police Deviance*, ed. Thomas Barker and David L. Carter. 3rd ed. Cinciannati: Anderson Publishing.

Wilson, James Q. 1968. *Public Opinions on Police Misuse of Force: A New York Study. Report to the Governor*. Vol. 3. Albany, NY: New York State Commission on Criminal Justice and Use of Force.

Willis, James J., Stephen D. Mastrofski, David Weisburd, and Rosann Greenspan. 2003. *Compstat and Organizational Change in the Lowell Police Department: Challenges and opportunities*. Washington, DC: The Police Foundation.

Winfree, Thomas L., Jr. and Carol T. Griffiths. 1977. "Adolescent Attitudes toward the Police." In *Juvenile Delinquency: Little Brother Grows Up*, ed. Theodore N. Ferdinand. Beverly Hills, CA: Sage Publications.

Witt, James W. 1973. "Non-coercive Interrogations and the Administration of Justice: The Impact of Miranda on Police Effectuality." *Journal of Criminal Law and Criminology* 64: 320–32.

Worden, Robert E. 1989. "Situational and Attitudinal Explanations of Police Behavior: A Theoretical Reappraisal and Empirical Assessment." *Law and Society Review* 23: 667–711.

———. 1995. "The Causes of Police Brutality: Theory and Evidence on Police Use of Force." In *And Justice for All: Understanding and Controlling Police Abuse of Force*, ed. William A. Geller and Hans Toch. Washington, DC: Police Executive Research Forum.

Wortley, Scott, John Hagan, and Ross Macmilian. 1997. "Just Deserts? The Racial Polarization of Perceptions of Criminal Injustice." *Law and Society Review* 31: 637–76.

Yale Law Journal. 1979. "Project: Suing the Police in Federal Court." *Yale Law Journal* 88: 781–824.

Yeo, Helen, and Tracey Budd. 2000. Policing and the Public: Findings from the 1998 British Crime Survey. Home Office Research: Research Findings No. 113. Available at http://www.homeoffice.gov.uk/rds/index.htm.

Zimring, Franklin E., and Gordon Hawkins. 1973. *Deterrence: The Legal Threat in Crime Control*. Chicago: University of Chicago Press.

Zingraff, Matthew T., Marcinda Mason, William Smith, Donald Tomaskovic-Devey, Patricia Warren, Harvey L. McMurray, and Robert C. Fenlon. 2000. *Evaluating North Carolina State Highway Patrol Data: Citation, Warnings, and Searches in 1998*. Raleigh, NC: North Carolina Department of Crime Crontrol and Public Safety.

PART IV

JUVENILE JUSTICE

CHAPTER 20

JUVENILE JUSTICE

BARRY C. FELD AND DONNA M. BISHOP

FOR more than a century, two competing cultural conceptions of youth have animated juvenile and criminal justice policies. On the one hand, policymakers may view children as immature, innocent, vulnerable, and dependent. On the other hand, they may characterize youths as mature, responsible, and almost adultlike. These competing perceptions of children affect judgments about their culpability—e.g., degree of criminal responsibility and appropriate treatment or punishment—and questions about their competence—youths' ability to understand and participate in the legal process. Questions about culpability focus on youths' judgment, risk perceptions, and self-control, which influence policies about appropriate intervention, e.g., treatment or punishment. Questions about competence focus on youths' decision-making capacities and how developmental limitations affect their ability to exercise rights. These competing views of youths' competence and culpability have influenced juvenile courts' procedure and substance from their inception.

At the beginning of the twentieth century, Progressive Era reformers emphasized youths' immaturity and vulnerability, and created a separate justice system to shield children from the stigmatizing punishments of the criminal courts and the corrupting influence of adult jails and prisons. They characterized children as irresponsible and incompetent, and replaced the criminal-punitive model of criminal justice with a civil-therapeutic one for young people. According to the Progressives' vision, the juvenile court would identify the sources of youths' problem behaviors and act *in loco parentis* to provide care and supervision to promote their development into responsible and law-abiding adults (Zimring 2000*a*).

By the end of the twentieth century, lawmakers had adopted harsh, get-tough policies that equated adolescents' culpability with that of adults. In the late 1980s and early 1990s, almost every state revised its laws to prosecute more and younger juveniles in criminal court, and to punish delinquents more severely in juvenile court (Torbet et al. 1996). These changes reflect a fundamental cultural and legal reconceptualization of youths from innocent and dependent children to responsible and autonomous adultlike offenders. Politicians' sound bites—"old enough to do the crime, old enough to do the time"—exemplify the reformulation of adolescents, hold them criminally responsible for their actions, and reject youthfulness as a mitigating factor in sentencing (Feld 2008).

Over the past century, several forces have converged at different times to produce these wide oscillations in the social construction of adolescence and juvenile and criminal justice policy—e.g., from rehabilitative treatment to harsh punishment; from a focus on the offender to an emphasis on the offense; from broad policies of inclusiveness to equally broad "front end" diversion policies and overreaching, exclusionary "back end" transfer policies (Bernard 1992; Feld 2003a). Moreover, juvenile justice practices "in action" differ markedly from the law "on the books," and the historical disjunction between rhetoric and reality has provided impetus for significant system reforms (Feld 2003b).

The idea of childhood is socially constructed, and throughout the twentieth century the juvenile court has been one arena in which public officials have contested its meaning. The court's jurisdictional boundaries, transfer methods, and delinquency sanctions have evolved with and changed as a result of broader social and political forces that have affected both youth and crime policy. In response to a media-generated panic about increasing youth violence, politicians in the 1980s and 1990s characterized youths as responsible and adultlike, and consigned them to criminal courts, a construction and response quite at odds with the Progressives' view of children as innocent and vulnerable. Confronted with harsh policies that equated youths and adults, the John D. and Catherine T. MacArthur Foundation sponsored an ambitious research program to identify the sources and nature of differences in competence and culpability between adolescents and adults (Scott and Steinberg 2008). The research identifies substantial differences between youths' and adults' thinking, behavior, and self-control. Although adolescents develop adultlike cognitive capacities by their mid-teens, their judgment and impulse control does not approximate that of adults for nearly another decade. These differences have direct relevance for considerations of competence and culpability.

This chapter examines juvenile justice policy and practice with a special focus on changes over the past quarter-century that have both challenged and reasserted juvenile courts' founding principles that children do indeed differ from adults. Section I provides an overview of the early juvenile court—its philosophical underpinnings and historic mission. Section II examines the "due process revolution" of the 1960s and assesses its intended and unintended consequences. Section III focuses on punitive shifts in juvenile justice policies during the 1980s and 1990s. It identifies the structural and political sources of "get tough" policies, examines the reformulation of adolescents' culpability, and explores their impact on juvenile justice administration.

Section IV examines the contemporary juvenile court and recent responses to juvenile courts' historical deficiencies and the punitive overreaction of the 1990s. It assays how new research on adolescent competence and culpability has implicated critical issues in juvenile justice administration and influenced youth crime policy.

The main points and conclusions of this chapter are:

- For the past century, policymakers have chosen from two competing images of youth—immature and vulnerable vs. mature and responsible—to rationalize juvenile justice policies.
- In the 1980s and 1990s, politicians equated adolescents' and adults' competence and culpability and advocated punitive get-tough laws to punish and deter young offenders.
- These punitive policies led to the transfer of more and younger juveniles to the criminal justice system for prosecution and confinement as adults and to tougher sentences for delinquents. These policies repudiated the founding principles of the juvenile court that viewed children as categorically different from adults and placed them in a separate judicial system.
- The MacArthur Foundation's research on adolescents' competence and culpability demonstrates clear differences between youths and adults in thinking, behavior, and self-control. Recent neuroscience research provides a biological explanation for social scientists' observations about how children differ from adults. Because of these differences, many get-tough policies have produced irrational, counterproductive results.
- The renewed appreciation of adolescents' developmental differences and diminished criminal responsibility encouraged the Supreme Court in *Roper v. Simmons* (2005) to abolish the death penalty for offenders younger than eighteen years of age and in *Graham v. Florida* (2010) to prohibit imposition of life without parole sentences on non-homicide juvenile offenders.
- Youths' impaired capacity to exercise rights, to participate in the juvenile or criminal process, and to make legal decisions requires a reappraisal of procedural safeguards for youths in both systems.

I. The Progressive Juvenile Court: 1899–1960s

The social history of the Progressive Era and the creation of a separate juvenile justice system is an oft-told tale (e.g., Rothman 1980; Feld, 1999; Tanenhaus 2004; Platt 2009). Social changes associated with economic modernization, immigration, and urbanization modified the roles of women and children. The idea of childhood is socially constructed, and during this period the upper and middle classes promoted an image of children as vulnerable, fragile, and dependent innocents (Ryerson 1978; Platt 2009). Progressive reformers embraced the new construction of childhood and enacted a number of child-centered reforms—juvenile court, child labor laws, social welfare laws, and compulsory school attendance laws—that both reflected and advanced the changing imagery of childhood (Feld 1999).

Changes in ideological assumptions about the sources of crime and deviance influenced many Progressive criminal justice reforms. Positivism—the effort to identify antecedent factors that cause crime and delinquency—challenged the classic formulation of crime as the product of free-will choices (Rothman 1980). Positive criminology attributed criminal behavior to external forces and adopted informal, discretionary policies to rehabilitate offenders—probation, parole, indeterminate sentences, and the juvenile court (Allen 1964).

The juvenile court melded the new ideology of childhood with the new conception of social control, introduced a judicial-welfare alternative to criminal courts, removed children from the adult criminal justice system, and provided individualized treatment in a separate system. From juvenile courts' inception in 1899 and for the next seventy years, the court was firmly rooted in the doctrine of *parens patriae*—the state as parent and arbiter of child-rearing. Progressive reformers conceived of children as immature and irresponsible, and saw the juvenile court as a non-punitive child welfare system. To distinguish it from the criminal court, they closed proceedings to public scrutiny and adopted a euphemistic vocabulary. Juvenile court hearings concentrated on a child's background and welfare, and judges enjoyed wide discretion to administer their courts and supervise children (Allen 1964; Ryerson 1978; Tanenhaus 2004).

The juvenile court's rehabilitative mission required a specialized judge trained in social work and child development whose empathy and insight would enable him to make dispositions in the "best interests" of the child (Mack 1909). Proof that the child committed an offense—today viewed as a logical and necessary prerequisite to an inquiry into a child's needs and sentence—was a secondary consideration, as court personnel viewed an offense primarily as a symptom of a child's "real needs." Reformers exhibited little concern about protecting children from erroneous adjudications of delinquency because they believed the court delivered benign treatment from which children would benefit. Progressives thus defined the courts' jurisdiction expansively to include youths accused of crimes, noncriminal "status offenders" who were "at risk" to become delinquents, as well as abused and neglected children (Platt 2009).

Juvenile courts imposed indeterminate and nonproportional sentences, which they characterized as treatment and supervision rather than punishment and control. Dispositions focused on youths' future welfare rather than their past offenses and could continue for the duration of minority, e.g., until age twenty-one. The courts' founders opposed procedural safeguards, such as representation by defense counsel and the privilege against self incrimination, because they feared they would impede open communication between judge and child and interfere with the court's child welfare mission. They employed informal procedures, excluded lawyers and juries, and conducted confidential hearings (Feld 1999).

At its inception, the juvenile court was a fragile institution whose continued existence depended on garnering public and political support (Tanenhaus 2004). The criminal behavior of some young offenders—especially violent and chronic offenders—threatened that support (Tanenhaus 2004). While commission of a serious crime neither transformed a young person into a fully responsible adult nor rendered him a poor candidate for treatment, the public tended to view young violent offenders as sophisticated and adultlike, rather than as immature children, and pressed for harsh punishments (Tanenhaus 2000). Persistent recidivists posed an equally great challenge to the courts' legitimacy. Their failure to respond to prior intervention suggested that young people might be less amenable to rehabilitation than court advocates assumed. From their creation, juvenile courts transferred some serious and persistent young offenders to criminal court (Rothman 1980; Tanenhaus 2000). Although waiver of jurisdiction conflicted with the juvenile court's underlying principles of youths' diminished criminal responsibility and limited adjudicative competence, it proved politically expedient. By relinquishing authority over a few serious offenders, judges could placate public fear and political clamor and thus preserve juvenile courts' diversionary and rehabilitative role for the vast majority of young offenders.

From the juvenile court's inception, Progressive reformers intended it to discriminate in its intervention. They designed it to control poor and immigrant children, to assimilate and "Americanize" them, and to distinguish between "our children" and "other people's children" (Rothman 1980). Today, juvenile courts continue to process and confine a disproportionate number of racial and ethnic minorities, and these disparities remain one of the fundamental criticisms of contemporary juvenile justice (Feld 1999; McCord, Spatz-Widom, and Crowell 2001; Hawkins and Kempf-Leonard 2005). Similarly, reformers exhibited special concern about female offenders' "sexual precocity," and juvenile courts' status jurisdiction enabled them to respond to noncriminal behavior such as sexual activity, truancy, and immorality (Schlossman 1977; Ryerson 1978; Schlossman and Wallach 1978; Platt 2009). Gendered disparities in juvenile justice administration persist today (Feld 2009).

The Progressives situated the juvenile court on several cultural, legal, and criminological fault lines. They created binary distinctions between the juvenile and criminal justice systems: either child or adult; either immature and deserving of assistance or blameworthy and deserving of punishment; either devoid of rules and informal or formal and adversarial. Beginning in the 1960s, a rise in serious youth crime and Supreme Court decisions that addressed the reality of juvenile justice and corrections fostered a shift from the former to the latter of each binary pair.

II. The 1960s and the "Due Process Revolution"

In the decades prior to and after World War II, black migration from the rural South to the urban North increased minority concentrations in urban ghettos, made race a national rather than a regional issue, and provided political and legal impetus for the civil rights movement and constitutional reforms (Feld 1999; 2003a). Youth crime increased dramatically in the 1960s as the children of the baby boom began to reach adolescence, and as the Great Migration substantially increased urbanization of blacks and led to higher crime rates in minority areas (Zimring and Hawkins 1997). These broader structural and demographic changes impelled the Warren Court's civil rights decisions, criminal procedure rulings, and its "constitutional domestication" of the juvenile court during the 1960s. The Court's criminal procedure and juvenile justice decisions attempted to protect minority citizens and to limit the authority of the states. The Court adopted procedural safeguards and created per se rules to limit state power, constrain police discretion, and protect peoples' freedom. Unfortunately, the Court's criminal procedure and juvenile court decisions—because they coincided with rising crime rates, urban racial disorders, and concerns about racial disparities in justice administration—fueled conservative calls for "law and order" (Feld 1999, 2003a).

Juvenile court's idealistic vision of individualized treatments often fell far short of realization, but for nearly seventy years the public and policymakers ignored its institutional failures. The absence of procedural safeguards against wrongful convictions and judges' broad authority over delinquent and predelinquent youth—viewed as essential to the child-saving mission—fostered judicial arbitrariness, discriminatory decisions, and abuses of power. Almost all youth appeared in juvenile court without lawyers (Feld 1993). Probation caseloads were often extraordinarily high, and probation officers frequently were political appointees who lacked appropriate qualifications or training for their positions (Ryerson 1978). Juvenile institutions suffered from overcrowding, unsafe and unsanitary conditions, and poorly trained staff and high turnover (President's Commission on Law Enforcement and the Administration of Justice 1967). In many institutions, a rule of silence prevailed, recalcitrant inmates spent lengthy periods in isolation rooms, and staff-inmate and inmate-inmate violence was endemic (Feld 1976). In the 1960s, a series of reports—the most influential of which was the President's Crime Commission *Task Force Report on Juvenile Delinquency and Youth Crime* (1967)—revealed the deficiencies of juvenile courts and correctional institutions and the plight of juvenile offenders.

The Supreme Court in *In re Gault*, 387 U.S. 1 (1967), began to transform the juvenile court into a very different institution than the one contemplated by the

Progressives. *Gault* highlighted the disjunction between the rhetoric of juvenile rehabilitation—long used to justify differences between the procedural safeguards afforded criminal defendants and those available to delinquents—and the reality of juvenile correctional practice. In *Gault,* the Supreme Court engrafted some formal procedures at trial onto the juvenile court's individualized treatment approach with the observation that "Under our Constitution, the condition of being a boy does not justify a kangaroo court" (1967, 27–28). Despite juvenile courts' therapeutic rhetoric, *Gault* concluded that the reality of punitive confinement in juvenile institutions required fundamentally fair procedural safeguards: advance notice of charges, a hearing, assistance of counsel, an opportunity to confront and cross-examine witnesses, and the privilege against self-incrimination (Feld 1984). *Gault* asserted that adversarial procedural safeguards were essential to determine the factual accuracy of delinquency allegations and to limit the power of the state and insisted that their introduction would not impair juvenile courts' rehabilitative mission.

Gault endorsed juvenile courts' therapeutic goals, reaffirmed that juveniles differed from adults, and agreed that they should receive treatment. However, by mandating procedural safeguards, the Court envisioned youths as individuals competent to exercise legal rights and to participate in the adversarial system. Progressives eschewed procedural safeguards in juvenile courts because they viewed young people as immature and irresponsible, and because procedures would encumber rather than contribute to child welfare. Although *Gault* rejected those assumptions, whether juveniles actually are competent to exercise *Miranda* and other rights became an increasingly critical question as states adopted more punitive policies (Feld 2003*b*).

Several subsequent Supreme Court decisions further criminalized juvenile delinquency proceedings. In *In re Winship*, 397 U.S. 358 (1970), the Court required states to prove delinquents' guilt by the criminal law's standard of proof—beyond a reasonable doubt. In *Breed v. Jones*, 421 U.S. 519 (1975), the court applied the constitutional ban on double jeopardy based on the functional equivalence of criminal trials and delinquency proceedings. However, in *McKeiver v. Pennsylvania*, 403 U.S. 528 (1971), the Court refused to grant delinquents the constitutional right to a jury trial available to adult criminal defendants. *McKeiver* concluded that affording delinquents a jury trial would adversely affect the informality, flexibility, and confidentiality of juvenile court proceedings and could provide impetus to abandon the juvenile court experiment (Feld 2003*b*).

Despite *McKeiver*'s efforts to reaffirm foundational principles of treatment and rehabilitation, in the aftermath of the Court's due process decisions, judicial, legislative, and administrative changes have fostered a procedural and substantive convergence between juvenile and criminal courts. *Gault* and *Winship* unintentionally transformed the juvenile court from its original conception as a social welfare agency into a scaled-down version of the criminal court (Feld 1984; 1988*a*). By emphasizing procedural regularity to determine delinquency, the Court shifted juvenile courts' initial focus from assessing a youth's "real needs" to proving she committed a crime. Formalizing the connection between law violations and sanctions made explicit a relationship previously implicit, unacknowledged, and deliberately obscured.

Gault and *Winship*'s insistence on procedural safeguards in juvenile courts may have legitimated more punitive dispositions for young offenders. For example, *Gault*'s newfound right to counsel for delinquents made it imperative that prosecutors enter juvenile courts for the first time. Prosecutors established juvenile divisions and staffed them with traditionally trained attorneys who infused the juvenile court with a criminal law orientation. Warm, informal talks between judges, children, and parents in juvenile courts all but disappeared as court professionals talked over and about the child whom they relegated to a passive role. Moreover, providing a modicum of procedural justice legitimated greater punitiveness because once states granted even a semblance of procedural justice, they more readily departed from a purely rehabilitative model of the juvenile court. It is a historical irony that concern about racial inequality provided the initial impetus for the Supreme Court's focus on juveniles' procedural rights, because the existence of those procedures rationalized increasingly punitive penalties that fall most heavily on minority juvenile offenders.

By the early 1970s, both liberal and conservative critics of rehabilitation and indeterminate sentencing began to swing the penal policy pendulum toward retribution and determinate sentencing. Beginning in the mid-1960s, urban race riots, escalating crime rates, dissatisfaction with the treatment model in penology, and the emerging politics of crime prompted calls for a return to classical principles of criminal law (Beckett and Sasson 2000; Garland 2001; Feld 2003a). The influential publication by the American Friends Service Committee (1971), *Struggle for Justice*, exhorted courts and legislatures to rein in judicial discretion and return to "just deserts" as a remedy for the disparities associated with individualized treatment. Utilitarian justifications for treatment fared poorly. Evaluation of the effectiveness of treatment raised substantial doubts about clinicians' abilities to coerce behavioral change and highlighted the subjectivity inherent in therapeutic justice. In the 1970s, researchers published a series of negative appraisals of correctional treatment programs (e.g., Lipton, Martinson, and Wilks 1975; Wright and Dixon 1977; Sechrest, White, and Brown 1979). Martinson's (1974) celebrated conclusion that "nothing works" precipitated a sharp decline in support for juvenile courts' therapeutic rationale (Zimring 2000a). Although other research later challenged Martinson's negative assessment—pointing to methodological flaws in the research, weak evaluation designs, and poor program implementation, rather than the absence of viable treatment methods (e.g., Palmer 1991; Lipsey 1992)—those critiques received little attention from policymakers.

III. 1980s–1990s: The "Get Tough" Era

Macro-structural, economic, and racial demographic changes that occurred in American cities during the 1970s and 1980s, and the escalation in black youth homicide rates at the end of the 1980s provided the backdrop for states' adoption of get-tough juvenile justice policies in the early 1990s (Feld 1999). The Great Migration of blacks from the rural South to the urban North during the period between World Wars I and II concentrated large numbers of African Americans in inner-city ghettoes (Massey and Denton 1993). After World War II, private and governmental highway, housing, and mortgage policies encouraged suburban expansion and contributed to the growth of middle-class, predominantly white suburbs around increasingly poor and minority urban cores (Feld 1999; Massey and Denton 1993). Beginning in the 1970s, the transition from an industrial and manufacturing to an information and service economy reduced job prospects for unskilled urban dwellers. By the end of the 1980s, an impoverished black underclass was trapped in the inner cities (Wilson 1987). The introduction of crack cocaine combined with the proliferation of guns sparked turf wars in urban neighborhoods over control of lucrative drug markets, and rates of black youth homicide sharply escalated (Blumstein and Cork 1996; Zimring 1998; Cork 1999; Feld 1999).

The upsurge in juvenile gun violence that began in the mid-1980s and peaked in 1994 provided the political impetus to transform juvenile justice policies. The media responded to the urban, predominately black youth gun violence with heavy and sensationalized coverage (Feld 2003a). Media portrayals of young offenders shifted dramatically from the traditionally benign images of immature, misguided youth to menacing portraits of cruel and remorseless adolescent "super-predators" (DiIulio 1995). Political scientist John DeIulio (1995, 23) famously claimed that "Americans are sitting atop a demographic crime bomb," and others warned of a coming "blood bath" of youth violence (Fox 1996).

A moral panic ensued in which politicians exploited public fears of crime for electoral advantage (Feld 1999, 2003a). Conservative politicians and the mass media pushed crime to the top of the political agenda and focused on violence and gun crimes to promote broader get-tough policies. Politicians, fearful of being labeled "soft on crime," tried to outdo their opponents in the competition to crack down on youth crime. These political responses sharply challenged the underlying assumptions that had animated the earlier juvenile court movement. The public and politicians no longer viewed young offenders as innocent and dependent children, but rather as responsible and autonomous adultlike offenders (Feld 1999; Garland 2001). Characterizing juvenile offenders as adultlike, incipient career criminals gave traction to sound-bite crime policies—"adult crime, adult time." Legislators touted the utility of punishment both as a deterrent and as a means to protect public safety, applied harsh adult sanctions to youths who were by no means "worst case" offenders, and enacted unprecedented punitive reforms.

Beginning in the 1980s, juvenile justice policy dramatically shifted away from the *parens patriae* mission to nurture miscreant youths to an unabashed emphasis on punishment (Feld 1988*a*; Torbet et al. 1996). Legislatures in nearly every state amended their juvenile code purpose clauses to endorse "punishment," "holding youth accountable," and "protecting the public safety" as new juvenile justice goals (Feld 1988*a*; Torbet et al. 1996). Legislatures in nearly half the states adopted offense-based sentencing provisions to restrict juvenile court judges' sentencing discretion (Feld 1998). Some states adopted sentencing guidelines to impose presumptive, determinate, and proportional sentences based on age, offense seriousness, and prior record (Feld 1998). Others adopted mandatory minimum sentencing provisions that prescribed minimum periods of confinement or levels of secure placement keyed to the seriousness of the offense. These measures use principles of proportionality to rationalize sentences, to increase the penal bite of juvenile sanctions, and to demonstrate symbolically legislators' toughness.

States also took steps to facilitate the transfer of more and younger juvenile offenders to criminal court for prosecution and punishment as adults (Torbet et al. 1996; Feld and Bishop 2011). Historically, juvenile court judges waived youths to criminal court only if they concluded after investigating the child's background—e.g., his clinical needs and assessments, family circumstances, offense and prior record—that he was too dangerous to retain in the juvenile system or was not amenable to treatment. Because politicians perceived juvenile court judges as reluctant to waive serious offenders, they enacted alternative procedures to bypass juvenile courts or to sharply restrict judges' waiver discretion (Feld 2000*a*).

In fifteen states, lawmakers shifted to prosecutors authority to choose the forum—juvenile or criminal court—in which a case would be tried and allowed them to direct file—transfer a case—without any hearing or judicial review (Snyder and Sickmund 2006). Most states statutorily excluded some serious or violent crimes from juvenile court jurisdiction, often without regard to the offender's age. In some states, children as young as ten may be tried as adults. Others limited judges' discretion by making judicial waiver mandatory or presumptive if prosecutors charged youths with serious crimes. Many states adopted "once an adult, always an adult" provisions that amplified the impact of these other provisions. Some states lowered their juvenile courts' maximum age of jurisdiction and converted all youths above the new, lower-age threshold into criminals (Feld 2000*a*). Analysts estimate that annually states try in criminal courts about 250,000 youths who committed their crimes when they were under eighteen, many of whom were neither serious nor chronic offenders (Snyder and Sickmund 2006).

For decades, studies have consistently reported racial disparities in juvenile court sentencing and waiver decisions, which have been exacerbated by the recent get-tough reforms (Bortner, Zatz, and Hawkins 2000; Bishop 2005; Human Rights Watch 2005; Poe-Yamagata and Jones 2007). As a result of successive screenings, differential processing, and cumulative disadvantage, minority youths comprise the majority of juveniles transferred to criminal court and three-quarters of all youths under age eighteen who enter prison (Juskiewicz 2000; Poe-Yamagata and Jones 2007).

Criminal court judges apparently do not mitigate the sentences imposed on youths convicted in criminal court on account of their youthfulness and immaturity. Indeed, judges imposed harsher sentences on waived adolescents than they imposed on comparable young adult defendants (Kurlychek and Johnson 2004, 2010; Feld and Bishop 2011). Except as noted below, criminal sentencing laws did not regard even the most extreme penalties to be inconsistent with youth. Until the Supreme Court's decision in *Roper v. Simmons*, 543 U.S. 551 (2005), some states imposed the death penalty on offenders as young as sixteen. And today, in contravention of the U.N. Convention on the Rights of the Child,[1] several thousand individuals serve sentences of life without possibility of parole (LWOP) for offenses they committed as juveniles (Human Rights Watch 2005).[2] Only three other countries (none in Europe) permit juvenile LWOP sentences, but they have imposed them only in about a dozen cases worldwide (Human Rights Watch 2005, 5).

In sum, at the close of the twentieth century, the United States had embraced policies that expanded the reach and bite of transfer laws, and increased the punitive powers of juvenile courts. These shifts challenged, if not repudiated, the basic ideas of youthful immaturity and malleability that provided the critical jurisprudential underpinnings of the juvenile court.

IV. 2000–2010: Reassessing Adolescents' Competence and Culpability

Nearly a century after its creation, widespread public, policymaker, and political dissatisfaction with the juvenile justice system produced contradictory impulses. Some politicians advocated get-tough policies and criticized juvenile courts for failing to adopt harsher, retributive strategies to hold young offenders accountable and to punish them just like adults. Supporters of juvenile courts criticized them for failing to meet the needs of their clientele, many of whom suffered from psychological problems, educational deficits, poverty, and abuse (Scott and Steinberg 2008). Others condemned the racial disparities in juvenile justice administration that produced disproportionate minority confinement (McCord, Spatz-Widom, and Crowell 2001; Hawkins and Kempf-Leonard 2005). The public perceived the juvenile court as incapable of rehabilitating offenders, reducing youth crime, or protecting the public safety (Feld 2003*a*).

Beginning in the mid-1990s, the John D. and Catherine T. MacArthur Foundation funded a Network on Adolescent Development and Juvenile Justice (ADJJ), sponsored extensive developmental psychological research on youths' thinking and behavior, and provided an evidence-based rationale for juvenile justice policy (Scott and Steinberg 2008; http://www.adjj.org). Created in response to the get-tough policies of the 1990s, the ADJJ Network conducted interdisciplinary research to examine developmental differences between how young people and adults think and act, and to consider the implications of adolescents' immature judgment for juvenile and criminal justice policy. The MacArthur research program focused on three broad themes: (1) adolescents' legal competence; (2) youths' criminal culpability; and (3) their treatment responsiveness and potential for change. Research on competence focused on how adolescents think, their decision-making capacities, and how their limitations affect their ability to participate in the justice systems. Research on culpability focused on adolescents' maturity of judgment and criminal responsibility, and provided a rationale for categorical mitigation of sanctions for adolescents. The ADJJ Network has published a series of edited books and monographs, and its research is encouraging a re-examination and amelioration of some of the harsher get-tough policies enacted previously (e.g., Grisso and Schwartz 2000; Fagan and Zimring 2000; Hawkins and Kempf-Leonard 2005; Scott and Steinberg 2008). The MacArthur Foundation is collaborating with policymakers and stakeholders in several states to implement developmentally appropriate juvenile justice policies that reflect current knowledge about adolescents' culpability and competence.

A. Adolescents' Diminished Culpability

In 2005 the Supreme Court in *Roper v. Simmons*, 543 U.S. 551 (2005) overruled *Stanford v. Kentucky*, 492 U.S. 361 (1989), and categorically barred states from executing youths for crimes committed prior to eighteen years of age. Changes in state laws and jury verdicts provided evidence of an emerging national consensus against executing juveniles. The *Roper* majority also conducted a proportionality analysis of adolescents' culpability and offered three reasons why states could not punish youths whom they found to be criminally responsible as severely as adults. First, juveniles' immature judgment and lesser self-control caused them to act impulsively without full appreciation of consequences and reduced their culpability (*Roper* 2005). Second, juveniles' greater susceptibility than adults to negative peer influences diminished their criminal responsibility (*Roper* 2005). Third, juveniles' personalities are more transitory and less well-formed, and their crimes provide less reliable evidence of a "depraved character" than do those of adults (*Roper* 2005). These developmental characteristics correspond with traditional justifications to mitigate punishment such as diminished capacity, duress and provocation, and lack of bad character (Scott and Steinberg 2003; 2008). *Roper* recognized both adolescents' diminished responsibility for past offenses and their unformed and perhaps redeemable character in the future. Juveniles' immature judgment, susceptibility to negative influence, and transitory character also negated retributive and deterrent justifications for the death penalty (*Roper* 2005).

The most substantial differences between the majority and dissenting justices in *Roper* concerned whether to bar the death penalty categorically or to allow juries to assess juveniles' culpability individually (Feld 2008). Although two dissenting opinions urged individualized evaluations, Justice Kennedy opted for a categorical ban.

> The differences between juvenile and adult offenders are too marked and well understood to *risk* allowing a youthful person to receive the death penalty despite insufficient culpability. An *unacceptable likelihood* exists that the brutality or cold-blooded nature of any particular crime would overpower mitigating arguments based on youth as a matter of course, even where the juvenile offender's objective immaturity, vulnerability, and lack of true depravity should require a sentence less severe than death. (*Roper* 2005, 572–73)

Justice Kennedy noted that psychiatrists refrain from diagnosing patients younger than eighteen years of age with "antisocial personality disorder" because the psychiatrists lacked clinical tools with which to differentiate between immature juveniles and the "rare juvenile offender whose crime reflects irreparable corruption" (*Roper* 2005, 573). Because jurors might ignore the mitigating role of youthfulness when confronted with a brutal murder, *Roper* used age as a conclusive proxy for reduced culpability and disallowed them to make judgments that trained professionals eschewed.

Roper offered three reasons—immature judgment, susceptibility to negative peer influences, and transitional identities—to support its conclusion that juveniles are categorically less criminally responsible than adults. Although differences between adolescents and adults seem intuitively obvious—"as any parent knows"— *Roper* did not cite scientific evidence to bolster its decision (*Roper* 2005; Denno 2006). However, developmental psychological and neuroscience research corroborates *Roper*'s observations about adolescents' immature decision making, limited self-control, and reduced culpability and its implication for sentencing youths.

Sentencing theory apportions deserved punishment to the seriousness of the offense (von Hirsch 1976, 1985; Frase 2005). Two elements—harm and culpability— define a crime's seriousness and the punishment its perpetrator deserves. An offender's age does not affect the harm caused—a fifteen-year-old can inflict the same injuries as an adult (van den Haag 1975). However, an offender's ability to appreciate the wrongfulness of her actions and to control her behavior increases with age and affects evaluations of culpability (Zimring 2000b; Brink 2004). Although states may hold youths accountable for their harms, *Roper* limited somewhat the severity of the sentence they could impose because of diminished responsibility. Even after youths can distinguish right from wrong, their decisions are not as blameworthy as adults' and warrant less severe punishment (Feld 1997; Scott and Grisso 1997; Zimring 2000b).

Developmental psychologists study how children's thinking and behavior change as they mature. By mid-adolescence, most youths can distinguish right from wrong and can reason similarly to adults (Scott 1992; Steinberg and Cauffman 1999; Scott and Steinberg 2008). For example, youths and adults use comparable reasoning processes to make informed consent medical decisions (Morse 1997). But the ability to make good choices when provided with complete information under laboratory conditions differs from the ability to make good decisions under stressful conditions with incomplete information (Cauffman and Steinberg 1995; Steinberg and Cauffman 1996; Spear 2000). Emotions play a significant role in decision making, and researchers distinguish between conditions of "cold cognition" and "hot cognition" (Dahl 2004; Aronson 2007). Mood volatility, an appetite for excitement, and stress adversely affect the quality of adolescents' decisions (Scott 1992; Steinberg and Cauffman 1996).

Research sponsored by ADJJ Network reports a disjunction between youths' cognitive abilities and their maturity of judgment (www.adjj.org; Feld 2008; Scott and Steinberg 2008). Even though adolescents by about age sixteen exhibit cognitive abilities comparable with adults, they do not develop psycho-social maturity, capacity to exercise self-control, and competence to make adult-quality decisions until their early-twenties (Scott, Reppucci, and Woolard 1995; Scott and Steinberg 2003; Feld 2008). The "Immaturity Gap" represents the cleavage between adolescents' intellectual maturity—which reaches near-adult levels by age sixteen—and psycho-social maturity of judgment which may not emerge fully for another decade (Feld 2008; Scott and Steinberg 2008).

Roper highlighted adolescents' immature judgment rather than their cognitive ability to distinguish right from wrong. Youths' immature judgment in several domains—perceptions of risk, appreciation of future consequences, self-management, and ability to make autonomous choices—distinguishes them from adults (Morse 1997; Scott and Steinberg 2003). Youths' bad choices are categorically less blameworthy than those of adults because the differences in knowledge and experience, short-term versus long-term time perspectives, attitude toward risk, and impulsivity are normal features of adolescent development (Scott, Reppucci, and Woolard 1995; Morse 1997; Scott and Grisso 1997; Scott and Steinberg 2003).

To exercise good judgment and self-control, a person must be able to think ahead, delay gratification, and restrain impulses. Adolescents act more impulsively, fail to consider long-term consequences, and engage in riskier behavior than do adults. Their propensity to take risks is reflected in higher incidences of accidents, suicides, unsafe-sexual practices, and criminal activity (Scott 1992; Spear 2000). To calculate risks, a person has to identify potential positive and negative outcomes, estimate the likelihood of occurrence, and then apply value preferences to optimize outcomes (Furby and Beyth-Marom 1992). To a greater extent than adults, adolescents underestimate the amount and likelihood of risks, employ a shorter time frame in their calculus, and focus on gains rather than losses (Furby and

Beyth-Marom 1992; Grisso 2000; Scott 2000). Juveniles fifteen years of age and younger act more impulsively than do older adolescents, but even sixteen- and seventeen-year-old youths fail to exhibit adult levels of self-control (adjj.org). Adolescents possess less information and consider fewer options than adults do when they make decisions because of inexperience (Scott 2000). While youths and adults solve simple problems similarly, the length of time used to solve complex problems increases with age (adjj.org).

Adolescents' risk perception actually *declines* during mid-adolescence and then gradually increases into adulthood—sixteen- and seventeen-year-olds perceive fewer risks than do either younger or older research subjects (adjj.org). Mid-teens are the most present-oriented of all age groups, and future orientation gradually increases into the early twenties (adjj.org). Youths weigh costs and benefits differently than do adults and apply different subjective values to outcomes that affect their choices (Scott and Steinberg 2008). A study of peoples' ability to delay gratification reports that adolescents more often opt for an immediate, but smaller, reward, whereas adults delay a reward unless the immediate value only is slightly discounted (adjj.org).

Youth also view *not* engaging in risky behaviors differently than do adults (Scott 1992; Scott and Steinberg 2003, 2008). They engage in risky behavior for heightened sensations, excitement, and an adrenaline rush (Scott and Grisso 1997; Spear 2000). Their appetite for risk and novel sensations peaks at ages sixteen and seventeen and then declines. The widest divergence between perception of and preference for risk occurs during mid-adolescence when youths' rates of criminal activity also increase (adjj.org). Youths' feelings of invulnerability and immortality heighten these risk proclivities (Furby and Beyth-Marom 1992).

Youths' immature judgment and impaired self-control are associated with neurobiological differences between adolescent and adult brains. Neuroscience research corroborates developmental psychologists' observations and provides an additional basis to find youths' criminal responsibility diminished (Maroney 2009). Differences between adolescents' and adults' thinking and behavior reflect basic neurobiological differences in the human brain, which does not fully mature until the early twenties (Spear 2000; Sowell et al 2001, 2002; Dahl 2004; Scott and Steinberg 2008). Adolescents simply do not have the physiological capacity of adults to exercise judgment or control impulses (Dahl 2004; Gruber and Yurgelun Todd 2006). The prefrontal cortex (PFC) of the frontal lobe of the brain operates as the Chief Executive Officer to control advanced cerebral activities (Kandel et al. 2000). Executive functions include reasoning, abstract thinking, planning, anticipating consequences, and impulse control (Aronson 2009). During adolescence and into the early twenties, increased myelination of the PFC improves executive functions and reasoning ability. By contrast, the amygdala—the limbic system at the base of the brain—controls instinctual behavior, such as the "fight or flight" response (Kandel et al 2000). Adolescents rely more heavily on the amygdala and less heavily on the PFC than do adults when they experience stressful situations. Their impulsive behavior reflects a gut reaction rather than sober reflection (Arrendondo 2003). Novel circumstances and aroused emotions especially challenge youths' ability to exercise self-control and to resist impulsive decisions.

Neuroscience research provides a hard-science explanation for social scientists' observations about adolescents' behavior and self-control. Adolescents' immature brains do not provide a deterministic excuse for criminal behavior (Maroney 2009). Scientists have not established the links between immature brain structure and function and their impact on real-life decisions or behavior under stressful conditions, nor have they developed bases on which to differentiate among offenders founded on brain development (Morse 2006; Aronson 2007; Maroney 2009). Rather, neuroscience research enhances our understanding of how and why juveniles think and behave differently from adults, and furnishes another basis to mitigate their punishment.

Roper's rationale of adolescents' diminished responsibility has wider implications for sentencing youth. A juvenile's criminal responsibility is just as diminished when states impose LWOP or other lengthy sentences as it is when they execute him (Brink 2004; Feld 2008). The Supreme Court's capital punishment jurisprudence insisted that "death is different" (*Eddings* 1982; *Harmelin* 1991; *Graham* 2010). However, there are no developmental or penological features that distinguish youths' diminished criminal responsibility for purposes of the death penalty from their reduced culpability when states impose other harsh sentences (Zimring 1998). Forty-two states permit judges to impose an LWOP sentence on any offender—adult or juvenile—convicted of serious offenses—e.g., murder or rape—and twenty-seven states require mandatory sentences for offenders convicted of those crimes.

Mandatory LWOP sentences preclude consideration of youthfulness as a mitigating factor (Human Rights Watch 2005; Nellis and King 2009). Several states abrogated the common-law infancy defense for very young children and removed the only substantive criminal law protections for youth (Feld 2008). Appellate courts regularly uphold LWOP sentences and long terms of imprisonment imposed on youths as young as twelve years of age, and reject juveniles' pleas to consider youthfulness as a mitigating factor (Human Rights Watch 2005; Feld 2008; Deitch et al 2009). About one of every six juveniles who received an LWOP sentence was fifteen years of age or younger when they committed their crimes (Human Rights Watch 2005). More than half (59 percent) of juveniles who received an LWOP sentence had no prior criminal convictions (Human Rights Watch 2005). More than one quarter (26 percent) of youths received an LWOP sentence for a felony murder to which they were an accessory rather than the principal (Human Rights Watch 2005). In addition to the several thousand youths serving LWOP sentences, criminal court judges have imposed life sentences on an additional 6,807 juveniles (Nellis and King 2009). Although the Court's death penalty jurisprudence defines youthfulness as a mitigating factor, trial judges perversely treat it as an aggravating factor and sentence juveniles more severely than young adults convicted of similar crimes (Kurlychek and Johnson 2004, 2010; Snyder and Sickmund 2006). Youths convicted of murder are more likely than adult murderers to enter prison with LWOP sentences (Human Rights Watch 2005).

In *Graham v. Florida*, 130 S.Ct. 2011(2010), the Court applied *Roper's* diminished responsibility rationale to youths convicted of non-homicide crimes whom judges sentenced to life without parole. Historically, the Court's Eighth Amendment proportionality analyses had distinguished between capital sentences and long terms of imprisonment, and deferred to legislative decisions about deserved punishments (Feld 2008). However, *Graham* concluded that offenders who did not kill were "categorically less deserving of the most serious forms of punishment than are murderers." Because of juveniles' diminished responsibility, those who did not kill have "twice-diminished moral culpability. The age of the offender and the nature of the crime" categorically precluded the penultimate penalty for non-homicide crimes as well. *Graham* emphasized youths' immature judgment and reduced self-control, susceptibility to negative peer influences, and transitory personality development. *Graham* asserted that subsequent research in developmental psychology and neuroscience bolstered its *Roper* conclusion that adolescents' reduced culpability required somewhat mitigated sentences:

> [D]evelopments in psychology and brain science continue to show fundamental differences between juvenile and adult minds. For example, parts of the brain involved in behavior control continue to mature through late adolescence.

Graham's Eighth Amendment analyses referred to many factors—penal justifications for sentencing practices, *Roper's* intuition about adolescent developmental differences, states' laws and sentencing practices, and international law—and neuroscience provided one more piece of confirmatory data in the Court's holding (Maroney 2009).

Although *Graham* extended *Roper's* rationale of youths' diminished culpability, it granted the 129 youths convicted of non-homicide crimes and serving LWOP sentences limited relief. The Court only required states to "give defendants like Graham some meaningful opportunity to obtain release based on demonstrated maturity and rehabilitation," but cautioned that the opportunity for parole review "does not require the state to release that offender during his natural life." *Graham* distinguished the lesser seriousness of non-homicide crimes from murder and does not affect the seven thousand youths convicted of murder who serve LWOP or life sentences or others who serve very lengthy sentences (Nellis and King 2009).

B. Adolescents' Legal Competence

Contemporary delinquency proceedings have become much more procedurally formal than those envisioned a century ago. The increased legal complexity makes greater demands on children's ability to make legal decisions and to participate in proceedings. However, developmental psychologists questions youths' competence to understand and to participate or to waive rights. Adolescents' limited competence stems from many of the same developmental and neurobiological features reviewed above.

Progressive reformers envisioned a procedurally informal juvenile court that acted in the child's best interests. *Gault* (1967) granted delinquents a constitutional right to counsel and the Fifth Amendment privilege against self-incrimination, and initiated a procedural convergence between juvenile and criminal courts. *Gault* and its progeny made delinquency proceedings more formal and complex and require youths to make difficult legal decisions. Adolescents' adjudicative competency has become more critical as states' get-tough policies increased the direct and collateral consequences of delinquency adjudications (Feld 2003*b*).

Developmental psychologists have examined adolescents' adjudicative competence, their ability to exercise or waive *Miranda* rights or the right to counsel, and their capacity to participate in legal proceedings. The research questions whether juveniles possess the cognitive ability, psycho-social maturity, and judgment necessary to exercise legal rights. It convincingly indicates that younger and mid-adolescent youths exhibit substantial deficits in understanding and competence compared with adults. Many of the developmental features reviewed previously—impaired judgment, risk-calculus, short-term perspective, and the like—contribute to their reduced competence. The Supreme Court in *Graham* noted how these characteristics adversely affected juveniles' ability to exercise procedural rights and impaired their defense representation:

> [T]he features that distinguish juveniles from adults also put them at a significant disadvantage in criminal proceedings. Juveniles mistrust adults and have limited understandings of the criminal justice system and the roles of the institutional actors within it. They are less likely than adults to work with their lawyers to aid in their defense. Difficulty in weighing long-term consequences; a corresponding impulsiveness; and reluctance to trust defense counsel seen as part of the adult world a rebellious youth rejects, all can lead to poor decisions by one charged with a juvenile offense. These factors are likely to impair the quality of a juvenile defendant's representation. (*Graham* 2010).

This section reviews the legal contexts within which questions arise about adolescents' adjudicative competence—competence to stand trial and ability to waive *Miranda* and the right to counsel. Despite clear developmental differences between youths and adults, the Court and most states do not provide additional procedural safeguards to protect juveniles from their own immaturity and vulnerability. Instead, they use adult standards to gauge juveniles' competence to stand trial and to waive *Miranda* rights and counsel. Because of differences in ability and competence, formal equality produces practical inequality for juveniles in the justice system.

1. *Adolescents' Competence to Stand Trial*

As juvenile courts have become more formal and punitive, analysts increasingly question juveniles' ability to function in complex legal settings in which prosecutors and judges may impose significant consequences. As states transfer more and younger juveniles to criminal courts, judges face even more difficult questions about youths' competence to stand trial as adults because of developmental immaturity. Competence is the constitutional prerequisite to the exercise of other procedural rights and to assure a fair trial. To be competent to stand trial, a criminal defendant must have "sufficient present ability to consult with his lawyer with a reasonable degree of rational understanding [and have a] rational as well as factual under-standing of the proceedings against him," and have the capacity "to assist in preparing his defense" (*Dusky v. United States,* 362 U.S. 402 [1960]; *Drope v. Missouri,* 420 U.S. 162 [1975]). Judges evaluate a youth's competence by assessing her ability to "(1) understand the charges and the basic elements of the adversary system (under-standing), (2) appreciate one's situation as a defendant in a criminal prosecution (appreciation), and (3) relate pertinent information to counsel concerning the facts of the case (reasoning)" (Bonnie and Grisso 2000, 76).

Developmental psychologists argue that immaturity per se produces deficits of understanding, impairment of judgment, and inability to assist counsel similar to those produced by severe mental illness or developmental disability (Grisso 1997a, 1997b, 2000; Scott and Grisso 2005). For adolescents, generic developmental features adversely affect their ability to understand proceedings, to receive infor-mation, to communicate with and assist counsel, and to make rational decisions, and render them incompetent (Grisso 1997b; Scott and Grisso 2005). About half the states address juveniles' competency to stand trial in statutes, court rules of procedure or case law, and conclude that delinquents have a fundamental right not to be tried while incompetent (Scott and Grisso 2005).

Even after states recognize juveniles' right to a competency determination, they differ over the appropriate standard to apply. Some courts apply the adult competency standard in delinquency and criminal prosecutions because both proceedings may result in a child's loss of liberty. Other jurisdictions opt for a more relaxed competency standard in delinquency than in criminal proceedings, because juvenile hearings are less complex than criminal trials (Scott and Grisso 2005).

2. *Juveniles' Ability to Exercise Legal Rights: Miranda Rights*

After *Gault* applied the privilege against self-incrimination to delinquency proceed-ings, juveniles also must receive a *Miranda,* 384 U.S. 436 (1966) warning prior to custodial interrogation. The Court in *Haley v. Ohio,* 332 U.S. 596 (1948), and *Gallegos v. Colorado,* 370 U.S. 49 (1962) cautioned judges closely to scrutinize the effects of youthfulness and inexperience on the voluntariness of statements, and it excluded confessions extracted from fourteen- and fifteen-year-old youths. *Gault* reiterated the Court's concerns about the impact of youthfulness on the exercise of legal rights. However, in *Fare v. Michael C.*, 442 U.S. 707 (1979), the Court considered a *Miranda* waiver given by a sixteen-and-a-half-year-old who had several prior arrests. *Fare* repudiated the Court's earlier concern about juveniles' vulnerability to coercion and held that trial judges should use the adult standard—"knowing, intelligent, and voluntary" under the "totality of the circumstances"—to evaluate juveniles' waivers of rights. *Fare* rejected the view that developmental differences between juveniles and adults required different procedures and insisted that children, like adults, must assert legal rights clearly and unambiguously (Feld 2000b). The Court in *Yarborough v. Alvarado*, 541 U.S. 652 (2004) rejected youthfulness and inexperience as special factors when deciding whether juveniles are in custody and entitled to a *Miranda* warning.

As a result of *Fare* and *Alvarado*, federal constitutional law and the vast majority of states[3] treat juveniles as the functional equals of adults in the interrogation room. Just as with an adult, trial judges must decide whether a youth made a waiver of her rights "knowingly, intelligently, and voluntarily." The "totality of the circumstances" includes factors about the offender—e.g., age, education, IQ, and prior contacts with police—and circumstances surrounding the interrogation—e.g., the location, methods, and length of interrogation (Feld 2006a; 2006b). While appellate courts identify many factors for trial judges to consider, they remit the weighing of those factors to their discretion (Grisso 1980; Feld 2006a). In practice, most judges apply the totality standard very conservatively, find valid *Miranda* waivers whenever police testify that a juvenile said she understood her rights, and often fail to exclude even obviously invalid waivers and confessions (Feld 1984, 2006a). Coercive interrogation techniques, young age *and* mental deficiencies do not prevent trial judges from finding and appellate courts from upholding youths' *Miranda* waivers as voluntary (Feld 1984; 2006a). Trial judges admit confessions made by ten-year-old children and by illiterate or developmentally disabled juveniles whom psychologists characterize as incapable of abstract reasoning (see, e.g., *People v. Cheatham*, 551 N.W. 2d 355 [Mich. 1996]; Drizin and Leo 2004; Feld 2006a).

Although judges use the adult legal standard to gauge juveniles' waivers of rights, developmental and social psychologists question whether juveniles have the cognitive capacity or psycho-social maturity to make a valid waiver. The foremost research, by Thomas Grisso, reports that most juveniles simply do not understand a *Miranda* warning or counsel advisory well enough to waive rights in a knowing and intelligent manner (Grisso 1980; 1981; Feld 2000b). Without adequate understanding, juveniles are at a comparative disadvantage with adults to exercise rights. Juveniles most frequently misunderstood the right to consult with an attorney and to have a lawyer present when police questioned them (Grisso 1980, 1981). Younger juveniles exhibited even poorer understanding of their *Miranda* rights than did mid-adolescents (Grisso 1981). Even though juveniles sixteen years of age and older exhibited a level of understanding comparable with adults, substantial minorities of both groups failed to grasp at least some components of the standard warning.

Although *Miranda* focuses primarily on suspects' understanding of the words of the warning, a valid waiver of rights also requires the ability to appreciate legal consequences and to make rational decisions. Juveniles often fail to appreciate the significance of rights or to grasp the basic idea of a right as something they can exercise without adverse consequences (Grisso 1997a, 1997b; Grisso et al. 2003). They are more likely than adults to conceive of a right as something that authorities permit them to do, but which they may unilaterally retract or withhold (Grisso 2000). Children's lower social status and societal expectations of their obedience to authority may make them more vulnerable to interrogation techniques than adults. For example, when youth deal with authority figures, they may speak less assertively and use indirect patterns of speech to avoid conflict (Ainsworth 1993). During interrogation, youth respond more passively and acquiesce to police suggestions more easily (Kaban and Tobey 1999). Thus, *Fare's* requirement that juveniles invoke *Miranda* rights with adultlike technical precision conflicts with normal social responses and verbal styles of most delinquents.

Empirical studies of routine interrogations of older juveniles and the characteristics of defendants who gave proven false confessions shed light on police practices and developmental psychologists concerns about adolescents' vulnerability. Feld (2006a, 2006b) reported that 80 percent of the sixteen- and seventeen-year-old juveniles charged with a felony waived their *Miranda* rights. These rates are very similar to the high waiver rates reported in studies of adults (Leo 1996; Gudjonsson 2003). Once officers secured a *Miranda* waiver, they used the same two-pronged strategy they employed with adults to overcome suspects' resistance and to enable them more readily to admit responsibility.[4] Feld's (2006a, 2006b) research on older juveniles is remarkably congruent with Leo's (1996, 2008) observations of interrogation of adults. About the same proportion waived their *Miranda* rights, following which police used the same strategies and tactics to question them. These juveniles responded to those tactics, co-operated or resisted, and provided incriminating evidence at about the same rate as did adults. Police interrogated the vast majority of these juveniles for a brief period of time (Feld 2006b). In short, the law treats juveniles just like adults, and police question them just as they do older suspects.

Drizin and Leo (2004) examined 125 cases of proven false confessions based on DNA-exonerations. Three factors consistently contributed to police-induced false confessions—youthfulness, coercive interrogation techniques, and prolonged questioning. Youths' diminished competence relative to adults increased their susceptibility to psychological techniques and the concomitant risks of false confessions. Their limited understanding of rights or appreciation of legal consequences increases the likelihood that they will waive *Miranda* rights (Bonnie and Grisso 2000; Redlich and Goodman 2003; Redlich et al. 2004; Kassin and Gudjonsson 2005). Juveniles' imperfect ability to think strategically makes them more likely than adults to assume responsibility out of misguided feelings of loyalty to peers (Grisso et al. 2003). They have a greater tendency than adults to comply with authority figures and to acquiesce to police (Gudjonsson 2003; Tanenhaus and Drizin 2003). Interrogation techniques designed for adults—especially coercive or prolonged questioning—may prove especially problematic when deployed against young suspects. Police obtained 35 percent of all of the proven false confessions from youths younger than eighteen years of age and 19 percent from youths aged fifteen or younger, even though younger juveniles comprise a very small proportion of the serious offender population (Drizin and Leo 2004).

3. *Waivers of Counsel*

Gault (1967) likened the seriousness of a delinquency proceeding to a felony prosecution and granted juveniles a constitutional right to counsel. However, *Gault* only required a judge to advise a child and parent of a right to counsel and, if indigent, to have counsel appointed. The Court also noted that juveniles could waive counsel as long as they did so knowingly, intelligently, and voluntarily. Most states do not use special measures to protect youths from their own immaturity, such as mandatory appointment of counsel (Feld 1984, 1993). As with *Miranda* waivers, formal equality produces practical inequality—lawyers represent juveniles at lower rates than they do adult criminal defendants (Feld 1988*b*, 1991; Harlow 2000; Burrus and Kempf-Leonard 2002).

Waiver of counsel is the most common reason that so many juveniles are unrepresented (Feld 1989; ABA 1995; Cooper, Puritz, and Shang 1998; Berkheiser 2002).[5] As with *Miranda*, judges use the adult standard—knowing, intelligent, and voluntary—to gauge juveniles' waivers of counsel (*Fare v. Michael C.* 1979; *Johnson v. Zerbst*, 304 U.S. 458 [1938]; Berkheiser 2002). They consider the same factors—age, education, IQ, prior contacts with police, or experience with delinquency trials—to decide whether youths understood and voluntarily waived counsel (Feld 1984; 1989; 2006*a*). Many juveniles waive counsel without consulting with either a parent or an attorney (Berkheiser 2002). Judges are supposed to give a clear advisory of the right to counsel and then determine whether a child possesses sufficient ability to represent herself, whether she understands the charges, proceedings, and potential consequences, and whether she appreciates the disadvantages of waiving counsel (*In re Christopher H.*, 596 S.E.2d 500 [SC App. 2004]). Appellate cases reveal that judges frequently omit any counsel advisory, often neglect to create a record of a waiver colloquy, and readily accept waivers from obviously incompetent children (Berkheiser 2002).

Developmental psychological research on adolescents' adjudicative competence raises further doubts about juveniles' ability to exercise legal rights. As noted earlier, a defendant must have the ability to understand legal proceedings; to provide, receive, and understand information from counsel; and to make reasonable choices in order to be competent to stand trial (*Dusky v. United States*, 362 U.S. 402 [1960]; Bonnie and Grisso 2000; Grisso 2000). Grisso's research on adolescents' adjudicative competence, like his earlier research on youths' competence to exercise *Miranda* rights, found significant age-related differences in understanding and judgment (Grisso et al. 2003). Most juveniles younger than thirteen or fourteen years of age exhibited the same degree of impairment as severely mentally ill adult defendants and lacked basic ability to understand, assist, or participate in their defense (Bonnie and Grisso 2000; Grisso et al. 2003; Scott and Steinberg 2008). A significant proportion of juveniles younger than sixteen lacked competence to stand trial, to make legal decisions, or to assist counsel, and many older youths exhibited substantial impairments (Grisso et al. 2003). Even adolescents who may be legally competent in terms of formal understanding often make poorer legal decisions than do adults because of their more limited time-perspective, emphasis on short-term versus long-term consequences, and concern about peer approval (Scott and Grisso 1997*a*, 1997*b*; Steinberg and Cauffman 1999; Bonnie and Grisso 2000).

The research on juveniles' adjudicative competence reinforces studies of their ability to waive *Miranda* rights and counsel. Many juveniles simply do not understand the meaning of a *Miranda* warning or a counsel advisory well enough to make a valid waiver. Although older juveniles understood *Miranda* warnings about as well as adults, substantial minorities of both groups failed to grasp at least some elements of the warning (Grisso 1997*a*, 1997*b*). Even youths who understand the words of a *Miranda* warning or advisory of counsel may not appreciate the function or importance of rights as well as adults (Grisso 1980, 1997*a*, 1997*b*, 2003; ABA 1995). Research reports significant age-related differences between adolescents' and young adults' adjudicative competence, legal understanding, and quality of judgment (Bonnie and Grisso 2000; Grisso et al 2003). Low IQ scores interacted with age, and youths' with low IQs performed significantly worse than did either low-IQ adults or same-aged youths (Grisso et al 2003; Scott and Grisso 2005). And, low-IQ youths comprise a larger proportion of youths involved with juvenile courts than in the general population.

More than forty years after *Gault* granted delinquents a constitutional right to counsel, the delivery of quality legal services in juvenile courts remains problematic. Many juveniles, including those charged with serious crimes, waive their right to counsel (Feld 1993; Feld and Schaefer 2010). Since the late 1990s, the American Bar Association and the National Juvenile Defender Center have conducted a series of state-by-state assessments and report that many, if not most, juveniles appear without counsel. They also report that when juveniles are represented, their lawyers often provide substandard representation because of obstacles to effective advocacy such as inadequate support services, heavy caseloads, and a lack of investigators or dispositional advisors (Feld and Schaefer 2010). Moreover, regardless of how inadequately lawyers perform, juvenile courts seem incapable of correcting their own errors. Defense attorneys rarely, if ever, appeal adverse decisions and often lack a record with which to challenge an invalid waiver of counsel (Feld and Schaefer 2010).

The collateral consequences of delinquency convictions amplify the procedural deficiencies of juvenile courts (Feld 2003*b*). In addition to the direct consequences, states consider prior delinquency convictions to transfer youths to criminal and to enhance their criminal sentences as adults (Feld 2003*b*). In addition, delinquency convictions may provide the predicate for sex offender registration, while drug convictions may bar youths and their families from public housing.

V. CONCLUSION

Recent developmental psychological and neuroscience research has taught us scientifically much more than we previously knew about how children think and act, and how their thought processes differ from adults. And these studies reaffirm *Roper*'s intuition that juveniles differ from adults. The research findings reinforce the historic recognition that youths' legal competence and criminal responsibility are less than those of adults and support the rationale for a separate juvenile justice system (Scott and Steinberg 2008). After two decades of punitive, get-tough policies, it is appropriate to re-examine the implications of research on competence and culpability for sentencing youths and protecting their procedural rights.

Roper and *Graham*'s diminished responsibility rationale provide a broader foundation to formally recognize youthfulness as a categorical mitigating factor in criminal sentencing. Because adolescents lack the judgment, appreciation of consequences, and self-control of adults, they deserve shorter sentences when they cause the same harms. Adolescents' personalities are in transition, and it is unjust and irrational to continue harshly punishing a fifty- or sixty-year-old person for the crime that he, as an irresponsible child, committed several decades earlier.

Roper and *Graham*'s categorical treatment of youths' diminished criminal responsibility provides the rationale for a "youth discount" (Feld 1997, 1999, 2008). *Roper* and *Graham* used age as a proxy for reduced culpability because no better, more reliable bases exist on which to individualize sentences. Because all adolescents share general characteristics of immature judgment, impulsiveness, and lack of self-control, all young offenders in criminal courts should receive categorical reductions of adult sentences. A categorical rule of youthful mitigation is preferable to individualized sentencing discretion for two reasons. The first is our inability either to define or identify what constitutes adultlike culpability among offending youths. Despite developmental differences, clinicians lack the tools with which to assess youths' impulsivity, foresight, or preference for risk in ways that relate to maturity of judgment and criminal responsibility. The second reason to treat youthfulness categorically is the inability of judges or juries to fairly weigh an abstract consideration of youthfulness as a mitigating factor against the aggravating reality of a horrific crime. A substantial youth discount of the sentences imposed on adults provides a sliding scale of severity that corresponds with the increasingly diminished responsibility of younger offenders. A sliding scale of diminished criminal responsibility gives the largest sentence reductions to the youngest, least mature offenders. Recognizing youthfulness as a mitigating factor would preclude imposing LWOP and other lengthy sentences on younger offenders.

The decades since *Gault* have witnessed a procedural as well as substantive convergence between juvenile and criminal courts. The greater procedural formality and adversarial nature of delinquency proceedings reflects juvenile courts' shift in emphases from rehabilitating offenders to protecting public safety. Despite these changes, most states do not provide delinquents with procedural safeguards that provide formal or functional protections comparable to those of adult criminal defendants (Feld 2003*b*). Juveniles waive their *Miranda* rights and right to counsel at trial under a standard—"knowing, intelligent, and voluntary" under the "totality of circumstances"—that is unlikely to discern whether they actually understand and are competent to exercise the rights they relinquish. The high rates of waiver of counsel constitute an indictment of the entire delinquency process, because assistance of counsel is the essential prerequisite to the exercise of other procedural safeguards. The denial of jury trials calls into question the validity and reliability of delinquency adjudications, both for initial dispositions and for collateral use such as sentence enhancements (Feld 2003*b*). In short, states do not provide juveniles with special procedural safeguards to protect them from their own immaturity and vulnerability *nor* do they provide them with the full panoply of criminal procedural safeguards to protect them from punitive state intervention. Instead, juvenile courts assure that youths continue to "receive the worst of both worlds"—treating juvenile offenders just like adult criminal defendants when formal equality redounds to their disadvantage, and providing less effective juvenile court procedures when they provide an advantage to the state.

It will take political courage for legislators to enact laws that benefit easily demonized groups, such as young offenders. It will take even greater political courage when enacting responsible youth crime policy exposes a politician to a charge by her opponent that she is "soft on crime." Politicians overreacted during the 1990s and enacted get-tough waiver and criminal sentencing laws—offense exclusion, prosecutorial direct file, and mandatory LWOP sentences—that are inhumane, unjust, and counterproductive (CDC 2007). Public opinion supports policies to rehabilitate serious young offenders to reduce future crime, rather than simply to incarcerate them for longer periods (Nagin et al. 2006). Our greater scientific understanding of adolescent development, positive public support for less punitive policies, and low crime rates may strengthen legislators' resolve to promote just and sensible youth and crime policies. A juvenile justice system based on adolescents' diminished criminal responsibility and impaired adjudicative competence must provide youths with shorter sentences and greater procedural safeguards than they currently receive and protect them from harsh criminal justice policies.

NOTES

1. The U.N. Convention on the Rights of the Child [CRC] recognizes the special needs of children and their potential for rehabilitation. Because sentences of life without possibility of parole flatly contradict the idea that children have the potential to change, the CRC (Article 37a) provides that "Neither capital punishment *nor life imprisonment without possibility of release* shall be imposed for offences committed by persons below eighteen years of age."

2. Sixty percent of these youth were first offenders. The vast majority were convicted of murder, but more than one-quarter were convicted of felony murder, where a youth participated in a robbery or burglary during which a co-defendant committed murder without his knowledge or intent (Human Rights Watch 2005, 1–2).

3. Ten states mandate additional procedural requirements for juveniles beyond the "totality" approach endorsed by *Fare* (Feld 2006*a*, 2006*b*). These jurisdictions require the presence of a parent or other "interested adult" at a juvenile's interrogation as a prerequisite to a valid waiver of *Miranda* rights. These states presume that most juveniles lack competence to exercise *Miranda* rights unaided and require an adult's assistance. They assume that a parent's presence would enhance juveniles' understanding of rights, mitigate the dangers of unreliable statements, provide an independent witness of what occurs during interrogation, and reduce police coercion (e.g., *State v. Presha,* 748 A.2d 1108 [N.J. 2000]). Most commentators endorse parental-presence safeguards even though empirical research and experience provide substantial reason to question the validity of the assumptions or the rule's usefulness (Feld 2006*a*, 2006*b*).

4. Maximization techniques intimidate suspects and impress on them the futility of denial, while minimization techniques provide moral justifications or face-saving alternatives to enable them to confess (Leo 1996, 2008; Kassin and Gudjonsson 2004; Kassin 2005).

5. Several other factors contribute to juveniles' appearance without counsel. Public-defender legal services may be inadequate in non-urban areas (ABA 1995; Feld and Schaefer 2010). Judges may give cursory advisories, imply that a rights colloquy and waiver are just a legal technicality, and readily find waivers by juveniles in order to ease courts' administrative burdens (ABA 1995; Cooper, Puritz, and Shang 1998; Berkheiser 2002; Bookser 2004). Judges may not appoint counsel if they expect to impose a non-custodial sentence (Lefstein, Stapleton, and Teitelbaum 1971; Feld 1989; Burrus and Kempf-Leonard 2002).

REFERENCES

Adolescent Development and Juvenile Justice. John D. and Catherine T. MacArthur Foundation, available at www.http//adjj.org.

Ainsworth, Janet E. 1993. "In a Different Register: The Pragmatics of Powerlessness in Police Interrogation." *Yale Law Journal* 103: 259.

Allen, Francis A. 1964. "Legal Values and the Rehabilitative Ideal." In *The Borderland of the Criminal Law: Essays in Law and Criminology*. Chicago: University of Chicago Press.

American Bar Association. 1995. *A Call for Justice: An Assessment of Access to Counsel and Quality of Representation in Delinquency Proceedings*. Washington, DC: American Bar Association Juvenile Justice Center.

American Friends Service Committee. 1971. *Struggle for Justice*. New York: Hill and Wang.

Aronson, Jay D. 2007. "Brain Imaging, Culpability and the Juvenile Death Penalty." *Psychology, Public Policy and Law* 13:115.

———. 2009. "Neuroscience and Juvenile Justice." *Akron Law Review* 42: 917–29.

Arrendondo, David E. 2003. "Child Development, Children's Mental Health and the Juvenile Justice System." *Stanford Law and Policy Review* 14: 13.

Beckett, Katherine, and Theodore Sasson. 2000. *The Politics of Injustice: Crime and Punishment in America*. Thousand Oaks, CA: Pine Forge Press.

Berkheiser, Mary. 2002. "The Fiction of Juvenile Right to Counsel: Waiver in the Juvenile Courts." *Florida Law Review* 54: 577–686.

Bernard, Thomas. 1992. *Cycles of Juvenile Justice*. New York: Oxford University Press.

Bishop, Donna M. 2005. "The Role of Race and Ethnicity in Juvenile Justice Processing." In *Our Children, Their Children: Confronting Racial and Ethnic Differences in American Juveniles Justice* ed. Darnell F. Hawkins and Kimberly Kempf-Leonard. Chicago: University of Chicago Press.

Bishop, Donna M., Charles E. Frazier, Lonn Lanza-Kaduce, and Lawrence Winner. 1996. "The Transfer of Juveniles to Criminal Court: Does it Make a Difference?" *Crime and Delinquency* 42: 171–91.

Blumstein, Alfred, and Daniel Cork. 1996. "Linking Gun Availability to Youth Gun Violence." *Law and Contemporary Problems* 59: 5–24.

Bonnie, Richard, and Thomas Grisso. 2000. "Adjudicative Competence and Youthful Offenders." In *Youth on Trial: A Developmental Perspective on Juvenile Courts,* ed. Thomas Grisso and Robert G. Schwartz. Chicago: University of Chicago Press.

Bookser, Susanne M. 2004. "Making Gault Meaningful: Access to Counsel and Quality of Representation in Delinquency Proceedings for Indigent Youth." *Whittier Journal of Child and Family Advocacy* 3: 297–328.

Bortner, M. A., Marjorie S. Zatz, and Darnell F. Hawkins. 2000. "Race and Transfer: Empirical Research and Social Context." In *The Changing Borders of Juvenile Justice: Waiver of Adolescents to the Criminal Court,* ed. Jeffrey Fagan and Franklin E. Zimring. Chicago: University of Chicago Press.

Brink, David O. 2004. "Immaturity, Normative Competence and Juvenile Transfer: How (Not) to Punish Minors for Major Crimes." *Texas Law Review* 82: 1555.

Cauffman, Elizabeth, and Laurence Steinberg. 1995. "The Cognitive and Affective Influences on Adolescent Decision-Making." *Temple Law Review* 68: 1763.

Centers for Disease Control and Prevention, U.S. Department of Health and Human Services. November 30, 2007. "Effects on Violence of Laws and Policies Facilitating the

Transfer of Youth from the Juvenile to the Adult Justice System." Morbidity and
   Mortality Weekly Report, vol. 56, No. RR-9. Atlanta, GA: CDCP.
Cooper, N. Lee, Patricia Puritz, and Wendy Shang. 1998. "Fulfilling the Promise of *In
   re Gault*: Advancing the Role of Lawyers for Children." *Wake Forest Law Review*
   33: 651–79.
Cork, Daniel. 1999. "Examining Space-Time Interaction in City-Level Homicide Data:
   Crack Markets and the Diffusion of Guns Among Youth." *Journal of Quantitative
   Criminology* 15: 379–406.
Dahl, Ronald E. 2004. "Adolescent Brain Development: A Period of Vulnerabilities and
   Opportunities." *Annals of the New York Academy of Sciences* 1021: 1–22.
Deitch, Michele, Amanda Barstow, Leslie Lukens, and Ryan Reyna. 2009. *From Time Out
   to Hard Time: Young Children in the Adult Criminal Justice System.* Austin, TX. Lyndon
   B. Johnson School of Public Affairs.
Denno, Deborah W. 2006. "The Scientific Shortcomings of *Roper v. Simmons.*" *Ohio State
   Journal of Criminal Law* 3: 379–96.
DiIulio, John. 1995. The Coming of the Super-predators. *Weekly Standard*, November 19,
   23–29.
Drizin, Steven A., and Richard A. Leo. 2004. "The Problem of False Confessions in the
   Post-DNA World." *North Carolina Law Review* 82: 891.
Fagan, Jeffrey, and Franklin E. Zimring, eds. 2000. *The Changing Borders of Juvenile
   Justice: Waiver of Adolescents to the Criminal Court.* Chicago: University of
   Chicago Press.
Feld, Barry C. 1976. *Neutralizing Inmate Violence: Juvenile Offenders in Institutions.*
   Cambridge, MA: Ballinger.
———. 1984. "Criminalizing Juvenile Justice: Rules of Procedure for Juvenile Courts."
   Minnesota Law Review 69: 141–276.
———. 1988a. "The Juvenile Court Meets the Principle of Offense: Punishment,
   Treatment, and the Difference it Makes." Boston University Law Review
   68: 821–915.
———. 1988b. "*In re Gault* Revisited: A Cross-state Comparison of the Right to Counsel in
   Juvenile Court." *Crime and Delinquency* 34: 393–424.
———. 1989. "The Right to Counsel in Juvenile Court: An Empirical Study of When
   Lawyers Appear and the Difference They Make." *Journal of Criminal Law and
   Criminology* 79: 1185–346.
———. 1991. "Justice by Geography: Urban, Suburban, and Rural Variations in
   Juvenile Justice Administration." *Journal of Criminal Law and Criminology*
   82: 156–210.
———. 1993. *Justice fior Children: The Right to Counsel and the Juvenile Courts.* Boston:
   Northeastern University Press.
———. 1997. "Abolish the Juvenile Court: Youthfulness, Criminal Responsibility and
   Sentencing Policy." *Journal of Criminal Law and Criminology* 88: 68–136.
———. 1998. "Juvenile and Criminal Justice Systems' Responses to Youth Violence." In
   Youth Violence, edited by Michael Tonry and Mark H. Moore. Vol. 24 of *Crime and
   Justice: A Review of Research,* edited by Michael Tonry. Chicago: University of Chicago
   Press.
———. 1999. *Bad Kids: Race and the Transformation of the Juvenile Court.* New York:
   Oxford University Press.

———. 2000a. "Legislative Exclusion of Offenses from Juvenile Court Jurisdiction: A History and Critique." In *The Changing Borders of Juvenile Justice: Waiver of Adolescents to the Criminal Court,* ed. Jeffrey Fagan and Franklin E. Zimring. Chicago: University of Chicago Press.

———. 2000b. "Juveniles = Waiver of Legal Rights: Confessions, *Miranda*, and the Right to Counsel." In *Youth on Trial: A Developmental Perspective on Juvenile Courts,* ed. Thomas Grisso and Robert G. Schwartz. Chicago: University of Chicago Press.

———. 2003a. "Race, Politics and Juvenile Justice: The Warren Court and the Conservative 'Backlash.'" *Minnesota Law Review* 87: 1447–77.

———. 2003b. "The Constitutional Tension Between Apprendi and McKeiver: Sentence Enhancements Based on Delinquency Convictions and the Quality of Justice in Juvenile Courts." *Wake Forest Law Review* 38: 1111–224.

———. 2006a. "Juveniles' Competence to Exercise *Miranda* Rights: An Empirical Study of Policy and Practice." *Minnesota Law Review* 91: 26–100.

———. 2006b. "Police Interrogation of Juveniles: An Empirical Study of Policy and Practice." *Journal of Criminal Law and Criminology* 97: 219–316.

———. 2008. "A Slower Form of Death: Implications of *Roper v. Simmons* for Juveniles Sentence to Life Without Parole." *Notre Dame Journal of Law, Ethics, and Public Policy* 22: 9–65.

———. 2009. "Violent Girls or Relabeled Status Offenders? An Alternative Interpretation of the Data." *Crime and Delinquency* 55: 241–65.

Feld, Barry C., and Shelly Schaefer. 2010. "The Right to Counsel in Juvenile Court: Law Reform to Deliver Legal Services and Reduce Justice by Geography." *Criminology and Public Policy* 9: 327.

Feld, Barry C., and Donna M. Bishop. 2011. "Transfer of Juveniles to Criminal Court." In *Oxford Handbook on Juvenile Crime and Juvenile Justice*, ed. Barry C. Feld and Donna M. Bishop. New York: Oxford University Press.

Frase, Richard S. 2005. "Excessive Prison Sentences, Punishment Goals and the Eighth Amendment: 'Proportionality' Relative to What?" *Minnesota Law Review* 89: 571.

Fox, James Alan. 1996. *Trends in Juvenile Violnce: A Report to the United States Attorney General on Current and Future Rates of Juvenile Offending*. Washington, DC: U.S. Department of Justice.

Furby, Lita, and Ruth Beyth-Marom. 1992. *Risk-Taking in Adolescence: A Decision-making Perspective*. Washington, DC. Carnegie Council on Adolescent Development.

Garland, David. 2001. *The Culture of Control: Crime and Social Order in Contemporary Society*. Chicago: University of Chicago Press.

Grisso, Thomas. 1980. "Juveniles' Capacities to Waive *Miranda* Rights: An Empirical Analysis." *California Law Review* 68: 1134–66.

———. 1981. *Juveniles' Waiver of Rights: Legal and Psychological Competence* (New York: Plenum Press).

———. 1997a. "The Competence of Adolescents as Trial Defendants." *Psychology, Public Police and Law* 3: 3–11.

———. 1997b. "Juvenile Competency to Stand Trial: Questions in an Era of Punitive Reform." *Criminal Justice* (Fall 1997): 7.

———. 2000. "What We Know about Youths' Capacities as Trial Defendants." In *Youth on Trial: A Developmental Perspective on Juvenile Courts,* ed. Thomas Grisso and Robert G. Schwartz. Chicago: University of Chicago Press.

Grisso, Thomas, and Robert Schwartz, eds. 2000. *Youth on Trial: A Developmental Perspective on Juvenile Justice*. Chicago: University of Chicago Press.

Grisso, Thomas, Laurence Steinberg, JenniferWoolard, Elizabeth Cauffman, Elizabeth Scott, Sandra Graham, Fran Lexcen, N. Dickon Reppucci, and Robert Schwartz. 2003. "Juveniles' Competence to Stand Trial: A Comparison of Adolescents' and Adults' Capacities as Trial Defendants." *Law and Human Behavior* 27:333–63.

Gruber, Staci A., and Deborah A. Yurgelun-Todd. 2006. "Neurobiology and the Law: A Role in Juvenile Justice." *Ohio State Journal of Criminal Law* 3: 321.

Gudjonsson, Gisli H. 2003. *The Psychology of Interrogations and Confessions: A Handbook*. Wiley Series in Psychology of Crime, Policing, and Law. New York: Wiley.

Harlow, Caroline Wolf. 2000. *Defense Counsel in Criminal Cases*. Washington, DC: Bureau of Justice Statistics, U.S. Department of Justice.

Hawkins, Darnell F., and Kimberly Kempf-Leonard. 2005. *Our Children, Their Children: Confronting Racial and Ethnic Differences in American Juveniles Justice*. Chicago: University of Chicago Press.

Human Rights Watch/Amnesty International. 2005. *The Rest of Their Lives: Life Without Parole for Child Offenders in the United States*. New York: Amnesty International. http://hrw.org/reports/2005/us1005/.

Juskiewicz, Jolanta. 2000. "Youth Crime/Adult Time." http://www.buildingblocksforyouth.org/ycat/ycat.html.

Kaban, Barbara, and Ann E. Tobey. 1999. "When Police Question Children, Are Protections Adequate?" *Juvenile Center for Children and Courts* 1: 151.

Kandel, Eric R. et al., eds. 2000. *Principals of Neuroscience*. New York: McGraw-Hill Medical.

Kassin, Saul. 2005. "On the Psychology of Confessions." *American Psychologist* 60: 215.

Kassin, Saul, and Gisli H. Gudjonsson. 2004. "The Psychology of Confessions: A Review of the Literature and Issues." *Psychological Sciences in Public Interest* 5: 33.

Kurlychek, Megan, and Brian D. Johnson. 2004. "The Juvenile Penalty: A Comparison of Juvenile and Young Adult Sentencing Outcomes in Criminal Court." *Criminology* 42: 485–517.

———. 2010. "Juvenility and Punishment: Sentencing Juveniles in Adult Criminal Court." *Criminology* 48: 725–57.

Lefstein, Norman et al. 1969. "In Search of Juvenile Justice: Gault and Its Implementation," *Law and Society Review* 3: 491–562.

Leo Richard A. 1996. "Inside the Interrogation Room." *Journal of Criminal Law and Criminology* 86: 266.

———. 2008. *Police Interrogation in America*. Cambridge, MA: Harvard University Press.

Lipsey, Mark W. 1992. "Juvenile Delinquency Treatment: A Meta-Analytic Inquiry into the Variability of Effects." In *Meta-Analysis for Explanation*, ed. Thomas D. Cook, Harris Cooper, David S. Cordray, Heidi Hartmann, Larry V. Hedges, Richard J. Light, Thomas A. Louis, and Frederick Mosteller. New York: Russell Sage Foundation.

Lipton, Douglas, Robert Martinson, and Judith Wilks. 1975. *The Effectiveness of Correctional Intervention: A Survey of Treatment Evaluation Studies*. New York: Praeger.

Mack, Julian W. 1909. "The Juvenile Court." *Harvard Law Review* 23: 104–22.

Maroney, Terry A. 2009. "The False Promise of Adolescent Brain Science in Juvenile Justice." *Notre Dame Law Review* 85: 89–176.

Martinson, Robert. 1974. "What Works? Questions and Answers About Prison Reform." *Public Interest* 35: 22–54.

Massey, Douglas, and Nancy Denton. 1993. *American Apartheid: Segregation and the Making of the Underclass.* Cambridge, MA: Harvard University Press.

McCord, Joan, Cathy Spatz-Widom, and Nancy A. Crowell. 2001. *Juvenile Crime, Juvenile Justice.* Washington, DC: National Academy of Sciences.

Morse, Stephen J. 1997. "Immaturity and Irresponsibility." *Journal of Criminal Law and Criminology* 88: 15.

———. 2006. "Brain Overclaim Syndrome and Criminal Responsibility: A Diagnostic Note." *Ohio State Journal of Criminal Law* 3: 397.

Nagin, Daniel S., Alex R. Piquero, Elizabeth S. Scott, and Laurence Steinberg. 2006. "Public Preference for Rehabilitation Versus Incarceration of Juvenile Offenders: Evidence from a Contingent Valuation Study. *Criminology and Public Policy* 5: 627–52.

Nellis, Ashley, and Ryan S. King. "No Exit: The Expanding Use of Life Sentences in America." Washington, DC: The Sentencing Project.

Palmer, Ted. B. 1991. "The Effectiveness of Intervention: Recent Trends and Current Issues." *Crime and Delinquency* 37: 330–46.

Platt, Anthony M. 2009. The Childsavers: The Invention of Delinquency. New Brunswick, NJ: Rutgers University Press.

Poe-Yamagata, Eileen, and Michael A. Jones. 2007. "And Justice for Some." http://www.buildingblocksforyouth.org/justiceforsome/jfs.pdf.

President's Commission on Law Enforcement and the Administration of Justice. 1967. *Task Force Report on Juvenile Delinquency and Youth Crime.* Washington, DC: U.S. Government Printing Office.

Redlich, Allison D., Melissa Silverman, Julie Chen and Hans Steiner. 2004. "The Police Interrogation of Children and Adolescents." In *Interrogations, Confessions, and Entrapment,* ed. G. Daniel Lassiter. New York: Kluwer Academic/Plenum.)

Redlich, Allison D., and Gail S. Goodman. 2003. "Taking Responsibility for an Act Not Committed: The Influence of Age and Suggestibility." *Law and Human Behavior* 27:141.

Rothman, David J. 1980. *Conscience and Convenience: The Asylum and Its Alternative in Progressive America.* Boston: Little Brown.

Ryerson, Ellen. 1978. *The Best Laid Plans: America's Juvenile Court Experiment.* New York: Hill and Wang.

Schlossman, Steven. 1977. *Love and the American Delinquent: The Theory and Practice of "Progressive" Juvenile Justice.* Chicago: University of Chicago Press.

Schlossman, Steven, and Stephanie Wallach. 1978. "The Crime of Precocious Sexuality: Female Juvenile Delinquency in the Progressive Era." *Harvard Educational Review* 48:65–94.

Scott, Elizabeth S. 1992. "Judgment and Reasoning in Adolescent Decisionmaking." *Villanova Law Review* 37:1607.

———. 2000a. "Criminal Responsibility in Adolescence: Lessons from Developmental Psychology." In *Youth on Trial: A Developmental Perspective on Juvenile Courts,* ed. Thomas Grisso and Robert G. Schwartz. Chicago: University of Chicago Press.

———. 2000b. "The Legal Construction of Adolescence." *Hofstra Law Review* 29:547.

Scott, Elizabeth S., and Thomas Grisso. 1997. "The Evolution of Adolescence: A Developmental Perspective on Juvenile Justice Reform." *Journal of Criminal Law and Criminology* 88:137–89.

———. 2005. "Developmental Incompetence, Due Process, and Juvenile Justice Policy." *North Carolina Law Review* 83:793–846.

Scott, Elizabeth S., N. Dickon Reppucci, and Jennifer L. Woolard. 1995. "Evaluating Adolescent Decision Making in Legal Contexts." *Law and Human Behavior* 19:221.

Scott, Elizabeth S., and Laurence Steinberg. 2003. "Blaming Youth." *Texas Law Review* 81:799–840.

———. 2008. *Rethinking Juvenile Justice.* Cambridge, MA: Harvard University Press.

Sechrest, Lee B., Susan O. White, and Elizabeth D. Brown, eds. 1979. *The Rehabilitation of Criminal Offenders.* Washington, DC: National Academy of Sciences.

Snyder, Howard A., and Melissa Sickmund. 2006. *Juvenile Offenders and Victims: A National Report 2006.* Washington, DC: Office of Juvenile Justice and Delinquency Prevention.

Sowell, Elizabeth R. et al. 2002. "Development of Cortical and Subcortical Brain Structures in Childhood and Adolescence." *Developmental Medicine and Child Neurology* 44:4–16.

———. 2001. "Mapping Continued Brain Growth and Gray Matter Density Reduction in Dorsal Frontal Cortex: Inverse Relationships During Postadolescent Brain Maturation." *Journal of Neuroscience* 21:8819–829.

Spear, L. P. 2000. "The Adolescent Brain and Age-Related Behavioral Manifestations." *Neuroscience and Biobehavioral Reviews* 24:417.

Steinberg, Laurence, and Elizabeth Cauffman. 1996. "Maturity of Judgment in Adolescence: Psychosocial Factors in Adolescent Decision Making." *Law and Human Behavior* 20:249.

———. 1999. "The Elephant in the Courtroom: A Developmental Perspective on the Adjudication of Youthful Offenders." *Virginia Journal of Social Policy and Law* 6:389.

Tanenhaus, David S. 2000. "The Evolution of Transfer out of the Juvenile Court." In *The Changing Borders of Juvenile Justice: Waiver of Adolescents to the Criminal Court,* ed. Jeffrey Fagan and Franklin E. Zimring. Chicago: University of Chicago Press.

———. 2004. *Juvenile Justice in the Making.* New York: Oxford University Press.

Tanenhaus, David S., and Steven A. Drizin. 2003. "Owing to the Extreme Youth of the Accused: The Changing Legal Response to Juvenile Homicide." *Journal of Criminal Law and Criminology* 92:641.

Torbet, Patricia, Richard Gable, Hunter Hurst IV, Imogene Montgomery, Linda Szymanski, and Douglas Thomas. 1996. *State Responses to Serious and Violent Juvenile Crime.* Pittsburgh: National Center for Juvenile Justice.

Van den Haag, Ernest. 1975. *Punishing Criminals: Concerning a Very Old and Painful Question.* New York: Basic Books.

Von Hirsch, Andrew. 1976. *Doing Justice: The Choice of Punishments.* New York: Hill and Wang.

———. 1985. *Past or Future Crimes: Deservedness and Dangerousness in the Sentencing of Criminals.* New Brunswick: Rutgers University Press.

Wilson, William Julius. 1987. *When Work Disappears.* New York: Random House.

Wright, William F., and Michael C. Dixon. 1977. "Community Treatment of Juvenile Delinquency: A Review of Evaluation Studies." *Journal of Research in Crime and Delinquency* 19:35–67.

Zimring, Franklin E. 1998. *American Youth Violence.* New York: Oxford University Press.

———. 2000a. "The Common Thread: Diversion in Juvenile Justice." *California Law Review* 88:2477–495.

———. 2000b. "The Punitive Necessity of Waiver." In *The Changing Borders of Juvenile Justice: Waiver of Adolescents to the Criminal Court,* ed. Jeffrey Fagan and Franklin E. Zimring. Chicago: University of Chicago Press.

Zimring, Franklin E. and Gordon Hawkins. 1997. *Crime is Not the Problem: Lethal Violence in America.* New York: Oxford University Press.

PART V

PROSECUTION AND
SENTENCING

CHAPTER 21

....

PROSECUTION

....

CANDACE MCCOY

CRIMINAL prosecution differs across time and place, and the role of public prosecutors in it also varies. For instance, the practice of employing prosecuting attorneys to work as salaried representatives of the state is comparatively recent. In the United States, it was not until the late nineteenth century that local governments began to hire attorneys specializing exclusively in the prosecution of accused criminals. Before that, most trials were conducted before a judge and jury with the accused present, assisted perhaps by a privately hired defense attorney, with the victim serving as prosecuting witness. If the victim hired a private attorney to ensure that all favorable evidence would be presented to the jury, which happened rarely, that lawyer would have been the closest equivalent to a prosecutor (Friedman 1993, chap. 7).

By 1900, primarily as a result of the establishment of public police forces in the more densely populated cities of the eastern United States, cases involving nearly identical allegations keyed to particular sections of criminal codes were increasingly submitted to the urban courts. In response, local governments hired private attorneys to organize the evidence and litigate all these similar cases. Government payments for this work subsidized these attorneys' private law practices. Eventually this somewhat mechanical government work became sufficiently frequent that it could constitute a full-time law practice. At that point, it made economic sense for a local government simply to hire an attorney as a full-time employee. The public prosecutor was born (Fisher 2003, chap. 2). This development is in sharp contrast to the history of prosecution in Europe, which relied on a common legal code dating back to Roman civil law and was applied "top down" from a central authority to localities.

In England, development of public prosecution had followed a similar course as in the United States, insofar as a local tradition of addressing street crime produced a prosecutorial bar. Traditionally, trials were "do-it-yourself activities" for the accused and victims. In 1752 and 1754, Parliament passed laws providing for payment of the costs associated with helping a victim prepare for trial, and statutes of 1778 and 1818 extended these payments to all cases. These became lawyers' fees paid to private attorneys, and over the course of a century a prosecution bar developed (Langbein 2003). As Langbein points out, "there was no positive theory of private prosecution, no body of thought explaining or justifying it." It simply took shape in response to social and political changes of the Industrial Age, "a default system, accepted because to devise an effective alternative would have required the political community to confront a nest of divisive issues about financing and controlling a prosecutorial corps" (Langbein 2003, 12). To this day, these issues remain underexamined both in England and the United States, and political or sociological theory explaining why prosecution is what it is, and what it should be, is thin.

The purpose of this chapter is to urge scholars and policymakers alike to examine the questions: "Why is prosecution organized like it is, and why does it operate like it does?" Only when some thought is given to these baseline questions can the normative inquiry—"how *should* prosecution be organized and operated?"—be addressed adequately. A number of generalizations are relevant:

- Public prosecution is a function of the executive branch of government and operates within and contributes to its political environment.
- There are two major bodies of research literature about prosecution in common law countries: sociological and legal. There is very little literature from political science.
- The sociological literature on prosecution concentrates on the courtroom workgroup and the prosecutor as one member of it. Insights from this literature answer the questions "why is prosecution organized like it is, and why does it operate like it does?" by proposing that a local legal culture emerges from years of courtroom functioning, developing shared expectations of typical punishments for normal cases, and consensual methods of adjudicating those cases.
- The legal literature on prosecution concentrates on the adversarial system, or deviation from it, and answers the questions "why is prosecution organized like it is, and why does it operate like it does?" with reference to case law developments, historical explanations of changing legal standards, and rules (or the lack of them) guiding the exercise of prosecutorial discretion.
- The modern practice of prosecution includes the power to investigate crime, to charge, to plea bargain, to manage defendant cooperation and snitching,

to force defendants into "consent" agreements through "pre-bargains," and to influence sentencing significantly through management of facts eventually presented to judges.

- Prosecutors have become increasingly powerful over the past century due to the growth of plea bargaining in the first half of the twentieth century and also to the widespread adoption of mandatory sentencing laws (and, to a lesser degree, sentencing guidelines) constraining judicial power in the second half of the century. Although expeditious and developed to serve the interests of substantive justice, plea bargaining under contemporary legal standards is inherently coercive.

- A history of plea bargaining in the United States explains why prosecutors do what they do under current law.

- Internal controls include the adversary system itself, in which each defendant has a defense attorney who must hold the prosecutor to the standard of "proof beyond a reasonable doubt" required for conviction. This can be regarded as internal because it structures the working environment for the courtroom workgroup, of which the prosecutor is the most powerful member. Another internal control is management rules and guidelines promulgated and enforced within the office of the district attorney, guidelines that are themselves responsive to the courtroom environment and established procedural requirements.

- External controls include civil lawsuits (which are extremely rare, since prosecutors have absolute immunity from suit) and pressure from the electorate and political parties. Also, prosecutors are attorneys and are subject to professional discipline from the organized bar. While important for addressing the most extreme examples of prosecutorial malfeasance, these controls are not significant factors influencing the daily work of most prosecutors.

- The quality of justice would be improved in the United States if deeper inquiry into the sources of prosecutorial power were undertaken. Prosecutors are creatures of their local political jurisdictions, a fact that is traceable to the history and sociology described above.

- Local politics in the United States is radically decentralized. Thousands of small towns, townships, counties, and cities have their own prosecutorial corps, subject only to the broadest requirements of federal constitutional law and such controls as individual states may choose to impose. Efforts to develop and enforce a common professional standard of care for prosecutors, as have been undertaken for police and judges, will likely fail unless some political centralization occurs and/or unless the laws change.

- Necessary legal reforms include repeal of mandatory sentencing laws, regulation of the trial penalty, rejecting absolute immunity from lawsuit in favor of limited liability for unconstitutional "custom, policies, and practices," federal constitutional change of standards required for proof beyond a reasonable doubt in plea bargains, and assumption by states of stronger oversight of local prosecutors.

- All such legal reforms would necessarily be imposed "from the top down" onto localities, and the degree of their penetration into the daily work-world of local prosecution would likely be uneven. Nevertheless, unless American states are willing to undertake greater political centralization, such legal reforms are likely to be the only viable approaches to regulation of US prosecutorial power in the coming decades.

This chapter has six sections. The first discusses definition and the sources of prosecutorial power. Sections II and III survey the sociological and legal literatures on prosecution. The fourth discusses plea bargaining. Section V discusses the historical origins and development of public prosecution. The last section offers a general theory of prosecution.

I. Definition and Sources of Prosecutorial Power

A general definition of prosecution: the power of the state expressed in the executive's capacity to conduct criminal investigations, to initiate charges alleging violations of the law, to participate in guilty plea negotiations, and to serve as the state's representative in criminal trials. Usually, it is understood that the goals of prosecution are suppressing crime, achieving social regulation, maintaining political influence, and serving justice. Sometimes these goals conflict. Overall, prosecution is a system of social control determined by the goals of the political power to which the prosecutor is accountable.

In common law countries, prosecution is pursued within an adversarial model of adjudication. This adversarial system is premised on the theory that truth will emerge from a battle between opposing sides: the defendant and the state—or, prior to the invention of the public prosecutor, the defendant and the victim, "which derives from the origin of trials as substitutes for private out-of-court brawls." This system is believed to be most effective in finding the truth of what happened in any alleged criminal incident because "each side strive(s) as hard as it can, in a keenly partisan spirit, to bring to the court's attention the evidence favorable to that side" (Frank 1949, 80) The prosecutor serves as both an investigator of fact and as a partisan determined to get these facts before a judge and jury, and thus demonstrate that they amount to guilt beyond a reasonable doubt.

That there seems to be a conflict of interest inherent in having prosecutors both investigate facts and present them to the court—in those situations in which the facts upon investigation turn out to be favorable to the defendant—has not escaped critics' notice. The incentive for the partisan is to hide the facts that the investigator has unearthed. In the adversarial system, it is assumed that there is no conflict of interest because defense attorneys will be equally zealous, and discover and present the facts the prosecutor may have incentive to hide. Thus, the healthy operation of an adversarial system depends on strong defense attorneys who act as watchdogs on prosecutors.

Other nations that do not structure their criminal adjudication under an adversarial model keep the fact-finding and court advocacy functions of prosecution separate. The historical roots of continental European trials are in written civil codes (from *civitas*, or "political community," thus "civil law") as opposed to common procedures that developed naturally over time to address private disputes submitted to public officials for resolution. In countries that use an "inquisitorial" model of adjudication, the criminal code provides for a public official akin to an investigating magistrate, who prepares a *dossier* on each case. It contains all the evidence the magistrates finds, including all evidence from the police, and also the personal circumstances of the defendant's life (e.g., job, family, education, health). This dossier is delivered to the court, the defense attorney, and the prosecutor. Trials are conducted "on the dossier" and each side presents witnesses and argues about the meaning of particular pieces of evidence as found in the investigation. The judge may independently question attorneys on either side and the witnesses themselves. Under this model of adjudication, the prosecutor's role is quite different than that in adversarial systems. If the defendant is convicted, the judge then turns to the part of the dossier containing personal information about the defendant that may influence sentencing.

In sum, any theory of prosecution in common law countries such as the United States must begin with the historical observation that prosecution began in partisanship and later added the role of public official. Today, prosecutors are still expected to be vigorous partisans in court—crime controllers—as well as magisterial managers of the interests of justice and the public good (Tonry 1991; Zacharias and Green 2009). They play these roles with a very wide degree of latitude, or discretion.

Like all public officials, prosecutors derive their powers from the political structure that creates them and defines their functions. In the United States as elsewhere, public prosecution of crime is a function of the executive branch. But prosecution also serves as a bridge between the executive and judicial branches of government. Considering that the various court parts are spread over two different branches and are charged with the job of implementing the legislature's criminal code, it is scarcely surprising that courts as organizations are regarded as fragmented and that prosecutors as one part of the court organization are quite powerful, since they span two branches.

As members of the executive branch, prosecutors are important law enforcement officials. Without prosecutors, public police would be the only government agency assuring public safety. Without prosecutors, people accused of crime would not be brought to court. Here a dilemma of prosecutorial role appears: police handle most public safety matters, yet prosecutors are the law enforcement officers whose job it is to bring accused offenders to justice. Prosecutors' status as lawyers imposes a professional responsibility to adhere carefully to legal requirements that are not ordinarily the concerns of police, yet they are expected to be concerned primarily with law enforcement. It is often said that prosecutors must vigorously protect the public safety and simultaneously work in the interests of justice. Sometimes these missions can conflict (Felkenes 1975, contrasting prosecutors who are punishers versus those who are quasi-judicial; see application of this duality to wrongful convictions, Forst 2008 and Zacharias and Green 2009).

Another structural observation about prosecutorial power is that, like almost all governmental functions in the United States, the organization of prosecution is decentralized. Unlike countries in which state authority resides in one government, the federal structure of the United States produces a great number of municipal and state jurisdictions, each enforcing its own law, and a federal government prosecuting those crimes that are reserved to the federal authority under the US Code. Like public schools and police, courts are public institutions funded and managed by local—not federal—authorities. The office of the public prosecutor operates under relevant municipal directions and enforces the municipal code as well as state law, and prosecutors make criminal charges in local courts. Obviously, prosecutorial priorities and practices would vary under this decentralized system, which covers several thousand local court jurisdictions, because those jurisdictions themselves are sociologically and economically diverse. Accordingly, any effort to standardize prosecutorial practices will face great difficulty in application since formulating common office procedures, rules or guidelines must cover such a broad territory. The task would not be impossible, however, as the sentencing guidelines movement or the major reforms of local American policing since the 1980s can demonstrate. Both sentencing and policing are functions of highly decentralized public offices: judges and police officers.

In such a decentralized system, criminal justice agencies will likely develop their own ways of practice depending on a wide variety of locally relevant factors on the macro level (economics, demographics, political structure) and on the micro level (personalities, managerial philosophies). Church called this "local legal culture," and it is the source of variation in court practices, procedures, and outcomes (Church 1982). Generations of scholars have explored the idea of local legal culture, attempting to understand these factors and explain why prosecutors are what they are, and do what they do, in terms of empirically observable work patterns in local courthouses.

II. Sociological Literature
on Prosecution

The American tradition of social scientific study of courts can be traced to Roscoe Pound's descriptive work, *Criminal Justice in Cleveland* (1922), and was significantly advanced by Jacob (1965), Blumberg (1967a), and Eisenstein and Jacob (1976), among others. All these describe in detail how criminal cases are adjudicated from the point of police booking through sentencing, explaining the roles and work outcomes of each of the court professionals at each of the adjudicative stages. All concentrate on the prosecutor's position in the "courtroom workgroup." What the concept of "local legal culture" adds is that the norms of these workgroups vary, depending on their political and economic environments (Eisenstein, Fleming, and Nardulli 1998; Johnson 2006).

It is understood that a court as a functioning entity has several parts that are not necessarily well-coordinated. That is, in order to accomplish adjudication, each case will be prepared separately by a prosecutor (who at the beginning relies on police reports and grand jury investigations), a defense attorney (either private or publicly funded), and a judge. The state through its representative, the prosecutor, must prove guilt beyond a reasonable doubt in order to obtain convictions.

Sociologically, the prosecutor is a member of a courtroom workgroup, which traditionally included the opposing attorneys, the judge who decided matters of law, and the jury that decided matters of fact. With the exception of the jury, each court part has its own support staff. This is not a hierarchical organization in which the judge has authority over the other parts, but a collegial "horizontal" one in which the independent offices involved must consensually establish a working protocol among themselves, subject to continual renegotiation and updating (Feeley 1984). By being forced by law to take account of the defendant's perspective, this structure is intended to uphold traditional legal values of due process as well as provide crime control (Packer 1968).

Because it is a fundamental premise of the common law's adversary system that prosecutors and defenders must conduct separate investigations and be prepared to challenge each other vigorously so that the "truth" may emerge, this system thwarts organizational cooperation—and is conceptually opposed to it. Over time, however, the workgroup together brings a great volume of cases to conclusion, and in doing so "establish(es) expectations, practices, and informal rules of behavior of judges and attorneys," amounting to a legal culture (Church et al. 1978, 54). "A court's management culture is reflected in what is valued, the norms and expectations, the leadership style, the communication patterns, the procedures and routines, and the definition of success that makes the court unique. More simply: 'The way things are done around here'" (Ostrom et al. 2007, 5).

As these practices and behaviors are repeated and replicated, the sociologists explain, all court officials begin to develop a shared sense of what the characteristics of a typical crime are, and what the appropriate punishment for it should be. Sudnow named these phenomena the "normal crimes" to which a "going rate" of punishment would be applied (Sudnow 1965). Subsequent scholarship observed that a similar shared expectation of the "normal procedure" for adjudicating these crimes develops as the workgroup's preferred method of case processing, and that any of these normalities may change over time depending on external legal, political, or social pressures or reforms internal to the various court parts (McCoy 1993). We would expect the normal crimes, typical procedures, and going rates to vary depending on the characteristics of the political jurisdiction in which the court functions, as any speeding driver who knows whether to slow down depending on the town she is driving through intuitively understands.

Ostrom et al. (2007) recently studied twelve general jurisdiction courts in three very different states (California, Florida, and Minnesota) to describe differing court cultures and the effect that culture has on procedures and case dispositions. They explained court culture as a product of different values. Observing case management styles, judge-staff relations, change management, leadership, and internal organization in each court, they found that four "cultural archetypes" emerged. Each court could be described as either "communal, networked, autonomous, or hierarchical" (Ostrom et al. 2007, tables 2, 3). The courts approached such matters as speedy trial, plea bargaining, and allocation of funding differently depending on the values and corresponding organizational type that they thought were most important. Referring back to Church, the values were not about abstract principles of justice but were rather about "the right way to do things around here." Again, the local—and varied—meaning of justice in this description implies that prosecutors will learn and enforce the values that their electorate wants them to, not those that are enforced from any higher legal or moral authority.

The latest sociological research about prosecution concerns "community prosecution." In the policing profession, "community policing" throughout the 1990s had many meanings and many different manifestations depending on the communities under discussion. The rhetoric of community policing, particularly the problem-solving variety, has been applied to programs in which local prosecutors identify "problems" and seek to solve them through coordinated law enforcement and community services and civil code enforcement (Coles 2008). "Community-oriented" prosecutors are expected to reach out to local "stakeholders" such as business leaders, social service providers, and civic groups to identify which types of crime problems the prosecutors should target. Many such programs address low-level, quality-of-life crimes and neighborhood drug use and dealing, presumably because the "community" demands it (Goldkamp et al. 2003). This approach is essentially a policing strategy, not a prosecutorial one, though you may disagree. (To see the debate, read "Community Prosecution: Rhetoric or Reality?" Nugent-Borakove and Fanflik 2008).

The point is that prosecutors operate locally and are major political players in community life, a fact that has lately been emphasized and developed in crime control initiatives. When added to the earlier sociological accounts of the role of prosecutors in the courtroom workgroup, a picture of prosecutors as community representatives and advocates emerges. Under the sociological account of court functioning and norm development, the prosecutor's proper role is to serve as a law enforcement unit, liaise with the police, gather evidence and conduct more investigation as needed, and represent the government (called in legal proceedings "the state," "the commonwealth," or simply "the people") by advancing cases into court. In such a system, that player who controls the flow of work into the system will exercise great power, a power that is mindful of the need to serve the interests of the voters in the "community."

As the most powerful player in the courtroom workgroup, the prosecutor can significantly influence the disposition of criminal cases even more powerfully than the judge can, since judges work only with the cases prosecutors send to them. The sociological explanation of why prosecution functions as it does highlights the prosecutor's role both as workgroup member and powerful law enforcement agent, enforcing the law as understood by the electorate and elites of the relevant jurisdiction. Because jurisdictions have very different characteristics, prosecutorial practices will also vary.

III. Legal Literature about Prosecution

There is a well-developed body of literature about the *practice* of prosecution, which is part of the larger legal literature concerned with statutes, cases, interpretation, and application of law. Insofar as case law itself is normative, that literature may be regarded as providing a theory of why prosecutors do what they do. Generally, American case law and the legal literature commenting on it state that public prosecutors have extremely broad discretion to conduct their work as they deem necessary. It is very rare for any claim of "malicious prosecution" or prosecutorial misconduct to prevail (Poulin 1996). In the United States, prosecutors enjoy absolute immunity from civil suit,[1] including immunity against claims that their policies and practices on supervision, training, or information management violate constitutional rights or state law.[2] As for complaints that prosecutorial activities illegally affect particular groups of defendants, "the last successful claim of racially selective prosecution appears to have been *Yick Wo* v. *Hopkins*" in 1886 (Bibas 2009, n37). Because the law provides such wide power to prosecutors, it is rarely challenged, so there is little statutory law, case law or commentary defining the mission, practices, procedures, or strategies of prosecuting, other than the framework of criminal procedure itself under which all court actors must function.

This is not to say that the framework of criminal procedure does not produce a literature to which prosecutors are quite attentive and which explains how prosecutors work. To recount that huge body of case law here would be impossible and perhaps not exactly apt in answering the questions posed at the beginning of the chapter, which are "*why* do prosecutors do what they do," not *how*. The law prescribes how prosecutors must do their jobs, but the broader structure of adjudication in which they work is also defined and developed under law, and it is that structure that receives the attention of policymakers and scholars alike.

In particular, scholars have studied prosecutorial practices of charging and plea bargaining (see McCoy, 1993 for an overview of this literature up to 1985). Descriptions of these practices in the early half of the twentieth century generally describe them as antithetical to the adversary system, because increasingly they were moving toward the shared consensual model of courtroom workgroup functioning characterized by "going rates" and "normal punishments." But after the 1980s, politics intervened. In the United States, new legislation instituting guidelines sentencing, mandatory sentencing, and generally harsher punishments under *any* sentencing structure changed the dynamics of the court workgroup's practices. Prosecutorial power increased as judicial power decreased under guidelines sentencing (Stith and Cabranes 1998; Wright 2005) and, in a "get tough" political environment, representatives of law enforcement become increasingly powerful. Moreover, executive power has increased in general in the years since the 9/11 attacks on the World Trade Center in New York and on the Pentagon, leading one commentator to state that "the whole history of America since World War II caused an inertial transfer of power toward the executive branch" (Wills 2009). Scholars studying courts have updated the "courtroom workgroup" scholarship by analyzing how increased prosecutorial powers have changed the normal expectations of sentencing outcomes and "normal procedures" for achieving them. Qualitative observational studies have concluded that procedural regularities of charging and plea bargaining have become increasingly streamlined since the 1970s, that the trial penalty (the difference in punishment depending on whether the defendant pleads guilty or is convicted after trial) has increased, and that prosecutorial guidelines internal to the court organization have done little to rein in prosecutorial discretion (Bowen 2009).

In sum, the prosecutorial power is wide and deep, likely to vary in its exercise and products depending on the local politics in which it is embedded, and capable of driving the work of criminal courts. It is exercised under the legal framework called "case disposition," in which the police bring an arrested person to the prosecutor, the prosecutor charges that person with a crime or crimes as defined under the relevant criminal statutes, investigates the evidence in the case (in felony cases in most states, doing so with a grand jury), determines whether enough evidence exists to prove each charge, engages in plea negotiation with defense counsel, sets the terms of any plea bargain offer and agrees to a guilty plea bargain or not, and acts as the state's representative in the criminal trial if the case has not ended in a guilty plea. At each of these stages, the prosecutor has discretion to proceed or not, and if so how (Davis 2007).

IV. Prosecutorial Discretion in Charging and Plea Negotiation

Kenneth Culp Davis famously defined discretion as the capacity to choose between two or more equally permissible alternative courses of action (Davis 1969). Prosecutorial discretion in charging an arrested person with a crime is an excellent example. Police arrest suspected criminals and book them, officially stating the activity deemed to violate the law. Prosecutors receive this information from the police, supplement it with any other information available at this early stage of the process, and file a legal document with the court listing the crime or crimes to which the accused will be expected to answer—or not. In this "charging" they are guided by constitutional law, which requires that police had probable cause to arrest, and prosecutors will be expected to prove that they did; otherwise, a judge must dismiss the case. Charges are keyed to offenses as listed in the jurisdiction's criminal code, and there is good evidence that charge bargaining varies depending on how many options the criminal code presents (Wright and Engen 2007).

Immediately, alternate possibilities arise. Some prosecutors' offices have a policy of charging every crime at the highest level of severity to which the facts could apply, reasoning that if due to lack of probable cause a judge dismisses or reduces the charges later in the process, the fullest measure of public safety has been wrung from the arrest. Other prosecutors' offices will set charges only at that level of severity for which there is definitely probable cause, reasoning that obtaining the grand jury indictment will be easy, that it is unfair to hold an arrestee on scanty evidence, and that prosecutorial resources are best spent on cases that will produce solid convictions. Either of these approaches is legally permissible. Which approach a particular office will favor depends on the host of factors comprising the local legal culture.

Prosecutors even have wide discretion to decline to prosecute altogether, a choice that can be extremely powerful. The usual situation in a "normal felony" is that if a prosecutor decides not to pursue the felony arrest, it will simply not be referred to a grand jury and will either be "downgraded" to a misdemeanor charge or dropped altogether for lack of prosecution. (Some jurisdictions use preliminary hearings instead of grand jury indictments in deciding probable cause.) Usually, however, the reverse situation occurs: a prosecutor will vigorously demand that every person arrested for a felony crime must answer for it. But if the state can produce only weak evidence, the prosecutor has the power to agree to pursue only those less-serious charges for which the evidence is strongest.

This typical exercise of the power to charge or decline to charge appears quite straightforward. Clearly, it is strongly influenced by the prosecutor's prediction of what will happen in the case when its evidence is challenged by the defense and reviewed by the judge. But other uses of the power of *declination* (a term used in the federal system to indicate "decline to charge") only tangentially involve the court. These involve what I call "pre-bargains" and attorneys call "deferred prosecutions." In these cases, prosecutors have a target defendant under investigation and have enough evidence of wrongdoing to initiate charges against the target. But, for various reasons, they do not. Instead, they extract a negotiated guilty plea, which is held in abeyance while the target defendant corrects the criminality.

An example of this practice has emerged from the white-collar criminal conspiracies of recent years. Prosecutors investigate Wall Street dealings and determine that a corporation has been violating the law. Rather than press charges, they notify the officers of the corporation that they have sufficient evidence to do so but prefer to demand organizational reform and monitor the organization over time for compliance with the law. If the corporate officers admit guilt (to the prosecutors, not to a judge), the prosecutors will agree not to charge the organization or its officers with crimes. The corporation must undertake a set of reforms the prosecutors require and submit to monitoring by an outside firm appointed and paid for by the prosecutor's office. If the monitoring determines that the corporation is not in compliance, the prosecutors may initiate charges on the original crimes and make it known to the judge that the target has previously admitted guilt.

This guilty plea agreement—in exchange for a private guilty plea the prosecutor agrees not to charge the defendant with a crime—occurs even before the charging stage of criminal procedure and is thus a "pre-bargain," though the parties call it a "deferred prosecution agreement" (US Department of Justice 2009). This agreement raises concerns, of course, because: it is not transparent; it is an exercise of prosecutorial power never reviewed by a judge unless it "goes wrong"; it can cost a great deal of public money for the monitoring; and it establishes the public criminal prosecutor as an economic force in a field usually regarded as the province of regulatory agencies (in the case of white-collar investigations, the Securities Exchange Commission).[3] Yet it is an obvious outcome of the broad prosecutorial discretion to decide whether and what to charge. Further, "pre-bargaining" is not solely an American prosecutorial phenomenon. Recently in England, the Serious Frauds Office, a prosecuting arm of the English attorney general, was revealed to have attempted to strike a deal with the arms company BAE in which BAE would pay over 500 million pounds it was said to have paid in illegal bribes to representatives of foreign governments seeking British contracts. BAE was willing to admit some guilt but refused to agree to the bargain because it said the penalty amount was too high. The only way to know whether the amount was in fact too high would be to submit the matter to a court, but to do so would reveal the existence of the pre-bargain. The story was made public only through investigative reporting by *The*

Guardian (Leigh and Evans 2009). The matter was settled when the attorneys general of both England and Wales and the United States charged BAE with one count of making false statements about its compliance with anti-bribery laws. The huge military contracting firm immediately pled guilty and agreed to pay $400 million to the United States and $50 million to England and Wales. The firm was not itself convicted of bribery, allowing it to continue to contract with the two governments (Public Broadcasting System 2010; *Guardian* 2010). It is doubtful that the respective attorneys general would have made even the false-statements charge public, had not the investigative reporting revealed the existence of the pre-bargain. The value of BAE stock rocketed up at the news, since investors had feared the fines would be much larger.

Much more typical are pre-bargains involving street crime, exemplified in the 1978 Supreme Court case of *Bordenkircher* v. *Hayes*, 434 U.S. 357 (1978). In that case, a Kentucky statute prescribed punishments for felony crimes, but if the accused was a recidivist, the habitual offender provisions of the law required an additional five years mandatory prison time be added to the sentence. The local prosecutor Bordenkircher demanded that the defendant Hayes plead guilty to a charge of forging a check for $88.83 and be sentenced to five years in prison. If he would agree to do this, the prosecutor would not charge him as a "third strike" habitual offender, although he had been convicted of serious felonies twice before. But if he refused to plead guilty, the prosecutor would add the recidivism charge to the indictment. Hayes continued to claim he was innocent, had a trial, was convicted, and the mandatory sentence of life imprisonment was imposed. He appealed, stating that the prosecutor's demand of a "pre-bargain" was unconstitutional as a violation of his right to due process under the Fourteenth Amendment. If he chose to exercise his right to trial, he said, it should have been solely on the charge of forgery, for which the prosecutor had insisted on a guilty plea during the plea bargaining. The Supreme Court disagreed, stating that prosecutorial discretion in charging is almost unlimited. Even in this case, where the prosecutor candidly admitted that he was threatening to charge Hayes with the "three strikes" law in order to force him to give up his right to trial, the Supreme Court would not say that the prosecutor was vindictive or that the right to trial had been compromised.

Perhaps the most searing example of this dynamic, in which a prosecutor demands a guilty plea in return for refraining from bringing new charges, is the death penalty "stipulation." Prosecutors demand that accused murderers plead guilty, or the prosecutors will allege that the case facts are sufficiently aggravated to fit statutory requirements for imposing capital punishment (Hoffman, Kahn, and Fisher 2000). As between the judge, jury, and prosecutor, whether a murderer will be subject to the death penalty is a decision most significantly influenced by the prosecutor, according to empirical studies of states' capital punishment systems, and it is significantly affected by race-based factors such as race of victim and location of crime (Paternoster 1984; Zacharias and Green 2009).

The *Bordenkircher* case is presented in some detail here as an example of concerns that the charge bargaining process raises in local courts across the nation: the influence of mandatory sentencing on strategic decisions, the unavailability of recourse to challenge those decisions, and above all the wide scope of prosecutorial discretion in charging. *Bordenkircher* may be seen as an example not only of charge bargaining on charges for which the defendant has been indicted (by far the most typical situation), but also as an example of "pre-bargaining" in which the prosecutor threatens to bring more charges unless the defendant acquiesces to the government's requirements.

To understand these various permutations of plea bargaining, it may be helpful to review some basic definitions. *Plea bargaining* is "the process by which the defendant in a criminal case relinquishes the right to go to trial in exchange for a reduction in charge and/or sentence" (McCoy 1993, 50), and the reduction in severity may be accomplished in various ways, depending on the laws of the jurisdiction. Its form varies, sometimes involving charge bargaining, sentence bargaining, fact bargaining, or pre-bargaining, and sometimes a combination of these. *Charge bargaining* occurs when defendants agree to plead guilty in return for the prosecutor's promise to reduce the severity of a charge or drop some altogether. *Sentence bargaining* occurs when a guilty plea is promised in return for a lower punishment than would be expected had the defendant gone to trial and been convicted, and this may be an explicit agreement made with the participation of the judge or an implicit agreement that the judge will sentence with the typical punishment usually given in such a situation. *Fact bargaining* occurs when, under sentencing laws that affix particular punishments for facts involved in the crime (such as the vulnerability of the victim, or the amount of money stolen, etc.), the prosecutor and defender agree to bring to the court's attention only that evidence in the case that will produce the agreed-upon sentence. *Pre-bargaining* occurs when the defendant agrees to do something required by the prosecutor in return for the prosecutor's promise not to bring charges at all.

There is little judicial oversight of any of these types of bargaining. For example, consider charge bargaining. In return for a guilty plea, the prosecutor can oblige a judge to dismiss charges for lack of prosecution. More often, the parties will agree to reduce the severity of the charges that will be sent to the judge for approval and eventual conviction. In jurisdictions with sentencing guidelines,[4] prosecutors hold the greatest power within the courtroom workgroup, because sentences are calculated based upon the charges of conviction (Reitz 1998, confirmed empirically by Piel and Bushway 2007). Pre-bargaining may be regarded as a variant of charge bargaining, since it occurs when prosecutors agree to refrain from making formal charges in open court—judges will not even know that a case ever happened.

Sentence bargaining would be expected to be more shared among the courtroom workgroup because judges, not prosecutors, impose the sentences in all cases. For the going rate under normal procedures, the courtroom workgroup has arrived at an understanding about what a judge will normally do when the prosecutor and defense attorney state that a defendant will plead guilty to particular charges. The only job for the judge is to indicate whether the typical sentence for those charges will probably be imposed. In rare cases, the judge will indicate that the court will not accept the guilty plea or will probably impose a sentence other than the normally expected one. In such a rare case, the defendant may withdraw the plea, and the lawyers will attempt renegotiation. The form of sentence bargaining will vary depending on the sentencing law of the particular jurisdiction, and in a few states judges are permitted to participate in the actual bargaining sessions.

Fact bargaining is observable mostly in jurisdictions that have sentencing guidelines so detailed as to take account of particular facts of each case. Prosecutors and defenders will bargain over the statutory elements of each crime charged and what facts actually prove them. In return for a guilty plea, prosecutors may agree as to what facts they will bring to the judge's attention at sentencing (Stith and Cabranes 1998; Bibas 2001). The probation office, in its presentence report, is expected to police this process, though its success is likely to be limited if the defense and the prosecution have agreed on which facts were "proven" or not (Probation Officers' Advisory Group 1996).

State mandatory sentencing laws such as the repeat offender statute in the *Bordenkircher* case (a type which eventually morphed into "three strikes" laws) or "use a gun, go to prison," or for example, laws mandating years in prison for dealing drugs within 1,000 feet of a school, encourage pre-bargaining, charge bargaining, and fact bargaining. Because prosecutors hold the power to charge, they pre-bargain by threatening an arrestee with prosecution under the mandatory provisions unless the arrestee does something the prosecutor wants, such as testify against co-defendants. In charge bargaining under mandatory sentencing, once charges are actually made, the prosecutor can agree to drop those charges that require mandatory prison time, in return for a guilty plea (Heumann and Loftin 1975). In fact bargaining, in return for a guilty plea the prosecutor agrees with the defense attorney that a particular piece of evidence that would trigger the mandatory sentence will not be brought to the court's attention. Armed robbery becomes robbery; drug dealing within 1,000 feet of a school becomes simple dealing. This practice returns some discretion to judges because they are not constrained by the mandatory sentencing requirement, but prosecutors hold the greatest power over the cases because pre-bargaining, charge bargaining, and fact bargaining all control what a judge will see.

A variation on the plea-bargaining theme is "cooperation" or "snitching," in which a defendant will provide information or testimony against a co-defendant in return for a lower sentence. Although cooperation agreements are not plea bargains *per se* because they do not always involve a guilty plea on the part of the cooperator, they do give substantial concessions to the criminal suspect in return for important prosecutorial benefits. In cases involving wide criminal conspiracies such as drug cartel dealings, violent gang activities, or organized crime, the goal is to "flip" or "turn" criminals at the lower end of the organizational hierarchy from loyalty to the criminal organization to cooperation with law enforcement, protecting them as they provide useful information, testify at trial, or even put themselves at great risk in "wearing a wire" to get incriminating evidence (Natapoff 2009). Prosecutors acknowledge that these defendants, although guilty of serious crimes, provide services that are crucial in achieving conviction and punishment of others involved in the conspiracies. These are "little fish," used as a means to the end of convicting "the big fish," achieving a greater good than fully prosecuting the low-level offenders would have achieved. Of course, occasionally after a cooperation agreement has been reached, prosecutors learn they have been dealing with the "big fish" who deserves the most punishment but will as a result of the bargain receive the least. Nevertheless, if conducted carefully and under established guidelines, cooperation agreements are generally regarded as justifiable even apart from reasons of achieving individual case settlement, because they are used for the immediate purposes of advancing criminal investigation.

When considering the tremendous power that state and federal sentencing laws give to prosecutors in any system in which plea bargaining occurs in any of its various permutations, it might be said that judges have no power to influence plea bargains and thus to exercise some measure of oversight over prosecutors. That would be an overstatement. As pivotal members of the courthouse workgroup, to whom all the various officials eventually report, judges police the quality of evidence and are most influential in setting the going rate, because the attorneys negotiate based on their expectations of what the judge will do when the facts of the case and guilty plea agreement are brought to the court's attention. (The exception, of course, is pre-bargaining, in which no formal case is initiated in court.) Investigation of various sentencing laws in action has demonstrated that, when prosecutors agree to "hide the gun" in return for a guilty plea, or when defenders and prosecutors agree to circumvent three-strikes laws by arranging guilty pleas to charges that do not trigger the mandatories, they do so after judges have signaled their displeasure with the sentencing laws and their willingness to approve devices that circumvent the provisions (Zimring and Kamin 2001; Bazelon 2010).

The US Supreme Court has also signaled that judges cannot be ignored in the plea-bargaining process. In *Blakely v. Washington* (2004), a defendant had agreed to plead guilty under the state of Washington's strict sentencing guidelines to very serious charges of kidnapping and use of a weapon. The agreement to these charges did not include a finding of "deliberate cruelty," which would have lengthened the prison sentence. At the sentencing hearing, the judge on his own volition found that the defendant had acted with deliberate cruelty and added months to the prison time the attorneys had agreed upon in the plea bargain. Justice Scalia said that the "judge in this case could not have imposed the exceptional ninety-month sentence solely on the basis of the facts admitted in the guilty plea," but was correct under the Sixth Amendment to require that the unmentioned facts be brought into open court and proven beyond a reasonable doubt, and if proven be used to compute the sentence.

The *Blakely* judge was probably unusually active in intervening in the attorneys' plea bargain, but the case demonstrates that judges are usually aware of the facts of cases whether they are highlighted in the plea agreement or not. The court's presentence investigation aims to compile all the evidence, and judges see it before pronouncing sentence. The courtroom workgroup performs an intricate dance at this point, in which various players withdraw or engage depending on their values as to what appropriate punishment would be. The roles of each court actor in plea bargaining are well known. Alschuler's seminal descriptions and analyses of the practice, from a series of law review articles published in the 1970s and 1980s (Alschuler 1968, 1975, 1976, 1978, 1979, 1981, 1983) are almost as accurate today as they were then.

Nevertheless, there have been important changes in plea bargaining over the years. Although its forms have remained mostly static (with the exception of the increasing use of pre-bargaining over the past three decades), the substantive criminal law itself has changed, as has sentencing law. Indeterminate sentencing generally produced sentence bargaining, in which judges signaled the going rate and attorneys bargaining with their eyes on it. Twenty-nine states still have indeterminate structures, though almost all have tacked onto them mandatory sentencing for particular crimes. In the twenty-one states and federal system that have adopted forms of determinate sentencing, including guidelines ranging from broad to extremely specific, charge bargaining became more common. With the proliferation of mandatory provisions and detailed guidelines based on particular facts of the case (Virginia, Washington, and the federal system,) fact bargaining flourished. The result is that the prevalence of guilty pleas versus trial has increased steadily since the 1970s, and it is probable that the severity of the trial penalty has increased as well. Defendants now plead guilty to crimes carrying much more severe punishment than in the past, and the percentage of criminal cases concluded through guilty pleas has increased over recent decades from approximately 80 percent to 95 percent.

Heumann shows that the guilty plea rate in the federal system was approximately 90 percent from 1947 to 1950, then dropped below 80 percent in the late 1970s, then climbed steadily to 93 percent in 1998 (Heuman 2002, 633). By 2004 in city courts across the nation, the guilty plea rate was 97 percent. (Cohen and Kyckelhan 2010) The number of trials has decreased accordingly, prompting many commentators to mourn "the vanishing trial" (Galanter 2004). To evaluate this public policy, and to decide what its future should be, a political history of plea bargaining over the past century can show why prosecutors accrued such power and can point the way to appropriate guidance in the future.

V. Why and How Did Plea Bargaining Develop in the United States?

Most people who stop to think about the reasons plea bargains are ubiquitous in common law courts conclude that they are necessary evils.[5] The ideal is the full-blown adversary trial, in which prosecutors and defenders battle in front of a jury with a benevolent judge acting as referee. But the criminal jury trial has been abandoned as too complex, expensive, and uncertain. This may come as a surprise to fans of television shows like *Law and Order* and to law students, who almost exclusively study appellate decisions from cases that have actually been tried so as to learn common law principles and "black letter law," but finding a trial among the mass of cases prosecuted is like "finding a hippopotamus in the Bronx." The hippopotamus is indeed there—in the Bronx zoo—but like a trial he is an exotic creature who has little to do with normal life in the community (Koski 2003, 3–4, quoting Langbein).

This is not to disparage the considerable benefits of jury trials, but these are probably not being achieved very well in a system in which trials are exceedingly rare, perhaps because trial procedure is hopelessly encrusted with legalism that works to the detriment of "normal life" in the courtroom workgroup. Perversely, well-intended detailed rules expected to equalize the playing field in an adversarial system have become so heavy that the game is pushed underground (Kagan 2001, 96).

Historically, in the law governing guilty pleas—which are, after all, confessions—this has happened before. Langbein has gone so far as to compare the elaborate medieval rules about confessions and the use of torture to the modern plea-bargaining system. In medieval Europe, "conviction had to be based upon the testimony of two unimpeachable eyewitnesses . . . without [them], a criminal court could not convict an accused who contested the charges against him. Only if the accused *voluntarily* confessed could the court convict him without the eyewitness testimony" (Langbein 1978, 4) What followed is different "in degree, but not kind" from the plea-bargaining system. The accused was asked to confess. If he refused, torture ensued and a confession inevitably followed. (The modern equivalent, says Langbein, is the "trial penalty," in which an accused is presented with the "choice" of pleading guilty to the bargained sentence or going to trial and, if convicted, be sentenced with significantly more severe punishment than the prosecutor had promised in return for a confession.) To assure that the confession was "voluntary," the medieval accused would be brought into public court a few days after the torture and asked to reaffirm the confession. (The modern equivalent would be the court event in which prosecutors tell the judge the "factual basis" for a guilty plea, after which the accused affirms his intent to plead guilty and agrees that "no promises or concessions have been made," even though everybody in the courtroom knows this to be untrue.) If he recanted, he would be sent back for more torture. (If a modern defendant reverses his decision to plead guilty, more plea bargaining will ensue, and the trial penalty may increase.) Langbein points out that torture developed as an alternative to the medieval trial procedure that made it too difficult to convict guilty persons. He believes that the Anglo-American rules of evidence are similar. In our zeal to protect the rights of defendants, we have constructed a system so encrusted with arcane rules as to result in the actual denial of those rights:

> American plea bargaining, in like fashion, sacrifices just those values that the unworkable system of adversary jury trial is meant to serve: lay participation in criminal adjudication, the presumption of innocence, the prosecutorial burden of proof beyond reasonable doubt, the right to confront and cross-examine accusers, the privilege against self-incrimination. Especially in its handling of the privilege against self-incrimination does American criminal procedure reach the outer bounds of incoherence. (Langbein 1978, 7)

Perhaps, in time, historians will regard the modern rise of plea bargaining and death of the criminal trial as equivalent to the rise of equity in England in the 1600s. Equity, a system of court procedure serving as an alternative to common law pleading, developed to avoid the excesses of formal law. A rational system with its own principles, logic, and practices, it was well-regarded by the public, the parties, and the courts as providing a "rough justice" generally fairer than that of formal adversarial trial. However, unlike equity, which developed its own full-blown judge-dominated courts, plea bargaining is controlled mostly by prosecutors with the participation of the defense bar and thin oversight from the bench.

Although modern trials are complex, expensive, and uncertain, their complexity cannot immediately be reduced because law reform is so difficult. However, plea bargaining can at least reduce their uncertainly. Prosecutors plea bargain to get the "sure thing" of a conviction (Albonetti 1986), and defenders acquiesce as they manage their many cases by prioritizing according to how serious the case is and how likely they are to be able to prove reasonable doubt about the prosecution's evidence (Mather 1979). Plea bargaining has the added advantage of saving the state the costs of trial, which are considerable. These costs have increased steadily over the past 150 years in the United States as rules of evidence have become more complex and trial procedures more elaborate. A century ago, seating a jury through the *voir dire* process was easy: simply call the first twelve men on a list of voters in the last election and start the trial, which would usually be concluded in a matter of a few hours. Today, even *seating* a jury can take a full day or more. This simple example of how trials have become increasingly time-consuming and resource-draining helps explain why plea bargaining has replaced them.

Laymen usually state that saving the time and expense of trials is the reason that prosecutors plea bargain. Courtroom workers disagree; costs are not primarily on their minds while plea bargaining. Instead, the strength of proof in each case and the norms of probable punishments are uppermost. However, they are operating within an organizational structure that has its own imperatives and structures their work accordingly. It is generally believed that defendants have only one card to play: they can force the state to spend days in a trial courtroom, with all its associated salaries for judges and staff, public defenders, transcripts and tests, and prosecutorial effort. A defendant would be willing to trade this for a lower sentence, even though there may be weaknesses in the state's evidence against him, and he might not be convicted at trial. A trial could produce the same result as a plea bargain (or, indeed, even an acquittal). But in a great many cases, defendants have no realistic hopes of prevailing and might as well plead guilty and get on with the punishment. In this account, a defendant, like the attorneys, is also reducing uncertainty by avoiding trial and taking a "sure thing" of a negotiated sentence. Considerable expense is avoided, and this result is possible because *both sides* in the adversarial process (the prosecutor and the defender) have organizational incentives to be non-adversarial (Blumberg 1967*b*).

But what of the actual evidence? Without a public trial, there is no way to know whether the plea bargain was truly based on proof beyond a reasonable doubt, which is the constitutional requirement for conviction. A confession in the form of a guilty plea does not necessarily prove actual guilt—fatalism, mental weakness, youth or inexperience, "taking the fall" for others involved in the crime, desire to be released immediately from pretrial detention, and particularly contemplation of the trial penalty (discussed later) are all reasons that a person might plead guilty even if the state's evidence is not strong. Prosecutors, defenders, and scholars counter these criticisms by pointing out that attorneys prepare their cases with great attention to the strength of proof, and either side must be willing to compromise if the other can credibly cast doubt on the evidence offered. This, and not institutionalized leniency or coercive threats of harsher sentences, they claim, accounts for the reduced charges or sentences that plea bargaining produces. However, the benefits of opening the evidence before a judge—much less the public or victims—are significantly lessened. Plea bargaining eliminates the "publicness" of criminal procedure, moving the evidence and decision-making about it from the open courtroom and placing it behind the attorneys' closed doors. In a plea bargain, except for cursory review and approval of the agreement, neither judges, victims, nor the public have much capacity to weigh the actual strengths of the prosecution's case.

Considering that trials are indeed complex, uncertain, and expensive, it is not surprising that the caseload pressure explanation for the rise of plea bargaining in the late nineteenth century continues to hold the popular imagination. However, although this observation may make sense in the twenty-first century, trial procedure was not as onerous at the time that plea bargaining began. This has led scholars to question whether the roots of plea bargaining are to be found not in caseload pressure from too many trials for too many crimes but in something else. Heumann (1975) showed that at the time plea bargaining first developed as a primary mode of case disposition in the 1850s, courts had plenty of resources to conduct trials and were not inundated with high numbers of arrestees. Heumann found a different reason for the development of plea bargaining to be more compelling: workgroup expectations about what is likely to happen to cases of "normal crimes," given particular levels of credible proof. Coupled with the "reduction of uncertainty" argument, and also the fact (but not the *only* fact) that guilty pleas short-circuit trials, these combined reasons produce a cogent explanation for the rise of plea bargaining in common law nations worldwide in the twentieth century.

Recent scholarship has added more. Fisher's (2003) account of the rise of plea bargaining in Massachusetts in the late 1800s and early 1900s points to two other factors: courts increasingly responded to crime in a rational-legal mode characteristic of bureaucracies rather than the earlier individualized moralistic court-centered mode, and statutes providing mandatory penalties for vice crimes empowered prosecutors to extract guilty pleas.[6] These two explanations for the rise of plea bargaining supplement but do not contradict earlier accounts, adding a sociological "macro" explanation to the "micro" explanations focusing on the court as the unit of analysis. They draw attention to the way public institutions change over time, reflecting and also advancing the sensibilities of the age.

For example, a criminal procedure grounded in Enlightenment ideals, such as that set out in 1787 in the US Constitution, would be concerned with the "inalienable rights" of each individual accused. But with the advent of the modern industrial age, specialization of work functions, regularization of work product, and rational-legal bureaucratic organization became more prominent. Max Weber said:

> The decisive reason for the advance of bureaucratic organization has always been its purely technical superiority. . . . Precision, despatch, clarity, familiarity with the documents, continuity, discretion, uniformity, rigid subordination, savings in friction and in material and personal costs . . . the work of a salaried bureaucracy is not only more precise but in consequence often cheaper than that of a formally unpaid honorific official. . . . In particular, in the sphere of the administration of justice, it is normally the bureaucracy which first creates the basis for the introduction of a conceptually coherent and rational legal system . . . gradual introduction of rationally trained specialists to replace the earlier procedures tied to tradition or irrational preconceptions. (Weber 1922, 350, 352)

Weber was a European lawyer, probably the greatest legal sociologist of the twentieth century, and he had in mind the European inquisitorial system rather than the common law adversarial system when he applied his theories to adjudication.[7] He regarded bureaucratization of adjudication as historically inevitable and the source of legitimacy for the modern state. He was not referring to plea bargaining, which has never gained a foothold in Europe. He had in mind the inquisitorial method of trial on the dossier, described earlier. In contemporary Western Europe, every serious felony case is adjudicated in public with reference to the investigating magistrate's file. Non-serious felons do not face prison time and have the option of agreeing to pay fines and make restitution as required in the penal law; if they wish, they do this in much the same way as Americans pay traffic tickets or civil code violations: admitting that the facts alleged are true and mailing money to the court. In this way, European systems avoid the high costs of trials that common law countries would incur should all arrestees refuse to plead guilty. Since the bulk of criminal cases involve property crime or drug crime, removing them from the trial docket frees resources for trials of every person charged with a violent or repeat offense. These "penal orders" are controlled by prosecutors because they are criminal charges, and defendants are expected to agree to the charges on a take-it-or-leave-it basis. Most defendants take it. But if they do not, their cases are scheduled for full trial in which the potential punishment of fines and restitution, in the event of conviction, will not be higher than the penal order originally demanded (examples of prosecutorial dispositions in Europe may be found in Tonry and Frase [2001]).

In common law countries, the guilty plea process is an example of bureaucratized justice because it allowed prosecutors to categorize cases by degree of credible proof and to dispose of cases by dismissing charges in those with weak evidence, accepting guilty pleas to those with sufficient evidence to go to trial but perhaps not to convict, and to refuse to agree to lower sentences in cases with very strong evidence for the state. Abstract individual rights, such as the right to trial or the right not to self-incriminate, are not primary concerns as they were in the Enlightenment period.

Fisher's (2003) analysis of court records at the turn of the century sets the groundwork for a theory of prosecution: prosecutors do what they do, and are what they are, because they are government employees in an era in which the nation-state became increasingly powerful and their work took on the scientific, rational methodologies that characterized that period. Another history of plea bargaining in Massachusetts at about the same time, this one concentrating on Boston, focused on the effect of immigration and poverty in the Boston Brahmin–controlled city (Vogel 2005). Vogel's work supports Fisher's theory of prosecution: law enforcement in this period was given greater power as a means of bureaucratically controlling (sorting, categorizing, utilizing) the poor. A public police force was instituted in Boston in 1891, with the expectation that it would, among other jobs, enforce anti-vice laws and restore some order and decorum that the Brahmins believed had diminished since the influx of immigration changed the character of their city, suppressing the unruly but leaving the orderly available for work. Fisher points out that new laws prohibiting the sale of unlicensed alcohol and regulating saloon operations were passed: a graduated scale of offenses with corresponding mandatory fines. The newly established public prosecutors responded to alcohol-related arrests from the public police by agreeing to lower a charge one degree in return for a defendant's guilty plea. Because the penalties were mandatory, the prosecutor essentially set the sentence by offering the plea bargain, and judges were not involved; the defendants paid the fines and the cases ended. The prosecutor's power to control the great mass of cases alleging low-level criminality expanded with such arrangements, leading to diversion programs in which prosecutors agreed to dismiss cases if arrestees agreed to submit to programs for their "improvement." Here also are seen the origins of probation as a sentencing option (Fisher 2003).

In short, the origins of plea bargaining are historical, sociological, and political as much as they are economic. As the owners of the plea-bargaining process, public prosecutors have amassed great power from social changes. They now control the flow of cases into court systems nationwide, and they decide how to proceed with those cases under new sentencing laws, which grant them the discretion to decide the course of each defendant's case in a legal environment in which defenders and judges have less capacity to influence case outcomes.

Although the conditions that gave rise to plea bargaining may not be the conditions that drive it today, the practice has become institutionalized and regularized.[8] Even if we wanted to return to a system in which trials were used in a greater percentage of cases, by now public budgeting for courts has normalized around the expectation that almost every case will end in a guilty plea. Furthermore, it is clear that caseload no longer is the primary factor driving the plea-bargaining system, if it ever was. If the association between case overload and guilty pleas were so tight, guilty-plea rates would have dropped and trials would have become more common as the crime rate (and thus the caseload) plummeted nationwide in the early 1990s. Instead, over the course of the next two decades, and even as the crime rate fell and number of cases coming into courts reached low levels not seen since the 1950s, the guilty plea rate not only stayed high but increased.

Prosecutorial power has similarly increased, and prosecutorial discretion is mostly unbounded. A theory of why prosecutors do what they do today begins with Fisher's answer: "because they can" (Fisher 2003, 49).

VI. Toward a Theory of Prosecution

Perhaps the bleak picture presented here is too critical of prosecutorial power. There is no doubt that prosecutors are well-meaning public officials—good people doing the best they can, using the tools provided to them, to ensure public safety. The issues discussed in this chapter do not contradict this observation; they simply raise questions about whether the "tools provided" are appropriate. To determine what tools are best for the work at hand, it is necessary to ask larger questions about what goals prosecutors should be expected to achieve, which in turn rests on a theoretical explanation about where the institution of prosecution fits within a democratic, constitutionally created political structure.

I began with the observations that prosecutors are members of the executive branch, that they operate in an adversarial legal system, and that they are expected to exert coercive powers to serve objectives set by the government of which they are a part. These objectives are usually defined as providing public safety while simultaneously acting in a quasi-magisterial role concerned with "the interests of justice," though setting other goals would be possible. This model generally holds in common law countries of the English-speaking diaspora.

Whether prosecution *should* be organized like this is a different question. Its answer probably depends on whether the questioner believes that the institution of prosecution is performing well in its existing structure. Although it is radical to propose that the function of prosecution should be removed from the executive branch, there is great concern that executive power generally can be comparatively unconstrained, and that prosecution as one manifestation of it is particularly susceptible to overreach. This may be due to the fact that governments in the late twentieth century gave more and more power to any organization that claimed to repress crime and disorder, or it may be due to a growing imbalance in the adversary system, or both. Courts are supposed to provide a neutral field on which equally prepared and equally armed adversaries can battle until the spectators (either a judge or judge and jury) can determine the winner—the side that has given the most compelling account of the alleged crime. Increasingly, however, due to the operations of plea bargaining and changes in sentencing laws, the battle is weighted in favor of the prosecutor, and judges have little control over a game that they sometimes do not even know is being played.

In short, attempting to control prosecutorial discretion through well-established checks and balances inherent in the structure of democratic government and the operation of the adversary system in court is probably not working very well at this historical moment. But if the theory that adversarial structure produces the best court outcomes because partisanship promotes rigorous investigation and challenge of evidence is valid, the logical reform would be to strengthen adversarial procedure. Plea bargaining and, in the larger sense, consensual courtroom workgroup agreements about the value in procedure are antithetical to adversary processes. Plea bargaining would have to be changed radically, or some substitute for it that will provide adversarial evidentiary testing must be devised.[9] Explaining the various approaches to plea-bargaining reform would require a book in itself and is not attempted here, though surely it is fair to say that the problem of plea bargaining is the most important topic for any serious inquiry into the current state of prosecutorial powers. Nobody seriously suggests that plea bargaining can be abolished in the United States or Britain or other common law countries. Jurisdictions that claim to have done so have actually substituted one form of it for another (for example, eliminating charge bargaining but strengthening sentence bargaining, or shifting from sentence bargaining to fact bargaining). Plea bargaining has so clearly "triumphed," in Fisher's words, that reformers ask not how to end it in favor of bringing back the adversarial trial but how to regulate its worst features: the lack of opportunity to challenge evidence, the coercive use of the trial penalty, the hidden discretionary decisions of public prosecutors who are not accountable to or influenced by other public institutions, and ultimately the suspicion that victims of crime are not well served as "clients" of the adversarial prosecutor (McCoy 2005).

Changing the internal dynamics of court functioning so as to strengthen the power of other players—defenders and judges—is a recommendation based on the adversarial theory of truth-finding. It posits that adversary processes should not be subverted by mechanisms that take decision-making power away from courts and place it instead in the executive branch (or any branch, for that matter.) Reforms internal to the court system would structure the working environment for the courtroom workgroup, of which the prosecutor is now the most powerful member, so as to spread discretionary power more evenly among the various court players and require open court hearings (though not necessarily full trials) in which evidence would be challenged. If the theory of adversary process as truthfinder is to be supported, laws that empower prosecutors at the expense of judges and defenders would have to be repealed.[10] Mandatory sentencing is the obvious prime example.

It cannot be said that prosecutors are fully accountable to the adversary system, though they are in theory and though they work within a broad adversarial court structure. Plea bargaining, which is controlled by prosecutors, is not conducted in court. Plea bargains are brought into a courtroom only when the "done deals" are laid before a judge. Judges must assure that the defendant knows his rights, including the right to trial, and judges check to be sure there is a factual basis for each plea, and of course it is judges who, in fact, hear pretrial motions that can significantly affect plea negotiations. (For example, motions to suppress evidence due to illegal police actions can be mini-trials on their own.) But, when considering the great volume of cases in which prosecutors have charged (or not charged) defendants with crimes, there is no doubt that prosecutorial actions determine the final outcomes of a much greater number of cases than the comparatively very few in which judges are asked to hear pretrial motions or preside over trials.

The prosecutor's need to interact with judges and defenders has traditionally been regarded as the only powerful tool for achieving prosecutorial accountability to the law, but prosecutorial control over charging and plea bargaining skews the checks and balances of the adversarial system. Therefore, a set of reform possibilities is rooted in the goal of re-introducing some measure of power to judges (and perhaps defenders) by forcing the fact-finding back into court. These include bench trials, sometimes called "slow pleas of guilty," in which a judge holds a mini-trial, without a jury, concentrating only on contested facts that the prosecutor and defender bring to court (Schulhofer 1984; King et al. 2005) Some suggest that sentencing hearings after conviction might serve as "mini-trials" on contested facts in jurisdictions with strict sentencing guidelines. Some even suggest that common law countries should adopt aspects of the criminal procedure of continental European nations, in which explicit plea bargaining is almost never used and in which every serious felony case is subjected to a short, judge-dominated trial—even when a defendant prefers to plead guilty! Although the civil law system surely solves the problems of prosecutorial discretion and accountability, its differing trial procedures and very different rules of evidence[11] probably render it an impractical guide for incremental reform of common law systems.

Some critics call for changing the organizational culture of prosecution, which values win-loss records and hard-driving crime control at the expense of victims' and voters' concerns (Bibas 2009). Although outsiders and even enlightened prosecutors themselves can call for new management guidelines, incentive structures, training and promotion, and organizational development strategies, there is almost no external pressure on prosecutors to do this. Moreover, insofar as the adversarial theory of adjudication is supported, a campaign asking prosecutors to scale back use of the crime control tools that legislation has provided would be quixotic. Municipal government, in which the greatest amount of prosecutorial activity is exercised in the United States, is decentralized and has little reason to change. The strongest examples of prosecutorial guidelines are rules imposed from above, i.e., federal Department of Justice guidelines for US attorneys in charging and plea bargaining, or the *Brimage* guidelines on plea bargaining applied to all local New Jersey prosecutors in a state where local prosecutors are appointed by the governor/ executive, not elected locally (New Jersey Attorney General 2004). The great majority of prosecutors in the United States are locally elected and not accountable to a state office, which could require promulgation of such guidelines. They thus have little incentive to do so.

This failure of local prosecutors to adopt careful guidelines for charging and plea bargaining highlights the fact that American prosecution, like its police and schools, is highly decentralized. Adversarial theory assumes that prosecutors everywhere, as part of court workgroups, will function well in crime control and truth-seeking functions due to the very structure of adjudication itself, which is roughly uniform everywhere but conditioned in important ways by different state sentencing laws. But sociological insights about the nature of consensual courtroom workgroup decision making empirically undermine adversarial theory. In practice, the theory is not strongly supported, at least as the adversarial system currently operates. A search for a different theory that could better explain not only why prosecution operates as it does, but how it should operate, could begin.

But prosecution is seldom seen as a policy problem, despite ample evidence from the exposure of wrongful convictions all around the nation over the past two decades. Perhaps this is due to some fuzziness in prevailing political theory about the fundamental question of exactly to what (or who) prosecutors are supposed to be held accountable.

Accountability of any organization rests on connection to the people the organization serves. Profit-making companies are accountable to shareholders, schools are accountable to parents and local taxpayers, police are accountable to citizens and their elected representatives. To whom are prosecutors accountable? As elected officers, members of the executive branch of government, they are broadly accountable to the voters. But few citizens know enough of the daily work of these public servants to be able to review it meaningfully. Elections of prosecutors are usually (though not always) determined by the power of the political party to which the prosecutor belongs, not by the demonstrated superiority of a candidate's managerial skills, law enforcement philosophy, legal knowledge, or established methods of conducting charging, plea bargaining, or other prosecutorial functions.

In most states, prosecutors are popularly elected, meaning they are deeply embedded in the type of political structure the jurisdiction has built. Even in those few states and the federal system in which prosecutors are appointed, the political party holding the executive branch will appoint its own loyalists to the top job, and that person will hire assistant attorneys to staff the office as needed. For example, if a city still follows old-fashioned "political machine" politics, a prosecutor's loyalty to political patrons and their party will be paramount for advancing professional aspirations. By contrast, if a city has a civil-service and city-manager style of government, a prosecutor's career will be shaped by financial and performance benchmarks set by the city council and agency managers. None of these officials are likely to be closely involved in monitoring the daily work of the prosecutor's office. As long as the prosecutor stays within budget and responds to powerful constituencies' demands for law and order, city officials are unlikely to question the methods by which convictions are obtained. An extremely broad accountability to the voters is maintained, but prosecutorial discretion is scarcely limited.

In 1973 Malcolm Feeley wrote that "only two mechanisms are institutionalized to induce [court officials] to comply with formal rules and goals of the criminal justice system—normative inducements accruing from professionalism and the appellate procedures—and neither is very effective" (Feeley 1973, 422). Feeley was referring to police and judges as well as prosecutors. Since 1973, major reforms in controlling police discretion and judicial discretion have been undertaken, but prosecutorial discretion has not received such scrutiny. States passed new sentencing laws to control the discretion of judges, and theoretically could do so to control prosecutorial discretion, but this is unlikely. Public punitiveness can be focused on demanding that "lenient" judges be reined in, but it operates in the opposite direction for law-and-order prosecutors. Furthermore, sentencing guidelines were originally championed by the Left, not the Right, because they were seen as powerful tools for eliminating racial disparities in criminal procedures. Thirty years later, the Left is disenchanted with guidelines although there is evidence that they have indeed narrowed racial disparities somewhat (Spohn 2000). In short, there is no political will to insert prosecutorial guidelines into state laws.

The experience of police reform over the past thirty years may be more closely applicable to developing an agenda for prosecutorial reforms. Local police, like prosecutors, are radically decentralized and accountable mostly to local politics. An ambitious agenda of law reform beginning with the seminal Supreme Court case of

Monell v. Department of Social Services, 436 U.S. 658 (1978) rendered local police departments vulnerable to private civil lawsuits claiming denial of constitutional rights due to police "custom, policy, or practice." Over time, these lawsuits forced police nationwide to define their procedures, professionalize their training and supervision, and take account of federal constitutional requirements. The "private attorneys general" model of private lawsuits forcing social change is a mostly unnoticed success story of bringing local practices into compliance with "best practices" (McCoy 2010). The same could be done in the area of prosecution, but the Supreme Court would have to pierce the absolute immunity from lawsuit that prosecutors currently enjoy by making an exception allowing suit against the prosecutorial office (not the person) when federal constitutional rights are violated by prosecutorial "custom, policy, or practice." The Court explicitly declined to pierce the personal immunity of individual prosecutors in *Van de Kamp v. Goldstein,* 554 U.S. 942; 129 S.Ct. 25, though prosecutors' offices as organizations might arguably under some circumstances be subjected to "custom, policy, practice" analysis under section 1983 of the US Code, as police departments are.

Recall Langbein's observation: we need "a positive theory of private prosecution . . . a body of thought explaining or justifying it" (Langbein 2003, 12). We might begin by asking why we need trials, and then why—despite mouthing adversarial theory—we do not in fact use them much at all. Next, political theory explaining why decentralization is better than more centralized regulation must provide an explanation of why prosecutors are allowed to do what they do. "All politics is local," said Massachusetts congressman Tip O'Neill, and the sociologists of courtroom workgroups operating in local legal cultures agree. Why and how local political practices should be constrained by professional standards imposed from "above," whether from state governments or from federal constitutional requirements, is a question of political theory. Future research on prosecution will proceed from political theory, not sociological or legal/adversarial, because prosecutorial practices can be explained by reference to the political jurisdictions that sustain them.

NOTES

....

1. *Imbler v. Pachtman,* 424 U.S. 409; 96 S.Ct. 984 (1976).
2. *Van de Kamp v. Goldstein,* 554 U.S. 942; 129 S.Ct. 25.
3. "Pre-bargaining" in other types of crimes could preclude action from related regulatory agencies. For instance, an agreement with a pharmaceutical company to stop producing a particular drug in return for not facing criminal charges of child endangerment could usurp the role of the Food and Drug Administration. Any of a number of such scenarios can be hypothesized.

4. The federal sentencing guidelines attempted to preclude charge bargaining by simply grouping all counts of conviction into one "score" for purposes of determining the guidelines severity level. In practice, what happened was that prosecutors were able to pile on other facts regarded as relevant and thus convince a court to increase the sentencing severity based on those facts, rather than number of charges. This was possible under a separate guideline allowing prosecutors to increase penalties for any "relevant conduct."

5. In Canadian cities, the guilty plea rate is about 80 percent (Di Luca 2005). In England and Wales for 2008, it was 70 percent. Ministry of Justice, Judicial and Court Statistics 2008, ch. 6, 108–9, available at www.justice.gov.uk/publications/judicialandcourt-statistics. This is a rise since 2001 from 56 percent to 70 percent in 2008, a change which the British Ministry of Justice attributes to the fact that "early plea discounts" in sentencing severity are now offered to defendants. Nevertheless, the size of the trial penalty (difference in severity of sentence after guilty plea versus after trial) is regulated in England and Wales and cannot exceed 30 percent.

6. Fisher disagrees with Heumann on an important point. Although he agrees that case pressure is not the only reason plea bargaining took hold in the 1800s, he does find that courts were more burdened in providing trials than Heumann reported. That is because, he says, Heumann forgot to look at the total budget for these courts, in which civil litigation was increasing exponentially. It is possible that court budgets were directed towards providing trials in civil cases, leaving the comparatively light criminal case burden to be dealt with through guilty pleas.

7. See especially "Bureaucracy and the Law," pt. 3, chap. 6, of *Wirtschaft und Gesellschaft*: "Of course, and above all, the sure instincts of the bureaucracy for the conditions of maintaining its power . . . are inseparably fused with the canonization of the abstract and 'objective' idea of 'reasons of state' . . . Equality before the law and the demand for legal guarantees against arbitrariness demand a formal and rational 'objectivity of administration,' as opposed to the personally free discretion flowing from the 'grace' of the old patrimonial domination." Max Weber, *From Max Weber*, tran. and ed. and with an introduction by H. H. Gerth and C. Wright Mills (London: Routledge and Kegan Paul, 1948), 220.

8. The federal sentencing guidelines reduce the "count" by two to three points in return for a defendant's "acceptance of responsibility."

9. One approach would be to concentrate on the administrative nature of criminal adjudication, removing criminal prosecution from the adversarial system and treating criminal courts as administrative agencies subject to review under procedures similar to the Administrative Procedures Act. (See Barkow 2008–09).

10. Or, rather than repeal, it might be possible to pass new laws that would give judges more power over the outcomes of plea bargaining. An intriguing proposal is to pass state laws requiring judges to regulate the trial penalty by refusing to approve plea bargains if the recommended sentences exceed a "cap" determined for each offense level (see Covey 2008). Of course, any court could voluntarily adopt such a system even in the absence of new state laws.

11. The detailed dossier describing all elements of proof, which can be quite thick, is submitted to the trial court where it may be challenged by the prosecutor and defender. In an approach similar to the "stipulation to the facts" of bench trials, the attorneys vigorously challenge only those pieces of evidence that are weak for the opposing side. This means that victims often testify so that judges may assess their credibility, and each defendant is

expected to make a statement. The trial judge will have read the dossier beforehand and often questions witnesses and the attorneys from the bench. There are two lay-citizen "assessors," the closest equivalent to a jury, who may also question witnesses and the attorneys, and who will vote on the final question of guilt or innocence. Every felony case is tried, and these trials usually last an hour or two. In the United States, every jurisdiction permits bench trials, which, in practice, may resemble the European felony trial. Nationwide, about 2–3 percent of all trials are heard by judges without juries.

REFERENCES

Albonetti, Celesta. 1986. "Criminality, Prosecutorial Screening, and Uncertainty: Toward a Theory of Discretionary Decision-making in Felony Case Processing." *Criminology* 24: 623.

Alschuler, Albert W. 1968. "The Prosecutor's Role in the Plea Bargaining." *University of Chicago Law Review* 36: 50.

———. 1975. "The Defense Attorney's Role in Plea Bargaining." *Yale Law Review* 84: 1179.

———. 1976. "The Trial Judge's Role in Plea Bargaining." *Columbia Law Review* 76: 1059.

———. 1978. "Sentencing Reform and Prosecutorial Power: A Critique of Recent Proposals for 'Fixed' and 'Presumptive' Sentencing." *University of Pennsylvania Law Review* 126: 550.

———. 1979. "Plea Bargaining and Its History." *Columbia Law Review* 79: 1. (Simultaneously published in *Law and Society Review* 13:211 [1979]).

———. 1981. "The Changing Plea Bargaining Debate." *California Law Review* 69: 652.

———. 1983. "Implementing the Criminal Defendant's Right to Trial: Alternatives to the Plea Bargaining System." *University of Chicago Law Review* 50: 829.

Barkow, Rachel E. 2008–09. "Institutional Design and the Policing of Prosecutors: Lessons from Administrative Law." *Stanford Law Review* 61: 869.

Bazelon, Emily. 2010. "Arguing Three Strikes." *New York Times Sunday Magazine*, May 23, www.nytimes.com.

Bibas, Stephanos. 2001. "Judicial Fact-Finding and Sentence Enhancements in a World of Guilty Pleas." *Yale Law Journal* 110: 1097.

———. 2009. "Prosecutorial Regulation vs. Prosecutorial Accountability," *University of Pennsylvania Law Review* 157: 959.

Blumberg, Abraham S. 1967a. *Criminal Justice*. Chicago: Quadrangle Books.

———. 1967b. "The Practice of Law as a Confidence Game." *Law and Society Review* 1: 15.

Bowen, Deirdre. 2009. "Calling Your Bluff: How Prosecutors and Defense Attorneys Adapt Plea Bargaining Strategies in Response to Increased Formalization" *Justice Quarterly* 26: 2.

Church, Thomas W. 1982. *Examining Local Legal Culture: Practitioner Attitudes in Four Criminal Courts*. Washington, DC: US Department of Justice, National Institute of Justice.

Church, Thomas, Kenneth N. Chantry, Larry L. Sipes, National Center for State Courts, National Conference of Metropolitan Courts, et al. 1978. *Justice Delayed: The Pace of Litigation in Urban Trial Courts*. Williamsburg, VA: The National Center for State Courts.

Cohen, Thomas, and Travey Kyckelhan. 2010. *Felony Defendants in Large Urban Counties 2006*. Washington, DC: Department of Justice, Bureau of Justice Statistics.

Coles, Catherine. 2008. "Evolving Strategies in Twentieth-Century American Prosecution." In *The Changing Role of the American Prosecutor*, ed. John W. Worrall and M. Elaine Nugent-Borakove. Albany, NY: SUNY Press.

Covey, Russell D. 2008. "Fixed Justice: Reforming Plea Bargaining with Plea-Based Ceilings." *Tulane Law Review* 82: 1237–90.

Davis, Angela J. 2007. *Arbitrary Justice: The Power of the American Prosecutor*. New York: Oxford University Press.

Davis, Kenneth Culp. 1969. *Discretionary Justice*. Baton Rouge: Louisiana State University Press.

Di Luca, Joseph. 2005. "Expedient McJustice or Principled Alternative Dispute Resolution? A Review of Plea Bargaining in Canada." *Criminal Law Quarterly* 50: 14.

Eisenstein, James, Roy B. Fleming, and Peter F. Nardulli. 1988. *The Contours of Justice: Communities and their Courts*. Philadelphia: University of Pennsylvania Press. 2nd. ed. University Press of America, 1999.

Eisenstein, James, and Herbert Jacob. 1976. *Felony Justice: An Organizational Analysis of Criminal Courts*. Boston: Little, Brown.

Feeley, Malcolm M. 1973. "Two Models of the Criminal Justice System: An Organizational Perspective." *Law and Society Review* 7(3): 407–26.

———. 1984. *Court Reform on Trial: Why Simple Solutions Fail*. New York: Basic Books.

Felkenes, George T. 1975. "The Prosecutor: A Look at Reality." *Southwestern University Law Review* 98: 110.

Fisher, George T. 2003. *Plea Bargaining's Triumph: The History of Plea Bargaining in America*. Palo Alto, CA: Stanford University Press.

Forst, Brian. 2008. "Prosecution Policy and Errors of Justice." In *The Changing Role of the American Prosecutor*, edited by John W. Worrall and M. Elaine Nugent-Borakove. Albany: SUNY Press.

Frank, Jerome. 1949. *Courts on Trial*. Princeton, NJ: Princeton University Press.

Friedman, Lawrence M. 1993. *Crime and Punishment in American History*. New York: BasicBooks.

Galanter, Marc. 2004. "The Vanishing Trial: An Examination of Trials and Related Matters in Federal and State Courts." *Journal of Empirical Legal Studies* 1: 459.

Goldkamp, John S., Cheryl Irons-Guynn, and Doris Weiland. 2001. *Community Prosecution Strategies: Measuring Impact*. Washington, DC: Bureau of Justice Assistance. http://www.ncjrs.gov/pdffiles1/bja/192826.pdf.

Guardian (UK). 2010. "The BAE Files." February 7, www.guardian.co.uk/world/bae.

Heumann, Milton. 1975. "A Note on Plea Bargaining and Case Pressure." *Law and Society Review* 9: 515.

———. 2002. "Plea Bargaining: Process and Outcome." *Criminal Law Bulletin* 38 (September-October): 630.

Heumann, Milton, and Colin Loftin. 1975. "Mandatory Sentencing and the Abolition of Plea Bargaining." *Law and Society Review* 13: 515.

Hoffman, Joseph L., Marcy L. Kahn, and Steven W. Fisher. 2000. "Plea Bargaining in the Shadow of Death." *Fordham Law Review* 69: 2313.

Jacob, Herbert. 1965. *Justice in America: Courts, Lawyers and the Judicial Process*. Boston: Little, Brown.

Johnson, Brian D. 2006. "The Multilevel Context of Criminal Sentencing: Integrating Judge and County Level Influences in the Study of Courtroom Decision Making." *Criminology* 442: 259–98.

Kagan, Robert A. 2001. *Adversarial Legalism: The American Way of Law* Cambridge, MA: Harvard University Press.

King, Nancy, David A. Soulé, Sara Steen, and Robert R. Weidner. 2005. "When Process Affects Punishment: Differences in Sentences after Guilty Plea, Bench Trial, and Jury Trial in Five Guidelines States." *Columbia Law Review* 105(4): 959–1009.

Koski, Douglas D. 2003. *The Jury Trial in Criminal Justice.* Durham, NC: Carolina Academic Press.

Langbein, John. 1978. "Torture and Plea Bargaining." *Public Interest* 46: 3–22. (Distilled from Langbein, "Torture and Plea Bargaining," *University of Chicago Law Review*, 1978.)

———. 2003. *The Origins of Adversary Criminal Trial.* New York: Oxford University Press.

Leigh, David, and Rob Evans. 2009. "The Arms Firm, the SFO and the Inquiry that Refused to Go Away." *Guardian*, October 2, pp. 1 and 8–9.

Mather, Lynn. 1979. *Plea Bargaining or Trial?* Lexington, MA: Lexington Books.

McCoy, Candace. 1993. *Politics and Plea Bargaining: Victims' Rights in California* Philadelphia: University of Pennsylvania Press.

———. 2005. "Plea Bargaining as Coercion: The Trial Penalty and Plea Bargaining Reform." *Criminal Law Quarterly* 50(1–2): 67–107.

———. 2010. "How Civil Rights Lawsuits Improve American Policing." In *Holding Police Accountable*, ed. Candace McCoy. Washington, DC: Urban Institute Press.

Natapoff, Alexandra. 2009. *Snitching: Criminal Informants and the Erosion of American Justice.* New York: New York University Press.

New Jersey Attorney General. 2004. *Brimage Guidelines 2004 Revisions.* Trenton, NJ: Office of the Attorney General.

Nugent-Borakove, Elaine M., and Patricia L. Fanflik. 2008. "Community Prosecution: Rhetoric or Reality?" In *The Changing Role of the American Prosecutor*, ed. John W. Worrall and M. Elaine Nugent-Borakove. Albany, NY: SUNY Press.

Ostrom, Brian J., Charles W. Ostrom, Roger A. Hanson, and Matthew Kleiman. 2007. *Trial Courts as Organizations.* Philadelphia: Temple University Press.

Packer, Herbert. 1968. *The Limits of the Criminal Sanction.* Palo Alto, CA: Stanford University Press.

Paternoster, Raymond. 1984. "Prosecutorial Discretion in Requesting the Death Penalty: The Case of Victim-Based Discrimination." *Law and Society Review* 18: 437.

Piel, Anne Morrison, and Shawn D. Bushway. 2007. "Measuring and Explaining Charge Bargaining." *Journal of Quantitative Criminology* 2: 105–25.

Poulin, Anne Bowen. 1996. "Prosecutorial Discretion and Selective Prosecution: Enforcing Protection after *United States* v. *Armstrong*." *American Criminal Law Review.* 34: 1071.

Pound, Roscoe. 1922. *Criminal Justice in Cleveland.* Cleveland: The Cleveland Foundation, 2nd. ed. 1968, Montclair, NJ: Patterson Smith Publishing.

Probation Officers' Advisory Group to the US Sentencing Commission. 1996. "Probation Officers' Survey." *Federal Sentencing Reporter* 8(6): 303–13. This volume contains several articles commenting on the findings of the survey.

Public Broadcasting System. 2010. "BAE To Pay More Than 400 Million in US and UK Fines." American Public Radio, Public Broadcasting System, February 5.

http://www.pbs.org/frontlineworld/stories/bribe/2010/02/bae-to-pay-more-than-400-million-in-us-and-uk-fines.html.

Reitz, Kevin. 1998. "Modeling Sentencing Discretion in American Sentencing Systems." *Law and Policy* 20: 389–428.

Schulhofer, Stephen. 1984. "Is Plea Bargaining Inevitable?" *Harvard Law Review* 97: 1037.

Spohn, Cassia C. 2000. "Thirty Years of Sentencing Reform: The Quest for a Racially Neutral Sentencing Process." *Crime and Justice 2000*. Washington, DC: National Institute of Justice. http://www.ncjrs.gov/criminal_justice2000/vol_3/03i.pdf.

Stith, Kate, and Jose A. Cabranes. 1998. *Fear of Judging: Sentencing Guidelines in the Federal Courts*. Chicago: University of Chicago Press.

Sudnow, David. 1965. "Normal Crimes: Sociological Features of the Penal Code in a Public Defender's Office." *Social Problems* 12: 255.

Tonry, Michael. 1991. "Public Prosecution and Hydro Engineering." *Minnesota Law Review* 75: 971.

Tonry, Michael, and Richard S. Frase. 2001. *Sentencing and Sanctions in Western Countries*. New York: Oxford University Press.

United States Department of Justice. 2009. "UBS Enters Into Deferred Prosecution Agreement." Washington, DC: United States Department of Justice. http://www.justice.gov/opa/pr/2009/February/09-tax-136.html.

Vogel, Mary E. 2005. *Coercion to Compromise: Plea Bargaining, the Courts, and the Making of Political Authority*. New York: Oxford University Press.

Weber, Max. 1922/1956. *Wirtschaft und Gesellschaft*. 4th ed. Tubingen: University of Turbingen. Available in Weber, *Selection in Translation*. 1978. "The Development of Bureaucracy and its Relation to Law." Ed. W. G. Runciman. Trans. Eric Matthews. London: Cambridge University Press,

Wills, Garry. 2009. "Entangled Giant." *New York Review of Books,* October 8, p. 1.

Worrall, John W., and M. Elaine Nugent-Borakove, eds. 2008. *The Changing Role of the American Prosecutor*. Albany, NY: SUNY Press.

Wright, Ronald F. 2005. "Prosecutorial Discretion and Its Challenges: Sentencing Commissions as Provocateurs of Prosecutorial Self-Regulation." *Columbia Law Review* 105: 1010.

Wright, Ronald F., and Rodney L. Engen. 2007. "Charge Movement and Theories of Prosecutors." *Marquette Law Review* 91: 9–38.

Zacharias, Fred C., and Bruce A. Green. 2009. "The Duty to Avoid Wrongful Convictions: A Thought Experiment in the Regulation of Prosecutors." *Boston University Law Review* 89: 1.

Zimring, Franklin, and Sam Kamin. 2001. *Punishment and Democracy: Three Strikes and You're Out in California*. New York: Oxford University Press.

CHAPTER 22

....

SENTENCING

....

BRIAN D. JOHNSON

Sentencing decisions arguably exert more influence over life and liberty than any other stage of the criminal justice system. The sentencing decision represents the culmination of the formal justice process—it is here that the criminal law is translated into criminal punishment. In this process, myriad tensions are negotiated and resolved, balancing the often contradictory goals of uniformity and individuality in punishment, of individual freedom and community protection, and of local court resources and organizational constraints.

The goals of criminal sentencing are inherently diverse and often contradictory. Judges at sentencing are charged with balancing concerns for community protection and public safety with individual reformation and offender needs. They are asked to balance the culpability of individual offenders with the goals of crime reduction and crime prevention in society, and increasingly they are asked to consider larger organizational and systemic goals such as concern for correctional resources or the disparate effects of their sentences on specific demographic groups in society.

For much of the twentieth century sentencing practices in the United States remained essentially unchanged. Recent decades, however, have witnessed a revolution in sentencing reform, with a series of transformative innovations aimed at creating greater uniformity, greater equality, and increased severity in sentencing. These changes have fundamentally altered the contours of contemporary punishment, redefining the structural and philosophical determinates of sentencing policy and contributing to dramatic growth in American prison populations. Contemporary reform movements have reconfigured the structure and goals of sentencing and created a variegated mix of differentiated sentencing systems across U.S. jurisdictions. This process of sentencing reform is ongoing—it continues to fuel ideological conflicts and stir heated policy debates, making sentencing in America one of the most politically charged and volatile issues in contemporary criminal justice.

Prior to the 1970s, sentencing systems were premised on rehabilitative ideals that emphasized individualized punishments tailored to the unique needs of individual offenders. Terms of confinement were often flexible and uncertain, involving wide ranges, with broad minimum and maximum terms that provided for substantial flexibility in determining when an offender had been rehabilitated and when he or she was therefore ready to be released back into society. This approach dated back to the mid-nineteenth century and was known as "indeterminate sentencing" because it produced sentences that were often uncertain and unpredictable. Judges decided the type and range of punishment, but release decisions were made by prison authorities or parole boards, who exercised considerable discretion in determining the final term of imprisonment.

Inherent in the era of indeterminate sentencing was a belief that criminal justice officials could be trusted to reform criminal offenders—judges were viewed as uniquely qualified to assess individual punishment and rehabilitative needs. With the exception of statutory maximums, judges determined sentencing outcomes carte blanche, without written reasons, systematic oversight, or appellate review (Frankel 1973). Parole boards exercised similar unfettered discretion in the determination of actual release dates from prison. Although this approach dominated criminal sentencing for nearly a century, a number of important events coincided during the 1960s and 1970s to raise serious concerns about its efficacy.

Prison conditions came under attack, race riots erupted in several cities, and a countercultural youth movement emerged in conjunction with anti–Vietnam War sentiments to help fuel a growing mistrust of government (Kerner Commission 1968). As part of the larger civil rights movement, a due process revolution swept through the justice system, criticizing the unbridled discretion of judges and parole officials and emphasizing heightened concerns over unwarranted disparities in punishment. Perhaps most famously, Judge Marvin Frankel published a scathing critique of indeterminate sentencing that questioned judicial training, oversight, and rationality in sentencing, claiming that the "almost wholly unchecked and sweeping powers" of judges "are terrifying and intolerable for a society that professes devotion to the rule of law" (Frankel 1973, 5). Violent crime was also on the rise, with some commentators identifying rehabilitative sentencing practices as the putative cause and arguing for a philosophical shift toward increased crime control (Wilson 1975). At the same time, empirical evidence suggested rehabilitation was ineffective, with one particularly influential report concluding that with few and isolated exceptions, "nothing works" in corrections (Lipton, Martinson, and Wilks 1975). Although its conclusions were largely taken out of context, this report served as a sounding board for criminal justice pundits and reform-minded politicians bent on change.

Ultimately, the confluence of these social forces fueled the flames of criminal justice reform and placed a new "get tough" sentencing philosophy at the forefront of political discourse in the United States. An unusual alliance of interest groups emerged, including both civil rights advocates and political liberals on the Left who were concerned with inequality in sentencing, and crime-control proponents and political conservatives on the Right who were concerned with undue leniency. United in public dissatisfaction with the justice system, this bipartisan coalition worked for striking reform in American sentencing systems. Although rehabilitation programs in practice were often underfunded and poorly implemented, rehabilitation as the core philosophical foundation of sentencing was abandoned, producing a policy void in sentencing that in many ways has yet to be filled today. An array of sentencing innovations were soon implemented, collectively known today as "determinate sentencing," which attempted to address concerns with disparity, inequity, and leniency in punishment.

Determinate sentencing reforms came in sundry forms, but they shared the common goal of constricting the sentencing discretion of judges and parole officials in order to limit inconsistency and uncertainty in punishment. Early reform efforts included statutory determinate sentencing systems, in which legislatures prescribed specific criminal penalties for specific crimes, as well as parole guidelines and voluntary sentencing guidelines—the former attempted to structure the discretion of parole boards, and the latter provided for nonbinding sentencing recommendations to which judges could voluntarily choose to adhere. These early reform efforts were not widely adopted, but subsequent sentencing innovations were introduced that have become extremely influential. A number of jurisdictions have established permanent sentencing commissions and promulgated legally binding "presumptive" guidelines, which more formally structure judicial sentencing discretion. Several jurisdictions have completely or partly abolished parole and passed "truth-in-sentencing" laws that require offenders to serve the vast majority of their nominal sentences, and every state has passed mandatory minimum sentencing provisions, such as three-strikes laws, that establish fixed minimum terms of imprisonment for select offenses or offenders.

One unforeseen consequence has been a carceral explosion unprecedented in the history of the nation. Since 1970 the American incarceration rate, adjusted for population growth, has roughly quintupled. As of 2008, more than 2.4 million people—more than 1 percent of the adult population—are behind bars (Bureau of Justice Statistics 2008), making the United States the world leader in incarceration (Mauer 2006). Moreover, public expenditures on corrections have also quintupled, and more new prisons have been built in recent decades than in the entire preceding history of the nation (Ruth and Reitz 2003). Contemporary prison growth in large part reflects recent policy initiatives that have increased arrests and incarcerations for drug crimes as well as length of stay and time served for other offenses (Blumstein and Beck 1999). Notably, the effects of modern prison growth have been disproportionately visited upon racial and ethnic minorities. Growth in African American imprisonment continues to outpace whites, with current imprisonment rates that are seven to eight times higher (Mauer 2006).

Many commentators have noted that financially, socially, and morally this rate of imprisonment cannot continue unabated. The pendulum of punishment is therefore beginning to show signs of swinging away from the law-and-order crime control policies of the 1980s and 1990s, back toward more offender-based rehabilitative and restorative sentencing principles. A nascent social movement has emerged emphasizing increased use of community corrections, sentencing alternatives, and rehabilitative correctional treatments (MacKenzie 2006), though most jurisdictions have yet to fully embrace them.

The revolution in determinate sentencing innovations has spurred a new wave of scholarly research on criminal sentencing and sentencing policy. Increased support has emerged for evidence-based sentencing and corrections, suggesting that empirical research may take on a heightened importance in continuing reform efforts. A number of studies assess the effects of sentencing reform efforts on fairness and equality in punishment as well as their effects on distended prison populations. Continued concern over issues of social inequality in sentencing has produced a spate of studies focusing on racial, ethnic, and gender disparity, and an increased emphasis on uniformity in sentencing has fueled an emergent interest in geographic disparity in punishment. Collectively, current work identifies a number of directions for future research, and it leads to several important insights regarding the desirable and undesirable consequences of current sentencing policy in America.

Contemporary sentencing research supports the continued use of sentencing guidelines as a promising approach for structuring sentencing discretion and managing the size of correctional populations, although evidence suggests that unwarranted sentencing disparities have not been eliminated. Racial and ethnic factors continue to be associated with incarceration and with discretionary outcomes like guidelines departures, particularly in drug cases. Gender effects are even more pronounced, and recent evidence suggests these disparities persist in jurisdictions with sentencing guidelines. Moreover, sentences continue to vary considerably across locations, raising important questions about jurisdictional differences in punishment. Future research efforts are needed that begin to collect and analyze new and unique sources of sentencing data, with a focus on examining new outcomes of interest, incorporating additional court actors besides the sentencing judge, and evaluating ongoing changes in contemporary sentencing policy across diverse jurisdictions, both nationally and internationally.

Assessing the current state of knowledge on criminal sentencing and sentencing policy leads to several general conclusions and specific policy recommendations:

- First, sentencing guidelines offer a promising approach for constraining judicial discretion and altering existing sentencing patterns. When tied to correctional resources they also offer an effective tool for managing correctional populations.

- Second, sentencing guidelines have not altogether eliminated judicial sentencing discretion or disparity between offenders or among courts. Research suggests that race, ethnicity, and gender continue to influence sentencing, at least for some offenders convicted of some crimes in some court contexts. The focus of future research should be on explaining how, why, and where unwarranted disparity is most prominent.
- Third, the scope and application of mandatory sentencing provisions need to be dramatically reduced. They should be limited to only the most serious, violent offenders, and mandatory sentences that require long sentences for drug and other nonviolent offenders should be repealed. Such restrictions would have important salutary effects on both distended prison populations and racial disproportionality in imprisonment.
- Fourth, very little is known about prosecutorial discretion in sentencing. Sentencing guidelines are likely to shift sentencing discretion from judges to prosecutors, though little empirical evidence exists that this has resulted in increased disparities in charging or plea bargaining. Improved information on the many important decisions of prosecutors, however, is sorely needed to better assess the necessity of increased prosecutorial oversight and regulation in the future.
- Fifth, increased use of well-managed community punishments offer a useful approach for addressing high prison costs and prison overcrowding, and for restricting our current reliance on incarceration as the primary sentencing option. Intermediate sanctions provide a more dynamic range of punishment options and can be built into sentencing guidelines to effectively regulate their use.
- Sixth, problem-solving diversionary courts may also represent a promising policy approach for diverting certain categories of offenders from incarceration. The use of drug courts in the sentencing of drug offenders in particular has shown promising results, though few evaluations currently exist for other types of problem-solving courts.

This chapter reviews the contemporary state of knowledge on criminal sentencing and sentencing systems in the United States. It begins with a discussion of the major sentencing innovations that have been enacted over the past four decades. These include parole abolition and truth-in-sentencing laws, statutory determinate sentencing, mandatory minimum sentences, and state and federal sentencing guidelines, along with a brief discussion of recent constitutionality issues in federal sentencing. Next, it discusses contemporary research evidence for consistency, uniformity, and equality in sentencing, focusing particularly on the evidence concerning racial, ethnic, gender, socioeconomic, and geographic disparities in punishment. Research assessing the effect of modern sentencing reforms is also reviewed, followed by a discussion of evidence-based policy recommendations. I conclude with an analysis of future directions for research on criminal sentencing.

I. Modern Determinate Sentencing Systems

Although a slight majority of states still operate under indeterminate sentencing systems, a distinct shift in sentencing has occurred that has fundamentally altered the modern terrain of punishment in America today. Indeterminate sentencing was premised on the notion that judges required unconstrained sentencing latitude to craft individual sentences to reform offenders effectively. Parole boards similarly required broad discretion to determine when offenders were rehabilitated and ready for release. With the abandonment of rehabilitation as the core sentencing rationale in the 1970s, though, the theoretical justifications and structural foundations for individualized punishment came under attack. Why should judges have broad, unquestioned sentencing discretion if individualized sentences lacked rehabilitative efficacy? Why should parole boards determine release dates if individual reformation was a myth? Should rules not be in place to avoid capriciousness and create greater equality and uniformity in punishment? Why should the public abide the disingenuousness of incarceration terms that were often only a fraction of the prodigious nominal terms of confinement pronounced at sentencing? These and related questions swelled in the rising tide of public opinion against rehabilitation in punishment and helped forge a series of new "determinate" sentencing innovations in the years to come.

The fall of rehabilitation also created a sharp and unexpected void in punitive philosophy. The solution that emerged, in part, was a reliance on a new "justice model" of punishment in which the goal of sentencing would be certain, fair, and proportional punishments. This new philosophy of punishment emphasized "just deserts"—or deserved justice—in which the goal of sentencing was to fit the punishment to the offense rather than the offender (Von Hirsch 1976). If rehabilitation was no longer the explicit goal of punishment, then indefinite terms of incarceration had little justification, and fixed and equal sentences reflecting offense severity and the prior offending history of the offender seemed preferable. Under just deserts, uniformity began to replace individualization as the paradigm regnant in sentencing, although no single purpose for punishment emerged; instead, sentencing policy often combined overlapping interest in deterrence, incapacitation, retribution, and crime control along with concerns for rehabilitation.

The emergence of just deserts as a philosophy of punishment was at the heart of a much larger structural shift toward "determinate sentencing." Although determinate sentencing reforms came in many forms, at their core were attempts to cabin judicial discretion and to create more uniform, fixed, and known terms of punishment. Determinate sentencing reforms attempted to address public perceptions of bias, disingenuousness, and capriciousness. Under determinate sentencing, systemic decision making is substituted for individualism, with narrow sentencing ranges or specific punishments replacing broad sentencing ranges, and with time served more directly tied to the pronounced sentence rather than the post hoc decisions of parole boards. Under this model, sentencing considerations emphasize greater uniformity, neutrality, certainty, predictability and severity in punishment, rather than focusing primarily on the rehabilitation of offenders.

A. Modern Sentencing Innovations

Although determinate sentencing innovations all shared at least some of these core concerns, they have taken various forms, leaving some commentators to note that sentencing philosophies today lack a strong, unifying organizational and policy-oriented goal structure (Reitz 2001). Determinate sentencing is often contrasted with indeterminate sentencing, but most modern sentencing systems are hybrids that are neither purely determinate nor purely indeterminate. Different jurisdictions have enacted varying degrees of sentencing reform, often with little consideration for their overlapping application.

1. *Truth-in-Sentencing and Parole Abolition*

A number of jurisdictions have taken explicit steps to address the disjuncture between sentences imposed on offenders by the court and the time that offenders spend incarcerated. Under indeterminate sentencing, parole boards typically considered offenders for early release after as little as one-third of the nominal sentence was served. Exact periods of confinement were therefore uncertain and unpredictable. "Good-time" reductions for satisfactory prison behavior, earned-time incentives for educational or vocational programs, and time reductions associated with prison crowding also contributed to shorter terms of confinement than those pronounced by the court. As part of the determinate sentencing revolution, many jurisdictions passed "truth-in-sentencing" laws in an attempt to increase the correspondence between the pronounced sentence and the sentence served.

Truth-in-sentencing laws attempt to reduce the discrepancy between the sentence imposed and the actual term of imprisonment by requiring offenders to serve a substantial, minimum portion of their sentence before being eligible for release. According to the Bureau of Justice Statistics, forty-one states had passed truth-in-sentencing laws by 1999, with twenty-six states and the District of Columbia conforming to federal incentive grants that require offenders convicted of serious violent crimes to serve at least 85 percent of their nominal sentence (Bureau of Justice Statistics 1999). Truth-in-sentencing laws vary notably among jurisdictions. Some states, like Maryland, Indiana, Nebraska and Texas, require qualifying offenders to serve a minimum of 50 percent of their sentences, whereas others, like Idaho, Nevada, and New Hampshire, mandate that offenders serve the full 100 percent. Very often, truth-in-sentencing laws specifically target violent offenders, with nearly all states establishing minimum standards that require offenders to serve somewhere between 50 percent and 100 percent of their sentence.

A number of states have also fully or partly abolished discretionary parole release in an attempt to increase predictability, certainty, and transparency in punishment. At the turn of the twenty-first century, fourteen states had abolished discretionary parole for all offenders and several other states had limited its application, often precluding the possibility of parole in the case of specific categories of serious, violent, or repeat offenders (Bureau of Justice Statistics 1999). In some states, parole boards have been retained but their duties have been redefined to provide oversight to offenders serving terms of post-incarceration supervised release. Collectively, truth-in-sentencing and parole abolition have significantly contributed to increased time served, particularly for violent offenders, which has played a key role in fueling the unprecedented growth in contemporary state and federal prison populations (Blumstein and Beck 1999).

2. *Statutory Determinate Sentencing*

In many jurisdictions, parole abolition and truth-in-sentencing were enacted along with broader policy efforts designed to achieve additional goals of sentencing reform. Among the earliest determinate sentencing reforms were attempts to codify sentencing discretion in state criminal codes. In the 1970s a number of states, including California, Illinois, Arizona, and Colorado, experimented with statutory determinate sentencing systems, in which criminal punishments for specific crimes were fixed by legislative statutes. California still follows a statutory system in which each criminal offense carries with it three potential punishments—the middle punishment is assumed appropriate under normal circumstances, with a lesser or greater punishment available if mitigating or aggravating circumstances exist. The sentencing judge must provide reasons on record for selecting a mitigating or aggravating sentence.

Other states that have enacted statutory determinate sentencing provide ranges of punishments for each crime, which vary in their degree of determinacy. Although statutory determinate sentencing offers one mechanism for increasing uniformity in sentencing, it is built upon the assumption that state legislatures are well equipped to make standardized sentencing determinations. In reality, elected officials are unlikely to have the expertise, available time, or legal knowledge to adequately codify, monitor, and regulate systems of fixed determinate punishments. Perhaps for this reason, no state has adopted a new statutory system of determinate sentencing since they were first introduced in the 1970s and early 1980s (although Florida did replace its sentencing guidelines with statutory presumptions for minimum sentences in 1998).

3. *Mandatory Minimum Sentencing*

Mandatory minimums are legislatively determined minimum sentences that uniformly apply to specific offenses or offenders. Judges are legally bound to sentence offenders to at least the mandatory minimum, with discretion to sentence them up to the statutory maximum. Mandatory sentences can also restrict parole or early-release eligibility, such as in the case of certain mandatory life sentences that preclude the possibility of parole release.

In 1970, at the height of the indeterminate sentencing movement, Congress categorically repealed all mandatory minimum sentences. Since that time, every state has reenacted them, making them the most prolific of modern sentencing reforms. Today the federal system alone has more than one hundred mandatory minimums (Tonry 1996). In part, the popularity of mandatory minimums reflects the fact that it is much easier to legislate specific laws tied to specific offenses than it is to design and implement a comprehensive system of statutory punishments for all crimes. Mandatory minimums have also enjoyed historically high levels of public support, making them a politically popular sentencing innovation.

Most mandatory sentences target violent, drug, or firearms offenses, or apply to "habitual" offenders, such as the "three-strikes laws" that require twenty-five years to life imprisonment for third-time felons. Some commentators point out that mandatory minimum sentences serve important political and symbolic goals, though they have been widely criticized for their ineffectiveness, selective application, and their procrustean and draconian approach to punishment (Tonry 1996). In jurisdictions with sentencing guidelines, mandatory sentences often conflict with prescribed guidelines ranges, introducing conflict between legislative and commission-based punishments. Despite their proliferation, mandatory minimum laws have existed for centuries, though in much more modest fashion, and their effects on sentencing are restricted to specific offenses or offenders.

4. *Sentencing Commissions and Sentencing Guidelines*

In an eloquent diatribe against indeterminate sentencing, Judge Frankel proposed as an alternative the creation of a new administrative body—the sentencing commission—that would be charged with establishing and monitoring a system of uniform sentencing recommendations (Frankel 1973). Frankel argued that unlike the state legislature, an administrative commission of sentencing experts would be able to develop special competency regarding appropriate punishments while remaining isolated from short-term political pressures. He argued that judges lacked the requisite training and accountability for their punishment decisions, and he proposed that a standardized system of recommendations, or "sentencing guidelines," be created to provide benchmarks for judges to increase uniformity, equity, and accountability in punishment.

5. *State Sentencing Guidelines*

Since the early 1980s, state sentencing guidelines have become a popular vehicle for enacting large-scale sentencing reform. At least twenty-one states currently operate sentencing guidelines (Kauder and Ostrum 2008), with more than half of the states experimenting with guidelines at one time or another. Like other determinate sentencing reforms, sentencing guidelines constrain judicial sentencing discretion, but unlike other reforms they typically rely on a sentencing commission as a specialized administrative body to structure and oversee judicial sentencing practices. Most sentencing guidelines today are set up as two-dimensional grids that include a measure of the seriousness of the current offense on one axis, along with a measure of the prior criminal record of the offender on the other. Sentencing decisions are determined, then, by the intersection of these two core sentencing criteria, with more serious crimes and longer criminal histories resulting in more severe recommended punishments.

Although all sentencing guidelines are founded on similar core ideas, their jurisdictional permutations have been diverse. Guidelines systems differ in their complexity, their sentencing ranges, the extent to which they constrain judicial sentencing discretion, whether or not discretionary parole release is retained, the types of crimes and sentencing options they control, the philosophies of punishment they emphasize, and the extent to which they deviate from past sentencing practices (Frase 2005). Table 22.1 summarizes several of the major components of extant guidelines systems. Some guidelines, like those in Minnesota, govern only prison sentences for felony offenses, whereas others, like those in Pennsylvania, cover a broad range of sentencing options, including jail, prison, and intermediate sanctions, for both felony and misdemeanor offenses. A few states, like Delaware and Ohio, have created narrative rather than grid-based guidelines and other states, like Maryland, have developed separate sentencing matrices for different categories of crime. Although there has been some discussion of creating three-dimensional guidelines that incorporate other factors such as offender culpability or amenability to treatment, no state has yet taken this approach.

State guideline systems can be broadly categorized along two continuums, one ranging from "mandatory guidelines" to "voluntary guidelines" and one ranging from "descriptive" to "prescriptive" guidelines. Mandatory guidelines legally mandate judges to uniformly sentence within prescribed ranges, although few guidelines are truly mandatory. Many guidelines instead are "presumptive," meaning

Table 22.1. Summary of Sentencing Guidelines Systems

Jurisdiction	Scale: Voluntary (1) vs. Mandatory (12)	Initial Effective Date	Major Structural Features					Also Regulates		
			Perm. Sent. Comm.	Resource Impact Assessments	Appeals or Other Enforcement	Parole Release Abolished	Intermediate Sanctions	Misdem. Offenses	Revocation of Probation	Supervised Rel./Parole
Utah	6	01/1979	1983	1993	reasons	mostly	some	some		some
Alaska	3	01/1980			X	X			some	
Minnesota	11	05/1980	X	X	X	X				some
Pennsylvania	9	07/1982	X	some	some		1994	X		
Maryland	7	07/1983	1996	1996	reasons			X		
Florida	Not rated	10/1983	until 1998	1988–1998	some	X				
Michigan	8	01/1984	1995–2002	1995–1997	some, 1999		some			
Washington	10	07/1984	X	X	X	X	some		some	
Delaware	6	10/1987	X	X	reasons	1990	X	X	some	
Federal	Not rated	11/1987	X	some	X	X	some	some	X	X
Oregon	10	11/1989	X	X	X	X	X			some
Tennessee	3	11/1989	until 1995	until 1995	some	some	X	X		
Virginia	6	01/1991	1995	1995	reasons	1995	some		some	
Kansas	10	07/1993	X	1995	X	X				some
Arkansas	4	01/1994	X	X	reasons	some	X			
North Carolina	12	10/1994	X	X	some	X	X	X		some
Wisconsin	1	1985, 1995	X	X						
Ohio	1	07/1996	X	X		X			some	some
Missouri	2	03/1997	X	X		some				
Louisiana	5	1/1992	X				some			
Massachusetts	7	01/1994	X	X	X		X	X		X
D.C.	3	06/2004	X	some		X			some	some
Alabama	3	10/2006	X	X						some

Note: Adapted from Frase (2005) and Kauder and Ostrum (2008) judges are legally required to follow them unless extenuating circumstances exist, in which case they may "depart" from the recommended ranges. Presumptive guidelines typically require explicit written justification for departures, which are often subject to appellate review. Voluntary guidelines, on the other hand, provide sentencing recommendations that are not legally binding. Judges are encouraged to conform to the guidelines, but they are not required to do so. Presumptive guidelines place a higher level of control over judicial sentencing discretion than voluntary guidelines. Descriptive guidelines are based on past sentencing practices, attempting to codify existing sentencing behaviors, whereas prescriptive guidelines "prescribe" new sentencing patterns that differ from past practices in substantively meaningful ways. State guidelines systems in practice vary considerably in the extent to which judges must follow them and in the degree to which their sentence recommendations are representative of past sentencing practices (Kauder and Ostrum 2008).

In general, state sentencing guidelines have been favorably received by practitioners, policymakers, and academics alike. Frase (2000, 425), for instance, concludes that "state sentencing guidelines have proven to be much better than any other sentencing system that has been tried or proposed." Not all sentencing guidelines, however, have enjoyed unqualified success. Some states, like Wisconsin, have created sentencing commissions only to see them subsequently repealed then reinstated, and other states have been unsuccessful in their attempts to promulgate guidelines altogether. Several states, including New Mexico, Oklahoma, Iowa, and New Jersey, are currently working to establish sentencing guidelines. By far the most controversial sentencing guidelines, though, have been the federal guidelines, which differ substantially from state systems.

6. *Federal Sentencing Guidelines*

The federal guidelines took a unique approach to sentencing reform that has been heavily criticized on several fronts. First, the federal guidelines were based on a detailed and complex sentencing calculus, involving myriad calculations and numerous specific sentencing adjustments, which resulted in a uniquely technical, abstract, and complicated guidelines system. Second, the federal guidelines were designed to be especially rigid in their application, creating narrow ranges, expressly restricting use of sentencing considerations such as family, education, employment and community ties, and limiting the judge's ability to depart from the guidelines to circumstances not adequately accounted for by the commission. The guidelines substantially restricted judicial discretion, displacing it to federal probation officers and federal prosecutors. Third, the federal guidelines increased federal punishments and dramatically reduced the use of probation, limiting it as a sentencing option to only 23 of the 258 cells in the guidelines. Fourth, the guidelines created an unusual departure mechanism for "substantial assistance" to the government, which required a motion from the prosecutor to earn an often-sizable sentencing discount for offenders who assisted in the prosecution of another federal case. And fifth, the federal guidelines were based on real-offense sentencing, which meant that the judge at sentencing must consider all "relevant conduct" related to the offense, including acquitted and uncharged offense behaviors. For these and other reasons, the federal guidelines have been labeled overly rigid, harsh, and constraining, as well as too complex and mechanical in their application (Stith and Cabranes 1998). One prominent scholar referred to them as the "most controversial and disliked sentencing reform initiative in U.S. history" (Tonry 1996, 72).

Whereas most state guidelines systems have ten to fifteen levels of offense severity, the federal guidelines have forty-three levels. Their application involves detailed calculations and complex sentencing adjustments. Each offense type has a base offense-level that is applied, which can be subsequently altered through the application of general and offense-specific adjustments. General adjustments include such things as mitigating and aggravating offense roles, discounts for "acceptance of responsibility," and enhancements for vulnerable victims and obstruction of justice. Numerous "offense-specific" adjustments also apply under the federal guidelines. Drug offenders, for instance, may receive specific enhancements for possession of a firearm or distribution of drugs in prison, or they may receive a discount under the "safety valve" provision that removes mandatory minimums for first-time minor offenders. Final offense severity scores also vary according to such things as the quantity and type of drugs, the amount of loss in financial crimes, and even criminal history considerations, such as special offense-level enhancements for career criminals, terrorism, and hate crimes.

Although these examples scarcely scratch the surface of the complexity of federal sentencing, they illustrate the dynamic and complex processes involved in applying the federal guidelines. Some critics suggest the guidelines are "a labyrinthine system of rules devised by a distant and alien administrative agency" that "sacrifice comprehensibility and common sense on the altar of pseudo-scientific uniformity" (Stith and Cabranes 1998, 5). The unparalleled degree of complexity in federal sentencing was rooted in the desire to create a sentencing system that would fully account for all relevant considerations at sentencing. As others have noted, however, it is impractical if not impossible to reduce the full complexity of individuals and their behavior to a simple two-dimensional mathematical calculus (Tonry 1996).

The complexity and rigidity of the federal guidelines have also led to geographical variation in the ways they are applied. Research on federal departures, for instance, shows that their use varies dramatically across federal districts. The guidelines often invoke vague definitions, for instance between a "minor" and "minimal" role in the offense, resulting in fact bargaining over the types of discounts and enhancements to be applied (Nagel and Schulhofer 1992). Similarly, research confirms that the relative definition of what qualifies as "substantial assistance" is far from uniform (Johnson, Ulmer, and Kramer 2008), and substantial assistance departures have been further questioned on philosophical grounds because they arguably reward more culpable and experienced offenders who have more useful information to divulge.

Since their inception in 1987, the federal sentencing guidelines have faced a number of important legal challenges (Frase 2007). The guidelines were first criticized on grounds that they violated the "separation of powers" clause in the U.S. Constitution. The U.S. Sentencing Commission (USSC) is lodged within the judicial branch of government, and critics maintained that because it was a bureaucratic administrative agency with lawmaking power, it was in fact performing legislative duties. In 1989 the Supreme Court ruled that the USSC did not violent the separation of powers and the federal guidelines were legally upheld (*Mistretta v. United States*, 488 U.S. 361 [1989]). A series of other important Supreme Court decisions involving U.S. sentencing systems followed (see Frase 2007; USSC 2008) until January 2005 when federal sentencing was fundamentally restructured.

The watershed case was *Booker* (*U.S. v. Booker*, 543 U.S. 220 [2005]). Because the federal guidelines are based on real offense sentencing, offenders can be punished for all offense-related behaviors, even those not formally charged or not resulting in conviction. Known as "relevant conduct," these factors include the magnitude of harm, individual motivation for the crime, total amount of drugs or lost goods, and similar offense-related considerations. Real offense sentencing was implemented by the architects of the federal guidelines in an attempt to limit the influence of charge bargaining in federal court. Importantly, though, the standard of evidence for proving relevant conduct is lower than for conviction—the judge needs only a "preponderance of the evidence" to apply guidelines adjustments at sentencing, rather than the stricter legal standard of "beyond a reasonable doubt" used for conviction.

In practice, this meant that federal judges were permitted to enhance punishments above the upper range of the applicable guidelines based on relevant conduct behaviors that were not subjected to the same legal standard of proof guaranteed by the Sixth Amendment. The Supreme Court's five-to-four decision in *Booker* ruled that the imposition of a sentence above the upper guidelines range based on only a preponderance of the evidence violated an offender's constitutional right to a jury by not providing for a jury determination of the sentencing facts. Confronted with this dilemma, the Court elected to treat the federal guidelines as "advisory" rather than abandon them. Federal judges now must consult the federal sentencing guidelines, but they are no longer legally mandated to impose sentences within the recommended ranges. Recent Court rulings, however, have established a "presumption of reasonableness" for sentences that fall within federal guidelines ranges (*Rita v. U.S*, 127 S.Ct. 2456 [2007]). The full effect of these landmark changes in federal sentencing has yet to be realized. Preliminary evidence suggests that judges have begun to sentence offenders outside the federal guidelines with increasing frequency, but federal sentencing practices otherwise have not been dramatically altered (Hofer 2007).

The experience of the federal sentencing guidelines highlights some of the potential pitfalls in the implementation of sentencing guidelines, but for the most part guidelines represent a modern sentencing innovation that has been well received. Guidelines systems continue to evolve, with increased efforts to diversify, incorporate intermediate punishments, and improved resource management functions. The extent to which sentencing guidelines and other recent sentencing innovations have successfully achieved the original goals of sentencing reform, though, including increased uniformity and equality in punishment, remains a central topic of scholarly research on criminal sentencing.

II. Research on Criminal Sentencing

Post-sentencing reform discourse has focused primarily on the effectiveness of guidelines systems in eliminating idiosyncratic sentencing practices, increasing uniformity, and reducing unwarranted disparities. Although sentencing guidelines are generally viewed as having reduced unwarranted disparity, empirical research continues to unearth significant differences along racial, ethnic, gender, and geographic lines. Far less research has attempted to codify the effects of sentencing reform on other outcomes of interest, such as prison populations or crime rates. Overall, sentencing guidelines that are tied to correctional resources and incorporate intermediate sanctions seem to offer the most promising approach for future reforms.

A. Unwarranted Disparities in Sentencing

Contemporary sentencing research is dominated by empirical studies of individual sentencing disparity, typically focusing on racial or gender differences in punishment and the extent to which they can be accounted for by guidelines factors like offense severity and prior record (Blumstein et al. 1983). The implicit assumption is often that unaccounted-for disparity is symptomatic of discrimination in the justice system, but importantly, "disparity" is distinct from "discrimination," with the former defined as observed differences in punishment and the latter by observed differences attributable to prejudice or bias on the part of court actors or the system as a whole. Research on sentencing disparity abounds, but relatively few studies explicitly measure "discrimination," in part because of the inherent difficulties involved in this rare breed of research. Collectively, current work suggests that individual offender characteristics continue to influence criminal sentencing decisions, but these effects are typically small compared with legal considerations like the severity of the current offense and the prior record of the offender.

1. *Racial and Ethnic Disparity*

Conclusions regarding the relative importance of racial and ethnic considerations in sentencing have varied over time, but contemporary research suggests that both race and ethnicity continue to influence sentencing decisions, particularly for young, unemployed offenders and in drug cases. Racial and ethnic disparity tends to be associated primarily with the incarceration decision, as well as outcomes involving a high degree of discretion, such as judicial departures from sentencing guidelines. Despite these conclusions, racial and ethnic effects are typically small in magnitude relative to legal characteristics of the case.

Since at least the 1930s, criminologists have been preoccupied with the study of racial and ethnic disparities in sentencing (Sellin 1928), with scholarly treatments of racial inequality and discrimination in the justice system abounding (Blumstein et al. 1983). Research on racial disparity in sentencing has advanced through four distinct waves (Zatz 1987). Wave 1 consisted of studies done prior to 1960 in which simplistic methods with insufficient legal controls produced strong evidence of racial disparity in sentencing. Wave 2 occurred in the 1960s and introduced stronger legal controls that largely explained these early race differences. Wave 3 in the 1970s provided advances in data sources and analytical techniques, and revealed more subtle and indirect racial disparities. Wave 4, starting in the 1980s, has focused on the degree to which racial and ethnic disparities have been ameliorated or exacerbated under modern determinate sentencing innovations.

Although findings remain somewhat equivocal, the weight of contemporary evidence suggests that minority defendants are often disadvantaged, particularly for certain sentencing decisions and in certain contexts (Spohn 2000). Black and Hispanic offenders, in particular, are often more likely to be incarcerated, and they are less likely to benefit from downward departures from sentencing guidelines (Mitchell 2005). In general, racial disparities are greatest for black and Hispanic offenders who are young, male, and unemployed (Spohn and Holleran 2000), and for those convicted of drug offenses, especially in federal court (Steffensmeier and Demuth 2000). For instance, one recent meta-analysis of sentencing disparity reviewed seventy-one studies and concluded that although the magnitude of race effects is small compared to other factors like offense seriousness, the evidence indicates that "unwarranted racial disparities persist" in sentencing (Mitchell 2005, 439).

Some research finds variations in racial and ethnic disparities in additional case processing decisions and across jurisdictions. For instance, recent work finds that minority offenders are given higher bail amounts that they are less able to pay, which translates into increased severity at sentencing (Demuth 2003). There is also some evidence that the race of the victim influences sentencing. Several studies demonstrate important racial disparities in capital punishment in the United States, with black offenders who target white victims most likely to receive the death penalty (Paternoster and Brame 2008). Few studies outside of capital punishment investigate victim characteristics, however, so this represents a priority for future research.

Recent empirical work also suggests that racial and ethnic disparity varies along other sentencing dimensions. For instance, studies report significant variation in these effects across crime types (Steffensmeier and Demuth 2000), modes of conviction (Johnson 2003), and organizational court contexts (Ulmer and Johnson 2004). Theoretical explanations for racial disparities in punishment generally suggest that organizational time and information constraints lead judges and other court actors to rely on an attribution process, which invokes criminal stereotypes and past experiences that disadvantage minority defendants (Albonetti 1991). Few studies, however, actually attempt to measure these underlying theoretical constructs. One notable exception is the work of Bridges and Steen (1998), which found observed racial differences in juvenile punishments were largely accounted for by racial attributions—probation officers were more likely to attribute the criminal behavior of minority youth to internal causes, whereas criminality for white youth was more often attributed to external social forces. Additional research of this kind is needed that moves beyond simple comparisons of racial groups and begins to capture the underlying decision-making processes of different criminal court actors at sentencing.

Taken as a whole, contemporary research on racial and ethnic disparity indicates that black and Hispanic offenders are often disadvantaged at sentencing, although racial disparity and discrimination is far from systemic—it does not characterize every decision in every court but rather appears to be tied to some decisions for some offenders who commit particular offenses in certain contexts. The goal of future research, therefore, should be to begin to identify and investigate the underlying causes of observed differences as well as the particular sentencing contexts in which racial and ethnic inequalities are most egregious and most pronounced.

2. *Gender Disparity*

An equally extensive literature examines gender disparities in sentencing, with results that are often less ambiguous than for race and ethnicity. The majority of studies conclude that female offenders are treated with relative leniency at sentencing, even after the implementation of modern sentencing reforms like guidelines (Zatz 2000; Blackwell, Holleran, and Finn 2008). While there are exceptions, most studies find that females are less likely to be incarcerated and that they are more likely to benefit in decisions that involve a high degree of sentencing discretion, such as departures from sentencing guidelines. The results for length of incarceration are less conclusive but also tend to favor female defendants (Daly and Bordt 1995; Zatz 2000).

Some work also suggests that race or ethnicity and gender mutually condition one another at sentencing. For instance, Steffensmeier and Demuth (2006) report that racial and ethnic disparities primarily characterize the sentencing of male rather than female offenders, but that gender matters across all racial and ethnic groups. Related work suggests gender differences at sentencing are reflective of earlier case processing decisions such as pretrial detention (Kruttschnitt and Green 1984). Overall, gender differences tend to be more pronounced than racial and ethnic differences. For instance, in their summary of research, Daly and Bordt (1995, 143) concluded that "sex effects favoring women are far more frequent than race effects favoring whites."

Theoretical explanations of gender differences in punishment range from practical considerations involving family roles, child-rearing responsibilities, economic dependencies, and gendered health-care concerns to arguments that judges are socialized to treat female offenders paternalistically or chivalrously at sentencing (Daly 1994; Zatz 2000). Relatively few studies, however, explicitly measure these intervening theoretical processes, so it is difficult to draw firm conclusions. Additional qualitative research is needed to better investigate the underlying reasons for gender differences in sentencing. In part, judges may simply view male offenders as more culpable or more dangerous in light of their increased involvement in serious and violent crime. The effects of gender may also depend on other considerations, like social contexts or types of crime. For instance, some scholars have suggested that sex disparities reflect attributions about gender-appropriate behaviors (Nagel and Hagan 1982), and some research supports this claim finding less "respectable" women tend to receive harsher sentences (Kruttschnitt 1982).

3. Socioeconomic Disparity

Research on the effects of socioeconomic factors in sentencing is anemic compared with studies of race and gender. Adequate indicators of social and economic standing are routinely missing from public sentencing data and, when available, are often poorly measured (Zatz 2000). Moreover, because convicted offenders typically come from lower socioeconomic ranks, studies of social class tend to suffer from a lack of variation on indictors of socioeconomic status. Given the limitations and dearth of work examining socioeconomic effects in sentencing, it is difficult to draw firm conclusions about its importance, but studies that include measures of class status tend to find evidence that lower-class citizens receive more severe punishments (Zatz 2000).

Much of the work on socioeconomic status relies on coarse proxies, such as educational attainment or employment status. For instance, Chiricos and Bales (1991) concluded that unemployment exerts significant independent effects on judicial decisions regarding both pretrial and post-sentencing incarceration. Moreover, they found that employment status demonstrated the strongest effects for young, black males. More recent work concurs, finding that socioeconomic factors are intimately tied to the race and gender of the offender. Spohn and Holleran (2000), for instance, report that unemployed black and Hispanic males are more likely to be sentenced to incarceration relative to employed white males. Education has also been found to affect sentencing, with more educated offenders more likely to receive beneficial departures below federal sentencing guidelines ranges (Johnson, Ulmer, and Kramer 2008).

Overall, research on socioeconomic influences remains limited so overarching conclusions should be drawn cautiously. The few studies that have employed more sophisticated measures of socioeconomic status are now dated and provide mixed results (see Chiricos and Waldo, 1975; Hagan, Nagel, and Albonetti 1980). Current work collectively suggests that socioeconomic status, particularly in conjunction with race and gender, may influence sentencing decisions, producing less favorable outcomes for lower-class offenders, but future research is needed that investigates this issue in greater depth with improved methods and measures.

4. *Geographical Variation in Sentencing*

In addition to reducing individual sentencing disparities, another core goal of modern sentencing reform was to create greater uniformity in punishment among courts (USSC 2004). Both qualitative and quantitative studies suggest that localized cultural norms result in distinct case-processing strategies that color the relative salience and interpretation of core criteria in sentencing (Ulmer and Johnson 2004). The likelihood of incarceration, average sentence length, and use of discretionary departure provisions have all been shown to vary significantly across jurisdictions, often in accord with organizational characteristics of the local court environment.

In part, disparate findings regarding individual offender characteristics across studies may reflect environmental differences among courts. Future research on individual disparities in sentencing will benefit tremendously from shifting the focus away from whether race, gender, and other considerations in sentencing matter, to where, when, and how they matter across decision-making contexts. Early work in political science argued that local political, legal, and organizational environments interact with court workgroup dynamics to establish localized punishment norms that create jurisdictional variations in punishment (Eisenstein and Jacobs 1977; Eisenstein, Flemming, and Nardulli 1988). According to this perspective, distinct "court communities" emerge over time that result in differing approaches to case processing and sentencing among courts.

Large-scale, systematic empirical research on intercourt variations in sentencing practices, however, represents a relatively modern research endeavor. Recent work offers some evidence that individual sentencing considerations can vary substantially across courts. Organizational factors such as the size, caseload, and departure rate of the court, along with the availability of local correctional resources, have all been tied to individual sentencing decisions (Ulmer and Johnson 2004; Johnson 2005). Contextual effects in punishment are often subtle and indirect, and they typically account for a small proportion of the total variation in sentencing, but they can be quite consequential when considered in concert with other individual considerations in sentencing. Additional contextual sentencing considerations include the background characteristics of sentencing judges (Johnson 2006), racial population dynamics (King and Wheelock 2007), local political contexts (Helms and Jacobs 1999), and the degree of diversity in local courtroom workgroups (Ward, Farrell, and Rousseau 2009), though empirical work in each of these areas is not well developed, and these findings remain mixed.

Much of this work assumes that intercourt variation in sentencing is undesirable, yet there may be important reasons for court workgroups to develop unique local sentencing standards. Given regional variations in caseloads, public values, attitudes toward crime, and other locally determined sentencing considerations, some degree of cross-court variation in punishment may be necessary to achieve just sentencing outcomes. Future research is needed that further examines the underlying causes of interjurisdictional variations in sentencing to better address this emerging concern.

B. The Effects of Sentencing Reform

Relative to the expansive literature on extralegal disparities in criminal sentencing, surprisingly little empirical research attempts to quantify the effects of modern sentencing reforms. Some research suggests that sentencing guidelines affect state-level incarceration and prison admission rates, with little effect from other reforms like mandatory minimums and truth-in-sentencing (Sorensen and Stemen 2002), whereas other work finds little overall effect of determinate sentencing reforms on existing prison populations (Marvell and Moody 1996). A number of studies demonstrate not only that sentencing guidelines are an effective mechanism for altering past sentencing practices but also that sentencing commissions provide a useful bureaucratic structure for implementing these changes (Tonry 1996).

In some states, sentencing commissions have also been able to use guidelines systems to achieve systemic goals, like effective management of growing correctional populations (Frase 2005). Many states now routinely conduct computer projections on prison populations in order to evaluate the influence of potential changes to their sentencing guidelines or other proposed sentencing changes. In some cases, resource management concerns have been the primary motivating factor behind the establishment of state sentencing guidelines.

Too few evaluations have been conducted comparing sentencing patterns before and after the implementation of sentencing guidelines. Early work of this sort suggested that racial and gender disparities were significantly reduced by state guidelines. For instance, evaluations in Minnesota found that extralegal offender disparity had been curtailed and that the guidelines did not result in dramatic changes in charging practices in that state (Miethe and Moore 1985; Miethe 1987). However, follow-up work has since suggested that the reduction in disparity dissipated over time (Stolzenberg and D'Allessio 1996), and more recent work now identifies other key decisions, such as departures from sentencing guidelines, that have the potential to reintroduce disparities into sentencing under guidelines (Johnson 2005).

A number of more recent guidelines evaluations have also concluded that meaningful sentencing disparities remain under guidelines systems. Koons-Witt (2002), for instance, re-examined gender disparity before and after the passage of Minnesota's guidelines and concluded that although gender did not have direct effects on punishment, women with dependent children were treated with special leniency in both time periods. She concluded that issues of substantive justice continue to affect sentencing under the Minnesota guidelines. Similarly, Sims-Blackwell, Holleran, and Finn's recent evaluation of gender disparity under the Pennsylvania guidelines concluded that "Pennsylvania's structured sentencing model has not affected the sex-sentencing relationship in that state" (2008, 399).

Two recent evaluations of sentencing reform in Ohio concurred, finding that the sentencing guidelines in that state produced few uniform changes over time. Although racial disparity in charging was reduced, disparity in imprisonment increased (Wooldredge, Griffin, and Rauschenberg 2005) and the effects of gender on imprisonment remained unchanged before and after the passage of Ohio's guidelines (Griffin and Wooldredge 2006). In general, there has also been little evidence that the introduction of guidelines has significantly increased disparities associated with prosecutorial decision making as some initially feared, although empirical studies of this ilk remain rare (Miethe 1987; Wooldredge and Griffin 2005).

Early evaluations of the federal guidelines reported that they were successful in reducing disparity (USSC 1991), but these conclusions have also been challenged on several grounds (Tonry 1996). Few independent evaluations of pre/post differences in federal sentencing exist, although one evaluation concluded that under the federal guidelines, "Special treatment, not equal treatment persists" (Nagel and Johnson 1994). Moreover, conclusions drawn from early guidelines evaluations may have limited applicability today in the wake of recent Supreme Court decisions that have transformed the federal guidelines from presumptive to advisory. A clear priority of future research on federal sentencing is to investigate the effects of this structural shift on federal sentencing practice.

Scholarly consensus generally concludes that sentencing guidelines have achieved many of their goals (Tonry 1996; Frase 2005). Much of this research, however, is now dated, and it has focused on only a limited number of guidelines systems. Relatively few studies investigate the long-term impact of sentencing guidelines, and results from current work are inherently difficult to generalize across research contexts. As Bushway and Piehl (2007) argue, it is important for analyses of sentencing reforms to account explicitly for jurisdictional variation in the institutional settings in which different sentencing policies are enacted. As different states enact and revise guidelines systems, unique opportunities will continue to arise for researchers to assess the effects of policy changes on sentencing practices across jurisdictions. The recent Supreme Court decisions in *Booker* and *Blakely* (*Blakely v. Washington* 124 S. Ct. 2531 [2004]) provide examples of important natural experiments for examining the effects of policy changes in sentencing, so future research should take advantage of these and related changes both within and across jurisdictions.

Overall, commission-based regulation of sentencing guidelines has proven to be an effective mechanism for altering punishment patterns and implementing other policy initiatives such as correctional management goals (Tonry 1996). In part, the apparent success of guidelines and sentencing commissions stems from their broad appeal across multiple constituencies. Legal advocates, civil libertarians, and liberal scholars laud guidelines for encouraging greater consistency, uniformity, and intentionality in sentencing; crime control advocates, law enforcement agents, and conservative scholars support them for the certainty and severity of punishment they provide. Practitioners, including correctional officials, prosecutors, and even judges increasingly support sentencing guidelines because they reduce uncertainty in sentencing, increase predictability in corrections, and allow for improved resource management. Given the current breadth of their political support, the continued dissemination of state sentencing guidelines in the United States shows little sign of abating at this time, although this process remains far from complete in many U.S. jurisdictions.

C. Evidence-Based Policy Recommendations

The collective research on sentencing provides several directions for useful evidence-based policy reform. First, research findings suggest that commission-based sentencing guidelines have a lot to offer the future of punishment in the United States. They have proven to be effective tools for tailoring criminal punishments and for managing correctional populations. There is some suggestion that guidelines may also serve to create greater uniformity and fairness in sentencing, though this remains a source of debate. A select number of states have also recently introduced intermediate sanctions into their guidelines structures with some success (Tonry 1998). One lesson from prior work is that sentencing guidelines must be tailored to the unique local and historical circumstances of the jurisdiction in which they are enacted. It is unlikely that "one size fits all" will ever apply to state sentencing systems, given state diversity in their constituencies, legal codes, and historical and cultural sentencing norms. Overall, guidelines that are administered by sentencing commissions, are tied to correctional resources, and explicitly provide for alternatives to incarceration seem to hold the most promise for future policy development.

Second, there is convincing evidence that other sentencing innovations, particularly mandatory minimums, are less successful in achieving the goals of sentencing reform. Research indicates that mandatory sentences have been selectively applied in only a fraction of cases that are technically eligible (Tonry 1996, 2009). As Reitz (2001) suggests, the "hyper-determinacy" of mandatory sentences is often circumvented by a prosecutorial decision-making process that is exempt from public scrutiny and official review. There is also evidence that mandatory penalties are ineffective deterrents of future crime (Zimring, Hawkins, and Kamin 2003; Tonry 2009), and that they have contributed to stark racial disproportionality in imprisonment (Tonry 1995; Mauer 2001). The latter issue is particularly important and perhaps best illustrated by the notorious discontinuity between mandatory minimum penalties for crack and powder cocaine. In the federal system, an offender traditionally had to have 500 grams of powder cocaine, predominantly used by white offenders, to trigger the same five-year mandatory sentence attached to only 5 grams of crack cocaine, predominantly used by African Americans. This "100:1" ratio in punishment has been heavily criticized (Tonry 1995), and although federal guidelines penalties for crack cocaine have been recently reduced (USSC 2007) they remain excessively severe. A core policy concern surrounding mandatory minimums is their breadth of application, particularly for drug crimes—they have proven easy to enact but difficult to repeal. Future policy efforts should therefore be targeted at narrowing the scope of existing mandatory laws and restricting their application to only the most serious violent crimes, for which there is some general consensus that long prison sentences are appropriate.

Third, prior work repeatedly identifies the expanding role of the prosecutor as a key unregulated element in sentencing. Sentencing reform has exclusively targeted the discretion of judges and correctional officials with virtually no effort to investigate, monitor, or constrain the discretion of public prosecutors. In most jurisdictions, prosecutors retain the wholly unchecked discretion to dismiss charges outright, determine initial charges, engage in charge or sentence negotiations via plea bargaining, and invoke certain mandatory minimum sentencing provisions. In many cases, these charging decisions have direct consequences for the type and availability of punishments at sentencing. Research on prosecutorial charging is relatively dated and surprisingly sparse. It provides only limited and mixed evidence for charging disparity, but select studies have identified important racial, gender, and related disparities in prosecutorial decision-making outcomes (LaFree 1980; Paternoster 1984; Albonetti 1992).

Although there is a delicate balance between providing needed oversight and creating hyperformality in the punishment process, prosecutorial decision making requires, at the very least, additional future inquiry and investigation. The discretionary powers of the public prosecutor are immense and remain largely immune from public and legal oversight. Although overregulation is no panacea for discretionary decision making, prosecutorial screening and case-processing guidelines may hold the key to producing greater consistency and fairness in prosecution and punishment (Forst 1999). Future policy initiatives need to mandate the collection of relevant data from prosecutors' offices regarding their initial screening and charging decisions in order to assess the need for prosecutorial reform. To the extent that inequitable outcomes result from inconsistent or biased charging practices, prosecutorial charging guidelines akin to existing state sentencing guidelines could be developed and enacted across jurisdictions. Such an approach has already been applied to prosecutors in the Netherlands (Tak 2001).

Fourth, well-implemented, community-based intermediate sanctions offer a potentially useful approach for increasing proportionality in punishment and for reducing prison costs and overcrowding associated with overreliance on incarceration as a primary sentencing option. Intermediate sanctions encompass a broad array of punishment options, such as electronic monitoring, intensive supervision, drug and alcohol treatments, and day-reporting centers among others, that theoretically fall between probation and incarceration on the punishment severity continuum (Tonry and Morris 1990). Although structuring the use of intermediate sanctions is a formidable challenge, several states have demonstrated that it is possible to develop sentencing guidelines that incorporate community-based intermediate punishment options into their formal sentencing structure. At least seven states have formally incorporated intermediate sanction provisions into their guidelines to structure the sentencing of offenders to community-based punishments, with several other states partially regulating the use of alternative sanctions.

Different states have taken different approaches to intermediate punishments. North Carolina and Pennsylvania, the earliest states to incorporate them into their sentencing guidelines, have developed clusters of punishment cells, or different "sentencing zones," in which intermediate punishments can be used in lieu of or in conjunction with probation and incarceration. This approach has been followed in Massachusetts. Other states, like Washington, have developed specific "structured sentencing alternatives" or "categorical exceptions" that offer sentencing reductions or community-based alternatives to specific offender groups, such as nonviolent offenders with no previous felony convictions (Engen et al. 2003). Structuring intermediate punishments through sentencing guidelines helps to increase punishment options, assuage fiscal and spatial constraints on overcrowded prisons, and address concerns over judicial misapplication of sentencing alternatives to inappropriate offenders. Still, relatively little guidance is currently provided for choosing among available alternatives, so further refinements in the structuring of these options is needed. For instance, sentencing presumptions regarding how and when to substitute community punishments for incarceration should be pursued in future reforms. Overall, incorporation of intermediate sanctions into sentencing guidelines, particularly as a substitute for imprisonment, offers a promising policy initiative, though additional experimentation and research is clearly needed in this area.

Finally, one recent development in contemporary sentencing policy has been the emergence and rapid dissemination of specialized courts, or problem-solving courts, in many U.S. jurisdictions. To some degree this reflects the development of restorative justice principles as a new philosophy of punishment in sentencing (Daly 2000). Problem-solving courts emerged with the implementation of the first drug court in Dade County, Florida in 1989, which was designed to combine the efforts of justice and treatment professionals to provide intensive community-based treatment, management, and supervision of felony drug offenders. The general concept of problem-solving courts has since rapidly spread, with drug courts being established in every state and numerous other specialized courts being developed in other areas, including domestic violence, mental health, guns, community, teen, and family courts. Initial research evidence on drug courts has been very positive (MacKenzie 2006), but few evaluations have been conducted on other specialized courts, and some care must be exercised in assuming that the principles developed for drug offenders will naturally translate to other domains. Still, problem-solving courts currently hold considerable promise as a relatively recent policy initiative in criminal sentencing.

D. Future Directions

Historically, sentencing research has provided a wealth of knowledge about the factors that best predict judicial decision making in criminal courts. Although this research has advanced considerably in recent years (Zatz 1987) it will continue to benefit from the pursuit of several emerging areas, including empirical examinations of new outcomes of interest, investigation of additional forms of sentencing disparity, efforts to better understand the underlying causes of disparate punishment, incorporation of improved measures of social context and additional court actors besides the sentencing judge, and increased use of comparative policy-based analysis.

First, future work must continue to identify and investigate important punishment decisions in addition to those traditionally examined. The standard approach has been to focus almost exclusively on incarceration and sentence length. These are both important outcomes, but they capture only a small portion of the full range of decisions that comprise criminal sentencing. Recent empirical literature has therefore begun to examine additional outcomes of interest, such as distinctions between jail and prison sentences (Holleran and Spohn 2004), judicial decisions to depart from sentencing guidelines (Johnson 2005), the judicial use of intermediate sanctions (Engen et al. 2003), bail decisions (Demuth 2003), the application of habitual offender or mandatory minimum laws (Crawford, Chiricos, and Kleck 1998; Ulmer, Kurlychek, and Kramer 2007), and the withholding of adjudicated guilt in criminal cases (Bontrager, Bales, and Chiricos 2005). This research sets a useful precedent that acknowledges the full range of consequential decisions that judges and other court actors engage in, and it suggests that the ongoing investigation of additional outcomes will continue to pay dividends to research and policy interests in future work.

Second, extant research should continue to expand its ken to include additional forms of seldom-examined sentencing disparity. With regard to race, little research examines sentencing disparity among racial and ethnic groups other than those that are the most sizable. Only a few studies examine sentencing outcomes for Asian Americans (Johnson and Betsinger 2009) or American Indian offenders (Bynum and Paternoster 1984; Alvarez and Bachman 1996), and virtually no research examines important differences within racial and ethnic groups, such as among Hispanic groups of different nationalities. Recent arguments also call for incorporation of additional sentencing factors, such as family and socioeconomic information, drug and alcohol histories, and additional victim and incident characteristics. Much sentencing research relies heavily on publicly available guidelines data (Wellford 2007), with few attempts to use other methods of data collection. For instance, surveys of court actors represent a useful but underused tool for investigating various aspects of different court decision-making processes. Independent collection of additional information and additional types of data therefore offers an important direction for continuing to improve research on understudied elements in sentencing.

Third, research on sentencing would benefit from increased attention to the underlying causes of differential treatment in sentencing. Sentencing researchers need to begin thinking outside of the traditional sentencing paradigm, which has long been guided by relative comparison of "legal" and "extralegal" sentencing factors. Legal factors are those that judges are legally authorized to consider in sentencing, such as the severity of the offense or the criminal history of the offender, whereas extralegal factors are those legally prohibited or not ordinarily relevant to the purposes of sentencing, such as race, gender, or socioeconomic status. Traditionally, studies emphasize the primacy of extralegal predictors as evidence that the system is biased or they highlight the importance of legal influences to argue the converse. Too seldom, though, is adequate consideration given to when and why extralegal effects emerge or how these differences are best explained. For instance, some research suggests that extralegal disadvantages are codified in legal criteria like prior record scores (Bushway and Piehl 2007). In general, a broader approach is necessary in terms of testing more nuanced theoretical frameworks, better analyzing the indirect and interactive effects of legal and extralegal considerations, and improving investigations into the larger societal consequences of criminal sentencing in related domains like family, schooling, employment, and public health.

Fourth, future research should continue to incorporate improved measures of both social contexts and criminal court actors in analyses of sentencing. Recent work demonstrates an increased recognition of the importance of social contexts in punishment, or what Sampson and Lauritsen (1997, 349) have labeled "a deeper appreciation for the salience of macro-social contexts." One emerging conclusion, in line with the "court community" perspective discussed above, is that sentencing outcomes and sentencing disparity often vary across court contexts (Ulmer and

Johnson 2004). It is increasingly important, then, for future work to focus not only on whether disparities exist but also on how they are mitigated or aggravated by courtroom social, political, and legal environments.

Additional research is also needed that better integrates the influence of different court actors, such as the prosecutor, into the sentencing process. In order to draw firm conclusions about the magnitude of disparity or the ability of guidelines to ameliorate it, future work will need to assess better the cumulative impacts of race, ethnicity, gender, and other factors across the multiple stages of criminal case processing. Studies of this sort remain rare and are often limited to specific offense types or specific jurisdictions, so little remains known about the overall degree to which observed disparities in sentencing are counterbalanced, nullified or accentuated by earlier case processing decisions (Zatz 1987).

We know especially little about the expanding role of prosecutors under determinate sentencing systems (Miethe 1987; Wooldredge and Griffin 2006), or the ways that prosecutorial decisions influence, or are influenced by, final sentencing decisions in criminal court, so these are especially important future priorities. A few studies have begun to empirically investigate court workgroup dynamics. For instance, Haynes, Ruback, and Cusik (2010) recently examined the role of workgroup similarity and stability in punishment, and Ward, Farrell, and Rousseau (2009) examined the effect of workgroup diversity on racial and ethnic disparity in sentencing. These innovative studies highlight important directions for future research to continue to incorporate more nuanced and detailed measures of important social, cultural, and organizational influences in punishment.

Finally, although still relatively rare, modern sentencing research highlights the need for research assessing the effects of contemporary policy reforms both within and across jurisdictions. One approach has been to compare sentencing practices in different states. For instance, Piehl and Bushway (2007) contrast charging and sentencing behaviors in a voluntary guidelines state (Maryland) with a presumptive guidelines state (Washington). Their results suggest that charging practices differ in the two contexts and in ways that likely obscure conclusions regarding disparity in guidelines sentencing. A second approach has been to examine policy changes within a single sentencing system. For instance, Crow and Bales (2006) examined the effects of sentencing reform in Florida where key policy changes occurred in the structure of state sentencing guidelines. They found that policy changes were associated with substantial shifts in overall punishment severity and in the relative importance of individual sentencing considerations. Given the diversity of sentencing systems and the frequency of revisions to existing state guidelines, both within- and across-jurisdictional comparisons provide important avenues for future research on the policy impact of evolving sentencing systems in the United States. Important discretion also exists in the ways that guidelines are created and applied, which requires the explicit focus of sentencing researchers in future work as well (Bushway and Piehl 2007).

The majority of contemporary research on criminal sentencing has been limited to a handful of sentencing guidelines states, predominantly Minnesota, Pennsylvania, and Washington State. Dozens of other states have recently implemented guidelines, yet little research exists in these diverse contexts. Moreover, the majority of states still operate under indeterminate sentencing schemes that have only rarely been the focus of contemporary research. Studies that take a comparative approach, for example contrasting outcomes in determinate and indeterminate state systems, hold the potential to make important, unique contributions in future work.

Sentencing research would also benefit greatly from a broader international perspective. As one scholar noted, "Perhaps the most glaring gap in the literature is that almost all of the research on sentencing disparity is limited to the contemporary North American—particularly U.S.—context" (Ulmer 2005, 1501). Despite substantial similarity in the core elements of Western justice systems, important variation exists in the specific punishment policies of different nations (Tonry 2001). For instance, the United States is characterized by higher incarceration rates and longer terms of imprisonment than other Western nations. Variation in punishment policies and practices offer important opportunities for comparative research, yet only a few studies have examined sentencing in other Western nations (Tonry and Frase 2001), much of which is limited to Great Britain (Ashworth 2001), Australia (Snowball and Weatherburn 2007), or the Netherlands (Tak 2001; Johnson, van Wingerden, and Nieuwbeerta, 2010). International research is becoming ever more important in the global world of penal policy, so comparative approaches in future research will offer special utility for advancing knowledge on diverse sentencing practices and policies across nations. These and related ventures, though far from comprehensive, all represent innovative, promising, and important directions for future research.

III. Conclusion

The contemporary landscape of criminal sentencing has been fundamentally deconstructed and reassembled over the past three decades. The juggernaut of modern sentencing reform has left in its wake a patchwork medley of sentencing systems, some that retain the elements of bygone indeterminate sentencing, some that have been redefined in terms of determinate sentencing, and some that teeter on the edge of a new breed of experimental sentencing reforms, emphasizing emerging paradigms such as restorative justice meted out in specialized courts. In most cases, modern sentencing systems combine elements of the past with visions of the future, but as of yet no clear dominant systemic sentencing paradigm has emerged.

Recent years have seen evidence that the tough-on-crime movement in the United States is beginning to subside, in part because sustained growth in American corrections along the lines of past decades is no longer tenable, and in part because of growing evidence in support of rehabilitative correctional programs (MacKenzie 2006).

These changes introduce an emerging public policy dilemma between established determinate sentencing structures that now exist in many states and the emerging social movement that is beginning to increasingly emphasize offender-based sentencing options and community punishments, at least for some defendants and for some crimes (Reitz 2001). Emerging restorative justice approaches emphasize reparation over retribution and individual accountability over proportionality. It will therefore be the challenge of future policy to balance the goals of equity and uniformity within structured sentencing frameworks with the emerging emphasis on individualized rehabilitative approaches to criminal punishment. The research community will play a crucial role in this process—effective implementation of future sentencing initiatives will require the redoubled efforts of social scientific research to clearly establish the best evidenced-based sentencing policies for fair and effective sentencing practices.

This process may also require new initiative on the part of sentencing researchers. It is often easy to be swept up in the inexorable current of comfortable research agendas—applying similar theories to similar research questions, executed on known, available datasets. This is not to deny the vast contributions of past work, but rather to emphasize that the greatest gains in future research will be made by asking new and innovative research questions, by identifying and investigating emergent policy developments, by seeking out and collecting new, untapped sources of sentencing data, and by applying rigorous analytical tools and methodologies, particularly in cross-jurisdictional, international, and comparative contexts. Such endeavors hold the greatest promise to provide new insights to policymakers, practitioners, and academics alike in coming decades, which are likely to continue to emphasize innovative sentencing policy reforms. The directions that future reforms take will likely depend on a host of factors, including changes in crime rates, economic conditions, correctional budgets, prison crowding, and technological innovations, as well as the national political climate and the influence of popular media, but sentencing guidelines have already proven to be highly adaptable and attractive to diverse interest groups so they are likely to continue to spread among jurisdictions as a cornerstone of future evidence-based policy reforms.

REFERENCES

Albonetti, Celesta. 1991. "An Integration of Theories to Explain Judicial Discretion." *Social Problems* 38:247–66.

Alvarez, Alexander, and Ronet D. Bachman. 1996. "American Indians and Sentencing Disparity: An Arizona Test." *Journal of Criminal Justice* 24(6):549–61.

Ashworth, Andrew. 2001. "The Decline of English Sentencing and Other Stories." In *Sentencing and Sanctions in Western Countries*, ed. Michael Tonry and Richard S. Frase. New York: Oxford University Press.

Blackwell, Brenda S., David Holleran, and Mary A. Finn. 2008. "The Impact of the Pennsylvania Sentencing Guidelines on Sex Differences in Sentencing." *Journal of Contemporary Criminal Justice* 24: 399–418.

Blumstein, Alfred, and Allen J. Beck. 1999. "Population Growth in U.S. Prisons, 1980–1996." In *Prisons*, edited by Michael Tonry and Joan Petersilia. Vol. 26 of *Crime and Justice: A Review of Research*, edited by Michael Tonry. Chicago: University of Chicago Press.

Blumstein, Alfred, Jacqueline Cohen, Susan E. Martin, and Michael Tonry. 1983. *Research on Sentencing: The Search for Reform,* vol. 1. Washington: National Academy Press.

Bontrager, Stephanie, William Bales, and Theodore Chiricos. 2005. "Race, Ethnicity, Threat and the Labeling of Convicted Felons." *Criminology* 43: 589–622.

Bridges, George S., and Sara Steen. 1998. "Racial Disparities in Official Assessments of Juvenile Offenders: Attributional Stereotypes as Mediating Mechanisms." *American Sociological Review* 63: 554–70.

Bureau of Justice Statistics. 1999. *Truth in Sentencing in State Prisons*. Washington, DC: U.S. Government Printing Office.

———. 2008. *Prisoners in 2007*. Washington, DC: U.S. Government Printing Office.

Bushway, Shawn D., and Anne Morrison Piehl. 2007. "Social Science Research and the Legal Threat to Presumptive Sentencing Guidelines." *Criminology and Public Policy* 6: 461–82.

Bynum, Tim, and Raymond Paternoster. 1984. "Discrimination Revisited: An Exploration of Frontstage and Backstage Criminal Justice Decision Making." *Sociology and Social Research* 69: 90–108.

Chiricos, Theodore G., and William D. Bales. 1991. "Unemployment and Punishment: An Empirical Assessment." *Criminology* 29: 701–24.

Chiricos, Theodore G., and Gordon P. Waldo. 1975. "Socioeconomic Status and Criminal Sentencing: An Empirical Assessment of a Conflict Proposition." *American Sociological Review* 40: 753–72.

Crawford, Charles, Theodore Chiricos, and Gary Kleck. 1998. "Race, Racial Threat, and Sentencing of Habitual Offenders." *Criminology* 36: 481–512.

Crow, Matthew S., and William Bales. 2006. "Sentencing Guidelines and Focal Concerns: The Effect of Sentencing Policy as a Practical Constraint on Sentencing Decisions." *American Journal of Criminal Justice* 30: 285–304.

Daly, Kathleen. 1994. *Gender, Crime, and Punishment*. New Haven, CT: Yale University Press.

———. 2000. "Revisiting the Relationship between Retributive and Restorative Justice." In *Restorative Justice: From Philosophy to Practice*, ed. Heather Strang and John Braithwaite. Aldershot, UK: Dartmouth University Press.

Daly, Kathleen, and Rebecca Bordt. 1995. "Sex Effects and Sentencing: An Analysis of the Statistical Literature." *Justice Quarterly* 12: 141–75.

Demuth, Stephen. 2003. "Racial and Ethnic Differences in Pretrial Release Decisions and Outcomes: A Comparison of Hispanic, Black, and White Felony Arrestees." *Criminology* 41: 873–908.

Eisenstein, James, and Herbert Jacob. 1977. *Felony Justice: An Organizational Analysis of Criminal Courts.* Boston: Little, Brown.

Eisenstein, James, Roy Flemming, and Peter Nardulli. 1988. *The Contours of Justice: Communities and Their Courts.* Boston: Little, Brown.

Engen, Rodney, Randy Gainey, Robert Crutchfield, and Joseph Weis. 2003. "Discretion and Disparity Under Sentencing Guidelines: The Role of Departures and Structures Sentencing Alternatives." *Criminology* 41: 99–130.

Forst, Brian. 1999. "Prosecution." In *Crime: Public Policies for Crime Control,* ed. James Q. Wilson and Joan Petersilia. Oakland, CA: Institute for Contemporary Studies Press.

Frankel, Marvin. 1973. *Criminal Sentences: Law without Order.* New York: Hill and Wang.

Frase, Richard. 2000. "Is Guided Discretion Sufficient? Overview of State Sentencing Guidelines." *St. Louis University Law Journal* 44: 425–30.

———. 2005. "State Sentencing Guidelines: Diversity, Consensus, and Unresolved Policy Issues" *Columbia Law Review* 105: 1190–232.

———. 2007. "The Apprendi-Blakely Cases: Sentencing Reform Counter Revolution?" *Criminology and Public Policy* 6: 403–31.

Griffin, Timothy, and John Wooldredge. 2006. "Sex-based Disparities in Felony Dispositions Before versus After Sentencing Reform in Ohio." *Criminology* 44: 893–923.

Hagan, John, Ilene H. Nagel, and Celesta Albonetti. 1980. "The Differential Sentencing of White-Collar Offenders in Ten Federal District Courts." *American Sociological Review* 45: 802–20.

Haynes, Stacy H., Barry Ruback, and Gretchen R. Cusik. 2010. "Courtroom Workgroups and Sentencing: The Effects Of Similarity, Proximity, and Stability." *Crime and Delinquency* 56: 126–61.

Helms, Ronald, and David Jacobs. 1999. "Collective Outbursts, Politics, and Punitive Resources: Toward a Political Sociology of Spending on Social Control." *Social Forces* 77: 1497–523.

Hofer, Paul J. 2007. "*United States v. Booker* as a Natural Experiment: Using Empirical Research to Inform the Federal Sentencing Policy Debate." *Criminology and Public Policy* 6: 433–60.

Holleran, David, and Cassia Spohn. 2004. "On the Use of the Total Incarceration Variables in Sentencing Research." *Criminology* 42: 211–41.

Johnson, Brian D. 2003. "Racial and Ethnic Disparities in Sentencing Departures across Modes of Conviction." *Criminology* 41: 449–90.

———. 2005. "Contextual Disparities in Guidelines Departures: Courtroom Social Contexts, Guidelines Compliance, and Extralegal Disparities in Criminal Sentencing." *Criminology* 43: 761–96.

———. 2006. "The Multilevel Context of Criminal Sentencing: Integrating Judge and County Level Influences." *Criminology* 44: 259–98.

Johnson, Brian D., Jeffery T. Ulmer, and John H. Kramer. 2008. "The Social Context of Guidelines Circumvention: The Case of Federal District Courts." *Criminology* 46: 737–83.

Johnson, Brian D., and Sara Betsinger. 2009. "Punishing the 'Model Minority': Asian American Criminal Sentencing Outcomes in Federal District Courts." *Criminology* 47(4): 1045–90.

Johnson, Brian D., Sigrid van Wingerden, and Paul Nieuwbeerta. 2010. "Sentencing Homicide Offenders in the Netherlands: Offender, Victim and Situational Influences in Criminal Punishment." *Criminology* 48(4): 601–38.

Kauder, Neal, and Brian Ostrum. 2008. "State Sentencing Guidelines: Profiles and Continuum." NCSC Report, July 2008. Williamsburg, VA: National Center for State Courts.

Kerner Commission. 1968. *Report of the National Advisory Commission on Civil Disorders.* Washington, DC: U.S. Government Printing Office.

King, Ryan D., and Darren Wheelock. 2007. "Group Threat and Social Control: Race, Perceptions of Minorities and the Desire to Punish." *Social Forces* 85(3): 1255–80.

Koons-Witt, Barbara A. 2002. "The Effect of Gender on the Decision to Incarcerate Before and After the Introduction of Sentencing Guidelines." *Criminology* 40: 297–328.

Kruttschnitt. Candace. 1982. "Women, Crime, and Dependency: An Application of the Theory of Law." *Criminology* 19: 495–513.

Kruttschnitt, Candace, and Donald E. Green. 1984. "The Sex-sanctioning Issue: Is It History?" *American Sociological Review* 49: 541–51.

LaFree, Gary D. 1980. "The Effect of Sexual Stratification by Race on Official Reactions to Rape." *American Sociological Review* 45: 842–54.

Lipton, Douglas, Robert Martinson, and Judith Wilks. 1975. *The Effectiveness of Correctional Treatment: A Survey of Treatment Evaluation Studies.* New York: Praeger.

MacKenzie, Doris L. 2006. *What Works in Corrections: Reducing the Criminal Activities of Offenders and Delinquents.* New York: Cambridge University Press.

Marvell, Thomas B. and Carlisle E. Moody. 1996. "Determinate Sentencing and Abolishing Parole: The Long-term Impacts on Prisons and Crime." *Criminology* 34: 107–28.

Mauer, Marc. 2001. "The Causes and Consequences of Prison Growth in the United States." *Punishment and Society* 3: 9–20.

———. 2006. *Race to Incarcerate.* New York: The New Press.

Miethe, Terence 1987. "Charging and Plea Bargaining under Determinate Sentencing." *Journal of Criminal Law and Criminology* 78: 155–76.

Miethe, Terence, and Charles Moore. 1985. "Socioeconomic Disparities under Determinate Sentencing Systems: A Comparison of Preguideline and Postguideline Practices in Minnesota." *Criminology* 23: 337–63.

Mitchell, Ojmarrh. 2005. "A Meta-Analysis of Race and Sentencing Research: Explaining the Inconsistencies." *Journal of Quantitative Criminology* 21: 439–66.

Nagel, Ilene H., and John Hagan. 1982. "Gender and Crime: Offense Patterns and Criminal Court Sanctions." In *Crime and Justice: A Review of Research*, vol. 4, edited by Michael Tonry and Norval Morris. Chicago: University of Chicago Press.

Nagel, Ilene H., and Barry L. Johnson. 1994. "The Role of Gender in a Structured Sentencing System: Equal Treatment, Policy Choices, and the Sentencing of Female Offenders under the United States Sentencing Guidelines." *Journal of Criminal Law and Criminology* 85: 181–221.

Nagel, Ilene H., and Stephen J. Schulhofer. 1992. "A Tale of Three Cities: An Empirical Study of Charging and Bargaining Practices under the Federal Sentencing Guidelines." *Southern California Law Review* 66: 501–66.

Paternoster, Raymond. 1984. "Prosecutorial Discretion in Requesting the Death Penalty: The Case of Victim-Based Discrimination." *Law and Society Review* 18: 437–78.

Paternoster, Raymond, and Robert Brame. 2008. "Reassessing Race Disparities in Maryland Capital Cases." *Criminology* 46(4): 971–1008.

Piehl, Anne M., and Shawn D. Bushway. 2007. "Measuring and Explaining Charge Bargaining." *Journal of Quantitative Criminology* 23: 105–25.

Reitz, Kevin R. 2001. "*The Disassembly and Reassembly of U.S. Sentencing Practices.*" In *Sentencing and Sanctions in Western Countries*, ed. Michael Tonry and Richard S. Frase. New York: Oxford University Press.

Ruth, Henry S., and Kevin R. Reitz. 2003. *The Challenge of Crime: Rethinking Our Response.* Cambridge, MA: Harvard University Press.

Sampson, Robert J., and Janet L. Lauritsen. 1997. "Racial and Ethnic Disparities in Crime and Criminal Justice in the United States." *Crime and Justice* 21: 311–74.

Sellin, Thorsten. 1928. "The Negro Criminal: A Statistical Note." *Annals of the American Academy of Political and Social Science* 140: 52–64.

Sims-Blackwell, Brenda, David Holleran, and Mary A. Finn. 2008. "The Impact of the Pennsylvania Sentencing Guidelines on Sex Differences in Sentencing." *Journal of Contemporary Criminal Justice* 24: 399–418.

Snowball, Lucy, and Don Weatherburn. 2007. "Does Racial Bias in Sentencing Contribute to Indigenous Overrepresentation in Prison?" *Australian and New Zealand Journal of Criminology* 40: 272–90.

Sorensen, Jon, and Don Stemen. 2002. "The Effect of State Sentencing Policies on Incarceration Rates." *Crime and Delinquency* 48: 456–75.

Spohn, Cassia. 2000. "Thirty Years of Sentencing Reform: The Quest for a Racially Neutral Sentencing Process." *Criminal Justice: The National Institute of Justice Journal* 3:427–501.

Spohn, Cassia, and David Holleran. 2000. "The Imprisonment Penalty Paid by Young Unemployed Black and Hispanic Male Offenders." *Criminology* 38: 281–306.

Steffensmeier, Darrell, and Stephen DeMuth. 2000. "Ethnicity and Sentencing Outcomes in U.S. Federal Courts: Who is Punished More Harshly?" *American Sociological Review* 65: 705–29.

Steffensmeier, Darrell, and Stephen Demuth. 2006. "Does Gender Modify the Effects of Race-Ethnicity on Criminal Sanctioning? Sentences for Male and Female White, Black, and Hispanic Defendants." *Journal of Quantitative Criminology* 22(3): 241–61.

Stith, Kate, and Jose Cabranes. 1998. *Fear of Judging: Sentencing Guidelines in the Federal Courts.* Chicago: University of Chicago Press.

Stolzenberg, Lisa, and Stewart J. D'Allessio. 1996. "The Unintended Consequences of Linking Sentencing Guidelines to Moody and Marvell Prison Populations: A Reply to Moody and Marvell." *Criminology* 34: 269–79.

Tak, Peter J. 2001. "*Sentencing and Punishment in the Netherlands.*" In *Sentencing and Sanctions in Western Countries*, ed. Michael Tonry and Richard S. Frase. New York: Oxford University Press.

Tonry, Michael. 1995. *Malign Neglect.* New York: Oxford University Press.

———. 1996. *Sentencing Matters.* New York: Oxford University Press.

———. 1998. "*Intermediate Sanctions in Sentencing Guidelines.*" In *Crime and Justice: A Review of Research,* vol. 23, edited by Michael Tonry. Chicago: University of Chicago Press.

———. 2001. *"Punishment Policies and Patterns in Western Countries."* In *Sentencing and Sanctions in Western Countries*, ed. Michael Tonry and Richard S. Frase. New York: Oxford University Press.

———. 2009. "Mandatory Penalties." In *Crime and Justice: A Review of Research,* vol. 38, edited by Michael Tonry. Chicago: University of Chicago Press.

Tonry, Michael, and Richard S. Frase, eds. 2001. *Sentencing and Sanctions in Western Countries*. New York: Oxford University Press.

Tonry, Michael, and Norval Morris. 1990. "Introduction." In *Crime and Justice: A Review of Research,* vol. 3, edited by Michael Tonry and Norval Morris. Chicago: University of Chicago Press.

Ulmer, Jeffery T. 2005. "Sentencing and Sentencing Disparities." In *The Encyclopedia of Criminology,* edited by Richard Wright and J. Mitchell Miller. New York: Routledge.

Ulmer, Jeffery T., and Brian D. Johnson. 2004. "Sentencing in Context: A Multilevel Analysis." *Criminology* 42:137–77.

Ulmer, Jeffery T., Megan Kurlychek, and John H. Kramer. 2007. "Prosecutorial Discretion and the Imposition of Mandatory Minimum Sentences." *Journal of Research in Crime and Delinquency* 44: 427–58.

United States Sentencing Commission (USSC). 1991. *The Federal Sentencing Guidelines: A Report on the Operation of the Guidelines System and Short-Term Impacts on Disparity in Sentencing, Use of Incarceration, and Prosecutorial Discretion and Plea Bargaining.* Washington, DC: U.S. Government Printing Office.

———. 2004. *Guidelines Manual. Section 3E1.1.* Washington, DC: United States Sentencing Commission.

———. 2007. *Cocaine and Federal Sentencing Policy.* Report to Congress, May 2007. Washington, DC: United States Sentencing Commission.

———. 2008. *Supreme Court Cases on Sentencing Issues.* Office of General Counsel. Washington, DC: United States Sentencing Commission.

Von Hirsch, Andrew. 1976. *Doing Justice: Report of the Committee for the Study of Incarceration.* New York: Hill and Wang.

Ward, Geoff, Amy Farrell, and Danielle Rousseau. 2009. "Does Racial Balance in Workforce Representation Yield Equal Justice? Race Relations of Sentencing in Federal Court Organizations." *Law and Society Review* 43(4): 757–806.

Wellford, Charles F. 2007. "Sentencing Research for Sentencing Reform." *Criminology and Public Policy* 6: 399–402.

Wilson, James Q. 1975. *Thinking About Crime.* New York: Random House.

Wooldredge, John, Timothy Griffin, and Fritz Rauschenberg. 2005. "(Un)anticipated Effects of Sentencing Reform on the Disparate Treatment of Defendants." *Law and Society Review* 39: 835–73.

Wooldredge, John, and Timothy Griffin. 2005. "Displaced Discretion under Ohio Sentencing Guidelines." *Journal of Criminal Justice* 33: 301–16.

Zatz, Marjorie. 1987. "The Changing Forms of Racial/Ethnic Bias in Sentencing." *Journal of Research in Crime and Delinquency.* 24: 69–92.

———. 2000. "The Convergence of Race, Ethnicity, Gender, and Class on Court Decisionmaking: Looking Toward the 21st Century." *Criminal Justice: The National Institute of Justice Journal* 3: 503–52.

Zimring, Frank, and Gordon Hawkins, and Sam Kamin. 2003. *Punishment and Democracy: Three Strikes and You're Out in California.* New York: Oxford University Press.

CHAPTER 23

MANDATORY PENALTIES

MICHAEL TONRY

THREE important things need to be understood about mandatory penalties. The first is that the term is a misnomer. No penalty is mandatory. A statute may say that anyone convicted of, say, armed robbery must be sentenced to a prison term of at least five years, but that does not mean that all arrested armed robbers will receive five-year sentences. Even if all the necessary facts can be proven, prosecutors may charge the offender with a different offense—such as unarmed robbery, theft, or assault—not affected by the seemingly mandatory penalty. Or prosecutors may invite a guilty plea to, say, assault or simple robbery, in exchange for dismissal of the armed-robbery charge. Or the judge or a jury, knowing that an armed-robbery conviction will trigger a five-year prison term, may decide to convict the defendant of some other offense. A mandatory penalty is "mandatory" only when the prosecutor files the necessary charge and does not dismiss it later on in plea negotiations, and when the defendant is convicted of the designated offense and not some other one. If practitioners believe a penalty seemingly mandated by law is too severe or is otherwise inappropriate, they can figure out ways to avoid its application, and often do.

The second thing to understand is that mandatory penalties generally do not deter crime as their proponents expect or claim they will. The principal argument made in their favor is that, precisely because they are mandatory, their existence will prevent crime: would-be offenders will be deterred by the threatened punishment. There is no credible evidence that this is true. A significant body of research on the effects of mandatory penalty laws shows that their enactment and application do not discernibly reduce crime rates. A larger body of research on the deterrent effects of criminal sanctions is generally consistent with that conclusion.

The third thing to understand, perhaps the most surprising and striking, is that the first two points have been widely understood for at least two centuries. In eighteenth-century England, pickpockets regularly plied their trade among the crowds assembled to watch the hangings of pickpockets, and judges and juries regularly circumvented mandatory death penalty statutes (Teeters and Hedblom 1967; Hay et al. 1975). Evidence has steadily accumulated since then that practitioners try to avoid imposing sentences they consider unjust and that it is unrealistic to expect mandatory penalty laws to be effective deterrents.

Why then do legislators enact such laws? One reason is that they do not know their history and reason that, since they themselves are deterred from speeding by the presence of police cars, would-be offenders must be deterred by threatened mandatory penalties. The analogy is inapt, however, because a statute specifying sentences for crime is not a police car parked alongside the highway. Would be offenders may not know there is a mandatory penalty law, they do not expect to be caught, and they may not be the kind of people who think about likely penalties at all.

Other reasons why such laws are enacted are that legislators may have primarily ideological or political objectives in mind. They want to show that they are tough on criminals and tough on crime, and hope that will help them get re-elected. Or they may have expressive motives. They may understand that mandatory penalty laws do not achieve their nominal aims but want to assure the public that they understand that people are fearful and angry about crime. Enactment of a seemingly severe sentencing law may be a primarily symbolic act meant to assure voters that legislators recognize their anxiety and want to express solidarity with them.

Policy analysts, researchers, and judges have long agreed that mandatory penalties are a bad idea. Nearly every authoritative nonpartisan law reform organization that has considered the subject, including the American Law Institute (1962, 2007), the American Bar Association (e.g., 1968, standard 2.3; 1994, standard 18–3.21[b]), the Federal Courts Study Committee (1990), and the U.S. Sentencing Commission (1991) have opposed enactment, and favored repeal, of mandatory penalties. In 2004, an American Bar Association commission headed by the conservative U.S. Supreme Court Justice Anthony Kennedy called upon states, territories, and the federal government to repeal mandatory minimum sentence statutes (Kennedy 2004).

Mandatory sentencing laws for felonies take a number of forms. Typical laws specify minimum prison sentences for designated violent and drug crimes (e.g., minimum five years' imprisonment for selling ten grams of crack cocaine). Others require that incremental penalties be imposed on convicted offenders meeting specified criteria (e.g., anyone convicted of an offense involving a firearm must receive two years' imprisonment in addition to that imposed for the basic offense). Sometimes they specify minimum sentences to be imposed on people convicted of a particular offense who have prior felony convictions. Three-strikes laws, for example, are mandatory sentencing laws. Typically they provide that anyone convicted of a designated (usually violent or drug) crime, who has previously twice been convicted of similar crimes, be sentenced to a prison sentence of twenty-five years or more.

Several other kinds of "mandatory" sentencing laws are not addressed in this article. I do not discuss mandatory sentences for misdemeanors; a common example is laws that mandate short jail terms for some drunk-driving offenses. I do not discuss laws that use the word "mandatory" but do not mean it. "Mandatory life" sentences for murder are legally required in England and in some Australian states. The terminology, however, is misleading. In most cases, the judge also indicates how long the offender should be held before release on parole. Utterance of the words "mandatory life imprisonment" is obligatory; a life spent behind bars seldom is.

No one who has lived in the United States, however, can be unaware that conservative politicians for three decades consistently promoted passage of more and harsher mandatory sentence laws. Moderate and liberal politicians, most famously former president Bill Clinton, from the mid-1980s on more often than not followed suit. Between the mid-1970s and the early 1980s, every American state but one enacted at least one new mandatory penalty law (Shane-DuBow, Brown, and Olsen 1985). Most adopted many such laws for violent, sexual, and drug offenses and for "career criminals."

The U.S. Congress repeatedly, between 1984 and 1996, enacted new mandatory sentencing laws and increased penalties under existing ones (Austin et al. 1994). The first "three strikes and you're out" law was enacted by referendum in Washington State and was followed most famously in California in 1994 but also by more than twenty-three other states and the federal government (Dickey and Hollenhorst 1999). The pace of new enactments has slowed. Except in Alaska in 2006, no new three-strikes laws were enacted in American states after 1996 (Chen 2008, table 1). In some states, the scope of mandatory penalty laws has been narrowed, though only slightly, and in a few states judges were given new discretion to impose some other sentence in narrowly defined categories of cases (Butterfield 2003; Steinhauer 2009). In 2007, the U.S. Sentencing Commission changed its guidelines to narrow the ramifications of mandatory penalties for drug crimes. Taken as a whole, though, as Adam Liptak (2007, A21) noted of the U.S. Sentencing Commission changes, these changes only nibble at the edges: "The sentencing commission's striking move . . . will have only a minor impact. Unless Congress acts, many thousands of defendants will continue to face vastly different sentences for selling different types of the same thing." No major laws have been repealed, no major laws have been enacted retroactively to shorten the sentences of the hundreds of thousands of prisoners serving time under mandatory minimum laws, and most new laws narrowing their scope have been restrictively drafted to cover only minor offenses and offenders.

The decent thing to do would be to repeal all existing mandatory penalties and to enact no new ones. If that is politically impracticable, there are ways to avoid or ameliorate the foreseeable dysfunctional effects of mandatory penalties. First, make penalties presumptive rather than mandatory. Second, add "sunset provisions" providing that the laws lapse and become presumptive after three to five years, and include such provisions in any new mandatory minimum sentencing laws. Third, limit lengthy prison terms—whether or not subject to mandatory penalties—to serious crimes such as grievous assaults causing serious injury, aggravated rape, murder, and flagrant financial crimes. Fourth, authorize correctional officials to reconsider release dates of all offenders receiving prison sentences exceeding a designated length (say five or ten years).

This chapter summarizes research on the implementation, operation, and deterrent effects of mandatory sentencing laws.[1] Section I examines research before 1970. Section II examines the major empirical evaluations in the United States since then. Section III summarizes the small literature in other countries, primarily Australia, Canada, England and Wales, and South Africa. Although the mandatory penalties are much less harsh in those countries and the research is less extensive, the findings are indistinguishable from those in the United States. Section IV briefly examines research on deterrent effects. Section V tries to make sense of these findings and to outline their policy implications.

A number of robust conclusions emerge from research concerning mandatory penalties in the United States, Australia, Canada, England and Wales, and South Africa:

- "Mandatory" penalties are only as mandatory as prosecutors and judges (and occasionally juries) allow them to be.
- Mandatory penalties generate stark disparities between comparable cases when sometimes they are applied, resulting in lengthy prison sentences for affected offenders, and sometimes they are circumvented, usually resulting in much shorter sentences for those offenders.
- Mandatory penalties encourage hypocrisy among criminal court practitioners who often feel that justice requires that they impose a different sentence than the seemingly applicable law mandates. This forces the relevant decisions into the shadows of corridors and behind locked doors rather than in the open courtroom where they belong.
- There is no credible evidence that enactment or application of mandatory penalties reduces crime rates.

I. Mandatory Penalties before 1970

The foreseeable problems in implementing mandatory penalties have been well known for two hundred years. "Nullification," a term in common usage for more than two centuries, encapsulates the process by which judges and juries refuse to enforce laws or apply penalties that they consider unjust. Oliver Wendell Holmes Jr. (1889) described the jury's capacity to nullify harsh laws as among its principal virtues. Harvard Law School dean Roscoe Pound claimed that "jury lawlessness is the great corrective of law in its actual administration" (1910, 18).

A. Eighteenth-Century England

The death penalty debate in eighteenth- and nineteenth-century England is strikingly similar to contemporary American debates about mandatory penalties. At the end of the eighteenth century, Edmund Burke declared "that he could obtain the consent of the House of Commons to any Bill imposing the punishment of death" (Select Committee on Capital Punishment 1930, paras. 10, 11). Samuel Romilly, England's most celebrated nineteenth-century death penalty opponent, repeatedly called for repeal of capital punishment laws because they were applied erratically and unfairly and because the erratic application inevitably undermined whatever deterrent effects they might possibly have had (Romilly 1820).

Between 1714 and 1830, the British Parliament created 156 new capital offenses. By 1819 British law recognized 220 capital offenses, most of them property crimes. During the same period, however, the number of executions steadily declined (Hay 1975). Judges and juries went to extreme lengths to avoid imposing death sentences. Juries often refused to convict. A variant, with twentieth-century echoes, was to convict of a lesser offense. According to a 1930 report of the British Select Committee on Capital Punishment, describing eighteenth-century practices, in vast numbers of cases the sentence of death was not imposed, or if imposed was not carried out. For one thing, juries in increasing numbers refused to convict. A jury would assess the amount taken from a shop at 4s. [shillings] 10d. [pence] so as to avoid the capital penalty that fell on a theft of 5s. In the case of a dwelling, where the theft of 40s was a capital offense, even when a woman confessed that she had stolen a larger amount, the jury notwithstanding found that the amount was only 39s. And when later, in 1827, the legislature raised the capital indictment to £5, the juries raised their verdicts to £4 19s (Select Committee on Capital Punishment 1930, para. 17). As more capital offenses were created, the courts adopted increasingly narrow interpretations of procedural, pleading, and evidentiary rules. Seemingly well-founded prosecutions would fall because a name or a date was incorrect or a defendant was wrongly described as a "farmer" rather than as a "yeoman" (Radzinowicz 1948–68, vol. 1, 25–28, 89–91, 97–103; Hay 1980, 32–34).

Even among those sentenced to death, the proportion executed declined steadily. According to the Select Committee on Capital Punishment, "The Prerogative of the Crown [pardon] was increasingly exercised. Down to 1756 about two-thirds of those condemned were actually brought to the scaffold; from 1756 to 1772 the proportion sank to one-half. Between 1802 and 1808 it was no more than one-eighth" (1930, para. 21). Most of those pardoned received substituted punishments of a term of imprisonment or transportation (Stephen 1883, vol. 1, chap. 13).

B. America in the 1950s

The American Bar Foundation Survey of the Administration of Criminal Justice in the United States in the 1950s confirmed the lessons from eighteenth-century England. Frank Remington, director of the eighteen-year project, noted: "Legislative prescription of a high mandatory sentence for certain offenders is likely to result in a reduction in charges at the prosecution stage, or if this is not done, by a refusal of the judge to convict at the adjudication stage. The issue . . . thus is not solely whether certain offenders should be dealt with severely, but also how the criminal justice system will accommodate to the legislative charge" (1969, xvii).

The survey's findings are exemplified by three processes the reports described. First, Donald Newman described how Michigan judges dealt with a lengthy mandatory minimum for drug sales:

> Mandatory minimums are almost universally disliked by trial judges. . . . The clearest illustration of routine reductions is provided by reduction of sale of narcotics to possession or addiction. . . . Judges . . . actively participated in the charge reduction process to the extent of refusing to accept guilty pleas to sale and liberally assigning counsel to work out reduced charges. . . . To demonstrate its infrequent application, from the effective date of the revised law (May 8, 1952) to the date of tabulation four years later (June 30, 1956), only twelve sale-of-narcotics convictions were recorded in Detroit out of 476 defendants originally charged with sale. The remainder (except a handful acquitted altogether) pleaded guilty to reduced charges. (Newman 1966, 179)

Second, Newman described efforts to avoid fifteen-year mandatory maximum sentences for breaking-and-entering and armed robbery:

> In Michigan conviction of armed robbery or breaking and entering in the nighttime (fifteen-year maximum compared to five years for daytime breaking) is rare. The pattern of downgrading is such that it becomes virtually routine, and the bargaining session becomes a ritual. The real issue in such negotiations is not whether the charge will be reduced but how far, that is, to what lesser offense. . . . [A]rmed robbery is so often downgraded that the Michigan parole board tends to treat a conviction for unarmed robbery as *prima facie* proof that the defendant had a weapon. And the frequency of altering nighttime burglary to breaking and entering in the daytime led one prosecutor to remark: "You'd think all our burglaries occur at high noon." (1966, 182)

Third, Robert O. Dawson described "very strong" judicial resistance to a twenty-year mandatory minimum for sale of narcotics:

All of the judges of Recorder's Court, in registering their dislike for the provision, cited the hypothetical case of a young man having no criminal record being given a twenty-year minimum sentence for selling a single marijuana cigarette. Charge reductions to possession or use are routine. Indeed, in some cases, judges have refused to accept guilty pleas to sale of narcotics, but have continued the case and appointed counsel with instructions to negotiate a charge reduction. (1969, 201)

These findings from the American Bar Foundation Survey differ in detail from those of eighteenth-century England, but only in detail. When the U.S. Congress repealed most mandatory penalties for drug offenses in 1970, it was merely acknowledging enforcement problems that had long been recognized (U.S. Sentencing Commission 1991).

II. Mandatory Penalties since 1970

Between 1975 and 1996, mandatory minimums were America's most frequently enacted sentencing law changes. By 1983, forty-nine of the fifty states (Wisconsin was the lone holdout) had adopted mandatory sentencing laws for offenses other than murder or drunk driving (Shane-DuBow, Brown, and Olsen 1985, table 30). By 1994 every state had adopted mandatory penalties; most had several (Austin et al. 1994). Most mandatory penalties apply to drug offenses, murder or aggravated rape, felonies involving firearms, or felonies committed by people who have previous felony convictions. Between 1985 and mid-1991, the U.S. Congress enacted at least twenty new mandatory penalty provisions; by 1991, more than sixty federal statutes subjected more than one hundred crimes to mandatory penalties (U.S. Sentencing Commission 1991, 8–10).

More followed, including the federal three-strikes law, in the next few years. Few if any new mandatory penalty laws were enacted after 1996. The experience in most states in the late 1980s and early 1990s was similar. In Florida, for example, seven new mandatory sentencing laws were enacted between 1988 and 1990 (Austin 1991, 4). In Arizona, mandatory sentencing laws were so common that 57 percent of felony offenders in fiscal year 1990 were potentially subject to mandatory sentencing provisions, although in the vast majority of cases defendants were allowed to plead guilty to offenses not subject to minimums (Knapp 1991, 10).

Few new mandatory penalty laws have been enacted since the mid-1990s. The National Conference of State Legislatures publishes annual reports titled "State Crime Legislation in [e.g.] 2006"; these describe minor changes in state mandatory penalty laws since the mid-1990s but no major new ones (http://www.ncsl.org).

There have been only a handful of evaluations of the implementation of mandatory penalty laws. One is an evaluation of the "Rockefeller Drug Laws" (Joint

Committee on New York Drug Law Evaluation 1978). One concerns a Michigan law requiring imposition of a two-year mandatory prison sentence on persons convicted of possession of a gun during commission of a felony (Loftin and McDowall 1981; Loftin, Heumann, and McDowall 1983). Two concern a Massachusetts law requiring a one-year prison sentence for persons convicted of carrying a firearm unlawfully (Beha 1977; Rossman et al. 1979). During the 1990s, ambitious evaluations assessed the effects on case processing of federal mandatory penalties and a 1994 Oregon referendum that mandated lengthy minimum prison sentences for people convicted of any of twenty-one designated crimes.

I discuss these slightly elderly evaluations for the simple reason that there are few more recent ones. The National Institute of Justice (NIJ), the research unit of the U.S. Department of Justice, has only twice made sentencing a primary research focus—in the early to mid-1980s and the mid-1990s. Most ambitious projects were NIJ–funded and date from those periods.

A. New York's Rockefeller Drug Laws

The "Rockefeller Drug Laws" took effect on September 1, 1973. They mandated lengthy prison sentences for narcotics offenses and included statutory limits on plea bargaining. The key findings were these: drug felony arrests, indictment rates, and conviction rates all declined. For those who were convicted, however, the likelihood of being imprisoned and the average length of prison term increased. The two preceding patterns canceled each other out, and the likelihood that a person arrested for a drug felony was imprisoned was about the same after the law took effect as before—around 11 percent. The proportion of drug felony dispositions resulting from trials tripled between 1973 and 1976, and the average time for processing of a single case doubled. Practitioners made vigorous efforts to avoid application of the mandatory sentences in cases in which they viewed those sentences as being too harsh; the remaining cases were dealt with as the law dictated (Joint Committee on New York Drug Law Evaluation 1978; Blumstein et al. 1983, 188–89).

B. Massachusetts's Bartley-Fox Law

Massachusetts's Bartley-Fox Amendment required imposition of a one-year mandatory minimum prison sentence, without suspension, furlough, or parole, for anyone convicted of unlawful carrying of an unlicensed firearm. An offender need not have committed any other crime. Two major evaluations were conducted (Beha 1977; Rossman et al. 1979). James Beha's (1977) analysis was based primarily on comparisons of police and court records for the six-month periods before and after the law's effective date. David Rossman and his colleagues (1979) dealt with official records from 1974, 1975, and 1976 supplemented by interviews with police, lawyers, and court personnel. One important finding was that police altered their behavior in ways aimed at limiting the law's reach. They became more selective about whom to frisk; the absolute number of reports of gun incidents taking place out of doors decreased, which meant a concomitant decrease in arrests, and the number of weapons seized without arrest increased substantially (Carlson 1982, 6).

There were four other major findings. Outcomes favorable to defendants, including both dismissals and acquittals, increased significantly. Of persons convicted of firearms carrying charges in Boston Municipal Court, appeal rates increased radically, from 21 percent in 1974 to 94 percent in 1976 (Beha 1977). The percentage of defendants who entirely avoided a conviction rose from 53.5 percent in 1974 to 80 percent in 1976 (Carlson 1982). Of that residuum of offenders who were finally convicted, the probability of receiving a custodial sentence increased from 23 percent to 100 percent (Carlson 1982).

C. The Michigan Felony Firearms Statute

The Michigan Felony Firearms Statute created a new offense of possessing a firearm while engaging in a felony and specified a two-year mandatory prison sentence that could not be suspended or shortened by release on parole and that had to be served consecutively to a sentence imposed for the underlying felony. The law took effect on January 1, 1977. The Wayne County prosecutor banned charge bargaining in firearms cases and took measures to enforce the ban, suggesting that the likelihood of circumvention should have been less than was experienced in New York and Massachusetts.

Heumann and Loftin (1979) observed a strong tendency in Wayne County toward early dismissal of charges other than on the merits. They interpreted this as evidence of efforts to avoid applying the mandatory penalties. Consistent with the Massachusetts findings that mandatory sentences reduce the probability of convictions, conviction probabilities declined for serious assaults and robberies (Loftin, Heumann, and McDowall 1983, 295).

Effects on sentencing severity were assessed in two ways. Using quantitative methods, Loftin, Heumann, and McDowall (1983) concluded that the statute did not generally increase the probability that prison sentences would be imposed, but for those receiving prison sentences, it increased the expected lengths of sentences for some offenses (297–98). Using simpler tabular analyses, they concluded that, overall, the percentage of defendants vulnerable to the firearms law who were incarcerated did not change markedly (Heumann and Loftin 1979).

Unexpectedly, the percentage of cases resolved at trial (rather than by plea bargain) jumped. Heumann and Loftin explain this as an innovative adaptive response to the mandatory penalty law: the "waiver trial." The judge would convict the defendant of a misdemeanor rather than the charged felony (the firearms law applied only to felonies) or would simply, with the prosecutor's acquiescence, acquit the defendant on the firearms charge. Either approach eliminated the threat of a mandatory sentence. Another device for nullifying the mandatory sentencing law was to decrease the sentence that otherwise would have been imposed by two years and then add the two years back on the basis of the firearms law (Heumann and Loftin 1979, 416–24).

D. Federal Mandatory Penalties

The U.S. Sentencing Commission report, *Mandatory Minimum Penalties in the Federal Criminal Justice System*, demonstrated that mandatory minimum sentencing laws shifted discretion from judges to prosecutors, resulted in higher trial rates and lengthened case processing times, failed to acknowledge salient differences between cases, and often punished minor offenders more harshly than anyone involved believed warranted. Heavy majorities of judges, defense counsel, and probation officers disliked mandatory penalties; prosecutors were about evenly divided. Judges and lawyers often circumvented mandatory sentences.

Analyses of sentencing data revealed a number of not unexpected patterns. First, prosecutors often did not file charges that carried mandatory minimums when the evidence would have supported such charges. Second, prosecutors used mandatory provisions tactically to induce guilty pleas. Third, mandatory penalties increased trial rates and thereby increased work loads and case processing times. Fourth, judges were often willing to work around, and under, the mandatory penalties. Forty percent of defendants whose cases the commission believed warranted mandatory minimums received shorter sentences than applicable statutes specified. Mandatory minimum defendants received downward departures 22 percent of the time. The commission observed that "the increased departure rate may reflect a greater tendency to exercise prosecutorial or judicial discretion as the severity of the penalties increases" (U.S. Sentencing Commission 1991, 53).

No category of federal court practitioners, including prosecutors, much liked mandatory minimum sentencing laws (U.S. Sentencing Commission 1991, chap. 6). Among forty-eight defense counsel, only one had anything positive to say, and he also had negative comments. Probation officers were also overwhelmingly hostile. Only among prosecutors was sentiment more favorable; even among them, however, thirty-four of sixty-one were wholly (23) or partly (11) negative. The most common complaints by all three groups were that the mandatory penalties were too harsh, resulted in too many trials, and eliminated judicial discretion. A mail survey showed that 62 percent of judges, 52 percent of private counsel, and 89 percent of federal defenders wanted mandatory penalties for drug crimes eliminated.

E. Oregon's Measure 11

Oregon's Measure 11, adopted by voters in a referendum in 1994, required imposition of mandatory minimum prison sentences from seventy to three hundred months on anyone (including children as young as fifteen) convicted of any of sixteen designated crimes. The law's coverage was later extended to five additional crimes.

A person who knew nothing about how courts operate might expect that anyone who committed those twenty-one crimes would receive the mandated sentences. RAND Corporation evaluators understood how courts operate (Merritt, Fain, and Turner 2006). They supposed that judges and lawyers would alter previous ways of doing business, especially in filing charges and negotiating plea bargains, to achieve results that seemed to them sensible and just. To find out whether they were right, they interviewed a considerable number of practitioners, analyzed data on sentences for offenses subject to Measure 11 and lesser related offenses for periods before and after Measure 11 took effect, and conducted another round of interviews to test their readings of the statistical analyses.

On the basis of the research summarized to this point in this chapter, they expected that, compared with sentencing patterns prior to adoption of Measure 11, relatively fewer people would be convicted of Measure 11 offenses and more of non–Measure 11 offenses, those convicted of Measure 11 offenses would receive harsher sentences, and jury trial rates would rise for a while and then return to prior levels. The rationales were that practitioners would divert some cases that would once have been Measure 11 offenses into less serious offense categories, that the remaining Measure 11 cases would be of greater average seriousness than before the law changed, and that the threat of harsher sentences would for a while cause more defendants to take their chances on a trial rather than plead guilty (but new "going rates" would in due course be established and guilty plea rates would return to normal).

The research confirmed the hypotheses and in addition showed that sentences for non–Measure 11 offenses also became harsher, that the mandatory minimums increased prosecutors' power, and that the changed sentencing patterns resulted primarily from changes in charging (fewer Measure 11 crimes, more lesser crimes) and plea bargaining (fewer pleas to initially charged offenses, more to lesser included offenses).

The only other major related evaluation was carried out in New Jersey by Candace McCoy and Patrick McManimon (2004). They examined sentencing patterns and case processing in New Jersey after enactment of a "truth-in-sentencing" law requiring people convicted of designated offenses to serve 85 percent of the announced sentence. This was not a mandatory minimum sentence law but similar hypotheses apply: that power would be shifted to prosecutors, that charging and bargaining patterns would change to shelter some defendants from the new law, that sentences would be harsher for those not sheltered, and that new plea negotiation "going rates" would be established. Each of the hypotheses was substantiated.

Nothing found in any of these studies contradicts findings from earlier periods. Nothing in these post-1970 findings would surprise the authors of the American Bar Foundation Surveys or observers of eighteenth-century English courts.

III. Mandatory Penalties in Other Countries

No Western country besides the United States has adopted a large number of broad-based mandatory penalties. The small literature concerns Australia, Canada, England and Wales, and South Africa. No ambitious evaluations comparable to those discussed in section II have been undertaken. There have been efforts, however, to take stock of their effects. The most recent and comprehensive is a report by the Sentencing Advisory Council of the Australian State of Victoria. Its conclusions are in line with every other major analysis:

> Ultimately, current research in this area indicates that there is a very low likelihood that a mandatory sentencing regime will deliver on its [deterrent] aims. . . . There is, in any case, ample evidence that mandatory sentencing can and will be circumvented by lawyers, judges, and juries both by accepted measures (such as plea bargaining) and by less visible means. The outcome of this avoidance is to jeopardize seriously another aim of mandatory sentencing; that is, to ensure that proportionate and consistent sentences are imposed. (Sentencing Advisory Council 2008, 21)

A. England and Wales

By American standards, some other countries' mandatory penalty laws are not mandatory at all. Three mandatory sentence laws were enacted in England and Wales as part of the Crime (Sentences) Act 1997. The first provided for an automatic life sentence (though affected offenders remained eligible for parole release) for a second serious violent or sexual offense unless there were "exceptional" circumstances. The other two specified a minimum seven-year sentence for third-time trafficking in class A drugs and a minimum three-year sentence for third-time domestic burglary. These laws, however, provided that judges could impose a lesser sentence if they concluded that imposition of the mandatory sentence would be unjust "in all the circumstances." Andrew Ashworth (2001), the preeminent British sentencing scholar, argued that that provision emasculated the law. The Court of Appeal, in an opinion by Lord Chief Justice Wolfe, in a case involving mandatory life sentences for second serious violent or sexual crimes, ruled that a finding that the offender "was not felt to present a significant risk to the public" would satisfy the "exceptional circumstances" test (Jones and Newburn 2006, 787). Cavadino and Dignan observed that the decision would "presumably allow sentencers to avoid passing life sentences in many—perhaps most—of these 'two-strikes'" cases (2002, 106). The mandatory life sentence for a second violent or sexual offense was repealed as part of the Criminal Justice Act 2003.[2]

B. South Africa

The South African laws were enacted in 1997 at a time of rapidly rising crime rates, ostensibly as an interim measure and with a two-year sunset clause.[3] They provided for mandatory minimums for certain serious offenses and minimum ten-, twenty-, and thirty-year sentences for first, second, and third rapes, respectively, and for specific types of murder. Similar to the English law, the initial proposed law provided that courts could impose less severe sentences if there were "circumstances" that would justify them. Before the departure criterion was enacted, it was redefined to require a more restrictive finding of "substantial and compelling circumstances." Constitutional challenges were raised. In *S. v. Malgas*, 2 SA 1222 (2001), the South African Supreme Court of Appeal, not unlike the English Court of Appeal before it, broadened the departure test: "'Substantial and compelling circumstances' may arise from a number of factors considered together—taken one by one, these factors need not be exceptional. If the sentencing court considers all the circumstances and is satisfied that the prescribed sentence would be unjust, as it would be 'disproportionate to the crime, the criminal, and the needs of society,' the court may impose a shorter sentence" (1234–35).

In the aftermath of *Malgas*, South Africa is repeating an old American story. Stephan Terblanche (2003), the preeminent South African sentencing scholar, has argued that minimum sentence legislation has worsened disparities and inconsistencies in South African sentencing. Evaluations have shown that judges depart from the mandatory minimums in a majority of cases (O'Donovan and Redpath 2006). There is evidence that circumvention of the law is widespread (Roth 2008, 169–70) and that sentences for those not benefitting from departures became harsher after the 1997 law was enacted (Sloth-Nielsen and Ehlers 2005). The most comprehensive examination of the effects of South Africa's mandatory penalties concluded that, because of *Malgas*, the laws did not substantially increase constraints on judicial discretion. The study documented increased inconsistency in sentencing and increases in court costs and delays (O'Donovan and Redpath 2006, 81–84).

C. Australia

Three-strikes laws in Western Australia and the Northern Territory attracted considerable attention in Australia even though, by American, English, and South African standards, they were mild (Hogg 1999; Law Council of Australia

2001). The Northern Territory, which traditionally has much the highest imprisonment rates in Australia, enacted a mandatory penalty law in 1997 for a broad
range of low-level offenses, including theft, receiving stolen property, criminal
damage, and unlawful use of a vehicle. First-time adult offenders faced a
mandatory minimum fourteen-day prison sentence, second-timers a minimum
ninety days, and third-timers a minimum of a year. A twenty-eight-day detention
term was mandated for fifteen- and sixteen-year-olds convicted of a second or
subsequent offense. In 1999 sexual and violent offenses were made subject to
mandatory penalties.

As in the English and South African laws, an "exceptional circumstances" provision in all these laws allowed judges to avoid imposing the minimum sentences on
adults when they made appropriate findings (Brown 2001). Johnson and Zdenkowski (2000), in an assessment of the effects, concluded that discretion had been
shifted from judges to prosecutors and that more case dispositions moved out of the
spotlight and into the shadows as defense lawyers negotiated charge dismissals and
agreements to permit informal dispositions (e.g., restitution). The mandatories for
property offenses were repealed in 2001. The mandatories for violent and sexual
offenses remained in effect in 2007 (Warner 2007).

Western Australia enacted two mandatory penalty laws. The first, in 1992, was
precipitated by a rash of automobile thefts by juveniles that produced police chases
and sixteen related traffic deaths in eighteen months. It mandated indeterminate
(parolable) detention in addition to at least eighteen months' imprisonment. Only
two juveniles were sentenced to indeterminate detention under the law. An evaluation by the Western Australian Crime Research Centre concluded that the law's
enactment had no effect on rates of automobile theft (Broadhurst and Loh 1993).
The law was repealed in 1994 (Brown 2001; Warner 2007).

A 1996 three-strikes law in Western Australia subjected people convicted for
the third and subsequent times of household burglary to a twelve-month minimum sentence to confinement. An Australian judge observed that such adult
offenders already typically received eighteen- to thirty-six-month sentences,
making the mandatory penalty "less than the term of an imprisonment that an
adult might have expected before the law was changed" and therefore largely symbolic (Yeats 1997, 375). The burglary three-strikes law remained in effect in 2007.
Kate Warner observed: "The heat seems to have gone out of the debate, perhaps
because in practice it has little effect on adults and the courts have circumvented
mandatory detention for juveniles by imposing Conditional Release Orders" (2007,
337). Neil Morgan's evaluation concluded that "there is compelling evidence from
Western Australia that neither the 1992 nor the 1996 laws achieved a deterrent
effect. . . . There was a leap in residential burglaries immediately after the introduction of the new [1996] laws at precisely the time when the greatest reduction would
have been expected" (2000, 172).

D. Canada

Canada is a federal country in which the criminal code and its sentencing laws are federal, but prosecutions are handled in provincial courts. There have been three major recent sets of mandatory penalties.[4] A minimum sentence of seven years was mandated for importation of narcotics, but this was declared unconstitutional by the Canadian Supreme Court because it was "grossly disproportionate to what the offender deserves" in the case before the court (*R v. Smith*, 34 C.C.C. 3d 97 [1987], at 139). New mandatories for drug importation were not enacted. A 1996 law mandated minimum four-year prison sentences for offenders committing any of ten violent crimes with a firearm. Cheryl Webster and Anthony Doob, after analyzing data on Canadian prison populations, concluded: "While the mandatory minimum sentences for violent crimes did in fact increase the sentences that *some* offenders received, it is likely that the 'new' sanction would not significantly differ from one that would have been handed down under the prior legislation for most offenders. . . . It is probable they would already have been dealt with in a harsh manner by Canadian judges" (2007, 317; emphasis in original). Legislation introduced in 2006 (Bill C-10, 39th Parliament, 1st sess.) requires a five-year mandatory minimum for gang-related gun crimes or gun use in relation to designated serious crimes and a longer minimum for second convictions. It applies only to handguns and involves only marginally more severe punishments than the 1996 legislation. Doob and Webster (2009) describe it, like its 1996 predecessor, as a primarily symbolic tough-on-crime initiative of a conservative government.

None of the laws in Canada, England, South Africa, and Australia are as severe as the harsher American laws and few are as rigid. To a considerable extent these countries have recognized the foreseeable nullification problems that face all rigid or severe sentencing laws by creating "exceptional circumstance" authority for judges to depart openly and accountably. The South Africans, however, have replicated the American pattern of stark and unjust disparities that result when some like-situated offenders benefit from low-visibility circumvention of severe laws and others go to prison for many years.

III. DETERRENT EFFECTS

One claim often made for mandatory minimum sentence laws is that their enactment and enforcement deter would-be offenders and thereby reduce crime rates and spare victims' suffering. This claim, if true, makes a powerful case. Unfortunately, the accumulated evidence shows that it is not true.

There are three kinds of sources of relevant evidence. First, governments in many countries have asked advisory committees or national commissions to survey knowledge of the deterrent effects of criminal penalties in general. Second, a sizable number of comprehensive reviews of the literature on deterrence have been published. Third, evaluations have been conducted of the deterrent effects of newly enacted mandatory penalty laws. The third of these is most narrowly relevant to the subject of this chapter, so I only briefly summarize the first two literatures.

A. National Advisory Bodies

No one doubts that society is safer having some criminal penalties rather than none at all, but that choice is not in issue. On the real-world question of whether increases in penalties significantly reduce the incidence of serious crimes, the consensus conclusion of governmental advisory bodies in many countries is possibly, a little, at most, but probably not.

After the most exhaustive examination of the question ever undertaken, the National Academy of Sciences Panel on Research on Deterrent and Incapacitative Effects concluded: "In summary . . . we cannot yet assert that the evidence warrants an affirmative conclusion regarding deterrence" (Blumstein, Cohen, and Nagin 1978, 7). Daniel Nagin of Carnegie Mellon University, a principal draftsman of the report, was less qualified in his assessment: "The evidence is woefully inadequate for providing a good estimate of the magnitude of whatever effect may exist. . . . Policymakers in the criminal justice system are done a disservice if they are left with the impression that the empirical evidence . . . strongly supports the deterrence hypothesis" (1978, 135–36). The National Academy of Sciences Panel on Understanding and Controlling Violence reached a similar conclusion in 1993. After documenting that the average prison sentence per violent crime tripled between 1975 and 1989, the panel asked, "What effect has increasing the prison population had on violent crime?" and answered, "Apparently very little" (Reiss and Roth 1993, 6).

Similar bodies in other Western countries have reached similar conclusions. British Prime Minister Margaret Thatcher's Conservative government created a Home Office advisory committee on criminal penalties. The resulting white paper expressed skepticism about the deterrent effects of penalties: "Deterrence is a principle with much immediate appeal. . . . But much crime is committed on impulse, given the opportunity presented by an open window or unlocked door, and it is committed by offenders who live from moment to moment; their crimes are as impulsive as the rest of their feckless, sad, or pathetic lives. It is unrealistic to construct sentencing arrangements on the assumption that most offenders will weigh up the possibilities in advance and base their conduct on rational calculation" (Home Office 1990, 6).

The same conclusions were earlier reached by the Canadian Sentencing Commission: "Evidence does not support the notion that variations in sanctions (within a range that reasonably could be contemplated) affect the deterrent value of sentences. In other words, deterrence cannot be used with empirical justification, to guide the imposition of sentences" (1987, xxvii).

Negative findings concerning the deterrent effects of penalties are not unique to English-speaking countries. A report issued by the Finnish Ministry of Justice's National Research Institute of Legal Policy explained: "Can our long prison sentences be defended on the basis of a cost/benefit assessment of their general preventative effect? The answer of the criminological expertise was no" (Törnudd 1993, 4).

B. Surveys of the Literature

The critical question is whether marginal changes in sanctions have measurable deterrent effects. The heavy majority of broad-based reviews reach similar conclusions that no credible evidence demonstrates that increasing penalties reliably achieves marginal deterrent effects. A few reviews by economists, relying solely on work by economists, come out the other way (e.g., Lewis 1986; Levitt 2002; Levitt and Miles 2007). They have been convincingly refuted. I quote the conclusions of the most influential recent surveys of the evidence.

Daniel Nagin, in 1998, revisiting the work of the 1978 National Academy of Sciences panel twenty years later, observed that he "was convinced that a number of studies have credibly demonstrated marginal deterrent effects," but concluded that it was "difficult to generalize from the findings of a specific study because knowledge about the factors that affect the efficacy of policy is so limited" (1998, 4).

Andrew von Hirsch and his colleagues (1999), in a survey of the literature commissioned by the Home Office of England and Wales, concluded that "there is as yet no firm evidence regarding the extent to which raising the severity of punishment would enhance deterrence of crime" (52).

Anthony Doob and Cheryl Webster, in 2003, in yet another major review of the literature, noted some inconclusive or weak evidence of marginal deterrence, but they concluded: "There is no plausible body of evidence that supports policies based on this premise [that increased penalties reduce crime]. On the contrary, standard social scientific norms governing the acceptance of the null hypothesis justify the present (always rebuttable) conclusion that sentence severity does not affect levels of crime" (2003, 146).

Finally, a meta-analysis by Travis Pratt and his colleagues (2006) produced a main finding on deterrence, one "noted by previous narrative reviews of the deterrence literature," that "the effects of severity estimates and deterrence/sanctions composites, even when statistically significant, are too weak to be of substantive significance)" (379).

C. Mandatory Penalty Evaluations

Two literatures are germane. Evaluations of mandatory minimum laws in the 1970s and 1980s focused on effects on sentencing outcomes and court processes. These generally conclude that deterrent effects cannot be shown to be associated with passage and implementation of mandatory penalty laws. A second literature, all focused on California in the 1990s, examines the effects on crime rates of changes in California sentencing laws. Most of it concerns the three-strikes law. The divide in California between some economists and other social scientists is stunning. Work by non-economists and some economists concludes that no crime-preventive effects can be shown. Work by other economists concludes that the new laws have had significant deterrent effects.

1. *Mandatory Minimum Evaluations*

No individual evaluation has demonstrated crime reduction effects attributable to enactment or implementation of a mandatory minimum sentence law. One analysis combined data from four studies that had not found deterrent effects and concluded that a small deterrent effect could be shown. For reasons given below, the finding is not credible.

The evaluators of the Rockefeller Drug Laws expended most of their efforts trying to identify effects on drug use or drug-related crime. They found none (Joint Committee on New York Drug Law Evaluation 1978).

A number of studies were made of the crime-preventive effects of the Massachusetts law requiring a one-year minimum sentence for people convicted of possession of an unregistered firearm. The studies concluded that it had either no deterrent effect on the use of firearms in violent crimes (Beha 1977; Rossman et al. 1979; Carlson 1982) or a small short-term effect that quickly disappeared (Pierce and Bowers 1981).

Studies in other states reached similar results. An evaluation of the mandatory sentencing law for firearms offenses in Detroit, Michigan, concluded that "the mandatory sentencing law did not have a preventive effect on crime" (Loftin, Heumann, and McDowall 1983). Assessments of the deterrent effects of mandatory penalty laws in Tampa, Jacksonville, and Miami, Florida, "concluded that the results did not support a preventive effect model" (Loftin and McDowall 1984, 259). An evaluation of the crime-preventive effects of mandatory penalty laws in Pittsburgh and Philadelphia, Pennsylvania concluded that the results "do not strongly challenge the conclusion that the statutes have no preventive effect" (McDowall, Loftin, and Wiersema 1992, 382).

One analysis based on evaluation data concluded that mandatory penalties had deterrent effects. McDowall, Loftin, and Wiersema (1992), the team of researchers who conducted the Michigan, Florida, and Pennsylvania deterrence analyses, combined the data from the sites in three states and concluded that mandatory penalties for gun crimes reduced gun homicides but not assaults or robberies involving guns.

This is counterintuitive and must be wrong. Homicides by definition are lethal assaults, and the ratios of assaults and robberies that involve guns and result in deaths should be relatively stable, assuming there have been no substantial changes in the lethality of available weapons. If the proportions of assaults and robberies involving guns decline, gun homicides should decline commensurately, and vice versa. If a deterrent effect can be shown for relatively small numbers of homicides, it should be much easier to demonstrate for vastly larger numbers of assaults and robberies. The analysis found no such effect.

2. California Studies

The gap between politics and knowledge concerning the effects of California's three-strikes law has been enormous. Most credible empirical assessments of the law's effects on crime rates and patterns have concluded that none can be shown.

a. California Government Views.

a. *California Government Views.* Although it took a dozen years, some agencies of California government eventually expressed views consistent with those of (most) researchers. It was a long time coming. In 1999 the California secretary of state Bill Jones claimed: "After five years, we now have strong statistical data to show the law is working as intended. California's murder and robbery rates are down by 50 percent [and] the overall crime rate in California has declined 38 percent. . . . It is clear that the implementation of the Three Strikes and You're Out Law has made a considerable positive impact on the incidence of crime and California" (Secretary of State 1999, 1, 3).

By 2004, when the accumulation of studies suggesting otherwise had become huge, even the California District Attorneys Association expressed more cautious views: the "dramatic drop in California's crime rate might be properly attributable to several substantial factors. It is counterintuitive, however, to think that incarcerating violent recidivist felons for longer periods (whether under the two- or three-strikes provisions of this law) was not one of them" (2004, 21).

In 2005, however, the Legislative Analyst's Office, after presenting an analysis showing that the declines in overall and violent crime rates in the four counties in which the law was most often applied and the four in which it was least often applied were indistinguishable, concluded: "For now, it remains an open question as to how much safer California's citizens are as a result of Three Strikes" (33).

b. California Impact Assessments.

b. *California Impact Assessments.* Many three-strikes laws are not, strictly speaking, mandatory minimum sentence laws. Under California's, for example, both prosecutors and judges can "strike" the prior convictions that trigger the law's mandatory minimum sentences.

In a longer article (Tonry 2009, table 3), I summarize and discuss the findings of fifteen efforts to assess the crime-preventive effects of California's three-strikes law. Only two, both by economists, concluded that the three-strikes law reduced California crime rates (Chen 2000; Shepherd 2002). Chen's findings were weak, and her conclusions were hedged.[5] Three econometric studies (Marvell and Moody 2001; Kovandzic, Sloan, and Vieraitis 2002; Moody, Marvell, and Kaminski 2003) concluded that enactment of three-strikes laws produced *increases* in homicide rates.

Shepherd (2002) produced the only assessment finding significant effects: "During the first two years after the legislation's enactment, approximately eight murders, 3,952 aggravated assaults, 10,672 robberies, and 384,488 burglaries were deterred in California by the two- and three-strikes legislation" (174).

The fundamental problem with Shepherd's analysis is that she assumes to be true something that other social scientists investigate—that increased penalties reduce crime rates. She observes that her "model predicts that offenses covered by two- and three-strikes legislation will be deterred" (2002, 173). That economists' models are often devised to confirm their assumptions ("predictions") may be why they so often find deterrent effects and why other economists can pick the models apart (e.g., Ayres and Donohue 2003*a*, 2003*b*; Donohue and Wolfers 2005; Donohue 2006). In the case of California's three-strikes law, however, Shepherd is an outlier; other economists' analyses concur with the no-deterrent-effect conclusions of non-economists (Marvell and Moody 2001; Kovandzic, Sloan, and Vieraitis 2002; Moody, Marvell, and Kaminski 2003).

No matter which body of evidence is consulted—the general literature on the deterrent effects of criminal sanctions, work more narrowly focused on the marginal deterrence hypothesis, or the evaluation literature on mandatory penalties—the conclusion is the same. There is little basis for believing that mandatory penalties have any significant effects on rates of serious crime.

V. Undoing the Harm

The policy and human rights implications of this two-century-old body of knowledge are clear. Mandatory penalties are a bad idea. They often result in injustice to individual offenders. They undermine the legitimacy of the courts and the prosecution system by fostering circumventions that are willful and subterranean. They undermine achievement of equality before the law when they cause comparably culpable offenders to be treated radically differently when one benefits from practitioners' circumventions and another receives a mandated penalty that everyone immediately involved considers too severe. And the clear weight of the evidence is, and for nearly forty years has been, that there is insufficient credible evidence to conclude that mandatory penalties have significant deterrent effects (Federal Judicial Center 1994).

The instrumental arguments against mandatory penalties are clear. First, they increase public expense by increasing trial rates and case processing times. Second, in every published process evaluation, judges and prosecutors were shown to have devised ways to circumvent application of the mandatory penalties.

The normative arguments against mandatory penalties are also straightforward. First, simple justice: because of their inflexibility, such laws sometimes result in imposition of penalties in individual cases that everyone involved believes to be unjustly severe. Second, perhaps more importantly, mandatory penalties encourage hypocrisy on the part of prosecutors and judges. The hypocrisies that mandatory penalties engender are what most troubles prosecutors and judges. Plea bargaining may be a necessary evil, an essential lubricant without which the machinery of justice would break down, but it is typically routinized. Armed robbery is pled down to robbery, aggravated assault to assault, theft 1 to theft 2. Prosecutors, defense counsel, judges, probation officers—all who are involved—know what is happening, understand why, and acknowledge the legitimacy of the reasons.

Judges, prosecutors, and defense counsel must live with their own consciences and with their shared views of the bounds of fair treatment of offenders. They must also keep the courts functioning. That they sometimes devise ways to avoid application of laws they believe to be undeservedly harsh should come as no surprise.

In a sensible world of rational policymaking, no mandatory penalty laws would be enacted. Those that exist would be repealed. That would be the simplest way to address the problems revealed by the literature and canvassed in this chapter. That is not the world we live in. There are other ways the problems could be addressed or at least diminished. First, much of what legislators hope to accomplish with mandatory sentencing laws could be achieved by making such laws presumptive or—following the pattern of other English-speaking countries—by adding provisions authorizing judges to impose some other sentence when they believe justice would thereby be served. Second, "sunset clauses" should be included in all future mandatory penalty laws, and they should be added to all existing ones. Sunset clauses provide for automatic repeal of a statute at a fixed time unless a new law is enacted to extend its life. With sunset clauses in place, legislators unwilling to take responsibility for voting to repeal a mandatory penalty law—lest they be vulnerable to being accused of "being soft on crime"—may feel able more comfortably acceding to its lapse. Third, if legislators are unwilling to repeal mandatory penalty laws or to ameliorate their effects, they should at very least greatly narrow their scope to include only patently serious crimes such as homicide and aggravated rape. Fourth, correctional or parole authorities should be authorized periodically to reconsider lengthy sentences (say five or ten years) and to release prisoners. The argument for administrative reconsideration of lengthy mandatory sentences parallels the argument for sunset clauses—some decisions present such difficult political problems for elected officials that it is better to eliminate the need to make them. Permitting corrections or parole officials to decide when a prisoner under lengthy sentence has served long enough would remove those decisions from the public eye.

Mandatory penalties is not a subject on which research has counted for much in the United States for the past thirty years. Policy debates neither waited for nor paid much attention to research results. We now know what we are ever likely to know, and what our predecessors knew, about mandatory penalties. They do little good and much harm.

NOTES

1. I draw heavily on an earlier, considerably longer survey of knowledge concerning mandatory penalties (Tonry 2009).
2. The story of the enactment and experience with the English laws is told most fully by Jones and Newburn (2006).
3. The mandatory penalties remained in effect in mid-2009 after a series of two-year extensions. Van zyl Smit (2000) tells the tale in considerable detail.
4. Crutcher(2001)provides a detailed account of the history of mandatory penalties in Canada.
5. "The approach taken in California has not been dramatically more effective at controlling crime than other states' efforts. . . . [California's law] is not considerably more effective at crime reduction than alternative methods that are narrower in scope" (Chen 2008, 362, 365).

REFERENCES

American Bar Association. 1968. *Sentencing Alternatives and Procedures.* Chicago: American Bar Association.
———. 1994. *American Bar Association Standards for Criminal Justice: Sentencing Alternatives and Procedures.* 3rd ed. Washington, DC: American Bar Association.
American Law Institute. 1962. *Model Penal Code (Proposed Official Draft).* Philadelphia: American Law Institute.
———. 2007. *Model Penal Code: Sentencing (Tentative Draft No. 1).* Philadelphia: American Law Institute.
Ashworth, Andrew. 2001. "The Decline of English Sentencing and Other Stories." In *Sentencing and Sanctions in Western Countries,* ed. Michael Tonry and Richard Frase. Oxford: Oxford University Press.

Austin, James. 1991. *The Consequences of Escalating the Use of Imprisonment: The Case Study of Florida.* San Francisco: National Council on Crime and Delinquency.

Austin, James, Charles Jones, John Kramer, and Phil Renninger. 1994. *National Assessment of Structured Sentencing.* Washington, DC: U.S. Department of Justice, Bureau of Justice Assistance.

Ayres, Ian, and John J. Donohue. 2003*a*. "The Latest Misfires in Support of the 'More Guns, Less Crime' Hypothesis." *Stanford Law Review* 55: 1371–98.

———. 2003*b*. "Shooting Down the 'More Guns, Less Crime' Hypothesis." *Stanford Law Review* 55: 1193–312.

Beha, James A., II 1977. "'And Nobody Can Get You Out': The Impact of a Mandatory Prison Sentence for the Illegal Carrying of a Firearm on the Use of Firearms and on the Administration of Criminal Justice in Boston." *Boston University Law Review* 57:96–146 (pt.1); 57: 289–333 (pt. 2).

Blumstein, Alfred, Jacqueline Cohen, Susan Martin, and Michael Tonry, eds. 1983. *Research on Sentencing: The Search for Reform.* Washington, DC: National Academy Press.

Blumstein, Alfred, Jacqueline Cohen, and Daniel Nagin, eds. 1978. *Deterrence and Incapacitation: Estimating the Effects of Criminal Sanctions on Crime Rates.* Washington, DC: National Academy of Sciences.

Broadhurst, Roderic, and Nini Loh. 1993. "The Phantom of Deterrence: The Crime (Serious and Repeat Offenders) Sentencing Act." *Australian and New Zealand Journal of Criminology* 26(3): 251–71.

Brown, David. 2001. "Mandatory Sentencing: A Criminological Perspective." *Australian Journal of Human Rights* 7(2): 31–51.

Butterfield, Fox. 2003. "With Cash Tight, States Reassess Long Jail Terms." *New York Times*, November 10, p. A1.

California District Attorneys Association. 2004. *Prosecutors' Perspectives on California's Three Strikes Law: A 10-Year Retrospective.* Sacramento: California District Attorneys Association.

Canadian Sentencing Commission. 1987. *Sentencing Reform: A Canadian Approach.* Ottawa: Canadian Government Publishing Centre.

Carlson, Kenneth. 1982. *Mandatory Sentencing: The Experience of Two States.* Washington, DC: U.S. Government Printing Office.

Cavadino, Michael, and James Dignan. 2002. *The Penal System: An Introduction.* 3rd ed. London: Sage.

Chen, Elsa Y. 2000. "'Three Strikes and You're Out' and 'Truth in Sentencing': Lessons in Policy Implementation and Impacts." PhD diss., Department of Political Science, University of California, Los Angeles.

———. 2008. "Impacts of 'Three Strikes and You're Out' on Crime Trends in California and throughout the United States." *Journal of Contemporary Criminal Justice* 24: 345–70.

Crutcher, Nicole. 2001. "Mandatory Minimum Penalties of Imprisonment: An Historical Analysis." *Criminal Law Quarterly* 44(3): 279–309.

Dawson, Robert O. 1969. *Sentencing.* Boston: Little, Brown.

Dickey, Walter, and Pamela Hollenhorst. 1999. "Three Strikes Laws: Five Years Later." *Corrections Management Quarterly* 3(3): 1–18.

Donohue, John J. 2006. "The Death Penalty: No Evidence for Deterrence." *Economists' Voice* 3(5): 1–6.

Donohue, John J., and Justin Wolfers. 2005. "Uses and Abuses of Empirical Evidence in the Death Penalty Debate." *Stanford Law Review* 58: 791–846.

Doob, Anthony, and Cheryl Webster. 2003. "Sentence Severity and Crime: Accepting the Null Hypothesis." In *Crime and Justice: A Review of Research*, vol. 30, edited by Michael Tonry. Chicago: University of Chicago Press.

Doob, Anthony, and Cheryl Webster. 2009. "Under Siege? Assessing the Future for Canada's Stable Rate of Imprisonment." In *International and Comparative Criminal Justice and Urban Governance: Convergence and Divergence in Global, National and Local Settings*, ed. Adam Crawford. Cambridge: Cambridge University Press.

Federal Courts Study Committee. 1990. *Report*. Washington, DC: Administrative Office of the U.S. Courts.

Federal Judicial Center. 1994. *The Consequences of Mandatory Minimum Prison Terms: A Summary of Recent Findings*. Washington, DC: Federal Judicial Center.

Hay, Douglas. 1975. "Property, Authority, and the Criminal Law." In *Albion's Fatal Tree: Crime and Society in Eighteenth Century England*, ed. Douglas Hay, Douglas, Peter Linebaugh, and E. P. Thompson. New York: Pantheon.

———. 1980. "Crime and Justice in Eighteenth and Nineteenth Century England." In *Crime and Justice: A Review of Research*, vol. 2, edited by Norval Morris and Michael Tonry. Chicago: University of Chicago Press.

Hay, Douglas, Peter Linebaugh, John G. Rule, E. Thompson, and Cal Winslow. 1975. *Albion's Fatal Tree: Crime and Society in Eighteenth-Century England*. New York: Pantheon.

Heumann, Milton, and Colin Loftin. 1979. "Mandatory Sentencing and the Abolition of Plea Bargaining: The Michigan Felony Firearms Statute." *Law and Society Review* 13: 393–430.

Hogg, Russell. 1999. "Mandatory Sentencing Laws and the Symbolic Politics of Law and Order." *University of New South Wales Law Journal* 22(1): 263–79.

Holmes, Oliver Wendell, Jr. 1889. "Law in Science and Science in Law." *Harvard Law Review* 12:443–63.

Home Office. 1990. *Crime, Justice, and Protecting the Public*. London: Home Office.

Johnson, Dianne, and George Zdenkowski. 2000. *Mandatory Injustice: Compulsory Imprisonment in the Northern Territory*. Sydney: Centre for Independent Journalism.

Joint Committee on New York Drug Law Evaluation. 1978. *The Nation's Toughest Drug Law: Evaluating the New York Experience*. Project of the Association of the Bar of the City of New York and the Drug Abuse Council, Inc. Washington, DC: U.S. Government Printing Office.

Jones, Trevor, and Tim Newburn. 2006. "Three Strikes and You're Out: Exploring Symbol and Substance in American and British Crime Control Policies." *British Journal of Criminology* 46(5): 781–802.

Kennedy, Anthony, chairman. 2004. *American Bar Association Justice Kennedy Commission Report with Recommendations to the ABA House of Delegates, August 2004*. Chicago: American Bar Association.

Knapp, Kay A. 1991. "Arizona: Unprincipled Sentencing, Mandatory Minimums, and Prison Crowding." *Overcrowded Times* 2(5): 10–12.

Kovandzic, Tomislav, John Sloan, and Lynne Vieraitis. 2002. "Unintended Consequences of Politically Popular Sentencing Policy: The Homicide Promoting Effects of 'Three Strikes' in U.S. Cities (1980–1999)." *Criminology and Public Policy* 1(3): 399–424.

Law Council of Australia. 2001. *The Mandatory Sentencing Debate*. Canberra: Law Council of Australia.

Legislative Analyst's Office, California Legislature. 2005. *A Primer: Three Strikes: The Impact after More than a Decade*. Sacramento: Legislative Analyst's Office.

Levitt, Steven D. 2002. "Deterrence." In *Crime: Public Policies for Crime Control*, ed. James Q. Wilson and Joan Petersilia. Oakland, CA: Institute for Contemporary Studies Press.

Levitt, Steven D., and Thomas J. Miles. 2007. "Empirical Study of Criminal Punishment." In *Handbook of Law and Economics* vol. 1, ed. A. Mitchell Polinsky and Steven Shavell. Amsterdam: Elsevier.

Lewis, Donald E. 1986. "The General Deterrent Effect of Longer Sentences." *British Journal of Criminology* 26(1): 47–62.

Liptak, Adam. 2007. "Whittling Away, but Leaving a Gap." *New York Times*, November 17, p. A21.

Loftin, Colin, Milton Heumann, and David McDowall. 1983. "Mandatory Sentencing and Firearms Violence: Evaluating an Alternative to Gun Control." *Law and Society Review* 17: 287–318.

Loftin, Colin, and David McDowall. 1981. "'One with a Gun Gets You Two': Mandatory Sentencing and Firearms Violence in Detroit." *Annals of the American Academy of Political and Social Science* 455(1): 150–67.

———. 1984. "The Deterrent Effects of the Florida Felony Firearm Law." *Journal of Criminal Law and Criminology* 75: 250–59.

Marvell, Thomas B., and Carlisle E. Moody. 2001. "The Lethal Effects of Three Strikes Laws." *Journal of Legal Studies* 30(1): 89–106.

McCoy, Candace, and Patrick McManimon. 2004. "New Jersey's 'No Early Release Act': Its Impact on Prosecution, Sentencing, Corrections, and Victim Satisfaction." Final report (unpublished), National Institute of Justice, Washington, DC (obtainable from the National Criminal Justice Reference Service).

McDowall, David, Colin Loftin, and Brian Wiersema. 1992. "A Comparative Study of the Preventive Effects of Mandatory Sentencing Laws for Gun Crimes." *Journal of Criminal Law and Criminology* 83: 378–94.

Merritt, Nancy, Terry Fain, and Susan Turner. 2006. "Oregon's Get Tough Sentencing Reform: A Lesson in Justice System Adaptation." *Criminology and Public Policy* 5(1): 5–36.

Moody, Carlisle E., Thomas B. Marvell, and Robert J. Kaminski. 2003. "Unintended Consequences: Three-Strikes Laws and the Murders of Police Officers." Cambridge, MA: National Bureau of Economic Research.

Morgan, Neil. 2000. "Mandatory Sentences in Australia: Where Have We Been and Where Are We Going?" *University of New South Wales Law Journal* 24(3): 164–83.

Nagin, Daniel S. 1978. "General Deterrence: A Review of the Empirical Evidence." In *Deterrence and Incapacitation*, ed. Alfred Blumstein, Jacqueline Cohen, and Daniel Nagin. Washington, DC: National Academy Press.

Nagin, Daniel S. 1998. "Criminal Deterrence Research at the Outset of the Twenty-first Century." In *Crime and Justice: A Review of Research*, vol. 23, edited by Michael Tonry. Chicago: University of Chicago Press.

Newman, Donald. 1966. *Conviction*. Boston: Little, Brown.

O'Donovan, Michael, and Jean Redpath. 2006. *The Impact of Mandatory Sentencing in South Africa*. Capetown: Open Society Foundation.

Pierce, Glen L., and William J. Bowers. 1981. "The Bartley-Fox Gun Law's Short-Term Impact on Crime in Boston." *Annals of the American Academy of Political and Social Science* 455(1): 120–32.

Pound, Roscoe. 1910. "Law in Books and Law in Action." *American Law Review* 44: 12–36.

Pratt, Travis C., Francis T. Cullen, Kristie R. Blevins, Leah H. Daigle, and Tamara D. Madensen. 2006. "The Empirical Status of Deterrence Theory: A Meta-analysis." In *Taking Stock: The Status of Criminological Theory*, ed. Francis T. Cullen, John Paul Wright, and Kristie R. Blevins. New Brunswick, NJ: Transaction.

Radzinowicz, Leon. 1948–68. *A History of English Criminal Law and Its Administration from 1750.* 4 vols. London: Stevens.

Reiss, Albert J., Jr., and Jeffrey Roth, eds. 1993. *Understanding and Controlling Violence.* Washington, DC: National Academy Press.

Remington, Frank. 1969. "Introduction." In *Sentencing*, ed. Robert Dawson. Boston: Little, Brown.

Romilly, Sir Samuel. 1820. "Sir Samuel Romilly's Speeches." In *Criminal Law and Its Administration*, ed. Jerome Michael and Herbert Wechsler. Chicago: Foundation Press.

Rossman, David, Paul Froyd, Glen Pierce, John McDevitt, and William Bowers. 1979. *The Impact of the Mandatory Gun Law in Massachusetts.* Report to the National Institute of Law Enforcement and Criminal Justice. Washington, DC: U.S. Government Printing Office.

Roth, Sandra. 2008. "South African Mandatory Minimum Sentencing: Reform Required." *Minnesota Journal of International Law* 17: 155–82.

Secretary of State, State of California. 1999. *Three Strikes and You're Out: Five Years Later.* Sacramento: California Secretary of State.

Select Committee on Capital Punishment. 1930. *Report.* London: H.M. Stationery Office.

Sentencing Advisory Council. 2008. *Sentencing Matters: Mandatory Sentencing.* Melbourne: Sentencing Advisory Council.

Shane-DuBow, Sandra, Alice P. Brown, and Erik Olsen. 1985. *Sentencing Reform in the United States: History, Content, and Effect.* Washington, DC: U.S. Government Printing Office.

Shepherd, Joanna M. 2002. "Fear of the First Strike: The Full Deterrent Effect of California's Two-and Three-Strike Legislation." *Journal of Legal Studies* 31(1): 159–201.

Sloth-Nielsen, Julia, and Louise Ehlers. 2005. "Assessing the Impact: Mandatory and Minimum Sentences in South Africa." *South African Crime Quarterly* 14(December): 15–22.

Steinhauer, Jennifer. 2009. "To Cut Costs, States Relax Prison Policies." *New York Times*, March 24, p. A1.

Stephen, James Fitzjames. 1977. *A History of the Criminal Law of England.* New York: Franklin. (Originally published 1883. London: Macmillan).

Teeters, Negley K., with Jack H. Hedblom. 1967. *Hang by the Neck: The Legal Use of Scaffold and Noose, Gibbet, Stake, and Firing Squad from Colonial Times to the Present.* Springfield, IL: Thomas.

Terblanche, Stephan. 2003. "Mandatory and Minimum Sentences: Considering S. 51 of the Criminal Law Amendment Act of 1997." *Acta Juridica* (2003): 194–220.

Tonry, Michael. 2009. "Mandatory Penalties." In *Crime and Justice: A Review of Research*, vol. 39, edited by Michael Tonry. Chicago: University of Chicago Press.

Törnudd, Patrik. 1993. *Fifteen Years of Declining Prisoner Rates*. Research Communication no. 8. Helsinki: National Research Institute of Legal Policy.

U.S. Sentencing Commission. 1991. *Special Report to the Congress: Mandatory Minimum Penalties in the Federal Criminal Justice System*. Washington, DC: U.S. Sentencing Commission.

van zyl Smit, Dirk. 2000. "Mandatory Sentences: A Conundrum for the New South Africa?" *Punishment and Society* 2: 197–212.

von Hirsch, Andrew, Anthony E. Bottoms, Elizabeth Burney, and Per-Olof H. Wikström. 1999. *Criminal Deterrence and Sentence Severity: An Analysis of Recent Research*. Oxford: Hart.

Warner, Kate. 2007. "Mandatory Sentencing and the Role of the Academic." *Criminal Law Forum* 18(3–4): 321–47.

Webster, Cheryl Marie, and Anthony N. Doob. 2007. "Punitive Trends and Stable Imprisonment Rates in Canada." In *Crime, Punishment, and Politics in Comparative Perspective*, edited by Michael Tonry. Vol. 36 of *Crime and Justice: A Review of Research*, edited by Michael Tonry. Chicago: University of Chicago Press.

Yeats, Mary Ann. 1997. "'Three Strikes' and Restorative Justice: Dealing with Young Repeat Burglars in Australia." *Criminal Law Bulletin* 8: 369–85.

CHAPTER 24

....

CAPITAL PUNISHMENT

....

RAY PATERNOSTER

FOR as long as there have been civilizations with legal systems authorized to inflict punishment for wrongdoing, there have been death penalties. The death penalty was a possible punishment for numerous crimes in the Code of Hammurabi (*codex Hammurabi*) of Babylon around 1790 BCE, including for such crimes as stealing the son of another, making an accusation of a capital crime that was not proven, robbery, and rape. Three centuries earlier, the Code of Ur-Nammu of Sumeria (Mesopotamia or modern-day Iraq) declared that death would be the punishment for crimes such as murder, robbery, adultery, and rape. Under the laws of Draco in seventh-century BCE Greece, capital punishment was imposed for murder, treason, arson, and rape. Provisions for capital punishment were included in the legal codes of ancient China, the Roman Empire, and the monarchies of Europe during the Middle Ages (Edwards 2007). Under the English "Bloody Codes" of the 1700s, more than two hundred offenses were punishable by death. Even before it became a country, the United States embraced the death penalty. Capital punishment dates from at least 1608 when Captain George Kendall of the Jamestown Colony in Virginia was executed for allegedly being a Spanish spy.

The death penalty has existed in the United States since the 1600s (Banner 2002). There were no very accurate historical records prior to 1930, so historians can make only educated guesses about the number of executions. It has been estimated that there have been more than 16,000 executions on US soil since 1608, including approximately 1,200 since the mid-1970s when the modern era of capital punishment began. Although the United States is not alone among modern countries in using capital punishment, it is the only Western democracy to do so. Japan and

India retain the death penalty, but many countries that use it are non-democratic regimes, such as China, Saudi Arabia, Kuwait, North Korea, and Iran.

However, to say that America is a capital punishment country overlooks that there is great variation within the United States. Some states do not have the death penalty at all; some have it on their books but use it infrequently. Others, such as Texas, Virginia, and Oklahoma, use it often. Even within active death penalty states, however, there is tremendous variation; about two-thirds of the counties in both Texas and Oklahoma, for example, have not sent anyone to death in the modern era. The death penalty in the United States is, moreover, regionalized. From the mid-1970s until the present about 80 percent of all executions in the United States have taken place in southern states.

In this chapter I review the landscape of capital punishment as it now exists. Section I discusses the use of capital punishment internationally. A movement away from its use has frequently not occurred because of popular sentiment against it, but for economic and political reasons—mainly that membership in the European Union and Council of Europe requires the abolition of the death penalty. In section II, I review the use and characteristics of capital punishment in the United States. Section III discusses issues of race, and section IV examines major supreme court decisions. Section V reviews arguments for and against capital punishment. Section VI discusses problems in the administration of capital punishment. Section VII discusses life without the possibility of parole.

Many controversies about the death penalty have made their way into the courts. There have been numerous US Supreme Court decisions concerning the constitutionality of capital punishment and particular forms of it, such as whether death by firing squad is a constitutional punishment (*Wilkerson v. Utah* 99, U.S. 130 [1878]), or death by electrocution, (*In re Kemmler,* 136 U.S. 436 [1890]). In recent years this issue has arisen with respect to whether lethal injection is a constitutional form of punishment, and at least for now the Court says it is (*Baze v. Rees,* 553 U.S. 35 [2008]). Since the modern era of capital punishment began in 1976, the Court has taken on the task of deciding for what crimes capital punishment may be imposed (rape? murder? kidnapping?) and for what kinds of people (the mentally ill? the retarded? the young?). The Court has also given state courts guidance on procedures for capital trials and appeals. An extensive series of cases that I examine only briefly concerns how juries should be selected, what kinds of evidence can be used, whether there should be separate hearings for guilt and penalty, and standards for the quality of legal representation in capital cases.

Other issues that surround the death penalty concern whether it is an effective deterrent to crime—many people believe it is, but most scholars do not. It is, however, difficult to measure the deterrent effect of executions on homicides because there are so few of the former and many more of the latter. Retentionists argue that it costs a great deal more to hold people in prison for the rest of their lives than to execute them. The abolitionists counter that capital trials are anything but normal, that their uniqueness causes them to be lengthy and contested rituals, which necessitates equally lengthy and careful review processes. Supporters push religious commands and the moral doctrine of "an eye for an eye," while opponents warn us that the death penalty is subject to human error and the risk of execution of an innocent person.

A number of concrete problems plague capital punishment. Within the last decade questions have been raised about the adequacy of counsel in capital cases, the quality of scientific evidence and the treatment of scientific evidence in state crime labs, and the possibly unprofessional and unethical behavior of the police and prosecution in some capital cases. These issues in turn have raised questions about the conviction and execution of innocent persons. Innocent persons have been convicted of capital crimes and sentenced to death—about 138 people in twenty-six states have been released from death rows since 1973 (Death Penalty Information Center 2010). In 2000, the frequency of the falsely convicted and issues about the day-to-day fairness of Illinois' capital punishment system led Governor George H. Ryan to declare a moratorium on executions in that state, and to establish a special commission to investigate how Illinois goes about the business of trying capital cases. Other states, including Maryland and New Jersey, followed with their own moratoriums so studies could be conducted of the operation of the death penalty in those states.

In recent years there has been a dramatic decline in the number of death sentences imposed. This may reflect the public's growing concern with the death penalty's problems but also statutory changes in many states. Most states now have "life without the possibility of parole" (LWOP) provisions as a more compelling or at least less objectionable alternative to capital punishment. I discuss LWOPs and examine the implications they may have for the use of capital punishment.

The chapter concludes with a discussion of what might be fruitful and important areas for future research, and a look at what the future of the death penalty might be. One area for future research is the use of victim impact statements in capital hearings. While victim impact statements allow family members and others to convey to the sentencer the extent of the harm done, there is some concern that such testimony may inflame the emotions of the jury and bias the sentence toward death. The Supreme Court thus far has been unwilling to limit victim impact evidence, but it may need to revisit the issue. Another important area of future research is getting an accurate understanding of exactly how much it costs to have a system of capital punishment.

There is controversy and disagreement about what the future holds. Some scholars argue that the inevitable progress of civilization will bring an end to capital punishment. They point to the growing number of countries that have abandoned the death penalty to support their position, and the decline in the number of death sentences and the number of executions in the United States over the past ten years. Another view is that the increase in the number of countries that have abolished the death penalty results largely from political considerations and that those countries that retain the death penalty are not likely to give it up. China, for example, will likely retain the death penalty at least for a while and not be susceptible to diplomatic or economic pressure to abolish it. A majority of other retentionist countries are Islamic countries, which are likely to retain capital punishment as part of Sharia law.

The death penalty in the United States is substantially a state and not a federal concern, used mainly (80 percent) in southern states that seem unlikely to yield to diplomatic pressures or overtures about "civilization and progress." Support for capital punishment has consistently been around 65 percent of the American public since 2000. This more pessimistic view is that the number of death sentences and executions may continue to decline in the United States and around the world, but the death penalty is not likely to disappear anytime soon.

A number of conclusions can be drawn:

- There has been a steady decline in the number of countries using capital punishment in recent years, but it is still imposed in some countries, particularly in Islamic countries and in Asia.
- There has been a movement in Europe to abolish the death penalty to honor human rights.
- There have been approximately 16,000 executions in the United States, about 1,200 since 1977.
- The number of death sentences and the number of executions have been declining in the United States since the 1990s.
- The use of the death penalty varies greatly from state to state and within a state.
- Historically and today there is a close relationship between capital punishment and race.
- Common justifications of the death penalty are that it saves money, is necessary to deter crime, and is morally required. Each is controversial.
- There have been a number of problems with the death penalty in application—racial disparity, poor lawyers, executing or convicting the innocent, and prosecutorial/law enforcement misconduct.
- An alternative to the death penalty is life without parole, but it too comes with problems.
- The death penalty is likely to be with us for the foreseeable future.

I. The Death Penalty Internationally

The death penalty has been a frequently inflicted punishment in different countries, with different political regimes, in different parts of the world. Every form of government (democracy, oligarchy, monarchy, military junta), in every historical period and virtually every country has used the death penalty. Even the Vatican used capital punishment until it was abolished in 1969. There has, however, been a worldwide movement in the past three decades away from capital punishment toward some form of life imprisonment as the most serious punishment (Amnesty International 2009; Death Penalty Information Center 2010). As of December 2010, ninety-five countries had abolished the death penalty altogether, nine had abolished it for "ordinary crimes" (murder, kidnapping, rape) but retained it for other offenses such as treason, and thirty-five had not officially abolished the death penalty but had not executed anyone in the previous ten years. In total, 139 countries had abolished the death penalty for all offenses, for ordinary crimes, or in practice, although it still may exist in the law. Fifty-eight countries retained the death penalty for ordinary criminal offenses. Among these are China, Japan, Libya, Egypt, Iran, Afghanistan, Pakistan, Saudi Arabia, Vietnam, North Korea, and the United States. Over the past five years, the greatest number of executions has occurred in China, with lesser numbers in Iran, Saudi Arabia, and Pakistan. Within the past several years just five countries have imposed about 90 percent of all the executions: China, Iran, Saudi Arabia, Pakistan, and the United States.

Historically, there have been many methods of imposing the death penalty. Socrates was put to death in ancient Greece by drinking poison. In various Chinese dynasties executions were carried out by slicing the body with many cuts until death occurs (death by 1,000 cuts), cutting the person in half, boiling in water, hanging, and being buried alive (Lu and Miethe 2007). In Rome, executions were carried out by crucifixion, mauling by wild beasts in the arena, and being burned (Edwards 2007). European countries moved from brutal forms of execution such as being pulled apart by horses, boiling in oil or water, or breaking on the wheel or rack in the European medieval period to hanging by the eighteenth and nineteenth centuries (Ruff 2001).

Even today many different methods of execution are used. China has in recent years moved increasingly to lethal injection, but it still carries out many executions with a bullet to the head. Thailand uses a 9 mm machine gun on most of its condemned prisoners. Stoning is allowed in Iran, Saudi Arabia, and other Islamic countries. Beheading is permitted in Saudi Arabia and in the United Arab Emirates. Immurement (being left to die of starvation or dehydration) and having a wall fall on the condemned has been used in Afghanistan.

Over the past thirty years, there has been an international movement away from the death penalty and toward substitution of some form of life sentence as the most severe punishment. Since 1976, more than one hundred and four countries have abolished capital punishment for all crimes or for all ordinary crimes. A majority of countries are abolitionist in some form. The movement toward a more abolitionist position has not come about because of a groundswell of popular sentiment but for more pragmatic political and economic concerns. For example, Protocol 13 of the European Convention of Human Rights bans the death penalty under all circumstances. A number of countries that have recently abolished the death penalty have done so to qualify for membership in the European Union [Bosnia-Herzegovina (in 2001), Bulgaria (in 1998), the Czech Republic (in 1990), Hungary (in 1990), Lithuania (in 1998), Poland (in 1997), the Slovak Republic (in 1990), Ukraine (in 1999), Serbia (2002), Montenegro (2002), Estonia (1998), Latvia (in 1999), Turkey (in 2002), Armenia (in 2003).

A good argument can be made that the recent trend toward abolition has not occurred because of popular support for abolition but in spite of a lack of support for it (Zimring and Hawkins 1986; Marshall 2000; Zimring 2003). When Great Britain abolished the death penalty in 1965, a majority of the citizens in public opinion polls indicated that they were in favor of it for some crimes. Zimring (2003) reported that public opinion polls taken ten years after abolition showed that more than 80 percent of British respondents would like to see the death penalty reinstated. Another poll taken in Britain in 2003 revealed that 55 percent of those polled were in favor of the death penalty for murder (Death Penalty Information Center 2009). When the Federal Republic of Germany (West Germany) abolished the death penalty, 74 percent of its public was in favor of capital punishment, and only 21 percent favored abolition (Noelle and Neumann 1967). A majority of the French population was in favor of the death penalty when it was abolished by a left-of-center government in 1981 (Marshall 2000; Steiker 2002). When the death penalty was abolished in many European countries, popular support was quite high, and it was not until *after* abolition that it began to decline.

Hood and Hoyle (2009) have recently argued that a "new dynamic" has emerged in the international community, which recognizes capital punishment as a denial of human rights. Most are optimistic that this will eventually lead to "the final elimination of the death penalty worldwide" (1). There are reasons to be skeptical. Many countries that moved toward abolition did so primarily for economic and political reasons, and in opposition to public opinion. For example, Hood and Hoyle noted that Albania "moved quite rapidly toward abolishing the death penalty *as it prepared for membership in the Council of Europe*" and in the face of great public support for the death penalty (emphasis added, 11, 24). They also noted how Poland's abolition of the death penalty was motivated by "political will, official inquiry, and the influence of United Nations policy," but not that it came at the behest of public support for the human rights of murderers. Ukraine abolished capital punishment by legislative fiat with support from the Supreme Court of Ukraine, but did so in the face of public opposition (2009, 12). A similar antidemocratic process unfolded in Lithuania, which adopted abolition in the hopes of enjoying EU or EC membership when public support for abolition hovered around 20 percent (23).

It is not clear how successful the international abolitionist movement will be. Neither diplomatic pressure nor economic incentives is likely to bring many

Islamic countries into the abolitionist club. Saudi Arabia, Iran, Iraq, Yemen, and Pakistan will likely continue to use the executioner. The situation in East Asia is less clear. Johnson and Zimring (2009) hold hope for countries such as Japan, China, Vietnam, and North Korea to become abolitionist in part because retaining capital punishment prevents them from being seen as "decent" by other major powers. While this may be true of Japan, it is not clear that China, for example, will be overly concerned with its reputation in the West (remember Tiananmen Square?). They also suggest that economic interests may lead China to modify its current retentionist policy, but it seems more likely that the world will depend more on China economically than the other way around. Even if there is public support for abolition in China, and evidence indicates this is not true (Oberwittler and Qi 2008), the Chinese government seems able to resist it. While the number of executions in China and elsewhere in Asia may continue to decline it is not easy to see it being abolished at any time soon. The United States is consistently fifth or sixth on the list of the most frequently executing countries. Southern states are unlikely to bow to European Union or other diplomatic pressure to abolish the death penalty out of regard for human rights. While both death sentences and executions here may decline, it is doubtful that they will soon disappear.

II. The Death Penalty in the United States

The United States is a death penalty country. Beginning in 1967, there was a ten-year moratorium while federal courts sorted out various constitutional issues. Executions resumed in January 1977 when Gary Gilmore was put to death by firing squad in Utah. From 1977 to the end of 2010 there were 1,234 executions in the United States, all but three carried out by the states (Death Penalty Information Center 2010). Figure 24.1 shows the number of executions per year since the modern era of capital punishment began in 1976.

Not all states have the death penalty. Table 24.1 shows which states do and do not, and the number of executions from 1976 to 2010 in that state. Executions are not evenly distributed. Figure 24.2 illustrates that about 82 percent of all executions since 1976 have taken place in southern states. Almost half (46 percent) occur in Texas and Virginia. Figure 24.3 shows the annual per capita number of death sentences imposed in the United States since 1977. The number of death sentences peaked in the mid-1990s and has been declining since then. At the end of 2010, there were about 3,300 persons on death rows, 98 percent of whom are male. The racial breakdown is shown in figure 24.4. About 44 percent are white and 42 percent are black.

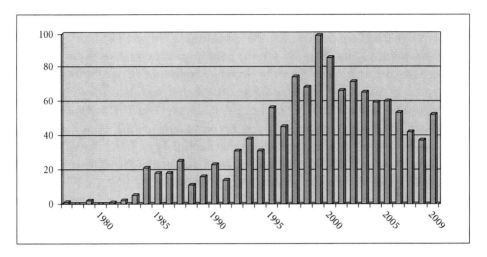

Figure 24.1. Number of Annual Executions in the U.S. from 1975–2009
Source: Death Penalty Information Center.

Table 24.1. Death Penalty and Non-Death Penalty States in the U.S., and the Number Executed between 1976–2009

Death Penalty States (35)

Alabama (44)	Florida (68)	Louisiana (28)	New Hampshire (0)	South Dakota (1)
Arizona (23)	Georgia (46)	Maryland (5)	North Carolina (43)	Tennessee (6)
Arkansas (27)	Idaho (1)	Mississippi (10)	Ohio (34)	Texas (449)
California (13)	Illinois (12)	Missouri (67)	Oklahoma (93)	Utah (6)
Colorado (1)	Indiana (20)	Montana (3)	Oregon (2)	Virginia (105)
Connecticut (1)	Kansas	Nebraska (3)	Pennsylvania (3)	Washington (4)
Delaware (14)	Kentucky (3)	Nevada (12)	South Carolina (42)	Wyoming (1)

Non-Death Penalty States (15)

Alaska	Massachusetts	New Mexico*	Vermont
Hawaii	Michigan	New York	West Virginia
Iowa	Minnesota	North Dakota	Wisconsin
Maine	New Jersey	Rhode Island	District of Columbia

* New Mexico abolished the death penalty in 2009, but had executed 1 person prior to that and there are two persons who remain on New Mexico's death row as of this date.

Most executions are by lethal injection. Of the 1,234 executions since 1977, 86 percent were performed with lethal injection. There are, however, authorized alternatives. Depending on when and where the death sentence was imposed and the condemned's preference, as of 2010 it was still possible for the death penalty to be carried out by electrocution, hanging, firing squad, or lethal gas.

A majority of states retain the death penalty, but there is great variation in how often they use it. Some states have capital punishment "on the books" but rarely

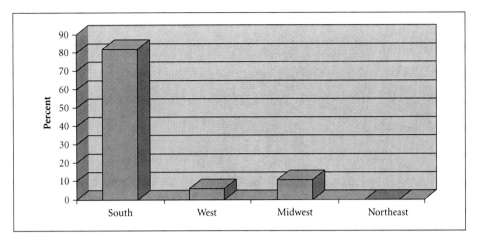

Figure 24.2. Executions in the U.S. by Region: 1976–2009
Source: Death Penalty Information Center.

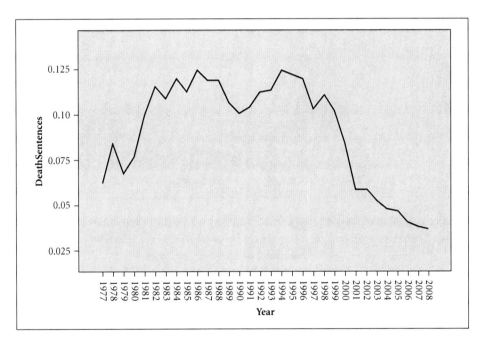

Figure 24.3. Death Sentences in the U.S. per 100,000 People: 1977–2008
Source: Death Penalty Information Center.

execute anyone. Figure 24.5 shows the diverse execution rates in states that had capital punishment on their statutes at the end of 2008. Perhaps we should not be too surprised. After all, states vary considerably across a number of other important dimensions including the form and structure of their death penalty law, the crime rate, the educational level of the population, how politically or religiously

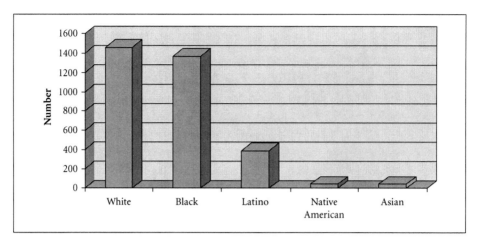

Figure 24.4. Racial Composition of Death Rows – 2009
Source: Death Row U.S.A., Summer 2009.

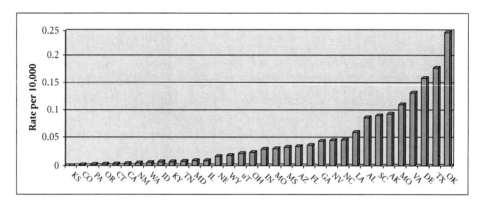

Figure 24.5. Rate of Executions (per 10,000 pop.) for Death Penalty States – 1977–2008
Source: Death Penalty Information Center. Rates represent the number of executions in the state from
1977–2008 divided by 2008 state population.

conservative the citizens are, the financial ability of the state to pay for capital trials, the extent of urbanization, and a number of other factors.

What may be considerably more surprising, however, is that there is at least as much if not more variation in the inclination to impose the death penalty *within* death penalty states as there is *between* death penalty states. In other words, a death penalty state may not be a death penalty *state*. For example, Texas is the most active death penalty state by far. There have been approximately four hundred executions in Texas since 1977, about 37 percent of the total number of executions for all states and three times more than in the next highest state (Virginia). Few would doubt that Texas is a "real" death penalty state. However, there is substantial variation among counties in Texas.

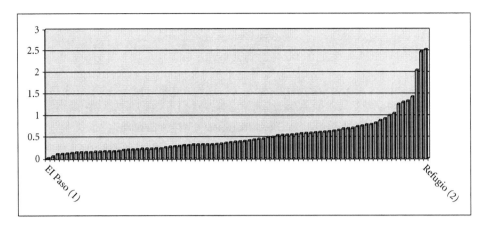

Figure 24.6. Execution Rate (per 10,000 pop.) for Texas Counties – 1977–2007
Source: Texas Department of Criminal Justice and Texas Department of State Health Services.
Rates represent the number of executions in the state from each county 1977–2007 divided by 2007
county population.

Of the 254 Texas counties, two-thirds have not had an execution since 1976.[1] Among the minority of counties in Texas that have had executions, the rate at which executions occur varies dramatically. There is more variability in the risk of execution within Texas than there is across all death penalty states in the United States, even though the law is the same throughout Texas.[2] Texas, of course, is not the only death penalty state to show this kind of variation.

Capital punishment is a regional punishment. Again, the vast majority of executions are performed in southern states. Even within the South there is much variation across jurisdictions and within death penalty states. The death penalty in the United States, though subject to state law, is very much a local phenomenon.

III. CAPITAL PUNISHMENT AND RACE IN AMERICA

The relationship between the death penalty and race dates at least to the Slave Codes that regulated and controlled virtually all aspects of African American life. The Louisiana Slave Code of 1806 is instructive: "The master may sell him, dispose of his person, his industry and his labor: he can do nothing, possess nothing, nor acquire anything but what must belong to his master" (Stampp 1956, 197). The codes described the rules of etiquette that must exist between black and white, sometimes providing that a slave could not talk back to nor scowl, roll their eyes at, or smirk at a white person. When blacks approached whites on the street they had to move out of the way and cast their eyes downward; black men had to take off their hats. Slaves had to have special passes to be off the plantation, could not assemble in groups, and could not own weapons or farm tools. They could not marry or form legal contracts. The criminal laws of the southern states often had different crimes and different punishments for blacks—slave or free. Blacks could be put to death for robbery, rebellion, talking about a rebellion, or assaulting a white person.

Slave codes did not disappear with the end of the Civil War and the Emancipation Proclamation but continued in only slightly altered form as Black Codes (Foner and Mahoney 1983). The black codes severely restricted the labor of newly freed blacks. Those who were unemployed or refused to sign labor contracts with white overseers could be convicted as vagrants. A long list of potentially capital crimes for blacks did not exist for whites. The formality and brutality of the law for blacks was complemented by the brutality of mob actions and lynchings (Tolnay and Beck 1995). The further separation of the races and forceful control of blacks continued with Jim Crow laws adopted by southern states in the late 1800s and continued well into the middle of the twentieth century.

Given this history, it is not surprising that use of capital punishment has been related to race. In the years 1930–67, about one-half of all those executed were African American, and 90 percent of those were executed for rape (Paternoster, Brame, and Bacon 2008). Black defendants fared worse at every point in the criminal justice system, particularly when they crossed racial boundaries and killed a white victim. Garfinkel (1949), for example, found that black offenders who killed white victims were substantially more likely to be indicted for first-degree murder than were others. Johnson (1941) found that black offenders in Virginia and North Carolina who killed whites were more likely to be indicted for first-degree murder, convicted of first-degree murder, and sentenced to death. Black offenders were also less likely than whites to have their death sentences commuted.

Marvin Wolfgang and Marc Riedel (1973) collected information on 300 rape convictions from 230 counties in eleven southern states. They found that black offenders in serious rape cases with white victims were more than twenty times more likely to be sentenced to death than all others. A study of Georgia in 1945–65 found that the combination of a black offender and white victim was the most important predictor of a death sentence among 361 convicted rapists (Wolfgang and Riedel 1975).

One aim of US Supreme Court decisions, beginning with *Gregg v. Georgia* (428 US 153 [1976]), was that procedural reforms of state death penalty statutes would reduce racial disparity. The problem, however, persists. Numerous studies of racial disparity and capital punishment have been conducted in states since 1976: California, Colorado, Florida, Georgia, Kentucky, Maryland, Mississippi, Nebraska, New Jersey, North Carolina, Pennsylvania, and South Carolina. Most studies show that offenders who killed white victims (and in some cases *particularly* if the offender was black) were more likely to be charged with a capital crime, sentenced to death, and executed. A review by the US General Accounting Office of twenty-eight capital punishment studies showed that killing a white victim influenced who was sentenced to death (U.S. GAO 1990). The most comprehensive study was by David Baldus and his colleagues of the Georgia capital sentencing system (Baldus et al. 1990). They examined over 2,000 homicide indictments in Georgia and collected detailed information about the homicide, the offender, and the victim. After holding important case characteristics constant, they estimated that a killer of a white victim was four times more likely to be sentenced to death than a killer of a nonwhite victim. The evidence of racial disparity was even greater in the cases that were at the mid-range of aggravating circumstances.

The Baldus study was used as the basis for an appeal, *McCleskey v. Kemp* (481 U.S. 279 [1987]), to the US Supreme Court. A majority of the Court rejected McCleskey's claim of racial discrimination. The most important finding was that general statistical evidence such as that presented by the Baldus study could not be the basis for a claim (like McCleskey's) that *he* was discriminated against in his own case. The Court held that defendants must prove that the specific decision-makers in their case acted with discriminatory intent or purpose. The Baldus data, the Court argued, simply showed a disparate outcome; to be successful in their claims offenders must prove a discriminatory intent. The Court observed that the racial disparity found in Georgia by the Baldus study was not sufficiently large enough to warrant a finding of racial discrimination, that "at most, the Baldus study indicates a discrepancy that appears to correlate with race" (Baldus et al. 1990, 1777). The Court suggested that evidence such as that amassed by the Baldus study be presented to state legislatures rather than to federal courts.

In a blistering dissent, Justice Brennan argued that the evidence presented proved that race *matters* for capital sentencing in Georgia, that it is shaped by our nation's history of racial conflict, and that justice requires that it not be denied:

> It is tempting to pretend that minorities on death row share a fate in no way connected to our own, that our treatment of them sounds no echoes beyond the chambers in which they die. Such an illusion is ultimately corrosive, for the reverberations of injustice are not so easily confined. The destinies of the two races in this country are indissolubly linked together . . . and the way in which we choose those who will die reveals the depth of moral commitment among the living. (*McClesky v. Kemp*, 481 U.S. 279, 344 [1987])

General statistical evidence on racial disparities in the administration of capital punishment was presented to federal and state legislatures. At the federal level, an unsuccessful attempt was made to enact the Racial Justice Act. One of the proposed provisions would allow capital defendants in state cases to present Baldus-type general statistical studies about the patterning of race in capital cases to federal courts as evidence of racial discrimination. They would not have to meet the *McCleskey* burden of showing an intent to discriminate in the individual's case. Although introduced in both houses of Congress in 1988, and supported by the American Bar Association and numerous civil rights and civil liberties groups, the proposed law was not enacted. Some states, however, have passed their own versions. Most recently, in August 2009 North Carolina passed a Racial Justice Act, which allows death-row inmates to challenge racial bias in the state's death penalty system by use of general statistical studies. Prosecutors would then have the opportunity to rebut the claim that the statistical disparities indicate racial bias. If proven, a judge could overturn the death sentence or prevent prosecutors from seeking the death penalty.

IV. Constitional History of the Death Penalty

The US Supreme Court declared capital punishment unconstitutional as practiced in 1972 but authorized it under certain specified conditions in 1976. Since 1976 the Court has regulated how state death penalties are imposed. It addressed procedures state capital trials must observe, such as bifurcated hearings, allowing virtually unlimited evidence in mitigation, standards for jury selection, effective legal representation, appeals, and appellate representation for indigent offenders. It also specified the kinds of crimes and the kinds of criminals who may be eligible for death. For example, the Court ruled that the death penalty was not warranted in the case of rape or kidnapping if no life was taken, and that accomplices could face a death sentence if they played a major role in the crime and demonstrated a "reckless disregard for human life." The Court ruled on whether juveniles and the mentally retarded may be executed and whether the mentally ill may be put to death.

It is impossible adequately to discuss all Supreme Court decisions about the death penalty (see Paternoster et al. 2008). The best starting point is *Furman v. Georgia* (408 U.S.238 [1972]). It was decided by a five-to-four vote, and each justice wrote his own opinion. A majority voted to strike down the death penalty statutes that then existed, but for different reasons.

State death penalty statutes then were "unitary." Both guilt and penalty were decided at the end of one trial. Jurors were given virtually unlimited discretion in deciding which capital defendants should live and which should die. Two of the justices in the majority (Justices Brennan and Marshall) would have completely abolished the death penalty in any form. The other three justices opposing the death penalty objected to how existing statutes operated. Justice Stewart argued that existing procedures risked that death sentences be imposed on the basis of caprice, rather than reason, and analogized the imposition of the death penalty to being struck by lightning—it doesn't strike the deserving, just the unlucky. Justice White argued that existing statutes gave jurors so much discretion that too few death sentences were handed down to establish a deterrent effect; the death penalty served no legitimate state purpose and was simply the "needless extinction of human life." Justice Douglas objected on equal protection grounds, arguing that jurors had so much unguided discretion that it was likely that they employed suspect factors, such as race and social class, in making their decisions. The four justices in the minority argued that the existing laws were constitutionally acceptable.

The *Furman* decision had one practical effect. It emptied death rows across the United States as all death sentences were converted to life sentences. It did not, however, spell the end of capital punishment.

State legislators crafted new statutes. They took two general forms. Some states sought to create mandatory statutes. Although they differed in detail, these statutes mandated a death sentence upon the conviction of a designated type of murder (say, murder during the commission of a kidnapping, armed robbery, or rape). This solution was simple but crude—it completely eliminates jury discretion.

The second solution was to provide a list of factors to be considered. Guided discretion death statutes identified factors that argued for (e.g., the killing of a police officer) and against a death sentence (e.g., the offender has no prior history of violent offenses). Jurors had to find at least one aggravating factor in order to impose death but had to balance all aggravating factors against the mitigating factors. Most new laws provided for bifurcated capital hearings (separate hearings on guilt and penalty) and an automatic appeal of all death sentences.

In 1976 the Supreme Court considered five cases involving various approaches. It ruled in *Gregg v. Georgia* (428 U.S. 153 [1976]), *Proffitt v. Florida* (428 U.S. 242 [1976]), and *Jurek v. Texas* (428 U.S. 262 [1976]) that guided discretion statutes were constitutionally permissible, but in *Woodson v. North Carolina* (428 U.S. 280 [1976]) and *Roberts v. Louisiana* (428 U.S. 325 [1976]) that mandatory death statutes were not. The Court objected to mandatory death statutes for several reasons. One was that they moved the problem of jury discretion to an earlier point (jurors not wanting to impose death could convict the person of a non-capital crime). A second was that they did not allow jurors to hear all possible reasons why a given person should or should not be sentenced to death.

A. Procedural Reforms

In *Gregg, Proffitt,* and *Jurek,* the Court did not lay down specific procedures that states must follow. It did, however, suggest two principles that such procedures should honor—death sentences should be consistent (like cases should be treated alike) and should be individualized (the sentence should reflect the defendant's unique culpability). In addition, it suggested possible ways to conduct a proper capital trial. These included a bifurcated hearing, a set of statutory aggravating circumstances, any one of which would make an offense death-eligible (for example, the murder was committed during an armed robbery), a way to hear mitigating factors, a weighing of aggravating against mitigating circumstances, and appellate review. The Court did not require these things, but if a state statute had them, it would likely pass constitutional scrutiny.

The Court later considered the information a capital sentencing jury could hear. In *Lockett v. Ohio* (438 U.S. 586 [1978]), the Court ruled that a state must allow the defendant to introduce as a mitigating factor any aspect of his character or record and any circumstances about the offense that might support a sentence less than death. In *Skipper v. South Carolina* (106 S. Ct. 1669 [1986]), the Court determined that behavior in jail before and during trial is relevant mitigating evidence. In *Booth v. Maryland* (107 S. Ct. 2529 [1987]), it ruled that victim impact evidence could not be used during the penalty phase because it encouraged the sentencer to base its decision on emotion and sympathy rather than a rational consideration of the character of the defendant and the characteristics of the offense. It reaffirmed this position two years later in *South Carolina v. Gathers* (109 S. Ct. 2207 [1989]). In *Strickland v. Washington* (466 U.S. 668 [1984]), the Court defined the requirements for effective assistance of counsel in state capital trials.

Beginning in the mid-1980s, however, the Court backed away from some of the procedures it suggested in previous cases were essential. In *Zant v. Stephens* (103 S. Ct. 2733 [1983]) and *Barclay v. Florida* (103 S. Ct. 3418 [1983]), the Court ruled that the only function served by a statutory aggravating circumstance is to narrow the range of cases in which a sentence of death could be imposed. Once the sentencer found an aggravating circumstance, it had virtually unlimited discretion. In *Barefoot v. Estelle* (103 S. Ct 3383 [1983]), it accepted that predictions by a psychiatrist on behalf of the state that a defendant will commit violent crimes in the future would more often be wrong than right, but decided the solution was to let the defense introduce its own expert evidence. In *Pulley v. Harris* (465 U.S. 37 [1984]), it ruled that proportionality review of death sentences by state appellate courts was not constitutionally required. In *Payne v. Tennessee* (501 U.S. 808 [1991]), the Court "corrected the imbalance" in favor of the defendant's use of mitigating evidence that it thought *Lockett* gave by overturning its own *Booth* decision and permitting victim impact evidence at the penalty hearing. The Court recently (in *Kelly v. California*, 129 S. Ct. 564 [2008]) declined the opportunity to place restrictions upon the kind of evidence that may be used (written and oral statements are permitted as are cards, letters, photographs, and elaborate videos that portray the life of the one who was murdered), and it has placed no clear limits on what "harm" may be argued as being due to the offense (family breakups that occurred months or more after the crime is permitted), or who may speak for the victim (family, friends, neighbors). Even an undefined "law enforcement community" may be taken as being harmed by the offense.

B. Substantive Reforms

The post-*Gregg* Supreme Court provided limitations on the nature of death-eligible crimes. *Gregg* laid out a framework by holding that only capital crimes characterized by at least one statutory aggravating circumstance would be death eligible. In *Coker v. Georgia* (433 U.S. 584 [1977]), the Court held that the death penalty was disproportionate and therefore unconstitutional for the rape of an adult woman. In *Eberheart v. Georgia* (433 U.S. 917 [1977]), it forbade capital punishment for kidnapping when there was no loss of life.

The Court authorized death for some accomplices. In *Enmund v. Florida* (458 U.S. 782 [1982]), a defendant was sentenced to death under Florida law for an armed robbery-murder in which the defendant was sitting in a get-away car when his co-defendant robbed and killed the two victims. The Court overturned Enmund's death sentence as disproportionate, stating that the Eighth Amendment's prohibition against cruel and unusual punishment prohibits the death penalty being imposed on defendants who did not take a life, attempt to take a life, or intend to take a life, and whose participation in the crime was relatively minor.

What about the cases in which a defendant did not take, attempt to take, or intend to take a life, but whose involvement in the crime was more extensive? In *Tison v. Arizona* (107 S. Ct. 1676 [1987]), three sons smuggled guns into the Arizona State Prison to assist their father in escaping. During the escape the father killed four people under circumstances in which the sons had no basis for expecting him to do that. The father died while escaping. Two sons were captured, convicted, and sentenced to death. A majority of the Court took the position that the sons' supplying weapons and helping their father escape demonstrated a "reckless disregard for human life" and, accordingly, that they could be executed.

The latest important case on this subject is *Kennedy v. Louisiana* (129 S. Ct. 1 [2008]). *Coker* had decided that the rape of an *adult woman* was not a death-eligible offense. Some states revised their definitions of capital crime to include the nonfatal rape of a minor. Louisiana in 1995 provided for the death penalty for the rape of child under the age of twelve. Patrick O. Kennedy was convicted and sentenced to death for the brutal rape of his eight-year-old stepdaughter. In a five-to-four decision, the US Supreme Court held that the Eighth Amendment's "cruel and unusual" punishment clause prevents the imposition of the death penalty even in the rape of a child if it did not result or was not intended to result in the death of the victim.

C. Treatment of Special Groups

The US Supreme Court has identified groups of people who *may not* be sentenced to death. The principal cases concerned offenders whose crimes occurred before their eighteenth birthday and the mentally ill and mentally retarded.

When *Gregg* was decided, no state outright prohibited the execution of a defendant who was mentally retarded when he committed his offense. Mental retardation was treated as one of a number of possible mitigating circumstances the jury could consider. From 1977 until 1989, there were thirty-four executions in which there was evidence that the defendant was of deeply subnormal intelligence at the time of the offense. During this some eighteen states prohibited the execution of the mentally retarded. The first major Supreme Court decision was *Penry v. Lynaugh* (109 S. Ct. 2934 [1989]). Johnny Paul Penry was convicted and sentenced to death by a Texas trial court for rape and murder. At the time of his trial, Penry's mental competence was examined by a psychologist who testified that Penry had an IQ in the mid-fifties, the mental capacity of a six- and a half-year-old child, and the social maturity of a nine- or ten-year-old. The Court ruled that the Eighth Amendment did not prohibit the execution of the mentally retarded. Mental retardation and diminished mental capacity in general were to be treated as mitigating factors.

The Court re-examined the issue in *Atkins v. Virginia* (536 U.S. 304 [2002]). Daryl Atkins was convicted by a Virginia jury of murder, abduction, and armed robbery and sentenced to death despite testimony that Atkins was mildly retarded and had an IQ of fifty-nine. The Court reviewed the case and, overturning *Penry*, held that the mentally retarded as a class could not be subject to the death penalty.

What had happened in the years since *Penry*? The most significant difference was that a number of states had prohibited the execution of the mentally retarded and no state changed from not allowing the penalty to permitting it. This one-way change of legislative heart was significant to the Court because it signaled that the moral sentiments of society had evolved, and it was no longer found acceptable to execute the mentally retarded.

The second suspect category considered was that of juveniles. From 1977 through March 2005, seven states executed twenty-two juveniles, all but one of whom was seventeen years old at the time of the crime (the other was sixteen). In previous decisions, the Supreme Court drew a "line in the sand" by providing the states with a minimum age below which one could not be executed.

In *Thompson v. Oklahom*a (787 U.S. 815 [1988]) the Supreme Court held that the execution of a person who was fifteen years old at the time their crime was committed was unconstitutional under the Eighth Amendment. In *Stanford v. Kentucky* and *Wilkins v. Missouri* (494 U.S. 361 [1989]), however, the Court upheld the execution of people who were sixteen and seventeen years old.

The Court ended the practice of executing juveniles in March 2005 in *Roper vs. Simmons* (125 S. Ct. 1183 [2005]). It examined state practices with respect to the death penalty for juveniles, and concluded that the trend in state (and international) law was to treat juveniles as persons needing the same kind of special protection as the mentally retarded.

The issue of the execution of the mentally ill first came before the US Supreme Court in *Ford v. Wainwright* (477 U.S. 399 [1986]). Ford was mentally competent when he committed his crime, convicted, and sentenced to death in Florida in 1974. After more than ten years on death row, however, Ford's mental state had substantially deteriorated to the point where he not only thought he was Pope John Paul III but believed that the death penalty could not given to him because he controlled the governor of Florida through mental telepathy. The Supreme Court ruled that executing a person who at the time of his execution was mentally ill is cruel and unusual punishment. In a concurring opinion, Justice Stewart raised the question whether a state could medicate an insane person to the point that he became competent enough to be put to death. At the time of this writing, the question remained open.

V. Common Justifications

Many arguments are made in defense of the death penalty: a financial argument, a deterrence argument, an incapacitation argument, a religious argument, a moral argument, and a democratic argument. With the exception of the moral and religious arguments, these arguments can be subjected to empirical test. The empirical evidence is not always clear, but it does seem safe to conclude that there is no consistent and substantial evidence that the death penalty is cheaper, a better general deterrent, significantly better at incapacitating, nor is it justified by religious principles compared with life imprisonment without possibility of parole (LWOP).

A. Money

The financial argument is that executing convicted capital offenders is less of a drain on taxpayer dollars than the LWOP sentence. It is fairly expensive to keep an inmate in a secure penitentiary for life—we can estimate yearly costs at about $25,000, due to the high security that a "lifer" convicted of murder might need. With a life sentence, the total cost might be between $1 million to $1.5 million per life inmate. The appropriate comparison, however, is not between the cost of an execution and the cost of life imprisonment but the cost of maintaining a system of capital punishment vs. maintaining one that includes only a life sentence. Capital trials are substantially more expensive than non-capital trials at every stage. There are more pretrial motions, greater investigative costs, longer and more expensive jury selection, are more motions during trial, guilt, penalty, and appeal phases. Various state supreme courts and the US Supreme Court have simplified the appellate process, but this must be weighed against the finding that major trial errors occur in about two-thirds of all capital cases, necessitating a new guilt phase, penalty phase, or both (Liebman et al. 2000; 2002). Another reason for the high cost of the death penalty is the long length of stay on death row. Figure 24.7 shows the number of months between capital sentencing and execution from 1977 to 2007. The average length of time on death row has tripled from about 50 months to about 150 months.

Various researchers have estimated the costs of capital punishment. In North Carolina, Cook and Slawson (1993) estimated that a capital case costs about $250,000 more than a comparable non-capital case. Overall, they estimated that from pretrial to execution the cost of a capital case is about $2 million. A Kansas legislative committee estimated that the cost of a death penalty case was about $1.26 million while a comparable life case was $740,000. This was mainly because trial costs in death penalty cases were estimated to be sixteen times greater than in life cases, and appellate costs were twenty-one times greater (Legislative Post Audit Committee 2003). A study by the Urban Institute of the cost of the death penalty in Maryland found that a death-eligible case in which death was sought cost about $1.8 million compared with $1.1 million for a death-eligible case for which the state sought a life sentence (Roman et al. 2008). Baicker (2004) estimated that in the period 1983–99, it cost approximately $2 million per death penalty case and that to pay for death penalty prosecutions county governments have had to raise taxes or cut back on spending in other areas. High prosecution costs are frequently cited by local prosecutors as a reason they decide not to prosecute as a capital offense a crime that by statute is death eligible. Studies of other states and the federal death penalty system have found what both supporters and critics of the death penalty acknowledge—that it is a very, very

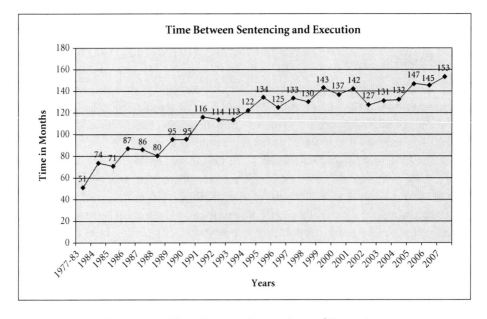

Figure 24.7. Time Between Sentencing and Execution
Source: Death Penalty Information Center.

expensive system to maintain and more costly than if LWOPs were the most severe penalty that could be imposed (Death Penalty Information Center 2009).

B. General Deterrence

Thorsten Sellin (1959) reasoned that if the death penalty deters murder, then a state that supports it should have lower homicide rates on average than a comparable state that does not. He compared the homicide rates of death penalty and non–death penalty states that were geographically contiguous and would, he reasoned, be comparable to each other in respects that would affect their homicide rate (such as urbanization, the age distribution of the population, and average education of the population). Some of his findings are summarized in figure 24.8. In comparing three states of the Upper Midwest, for example, Sellin found that that the two death penalty states (Indiana and Ohio) did not have lower homicide rates than the one state without the death penalty (Michigan). Iowa, another state that had the death penalty, did not have a lower homicide rate than two states next to it, Minnesota and Wisconsin, which did not have the penalty. Maine, a non–death penalty state, had a homicide rate not much different from New Hampshire and Vermont, two death penalty states. Rhode Island's homicide rate was not much different from that of Massachusetts and Connecticut, two states with which it shared a border but which (unlike Rhode Island) were death penalty states. Sellin made other kinds of comparisons as well. For example, for states that shifted from being a death penalty state to being a non–death penalty state he compared the homicide rates before and after the abolition. He made similar comparisons for states that shifted from being abolitionist to being death penalty states, with the expectation that homicide rates would drop. In these over-time comparisons, Sellin found no strong or consistent evidence to suggest that the presence or absence of the death penalty made any difference.

Sellin's was the prevailing view until Isaac Ehrlich (1975), using sophisticated econometric models, concluded that each execution from 1933 to 1969 prevented seven or eight murders. Ehrlich's findings caused a stir, and other scholars immediately tried to replicate and verify his results. Critics concluded that his findings were fragile and disappeared when some years were removed from his data, or if a slightly different model was estimated (Blumstein, Cohen, and Nagin 1978).

By the 1980s interest in the deterrent effect of capital punishment waned. It revived in the late 1990s mainly among economists who used new statistical tools and new data sets to examine the effect of executions since 1977. These studies produced fascinating but inconsistent results. Mocan and Gittings (2003) reported that each execution from 1977 to 1997 prevented five murders, as did Shepherd (2004). Dezhbakhsh, Rubin, and Shepherd (2003) reported that each execution prevented eighteen murders. Other studies found no evidence of deterrence, and two of the most comprehensive analyses argued strongly that there was no evidence for a deterrent effect for the death penalty (Berk 2005; Donohue and Wolfers 2006). Donohue

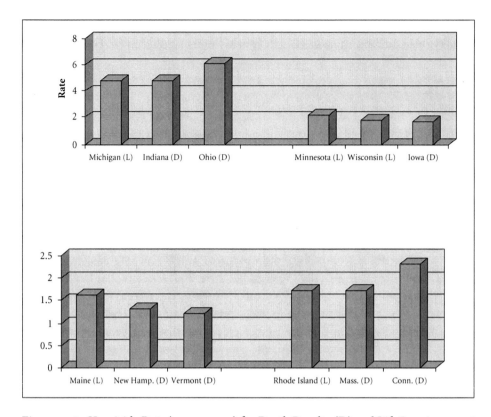

Figure 24.8. Homicide Rate (per 100,000) for Death Penalty (D) and Life Imprisonment (L) States

and Wolfers' study is very comprehensive with details about what statistical assumptions were made by researchers, how variables were measured, and the effects of these decisions on the results. They concluded (2006, 843) that the best conclusion is that the deterrence question cannot be answered: "The estimated effects of capital punishment on homicide rates change dramatically even with small changes in econometric specifications. Aggregating over all our estimates, it is entirely unclear even whether the preponderance of the evidence suggests that the death penalty causes more or less murder." To this day, the deterrent effect of the death penalty remains a controversial and contested question.

C. Incapacitation

A related argument is that capital punishment is necessary to protect the public because it is the only way to prevent those who have already murdered from murdering again. To save future innocent murder victims, the argument goes, we should execute killers so they will not kill again. The risk that a murderer might be released on parole or escape from prison and kill someone in the community or kill an inmate or correctional officer behind bars is not great, but it is greater than zero.

Kenneth McDuff of Texas was under three death sentences for the murders of three teenagers until his death sentences were commuted to life sentences by the *Furman* decision. Because of overcrowding in Texas prisons, McDuff served a little more than twenty years and was released under parole supervision. He murdered two more women, was convicted, and given two more death sentences. This time the sentences were carried out, and McDuff was executed. His last two victims would be alive if *Furman* had not spared McDuff's life.

Kenneth McDuff is an extremely rare case, but opponents of capital punishment must acknowledge that it will effectively prevent a murderer from committing another crime. However, had McDuff been sentenced to an LWOP sentence, which Texas did not have at that time, he would not have been released and would not have murdered again. In order to protect the public effectively then, we may not have to resort to capital punishment. The argument may quickly be raised that an inmate with an LWOP may nevertheless murder again by killing a fellow inmate or correctional officer. Marquart and Sorensen (1988) studied the future criminal behavior of 239 inmates from around the country whose death sentences were commuted to life under the *Furman* decision and found that only six had gone on to commit another murder in prison.

D. Religion

It is often observed that some religions provide justification for the death penalty. For example, some Christians point to biblical scripture such as the book of Genesis where God announces to Noah that "whoever sheds the blood of man, by man shall his blood be shed." A Muslim could point to text in the Quran where it is stated that adulterers and apostates should be put to death. A Jew could appeal to Mosaic Law and the writings in the Pentateuch or the Torah where some thirty offenses are punishable by death.

The problem with relying on a religious justification for the death penalty is that most religious texts can also be used to support opposition to the death penalty. For example, Christians can cite the teaching of Jesus in the Sermon on the Mount (Matthew 5:38–39) "You have heard that it was said, 'an eye for an eye and a tooth for a tooth.' But I say to you, do not resist the one who is evil. But if any one strikes you on the right cheek, turn to him the other also." While the death penalty is consistent with Islamic law, the Quran (17:33) also speaks to the need to forgive those who have wronged us rather than to strike back with equal might. And while Mosaic Law permitted the death penalty, its use was so carefully qualified (there had to be two eyewitnesses to the crime, for example) that it was rarely used.

Today, many religions, with the exception of evangelical Protestant denominations, condemn use of the death penalty. The Roman Catholic Church opposes capital punishment as part of a culture of death (as it does abortion). It was explicitly condemned by Pope John Paul II in 1995 in his *Evangelium Vitae*. The Episcopal Church, the Presbyterian Church (USA), and the American Baptist Church all oppose the death penalty as do Conservative and Reform Judaism. A few church organizations do still support capital punishment including the Southern Baptist Convention, Missouri Synod of the Lutheran Church, the Orthodox Presbyterian Church, and Orthodox Judaism. That Islam supports the death penalty is vividly seen by the number of executions in places like Iran, Pakistan, and Saudi Arabia. Both sides of the capital punishment debate can find support for their position in some religious teaching (Association of Religious Data Archives 2009).

E. Morality

One of the most common justifications for the death penalty is morality. It is derived from a concept of retribution that argues that murderers should be executed because they deserve it. Here "just desert" is understood to imply that capital punishment is the only morally fitting punishment to visit upon one who has taken the life of another. Modern retributive positions in support of the death penalty have been endorsed by Walter Berns (1979) and Ernst van den Haag (1975, 1978). The retributive justification is simple—murderers have taken an innocent life; they should be punished in exact proportion to the harm and the only way to do that is by taking the murderer's life. Capital punishment is morally correct in this view and needs no further, instrumental justification.

Those who would oppose capital punishment might acknowledge that a murderer deserves severe punishment but may disagree as to what that punishment should be. Some retributive writers reject the Berns and van den Haag equality-based retribution and argue instead for a proportionality-based retribution. Under this view, the amount of punishment must be severe and severe enough that it does not trivialize the harm produced by the crime, and it must be consistent with other moral principles of the society (Reiman 1986; Bedau 2004). A modern retributive position, therefore, is that life imprisonment without the possibility of parole is a more appropriate punishment for the most severe crimes than is capital punishment.

F. Democratic Values

The democratic argument is that the public demands the death penalty. Those who support capital punishment can point to a body of evidence that the public is on their side. Figure 24.9 shows the results of a series of Gallup public opinion

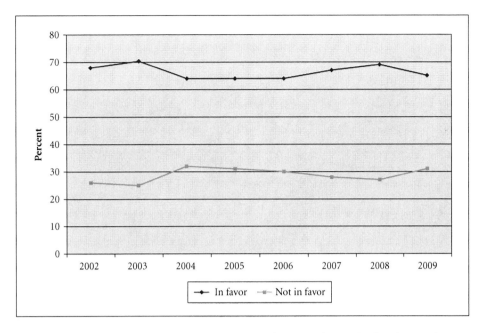

Figure 24.9. Percent of Americans in Favor of the Death Penalty for Those Who
Commit Murder
Source: Gallup 2009.

polls since 2002. People were asked, "Are you in favor of the death penalty for a
person convicted of murder?" A majority of Americans have consistently
favored the use of capital punishment for those who commit murder, and this
percentage has not changed much. Sixty-eight percent of the public supported
death for murderers in 2002 and 65 percent agreed in 2009. This is strong evidence of support since 59 percent of those polled in 2009 also believed that an
innocent person has been executed within the past five years. It would be difficult to argue that Americans want to abolish the death penalty based upon these
poll findings.

Critics of the death penalty argue, however, that public opinion surveys that
ask respondents if they favor the death penalty exaggerate support for capital punishment. They assert that the right question is whether respondents would favor
death over some other alternative punishment such as life in prison. When the
Gallup polling organization asks people if they would prefer death or life without
parole for those convicted of murder, roughly the same percent support LWOP as
do death (See figure 24.10). In 2006, 48 percent of those polled favored LWOP
while only 46 percent favored the death penalty for those convicted of murder.
Over the past twenty years, support for LWOP as the preferred penalty for murder
has increased.

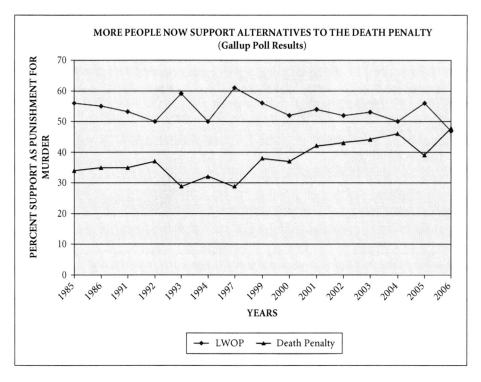

Figure 24.10. Preference for Life Without Parole vs. the Death Penalty
Source: Death Penalty Information Center.

VI. Problems in Administering the Death Penalty

If we were to design a system of capital punishment without knowing whether we personally would ever be caught up in it, we would likely want to build one that was fair and produced fair outcomes. By *fair procedures* we would want things like impartial law enforcement officers investigating the case, and prosecutors who willingly share any exculpatory evidence they uncover. We would want the evidence presented to be objective and free of bias or distortion, we would want competent defense attorneys defending cases, and we would want avenues to appeal any errors. By *fair outcomes*, we would like to have a death penalty system that culls only the "worst of the worst" offenders, and that the death be reserved only for those who commit the most heinous and egregious offenses. While this is what we may want in our death penalty system, we have to balance that against the knowledge that any piece of machinery built and operated by human beings is going to have some problems in working properly. The complicated machinery of the death penalty is no exception.

A. Executing the Innocent

While there has been no unambiguously documented case of an innocent person being executed, there are cases where the issue remains in doubt. Cameron Todd Willingham was executed in Texas in 2004. Willingham was convicted of setting fire to his house resulting in the death of his three children. Local and state fire investigators testified that "scientific evidence" (burn and pour patterns on the house floors and a spider "shatter pattern" on some glass that investigators claim showed that a fire accelerant had been used to set the fire) showed that the blaze had been deliberately started. To the moment of his execution Willingham, who refused an offer to plead guilty in exchange for a life sentence, protested his innocence. The year after Willingham was executed, Texas created the Forensic Science Commission to investigate charges of scientific mistakes or misconduct in Texas criminal cases, and the panel began looking into the Willingham case. It commissioned Craig Beyler, a nationally recognized fire expert, to examine the evidence in the Willingham case. Beyler's unambiguous conclusion was that there was no way that arson could be established by the evidence.

Since 1973, 138 people in twenty-six different states convicted of a capital crime have later been found to be innocent (none of these were executed). From 1973 to 1999, there was an average of 3.1 exonerations per year, but from 2000 to 2007, there has been an average of 5 exonerations per year. With twenty-six different states having at least one exoneration, almost 75 percent of death penalty states have convicted an innocent person. The problem with innocents being convicted appears endemic.

Some argue that the discovery of the innocence of these people before they were executed shows that the system "works." However, we have the troubling fact that many of these eventually exonerated were not found to be innocent because of actions on the part of legal officials. The case of Anthony Porter is a good example. Porter was convicted of two murders in Chicago in 1983 and sentenced to death. He was within two days of being put to death in 1998 when the Illinois Supreme Court granted him a stay. Porter's case was taken up by a Northwestern University journalism professor and his students. After their extensive investigation and the work of a private investigator, the students identified the real killer, who confessed to the crime. Porter had spent nearly fifteen years of his life and came within fifty hours of being executed before he was exonerated.

B. Ineffective Counsel

Capital defendants have had a right to effective assistance of counsel since 1932 in the *Powell v. Alabama* case (involving the "Scottsboro boys"). It has never been precisely clear what "effective counsel" in capital cases means. The US Supreme Court in *Strickland v. Washington* (466 U.S. 668 [1984]) tried to provide some criteria by setting up a two-pronged test: ineffective counsel are deficient under "prevailing professional norms," and perform so poorly at trial that it prejudices the outcome of the case (the outcome would have been different with a different lawyer).

The extensiveness of the problem of incompetent defense counsel was revealed by James Liebman and his colleagues (Liebman et al. 2000, 2002). They followed up 5,760 death sentences imposed from 1973 to 1995 and found two important things. First, errors in 68 percent of cases required that the conviction or the penalty be overturned. Second, one of the two primary reasons for the errors was the incompetence of defense lawyers.

Here are a few examples. A Texas murder suspect, George McFarland, was represented by defense counsel John Benn. The seventy-two-year-old Been had not tried a capital case in Texas for twenty years, spent only four hours preparing for the trial, never examined the crime scene, never interviewed a witness, filed no motions in the case, and visited his client only twice before trial. Further, according to newspaper reporters who attended the trial, Mr. Benn appeared to be asleep for most of the trial. The judge dismissed the significance of Mr. Benn's sleeping arguing that "the Constitution says everyone's entitled to the attorney of their choice . . . [it] doesn't say that the lawyer has to be awake" (*McFarland v. State*, 928 S.W.2d 482 [Tex. Crim. App.], [1996]).

In a Georgia case, the defendant's court-appointed lawyer barely defended his client and presented almost no mitigating evidence during the penalty phase. The only comments the attorney made to the jury were:

> You have got a little ole nigger man over there that doesn't weigh over 135 pounds. He is poor and he is broke. He's got a court appointed lawyer. . . . He's ignorant. I will venture to say that he has an IQ of not over 80. *Isaacs & Dungee v. Kemp*, (778 F.2d 1482 [11th Cir. 1985]), *cert. denied*, (476 U.S. 1164 [1986])

Had the attorney bothered to investigate, he would have discovered that his client was not merely "ignorant" with an IQ "not over 80" but borderline mentally retarded with an IQ of about 68.

An indication of how widespread incompetent counsel is in capital cases was revealed in a study reported in the *National Law Journal* (1990). The authors examined the quality of defense counsel in six southern states and found that lawyers in Texas who had tried a death penalty case were nine times more likely to have been professionally disciplined than non-capital lawyers in the state, and in Georgia and Alabama twenty-six times more likely. In Louisiana they were forty-seven times more likely to have been disbarred, suspended from their law practice, or otherwise professionally disciplined.

C. Misconduct

In *Berger v. United States* (295, U.S. 78 [1936]), the US Supreme Court held that "the prosecutor's interest in a criminal prosecution is not that it shall win a case, but that justice shall be done. . . . While he may strike hard blows, he is not at liberty to strike foul ones." This implies that prosecutors and law enforcement officers are not free to do what they please to make their case, but must pursue justice and must do so without "striking foul blows." Easier said than done, for in the pursuit of justice or "the truth" prosecutors and law enforcement officers make mistakes. They are under great pressure to solve serious, brutal crimes, and sometimes that pressure leads them to ignore or underweight evidence, which they might not normally have accepted or might have questioned more skeptically. They may develop theories about a case based upon an initial suspect, and their eyes may become closed to evidence exculpating their initial suspect or evidence that points in a different direction. As a result, mistakes are made. Liebman and his colleagues discovered that mistakes made by prosecutors and police were one of the two most frequent sources of legal error.

The case of Rolando Cruz is a good example. Chicago police and prosecutors were under great pressure to find the murderer of ten-year-old Jeanine Nicarico, a case that had remained unsolved for years. Cruz and Alejandro Hernandez implicated each other in the crime in order to get a $10,000 reward. The pressure the police and prosecutors were under to solve the case, and perhaps their own belief in his guilt, may have led police to concoct a story that Cruz not only confessed to the killings during interrogations but that he had "visions" and saw things about the crime that only the killer would have known. Perhaps bolstered by the police's confidence that they had the right man, prosecutors saw no reason to investigate other suspects such as Brian Dugan, who had also confessed to the crime. After several mistrials of Cruz, a Chicago police officer asserted that police had lied about Cruz's visions and confession. Even after this, however, Chicago prosecutors continued to believe that Cruz was involved. These examples are not isolated. Liebmann and colleagues found that prosecutorial suppression of possibly exculpatory evidence comprised about 20 percent of all the reversals they studied.

D. Jailhouse "Snitches" and Junk Science

In many capital cases reversed on appeal, the prosecution relied on testimony from jail-house informants or "snitches," or on "junk science." Northwestern University's Center for Wrongful Convictions documented that a snitch had been used by the prosecution to bolster their case in respect to 51 of the 111 persons (46 percent) who had been exonerated of a capital crime up to the end of 2004 (Northwestern University 2005).

Frequently, exonerated persons are found to have been the victims of junk science—scientific findings of doubtful credibility. For example, Ray Krone of Phoenix, Arizona was convicted and sentenced to death for the murder of Kim Ancona, a cocktail waitress. Krone was convicted in part because a state expert testified that bite marks found on Ancona matched teeth impressions from Krone. Testimony from the same expert was used to convict Robby Lee Tankersley of the rape and murder of a Yuma, Arizona, woman. The problem is that bite marks or tooth impressions are not unique identifiers like fingerprints and can change over time. The American Board of Forensic Odontology is so skeptical of their validity that it has urged its members to use great caution in providing testimony about teeth impressions. Krone was subsequently exonerated when DNA evidence proved he could not have been the killer.

Ronald Keith Williamson was convicted and sentenced to death in Ada, Oklahoma, for the rape and murder of Debbie Sue Carter. Williamson's conviction was secured in part by a snitch and in part by the testimony of an Oklahoma forensic scientist who claimed that hairs found at the scene "matched" those of Williamson. Hair matching is notoriously inaccurate, and another state expert who analyzed hair fibers from the scene found no "match" to Williamson, but her findings were buried for more than ten years. Williamson came within five days of being executed before DNA tests exonerated him, but not before he had spent eleven years in prison.

All of these problems leave you wondering, "What can we possibly do, murderers deserve a severe penalty, but I just don't know about the death penalty. There seem to be so many things that can and do go wrong, but what other choice do we have?" One other choice is life in prison without the possibility of parole.

VII. LWOP

Some death penalty opponents argue that the maximum punishment should be life without the possibility of parole. An LWOP sentence is available in all thirty-five states that have the death penalty and in fourteen of fifteen states that do not have it (Alaska is the only exception). Figure 24.3 showed the death sentencing rate per 100,000 population in the United States from 1977 until 2008. Since 1996 there has been a dramatic decline. By 2008 the rate was lower than at any time since 1977. During approximately the same time period, the number of LWOPs increased from 12,453 in 1992 to 41,095 in 2008, an increase of 230 percent (Nellis and King 2009).

The public appears to support the use of LWOP sentences for murderers, and this sentence offers many advantageous alternatives to the death penalty. It is arguably no worse (and likely no better) a deterrent to murder, it is almost as effective at incapacitating, it is an onerous penalty that reflects society's condemnation of murder, and it is likely to be less burdensome on taxpayers. In addition, there is one undeniable advantage of LWOP—mistakes can be corrected. A problem with the death penalty that concerns many Americans is the possibility that an innocent person may be wrongly executed. The decline in the number of death sentences and increase in the number of LWOP sentences may be an effect of that concern.

The United States is one of a handful of countries that imposes LWOPs on children (Amnesty International 2005). All countries except the United States and Somalia have ratified the Convention on the Rights of the Child, which explicitly forbids life imprisonment without parole for offenses committed by persons below eighteen years of age. There are now more than 1,700 people in state prisons in the United States serving LWOP sentences for crimes committed as children (Nellis and King 2009). Other countries with LWOPs include Australia, Denmark (although one serving a real life sentence may apply for a pardon and reduction in sentence after serving twelve years), England, France, North Korea, Nigeria, Malaysia, and the Netherlands (though a person can apply for a royal decree, which can reduce the sentence).

Most Western European countries do not have LWOPs, and those that do use it only rarely. This is not the case in the United States. The Sentencing Project in 2008 reported that there were more than 40,000 inmates (1,333 of whom were women) serving LWOP terms, an increase of 22 percent since 2003 and an increase of 230 percent since 1992. In six states (Illinois, Iowa, Louisiana, Maine, Pennsylvania, and South Dakota) and the federal system, all life sentences were LWOP sentences (Nellis and King 2009). The racial disparities seen in death penalty statistics are also noticeable for LWOPs. Although African Americans comprise about 45 percent of all life *with* parole sentences, they make up 56 percent of all LWOP sentences. For juvenile LWOP sentences, about 47 percent of all life *with* parole sentences were African American while 56 percent of all LWOP sentences are African American.

VIII. Conclusion

Most countries that retain the death penalty are likely to continue to do so. Over the past twenty years, most countries that abolished the death penalty did so in order to be eligible for membership in the European Union. Many that retain the death penalty are either Islamist or anti-democratic (China, Iran, North Korea) and are unlikely to abolish their death penalties. Many countries officially have the death penalty (sixty-two as of 2009), but most executions occur in just a few—China, Iran, Saudi Arabia, Pakistan, the Sudan, and the United States.

It is unlikely that the situation will change much in the United States either. The number of death sentences will likely continue to decline as the public continues to be concerned about the possibility of executing innocents and other problems with the death penalty. Public concern about executing innocents is fueled by the constant drip of death row exonerations. It is likely that there will continue to be a few each year, enough perhaps to keep the public wary of an innocent person being put to death, although a majority already believes that this has happened. It is doubtful if those states that contribute most to the execution numbers will stop their practice. High execution states are southern states that historically have used the death penalty. We will likely see something similar to what occurred during from the 1950s to the 1960s when the number of executions was reduced each year to a handful.

Lawyers will continue to attack the death penalty, and scholars will continue to study it. One area where interests may converge is execution of the mentally ill. The American Civil Liberties Union has estimated that about 10 percent of the more than 3,400 offenders on death row have a severe mental illness (Malone 2005), but many of these illnesses are not severe enough to meet the current standard. Devising a standard for the execution of the mentally ill will not be easy because unlike youth (age) and mental retardation (IQ), where to draw the line with mental illness is much more elusive.

Another area where research and public policy interests converge is cost. Since many states and counties have recently faced large budget deficits, it is not clear that they will be able to afford the death penalty. Unfortunately, it is not exactly clear how much money the death penalty costs or what is achieved in return via crime control. While cost *estimates* have been made, there has been no systematic study of the cost of the death penalty because no one tracks the costs at each step of the capital process.

Another important area for research concerns the effects of victim impact evidence in capital cases. In all capital punishment states, family members, relatives, even friends and co-workers of the slain victim can present written and oral testimony at the sentencing hearing on the impact the murder has had on their lives. These statements include assessments by survivors about the value of the victim and how much they are missed, the impact the murder has had on the lives and physical and emotional health of the survivors, and sometimes an impassioned plea as to what sentence the family would like to see imposed. These are touching, highly emotional statements that are virtually impossible for the defense to rebut and may have a volatile impact on the emotions and sympathies of the sentencer. Research in behavioral economics about the "identified victim" indicates that sympathy is more easily generated for a victim who is clearly and saliently identified than for one whose life is not so clearly portrayed. Victim impact statements are sometimes presented to the jury in written form, sometimes by live testimony, and other times in elaborate videos that depict the life of the slain victim complete with heart-wrenching background music. The Supreme Court has recently decided (*Kelly v. California* 129 S. Ct. 564 [2008]) against any attempt to regulate these victim-impact statements but the question remains whether their effect on the defendant is highly prejudicial. Like many things about the death penalty, it remains highly controversial.

NOTES

1. When I refer to an executing being "in" a county, I refer to the county where the case was tried, not the county where the actual execution occurred.

2. One way to compare heterogeneity is to calculate the coefficient of variation (CV), which is the ratio of a standard deviation to its mean. For execution rates across death penalty states in figure 1 the CV is 1.365, for the state of Texas it is 2.141.

REFERENCES

Amnesty International. 2005 "For the Rest of Their Lives: Life without Parole for Child Offenders in the United States." Available at http://www.amnestyusa.org/countries/usa/clwop/report.pdf.

———. 2009. *Amnesty International Report-2005: The State of the World's Human Rights.* London: Amnesty International Publications.

Association of Religious Data Archives 2009 Available at http://www.thearda.com/.

Baicker, Katherine. 2004. "The Budgetary Repercussions of Capital Convictions." *Advances in Economic Analysis and Policy* 4(1): Article 6.

Baldus, David C., George G. Woodworth, and Charles A. Pulaski, Jr. 1990. *Equal Justice and the Death Penalty.* Boston: Northeastern University Press.

Banner, Stuart. 2002. *The Death Penalty: An American History.* Boston: Harvard University Press.

Bedau, Hugo A. 2004. "An Abolitionist's Survey of the Death Penalty in America Today." In *Debating the Death Penalty*, edited by Hugo A. Bedau and Paul G. Cassell, 15–50. New York: Oxford University Press.

Berk, Richard. 2005. "New Claims about Executions and General Deterrence: Déjà vu All Over Again." *Journal of Empirical Legal Studies* 2: 303–30.

Berns, Walter. 1979. *For Capital Punishment.* New York: Basic Books.

Cook, Philip J., and Donna B. Slawson. 1993. *The Cost of Processing Murder Cases in North Carolina.* Durham, NC: Sanford Institute of Public Policy, Duke University.

Death Penalty Information Center. 2009. Available at http://www.deathpenaltyinfo.org/.

Death Row U.S.A. 2009. Summer 2009. New York: NAACP Legal Defense and Education Fund. Available at http://www.naacpldf.org/content/pdf/pubs/drusa/DRUSA_Summer_2009.pdf.

Dezhbakhsh, Hashem, Paul H. Rubin, and Joanna Shepherd. 2003. Does Capital Punishment Have a Deterrent Effect? New Evidence from Post-moratorium Panel Data. *American Law and Economics Review* 5: 344–76.

Donohue, John J., and Justin Wolfers. 2006. Uses and Abuses of Empirical Evidence in the Death Penalty Debate. *Stanford Law Review* 58: 791–846.

Edwards, Catherine. 2007. *Death in Ancient Rome.* New Haven, CT: Yale University Press.

Ehrlich, Isaac. 1975. "The Deterrent Effect of Capital Punishment: A Question of Life and Death." *American Economic Review* 65: 397–417.

Foner, Eric, and Olivia Mahoney. 1995. *America's Reconstruction: People and Politics After the Civil War*. New York: Harper Collins.

Gallop Organization. 2006. http://www.gallup.com/home.aspx.

Garfinkel, Harold. 1949. "Research Note on Inter- and Intra-racial Homicides." *Social Forces* 27: 369–80.

Hood, Roger, and Carolyn Hoyle, 2009. Abolishing the Death Penalty Worldwide: The Impact of a "New Dynamic." In *Crime and Justice: A Review of Research,* vol. 38, edited by Michael Tonry. Chicago: University of Chicago Press.

Johnson, David T., and Franklin P. Zimring. 2009. *The Next Frontier: National Development, Political Change, and the Death Penalty in Asia.* New York: Oxford University Press.

Johnson, Guy. 1941. "The Negro and Crime." *Annals of the American Academy of Political and Social Science* 217: 93–104.

Kant, Immanuel. 1965. *The Metaphysical Elements of Justice.* Indianapolis:Bobbs-Merrill.

King, Linda Randa. 1997. *Society's Final Solution.* Lanham, MD: University Press of America.

Klein, Lawrence R., Brian Forst, and Victor Filatov. 1978. "The Deterrent Effect of Capital Punishment: An Assessment of the Estimates." In Deterrence and Incapacitation: Estimating the Effects of Criminal Sanctions on Crime Rates, ed. Alfred Blumstein, Jacqueline Cohen and Daniel S. Nagin. Washington, DC: National Academy Press.

Legislative Post-Audit Committee. 2003. *Costs Incurred for Death Penalty Cases: A K-Goal Audit of the Department of Corrections.* Legislative Division of Post Audit, Legislature of Kansas.

Liebman, James J., Jeffrey Fagan, Valerie West, and J. Lloyd. 2000. "Capital Attrition: Error Rates in Capital Cases, 1973–1995." *Texas Law Review* 78: 1839–65.

Liebman, James J., Jeffrey Fagan, Valerie West, Andrew Gelman, Garth Davies, and Alexander Kiss. 2002. *A Broken System Part II: Why There is So Much Error in Capital Cases and What Can Be Done about It.* New York: Columbia University School of Law.

Lu, Hong, and Terence D. Miethe. 2007. *China's Death Penalty: History, Law, and Contemporary Practice.* New York: Routledge.

Malone, Dan. 2005. "Cruel and Inhumane: Executing the Mentally Ill." Amnesty International Magazine, Fall. Available at http://www.amnestyusa.org/amnesty-magazine/fall-1005/page.do?id=1105178.

Marquart, James, and Jonathan Sorensen. 1988. "Institutional and Post-release Behavior of Furman-commuted Inmates in Texas." *Criminology* 26: 677–93.

Mauer, Marc, Ryan King, and Malcolm C. Young. 2005. *The Meaning of "life": Long Prison Sentences in Context.* Washington, DC: The Sentencing Project. Available at http://www.sentencingproject.org/doc/publications/inc_meaningoflife.pdf.

Mocan, H. Naci, and R. Kaj Gittings. 2003. Getting Off Death Row: Commuted Sentences and the Deterrent Effect of Capital Punishment. *Journal of Law and Economics* 46: 453–78.

National Law Journal. 1990. "Fatal Defense, Death Row Defense: Lawyers in Trouble." June 11.

Nellis, Ashley, and Ryan S. King. 2009. *No Exit: The Expanding Use of Life Imprisonment in America.* Washington, DC: The Sentencing Project. Available at http://www.sentencingproject.org/doc/publications/inc_noexit.pdf.

Northwestern University. 2005. "The Snitch System." Northwestern University Law School: Center on Wrongful Convictions. Available at http://www.law.northwestern.edu/wrongfulconvictions/issues/causesandremedies/snitches/SnitchSystemBooklet.pdf.

Oberwitler, Dietrich, and Shenghui Qi. 2008. "Public Opinion on the Death Penalty in China: Results from a General Population Survey Conducted in Three Provinces in 2007/08." *Max Planck Institute for Foreign and International Criminal Law*. Unpublished manuscript. Available at http://www.mpicc.de/ww/en/pub/forschung/forschungsarbeit/kriminologie/death_penalty.htm.

Paternoster, Raymond, Robert Brame, and Sarah Bacon. 2008. *The Death Penalty: America's Experience with Capital Punishment*. New York: Oxford University Press.

Reiman, Jeffrey H. 1985. "Justice, Civilization, and the Death Penalty: Answering van den Haag." *Philosophy and Public Affairs* 14: 115–48.

Roman, John, Aaron Chalfin, Aaron Sundquist, Carly Knight, and Askar Darmenov. 2008. *The Cost of the Death Penalty in Maryland*. Washington, DC: The Urban Institute.

Ruff, Julius R. 2001. *Violence in Early Modern Europe: 1500–1800*. Cambridge: Cambridge University Press.

Sellin, Thorsten. 1959. *The Death Penalty*. Philadelphia: The American Law Institute.

Shepherd, Johanna M. 2004. "Murders of Passion, Execution Delays and the Deterrence of Capital Punishment." *Journal of Legal Studies* 33: 283–321.

Stampp, Kenneth M. 1956. *The Peculiar Institution*. New York: Alfred A. Knopf.

Tolnay, Stewart E., and E. M. Beck. 1995. *A Festival of Violence: An Analysis of Southern Lynchings, 1892–1930*. Urbana: University of Illinois Press.

United States General Accounting Office 1990 Death Penalty Sentencing: Research Indicates Pattern of Racial Disparities. Washington, DC, U.S. General Accounting Office. Available at http://gao.gov/.

Van den Haag, Ernest. 1975. *Punishing Criminals: Concerning A Very Old and Painful Question*. New York: Basic Books.

———. 1978. "In Defense of the Death Penalty: A Legal-Practical-Moral Analysis." *Criminal Law Bulletin* 14: 51–68.

Welsh-Huggins, Andrew. 2009. "Ohio Death Sentences Declining." Associated Press article available at http://www.ohio.com/news/37428319.html.

Wolfgang, Marvin E., and Marc Riedel, 1973, Race, Judicial Discretion, and the Death Penalty. *Annals of the American Academy of Political and Social Science* 407: 119–33.

———. 1975. "Rape, Race, and the Death Penalty in Georgia." *American Journal of Orthopsychiatry* 45: 658–68.

Zimring, Franklin E. 2003. *The Contradictions of American Capital Punishment*. New York: Oxford University Press.

PART VI

CORRECTIONS

CHAPTER 25

JAILS AND PRETRIAL RELEASE

BRANDON K. APPLEGATE

A critical point in the process of criminal justice is reached shortly after someone suspected of a crime is arrested. Unless the charge is minor (and the suspect meets certain other criteria), he or she is typically booked into a detention facility—a jail. The defendant may remain in the jail until the final disposition of his or her case or may be released back to the community pending such an outcome. The stakes are high—personal liberty for the accused, risk of potential danger to the community, and the very ability to proceed against the defendant for the judicial process. The volume is also remarkable. According to the latest estimates from the Bureau of Justice Statistics, the average daily inmate population of all local jails in the United States stood at more than 776,500 (Minton and Sabol 2009). This figure is dwarfed, however, by the number of bookings that jails handle each year—approximately 13.4 million (Sabol, Minton, and Noonan 2009). Thus, jailing and pretrial release are vital concerns in criminal justice.

There are ostensible benefits to holding criminal defendants in jail until the final adjudication of their cases. It has been asserted that detention assures appearance for court proceedings, incapacitates defendants from committing crimes against free citizens, and presents the possibility of participation in reha-bilitative, educational, vocational, or other institutional treatment programs. Critics, however, point out that pretrial release is more consistent with the pre-sumption of innocence prior to conviction. Thus, by releasing defendants while their cases progress, liberty is restored to citizens who have not yet been con-victed of a crime. Moreover, pretrial release may allow defendants to participate more fully in preparing their defense and to maintain community ties including connections to family and employment. Compared to incarceration, pretrial release may also be less stressful for the accused and, in addition, is less costly for correctional departments. In some cases, release is used as an emergency measure to reduce jail crowding.

Throughout this chapter, consideration is given to the structure and function of institutions as well as to decision points in the progression of criminal cases. Pretrial defendants account for about 63 percent of local jail inmates (Minton and Sabol 2009). Importantly, jails also hold inmates who have been convicted and are serving a sentence usually of a year or less, individuals who were previously convicted and are now facing charges of violating probation or parole conditions, and small numbers of inmates who are being held for a variety of other reasons. Jails, therefore, must be viewed as organizational entities whose responsibilities extend beyond pretrial detention. Similarly, pretrial supervision programs have become an important component of pretrial release. The proliferation of these programs requires that any consideration of pretrial release move beyond the initial exercise of discretion to release or detain defendants.

Several important themes emerge in an examination of research on jails:

- Jail incarceration rates have risen dramatically, currently reaching 258 inmates per 100,000 citizens.
- More than 60 percent of jail inmates are being held pretrial.
- Conditions of early jails were dismal, while contemporary jails have more humane living conditions.
- Podular/direct supervision jails may reduce misbehavior among inmates and improve working conditions for jail officers.
- Jail inmates have abnormally high rates of mental disorders, distress, suicide, and self-injury. The experience of being jailed contributes to these problems.

A number of conclusions can be drawn from the literature on pretrial release:

- Reform movements in pretrial release focused on appearance at trial in the 1960s and danger to the community in the 1970s and 1980s.
- Defendants at the federal level are detained before trial at more than one and one-half times the rate of defendants in state courts. Bail is the most common method of release.
- Offense-related variables are the strongest predictors of release decisions. The evidence on whether defendant's race, ethnicity, and sex are related to release is mixed.
- Pretrial misconduct occurs at higher rates among defendants with weaker community ties and more extensive criminal justice involvement. It is unclear what impact pretrial supervision has on misconduct.

Section I provides an overview of the jail inmate population. Data reveal the current makeup and important shifts in inmate characteristics. In section II, I discuss the historical development of jails and pretrial release. I review the empirical evidence on contemporary pretrial release issues in section III, including trends in pretrial release and detention, correlates of release decisions, and dimensions of supervision and misconduct among released defendants. Section IV turns to contemporary jail issues of direct supervision in new generation facilities, mental health, and adjustment to jail confinement. Section V concludes with a discussion of policy implications and fruitful directions for future research.

I. The Jail Inmate Population

The United States has increased the number of prisoners held in local jails at a remarkable rate. The 1880 decennial census provides the earliest reliable national estimate of the extent of jail incarceration—18,686 inmates, or 37 inmates for every 100,000 people in the US population (Cahalan and Parsons 1986). Because the US Census Bureau subsequently counted only sentenced inmates, data for the next several decades are not directly comparable. Over the following century, however, the jail inmate population increased nearly tenfold; by 1980, jails held an estimated 182,800 inmates (Snell 1995). A portion of this shift can be attributed to broader growth in the American population. Controlling for the country's expansion reveals a more modest, but still considerable, rise in jail use. The incarceration rate per 100,000 citizens increased by 2.5 times from 1880 to 1983 (Cahalan and Parsons 1986). During the 1980s and 1990s, the extent to which people were held in American jails rose more dramatically. In the ten-year period from 1983 to 1993, the number of inmates doubled from 223,551 to 459,804 (see figure 25.1). Similarly, the incarceration rate went from 96 to 188 per 100,000 (Perkins, Stephan, and Beck 1995). More recently, growth has slowed. From year 2000 to 2008, the average annual growth rate—2.9 percent—was less than half what it had been during the preceding two decades. Still, as of midyear 2008, 785,556 people—one out of every 387 U.S. citizens—were held in a local jail (Minton and Sabol 2009) (see figure 25.2).

A few trends in the makeup of the inmate population should be noted. First, the extent to which the inmate population is comprised of those who have been convicted has declined over time. In the late 1800s three-quarters of jail inmates had been sentenced. By 1970, however, less than half were convicted (Cahalan and Parsons 1986). Since 2003 this figure has stood below 40 percent, and the most recent assessment places it at 37.1 percent (Minton and Sabol 2009). Thus, a strong majority of inmates in local jails are being held pretrial. Second, women as a proportion of all jail inmates have increased in the past few decades. In 1970, they were 5

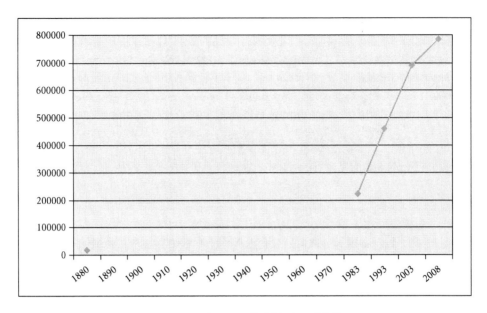

Figure 25.1. Persons Held in Local Jails
Source: Cahalan and Parsons 1986; Beck and Karberg 2001; Minton and Sabol 2009.

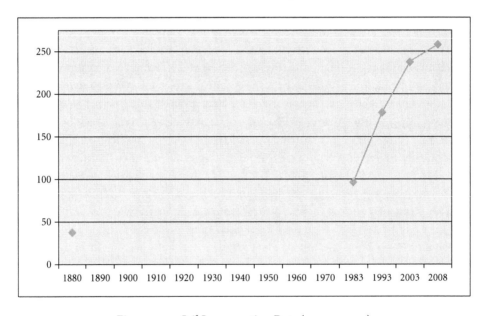

Figure 25.2. Jail Incarceration Rate (per 100,000)
Sources: Cahalan and Parsons 1986; Perkins, Stephan, and Beck 1995; Minton and Sabol 2009.

percent of the population (Cahalan and Parsons 1986); by 2008 they made up 12.7 percent of jail inmates (Minton and Sabol 2009). Third, comparisons across time are complicated by classification issues, but the racial composition of the inmate population appears to have been fairly stable recently, while ethnicity has shifted.

Counts produced in the late 1970s and early 1980s of whites and blacks included those who were of Hispanic origin. About 57 percent of inmates were white and 40 percent were black. Ten percent were Hispanic (Cahalan and Parsons 1986). More recently, inmates have been classified differently; Hispanics are not accounted within racial groups. Thus, in 2008, 42.5 percent of inmates were non-Hispanic whites, 39.2 percent were non-Hispanic blacks, and 16.4 percent were Hispanic (Minton and Sabol 2009). These figures (see table 25.1) are more or less the same as they were at the start of the decade (Beck and Karberg 2001).

A number of scholars have offered explanations for the high imprisonment rate in the United States.[1] One possibility is that imprisonment increased in step with rising crime. When the United States is considered alone, this explanation seems plausible as the rate of crime, particularly violent crime, was high during the 1980s and 1990s. Cross-national comparisons reveal, however, that America was not unique in its experience with crime. Other Western nations also experienced rising crime, but their incarceration rates did not follow the trend of dramatic increase experienced in the United States. Tonry (2008) observes that, taking jails and prisons together, the incarceration rate of the United States was quite similar to that of other Western nations in the early 1970s but was five to ten times higher by 2005.

In somewhat similar fashion, placing responsibility on public opinion falls short. The citizens of other nations hold opinions on crime and punishment that are fairly similar to those of the American public (Roberts et al. 2002). Similar estimates of the amount of crime, beliefs about trends in crime, and opinions on what ought to be done with offenders cannot explain why the United States charted a distinctly different path with policies leading to incarceration. Notably, there is also good evidence that public opinion in the United States has often followed, not led, efforts to "get tough" with offenders (Beckett 1997).

Theories that delve more deeply into the structure and culture of American society offer more promising explanations. Garland (2001) contends that recent

Table 25.1. Trends in Jail Inmate Characteristics

	Sex		Race[a]			% White Non-Hispanic	% Black Non-Hispanic	% Hispanic
	% Unconvicted	% Male	% Female	% White	% Black	% Hispanic			
1970	52	95.0	5.0	56	41	6			
1988	51	91.1	8.9				43.3	40.5	15.0
1998	57	89.2	10.8				41.3	41.2	15.5
2008	63	87.3	12.7				42.5	39.2	16.4

Note: Races other than White, Black, and Hispanic are not shown. In 1970, Hispanic jail inmates were included in counts of White and Black jail inmates.

Sources: Cahalan and Parsons (1986); Perkins, Stephan, and Beck (1995); Gilliard (1999); Minton and Sabol (2009).

periods of increased incarceration reflect certain post-modern realities. In his view, preoccupations with uncertainty, danger, and risk (in concert with governmental limitations in effecting lower crime rates) have resulted in policymakers trying to "do something" to reassure the public. Tonry (2004) points out, however, that Garland's explanation still does not account for cross-national differences. In his 2007 presidential address to the American Society of Criminology, Tonry (2008, 4) argued that U.S. imprisonment policies were possible because of weak human rights concerns born of "the paranoid style in American politics, religious fundamentalism, an obsolete constitutional system, and the history of American race relations." That is, uniquely American political processes and contemporary sensibilities about crime account for the incomparable use of incarceration (also see Tonry 2004).

II. Historical Developments

The roots of modern American jails are usually traced to twelfth-century England. Mainly, the early English jail was used to detain people until the next time a judge visited a county, and defendants could then be brought to trial. Sometimes this meant being held in jail for months or years before being tried. Jails also incarcerated people who had been convicted and fined but were unable to pay. Rather than this period in jail serving as punishment in lieu of the fine, convicts were simply held indefinitely until they or someone else paid their fine. At this time, incarceration only rarely served as the punishment for offenders after they had been convicted, a practice that persisted for several centuries (Moynahan and Stewart 1980).

Despite the lack of punitive intent, many inmates found the conditions of these jails barely livable. Because the facilities generally were not very secure, inmates might be chained to each other or to a wall or the floor, especially at night. Jails were cold, dark, wet, and commonly comprised a single space, prohibiting segregation by sex or age. Disease was always a concern, and many people died while in jail (McConville 1995). Rather than being funded by the government, jails operated on the basis of inmate fees. Inmates were charged for food, water, bedding, clothing, and even for being admitted to and released from the jail. Often indigent inmates did not live to be released, but inmates with the ability to pay substantial sums enjoyed fine food, comfortable quarters (perhaps in the keeper's own house), entertainment, beer, and even having their family and servants live with them.

Jails remained largely unchanged in England from the twelfth through the seventeenth century, so it is not surprising that early colonial American jails shared many of these characteristics. Colonists began building jails shortly after their arrival in America, around the mid-1600s. Most of these facilities operated with inmate fees and consisted of a single room with no provision for separating inmates. Jails also continued to house, almost exclusively, defendants who were awaiting trial and those who had been found guilty and were waiting to be punished. Incarceration in jail itself still was not considered punishment (Rothman 1971).

The origin of a right to be released pending trial via bail also can be traced to England. The 1689 English Bill of Rights laid the foundation for including a right to bail in early American laws (Goldfarb 1965). The Judiciary Act of 1789 established the judicial branch of the United States federal government but also asserted a presumption of bail for offenses where the possible punishment was not death. Two years later, the Eight Amendment to the US Constitution prohibited the imposition of excessive bail. Even so, bail was often set above a defendant's ability to pay, assuring detention until the resolution of his or her case.

In the following century, several substantial changes occurred in the use and operation of jails. By the 1800s, most jails had shifted from being used almost exclusively for pretrial detention to also providing punishment in the form of incarceration to offenders who had been convicted of minor crimes (Moynahan and Stewart 1980). Jails continued to hold children, slaves, the mentally ill, and debtors, but during this century they began to separate male and female inmates. Modest improvements in the conditions of confinement also were introduced, including improved ventilation and lighting, heat, and abolishment of the inmate fee system.[2]

Throughout the twentieth century, improvements in the construction, operation, and conditions of US jails continued. Reforms, however, were achieved in small, irregular steps, perhaps owing to local level control and operation of jails (Mattick 1974). Early in the century, Fishman (1923) recounted observations of South Carolina jails that reflected many of the same deplorable conditions of earlier institutions: "In rainy weather, the water pours down into the jail in torrents . . . sewage not properly disposed of . . . floor and bedding dirty . . . jail improperly heated . . . scraps of decaying food lying around . . . the building has only two compartments, making it almost impossible to separate properly the inmates according to sex, race, and age" (241–44). These conditions were not unique to South Carolina or to the early part of the twentieth century. In the mid-1970s, Mattick (1974, 782) drew the conclusion that "jails everywhere are inadequate." While some critics called for abolition of jails, eventually the conversation turned to ways to improve jails. Much of the progress achieved on this front can probably be attributed to the contributions of national organizations interested in correctional work such as the American Prison Association, the American Correctional Association, the National Institute of Corrections, and others. The American Jail Association, for example, implemented several initiatives to support professionalization and improvement of local corrections, including facility accreditation standards, officer certification requirements, and training seminars (American Jail Association 2007). These organizations provided not only broad principles and ideals (Mattick 1974) but also conduits for cross-jurisdictional communication about jail standards.

Concerns about the conditions of local jails and about the fairness of pretrial detention spurred a reform movement in pretrial release in the 1960s. At this point, the predominant method of release before trial was through financial bond—defendants were released only if they posted cash or property as collateral meant to assure they appeared before the court for future hearings. When defendants were believed to be potentially dangerous, preventive detention was sought through a sub rosa process of setting higher bond amounts. Critics observed that such practices discriminated against poorer defendants, often resulted in arbitrary and highly inconsistent decisions about bond amounts, and probably resulted in detention of more defendants than necessary (Goldfarb 1965; Goldkamp 1985).

Discussion focused on how to enhance due process while still assuring appearance at trial. In an innovative effort to reform pretrial release practices, the Vera Institute of Justice implemented the Manhattan Bail Project in 1961. Project staff determined the strength of each defendant's community ties and developed recommendations regarding release or detention, based on the likelihood of appearance for subsequent court dates. The project demonstrated that many people could be released without bail and would still appear for trial (Vera Institute of Justice 2004). Shortly thereafter, the US federal government passed the Bail Reform Act of 1966, which established release on recognizance—releasing a defendant without the security of bail—as presumptive in noncapital cases. In addition, conditional release—the defendant must agree to certain conditions such as regular reporting and abstaining from alcohol and drugs—and deposit bail—the defendant was required to deposit a small percentage of the full bail amount with the court—emerged as more widely used options through the 1960s and 1970s (Thomas 1976).

A second reform movement in the 1970s and 1980s, however, had a different tone. As Goldkamp (1985) notes, the outcome of interest shifted from assuring appearance at trial to assuring the safety of the public. The danger that defendants might pose to the community if they were released served as the new foundation for reforming pretrial detention practices. The clearest expression of this new direction was the federal Bail Reform Act of 1984.[3] Although it retained the presumption of release on recognizance or on unsecured personal bond from the earlier act, this new legislation explicitly endorsed preventive detention in cases where it is judged that "no condition will reasonably assure . . . the safety of the community" (Federal Judicial Center 1993, 7). Thus, the imposition of high bail as an effort to keep potentially dangerous defendants confined was replaced by the ability to deny release altogether. The constitutionality of preventive detention based on a prediction of future dangerousness was subsequently upheld in *U.S. v. Salerno* 481 U.S. 739 (1987). The Supreme Court ruled that "preventing danger to the community is a legitimate regulatory goal" and that pretrial detention is a permissible means of pursuing it (at 747).

III. Contemporary Pretrial Release Issues

The decisions and processes that result in defendants returning to the community or remaining incarcerated until the final disposition of criminal cases account for a substantial portion of jail populations.

A. Pretrial Release and Detention Trends

An examination of recent patterns of pretrial release and detention reveals some useful insights. The U.S. Bureau of Justice Statistics' State Court Processing Statistics (SCPS) program gathers felony pretrial data biennially from a sample of the seventy-five largest counties in the United States. Cohen and Reaves's (2007) analysis of data from 1990 to 2004 shows that the portion of defendants detained before trial has remained largely stable. Averaged across this series, 38 percent of defendants have been detained until their cases were resolved. Moreover, the detention rate has varied little since 1990. At its lowest point in 1998, 36 percent were detained, and it reached its zenith, 43 percent, in 2004. The pattern is distinctly different, however, at the federal level. The proportion of federal defendants detained has increased steadily in recent years. In 1992, 38 percent of federal defendants were held in jail pending the outcome of their cases (Byrne and Stowell 2007). By 2008 the rate had reached 62.5 percent (Administrative Office of the United States Courts 2009). Thus, federal defendants are more likely to be detained, and the gap in detention rates between the federal and state systems has widened.

It is unclear what explains the difference in trajectories for pretrial detention at the state and federal levels. VanNostrand and Keebler (2009) show that the federal courts processed an increasing number of higher-risk defendants between 2001 and 2007, but federal courts detained a rising percentage of defendants at all risk levels across this period. Byrne and Stowell (2007, 37) contend that the increased rate of pretrial detention at the federal level reflects a "preoccupation with drugs, weapons, and immigration law violations" and control-oriented policy choices. Comparable analyses of state pretrial risk, detention, and policy trends are not available.

Although the existing data do not provide a clear explanation for growth in pretrial detention at the federal level and stasis at the state level, they suggest a possible cause of the gap: greater use of preventive detention with federal defendants. Scalia (1999) reports that 34 percent of federal defendants in 1996 were ordered detained pending adjudication of their cases. In contrast, for the same year SCPS data reveal 6 percent of state defendants were denied release (Hart and Reaves 1999). Use of preventive detention for felony defendants at the state level has not exceeded 7 percent since (Reaves 2001; Rainville and Reaves 2003; Cohen and Reaves 2006; Kyckelhahn and Cohen 2008).

Defendants who are not preventively detained may be handled through several mechanisms. Defendants may be released outright—release on own recognizance (ROR)—or if they meet certain conditions set by the court. The least restrictive alternatives include nonfinancial conditions—such as regular reporting, drug testing, or mental health treatment—and unsecured bond—a monetary bail amount is set but the defendant pays nothing unless he or she fails to appear in court. Financial conditions of release may require the defendant to post the entire bail amount—cash bond—or only a percentage, either to the court—deposit bond—or to a private bail bond agent—surety bond. Cohen and Reaves (2007, 2) note a "pronounced trend . . . in the type of release used" in American state courts between 1990 and 2004. At the beginning of this period, 40 percent of defendants secured a nonfinancial release. Twenty-four percent of defendants were released on financial conditions. By 2004, nearly the opposite was true—28 percent of defendants secured a nonfinancial release, and 36 percent were financial. Most of the difference is accounted for by the two most common release options. Use of ROR dropped, and surety bonds increased.

Looking at released defendants tells only a portion of the story. It does not reveal what conditions faced those who were not preventively detained but also were not released. The emerging dominance of financial releases could signal an increased ability to pay among defendants. Examining the conditions set for all defendants, however, calls this explanation into question. In 1990 only 53 percent of defendants had to meet a financial condition to be released. By 2004 this figure had reached 68 percent. Throughout the period, about half of those who had to "make bail" did so (Cohen and Reaves 2007). Thus, it appears that release on financial conditions grew due to greater reliance on financial requirements as a condition of release, not because of any change in the financial resources available to defendants.

B. Correlates of Pretrial Release

As noted earlier, two broad considerations structure decisions whether to release a defendant and what conditions to impose on that release: the risk of danger to the community, witnesses, and victims, and the risk of flight from prosecution. The particular factors that are legislatively or constitutionally established as legally relevant for making pretrial release decisions vary somewhat among jurisdictions, but several are nearly ubiquitous. Typical indicators of risk are the nature of the current offense, the weight of the evidence against the defendant, prior criminal record, prior failure to appear in court, residential stability, marriage and other family ties, and employment (Goldkamp 1985). Each of these factors ostensibly shapes whether the defendant is preventively detained, released without conditions, released with conditions, or required to post bail for release, and the bail amount if it is imposed.

It should not be surprising that empirical research typically shows offending-related variables to be among the most powerful predictors of pretrial release decisions and outcomes. Cohen and Reaves (2007), controlling for other variables, found that the predicted probability of release was lowest for defendants charged with murder (11 percent) or robbery (36 percent) and considerably higher for those facing fraud (76 percent) or driving-related felony charges (76 percent). Those who had been on probation or parole at the time they were arrested were less likely to be released as were those with a history of prior arrests, convictions, or failures to appear in court. Others similarly report that offense severity and prior criminal and court records emerge as the strongest correlates of pretrial release (Goldkamp 1979; Goldkamp and Gottfredson 1985; Gottfredson and Gottfredson 1988; Walker 1993; Steiner 2009).

For defendants who are offered release under financial or nonfinancial conditions, release is ultimately determined not only by the court's decision to offer release but also by the defendants' willingness and ability to meet those conditions.[4] Looking only at the final outcome—whether a defendant is in or out of jail—therefore, may obscure important correlates of prior steps in the pretrial process.

Recent studies by Demuth (2003; Demuth and Steffensmeier 2004) emphasize the need to distinguish decisions from outcomes. Separate models were estimated for predictors of preventive detention, imposing financial release conditions, setting of the bond amount, whether defendants who were offered release on bail remained in jail, and whether defendants were ultimately released pending adjudication. For the most part, Demuth's (2003; Demuth and Steffensmeier 2004) analyses affirmed that a more serious current offense, prior failure to appear, prior arrest or incarceration, and being under criminal justice supervision at the time of arrest consistently predicted not only eventual detention but also eligibility for release, setting of bail as a release condition, bail amount, and whether the defendant made bail. Offense type revealed one notable exception. Although defendants facing charges for assault, drug trafficking, or "other" property, violent, or drug offenses were more likely to have bail imposed and to have a higher bail amount, their odds of making bail were one-and-one-half to two times those of defendants facing charges for theft (the reference category in their analyses). It is unclear what explains the differential willingness or ability to make bail among these defendants.

In addition to legally relevant variables, scholars have also considered the potential impacts of race, ethnicity, and gender on pretrial release. A common concern raised in support of reforms in the 1960s was that bail as a requirement for release from jail disadvantaged lower income defendants. Because race has a long history of linkage with economic resources in the United States, financial release policies functioned particularly to the detriment of racial minorities (Goldfarb 1965). More recently, Demuth (2003; Demuth and Steffensmeier 2004) suggested that race, ethnicity, and gender may influence pretrial release because of their connection to judges' "focal concerns." Drawing on sentencing theory (see, Steffensmeier, Ulmer, and Kramer 1998), Demuth (2003, 225) proposed that status characteristics may be used as shorthand indicators as judges consider "blameworthiness, protection of the community, and practical constraints and consequences."

The empirical research on race, ethnicity, gender, and pretrial release is mixed. A handful of studies have found that minority status has no significant effect on pretrial release decisions once legally relevant variables are considered. Others, however, have revealed detrimental effects for minorities and men (Free 2002). For example, recent analyses of nationally representative data from the State Court Processing Statistics (SCPS) program show that, compared with whites, African Americans are more likely to be preventively detained. They are also less likely to make bail, and for those who are charged with a drug offense, African Americans are more likely to have bail imposed as a condition of release. The results are similar for Hispanic defendants, although they also tend to have higher bail amounts (Demuth 2003; Demuth and Steffensmeier 2004; Cohen and Reaves 2007; Schlesinger 2007; Steiner 2009). All decisions and outcomes are less restrictive toward women than men, with the greatest gaps appearing among Hispanic defendants (Demuth and Steffensmeier 2004). Thus, racial and ethnic minority defendants are less likely to be released pretrial than are white defendants, and men are more likely to be detained than are women. The classic concern that the financial demands of bail may work to the detriment of minorities still has merit. A portion of the differential release probabilities for whites compared to African Americans and Hispanics can be explained by bail amount or the defendant's willingness or ability to pay bail when it is offered as a release condition. The remainder, however, can be attributed to a more direct effect—differences in the likelihood of being preventively detained.

A shortcoming of these studies is that the SCPS data series does not include information on defendants' community ties. Marital status, family and friendship networks, employment, residential stability, and other indicators that a defendant is rooted in the local area are relevant to judges' assessments of flight risk. If racial or ethnic minorities or men show weaker community ties, this could at least partly explain their disparate pretrial release outcomes. In studies drawing on other data sets and introducing controls for community ties, the effects of race have been equivocal (Goldkamp and Gottfredson 1985; Petee 1994; Goldkamp et al. 1995; Turner and Johnson 2005). The work of Albonetti, Hauser, Hagan, and Nagel (1989), however, suggests that race may have an indirect influence on pretrial release. In their analysis of data from ten federal court districts—although the influence of marriage, employment and residence did not vary across racial groups—education and income reduced the restrictiveness of release outcomes more for white than for black defendants. Thus, the disadvantage of minority racial status may not operate alone but rather through the weight judges assign to other legally relevant factors in reaching decisions about release and conditions of release.

C. Pretrial Supervision, Risk, and Misconduct

When criminal defendants are released to the community rather than detained pending the outcome of their cases, risk of two types of misconduct becomes salient. First, the defendant may fail to appear for a scheduled court hearing. When this occurs, the judiciary's ability to pursue justice is hampered, and costs associated with rescheduling and possible reapprehension of the defendant are incurred.

Second, the defendant may commit new crimes, bringing harm to victims and the community, and also redoubling economic demands on the system should the defendant be re-arrested. There is substantial variation among jurisdictions in the extent to which defendants engage in misconduct while under pretrial release. In the federal courts, failures to appear (FTA) and re-arrests are remarkably rare. VanNostrand and Keebler (2009) report that of all defendants processed through the US federal courts between October 2001 and September 2007, 3.5 percent were re-arrested for a new crime and 3.5 percent failed to appear in court. Misconduct rates in the federal system have been this low for at least the past decade (Byrne and Stowell 2007). In contrast, Cohen and Reaves's (2007) analysis of SCPS data from 1990 through 2004 reveals an FTA rate of 23 percent and a re-arrest rate of 17 percent among cases processed in the largest counties in the United States. Rates reaching a third or more of defendants have been reported in individual local jurisdictions (Goldkamp and White 2006). The relatively lower rate of misconduct at the federal level is likely due at least in part to the greater use of pretrial detention. Presumably, the comparatively small portion of defendants released before trial in the federal court system are lower risk. Researchers, however, have yet to pursue systematic explanations of differences in pretrial misconduct across jurisdictions.

The bulk of the research on pretrial misconduct has been directed instead at understanding and predicting variations across individual defendants. The possible correlates that researchers have examined fall into several general domains; characteristics of the defendant's current charges, criminal history variables, community ties, and demographics are the most common. The particular operationalization of each correlate varies among studies, complicating direct comparisons. Even so, a few variables emerge from the literature as largely common predictors of pretrial misconduct. Defendants who are unemployed, do not have a telephone, have previously been arrested or convicted, and who have a prior FTA are more likely to be re-arrested or miss a scheduled court appearance (Goldkamp et al. 1995; Rhodes, Hyatt, and Scheiman 1996; Maxwell 1999; Cohen and Reaves 2007; Lowenkamp, Lemke, and Latessa 2008; Siddiqi 2009; VanNostrand and Keebler 2009). Although less often examined, prior incarcerations, current substance use, and a history of serious personal and legal problems related to drug use have also been identified as predictors of misconduct (Rhodes, Hyatt, and Scheiman 1996; Lowenkamp, Lemke, and Latessa 2008; VanNostrand and Keebler 2009). The literature shows that a host of other variables, including race, age, gender, marital status, residence, and aspects of the current offense sometimes are related to re-arrest and FTA but other times are insignificant (Goldkamp et al. 1995; Rhodes, Hyatt, and Scheiman 1996; Maxwell 1999; Cohen and Reaves 2007; Lowenkamp, Lemke, and Latessa 2008; Siddiqi 2009; VanNostrand and Keebler 2009).

A practical application of this research has been the development of objective risk-assessment tools. Three recent studies drawing on distinct data sets illustrate the modest success of these efforts. The largest undertaking, carried out by Van-Nostrand and Keebler (2009), drew on records of more than 575,000 defendants processed by the federal court system between 2001 and 2007. Using logistic regression analysis, the authors identified nine "statistically significant and policy relevant predictors" of failure during pretrial release: pending charges, prior misdemeanor arrests, prior felony arrests, prior FTAs, employment status, residence status, type of substance abuse, level of current charge, and type of offense for the current charge (VanNostrand and Keebler 2009, 22). Together, these variables were able to account for less than eight percent of the variation in misconduct among defendants. When the regression model was used to create a five-level risk classification system, meaningful distinctions in misconduct rates were revealed. Defendants at the lowest risk classification failed at a rate of 2.3 percent, compared with 15.5 percent for those at the highest risk level.[5]

The results produced by Siddiqi (2009) and Lowenkamp, Lemke, and Latessa (2008) are remarkably similar. Lowenkamp, Lemke, and Latessa (2008) developed an eleven-point risk score based on prior FTA, prior incarceration, residential stability, employment, drug use, and drug-related problems among defendants referred to five pretrial services agencies. The correlation of risk scores with FTA (.26) and re-arrest (.24) indicate a minimal ability to explain variation in misconduct (about 6 to 7 percent), but those at the lowest risk classification were far less likely to fail to appear (2.1 percent) or be re-arrested (4.3 percent) than those at the highest risk level (33 percent for both types of misconduct).

Finally, examining more than 26,000 defendants from New York City released in 2001, Siddiqi (2009) identified some of the same predictors as VanNostrand and Keebler (2009), such as prior FTA, prior arrest, and unemployment. After eliminating additional variables on which he argued policy should not be based—race, age, borough—Siddiqi was able to explain 7 percent of the variation in rates of misconduct, which included FTA and arrest for a violent offense. Siddiqi's (2009) risk-assessment instrument shows an ability to distinguish low-risk from high-risk cases, with defendants at the high end engaging in misconduct six times more often than those at the low end.

An important aspect of pretrial misconduct involves the type of release. Ostensibly, defendants released on their own recognizance (ROR) should pose the lowest risk. Higher-risk defendants face conditions of release—bail, supervision, and other restrictions—to encourage appearance in court and discourage criminal behavior. The available evidence, however, suggests that this system does not effectively equalize the rate of misconduct across defendants. Block (2005) reports that felony defendants in California released on surety bond failed to appear less often (20.1 percent) than those released on their own recognizance or on conditional release (31.8 percent). Using a more sophisticated analysis that controlled for other variables, Cohen and Reaves (2007) also found FTA rates to be lower for surety, deposit, property, and full cash bond than for ROR. For risk of re-arrest, however, all types of release were statistically indistinguishable except for unsecured bond and emergency release, which were both higher. Intriguingly, VanNostrand and Keebler (2009) found that federal defendants who were required to meet certain supervision conditions—drug testing, drug treatment, electronic monitoring, and housing restrictions—engaged in misconduct at higher rates than defendants for whom release was not contingent on supervision.

Moving beyond the type of release, some researchers have examined the effect of particular conditions of release on misconduct. The largest body of work has concentrated on drug testing as a condition of pretrial release. Emerging in the 1980s, the practice of monitoring defendants released pending trial for drug use was instigated by concerns about a high level of substance use among arrestees (National Institute of Justice 2003) and a general trend toward control and surveillance for offenders in the community (Cullen, Wright, and Applegate 1996). Based on a 2001 national survey, Clark and Henry (2003) report that 77 percent of pretrial services agencies currently conduct drug testing on defendants released under their supervision.

The research literature, however, suggests that drug testing may not be an efficient use of resources (Belenko, Mara-Drita, and McElroy 1992). Experimental studies comparing defendants released with drug testing as a condition versus those without such a condition tend to show equivalent rates of re-arrest and FTA (Cullen, Wright, and Applegate 1996). Moreover, knowing which defendants have used drugs and which have tested negative for substance use appears to be of little value to pretrial supervision. Rhodes and his colleagues (1996) re-analyzed data from eight prior studies. Although they found that positive tests for two individual drugs were related to misconduct—heroin for re-arrest and cocaine for FTA—they concluded that "no evidence supports the general assertion that arrestees who test positive pose greater risks of pretrial misconduct than arrestees who test negative" (Rhodes, Hyatt, Scheiman; 1996, 340). Drug test results add little to our ability to predict FTA or re-arrest once other variables such as criminal history and community ties have been considered.

Beyond drug testing, relatively little attention has been devoted to the content of pretrial supervision. Clark and Henry's (2003) survey shows what components are common. Pretrial services programs conduct interviews with defendants to assess their release risk. Nationally, 95 percent of programs report trying to verify defendants' information, but Siddiqi's (2009) study raises questions about the success of these efforts—only 28 percent of defendants' information about community ties was verified by pretrial services personnel in his New York City study. Nearly all pretrial services programs supervise defendants through telephone or in-person contacts, more than eight in ten refer defendants to substance abuse treatment or mental health services, and nearly 80 percent attempt to contact defendants who fail to appear in court (Clark and Henry 2003).

Data revealing the extent to which these practices affect pretrial misconduct for the most part do not exist. A series of analyses reported by Goldkamp and White (2006) comprise a notable exception. In separate experiments in Philadelphia, the researchers assessed the effect of enhanced assistance from pretrial services personnel at the initial court appearance, contact after arraignment, more frequent contact with defendants, reminders about upcoming court dates, and following up on defendants who missed appointments. The results revealed no reduction in misconduct for the experimental groups who were assigned to receive these services compared to the control groups who were not. The authors note, however, that implementation of the enhanced pretrial supervision services often fell far short. Some results suggest that when defendants did receive the assigned service, outcomes improved. For example, when pretrial services staff were able to reach defendants by telephone to remind them of an upcoming appointment, rates of re-arrest and FTA were cut by one-third or more. Unfortunately, the number of defendants involved in these analyses was small, and the degree of implementation was not randomly assigned, raising the possibility that something other than the supervision component affected misconduct levels.

IV. Contemporary Jail Issues

American Jails before 1975 were not especially nice places in which to live or work. Beginning in the mid-1970s, new types of jails were established. Whether the new jails achieved their aims is not entirely clear. Whether in old- or new-style jails, many inmates have difficulty adapting. This may in part be because many are afflicted by pre-existing mental health conditions.

A. The New Generation Jail Philosophy

One of the most notable twentieth-century innovations in jail design and management was initiated in the 1970s. The US Federal Bureau of Prisons embarked on an effort to design jails that would better meet basic inmate needs—such as privacy and security—and encourage more pro-social behavior (Gettinger 1984). Traditionally, jail inmates were held in open barracks or in cells arranged linearly along a corridor (Wener, Frazier, and Farbstein 1985). Surveillance by officers occurred intermittently and remotely because they were separated from the inmates by physical barriers.

By contrast, the new generation architectural design placed inmates into self-contained living units that were triangular or wedge-shaped. In combination with the architectural layout, stationing officers within the unit allowed them a direct line of sight into all areas of the unit at all times. The furnishings in new generation living units also differed. Rather than "vandal proof" stainless steel and concrete fixtures that are permanently affixed, the pods included carpeting, porcelain lavatories, moveable furniture that may be padded or plastic, and other "soft" fixtures.

The physical features lend themselves to expression of a unique inmate management approach, which also distinguishes new generation jails from traditional facilities. Correctional officers' work in traditional facilities has been characterized as "fragmented, routinized, and menial" or as "bureaucratic chores that require little or no judgment, initiative, or skill on the part of the officer" (Zupan and Menke 1988, 615). In such units, officers are often relegated to patrolling corridors, conducting counts, escorting inmates from one area to another, and attempting to maintain order. Personal security is obtained by physical separation from inmates, and authority is frequently shared with inmates through tacit agreements where guards ignore minor rule violations in exchange for inmates' general compliance (Zupan 1991; see also Sykes 1958). Direct supervision, by contrast, requires well-developed interpersonal skills, creativity in managing inmates, and independence. Zupan (1991) has identified several dimensions of officer behavior essential to effective direct supervision, including proactively addressing conflicts, building rapport, treating all inmates fairly, balancing discretion and consistency, and actively engaging with inmates.

The first new Bureau of Prisons facilities, located in San Diego and New York, opened in 1974, and a third metropolitan correctional center opened in Chicago in 1975 (Nelson and Davis 1995). Because the new facilities were a radical departure from traditional jails, observers initially had reservations about whether they could be operated safely (Wener 2005). Following early reports of reduced violence, graffiti, vandalism, and other incidents in the federal facilities (e.g., Wener and Olsen 1980) and especially in New York City's redesigned version of "The Tombs," new generation jails were embraced more widely (Wener 2005). In a sample drawn in 1999, twenty-five years after the first new generation jails opened, more than one in five medium and large jails reported that they operate a new generation facility (Tartaro 2002b).

Much of the impetus to adopt new generation jail principles arose from the promise of reduced inmate misbehavior. The literature, however, is less than clear that this promise has been fulfilled. Research suggests that inmates held in new generation jails feel satisfied with the facilities (Wener and Olsen 1980; Wener, Frazier, and Farbstein 1985), experience less stress and feel safer (Zupan and Stohr-Gillmore 1988; Zupan 1991; Williams, Rodeheaver, and Huggins 1999), and may experience lower rates of recidivism following release (Applegate, Surette, and McCarthy 1999) than inmates housed in traditional jails. The evidence on inmate misbehavior while incarcerated is mixed but suggests that rates of at least some types of infractions may be lower in new generation than in traditional jails (Wener and Olsen 1980; Bayens, Williams, and Smykla 1997; Senese 1997; Williams, Rodeheaver, and Huggins 1999; cf. Keller and Wang 2005).

Whether new generation jails provide a superior work experience for jail officers also is unclear. Among the evidence for positive effects, officers in new generation jails tend to see the facility as cleaner, less crowded, having fresher air, and being more temperate (Farbstein and Wener 1989; Williams, Rodeheaver, and Huggins 1999). Some studies also suggest that new generation jail officers are more satisfied with their jobs, believe there is greater opportunity for advancement, think the staff has better control of the unit, and see the facility as safer (Houston, Gibbons, and Jones 1988; Zupan and Menke 1988; Farbstein and Wener 1989; Zupan 1991; Williams, Rodeheaver, and Huggins 1999). Other assessments, however, have found that staff are no more satisfied with their jobs, do not feel any safer, are no less stressed, and are no different from staff in linear jails on several dimensions of perceived job enrichment (Houston, Gibbons, and Jones 1988; Zupan and Menke 1988; Zupan 1991; Williams, Rodeheaver, and Huggins 1999; Yocum et al. 2006; Applegate and Paoline 2007).

Two factors suggest caution in interpreting the results of evaluations of new generation jails. First, the research designs employed have been relatively weak. The earliest evaluations assessed inmates and staff in new generation jails with no basis for comparison. More recent studies have used pre/post designs or have gathered data from a very small number of traditional jails to compare with data from a very small number of new generation facilities. The risk is that variables other than new generation design may account for observed differences; equally problematic, true effects of new generation innovations may be obscured. Second, evidence suggests that new generation jails have only partially implemented the physical and supervisory dimensions of the philosophy. In two studies of new generation jails, Tartaro (2002*a*, 2006) found considerable variation in use of soft furnishings and in the extent to which officers were posted within the inmate living areas. Incomplete implementation might explain the evidence of less than optimal results for inmates and staff.

B. Mental Health and Adjustment to Jail

The alternative design and operation of new generation jails raises the issue of how the institution affects inmates. A large body of literature exists regarding the impact of long-term incarceration in prison (see, for example, Johnson and Toch 1982; Stohr and Hemmens 2004). The adaptive response of individuals to comparatively shorter incarceration in jails, however, has received far less empirical and theoretical attention. Even so, information can be drawn together to paint a portrait of the jail experience.

More than twenty-five years ago, Gibbs (1982, 99) observed that detention in jail is "unusually disruptive, debilitating, and even traumatic." He identified four areas where jail inmates experience problems. First, Gibbs argued, inmates experience entry shock—those booked for the first time and those who have been to jail before are struck by the abrupt and dramatic change in their status from free citizens on the street to jail inmates. The second problem area, maintaining outside links, arises from a need to feel that one's connections to the outside world have not been completely severed. Family and friends are important sources of emotional as well as tangible support. Third, Gibbs noted that concerns about stability and safety grow out of the tremendous uncertainty that accompanies detention in jail. Jail inmates often have little information about how long they may be in jail, the legal status of their case, the competence of their attorney, whether they will be able to secure release on bond, and many other aspects of their situation over which they have virtually no control. Their physical safety may also be threatened as they are thrust into close contact with other inmates who are also stressed and may be violent. Finally, Gibbs (1982, 101) suggested that inactivity is a problem for inmates, noting that "jails are notoriously boring places."

Recent data illustrate that signs of distress are highly prevalent among jail inmates. Drawing on data collected in 2002 from a nationally representative sample, James and Glaze (2006) report that 64 percent of jail inmates had a recent history of mental health problems or had symptoms of a mental disorder. The most common symptoms were for a mania disorder—found among more than half of the inmates surveyed—but symptoms of depression and psychosis were also reported by more than 25 percent of local jail inmates. The survey was not designed to result in clinical diagnoses of mental illnesses, and estimates of the prevalence of serious mental illness among incarcerated populations are much lower (Abram and Teplin 1991). Still, mental health problems are found at markedly higher rates among jail inmates than among the general population (Lindquist and Lindquist 1997; James and Glaze 2006), and jail administrators assert that mentally ill inmates pose significant operational challenges (Borum and Rand 2000).

Jail inmates also manifest troubling levels of physical signs of psychological distress. Some authors suggest that suicidal and self-injurious behaviors are symptoms of an underlying psychological disorder, while others argue that they result from inmates' efforts to manipulate their environment (Thomas et al. 2006), views that are also held by mental health professionals in corrections (DeHart, Smith, and Kaminski 2009). In either case, inmates' psychological or environmental resources are outstripped by their personal needs in jail. In 2002 nearly one-third of deaths of inmates in US jails were suicides, a rate of 47 per 100,000 inmates. The situation has improved considerably—in 1983 the suicide rate was 129 per 100,000 and accounted for 56 percent of jail inmate deaths. Even so, the jail suicide rate for 2002 was three times the rate found in state prisons and nearly three times the rate of suicides among the general population (Mumola 2005). Although national data on self-injury are not available and estimates typically suggest that less than 5 percent of inmates intentionally physically harm themselves (Young, Justice, and Erdberg 2006), self-injury among inmates is gaining recognition as a serious problem in correctional institutions. These intentional injuries can include anything from cutting, biting, and burning oneself to swallowing harmful objects (DeHart, Smith, and Kaminski 2009).

The observation of prevalence rates alone cannot explain why so many jail inmates show symptoms of mental illness or distress. It has been suggested that the high rates of mental health problems found among jail inmates reflect pre-existing conditions among the types of people who are arrested and detained—an importation model. There appears to be some validity to this position. People with mental illness, drug dependence, and other deficits may be more likely to come to the attention of the police, to be arrested, and to remain in jail (Irwin 1985; Lamb and Weinberger 1998; Cox et al. 2001). The widespread efforts to divert nonviolent mentally ill offenders, particularly those who also suffer from substance dependence, prior to or immediately after booking into jail, underscores that psychological deficits exist for many offenders prior to incarceration. To date, the research on diversion from jail into the mental health system has revealed marginal success (Steadman and Naples 2005). Improved quality of services and coordination between the mental health and criminal justice systems, however, show promise for reducing economic costs and recidivism by directing individuals toward more appropriate avenues of care (Lamberti et al. 2001; Mire, Forsyth, and Hanser 2008).

The mental health issues revealed among jail inmates are not solely due to pre-existing conditions. Two findings from a small but telling set of studies suggest that institutionalization also contributes to mental health problems—the experience of going to jail has an independent effect on levels of psychological distress. First, several dimensions of mental distress symptoms increase following admission to jail. Gibbs (1987) and Lindquist and Lindquist (1997) present data showing that symptoms of depression, anxiety, psychoticism, somatization, general distress, and other mental disturbances are consistently higher after a person is in jail than they are for the period immediately preceding incarceration. Second, symptoms of a mental health disorder increase when inmates' needs exceed the supply of resources available in jail to meet those needs (Gibbs 1991; Lindquist and Lindquist 1997). Thus, the jail environment itself plays a role in the extent to which inmates experience mental health problems.

Some detainees do not find being in jail vastly stressful. Fleisher (1995) observed that the most marginalized street criminals in his ethnographic study frequently embraced going to jail as a convenient way to get access to needed housing, medical, and other services. Even though the jail offers something of a sanctuary for these offenders, the reliance on jail for support serves to maintain and exacerbate their separation from supportive social networks. Thus, while these street-level offenders may find jail to be a useful resource for meeting immediate needs, it provides a poor long-term solution.

Maintaining contact with people in the outside world can insulate inmates against the psychological distress of being arrested and held in jail. Families provide resources, information about life on the outside, and encouragement to participate in rehabilitative services (Hairston 1988). Inmates who are not visited by their families show greater feelings of loneliness, isolation, guilt, anger, and despair (Gordon and McConnell 1999; Wooldredge 1999). In addition to the ability of family members to assist inmates with financial, legal, employment, and other functional challenges, maintaining connections to family, especially to spouses and children, is among the most important concerns for recently incarcerated men and women (Weisheit and Klofas 1990; Hairston 1991). For inmates who are not released pretrial or are sentenced to jail, visitation is an important avenue for maintaining connections. Researchers have found, however, that many jails are hesitant to make information about visitation procedures available, and empirical evidence suggests that some jails' practices and policies impede inmate-family connections (Sturges 2002; Arditti 2003; Hairston 2004; Sturges and Hardesty 2005; Sitren et al. 2009).

V. Policy Implications and Future Research

The issues reviewed above suggest some new directions for policies on pretrial release and jails. They also reveal areas where additional research is needed. Below, four policy recommendations and several high-priority research issues are outlined.

A. Policy Recommendations

First, judges, pretrial services personnel, and other key actors should reconsider whether high rates of pretrial detention at the federal level are necessary. Overall release rates in the federal court system are 20 percentage points lower than in the state courts, and use of preventive detention is five times higher. Officials should look closely at whether the increasingly restrictive policies that led to this situation (Byrne and Stowell 2007) are necessary to secure community safety and the appearance of defendants at trial.

Second, drug testing should be eliminated as a component of pretrial release. Once other factors are taken into consideration, positive drug tests do not add to our ability to predict misconduct. Some might suggest that what is needed are better tests. Urinalysis, probably the most common method of testing pretrial releasees for drug use, cannot distinguish between one-time or occasional use versus dependence. It is the latter that appears to be the more important consideration (Lowenkamp et al. 2008). Better testing, however, is prohibitively expensive. Moreover, self-reported drug use is at least as good a predictor of misconduct as are tests, is less costly, and can be used to produce a detailed profile of current and past use and dependence (Belenko, Mara-Drita, and McElroy 1992). Understanding each defendant's pattern of drug and alcohol use could help to shift pretrial supervision from merely monitoring or surveillance of releasees to planning reformative interventions.

Third, jail planners and administrators should seek ways better to meet the psychological needs of inmates and should coordinate more fully with mental health providers for inmates with serious psychological problems. Some readers may balk at the suggestion that jails should be more supportive: Should they not be punitive? Several considerations counter this argument. Three in five jail inmates have not been convicted of a crime—they do not yet legally deserve punishment. Jail environments that meet inmates' needs can reduce maladaptive behavior (Gettinger 1984). Rates of suicide and self-injury could decline, and the research on new generation jails suggests that inmate misconduct might be reduced while realizing additional benefits for jail officers and facilities (Wener 2006). Further, more austere jail facilities do not result in lower recidivism once inmates are released (Applegate, Surette, and McCarthy 1999). Regarding severely mentally ill persons brought to jail, more concerted efforts to secure high-quality treatment could help break the cycle of arrest, temporary improvement in psychological functioning, decompensation, and re-arrest (Cox et al. 2001; Mire, Forsyth, and Hanser 2008).

Fourth, jails should seek ways to facilitate supportive and pro-social relationships between inmates and those outside jail. Some changes would be relatively simple, such as making visitation policies readily available to inmates and to their friends and family members. Other changes may require more effort, resources, and coordination with outside agencies. Although most of the recent attention on inmate re-entry has focused on prisons, scholars, practitioners, and policymakers have also begun to recognize that most jail inmates will return to the community (Solomon et al. 2008). Maintaining existing links with the outside world, forging new ties, and addressing the host of deficits faced by many jail inmates promise to ease this transition.

B. Future Research

A number of aspects of jails and pretrial release are ripe for additional research. Greater empirical analyses would not only enhance basic understanding of these institutions and the processes associated with them, but it would also result in further recommendations for criminal justice policy.

Recent work that has examined each decision point in the process of pretrial release—preventive detention, release on recognizance, setting of bail or other release conditions, setting of bail amount, and ultimately whether the defendant is released—adds substantially to our understanding of cumulative effects and the points at which the defendant's race matters (Demuth 2003; Demuth and Steffensmeier 2004). It would now be useful to examine narrower issues in more detail. Scholars should assess the determinants of who makes bail when it is set as a condition of release. In particular, the assumption that defendants who are held on bail cannot afford to pay should be subjected to empirical investigation. The importance of this work is highlighted by recent calls for expanded use of surety bond (Block

2005) and by the trend toward greater reliance on financial requirements as a condition of release (Cohen and Reaves 2007).

Other studies should determine the extent to which dimensions of community ties can account for racial, ethnic, and gender differences in release probabilities (Cohen and Reaves 2007). The salience of this work is twofold. First, it would reveal the extent to which disparities can be explained by legally relevant variables. Second, if community ties are related to the greater likelihood of pretrial detention among minorities and men, there is still the question of whether these legal factors are appropriate and necessary considerations. If they do not add substantially to predicting valid outcome concerns—failure to appear and re-arrest—an argument could be made that using them to make release decisions amounts to de facto discrimination.

A related line of research should examine pretrial misconduct. Aggregate-level studies seeking to explain differential rates of failure to appear and re-arrest across jurisdictions could be very enlightening. At the individual level, scholars should continue to seek better predictors of misconduct. As noted, the existing efforts have resulted in only a modest ability to classify defendants by risk. More rigorous experiments on the effects of supervision, such as those carried out by Goldkamp and White (2006), also should be included in this line of work.

An important part of the agenda for future research on jails would include efforts to understand their dramatic expansion since the early 1980s. Earlier in this essay, explanations for the high rate of incarceration in the United States were discussed. Jails, however, merit separate consideration. Several characteristics distinguish jails from prisons in potentially relevant ways. Most jails are locally administered; as a whole, they admit and release far more people each year; at any one time, they house less than half as many inmates; most of their inmates are held for a much shorter time; and more than half of their inmates are being held pretrial. Studies that look at how jails "fit" into the context of criminal justice operations and culture in local jurisdictions may be useful to understanding the size of the local incarceration enterprise (Welsh 1995; Davis et al. 2004). Taking a broader view, however, may be necessary to understand fully why jail growth over the past several decades was so dramatic and widespread.

Traditionally, jails have been stressful and dangerous for staff and inmates alike. New generation jail designs and operations hold promise for alleviating many of those problems for officers and inmates. The existing research shows equivocal results about the effects of new generation jails, but also reveals that principles of this innovation often have been only partially implemented. The available research, however, does not show whether fidelity of implementation conditions the effect of new generation jails, nor does it reveal which elements of new generation designs and operations are most critical. Researchers should design and carry out more rigorous analyses to address these issues.

Additional studies should be conducted on the effects of congruence between inmate needs and environmental resources to meet those needs. The existing work in this area is somewhat dated and is based on a single methodological approach (Gibbs 1991; Lindquist and Lindquist 1997). Scholars need to expand this work to encompass different jail environments, different types of inmates, and different ways of assessing inmates' concerns. How jails can be structured and operated to alleviate problems is a broad concern and fits well into the contemporary emphasis on offender re-entry. An eye should be turned toward assessing what approaches help to relieve deficits and develop competencies for successful re-entry to the community.

NOTES

1. The theoretical perspectives discussed here were derived from consideration of incarceration rates, combining prisons and jails. Jails are distinct in ways that may be relevant and may merit separate theoretical explanations for jail population growth.

2. Some jurisdictions have returned to billing sentenced jail inmates for incarceration. Klamath County in Oregon, for example, began charging $60 per day in 2003, though other jurisdictions typically charge lower fees (Loew 2009).

3. Although this federal law is well known, earlier legislation had already marked the turn toward concerns about danger. In 1970 Washington, DC, had passed a preventive detention law, and by 1984 more than half of the states had followed this lead (Walker 1993; also see Goldkamp 1985).

4. Most scholars imply that defendants held on bail are unable to pay the amount necessary to secure their release. While this interpretation likely is accurate in many cases, it is also possible that some defendants could "make bail" but choose not to do so. Additional data would be necessary to disentangle willingness to meet financial release conditions from financial ability.

5. The authors do not report the number of cases included in the logistic regression analysis, but risk classifications are reported for 172,515 of the 575,178 cases in the study.

REFERENCES

Abram, Karen M., and Linda A. Teplin. 1991. "Co-Occurring Disorders among Mentally Ill Jail Detainees: Implications for Public Policy." *American Psychologist* 46: 1036–45.

Administrative Office of the United States Courts. 2009. *2008 Annual Report of the Director: Judicial Business of the United States Courts.* Washington, DC: US Government Printing Office. http://www.uscourts.gov/judbususc/judbus.html.

Albonetti, Celesta A., Robert M. Hauser, John Hagan, and Ilene H. Nagel. 1989. "Criminal Justice Decision Making as a Stratification Process: The Role of Race and Stratification Resources in Pretrial Release." *Journal of Quantitative Criminology* 5: 57–82.

American Jail Association. 2007. *Who's Who in Jail Management*, 5th ed. Hagerstown, MD: American Jail Association.

Applegate, Brandon K., Raymond Surette, and Bernard J. McCarthy. 1999. "Detention and Desistance from Crime: Evaluating the Influence of a New Generation Jail on Recidivism." *Journal of Criminal Justice* 27: 539–48.

Applegate, Brandon K., and Eugene A. Paoline III. 2007. "Jail Officers' Perceptions of the Work Environment in Traditional Versus New Generation Facilities." *American Journal of Criminal Justice* 31: 64–80.

Arditti, Joyce. 2003. "Humanizing Family Visiting in Corrections Settings." *American Jails* 17, no. 5: 9–17.

Bayens, Gerald J., Jimmy J. Williams, and John O. Smykla. 1997. "Jail Type Makes a Difference: Evaluating the Transition From a Traditional to a Podular, Direct Supervision Jail Across Ten Years. *American Jails* 11, no. 2: 32–39.

Beck, Allen J., and Jennifer C. Karberg. 2001. *Prison and Jail Inmates at Midyear 2000.* Washington, DC: Bureau of Justice Statistics.

Beckett, Katherine. 1997. *Making Crime Pay: Law and Order in Contemporary American Politics.* New York: Oxford University Press.

Belenko, Steven, Iona Mara-Drita, and Jerome E. McElroy. 1992. "Drug Tests and the Prediction of Pretrial Misconduct: Findings and Policy Issues." *Crime and Delinquency* 38: 557–82.

Block, Michael K. 2005. "The Effectiveness and Cost of Secured and Unsecured Pretrial Release in California's Large Urban Counties: 1990–2000." Unpublished manuscript, University of Arizona. http://www.pretrial.org/AnalysisAndResearch/PublishedResearch/Pages/publishedresearch.aspx.

Borum, Randy, and Michelle Rand. 2000. "Mental Health Diagnostic and Treatment Services in Florida's Jails." *Journal of Correctional Health Care* 7: 189–207.

Byrne, James, and Jacob Stowell. 2007. "The Impact of the Federal Pretrial Services Act of 1982 on the Release, Supervision, and Detention of Pretrial Defendants." *Federal Probation* 71, no. 2: 31–38.

Cahalan, Margaret W., and Lee Anne Parsons. 1986. *Historical Corrections Statistics in the United States 1850–1984.* Washington, DC: Bureau of Justice Statistics.

Clark, John, and D. Alan Henry. 2003. *Pretrial Services Programming at the Start of the 21st Century: A Survey of Pretrial Services Programs.* Washington, DC: Bureau of Justice Assistance.

Cohen, Thomas H., and Brian A. Reaves. 2006. *Felony Defendants in Large Urban Counties 2002.* Washington, DC: Bureau of Justice Statistics.

Cohen, Thomas H., and Brian A. Reaves. 2007. *Pretrial Release of Felony Defendants in State Courts.* Washington, DC: Bureau of Justice Statistics.

Cox, Judith F., Pamela C. Morschauser, Steven Banks, and James L. Stone. 2001. "A Five-Year Population Study of Persons Involved in the Mental Health and Local Correctional Systems: Implications for Service Planning." *Journal of Behavioral Health Services and Research* 28: 177–87.

Cullen, Francis T., John Paul Wright, and Brandon K. Applegate. 1996. "Control in the Community: The Limits of Reform?" In *Choosing Correctional Options That Work: Defining the Demand and Evaluating the Supply*, ed. Alan T. Harland. Thousand Oaks, CA: Sage.

Davis, Robin King, Brandon K. Applegate, Charles W. Otto, Raymond Surette, and Bernard J. McCarthy. 2004. "Roles and Responsibilities: Analyzing Local Leaders' Views on Jail Crowding from a System Perspective." *Crime and Delinquency* 50: 458–82.

DeHart, Dana D., Hayden P. Smith, and Robert J. Kaminski. 2009. "Institutional Responses to Self-Injurious Behavior among Inmates." *Journal of Correctional Health Care* 15: 129–41.

Demuth, Stephen. 2003. "Racial and Ethnic Differences in Pretrial Release Decisions and Outcomes: A Comparison of Hispanic, Black, and White Felony Arrestees." *Criminology* 41: 873–907.

Demuth, Stephen, and Darrell Steffensmeier. 2004. "The Impact of Gender and Race-Ethnicity in the Pretrial Release Process." *Social Problems* 51: 222–42.

Farbstein, Jan, and Richard Wener. 1989. *A Comparison of "Direct" and "Indirect" Supervision of Correctional Facilities: Final Report*. Washington, DC: National Institute of Corrections.

Federal Judicial Center. 1993. *The Bail Reform Act of 1984* 2nd ed. Washington, DC: Federal Judicial Center.

Fishman, Joseph F. 1923. *Crucibles of Crime: The Shocking Story of the American Jail*. New York: Cosmopolis.

Fleisher, Mark S. 1995. *Beggars and Thieves: Lives of Urban Street Criminals*. Madison, WI: University of Wisconsin Press.

Free, Marvin D., Jr. 2002. "Race and Presentencing Decisions in the United States: A Summary and Critique of the Research." *Criminal Justice Review* 27: 203–32.

Garland, David. 2001. *Culture of Control: Crime and Social Order in Contemporary Society*. Chicago: University of Chicago Press.

Gettinger, Stephen H. 1984. *New Generation Jails: An Innovative Approach to an Age-Old Problem*. Washington, DC: National Institute of Corrections, US Department of Justice.

Gibbs, John J. 1982. "The First Cut is the Deepest: Psychological Breakdown and Survival in the Detention Setting." In *The Pains of Imprisonment*, ed. Robert Johnson and Hans Toch. Beverly Hills, CA: Sage.

Gibbs, John J. 1987. "Symptoms of Psychopathology among Jail Prisoners: The Effects of Exposure to the Jail Environment." *Criminal Justice and Behavior* 14: 288–310.

———. 1991. "Environmental Congruence and Symptoms of Psychopathology: A Further Exploration of the Effects of Exposure to the Jail Environment." *Criminal Justice and Behavior* 18: 351–74.

Gilliard, Darrell K. 1999. *Prison and Jail Inmates at Midyear 1998*. Washington, DC: Bureau of Justice Statistics.

Goldfarb, Ronald. 1965. *Ransom: A Critique of the American Jail System*. New York: Harper and Row.

Goldkamp, John S. 1979. *Two Classes of Accused: A Study of Bail and Detention in American Justice*. Cambridge, MA: Ballinger.

———. 1985. "Danger and Detention: A Second Generation of Bail Reform." *Journal of Criminal Law and Criminology* 76: 1–74.

Goldkamp, John S., and Michael R. Gottfredson. 1985. *Policy Guidelines for Bail: An Experiment in Court Reform*. Philadelphia: Temple University Press.

Goldkamp, John S., Michael R. Gottfredson, Peter R. Jones, and Doris Weiland. 1995. *Personal Liberty and Community Safety: Pretrial Release in the Criminal Court*. New York: Plenum.

Goldkamp, John S., and White, Michael D. 2006. "Restoring Accountability in Pretrial Release: The Philadelphia Pretrial Release Supervision Experiments." *Journal of Experimental Criminology* 2: 143–81.

Gordon, Jill, and Elizabeth McConnell. 1999. "Are Conjugal and Familial Visitations Effective Rehabilitative Concepts?" *Prison Journal* 79: 119–36.

Gottfredson, Michael R., and Denise M. Gottfredson. 1988. *Decision Making in Criminal Justice: Toward the Rational Exercise of Discretion.* 2nd ed. New York: Plenum.

Hairston, Creasie F. 1988. "Family Ties During Imprisonment: Do They Influence Future Criminal Activity?" *Federal Probation* 52, no. 1: 48–52.

———. 1991. "Mothers in Jail: Parent-Child Separation and Jail Visitation." *Journal of Women and Social Work* 6:9–38.

———. 2004. "Prisoners and Families: Parenting Issues during Incarceration." In *Prisoners Once Removed*, ed. Jeremy Travis and Michelle Waul. Washington, DC: Urban Institute Press.

Hart, Timothy C., and Brian A. Reaves. 1999. *Felony Defendants in Large Urban Counties 1996.* Washington, DC: Bureau of Justice Statistics.

Houston, James G., Don C. Gibbons, and Joseph F. Jones. 1988. "Physical Environment and Jail Social Climate." *Crime and Delinquency* 34: 449–66.

Irwin, John. 1985. *The Jail: Managing the Underclass in American Society.* Berkeley: University of California Press.

James, Doris J., and Lauren E. Glaze. 2006. *Mental Health Problems of Prison and Jail Inmates.* Washington, DC: Bureau of Justice Statistics.

Johnson, Robert, and Hans Toch, eds. 1982. *The Pains of Imprisonment.* Beverly Hills, CA: Sage.

Keller, Mark, and Hsiao-Ming Wang. 2005. "Inmate Assaults in Texas County Jails." *Prison Journal* 85: 515–34.

Kyckelhahn, Tracey, and Thomas H. Cohen. 2008. *Felony Defendants in Large Urban Counties 2004.* Washington, DC: Bureau of Justice Statistics.

Lamb, H. Richard, and Linda E. Weinberger. 1998. "Persons with Severe Mental Illness in Jails and Prisons: A Review." *Psychiatric Services* 49: 483–92.

Lamberti, J. Steven, Robert L. Weisman, Steven B. Schwarzkopf, Nancy Price, Rudo M. Ashton, and John Trompeter. 2001. "The Mentally Ill in Jails and Prisons: Towards an Integrated Model of Prevention." *Psychiatric Quarterly* 72: 63–77.

Lindquist, Christine H., and Charles A. Lindquist. 1997. "Gender Differences in Distress: Mental Health Consequences of Environmental Stress among Jail Inmates." *Behavioral Sciences and the Law* 15: 503–23.

Lowenkamp, Christopher T., Robert Lemke, and Edward Latessa. 2008. "The Development and Validation of a Pretrial Screening Tool." *Federal Probation* 72, no. 3: 2–9.

Loew, Tracy. 2009. "Debt to Society Costs $60 a Night." *USA Today*, May 28, 1A.

Mattick, Hans. 1974. "The Contemporary Jails of the United States: An Unknown and Neglected Area of Justice." In *Handbook of Criminology*, ed. Daniel Glaser. Chicago: Rand McNally.

Maxwell, Sheila R. 1999. "Examining the Congruence Between Predictors of ROR and Failures to Appear." *Journal of Criminal Justice* 27: 127–41.

McConville, Sean. 1995. "Local Justice: The Jail." In *The Oxford History of the Prison: The Practice of Punishment in Modern Society*, ed. Norval Morris and David J. Rothman. New York: Oxford University Press.

Minton, Todd, and William J. Sabol. 2009. *Jail Inmates at Midyear 2008—Statistical Tables.* Washington, DC: Bureau of Justice Statistics.

Mire, Scott, Craig J. Forsyth, and Robert Hanser. 2008. "Jail Diversion: Addressing the Needs of Offenders with Mental Illness and Co-Occurring Disorders." *Journal of Offender Rehabilitation* 45: 19–31.

Moynahan, James M., and Earle K. Stewart. 1980. *The American Jail: Its Development and Growth*. Chicago: Nelson-Hall.

Mumola, Christopher J. 2005. *Suicide and Homicide in State Prisons and Local Jails*. Washington, DC: Bureau of Justice Statistics.

National Institute of Justice. 2003. *2000 Arrestee Drug Abuse Monitoring: Annual Report*. Washington, DC: National Institute of Justice.

Nelson, W. Raymond, and Russell M. Davis. 1995. "Podular Direct Supervision: The First Twenty Years." *American Jails* 9, no. 3: 11–22.

Perkins, Craig A., James J. Stephan, and Allen J. Beck. 1995. *Jails and Jail Inmates 1993–94*. Washington, DC: Bureau of Justice Statistics.

Petee, Thomas A. 1994. "Recommended for Release on Recognizance: Factors Affecting Pretrial Release Recommendations." *Journal of Social Psychology* 134: 375–82.

Rainville, Gerard, and Brian A. Reaves. 2003. *Felony Defendants in Large Urban Counties 2000*. Washington, DC: Bureau of Justice Statistics.

Reaves, Brian A. 2001. *Felony Defendants in Large Urban Counties 1998*. Washington, DC: Bureau of Justice Statistics.

Rhodes, William, Raymond Hyatt, and Paul Scheiman. 1996. "Predicting Pretrial Misconduct with Drug Tests of Arrestees: Evidence from Eight Settings." *Journal of Quantitative Criminology* 12: 315–48.

Roberts, Julian V., Loretta J. Stalans, David Indermauer, and Michael Hough. 2002. *Penal Populism and Public Opinion: Lessons from Five Countries*. New York: Oxford University Press.

Rothman, David J. 1971. *The Discovery of the Asylum: Order and Disorder in the New Republic*. Boston, MA: Little, Brown.

Sabol, William J., Todd Minton, and Margaret Noonan. 2009. "Recent Findings from the Bureau of Justice Statistics on Local Jails." Presented at the annual conference of the American Jail Association, Louisville, KY, April 28.

Scalia, John. 1999. *Federal Pretrial Release and Detention 1996*. Washington, DC: Bureau of Justice Statistics.

Schlesinger, Traci. 2007. "The Cumulative Effects of Racial Disparities in Criminal Processing." *Journal of the Institute of Justice and International Studies* 7: 261–78.

Senese, Jeffrey D. 1997. "Evaluating Jail Reform: A Comparative Analysis of Podular/Direct and Linear Jail Inmate Infractions." *Journal of Criminal Justice* 25: 61–73.

Siddiqi, Qudsia. 2009. *Predicting the Likelihood of Pretrial Failure to Appear and/or Rearrest for a Violent Offense Among New York City Defendants: An Analysis of the 2001 Dataset*. New York: New York City Criminal Justice Agency, Inc. http://www.nycja.org/research/research.htm.

Sitren, Alicia H., Hayden P. Smith, Brandon K. Applegate, and Laurie A. Gould. 2009. "Jail Visitation: An Assessment of Organizational Policy and Information Availability." *Southwest Journal of Criminal Justice* 5: 207–20.

Snell, Tracy L. 1995. *Correctional Populations in the United States 1993*. Washington, DC: Bureau of Justice Statistics.

Solomon, Amy L., Jenny W. L. Osborne, Stefan F. LoBuglio, Jeff Mellow, and Debbie A. Mukamal. 2008. *Life After Lockup: Improving Reentry from Jail to the Community*. Washington, DC: Urban Institute. http://www.urban.org.

Steadman, Henry J., and Michelle Naples. 2005. "Assessing the Effectiveness of Jail Diversion Programs for Persons with Serious Mental Illness and Co-Occurring Substance Use Disorders." *Behavioral Sciences and the Law* 23: 163–70.

Steffensmeier, Darrell, Jeffery Ulmer, and John Kramer. 1998. "The Interaction of Race, Gender, and Age in Criminal Sentencing: The Punishment Cost of Being Young, Black, and Male." *Criminology* 36: 763–98.

Steiner, Benjamin. 2009. "The Effects of Juvenile Transfer to Criminal Court on Incarceration Decisions." *Justice Quarterly* 26: 77–106.

Stohr, Mary K., and Craig Hemmens, eds. 2004. *The Inmate Prison Experience*. Upper Saddle River, NJ: Prentice-Hall.

Sturges, Judith E. 2002. "Visitation at County Jails: Potential Policy Implications." *Criminal Justice Policy Review* 13: 32–45.

Sturges, Judith E., and Katherine N. Hardesty. 2005. "Survey of Pennsylvania Jail Wardens: An Examination of Visitation Policies within the Context of Ecosystem Theory." *Criminal Justice Review* 30: 141–54.

Sykes, Gresham. 1958. *The Society of Captives*. Princeton, NJ: Princeton University Press.

Tartaro, Christine. 2002a. "Examining Implementation Issues with New Generation Jails." *Criminal Justice Policy Review* 13: 219–37.

——. 2002b. "The Impact of Density on Jail Violence." *Journal of Criminal Justice* 30:499–510.

——. 2006. "Watered Down: Partial Implementation of the New Generation Jail Philosophy." *Prison Journal* 86: 284–300.

Thomas, Jim, Margaret Leaf, Steve Kazmierczak, and Josh Stone. 2006. "Self-Injury in Correctional Settings: "Pathology" of Prisons or of Prisoners?" *Criminology and Public Policy* 5: 193–202.

Thomas, Wayne H. 1976. *Bail Reform in America*. Berkeley, CA: University of California Press.

Tonry, Michael. 2004. *Thinking About Crime: Sense and Sensibility in American Penal Culture*. New York: Oxford University Press.

Tonry, Michael. 2008. "Crime and Human Rights—How Political Paranoia, Protestant Fundamentalism, and Constitutional Obsolescence Combined to Devastate Black America: The American Society of Criminology 2007 Presidential Address." *Criminology* 46: 1–34.

Turner, K. B., and James B. Johnson. 2005. "A Comparison of Bail Amounts for Hispanics, Whites, and African Americans: A Single County Analysis." *American Journal of Criminal Justice* 30: 35–53.

VanNostrand, Marie, and Gina Keebler. 2009. *Pretrial Risk Assessment in the Federal Court*. Washington, DC: Office of the Federal Detention Trustee.

Vera Institute of Justice. 2004. *A Short History of Vera's Work on the Judicial Process*. New York: Vera Institute of Justice.

Walker, Samuel. 1993. *Taming the System: The Control of Discretion in Criminal Justice 1950–1990*. New York: Oxford University Press.

Weisheit, Ralph A., and John M. Klofas. 1990. "The Impact of Jail: Collateral Costs and Affective Response." *Journal of Offender Counseling, Services and Rehabilitation* 14: 51–65.

Welsh, Wayne N. 1995. *Counties in Court: Jail Overcrowding and Court-Ordered Reform*. Philadelphia: Temple University Press.

Wener, Richard. 2005. "The Invention of Direct Supervision." *Corrections Compendium* 30, no. 2: 4–7, 32–34.

——. 2006. "Effectiveness of the Direct Supervision System of Correctional Design and Management: A Review of the Literature." *Criminal Justice and Behavior* 33: 392–410.

Wener, Richard, William Frazier, and Jay Farbstein. 1985. "Three Generations of Evaluation and Design of Correctional Facilities." *Environment and Behavior* 17: 71–95.

Wener, Richard, and R. Olsen. 1980. "Innovative Correctional Environments: A User Assessment." *Environment and Behavior* 12: 478–93.

Williams, James L., Daniel G. Rodeheaver, and Denise W. Huggins. 1999. "A Comparative Evaluation of a New Generation Jail." *American Journal of Criminal Justice* 23: 223–46.

Wooldredge, John. 1999. "Inmate Experiences and Psychological Well-Being." *Criminal Justice and Behavior* 26: 235–51.

Yocum, Rich, Jon Anderson, Teresa Da Vigo, and Shawn Lee. 2006. "Direct-Supervision and Remote-Supervision Jails: A Comparative Study of Psychosocial Factors." *Journal of Applied Social Psychology* 36: 1790–812.

Young, Myla H., Jerald V. Justice, and Philip Erdberg. 2006. "Risk of Harm: Inmates Who Harm Themselves While in Prison Psychiatric Treatment." *Journal of Forensic Sciences* 51: 152–56.

Zupan, Linda L. 1991. *Jails: Reform and the New Generation Philosophy*. Cincinnati, OH: Anderson.

Zupan, Linda L., and Ben A. Menke. 1988. "Implementing Organizational Change: From Traditional to New Generation Jail Operations." *Policy Studies Review* 7: 615–25.

Zupan, Linda L., and Mary K. Stohr-Gillmore. 1988. "Doing Time in the New Generation Jail: Inmate Perceptions of Gains and Losses." *Policy Studies Review* 7: 626–40.

CHAPTER 26

PROBATION AND COMMUNITY PENALTIES

STAN C. PROBAND

PROBATION is an improbable stepchild of modern American correctional systems. Its traditional function of providing support and services for offenders was out of step with the politicization of criminal justice policymaking that began in the mid-1970s and that movement's emphasis on continual increases in the severity of punishment and its lack of sympathy with the plights or interests of convicted offenders.

Probation nonetheless remains the most common form of correctional supervision. Well over half of sentenced offenders, over four million at any one time in recent years, are under the control of probation agencies. More than two million people are sentenced to probation each year, and more than two million are discharged. Most complete their sentences successfully. Only about one-sixth are imprisoned for new crimes or breaches of probation conditions. Many of the latter have violated only technical conditions such as by not appearing for a scheduled meeting or failing a drug test.

Supporters have in recent decades repeatedly tried to reinvigorate probation and to strengthen its role and its standing, both because they believe in its mission to help offenders put their offenses behind them, and because they believe imprisonment is harmful and should be used only as a last resort. A wide range of new or expanded sanctions, including intensive forms of probation, house arrest, electronic monitoring, community service, day fines, and boot camps,[1] were established beginning in the 1970s. Some have survived. Some have not. Few are used primarily as they were intended to be used—as alternatives to imprisonment. Most are instead used mostly for offenders who would not otherwise have been sent to prison. Those who are sentenced to newer community penalties are often supervised so closely that many breaches of conditions are identified, and many of those in breach are then sent to prison when the community penalty is revoked. The more punitive attitudes of recent decades have affected probation as they have affected other criminal justice institutions. Probation's traditional helping mission has been contrary to the temper of the times.

There may be hope for probation's future. Concern for offenders' well-being, and greater flexibilities in dealing with them, have been re-entering the criminal justice system, most notably through the prisoner re-entry and drug court movements. Both focus on preventing re-offending rather than on helping offenders, but both aim to address offenders' human and social needs in order to strengthen their capacities for living conventional, law-abiding lives. Re-entry programs often target social services and treatment programs on offenders' deficits. Drug courts have generally rejected zero-tolerance approaches and view relapses as almost inevitable human failings, and thus part of any long-term recovery. Think of nicotine addiction, alcoholism, or obesity as parallels. Almost no one stops smoking, overcomes alcohol's call, or radically alters eating habits in one go or in several.

A number of generalizations can be offered:

- Probation is by far the most frequently imposed criminal sanction.
- Only one-sixth of probationers are sent to prison for new crimes or for breaches of technical conditions.
- Most "new" community penalties have failed to operate as alternatives to imprisonment.
- Probation agencies more than other corrections agencies have suffered in recent decades from a fall in standing and insufficient resources.
- The social work ethos of probation that was dominant before 1975 has in large part been supplanted by a tougher law enforcement ethos, partly because probation personnel have been affected by general cultural changes and have become more punitive in their views, partly because agencies have attempted to adapt their missions to accord with prevailing attitudes, and partly because of changing recruitment patterns.

The following discussion of probation and community penalties is organized in four sections.[2] The first provides a brief history of the evolution of probation since 1970. The second discusses the scale of probation. Whether or not it is fashionable, it is frequently imposed. The third section offers a brief survey of knowledge concerning the effectiveness of community penalties in widespread use. The fourth discusses possible futures for probation.

I. A BRIEF HISTORY OF PROBATION, 1970–2010

Probation and probation agencies have been more affected by changes in the politics of crime control in the United States in the past forty years than any other component of the criminal justice system. Policing strategies have been characterized by a shift away from a professional model of policing to incorporate newer conceptions of community and problem-solving policing, and have incorporated new technologies and methods, but the core mission is still understood to be to prevent, investigate, and otherwise respond to crime. Prosecutors and judges have been affected by the shift away from individualized and indeterminate sentencing, and the ensuing guidelines, mandatory penalties, and greater severity in punishment. However, the core mission continues to be prosecute and try alleged offenders, and to determine appropriate punishments. Prisons have decreased investment in treatment and training programs and personnel, but the core mission continues to be to hold inmates in safe and appropriately secure conditions until their sentences have expired. Parole agencies, although their authority has been reduced and they have become more risk-averse about releasing eligible inmates from prison, retain as their core missions release of selected prison inmates before expiration of their sentences, supervision of those released, and revocation of parole of those who have misbehaved.[3] Important details have changed, but the day-to-day activities of individual police, prosecutors, judges, prison officials, and parole board members were little different in 2010 than they had been in 1970, or in the fifty years before that.[4]

Probation is different.[5] Its mission and ethos changed. In 1970, probation had four core functions. The first was provision of social services and sympathetic support to help probationers obtain services, find jobs, and lay foundations for future lives as law-abiding citizens. The second was to prepare presentence investigation reports to be considered by judges in determining appropriately individualized sentences in individual cases.

The third was to allow judges sometimes to impose sentences that were punitive in form but not in substance. Criminal convictions should be followed by punishments, but some offenders are highly unlikely to re-offend and have no need for social services. Offenders would be sentenced to purely nominal supervision and otherwise be allowed to get on with their lives. The late Norval Morris used to describe this function as appearing to do something while doing nothing.[6]

The fourth was sometimes to respond to probationers' failures to observe probation conditions, including by committing new crimes, by initiating proceedings for revocation of probation, and by imposition of a different sentence by the judge.

Because the primary aim was provision of social welfare services, probation offices often saw themselves as being as much or more social welfare than criminal justice agencies. Professional probation officers often were trained social workers.

Many individual probation officers and officials had earlier in their lives attended seminaries with the intention of being clergymen. The prevailing ethos was one of provision of social welfare services to troubled people. The systems of individualized, indeterminate sentencing that were ubiquitous in the United States from 1930 to 1975 (Rothman 1981) were sometimes said to reflect a "rehabilitative ideal." Probation systems dealt with vastly larger numbers of offenders than did prisons and jails, and thus were meant to be the primary agents of rehabilitation.

The preceding description is, of course, idealized. In a country then and now lacking a well-developed social welfare system for its general population, sufficient resources were seldom available for probation officers to provide the support and services they believed offenders needed. This is hardly surprising: a political culture in which disadvantaged law-abiding people are not assured adequate housing, minimum income, or state-supported drug treatment or mental health service is unlikely to be a place where those resources are adequately provided for offenders. In retrospect, it is clear that rehabilitative know-how often was lacking. Personnel also often fell far short of the ideal. The Federal Probation Service in many places was highly professional and hired people with appropriate training. This was true in some states also, especially in California, Minnesota, and Wisconsin. However, in other states, probation systems were fragmented, and in many places probation officers worked for and were hired by local court systems. This meant that officers often were hired for reasons primarily of political patronage or personal connections, and many lacked relevant professional training and background. The social work ethos nonetheless was important, and many departments and officers struggled to provide probationers the support they believed was needed.

The social work ethos did not disappear after 1975, but the primary emphasis shifted from service provision to surveillance, for three important reasons. The "Nothing Works" movement, symbolized by that interpretation of Robert Martinson's famous article "What Works? Questions and Answers about Prison Reform," led to a decrease in investment in treatment services and programs. Martinson did not conclude that "nothing works." He instead concluded that the findings of evaluation research, much of it methodologically weak, did not justify a conclusion that rehabilitative correctional services could be shown to be effective at reducing recidivism. That conclusion is not incompatible with the existence of effective programs, with the possibility that better-designed evaluations would show that some programs are effective (as has since been shown to be true), or with the possibility that some probation services improve probationers' lives and social functioning irrespective of whether they reduce recidivism. Nonetheless, the rhetorical question in Martinson's title, coupled with his discouraging conclusions, almost invited a general view that nothing works.[7]

The second reason probation changed is that prevailing sensibilities and political attitudes changed. Criminal justice issues moved from the fringes of American politics to the center. Partly as a result, rehabilitation fell from favor as a primary objective and was replaced by retribution and crime prevention.

The politicization of American criminal justice policy began with an emphasis on "crime in the streets" by Barry Goldwater, the unsuccessful Republican presidential candidate in 1964 (Weaver 2007; Lowndes 2008). By the late 1970s and for the following twenty years, "law and order" became one of the two or three most effective partisan issues in American politics, with Republican and conservative candidates regularly accusing judges and parole boards of "leniency" and calling for more use of imprisonment and longer sentences (Edsall and Edsall 1991; Black and Black 2002). The law-and-order movement found its guiding intellectual voice in James Q. Wilson's *Thinking about Crime* (1975). Wilson observed that the criminal justice system lacked the resources or capacity to rehabilitate criminals or to address the root causes of crime. He urged instead that near-exclusive attention be given to preventing crime and victimization, and that primary strategic emphasis be given to deterrence and incapacitation. Between the mid-1970s and mid-1990s, policymakers responded with a plethora of "tough-on-crime" legislation, including parole abolition, mandatory penalty, truth-in-sentencing, three-strikes, and life-without-possibility-of-parole laws. The imprisonment rate increased by a factor of five after 1973, rising from 160 per 100,000 population to nearly 800 in 2011. During some years in the 1970s and 1980s, and occasionally afterwards, public opinion surveys showed that crime, drugs, or both were among the public policy issues that most worried citizens. More than 80 percent of citizens in many years expressed the belief that judges were too lenient.

The third reason probation changed radically is that the first two developments altered the financial, cultural, and political environment within which it operated. Prisons and jails are much more expensive to operate than probation departments, and the number of prisoners increased by eight to ten times after 1973 (more than the imprisonment rate because the national population increased substantially). Numerous lawsuits in federal courts about the deleterious effects on inmates of overcrowded prisons forced states greatly to increase the number of prisons. In legislative battles over budget priorities, unfashionable probation lost out to politically popular prisons.

Probation department budgets were undermined by the effects of the Nothing Works movement. If rehabilitative programs are ineffective, why spend money on them or allocate scarce resources to running them?

Probation departments were also affected to a major extent by the changed criminal justice logic that James Q. Wilson represented. Because probationers as a legal matter are not ordinary autonomous citizens but are technically in a form of state custody, many constitutional criminal procedure protections do not apply to them. Most notably, probation officers can make unannounced visits to probationers' homes, and may search them without obtaining a search warrant. When criminal justice emphasis shifted from rehabilitation to deterrence and incapacitation, to many people it seemed natural that probation officers would become more akin to police officers and act aggressively to monitor offenders who might reoffend. This logic led in many states to passage of legislation authorizing probation officers to carry firearms. In some places it led to creation of joint probation-police operations in which police, who cannot ordinarily search private residences without warrants issued by judges, could take advantage of probation officers' powers and conduct warrantless searches.

Finally, the attitudes of many probation officers changed. In a time when few people were especially sympathetic to offenders' interests, and most supported harsh anti-crime policies, many probation officers felt or came to feel the same way and willingly collaborated in probation's change in emphasis (Tonry 1991). Probation recruitment also changed as its social work ethos weakened and probation officers' functions grew closer to those of police officers. Social workers and former seminary students less often became probation officers. Increasing numbers came from law enforcement backgrounds or were graduates of criminal justice programs. New generations of probation officers, whatever their backgrounds, were socialized into professional cultures that emphasized surveillance, offender compliance with conditions, and crime prevention over provision of social services. One stark sign of this was a difference in attitudes and practices concerning new minor crimes or indications of drug use. In earlier times, many probation officers would often have seen such occurrences as signs the probationer was having problems and needed more help, or as temporary lapses by a probationer who was generally successfully rebuilding a conventional life, and elected not to initiate revocation proceedings or to bring the apparent offense to police attention. Such attitudes became much less common in the 1980s and 1990s, resulting in much higher levels of revocation.[8]

People who believed in probation's service ethos, or who believed that too many minor offenders were being sent to prison initially or following revocations, did not give up. One sign of this was a succession of efforts to reinvent probation under new names. In the 1970s, many new restitution and community service programs and more intensive forms of supervision were initiated under the rubric "alternatives to correction." Evaluations also showed—a finding that recurred in community penalty evaluations for the following twenty years—that judges seldom sentenced people to the new programs who would otherwise have been sent to prison but used them instead for people who otherwise would have received a less demanding probation sentence. The new programs simply were not considered by judges, prosecutors, and many elected officials to be punitive enough to serve as appropriate alternatives to imprisonment (Morris and Tonry 1990).

The reformers' solution was partly semantic—to use a term, "intermediate sanctions" or "intermediate punishments" that sounded more punitive—and partly substantive. New sanctions were developed—house arrest, electronic monitoring, boot camps, intensive forms of probation—which were more intrusive and punitive. Proponents hoped this would lead judges to see them as punitive and use them in place of prison sentences. Evaluations generally showed the new programs to be no less effective than prison at reducing recidivism and less expensive if run well, but also that judges tended once again to use them as harsher sentences for people who otherwise would have been sentenced to probation rather than as substitutes for imprisonment. And, the punitive attitudes of the time often resulted in high revocation rates, which undermined achievement of the goal of reducing prison use. The intermediate sanctions efforts succeeded in making sentences supervised by probation officers more punitive, but not in reducing re-offending or diverting large numbers of people from prison (Morris and Tonry 1990; Petersilia and Turner 1993).

And so "community penalties," part of the title of this article. The semantic logic of "intermediate punishments" failed to legitimate non-incarcerative sentences in practitioners' and policymakers' minds any more successfully than "alternatives to incarceration" had. At day's end, only prison sentences were seen as sufficiently punitive to be used for nontrivial crimes. Community penalties is descriptive and does not carry the stigma of "leniency" that bedeviled probation in the 1970s and does to this day.

II. The Scale of Probation

Probation may not be a fashionable sentencing option, but it is by far the most common. On December 31, 2008, probationers constituted 4, 271,000 of the 7,308,000 people held in jails or state and federal prisons, or supervised by probation or parole agencies. Nearly 2 percent of the American population was on probation. The number of probationers increased at a rate of 1.4 percent a year between 2000 and 2008. The 400,000 increase during those years slightly exceeded the 370,000 increase in the number of people behind bars.

Figure 26.1 shows total numbers of people under control of the four correctional institutions since 1980. Crime rates in America have been falling since 1991, but that has had no effect on the numbers of people under justice system control. Probation numbers have increased vastly more in absolute and rate-of-increase terms than have parole populations. There are many fewer parolees in absolute numbers because they have by definition been released from custodial institutions, and almost all parole programs deal only with prison populations (few people are paroled from local jails). The lower rate of growth for parole is attributable to abolition of parole release altogether in some American jurisdictions, by passage in the federal system and more than half of the states of "truth-in-sentencing" laws that require many prisoners to serve at least 85 percent of their nominal sentences, and by increased risk averseness in recent decades of parole boards, which have released proportionately many fewer eligible prisoners than in earlier times and have released them later in their terms.

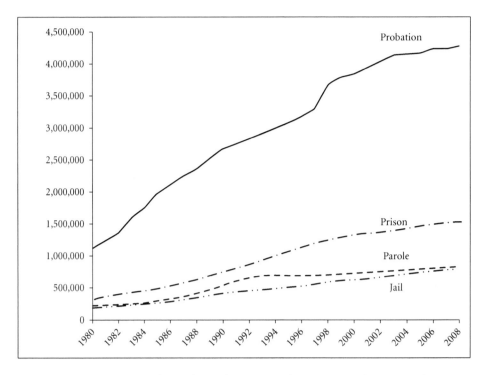

Figure 26.1. Annual Numbers of Persons under Sentence of Prison, Jail, Probation, or Parole 1980–2008

Sources: Sourcebook of Criminal Justice Statistics, table 6.1 (Bureau of Justice Statistics 2006, http://albany.edu/sourcebook/csv/t612006.csv); *Probation and Parole in the United States 2008* (Glaze, Bonczar, and Cooper 2009).

Correctional population trends are shown in a different way in table 26.1. It shows the numbers of people under control of the four correctional institutions in 1990, 2000, and 2008, together with the percentage increases in each over time. The probation population has increased by nearly 60 percent since 1990. The percentage increases have been greater for jail and prison inmates, but in absolute numbers almost twice as many people are on probation as are in confinement.

Probationers are whiter and more female than prison and jail inmates. Fifty-six percent of probationers in 2008 were non-Hispanic white, 29 percent were non-Hispanic black, and 13 percent were Hispanic.[9] Among prisoners, barely a third were non-Hispanic white, 38 percent were non-Hispanic black, and 20 percent were Hispanic.[10] Twenty-four percent of probationers were women, compared with only 7 percent of prisoners.

The reasons for the gender difference between prisoners and probationers are well understood. Women commit many fewer serious crimes than do men, and accordingly are less often sent to prison. In addition, all else being equal, female offenders are less often sentenced to imprisonment than male offenders, and for shorter terms.[11]

Table 26.1. Change Over Time in Number of Persons Under Custody of Probation, Parole, Prison or Jail, 1990–2008

Year	Probation	Parole	Jail	Prison
1990	2,670,234	531,407	405,320	743,382
2000	3,826,209	723,898	621,149	1,316,333
2008	4,207,917	828,169	785,556	1,518,559
Change from 1990–2008	59.9 percent	55.8 percent	93.8 percent	104.3 percent

Sources: Bureau of Justice Statistics, Sourcebook of Criminal Justice Statistics. 2006. "Adults on probation, in jail or prison, and on parole United States, 1980–2006, Table 6.1." Washington D.C.: U.S. Department of Justice, U.S. Government Printing Office. Glaze, Lauren E., Thomas P. Bonczar, and Matthew S. Cooper. 2009. *Probation and Parole in the United States 2008*. Washington D.C.: U.S. Department of Justice, U.S. Government Printing Office.

The reasons for the stark racial and ethnicity differences are equally well known but are more contentious. To some degree, blacks and Hispanics commit relatively more violent crimes than whites, which explains part of the disparity in imprisonment. However, other major factors are racial profiling by police, the effects of conscious and unconscious bias against black offenders, the "War on Drugs" emphasis on arrests of inner-city, street-level drug dealers, and sentencing laws that punish offenses more often committed by blacks and Hispanics especially severely (Tonry and Melewski 2008; Spohn, chap. 11, this volume).

Probation sentences are mostly imposed for minor offenses. Only 19 percent of probationers in 2008 had been convicted of violent crimes. Twenty-five percent were convicted of property crimes, 29 percent of drug crimes, and most of the rest of low-level, public order offenses.[12]

The huge absolute and steadily increasing numbers of probationers are partly attributable to a way of thinking that undergirds the failure of the alternatives to incarceration and intermediate punishments initiatives of the 1970s and 1980s–90s. Throughout the period beginning in 1970, data systems and most operating agencies have continued to classify all non-incarcerative punishments under the common term "probation." In practice, many offenders who are sentenced to pay a fine are sentenced to probation with the condition that they pay the fine. People sentenced to community service, house arrest, community-based drug treatment, and electronic monitoring receive those sanctions as conditions of probation. All are classified as probationers. Other countries' legal systems count their sentenced populations in terms of different punishments. The four large Scandinavian countries, for example, report sentence data separately for prison sentences, suspended prison sentences, probation, community service, fines, treatment programs, and various combinations (Lappi-Seppälä 2007, table 9).

The American pattern of counting everything but prison or post-prison (parole) as probation may offer a clue as to why newer community sanctions such as house arrest and community service did not catch on as prison alternatives. If probation is by many considered per se to be "lenient," other sanctions considered to be forms of probation were likely tarred with the same brush. Hawken and Kleiman (2009, 8) express this in commenting on probation sentences: "[I]t is common for offenders and officials alike to treat a probation sentence as representing something less than actual punishment. That limits the value of probation as a sanction, leading to the possible incarceration of offenders who might otherwise be well-managed under community supervision."

Most probationers serve short terms, often less than a year. This is because nearly half of those on probation at any one time have been convicted of misdemeanors. Turnover is enormous. In 2008, 2,370,000 people began probation sentences, and 2,340,000 completed them. Of those, 63 percent did so satisfactorily, 10 percent were "unsatisfactory" (often because a fine had not been paid), and 17 percent had been sent to prison following either revocation of probation or conviction of a new offense. By contrast, among people exiting parole sentences in 2008, only 49 percent successfully completed their terms satisfactorily, 25 percent were re-imprisoned following revocations, 9 percent were imprisoned following new convictions, and 11 percent absconded (Glaze and Bonczar 2009, tables 3, 5).

High rates of breach of parole conditions should not be surprising, especially in recent years. Lower breach rates for probationers are also not surprising as they typically deal with less serious offenses and less chronic offenders. Most serious and chronic offenders come from socially and economically disadvantaged segments of the population, lack work skills and family support systems, and have poor job prospects. These are the characteristics that in every country are associated with offending and lower-than-average ability to conform to bureaucratic expectations. Breaches can consist of a wide range of actions including failing to attend a scheduled meeting with a probation officer, failing a drug test, and committing a new crime. Whether breaches are acted upon depends on the individual officer. In a time when the probation ethos has shifted from service provision to surveillance, officers are much more likely than in earlier times to initiate revocations when breaches occur, and to initiate revocations on the basis of actions (e.g., failing to attend a meeting) that are not criminal.

An evaluation report on Project Hope, a well-known community penalty program in Hawaii, provides an illustration of this mind-set: "Under HOPE, offenders who violate the terms of probation are immediately arrested and are brought before a judge. . . . Under HOPE *every* positive drug test and every missed probation appointment is met with a sanction" (Hawken and Kleiman 2009, 9). Were that the policy throughout the United States, parole revocation rates would be even higher than they are, and probation revocation rates would increase dramatically.

III. Varieties of Probation and Community Penalties

Surprisingly little research on probation has been done in recent years. Much the best and most comprehensive overview (Petersilia 1997), published more than a decade ago, remains the best depiction of what probation officers do. Many evaluations of alternatives to corrections and intermediate sanctions appeared in the 1980s and early 1990s, many funded by the U.S. Department of Justice. Their results are summarized in Tonry and Lynch (1996), Sherman et al. (2002), and MacKenzie (2006). Since then, most research on community corrections programs has focused on re-entry programs for released inmates (see Petersilia, chap. 30, this volume) or on classification of offenders for risk (see Cullen and Smith, chap. 6, this volume). Because the literature on the effectiveness of particular kinds of community sanctions is now familiar, this section begins by describing probation officers' core activities and then briefly describes the classic work on widely available sanctions.

A. Pre-sentence Investigation Reports

During the era of indeterminate sentencing that ended in the mid-1970s, preparation of pre-sentence investigation reports (PSIs) in individual cases was a core activity of probation officers (e.g., Clear, Clear, and Burrell 1988). Judges were expected to individualize sentences in individual cases to take account of the causes of the offender's behavior, rehabilitative needs, and unusual risks of re-offending. The judges lacked sufficient knowledge of the offender's life and circumstances to make that possible. It was the probation officer's job to dig up the information for the judge and often to recommend what should be done.

Probation officers still prepare PSIs, but much less often in earlier times. Partly this results from the change of ethos. If sentencing's aim is not primarily rehabilitative but is instead expected to make sentences proportionate to the offender's culpability, then judges do not need detailed biographical information on the offender's life. This results partly from the adoption of sentencing guidelines and mandatory penalty laws that limit judges' discretion and partly from the reality that 95–98 percent of offenders plead guilty, usually with an understanding of what the sentence will be. PSIs remain an important probation activity, but a much less central one than in earlier times (Petersilia 1997).

B. Nominal Probation

One core function of probation has long been to give the appearance of doing something punitive to minor offenders while doing nothing at all, or very little. The change of the governing probation ethos makes it less likely that probation officers would simply let probationers alone. More punitive attitudes mean that officers more often monitor probationers to make sure they are not violating technical conditions. Some probation offices do, however, recognize a category of probationers who require no or nominal supervision and allow them to serve their terms without supervision or subject only to the condition that they send in a postcard or make a phone call every few months to verify their whereabouts (Petersilia 1997).

Doing little or nothing makes sense for many minor offenders in any case. It is a waste of resources to supervise people closely who present no significant risks to the community. This may be why national probation caseload statistics typically show that 8–9 percent of the caseload is "inactive" (Glaze and Bonczar 2009, table A5).

In many European countries, the suspended prison sentence—the functional equivalent of nominal probation—is one of the most frequently imposed punishments (Weigend 2001 [Germany]; Lappi-Seppälä 2001, 2007 [Denmark, Finland, Norway, Sweden]). The logic is that being charged and convicted are disturbing and stigmatizing experiences, and by themselves constitute a considerable burden for a citizen to bear.

C. Management for Risk

To a considerable extent, the focus of all correctional institutions has shifted away from emphases on rehabilitation of offenders, or on imposition of sentences proportionate to the culpability expressed by the offender's crime, toward management of risk. Incapacitation of dangerous or incorrigible offenders has become a recurring theme in sentencing (think of three-strikes, mandatory penalty, and dangerous offender laws); parole boards have become much more risk-averse in making release decisions; and community corrections agencies have shifted emphasis from service provision to surveillance and to taking action when breaches occur.

The principal criterion used to measure the effectiveness of community penalties is re-offending. A huge amount of effort has gone into efforts to determine what programs are most effective, or effective at all by that criterion. Systematic efforts have been made in meta-analyses of program effects (e.g., Lipsey 2009), systematic reviews (MacKenzie 2006; Lipsey and Cullen 2007), and comprehensive surveys of the evidence (Bourgon et al. 2009; Cullen and Smith, chap. 6, this volume) to document what is and is not effective in those terms.

The most important work has been done in Canada, based on extensive evaluations of operating programs and attempts to identify the circumstances and management practices best attuned to reducing re-offending. A recent review of the effects of Canada's Risk, Need, and Responsivity (RNR) program provides an especially comprehensive review of the evidence (Bourgon et al. 2009). One of RNR's strongest prescriptions is that intensity of service provision should vary directly with the risks offenders present, on the sensible rationale that scarce resources should be expended where they are needed most and can have the greatest effect. One implication is that the long-time nominal probation approach made, and makes, a great deal of sense for low-risk offenders.

D. Intensive Probation

According to the logic of the Canadian RNR model, programs of intensive supervision (ISP) probation should produce better effects than regular probation. Many such programs, often on a pilot basis with federal funding, were established and evaluated in the 1980s. A major multisite evaluation, much the most ambitious ever undertaken, was carried out by the RAND Corporation (Petersilia and Turner 1993). Its most distinctive feature was that all the evaluations of separate programs used an experimental research design. Probationers were randomly assigned to the experimental program or to "the normal sentence" to assure that the groups whose experiences were compared were comparable. The evaluation found no evidence that participation reduced re-offending rates. This was in the period, however, after the probation social work ethos had shifted. The ISP programs offered close surveillance to detect noncompliance with conditions, but offered little access to treatment programs. The researchers detected signs that those few programs which did provide some greater access to treatment had better success.

E. Financial Penalties

In so capitalistic a society as the United States, it might be expected that financial penalties would be widely used as a criminal sanction. In many countries in Europe (e.g., Germany, Austria, and throughout Scandinavia), "day fines" are the most commonly imposed sanction, including for many serious and violent crimes. The number of day fines is based on the seriousness of the crime, and the daily amount is tailored to the offender's income and assets. In the United States, by contrast, except for white-collar crimes, fines are seldom used as a sole sanction except for minor behaviors such as traffic and routine regulatory offenses. In 2006, the most recent year for which data are available, 96 percent of felons were sentenced to prison or probation; of these, 38 percent also were ordered to pay fines (Rosenmerkel, Durose, and Fatole 2009, table 1.5). The fine as a sole punishment for nontrivial crimes basically does not exist in the United States except in federal courts dealing with business crimes.

Pilot day-fine projects, funded by the federal government, were established in the United States in the 1980s. Although, the pilots were meant, on the European model, to test the use of day fines as prison alternatives, no participating jurisdiction was able to persuade judges to use them in that way. The pilots all failed and the day-fine programs were abandoned. The stories are told in detail in Morris and Tonry (1990, chap. 5).

F. Community Service

The community service story is not unlike that of day fines. Community service was first used as an alternative to imprisonment in California state courts in the 1960s to provide an alternative to imprisonment for welfare recipients who were sentenced to fines they could not pay. Rather than send them to prison for nonpayment, judges ordered them to perform community service, in effect a "fine on time." Pilot projects were established throughout the United States, and a few had promising results: judges used them in place of imprisonment about half the time; most people receiving the sentence satisfied their obligations (e.g., McDonald 1986). Governments in other countries, including England, Scotland, and the Netherlands, were impressed by the American successes and established successful programs inspired by the American models. In the United States, however, the pilot projects withered away. Community service is seldom used as a stand-alone sentence in place of imprisonment, but as one among many conditions of probation. The stories are told in detail in Morris and Tonry (1990, chap. 6).

Probation's story since the mid-1970s has not been a happy one. New programs, sometimes under new names, and often supported by federal pilot funding, were established in many forms in many places. They faced the twin obstacles of inadequate investment in services and treatment facilities partly precipitated by the nothing-works mentality, heightened emphasis on surveillance, strict enforcement of conditions, and quick revocation. Unsurprisingly in retrospect, most failed to achieve their goals.

IV. THE FUTURE OF PROBATION

The future of probation may be importantly shaped by what happens in coming years with programs launched as part of the prisoner re-entry movement. The movement, begun in the late 1990s, was heralded by a publication by Jeremy Travis (2000), then director of the U.S. National Institute of Justice. He observed that the vast majority of people sentenced to imprisonment are eventually released. By the late 1990s, the annual number of released prisoners exceeded a half-million. Two-thirds of people released from prison each year are re-arrested within three years (Langan and Levin 2002). Thus, Travis observed, if governments are serious about crime prevention, they should work to reduce the odds that people released from prison will re-offend. That argument caught on. The federal government has since early in this century funded state re-entry pilot projects, and most states have established re-entry task forces and new programs. Joan Petersilia (chap. 30, this volume) describes progress to date.

The social work ethos, though much more powerfully focused on preventing re-offending, is slipping back into the American criminal justice system. If it makes sense to worry about strengthening the work skills and cognitive functioning of people released from prison, reducing their drug dependence and use, and tailoring individualized approaches to address the problems in their lives that led to their offending, it makes sense to do the same things with probationers.

A similar observation can be made about drug and other specialty courts, which individualize regimes to meet individual offenders' needs, and thus view their relapses as part of the problem to be solved. Probation may have a future.

NOTES

1. Boot camps are often, for some reason, listed among alternatives to imprisonment, even though they are not alternatives. At best they offer short, intensive prison experiences in place of longer terms. In any case, the evidence is clear that they do not reduce re-offending rates (Wilson, MacKenzie, and Mitchell 2008).

2. This chapter is less detailed than many in this handbook because much that it might discuss is dealt with elsewhere in this volume (e.g., treatment and rehabilitation [Cullenand Smith, chap. 6], drug and other specialty courts [Mitchell, chap. 27], drug dependence [Caulkins and Kleiman, chap. 10], sentencing [Johnson, chap. 22]), parole and re-entry [Petersilia, chap. 30]).

3. Parole agencies most nearly resemble probation agencies in the respects discussed in this chapter, including the shift away from a social-service provision orientation in supervision and toward a surveillant and punitive orientation. To some extent the effects of that shift are being ameliorated by the prisoner re-entry movement. Joan Petersilia discusses these developments in her chapter in this volume and in Petersilia (2003).

4. Developments concerning other criminal justice agencies are discussed in other chapters in this volume in Kutnjak Ivković (19), Mastrofski and Willis (16), Reisig (18), and Sherman (17, police), McCoy (21, prosecution), Johnson (22, sentencing), Jewkes (28, prisons), and Petersilia (30, parole and re-entry).

5. This introduction provides a short history of the evolution of American probation since the 1960s. It draws on a number of basic sources (Morris and Tonry 1990; Champion 2007; Abadinsky 2008; Clear, Cole, and Reisig 2010). All but the first of these are undergraduate textbooks. Except for David Rothman's classic *Conscience and Convenience* (1981), which discusses probation as one of several main topics, works on the history of American probation are conspicuous in their absence. This is in marked contrast to England and Wales, where three major histories have appeared since 2006: Whitehead (2006); Gard (2007); Burke and Mair (2010).

6. For example, "[T]here may well be many times when nominal probation, giving the appearance but not the reality of punishment, is exactly what's wanted. Sometimes, for some offenses and offenders, prosecution, or the entry of conviction, that may be enough" (Morris and Tonry 1990, 6).

7. That interpretation of Martinson's work influenced developments in many countries, including Denmark (Kyvsgaard 2004), Germany (Albrecht 2004), and the Netherlands (Junger-Tas 2004).

8. The account given here of changes in American probation since the 1960s was paralleled in England and Wales, with the important differences that the social work ethos was not seriously attacked until the early 1990s, and remains much more powerful in England and Wales than it became in the United States. English judges retain much more discretion to individualize sentences than do American judges, and presentence investigation reports remain important (Burke and Mair 2010).

9. These numbers understate the true percentages for blacks. Before the mid-1990s, the Bureau of Justice Statistics (BJS) reported racial classifications for all offender groups, and separately reported the Hispanic percentage. This is how the Bureau of the Census continues to report demographic data. Since the mid-1990s, BJS has reported data for white, black, Hispanic, and other groups, combining black and white Hispanics into one category. The effect is to reduce the true black percentages by approximately 10 percent.

10. For a detailed discussion, see Spohn (in this volume).

11. For detailed discussion of these issues, see Gartner (in this volume).

12. The numbers concerning this and the preceding two paragraphs come from Glaze and Bonczar (2009). Prison numbers come from Sabol, West, and Cooper (2009).

REFERENCES

Abadinsky, Howard. 2008. *Probation and Parole: Theory and Practice*, 10th ed. Englewood Cliffs, NJ: Prentice-Hall.

Albrecht, Hans-Jörg. 2004. "Youth Justice in Germany." In *Youth Crime and Youth Justice: Comparative and Cross-national Perspectives*, edited by Michael Tonry and Anthony N. Doob. Vol. 31 of *Crime and Justice: A Review of Research*, edited by Michael Tonry. Chicago: University of Chicago Press.

Black, Earl, and Merle Black. 2002. *Southern Republicans*. Cambridge, MA: Harvard University Press.

Bourgon, Guy, James Bonta, Tanya Rugge, Terri-Lynne Scott, and Annie K. Yessine. 2009. *Translating "What Works" into Sustainable Everyday Practice: Program Design, Implementation and Evaluation*. Ottawa: Public Safety Canada.

Burke, Lol, and George Mair. 2010. *Short History of Probation*. Cullompton, Devon, UK: Willan.

Caulkins, Jonathan, and Mark Kleiman. In this volume, chap. 10, "Drugs and Crime."

Champion, Dean J. 2007. *Probation, Parole and Community Corrections*, 6th ed. Englewood Cliffs, NJ: Prentice-Hall.

Clear, Todd R., Val B. Clear, and William D. Burrell. 1988. *Offender Assessment and Evaluation: The Pre-Sentence Investigation Report*. Cincinnati, OH: Anderson.

Clear, Todd R., George F. Cole, and Michael D. Reisig. 2010. *American Corrections*, 9th ed. Belmont, CA: Wadsworth.

Edsall, Thomas, and Mary Edsall. 1991. *Chain Reaction: The Impact of Race, Rights, and Taxes on American Politics*. New York: Norton.

Gard, Raymond. 2007. *Treatment in the Open: A History of Probation and Corporal Punishment in the Courts of England and Wales, 1900 to 1950*. Germany: VDM Verlag Dr. Mueller e.K.

Gartner, Rosemary. In this volume, chap. 12, "Sex, Gender, and Crime."

Glaze, Lauren C., and Thomas P. Bonczar. 2009. *Probation and Parole in the United States, 2008*. Washington, DC: Bureau of Justice Statistics, U.S. Department of Justice.

Hawken, Angela, and Mark Kleiman. 2009. *Managing Drug Involved Probationers with Swift and Certain Sanctions: Evaluating Hawaii's HOPE*. Final Report to the National Institute of Justice, U.S. Department of Justice (grant no. 2007-IJ-CX-0033; obtainable from the National Criminal Justice Reference Service).

Ivković, Kutnjak, Sanja. In this volume, chap.19, "Legitimacy and Lawful Policing."

Jewkes, Yvonne. In this volume, chap. 28, "Prisons."

Johnson, Brian. In this volume, chap. 22, "Sentencing."

Kyvsgaard, Britta. 2004. "Youth Justice in Denmark." In *Youth Crime and Youth Justice: Comparative and Cross-national Perspectives,* edited by Michael Tonry and Anthony N. Doob. Vol. 31 of *Crime and Justice: A Review of Research,* edited by Michael Tonry. Chicago: University of Chicago Press.

Junger-Tas, Josine. 2004. "Youth Justice in the Netherlands." In *Youth Crime and Youth Justice: Comparative and Cross-national Perspectives,* edited by Michael Tonry and Anthony N. Doob. Vol. 31 of *Crime and Justice: A Review of Research,* edited by Michael Tonry. Chicago: University of Chicago Press.

Langan, Patrick A., and David J. Levin. 2002. *Recidivism of Prisoners Released in 1994*. Washington, DC: U.S. Department of Justice, Bureau of Justice Statistics.

Lappi-Seppälä, Tapio. 2001. "Sentencing and Punishment in Finland: The Decline of the Repressive Ideal." In *Sentencing and Sanctions in Western Countries*, ed. Michael Tonry and Richard Frase. New York: Oxford University Press.

Lappi-Seppälä, Tapio. 2007. "Penal Policy in Scandinavia." In *Crime, Punishment, and Politics in Comparative Perspective*, edited by Michael Tonry. Vol. 36 of *Crime and Justice: A Review of Research,* edited by Michael Tonry. Chicago: University of Chicago Press.

Lipsey, Mark W. 2009. "The Primary Factors that Characterize Effective Interventions with Juvenile Offenders: A Meta-Analytic Overview." *Victims and Offenders* 4: 124–47.

Lipsey, Mark W., and Frank Cullen. 2007. "The Effectiveness of Correctional Rehabilitation: A Review of Systematic Reviews." *Annual Review of Law and Social Science* 3: 297–320.

Lowndes, Joseph. E. 2008. *From the New Deal to the New Right: Race and the Southern Origins of Modern Conservatism*. New Haven, CT: Yale University Press.

MacKenzie, Doris Layton. 2006. *What Works in Corrections. Reducing the Criminal Activities of Offenders and Delinquents*. New York: Cambridge University Press.

Martinson, Robert. 1974. "What Works? Questions and Answers About Prison Reform," *The Public Interest* (Spring): 22–54.

Willis, Mastrofski, Stephen, D., and James J. Willis. In this volume, chap. 16, "Police Organization."

McCoy, Candace. In this volume, chap. 21, "Prosecution."

McDonald, Douglas C. 1986. *Punishment without Walls*. New Burnswick, NJ: Rutgers University Press.

Mitchell, Ojmarrh. In this volume, chap. 27, "Drug and Other Specialty Courts."

Morris, Norval, and Michael Tonry. 1990. *Between Prison and Probation: Intermediate Punishments in a Rational Sentencing System*. New York: Oxford University Press.

Petersilia, Joan. 1997. "Probation in the United States." In *Crime and Justice: A Review of Research,* vol. 22, edited by Michael Tonry. Chicago: University of Chicago Press.

———. 2003. *When Prisoners Come Home: Parole and Prisoner Reentry.* New York: Oxford University Press.

———. In this volume, chap. 30, "Parole and Re-entry."

Petersilia, Joan, and Susan Turner. 1993. "Intensive Probation and Parole." In *Crime and Justice: A Review of Research*, vol. 17, edited by Michael Tonry. Chicago: University of Chicago Press.

Reisig, Michael. In this volume, chap. 18, "Community and Problem-Solving Policing."

Rothman, David J. 1981. *Conscience and Convenience: The Assylum and its Alternatives in Progressive America.* Boston: Little, Brown.

Rosenmerkel, Sean, Matthew Durose, and Donald Fatole Jr. 2009. *Felony Sentences in State Courts, 2006—Statistical Tables.* Washington, DC: U.S. Department of Justice, Bureau of Justice Statistics.

Sabol, William, J., Heather C. West, and Matthew Cooper. 2009. *Prisoners in 2008.* Washington, DC: Bureau of Justice Statistics, U.S. Department of Justice.

Sherman, Lawrence W., David P. Farrington, Brandon C. Welsh, and Doris Layton MacKenzie, eds. 2002. *Evidence-Based Crime Prevention.* London: Routledge.

Sherman, Lawrence W. In this volume, chap. 17, "Police and Crime Control."

Smith, Paula, and Frank Cullen. In this volume, chap. 6, "Treatment and Rehabilitation."

Spohn, Cassia. In this volume, chap. 11, "Race, Ethnicity, and Crime."

Tonry, Michael. 1991. "Stated and Latent Functions of Intensive Supervision Probation," *Crime and Delinquency* 36: 174–91.

Tonry, Michael, and Mary Lynch. 1996. "Intermediate Sanctions." In *Crime and Justice: A Review of Research,* vol. 20, edited by Michael Tonry. Chicago: University of Chicago Press.

Tonry, Michael, and Matthew Melewski. 2008. "The Malign Effects of Drug and Crime Control Policies on Black Americans." In *Crime and Justice: A Review of Research,* vol. 37, edited by Michael Tonry. Chicago: University of Chicago Press.

Travis, Jeremy. 2000. *But They All Come Back: Rethinking Prisoner Reentry.* National Institute of Justice: U.S. Department of Justice, National Institute of Justice.

Weaver, Vesla Mae. 2007. "Frontlash: Race and the Development of Punitive Crime Policy." *Studies in American Political Development* 21 (fall): 230–65.

Weigend, Thomas. 2001. "Sentencing and Punishment in Germany." In *Sentencing and Sanctions in Western Countries*, ed. Michael Tonry and Richard Frase. New York: Oxford University Press.

Whitehead, Philip, and Roger Statham. 2006. *The History of Probation: Politics, Power and Cultural Change*, 1876–2005. Crayford, UK: Shaw.

Wilson, David B., Doris L. MacKenzie, and Fawn Ngo Mitchell. 2008. *Effects of Correctional Boot Camps on Offending.* Campbell Collaboration: Administration of Justice Program, George Mason University.

Wilson, James Q. 1975. *Thinking about Crime.* New York: Basic Books.

CHAPTER 27

DRUG AND OTHER SPECIALTY COURTS

OJMARRH MITCHELL

SINCE the 1970s, prevailing correctional practices in the United States largely have abandoned the philosophy of rehabilitation, which had long served as the foundation of American corrections (Beckett 1997; Tonry 2004; Western 2006). Individualized treatment increasingly was viewed as ineffective, and the highly discretionary nature of sentencing and parole decisions were assailed as too lenient, discriminatory, or both. Individualized treatment was replaced with punitive sanctions designed to deter, incapacitate, and punish offenders. The discretion of judges and correctional officials was limited by sentencing guidelines, mandatory minimum sentences, and the abolition of discretionary parole release. As a result of these changes, the probability of being sentenced to prison and time served in prison increased, and both of these changes were most dramatic for drug offenses (e.g., Blumstein and Beck 1999; Western 2006, 45). Along with the increased punitiveness of courts and corrections, police dramatically increased the number of arrests for drug offenses, particularly of low-level drug offenders (e.g., Mitchell 2009). The end result has been an unprecedented number of offenders incarcerated, particularly drug offenders.

Cutting against this grain has been the rise of specialty courts (also known as "problem solving courts"), which combine individualized treatment with relatively strict community supervision and judicial oversight to combat specific crime problems. Drug courts were the first manifestation of specialty courts and are still the most prominent. The success of drug courts has led to the drug court model being applied to other crime problems such as domestic violence and mentally ill offenders.

The rapid growth in the number and various manifestations of specialty courts makes it accurate to characterize this growth as a "movement."

The first drug court was established in Miami-Dade County, Florida in 1989 (Nolan 2001; Goldkamp 2002). A boom in crack cocaine use and the War on Drugs' emphasis on arresting low-level drug offenders flooded the Miami's criminal justice system. The influx overwhelmed Miami-Dade's criminal justice system, and a commission was tasked with studying this problem. This commission included judges Herbert Klein and Gerald Wetherington, as well as State Attorney Janet Reno and Public Defender Bennett Brummer. This commission designed a specialized court for drug offenders as a partial solution to the problems presented by the influx of drug offenders. The hallmarks of this court were its use of diversionary, nonadversarial case processing, community-based drug treatment monitored by the court, and sanctions for noncompliance with the treatment plan.

Miami-Dade's innovative drug court was viewed as a success and its approach has been widely adopted. Just five years after the establishment of the first drug court, 40 drug courts were in operation; five years later, 472 were in operation. Currently, there are more than 2,100 drug courts in operation with every state operating at least one. The proliferation of the drug court model is not confined to the United States; drug courts have caught on internationally as well. Drug courts proliferated not only in number but also in type. Whereas drug courts were originally designed for adult illicit substance-abusing offenders, these courts also have been developed for juveniles and chronic drunk drivers. Moreover, the problem-solving approach that underlies drug courts has been applied to other common criminal justice problems and populations.

A large body of research assesses the effectiveness of drug courts for adult offenders. These evaluations find considerable evidence of drug courts' effectiveness in reducing recidivism. An ongoing synthesis of these evaluations finds that the average size of drug courts' treatment effect translates into an approximately 13 percentage point reduction in recidivism. This average effect may appear modest, but it is larger than the average effect of any other common criminal justice-based drug treatment program.

The evidence assessing the effects of other kinds of specialty courts is relatively scant but rapidly growing. The existing evaluations of non-drug specialty courts generally have produced mixed results. Given the mixed results of such evaluations and the modest number of such evaluations, it is premature to draw definitive conclusions about these courts' effects.

Drug courts proliferated in response to the increasing number of offenders entering the criminal justice system with identifiable drug problems, the availability of funding to start such courts, and the ability of drug courts to "hold offenders accountable"—a notion that fit prevailing sensibilities. Drug courts have been effective because they target a well-known risk factor for continued criminal conduct, use treatment services known to be effective in reducing substance use, and "coerce" offenders into maintaining their involvement in treatment, which is a robust predictor of treatment success. Other specialty courts, however, lack one or more of these features, and as a result may prove less effective in reducing criminal conduct than drug courts. The expansion of specialty courts must include aggressive efforts to evaluate their effectiveness and establish sets of best practices, in order to prevent the specialty court movement from becoming the latest failed effort at individualizing treatment for offenders.

A number of conclusions can be drawn from the current evidence:

- Specialty courts combine individualized treatment with the moral and legal authority of the court to form potentially powerful interventions.
- Specialty courts, especially drug courts, have grown in number rapidly in the past 20 years and now operate in every state.
- The expansion of specialty courts is explained by their perceived effectiveness, fit to prevailing sensibilities about crime, the availability of federal funds, and the perceived growth in the number of offenders with identifiable crime-related problems.
- The large number of evaluations of drug courts for adult offenders are generally methodologically weak, but a few very rigorous evaluations have been conducted. These evaluations provide credible evidence of the effectiveness of these courts in reducing recidivism.
- Further, the average size of drug courts' treatment effects is larger than any other common criminal justice based drug treatment intervention.
- It is unclear why some drug courts produce larger effects than others. The next wave of research needs to address this issue theoretically and empirically.
- The effectiveness of other specialty courts in reducing recidivism is an open question. Evaluations of juvenile drug courts, domestic violence courts, and mental health courts all provide mixed evidence of effectiveness. DWI courts have a small but relatively consistent body of research demonstrating their effectiveness. More research concerning best court practices and examining these courts' effectiveness is needed.

This article is organized into four sections. Section I defines specialty courts, and traces their growth in number and types. This section also explores the factors that sparked the specialty court movement. Section II examines drug courts, the most popular and prominent type of specialty court. This section outlines key features of the drug court model, reviews the evidence of their effectiveness in reducing criminal behavior, and identifies neglected issues. Section III considers other manifestations of specialty courts and the emerging research evaluating the effectiveness of these courts. Section IV probes the policy implications of specialty court research and what this body of research suggests about the long-term viability of the specialty court movement.

I. Specialty Courts and Their Rise

There is no widely agreed upon definition of "specialty courts." However, their philosophy is clear. Specialty courts are based on the beliefs that courts "can and should play a role in trying to solve problems" that fuel caseloads, "outcomes—not just process and precedents—matter," and the coercive power of courts "can change people's behavior" (Kaye 1999, 3). Most often specialty courts put this philosophy into practice by targeting a specific problem behavior (e.g., drug use, domestic violence, mental illness), abandoning the usual adversarial court process in favor of a collaborative approach, developing individualized interventions for offenders, and using the courts' coercive power to compel and monitor compliance with individualized treatment plans. Hence, one possible definition is that specialty courts are courts or special court dockets in which court actors (e.g., judges, prosecutors, defense attorneys, probation officers, treatment providers) collaboratively use the court's authority to monitor offenders' compliance with individualized interventions designed to ameliorate a specific problem. Several types of innovative courts fall under this definition including drug, DWI, mental health, community, domestic violence, gun, homelessness, and re-entry courts. This definition excludes other special court dockets such as teen, truancy, and child-support courts, which usually lack the treatment component vital to specialty courts.

Drug courts first put the underlying philosophy of specialty courts into practice by using the united efforts of court actors to solve the substance abuse problems of eligible drug-involved offenders. These efforts focus on achieving the short-term goals of treatment engagement, treatment attendance, and "clean" drug tests—all in effort to achieve the long-term goal of drug abstinence and law-abiding behavior.

Drug courts, however, are far from the only manifestation of specialty courts. Mental health courts are another prominent example. Mental health courts use the collaborative efforts of court agents to intervene in the cycle of recurring criminal behavior among offenders with identifiable mental health issues (McNiel and Binder 2007; Huddleston, Marlowe, and Casebolt 2008). Domestic violence courts are also relatively common. What's different about domestic violence courts is that they use a heavier dose of punishment (actual and threatened) in combination with treatment than other kinds of specialty courts (Gover, MacDonald, and Alpert 2003). Community courts are an emerging type of specialty court, but they are much less popular than other specialty courts (Huddleston, Marlowe, and Casebolt 2008). Community courts focus on solving local crime problems, particularly "quality of life" crime problems (e.g., vandalism, minor theft, prostitution) and the problems of the offenders committing these crimes (Lee 2000). An additional goal of community courts is to get offenders to repair the harm done to the affected community. Still other manifestations of specialty courts are the recent initiations of gun (see e.g., Sheppard and Kelly 2002) and re-entry courts (see e.g., Farole 2003).

A. The Specialty Court Movement

The specialty court movement began with drug courts in 1989 in Dade County, Florida. Since then, the number of drug courts has grown exponentially (see figure 27.1). By 2004, the number of operating drug courts stood at over 1,600. The most recent data indicate that there were more than 2,100 in operation in 2007 (Huddleston, Marlowe, and Casebolt 2008). Every state and US territory, except the Virgin Islands, had at least one operating drug court. Drug courts have also spread to other nations including Canada, the United Kingdom, New Zealand, Australia, South Africa, Bermuda, and Jamaica (Berman and Feinblatt 2005).

The types of drug courts have also increased. Originally, drug courts primarily served adult offenders with illicit substance abuse problems ("traditional" drug courts). In recent years, drug courts have been extended to juveniles and to offenders charged with driving while under the influence of alcohol. The drug court model also has begun to make inroads in federal and tribal jurisdictions. Further, the drug court model has been applied outside of criminal courts; family drug courts are a relatively new development that handle family court issues (parental rights, allegations of neglect, and so forth) in cases in which drug abuse is determined to be a factor.

The growth in the types of non-drug related specialty court is also noteworthy. As of year-end 2007, there were 601 operational "other specialty" (i.e., non-drug)

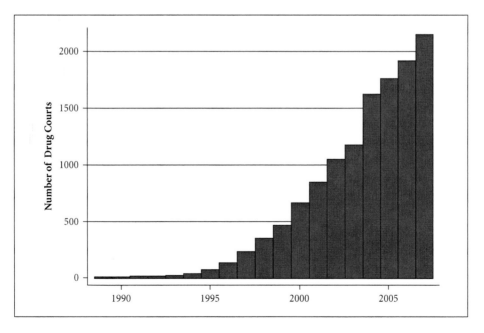

Figure 27.1. Number of U.S. Drug Courts, 1989–2007
Source: Huddleston, Marlowe, and Casebolt 2008.

courts operating in all but thirteen states (Huddleston, Marlowe, and Casebolt 2008, 18–19).[1] The most common of these were mental health courts (219), domestic violence courts (185), homelessness courts (37), and community courts (30). Remarkably, the total number of these other specialty courts grew from 229 in 2004 to 601 in 2007, a nearly 62 percent increase (Huddleston, Freeman-Wilson, and Boone 2004; Huddleston, Marlowe, and Casebolt 2008). Clearly, the growth of specialty courts is not confined to drug courts.

B. Explaining the Growth of Drug Courts and the Revitalization of Individualized Treatment

Numerous rigorous evaluations of drug courts now support their effectiveness, but initially they spread without strong evidence of their effectiveness. Undoubtedly, there were early indications of the efficacy of drug courts, but this evidence was largely anecdotal and impressionistic, based primarily on the enthusiastic support of judges and other court actors involved in early drug courts. Only a handful of drug court evaluations existed prior to the enactment of the Violent Crime Control Act of 1994, which spurred their proliferation. Thus, Congress and local jurisdictions blessed the drug court model without strong scientific evidence of these courts' effectiveness. Given this lack of empirical evidence, what explains the rapid proliferation of drug courts across the United States? Why did so many jurisdictions adopt this model bearing the burden of significant implementation costs without strong evidence that it worked? At least three factors explain it: need, ideological fit, and federal and private funding.

Many jurisdictions implemented drug courts out of sheer need. The cocaine/crack cocaine epidemic of the mid to late1980s, combined with the War on Drugs' increased emphasis on low-level drug offenders, flooded the courts and crowded correctional facilities. Many of these offenders were re-arrested and re-processed through the system shortly after being released. Drug courts provided jurisdictions an innovative and potentially effective means of dealing with the surge in the number of drug offenders and the chronic nature of their criminal behavior.

A second important factor was the drug courts' fit with prevailing sensibilities about crime and punishment. Since the 1970s, American penal philosophy has moved away from rehabilitation towards a punitive amalgam of deterrence, incapacitation, and retribution. In the 1980s, drug offenders became a target of these punitive penalties, as public concern about drug use and drug-related crime rose dramatically (e.g., see Beckett 1997; Reinarman and Levine 1997). The prevailing punitive philosophy of the time is best summarized by the White House's first National Drug Control Strategy (ONDCP 1989) that stated: "To prevent people from using drugs, drug enforcement activities must make it increasingly difficult to engage in *any* drug activity with impunity . . . we need a national drug law

enforcement strategy that casts a wide net and seeks to ensure that *all drug users*—
whatever its scale—face the risk of criminal sanction" (18, emphasis added). Such
sentiment meshed well with the larger Reagan/Bush philosophy of user accountability: "[I]n a free society we're all accountable for our actions. If this problem is
to be solved, drug users can no longer excuse themselves by blaming society. As
individuals, *they're responsible*" (Reagan, August 4, 1986, emphasis added). The
intended result of this philosophy was clear: "Making streets safer and drug users
more accountable for their actions *requires the criminal justice system to expand*
and reform in an unprecedented way. Effective street-level enforcement means
dramatically increasing the number of drug offenders arrested" (ONDCP 1989, 24,
emphasis added). Undoubtedly, the criminal justice system expanded greatly in
the 1980s and 1990s with increases in drug arrests as a primary factor, but the
effectiveness of employing punitive sanctions against low-level drug offenders, and
drug-involved offenders more generally, was already becoming questionable by the
late 1980s. Many drug-involved offenders were unresponsive to punitive sanctions—
as soon as they were released, they returned to drug use and other criminal activity,
which often resulted in quick returns to the criminal justice system.

Just as American courts and corrections took a decidedly punitive turn toward
drug offenders, the evidence of the effectiveness of drug treatment was burgeoning.
Evaluations of drug-abuse treatment found that several of the most commonly used
treatment modalities were effective in reducing drug use and/or criminal activity.
For example, national data from the Drug Abuse Reporting Program and the Treatment Outcome Prospective Study (TOPS) both found considerable evidence supporting the effectiveness of therapeutic communities, methadone maintenance, and
intensive outpatient treatment programs in reducing drug use, crime, or both (e.g.,
Simpson 1982; Hubbard, Marsden, et al. 1984; Hubbard, Rachel, et al. 1989; Anglin
and Hser 1990; Simpson 1990). Despite this evidence, many policymakers rejected
traditional forms of drug treatment and embraced punitive sanctions as the solution to drug problems, and policymakers who continued to embrace rehabilitation
feared being labeled "soft on crime."

In this political and social environment the drug court model was a perfect
compromise. The drug court model bound the potential effectiveness of drug treatment together with rigorous programmatic demands and criminal justice supervision, which held offenders accountable. Proponents of "tough on crime" approaches
to drug problems were able to support drug courts and maintain face, as drug courts
closely supervise and hold offenders accountable. Supporters of rehabilitation and
pragmatists were able to support drug courts, as they use treatment programs demonstrated to be effective outside of the drug court context. Compassionate but
tough, drug courts were attractive to policymakers of all ilk.

A third factor that cannot be overlooked was the availability of funding, especially federal funding. Over $80 million in federal funding was made available for
drug court expansion between 1989 and 1997 (GAO 1997, 6). The bulk (40 percent)

came from Title V of the Violent Crime Control and Law Enforcement Act of 1994, which authorized $1 billion over six years for drug court programs; only a fraction of these authorized federal funds were actually appropriated (GAO 1997, 41).[2] The GAO estimates during this period that another $45 million was supplied to drug courts from local, state, and nongovernmental sources. Combined, this $125 million dollars in federal and private funding may not appear to be a lot of money for an innovation of this sort, but given that there were only 230 drug courts in operation in 1997, this figure is substantial; if one assumes the convenient fiction that these 230 courts received these funds evenly, then each court received more than a half million dollars. Another clear indicator of the federal government's role in promoting drug courts comes from the federal Drug Court Program Office (DCPO), which reported that 275 drug courts became operational with support for DCPO funds between 1995 and 2000 (DCPO 2000).

Federal support of drug courts continues to this day, largely through the DCPO. Between fiscal year 2002 and 2008, more than $100 million was awarded to state and local agencies from the Drug Court Discretionary Grant Program alone. And in fiscal year 2009, another $40 million was made available (BJA 2009). These are not the only federal funds available in 2009; another $23 million dollars is available from the Centers for Substance Abuse Treatment. Clearly, the federal government made a concerted effort to stimulate the proliferation of drug courts by making federal funds available for such courts. The availability of these funds is itself a testament to the political popularity of drug courts and the belief that drug courts offer an effective solution to many offenders' drug problems.

II. Drug Courts

The extraordinary growth in specialty courts sparks several questions. How do these courts operate? Who is eligible for them? And are they effective in dealing with their targeted problems?

A. The Drug Court Model

Prior to the advent of drug courts, drug-involved offenders were processed through the criminal justice system via standard processes. Arrested drug offenders were booked, arraigned, charged, prosecuted, convicted, and often incarcerated with little, if any, concerted effort to treat the underlying substance abuse issues that fueled their criminal conduct. Drug courts grew out of court actors' frustrations with the seemingly perpetual cycle of arresting and prosecuting drug offenders only to have them quickly reappear in the system.

The drug court model combines drug treatment with the legal and moral authority of the court to break the cycle of drug use and drug-fueled crime. In a nutshell, a prototypical drug court operates as follows. Shortly after arrest, drug-involved offenders who appear to be eligible are identified and screened for program eligibility. Arrestees deemed eligible are offered entry into the drug court with the promise that the charges against them will be reduced or dismissed upon successful program completion. Arrestees who agree to enter the drug court become drug court "clients." Once in the drug court, clients have their cases handled nonadversarially with court actors working collaboratively to promote treatment success. As a condition of program entry, drug court clients agree to abide by the court's demands, which typically include frequent urine testing, treatment attendance, and appearance before the court for status hearings. These status hearings are crucial as it is here that the drug court judge and clients interact directly, and it is in these hearings where judges in collaboration with other court actors most nakedly use the coercive authority of the court. The court uses various rewards (e.g., praise, tokens of achievement) and sanctions (e.g., increased treatment attendance or urine testing, short jail stays) to compel compliance to program requirements. Compliant clients advance through three or more progressively less-intense stages before completing the drug court, which typically takes at least one year. Ultimately, successful drug court clients are acknowledged at a formal graduation ceremony.

The drug court model begins with early identification of eligible arrestees. Early identification of arrestees eligible for drug court is believed to be essential, because for many being arrested is a traumatic event. The trauma of arrest "can force substance using behavior into the open, making denial difficult" (National Association of Drug Court Professionals 1997, 5). In this window of opportunity, arrestees are believed to be receptive to treatment initiation.

Drug court eligibility requirements vary widely. In the majority of jurisdictions, however, eligibility is restricted to nonviolent offenders with evidence of substance dependence. Most commonly, nonviolent offenders are defined as offenders neither charged with, nor previously convicted of, a serious violent offense. Not all jurisdictions have this criterion, but the vast majority do, in part because this is necessary to be eligible for federal drug court funding.[3] Many courts also exclude arrestees charged with drug trafficking offenses, with three or more prior felony convictions, or with serious mental health issues (see e.g., Kalich and Evans 2006). In the end, most eligible offenders are charged with drug or property offenses and have relatively few prior felony convictions. Eligible arrestees are given the Machiavellian choice of participating in the community-based drug treatment of the drug court or staying in the traditional court process and risking incarceration.

Typically, arrestees who agree to participate have their criminal charges processed by the court in one of two ways. In the first method, defendants waive their rights to a speedy trial and enter the drug court treatment program. If they successfully complete the program, the charges against them are dismissed. Clients who fail to complete the program are prosecuted. This method of processing is commonly referred to as "pre-plea" or "diversionary" processing. In the second method of processing ("post-plea" processing), the court adjudicates the charges against the defendant; if the defendant is found guilty, the defendant then enters the drug court program, and sentencing is either withheld until participation in the drug court is complete or the sentence is pronounced but suspended until participation is complete. Clients who successfully complete the program typically receive a sentence of time served or serve a term of probation (GAO 1997; Marlowe et al. 2006a; Wilson, Mitchell, and MacKenzie 2006). Some courts use both methods of case disposition for different groups of offenders. For example, Delaware used the diversionary approach with youthful, less criminally involved offenders, and the post-plea approach with more serious offenders. Those on the diversionary track were required to participate in drug court for six to twelve months. The more serious offenders on the post-plea track were required to be involved for longer periods of time.

Early drug courts predominately used the pre-plea model (see GAO 1997; Huddleston, Marlowe, and Casebolt 2008). In recent years, however, drug courts have moved toward the post-plea model. A 2005 survey revealed that 59 percent of drug courts use the post-plea method, 7 percent use the pre-plea method, and 19 percent used both methods (Huddleston, Marlowe, and Casebolt 2008, 4–5).

Regardless of method of court processing, drug court clients are assessed, and a treatment plan is developed that matches the needs and problems of the offender. Available treatment options vary widely but include detoxification, group and individual counseling, drug education, cognitive-behavioral therapy, mental health treatment, pharmacological treatments, among many others. These options can be delivered in outpatient or inpatient settings. Treatment options also include services linking clients to medical treatment, housing, and employment. Over time as clients' needs change, treatment plans are reassessed and modified as necessary.

Drug court treatment is typically organized into three or more progressively less-intensive stages. In the first stage, clients are required to attend treatment programming several times a week, submit to urine testing at least weekly, and appear frequently before the court for status hearings. This first stage usually is designed to last thirty to ninety days. Before clients advance to the next stage they must demonstrate sustained abstinence and completion of each stages' requirements. In subsequent stages the frequency of treatment programming, urine testing, and status hearings are gradually reduced, but the length of these subsequent stages is often increased. The minimum length of time necessary to complete drug court programming is typically a year, but in some diversionary (pre-plea) drug courts the minimum duration of successful treatment is six months and in some post-plea courts the minimum duration is two or more years. These are minimum times to completion; actual time to completion is considerably longer, because most drug court clients are sanctioned for setbacks.

An important component of the drug court model is the use of graduated sanctions. Offenders are required to attend status hearings periodically throughout their participation in drug court, and status hearings are also required if a violation of drug court rules is alleged. In these hearings, treatment providers and drug court administrators inform the judge of each client's treatment progress (e.g., record of treatment attendance, number drug tests taken, and the result of each), and based upon these reports the judge takes appropriate action. Drug courts often use predetermined schedules of sanctions in deciding the appropriate response. Initial or minor deviations from the treatment plan may be met with increased drug testing, treatment attendance, and other measures. More serious or continued infractions may result in short jail stays. And the most serious or persistent infractions are met with termination from the drug court.

It is important to emphasize that the program requirements for drug courts are strict and clients are closely monitored for adherence to the demands of the program. Perhaps the best evidence of the rigor of the drug court model is that most drug court clients do not successfully complete them. For example, a GAO survey of drug courts operating at the end of 1996 found that "about 48 percent" of drug court clients successfully completed the program (GAO 1997, 56). Likewise, Belenko's (2001) review of drug court evaluations found an average graduation rate of 47 percent with a range of 36 percent to 60 percent. Thus, the best estimate of drug court graduation rates is just under 50 percent. The remaining clients are terminated for noncompliance such as a new felony arrest, failure to abstain from drug use, failure to attend treatment, failure to attend status hearings, or absconding completely. Another small but nontrivial group of offenders who initially agree to participate is terminated after voluntarily deciding to quit.[4] Other evidence of drug courts' rigor is found in the declinations to participate of many eligible offenders.

The key components of drug courts are thus (1) collaborative, nonadversarial, outcome-driven court processing; (2) early identification of eligible offenders; (3) drug treatment integrated into criminal justice case processing; (4) urine testing; (5) judicial monitoring; and (6) the use of graduated sanctions and rewards. These components combine to form individualized interventions that simultaneously provide drug treatment to drug-abusing offenders and hold them accountable for their behavior.

B. The Effectiveness of Drug Courts in Reducing Recidivism

Several notable prior reviews of this body of research have been conducted (e.g., GAO 1997; Belenko 2001; GAO 2005; Wilson, Mitchell, and MacKenzie 2006). The GAO (1997) examined twenty drug court evaluations and noted the general lack of methodological rigor. For example, many evaluations did not include a comparison group and most evaluations examined recidivism only during the period of program participation. Most important, the GAO's review found drug courts' effects to be inconsistent. The GAO concluded that the evidence supporting the effectiveness of drug courts was "insufficient." Belenko's (2001) larger synthesis of thirty-seven evaluations echoed many of the GAO's findings. Belenko noted the lack of rigor in this body of research and the short recidivism tracking periods used in most evaluations. However, based on this larger set of evaluations, Belenko cautiously supported the recidivism-suppressing effects of drug courts. In 2005 the GAO updated its review of drug court evaluations, and this time concluded that the evidence indicated that drug courts reduce recidivism in the period of time corresponding to the drug court treatment, but drug courts' effects on recidivism beyond this period and on drug use were questionable. Most recently, Wilson and colleagues (2006) synthesized the findings of fifty-five drug court evaluations. These authors tentatively concluded that drug court participants have lower rates of recidivism (drug and non-drug offending) than similar offenders who did not participate in drug courts. These findings held for evaluations that measured recidivism during and after program participation. Like the earlier reviews, Wilson and colleagues' findings were tempered by the generally weak methodological rigor of these evaluations. Taken together, evaluations reveal growing support for the effectiveness of drug courts, particularly during the period of program participation, but the effects of drug court participation on measures of drug offending (and in the long term) are uncertain.

The review below is an update of an ongoing quantitative review (i.e., meta-analysis) being conducted by Wilson and colleagues (see Wilson, Mitchell, and MacKenzie 2006). The evaluation literature has expanded significantly since the last analysis was conducted. Here I focus on the effects of drug courts on different types of recidivism (drug and non-drug offending) over time, and by methodological rigor. Currently, ninety evaluations that compare drug court clients to drug-using offenders who did not participate in a drug court program (i.e., two-group designs) on at least one measure of recidivism have been identified. Thus far seventy-five of these evaluations have been coded on measures capturing key features of the drug court program, sample, and methodology used in each evaluation.

1. *Describing Extant Drug Court Evaluations*

Of the seventy-five coded evaluations, most evaluated traditional drug courts (i.e., drug courts designed for adult illicit substance users). Eighty percent (sixty of the seventy-five) assessed the effectiveness of traditional drug courts. Eight evaluations examined the effectiveness of DWI courts. Another seven evaluated the effectiveness of juvenile drug courts. Table 27.1 summarizes key features of these seventy-five evaluations by type of drug court. The majority of these evaluations are unpublished technical reports produced by government or private research entities. All included at least one measure of recidivism. Half also included some measure of drug re-offending such as drug use or, more commonly, re-arrest on a drug charge. Very few evaluations assessed drug courts' effects on non-crime outcomes such as employment, welfare use, or physical health (not shown in table 27.1). Further, most evaluations used measures of recidivism that followed research participants for no more than two years, and most often the period of recidivism tracking overlapped completely or partially with the period of drug court participation.

In terms of programmatic and sample features, the evaluated drug courts shared commonalities but also varied considerably. Evaluations of traditional and juvenile drug courts revealed that such courts varied widely in the method of disposition. There was an approximately even split between pre-plea, post-plea, and mixed-plea methods of disposition. Evaluations of DWI courts uniformly used the post-plea method in those evaluations where disposition method could be discerned. The evaluations exhibited relatively little variation in terms of sample characteristics. Overwhelmingly, the samples were male and nonviolent offenders. Thus, existing evaluations primarily assess the effectiveness of drug courts in samples of nonviolent, male offenders.

Another noteworthy feature of this body of research is its lack of methodological rigor. Each of the evaluations' methodological rigor was rated by two trained coders. Evaluations were placed into four categories: (1) uncompromised randomized experiments, (2) rigorous quasi-experiments/compromised randomized experiments, (3) standard quasi-experiments, and (4) weak quasi-experiments. The term "uncompromised" randomized experiments refers to evaluations without large overall or differential attrition problems. (Compromised randomized experiments had such attrition problems.) "Rigorous" quasi-experiment typically used subject-level matching on key variables or propensity score matching. "Standard" quasi-experiments used either a historical comparison group who met drug court eligibility criteria constructed from archival data or a group of offenders who were eligible but not referred to the drug court program. Most commonly, "weak" quasi-experimental designs involved comparing drug court clients to drug offenders who were eligible for participation in a drug court but declined participation ("refusers") or were referred to the drug court but were rejected by drug court administrators ("rejects"). Such designs have questionable internal validity because refusers and rejects are likely to differ on factors like pre-treatment motivation, perceived seriousness of drug problem, and self-efficacy, among many other potentially important factors. Therefore, any differences found by such studies are susceptible to selection bias and their results are open to alternative explanations (e.g., differences are produced by differences in pre-treatment motivation—not drug court participation).

The three types of drug courts varied substantively in methodological rigor. Among evaluations of traditional drug courts, uncompromised randomized experiments were rare (5 percent of evaluations). Rigorous quasi-experiments were considerably more common (25 percent). Yet, most evaluations are rated as standard (50 percent) or weak (20 percent) quasi-experiments. Juvenile drug courts were

Table 27.1. Key Features of Evaluation, Court, and Sample

	Traditional Drug Court[a] (k = 60)	Juvenile Drug Court (k = 7)	DWI Drug Court (k = 8)
Variable	Frequency (%)	Frequency (%)	Frequency (%)
Time period			
1989–1993	1 (2%)	0 (0%)	0 (0%)
1994–1998	14 (23%)	1 (14%)	0 (0%)
1999–2003	30 (50%)	2 (29%)	1 (13%)
2004 or later	14 (23%)	2 (29%)	6 (75%)
Undated	1 (2%)	2 (29%)	1 (13%)
Publication status			
Published	23 (38%)	1 (14%)	3 (63%)
Unpublished	37 (62%)	6 (86%)	5 (38%)
Outcome measure			
General recidivism only	32 (53%)	3 (53%)	2 (25%)
Includes drug outcome	28 (47%)	4 (57%)	6 (75%)
Max length of follow-up			
12 or less months	18 (30%)	3 (43%)	2 (25%)
12–24 months	17 (28%)	2 (29%)	5 (63%)
24–36 months	9 (15%)	1 (14%)	0 (0%)
36+ months	3 (5%)	0 (0%)	1 (13%)
Unknown max., min. known	7 (12%)	0 (0%)	0 (0%)
No information/unclear	6 (10%)	1 (14%)	0 (0%)
Follow-up Tx overlap			
Complete overlap	12 (20%)	3 (43%)	2 (25%)
Partial overlap	28 (47%)	2 (29%)	4 (50%)
No overlap	19 (32%)	2 (29%)	1 (13%)
No information/Unclear	1 (2%)	0	1 (13%)
Method of disposition			
Pre-plea	18 (30%)	1 (14%)	0 (0%)
Post-plea	18 (30%)	1 (14%)	2 (25%)
Mixed/Other	11 (18%)	1 (14%)	0 (0%)
No information/Unclear	13 (22%)	4 (57%)	6 (75%)
Gender composition			
All male (90%+ male)	0 (0%)	0 (0%)	1 (13%)
Mostly male (60–90% male)	49 (82%)	7 (100%)	5 (63%)
Approx. equal (59–40% male)	2 (3%)	0 (0%)	0 (0%)
Mostly female (39–10% male)	0 (0%)	0 (0%)	0 (0%)
All female (<10% male)	1 (2%)	0 (0%)	0 (0%)
No information/Unclear	8 (13%)	0 (0%)	2 (25%)
Offender type			
Only non-violent offenders	55 (92%)	7 (100%)	4 (50%)
Includes violent offenders	5 (8%)	0 (0%)	0 (0%)
No information/Unclear	0 (0%)	0 (0%)	4 (50%)
Methodological rigor			
Weak quasi-experiment	12 (20%)	2 (29%)	1 (13%)
Standard quasi-experiment	30 (50%)	2 (29%)	3 (38%)

(*Continued*)

Table 27.1. (*Continued*)

	Traditional Drug Court[a] ($k = 60$)	Juvenile Drug Court ($k = 7$)	DWI Drug Court ($k = 8$)
Rigorous quasi-experiment	15 (25%)	3 (43%)	1 (13%)
Uncompromised random experiment	3 (5%)	0 (0%)	3 (38%)

[a]Includes drug courts that include some offenders charged/convicted of driving under the influence.

almost evenly split between the three lowest method scores. No uncompromised randomized experiments have been conducted in these courts, although two evaluations compromised by large differential attrition problems have been conducted (Dickie 2000, 2001). The DWI courts had the highest typical method score; half of coded evaluations were rated as either uncompromised experiments (38 percent) or rigorous quasi-experiments (13 percent).

The existing research is sufficient primarily in addressing the effectiveness of traditional drug courts on relatively short-term measures of recidivism (two years or less). The large number of such evaluations inspires confidence in their collective findings. Yet, at the same time, the generally weak methodological rigor evident in evaluations of traditional drug courts compromises confidence in these evaluations' findings, and makes it necessary to examine whether evidence of drug courts' effectiveness is confined to only weaker evaluations. The modest number of juvenile drug and DWI court evaluations makes drawing firm conclusions about their effectiveness difficult. The effectiveness of each type of court is assessed below.

2. Results

It is difficult to describe the results of these seventy-five evaluations accurately within the page constraints of this article using a traditional narrative literature review. Moreover, traditional narrative reviews have been demonstrated to systematically underestimate treatment effects (Mann 1994). Instead, the results of these evaluations are summarized by using quantitative synthesis methods, also known as meta-analysis.

At the heart of a meta-analytic synthesis of research is the concept of an effect size. In the present context, effect sizes quantify differences between drug court participants and nonparticipants in a standardized format that enables comparisons across evaluations. Specifically, the odds ratio effect size is used, because most of the outcomes were dichotomous. For all of the drug court evaluations included in this review, odds ratio effect sizes were calculated using each evaluation's most general measure of recidivism that had the longest recidivism tracking period. In evaluations that included drug outcomes, odds ratios for these outcomes were also calculated (for a detailed discussion of outcome coding see Wilson, Mitchell, and MacKenzie 2006). For readers who are not familiar with odds ratios and to facilitate interpretation of these findings, odds ratio effect sizes are converted into percentages in several places.[5]

Forty-four of the sixty (90 percent) evaluations of traditional drug courts had odds ratio effect sizes greater than 1.0, indicating lower recidivism for drug court participants. The random effects mean effect size (see table 27.2) for traditional drug courts is 1.69 (95 percent C.I. 1.51–1.91). A mean effect size of this magnitude suggests that if 50 percent of participants recidivated, then approximately 63 percent of nonparticipants recidivated. And if the assumption of a 50 percent recidivism rate for the treatment group is reasonable, then this mean effect size suggests that participation in a drug court reduces recidivism by 13 percentage points. A similar mean effect size is found for drug outcomes (1.59 with 95 percent C.I. 1.31–1.92).

In seven of the eight DWI court evaluations, court participants had lower recidivism rates than comparisons (i.e., odds ratio larger than 1.0). In comparison with traditional drug courts, DWI courts had somewhat larger mean effect sizes for both types of outcomes but much wider confidence intervals due to the small number of DWI evaluations. And despite the modest number of such evaluations, the mean effect size for both outcomes is statistically significant.

Likewise, in six of the seven juvenile drug court evaluations, court participants had lower recidivism rates than comparisons. However, while the mean effect sizes for juvenile drug courts on both general and drug recidivism outcomes are greater than 1.0 (indicating lower recidivism for court participants), these mean effect sizes are not statistically significant. This lack of statistical significance appears to be a function of the modest number of evaluations and the small sample sizes typically used (most had total sample sizes less than two hundred).

The magnitude of these treatment effects may strike some readers as modest, but it is important to note that these mean effect sizes are larger than that of any other widely applied criminal justice based drug treatment program. For example, a recent meta-analytic synthesis of incarceration-based drug treatment found that the random effects mean odds ratio for such drug interventions on general measures of recidivism was 1.37 (95 percent C.I. 1.24–1.51; Mitchell, Wilson, and

Table 27.2. Random effects mean effect size by type of court and type of outcome

	Traditional drug court		Juvenile drug court		DWI court	
Outcome	Mean (95% CI)	k	Mean (95% CI)	k	Mean (95% CI)	k
General recidivism	1.69* (1.51–1.91)	60	1.53 (0.92–2.55)	7	1.79* (1.27–2.50)	8
Drug recidivism	1.59* (1.31–1.92)	28	1.71 (0.47–6.19)	4	2.19* (1.02–4.68)	6

* $p<.05$; i.e., null hypothesis of a random effects mean equal to zero is rejected at .05 level of statistical significance.

MacKenzie 2007). The mean effect size for drug courts on general measures of recidivism also is larger than that of prison-based therapeutic communities (random-effects mean of 1.38 with a 95 percent C.I. 1.17–1.62 [Mitchell, Wilson, and MacKenzie 2007, 362]). And another recent meta-analysis of criminal justice based drug treatment interventions administered in the community (e.g., Treatment Alternatives to Street Crime or TASC programs) also indicated more modest treatment effects (Chanhatasilpa, MacKenzie, and Hickman 2000). While such comparisons are obviously complicated by differences in sample characteristics (e.g., perhaps incarceration-based treatment programs treat clients with more severe problems) and research methodology, drug courts' average treatment effect appears substantively larger than that of any other type of criminal justice—based drug treatment program.

Coded features of the traditional drug courts evaluations' were used to "explain" variation in the magnitude of treatment effects (see table 27.3). Perhaps the most important finding is that the mean effect size for traditional drug courts does *not* statistically differ by methodological rigor. This finding indicates that traditional drug courts' effects are *not* confined to methodologically weak evaluations. While the mean effects do not statistically differ by methodological rigor, evaluations with the lowest methodological rating had the lowest average treatment effects and the most rigorous evaluations had the largest treatment effects. Thus, the strongest evidence of traditional drug courts' effectiveness is found in evaluations with the greatest rigor.

Another important issue concerns the duration of drug courts' effects. Several of the early reviews questioned the long-term effects of drug courts on recidivism outcomes and whether drug courts' effects persist after drug court participation ends (see, e.g., GAO 1997; Belenko 2001). Two of the coded features were used to address these issues: the maximum length of the recidivism observation period; and the whether the observation period for the recidivism measure overlaps completely, partially, or not at all with the period of participation in the drug court. The analyses reported in table 27.3 indicate that drug courts' recidivism suppressing effects diminish as the length of recidivism tracking period increases. The treatment effects are highest (mean odds ratio of 1.88) in evaluations that follow research participants for twelve to twenty-four months, but they shrink as the tracking period becomes longer. Yet, even in those evaluations that track recidivism for more than three years, the recidivism of treatment participants is still statistically lower than that of comparisons (mean odds ratio of 1.23). A related but distinct question concerns the persistence of drug courts' effects after program participation ends. Surprisingly, treatment effects are longer (1.65) in evaluations that examined recidivism only after treatment participation ended than in evaluations where the recidivism tracking period and period of active involvement in drug court overlap. Subsequent analyses (not shown) reveal that evaluations, which examined only post-program recidivism, typically had short tracking periods of two years or less. When only effect

Table 27.3. Moderator analysis for traditional drug courts' effect sizes

Variable	Mean ES	95% CI	k
Publication status*			
Published	1.69	1.54–1.85	23
Unpublished	1.36	1.28–1.43	37
Max length of follow-up*			
12 or less months	1.45	1.32–1.59	18
12–24 months	1.88	1.67–2.13	17
24–36 months	1.42	1.24–1.64	9
36+ months	1.23	1.14–1.34	3
Follow-up-Treatment overlap*			
Complete overlap with treatment period	1.33	1.17–1.51	12
Partial overlap with treatment period	1.40	1.32–1.48	28
No overlap with treatment period	1.65	1.48–1.84	19
Method of disposition*			
Pre-plea	1.66	1.51–1.83	18
Post-plea	1.52	1.38–1.69	18
Mixed/Other	1.22	1.14–1.32	11
No Information	1.70	1.47–1.95	13
Gender composition			
All male (90%+ male)	—	—	—
Mostly male (60–90% male)	1.47	1.39–1.54	49
Approx. equal (59–40% male)	1.32	0.85–2.04	2
Mostly female (39–10% male)	—	—	—
All female (<10% male)	1.62	0.97–2.71	1
Offender type			
Non-violent offenders	1.47	1.40–1.55	55
Includes violent offenders	1.20	1.05–1.38	5
Methodological rigor			
Weak quasi-experiment	1.33	1.17–1.51	12
Standard quasi-experiment	1.42	1.33–1.51	30
Rigorous quasi-experiment	1.54	1.40–1.69	15
Uncompromised random experiment	1.47	1.10–1.95	3

* $p<.05$; i.e., null hypothesis of equal category means is rejected at .05 level of statistical significance.

sizes from evaluations that track recidivism for two years or less are considered, the mean effect sizes for complete, partial, and no overlap are statistically and virtually identical (all approximately 1.59). Thus, the recidivism-reducing effects of traditional drug courts do persist beyond the period of treatment, but these effects diminish with time, particularly after three years.

These findings offer substantial support for the effectiveness of drug courts, especially traditional drug courts, in recidivism outcomes. Evidence of the effectiveness of all three types of drug courts is found in the above summary, but it is weakest for juvenile drug courts and most robust for traditional drug courts. Evidence of traditional drug courts' effectiveness is strongest in more rigorous evaluations. These effects last beyond the period of program participation but diminish over time. And perhaps most important, the magnitude of drug courts' effects are larger than other widely adopted criminal justice—based drug treatment programs. Based in large part on such findings, several scholars have concluded that the effectiveness of drug courts is a settled issue (e.g., see Marlowe et al. 2006b).

Why are drug courts effective? The answer is that the drug court model capitalizes on four remarkably consistent research findings. First, the frequency of drug use is positively and strongly related to the frequency of (non-drug use) offending (see e.g., Ball, Schaffer, and Nurco 1981; Johnson et al. 1985; Nurco et al. 1988). Second, substance-abuse treatment is effective in reducing both drug use and criminal activity (e.g., see Simpson 1982; Hubbard, Freeman-Wilson, et al. 1984; Hubbard, Rachel, et al. 1989; Anglin and Hser 1990; Simpson 1990). Third, substance-abuse treatment increases in effectiveness as time in treatment increases (e.g., see Simpson 1979; Anglin and Hser 1990; Wexler, Falkin, and Lipton 1990; Peters, Haas, and Hunt 2001). Fourth, substance-abuse treatment is just as effective with coerced participants as voluntary treatment seekers (e.g., see Anglin, Brecht, and Maddahian 1990; Farabee, Prendergast, and Anglin 1998). The drug court model capitalizes on these research findings by combining substance-abuse treatment with the coercive power of the court. Court actors provide drug court clients with incentives and sanctions all designed to compel offenders to initiate, stay in, and complete drug treatment.

C. Unresolved Issues

The literature assessing the effectiveness of drug courts is large and robust. It finds considerable evidence of drug courts' effectiveness in reducing criminal behavior. An implication is that the marginal benefit of additional evaluations of traditional drug courts, especially evaluations using weak or standard quasi-experimental designs, is likely to be exceedingly small. The need, if there is one, is for more evaluations using experimental designs—the results of such research hold the promise of convincing even the staunchest drug court critics of their effectiveness.

The most fundamental unresolved issue in drug court research is why some drug courts are more effective than others. What practices, characteristics, and features cause some drug courts to produce large recidivism suppressing effects, while others have no such effects? Longshore and colleagues (2001) offer an interesting and insightful framework for addressing such questions. They argue that the most effective drug courts exert more *leverage* (i.e., the consequences of failing are more severe), have less *population severity* (in terms of severity of drug use, criminal involvement, or both), more *program intensity* (e.g., more frequent drug tests), more *predictability* in that clients "know how the court will respond if they are compliant or noncompliant" (16), and more *rehabilitative emphasis*, as opposed to punitive emphasis (e.g., a relatively large number of positive drug tests are required before an intermediate sanction like a short jail stay is ordered). Using such a framework could prove useful in examining the variable effects of drug courts.

Another important unresolved issue concerns whether the traditional drug court model can be expanded to more serious offenders and maintain its impressive results. Drug courts throughout the United States have almost uniformly restricted drug court eligibility to nonviolent offenders—largely due to federal regulations that require this provision to receive federal funds. Drug courts restrict program eligibility in other ways as well. For example, in many courts offenders convicted of distribution or sales offenses are excluded. Given that a large proportion of drug distribution and sales offenses are committed by drug users trying to support their expensive habits (see e.g., Johnson et al. 1985), such policies may exclude a substantial population of offenders who could benefit from drug court treatment. Likewise, many courts also exclude drug-abusing offenders with extensive criminal histories and serious mental health issues. While such offenders are obviously more of a risk to public safety, offering effective drug treatment to such offenders holds the promise of producing large reductions in re-offending. Further, there is some evidence that expanding the drug court model to broader populations of offenders can be effective. Perhaps the most prominent example of this is found in the research of Adele Harrell and colleagues who evaluated the National Demonstration of the Breaking the Cycle (BTC) project. This project applied a relatively weak version of the drug court model to all drug-abusing offenders arrested on felony charges in three sites (Tacoma, Washington;, Birmingham, Alabama; and Jacksonville, Florida). In spite of partial program implementation, the evaluation found that participation in the BTC was associated with reductions in criminal behavior (Harrell et al. 2002; Mitchell and Harrell 2006).

A related unresolved issue concerns the effectiveness of expanding the traditional drug court to juveniles and DWI offenders. The review of juvenile drug court and DWI court evaluations reveals that both types of courts show promise, but their effectiveness is unsettled. The implications are clear. First, more evaluations of juvenile drug courts are needed. There is an especially sharp need for evaluations of juvenile drug courts of the highest quality (i.e., uncompromised randomized experiments). Second, while the existing research suggests that DWI courts do reduce recidivism, the relatively small number of such evaluations indicates a need for additional evaluations.

III. Beyond Drug Courts

The success of the drug court model has led to the development of other specialty courts. The two most common of such specialty courts are domestic violence and mental health courts. Considerably less common are types of specialty courts such as community and re-entry courts. This section focuses on describing the practices of domestic violence courts and mental health courts, and their effectiveness in reducing criminal behavior.

A. Domestic violence courts

Domestic violence court is a term often applied to any court or court docket that focuses on domestic violence cases. Some "domestic violence courts" are administrative. These administrative courts focus on issues like speedy adjudication of such cases or ensuring that domestic violence is punished appropriately. The term "domestic violence court" is also applied to courts that parallel the drug court model in that they create separate courts or court dockets for such cases, bring together court actors from multiple agencies in a collaborative effort to tailor an intervention for each case, integrate a treatment component into the court process, and closely monitor offender compliance with the intervention. I focus on the latter.

Domestic violence courts emerged as public awareness of domestic violence increased and in response to the need to deal with such cases more effectively. The public's increasing awareness of domestic violence issues has led to police adopting tactics like mandatory arrest laws, which in turn caused a surge in domestic violence cases. Between 1989 and 1998, domestic violence cases in state courts rose 178 percent (Ostrom and Kauder 1999). Yet, traditional court systems' handling of such cases was viewed unfavorably, as conviction rates were often low and sentences were short.

Reformers seized upon the drug court model. While there is considerable variation in the practices of domestic violence courts, most often they bring together and coordinate multiple criminal justice and social service agencies in an effort to hold offenders accountable and to solve a specific crime problem. While treating the batterer is a concern of domestic violence courts, a larger concern is victim safety, which is often achieved through efforts to ensure offenders are convicted of their crimes, sanctioned appropriately, and closely monitored in the community. Thus, a key difference between domestic violence and drug courts is that domestic violence courts often have a more punitive approach.

As an example of a domestic violence court, consider Lexington County's (South Carolina) court evaluated by Gover, MacDonald, and Alpert (2003). All nonfelony battery cases were referred to a specialized court, which combined the efforts of local police and prosecutors with the help of a victims' advocate, and mental health counselors who assigned offenders to appropriate treatment programs. Upon conviction, the court suspended jail sentences in exchange for successful completion of a twenty-six-week batterer intervention. The goals of this intervention were to "hold perpetrators of domestic violence accountable through increasing fines and time spent in jail, ... improve victim safety, ... [and to] reduce recidivism" (114–15).

Evaluations of domestic violence courts are few in number but increasing rapidly. Results are mixed with approximately even numbers of evaluations finding reductions in recidivism (e.g., Goldkamp et al. 1996; Gover, MacDonald, and Alpert 2003; Harrell et al. 2006; Harrell et al. 2007 [Massachusetts site]) and finding no reductions (Newmark et al. 2001; Peterson 2003, 2004; Harrell et al. 2007 [Michigan]). Determining the effectiveness of domestic violence courts is complicated by the focus on victim safety via close monitoring of offenders; this may increase the likelihood of re-arrest, probation revocation, and re-conviction. Thus, evaluations that use official criminal justice measures of recidivism like re-arrest may confound the *effects* of the intervention with the *actions* of the intervention itself. As a result, evaluations using self-reported victimization are preferred. Yet, even when such measures are considered, the effects of domestic violence courts are mixed (e.g., Harrell et al. 2007).

B. Mental Health Courts

Mental health courts intervene with a problem population. The number and proportion of offenders in jail and prison with mental health issues have increased dramatically over the past thirty years, as de-institutionalization of the mentally ill has been more popular (The Sentencing Project 2002). It is estimated that appropriately 16 percent of offenders in state prisons, local jails, and on probation are mentally ill (Ditton 1999). In some states jails and prisons house more people with mental illness than do mental hospitals (Torrey 1995). Upon release from incarceration, offenders with mental illnesses typically are not linked to mental health resources in the community; they often also lack resources and social support. These factors increase the likelihood of re-offending and re-involvement with the criminal justice system.

Mental health courts apply the drug court model. Mentally ill offenders, typically charged with misdemeanors, are diverted out of the traditional court process into a separate court docket, where dedicated court actors and mental health professionals work collaboratively to tailor an appropriate intervention to each case. Participation is voluntary but, once enrolled in the program, adherence to the treatment plan and the court's rules is closely monitored. Offenders who successfully complete the intervention are rewarded with dismissed charges or reduced sanctions.

The spread of mental health courts is occurring much faster than the accumulation of evidence supporting their effectiveness. The first mental health court began operation in Broward County, Florida, in 1997 (Boothroyd et al. 2005). Currently, more than two hundred operate in at least thirty-five states (Huddleston, Marlowe, and Casebolt 2008). Like drug courts, the proliferation of mental health courts has been spurred by federal legislation appropriating funds for such courts. Congress passed America's Law Enforcement and Mental Health Project Act in 2000 and the Mentally Ill Offender Treatment and Crime Reduction Act of 2004, both of which provide funding for mental health courts.

Only a handful of court evaluations are available. The majority support the effectiveness of mental health courts in reducing criminal behavior. In one of the earliest evaluations, Trupin and Richards (2003) compared voluntary participants in Seattle's mental health courts with a group of eligible offenders who chose not to participate. Approximately nine months after beginning the program, participants had fewer jail bookings than nonparticipants. An evaluation of a mental health court operating in San Francisco also found considerable evidence of effectiveness in reducing recidivism. McNiel and Binder's (2007) found that the likelihood of program participants being charged with any new crimes "was about 26 percent lower than that of comparable individuals who received treatment as usual, and the likelihood of mental health court participants being charged with new violent crimes was 55 percent lower" than that of the comparison group (1401). Likewise, an evaluation of a mental health court in an unnamed county in the southeastern United States conducted by Moore and Hiday (2006) found that court participants had fewer re-arrests and reduced severity of re-arrests, but the prevalence of re-arrest was not statistically different from that of the comparison group.

Several evaluations have found less support for these courts' effectiveness. An evaluation of Broward County's mental health court conducted by Christy and colleagues (2005) found that, one year after program entry, participants and nonparticipants were not statistically different on a host of re-arrest measures (e.g., proportion re-arrested, number of re-arrests, time to re-arrest). Another study of the same court found no differences between court participants and nonparticipants on symptoms of mental health problems as measured by the Brief Psychiatric Rating Scale (Boothroyd et al. 2005). The only randomized experimental evaluation of a mental health court (Cosden et al. 2005) found that after one year, participants had fewer new convictions than the control group, but after two years the two groups exhibited no statistically significant differences on any of the measures of criminal activity. Taken as a whole, evaluations of mental health courts are promising, but confidence in their cumulative findings is undermined by the small number of evaluations.

C. Non-Drug Specialty Courts: Boom or Bust?

Like drug courts before them, domestic violence and mental health courts are spreading rapidly. Their proliferation has been spurred by rising public concern about the problems they address, the fit between these courts' practices and prevailing sensibilities about crime (i.e., offender accountability), and federal aid to local jurisdictions adopting these courts. Yet, research assessing these courts' effectiveness is scant, mixed, and unconvincing.

History reveals that many criminal justice innovations that find initial public appeal and governmental support fail to reduce criminal behavior and eventually lose popularity. Intensive supervision probation (ISP) and boot camp programs are two recent examples. It remains to be seen whether domestic violence and mental health courts will meet the same fate, or will find both popular and empirical support, like drug courts. Given that these courts are based on the drug court model, it would be easy to assume that domestic violence and mental health courts eventually will be found to be effective. However, unlike drug courts, which build on four long-standing, bedrock findings that appear to be central to their effectiveness, domestic violence and mental health courts have no such foundation. Thus the assumption that non-drug specialty courts will eventually be shown to have the same sort of consistent crime-suppressing effects as drug courts is more dubious than might appear at first glance.

IV. Conclusion

The rapid proliferation of drug courts across the United States has been remarkable. In less than twenty years, drug courts have gone from a solitary court in one jurisdiction to a national phenomenon with thousands in operation, and at least one in every state and territory.

The vast majority of evaluations find that drug court participants have lower recidivism than nonparticipants, and often these differences are considerable. Cumulatively, this body of research finds that the magnitude of drug courts' effects on recidivism is larger than any other widely applied criminal justice—based drug treatment program. While this evidence is not impervious to criticisms regarding its rigor, the debate about the effectiveness of "traditional" drug courts (i.e., courts focusing on adult illicit substance abusers) is nearing a close. The evidence strongly suggests that drug courts work.

The clearest policy implication of this research is that continued funding, development, and operation of traditional drug courts is warranted. Another implication is that continued evaluations, particularly nonexperimental evaluations, add very little to the existing research base. The most useful future research will either apply randomized experimental methodologies, focus on establishing which court features and practices distinguish more effective drug courts from less effective ones, or will utilize both.

Existing research suggests that dedicated DWI courts are effective in reducing recidivism, but the number of such evaluations urges caution. The evidence of the effectiveness of juvenile drug courts is even shakier. The obvious implication is that evaluations of these nontraditional drug courts are a research priority. Further, the success of traditional drug courts begs the question: Could the traditional drug court model be effectively applied to offenders typically ineligible (such as violent offenders and offenders with extensive histories of serious offending)? Existing evidence suggests that loosening the strict eligibility criteria characteristic of many drug courts could yield sizable reductions in recidivism.

Domestic violence and mental health courts are spreading rapidly across the United States. Given the seriousness of domestic violence and the sheer number of offenders with mental health issues, continued funding of such courts is justifiable. Yet, it is important for evaluation research to keep pace. The most useful future evaluation research of non-drug specialty courts will seek not only to address the effects of these courts on multiple outcomes but also detail the practices of the evaluated courts, so a set of best practices can be identified. Ultimately, for the specialty court movement to continue to grow and to survive in the long term, the effectiveness of non-drug specialty courts must to be established.

NOTES

1. This number excludes teen courts, truancy, and child-support courts, all of which do not fit the definition of specialty courts.

2. It is ironic that the bulk of federal funding for drug courts comes from the Violent Crime Control Act of 1994, as the Act forbids the distribution of funds to drug courts that allow clients with current charges or prior convictions involving serious *violence*.

3. According to a 1997 US General Accounting Office (GAO) report, approximately 80 percent of drug courts operating at the end of 1996 received federal funds (GAO 1997, 38).

4. According to the 1997 GAO report, 3.5 percent of clients voluntarily quit drug court programming (55).

5. Note that whenever odds ratios were converted to percentages, it was arbitrarily assumed that one group had a 50 percent recidivism rate. This assumption was made purely for computation convenience. The drawback with this convenient assumption is that if any other recidivism rate had been assumed, then the percentage differences between groups would be smaller.

REFERENCES

Anglin, M. Douglas, Mary-Lynn Brecht, and Ebrahim Maddahian. 1990. "Pretreatment Characteristics and Treatment Performance of Legally Coerced Versus Voluntary Methadone Maintenance Admissions." *Criminology* 27: 537–57.

Anglin, M. Douglas, and Yih-Ing Hser. 1990. "Treatment of Drug Abuse." In *Drugs and Crime*, ed. Michael Tonry and James Q. Wilson. Vol. 13 of *Crime and Justice: A Review of Research,* edited by Michael Tonry. Chicago: University of Chicago.

Ball, John C., John W. Shaffer, and David N. Nurco. 1981. "The Criminality of Heroin Addicts: When Addicted and When Off Opiates." In *The Drugs-crime Connection*, edited by James A. Inciardi. Beverly Hills, CA: Sage Publications.

Beckett, Katherine. 1997. *Making Crime Pay*. New York: Oxford University Press.

Belenko, Steven R. 2001. *Research on Drug Courts: A Critical Review 2001 Update*. New York: National Center on Addiction and Substance Abuse.

Berman, Greg, and John Feinblatt. 2005. *Good Courts: The Case for Problem-Solving Courts*. New York: New Press.

Blumstein, Alfred, and Allen J. Beck. 1999. "Population Growth in U.S. Prisons, 1980–1996." In *Prisons*, edited by Michael Tonry and Joan Petersilia. Vol. 26 of *Crime and Justice: A Review of Research*, edited by Michael Tonry.Chicago, IL: University of Chicago Press.

Boothroyd, Roger A., Cynthia Calkins Mercado, Norman G. Poythree, Annette Christy, and John Petrila. 2005. "Clinical Outcomes of Defendants in Mental Health Courts." *Psychiatric Services* 56: 829–34.

Bureau of Justice Assistance. 2009. "BJA Programs: Drug Court Discretionary Grant Program Office of Justice Programs." http://www.ojp.usdoj.gov/BJA/grant/drugcourts. html.

Chanhatasilpa, Chanchalat, Doris L. MacKenzie, and Laura J. Hickman. 2000. "The Effectiveness of Community-Based Programs for Chemically Dependent Offenders: A Review and Assessment of the Research." *Journal of Substance Abuse Treatment* 94: 383–93.

Christy, Annette, Norman G. Poythress, Roger A. Boothroyd, John Petrila, and Shabnam Mehra. 2005. "Evaluating the Efficiency and Community Safety Goals of the Broward County Mental Health Court." *Behavioral Sciences and the Law* 23:227–43.

Cosden, Merith, Jeffrey K. Ellens, Jeffrey L. Schnell, and Yasmeen Yamini-Diouf. 2005. "Efficacy of a Mental Health Treatment Court with Assertive Community Treatment." *Behavioral Sciences and the Law* 23: 199–214.

Dickie, J. L. 2000. *Summit County Juvenile Drug Court: Evaluation Report July 1, 1999–June 30, 2000*. Akron, OH: The Institute for Health and Social Policy, University of Akron.

———. 2001. *Summit County Juvenile Drug court: Evaluation Report July 1, 2000–June 30, 2001*. Akron, OH: The Institute of Health and Social Policy, University of Akron.

Ditton, Paula M. 1999. *Mental Health and Treatment of Inmates and Probationers*. Washington, DC: Bureau of Justice Statistics.

Drug Court Program Office. 2000. *About the Drug Courts Program Office*. Washington, DC: Drug Courts Program Office.

Farabee, David, Michael Prendergast, and M. Douglas Anglin. 1998. "The Effectiveness of Coerced Treatment for Drug-Abusing Offenders." *Federal Probation* 62: 3–10.

Farole, Donald J., Jr. 2003. *The Harlem Parole Reentry Court Evaluation: Implementation and Preliminary Impacts*. New York: Center for Court Innovation.

Gebelein, Richard S. 2000. *The Rebirth of Rehabilitation: Promise and Perils of Drug Courts, Papers From the Executive Sessions on Sentencing and Corrections*. Washington, DC: National Institute of Justice.

Goldkamp, John S. 2002. "The Impact of Drug Courts." *Criminology and Public Policy* 2: 197–206.

Goldkamp, John S., Doris Weiland, Mark Collins, and Michael White. 1996. *The Role of Drug and Alcohol Abuse in Domestic Violence and Its Treatment: Dade County's Domestic Violence Court Experiment, Final Report*. Philadelphia: Crime and Justice Research Institute.

Gover, Angela R., John M. MacDonald, and Geoffrey P. Alpert. 2003. "Combating Domestic Violence: Findings from an Evaluation of a Local Domestic Violence Court." *Criminology and Public Policy* 3: 109–32.

Harrell, Adele, Ojmarrh Mitchell, Alexa Hirst, Douglas Marlowe, and Jeffery Merrill. 2002. "Breaking the Cycle of Drugs and Crime: Findings from the Birmingham BTC Demonstration." *Criminology and Public Policy* 1: 187–216.

Harrell, Adele, Lisa Newmark, Christy Visher, and Jennifer Castro. 2007. *Final Report on the Evaluation of the Judicial Oversight Demonstration.* Washington, DC: The Urban Institute.

Harrell, Adele, Megan Schaffer, Christine DeStefano, and Jennifer Castro. 2006. *The Evaluation of the Milwaukee's Judicial Oversight Demonstration.* Washington, DC: The Urban Institute.

Hubbard, Robert L., Mary Ellen Marsden, J. Valley Rachel, Henrick J. Harwood, Elizabeth R. Cavanaugh, and Harold M. Ginzburg. 1989. *Drug Abuse Treatment: A National Study of Effectiveness.* Chapel Hill: University of North Carolina Press.

Hubbard, Robert L., J. Valley Rachel, S. Gail Craddock, and Elizabeth R. Cavanaugh. 1984. "Treatment Outcome Prospective Study (TOPS): Client Characteristics and Behaviors Before, During, and After Treatment." In *Drug Abuse Treatment Evaluation: Strategies, Progress, and Prospects*, edited by F. M. Tims and J. P. Ludford. Washington, DC: National Institute on Drug Abuse.

Huddleston, C. West, III, Karen Freeman-Wilson, and Donna L. Boone. 2004. *Painting the Current Picture: A National Report Card on Drug Courts and Other Problem Solving Courts in the United States.* Alexandria, VA: National Drug Court Institute.

Huddleston, C. West, III, Douglas B. Marlowe, and Rachel Casebolt. 2008. *Painting the Current Picture: A National Report Card on Drug Courts and Other Problem-Solving Court Programs in the United States.* Washington, DC: National Drug Court Institute.

Johnson, Bruce D., Paul J. Goldstein, Edward Preble, James Schmeidler, Douglas S. Lipton, Barry Spunt, and Thomas Miller. 1985. *Taking Care of Business: The Economics of Crime by Heroin Abusers.* Lexington, MA: Lexington Books.

Kalich, DeAnn M., and Rhonda D. Evans. 2006. "Drug Court: An Effective Alternative to Incarceration." *Deviant Behavior* 27: 569–90.

Kaye, Judith S. 1999. "Making the Case for Hands-On Courts." *Newsweek*, October 11, 13.

Lee, Eric. 2000. *Community Courts: An Evolving Model.* Washington, DC: Bureau of Justice Assistance.

Longshore, Douglas, Susan W. Turner, Andrew Morral, Adele Harrell, Duane McBride, Elizabeth Deschenes, and Martin Iguchi. 2001. "Drug Courts: A Conceptual Framework." *Journal of Drug Issues* 31: 7–26.

Mann, Charles C. 1994. "Can Meta-Analysis Make Policy?" *Science* 266: 960–62.

Marlowe, Douglas B., David S. Festinger, Patricia A. Lee, Karen L. Dugosh, and Kathleen M. Benasutti. 2006a. "Matching Judicial Supervision to Clients' Risk Status In Drug Court." *Crime and Delinquency* 52: 52–76.

Marlowe, Douglas B., Cary Heck, C. West Huddleston III, and Rachel Casebolt. 2006b. "A National Research Agenda for Drug Courts: Plotting the Course for Second-Generation Scientific Inquiry." *Drug Court Review* 5: 1–32.

McNiel, Dale E., and Renee L. Binder. 2007. "Effectiveness of a Mental Health Court in Reducing Criminal Recidivism and Violence." *American Journal of Psychiatry* 164: 1395–403.

Mitchell, Ojmarrh. 2009. "Ineffectiveness, Financial Waste, and Unfairness: The Legacy of the War on Drugs." *Journal of Crime and Justice* 32(2): 1–19.

Mitchell, Ojmarrh, and Adele Harrell. 2006. "Evaluation of the Breaking the Cycle Demonstration Project: Jacksonville, FL and Tacoma, WA." *Journal of Drug Issues* 36: 93–114.

Mitchell, Ojmarrh, David B. Wilson, and Doris L. MacKenzie. 2007. "Does Incarceration-Based Drug Treatment Reduce Recidivism? A Meta-Analytic Synthesis of the Research." *Journal of Experimental Criminology* 3: 353–75.

Moore, Marlee E., and Virginia Aldige Hiday. 2006. "Mental Health Court Outcomes: A Comparison of Re-Arrest and Re-Arrest Severity between Mental Health Court and Traditional Court Participants." *Law and Human Behavior* 30: 659–74.

National Association of Drug Court Professionals. 1997. Defining Drug Courts: The Key Components. Washington, DC: Bureau of Justice Assistance.

Newmark, Lisa, Mike Rempel, Kelly Diffily, and Kamala Mallik Kane. 2001. *Specialized Felony Domestic Violence Courts: Lessons on Implementation and Impacts for the Kings County Experience*. Washington, DC: The Urban Institute.

Nolan, James L. 2001. *Reinventing Justice: The American Drug Court Movement*. Princeton, NJ: Princeton University.

Nurco, David N., Thomas E. Hanlon, Thomas W. Kinlock, and Karen R. Duszynsi. 1988 "Differential Criminal Patterns of Narcotic Addicts Over an Addiction Career." *Criminology* 26: 407–23.

Ostrom, Brian J., and Neal B. Kauder. 1999. *Examining the Work of State Courts, 1998: A National Perspective from the Court Statistics Project*. Williamsburg, VA: National Center for State Courts.

Peters, Roger H., Amie L. Haas, and W. Michael. Hunt. 2001. "Treatment 'Dosage' Effects in Drug Court Programs." *Journal of Offender Rehabilitation* 33: 63–72.

Peterson, Richard R. 2003. *The Impact of Case Processing on Re-arrests Among Domestic Violence Offenders in New York City*. New York: New York City Criminal Justice Agency.

———. 2004. *The Impact of Manhattan's Specialized Domestic Violence Court*. New York: New York City Criminal Justice Agency.

Reagan, Ronald. *Remarks at a White House Briefing for Service Organization Representatives on Drug Abuse, July 30, 1986*. Ronald Reagan Presidential Library 1986. http://www.reagan.utexas.edu/archives/speeches/1986/073086a.htm.

Reinarman, Craig, and Harry G. Levine. 1997. "The Crack Attack: Politics and Media in the Crack Scare." In *Crack in America: Demon Drugs and Social Justice*, ed. C. Reinarman and H. G. Levine. Berkeley: University of California Press.

The Sentencing Project. 2002. *Mentally Ill Offenders in the Criminal Justice System: An Analysis and Prescription*. Washington, DC: The Sentencing Project.

Sheppard, David, and Patricia Kelly. 2002. *Juvenile Gun Courts: Promoting Accountability and Providing Treatment*. Washington, DC: Office of Juvenile Justice and Delinquency Prevention.

Simpson, D. Dwayne. 1979. "The Relation Of Time Spent In Drug Abuse Treatment To Posttreatment Outcome." *American Journal of Psychiatry* 136: 1449–53.

———. 1982. "Effectiveness of Treatment for Drug Abuse: An Overview of the DARP Research Program." *Advances in Alcohol and Substance Abuse* 2: 7–29.

———. 1990. *Opioid Addiction and Treatment: A 12-Year Follow-Up*. Malabar, FL: Robert E. Krieger.

Tonry, Michael. 2004. *Thinking about Crime: Sense and Sensibility in American Penal Culture*. New York: Oxford.

Torrey, E. Fuller. 1995. "Jails and Prisons: America's New Mental Hospitals." *American Journal of Public Health* 85: 1611–613.

Trupin, Eric, and Henry Richards. 2003. "Seattle's Mental Health Courts: Early Indicators of Effectiveness." *International Journal of Law and Psychiatry* 26: 33–53.

US General Accounting Office (GAO). 1997. *Drug Courts: Overview Of Growth, Characteristics, and Results*. Washington, DC: United States General Accounting Office.

———. 2005. *Adult Drug Courts: Evidence Indicates Recidivism Reductions and Mixed Results for Other Outcomes*. Washington, DC: United States General Accounting Office.

US Office of National Drug Control Policy (ONDCP). 1989. *National Drug Control Strategy*. Washington, DC: Office of National Drug Control Policy, Executive Office of the President.

Western, Bruce. 2006. *Punishment and Inequality in America*. New York: Russell Sage Foundation.

Wexler, Harry K., Gregory P. Falkin, and Douglas S. Lipton. 1990. "Outcome Evaluation of a Prison Therapeutic Community for Substance Abuse Treatment." *Criminal Justice and Behavior* 17: 71–92.

Wilson, David B., Ojmarrh Mitchell, and Doris L. MacKenzie. 2006. "A Systematic Review of Drug Court Effects on Recidivism." *Journal of Experimental Criminology* 2: 459–87.

CHAPTER 28

....

PRISONS

....

YVONNE JEWKES

NEARLY ten million people are held in penal institutions throughout the world (Walmsley 2009). The United States heads the world prison population table with a rate of 756 prisoners per 100,000 of the national population and England and Wales is the biggest user of imprisonment in Europe with 153 inmates per 100,000 of the general population (Walmsley 2009). Imprisonment is, however, but one stage of the journey that offenders committed to custody make. Prison has been described as a "sophisticated sausage machine" (Caird 1974, 9), and it is not surprising that the more people who are stuffed in at one end, the more problems are created at the other. The efficiency and effectiveness of probation services, parole supervision, and re-entry programs are severely compromised as prison populations continue to rise unchecked, and high re-offending rates in the United States and the United Kingdom indicate that imprisonment has a criminogenic effect (Nagin, Cullen, and Jonson 2009). Further, the extent to which periods in custody have become a normalized and anticipated part of the lifecourse for sections of the population, resulting in devastating socio-economic consequences for certain (mostly minority ethnic) communities suggests that imprisonment has become an inevitable, enduring, and inarguable feature of punishment in both countries.

In its exploration of why the United States and the United Kingdom have acquired such a deep cultural attachment to the prison, this chapter is divided into four sections. Section I introduces the history of prisons and the development of imprisonment as the primary means of punishment in Western industrialized nations. It paints the history of imprisonment with very broad brushstrokes, highlighting a few key moments in the development of the prison that leave a persistent legacy and continue to shape our understanding of prisons today (a much more detailed history of imprisonment in the West can be found in Morris and Rothman

[1995]). Section II explores recent history (since the 1960s) and attempts to account for the dramatic increases and racial disparities in the US prison population during a period when overall crime rates were declining. Section III examines the sociological and psychological literature on the "effects" of imprisonment and considers the particular problems of drugs, mental illness, and suicide in prisons. Section IV reflects on some of the most salient and challenging issues that are raised.

The main conclusions are as follows:

- Since the end of the eighteenth century, the prison has been the predominant form of punishment in the West. The history of imprisonment in the United States and the United Kingdom is a broadly shared history with each country exporting penal philosophies and practices to the other.
- Since the 1970s, both nations have introduced penal policies and laws that have criminalized greater numbers of people and had a disproportionate impact on young, black males from impoverished urban areas. Despite generally falling levels of crime, imprisonment has become a central feature of neopopulist politics, which has come to dominate political debate and policy formulation. Yet the fact that different states in the United States and different countries across Europe experience similar crime rates, but still have markedly varying incarceration rates, challenges the orthodoxy that mass imprisonment is unavoidable or is always desirable to the general populace.
- Sociological and psychological academic research has, on the whole, reached quite different conclusions about the effects of imprisonment. While psychologists have largely concluded that imprisonment is not especially harmful to the individual, scholars from the sociological tradition have argued that prison is a painful, debilitating, and stigmatizing experience, which requires the prisoner to adopt certain coping and adaptation skills in order to survive. In addition, it has been found that adverse effects are felt, not only by the prisoner but by their partner, children, family, and the community at large. Post-release offending, drug misuse, mental illness, and suicide are all disproportionately high among prison inmates; again having devastating consequences not only for the individual in custody but also for their family and for society.
- Prisons are heavily symbolic institutions, and the populist media perpetuate the notion that people commit crimes because "they" are not like "us." While evidence (e.g., from the Social Exclusion Unit 2002) shows that most of the people processed through the criminal justice system are excluded from the full range of goods, services, and rights associated with citizenship, their experiences of marginalization and deprivation are underplayed in political, policy and popular discourses.

I. A Brief Historical Overview

Most penal histories start at the end of the eighteenth century when imprisonment—of the mind and soul of the offender, as well as the body—became the predominant form of punishment in Western society (Foucault 1977). Before this time the gaol, or jail, was purely a place of detention for an indiscriminate mix of people awaiting trial or execution or committed for debt. Imprisonment was essentially a profit-making enterprise with fees charged for admission, discharge, food, clothing, lodgings, removing irons prior to a court appearance, and the "tap" (an alehouse for prisoners and visitors). Liquor was an especially sought-after commodity; in both England and America it was common for the jailer or sheriff to provide a bar charging inflated prices.

When a new jail was opened in 1773 in Pennsylvania, conditions were initially held to be a little better than previously because gallons of spirits were brought into the prison daily, and it was common for women to get arrested in order to gain access to the male prisoners. However, prisoners would barter their clothes for liquor or be forcibly stripped upon entering by other inmates seeking funds for the bar, leaving the majority of inmates impoverished, starving, and prone to disease (McConville 1998).

Mental illness has also been a defining feature of incarceration throughout history. In England, as early as 1774, local justices were obliged to appoint a resident medical officer to each prison, although it was not until 1861 that concerns about the suitability of prison for the mentally disordered precipitated the opening of a wing for mentally ill criminals at the Bethlem Hospital in London, followed two years later by the opening of Broadmoor asylum. However, these initiatives did not herald an end to the punishment of the mentally ill as contemporaneously special provision was being created within the prison system for those who were not to be transferred to hospital (Senior and Shaw 2007).

Three related processes gradually started to affect imprisonment in the early nineteenth century. First, there was growing public awareness of the appalling conditions within prisons.

Second, the emergence of "Enlightenment thinking" in Europe meant that punishment became viewed as something that could be guided by reason. Several scholars have characterized this period as a transitional one in which disciplinary institutions (prisons, schools, factories, etc.) came to control and regulate populations. Most notably, Michel Foucault (1977) contrasts the horrific public torture and execution of Damiens, hung, drawn, and quartered for attempted regicide in 1759, with the minutely detailed timetable of a reformatory for young offenders at Mettray in France eighty years later. For Foucault this demonstrates a fundamental change in punishment, from public bodily punishment in the eighteenth century, to the highly regulated prison in which the mind and soul of the offender is the central concern of the institution by the mid-nineteenth century (see also Rothman 1971).

Third, the efforts of a number of reform-minded individuals had a profound impact on the way that prisons were conceived. The Englishman John Howard (1726–90) shaped thinking about punishment beyond his own country, and in both England and the United States there began the establishment of a different kind of penal institution in which prisoners were classified, held in separate cells, and routinized through a timetable. The new institutions were clean, secure, and constructed around the belief that through hard work, religion, and solitude the prisoner could be transformed into a law-abiding citizen. By 1787 these ideas had strongly influenced a small group of concerned citizens in Pennsylvania, including Benjamin Franklin and Benjamin Rush. With a group of well-meaning Quakers and philanthropists, they set up the Philadelphia Society for Alleviating the Miseries of Public Prisons, which followed Howard's lead in advocating solitary confinement and hard labor as the most effective means for reforming criminals.

Religion was central to the nineteenth-century prison regime. During the 1820s and 1830s, two contrasting methods of faith-based reformatory prison regime emerged: the separate system (or "Pennsylvania system"), which was advocated by the Philadelphia Society and received strong approval from the recently appointed government Inspectors in England; and the silent system, exemplified by the regime at Auburn Prison in New York, which opened in 1819. Under the separate system prisoners would be kept apart at all times, held alone in separate cells where they would work, sleep, and take meals. The only time they were permitted to leave their cells was to attend chapel, when their faces would be masked, or for exercise during which they might be sent to separate exercise yards. Under the silent system, prisoners were put to hard labor and had to remain silent at all times. The aim of both the separate and the silent system was to avoid any contaminating influence, particularly for young or first-time offenders from more hardened criminals.

Although a benign faith in reformation underpinned penal systems in this era (both the Pennsylvania and the Auburn systems embodied a treatment philosophy not only in their programs but also in their architectural designs), the prisons that were established after them found it increasingly difficult to adhere to their ideals. Many became overcrowded, mismanaged, and violent, leading to greater political interference and external investigation. Gustave de Beaumont and Alexis de Tocqueville, whose mission was encapsulated in the title of their work, *On the Penitentiary System in the United States, and Its Application in France* (1833), observed that while some of the American penitentiaries they visited might serve as models elsewhere, others were "everything which ought to be avoided."

The goal of reform also became increasingly elusive in English prisons, and by the second half of the nineteenth century took a back seat altogether in what has been characterized as a period of cold barbarity (Soothill 2007, 38). Increasing public fears about dangerous criminals were driven by discussions of offenders and prisons in parliamentary debates, newspapers, and novels. Between the Gladstone Inquiry of 1895 and the "golden era" of prison reform ushered in by Alexander Paterson, prison commissioner in England and Wales, in 1922, the penal estate expanded to accommodate felons who could no longer be transported to the colonies and young offenders who were viewed as sufficiently malleable to respond positively to treatment and hard work—an approach that underpinned the earlier Borstal system which was a penal regime for delinquent boys. With an emphasis on physical labor, moral reformation and discipline backed by corporal punishment, borstals were named after the first such institution in Borstal, Kent, established in 1902. They existed in this name for eighty years before being renamed youth custody centres, which in turn evolved into the contemporary young offender institution.

In the United States, similar concerns at the end of the nineteenth century, and related anxieties about discipline, security, and overcrowding, led prison administrators to introduce the practice of *prison industry*; a precursor to today's privatized prisons. They increased the number of prison workshops in an effort to impose discipline and ease the problems of overcrowding (at least during daylight hours), and succeeded not only in offsetting some of their expenses but also showing some profit. The industrial prison was exemplified by San Quentin in California, Sing Sing in Ossining, New York, and the Illinois State Penitentiary at Statesville. Chain gangs also proliferated at this time, particularly in America's southern states.

The industrial prison came to an abrupt end during the Great Depression, when jobs became scarce across the United States, and legislation was passed that first curtailed and then prohibited convict labor. Since that time, the argument that prison labor deprives the "respectable" working class of economic opportunity has held sway in the United States, unlike in some other countries, such as Japan, where prison labor is viewed as an intrinsic element of an individual's journey to character reformation. In England and Wales, the work offered to prisoners has been designed to keep idle hands and minds occupied and has remained, on the whole, menial, repetitive, and poorly paid (on average around £10 [US$15.60] for a thirty-two-hour week; well below the legal minimum wage of £5.80[US$9.05] per hour).

Rehabilitative thinking underpinned penal policy throughout much of the twentieth century, especially in the 1950s, 1960s, and early 1970s when the welfarist model resulted in judicial proceedings being influenced by a new raft of professional experts, including social workers, psychologists, health professionals, and academics. In the United States, California, Minnesota, and Wisconsin rivaled countries such as the Netherlands and Sweden for innovation in rehabilitative programs (Rothman 1980), although by the mid-1970s treatment was coming to be seen as further expression of repressive disciplinary tendencies. The retributive or just deserts model was especially critical of rehabilitation's emphasis on what it saw as excessive intervention and denying offenders their due rights (von Hirsch 1976). It also opposed the use of indeterminate sentencing whereby prisoners would be treated for as long as it took to make them better.

The rehabilitative ideal was finally sunk by a doctrine that, in the mid- to late 1970s, had a swift and profound impact on expert knowledge, policy, and practice. The originator of this groundbreaking idea was Robert Martinson who, after analyzing 231 studies of treatment programs in the United States, concluded that: "with few and isolated exceptions, the rehabilitative efforts that have been reported so far have had no appreciable effect on recidivism" (1974, 25). Martinson's famous research is commonly, though somewhat misleadingly, paraphrased as concluding that "nothing works."

Liberals, like Martinson, found the idea that "nothing works" attractive because it could be employed to support a reduction in the use of imprisonment. However, it was equally appealing to conservatives, who used Martinson's findings to support their calls for longer sentences, more brutal regimes, and capital punishment.

Across many penal systems in the English-speaking world, educational and psychological programs were starved of funds and closed. There followed a long period when prisons became little more than warehouses; a problem exacerbated by the dramatic rises in prison populations that occurred on both sides of the Atlantic from the mid-twentieth century. Deprived of any kind of meaningful occupation, inmates' frustration led to rioting and interpersonal violence, culminating in the infamous riot at Attica State Prison in 1971 during which thirty-nine individuals, including ten staff, died (Useem and Kimball 1991).

In 1968 the US Supreme Court ruled that prisoners could sue the government for holding them in unsatisfactory conditions, and by 1991 prisons in forty states had been found unconstitutional in this regard (Mehigan and Rowe 2007). This placed a duty on prison administrators to improve conditions but did nothing to address the funding shortfall that had led to the overcrowding in the first place. When private firms started actively lobbying to be granted contracts to manage correctional facilities, the time seemed right—given rising imprisonment rates and a punitive public mood—to admit that prisons were no longer required to rehabilitate or train inmates but simply to incapacitate them, and subsequently hand them over to private sector management (Mehigan and Rowe 2007). Since then the United States has successfully—though controversially—exported the concept of prison privatization to many other Western countries, while expanding its own inmate population to previously unimaginable levels (see the collection edited by Morris and Rothman 1995 for several useful contributions on the histories of imprisonment in the United States, England, and elsewhere).

II. Recent History and the Growth of the US Prison Population

Recent history has been replete with shocking statistics about the US prison population. To take just two of the most frequently cited: one in every one hundred adult Americans is in custody; and almost half of the world's prisoners are in the United States. The majority of the US's 2.3 million inmates (62.6 percent) are held in state or federal correctional facilities; 32.4 percent are held in local jails; the remaining 5 percent are divided among other types of correctional facilities, including military and juvenile detention centers (Sabol, West, and Cooper 2009). Wacquant puts these numbers into context:

> To gauge how extreme this scale of confinement is, suffice it to say that it is about 40 percent higher that South Africa's at the height of the armed struggle against apartheid and six to twelve times the rate of the countries of the European Union, even though the latter have also seen their imprisonment rate rise rapidly over the past two decades. During the period 1985–1995, the United States amassed nearly one million more inmates at a pace of an additional 1,631 bodies per week, equivalent to incorporating the confined population of France every six months. (Wacquant 2005, 5)

While these trends are exceptional, there is a perception that where America leads, other English-speaking nations follow on matters of penal policy (Jones and Newburn 2005). The US experience is merely a more extreme version of what is occurring in England and Wales, where the prison population has more than doubled from 40,000 to 84,000 since 1971, making it the most imprisoning country in Europe. But what accounts for these trends?

A simple explanation that the general public and politicians often adhere to is that there is a direct relationship between crime rates and imprisonment: when crime increases, so does imprisonment, and high levels of imprisonment then lead to a reduction in crime. However, this does not accord with reality:

> Imprisonment rates and severity of punishment move independently from changes in crime rates, patterns, and trends. Governments decide how much punishment they want, and these decisions are in no simple way related to crime rates, patterns, and trends. This can be seen by comparing crime and punishment trends in Finland, Germany, and the United States between 1960 and 1990. The trends are close to identical . . . yet the U.S. imprisonment rate quadrupled in that period. The Finnish rate fell by 60 percent and the German rate was broadly stable. (Tonry 2004, 14)

Just as changes in levels of imprisonment cannot be explained in terms of crime rates, they also cannot be explained by reference to variations in demographic factors, rises in the general population, or criminalization of lots of different sections of the population. Sentencing and release policies, not crime rates, determine the numbers of persons in prison, a point illustrated by examining incarceration rates and crime rates in the three largest American states between 1991 and 1998. Texas experienced a 144 percent increase in incarceration despite a 35 percent drop in crime rates; California had a 44 percent rise in its incarceration rate with a 36 percent drop in crime rates; New York saw its incarceration rate increase by only 24 percent, yet nonetheless experienced a drop in crime rates of 43 percent (Alexander 2009). Further, the prison population is not one that reflects the broad diversity of the community and the burdens of criminalization fall disproportionately on certain groups, revealing much about prevailing power structures and inequalities.

Garland (2001) has suggested that that in order to understand why the United States and the United Kingdom have developed such a profound attachment to the prison system, we must look to the broader social and political shifts that have transformed both nations since the 1950s. First, both countries have witnessed profound social, cultural, and economic changes, including—in the 1950s and 1960s—rapid developments in industry, technology, and media, and the expansion of economic prosperity and consumerism, followed in the 1970s and 1980s by a period of economic depression, industrial erosion, and the rise of feminized service sectors.

Second, there occurred political transformations that underpinned a whole new social terrain of group relations and social attitudes. Though these were long-term processes, it was throughout the 1980s and 1990s that a fundamental and quite rapid shift occurred in which those who had once supported welfare state policies came to view them as expensive luxuries, which were not only no longer affordable to the hard-working tax-payer but were increasingly going to an undeserving and increasingly dangerous underclass. Garland argues that the neopopulist political agendas of President Reagan in the United States and Prime Minister Thatcher in the United Kingdom created a new moral climate that blamed crime on 1960s permissiveness and sought radical changes in the structure of families, households, and entire communities. At precisely the same time as individuals were being offered market choices and freedoms from social constraint, they were being pulled back by social and political policies that sought to return them to the values of family, work, abstinence, and self-regulation. This new moral ethos was supported by a reinvigorated politics of law and order, which became disproportionately targeted at the most vulnerable and excluded groups in society. In other words, a key outcome of the politics of the 1980s and 1990s was a profound hardening of social divisions: old solidarities and collective identities were cast aside, and as the relatively affluent enjoyed even greater wealth and personal freedoms, new schisms emerged to justify increasingly vigorous methods of control and repression aimed at the already marginalized and disenfranchised.

Another consequence of the Reagan/Thatcher era was a reduction in the role of government across a wide range of social institutions and encouragement of private companies to finance, build, and manage prisons, schools, and hospitals. Some critics of private prisons argue that these institutions are morally repugnant because, although individuals who break society's rules must be punished, it is morally wrong to make those who deliver this punishment wealthier according to the quantum of pain they deliver (Ryan and Ward 1989). Critics also claim that the idea of private prisons was sold by the New Right on the untested assertion that they would reform offenders more effectively than state-run prisons, where recidivist rates have historically been high. However, operating costs must be kept low in the private sector in order to make savings for government and profits for shareholders, and this, critics claim, has been achieved largely by reducing staffing, keeping wages suppressed, and compromising on living conditions for inmates and on working conditions for staff.

Vanessa Barker (2009) identifies, as does Garland, the 1960s through the 1990s as a critical period in the trajectory of penal expansion, although Barker offers a more nuanced analysis than does Garland, highlighting the disparities in use of imprisonment *between* states. For example, Barker argues that the shock of high crime in the 1960s and 1970s resulted in an emotive, passionate, and punitive approach to crime control in California where Ronald Reagan was then governor. As crime became associated with moral depravity, and as policy emphasized the suffering experienced by victims, all notions of rehabilitating offenders were abandoned as retribution became the main goal of punishment.

In contrast, Washington state faced up to immense problems within its penal system by recognizing that its prisons had become too expensive and too ineffective; mere warehouses holding an undifferentiated mass of inmates. In response, state officials adopted the principle of parsimony. While California used imprisonment extravagantly and with the aim of invoking pain on the offender to restore equilibrium, Washington diverted offenders away from prison via a strategy of decriminalization of some offenses and minimum use of custody. Despite succumbing to some populist and punitive measures, including "three strikes" legislation, "Hard Time for Armed Crime," and juvenile justice reforms that allow violent offenders aged sixteen and seventeen to be tried as adults, Barker maintains that Washington has not fundamentally changed its penal philosophies and still has a low incarceration rate compared to other American states.

While the explanations offered by Garland and Barker are not without flaws (see Tonry 2009, for a critique), there is a degree of consensus that what occurred in New York in this critical period had a significant impact not only on its own prison population but also on use of imprisonment across the United States. In New York the perceived root cause of much crime was tackled via a series of far-reaching and draconian drug laws, the result being that "today, violent and drug offenders make up over 83 percent of New York's prison population, 53.4 percent and 30 percent, respectively" (Barker 2009, 127).

However, while the New York authorities effectively decriminalized many other types of offenses, leading to a relatively modest rise in use of imprisonment, the US government's nationwide "war on drugs" did not run parallel to any decriminalization strategies and resulted not only in an intensification of punishments for drug offenses but also a swelling of the population available for processing by the criminal justice system. These outcomes combined to ensure that the criminal justice system swallowed up in even greater numbers than previously its traditional constituency of young, black, poorly educated males from large, deprived urban areas (Caplow and Simon 1999). This phenomena has been termed "mass imprisonment," and it has two main characteristics: first, the sheer number of people in prison, and second, the social concentration of imprisonment's effects: "Imprisonment becomes *mass imprisonment* when it ceases to be the incarceration of individual offenders and becomes the systematic imprisonment of whole groups of the population" (Garland 2001, 1–2). For the social groups most disproportionately targeted, imprisonment has become part of the socialization process; "a regular, predictable part of experience, rather than a rare and infrequent event" (1–2).

Over the last twenty years, concerns about the ethnic composition of America's incarcerated population have also underpinned discussion of the two monoliths of America's cruel and unusual punishment system: the supermax, and death row. Supermaxes are purpose-built, maximum-security prisons where inmates are held in conditions not unlike their nineteenth-century predecessors. The pointless cruelty of the treadwheel may have disappeared, but physical isolation, sensory deprivation, and the provision of minimum food requirements are equally intended to break prisoners' spirit and will (Pratt et al. 2005). The supermax takes the administrative task of processing prisoners through the system to new depths of impersonal brutality, particularly in those states where it converges with death row. The social exclusion of predominantly African American men is underlined in the most potently symbolic fashion. It is arguable that all custodial environments are repositories for the fears and anxieties of the wider social group, but the supermax and death row combine to represent the most graphic illustration of "toxic waste management" in contemporary advanced Western societies (Lynch 2005).

The supermax may be illustrative of a new punitive turn, which also encompasses a range of penal developments introduced in the United States and the United Kingdom; among them, indefinite detention strategies, shaming punishments such as registers for sex offenders, and the return of chain gangs in some states. However, in countries that have lower prison populations than those of the United States and the United Kingdom, there may be aspects of penal procedure and organizational practice that mask the punitive behind the seemingly progressive. For example, Italy has one of the lowest rates of convicted prisoners in Europe, and has a reputation for leniency and measures of mercy and conditional forgiveness, but its conviction and custody rates of foreign-born offenders are increasing, and it has one of the highest average detention periods (Nelken 2005). Canada, meanwhile, has a reputation for being moderate and progressive (prisons are becoming smaller, and a "needs" discourse has been introduced, explicitly directed at specific prison populations such as inmates from minority ethnic backgrounds), but its treatment philosophy echoes the punitive rhetoric of countries, such as the United Kingdom, by requiring prisoners to acknowledge responsibility for what they have done before accepting them onto any treatment programs (Moore and Hannah-Moffat 2005).

One of the most interesting penal experiments of recent years has taken place in Finland, which, in the last four decades, has gone from being among the highest prison populations in Europe to the lowest and where, even in the most "secure" closed prisons (such as Hämeenlinna, sixty miles from Helsinki) the regime is strict but not oppressive, with plenty of opportunities to work and study. With a legacy of Soviet influence on the country, Finland in the 1960s recognized its high (certainly high in relation to its Scandinavian neighbors) prison population as a problem and introduced a series of legal reforms explicitly designed to reduce it. These formal initiatives were backed up by a willingness on the part of civil servants, the judiciary, and the prison authorities to use all available means to bring down prisoner numbers and by widespread public support for community service orders, which were introduced in 1989 (Lappi-Seppälä 2000, 2008).

Yet, like other Scandinavian countries, Finland's young people appear to have a weaker commitment to the progressive policies of their parents' generation, and there are fears that the low imprisonment rates and high tolerance levels characteristic of this region may be in jeopardy (Bondeson 2005). These emerging signs of strain are, to a significant degree, fuelled by an expanding and increasingly strident media who are perceptibly changing public views of crime and punishment.

In most Western democracies there is, then, to a greater or lesser degree, tension between prison reformers' demands for humane and rehabilitative punishments and public expectations about what prisons should be, which are frequently shaped by the popular press. It is somewhat ironic that the UK press persists in falsely painting a picture of prisons as "holiday camps," when some prisoners still do not have adequate twenty-four-hour-a-day access to toilets, and few would contest that integrated sanitation is not ideal in an 8-x-10-foot cell shared by more than one man. Meanwhile, in the United States, pressure of numbers has resulted in many prisons becoming little more than human filing cabinets as inmates are stacked up in multiple-tiered bunks in shared dormitories with no hope of any personal, private space.

III. The Effects of Imprisonment: Sociological and Psychological Schisms

The developments described earlier—a return to retributive, ostentatious punishment; an inexorably rising prison population; the overrepresentation of young black men in prison; a commitment to privatization and profit-driven punishment; and a level of penal populism that mitigates against any politician voicing disquiet about these issues—combine to produce the kinds of environments that eighteenth- and nineteenth-century prison inmates might recognize. In turn, this suggests that we are returning to a two-hundred-year-old model of citizenship and human rights when it comes to those who offend. Little wonder that academic interest in the effects of imprisonment and the psychological and physical pains it induces has recently been revived after an absence of several decades (see, for example, Liebling and Maruna 2005). Of course, the effects of imprisonment will differ in intensity depending on the type of prison an individual is held in, the length of sentence, pre-prison experiences, the individual's physical and mental well-being, and their ties to family and other outside influences. It hardly needs stating that imprisonment will be experienced somewhat differently by an inmate in a Scandinavian open prison compared to someone held in an American supermax. It is also arguable, however, that to some extent at least a prison is a prison is a prison (King 2007). The "pains of imprisonment" (Sykes 1958) are thus usually conceptualized by degree of deprivation and discomfort experienced, and the disparities are referred to as depth (Downes 1988) and weight (King and McDermott 1995) of imprisonment. These two measures combine to characterize the burden that incarceration imposes on prisoners as becoming heavier as they penetrate deeper into the various levels of security and control imposed.

The idea that prisoners will experience certain pains of imprisonment was explored in a number of classic twentieth-century prison studies in the sociological tradition, which are usually discussed in a linear, chronological fashion. From this work emerges a pattern of common deprivations that typically afflict inmates and require carefully constructed responses, both individual and social, in order to survive with the sense of self intact. The overriding theme of this branch of penology (commonly known as the *deprivations literature*) is that key to social-psychological survival is prisoners' ability to adapt to life inside through a variety of coping strategies. One of the first studies was conducted by Donald Clemmer while he was employed as a guard at Menard prison in Illinois (he went on to be the director of the District of Columbia's prison system and the president of the American Correctional Association). *The Prison Community* ([1940]1958) was a landmark text because it introduced the idea that prisoners adhere to an inmate code that helps them to survive their sentence; subsequently summarized by Sykes and Messinger (1960, 8) as a fivefold set of rules: never rat [grass] on a con; play it cool and do your own time; don't exploit or steal from other prisoners; don't show weakness—be tough; be a man; and be sharp—don't ever side with prison officers and authorities.

Sykes himself went on to write what is frequently described as the most influential work on prisons, *The Society of Captives: A Study of a Maximum Security Prison* (1958). Based on research conducted in the New Jersey State Prison in Trenton, Sykes discusses five deprivations that are inflicted upon inmates, which constitute the defining characteristics of confinement: the deprivation of liberty, goods and services, heterosexual relationships, autonomy, and security are more than mere frustrations; they are experienced as a set of threats or attacks directed against the very foundation of the prisoner's being. One way for prisoners to diminish the pain of imprisonment, however, is to form a cohesive response to the harshness of prison life. Social solidarity between inmates manifests itself in the formal and informal codes they adopt and in the special language or "argot" they use. It is in such displays of autonomy, tolerated by the prison authorities, that prisoners develop ways of coping with imprisonment, and the delicate balance of power between staff and inmates is negotiated. In Sykes' view, prison officials might be granted a level of power without equal in contemporary society, but even in prison, power is never total.

Offering an alternative view, the Norwegian penologist Thomas Mathiesen (1965) found little evidence of the degree of social cohesion that Sykes describes, and claimed that the prison environment constitutes a "disrupted" society in which inmates are essentially weak and lonely individuals, subject to an enforced dependency on their custodians.

Erving Goffman has also been a significant influence on prison studies, popularizing the term "total institution" and alerting scholars to the particular trauma that many inmates experience on entry to a closed institution (asylums, monasteries, army barracks, and the like, as well as prisons). For Goffman, the symbolic significance of entry from the free community to the total institution goes well beyond the bureaucratic requirements of the establishment and can be described as "mortification of self" or "civil death" (Goffman 1961, 25).

The effects of long-term imprisonment have been a particularly productive focus for research. In another classic study, describing the minutiae of everyday life in a high-security prison in the north of England, Cohen and Taylor (1972) suggest that civil death can be a prolonged experience as some long-term prisoners fear the possibility of "turning, or being turned, from a live person into a dead thing, into a stone, into a robot, an automaton, without personal autonomy of action, and without subjectivity" (1972, 109). Johnson and Toch (1982) surmise that the main factors that give rise to this fear are the inability to counter the unfavorable definitions of oneself, which are continually offered by those who work within the prison system, and by external agencies such as the public, politicians, and the media; the decreasing ability over a long period to mark time resulting in a fear of losing other cognitive faculties as well; and the dependency that long-term imprisonment instills in inmates, so that they assume an uncharacteristically passive role and fear losing the capacity to think and act for themselves.

As in any organization, a climate of fear and vulnerability is bound to lead to the exploitation of weaker individuals by more powerful ones, and in prison, the illusion of power often rests on outward displays of intimidation and violence, leading Hans Toch (1975, 146) to describe manliness as the prison-coping strategy par excellence. Physical jostling for positions of power is common among groups of men generally, but a hypermasculinity is perhaps especially visible in prisons because they are such blatantly status-depriving environments. However, Toch also reminds us that the establishment and maintenance of a tough façade can be a great source of pressure, and while many inmates go to extraordinary lengths to conform to the hegemonic masculine ideal, their manly self-portraits crumble, indeed are "relinquished with gratitude" during conversations with researchers and other visitors to prisons (Toch 1975, 15).

In contrast to the sociological literature that has characterized imprisonment as brutal and damaging, research from psychology using methods such as structured questionnaires and psychometric tests has largely concluded that the effects of imprisonment are negligible and that there is no causal relationship between length of time spent in prison and deterioration of mental faculties (Banister et al. 1973; Bukstel and Kilmann 1980) or that prisoners cope surprisingly well with confinement after an initial period of distress or disorientation (Zamble and Porporino 1988). At worst, a prison sentence is experienced as a period of stasis or "deep freeze." Bukstel and Kilmann (1980, 478) have gone so far as to state that those prisoners on death row find confinement "quite stressful." For Alison Liebling, who has conducted many sociologically informed studies of prisoner suicide, this kind of bland understatement illustrates the failure of psychological research to ask the right questions. She argues that psychological studies of prison effects have

> proceeded without sufficient affective understanding, in deference to record-based measurement. Such studies rarely follow prisoners after release, and they rarely investigate psychological or emotional distress and disability. . . . They look instead at skills and personality traits, omitting to consider those who have not survived (or who have almost not survived) the prison experience. It is by this route that such research has been able to conclude that imprisonment is not harmful. (Liebling 1999, 287)

Moreover, such studies have failed to appreciate that prison is not a uniform experience; they have tended to omit specific groups from their samples (including women and those segregated and/or isolated for long periods), they have ignored the potential cumulative effects of repeated short periods of time spent in custody, and they have perpetuated the popular myth that many inmates cope better with institutional life than with freedom (see Liebling 1999, for a more detailed exploration of the sociological and psychological "coping" literature and its usefulness in understanding prisoner suicide).

It must also be remembered that the effects of imprisonment extend beyond the confined individual at the time of their sentence. Tonry and Petersilia (1999) highlight six collateral effects of imprisonment: (1) effects on prisoners while confined; (2) effects on prisoners' relationships and employment after release; (3) effects on their physical and mental health; (4) effects on prisoners' future criminal behavior; (5) effects on their spouses or partners and children; and (6) effects on the wider community. Limitations of space preclude discussion of all of these, but the effects of parental imprisonment on children have recently been the focus of renewed interest in academic scholarship. As prison numbers have soared, the number of children experiencing the imprisonment of a parent has increased, and effects including antisocial behavior, offending, mental health problems, drug abuse, school failure, and future unemployment also appear to have risen commensurately (Murray and Farrington 2008). The trauma of child-parent separation, the economic burden that imprisonment frequently entails, and the social stigma that having a parent in prison carries combine to have a profound effect on children's well-being. Children may be particularly adversely affected if they have a mother in prison, if parents are imprisoned frequently or for longer periods of time, or if they are imprisoned in punitive conditions. In the United States, black children are nine times more likely and Hispanic children three times more likely than white children to have an imprisoned parent. Studies have also suggested that prisoners' children are at higher than usual risk of future criminality, thus repeating patterns of incarceration through generations of families (Murray and Farrington 2005).

A. Drugs, Mental Illness, and Suicide in Prisons

One of the biggest differences between Sykes's influential 1958 study and contemporary research into prison cultures and communities is the overwhelming presence of drugs in today's prisons; indeed Class A drugs have been described as the key motor of social dynamics in prison (Crewe 2005). Whether interpreted as a dangerous and maladaptive response to confinement or an understandable aid to doing time, the fact is that prisons accommodate a high percentage of offenders whose drug use has become problematic. Moreover, drugs, and the ruthlessly dog-eat-dog environment they engender, have arguably destroyed any likelihood of the kind of inmate solidarity that Sykes claims is one of the key factors in coping with imprisonment. There are several reasons why people take drugs in prison, ranging from self-medication and time-management (taking drugs can allow the user to slip away from the realities of their physical surroundings and structural inequalities) to (fragile) networking, status, and economic power (in prisons, drugs are associated with anti-authoritarian, entrepreneurial, macho risk-taking, and can provide many social pay-offs as well as bringing personal financial reward).

Illicit drugs are implicated in the incarceration of three-quarters of all inmates in the United States. Sixty-five percent (1.5 million) meet the DSM-IV medical criteria for alcohol or other drug abuse and addiction; a further 20 percent (458,000), while not meeting the DSM-IV criteria, were nonetheless substance-involved at the time of their offense (CASA 2010). In addition to the inmates who were convicted of a drug law violation, 54.3 percent of alcohol law violators, 77.2 percent of those who committed a property crime, 65.4 percent of inmates who committed a violent crime, and 67.6 percent of those sentenced for other crimes either committed their offense to get money to buy drugs, were under the influence of drugs at the time of the offense, had a history of regular drug use, or had a drug use disorder (CASA 2010).

A similar picture emerges in the United Kingdom, where studies report that between 60 to 70 percent of prisoners have misused drugs in the twelve months prior to imprisonment. Class A drugs such as heroin, crack, or cocaine have been used by 47 percent of prisoners in the twelve months prior to imprisonment, although at some inner city prisons, 80 percent of prisoners are found to have Class A drugs in their system on reception (Wheatley 2007). Using a crude estimate of problematic drug use, Wheatley surmises that in England and Wales, half the prison population (i.e., 42,000 prisoners) is made up of drug abusers at any one time (Wheatley 2008). Part of the reason that drugs have reached such epic proportions is that prison authorities have been extremely slow to respond. Further, it is estimated that just 10 percent of prisoners receive treatment for their drugs use in England and Wales (Wheatley 2007); and 11 percent do so in the United States (CASA 2010).

Once again the racial disparities are startling. Research published in May 2000 by Human Rights Watch found that in the United States blacks comprised 62.7 percent and whites 36.7 percent of all drug offenders admitted to state prison, even though federal surveys and other data show clearly that this variance bears scant relation to racial differences in drug offending:

> The war on drugs has been waged disproportionately against black Americans. . . . There are, for example, five times more white drug users than black. Relative to population, black men are admitted to state prison on drug charges at a rate that is 13.4 times greater than that of white men. In large part because of the extraordinary racial disparities in incarceration for drug offenses, blacks are incarcerated for all offenses at 8.2 times the rate of whites. One in every 20 black men over the age of 18 in the United States is in state or federal prison, compared to one in 180 white men. (Human Rights Watch 2000)

Put simply, drug use by white individuals of all social classes has increased since the late 1970s, but their drugs of choice (e.g., powder cocaine) have not received the media and political attention that catalyzed the war on drugs in the mid-1980s when crack cocaine spread throughout low-income minority neighborhoods, which were already seen as dangerous and threatening (Reinarman and Levine 1997).

Drug misuse is also intrinsically linked to mental illness, as illustrated by the statistic that one-quarter (24.4 percent) of prison and jail inmates in the United States have *both* a substance use disorder and a co-occurring mental health problem (CASA 2010). And although one-third (32.9 percent) of the US prison population has a diagnosis of mental illness alone (CASA 2010), there may be many more mentally ill prisoners who remain undiagnosed. In England and Wales, 64 percent of male and 50 percent of female sentenced prisoners have a personality disorder.

Psychotic disorders are represented in prison at fourteen times the level as in the general population for men, and twenty-three times the level for women (PRT 2004). Prisoners' mental health is underresearched, and relatively little knowledge about the lives of inmates suffering from psychotic disorders exists outside the psychological and psychiatric fields. We can say with some certainty, however, that prison regimes do little to address the mental health needs of prisoners. The Prison Reform Trust reports that 28 percent of sentenced male prisoners with evidence of psychosis spend twenty-three or more hours a day in their cells—more than twice the proportion of those without mental health difficulties—and sufferers are twice as likely to be refused treatment for mental health problems inside prison than outside it (PRT 2004). In both the United Kingdom and United States, one in ten prisoners are ex-military personnel and, once again, there has been very little research conducted on the relationship between veterans and offending, or on the particular psychological problems, such as post-traumatic stress disorder, they might experience.

In recent years there has been a convergence of penal and medical discourses in an attempt to bridge the gap between clinical and actuarial assessments of the most dangerous offenders, but there are problems associated with attempts to control so-called dangerous populations within the penal system, especially when risk management replaces treatment. One of the outcomes of our current preoccupation with notions of risk and dangerousness, especially when driven by a populist agenda, is that indeterminate sentencing has become a common feature of penal policy. In England and Wales, greater use of protective custody has resulted in a number of new penal sanctions, including "imprisonment for public protection" and "whole life tariffs" (nineteen of which were imposed in the first decade of this century, doubling the previous number of prisoners who will never be released).

American jurisdictions, meanwhile, have increased use of life sentences without the possibility of parole (LWOPs). According to a recent report (Nellis and King 2009), 29 percent of persons serving a life sentence (41,095) have no possibility of parole, and 1,755 were juveniles at the time of the crime. Breaking these figures down by state, the report notes that in five states (Alabama, California, Massachusetts, Nevada, and New York) at least one in six prisoners is serving a life sentence. Five states (California, Florida, Louisiana, Michigan, and Pennsylvania) each have more than 3,000 people serving life without parole; and in six states (Illinois, Iowa, Louisiana, Maine, Pennsylvania, and South Dakota) *all* life sentences are imposed without the possibility of parole. In line with other extravagant uses of imprisonment described in this article, the dramatic growth in life sentences and LWOP is not primarily a result of higher crime rates but of policy changes that have imposed harsher punishments and restricted parole consideration, and they disproportionately affect black people: 66 percent of all persons sentenced to life are nonwhite, and 77 percent of juveniles serving life sentences are nonwhite. In addition, the United States is the only Western country that retains the death penalty.

Elsewhere I have characterized the loss of control over significant life events that imprisonment entails as comparable to the experience of chronic or terminal illness, especially when perceived by the patient as dying "prematurely" (Jewkes 2005). In such circumstances some prisoners not only fail to cope but fail to see why they *should* cope. Experiencing imprisonment as a kind of bereavement for oneself and confined in environments, which can be volatile and disorientating, it is unsurprising that rates of self-harm and suicide are far higher in prisons than in the community.

The predominant risk factors in suicide and self-harm generally are: adverse life events, poor interpersonal relationships, weak attachment to education and employment, alcohol and drug misuse, mental disorder and socio-economic disadvantage; all of which make the prison population one that is carefully selected to be at risk of suicide (Liebling 1992). Moreover, while prisoners at risk of suicide share many common characteristics with the at-risk population in society at large, one prison-specific risk factor is the chronic levels of overcrowding (which has also been linked to self-harm, drug use, and mental health problems). The worst prisons for overcrowding are those that hold high numbers of remand (pre-trial) prisoners, and prison suicides occur disproportionately among unsentenced prisoners. Around half occur within one month of entry into custody when anxiety and distress levels are elevated; only about a quarter of those who die by suicide have been identified as being at risk despite most prisoners having experienced chronic depression prior to the act (Liebling 2007).

Illustrating the links between all the problems identified in this section, a study of randomly sampled prisoners in twelve prisons in England and Wales found that 48 percent of prisoners who had attempted suicide reported problematic drug use, 57 percent had experienced a personality disorder, and 84 percent had experienced a neurotic disorder in the previous year. Immediate triggers were problems with medication, transfers to another prison, losing custody of children, problems with bullying, flashbacks to previous abuse, and a lack of trust in those around them. Interestingly, suicide is one of the few problems associated with imprisonment that does not adversely affect the black inmate population. In line with suicides in the wider community, it is young, white men who are most at risk (Liebling 2007).

IV. Current Issues and the Future of Imprisonment

This article has demonstrated that rates of imprisonment bear no direct correlation to offending rates and that if prison can be said to work, it is primarily in the sense of satisfying media-driven public demands for tougher sentences in the context of false perceptions that violent, indiscriminate crime is inexorably rising. Incarceration appears to have a negligible deterrent effect and—as a consequence of antisocial prison experiences, stigma experienced on release, etc.—may have a criminogenic effect on future behavior (Nagin, Cullen, and Jonson 2009). Otherwise, prison "works" by keeping a relatively small number of extremely dangerous individuals in custody (and therefore off the streets) while at the same time incarcerating large numbers of vulnerable individuals with specific problems that the prison system is ill-equipped to deal with.

As both the United States and United Kingdom appear to be returning to pre-Enlightenment ideas about expressive forms of punishment, there are a number of issues that should arguably dominate the agenda for research on imprisonment in the forthcoming decade. Given the many human rights issues raised in this chapter (high levels of drug use, mental illness, suicide and self-harm; low commitment to providing prisoners with meaningful activity, appropriately waged labor etc.), questions of legitimacy are inevitably raised. Over the last decade, prisoners in the United Kingdom have been among the most enthusiastic followers of European legislation, which was not designed with their circumstances in mind but has, nonetheless, affected prison law in numerous ways. The European Commission and Court of Human Rights has been particularly significant given the populist punitiveness that characterizes penal debate in the United Kingdom. To cite one example, the British public regard the issue of prisoners' enfranchisement as a controversial issue, as witnessed by a recent BBC poll, which found that 95 percent of respondents thought that prisoners' should not be allowed to vote. However, following 140 years of disenfranchising prisoners, a case brought by an English prisoner in 2004 (*Hirst v. UK*) went before the European Court of Human Rights, which deemed the government's stance unlawful. Greeting the news with less than enthusiasm, a Ministry of Justice spokesman declared that "*some* degree of voting being extended to *some* serving prisoners is legally unavoidable" and suggested that voting rights might be granted to prisoners serving less than four years or even just to those serving less than one year. Even though this might mean that only about 28,000 prisoners in the United Kingdom would be eligible to vote, the move is considered so controversial that one newspaper speculated that the Ministry had deliberately timed the announcement to coincide with the Easter parliamentary recess so as to draw minimum attention to it (*Telegraph* April 9, 2009).

For prisoners in the United States, however, any notion of human rights is virtually meaningless. Michael Tonry explains the problem:

> Unlike most European countries and Canada, [the United States] refuses to acknowledge the moral force of international human rights conventions and declarations, or to incorporate them into its laws. Fifty years ago, United States' governments were world leaders in promoting human rights values, the imprisonment rate was stable and in line with those of other Western democracies, capital punishment was falling into disuse, and the U.S. Supreme Court was

admired throughout the world for its extension of human rights protections to criminal suspects. Something went terribly wrong (Tonry 2009, 379).

For many academic scholars the thing that went terribly wrong was a political appeal to notions of "self" and "other." In the United States and the United Kingdom a conservative moral agenda has dominated for more than two decades, which in matters of crime and deviance has emphasized deterrence and repression, and voiced support for more prisons and a tougher criminal justice system. While Tonry remains unconvinced by arguments about media-propelled populist punitiveness (and there are certainly many studies that bear out that the public are actually much less retributive than they are usually held to be), I would argue that we live in a society where political process and media discourse are indistinguishable and mutually constitutive, and that in both countries, it is outsiders who provide the others against whom we measure ourselves (Jewkes 2010). Popular media discourses operate as sites of inclusion and exclusion, and demonization exists along a spectrum of deviance with, at one end, "stigmatized others" who are portrayed as gradually but steadily corrosive of the fabric of society (as opposed to immediately and acutely threatening to the personal safety of its individual members); drugs offenders, welfare recipients, and illegal immigrants are examples. At the other end of the spectrum are "absolute others" who have committed crimes perceived as so heinous that their complete dislocation from the rest of society is presented as natural, even necessary (Greer and Jewkes 2005). Official response to absolute others is exemplified by the "war on terror" that has dominated the political agendas of both America and Britain since 2001 and which found its physical form in the American prison camp at Guantanamo Bay, Cuba, and Belmarsh Detention Centre in England.

For Tonry, this political paranoia about the enemy within has been supplemented in the United States by recurring episodes of religious-based intolerance, which has further cemented a xenophobic attitude toward immigrants and individuals of minority ethnic groups. Added to this, he notes that all other Western countries, apart from the United States and Britain, have entrenched bills of (human) rights. While the United States famously has had a constitutional Bill of Rights since the late eighteenth century, protecting freedom of speech, exercise of religion, and the like from state intervention, in relation to crime the courts tend to yield to the elected branches of state government. Similarly, and as already noted, while Britain must adhere to the directives of the European courts, governments may do so with minimum commitment and enthusiasm, for example, in relation to prisoners' rights. Most importantly, all these trends have been underpinned by criminal justice systems that discriminate against black people. In particular, the emphasis on penal sanctions for drug offenses highlighted earlier cannot be divorced from long-standing public association of racial minorities with certain criminalized activities (Tonry 1995, 2009).

Of course, the histories of race relations in the United States and the United Kingdom are very different, and this is not the time to dwell on the detail of racial stratification and discriminatory justice practices over the last two centuries in each country. But it is well documented that in both nations, there has been a racialization of crime and violence in the collective consciousness by political entrepreneurs seeking to jump on a bandwagon that casually brackets populist racial associations with crime and punishment (Tonry 1995, 2009). In the United States, the "war on drugs" (on certain drugs, anyway) had a devastating impact resulting in the mass imprisonment of young, disadvantaged, inner-city members of minority groups. By the 1980s black people made up half of the prison population, compared with only 12 percent of the US population, and had an imprisonment rate seven times higher than the white rate (Tonry 1995, 2009).

In the United Kingdom, the rate of black offenders in prison is also around seven times higher than their white counterparts and is rising much faster than that of white prisoners. Between 1993 and 2003, the white prison population increased by 48 percent; Asian prisoners, by 73 percent; and black prisoners by 138 percent (Home Office 2004). In addition, recent years have witnessed an overt racialization in political and media discourses of serious violent offenses, particularly those carried out by individuals on parole, and notions of potential "dangerousness" have come to be applied indiscriminately. As Foucault (1988) suggests, we judge the criminal, not the crime, and for all our "postmodern" sophistication, the beginning of the twenty-first century finds us still falling back on the positivist discourses of the nineteenth century. Attributing criminality, irrationality, and even animality to those who lead unconventional lifestyles, people from different ethnic backgrounds to our own, and people with mental illnesses, a "winner-loser" casino culture is created (Reiner, Livingstone, and Allen 2001, 177), and it is perhaps not surprising that these are the very groups who are overrepresented in our prison populations.

REFERENCES

Alexander, Elizabeth. 2009. "Michigan Breaks the Political Logjam: A New Model for Reducing Prison Populations." American Civil Liberties Union (Nov.): 4. http://www.aclu.org/files/assets/2009-12-18-MichiganReport.pdf.
Banister, P. A., F. V. Smith, K. J. Heskin, and N. Bolton. 1973. "Psychological Correlates of Long-Term Imprisonment. I. Cognitive Variables." British Journal of Criminology 13(4): 312–22.
Barker, Vanessa. 2009. Politics of Imprisonment: How the Democratic Process Shapes the Way America Punishes Offenders. New York: Oxford University Press.
Bondeson, Ulla. 2005. "Levels of Punitiveness in Scandinavia: Description and Explanations." In The New Punitiveness: Trends, Theories, Perspectives, edited by. John Pratt et al. Devon: Willan.
Bukstel, Lee H., and Peter R. Kilmann. 1980. "Psychological Effects of Imprisonment on Confined Individuals." Psychological Review 88: 469–93.

Caird, Rod. 1974. *A Good and Useful Life: Imprisonment in Britain Today*. London: Hart-Davis.

Caplow, Theodore, and Jonathan Simon. 1999. "Understanding Prison Policy and Population Trends." In *Prisons*, edited by Michael Tonry and Joan Petersilia. Vol. 26 of *Crime and Justice: A Review of Research*, edited by Michael Tonry. Chicago: University of Chicago Press.

Clemmer, Donald. [1940]1958. *The Prison Community*, 2nd ed. New York: Holt, Rinehart and Winston.

Cohen, Stanley, and Laurie Taylor. 1972. *Psychological Survival: The Experience of Long-Term Imprisonment*. Harmondsworth: Penguin.

Crewe, Ben. 2005. "Prisoner Society in the Era of Hard Drugs." *Punishment and Society* 7(4): 457–81.

de Beaumont, Gustave, and Alexis de Tocqueville. 1833. *On the Penitentiary System in the United States, and Its Application in France*. Philadelphia: Carey, Lea and Blanchard.

Downes, David. 1988. *Contrasts in Tolerance: Post-War Penal Policy in the Netherlands and England and Wales*. Oxford: Clarendon Press.

Foucault, Michel. 1977. *Discipline and Punish: the Birth of the Prison*. London: Penguin.

———. 1988. *Politics, Philosophy, Culture: Interviews and Other Writings 1977–1984*. London: Routledge.

Garland, David. 2001. *The Culture of Control: Crime and Social Order in Contemporary Society*. Oxford: Oxford University Press.

Goffman, Erving. 1961. *Asylums: Essays on the Social Situation of Mental Patients and Other Inmates*. London: Penguin.

Greer, Chris, and Yvonne Jewkes. 2005. "Images and Processes of Social Exclusion." *Social Justice* 32(1):20–31.

Home Office. 2004. *Statistics on Race and the Criminal Justice System*. London: Home Office.

Human Rights Watch. 2000. "United States Punishment and Prejudice: Racial Disparities in the War on Drugs." Vol. 12, no. 2, May. http://www.hrw.org/legacy/reports/2000/usa/Rcedrg00.htm#P54_1086.

Jewkes, Yvonne. 2005. "Loss, Liminality and the Life Sentence: Managing Identity Through a Disrupted Lifecourse." In *The Effects of Imprisonment*, edited by. Alison Liebling and Shadd Maruna. Devon: Willan.

———. 2010. *Media and Crime*. 2nd ed. London: Sage.

Johnson, Robert, and Hans Toch, eds. 1982. *The Pains of Imprisonment*. London: Sage.

Jones, Trevor, and Tim Newburn. 2005. "Comparative Criminal Justice Policy-making in the US and UK: The Case of Private Prisons." *British Journal of Criminology* 45(1): 58–80.

King, Roy D. 2007. "Imprisonment: Some International Comparisons and the Need to Revisit Panopticism." In *Handbook on Prisons*, edited by. Yvonne Jewkes. Devon: Willan

King, Roy D., and Kathleen McDermott. 1995. *The State of Our Prisons*, Oxford: Clarendon Press.

Lappi-Seppälä, Tapio. 2000. "The Fall of the Finnish Prison Population." *Journal of Scandinavian Studies in Criminology and Crime Prevention* 1(1): 27–40.

———. 2008. "Trust, Welfare, and Political Culture: Explaining Differences in National Penal Policies." In *Crime and Justice: A Review of Research*, vol. 37, edited by Michael Tonry. Chicago: University of Chicago Press.

Liebling, Alison. 1992. *Suicides in Prison*. London: Routledge.

———. 1999. "*Prison Suicide and Prisoner Coping*." In *Prisons*, edited by Michael Tonry and Joan Petersilia. Volume 26 of *Crime and Justice: A Review of Research*, edited by Michael Tonry. Chicago: University of Chicago Press.

———. 2007. "Prison Suicide and Its Prevention." In *Handbook on Prisons*, edited by Yvonne Jewkes. Devon: Willan.

Liebling, Alison, and Shadd Maruna, eds. 2005. *The Effects of Imprisonment*. Devon: Willan.

Lynch, Mona. 2005. "Supermax Meets Death Row: Legal Struggles around the New Punitiveness in the US." In *The New Punitiveness: Trends, Theories, Perspectives*, edited by John Pratt et al. Devon: Willan.

McConville, Sean. 1998. "Local Justice: The Jail." In *The Oxford History of the Prison: The Practice of Punishment in Western Society*, edited by Norval Morris and David J. Rothman. Oxford: Oxford University Press.

Martinson, Robert. 1974. "What Works? Questions and Answers about Prison Reform." *Public Interest* 35(Spring): 22–54.

Mathiesen, Thomas. 1965. *The Defences of the Weak: A Sociological Study of a Norwegian Correctional Institution*. London: Tavistock.

Mehigan, James, and Abigail Rowe. 2007. "Problematizing Prison Privatization: An Overview of the Debate." In *Handbook on Prisons*, edited by Yvonne Jewkes. Devon: Willan.

Moore, Dawn, and Kelly Hannah-Moffat. 2005. "The Liberal Veil: Revisiting Canadian Penality." In *The New Punitiveness: Trends, Theories, Perspectives*, edited by John Pratt et al. Devon: Willan.

Morris, Norval, and David J. Rothman. 1995. *The Oxford History of the Prison: The Practice of Punishment in Western Society*, New York: Oxford University Press.

Murray, Joseph, and David P. Farrington. 2005. "Parental Imprisonment: Effects on Boys' Antisocial Behaviour and Delinquency Through the Life-Course," *Journal of Child Psychology and Psychiatry* 46(12): 1269–78.

———. 2008. "The Effects of Parental Imprisonment on Children." In *Crime and Justice: A Review of Research, vol. 37*, edited by Michael Tonry. Chicago: University of Chicago Press.

Nagin, Daniel S., Francis T. Cullen, and Cheryl Lero Jonson. 2009. "Imprisonment and Reoffending." In *Crime and Justice: A Review of Research, vol. 38*, edited by Michael Tonry. Chicago: University of Chicago Press.

National Center on Addiction and Substance Abuse at Columbia University (CASA). 2010. "Behind Bars II: Substance Abuse and America's Prison Population" http://www.casacolumbia.org/templates/publications_reports.aspx.

Nelken, David. 2005. "When Is a Society Non-Punitive? The Italian Case." In *The New Punitiveness: Trends, Theories, Perspectives*, edited by J. Pratt et al. Devon: Willan.

Nellis, Ashley, and Ryan S. King. 2009. "No Exit: The Expanding Use of Life Sentences in America." The Sentencing Project: Washington, DC. http://www.sentencingproject.org/doc. . .inc_noexit.pdf.

Pratt, John, David Brown, Mark Brown, Simon Hallsworth, and Wayne Morrison, eds. 2005. *The New Punitiveness: Trends, Theories, Perspectives*. Devon: Willan.

Prison Reform Trust (PRT). 2004. "Prison Reform Trust Factfile." www.prisonreformtrust.org.uk.

Reinarman, Craig, and Harry G. Levine. 1997. *Crack in America: Demon Drugs and Social Justice*. Berkeley: University of California Press.

Reiner, Robert, Sonia Livingstone, and Jessica Allen. 2001. "Casino Culture: Media and Crime in a Winner-Loser Society." In *Crime, Risk and Justice: the Politics of Crime Control in Liberal Democracies*, edited by Kevin Stenson and Robert R. Sullivan. Devon: Willan.

Rothman, David J. 1971. *The Discovery of the Asylum: Social Order and Disorder in the New Republic*. Boston: Little, Brown.

———. 1980. *Conscience and Convenience: The Asylum and its Alternatives in Progressive America*. Boston: Little, Brown.

Ryan Michael, and Tony Ward. 1989. *Privatization and the Penal System: The American Experience and the Debate in Britain* Milton Keynes: Open University Press.

Sabol, William, J., Heather C. West, and Matthew Cooper. 2009. "*Bureau of Justice Statistics: Prisoners in 2008*." Washington, DC: U.S. Department of Justice http://www.ojp.usdoj.gov/bjs/pub/pdf/p08.pdf.

Senior, Jane, and Jenny Shaw. 2007. "Prison Healthcare." In *Handbook on Prisons*, edited by Yvonne Jewkes. Devon: Willan.

Social Exclusion Unit. 2002. *Reducing Re-Offending by Ex-Prisoners*. London: Social Exclusion Unit.

Soothill, Keith. 2007. "Prison Histories and Competing Audiences: 1776–1966." In *Handbook on Prisons*, edited by Yvonne Jewkes. Devon: Willan.

Sykes, Gresham. 1958. *The Society of Captives: A Study of a Maximum Security Prison*. Princeton, NJ: Princeton University Press.

Sykes, Gresham, and Sheldon Messinger. 1960. "The Inmate Social System." In volume 3 of *Crime and Justice*, edited by Leon Radzinowicz and Marvin Wolfgang. New York: Basic Books.

Toch, Hans. 1975. *Men in Crisis*. Chicago: Aldine.

Tonry, Michael. 1995. *Malign Neglect: Race, Crime, and Punishment in America*. New York: Oxford University Press.

———. 2004. *Thinking about Crime: Sense and Sensibility in American Penal Culture*. Oxford: Oxford University Press.

———. 2009. "Explanations of American Punishment Policies: A National History." In *Punishment and Society* 11(3): 377–94.

Tonry, Michael, and Joan Petersilia. 1999. "American Prisons at the Beginning of the Twenty-first Century." In *Prisons*, edited by Michael Tonry and Joan Petersilia. Volume 26 of *Crime and Justice: A Review of Research*, edited by Michael Tonry. Chicago: University of Chicago Press.

Useem, Bert, and Peter Kimball. 1991. *States of Siege: U.S. Prison Riots 1971–1986*. New York: Oxford University Press.

von Hirsch, Andrew. 1976. *Doing Justice: The Choice of Punishments*. New York: Hill and Wang.

Wacquant, Loïc. 2005. "The great Penal Leap Backward: Incarceration in America from Nixon to Clinton." In *The New Punitiveness: Trends, Theories, Perspectives*, edited by J. Pratt et al. Devon: Willan.

Walmsley, Roy. 2009. "World Prison Population List." 8th ed. http://www.kcl.ac.uk/depsta/law/research/icps/downloads/wppl-8th_41.pdf.

Wheatley, Michael. 2007. "Drugs in Prison." In *Handbook on Prisons*, edited by Yvonne Jewkes. Devon: Willan.

———. 2008. "Drugs." In *Dictionary of Prisons and Punishment*, edited by Yvonne Jewkes and Jamie Bennett. Devon: Willan.

Zamble, Edward, and Frank J. Porporino. 1988. *Coping, Behaviour and Adaptation in Prison Inmates*. New York: Springer-Verlag.

CHAPTER 29

......

WOMEN'S PRISONS

......

CANDACE KRUTTSCHNITT

WOMEN have always been a relatively small proportion of the prison population. In about 80 percent of the prison systems throughout the world, they comprise between 2 and 9 percent of the total prison population (Walmsley 2009). Yet, in some contexts (the United States, England, the Netherlands) their growth rates over the past two decades have outstripped those for men. Some of the factors that have contributed to the growing numbers of women behind bars are similar to those of men, but others are unique to female offenders, reflecting how society's conception of women's criminality and the types of women deserving of punishment, changes over time. Just as crime by women was long thought to be etiologically distinct from that of men, prisons for women, until very recently, have focused on distinctly feminine treatments girded by conceptions of women criminals as misfits or victims.

The development of the reformatory for female offenders came about when women offenders were no longer seen as "monsters of depravity" but instead as "childlike and wayward, more sinned against than sinners" (Rafter 1990, 49; see also Freedman 1981). This perspective of the female offender—that she was first and foremost "a victim"—persisted into the last decade of the twentieth century when custodial priorities for women began to shift from feminization and domestication to security and control (Sloop 1996; Carlen 1999). Women were now seen as serious offenders and potential troublemakers who needed to be held responsible for their own reform. Although this transition has been uneven and in some contexts incomplete (see e.g., Kruttschnitt and Gartner 2005; Silberman 2007), it is intimately linked to notions about the causes of female criminality and, more broadly, changes in gender relations.

Reformatories for women built after World War I upheld a dual system of corrections based on sex. Women were channeled into programs that would prepare
them to be good wives and mothers once they were released (Freedman 1981). These
institutions were often set in remote, rural locations to maximize the potential for
both controlling and domesticating women (Carlen 1983; Cooper 1993; Smith 1990;
Zedner 1991). The remnants of the second wave of the women's movement, however,
impinged on this rather neglectful and paternalistic attitude toward female prisoners. Perhaps nowhere is this more evident than in Canada in the late 1980s where
efforts were made to empower women prisoners and "feminize the discourse of
imprisonment" (Hannah-Moffat 1999, 2001; Shaw 1992). In other contexts, the
parity movement in society took the form of "equality with a vengeance" with
women's conditions of confinement increasingly looking like men's, despite their
well-acknowledged lower security risk (Kruttschnitt and Gartner 2005; Rierdan
1997; Worrall 2002).

This article summarizes what is known today about women's imprisonment
while being mindful of this historical and social backdrop. In so doing, it paints a
picture that offers little reason for optimism. In many contexts, the rate of women's
imprisonment continues to outstrip that of men's, yet few scholars are addressing
what might account for this situation. Recent evidence also suggests that conditions
of confinement for women have hardened, even as documentation of women
offenders' particular vulnerabilities grows. In addition, knowledge of what works to
reduce female recidivism remains sparse.

Factors that may be particularly important to understanding women's imprisonment today include the following:

- While the growth in women's imprisonment in the United States rose most
  dramatically between 1980 and 2000, women's incarceration rates continue
  to increase.
- Black women have been hit hardest by the surge in imprisonment in the United
  States, but over the last decade there is some evidence that this may be changing.
- Some of the factors that may be particularly important in understanding the
  growth of women's imprisonment in the United States include the move to
  presumptive sentencing, increasing rates of parole revocation, and the
  feminization of poverty.
- England and Wales, Australia, and the Netherlands also experienced notable
  increases in the number of women being sent to prison (albeit to a much
  lesser extent than in the United States) and, in all of these countries, racial
  minorities are overrepresented in the female prison population.
- Penologists studying women prisoners today have quite different concerns
  than they did in the past. These include the use of risk-assessment tools on
  female offenders, their unique vulnerabilities and agency, and the need for
  more gender-responsive programs.

- Relatively little is known about the effectiveness of programs in women's prisons, and virtually none of the prisoner re-entry research focuses on females.
- Future research needs to examine not only "what works" for female offenders but also whether more of these offenders would be better served by community-based placements.

This article has four sections. The first discusses changing patterns of imprisonment of women and men in the United States. The second considers trends cross-nationally. Section III discusses women's experiences as prisoners. I discuss important areas for future research and policy in section IV.

I. U.S. Data on the Imprisonment of Women and Men

Roughly one-third of the women being held in penal institutions throughout the world are in U.S. prisons (Walmsley 2009). At year-end 2007, there were 114,420 women and 1,598,316 men under state and federal correctional authorities' jurisdiction, and 105,500 women and 1,427,300 men in custody (Bureau of Justice Statistics 2008).[1] Women's incarceration rates rose most dramatically between 1980 and 2000 (rising from 11 to 59 per 100,000 females). Since 2001 they have continued to grow, albeit more slowly.[2] By midyear 2008, women's incarceration rate had risen to 69 per 100,000 females (see figure 29.1 and table 29.1). The comparable data for males also indicates substantial changes in their incarceration rates since 1980 but, relative to women, a more modest growth rate over the past decade (see table 29.2).

While much of the growth in women's imprisonment between 1980 and 2000 was due to a larger proportion of women being sent to prison for drug law violations than for violent or property crimes, there is some evidence that this may be changing. Table 29.3 shows that there has been a slight decline since 2001 in the percentge of the female prison population incarcerated for drugs and a steady increase in those confined for violent offenses. For males, the trends for violent offenders (the largest proportion) remain consistent over time, with some shift in the proportion of individuals convicted of property crimes and drug law violations occurring between 1986 and 1991 but remaining relatively stable throughout the first decade of the twenty-first century.

Just as the offender composition of the prison population changed over time, so also did its racial composition, albeit in some unexpected ways. Table 29.4 reveals that in 1990, the incarceration rate for black women (117) was six times greater than the rate for white women (19). Hispanic women's incarceration rate (56) was roughly

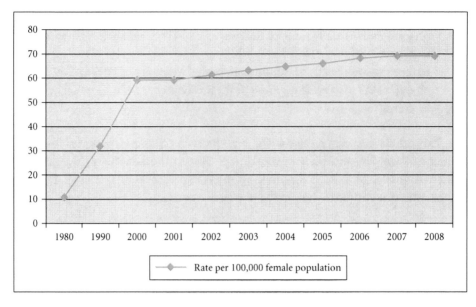

Figure 29.1. Rate per 100,000 female population of sentenced female prisoners
under jurisdiction of U.S. state and federal correctional authorities on Dec. 31,
1980–2007 and on June 30, 2008
(See table 29.1 for data and sources).

Table 29.1. Data for Figure 1

Year	No. of Females	Rate
1980	12,331	11
1990	40,564	32
2000	85,044	59
2001	85,184	59
2002	89,066	61
2003	92,571	63
2004	95,998	65
2005	98,688	66
2006	103,343	68
2007	105,688	69
2008	106,410	69

Source:—Bureau of Justice Statistics 2000a, fig. 6.2; Bureau of Justice Statistics 2009, table 8; U.S. Census Bureau 2009.

three times greater than white women's but only half as large as black women's. Between 1990 and 2000, the imprisonment rate for black women increased the most, followed by Hispanic and white women. After 2000, however, there were notable declines in the numbers of black women and men and Hispanic males being sent to prison. While it is unclear what caused this sudden shift, it may be related to

Table 29.2.   Incarceration Rates in State and Federal Prisons by Gender, 1980–2008 No. of Prisoners per 100,000 Residents*

Year	Total	Male	Female
1980	139	275	11
1990	297	564	31
2000	472	900	59
2001	472	900	59
2002	480	913	61
2003	485	923	63
2004	490	929	65
2005	495	938	66
2006	504	954	68
2007	509	961	69
2008	507	957	69

Source:—Bureau of Justice Statistics 1995, table 11; Bureau of Justice Statistics 2009, Table 6 and Table 8; U.S. Census Bureau 2009.

*Based on census estimates of the U.S. resident population on July 1 of each year and adjusted for census undercount. Sentenced prisoners are those with a sentence of more than one year.*Based on sentenced female prisoners under jurisdiction of U.S. state and federal correctional authorities on Dec. 31, 2000–2007 and on June 30, 2008.

Table 29.3.   Most Serious Offense of State Prison Inmates by Gender, 1986–2005 Percent of Prison Inmates

	1986	1991	2001	2002	2003	2004	2005
	F M	F M	F M	F M	F M	F M	F M
Violent	40.7 55.2	32.2 47.4	32.0 50.5	33.0 51.7	34.8 53.0	34.0 53.4	35.4 54.3
Property	41.2 30.5	28.7 24.6	26.2 18.8	28.7 19.9	30.0 20.2	30.9 20.1	28.6 18.5
Drugs	12.0 8.4	32.8 20.7	30.4 19.7	31.5 20.7	29.1 19.3	28.7 18.9	28.7 18.9
Public Order	5.1 5.2	5.7 7.0	10.9 10.7	6.1 7.1	5.3 7.0	5.5 7.1	6.1 7.7

Source:—Bureau of Justice Statistics 1994, table 2; Bureau of Justice Statistics 2003, Table 15; 2004, Table 13; 2005, Table 13; 2007, Table 11; 2008, Appendix Table 11.

Note:—All columns do not add to 100 percent because they exclude "other/unspecified" offenses (which include juvenile offenses and unspecified felonies).

the overall declines in incarceration rates in a number of states that imprison a large number of blacks and Hispanics (e.g., New York, New Jersey, Maryland, Illinois, Oklahoma; see Bureau of Justice Statistics 2008, figure 29.2). It may also be related to shifts in national drug policy. Nonetheless, the incarceration rate for black women in the United States remains remarkably high (150 per 100,000 residents at year-end 2007), exceeding the total imprisonment rate of almost all European countries, except Spain, and the male incarceration rate in selected nations (Denmark, Finland, Italy, Norway, Sweden, and Switzerland) in 2007.[3]

Table 29.4. Imprisonment Rates for Sentenced Prisoners, December 31, 1990, 2000, 2006, and 2007

	Imprisonment rate per 100,000				
	U.S. residents				Change
	1990	2000	2007	1990–2000	2000–2007
Total[a]	297[c]	478	506	181	28
Male[a]	564[d]	915	955	351	40
White[b]	338	410	481	72	71
Black[b]	2,234	3,188	3,138	954	-50
Hispanic or Latino	1,016[d]	1,419	1,259	403	-160
Female[a]	31[d]	59	69	28	10
White[b]	19	33	50	14	17
Black[b] 117	117	175	150	58	-25
Hispanic or Latino	56[d]	78	79	22	1

Note: Imprisonment rates are based on U.S. Census Bureau population estimates per 100,000 U.S. residents. Resident population estimates are as of January 1 in each year following the reference year.

[a]Includes American Indians, Alaska Natives, Asians, Native Hawaiians, other Pacific Islanders, and persons identifying two or more races.

[b]Excludes persons of Hispanic or Latino origin.

[c]Rate is based on U.S. resident population on December 31, 1990.

[d]Rate is based on U.S. resident population on July 1, 1990.

Source:—Bureau of Justice Statistics 2008, table 6; Bureau of Justice Statistics 2000*b*, table 1.9 and table 1.10.

Explanations for the Changing Patterns of Women's Imprisonment

Numerous explanations have been put forth for the rapid rise in imprisonment that took place primarily in the United States, and to a lesser extent in England and Australia, over the past three decades (see Tonry 2004, 23–27). For example, some argue that crime became a tool used by an expanding but largely ineffective government to restore the public's confidence in the state (Caplow and Simon 1999). Others have narrowed this broad paradigm by focusing on the politicians and the media, which used crime to further their own interests and garner public support for more punitive crime policies (Beckett 1997). And still others posit that the key to the growth in imprisonment is the development of the risk society and the attending actuarial tools designed to reduce social insecurities about crime and victimization (Feeley and Simon 1992; Simon 1993). It is Garland's (2001) thesis of the "culture of control," however, that has garnered the most attention in its sweeping account of the role of these, and other, social changes. He maintains that in the context of the insecurities of postmodern society and high crime rates, the state focused on punishment as a means of "authoritative intervention" and in so doing created a culture of control—a society focused on demonizing and punishing a new "dangerously alien class" (Garland 2000). In so doing, he also acknowledges variability in the new penal discourse and its implementation—a point well documented by other scholars (Haney 1996; Lynch 1998; O'Malley 1992, 1999; Vuolo and Kruttschnitt 2008) and one that is particularly important in the case of women offenders where remnants of the rehabilitative philosophy have been difficult to dislodge. Nevertheless, what is strikingly absent from all of this scholarly discourse is an explanation for why women's imprisonment rates have been growing at a faster rate than the imprisonment rates for men. Here, I point to several factors that might help address this omission.

In a previous review of women's imprisonment, Kruttschnitt and Gartner (2003) noted that both the war on drugs and sentencing reforms had a disproportionate impact on the growth of women's imprisonment. However, the recent stabilization and even slight decline in the proportion of women serving time for drug law violations, despite their increasing imprisonment rate, suggests that the drug war may no longer be a viable explanation. This is especially important for women of color who accounted for a disproportionate share of the growth in prison admissions for drug crimes (Bureau of Justice Statistics 2000a). Arrest data indicate that between 1999 and 2005, the proportion of blacks arrested for a drug offense declined from 40 percent to 33 percent, and between 1998 and 2004 the black proportion of drug convictions declined 13 percent (Mauer 2009). Accordingly, a more viable explanation may be related to the way in which changes in sentencing laws have had a disproportionate effect on women. Tougher sentencing laws (Auerhahn 2008) or the combination of presumptive sentences and mandatory-minimum sentences (Spelman 2009) affect women convicted of nonviolent offenses as much or more than those convicted of violent offenses because prior record aggravates sentence length. That is, whereas in the past a judge may have decided that a lengthy record of minor offenses would not warrant a prison sentence, under presumptive sentencing this can result in a prison sentence even if the offense of conviction is relatively minor, as it frequently is for women (see also Player 2005; Gelsthorpe 2007). The effect of limiting discretion in the sentencing of women offenders was illustrated particularly well in a recent examination of the discretionary component of the federal sentencing guidelines. Here it was revealed that in cases where prosecutors and judges have the ability to exercise discretion, they are significantly more likely to reduce the sentence of female offenders than of male offenders (Spohn and Fornango 2009, 836–37).

Parole may also play a large part in the increasing imprisonment rate for women. Caplow and Simon (1999, 102) argued that one of the most important contributors to the growth in the prison population in the United States has been parole violators; parole, in their view, is no longer an alternative to prison but rather a route to prison, and this is especially true for female offenders. The percentge of female parolees steadily increased from 8 percent in 1990 to 12 percent in 2007 (Petersilia 1999; Glaze and Bonczar 2008). Further, during the period that produced the largest increase in state prison populations (1983–96) data from multiple states indicate that female prison dischargees and parolees were increasingly being returned to prison (Greenfeld and Snell 1999). This is most dramatically illustrated in California, a state known for returning a particularly large proportion of their parolees to prison or jail (Glaze and Bonczar 2007). In 1980 women comprised only 3 percent of the felon parole violators in California, but by 2007 they represented almost 10 percent of this population (California Department of Corrections 2001; California Department of Corrections and Rehabilitation 2008).

Why are women increasingly being returned to prison for parole violations? Some argue that this occurred because of the "piling on of sanctions" (Blomberg 2003), or the increasingly arduous conditions of community supervision, which make it inevitable that offenders, and especially female offenders, will be recycled back into the prison population (Carlen and Tombs 2006). Female parolees have several disadvantages relative to their male counterparts. They are more likely to have a substance abuse problem and, even though the majority of them have one or more dependent children, they are more likely to have been unemployed or homeless prior to imprisonment (Bureau of Justice Statistics 2000b, 2000c). These disadvantages, coupled with the decline in services and resources for parolees (Petersilia 1999), may make meeting standard parole conditions (maintaining employment, reporting regularly to a parole officer, and notification of address changes) increasingly difficult for women offenders.

A final factor that is particularly relevant to the imprisonment of women is the shift that occurred in welfare policies. There is considerable empirical evidence of a negative relationship between welfare expenditures and incarceration rates in the United States and other Western industrialized nations (Beckett and Western 2001; Downes and Hansen 2006). The central premise here is that a single policy has developed to govern the socially marginal sector of the population. Wacquant (2008) has been most vocal in arguing that the simultaneous demise of the welfare state and growth of the penal state are not a coincidence but rather a development designed to control marginal populations.

But how can the decline in the number of welfare recipients help us understand the rise in women's risk of imprisonment?[4] At this point, the link is more discursive than causal because, as Haney (2004) notes, the substantial literature on welfare and penal policy ignores gender, and the research on gender and the welfare state leaves out punishment. Haney (2004) attempts to redress this omission by drawing parallels between the policies, discourses, and practices of the welfare and prison systems: the move to decentralization, privatization, and managerialism; the adoption of responsibilization and empowerment discourse; and the coexistence of punitive and therapeutic approaches in each system. Both systems, she concludes, serve to control women by giving them contrasting and ambivalent models of appropriate behavior (see also McCorkel 2004).

Despite these important arguments, it may be the "feminization of poverty" that provides the strongest explanatory link in the welfare paradigm. Cuts in welfare

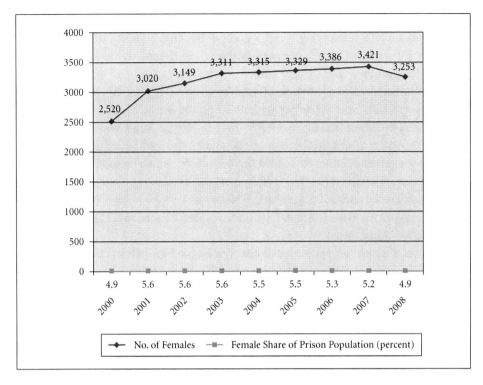

Figure 29.2. Total Sentenced Population in Custody, England and Wales December 31, 2000–2008

Sources:—Elkins, Olagundoye and Rogers 2001, Table B; Gray and Rogers 2002, Table A; Hollis and Goodman 2003, Table A; Home Office 2005, Table 1; Home Office 2007, Table 1; Ministry of Justice 2009, Table 1.

benefits (with the adoption of the Personal Responsibility and Work Opportunity Reconciliation Act of 1996), and the growth in low-paying, minimum-wage jobs resulted in more women turning to crime (including drug trafficking) to survive (Heimer 2000; Sudbury 2002; Holtfreter, Reisig, and Morash 2004; Kruttschnitt and Gartner 2005, 8–38).

II. Women's Imprisonment from a Cross-National Perspective

In several Western industrialized nations, the patterns observed in women's incarceration rates in the United States are much less pronounced.[5] Figure 29.2 shows that the number of sentenced women prisoners in England and Wales, and their proportional share of the prison population, rose from 2000 to 2003, leveled off in 2005 and thereafter went into a gradual decline. Notably, this has not been the case for male prisoners whose numbers continued to increase into 2008 (Elkins, Olagundoye, and Rogers 2001; Gray and Rogers 2002; Home Office 2005, 2007). What does remain remarkably similar to the U.S. case, however, is the shift in the proportion of women being sent to prison for a drug offense. In 2000, roughly 40 percent of the imprisoned women in England and Wales were there for drug law violations, and this held until 2003 when the number of imprisoned drug offenders began to decline. By 2008 drug offenders represented only 27 percent of the sentenced female prisoners. Also, as is true of the United States, this decline in drug offenders was offset by a gradual increase in the proportion of women being held for violent offenses (Elkins, Olagundoye, and Rogers 2001; Gray and Rogers 2002; Home Office 2007).

Australia is another country that has experienced growth in both the male and female prison populations. As in the United States, the growth rates until recently have been greater for females than males: between 1998 and 2008, the number of female prisoners increased by 72 percent but the number of male prisoners increased by only 37 percent (Australian Institute of Criminology 2009). Of course, the base rate for this increase is considerably smaller for females than it is for males, thereby inflating the female percentage increase. As is true in England, data from 2007 to 2008 indicate that the number of male prisoners increased by 2 percent, but the number of female prisoners declined by 1 percent (Australian Institute of Criminology 2009). Although long term data on the offense composition of offender populations are unavailable, recent data suggest that the largest share of the female prison population is imprisoned (in roughly equal proportions) for illicit drugs and "acts intended to cause injury" (Australian Bureau of Statistics 2008).

In other countries, it is more difficult to assess gender-specific trends, but there is some evidence that the Netherlands has experienced not only a marked increase in their incarceration rate (Downes 2007) but also sustained growth in number of women being sent to prison.[6] The population of imprisoned women doubled between 1995 and 2005, from 420 to 816, while the population of male prisoners increased at a substantially lower rate (about 60 percent; Eggen and Kalidien 2008). Evidence also suggests that the noted increase in the female incarceration rate may be due to the targeting of drug offenders (Slotboom et al. 2008). Whether this trend will begin to reverse itself, as it may be doing in the United States and England and Wales remains to be seen.

The magnitude of women's imprisonment in the United States is unsurpassed. While increases have occurred in other nations, and may be related to the adoption of more punitive policies particularly with regard to drug trafficking, no other country's female incarceration rate comes close to that of the United States.[7] What may, however, unite female penality across many Western countries is the overrepresentation of minorities. When the female prison population in the United States increased dramatically during the 1990s, it had a disproportionate effect on women of color, doubling the incarceration rate for black women. In England, the proportion of foreign nationals, three-quarters of whom are nonwhite, has been growing (Morgan and Liebling 2007). Among women prisoners, foreign nationals now represent almost one-quarter (22.5 percent) of the prison population. In the Netherlands, they represent one-third of the female prison population (Aebi and Delgrande 2009). In Western Australia, Aboriginals account for a disproportionate share of the prison population, representing only 2.5 percent of the state's population but more than 50 percent of the female prison population (Goulding 2007).

Some have argued that these trends represent the global effects of a U.S.–led war on drugs (Sudbury 2002). As the United States begins to back-off arresting and prosecuting a disproportionate number of minority drug offenders, it will be interesting to see whether other nations do the same and whether the number of foreign national and minority offenders in women's prisons decline.

III. The Nature of Women's Imprisonment

As scholars of penal history have long noted, fundamental assumptions about women's unique nature have had a remarkable impact on their conditions of confinement, making them both more remote and seemingly gentler but, at the same time, more demanding than those designed for men (Freedman 1981; Dobash, Dobash, and Gutteridge 1986; Rafter 1990; Zedner 1991). It is impossible to recount the history of women's imprisonment in this brief article. Instead, I draw attention to some of the historical characterizations of women's carceral experiences over the past century to provide a backdrop for the more current discourse and policy concerns that have been raised. These include:

> Paternalistic attitudes toward women inmates held by staff and reformers;
> Domesticity as a prison industry;
> Lesser security but greater enforcement for violating prison infractions;
> Therapeutic treatment reinforcing gendered ideologies;
> Prisoners' (homo)sexuality and affective relations; and
> The lack of aggression and violence among prisoners.

A. The New Penality and Its Effect on Women Prisoners

Penologists have characterized the last third of the twentieth century as a time of unusual changes in the techniques, objectives, and discourse of punishment. Most often this includes an acknowledgment of the expansion of the prison population due, in large part, to the demise of rehabilitation and the focus on public safety and victims' rights, which ushered in presumptive sentences and "truth in sentencing" laws. Less often, at least in the United States, has it included a detailed assessment of the conditions of confinement. As Simon (2000, 285) so aptly put it, "just when the experience of imprisonment is becoming a normal pathway for significant portions of the population, the pathways of knowledge that made experiences of incarceration visible are closing." Notable exceptions, however, can be found in the studies of selected women's prisons.

Two studies serve to document how the more instrumental aspects of prison life have changed for women. Rierden's (1997) study of Niantic Correctional Institution in Connecticut (which opened in 1918 during the rehabilitative era) records how prison life changed when a new facility was built across the street to accommodate expanding numbers. The new maximum security facility mandated that prisoners be confined in their cells unless they were at work or in class. The attitudes of staff also changed as they shifted from a rehabilitative rhetoric to one of responsibilization—or the notion that prisoners must take responsibility for changing their lives even if they have few avenues in prison for achieving this goal. Owen's (1998) quasi-ethnography of one of the largest and newest facilities for women prisoners in California also chronicles how growth in the female prison population is shaping the current conditions of confinement. Managing perpetual overcrowding (and the need for privacy) and lengthy terms of confinement are central elements of women's experience, which are structured by the relationships they develop inside and outside of the prison.

Several other studies offer insights into how women cope with what is often described as an incomplete transformation in penal goals and ideologies. Kruttschnitt and Gartner (2005), studying the oldest and newest prisons for women in California, revealed evidence of both continuity and change in women's carceral lives. Women responded to prison life in both the old rehabilitative prison and the new institution in very similar and predictable ways: some isolated themselves from other prisoners; others adapted well to both prisoners and staff; and others associated with only a small cadre of prisoners and eschewed staff. But these different modes of adaption were not randomly distributed across prisons. In the newest prison, which embodied many of the values and goals of the new penology, women were more likely to openly reject their conditions of confinement.

Silberman (2007), focusing on the only maximum security prison for women in Pennsylvania, observed considerable conflict between the old, gendered assumptions about women offenders and what he describes as a new emphasis on "emotional control." While the programs offered to the prisoners (sewing, cosmetology, parenting classes) resonate with the reformatory era, they also clashed with the growing custodial emphasis that included mandatory therapy. Women were now expected to take responsibility for their addictions, mental health issues, and prior experiences of victimization.

Similar contradictions in women's penal reform have been documented in Canada and England. Hannah-Moffat (2000, 2001) dissected the strategies recommended for women prisoners by the Task Force on Federally Sentenced Women in Canada (see also Shaw 1992). In so doing, she illustrates how they are linked to preexisting relations of power. Women prisoners are now characterized as responsible actors, even though the carceral regime that they inhabit is designed to limit their autonomy and choices. In England, recent recommendations for incarcerating fewer women, and making greater use of community sanctions, have seemingly been neutralized by judicial faith in the ability of prison programs "to de-victimize and empower women in prison" (Carlen 2002b, 277; Carlen and Tombs 2006).

1. Risk Assessment

The growing use of risk-assessment instruments on women offenders is an important component of the recent critical scholarship on women's imprisonment in Canada (Hannah-Moffat 1999, 2005), the United Kingdom (Carlen and Tombs 2006; Hudson 2002), and, to a lesser extent, the United States. Risk-assessment interventions serve multiple purposes but generally they encompass: predicting misconduct in prison so the appropriate security can be provided, and identifying offender needs and appropriate interventions to address these needs to reduce recidivism.

There is considerable controversy over the appropriateness of using risk tools on females that were developed and used on male offenders. The Level of Supervision Inventory-Revised (LSI-R) was developed by Andrews and Bonta (1995) and its predictive validity tested using studies of male offenders (Motiuk, Bonta, and Andrews 1986; Bonta and Motiuk 1990; Loza and Simourd 1994). Proponents of this tool, however, argue that it can be used on both women and men because etiological factors are gender neutral. Initial studies of recidivism using female offenders supported this notion (Lowenkamp, Holsinger, and Latessa 2001) as did studies of prison violence (Harer and Langan 2001). A recent meta-analysis of recidivism also revealed that the relationship between the LSI-R and recidivism for females was statistically and practically similar to that found for males (Smith, Cullen, and Latessa 2009, 198).[8]

Feminists who are critical of this instrument are less concerned with the empirical results (or its predictive ability) and more with the paradigm that underscores it: the use of a male norm, which assumes that men and women have the same needs and risks; viewing risk (or need) as a static category that "limits our understanding of how gender constitutes what we define as risk as well as the categories used to identify and assess levels of risk" (Hannah-Moffat 2009, 1406);[9] and the failure to acknowledge the important work being done to establish gender-responsive models (Holtfreter, Reisig, and Morash 2004; Morash 2009). This includes empirical work, which suggests that for women, needs may well be distinct from risks, and certain needs have no relationship to recidivism (Holt-freter and Morash 2003).

2. *Vulnerability*

Related to the issue of women's unique needs is the question of whether they are particularly vulnerable to the "pains of imprisonment" because of their maternal responsibilities and (relative to male prisoners) high rates of prior drug use, and physical and sexual abuse (Bureau of Justice Statistics 1999*a*, 1999*b*; Berry and Eigenberg 2003). However, while there is abundant evidence from studies con-ducted in England, Australia, Canada, and the United States that women prisoners (both pretrial and sentenced) have a greater prevalence of most mental disorders than women in the community, it is not clear whether their rates of mental disorder are higher than those of male prisoners (Ogloff and Tye 2007).[10] An important byproduct of these indicators of vulnerability is self-injury, and female prisoners are more likely to self-injure than male prisoners. Most of the research on self-injury and suicide among women prisoners has been conducted in the United Kingdom and Canada, and focuses primarily on background risk factors. These include sub-stance abuse, family disruption, physical or sexual abuse, and personality disorders (Kruttschnitt and Gartner 2003, 35–39; Borrill et al. 2005; Thomas et al. 2006).

Less well researched is the effect of conditions of confinement on self-injury and suicide. One study, which compared self-harm and suicide ideation among women incarcerated in two California prisons and three prisons in the United Kingdom, found that both of these indicators of vulnerability were higher in the United Kingdom even when a variety of covariates that might explain this relation-ship (e.g., prior mental health treatment, prior self harm, drug use, and sentence length) were controlled (Kruttschnitt and Vuolo 2007). The elevated rates of self-harm and suicide ideation in the United Kingdom may be a result of the transitional state of the Prison Service in England—where correctional officers are spending increasing amounts of time meeting managerial targets, and prisoners are spending increasing amounts of time alone in their cells (see also Borrill et al. 2005).

Similar concerns have been raised in Canada where the Correctional Services (1990) adopted an ostensibly feminist policy for women prisoners—Creating Choices—in response to a prison suicide. Yet in this new policy, self-injury is viewed as an institutional security risk, and women are disciplined for harming themselves (Kilty 2006) despite the evidence that shows that isolation increases the risk of self-harm and suicide (Liebling 1994; Thomas et al. 2006).

3. *Agency*

Self-harm has also been viewed as "an attempt to resist the power of the prison and to demonstrate personal agency" (Kilty 2006, 165).[11] The notion that women offenders are actively constructing and making sense of their lives is an increasingly important component of feminist scholarship (Daly and Maher 1998; Gaarder and Belknap 2002; Kruttschnitt and Carbone-Lopez 2006), even in the carceral context. Bosworth (1996, 1999, 130) was one of the first scholars to explicitly address how power is negotiated in women's prisons. Conducting fieldwork in three women's prisons in England, she used the concept of agency to denote both women's identity and their ability to act.[12] Drawing heavily on Goffman's (1969) institutional analysis of performance as identity management, she argued that women use different aspects of their identity—ethnicity, age, sexuality, and femininity—and their culture (food, dress, and religion) to assert independence from the prison regime. Women confront the penal regime's infantalization of them by attending to their physical appearance, which sometimes also invoked aspects of their cultural identity and, in other cases, by developing lesbian relationships. Agency in this context, then, does not have to involve direct challenges to authority or political action; rather, it can be seen in the subjective and expressive elements of power (Bosworth and Carrabine 2001).

Other scholars argue that Bosworth gives too much weight to women prisoners' agency and to the notion that identity can alter existing relations of penal power. Instead they call attention to the transformative power prisons have in redefining how a prisoner's agency is understood—whether through viewing noncompliance with therapeutic or medical interventions as "difficult to manage" or "risky" behavior, or through viewing women's self-defined political resistance and political identity as mere criminality (Carlen 1994, 2002a; Hannah-Moffat 2001; Corcoran 2006). The question of whether agency or structure is more important in determining women's carceral experiences has yet to be fully fleshed out, but one study of racial identity in women's prisons in California and the United Kingdom suggests that both come into play. Women's own histories and the political coordinates of where these histories are worked out shape responses to the prison environment (Kruttschnitt and Hussemann 2008).

B. Programming

The diversity of women's prison experiences, their growing numbers in the prison system, and the fact that the vast majority will eventually be released has led to a range of concerted efforts to find out "what works" for women offenders. Both scholars and policymakers have advocated "gender responsive" strategies for women (Bloom, Owen, and Covington 2003; United Nations, Office on Drugs and Crime 2008; Van Voorhis et al. 2008). Gender responsiveness is defined as "creating an environment . . . that reflects an understanding of the realities of women's lives and addresses the issues of women" (Bloom, Owen, and Covington 2003, v).

This perspective was developed, in large part, as a response to the use of empirical assessment tools, like the LSI-R which was derived to predict recidivism or serious misconduct of male prisoners, on female prisoners. It is argued that such tools "overclassify women" (i.e., place them in unnecessarily restrictive regimes) and fail to address the specific needs of female offenders (i.e., mental health, substance use, abuse, parenting, self esteem, poverty; see e.g., Farr 2000). Evidence to support these claims, at least with respect of recidivism, is equivocal. Based on an eighteen-month follow-up of women in Minnesota and Oregon, the LSI-R was found to work well for women who were relatively financially stable and whose offending context was similar to males. However, for women who exhibited more traditionally "gendered pathways" into crime (i.e., drugs, abuse, and street crimes such as prostitution), the LSI-R underclassified the risks and needs of low-risk offenders and overclassified those of high-risk women (Reisig, Holtfreter, and Morash 2006).

Two new gender-responsive assessment tools have been developed to address these problems. One is a trailer that supplements the existing LSI-R, and the other is a stand-alone risks-and-needs-assessment tool specifically designed for women offenders (Van Voorhis et al. 2008). These tools were tested on three prison samples, three probation samples, and two pre-release samples. They were correlated with misconduct for inmates (after six or twelve months depending on the site) and new offenses for the community-based samples (after twelve or twenty-four months depending on the site and on whether it was a re-arrest or a new period of incarceration). The results vary by site. In some locations the addition of the gender-responsive items to the LSI-R produced substantially stronger relationships between the risk scale and the outcome by comparison to the gender-neutral LSI-R. A measure of the ratio of true positives to false positives ("prediction hits") also indicated that the gender-responsive items, relative to the gender-neutral items, improves the predictive validity of the risk-assessment tool for women but the overall difference is modest.[13]

The development of gender-responsive risks and needs-assessment tools go hand in hand with the call for gender-responsive programs in women's prisons. As noted in a previous review of women's imprisonment, most of the gender-specific services and programs are community based, providing pre-release planning, alternatives to incarceration, or services for homeless women (Kruttschnitt and Gartner 2003, 45–49). Relatively little is known about the effectiveness of programs operating in women's prisons largely because either there have been problems with program implementation (see e.g., Schram and Morash 2002) or they have not been evaluated, or the evaluations are flawed. They lack random assignment, adequate sample sizes, measures of attrition, and decent follow-up periods (see e.g., Nee and Farman 2005, 2007; Johnson and Zlotnick 2008). There are, of course, some exceptions.

Two programs have focused on in-prison behavioral adjustments for women. Comparing a treatment and control group after twelve weeks, women who participated in a parenting program (the treatment) showed increased knowledge of child development, changes in their attitudes toward corporal punishment, a greater acceptance of parenting responsibilities, and more empathy toward a child's needs

(Sandifer 2008). Another program focused on the question of whether treatment engagement differs for males and females. Although the evaluators did not use random assignment, they enrolled 2,774 individuals in twenty prison-based treatment programs in five states. In so doing, they found that psychosocial issues (depression, anxiety, decision making) were more negatively related to treatment engagement for women than for men (Staton-Tindall et al. 2007).

Two other programs provide some insight into the effectiveness of substance-abuse treatment programs for women prisoners. Because these programs often fail to consider women's diagnostic profiles, Sacks and colleagues (2008) examined whether women with more dysfunctional symptoms and behaviors at Time 1 do better in a therapeutic community than in a cognitive-behavioral treatment program.[14] Using a longitudinal design that evaluated randomly selected participants at five points (entry into prison treatment, prison discharge, and six, twelve, and eighteen months post-release), they found that treatment in a therapeutic community was more effective than treatment in a cognitive-behavioral program in addressing substance abuse and mental health symptoms.

Further support for the effectiveness of therapeutic communities for women can be found in the drug rehabilitation program, Forever Free. Forever Free is a voluntary four-month, in-prison residential treatment program for substance abuse; it also contains a voluntary community residential treatment segment while women are on parole. One year after release, women who had participated in the Forever Free program reported significantly lower rates of re-arrest and conviction for new offenses and drug use relative to women who participated in the Life Plan for Recovery program (an eight-week, substance-abuse education course).[15] Their employment histories, psychological functioning, and relationships with children were also significantly better than those of the women in the comparison group (see Prendergast, Hall, and Wellisch 2002).

C. Prisoner Re-entry

The enormous growth in the prison population in the United States has generated substantial concern about the consequences of trying to reintegrate prisoners back into their communities once they are released (Pattillo, Weiman, and Western 2004; Travis and Visher 2005). But relatively little "re-entry" research has focused on female prisoners. We know that women prisoners who are facing release express considerable concern and anxiety about housing, employment, family reunification, and substance-abuse problems (Severance 2004). This is underscored in the qualitative accounts of the lives and experiences of female ex-prisoners (see Kruttschnitt and Gartner 2003, 53–55).

Why then has so little been done to assess the factors that are important for women in making a transition from prison back into the community? Petersilia (2004, 4), addressing the general lack of "what works" research in the area of reintegration, suggests two reasons. First, the Canadian "cognitive restructuring and risk responsivity" approaches have failed to catch on in the United States because of its sociological (versus psychological) tradition, which focuses more on programmatic rather than individualistic results. As we have seen, this is particularly important in the case of women offenders because risk responsivity has been heavily criticized for not being sensitive to women's needs. While cognitive restructuring programs have been particularly popular in the British government's approach to dealing with women offenders (Home Office 2000; Kendall 2002), it is not clear whether they are an effective tool in reducing recidivism.

The second reason encompasses the broader concern with the lack of solid scientific evidence about recidivism. Just as relatively few prison programs are rigorously evaluated (i.e., using large samples with random assignment and adequate follow-ups), there is also relatively little scientific evidence about the effectiveness of re-entry programs (see, e.g., Hartwell 2001).[16]

The *Returning Home* study examined the process of prisoner re-entry in Baltimore, Maryland by surveying 324 male and female prisoners thirty to ninety days prior to their release and approximately four to six months after release. While it documents the importance of work-release programs for finding subsequent employment, and the roles of drugs and physical and mental health conditions in reoffending, it is silent on the question of whether and how these experiences are gendered (Visher et al. 2004). More generally, the Maryland project demonstrated that a large proportion of prisoners return to communities that are socially and economically disadvantaged, and to families with substance-abuse problems. It might be worth considering whether the concept of prisoner reintegration (which underlies most re-entry programs) is faulty. As Carlen and Tombs (2006) suggest, this concept assumes that offenders were integrated into their communities before entering prison.

IV. CONCLUSIONS

Several years ago, Rosemary Gartner and I surveyed knowledge about women's imprisonment. We concluded with the following observation and question: "There is some evidence that the rate of increase in imprisonment in the United States is slowing, but does this extend to women and will it occur in other countries where the female prison populations are on the rise?" (Kruttschnitt and Gartner 2003, 61). Today it appears that while the overall growth in imprisonment in the United States has slowed down, the growth rate for women in the United States and in other selected countries continues to exceed that of men. This suggests several important areas for future research and policy concern.

First, we need to know more about the factors that are influencing this elevated growth rate in women's imprisonment. Drug law violations have long been considered the primary culprit in the United States and elsewhere, but though this may be changing, the number of women behind bars continues to grow. I have suggested here that, at least with regard to the United States, shifts in sentencing policies, parole revocation decisions, and welfare programs may have been particularly detrimental for female offenders. But, virtually no research has focused on these factors as explanatory components of the rise in the female imprisonment rate. If they are shown to be important determinants, consideration could be given to legislative and community-based alternatives that might reduce the female imprisonment rate. For example, presumptive sentencing policies, which put more women with lengthy but not particularly serious records behind bars, and parole revocations, which are based on minor violations rather than on new offenses, could be offset by a greater use of community-based facilities rather than penal institutions.

Second, the current characterizations of women's prison lives suggest considerable instability as conceptions about the appropriate conditions of confinement and treatment modalities become increasingly gender-neutral. Prison crowding has brought about a new wave of prison construction and one that pays scant attention to the sex of its occupants. Interestingly, this has also been matched with the development of new tools for assessing risk that are also thought to be effective regardless of the offender's sex. The ongoing controversy over using gender-neutral risk-assessment tools is not likely to wane quickly, but it may be misplaced. We have long known that women prisoners are generally not a high-risk group, whether the outcome of concern is prison violence or recidivism.

This brings me to a final recommendation. Much of the concern and policy efforts to address the growing numbers of women in prison have focused on gender-responsive programming. This has served to call attention to some of the unique factors in women offender's backgrounds—a history of abuse, poor parenting skills, low self esteem—and others that are critical to *all* offenders—poverty, the lack of job skills, and substance-abuse issues—but it has not served to increase the level of attention being directed to scientific evaluations of "what works" for women. Isn't this the next step?

NOTES

1. National Prisoner Statistics distinguish between prisoners in custody and prisoners under jurisdiction. Prisoners under custody refers to those who are being held in a state or federal facility. Jurisdiction refers to the state or federal system having legal authority over a prisoner. It includes not just those individuals in prison facilities but individuals who

have been released from prison but who are still under a correctional sentence (e.g., individuals on parole, residing in a halfway house or a treatment center).

2. Incarceration rate refers to the number of prisoners sentenced to more than one year, under state or federal jurisdiction, per 100,000 U.S. residents.

3. The European incarceration rates for males and females were calculated using Council of Europe data (Aebi and Delgrande 2009) on the number of male and female prisoners held in each country and Eurostat, which contains population data on each country for 2007.

4. By 2000 the number of people receiving welfare benefits in the United States (most of whom are women) fell 53 percent (Lichter and Jayakody 2002), and the imprisonment rate for women increased fivefold since 1980 (see table 1, this chapter).

5. Here we are limited in the number of countries we can examine because many nations do not keep systematic records over time on the female imprisonment rate.

6. In a previous review of women's imprisonment, Kruttschnitt and Gartner (2003, 13–15) tried to assess trends in the female prison population in Canada but noted both that the data are incomplete and are not comparable to the data reported for the United States and England and Wales because they are based on admissions rather than one-day counts. Nevertheless, Canada remains an intriguing case because it has avoided the punitive tendencies that have characterized the United States, and to a lesser extent England and Wales and Australia (see Webster and Doob 2007).

7. In 2007 the U.S. female incarceration rate was 69 per 100,000. By comparison, estimated imprisonment rates per 100,000 for females in selected European countries are: Denmark 6.5; England and Wales 15.8; Finland 9.4; France 7.6; Germany 10; Italy 6.9; Netherlands 11.8; Norway 8.5; Spain 25.4; Sweden 8.7; Switzerland 8.3 (see note #3 above).

8. A total of twenty-five studies were included in this analysis but only ten of these studies were published. Further, nine of the data sets used in the analysis came from one researcher who argued that the LSI-R is a gender-neutral instrument.

9. For example, Hannah-Moffat (2006, 188) argues that self-injury (traditionally viewed as a reaction to past trauma or a means of self-medicating) is now considered "difficult to manage" behavior and is undifferentiated from assaultive behavior.

10. This finding is based on studies that have been matched on demographic factors (e.g., age, education, income) that might explain the differences in the mental health of prison and community samples.

11. Agency is generally used to refer to "knowing self-direction" (Abrams 1995, 306, n11). In the prison context, it has also been used to direct attention to the ways in which women use their identities to deflect existing power relations (Bosworth 1999, 95).

12. No attempt is made in her work to understand how contextual variations might have affected the ways in which women resisted institutional control.

13. In the prison samples in Colorado, Missouri, and Minnesota, the AUC (area under the curve) values for gender-neutral assessments are respectively .59, .61, and .68; for the gender responsive assessments, they are .62, .65, and .70 (Van Voorhis et al. 2008, table 3).

14. A therapeutic community is based on the assumption that individuals must be removed from the general prison population and placed in a separate area, which is conducive to positive behavioral change.

15. The women in the two programs had similar demographic and criminal history profiles.

16. Seiter and Kadela (2003) reviewed the effectiveness of prisoner re-entry programs using the Maryland Scale of Scientific Method. While their findings indicate that there is solid evidence that vocational training and work release programs improve job skills and reduce recidivism, as do drug rehabilitation programs, it is not clear what proportion of the programs they evaluated included female prisoners.

REFERENCES

Abrams, Kathleen. 1995. "Sex Wars Redux: Agency and Coercion in Feminist Legal Theory." *Columbia Law Review* 95: 304–76.

Aebi, Marcelo F., and Natalia Delgrande. 2009. *SPACE I: Survey 2007*. Strasbourg: Council of Europe. http://www.coe.int/t/e/legal_affairs/legal_co-operation/prisons_and_alternatives/Statistics_SPACE_I/.

Andrews, Don A., and James Bonta. 1995. *The Level of Service Inventory-Revised*. Toronto: Multi-Health Systems.

Auerhahn, Kathleen. 2008. "Using Simulation Modeling to Evaluate Sentencing Reform in California: Choosing the Future." *Journal of Experimental Criminology* 4: 241–66.

Australian Bureau of Statistics. 2008. *Prisoners in Australia, 2008*. Canberra: Australian Bureau of Statistics.

Australian Institute of Criminology. 2009. *Crime and Criminal Justice Statistics: Age and Gender of Prisoners*. Canberra: Australian Government, Australian Institute of Criminology.

Beckett, Katherine. 1997. *Making Crime Pay: Law and Order in Contemporary American Politics*. New York: Oxford University Press.

Beckett, Katherine, and Bruce Western. 2001. "Governing Social Marginality: Welfare, Incarceration, and the Transformation of State Policy." In *Mass Imprisonment: Social Causes and Consequences*, ed. David Garland. London: Sage.

Berry, Phyllis E., and Helen M. Eigenberg. 2003. "Role Strain and Incarcerated Mothers: Understanding the Process of Mothering." *Women and Criminal Justice* 15: 101–19.

Blomberg, Thomas G. 2003. "Penal Reform and the Face of 'Alternatives.'" In *Punishment and Social Control*, 2nd ed., ed. Thomas G. Blomberg and Stanley Cohen. Hawthorne, NY: Aldine de Gruyter.

Bloom, Barbara, Barbara Owen, and Stephanie Covington. 2003. *Gender-Responsive Strategies: Research, Practice, and Guiding Principles for Women Offenders*. Washington, DC: U.S. Department of Justice, National Institute of Corrections.

Bonta, James, and Lawrence L. Motiuk. 1990. "Classification to Halfway Houses: A Quasi-Experimental Evaluation." *Criminology* 28: 497–506.

Borrill, Jo, Louisa Snow, Diana Medlicott, Rebecca Teers, and Jo Paton. 2005. "Learning from 'Near Misses': Interviews with Women Who Survived an Incident of Severe Self-harm in Prison." *Howard Journal* 44: 57–69.

Bosworth, Mary. 1996. "Resistance and Compliance in Women's Prisons: Toward a Critique of Legitimacy." *Critical Criminology* 7: 5–19.

———. 1999. *Engendering Resistance: Agency and Power in Women's Prisons*. Aldershot: Ashgate.

Bosworth, Mary, and Eamonn Carrabine. 2001. "Reassessing Resistance: Race, Gender and Sexuality in Prison." *Punishment and Society* 3: 501–15.

Bureau of Justice Statistics. 1994. *Women in Prison*. NCJ-145321. Washington, DC: U.S. Department of Justice, Bureau of Justice Statistics.

———. 1995. *Prisoners in 1994*. NCJ-151654. Washington, DC: U.S. Department of Justice, Bureau of Justice Statistics.

———. 1999a. *Prior Abuse Reported by Inmates and Probationers*. NCJ-172879. Washington, DC: U.S. Department of Justice, Bureau of Justice Statistics.

———. 1999b. *Special Report: Substance Abuse and Treatment, State and Federal Prisoners, 1997*. NCJ-172871. Washington, DC: U.S. Department of Justice, Bureau of Justice Statistics.

———. 2000a. *Sourcebook of Criminal Justice Statistics*. Washington, DC: U.S. Department of Justice, Bureau of Justice Statistics.

———. 2000b. *Correctional Populations in the U.S., 1997*. NCJ-177613. Washington, DC: U.S. Department of Justice, Bureau of Justice Statistics.

———. 2000c. *Incarcerated Parents and Their Children*. NCJ-182335. Washington, DC: U.S. Department of Justice, Bureau of Justice Statistics.

———. 2003. *Prisoners in 2002*. NCJ-200248. Washington, DC: U.S. Department of Justice, Bureau of Justice Statistics.

———. 2004. *Prisoners in 2003*. NCJ-205335. Washington, DC: U.S. Department of Justice, Bureau of Justice Statistics.

———. 2005. *Prisoners in 2004*. NCJ-210677. Washington, DC: U.S. Department of Justice, Bureau of Justice Statistics.

———. 2007. *Prisoners in 2006*. NCJ-219416. Washington, DC: U.S. Department of Justice, Bureau of Justice Statistics.

———. 2008. *Prisoners in 2007*. NCJ-224280. Washington, DC: U.S.Department of Justice, Bureau of Justice Statistics.

———. 2009. *Prison Inmates at Midyear 2008—Statistical Tables*. NCJ-225619. Washington, DC: U.S. Department of Justice, Bureau of Justice Statistics.

California Department of Corrections. 2001. *Historical Trends 1980–2000*. Sacramento: California Department of Corrections, Offender Information Services Branch, Data Analysis Unit.

California Department of Corrections and Rehabilitation. 2008. *California Prisoners and Parolees 2007*. Sacramento: Department of Corrections and Rehabilitation, Offender Information Services Branch, Estimates and Statistical Analysis Section, Data Analysis Unit.

Caplow, Theodore, and Jonathan Simon. 1999. "Understanding Prison Policy and Population Trends." In *Prisons*, edited by Michael Tonry and Joan Petersilia. Vol. 26 of *Crime and Justice: A Review of Research*, edited by Michael Tonry. Chicago: University of Chicago Press.

Carlen, Pat. 1983. *Women's Imprisonment: A Study in Social Control*. London: Routledge and Kegan Paul.

———. 1994. "Why Study Women's Imprisonment? Or Anyone Else's?" *British Journal of Criminology* 34(Special Issue):131–40.

————. 1999. "Women's Imprisonment in England, Current Issues." In *Harsh Punishment: International Experiences of Women's Imprisonment*, ed. Sandy Cook and Susanne Davies. Boston: Northeastern University Press.

————. 2002*a*. "New Discourses of Justification and Reform for Women's Imprisonment in England." In *Women and Punishment: The Struggle for Justice*, ed. Pat Carlen. Cullompton, Devon, UK: Willan.

————. 2002*b*. "Carceral Clawback: The Case of Women's Imprisonment in Canada." *Punishment and Society* 4: 114–21.

Carlen, Pat, and Jacqueline Tombs. 2006. "Reconfigurations of Penality: The Ongoing Case of the Women's Imprisonment and Reintegration Industries." *Theoretical Criminology* 10: 337–60.

Cooper, Sheelagh. 1993. "The Evolution of the Federal Women's Prison." In *Conflict with the Law: Women and the Canadian Criminal Justice System*, ed. Ellen Adelberg and Claudia Currie. Vancouver: Press Gang Publishers.

Corcoran, Mary. 2006. *Out of Order: The Political Imprisonment of Women in Northern Ireland 1972–1998*. Cullompton, Devon, UK: Willan.

Correctional Services of Canada. 1990. *Creating Choices: The Report of the Task Force on Federally Sentenced Women*. Ottawa: Correctional Services of Canada.

Daly, Kathleen, and Lisa Maher. 1998. "Crossroads and Intersections: Building from Feminist Critique." In *Criminology at the Crossroads: Feminist Readings in Crime and Justice*, ed. Kathleen Daly and Lisa Maher. New York: Oxford University Press.

Dobash, Russell P., R. Emerson Dobash, and Sue Gutteridge. 1986. *The Imprisonment of Women*. Oxford: Basil Blackwell.

Downes, David. 2007. "Visions of Penal Control in the Netherlands." In *Crime, Punishment, and Politics in Comparative Perspective*, edited by Michael Tonry. Vol. 36 of *Crime and Justice: A Review of Research*, edited by Michael Tonry. Chicago: University of Chicago Press.

Downes, David, and Kirstine Hansen. 2006. "Welfare and Punishment in Comparative Perspective." In *Perspectives on Punishment. The Contours of Control*, ed. Sarah Armstrong and Lesley McAra. New York: Oxford University Press.

Eggen, A.Th. J., and S. N. Kalidien. 2008. *Crime and Law Enforcement 2008*. Den Haag: Boom Juridsiche Uitgevers, CBS, WODC.

Elkins, Mike, Jide Olagundoye, and Keith Rogers. 2001. *Prison Population Brief England and Wales: December 2000*. London: Home Office, Research, Development and Statistics Directorate.

Farr, Kathryn Ann. 2000. "Classification for Female Inmates: Moving Forward." *Crime and Delinquency* 46: 3–17.

Feeley, Malcolm M., and Jonathan Simon. 1992. "The New Penology: Notes on the Emerging Strategy of Corrections and its Implications." *Criminology* 30: 449–79.

Freedman, Estelle B. 1981. *Their Sisters' Keepers: Women's Prison Reform in America, 1830–1930*. Palo Alto, CA: Stanford University Press.

Gaarder, Emily, and Joanne Belknap. 2002. "Tenuous Borders: Girls Transferred to Adult Court." *Criminology* 40: 481–518.

Garland, David. 2000. "The Culture of High Crime Societies: Some Preconditions of Recent 'Law and Order' Politics." *British Journal of Criminology* 40: 347–75.

————. 2001. *The Culture of Control: Crime and Social Order in Contemporary Society*. Chicago: University of Chicago Press.

Gelsthorpe, Loraine. 2007. "Gender and Sentencing." In *What Works with Women Offenders*, ed. Rosemary Sheetan, Gill McIvor, and Chris Trotter. Devon, UK: Willan.

Glaze, Lauren E., and Thomas P. Bonczar. 2007. *Probation and Parole in the United States, 2006.* NCJ 220218. Washington, DC: U.S. Department of Justice, Bureau of Justice Statistics.

———. 2008. *Probation and Parole in the United States, 2007.* NCJ224707.Washington, DC: U.S. Department of Justice, Bureau of Justice Statistics.

Goffman, Erving. 1969. *The Presentation of Self in Everyday Life.* London: Allen Lane.

Goulding, Dot. 2007. *Recapturing Freedom.* Sydney: Hawkins Press.

Gray, Carly, and Keith Rogers. 2002. *Prison Population Brief England and Wales: December 2001.* London: Home Office, Research, Development and Statistics Directorate.

Greenfeld, Lawrence A., and Tracy L. Snell. 1999. *Women Offenders.* U.S. Department of Justice Statistics. Special Report. NCJ175688. Washington, DC: U.S. Department of Justice, Bureau of Justice Statistics.

Haney, Lynne. 1996. "Homeboys, Babies, and Men in Suits: The State and the Reproduction of Male Dominance." *American Sociological Review* 61: 759–78.

———. 2004. "Introduction: Gender, Welfare, and States of Punishment." *Social Politics* 11:333–62.

Hannah-Moffat, Kelly. 1999. "Moral Agent or Actuarial Subject: Risk and Canadian Women's Imprisonment." *Theoretical Criminology* 3:71–94.

———. 2000. "Prisons that Empower: Neo-liberal Governance in Canadian Women's Prisons." *British Journal of Criminology* 40: 510–31.

———. 2001. *Punishment in Disguise: Penal Governance and Federal Imprisonment of Women in Canada.* Toronto: University of Toronto Press.

———. 2005. "Criminogenic Needs and the Transformative Risk Subject." *Punishment and Society* 7: 29–51.

———. 2006. "Pandora's Box: Risk/Need and Gender-responsive Corrections." *Criminology and Public Policy* 5: 183–92.

———. 2009. "Gridlock or Mutability: Reconsidering 'Gender' and Risk Assessment." *Criminology and Public Policy* 8: 209–19.

Harer, Miles D., and Neal P. Langan. 2001. "Gender Differences in Predictors of Prison Violence: Assessing the Predictive Validity of a Risk Classification System." *Crime and Delinquency* 47: 513–36.

Hartwell, Stephanie. 2001. "Female Mentally Ill Offenders and their Community Reintegration Needs: An Initial Examination." *International Journal of Law and Psychiatry* 24: 1–11.

Heimer, Karen. 2000. "Changes in the Gender Gap in Crime and Women's Economic Marginalization." In *Criminal Justice 2000: The Nature of Crime, Continuity and Change*, vol. 1, ed. Gary LaFree. Washington, DC: National Institute of Justice.

Hollis, Veronica, and Michelle Goodman. 2003. *Prison Population Brief England and Wales: December 2002.* London: Home Office, Research, Development and Statistics Directorate.

Holtfreter, Kristy, and Merry Morash. 2003. "The Needs of Women Offenders: Implications for Correctional Programming." *Women and Criminal Justice* 14: 137–60.

Holtfreter, Kristy, Michael D. Reisig, and Merry Morash. 2004. "Poverty, State Capital, and Recidivism among Women Offenders." *Criminology and Public Policy* 3: 185–208.

Home Office. 2000. *Searching for "What Works": An Evaluation of Cognitive Skills Programmes.* RDS Findings 306. London: Home Office.

———. 2005. *Population in Custody Monthly Tables: December 2004 England and Wales.* London: Research, Development and Stastics Directorate, National Offender Management Service.

———. 2007. *Population in Custody Monthly Tables: December 2006 England and Wales.* London: Research, Development and Statistics Directorate, National Offender Management Service.

Hudson, Barbara. 2002. "Gender Issues in Penal Policy and Penal Theory." In *Women and Punishment: The Struggle for Justice*, ed. Pat Carlen. Collumpton, Devon, UK: Willan.

Johnson, Jennifer E., and Caron Zlotnick. 2008. "A Pilot Study of Group Interpersonal Psychotherapy for Depression in Substance-abusing Female Prisoners." *Journal of Substance Abuse Treatment* 34: 371–77.

Kendall, Kathleen. 2002. *"Time to Think Again about Cognitive Behavioural Programmes."* In *Women and Punishment: The Struggle for Justice*, ed. Pat Carlen. Cullompton, Devon, UK: Willan.

Kilty, Jennifer M. 2006. "Under the Barred Umbrella: Is There Room for a Women-centered Self-injury Policy in Canadian Corrections?" *Criminology and Public Policy* 4: 161–82.

Kruttschnitt, Candace, and Kristin Carbone-Lopez. 2006. "Moving beyond the Stereotypes: Women's Subjective Accounts of Their Violent Crime." *Criminology* 44: 321–48.

Kruttschnitt, Candace, and Rosemary Gartner. 2003. "Women's Imprisonment." In *Crime and Justice: A Review of Research*, vol. 30, edited by Michael Tonry. Chicago: University of Chicago Press.

———. 2005. *Marking Time in the Golden State: Women's Imprisonment in California.* New York: Cambridge University Press.

Kruttschnitt, Candace, and Jeanette Hussemann. 2008. "The Micropolitics of Race and Ethnicity in Women's Prisons in Two Political Contexts." *British Journal of Sociology* 59: 709–28.

Kruttschnitt, Candace, and Mike Vuolo. 2007. "The Cultural Context of Women Prisoners' Mental Health: A Comparison of Two Prison Systems." *Punishment and Society* 9: 115–50.

Lichter, Daniel, and Rukamalie Jayakody. 2002. "Welfare Reform: How Do We Measure Success?" *Annual Review of Sociology* 28: 117–41.

Liebling, Alison. 1994. "Suicides among Women Prisoners." *Howard Journal* 33: 1–9.

Lowenkamp, Christopher T., Alexander M. Holsinger, and Edward J. Latessa. 2001. "Risk/Need Assessment, Offender Classification, and the Role of Childhood Abuse." *Criminal Justics and Behavior* 28: 543–63.

Loza, Wagby, and David J. Simourd. 1994. "Psychometric Evaluation of the Level of Supervision Inventory (LSI) among Male Canadian Federal Offenders." *Criminal Justice and Behavior* 21: 468–80.

Lynch, Mona. 1998. "Waste Managers? The New Penology, Crime Fighting, and Parole Agent Identity." *Law and Society Review* 32: 39–70.

Mauer, Marc. 2009. *The Changing Racial Dynamics of the War on Drugs.* Washington, DC: The Sentencing Project.

McCorkel, Jill. 2004. "Criminally Dependent? Gender, Punishment, and the Rhetoric of Welfare Reform." *Social Politics* 11: 386–410.

Ministry of Justice. 2009. *Population in Custody Monthly Tables: December 2008 England and Wales.* London: Ministry of Justice.

Morgan, Rod, and Alison Liebling. 2007. "Imprisonment: An Expanding Scene." In *The Oxford Handbook of Criminology*, 4th ed., ed. Mike Maguire, Rod Morgan, and Robert Reiner. Oxford University Press.

Morash, Merry. 2009. "A Great Debate over Using the Level of Service Inventory-Revised (LSI-R) with Women Offenders." *Criminology and Public Policy* 8: 173–81.

Motiuk, Lawrence L., James Bonta, and Don A. Andrews. 1986. "Classification in Correctional Halfway Houses: The Relative and Incremental Predictive Criterion Validities of the Megargee-MMPI and LSI systems." *Criminal Justice and Behavior* 13: 33–46.

Nee, Claire, and Sarah Farman. 2005. "Female Prisoners with Borderline Personality Disorder: Some Promising Treatment Developments." *Criminal Behaviour and Mental Health* 15: 2–16.

———. 2007. "Dialectical Behaviour Therapy as a Treatment for Borderline Personality Disorder in Prisons: Three Illustrative Case Studies." *Journal of Forensic Psychiatry and Psychology* 18: 160–80.

Ogloff, James, and Christine Tye. 2007. "Responding to the Mental Health Needs of Women Offenders." In *What Works with Women Offenders*, ed. Rosemary Sheehan, Gil McIvor, and Chris Trotter. Cullompton, Devon, UK: Willan.

O'Mally, Pat. 1992. "Risk, Power, and Crime Prevention." *Economy and Society* 21: 252–75.

———. 1999. "Volatile and Contradictory Punishment." *Theoretical Criminology* 3: 175–96.

Owen, Barbara. 1998. *In the Mix: Struggle and Survival in a Women's Prison*. Albany: State University of New York Press.

Pattillo, Mary, David Weiman, and Bruce Western. 2004. *Imprisoning America: The Social Effects of Mass Incarceration*. New York: Russell Sage Foundation.

Petersilia, Joan. 1999. "Parole and Prisoner Re-entry in the United States." In *Prisons*, edited by Michael Tonry and Joan Petersilia. Vol. 26 of *Crime and Justice: A Review of Research*, edited by Michael Tonry. Chicago: University of Chicago Press.

———. 2004. "What Works in Prisoner Reentry? Reviewing and Questioning the Evidence." *Federal Probation* 68: 1–8.

Player, Elaine. 2005. "The Reduction of Women's Imprisonment in England and Wales." *Punishment and Society* 7: 419–39.

Prendergast, Michael, Elizabeth Hall, and Jean Wellisch. 2002. *Outcome Evaluation of the Forever Free Substance Abuse Treatment Program: One-Year Postrelease Outcomes*. Final Report to NIJ, NCJ 199685. Washington, DC: U.S. Department of Justice, Bureau of Justice Statistics.

Rafter, Nichole Hahn. 1990. *Partial Justice: Women, Prison and Social Control*. 2nd ed. New Brunswick, NJ: Transaction.

Reisig, Michael D., Kristy Holtfreter, and Merry Morash. 2006. "Accessing Recidivism Risk across Female Pathways to Crime." *Justice Quarterly* 23: 384–405.

Rierden, Andi. 1997. *The Farm: Life inside a Women's Prison*. Amherst: University of Massachusetts Press.

Sacks, Joann Y., Karen McKendrick, Zachary Hamilton, Charles M. Cleland, Frank S. Pearson, and Steven Banks. 2008. "Treatment Outcomes for Female Offenders: Relationship to Number of Axis I Diagnosis." *Behavioral Sciences and the Law* 26: 413–34.

Sandifer, Jacquelyn. 2008. "Evaluating the Efficacy of a Parenting Program for Incarcerated Mothers." *Prison Journal* 88: 423–45.

Schram, Pamela, and Merry Morash. 2002. "Evaluation of a Life Skills Program for Women Inmates in Michigan." *Journal of Offender Rehabilitation* 34: 47–70.

Seiter, Richard P., and Karen R. Kadela. 2003. "Prisoner Re-entry: What Works, What Doesn't and What's Promising." *Crime and Delinquency* 49: 360–88.

Severance, Theresa A. 2004. "Concerns and Coping Strategies of Women Inmates Concerning Release: 'It's Going to Take Somebody in My Corner.'" *Journal of Offender Rehabilitation* 38: 73–79.

Shaw, Margaret. 1992. "Issues of Power and Control: Women in Prison and Their Defenders." *British Journal of Criminology* 32: 438–52.

Silberman, Matthew. 2007. "The Muncy Way: The Reformatory Ideal at the End of the 20th Century." *Prison Journal* 87: 271–94.

Simon, Jonathan. 1993. *Poor Discipline: Parole and the Social Control of the Underclass, 1890–1990.* Chicago: University of Chicago Press.

———. 2000. "The 'Society of Captives' in the Era of Hyper-incarceration." *Theoretical Criminology* 4: 285–308.

Sloop, John M. 1996. *The Cultural Prison: Discourse, Prisoners, and Punishment.* Tuscaloosa: University of Alabama Press.

Slotboom, Anne-Marie, Catrien Bijleveld, S. Day, and A. van Giezen. 2008. *Detained Women in the Netherlands: Importation and Deprivation Factors and Detention Damage.* Amsterdam: Vrije Universiteit.

Smith, A. 1990. "Female Prisoners in Ireland, 1855–1878." *Federal Probation* 54: 69–81.

Smith, Paul, Francis T. Cullen, and Edward J. Latessa. 2009. "Can 14,737 Women be Wrong? A Meta-analysis of the LSI-R and Recidivism for Female Offenders." *Criminology and Public Policy* 8: 183–208.

Spelman, William. 2009. "Crime, Cash, and Limited Options: Explaining the Prison Boom." *Criminology and Public Policy* 8: 29–77.

Spohn, Cassia, and Robert Fornango. 2009. "U.S. Attorneys and Substantial Assistance Departures: Testing for Interprosecutor Disparity." *Criminology* 47: 813–46.

Staton-Tindall, Michele, Bryan R. Garner, Janis T. Morey, Carl Leukefeld, Jennifer Krietemeyer, Christine A. Saum, and Carrier B. Oser. 2007. "Gender Differences in Treatment Engagement among a Sample of Incarcerated Substance Abusers." *Criminal Justice and Behavior* 34: 1143–56.

Sudbury, Julia. 2002. "Celling Black Bodies: Black Women in the Global Prison Industrial Complex." *Feminist Review* 70: 57–74.

Thomas, Jim, Margaret Leaf, Steve Kazmierczak, and Josh Stone. 2006. "Self-injury in Correctional Settings: 'Pathology' of Prisons or of Prisoners?" *Criminology and Public Policy* 5: 193–202.

Tonry, Michael. 2004. *Thinking about Crime: Sense and Sensibilities in American Penal Culture.* New York: Oxford University Press.

Travis, Jeremy, and Christy Visher. 2005. *Prisoner Reentry and Crime in America.* New York: Cambridge University Press.

United Nations, Office on Drugs and Crime. 2008. *Handbook for Prison Managers and Policymakers on Women and Imprisonment.* New York: United Nations.

U.S. Census Bureau. 2009. *Table 3: Annual Estimates of the Resident Population by Sex, Race, and Hispanic Origin for the United States: April 1, 2000 to July 1, 2008.* NC-EST2008-03. Washington, DC: U.S. Census Bureau, Population Division.

Van Voorhis, Patricia, Emily Salisbury, Emily Wright, and Ashley Bauman. 2008. "Achieving Accurate Pictures of Risk and Identifying Gender Responsive Needs: Two New Assessments for Women Offenders." Unpublished Paper. Washington, DC: U.S. Department of Justice, National Institute of Corrections.

Visher, Christy, Vera Kachnowski, Nancy La Vigne, and Jeremy Travis. 2004. *Baltimore Prisoners' Experiences Returning Home*. Washington, DC: Urban Institute.

Vuolo, Mike, and Candace Kruttschnitt. 2008. "Prisoners' Adjustment, Correctional Officers, and Context: The Foreground and Background of Punishment in Late Modernity." *Law and Society Review* 42: 307–36.

Wacquant, Loic. 2008. "Ordering Insecurity: Social Polarization and the Punitive Upsurge." *Radical Philosophy Review* 11: 9–27.

Walmsley, Roy. 2009. *World Female Imprisonment List*. 8th ed. London: King's College London, International Centre for Prison Studies.

Webster, Cheryl Marie, and Anthony N. Doob. 2007. "Punitive Trends and Stable Imprisonment Rates in Canada." In *Crime, Punishment, and Politics in Comparative Perspective*, edited by Michael Tonry. Vol. 36 of *Crime and Justice: A Review of Research*, edited by Michael Tonry. Chicago: University of Chicago Press.

Worrall, Anne. 2002. "Rendering Women Punishable: The Making of a Penal Crisis." In *Women and Punishment: The Struggle for Justice*, ed. Pat Carlen. Cullompton, Devon, UK: Willan.

Zedner, Lucia. 1991. *Women, Crime, and Custody in Victorian England*. Oxford: Clarendon.

CHAPTER 30

PAROLE AND PRISONER RE-ENTRY

JOAN PETERSILIA

PAROLE and prisoner re-entry are once again at the forefront of America's debate on crime and punishment. Mass incarceration, severe prison crowding, and high recidivism have created a system in crisis. Within this context, parole—which refers to both a release mechanism and a method of community supervision—has come under intense scrutiny. If parole is effective, dangerous offenders remain in prison and those who are released are better prepared for re-entry. If parole resources are misdirected, community safety is threatened as prisoners return home with few resources and little surveillance.

This is not the first time that parole has garnered national attention, but the current interest is decidedly different. In the 1980s, parole was blamed for turning dangerous criminals loose and campaigns called for its abolition. By 2000, sixteen states had abolished discretionary parole release, and three out of four inmates released from prison were released automatically (and mandatorily) at the end of a prescribed prison term rather than through a parole hearing (Hughes, Wilson, and Beck 2001). But most of those released were still required to be on post-prison parole supervision, where they were subject to reporting and drug-testing requirements, often with few rehabilitation programs to assist their re-entry. The outcomes were predictable: most released prisoners failed and were returned to prison. Parole violators were often returned to prison for technical violations rather than new crimes, and after a few months, were released yet again. The continuous churning of parolees in and out of prison is now widely viewed as a waste of correctional resources.

Tough-on-crime conservatives and rehabilitation-oriented liberals are calling for reforming parole and reinvesting in re-entry services. Policymakers now acknowledge a central penological fact: like it or not, the vast majority of those in prisons today (nearly 95 percent) will eventually be released. If current incarceration and release trends continue, more than 750,000 prisoners will be coming home annually by the year 2011 (Pew Center on the States 2008). To keep prison populations and costs down, advocates hope that expanding ex-offender job training, substance abuse, and mental health counseling will reduce recidivism, and the greater use of alternative sanctions will divert lower-risk parolees from prison. President Obama and Congress recently appropriated funding for the Second Chance Act of 2007, the first-of-its-kind legislation authorizing money to improve services for people returning from prisons. Millions of dollars will be given to state and local projects to help reduce re-offending. President Obama hopes the investment will reduce recidivism, ultimately lowering the nearly $60 billion spent annually on the nation's corrections system (Bureau of Justice Statistics 2006).

If parole and re-entry investments prove effective and cost-beneficial, they may set the stage for broader discussions about crime, community penalties, and mass incarceration. If re-entry efforts fail, they will likely be regarded as just another "soft on crime" experiment that failed, fueling a return to a lock-'em-up paradigm. Which scenario proves true will depend on realistic expectations and an understanding of parole's history, current operations, needs of the parole population, and "what works" in re-entry programming.

This chapter provides an overview of these issues. Section I defines parole and provides a brief history of American parole development. It describes the changes that occurred to parole in the 1980s and 1990s, resulting in a decline of focus on rehabilitation and discretionary parole release. Section II describes the characteristics of the parole population, including their education, work, and substance abuse histories. Section III is devoted to the rehabilitation and surveillance aspects of modern parole systems. This section also outlines the many civil disabilities and legal restrictions governing a parolee's life after prison. Section IV summarizes parolee recidivism rates and the contribution of parolees to US crime rates. This section also explains the circumstances under which parole may be revoked and the pressure that such revocations place on current prison systems. Section V summarizes the principles of effective rehabilitation programs, drawing conclusions for re-entry program design. The final section provides thoughts on future research.

A number of conclusions emerge:

- Parole release and parole supervision have been part of America's criminal justice system for more than one hundred years, but both were significantly transformed during the 1970s and 1980s. Discretionary decision making gave way to rule-governed sentencing, and models of rehabilitation-focused casework were replaced with surveillance-oriented approaches. These shifts laid the groundwork for the parole system we have today.

- The quadrupling of the US prison population over the past twenty-five years has meant more prisoners coming home, placing increasing demands on parole agencies. Most inmates leave prison with their education, work, and substance-abuse issues unaddressed. Moreover, they are often stigmatized and deliberately excluded. Until recently, scholars and others have neglected to pay sufficient attention to the profound challenges posed by the prisoner re-entry phenomenon.
- Support and funding for parole agencies remain low, resulting in dangerously high caseloads, few services for offenders, and high recidivism rates. Parole supervision in most jurisdictions neither protects the public nor rehabilitates the offender.
- Studies have shown that some parole intervention programs, including drug treatment and vocational training, can decrease recidivism and save money in the long run. These programs are evidence that "something works" in community-based sanctions, and such programs should be replicated and rigorously evaluated.
- Without changes to parole practices and programs, parole violators—who now account for more than a third of all annual prison admissions—will continue to drive up prison populations, exacerbating costs and prison overcrowding. This new reality underscores the importance of rethinking the efficacy and purposes of parole release and supervision.
- There appears a resurgence of political and government interest in parole and prisoner re-entry. Current interest is not to abolish parole release or reduce programs, but rather to strengthen reintegration services. Ultimately, parole reform may pave the way for reducing mass incarceration in America.

I. Definition and Evolution of Parole

People often confuse probation, parole, and pardon. All three place offenders in the community after a criminal conviction, but they are quite different. *Probation* is a judge's sentence that allows a convicted offender to continue to live in the community after criminal conviction, with restrictions on activities and with supervision for the duration of the sentence. *Parole* refers to offenders who have spent time in prison and are released to complete the remainder of their sentence under supervision in the community. Parole is usually granted from authorities in the correctional system (i.e., a parole board), since responsibility for offenders passes from the judicial system to the correctional system upon imprisonment. Parolees are technically still in state custody; they have merely been granted the privilege of living in the community instead of prison. If parolees or probationers violate the rules of their release, they can be returned to incarceration. *Pardon* is an executive act granted by a governor or the president that legally excuses a convicted offender from penalty. Those who are pardoned are excused from any further supervision.

A. The Definition and Functions of Parole

Inmates are released from prison mandatorily or discretionarily. *Mandatory release* is release after a specified period of time, as required by law, and occurs in jurisdictions using determinate sentencing. In determinate sentencing, the offender is given a set amount of time to serve by the court. Determinate sentencing eliminates parole boards, although the exact requirements vary by state. *Discretionary release* is at the paroling authority's discretion, within boundaries established by the sentence and by law. Discretionary release occurs in states using indeterminate sentencing, where the sentence imposed does not state a specific period of time or release date but a range of time, such as "five-to-ten years." In a recent survey of paroling authorities, about a third (34 percent) reported they operated within a determinate sentencing system, a quarter (21 percent) operated within an indeterminate system, and the remainder (45 percent) used both determinate and indeterminate sentencing. But even in the determinate sentencing states, nearly all (75 percent) of the paroling authorities indicated that they have some authority to release prisoners prior to sentence completion, illustrating that even determinate sentencing structures incorporate a discretionary release determination (Kinnevy and Caplan 2008).

In those states that permit discretionary release, state laws give parole boards the authority to change, within certain limits, the length of a sentence that is actually served. Parole officials may also change the conditions under which convicted offenders are supervised, and they may release offenders from prison to supervision in the community or to an outside facility. Parole authorities can also issue warrants revoking parole and reincarcerating offenders who violate parole conditions. For jurisdictions with determinate sentencing and no discretion for the timing of release, the paroling authority may still determine conditions of release. They thus can have a direct effect on prison management. For example, they can increase the number of prisoners required to be on post-prison supervision or they can decrease, by policy, the number of parole revocations returned to prison. It is this gatekeeper role that makes paroling authorities so central to current debates about prisoner re-entry and prison crowding. As has been observed, "no other part of the criminal justice system concentrates such power in the hands of so few" (Rhine et al. 1991, 32–33).

According to a survey by the Association of Paroling Authorities International (APAI), just 212 individuals in the United States were serving full time on paroling authorities and another 94 were serving on a part-time basis in 2002 (Burke 2003). Yet, these 306 persons have the statutory authority to grant parole, set conditions of parole, supervise parolees, revoke parole, and discharge from parole. Some paroling authorities also handle petitions for pardons and commutation, including in death penalty cases. Given these widespread responsibilities, parole authorities play an incredibly powerful, though often unrecognized, role in criminal justice administration and public safety.

B. History of Parole Development

Parole is generally traced to Australian and Irish origins. The word itself refers back to the French for a spoken "word of honor." Chief credit for developing the early parole system is given to Alexander Maconochie (1787–1860), who was in charge of the English penal colony at Norfolk Island, 1,000 miles off the coast of Australia, and to Sir Walter Crofton (1815–97), who directed Ireland's prisons. Maconochie criticized definite prison terms and developed a system of rewards for good conduct, labor, and study. Through a classification procedure he called the "mark system," prisoners could progress through stages of increasing responsibility and ultimately gain freedom. Under his direction, task accomplishment, not time served, was the criterion for release.

Walter Crofton implemented Maconochie's mark system in the Irish Prison System in 1854. After instituting strict imprisonment, Crofton transferred offenders to "intermediate prisons" where they accumulated "marks" based on work performance, behavior, and educational improvement. Eventually they would be given tickets-of-leave and released on parole. Parolees submitted monthly reports to the police, and a police inspector helped them find jobs and oversaw their activities. The concepts of intermediate prisons, assistance, and supervision after release were Crofton's contributions to parole. Because of Crofton's experiment, many Americans referred to parole as the Irish system.

Zebulon Brockway (1827–1920), a Michigan penologist, is given credit for implementing parole in the United States. He proposed a two-pronged strategy for managing prison populations and preparing inmates for release: indeterminate sentencing (where inmates would earn release based on in-prison behavior) coupled with post-prison parole supervision. He put his proposal into practice in 1876 when he was appointed superintendent at the Elmira Reformatory in New York. He instituted a system of indeterminacy and parole release, and is commonly credited as the father of both in the United States. His ideas reflected the tenor of the times: a belief that criminals could be reformed, and that every prisoner's treatment should be individualized (information drawn from Rothman 1980; Morris and Rothman 1995; Morris 2002).

Indeterminate sentencing and parole spread rapidly through the United States. In 1907, New York became the first state to adopt all the components of a parole system: indeterminate sentences, a system for granting release, post-release supervision, and specific criteria for parole revocation. By 1930, all states and the federal government had such systems.

Parole seemed to make perfect sense. First, it was believed to contribute to prisoner reform, by encouraging participation in rehabilitation programs. Second, the power to grant parole was thought to provide prison officials with a tool for maintaining institutional control and discipline. The prospects of a reduced sentence in exchange for good behavior encouraged better conduct among inmates. Finally, release on parole, as a back-end solution to prison crowding, was important from the beginning. Indeterminate sentencing coupled with parole release was a matter of absolute routine and good correctional practice for most of the twentieth century (Simon 1993; Morris 2002; Petersilia 2003; Thompson 2008).

Despite its expanded usage, parole was controversial from the start. A Gallup poll conducted in 1934 revealed that 82 percent of US adults believed that parole was not strict enough and should not be as frequently granted (Gallup Organization 1998). Nonetheless, over time, the positivistic approach to crime and criminals—which viewed the offender as "sick" and in need of help—began to influence parole release and supervision. The rehabilitative ideal, as it came to be known, affected all of corrections well into the 1960s, and gained acceptance for the belief that the purpose of incarceration and parole was to change the offender's behavior rather than simply to punish. As Rhine (1996) notes, as the rehabilitative ideal evolved, indeterminate sentencing in tandem with parole acquired a newfound legitimacy. It also gave legitimacy and purpose to parole boards, which were supposed to be composed of "experts" in behavioral change, and it was their responsibility to discern that moment during confinement when the offender was rehabilitated and thus suitable for release.

In the early years, there were few standards governing the decision to grant or deny parole, and decision-making rules were not made public. One of the long-standing criticisms of paroling authorities is that their members are too often selected based on party loyalty and political patronage, rather than professional qualifications and experience. In his book *Conscience and Convenience*, David Rothman discussed the issue of discretionary decisions by parole boards. He reported that in the early twentieth century, parole boards considered primarily the seriousness of the crime in determining whether to release an inmate on parole. However, there was no consensus on what constituted a serious crime. "Instead," Rothman wrote, "each member made his own decisions. The judgments were personal and therefore not subject to debate or reconsideration" (Rothman 1980, 173). These personal preferences resulted in unwarranted sentencing disparities or racial and gender bias. Regardless of criticisms, the use of parole release grew, and instead of using it as a special privilege to be extended to exceptional prisoners, it began to be used as a standard mode of prison release, routinely considered upon completion of a minimum term of confinement. What had started as a practical alternative to executive clemency, and then came to be used as a mechanism for controlling prison growth, gradually developed a distinctively rehabilitative rationale, incorporating the promise of help and assistance as well as surveillance (Bottomley 1990).

By the mid-1950s, indeterminate sentencing coupled with parole release was well entrenched in the United States, and by 1977, 72 percent of all inmates released were as a result of parole boards' discretionary decisions (Bottomley 1990). And in some states, essentially everyone was released as a result of parole board decision making. For example, throughout the 1960s, more than 95 percent of all inmates released in Washington, New Hampshire, and California were released by parole boards (O'Leary 1974). Indeterminate sentencing coupled with parole release was a matter of absolute routine and good correctional practice for most of the twentieth century. But all that was to change during the late 1970s, gaining increasing strength in the 1980s and 1990s, when demands for substantial reforms in parole practice began to be heard.

C. The Decline of Rehabilitation and Discretionary Parole Release

The pillars of the American corrections systems—indeterminate sentencing coupled with parole release, for the purposes of offender rehabilitation—basically collapsed during the late 1970s and early 1980s. Attacks on indeterminate sentencing and parole release centered on three major criticisms. First, *there was little scientific evidence that parole release and supervision reduced subsequent recidivism*. Robert Martinson and his colleagues published the now-famous review of the effectiveness of correctional treatment and concluded: "With few and isolated exceptions, the rehabilitative efforts that have been reported so far have had no appreciable effect on recidivism" (1974, 25). Of the 289 studies they reviewed, just 25 (9 percent) pertained to parole, and yet their summary was interpreted to mean that parole supervision (and all rehabilitation programs) did not work. Once rehabilitation could not be legitimated by science, there was nothing to support the "readiness for release" idea, and, therefore, no role for parole boards or indeterminate sentencing.

Second, *parole and indeterminate sentencing were challenged on moral grounds as unjust and inhumane*, especially when imposed on unwilling participants. Research at the time showed there was little relationship between in-prison behaviors, participation in rehabilitation programs, and post-release recidivism. If that were true, then why base release dates on in-prison performance? Prisoners too argued that not knowing their release dates held them in "suspended animation" and contributed one more pain of imprisonment.

Third, indeterminate sentencing permitted parole authorities to use a great deal of *uncontrolled discretion in release decisions,* and these decisions often were inconsistent and discriminatory. Since parole boards had a great deal of autonomy and their decisions were not subject to outside scrutiny, critics argued that it was a hidden system of discretionary decision making that led to race and class bias in release decisions.

It seemed as if no one liked indeterminate sentencing and parole in the early 1980s, and the time was ripe for change. Crime control advocates denounced parole supervision as being largely nominal and ineffective; social welfare advocates decried the lack of meaningful and useful rehabilitation programs. Several scholars, for example, James Q. Wilson, Andrew von Hirsch, and David Fogel, began to advocate alternative sentencing proposals. These individuals had a major influence on both academic and policy thinking about sentencing objectives. Together they advocated a system with less emphasis on rehabilitation, and the abolition of indeterminate sentencing and discretionary parole release. Liberals and conservatives endorsed the proposals. The political left was concerned about excessive discretion that permitted vastly different sentences in presumably similar cases, and the political right was concerned about the leniency of parole boards. A political coalition resulted, and soon incapacitation and "just deserts" replaced rehabilitation as the primary goal of American prisons.

With that changed focus, indeterminate sentencing and parole release came under serious attack, and calls for "abolishing parole" were heard in state after state. In 1975, Maine became the first state to eliminate parole. The following year, California and Indiana established determinate sentencing and abolished discretionary parole release. By 2002, sixteen states had abolished discretionary parole release for nearly all offenders. In nineteen other states, parole authorities had discretion over a small and decreasing number of parole-eligible inmates. Likewise, at the federal level, the Comprehensive Crime Control Act of 1984 created the US Sentencing Commission and phased out discretionary parole for most federal prisoners in 1997 (Petersilia 2003).

The Bureau of Justice Statistics (BJS) reports that just 24 percent of all those who left state prison in 2000 were released by a discretionary paroling authority, the lowest figure since the federal government began compiling statistics on this issue (Hughes, Wilson, and Beck 2001). As shown in figure 30.1, mandatory releases (39 percent of all releases in 2000)—the required release of inmates at the expiration of a certain time period—now surpass discretionary parole releases. And if one adds the "expiration releases," where the inmate is released after serving his full sentence, there is even a bigger imbalance between discretionary parole and mandatory release (24 percent versus 58 percent). Mandatory parole generally occurs in jurisdictions using determinate sentencing statutes. Inmates are conditionally released from prison after serving a portion of their original sentence minus any good time earned. In mandatory parole systems, the release date is basically a matter of bookkeeping: one calculates the amount of time served plus good time and subtracts it from the prison sentence imposed. When the required number of months has been served, prisoners are automatically released. The "mandatory parole" refers to the manner in which they are released; these prisoners may or may not go on post-prison parole supervision. "Expiration of sentence" refers to instances where the prisoner has served to his maximum sentence date and the Department of Corrections no longer has any authority over him or her.

Proponents hoped that determinate sentencing with mandatory parole would make sentencing more consistent across offenders and offenses—and it has (Marvell and Moody 1996). It was also thought that abolishing parole would lengthen the

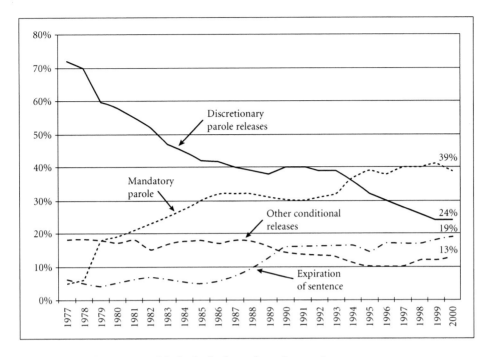

Figure 30.1. Method of release from State prison, 1977–2000

Note: Discretionary paroles are persons entering the community because of a parole board decision. Mandatory releases are persons whose release from prison was not decided by a parole board. Other conditional releases include commutations, pardons, and deaths. Expiration releases are those where the inmate has served his maximum court sentence

Source: Hughes, Wilson, and Beck 2001.

time inmates spent behind bars. After all, parole release was widely regarded as letting them out early. Solomon, Kachnowski, and Bhati (2005) did find that prisoners released to post-prison supervision served nearly a year less than those released without supervision (mandatorily), but it is not clear whether the longer prison terms served were the result of discretionary parole systems or the nature of the inmates' crime or institutional misconduct.

Opponents of parole also assert that there is no evidence that placing offenders on parole supervision helps reduce their recidivism rates. A recent controversial study by the Urban Institute, "Does Parole Supervision Work?", found no difference in the re-arrest rates of offenders released from prison with and without parole supervision. After statistically controlling for the offenders' demographic characteristics and criminal histories, the researchers found that 61 percent of mandatory parolees (those *without* supervision) were re-arrested, compared with 57 percent of discretionary (*with* supervision) parole releasees. Solomon, Kachnowski, and Bhati (2005, 37) concluded that, "Parole has not contributed substantially to reduced recidivism and increased public safety." This is not to say that parole supervision *couldn't* reduce recidivism, only that at the aggregate level in which it was studied, there was no evidence that it reduced re-arrests.

Interestingly, parolees themselves give supervision poor marks. Interviews with parolees for the Urban Institute's *Returning Home* study found that while the vast majority of parolees wanted help from their parole officers to find jobs and housing, only about half said their parole officer had been helpful to their transition or believed their supervision would help them stay out of prison. Instead, released prisoners cite family support as the most important factor in helping them say out of prison (La Vigne and Kachnowski 2005). It is not surprising that parolees don't find parole officers or supervision very helpful. In truth, parole officers are faced with increasingly large caseloads, have few treatment resources to offer parolees, and legal barriers parolees face make finding suitable housing and employment nearly impossible.

II. Parole Population Growth and the Characteristics of Parolees

Over the past generation, the rate of incarceration in America more than quadrupled, and on June 30, 2008, there were 1.54 million sentenced prisoners under state or federal jurisdiction (West and Sabol 2009). And except for those who die naturally or are executed in prison, everyone who goes to prison ultimately returns home. Nearly 95 percent of all state prisoners will eventually leave prison (Petersilia 2003). Estimates from the Department of Justice show that nearly one-half of all state inmates will be released within one year, and three-quarters will be released within five years (US Government Accountability Office 2001).

This huge exodus of prisoners has pushed parole populations to historic level. At yearend 2007, 824, 365 American adults were on parole—an increase of 3.2 percent over year-end 2006. Parolees represented 11 percent of the approximate 7.3 million persons who were "under correctional control" (incarcerated or on community supervision) (Bureau of Justice Statistics 2008).

Parole populations, like the prison population, are heavily influenced by just a few states. More than a quarter (27 percent) of *all* persons on parole in the United States were in California or Texas. California led the nation with 123,764 adults on parole at year-end 2007 (453 per 100,000 adult residents), followed by Texas with 101,748 (582 per 100,000 adult residents) (Glaze and Bonczar 2008). California is the only state with a universal parole policy, where *everyone* released from prison goes on parole supervision regardless of what they were convicted of, usually for a period of three years. This isn't true in other states. In Ohio, Massachusetts, and Florida, for example, just 40 percent of offenders released from prison get parole supervision (Petersilia 2008). These states supervise only their most risky prisoners. Regardless of whether ex-prisoners are on formal parole supervision, they all return home forever changed, often facing isolation, stigma, and a narrowed array of life chances.

A. Characteristics of Prisoners Coming Home and Preparation for Release

Inmates have always been released from prison, and in many ways their profiles have not changed much. Today's parole population is still mostly male (88 percent), although the number of females has risen steadily over the past decade. The average parolee is in his or her mid-thirties, with a median age of thirty-four. For both males and females, most parolees are members of racial or ethnic minorities (37 percent are black and 19 percent are Hispanic or Latino) (Glaze and Bonczar 2008).

Other inmate characteristics, however, are changing in ways that pose new challenges. The Bureau of Justice Statistics reported that 37 percent of *all* adults on parole in 2007 were convicted of drug crimes (Glaze and Bonczar 2008). Many states are reconsidering the harsh drug laws passed in the 1980s and 1990s, and accelerating releases for some drug offenders. Several states including Michigan, New York, and New Jersey are reforming their sentencing rules and rolling back mandatory sentences to allow low-level drug offenders to benefit from early parole (King 2007; Scott-Hayward 2009). The US Supreme Court recently upheld the right of judges to reject harsh federal sentencing guidelines for crack cocaine offenses and to impose more lenient sentences (*Kimbrough v. United States*, 552 U.S. 85 [2007]). The US Sentencing Commission also voted to allow judges retroactively to reduce drug sentences for some federal inmates, meaning that thousands of federal inmates—many with serious substance abuse histories—are walking out of prison doors (US Sentencing Commission 2007). The anticipated accelerated pace of drug-involved prison releases will strain parole and community resources even further.

Most of those released from prison today have serious social and medical problems. More than three-fourths of all prisoners have a history of substance abuse (one-fourth have histories of injection drug use), and one in six suffer from mental illness (Ditton 1999). Yet less than a third of exiting prisoners have received substance abuse or mental health treatment while in prison. And while some states have recently provided more funding for prison drug treatment, the percentage of state prisoners participating in such programs has been declining, from 25 percent a decade ago to about 10 percent in 2001 (Lynch and Sabol 2001). It isn't that the number of programs or number of participants have declined as much as it is that the prison population has increased so dramatically that the *percentage* participating has declined significantly.

A significant share of the prison population also lives with an infectious disease. Two to three percent of state prisoners are HIV-positive or have AIDS, a rate five times higher than that of the US population (Hammett, Harmon, and Rhodes 2002). According to the Centers for Disease Control, about 25 percent of *all* individuals living with HIV or AIDS in the United States had been released from a prison or jail that year (National Commission on Correctional Health Care 2002). Public health experts believe HIV will continue to escalate within prisons and eventually affect prevalence rates in the general community, as we incarcerate and release more drug offenders, many of whom engage in intravenous drug use, share needles, or trade sex for drugs.

An Urban Institute study showed that prisoners with health problems appear to have a more difficult re-entry process than others, as they are additionally confronted with the tasks of managing their health problems, obtaining health care, and keeping up with medications or appointments. Researchers found that 20 percent of those who had been receiving health services in prison are no longer being treated two months after release (Visher and Mallik-Kane 2007).

Few inmates have marketable skills or sufficient literacy to become gainfully employed at release. A third of all US prisoners were unemployed at their most recent arrest, and just 60 percent of inmates have a GED or high school diploma (compared to 85 percent of the US adult population). The National Adult Literacy Survey established that 11 percent of inmates, compared with 3 percent of the general population, have a learning disability, and 3 percent are mentally retarded (National Center for Education Statistics 1994). Again, despite evidence that inmates' literacy and job readiness has declined in the past decade, fewer inmates are participating in prison education or vocational programs. Just over 25 percent of all those released from prison in 2001 had participated in vocational training programs, and about a third of exiting prisoners will have participated in education programs—both figures down from a decade ago (Lynch and Sabol 2001).

In 2007, the nation spent about $47 billion in state general funds on corrections (which was 7 percent of all state general fund spending), yet spending on treatment equaled just 6 percent of the annual cost of housing a prisoner (American Correctional Association 2007; Pew Center on the States 2009).

The need for services for substance-abuse treatment and educational programming in prison has never been greater, but the percentage of prisoners receiving these services has declined. More punitive attitudes, combined with diminishing rehabilitation programs, means that more inmates spend their prison time "idle." Ironically, as inmate needs have increased and in-prison programs decreased, parole supervision and community services have also decreased for most returning prisoners.

III. The Parole and Re-entry Systems

Approximately 70 percent of those released from prison are placed on formal parole supervision. Most will be given a bus ticket, between $20 and $200, and told to report to their designated parole field office within a few days of release. In most states, parolees are legally required to return to the county of their last legal residence. The length of time spent on parole depends on the state and the conviction crime, but most parolees serve from one to five years (Petersilia 1999).

A. Conditions of Parole Supervision and Monitoring Compliance

All parolees are required to sign a parole contract stating that they agree to abide by certain conditions. Conditions generally can be grouped into standard conditions applicable to all parolees and special conditions that are tailored to particular offenders. Standard parole conditions are similar throughout most jurisdictions and include payment of supervision fees, finding employment, not carrying weapons, reporting changes of address and employment, not committing crimes, and submitting to search by the police and parole officers. Special conditions for substance abusers, for example, usually include periodic drug testing. Sex offenders and arsonists are commonly required to register with local law enforcement agencies.

Seeing that the parolee lives up to this parole contract is the principal responsibility of the parole agent. Bonczar (2008) recently reported that there were more than 65,000 full-time parole employees in the United States in 2007. About 14,000 of them were responsible for supervising parolees in the community. Parole agents are equipped with legal authority to carry and use firearms, and to search places, persons, and property without the requirements imposed by the Fourth Amendment (i.e., the right to privacy), to order arrests without probable cause, and to confine without bail. As Simon wrote, "The ability to arrest, confine, and in some cases imprison the parolee makes the parole agent a walking court system for those people directly affected" (Simon 1993, 193).

If parolees fail to live up to their conditions, they can be revoked and returned to prison to serve out the remainder of the original sentence or to serve a new sentence. Parole can be revoked for two reasons: the commission of a new crime, or the violation of the conditions of parole (a technical violation). Technical violations pertain to behavior that is not criminal, such as the failure to refrain from alcohol use or remain employed. In either event, the violation process is rather straightforward. Given that parolees are technically still in the legal custody of the prison or parole authorities, and as a result maintain a quasi-prisoner status, their constitutional rights are severely limited. When parole officers become aware of violations of the parole contract, they notify their supervisors, who make a recommendation to the parole authorities and can easily return a parolee to prison. Parolees do have some rights in revocation proceedings. Two US Supreme Court cases, *Morrissey v. Brewer* (408 U.S. 471 [1972]) and *Gagnon v. Scarpelli* (411 U.S. 778 [1973]), established minimum requirements for the revocation or parolee, forcing parole boards to conform to some standards of due process. Parolees must be given written notice of the nature of the violation and the evidence obtained, and they have a right to confront and cross-examine their accusers (del Carmen, Barnhill, and Bonham 2000).

Monitoring parolee behavior and delivering services is managed through case-loads (the number of parolees assigned to a single parole agent). Higher-risk pa-rolees are placed on smaller caseloads, which facilitate more intensive services and surveillance. Caseload assignment is usually based on a structured assessment of parolee risk, and an assessment of the needs or problem areas that have contributed to the parolee's criminality. By scoring personal information relative to the risk of recidivism, and the particular needs of the offender (i.e., a risk/need instrument), a total score is derived, which determines the particular level of parole supervision (for example intensive, medium, regular, administrative). Each jurisdiction has established policies that dictate the contact levels (times the officer will meet with the parolee). Officers may also contact family members of employers to inquire about the parolee's progress. The purpose of the contacts is to make sure that pa-rolees are complying with parole conditions.

The corrections field has struggled for some time with the question of the ideal caseload size for probation and parole officers. Unfortunately, substantial evidence now exists to show that simply reducing caseload size does not improve offender outcomes. In the 1980s, almost every jurisdiction in the United States experimented with some form of intensive supervision probation or parole (ISP). While the programs varied in terms of clientele served, all of them fea-tured smaller caseloads and stricter reporting requirements. The hope was that ISPs would provide more officer-offender interaction and services, and as a result that offender recidivism would decline. But a multisite ISP evaluation conducted by Petersilia and Turner (1993) found that offenders given intensive supervision were no likelier than other comparable offenders to commit new crimes but were likelier to have their parole and probation revoked because of technical condition violations (because of closer surveillance). Proponents hoped that ISPs would save money, but the combination of high revocation rates and related case-processing costs minimized the cost-effectiveness of the ISPs. But Petersilia and Turner did find one positive finding from the ISP evaluation: offenders who were on smaller caseloads *and* completed counseling, were employed, and paid restitution had lower re-arrest rates. This suggests that in-terventions that focus on diminishing behaviors associated with criminality are more important to reducing recidivism than simply increasing contacts between officer and offender.

The BJS recently reported that the average adult parole caseload was thirty-eight active parolees for each officer, but the average does not really describe the experiences of most parolees. Just two-thirds (68 percent) of adult offenders on parole in 2006 were required to have face-to-face contact with a parole officer at least once a month, including 14 percent who were required to have weekly face-to-face contact. An additional 17 percent of paroled offenders were required to meet with their parole officers less than once a month or to maintain contact by mail, telephone, or other means, and 13 percent of parolees were on "summary parole," on which they were no longer required to report on a regular basis (Bonczar 2008).

"Summary" parole is quite popular and is increasing in the United States because, even though the parolee has no formal reporting requirements, they are still considered to be in the custody of corrections agencies and their legal rights are severely limited. For example, California law requires each parolee to sign the standard Notice and Conditions of Parole, which informs each parolee that "you and your residence and any property under your control may be searched without a warrant by an agent of the Department of Corrections or any law enforcement officer" (Fama 2004, 363). The constitutional right to be free from unreasonable searches and seizures is virtually nonexistent while on parole. If a parolee is found to be in violation of parole conditions, they can easily be returned to prison as a parole violator without a criminal court proceeding.

For most parolees, supervision isn't particularly onerous; the system simply can't afford to do much monitoring for the majority of parolees under supervision. However, advances in technology have made the surveillance of high-risk parolees an around-the-clock intrusion. California, for example, places every high-risk sex offender on global position satellite (GPS) monitoring and has become the nation's leader when it comes to tracking offenders via the high-tech device. By 2008, California had a total of 4,800 high-risk sex offenders on GPS, half of *all* its sex offenders on parole. The considerable expansion of parole surveillance for sex offenders was mandated in 2006 by the passage of Proposition 83—also known as Jessica's Law, the toughest law in the nation—which focuses on sex offenders and requires that every paroled sex offender be monitored by GPS. High-risk sex offenders have lifelong GPS monitoring. They are also placed on reduced caseloads (40:1) and if they violate *any* parole condition (including living within 2,000 feet of a school or park) they are mandatorily returned to prison (California Attorney General 2006). So, "being on parole" provides very little meaningful surveillance for most parolees, but for others—particularly sex offenders—it can be quite arduous.

B. Rehabilitation Programs, the Cost of Parole Supervision, and Civil Disabilities

Although 70 percent of all persons under correctional control are on probation or parole, nearly nine out of ten correctional dollars goes to funding prisons. Nationally, the 2008 average annual cost of a year in prison was $29,000. In contrast, the average annual cost of parole supervision was $2,750. In California, with the nation's largest prison and parole population, the figures are dramatic: for every dollar California spends on prisons, it spent 15 cents on parole (Pew Center on the States 2009). Parole officers complain of growing paperwork and diminishing resources devoted to parolees.

The BJS survey of parole agencies reported that just 2 percent of all US parolees were participating in sex offender treatment programs in 2006, and about 5 percent were enrolled in a mental health treatment program run by a formally trained professional (Bonczar 2008). And of the fifty parole agencies studied in the survey, just seventeen agencies contracted for housing assistance, and twenty-five agencies had contracts to assist in parolee employment. But the existence of a contract doesn't necessarily mean that many parolees are being served. A recent study of all parolees released from California prisons in 2005 found that 56 percent—nearly two out of three parolees—didn't participate in *any* parole programming at all (California Department of Corrections and Rehabilitation 2007). It is no wonder that recidivism rates are so high. In a sense, we get what we pay for, and we have never chosen to invest sufficiently in parole or re-entry programs.

In addition to few treatment resources, parolees are also subject to a number of statutory restrictions or "civil disabilities" when they return home. Many restrictions are statutory, stemming from a common-law traditional that people who are incarcerated are "civilly dead" and have lost all civil rights (Travis 2005). Their criminal record may preclude them from voting or retaining their parental rights, and be grounds for divorce, and they may be barred from serving on a jury, holding public office, and owning firearms. In eleven states in 2004, ex-prisoners were permanently denied the right to vote (Manza and Uggen 2006). Employers are also increasingly forbidden from hiring parolees for certain jobs and are mandated to perform background checks for many others. The most common types of jobs with legal prohibitions against parolees are in the fields of child care, education, security, nursing, and home health care—exactly the types of jobs that are expanding. Since the mid-1980s, the number of barred occupations has increased dramatically.

Even if a parolee is not legally barred from a particular job, research shows that ex-offenders face bleak prospects in the labor market, with the mark of a criminal record representing an important barrier to finding work (Pager 2003). More than 60 percent of employers claim that they would not knowingly hire an applicant with a criminal background (Holzer, Raphael, and Stoll 2002). Overcoming the barriers that ex-offenders face in finding a job is critical to successful reintegration, since employment helps ex-prisoners be productive, take care of their families, develop valuable life skills, and strengthen their self-esteem and social connectedness. Research has also empirically established a positive link between job stability and reduced criminal offending. Lipsey's (1995) meta-analysis of nearly 400 studies found that the single most effective factor in reducing re-offending rates was employment.

IV. Revolving Door Justice: Inmates Release, Recidivism, and Prison Return

Staying out of prison is a lot harder than getting out. Regardless of how it is measured, the failure rate is very high among released prisoners (see table 30.1). The landmark BJS study of prisoners released in fifteen states in 1994 found that fully two-thirds (67 percent) were re-arrested and just over one-half (52 percent) were back in prison, serving time for a new prison sentence or for a technical violation of their release, within three years (Langan and Levin 2002). The "two-thirds re-arrest rate" after three years has been documented in the United States for about thirty-five years, ever since Daniel Glaser conducted his classic follow-up study of prisoners in *The Effectiveness of a Prison and Parole System* (1969). The Langan and Levin (2002) study also found that certain characteristics were associated with parole failure: black parolees had higher re-arrest rates, as did males in general, those with fewer prior arrests, those incarcerated for property offenses, and those who were younger at release (under twenty-five). The failure rate for prisoners who had been previously released on parole and were now being re-released was much higher (64 percent) than for prisoners being released to parole for the first time (21 percent) (Travis and Lawrence 2002).

Rosenfeld and his colleagues (2005), using data from the BJS recidivism study, calculated arrest probabilities by month for each of the thirty-six months after release. They adjusted the probability of arrest by subtracting out persons who were in jail, in prison, or dead during the month and therefore not eligible for arrest. Their results, shown in figure 30.2, reveal that the probability of arrest declines with months out of prison, and that the probability of arrest during the first month out of prison is roughly double that during the fifteenth month. As the figure also shows, arrest probabilities also differ by type of crime: prison releasees arrested on property or drug offenses are more likely to be arrested early in the post-release period than those arrested for violent offenses.

Table 30.1. Recidivism of Prisoners Released From State Prisons

Time After Release	Rearrested	Reconvicted	Returned to Prison	
			With or Without New Sentence	With New Sentence
6 months	29.9%	10.6%	NA	5%
1 year	44.1	21.5	NA	10.4
2 years	59.2	36.4	NA	18.8
3 years	67.5	46.9	51.8%	25.4

Source: Langan and Levin (2002)

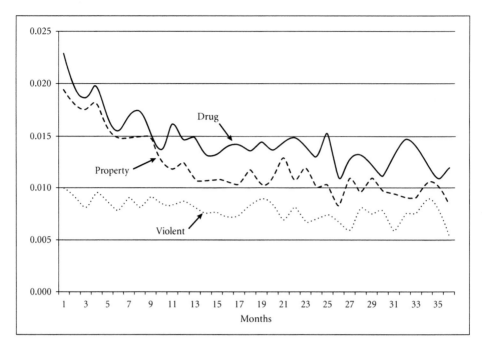

Figure 30.2. Probability of arrest for a violent, property, or drug crime 36 months after release from prison

Note: Probabilities adjusted for time off the street

Source: Rosenfeld, Wallman, and Fornango 2005.

Clearly, the first few months after prison release represent high crime risks, but Binswanger et al. (2007) also found that death rates for new prison releases—within the first days and weeks—are much higher than for matched demographic groups in the general population. The higher prisoner-release death rates (twelve times the average for the general population) were caused by high rates of homicide and drug overdoses. These results have led to calls to front-load parole services and surveillance so as to reduce these and other negative outcomes during the first six months after release (Petersilia 2003; Travis 2005; National Research Council 2008).

While individual recidivism rates have always shown high failure rates, until recently there was little attention paid to the overall amount of crime returning prisoners were responsible for. Rosenfeld, Wallman, and Fornango (2005) re-analyzed the BJS data and estimated that parolees accounted for 10 to 15 percent of all violent, property, and drug arrests between 1994 and 1997, and the share of total arrests attributable to released prisoners grew as general crime rates declined during the 1990s. In 1994 the arrests of prisoners released in the previous three years accounted for 13 percent of all arrests. By 2001 that figure had increased to more than 20 percent. If former prisoners are accounting for nearly one-fifth of all the nation's arrests, then investing in prisoner re-entry is unquestionably a matter of public safety. Such evidence has encouraged law enforcement organizations such as the International Association of Chiefs of Police (IACP) and the National District Attorneys Association to develop policies, training, and other tools that support effective prisoner re-entry (National District Attorneys Association 2005; La Vigne et al. 2006).

A. Parole Violators and Their Impact on Prison Populations

The BJS reports that about 50 percent of released prisoners will be returned to prison in the three years following release. Most of them will eventually be re-released and the revolving-door process will continually be repeated (Blumstein and Beck 2005). Prisoners refer to it as "doing a life term on the installment plan." The constant churning of parolees in and out of incarceration is a major contributor to the growing US prison population. As a percentage of all admissions to state prisons, parole violators more than doubled from 17 percent in 1980 to nearly 35 percent in 2006 (Sabol and Couture 2008). California had both the largest absolute number and the largest percentage increase of admissions for parole violations. In 2006, 65 percent of all admissions in California were for parole violations—not the result of new convictions (Grattet, Petersilia, and Lin 2008). Excluding California, parole violations represented slightly more than a quarter of all state prison admissions in 2006 (Sabol and Couture 2008).

In these budget-strapped times, many question the public safety benefits of violating parolees for technical violations. A technical parole violation is any violation of the conditions of parole other than a conviction for a new felony. Such violations include missing a meeting with a parole agent, being out after a curfew time, and, increasingly, failing a drug test. Hughes, Wilson, and Beck (2001) report that 16 percent of prisoners self-reported that they were returned to prison because they had a drug-related violation, 22 percent said they had absconded or otherwise failed to report to a parole officer, and 18 percent reported other reasons, such as failure to maintain employment.

One view is that imprisoning technical violators is an enormous and largely wasted expense. Processing admissions of parole violators takes as much time and costs as much money as processing admissions of new convictions—and for offenders who often will be in prison for only a few months. Many advocates argue that technical violations should not result in a return to prison and can be handled in the community with less drastic intermediate sanctions (Burke and Tonry 2006). The contrary view is that some violations, even of a procedural nature, are significant signs that a parolee is not respecting the terms of the parole contract and should suffer major consequences. This can also be a sign that even if the current violation is minor, if left unattended, it might lead to more serious ones.

Several states have begun to use parole violation decision making instruments to respond systematically to violations. The goal of such instruments is to differentiate technical violations and the response to them by the severity and risk posed by the offender. A recent survey by the APAI found that nineteen US agencies now use a decision matrix to decide which parole violators should be returned to prison (Kinnevy and Caplan 2008). Evaluations of matrices in Georgia, Kansas, Maryland, Texas, and New Jersey have demonstrated that such efforts can decrease prison admissions for technical parole violators and reduce disparities in parole decision making (Austin and Fabelo 2004; Burke 2004). The California Department of Corrections and Rehabilitation (CDCR) pilot-tested its own Parole Violation Decision Making Instrument (PVDMI) in 2008, and the results showed that the PVDMI increased consistency in decision making. California implemented the PVDMI statewide in 2009, and given that one third of *all* parole violators returned to prison in the United States come from California, this initiative has national implications.

Responding appropriately to parolee recidivism is one way to manage correctional resources better, but preventing parolees from failing in the first place is a more proactive strategy. That, however, begs the all-important question of whether we can implement re-entry programs to increase the odds of success.

V. Putting Science to Work: Promising Programs in Parole and Re-entry

No one believes that the current parole and re-entry system is working, but the $64,000 question is, Can we do better? Can we improve the outcomes for people returning from prison so that they are less likely to be re-arrested? Fortunately, the last decade has seen an explosion of interest in parole and prisoner re-entry, and the "what works?" literature has improved. It can no longer reasonably be said that rehabilitation doesn't work for prisoners and parolees. After extensively reviewing all of the literature, the National Research Council (2008, 82) concluded, " 'Nothing works' is no longer a defensible conclusion from assessment of program effects on re-entry outcomes."

A. What Works in Re-entry Programming?

Using a variety of techniques, researchers have developed a list of principles of effective intervention, and found that programs adhering to these principles significantly reduced recidivism, sometimes by as much as 30 percent (Andrews and Bonta 2006; Lowenkamp, Latessa, and Smith 2006). Petersilia (2004) recently summarized these principles and their applicability to re-entry programs:

- Treatment services should be behavioral in nature. Interventions should employ the cognitive behavioral and social learning techniques of modeling.
- Reinforcements in the program should be largely positive not negative.

- Services should be intensive, lasting three to twelve months (depending on need) and occupy 40–70 percent of the offender's time during the course of the program.
- Treatment interventions should be used primarily with higher-risk offenders, targeting their criminogenic needs (dynamic risk factors for change).
- The best strategy for discerning offender risk level is to rely on actuarial based assessments instruments.
- Conducting interventions in the community as opposed to an institutional setting will increase treatment effectiveness.
- In terms of staffing, there is a need to match styles and modes of treatment service to the learning styles of the offender (specific responsivity).

Important to our focus here, Lowenkamp et al. (2006) found that these principles apply to treatment within prisons as well as to community supervision programs.

B. Evidence-Based Program Implementation and Cost-Benefits

It is impossible to know the extent to which these evidence-based principles are being used in current parole and re-entry programs. Interest in prisoner re-entry over the last decade has fueled the development of hundreds of programs across the United States. Some re-entry programs are small and administered by community- and faith-based organizations, whereas other programs are large statewide initiatives, often administered by the state's corrections department. Some programs start inside the prison and continue into the community, whereas others begin when the prisoner has returned home. Some programs are residential, others involve day reporting, and still others involve a meeting every month or two. They rely on existing and volunteer community treatment services, primarily Alcoholics Anonymous and Narcotics Anonymous. The academic "what works" literature probably barely touches these programs, but these programs are delivering vital services and should not be dismissed, as they are the foot soldiers of the re-entry movement (for a review, see Petersilia 2004).

Many other re-entry programs are part of federally funded re-entry initiatives implemented in recent years. The "what works" literature is influencing their design and evaluations. The largest effort to implement evidence-based re-entry principles systematically is the federal government's Serious and Violent Offender Re-entry Initiative (SVORI). In 2003, sixty-nine agencies representing all fifty states received more than $110 million in federal funds to develop programs to improve the outcomes of serious and violent prisoners coming home (Lattimore et al. 2005). The federal government's SVORI goals were to improve a variety of outcomes, including family relationships, work, health, community integration, housing, and reduced crime. Programs were also encouraged to focus specifically on serious and violent offenders, or both. Most programs used a formal risk assessment tool to identify risks and needs, as recommended in the "what works" literature. Early outcome results appear promising. SVORI participants were more likely to receive services and participate in needed programs, and SVORI participants are doing better across a wide range of outcomes. Recidivism outcomes are not yet reported, but other outcomes, including housing, employment, mental health, and substance abuse, have improved. As Lattimore and Visher (2009, 7) recently reported to Congress, "In most cases, the difference in outcomes between those participating in SVORI programs and the comparison subjects indicates that SVORI program participation resulted in an improvement in outcomes."

The SVORI services generally resulted in improvements of 5 to 15 percent, so the findings align with previous research (Aos, Miller, and Drake 2006). It is important to note that most SVORI participants were repeat serious offenders (the males had an average of thirteen prior arrests), so that even relatively small reductions in recidivism rates can be quite cost-beneficial. For example, Aos, Miller, and Drake (2006) estimated that the average cognitive behavior therapy program in prison or the community reduces recidivism an average of 6.3 percent, and generates about $10,404 in life-cycle benefits associated with the crime reduction. Thus, per dollars of spending, cognitive therapy and several other parole and re-entry programs (e.g., vocational education, correctional industries, drug courts) produced favorable returns on investment.

In sum, it is possible to reduce offender recidivism in a cost-effective manner. The answer lies in investing in re-entry programs that incorporate "what works" principles, targeting those programs on specific offenders who can most benefit, and continually evaluating and revising program models as the science accumulates.

VI. Conclusions and Future Research

Parole and prisoner re-entry issues have captured the nation's attention, and the US parole system is entering another chapter in its history. Attacks on parole and community-based programs have virtually disappeared and have been replaced with calls for investing *more*, not less, in parole and prisoner re-entry. Where there was little scholarly attention paid to parole just ten years ago, the volume and visibility of work around parole and prisoner re-entry issues has grown to such an extent that it is now commonly referred to as a full-fledged movement (Petersilia 2009). And the re-entry momentum is likely to continue. President Obama recently asked Congress to allocate more funding for the Second Chance Act, and in his *Blueprint for Change in America*, he stated that he would "reduce crime recidivism by providing ex-offender support," and provide "job training, substance abuse and mental heath counseling to ex-offenders, so that they are successfully reintegrated into society" (Obama 2008, 53). He also promised to create a prison-to-work incentive program, reduce barriers to improve ex-offender employment rates, and give first-time, nonviolent offenders a chance to "serve their sentence, where appropriate, in the type of drug rehabilitation programs that have proven to work better than a prison term in changing bad behavior" (Obama 2008, 53). It appears that President Obama will question our dependence on mass incarceration as a response to crime, and if that proves true, evidence-based re-entry programs will surely be instrumental.

For all that has been learned about parole and re-entry in recent years, a number of important research questions remain. We now know a good deal about the needs of returning prisoners and have some evidence about the services they receive. However, much less research exists on the effectiveness of particular approaches to delivering services, and only a small number of studies have used rigorous scientific methods to test promising practices. The highest priority for future research is more credible program evaluations. To date, no studies have analyzed the differences among low-, medium-, and high-risk offenders using an experimental design. A recent panel of the National Research Council (2008, 82) concluded that while there is a great deal of experiential and practitioner knowledge with regard to the apparent efficacy of re-entry programs, "the challenge now is to subject these promising practices to rigorously designed evaluations." Rigorous program evaluations should accompany every significant re-entry initiative, and outcomes for these studies should focus not solely on recidivism but also on other behavioral outcomes, such as sobriety, stability in housing and employment, and attachment to families and communities. Our studies must also disaggregate the characteristics of the offender population so that we can design better programs for specialized populations, such as women, the elderly, sex offenders, or the mentally ill. A higher proportion of parolees in the future are likely to be comprised of one of these distinct population groups, and we know very little about how to deliver services to meet their specific needs.

Another priority for future research is to better understand the peak rates for recidivism that occur in the days and weeks immediately following release. Arrest rates decline over time after release from prison, especially for property and drug crimes. And, as noted, death rates for new prison releases are also very high. If we understood more about the first days and weeks after prison release, we might be able to intervene in order to reduce these and other negative outcomes. We also need to know whether policies that restrict the access of released prisoners to public housing and other forms of public assistance—including treatment services and other resources—affect recidivism and these early negative outcomes.

Researchers need to study more closely the recidivism process and particularly, the "black box" of parole violations and prison returns. The parole violation process is complex, and research suggests it is likely to be determined not just by a parolee's characteristic but also by the characteristics of the supervising agency, parole agents, and communities to which parolees return. Grattet, Petersilia, and

Lin (2008) recently completed a comprehensive study of parole violations in California and found that while offender and case characteristics were the most important factors in predicting parole outcomes, agent and community characteristics were also related to parole violations. Female agents, for example, appeared more forgiving of low-level criminal violations, particularly drug use and possession. Black parolees supervised by black agents had lower risks of technical parole violations; all other measured variables held statistically constant.

We also need a better understanding of how neighborhood characteristics affect the reintegration of offenders. Hipp et al. (2010) recently reported that the presence of more social service providers nearby (within two miles) led to lower recidivism rates and that this protective effect was particularly strong for African American and Latino parolees. They also found that parolees living in neighborhoods with higher levels of concentrated disadvantage experienced greater rates of recidivism, even after taking into account the individual characteristics of these parolees. This study highlights the importance of social context for successful reintegration. Research must move beyond simple statistical models that attempt to explain parolees' return to prison solely as a function of the parolees' background and behavior, since the characteristics of their agent, supervising agency, and community may be significant predictors as well.

Finally, researchers must study successful parolees in order to uncover the factors that encourage offenders to shift from formal social controls to informal social controls. Ultimately, parolees who make it shift from being accountable to programs and criminal justice agencies (e.g., police, parole) to being accountable to more informal social controls (e.g., families, neighbors). Ideally, formal criminal justice sanctions should act as "presses" to increase social bonds to law-abiding family members and conventional institutions. Ethnographic studies can identify how to promote positive social bonds between ex-convicts and community members.

We are now witnessing the start of a new ideological pendulum shift in US punishment policy. The emerging leadership of President Obama, a declining economy that is pressuring states to reduce incarceration, and a growing body of evidence identifying effective re-entry programs have created a window of opportunity for change. Parole and prisoner re-entry may well serve as a major conceptual framework for reorganizing criminal justice policy in the twenty-first century.

REFERENCES

American Correctional Association. 2007. *Directory*. Lanham, MD.
Andrews, Don, and James Bonta. 2006. *The Psychology of Criminal Conduct*, 4th ed. Cincinnati, OH: Anderson Publishing.

Aos, Steve, Marna Miller, and Elizabeth Drake. 2006. *Evidence-Based Public Policy Options to Reduce Future Construction, Criminal Justice Costs, and Crime Rates*. Olympia, WA: Washington State Institute for Public Policy.

Austin, James, and Tony Fabelo. 2004. *The Diminishing Returns of Increased Incarceration*. Washington, DC: JFA Institute.

Binswanger, Ingrid, Marc Stern, Richard Deyo, Patrick Heagerty, Allen Cheadle, Joann Elmore, and Thomas Koepsell. 2007. "Release from Prison—A High Risk of Death for Former Inmates." *New England Journal of Medicine* 356: 157–65.

Blumstein, Alfred, and Allen J. Beck. 2005. "Re-entry as a Transient State Between Liberty and Recommitment." In *Prisoner Re-entry and Crime in America*, edited by J. Travis and C. Visher. New York: Cambridge University Press.

Bonczar, Thomas P. 2008. *Characteristics of State Parole Supervising Agencies, 2006*. Washington, DC: Bureau of Justice Statistics.

Bottomley, Keith A. 1990. "Parole in Transition: A Comparative Study of Origins, Developments, and Prospects for the 1990s." In *Crime and Justice: A Review of Research*, vol. 12, edited by Michael Tonry and Norval Morris. Chicago: University of Chicago Press.

Bureau of Justice Statistics. 2006. *Justice Expenditure and Employment Extracts*. Washington, DC: US Department of Justice.

———. 2008. "One in Every 31 U.S. Adults Were in Prison or Jail or Probation or Parole in 2007." Press Release. December 11. Washington, DC: US Department of Justice.

Burke, Peggy. 2003. *A Handbook for New Parole Board Members*. Association of Paroling Authorities International. http://www.apaintl.org/content/en/pdf/CEPPParoleHandbook.pdf.

———. 2004. *Parole Violations Revisited*. Washington, DC: National Institute of Corrections.

Burke, Peggy, and Michael Tonry. 2006. *Successful Transition and Re-entry for Safer Communities: A Call to Action for Parole*. Silver Spring, MD: Center for Effective Public Policy.

California Attorney General. 2006. *Proposition 83 (Jessica's Law): Sex Offenders. Sexually Violent Predators*. Sacramento, CA: California Department of Justice.

California Department of Corrections and Rehabilitation. 2007. *Expert Panel on Adult Offender and Recidivism Reduction Programming: Report to the California State Legislature*. Sacramento, CA: California Department of Corrections and Rehabilitation.

del Carmen, Rolando, Maldine Barnhill, and Gene Bonham. 2000. *Civil Liabilities and Other Legal Issues for Probation and Parole Officers and Supervisors*. Washington DC: National Institute of Corrections.

Ditton, Paula. 1999. *Mental Health and Treatment of Inmates and Probationers*. Washington DC: Bureau of Justice Statistics.

Fama, Steve. 2004. *The California State Prisoners Handbook: A Comprehensive Practical Guide to Prison and Parole Law*. San Quentin, CA: The Prison Law Office.

Gallup Organization. 1998. *Gallup Surveys Pertaining to Parole (Special Request)*. New York: Gallup Organization.

Glaser, Daniel. 1969. *The Effectiveness of a Prison and Parole System*. Indianapolis, IN: Bobbs-Merrill.

Glaze, Lauren E., and Thomas P. Bonczar. 2008. *Probation and Parole in the United States, 2007—Statistical Tables*, edited by Bureau of Justice Statistics. Washington, DC: US Department of Justice.

Grattet, Ryken, Joan Petersilia, and Jeffrey Lin. 2008. *Parole Violations and Revocations in California*. Washington, DC: National Institute of Justice.

Hammett, Theodore, Patricia Harmon, and William Rhodes. 2002. "The Burden of Infectious Disease Among Inmates of and Releasees From US Correctional Facilities, 1997." *American Journal of Public Health* 92(11): 1789–94.

Hipp, John, Joan Petersilia, and Susan Turner. 2010. "Parolee Recidivism in California: The Effect of Neighborhood Context and Social Service Agency Characteristics." *Criminology* 48(2): 947–79.

Holzer, Harry, Steven Raphael, and Michael Stoll. 2002. *Can Employers Play A More Positive Role in Prisoner Re-entry?* Washington, DC: Urban Institute.

Hughes, Timothy A., Doris James Wilson, and Allen J. Beck. 2001. *Trends in State Parole, 1990–2000*. Washington, DC: Bureau of Justice Statistics.

King, Ryan S. 2007. *Changing Direction? State Sentencing Reforms 2004–2006*. Washington, DC: The Sentencing Project.

Kinnevy, Susan, and Joel Caplan. 2008. *Findings from the APAI International Survey of Releasing Authorities*. Philadelphia: University of Pennsylvania, Center for Research on Youth and Social Policy.

La Vigne, Nancy G., and V. Kachnowski. 2005. *Texas Prisoners' Reflections on Returning Home*. Washington, DC: Urban Institute.

La Vigne, Nancy G., Amy Solomon, Karen Beckman, and Kelly Dedel. 2006. *Prisoner Re-entry and Community Policing: Strategies for Enhancing Public Safety*. Washington, DC: Urban Institute.

Langan, Patrick, and David Levin. 2002. *Recidivism of Prisoners Released in 1994*. Washington, DC: Bureau of Justice Statistics.

Lattimore, Pamela K., C. A. Visher, L. Winterfield, C. Lindquist, and S. Brumbaugh. 2005. "Implementation of Prisoner Re-entry Programs: Findings from the Serious and Violent Offender Re-entry Initiative Multi-site Evaluation." *Justice Research and Policy* 7(2): 87–109.

Lattimore, Pamela K., and Christy Visher. 2009. *Assessment of the Serious and Violent Offender Re-entry Initiative*. Washington, DC: Urban Institute. http://www.urban.org/url.cfm?ID=901242.

Lipsey, Mark W. 1995. "What Do We Learn from 400 Research Studies on the Effectiveness of Treatment with Juvenile Delinquency?" In *What Works: Reducing Reoffending*, ed. J. McQuire. West Sussex, UK: John Wiley.

Lowenkamp, Christopher, Jennifer Pealer, Paula Smith, and Edward Latessa. 2006. "Adhering to the Risk and Need Principles: Does It Matter for Supervision-Based Programs?" *Federal Probation* 70(3): 3–8.

Lowenkamp, Christopher T., Edward J. Latessa, and Paula Smith. 2006. "Does Correctional Program Quality Really Matter? The Impact of Adhering to the Principles of Effective Intervention." *Criminology and Public Policy* 5(3): 575–94.

Lynch, James P., and William J. Sabol. 2001. *Prisoner Re-entry in Perspective*. Washington, DC: Urban Institute.

Manza, Jeff, and Christopher Uggen. 2006. *Locked Out: Felon Disenfranchisement and American Democracy*. New York: Oxford University Press.

Martinson, Robert. 1974. "What Works? Questions and Answers About Prison Reform." *Public Interest* 35: 22–35.

Marvell, Thomas B., and Charlisle E. Moody. 1996. "Determinate Sentencing and Abolishing Parole: The Long-Term Impacts on Prisons and Crime." *Criminology* 34(1): 107–28.

Morris, Norval. 2002. *Maconochie's Gentlemen: The Story of Norfolk Island the Roots of Modern Prison Reform*. New York: Oxford University Press.

Morris, Norval, and David J. Rothman, eds. 1995. *The Oxford History of the Prison: The Practice of Punishment in Western Society*. New York: Oxford University Press.

National Center for Education Statistics. 1994. *Literacy Behind Prison Walls*. Washington, DC: US Department of Education.

National Commission on Correctional Health Care. 2002. *The Health Status of Soon-To-Be-Released Inmates: A Report to Congress*. Washington, DC: National Institute of Justice.

National District Attorneys Association. 2005. *Policy Positions on Prisoner Re-entry Issues*. Alexandria, VA: National District Attorneys Association.

National Research Council. 2008. *Parole, Desistance from Crime, and Community Integration*. Washington, DC: National Academy of Sciences.

O'Leary, Vincent. 1974. "Parole Administration." In *Handbook of Criminology*, edited by D. Glaser. Chicago: Rand McNally Publishing.

Obama, Barack. 2008. *Blueprint for Change*. http://www.scribd.com/doc/4107302/Barack-Obamas-Blueprint-For-Change.

Pager, Devah. 2003. "The Mark of a Criminal Record." *American Journal of Sociology* 108: 937–75.

Petersilia, Joan. 1999. "Parole and Prisoner Re-entry in the United States." In *Prisons*, edited by Michael Tonry and Joan Petersilia. Vol. 26 of *Crime and Justice: A Review of Research,* edited by Michael Tonry. Chicago, IL: University of Chicago Press.

———. 2003. *When Prisoners Come Home: Parole and Prisoner Re-entry*. New York: Oxford University Press.

———. 2004. "What Works in Prisoner Re-entry? Reviewing and Questioning the Evidence." *Federal Probation* 68(2): 4–8.

———. 2008. "California's Correctional Paradox of Excess and Deprivation." In *Crime and Justice: A Review of Research*, vol. 37, edited by Michael Tonry. Chicago: University of Chicago Press.

———. 2009. "Transformation in Prisoner Re-entry: What a Difference a Decade Makes." In *When Prisoners Come Home: Parole and Prisoner Re-entry,* edited by Joan Petersilia. New York: Oxford University Press.

Petersilia, Joan, and Susan Turner. 1993. "Intensive Probation and Parole." In *Crime and Justice: A Review of Research*, vol. 17, edited by Michael Tonry. Chicago: University of Chicago Press.

Pew Center on the States. 2008. *One in 100: Behind Bars in America 2008*. Washington, DC: Pew Charitable Trusts.

———. 2009. *One in 31: The Long Reach of American Corrections*. Washington, DC: The Pew Charitable Trusts.

Rhine, Edward E. 1996. "Parole Boards." In *The Encyclopedia of American Prisons*, edited by M. McShane and F. Williams. New York: Garland.

Rhine, Edward, William Smith, Ronald Jackson, Peggy Burke, and Roger LaBelle. 1991. *Paroling Authorities: Recent History and Current Practice*. Laurel, MD: American Correctional Association.

Rosenfeld, Richard, Joel Wallman, and Robert Fornango. 2005. "The Contribution of Ex-Prisoners to Crime Rates." In *Prisoner Re-entry and Crime in America*, edited by J. Travis and C. Visher. New York: Cambridge University Press.

Rothman, David. 1980. *Conscience and Convenience: The Asylum and Its Alternatives in Progressive America*. Boston: Little, Brown.

Sabol, William, and Heather Couture. 2008. *Prison Inmates at Midyear 2007*. Washington, DC: Bureau of Justice Statistics.

Scott-Hayward, Christine. 2009. *The Fiscal Crisis in Corrections: Rethinking Policies and Practices*. New York: Vera Institute of Justice.

Simon, Jonathan. 1993. *Poor Discipline: Parole and the Control of the Underclass, 1890–1990*. Chicago: University of Chicago Press.

Solomon, Amy L., Vera Kachnowski, and Avinash Bhati. 2005. *Does Parole Work? Analyzing the Impact of Postprison Supervision on Re-arrest Outcomes*. Washington, DC: Urban Institute.

Thompson, Anthony C. 2008. *Releasing Prisoners, Redeeming Communities: Re-entry, Race, and Politics*. New York: New York University Press.

Travis, Jeremy. 2005. *But They All Come Back: Facing the Challenges of Prisoner Re-entry*. Washington, DC: Urban Institute.

Travis, Jeremy, and Sarah Lawrence. 2002. *Beyond the Prison Gates: The State of Parole in America*. Washington, DC: Urban Institute.

US Government Accountability Office. 2001. *Prisoner Releases: Trends and Information on Reintegration Programs*. Washington, DC: US Government Accountability Office.

US Sentencing Commission. 2007. "U.S. Sentencing Commission Votes Unanimously to Apply Amendment Retroactively for Crack Cocaine Offenses." Press Release. December 11. Washington, DC: US Sentencing Commission.

Visher, Christy, and Kamala Mallik-Kane. 2007. "Re-entry Experiences of Men with Health Problems." In *Public Health Behind Bars: From Prisons to Communities*, edited by R. B. Greifinger. New York: Springer.

West, Heather C., and William J. Sabol. 2009. *Prison Inmates at Midyear 2008: Statistical Tables*. Washington, DC: Bureau of Justice Statistics.

INDEX

....

"exceptional circumstances" provision, 741–742, 743, 744
excessive force, use of, 591–592
  causes of, 592–593
  data on, 593–595
  excessive force criminal cases, 605
  use of deadly force, 595
exclusionary rule, 603–604
expediency principle systems, 3, 15
experienced arrest certainty, 199
expiration parole releases, 932
expressive punishment policies and laws, 111–112
external validity, 64, 65

fact bargaining, 15, 676, 677, 679
Fagan, Jeffrey, 186
failures to appear (FTA) rates, 807, 808, 809
Fairness and Effectiveness in Policing: The Evidence (NRC), 519
Fare v. Michael C., 646, 647
Farrell, Amy, 722
Farrell, Graham, 143
Farrington, David P., 79, 131, 138, 142, 454
Federal Bureau of Investigation (FBI), 6–7, 10, 324, 348, 352–353
Federal Bureau of Prisons, U.S., 810
Federal Courts Study Committee, 731
federal firearm licensee (FFL), 431–432
federal legal systems, 12–13
federal mandatory penalties, 739
Federal Probation Service, 828
federal sentencing guidelines, 707–710
Feeley, Malcolm, 689
Fegley, Suzanne, 455
Felson, Marcus, 44
female offenders. *See* sex, gender, and crime; women's prisons
feminization of poverty, 904–905
Finland. *See* Scandinavian countries
Finn, Mary A., 716
Fisher, George T., 683, 684, 686–687, 691n5
Fishman, Janet E., 598
Fishman, Joseph F., 801
flagrant drug dealing, 294, 307–308
fleeing felon rule, 328, 329, 341n3
Florin, Paul, 146
Fogel, David, 932
Folger, Robert, 585
foot patrols, police, 547–549
Ford v. Wainwright, 774–775

forecasting criminal behavior, 514
forest plot analysis, 517–518
Forever Free program, 913
Fornango, Robert, 49, 557–558, 942
Foucault, Michel, 110–111, 117, 260, 874–875, 892
France, Anatole, 117, 264
Frankel, Marvin E., 164, 697, 704–705
Franklin, Benjamin, 875
Frase, Richard, 707
Freeman, Richard B., 461
Fridell, Lorie, 594, 601
Friedman, Lee, 69
Fry, Margaret, 215
fugitive slave laws, 98, 767–768
functional displacement, 141
Furman v. Georgia, 185, 337, 770–771, 779
Fyfe, James J., 593, 595, 598

Gagnon v. Scarpelli, 937
Galaway, Burt, 225
Gallegos v. Colorado, 646
Garfinkel, Harold, 768
Garland, David, 22, 23, 109–110, 219, 257, 258, 265–267, 799–800, 879, 880, 902–903
Gartin, Patrick R., 191, 527
Gartner, Rosemary, 903, 908, 914
gender. *See* sex, gender, and crime
gender disparity, in sentencing, 712–713, 716
gender gap in crime, 351
gender inequality model of violence, 367
gender responsiveness, 911–912
Gendreau, Paul, 159, 166, 167, 172
General Accounting Office (GAO), 337–338, 553, 769, 853–854
general deterrence, 179
general responsivity principle, 171
General Social Survey (Canada), 364, 386
geographical variations, in sentencing, 714–715
Gersh, Jeffrey S., 191
Gibbs, John J., 812–813, 814
Gill, Martin, 142
Gilmore, Gary, 763
Gittings, R. Kaj, 186, 777
Giuliani, Rudolph, 556–557
Glaser, Daniel, 941
Glaze, Lauren E., 813
global position satellite (GPS) monitoring, 939
Glueck, Sheldon and Eleanor, 352
Goffman, Erving, 884, 911
Goldberg v. Kelly, 105